KÖNIGSBERG
DUCAL
PRUSSIA
DANZIG
ELBING
RASTENBURG
ROYAL
PRUSSIA
MARIENWERDER
GRUDZIĄDZ
CHEŁMNO
TORUŃ
KUJAWY
P
O
L
A
N
D

•VILNIUS

•NOWOGRÓDEK
NIEŚWIEŻ •
KLECK •

LITHUANIA

WĘGRÓW •
GNIEZNO
BRZEŚĆ K.
WARSAW
• BRZEŚĆ L.
MIĘDZYRZECZ
POZNAŃ
ŚMIGIEL •
GREAT
BRZEZINY
WSCHOWA
POLAND
OSSIG •
PIOTRKÓW
LITTLE
POLAND
• LUBLIN
• WŁODZIMIERZ
LIEGNITZ •
• BRESLAU
JAUER•
• BRIEG
RAKÓW •
• LWÓW
• SANDOMIERZ
SILESIA
OLKUSZ
PIŃCZÓW
CRACOW
ROGÓW
PRAGUE
• LUCŁAWICE
GALICIA
BOHEMIA
OLOMOUC
MORAVIA
BRNO
TABOR
ROSSITZ
AUSTERLITZ
EIBENSCHITZ
AUSPITZ
ZNAIM
NICOLSBURG
HAPSBURG
PAUSRAM
FREISTADT
LINZ
AUSTRIA
VIENNA
UPPER
LOWER
HUNGARY
O
T
T
O
M
A
N
DEBRECEN
TRANSYLVANIA
NAGYVARAD
KOLOZSVÁR •
VESZPRÉM •
TORDA
MAROS-
VÁSÁRHELY
GYULAFEHÉRVÁR
• KLAGENFURT
NAGYSZEBEN
KRONSTADT •
Danube
PÉCS
TRIESTE
CAPODISTRIA
ZAGREB
TURKISH HUNGARY
E
M
P
I
R
E
NCONIA
RAGUSA

THE RADICAL REFORMATION

THE
RADICAL
REFORMATION

by

GEORGE HUNTSTON WILLIAMS

Philadelphia

THE WESTMINSTER PRESS

To

JAMES LUTHER ADAMS, Ph.D.

In Chicago, my first professor of theology
At Harvard, esteemed colleague in Christian ethics

On the occasion of his sixtieth birthday

and

On the occasion of their golden anniversary

To my parents

LUCY ADAMS WILLIAMS

Whose loving understanding of all individuals in their diversity
encouraged me in the study of their varied tongues, *and*

DAVID RHYS WILLIAMS, D.D.

Whose prophetic sermons opened for me the vision
of that world where thrones are crumbled and where kings are dust

CONTENTS

vii

ABBREVIATIONS

ARG	*Archiv für Reformationsgeschichte*
BFP	*Bibliotheca Fratrum Polonorum*
BHR	*Bibliothèque d'Humanisme et Renaissance*
BRN	*Bibliotheca Reformatoria Neerlandica*
CH	*Church History*
CR	*Corpus Reformatorum*
CS	*Corpus Schwenckfeldianorum*
DThC	*Dictionnaire de Théologie Catholique*
LCC	*The Library of Christian Classics*
ME	*Mennonite Encyclopedia*
ML	*Mennonitisches Lexikon*
MQR	*Mennonite Quarterly Review*
NAK	*Nederlandsch Archief vóor Kerkgeschiedenis*
ORP	*Odrodzenie i Reformacja w Polsce*
PL	*Patrologia Latina*
QFRG	*Quellen und Forschungen zur Reformations geschichte*
QGT	*Quellen zur Geschichte der Täufer*
SAW	*Spiritual and Anabaptist Writers*
VB	*Die Vadianische Briefsammlung*
WA	*Weimar Ausgabe, Luther's Works*
ZKG	*Zeitschrift für Kirchengeschichte*
ZSKG	*Zeitschrift für Schweizerische Kirchengeschichte*
ZW	Zwingli, *Sämtliche Werke*

PREFACE

There is no aspect of sixteenth-century research that is so alive with newly discovered and edited source materials and monographic revisions as the Radical Reformation. Indeed, the newly edited sources have almost the same significance for the interpretation of the whole of modern church history as the discoveries in the Dead Sea caves and in Upper Egypt are having for New Testament studies and early church history.

It would be premature to attempt at this stage a definitive account of the Radical Reformation. Nevertheless, the general reader in Reformation history is entitled to have before him a rough outline of the picture shaping up in the minds of the specialists. Even the specialists may be helped at this point in their archival and monographic burrowing by coming out for a moment to blink at the scene as a whole.

The proffered landscape may, at first glance, seem like a close-up of the crowded mounds of a prairie-dog town, but this will not be because we are surveying the life and work of a diminutive race of reformers and their followers. For good or ill, the Radicals were to shape the contours of the world that was to come after them far more than they or their Catholic and Protestant opponents realized.

The present narrative is greatly indebted to the recently completed *Mennonite Encyclopedia* in four volumes (1955–1959), the articles of which are in most cases based on the most recent monographic literature. Among the contributors and editors of that outstanding achievement to whom I am especially grateful for indirect and direct help and encouragement are Profs. Harold S. Bender, Cornelius Krahn, and Robert Friedmann. I am similarly indebted to Mrs. Selina G. Schultz of Washington, D.C., who is now bringing the nineteenth volume of the *Corpus Schwenckfeldianorum* to completion. Other colleagues and friends who have in varying ways helped in the writing of this book, and whom I should at this point like to mention are: Prof. Wiktor Weintraub, Dr. Walter Grossmann, and Mr. Ralph Lazzaro, of Harvard University; Profs. Franklin Littell, of the Perkins School of Theology, Southern Methodist University, Roland Bainton, of Yale University, and William Klassen, of Mennonite Biblical Seminary; Profs. Fritz Blanke, of the University of Zurich, and Ernst Staehelin, of the University of Basel; Dr. Jean Rott, of the National Library of Strasbourg, and Dr. Lech Szczucki, of the Warsaw Academy of Arts and Sciences; the Rev. Dr. Alexander St.-Ivanyi, of Lancaster, Massachusetts, and Father Joseph Alen, of Greenfield, Massachusetts; Drs. William Keeney, Irwin Horst, and Heinold Fast; Harvard Teaching Fellows Charles Gribble and Henry Birnbaum; my present and former students in varying stages of their achievements: Dr. Chalmers MacCormick, now of Wells College; Dr. J. Leo Garrett, now of Southern Baptist Theological Seminary; Dr. Marianka Fousek, John Tedeschi, Daniel Kratz, Rollin Armour, Alvin Beachy, Alton Templin, and Ernest Lashlee.

I am most grateful to my two research assistants, both of them candidates for the doctorate in theology at Harvard, the Rev. Harold Field Worthley and the Rev. Harold O. J. Brown. In addition to working with me in all phases of the book, both men kept in close touch with the work after my departure for Strasbourg.

My appreciation is also due to The Harvard Research Foundation for a grant that in 1956 helped me assemble the basic bibliography, and to Miss Elizabeth Abbot Smith of the First Parish, Arlington, Massachusetts, who, in 1960, in a very substantial way made possible the prosecution of this book and a related project.

There is an act symbolic of a new appreciation of the Radical Reformation in the fact that it is the leading press of the American sons of John Calvin which has undertaken the publication of this long history of the very men and movements he liked least, a history written, moreover, by a professor who, and in a university which, has spiritual connections with Calvin's principal foe, Michael Servetus. I wish, therefore, to express appreciation to Dr. Paul Meacham and the staff of The Westminster Press for their vision, encouragement, imagination, counsel, efficiency, and patience in helping me bring this complicated book through to completion. I should also like to express particular gratitude to my own revered teacher, colleague, and friend, Dr. John T. McNeill, for the care with which he has read a taxing manuscript in several stages of composition, and for the substance and precision of his comments. It was Dr. McNeill who first invited me to prepare the volume on the Radicals for The Westminster Press Library of Christian Classics. I hope that he will now feel that the delineation and the analysis of the Radical Reformation in this volume confirms his original surmise that the writings of some of these Radicals belong indeed among the classics of Christian testimony. The book is intended as a companion volume to the anthology of texts printed in The Library of Christian Classics, XXV: *Spiritual and Anabaptist Writers: Documents Illustrative of the Radical Reformation and Evangelical Catholicism,* edited by Angel M. Mergal and the present author.

This collection does not contain specimens of the work of our third main grouping, the Evangelical Rationalists, who grew out of Evangelical Catholicism, but titles of their writings are included in the "Bibliography of Material in English Translation Written by Representatives of the Radical Reformation (1524–1575)," *ibid.,* pp. 285–293. Readers of the present book are encouraged to make use of this bibliography of original sources in English translation and also of my "Studies in the Radical Reformation (1517–1618): A Bibliographical Survey of Research Since 1939," *Church History,* XXVII (1958), pp. 46–69, 124–160. It had been my plan to allow the bibliography of translations and the extensive bibliographical essay to serve as the remote footnoting, as it were, to the work now before us, which was originally projected as a comprehensive narrative free of all bibliographical references except for the acknowledgment and location of direct quotations from monographs and original sources. I have found it necessary, however, to expand the footnoting far beyond my original intention, without duplicating the effort that went into the two earlier bibliographies.

The book is so constructed that it should be possible to read it not only chapter by chapter but, by means of frequent cross references, also topically. Considerable importance has been attached to the specific Scriptural texts to which the Radicals appealed, and a Scriptural index supplements the main index. In general, the Christian names of the Reformation figures have been Anglicized. The titles of all sixteenth-century writings are rendered in English if they have been anywhere translated into English or have acquired standardized English designations; in Latin if that was the language of the original or if the Polish or Hungarian work has acquired a standardized Latin title; otherwise, in the modernized form of the Polish, Hungarian, German, Dutch, French, or Italian title.

A final word on capitalization. Typographical variations in such words as "anabaptist," "sacramentist," "unitarian," etc., are intentional, which will be apparent as the account unfolds.

GEORGE HUNTSTON WILLIAMS

Harvard Divinity School
Cambridge, Massachusetts

31 December 1961

Four centuries after the death of Caspar Schwenckfeld, Menno Simons, Laelius Socinus

INTRODUCTION

In the decade between the end of the sanguinary Great Peasants' War in Germany in 1525 and the collapse of the polygamous Biblical commonwealth of misguided peasants, artisans, and burghers in Münster in 1535, the gravest danger to an orderly and comprehensive reformation of Christendom was Anabaptism, which because of a profound disappointment with Martin Luther, Ulrich Zwingli, their clerical associates, and their magisterial supporters, withdrew into separatist conventicles. Anabaptists were regarded as seditious and heretical. The revival of the ancient Code of Justinian made this explicit. It was midway in the decade, at Speyer in April 1529, in the same diet at which (April 19) six princes and the delegations of fourteen Upper German towns first took the name "Protestant" as stout adherents of Luther's reforms, that an imperial law (April 22) was published against the Anabaptists, in which both Catholics and "Protestants" concurred. The following day a mandate of Charles V gave specific instructions to the higher officials of the Empire as to how to deal with the baleful combination of sedition, schism, and heresy combated long ago in the ancient imperial laws against the Donatists and other separatists and willful puritans. For a brief season, however, the Anabaptists were in otherwise respectable company, for the diet included in its censure also the sacramentarians, that is, the followers of Zwingli, because the Swiss seemed to be doing, in their interpretation and observance of the second of the two principal sacraments of the church—the Eucharist—what the Anabaptists were doing with the first—Baptism. By October of the same year, however, the Lutherans and the sacramentarians from Switzerland, along with representatives of the mediating position on the sacrament of the altar—notably, Martin Bucer of Strassburg—had met under the patronage of Landgrave Philip of Hesse at Marburg to compose the differences between the two reform movements issuing respectively from Wittenberg and Zurich. Although the two factions continued to disagree even violently on article 15 concerning the Lord's Supper, the over-all effect of the epoch-making colloquy was to extend the meaning of "Protestant" to include the Swiss and other pedobaptist sacramentarians. The Lutherans and the Zwinglians agreed at least, over against the Anabaptists, in interpreting the one sacrament, Baptism, as roughly equivalent to circumcision under the Old Covenant. They were alike disturbed by, and prepared to take stern measures against, the threat of the Anabaptists and the Spiritualists to the integrity and the durability of an orderly reformation with the sanction and support of the town councils, the princes, and the kings of Christendom. We may speak, therefore, of the Lutheran and Zwinglian movement and its analogues across the Channel and elsewhere as the Magisterial Reformation or, when one has in mind more its doctrine than its manner of establishment, as classical Protestantism.

It would be a mistake, of course, to assume that the theology of the Magisterial Reformation was incapable of propagation without the assistance of magistrates: witness the extraordinary conquests of the Huguenots in Catholic France, the Helvetians in Catholic Poland, and the Calvinists in the rise of the Dutch Republic; nevertheless, Reformed Christians, wherever they were compelled to organize in a hostile environment, presupposed or proposed a truly Christian state, and always carried the seed of a complete Christian commonwealth within the temporary and protective husks of their clandestine conventicles. They did not, on principle, eschew fighting for the word of God, given a favorable conjuncture of events.

Over against magisterial Protestantism, and its *provisionally* "sectarian" outposts in Catholic lands, stood the Anabaptists, who, with their determination to clear away the old abuses root and branch and at the same time to dispense with earthly magistrates and prelates, were only the first major threat of what proved to be a three-pronged movement constituting the Radical Reformation, the further definition and delineation of which constitutes the burden of this book.

This Radical Reformation was a loosely interrelated congeries of reformations and restitutions which, besides the Anabaptists of various types, included Spiritualists and spiritualizers of varying tendencies, and the Evangelical Rationalists, largely Italian in origin. In contrast to the Protestants, the exponents of the

Radical Reformation believed on principle in the separation of their own churches from the national or territorial state, although, in three or four instances (i.e., Müntzerites, Münsterites), they were misled into thinking that the regenerate magistrates from their own midst would prove more godly than Protestants or Catholics. With these exceptions, followers of the Radical Reformation in all three sectors denounced war and renounced all other forms of coercion except the ban, and sought to spread their version of the Christian life by missions, martyrdom, and philanthropy. No less confident than the fighting Calvinists that they were the chosen remnant of the Lord, having "through their covenant with God in a good conscience" worked out their own salvation in fear and trembling, these followers put their trust in the Lord of the quick and the dead, who would soon come and judge between the saints and the sinners.

In insisting on believers' baptism, or on the possession of the gifts of the Spirit, or on the experience of regeneration, and in being often quite indifferent to the general political and social order, the various exponents of the Radical Reformation not only opposed the Magisterial Reformation tactically and on principle but also clearly differentiated themselves from sixteenth-century Protestants, that is, the Lutherans and the Reformed (the Zwinglians and the Calvinists), on what constituted both the experience and the conception of salvation, and on what constituted the true church and proper Christian deportment. They saw in Luther's doctrine of salvation by faith alone a new indulgence system more grievous than that which he had attacked in ninety-five theses on the eve of the Reformation Era. They usually declined to use the theologically complementary term "sanctification," preferring, instead, to stress regeneration, or the new being in Christ, or the drive of the Spirit, or the quickening of the moral conscience, or, in veiled language, deification. In any event, the exponents and martyrs of the Radical Reformation, whether Anabaptists, Spiritualists, or Rationalists, were alike in their dissatisfaction with the Lutheran-Zwinglian-Calvinist forensic formulation of justification and with any doctrine of original sin and predestination that seemed to them to undercut the significance of their personal religious experience and their continuous exercise of those personal and corporate disciplines by which they strove to imitate in their midst what they construed from the New Testament texts to have been the life of the original apostolic community.

From the *Enchiridion of the Christian Soldier* of Erasmus in 1504 and the Sacramentist *Epistola Christiana* of Cornelius Hoen, through Benedetto of Mantova's anthological *Benefit of Christ's Death*, to the *De Jesu Christo servatore* of Socinus in 1578, the whole tapestry of the Radical Reformation was interwoven with a loosely twined bundle of threads that were giving a new configuration to the doctrine of salvation. In this explicit or more often merely implicit reconstruction or replacement of the Anselmian doctrine of the atonement, there was a characteristic stress on the divine compassion and an elaboration of a devout and detailed doctrine of the *imitatio Christi* or the discipleship of the reborn Christian, a corresponding alteration in the doctrine of the incarnation (variously formulated in terms of the celestial flesh of Christ), and frequently also an alteration in the traditional formulations of the relationship of the Father and the Son. The variations in incarnational theology cut across the whole Radical Reformation. The various stages in the explicit opposition to the Nicene doctrine of the Trinity were largely limited to the Evangelical Rationalists. In their intense eschatological convictions, some of the Spiritualists, many Anabaptists, and almost all of the Evangelical Rationalists adhered to the doctrine of the sleep or the death of the soul prior to the resurrection (psychopannychism).

The range and types of spirituality in the Radical Reformation suggest successively the rigor of the medieval monastery, the prim devotion of the Catholic Evangelicals, and the passion of the orders of the counter-reformed church far more than the hearty affirmation of life in all its vocational fullness that was characteristic of Lutheranism. Since there was, in fact, some continuity of Catholic Evangelism in Evangelical Rationalism, the brief interlude of Catholic Evangelism that burgeoned and then withered between 1500 and 1542 in the Romance lands has been included in the following account. Some of its early exponents joined the Protestants, others the Radical Reformation, while still others, after the introduction of the Roman Inquisition in 1542, turned their energies into the Counter Reform.

Constitutionally, the Radical Reformation was, of course, equally distant from classical (magisterial) Protestantism and Tridentine Catholicism. The reformers among the Old Believers and the Magisterial Reformers alike worked with the idea of *reformatio;* the Anabaptists, the Spiritualists, and the Rationalists labored under the more radical slogan of *restitutio.*

To be sure, the Protestants in their *reformatio* differed widely in the extent of their break from the medieval church.

To be specific, the progress of Lutheranism through a patchwork of territories and jurisdictions that seldom coincided even roughly with the medieval diocesan and provincial boundaries encouraged its leaders, in so many other respects conservative (where the Bible did not expressly speak against a traditional doctrinal formulation or institution), to minimize the significance of bishops and archbishops, so many of whom were, of course, temporal princes and thus integrally a part of the imperial constitution as prince-bishops and even imperial electors. With the expedient of the prince as *Notbischof,* Luther and his associates separated the whole question of polity from the core of essential Christian doctrine, although they were willing to utilize the office and traditions of episcopacy in organizing Lutheranism nationally, as in Sweden.

In contrast to Lutheranism, the Reformed churches (which began their career in breaking from episcopal authority with the sanction of the town councils) stressed polity as co-ordinate with doctrine; and, although basing the constitution of the Reformed Church (especially in Calvinism) on the polity of the New Testament, they unconsciously absorbed a good deal of the usage and political theory of the Swiss Confederation of city republics and reworked ecclesiologically the civic institutions of local councils and diets.

Over against Lutheranism and the Reformed Church, Cranmerian Anglicanism preserved episcopacy on principle, but primarily as a constitutional necessity in the magisterial reformation of a national kingdom, with its lords temporal and lords spiritual in the upper house of its Parliament, interpreted as at once the national diet and the national synod. Only belatedly did Anglicanism turn to the task of providing the threefold ministry of deacons, priests, and bishops with an adequate theology of orders.

Though the Magisterial Reformation was far from unified in its conception of the sacraments in general and the place of polity in particular, it was one in the general conviction that behind the national, territorial, and the cantonal church organizations there existed the one holy Catholic Church, made up of the predestined saints (Calvin) or the assembly of the true believers (Luther).

In contrast to the three major expressions of the Magisterial Reformation, the proponents of the Radical Reformation, for the most part, rejected the doctrine of absolute predestination and the doctrine of an invisible church, and took seriously the ordering of their churches, conventicles, or fellowships of regenerate saints on the principle of voluntary association.

The proponents of the Radical Reformation, espousing the faithful restoration of the apostolic church as it existed in the age of the martyrs before it was prudentially supported by Constantine, differed among themselves, however, on the procedure for restoring or reassembling such a church. They also differed on the question of the constitutional significance for Christians of the role of the judges and the kings in the Scriptures of the Old Covenant.

Of the three radical groups, the Anabaptists were most confident in being able to reproduce the structure of apostolic Christianity from the New Testament, supplemented by texts they regarded as comparably primitive, or authoritative, for instance, the descriptions of the early churches preserved by Eusebius of Caesarea, a spurious epistle of Clement of Rome, and the works of early fathers. The Anabaptists differed among themselves as to the degree to which the pattern and institutions of the people of the Old Covenant and their Scriptures were appropriable. The Anabaptists of Münster, for example, with their eschatological intensity, easily combined the readings of Daniel in the Old Testament and Revelation in the New Testament and thereby justified their reintroduction of the Old Testament constitution of warrior saints.

The Spiritualists likewise differed among themselves in their use of the Bible as a pattern for the church. Thomas Müntzer, with his zeal for prophetic reform of the whole of society, like the Anabaptist Münsterites, used the Old Testament in his blueprints for the reformation of church and commonwealth.

The contemplative Spiritualist Caspar Schwenckfeld, despairing of any valid *restitutio* without some clearer guidance from God than had been apparently given thus far, preferred, amidst the violent claims and counterclaims of Protestants, Catholics, and Anabaptists, to follow a "middle way" and to suspend the sacrament of the altar and interiorize it as an inward eucharist and communion until such a time as God himself would intervene and usher in the church of the Spirit. Other Spiritualists such as the Libertines and isolated Rationalists, suspended the use of all the sacraments (forerunners in this respect of the Quakers).

The Evangelical Rationalists from Camillo Renato to Faustus Socinus tended to be individualistic in their Christianity and were, like the Evangelical Spiritualists, distressed by the divisiveness and acrimony attendant upon the organization of religion; and some might have preferred the half-enunciated ideal of Erasmus, namely, a "Third Church," neither Protestant nor Catholic, devout but not doctrinaire. In Poland, Lithuania, and Transylvania, the Evangelical Rationalist ferment permeated the local reformed churches to create three well-integrated and inwardly disciplined ecclesiastical bodies, one of them destined to survive intact to the present day as the Unitarian Church in Rumania.

The doctrine of the inwardly disciplined but externally free "apostolic" church has therefore been rightly recognized as one of the common marks of the whole of the Radical Reformation.

A consideration of ecclesiology and polity must, of course, include specific reference to the theory and practice of the ministry and ordination thereto. The fact that the proponents of the Radical Reformation were frequently laymen has obscured the no less interesting fact that the movement was in part re-ordinationist as well as in its main sector ana-baptist. Among the Magisterial Reformers there were several who, like Zwingli, having already been ordained under the *ancien régime*, declined on principle to be reordained on becoming Protestant.

In contrast, within the Radical Reformation there are several instances of former priests who felt the need for a recommissioning and who finally repudiated their Catholic ordination (e.g., Menno Simons). In other instances, leaders to the end were obsessed with the question of a valid apostolic vocation, that is, the problem of being authentically sent to proclaim, to baptize, and to organize in the latter days of the world (e.g., Obbe Philips). In some cases the Radical Reformation leaders seemed to connect the continuity of missionary authority with the baptismal succession, at times with the direct outpouring of the Spirit. Thus, though many "lay" leaders within the Radical Reformation, such as Conrad Grebel, Schwenckfeld, and Socinus, were, so far as we know, never formally ordained, to overstress this would obscure the fact that the credentials of leadership in the Radical Reformation were at the beginning more often moral or charismatic than regular. The strongly re-ordinationist thrust within the Radical Reformation would, needless to say, become explicit only in the relatively few instances when a cleric of the old order became a leader in the new. Unordained monks and friars were, however, much more common among the recruits of the Radical Reformation than were ordained priests and prelates. Thus, a basic conflict over the conception of the nature of the church and polity between the Radical Reformation and the Magisterial Reformation came to be articulated in the debate between the two sides, not in terms of ordination, which was generally neglected, but rather in terms of formal, university theological education on the one side and apostolic, or prophetic or inspired, vocation on the other.

Akin to the prominence of the layman in the Radical Reformation and the functional extension of the priesthood of all believers in the direction of personal witness to Christ in missions and martyrdom, rather than in the diversification of the conception of vocation (as with Luther and Calvin), was the corresponding elevation of women to a status of almost complete equality with men in the central task of the fellowship of the reborn. Correlative with the enhanced role of women was the reconception of the medieval sacrament of marriage in the covenantal context of the Radical Reformation.

So much, then, by way of introduction for some of the traits common to the Radical Reformation.

Modern, and particularly American, Protestants, seeking to grasp the Radical Reformation as a whole, must try to see it as one of the two fronts against which classical Protestantism was seeking to establish its position, the other being Catholicism, which was renewing its strength and extending its global bounds.

With what they considered the papal Antichrist to their right, Luther and Melanchthon, Zwingli then Bullinger, Calvin and Cranmer, readily thought of their common foe to the left as a three-headed Cerberus and called the monster abusingly, without their wonted theological precision, almost interchangeably Libertinism, Anabaptism, Fanaticism. Today we are in a position to see much more clearly than they did the differences within the Radical Reformation. Indeed, historians within the denominational traditions surviving intact from the age of their martyrs, namely, the Mennonites, the Hutterites, the Schwenckfelders, and the (Transylvanian) Unitarians, and others in traditions indirectly dependent upon it—namely, the Quakers and the Baptists—have gone so far in the direction of distinguishing in the sixteenth century the Anabaptists and the Spiritualists and the Evangelical Rationalists that there is once again a great need to see the whole of the Radical Reformation synoptically, the better to understand both the general morphology of Christian radicalism and the classical formulation of Protestantism.

As a variegated episode in the general history of Christianity, the Radical Reformation may be said to extend from 1516, the year of Erasmus' edition of the Greek New Testament, to a cluster of events around 1578 and 1579, namely, the death of the leader of the Hutterites in their golden age (Peter Walpot); the death of the leader of the Transylvanian Unitarians (Francis Dávid); the arrival of Faustus Socinus in Poland and his conversion of Racovian, anti-Trinitarian Anabaptism in the direction of Socinianism; the official toleration of Mennonitism by William of Orange; and the Emden disputation between the Mennonites and the Reformed. By roughly this time, the Radical Reformation had eliminated its most obvious excesses, had softened its asperities, and had, moreover, come to differentiate and redefine quite clearly its own disparate impulses, settling down and consolidating inwardly in diverse and largely isolated sects and fellowships. Slowly gathering strength, bearers of their ideas and institutions or groups analogous to them were to become once again involved in general history, notably in the restructuring of English Christendom in the age of the Civil Wars and the Commonwealth. Again in our own times, when, in a new context at once secular and ecumenical, the European state churches are being disestablished, the large churchlike American denominations are being reorganized, and the younger churches of Asia and Africa are being challenged by renascent ethnic religions and the international religion of the proletariat, when, in short, the mission of the churches everywhere is being reconceived in a basically hostile or alienated environment, Christians of many denominations are finding themselves constitutionally and in certain other ways closer to the descendants of the despised sectaries of the Reformation Era than to the classical defenders of a reformed *corpus christianum*.

CHAPTER 1

REFORMED CATHOLICITY:
AN EVANGELICAL INTERLUDE

The shadow of the tragic figure of Charles, fifth in succession to the founder of the medieval Roman Empire, falls across the whole of Christendom as it was breaking asunder in the process of Protestant reformation, Catholic renewal, and the religious separatism of the Radical Reformers.

Born in Ghent in 1500, elected Emperor in 1519, crowned by the pope at Bologna in 1530, Charles abdicated in 1556, and lay dying in retirement at a monastery in Estremadura in 1558, at the end broken in spirit, as was the Christendom over which he had tried to preside with medieval dignity and devotion. He had been beset as Emperor from one side and the other by the Sultan in league with the *Rex christianissimus* of France, from another side by the pope, under various styles and policies acting as an ambitious Italian prince, and from another side by a university professor religiously rallying the latent nationalism of Germany. It could have been of little comfort to the abdicating Emperor that his great antagonist, the theological spokesman of the Reformation, had a decade earlier likewise ended his days in sorrow on the eve of the shattering religious civil war within the no longer sacred Empire of the German Nation.

To begin the history of the Radical Reformation with a reference to the pious Emperor whose tutor was the dour theologian destined to be the last non-Italian pope (Hadrian of Utrecht), whose magnificent imperial coronation in Bologna was to be the last at the hands of a pope, and whose ardent religious advisers were frequently incapable of making distinctions between Lutherans and Sacramentarians, to say nothing of Anabaptists and Spiritualists, demands immediate explanation.

Charles was favorable toward a kind of Catholic piety that had more in common with the theological fervor in Germany

1

than with papal urbanity. To this distinctive Catholic piety modern scholarship has finally assigned a name, Catholic Evangelism, gathering up therein a number of related movements on the slopes of the German crater.[1]

In so far as he understood Evangelism as irreproachably orthodox, Charles heeded and supported its exponents. But he was bigoted and ruthless toward everything he considered heresy, sedition, or dereliction of duty in high places.

Evangelism, a widespread outcropping of an undogmatic, ethically serious combination of medieval piety and humanistic culture, quickened by Luther's proclamation of salvation by faith alone (solafideism), but disturbed by his seeming antinomianism and programmatic neglect of the traditional means and patterns of personal sanctification, momentarily held high the hope of reforming a still Catholic Christendom—both its members and at long last even its papal head—and thus regaining the allegiance of the disaffected parts of Germany. Its foremost exponent was Charles's Netherlandish subject Desiderius Erasmus. Called Erasmianism, the movement manifested itself in several regional variants, specifically: in the Netherlands as "national-reformed, Biblical humanism," in France as Evangelism, in Spain as mystical, evangelical Illuminism, in Italy as Valdesianism (with perhaps disproportionate ascription of importance to a winsome exponent, John de Valdés), in Catholic Germany as "Expectancy,"[2] and in Poland as national Catholicism (which combined with Erasmianism the Christian nationalism of Hussitism and Slavic Orthodoxy). Catholic Evangelism began to disappear especially after the introduction of the Roman Inquisition in 1542. Its residual energies passed variously into Protestantism (William Farel, Gellius Faber, and Peter Martyr), the Counter Reformation (George Witzel, George Cassander, and Reginald Pole), and the Radical Reformation (Paracelsus, Andrew Modrzewski, and Bernardine Ochino).

We shall in the present chapter be limited to Spain and Italy and we shall introduce (Ch. 1.2.a) the chief exponent of Catholic Evangelism only in so far as he, through his Greek New Testament of 1516 and kindred work, was also the unwitting patron

---

[1] The best account, though limited to its Italian manifestations, with, however, a survey of the evolution of the term since its first use by Imbart de la Tour, is that of Eva-Maria Jung, "On the Nature of Evangelism in Sixteenth Century Italy," *Journal of the History of Ideas*, XIV (1953), 511–527.

[2] The term *"Expektantentum"* was first used by Ludwig von Pastor, *Die Reunionsbestrebungen während der Regierung Karls V* (Freiburg, 1879), 115. See further, Hubert Jedin in *Lexikon für Theologie und Kirche*, 2d ed. (Freiburg, 1959), 1254, 1318.

of much that was to prove decisive for the whole Radical Reformation; and we shall do so in the rather unexpected context of a chapter largely devoted to chronicling certain developments in Spain and Italy, the evocation of which may promote a fresh comprehension of the character of the Radical Reformation, for example: the rise of the national inquisition (Ch. 1.1) under Ferdinand of Aragon, who died in 1516, and the failure of the Fifth Lateran Council (Ch. 1.3.a), which terminated in 1517.

By beginning our narrative with Spain rather than Germany, we are emboldened moreover, in passing, to give a kind of symbolic prominence to another figure (Ch. 1.2.c), who may be taken as a representative embodiment of the diverse tendencies of the whole Radical Reformation.

Michael Servetus, of Navarre, was indeed the veritable effigy, for Catholic and Protestant alike, of all that seemed most execrable in the Radical Reformation: in his almost arrogant defense of the autonomy of reason or of conscience; in his martyr readiness to espouse anabaptism, anti-Trinitarianism, pacifism, and psychopannychism (soul sleep; Ch. 1.3.b); and in his apocalyptic sense of the urgency of engaging in a massive but irenic mission to the Jews and Moslems, combined with his prophetic susceptibility to the ethical implications of God's providence in the recurrent successes of Sultan Suleiman the Magnificent (1520–1566) against a moribund Christendom. This Spanish lawyer-physician, who, sometimes in lonely pseudonymity, sometimes in brash assaults, spun his captivating theological webs in the interstices of Catholic Evangelism, sectarianism, natural philosophy, and the occult, was to have the sorrowful distinction of being burned in effigy by the inquisition in Catholic Lyons and in the flesh in Reformed Geneva. Indeed, the intellectual and ethical tensions and conflicting compassions within this quixotically theological knight-errant were far closer empathetically to the deepest strains and fissures within Christendom as a whole than either its Catholic defenders or its Protestant reformers realized. Servetus felt the full impact of Renaissance humanism and natural philosophy in the West and of politically renascent Mohammedanism in the East.[3] In the microcosm of this proud and spiritually tormented heretic, the conflict of the Reformation Era was perhaps more faithfully mirrored than in Erasmus, Luther, or Charles.

To see Servetus as the shadowy obverse of Charles no less than as the open antagonist of Calvin is a new way of under-

[3] See Stephen A. Fischer-Galati, *Ottoman Imperialism and German Protestantism: 1521–1555* (Cambridge, 1959).

standing the Radical Reformation: as a major though abortive thrust of the Reformation Era rather than as a succession of marginal movements. But to understand Charles and Servetus, and especially the latter, and to be able to identify the Iberian strain in certain doctrinal and religio-political developments and episodes in the Radical Reformation as far away as Brussels in 1517 and Raków in 1579, we must glance back into the religious history of the Spain of Servetus, Valdés, and Charles.

More especially to understand the devout cruelty with which the sectarian heterodoxy of the Radical Reformation was to be suppressed in both Catholic and Protestant lands, we must examine the emergent pattern of the Spanish Inquisition, which will not have been far from the mind of Charles when as Emperor he revived at the diet of Speyer in 1529 the provision in the Code of Justinian for the capital punishment of rebaptizers, the Anabaptists (Ch. 10.1).

1. MARRANOS AND ALUMBRADOS:
THE SPANISH INQUISITION

Back in 1391 a long series of popular outbursts against the royally protected and often conspicuously wealthy or learned Jews had reached a climax in a widespread massacre in the three Spanish kingdoms (Castile, Aragon, Navarre). From that date on, conversion under duress was common. The Marranos (conversos, "new Christians") became an important ingredient in the Catholic population striving for religious homogeneity. Not a few prelates and noblemen could trace their ancestry to such converts, including notorious inquisitors. But of course many of the forced converts preserved their old religions under prudential disguises from generation to generation.

In 1478 Ferdinand, not yet king of Aragon (1479–1516), and Isabelle, queen in Castile (1474–1504), requested papal permission to restore the medieval inquisition in a royal form. The demand was prompted by four considerations: (1) the determination of the Catholic sovereigns to secure religious uniformity; (2) the failure of the policy of forced conversions of Jews and Moors; (3) the undisguised alarm that these forced converts, among whom there were erratic mystics (Alumbrados), would contaminate the faith; and (4) the temptation to tyrannize over and confiscate the property of selected enemies of the new royal authority among the nobility, and the secular and the regular clergy.

Besides both sincere and prudential converts, there survived into the reign of the joint Catholic sovereigns many Jews who had not made even outward obeisance. Ferdinand and Isabelle alleged as their reason for requesting a royal inquisition the threat of a Jewish uprising on Good Friday, 1478.

Their Inquisition was modeled both upon the system of the royal secret service and upon the medieval papal institution. The council of the Inquisition became the fifth of the five great councils by which the joint sovereigns ruled. At first there was a separate inquisitor-general for Aragon and for Castile.

A peculiarity of the Spanish Inquisition was thus the royal control exercised over it to bring about religio-political uniformity, the ruling passion of the peninsula, which had been long tripartite in religion and culture. The papacy had long granted to or indulged the Spanish rulers in the possession of powers and privileges in respect to the hierarchy and the religious orders which it vigorously contested when claimed by the Holy Roman Emperor and certain other European rulers. In 1482, Pope Sixtus IV even agreed to place with the ruler the right to nominate bishops and he acquiesced formally in the already venerable practice[4] of the royal placet, the royal approbation of any bull before its promulgation. Episcopal courts were thereupon limited by the threat of *recursus*, that is, the grant of recourse or appeal to a royal court. The king gained control of the three Spanish military orders by becoming ex officio their grand master.

The medieval papal Inquisition of Cathars had found its Dominical charter in the *Compelle intrare* of the unpopular banquet (Luke 14:23) long before construed by Augustine as a parable of the church making use of the coercive arm of the Empire. The Spanish Inquisition of Marranos took special satisfaction in interpreting literally the Dominical injunction of John 15:6: "If a man abide not in me, he is cast forth as a branch, and is withered; and men gather them, and cast them into the fire, and they are burned." But public burning was meted out only to a small percentage of the numerous suspects of the Inquisition.[5]

Before the application of torture, the suspect was first the subject of delation or rumor, then arrested, often in the dead of night, a notary making at the time an inventory of his possessions. The place of detention was often noisome, terrifyingly constrictive, and subterranean. A long time could elapse before the appearance at the trial. The object of the Inquisition proper was

---

[4] Alphonse XI, 1348.

[5] Juan Antonio Llorente (1756–1823), who wrote his famous *Histoire Critique de l'Inquisition d'Espagne* (Paris, 1817) in exile in France, gave circulation to exaggerated figures.

to secure an avowal of guilt. To be sure, the suspect was graciously permitted to name mortal enemies among the possible informants, and their evidence was thereupon discounted. He was also permitted to choose a counselor from a panel, although this person usually confined his defense to urging the suspect to make a clean confession of guilt. Torture was applied only in cases of inconsistent admissions or the refusal to name associates. The Inquisition was hardest upon lapsed heretics who had previously, after submitting to the prescribed penalties, sworn "with vehemence" that they would become loyal to the church, and upon heresiarchs, even though they might make a full confession. These more serious offenders were "relaxed" to the secular arm with a formal prayer for mercy.

The penitents, with the telltale penitential habits *(sanbenitos)* of various colors and devices, were marched in solemn procession to the market place on a feast day or on a royal or municipal festivity, and forty days of indulgence were granted to all who attended the public spectacle of faith. Behind the halberdiers came the penitents. Those to be lightly punished (flogging, galleys, exile, confiscation) came first, followed by the sword of justice and the inquisitors themselves, with the wretches to be "relaxed," at the rear. The auto-da-fé *(actus fidei)* began with a sermon, followed by the reading from two improvised pulpits of the individual misdeeds and sentences. The burning of the recalcitrants marked the climax of this cruel objectification of corporate faith.

In 1485, the surviving Jewish community was fatefully imperiled when certain enraged Marranos, some of them connected by marriage with noble families in Aragon, unwittingly gave impetus and further motivation to the detested institution by compassing the murder of the inquisitor of Aragon as he knelt near the high altar in the cathedral of Saragossa. The indiscriminate wrath of the old ethnic Christians was vented upon Jews and Marranos alike. Moreover, scarcely a noble family of Aragon survived the vindictiveness of the bestial masses without seeing at least one of its members disgraced at an auto-da-fé. Persecution reached a new peak after the conquest of Granada, when the policy of forced conformity became a national passion. On 30 March 1492 an edict was issued that gave the Jews four months to make a choice between conversion or banishment, a particularly somber prospect, for even submission to the rite of Baptism was no guarantee that a *converso* would be much more secure in his rights than before. Two wealthy Jews had offered Ferdinand three hundred thousand ducats in the hope of averting the

edict, and the king had been disposed to compromise. Suddenly
the inquisitor Thomas Torquemada (1420–1498), himself a
descendant of a *converso,* appeared with his crucifix and cajoled
the two sovereigns: "Behold the Crucified whom the wicked
Judas sold for thirty pieces of silver! If you approve the deed,
sell him for a greater sum!" About 160,000 Jews trudged out of
the land, most of them to North Africa, Italy, and the Levant.

Notable among the surviving but the suspected Marranos were
the Illuminists *(Alumbrados, Perfectos, Dejados).* Illuminism was
a school of practical piety that arose about 1500 among the Franciscans, many of whom were Marranos. It is not possible that the
majority of the *conversos* secretly adhered to Judaism. But it is
quite conceivable that among the scholarly Marranos, liberated
by choice or by force from the minute prescriptions of the Mosaic law, many might easily have been inclined to bypass also the
new Christian legalism and ceremonial in order to come into
direct contact with the God of Isaiah. Illuminism, which was the
foe of Spanish orthodoxy through the sixteenth century, was not
the monopoly of the *conversos,* but it was among them that it
found some of its most important proponents.[6]

Wycliffite ideas about predestination and reprobation, possibly
brought to Castile in the suite of Catharine of Gaunt, queen of
Henry III (d. 1406), are known to have attracted certain doctrinal poets among the *conversos* at court. The designation *Perfectos* may point to an Albigensian origin. Possibly Arabic
spirituality cropped out here in Christian guise, or Netherlandish
mysticism may have played a part in reinforcing the native movement. The goal of the Illuminist was absolute passivity, the
obliteration of the will before the sovereign will of God.
Through ecstasy, whereby the soul entered into direct contact
with the divine essence, the Illuminist regarded himself as
incapable of sin, a perilous doctrine susceptible of pious distortion. Illuminist quietism in some respects akin to Netherlandish Libertinism (Ch. 12.2) was nevertheless a characteristically
Spanish effort at recovering the sense of divine immediacy. Subjective and individualistic, it was at the opposite pole of that
Spanish religiosity which found corporate and cruel objectification in the auto-da-fé.

Since it had few literary exponents and concentrated on the
promotion of a quickened devotional life and effective Christian
living, it is difficult to ascertain whether or how far Illuminism

---

[6] Cf. Marcel Bataillon, *Érasme et l'Espagne* (Paris, 1937), 65 f. and the Harvard
Ph.D. thesis in progress by Carlos Fraker, "Certain Doctrinal Poets in Four-
teeth-Century Castile."

may have diverged from acceptable Catholic doctrine. An extreme form of Illuminist enthusiasm was that of one Brother Melchior, who in 1512 predicted an impending reformation of the political and religious order and the establishment of the New Jerusalem.[7] The inquisitors were hard put to distinguish between these heterodox mystics and the truly Catholic mystics, the pride of Spain's Golden Age. Cardinal Ximenes was favorably disposed toward the milder manifestations of Illuminism, unlike his successors of the Counter Reformation.[8] The main reason for the party's eventual condemnation by the Inquisition seems to have been the fact that they gathered in devotional conventicles, distinguishing themselves from the community of the faithful.[9] Illuminism, however, reasserted itself in the Spanish version of Erasmianism.

Ferdinand (idealized in *Il Principe*) had, on the eve of the Reformation, secured an enviable authority over the national episcopate and the monastic orders, and by means of the Inquisition control over even the inner life of his subjects. His unparalleled power over the church supplied the pattern of magisterial supervision and inquisition to lesser princes including Protestants to be and constituted also a threat to the papacy itself, which had originally sanctioned it. The practice of royal absolutism in the church, which could be condoned on the marches of Christendom, was fraught with hazard when the peninsula, politically unified, now emerged as the major power of Christendom.

On the death of Ferdinand in 1516, the pattern of his absolute monarchy fell to his grandson, Charles. A decade later, Rome would be sacked by imperial troops as though by Vandals, and a quarter of a century later the Inquisition would be renewed in Italy itself under papal authority but in the spirit of Spain, and would bring to a close the brief episode of humane Catholic Evangelism everywhere.

2. Erasmus: Patron of Evangelicals and Radicals

a. Desiderius Erasmus. The humanist of Rotterdam, who in 1516 entered the service of Charles as royal counselor at the Burgundian court in Brussels, and for this purpose was relieved by the pope in 1517 of his responsibilities as Augustinian canon, went through the Lutheran revolt from the same apostolic prince as the arbiter of Christian humanism for both sides. It is not so well recognized that he was also a patron of the Radical Ref-

[7] Cf. Bataillon, *op. cit.*, 69.
[8] *Ibid.*, 74.
[9] *Ibid.*, 180.

ormation. We may confine our reference to those features in the personality and work of Erasmus which have special significance for our narrative.

In the very year that Erasmus accepted his post as Burgundian counselor he published his epoch-making Greek New Testament with a classical Latin translation, and significantly began his long series of patristic editions with his first volume of his favorite, Jerome. Henceforth, the northern humanist was to do for the ancient Christian sources what his more classically oriented colleagues among the Italian humanists had been doing for the discovery, preservation, and publication of Greek and Roman literature. The works of Jerome were completed in nine volumes by 1518, of Hilary of Poitiers in 1523, of Epiphanius in 1524, of Irenaeus (so important for the Radical Reformation) and of Augustine in 1526, and of Chrysostom in 1530. Erasmus was to die supervising the printing of the works of Origen in the same town, Basel, where in the same year, 1536, Calvin (so at variance with both Erasmus and Origen on the questions of free will and predestination) would be bringing out his *Institutes*.

A notable feature of Erasmus' critical edition of the New Testament was the elimination from the traditional text of I John 5:7 of its initial Trinitarian phrase, "There are three that bear record in heaven: the Father, the Word, and the Holy Spirit, and these three are one." Not discovering it included in his Greek manuscripts or cited by the early fathers of the church, Erasmus expunged the verse current in the Vulgate translation. Moreover, in commenting on the Gospel of John, Erasmus observed that the term "God" in the New Testament, without further specificity, should be construed to apply to God the Father. Because of Erasmus, I John 5:7 was to be omitted from the older Anabaptist vernacular versions of the Bible.[10]

Erasmus, trained in the school of the *Devotio Moderna*, was not philosophically inclined, but belonged, generally speaking, to the scholastic *Moderni* (nominalists). Becoming specific on the dogma of Nicaea and the Fourth Lateran Council, he declared, "According to dialectical logic [in the context of nominalism], it is possible to say there are three gods, but to announce this to the untutored would give great offense."[11] In his Latin version of the New Testament he eschewed, in the Prologue to John's

---

[10] It was enclosed in parentheses in the Mennonite Biestkens Bible of 1560.
[11] Erasmus, *De libero arbitrio, Opera Omnia* (Lyons, 1706), IX, 1217C; cf. V, 500d; cited by Roland H. Bainton, "Michael Servetus and the Trinitarian Speculation of the Middle Ages," *Autour de Michel Servet et de Sébastien Castellion*, edited by Bruno Becker (Haarlem, 1953), 44 f.

Gospel, the Vulgate *Verbum* for the Greek *Logos,* and, under the guise of improved classical elegance, substituted for it the philosophically denuded and theologically neutral *sermo.* All the while, he insisted that he was disposed to leave theological subtlety on the doctrine of the Trinity to one side, remarking in his edition of Hilary of Poitiers, later to be employed by Servetus:

Is it not possible to have fellowship with the Father, Son, and Holy Spirit, without being able to explain philosophically the distinction between them and between the Nativity of the Son and the procession of the Holy Spirit? If I believe the tradition that there are three of one *natura*[!], what is the use of labored disputation? If I do not believe, I shall not be persuaded by any human reasons. . . . You will not be damned if you do not know whether the Spirit proceeding from the Father and the Son has one or two beginnings, but you will not escape damnation if you do not cultivate the fruits of the Spirit, which are love, joy, peace, patience, kindness, goodness, long-suffering, mercy, faith, modesty, continence, and chastity. . . . The sum of our religion is peace and unanimity, but these can scarcely stand unless we define as little as possible, and in many things leave each one free to follow his own judgment, because there is great obscurity on these matters.[12]

Not only in his stress upon the New Testament and ancient Christian sources and in his casualness about the Nicene-Lateran[13] formulation of the doctrine of the Trinity, but also in other doctrines and attitudes, Erasmus would be presently appealed to by diverse leaders of the Radical Reformation. This was true of his opposition to the monastic vow and his reconception of marriage (Ch. 20), his understanding of both Baptism and Communion (Ch. 2.1), his (qualified) pacifism, and his insistence on the practical freedom of the will. It must suffice in the present chapter to round out the picture with something on the last two features.

In his *Querela Pacis,* published the year after his Greek New Testament, Erasmus combined evangelical, classical, and prudential arguments for the restraint of war and the limitation of even the so-called "just" war.[14] He appealed to the Stoic idea of the

---

[12] Erasmus, *Epistolae,* edited by P. S. Allen, V; 173–192, No. 1334, 176 ff.; quoted by Roland Bainton, *Hunted Heretic: The Life and Death of Michael Servetus, 1511–1553* (Boston, 1953), 34.

[13] The reference here is to the patristic definition against Arius at the Council of Nicaea in 325 and the scholastic clarification of the same doctrine in 1215 at the Fourth Lateran Council, in connection with controversy between Joachim of Flora and Peter Lombard.

[14] See the analysis of Roland H. Bainton, "The *Querela Pacis* of Erasmus," *Archiv für Reformationsgeschichte* (henceforth: *ARG*), XVII (1951), 32–48.

harmony of the spheres, to the example of the irrational beasts that are never predatory on their own kind, and to the Stoic-patristic ideal of the unity of mankind, among whom reason and equity should prevail; and he vividly pointed up the futility and the inhumanity of actual warfare, as in his *Dulce bellum in-expertis* of 1525.

His conviction about man's capacity to use his own resources and specifically his free will to work out his own salvation was expounded in his first explicit attack on the predestinarianism of the Reformation in 1524, *Diatribe de libero arbitrio,* to which Luther replied in his celebrated delineation of the bondage of the will in the realm of salvation (1525). So deeply was Erasmus disappointed in the turn which Luther's reform was taking that he sadly declared: "I shall bear therefore with this [the medieval] Church until I shall see a better one."[15]

Erasmus nevertheless hoped he would be able in his program of returning to the sources so to freshen this church that, while it would retain an allegiance to the bishop of Rome, it would also be brought close to the ancient apostolic pattern and would then indeed constitute a "Third Church," different alike from the Renaissance-corrupted papacy of his own day and the belligerent and predestinarian Reformation church with which Erasmus could not make common cause. The "Third Church," with its slightly eschatological overtone, might be taken, if not as the slogan, at least as the program of Catholic Evangelism.

b. Erasmianism in Spain. Cardinal Ximenes, who had variously demonstrated his learning, his soldierly virtue, and his zeal for reform (for example, his opposition to Leo X's great indulgence, and his swift implementation of the meager reforming and educational canons of the Fifth Lateran Council [Ch. 1.3.a] even before its adjournment), on two occasions sought unsuccessfully to persuade Erasmus to make an extended visit to Spain. But Erasmianism, reinforced by certain impulses from local humanism and Illuminism, spread in Spain without the personal visit.

At the older Universities of Salamanca and Valladolid, and especially at Alcalá, the new foundation (1508) of Cardinal Ximenes, Biblical, classical, and grammatical studies had been flourishing well before the impact of Erasmus. Six professors of philology taught at Alcalá, where, according to Erasmus, the most signal accomplishments of European scholarship were being

---

[15] *"Fero igitur hanc Ecclesiam donec videro meliorem."* Erasmus, *De libero arbitrio, loc. cit.,* IX, 1258a. See Augustin Renaudet, *Érasme et l'Italie, Travaux d'Humanisme et Renaissance,* XV (Geneva, 1954), Book 4, entitled "Le problème de la 3ᵉ Église," 200 ff.

made, foremost among them the Complutensian (=Alcalan) Polyglot Bible, the Greek New Testament in 1514, the Hebrew text in 1517. Ximenes, the instigator, died just eight days after Luther posted his theses.

Erasmus' works were apparently not available in Spain before 1516. The first definite notice in 1518 is of the *Institutio principis christiani*.[16] In 1520 a Spanish translation of his *Querela Pacis* appeared. Spanish interest in his works rapidly increased when he was learnedly attacked by one of the Polyglot translators, Diego López Zúñiga, for certain features of his New Testament. Erasmus' edition differed from the Spanish in stressing the pre-eminence of the original Greek text, whereas in Alcalá the Greek text was printed facing the Latin of the authorized Vulgate. In spite of numerous attempts by his opponents to prove him a Lutheran, Erasmus sustained his reputation in Spain, especially when Charles arrived with a suite of Flemish humanists in 1522, and it was further enhanced when the *De libero arbitrio* (1524) revealed the point at which humanism, with its return to the sources, and reformation, by solafideism, parted company. In Spain as elsewhere it was recognized that Erasmian *philosophia Christi* was quite different from Lutheran justification by faith.

Thus differentiated, the Erasmian third party, in Spain as elsewhere in Romance lands, did not easily come apart in the tension between Rome and Wittenberg.

In many cases indigenous Illuminism and cosmopolitan Erasmianism found in Spain the same patron, as, for example, the Marquis of Villena, Don Pacheco, to whom John de Valdés dedicated his first extant work. Erasmus and the Illuminists coincided in their interpretation of the death of Christ as a glorious, not a sorrowful, event, and spurned the practice of meditating on the sufferings of the crucified Lord. In his annotations to the New Testament,[17] Erasmus says:

Jesus wanted his death to be glorious and not sad; he did not want us to weep over it, but to adore it, because he voluntarily faced it for the salvation of the whole world. . . . If Christ had wished us to grieve at his death after the vulgar fashion, why, when he was carrying his cross, did he reprove the daughters of Jerusalem?

These words were censured by the Sorbonne as impious, and the Spanish Inquisition condemned a similar tendency among the Illuminists.[18]

[16] Bataillon, *op. cit.,* 90.
[17] St. Luke, ch. 23, cited in Bataillon, *op. cit.,* 202.
[18] Bataillon, *op. cit.,* 202.

c. The Erasmian Brothers Valdés and Michael Servetus. The
hope of a Catholic Europe to save itself from shipwreck on the
rocks of nationalism and religious particularism was expressed
by twin followers of Erasmus, Alphonse and John de Valdés,
born near Toledo in the same year as the Emperor, 1500.[19] Significantly, it was Spain, which had never been a part of the Holy
Roman Empire, that was after 1517 the headquarters of the
attempt to preserve the theory and the usages of the Empire as a
universal society symbolically embracing all Christendom.

The two brothers played an important part, one in the administrative, the other in the religious, life of Charles's realms.
Sons of a distinguished family, they profited by an education
under the Italian humanist Peter Martyr d'Anghiera (1457–
1526). In 1520, Alphonse saw Charles crowned Emperor at
Aachen, and returned to Spain full of enthusiasm for the new
ruler. He recognized in the Lutheran movement a threat, not so
much to the church, as to the Empire. In 1524, Alphonse was
engaged by Charles as imperial secretary while his brother John
was still studying at the university in Alcalá. Sometime between
1527 and 1529, Alphonse published with John's collaboration
two dialogues (between Mercury and Charon; between Lactancio
and an Archdeacon) which were proimperial and antipapal in
tone, justifying the sack of Rome by imperial troops and casti-
gating the vices of the higher clergy: "To be a bishop means to
wear a white surplice, to say mass with a mitre on one's head,
and gloves and rings on one's fingers, to command one's clerics,
to protect one's incomes, and spend them at will, to have many
servants, to be anointed with salve, and to give benefices."[20] In
1531 a Spanish inquisitor would point out that the pages in
Mercurio y Carón on the life of perfected Christians had made
Alphonse suspect of affinity with the *Alumbrados*.

In 1529, John published, at Alcalá, *A Dialogue on Christian Doctrine*, actually a meditation on the Lord's Prayer, his
only religious work of which the original Spanish text survives.[21]
In it an idealized archbishop of Granada discusses with two
interlocutors (one of them the monk Eusebio, who is really

---

[19] Perhaps as early as 1498. See Domingo de Santa Teresa, *Juan de Valdés,
1498(?)—1541, su pensamiento religioso y las corrientes espirituales de su
tiempo,* Analecta Gregoriana, LXXXV (1957).
[20] *Diálogo entre Mercurio y Carón,* fo. xviii (1850), 72.
[21] *Diálogo de Doctrina Cristiana.* Virtually unknown before the unique copy
was brought to light in 1925, it may have been composed in 1526 when John
was in attendance at the court of Charles. Translated by Angel M. Mergal
in *Spiritual and Anabaptist Writers* (henceforth: *SAW*), edited by Angel
M. Mergal and George H. Williams (Philadelphia, 1957), 320 ff.

Valdés) the seven petitions of the Lord's Prayer. The archbishop begins by acknowledging the legitimacy of certain Illuminist practices, namely, praying without audible words, books, or beads, so long as this is a matter of spontaneous preference rather than a conventicular requirement. In commenting on the first petition, "Hallowed be thy name," Valdés enunciates a basic principle of Catholic Evangelism: "God's name is sanctified, when we sanctify ourselves." He does not interpret the petition for daily bread eucharistically, regarding it rather as "the heavenly bread" of grace, "from which eat only those to whom God has forgiven their sins." In a passage which anticipates his distinctive doctrine of the atonement (to be elaborated by Bernardine Ochino and then Faustus Socinus), a passage which incidentally throws light on the ethos and religious temper of his day, Valdés writes:

And something else should be kept in mind here: we are not worthy to have our sins forgiven just because we forgive our debtors, those who offend us, but because God wanted to forgive us through his infinite goodness and mercy; under these conditions we are forgiven. So, it is necessary to forgive our neighbors in order that God may forgive us, but let us not think that God forgives us because we forgive, because this will amount to attributing to ourselves what should be attributed only to God. I know some people that, even though thinking of themselves as very holy and wise, when they feel some enmity against somebody, not wishing to forgive them, they do not pray this part of the Pater Noster, but skip it.[22]

Concerning the persistence of evil and temptation even among those who regularly pray, Valdés expressly refers to Erasmus' recovery of the meaning that makes the most sense of the seventh petition: "Erasmus, in his translation of the New Testament, says: 'Deliver us from the evil *one*,' that is, from the devil." There is also, even in this early work, a phraseology which suggests the spirit of Luther as much as the leaven of Erasmus.

Valdés' *Dialogue* was immediately the occasion of a suit against him, but, because of the influence of his family and the favor of the Erasmian party, he was not directly condemned. His detractors thereupon started a second action against him, and he left for Naples, as yet free of the Spanish Inquisition. The *Dialogue* was condemned in his absence.[23]

The twin brothers Valdés were not alone among educated young Spaniards who pinned their hopes for a rejuvenated

[22] *SAW*, 326.
[23] John E. Longhurst, *Erasmus and the Spanish Inquisition: The Case of Juan de Valdés* (Albuquerque, 1950), 47 ff.

Europe on the young Emperor Charles, himself moved by a sense of Catholic destiny. After the sack of Rome in 1527, Charles resolved to make another attempt to rally the papacy to its ecumenical duties by accepting papal confirmation of his imperial dignity at a coronation in Bologna. On this festive occasion, there was present besides Alphonse de Valdés another thoughtful young Spaniard in the imperial suite, Michael Servetus.

At the age of fourteen, Servetus had come under the patronage of John de Quintana (d. 1534), a Franciscan, a doctor of the Sorbonne, and a member of the Cortes of Aragon. Quintana was a man of irenic spirit, prepared to make attempts to reconcile the Lutherans to the Roman Church. He enabled Servetus to spend the years 1528–1529 studying law at the University of Toulouse.

There, Servetus, as a Spaniard brought up in contact with Moriscos and Marranos, was taunted with charges of heterodoxy in the militantly orthodox university. He thereupon devoted much of his time to Biblical studies in an effort to reinforce his own orthodoxy in respect to Christology and the doctrine of the Trinity, theologically the chief points of controversy between Christendom and the two Semitic religions which, until 1492, had been so prominent. This research led him to the unexpected discovery that the doctrine of the Trinity was nowhere clearly enunciated in the Bible. It is also very likely that even at this early date he was at work on the problem of great concern to many earnest Spanish Catholics as to why the sacramental water of baptism so often had no potency with the Marranos, a problem which he would eventually solve in advocating complete immersion at Jesus' baptismal age of thirty (Ch. 11.1).

When Quintana was appointed chaplain to the Emperor in 1529, he took Servetus with him to Bologna for the reconciliation with Clement VII and for the double coronation. On 22 February 1530, the pope placed the iron crown of Lombardy on Charles's head, and two days later, on precisely his thirtieth birthday, in a kind of epiphany of the last Christian head of the disintegrating *corpus christianum,* Charles received the imperial diadem, while the Count Palatine, the only German prince present at the liturgical investment, carried the *Reichsapfel.* Never had this ancient symbol of universal Christian dominion been more aptly descriptive of a Holy Roman Emperor's global sway than at the coronation of the ruler of two hemispheres. And yet, within four months he would be confronting at Augsburg in the heart of Christendom that determined opposition of princes and divines who, in their support of Luther, had but recently taken the name Protestant. Within the decade, from his election as Emperor to his coronation, Charles had seen, without realizing it, that the Christian globe itself had become irrevocably severed into two hemispheres.

Servetus, whose legal studies had originally, as with Alphonse de Valdés, inclined him to favor the Emperor as at once the symbol and the executor of a united Christendom, was dismayed to see Charles humble himself before Pope Clement, who was "borne in pomp on the necks of princes . . . and adored in the open streets by all the people on bended knee, so that those who were able to kiss his feet or slippers counted themselves more fortunate than the rest, and declared that they had obtained many indulgences, and that on his account the infernal pains would be remitted for many years. O vilest of all beasts, most brazen of harlots!"[24]

Disappointed in the Emperor, Alphonse died of the plague in 1532, while John de Valdés and Servetus turned to a spiritual reform. Servetus, following the Spiritual Franciscans, predicted that the papacy would have to be destroyed as a precondition of the restoration of Christianity; he left Quintana and the imperial court, finally reaching Basel, where he lived for ten months with its Reformer John Oecolampadius. We shall overtake him there in Ch. 8.4 and John de Valdés in Naples in Ch. 21.2. We must now take note of the spiritual condition of Italy prior to the coronation and to the spread of Evangelism in Italy under Valdés' name and tutelage.

3. Stirrings of Reform and Dissent in Italy Before Valdesianism

a. The Abortive Fifth Lateran Council, 1512–1517. Numerous late medieval councils had shown the impossibility of reforming the church through its papal head. On the eve of the Reformation Era, the attempt was made to reform at least its members. The council was originally convened by Julius II (1503–1513), who, as a major Italian prince, was more disposed to expand the Papal States from the back of his war horse, in the military tradition of the pagan Julius, than to reform the apostolic see in the spirit of the first papal Julius. An initial act of the council was to move against the schismatic Council of Pisa (1511–1513) under French domination, and to abrogate the Pragmatic Sanction of Bourges.

[24] *Christianismi restitutio* (Vienne, 1553), 462; cited in Bainton, *Hunted Heretic,* 19 f.

In 1513, however, the new Pope Leo X (1513–1521) reached an understanding with Louis XII and persuaded him to drop his support of conciliarism through the instrumentality of the Council of Pisa in return for papal concessions, including the reinstatement of the cardinals degraded for supporting France at Pisa. In December 1514 the bull containing the new concordat was read in council. In 1516 the concordat itself was signed by Louis' successor, Francis I (1515–1547). It gave to the new king, instead of to the cathedral and monastic chapter as under the Pragmatic Sanction, the right to make nominations for almost all French bishoprics and archbishoprics, abbacies, and priories. Leo contented himself with the right of nominating to positions vacated through death of the incumbents while in Rome, and with the right of nomination in France itself in case the king should fail to nominate a technically qualified person within six months. This meant that Gallicanism was confirmed, but it was regal and not episcopal; and the control of the hierarchy was definitely placed in the hands of the monarch, exactly as was the case in Spain by another concordat. At the same time, Leo X condemned the conciliar theory and declared that the pope had full jurisdiction over all councils, their convocation, relocation, and adjournment.

Many had wistfully hoped for a thoroughgoing reform under Leo X, who was only thirty-seven at his elevation. Two Venetians of the Order of Camaldoli[25] had presented him with a long report, which was the most radical reform program of the conciliar era. But neither the council nor the pope was yet ready for so great a change. The reforming bull of 5 May 1514, *Supernae dispositionis arbitrio*, improved only slightly the situation in regard to the twin problems of revenue and pluralism. The Fifth Lateran Council, held in Rome under the eyes of successive popes, consisted almost entirely of Italians.

All the well-meant statements concerning a *reformatio capitis* had failed because of the lack of seriousness and decisiveness on the part of the two popes, themselves so much in need of reform.

b. Apocalypticism, Evangelism, and the New Religious Orders. After the council, the proto-Evangelical effort of a *reformatio membrorum* was resumed with special attention to conscientious prelates and parish priests. The older religious orders in Italy were likewise caught up in the reforming mood.

By contagion, the ladies of several great princely houses rose to pre-eminence for a season in their sponsorship of piety and reform throughout Italy. This reforming spirit which survived

[25] Thomas Giustiniani and Vincent Quirini.

the inconsequential Fifth Lateran Council was presently to be reinforced, among the theologically alert and the devout, in the Italian response to the German theological revolt. It is to be observed at the outset that Catholic. Evangelism in Italy, 1517–1542, which would presently go under the name of its principal abettor and spokesman as Valdesianism, was more closely related to Lutheranism than the analogous movement in Spain, which clearly antedated Luther. Besides Italian Evangelism, and the indigenous cloistral-parochial-diocesan reformation, which preceded it and then accompanied it, there was a third allied impulse in the opening quarter of the sixteenth century in Italy, namely, apocalyptic Spiritualism in the line of Joachim of Flora (d. 1202) and Jerome Savonarola (d. 1498).

In further interrelating these impulses it is pertinent to observe that Giles of Viterbo, the general of the Augustinian order and a precursor of Evangelism, had, in an apocalyptic sermon at the Fifth Lateran Council, coined also the classic formula of the Catholic idea of reformation: *"quod homines per sacra immutari fas est, non sacra per homines,"*[26] and that he had declared at the very outset of the sermon which inaugurated the council that the impending "renovation" and imminent "return to the sources" of the faith to be effected by the council seemed to him the very fulfillment of his twenty years of prophetic preaching. Not only did the council dash his hopes. It expressly condemned the itinerant preachers of apocalyptic Spiritualism,[27] of whom Giles was himself but a more refined representative! The devout and apocalyptic had henceforth in Italy to find other means for furthering their ideas.

Apocalyptic Spiritualism was the counterpart in Italy of the eccentric Illuminist apocalypticism of Brother Melchior in Spain (Ch. 1.1). The lay evangelists Johannes Baptista Italus and Francesco Meleto may be taken as representative of the swarm of inspired itinerants who prophesied the imminence of a better age, in their case to include the sudden conversion of Jews, Mohammedans, and distant pagans to the way of Christ.[28] A youthful visit to the East and a widespread prophecy that the

---

[26] Jean Hardouin, *Acta conciliorum,* IX (Paris, 1714), col. 1576.

[27] Leo's generalized opposition to apocalyptic preaching was approved by the council with only one bishop going on record in favor of preaching as the Spirit dictates. *Ibid.,* col. 1801 for the sole negative vote, and col. 1808 for Leo's specific statement on this head.

[28] Meleto appealed in his universalism to Ps. 19:6 (18:7): "And there is nothing hid from its [Christ's] heat." On Meleto and the movement which he typified, see Delio Cantimori, *Eretici Italiani del Cinquecento* (Florence, 1939), ch. ii. It is possible that Meleto and Baptista are identical.

year 1517 would mark the beginning of a major conversion of the Jews sustained them both in their apocalyptic ecumenicity. Itinerant preachers, filled with Joachimite yearnings for the age of the Spirit, they reanimated the dying echoes of Savonarola's pleas for civic righteousness, and occasionally spoke forth with classical allusions of the return of the age of gold. Condemned in general by the Lateran Council, Meleto himself was also condemned by name at the synod of Florence in 1517.[29] Baptista will tell his whole story of visions, arrests, and prophecies to the Reformers of Strassburg and summon both Luther and the Emperor's brother to penance (Ch. 10.3.a) in 1530.

Parallel to apocalyptic Spiritualism flowed the more placid stream of eleemosynary and contemplative Evangelism. It was just a year before the violent Dominican prophet Savonarola, scourging the papacy with the French rod of God's anger and the staff of his own apocalyptic indignation, was burned in Florence that there emerged in the neighboring republic of Genoa an entirely different kind of reform. It was in 1497 that the layman Ettore Vernazza established in Genoa the first of a rapidly spreading network of sodalities (*compagnie*) of Divine Love. Their original goal was charitable and devotional. The most famous *compagnia* was the Oratorio in Rome, established at the latest in 1517, as the Lateran Council came to its last session. It was made up of some sixty devout men of several walks of life.[30] A characteristic of the Oratorio and the other *compagnie* influenced by it was the stress on the editing of the patristic sources in disdainful preference to the "puddles of the neo-barbarians" (the Scholastics). This aristocratic sodality was animated by a rich spiritual discipline, by zeal for universal reform, and by a determination to fight heresy and schism with the sword of the spirit alone. When the swords of the imperial sackers of the Eternal City broke up their circle in 1527, the group in their dispersion kept in touch and invigorated with their zeal many local efforts of a kindred spirit.

Concerning the new Italian orders and reformed congregations of older orders, by far the most important development for our narrative is the ferment among the Franciscans and the rise of the Capuchin Order.

The late medieval struggle between the Conventual and the more radical Observant Franciscans had been consummated in

[29] Cantimori, *op. cit.*, 10.
[30] The Venetian Caspar Contarini, the most impassioned and irenic spokesman of Evangelism, and others long thought to have been among the members, were not. See now, Cistellini Antonio, *Figure della riforma pretridentina* (Brescia, 1948).

1517. But Pope Leo's definitive separation of the two did not
satisfy the more ardent Franciscans in their resolution to return
to the simplicities of Francis.

It is notable that the Capuchins, as before them the Observants, Spirituals, Celestines, and Clarenites, arose in the same
region of Italy, the March of Ancona. About 1525, Matthew
Serafini, of Bascio (1495–1552), desired not only to observe the
Rule of Francis to the letter but also to return to the original
garb of the saint. Coarse, brown, and provided with a pointed
cowl (*cappuccio*), it gave the reforming group their name of
Capuchins. Two brothers, Louis and Raphael, of Fossombrone,
joined Matthew Serafini as the first Capuchins. The patronage of
Evangelical Catherine Cibo, of Camerino, secured for them permission from her uncle, Clement VII, in 1526, to live as hermits
and wear their new garb.

They were devoted to poverty and to the ministry to the
poor and the sick. In their reaction to both scholasticism and
humanism, the Capuchins permitted none of their number to own
any more than three books. In 1528, in *Religionis zelus*, the pope
gave them permission to wear beards and to admit secular clerics
and laymen to their fellowship. They had to make an annual
report to the provincial chapter of the Conventual Franciscans;
and the provincial was entitled to visit them once a year. The
provincial of the Observants, John of Fano, sought to prevent
this secession, the very existence of which made the strict Observants of the Rule appear to be a second best; but he was unable
to do so and eventually joined the Capuchins himself. Victoria
Colonna, another Evangelical, in her turn used her influence with
Pope Paul III to protect the Capuchins from the aggression of the
Observants!

From the start the Capuchins were troubled by dissension.
Matthew of Bascio resigned after only two months as general, to
be succeeded by Louis of Fossombrone. He was replaced by
Bernard of Asti, who was succeeded by Bernardine Ochino, a
powerful Evangelical preacher of whom Charles V once said:
"That man is enough to make the stones weep." We shall deal
with him in Ch. 21.3.b as a major spokesman of Evangelical
Rationalism.

*c. Italian Philosophical Speculation on Immortality and the
Doctrine of the Trinity.* The only doctrinal question dealt with
by the abortive Fifth Lateran Council related to the problem of
the natural mortality of the soul.

The re-emergence of this problem, raised at this time in
humanist circles and in the medical and philosophical faculties

of the universities, was but an aspect of the general rationalism of the Italian Renaissance, which found expression, for example, in political theory and historiography (Niccolò Machiavelli and Francesco Guicciardini) and which also cropped out in another sector of doctrine, namely, in the incipient anti-Trinitarianism of certain philological, philosophical, and literary circles.

We shall take up briefly this early Italian anti-Trinitarianism after first attending to the problem of the natural mortality of the soul and the related theory of psychopannychism.

Northern Italy had been for some time prior to the Lateran Council the center of the discussion and debate over four divergent views in respect to survival after death, namely: (1) natural immortality, (2) the unconscious sleep of the soul (psychosomnolence), (3) the death of the soul with the body (thnetopsychism), and (4) the absorption of the rational soul into the universal Intellect. For reasons to be adduced later, we may embrace the second and third positions above (wherever combined with a Christian belief in the resurrection) as psychopannychism.[31] Since psychopannychism is destined to be one of the major doctrinal points at issue between John Calvin and several groups in the Radical Reformation, we appropriately take this occasion to supply the Italian background.

It was at the Council of Florence in 1439 that the Latin Church declared canonical, and thereupon temporarily imposed upon the Greek Church, a belief that had long been current in the West, namely, the belief in purgatory with the presupposition that the souls of the dead are *conscious* and are therefore capable of pain or joy even prior to the resurrection of their bodies. After the Council of Florence, fresh efforts were made to substantiate the Catholic tenet. Some of the new interest was humanistic and classical, some of it philosophical, specifically, Averroist, Thomist, and Platonic. A new impetus was given to speculation at the Academy in Florence by the Byzantine philosopher Gemistos Plethon, who brought in his own version of Platonism and indirectly stimulated others, such as Marsilio Ficino, with his use of ancient philosophy as a purifying and reforming force in the welter of late medieval religious life.

In the Platonic view, the mind that knows Truth must itself be an Idea, and as such immortal. But in the Venetian University

---

[31] The term means etymologically "the wakeful watch of the soul," but Calvin used it as a general designation for all views *not* consonant with his idea of the soul after death as capable of motion, feeling, vigor, and perception. John Calvin, *Psychopannychia*, edited by Walther Zimmerli (Leipzig, 1932), 35. See Ch. 23.1.

of Padua, where Aristotle was first taught in Greek in 1497, as also in the Universities of Ferrara and Bologna, the demonstrability of man's natural immortality was *philosophically* challenged, however firmly it might be held as an article of *revealed* truth. The Dominican Thomas de Vio (later Cardinal Gaetano), teaching at Padua, acknowledged in 1509 that Aristotle taught the mortality of the soul.

The basis of Paduan doubt was in general the prevalence of the Averroistic interpretation of Aristotle, which found no place for individual souls, but only for an eternal *rational soul,* in which each individual transiently participates. The only immortality within the Averroistic context was the impersonal absorption of the individual in the universal Intellect.

Of all the Aristotelians, it was Pietro Pomponazzi, of Mantua (1462–1524), professor successively at the Universities of Padua, Ferrara, and Bologna, who gave most clearly a new turn to the discussion in his famous *On the Immortality of the Soul* (1516), followed by his still more explicit *Apologia* (1517). Confronted by the choice between the impersonal immortality and collective Intellect of the Averroistic Aristotelians and the personal immortality promised by the Thomistic Aristotelians by their importing the doctrine of a special creation of each soul, Pomponazzi sought to safeguard the ethical dignity and the epistemological individuality of man in his natural mortality. Going back by way of the commentator Alexander of Aphrodisias to the Greek Aristotle,[32] Pomponazzi maintained that it was clearly possible to demonstrate by natural reason not only the mortality of the soul but also its individuality and dignity despite its transience. Each human being enjoys a unique place between the animals and the angels by virtue of his capacity for reflective knowledge and for ethical decisions in terms of universal concepts. In so far as the soul, operating through the whole body, is a mean between the mortal and the immortal, it may be said to participate in a temporary "immortality." Pomponazzi maintained that his philosophical views, mere deductions of human reason, were transcended by the divine revelation of a resurrection to come and needed to cause no ecclesiastical offense.

The received ecclesiastical view (now being challenged by Pomponazzi and his contemporaries with even more finality than by the Averroists) could not, of course, be content with an even-

---

[32] Aristotelians were divided in this period between the followings, respectively, of the two principal commentators on Aristotle—the Alexandrines and the Averroists. *On Immortality* is edited in translation in *The Renaissance Philosophy of Man,* by Ernst Cassirer *et al.* (Chicago, 1948), V.

tual resurrection from the dead; it insisted that each created soul, as the substantial form of the body, was capable of existing sentiently prior to the resurrection. This importation of natural theology into Catholic dogma was, in point of fact, much closer to Platonic philosophy than to the Bible. But the natural immortality of the soul had become so integral a part of the massive penitential and liturgical structure of Catholic moral theology that the philosophical threat to it moved Leo X, in the first year of his pontificate, to condemn in 1513, at the eighth session of the Fifth Lateran Council, the philosophical proofs and disproofs of immortality in the universities (*in universitatibus studiorum generalium*) and academic circles. Appealing to passages in Matthew and John and to the Clementine constitution against the Franciscan Peter Olivi at the Council of Vienne (1311), Leo's council asserted that the soul is naturally immortal and, as the substantial form of the body, is susceptible both of the pains of hell and purgatory and the bliss of paradise. The famous *Apostolici regiminis* reads in part:

In these our days . . . the sower of tares, the ancient enemy of the human race, has dared to sow and foster in the field of the Lord certain very pernicious errors, always rejected by the faithful, especially as to the nature of the reasonable soul (*anima rationalis*), that it is mortal, or one and the same in all men; and some, rashly philosophizing, declare this to be true, at least according to philosophy. Desiring to employ remedies appropriate to such a plague, We, with the approbation of the sacred council, condemn and reprobate all those who assert that the intellectual soul (*anima intellectiva*) is mortal, or one and the same in all men, and those who call these things in question, seeing that the soul is not only truly, and of itself, and essentially the form of the human body . . . but likewise is immortal, and, according to the number of bodies into which it is infused, singularly multipliable, multiplied, and to be multiplied. This manifestly appears from the gospel [Matt. 10:28], seeing that our Lord says, "They cannot kill the soul," and elsewhere [John 12:25], "He who hateth his soul in this world," etc., and also because he promises eternal rewards and eternal torments to those who are to be judged according to their merit in this life. . . .[33]

After the Fifth Lateran Council, a number of Catholic theologians continued the theme.

The key to the tangle of the Florentine Platonist, Paduan

[33] The text is printed in Mansi, *Concilia*, XXXII, coll. 842 f. See the presentation by F. Vernet in *DThC*, VIII:2, coll. 268 ff., and the discussion of A. Denifle (Catholic) vs. C. Stange (Protestant), contending that the purpose here of papal theology was not to prove by philosophical reasoning that the soul is immortal but, rather, to assert it as a dogma of the faith, in *Scholastik*, VIII (1933), 359–379.

Averroist, and papal definitions is furnished by the assertion of Pomponazzi that immortality cannot be proved philosophically, but can only be accepted on ecclesiastical authority.

The acceptance of the philosophical disproof of immortality combined with a vindication of life after death on the strength of revelation will be the mark of a hitherto largely unnoticed circle of Italian Evangelicals. Within the philosophical framework of the two Paduan conceptions of the soul's natural mortality (Averroist absorption in the collective Intellect and Pomponazzi's virtuous mortality), they will seek to rehabilitate the New Testament postulate (cf. I Thess. 4:13) of the death (thnetopsychism) or the unconscious sleep of the soul (psychosomnolence) in a lively expectation of the imminent resurrection of the virtuous, or, in other cases, the resurrection of both the virtuous and the wicked (the latter merely to hear the Final Judgment of Christ and thereupon to disappear). In either version, the Catholic system, with its purgatory, Masses for the dead, and penitential discipline, will be undermined.

Psychopannychism may be considered the Italian counterpart of Germanic solafideism and Swiss predestinarianism in contributing to the dismantlement of the medieval structures of sacramental grace and thus weakening, at the very outset of the Reformation Era, the grip of the papacy on the souls of men. It is for this reason that we have given attention to psychopannychism near the outset of our narrative of the Radical Reformation, because the discussion of the problem of immortality and the relationship of the soul to the body in the Fifth Lateran Council was symptomatic of the same kind of unrest in the Romance lands which broke out in Germany in connection with the indulgence system. Early representatives of psychopannychism and the apocalyptic eschatology connected with it were Camillo Renato and Michael Servetus. For the most part, Catholics and Protestants in the Reformation Era held to the *natural* immortality of the soul. But Martin Luther (for a portion of his reforming career and even then ambiguously), many of the Anabaptists (but not all the Swiss Brethren), some of the Spiritualists (including the Libertines), and later the Socinians constitute an important exception in adhering to psychopannychism. We shall have several occasions to refer to this recurrent feature of the Radical Reformation, the eschatologically undergirded doctrine of the sleep or the temporary death of the soul pending the resurrection.

Not only psychopannychism but also anti-Trinitarianism was to find its fullest ecclesiastical expression in Polish Socinianism and Hungarian Unitarianism. The leaders of these two parallel and closely interrelated movements, which we shall take up in Ch. 25 and elsewhere, were Italians or palpably dependent upon Italians. Although Servetus is commonly appealed to as the fountainhead of anti-Trinitarianism, it is well at this point in our narrative to take note of early indigenous Italian critics known to have directly influenced the later Radicals.

Lorenzo Valla, the exemplar of Italian philological rationalism, who exposed as a forgery the Donation of Constantine, also raised difficulties in respect to the formulation of the doctrine of the Trinity, especially in reference to Boethius' *De elegantiis linguae Latinae* (1442).[34] Laelius Socinus was later to cite the pertinent passage.[35]

Of perhaps even greater influence was the Arianizing tendency of the Florentine Academy under Savonarola's contemporary, the priest and Platonist, Marsilio Ficino (d. 1499), who in working on the Demiurge of the *Timaeus* was reminded of the close parallel with the Logos in the Prologue to John's Gospel and suggested a "Platonic" subordinationism. It was Cardinal Caspar Contarini who first pointed out the Arianizing tendency of the Platonic Academy, made up of *"sectatores complures homines doctos."*[36]

In reacting humanistically to the stylistic poverty of the Vulgate, Ficino made bold to translate *Verbum* as *sermo*, thereby sloughing off the whole traditional conception of Christ as the Eternal Word (*Logos, Verbum*) in a philosophical sense as the Mind and Instrument of God, and substituting the idea of Christ as merely the voice of God. Although Ficino, basing his thought allegedly on Paul, wrote of approaching the preached *sermo* with the same reverence as the Eucharistic *corpus*, he had started a train of thought that would equate the Word with the prophetic *vox* of the Old Testament, and even with rational *meditatio* and literary *scripta*, and which would inevitably render philosophically difficult the traditional conception of the Logos-Son as consubstantial with the Father. The usage of Ficino reappears in Erasmus (already noted in Ch. 1.2) and later in Sebastian Castellio, and in both Laelius and Faustus Socinus. Where the

---

[34] *Op. cit.* (Lyons, 1540), vi, 33, pp. 420–422; (Basel, 1540), 215.

[35] *Theses de filio Dei et Trinitate,* edited by Delio Cantimori in *Per la Storia degli Eretici Italiani del Secolo XVI in Europa* (Rome, 1937), 57 ff.; cf. Cantimori, *Eretici,* 239.

[36] Contarini, *Opera* (Paris, 1571), p. 550; noted and interpreted in a larger context by Delio Cantimori, "Anabattismo e Neoplatonismo nel XVI Secolo in Italia," Reale Accademia Nazionale dei Lincei, *Rendiconti della Classe di Scienze morali, storiche e filologiche,* Serie VI, XII (1936).

fathers had hypostasized the Logos as an eternal Person of the Godhead, the Radical Reformers in the tradition of Ficino will presently declare themselves unwilling to prolong the voice of God eternally and will instead insist upon Christ as wholly human but authoritative in his resonating echo of all the prophetic voices that had gone before and as the definitive allocution of God to all generations after him.

Moving about the circumference of the Empire, we have observed several rivulets of thought in Spain and Italy destined to join the churning vortex of the Radical Reformation, which was centered in Germany. We have taken note of psychopanny-chism; of an incipient anti-Trinitarianism represented by Ficino, Erasmus, and Servetus, resulting from the critical philological approach to the texts developed by Lorenzo Valla; of a disposition in John de Valdés to change the stress in the traditional formulation of the doctrine of the atonement; of a partly fused rationalistic (philological), apocalyptic, and "Joachimite" Spiritualism, of which Camillo Renato and Faustus Socinus will prove to be the most daring representatives; and of a pacifistic and tolerant mood, as with Erasmus, in Catholic Evangelism wherever it has appeared.[37]

We turn now to the Netherlands, where sacramentarianism, another ingredient of the Radical Reformation connected with Erasmus, had been endemic for centuries.

[37] The further sorting of this complex of tendencies in Italy will be selectively worked out in the Harvard Ph.D. thesis in progress by John Tedeschi.

CHAPTER 2

THE NETHERLANDISH SACRAMENTISTS
FROM WESSEL GANSFORT TO HINNE RODE

To go from Pomponazzi and psychopannychism in Italy to Wessel Gansfort and sacramentarianism in the Netherlands is not a standard transition in the historiography of the Reformation Era, nor to go back in time from the imperial coronation at Bologna in 1530 to the alterations in sacramental theology of the Brethren of the Common Life. But in a fresh account of the Radical Reformation, it is well to break away from the stereotyped fixation on the revolt against the Lutheran view of Spirit and Word (fanaticism) or against the medieval view of the sacrament of Baptism (anabaptism) as the first signs of radicalism.

We have briefly examined in Northern Italy the undermining of the elaborate medieval structure of indulgences and Masses for the dead implied in the philosophical repudiation of natural immortality and the concurrent reassertion of the Biblical teaching of soul sleep, or even death of the soul, prior to the general resurrection. We now turn to a development, indigenous to the Netherlands, which likewise sapped the Mass of its redemptive significance, the revolt against the sacrament of the altar as a repetitive sacramental sacrifice.

An articulate tradition of opposition to the doctrine of transubstantiation and the whole theology of, and devotional practices relating to, the sacrament of the altar was, in the Netherlands, called by the horrified ecclesiastical and magisterial authorities, somewhat misleadingly, "sacramentarianism," and its proponents "Sacramentists." A *sacramentarius* in the medieval period was one who held theologically that *any* of the sacraments was merely a sign involving no alteration either in the sacramental *res* (for example, the Eucharistic bread) or in the recipient (for example, the baptizand or ordinand). But the designation *sacramentarius* had come to mean primarily an opponent of the doctrine of the objective presence of the Eucharistic Christ in the sacrament of the altar.

In Dutch, the terms *sacramentisten* and *sacramentariërs* are used interchangeably. Henceforth, however, we shall make a distinction in English between the equivalents of these terms, using the former, "Sacramentists," to designate the Netherlandish group who held this doctrine and, *in addition,* certain other distinctive, related views, while we shall reserve the term "sacramentarians" solely in reference to the Lord's Supper and hence for those in and out of the Netherlands who held to a purely commemorative view of the Supper.

Luther and his followers designated as "sacramentarians" Andreas Bodenstein von Carlstadt, exiled from Wittenberg; Ulrich Zwingli, in Zurich; and Oecolampadius, in Basel. Since it was Zwingli who became, in the end, the outstanding spokesman for the view, the Sacramentists in the Netherlands were, in time, themselves often called Zwinglians; and, to compound the confusion of nomenclature, they were often, after 1517, called by the Netherlandish Catholic authorities even "Lutherans." But, of course, on precisely their attitude toward the sacrament of the altar the Netherlandish Sacramentists were a world apart from the consubstantiationist of Wittenberg. We shall endeavor to rectify and stabilize the appellations. The very fact that the Magisterial Reformation in Switzerland adopted the view of the Sacramentists as its own has tended to remove them from the general narrative of the Radical Reformation, to which they are now, up to a point, being restored.

It has long been recognized that the religious evolution of the Netherlands must be seen as moving from a late medieval Sacramentism, to about 1530; through Anabaptism, to about 1568; to the ascendancy of Calvinism thereafter. The endemic sacramentarianism of the Netherlands may indeed go far to explain why the Dutch were unable to accept the Reformation in its Lutheran form and eventually cast their lot with Calvinism.

The Sacramentists originally preferred for themselves the designation "Evangelicals" (*evangelischen*), analogous to, though probably not dependent on, Evangelism in the Romance lands, and have been, by modern scholarship, grouped with the Biblical humanists called also the Netherlandish "national-reformed."[1]

---

[1] Laurentius Knappert, *De opkomst van het Protestantisme* (The Hague, 1908), himself building on the work of J. G. de Hoop Scheffer, *Geschiedenis der Kerkhervorming in Nederland van haar opstaan tot 1531* (Amsterdam, 1873); J. Lindeboom, *De confessioneele ontwikkeling der reformatie in de Nederlanden* (The Hague, 1946), 34 ff.; J. Alton Templin is presently engaged in writing his Harvard Ph.D. thesis, "The Sacramentists in the Netherlands."

The Sacramentists of the Reformation Era were not always organized in conventicles, but they were aware of each other and mutually reinforced each other in time of persecution and in the hour of execution.

It is quite possible that Sacramentism in the Netherlands, rather than an outgrowth of skepticism, was the unwitting consequence of an earlier and excessive devotion to the sacrament of the altar, which induced a belief in the existence of and participation in the sacrament quite apart from a physical eating of the Host. Medieval theologians called this "spiritual communion," especially important in time of plague, famine, or isolation, but valid also in normal circumstances for the pious layman in his devotional exercises apart from the priestly ministrations. Along with this devout spiritualization of the sacrament, there was a prophetic-iconoclastic, even crude and libertarian, sacramentism which could be intermingled with the contemplative form in the later stages of the evolution of the two trends. Since the earnest sacramentarians could appeal to the Old Testament for sanction in their violence against alleged idolatry, it is never clear whether the scanty documentation from the inquisitorial chamber is describing an episode or movement nurtured by Augustinian-Johannine symbolism and Biblical humanism or prompted by the vagaries of a charismatically led, anticlerical iconoclasm. Sacramentarianism probably found different expressions in different classes.

The role of the religious sodalities and particularly of the chambers of rhetoric (*rederijkerskamers*) needs further investigation.[2] These were the rhetorical societies organized by the burghers for the festive celebrations of local saints and major events of the liturgical year, including the annual procession of the Corpus Christi. With a priest attached, with morality plays written and literary pieces delivered, the chambers were centers of fellowship which brought together contestants from all over the Burgundian realm in the annual *juwelen*. Without advancing an explanation, we may simply note that many Sacramentists and, later, Anabaptists were in some stage of their careers *rederijkers*.

The rise of sacramentarianism is surely as important in an account of the Radical Reformation as the emergence of antipedobaptism. The fact that sacramentarianism deprived one sacrament of its sacrificatory character *ex opere operato* and that anabaptism in contrast gave enhanced prominence to another

[2] See a preliminary sketch by Leonard Verduin, "The Chambers of Rhetoric and Anabaptist Origins in the Low Countries," *MQR*, XXXIV (1960), 192–196; for representative pieces, Leendert Meeuwis van Dis, *Reformatorische Rederijkerspelen uit de eerst helft van de zestiende eeuw* (Haarlem, 1937).

should not obscure the spiritualizing trait common to both processes. Moreover, in the alteration of the role of the two sacraments as *believers'* baptism and a *commemorative* communion, the two ordinances were brought close together in much the same eschatological joy and expectancy as in the pre-Constantinian church, when the bishop presided over an elaborate baptismal exorcism and ablution of converts that led directly to the paschal communion. With the ecclesiological shift in the role of the two sacraments in the Radical Reformation, a change took place also in the inherited views concerning the theology of justification, sanctification, the atonement, and the church, as we shall presently see.

1. MEDIEVAL SACRAMENTISM

For the rougher impulse in Netherlandish sacramentarianism, we cannot go all the way back in detail to the notorious heresiarch Tanchelm (d. 1115 or 1124), who exhorted his vast and devoted following not to partake of the sacrament of the priests, which he called a pollution, and not to heed the priests and bishops, nor to pay them tithes. He laid claim to being himself divine, through having the Spirit, and encouraged his followers, through a simulated marriage with an image of the Virgin, to suppose that their spokesman for a free (libertine) apostolic church sustained a special relationship to the Queen of heaven.[3] The fact that he crudely denounced the sacrament of the altar, that in the same area several priests and laymen in a more earnest spirit could renounce the official views of both the sacrament of the altar and pedobaptism,[4] and that Tanchelm could rally such multitudes of followers prepared to defend him with drawn swords, shows at once the antiquity and the extent of the sacramentarian impulse in the Netherlands. It must suffice to say that the whole bishopric of Utrecht (covering most of present-day Holland) might have defected had it not been for the tireless zeal of Norbert of Xanten, and that the first Sacramentist martyr in the Reformation Era (one Wendelmoet Claesdochter, Ch. 12.1) in the folk tradition of Tanchelm was as vituperative as she was brave.

The milder and devout form of sacramentarianism may be best represented by Wessel Gansfort (c. 1420–1489), whose *De sacra-*

---

[3] *Corpus documentorum inquisitionis Neerlandicae,* edited by Paul Frédéricq, I (Ghent/The Hague, 1889), 15 ff.
[4] Ivoy (now in the French department, Ardennes). *Ibid.,* 19, under date of 1112

mento eucharistiae[5] is the first major link in the chain of development, or recrudescence, of symbolist Eucharistic theology.

Trained at Deventer in the school of the Brethren of the Common Life and the *Devotio Moderna,* Gansfort was a bosom friend of Thomas à Kempis. While in his early twenties, Gansfort went to Cologne, where he learned about the sacramental theology of Rupert of Deutz (d. 1129 or 1135) and especially his doctrine of impanation. Rupert's doctrine that Christ would have become incarnate even if Adam had not fallen recurs in Gansfort, who copied out from Rupert:

We receive [in the Eucharist] the true divinity and humanity of Christ, who sitteth and reigneth in heaven, just as we may obtain the true spark of fire almost daily from the sun by the use of a small magnifying glass.

And elsewhere:

Unto him who has no faith except in the visible form of the bread and the wine, no benefit comes from the sacrifice; just as an ass, pricking up his unreasoning ears at the sound of a lyre, does indeed hear the sound but not the melody of the song.[6]

So much, directly from Rupert. Gansfort's doctrine of the atonement in terms of the cosmic struggle between the Lamb and the Dragon[7] was undoubtedly also influenced by Rupert's *De victoria Verbi Dei,*[8] wherein Rupert, holding that the Eucharist is no less necessary than baptism for redemption, declared that Christ descended into Hades for three days and three nights in order that the departed saints might receive his body, *in miro modo in illa specie, qua pependit in cruce.*[9] Whereas in the ancient church Christians considered themselves redeemed through baptism, Gansfort makes the sacrament of the Eucharist central and apparently the exclusive sacramental means of appropriating the grace of the redemptive action of Christ:

It is not by corruptible gold and silver, but by the precious blood of the Lamb, that we have been ransomed. . . from the hand of Satan, from destruction, from all the evil effect of our guilt and punishment;

---

[5] There is an English translation of *De sacramento eucharistiae* in Edward W. Miller and Jared W. Scudder, *Wessel Gansfort: Life and Writings* (New York/London, 1917), II, 1–70.

[6] Miller and Scudder, *Gansfort,* I, 55 f.; II, 320 and in general.

[7] *De causis, mysteriis et effectibus Dominicae incarnationis et passionis,* translated in Miller and Scudder, *Gansfort,* II, 109–147. Gansfort actually speaks of the incarnation as the fulfillment or completion of Christ.

[8] Migne, *Patrologia Latina* (henceforth: *PL*), 169, col. 1472c.

[9] We shall encounter this idea in the form of a Eucharistic *descensus* in Caspar Schwenckfeld and Servetus.

but how are we ransomed by his blood except by partaking of his blood and flesh through faith and piety born of faith? But how does such piety do its duty except through the degrees of increasing affection, until Christ shall have been fully found in us?[10]

Gansfort, of course, avows the doctrine of transubstantiation. The bread and wine become the body and blood of the Lord through being consecrated by the priest. This may be taken unto one's salvation if received worthily, or unto one's death if received unworthily. But there is a second inward and superior sacramental action, the sacrament received by the inner man, his faithful *commemoratio* of the fact that Christ has died for him personally[11] as he eats the flesh and blood of Christ spiritually. This inward rumination involves his intellect, will, and mind in recalling the life, precepts, and examples of Christ. Thus the more efficacious reception of the body and blood of Christ comes with the commemoration of him:

His memorial consists in the remembrance of him. The remembrance of his marvelous works provides food for them that fear him, because he that gives them food causes them to remember his marvelous works.[12]

He who believes in Christ truly eats his flesh. Stressing in combination John 3:36: "He who believes in the Son has eternal life," and ch. 6:54: "He who eats my flesh and drinks my blood has eternal life," and holding that it is in the second alone, the inward eucharist, that the *layman* receives both the flesh and the blood, Gansfort is prepared to write quite naturally of a Eucharist before the incarnation, not in type but in truth: "Hence, before the incarnation, the angels did eat his flesh, even as did the fathers in the wilderness through the spirit of the Son."[13] Even for Christians since the incarnation the spiritual sacrament is not dependent upon the physical bread at all: "Those who believe (*credere*) on him are they that eat (*edere*) his flesh." He goes on:

Now it is openly acknowledged that holy hermits had that life, though they hid in caves so many years. Therefore, Paul, the first hermit, did eat of the flesh of the Son of man even during the time when he did not see a single human being, not to speak of a priest,

---

[10] *De sacramento eucharistiae, loc. cit.,* 37 f. A major study of the whole of his theology is that of Maarten van Rhijn, *Wessel Gansfort* (The Hague, 1917).

[11] *De sacramento eucharistiae, loc. cit.,* 39; analyzed by van Rhijn, *Gansfort,* 213 ff. The distinctions modify and yet preserve Augustine's distinction between the bread of the Lord and the bread which is the Lord.

[12] *De sacramento eucharistiae, loc. cit.,* 59.

[13] *Ibid.,* 51.

celebrating the sacrament. But he did eat of it because he believed; and because he believed he frequently remembered; because he remembered he carefully considered; because he considered he ruminated; because he ruminated he tasted that it was sweet; because he tasted that it was sweet he desired; because he desired he hungered and thirsted; because he hungered and thirsted he knew that it was sweeter than honey and the honeycomb, he panted for it, he esteemed, he loved it, he pined with love, he was wounded by love for it.[14]

Indeed, it can be received by anyone, at any time, in any place, and hence can be said to be superior to the bread of the altar, which is confined to a particular place and time. Gansfort makes his point memorably, though without theological precision, when he recounts the story of a priest caught in an Alpine snowstorm and nourished through the winter by licking a stone after first observing, in his fatigue, several snakes doing the same. After his rescue in April, repeated searches for the nutritive Stone were in vain. The story obscurely implied that the concentrated remembrance of Christ, the Stone which the builders rejected, who himself in the wilderness refused the temptation to turn a stone into bread (Luke 4:3), sufficed for both physical and spiritual nourishment.[15] With all Gansfort's stress upon the superiority of *commemoratio* over physical *manducatio,* in a life of increasing Christlikeness in *philanthropia* and fraternal love[16] it was not much of a step to dispense with the priest and the Eucharistic elements altogether. This was the way of the Sacramentists, who stressed the commemorative Supper and turned decisively from the sacrificatory Mass and the doctrine of transubstantiation.[17]

On the eve of the Reformation Era the Eucharistic views of Gansfort, as well as overt sacramentarianism, which he himself, of course, would have disowned, must have widely permeated the Low Countries.

As early as the year 1510, a Dominican friar, one Wouter in Utrecht, made sharp criticism of the traditional practices,[18] though he temporarily recanted. Beginning in the year 1514, a Frisian priest, Gellius Faber, began to preach discreetly in a sacramentarian spirit, but would not leave the Old Church until the same

[14] *Ibid.,* 31.

[15] How the snakes could be included in the saving ordinance is not intruded into the story. *De sacramento eucharistiae, loc. cit.,* 39 f.

[16] *Ibid.,* 22, 32.

[17] These ideas bear some affinity to the *Imitatio Christi* (III, xiii, 1–2), which does not, however, transfer the idea of the flesh of Christ to the realm of personal meditation, as with Wessel.

[18] Frédéricq, *Corpus,* I, 497.

year in which Menno Simons would be making his break.[19]

The most notable exponent of the moderate position was, of course, Erasmus, whose deep familiarity with Augustinian symbolism and the primitive usages and pristine interpretations of the Supper as recorded in the Greek text of the New Testament prompted him to go farther than Gansfort in minimizing the importance of the real presence of scholastic theory and in affirming the identity of *credere* and *edere*. He contrasted the *pietas perfecta* of commemoration and the *pietas imperfecta* of the liturgical re-presentation of the body and the sacrifice.

Erasmus, to be sure, like Gansfort, affirmed the *corporea praesentia Christi* of the liturgical *repraesentatio,* but for him its saving efficacy was determined by the degree to which it could bring about the psychological process in the believer of commemorating the objective transaction of the cross.[20] Erasmus tended thus to free the faithful from the physical consumption at the Mass and to replace it with a spiritual communion. Thus the emphasis is no longer on the *corporea praesentia Christi* as such, but on the mystical and ethical appropriation of the saving Word of God. Erasmus stressed, in fact, the uselessness of the solely physical presence of Christ: Judas was close enough to him actually to kiss him. Erasmus was primarily interested in the cognitive and ethical appreciation of Christ, which alone was redemptive, although this inner appropriation might well be fostered by the *corporea praesentia Christi* at the Mass.

Besides the still nominally Catholic position of Erasmus, a view much more radical and outspoken in relation to the Catholic sacrament of the altar, in the tradition of the iconoclasts, is also documented on the threshold of the Reformation Era. In 1517, a certain Torreken van der Perre was lashed and otherwise disciplined at Oudenaarde for blaspheming the Blessed Sacrament; in 1518, at Brussels, one Lauken van Moeseke was racked for twelve days, had his tongue bored, and was thereupon decapitated for the same offense; and in 1519, at Antwerp, a house-

---

[19] In 1536. Faber joined the Sacramentist, "Zwinglian" wing of the Magisterial Reformation in the Low Countries and became in the end one of Menno's principal antagonists (Ch. 19.2). De Hoop Scheffer is responsible for fixing the date 1514, *op. cit.,* 59–61. Though challenged by K. Vos on the ground that Faber's name does not appear among the priests listed for the archbishopric of Utrecht, 1505–1518, J. Reitsma and J. Lindeboom place Faber's evangelical preaching as early as 1510; *Geschiedenis van de Hervorming der Nederlanden* (The Hague, 1949), 28.

[20] Gottfried Krodel, "Die Abendmahlslehre des Erasmus von Rotterdam und seine Stellung am Anfang des Abendmahlsstreites der Reformatoren," unpublished doctoral dissertation, Erlangen, 1955, esp. pp. 89–90, 91, 96–98.

wife, Kathelyne, suffered the somewhat less severe punishment of a pilgrimage to Rome for the same blasphemy.[21]

The commingling of the two sacramentarian streams, represented latterly by Torreken and Erasmus, constitutes the background of the Loist, the Libertine, in due course the Melchiorite, and the "national-reformed" ferment in the Netherlands, centering in dissatisfaction with the official sacramental theology. We shall also see the extent to which the Eucharistic theologies (and Christology) of Clement Ziegler and Melchior Hofmann (Ch. 11), of Carlstadt (Ch. 3.1) and Caspar Schwenckfeld (Ch. 5.5), draw respectively upon the same two or analogous currents of late medieval and Biblicohumanistic thought, the one expressing itself in iconoclastic fury against the adoration of the Host as idolatry, the other finding intense redemptive satisfaction in devout abstraction from the Host.

2. CORNELIUS HOEN AND HINNE RODE

In 1517 the Sacramentist Wouter again spoke out, discarded his friar's garb, and traveled through Holland, preaching "the truth of the gospel." This "Lutheran monk" fled to Strassburg around 1521, and may have shared his convictions with the gardener-preacher Clement Ziegler, a major figure in the rise of Strassburg sectarianism (Ch. 11.4). In any event, Wouter awakened an evangelical spirit in many of his Netherlandish adherents, among whom were Cornelius Hoen, John Sartorius, John de Bakker, and William Gnapheus, and largely opened the way for the still more radical sacramentarianism of the Anabaptists. At Delft, where Wouter lived for a time, a regular congregation of evangelical Sacramentists was organized, persisting well into the century.

Among the early Sacramentists, Cornelius Hoen, lawyer at the court of Holland at The Hague, may have heard Wouter's preaching in Delft as early as 1510. Emerging as an important mediator and formulator of the radical, or commemorative, Eucharistic theology, he credited Wouter with giving him "the sense of truth" around 1517, after he had read Gansfort, Erasmus, and Luther.

A major link in the chain of development in sacramentarian thought was Hoen's coming into contact with Gansfort's library. One Jacob Hoeck, canon and deacon at Naaldwijk and pastor in

---

[21] Frédéricq, *Corpus*, I, 514 f., 517 f. There are other instances on either side of the date 1517 preserved in the more recently edited Belgian martyrologies and local histories by A. L. E. Verheyden.

Wassenaar, a close friend and correspondent of Gansfort,[22] bequeathed his own library to a Martin Dorp, his nephew. Dorp, who had been professor of theology at Louvain since 1514, chose Hoen, a friend from student days (at the Hieronymus School of Utrecht), to examine the library for him. In it, Hoen found some of Gansfort's manuscripts, among them *De sacramento eucharistiae.* Hoen was fascinated by it and immediately shared the ideas with Dorp and their friends. Thereupon he proceeded to form his own more radical view of the Lord's Supper. It was decided that Gansfort's writings should be brought to the attention of Luther. For the undertaking, Hoen wrote his own *Epistola Christiana admodum,*[23] setting forth his view of the Lord's Supper as symbolic, with the word *est* meaning "signifies" in the crucial Eucharistic phrase of Matt. 26:26 and the canon of the Mass: *"Hoc est corpus meum."*

Hoen, concentrating on Gansfort's *commemoratio* and the inward superior sacrament, rejected transubstantiation and held that the Supper is a meal which signifies the promise of Christ to be with his followers. The meal was likened to a wedding ceremony (as with Gansfort) in which the bridegroom, Christ, gives his ring, the bread, as a pledge to his collective bride, the church, the one ever to belong to the other. Rejecting all other lovers, Christ and the covenanted member cling only to each other. The ring image derives from the parable of the prodigal son (Luke 15: 20–23), who received successively from his rejoicing father a kiss, a robe, a ring, new shoes, and a meal. Tertullian had long ago allegorized the robe as the garment of joy (the Holy Spirit), the ring as baptism, and the fatted calf as the Eucharist.[24] Though Hoen, the Dutch lawyer, unlike Tertullian, connected the ring with the bread of Communion, he may well have been influenced at this point by the lawyer-theologian of ancient North Africa.

Hoen goes on to say that the believer who trusts in the death of Christ as redemptive truly eats his flesh and drinks his blood. Indeed, Jesus himself says in John, ch. 6, that he is the bread of life and whoever believes in him abides in him. Jesus was saying by this that the one who believes in him has the true bread, Christ himself. The Scripture nowhere speaks of the miracle of transubstantiation, of which the Roman scholastics make so

[22] Albert Hardenberg, the biographer of Wessel Gansfort, records the events which brought Hoen into the history of the sacramentarians. The bulk of the *Vita* is translated in Miller and Scudder, *Gansfort,* II, 317–344.
[23] Edited by A. Eekhof, *De Avondmaalsbrief van Cornelis Hoen* (The Hague, 1917), and more recently in *CR,* XCI, 505 ff.
[24] In *De pudicia.*

much. The apostles did not say that Jesus gave them his literal blood and flesh. Even if he had done so himself, this would not give the priests power to do the same. Rather, Christ is seen and worshiped only in faith. He is not in the bread. Indeed, he sent the Paraclete for the very reason that he could not be corporally among his followers. The bread "signifies" his body. One can no more say that Christ is literally bread than that he is substantially a vine or a door. These are metaphors, not literal realities. Thus, there must be a distinction between the bread which is eaten and the Christ who is received by faith. Hoen argues that Christ has already given himself for men on the cross. On Calvary his body was offered up for the world. In anticipation of this action, he had instituted the Supper. But the commemorative elements are Christ only in the sense that the ring is the bridegroom—the covenantal dedication and the divine love are present with the signs thereof.

Though Hoen could speak of Christ's "offering" himself, he meant this, not in the sense of a sacrifice for sin, but in the same sense that the betrothed pair "offer" themselves to each other in marriage. Having rejected the penitential theology of the medieval church, Hoen found no place for a continuing sacrifice on the altar. Instead, the repetitively sacrificial, expiatory Mass has become a commemorative Supper, almost, as it were, a nuptial feast at which the pledge of faith and love is proclaimed. No longer is the atonement the commercial transaction of a ransom, but the covenantal transaction of a betrothal.

Hoen very much wished to share his discovery with Luther and get his judgment, but because of Hoen's advanced age, Hinne Rode, rector of the school of the Brethren in Utrecht, was chosen to make the journey instead.[25] Early in 1521, Rode carried with him the works of Gansfort which had come from Hoeck's library, others of Gansfort's acquired from the St. Agnes Cloister of Zwolle, and the *Epistola* of Hoen. Rode arrived in Wittenberg in late winter and left the works there in order that Luther could examine them and perhaps have them published.

Returning to Utrecht, Rode was soon dismissed from his office *"propter Lutherum."* We shall next meet him in Switzerland (Ch. 5.1).[26]

---

[25] Otto Clemen has succeeded in establishing an order of chronology for the events. "Hinne Rode in Wittenberg, Basel, Zürich und die frühesten Ausgaben Wesselscher Schriften," *Zeitschrift für Kirchengeschichte* (henceforth: *ZKG*), XVIII (1897), 346–372.

[26] Clemen observes that *"propter Lutherum"* in this case probably means "because of his contact with Luther."

Chapter 3

LUTHERAN SPIRITUALISTS:
CARLSTADT AND MÜNTZER

When Hinne Rode arrived in Wittenberg, he found Luther about to depart for his momentous appearance at Worms on 18 April 1521 before Charles at his first imperial diet.[1] The great episodes in the startling emergence of Luther, around whom titanic forces of destruction and renewal were surging, were vividly etched in the memories of all: the ninety-five theses on the indulgence system of 31 October 1517; the Leipzig disputation with John Eck, 27 June to 16 July 1519; the three great Reformation tracts, *To the Christian Nobility, On the Babylonian Captivity,* and *The Freedom of the Christian Man,* of August, October, and November 1520; and Luther's festive burning, on the morning of 10 December 1520, of the papal bull threatening him with excommunication, along with a copy of the canon law. In the excitement of these days, Rode must have felt himself privileged to receive any attention at all from Luther as to the merit of the works of Gansfort. Luther would surely have reacted emphatically against Hoen's interpretation of Gansfort's Eucharistic theology in the *Epistola.*[2] On 2 April, Luther, with a safe-conduct and accompanied by Nicholas Amsdorf and others, set out for Worms to stand against the Emperor.

With a papal bull of excommunication over him, *Dicet Romanum pontificem* of 3 January 1521, reinforced at Worms by the imperial ban signed by Charles on 26 May, Luther was

---

[1] Otto Clemen, *loc. cit.,* 357; A. Eekhof, *op. cit.,* xiv; van Rhijn, *Gansfort,* 259; and Hermann Barge, *Andreas Bodenstein von Carlstadt* (Leipzig, 1905), II, 150 n., all agree that Luther was still in Wittenberg when Rode arrived.

[2] This is a conjecture from the way in which Zwingli later worded the title page of the letter when he had it printed in 1525, *"apud quem omne iudicium sacrae scripturae fuit"* and from a subsequent letter of Zwingli to Luther: *"die epistel Honii . . . , von dero du wol weist."* Eekhof, *op. cit.,* xiv.

whisked off by his protector Frederick to live as Junker Jörg at the Wartburg. While Luther was occupying himself in seclusion for ten months with the translation of Erasmus' Greek text of the New Testament into German, the reform in Wittenberg was mainly in the hands of Andreas Bodenstein of Carlstadt.

1. CARLSTADT AND THE FIRST "PROTESTANT" COMMUNION

Carlstadt (so he was generally called) must have taken an interest in the Gansfort material and Hoen's letter, and may have been instrumental in having a selection of Gansfort's manuscripts, including *De sacramento eucharistiae,* published as a *Farrago*[3] in the first months of 1522.

Carlstadt (?1480–1541), a student at Erfurt and Cologne, came as a thoroughgoing Thomist to the University of Wittenberg (professor, 1505–1522). Within two years he had been elected dean of the faculty of arts, out of recognition for his first publication, *De intentionibus,* wherein he laboriously defended the reality of universals against the *Moderni.* By 1510 he had become a doctor of theology. Already a canon of the Castle Church of All Saints (*Allerheiligenstift*), he was now advanced to the second highest position therein, archdeacon. The Elector Frederick the Wise, enlarging the ancient foundation of his Saxon house both out of his interest in the relics and from concern for the economic enhancement of his newly founded university (1502), encouraged the ambitious Carlstadt to study briefly in Siena in 1516, where, by picking up a doctorate in both canon and civil law, he was able, on returning to All Saints', to become its provost. Despite some bitterness in the theological faculty for his neglect of canonical duties on his junket to Italy, he was elected their dean. In this capacity he became involved, along with Luther, with John Eck of Ingolstadt; and, when the Wittenberg party set out in July 1519, for the Leipzig disputation, Carlstadt occupied the first of two open wagons, encircled by his reference books, while the rector, Luther, and Melanchthon followed, all surrounded by nearly two hundred armed students and other supporters. Carlstadt's wagon broke down as they were reaching their destination, and the debater and his carefully assembled conciliar and theological tomes were dashed into the mud. This was all the more inauspicious for the reason that Carlstadt in the early spring had widely circulated a woodcut prepared by Lucas Cranach, with two wagons, one with a cross

---

[3] The full title is *Farrago rerum theologicarum uberrima.* Complete bibliographical detail in van Rhijn, *Gansfort,* lxi.

being drawn toward heaven and the other representing scholasticism on its way to hell.[4] With this bungled beginning, neither of the Wittenberg spokesmen was entirely successful; and from the double mishap may have dated Carlstadt's growing aversion to the ways of the academic world.

In any case, during Luther's absence at the Wartburg, Carlstadt turned boldly and forcefully to the more social and corporate aspects of reform in Wittenberg.

On Christmas Day, 1521, under considerable pressure from the populace, Carlstadt celebrated "the first Protestant communion." After a moving sermon, he read, without vestments, most of the Latin canon of the Mass,[5] but left out all reference to it as sacrifice and omitted the elevation of the Host; and the laity were communicated under both species.

Back of this momentous action was the mounting conviction of Carlstadt of the pre-eminence of the spirit over the letter, of grace over works, and of the common priesthood of all believers, a radicalism accelerated in the ambitious scholar and ecclesiastic by his provisional restoration to prominence in the turbulent affairs of the swift-paced, reformation-minded town. As dean of the faculty of theology, he had felt improperly displaced by Luther in the eyes of the world and was now glad of the opportunity to be for a season the chief spokesman in Wittenberg for the Reform.

As early as the summer semester of 1520, Carlstadt had avowed before a large audience his concern with Luther's neglect of the moral aspects of reform: "I am grieved by the bold deprecation of James [by Luther]," and elsewhere: "Beware that you do not take a paper and loveless faith for the greatest work." Although his earlier steps in breaking from the papal Church were by way of his attack on indulgences and the idea of purgatory, his departure from traditional scholastic Eucharistic theology had been first signalized in one of several theses, published around 1520, that it would be useful for the Mass to be sung in the language of the people.[6] Then, on 19 July 1521, he promoted one Christian Hoffmann to *baccalaureus biblicus*, one of whose theses was the demand for Communion in both kinds. About this time[7] Carlstadt composed his *Von beiden Gestalten der Heiligen Messe*. Herein, as heir of the medieval tradition of spiritual communion,

---

[4] Barge, *op. cit.*, I, 146.
[5] So, Barge, *op. cit.*, II, 175, n. 78.
[6] Thesis 28 in *XXXIII Conclusiones*, edited by Theodore Brieger, *ZKG*, XI (1890), 483.
[7] Barge, *op. cit.*, II, 147.

and perhaps influenced by Gansfort and Hoen as mediated by Rode, he was prepared to say:

I well know that thou canst for a lifetime remain without the sacrament and that it is required of none that the sacrament be taken once or frequently, so long as one stands and trusts firmly in the promises of Christ.[8]

On 20 October 1521 a commission made up of Carlstadt, Philip Melanchthon, and others sought to moderate the demands of the Augustinian friars stirred up by the Zwickau prophet Gabriel Zwilling (Ch. 3.2), who had moved much more swiftly in the Spiritualist direction, urging them to be content to have occasional Masses at their convent with Communion in both kinds for the laity. At the Castle Church of All Saints, originally endowed to assure votive Masses for deceased members of the Saxon ruling house, the new Spiritualism was represented by its new provost, Justus Jonas, also professor of canon law at the university. By 4 November 1521, the Sacrament was offered to the people in both kinds in the town or parish church, and on 3 December a mob of students entered the parish church, drove out the priest, and carried off the missals. In the midst of the turmoil the elector demanded an opinion of the university, which turned in a minority Catholic and a majority evangelical report. The latter, drawn up by Carlstadt, Melanchthon, and others, was content, however, to reject private Masses; and even on this point, Carlstadt, who was still more conservative than most of his evangelical colleagues, was disposed to find value for the celebrant at least in the saying of private Mass. Because of the conflicting reports, the elector decreed a return to the *status quo ante*.

It was consequently a surprise to all when Carlstadt announced on Sunday 22 December that he would distribute the Sacrament at All Saints under both kinds on New Year's Day. Carlstadt was apparently prompted to act boldly against the injunction of the elector under popular pressure coincident with a shift in his own convictions. The burghers had, on 17 December, submitted a six-article petition demanding, among other things, the elimination of obligatory Masses for the priest, of nuptial and votive Masses for the laity, and the regular extension of the chalice to the laity. On 24 December there was commotion in both the parish and the castle churches, and it was to forestall further outbreaks that Carlstadt thereupon advanced to Christmas Day his announced Communion service in both kinds.

[8] Quoted by Barge, *op. cit.*, II, 147.

He repeated this first "Protestant" Communion on New Year's Day, again on the first Sunday of 1522, and then on Epiphany. Unfortunately for the success of his deliberate and dignified simplification, the Zwickau prophets, led by Zwilling, took advantage of the reforming *Ordinance of the Town of Wittenberg,* published on 24 January, to become riotously bold in their iconoclasm. Although Carlstadt was not in direct contact with them, he was blamed for their vandalism, since his *Von Abtuung der Bilder,* which preceded the *Ordinance* by two days, had supplied the Old Testament arguments for the destruction of what was now construed as idolatry. Although the town stood by its *Ordinance,* in order to secure the elector's approval, Carlstadt was urged to give up his preaching. By the time Luther returned to Wittenberg on 6 March, Carlstadt was being swept swiftly into the side eddies of the Magisterial Reformation. For the moment he was limited to the giving of instruction at the university.

Luther, throwing his impounded energies into his famous series of sermons from 9 to 16 March (*Schonung der Schwachen,* on the theme "evangelical freedom is not a new law"), brought about the restoration of the Latin Mass with elevation of the Host and Communion in one kind. Only the sacrificial phrasings were eliminated, and also private Mass. (In his *Formula Missae et Communionis* of December 1523, Luther reinstituted Communion in both kinds, but the liturgy remained in Latin.) Carlstadt thereupon left Wittenberg for Orlamünde and its parish church, which he held as a prebendary of All Saints, but to which he now had himself congregationally called and therein installed as pastor. Here he turned to the task of expounding and, as he hoped, promoting his Spiritualist theology of the priesthood of all believers.

Up to this parting of the ways, despite jealousy and irritation on both sides, the two professorial colleagues had been in virtual agreement on the Eucharistic theology which was now dividing them in respect to expedients. Both Reformers had been brought to the point where, in their emphasis upon grace and faith and in the consequent introduction of subjectivity into the matter of Eucharistic reception, they had come close to depriving the sacrament of both its objectivity and, more seriously, its uniqueness in the redemptive experience of the Christian. According to both of them, Christ had given assurance of the forgiveness of sins in many other words and actions which a preacher might echo and expound from the pulpit without the need of his turning to the emblems on the altar. In fact, Luther, no less than Carlstadt, had,

early in his stress on salvation by faith alone, come to the conclusion that the true believer might dispense with the external
sacrament, which served mainly as the occasion for the regular
exercise of faith. Yet both Reformers up until their split in 1523
maintained somewhat inconsistently a doctrine of the real presence of Christ in the sacrament of the altar.

The conception of the Eucharistic sacrament in which the
claims were being concurrently made that, on the one side,
Christ himself was really, locally, objectively present for the
communicant, and, on the other, that his ill-defined presence
depended in some measure upon the faith of the communicant,
was an unstable theological compound which would necessarily,
in the new revolutionary situation, either resolve itself into its
components, as with Carlstadt, or, as with Luther, weight itself
down by means of revised scholastic materialization. Though
Luther had been, for a season, in his provisional Spiritualism and
accentuated fideism indifferent as to whether Communion should
be taken under one or two species, he would soon be resorting
to the doctrine of the ubiquity of Christ to explain his matured
views. Over against him, Carlstadt, now beginning to deny that
the elements were even signs or symbols of Christ's body and
blood, would presently distinguish between the two elements,
and interpret the wine as a reminder of the covenant of forgiveness and the bread as a reminder of the promise of the resurrection of the flesh. Jesus at the Last Supper in his verbal gesture
"Hoc est" pointed, according to Carlstadt, to his own body rather
than to the bread. This interpretation is one of the identifying
marks of the Carlstadtian strand in the tangled skein of
Eucharistic controversy from 1522 to 1529.

Challenged by Luther and confident that he could prove his
point, Carlstadt proceeded, between 1522 and 1524, to think
through his position and write. Luther himself, flushed by his
encounter, published in 1523 his *Vom Anbeten des Sakraments,*
undergirding his growing conviction in the real presence as an
essential part of Christian doctrine. By the end of the year,
Carlstadt was out with his *Vom Priestertum und Opfer Christi,*
in which he denied the real presence.

Luther preached at Jena. At Jena or Orlamünde between
22 and 24 August 1524, Luther and Carlstadt, apparently while
dining together, became locked in controversy, one of the
remembered features of the episode being Luther's having tossed
a coin to Carlstadt as a pledge of his willingness to have Carlstadt
fight out the Eucharistic issues boldly and prove his point if possible: "The more bravely you attack me, the more you will please

me!"[9] It is possible that at the same meal Carlstadt pressed upon Luther the Eucharistic theology contained in Hoen's *Epistola;*[10] but whether he did or not, it is clear that the sacramentarian view of Hoen and Zwingli, based upon a tropological interpretation of *est,* is substantially different from Carlstadt's now maturing Spiritualist conviction.

As an ardent exponent of the priesthood of all believers, Carlstadt, as a "new layman," had put aside his priestly vestments and his university insignia, and replaced academic theology with contemplation ("spiritual tribulation is a sacrament"),[11] proceeding to implement, in his responsive parish of Orlamünde, his conception of both Baptism and the Eucharist. He declined to baptize infants and may even, for a while, have suspended the Supper.[12] Although his stress on Old Testament righteousness brought him near to the Spiritualist egalitarianism of Thomas Müntzer (Ch. 3.2), he with his parish in Orlamünde had turned down, in July 1524, the invitation to join with Allstedt in a program of that socialization of the gospel which would presently be merged in part with the peasants' uprising. Even so, Carlstadt's theories alarmed Luther, who contrived his banishment from Electoral Saxony in September 1524; and, leaving for Basel, Carlstadt sojourned briefly at Rothenburg, where we shall meet him next (Ch. 4.2.b). We turn now from the sacramentarian leveler of Orlamünde to the belligerent prophet at Allstedt.

2. THOMAS MÜNTZER AND THE ZWICKAU PROPHETS

By the Magisterial Reformers, Thomas Müntzer was considered the personification of the social and religious unrest to which the new evangelical ideas could lead without the support and the constraint of reform-minded princes. A contemporary biography, sometimes ascribed to Melanchthon,[13] summed up

---

[9] *Luthers Werke, WA,* XV, 340.
[10] Hardenburg in his *Vita* of Gansfort, drawing purportedly upon reminiscences from the mouths of Melanchthon and the burgomaster of Constance, Thomas Blaurer, says that Hinne Rode was himself at the meal at which the gold guilder was tossed. This, of course, is a conflation of the visit of Rode to Wittenberg and of Luther to Jena. On this and other grounds, Clemen, *loc. cit.,* and Barge, *op. cit.,* II, 150, n. 8, dismiss it as entirely unworthy of credence.
[11] This was a thesis already put forward in 1520.
[12] *Wes sich Karlstadt mit Luther beredt zu Jena,* Acta Ienensa, 1524, *WA,* XV, 325; and *Ein Brief an die Christen zu Strassburg,* 1524, *ibid.,* 393 and n. 1.
[13] Reprinted by Otto Brandt, *Thomas Müntzer: Sein Leben und Seine Schriften* (Jena, 1933), 38.

and ever thereafter perpetuated the conservative view that Thomas Müntzer was a fierce fanatic, possessed of a demoniac spirit which finally hurled him into the leadership of the rebellious peasants of Middle Germany. According to this view he was the proponent of the superiority of the Spirit over Scripture, the fomenter of the Anabaptist heresy, the originator of the religious communism that led to the Münsterite experiment (Ch. 13), and the fierce pretender to the prophetic powers of an Elijah, proclaiming the end of the world. Modern scholarship has been able to remove successive layers of historical retouching of the original image of Thomas Müntzer and has been able to identify him as the principal spokesman of Revolutionary Spiritualism.

Born in Stolberg in the Harz Mountains in December, probably 1488 or 1489, wide-ranging in his studies—the Bible, the church fathers, the Rhenish mystics—Müntzer became a master and settled as provost in Frohse near Halle. From there, after meeting Luther at the Leipzig disputation, he became father confessor in a Bernardine convent,[14] where he made use of his relative leisure to read extensively. It was radical doubt as to the existence of God and the validity of Christ's message which plunged him into his reading. The decline of the church as a result of misdirection from its learned leadership, which was described in the fragment from Hegesippus (preserved by Eusebius of Caesarea in his *Ecclesiastical History*), made a lasting impression on him, fixing for him his basic conception of the church as a pneumatic community of explicit believers. He was also influenced by his careful study at this time of the acts of the Councils of Constance and Basel,[15] and the Pseudo-Joachimite commentary on Jeremiah. Under the influence of the latter he came to think of himself as a chosen instrument of God. Thus

---

[14] Beuditz (near Weissenfels).

[15] Annemarie Lohmann, *Zur geistigen Entwicklung Thomas Müntzers* (Leipzig/Berlin, 1931), 9. See also Lydia Müller, *Glaubenszeugnisse oberdeutscher Taufgesinnter*, I (Leipzig, 1938).

It is here (in connection with Müller) the place to point out that there are eight disparate volumes of Anabaptist source collections. All these *Quellen* concerning the *Täufer* (originally called in the series *Wiedertäufer*) have been assigned a Roman number (to date, I–VIII) and have been printed in Quellen und Forschungen zur Reformationsgeschichte, each with its separate number in this larger series. This more inclusive numbering will *not* be noted in subsequent bibliographical references. Instead, the eight volumes will be cited by the key words of their titles and their number in Quellen zur Geschichte der Täufer. Thus, Müller's book referred to will be cited as Müller, *Glaubenszeugnisse* (*QGT*, III), followed by the relevant pages.

when he was in May 1520 called temporarily to replace the
Erasmian pastor John Egranus in St. Mary's in the prosperous
and cultured town of Zwickau,[16] he became an eloquent interpreter of the Reformation movement in a socially radical way.
A book list among his remains is one indication of the intense
study that went into his sermon preparation. And when he was
reassigned, on the return of Egranus (October 1), to St. Catherine's, the parish of the humbler journeymen weavers and miners,
he became even more radical. Already he had won acclaim for his
denunciation of the opulent local Franciscans.

At this point he entered the circle of the three so-called
Zwickau prophets, drawing upon Taborite and Waldensian
principles (Chs. 9.1; 21.1), and preaching a radical Biblicism
characterized by direct revelation in visions and dreams, Spirit-
possession, the abandonment of infant baptism, belief in the millennium to be preceded by the ascendancy of the Turk as Antichrist, and possibly psychopannychism.

The first of the radical triumvirate in Zwickau was the weaver
Nicholas Storch, after whom the Zwickau prophets (Luther's
designation) were also called Storchites. With him were associated Thomas Drechsel and Marcus Thomas Stübner, who had
studied at Wittenberg, the only one of the three who had been
university educated. On 16 December 1521, they were expected
to appear before the town magistrates and divines to answer to
the charges of holding erroneous views of baptism and marriage.
They betook themselves, instead, to Wittenberg. With Stübner
as their more learned spokesman, they sought out Melanchthon
(in the absence of Luther) just two days after Carlstadt's
Protestant Communion service. Melanchthon was impressed by
their Biblical knowledge and at first receptive to some of their
ideas. On the basis of Mark 16:16, "He who believes and is baptized will be saved," the men from Zwickau argued against infant
baptism and found the Wittenbergers caught off guard. Then,
Melanchthon and Amsdorf (the latter having got an account of
the meeting) wrote to the elector concerning the visit and the
disturbing situation in prosperous Zwickau. They counseled the
elector not to suppress the movement by force, however, lest there
be rebellion and lest the Spirit of God be improperly restrained,
while in the meantime the university theologians were seeking
diligently to discern the spirits. Later, Melanchthon joined in
Luther's severer judgment of the *Schwärmer*. In the meantime

[16] It was three times as populous as contemporary Dresden; cf. Brandt, *op.
cit.*, 5.

Stübner had won Martin Cellarius and Dr. Gerhard Westerburg to their cause.[17]

Westerburg, destined to become an Anabaptist leader in the region of Cologne, was the son of a patrician family who had studied at the Universities of Cologne, 1514–1515, and Bologna, 1515–1517, acquiring the doctorate in both civil and canon law. A trip to Rome had introduced him to the evil conditions of the papacy. On his return to Germany he had entertained Nicholas Storch in his home, and then accompanied him to Wittenberg, where he met Luther and Cellarius in 1522. Through Storch he had become acquainted with the emerging opposition to infant baptism. Soon he was attracted to Carlstadt in Wittenberg, whose teachings concerning the Lord's Supper he adopted, and whose sister he married. He even moved to Jena in the neighborhood of Orlamünde in 1523–1524 to be nearer to him. He began his literary career as an enthusiastic advocate of the views of Carlstadt.

Martin Cellarius (Borrhaus), the other convert to Zwickau enthusiasm, had likewise been university educated, at Tübingen, where he had become a friend of his fellow student, Melanchthon, and at Ingolstadt, where he learned Hebrew from John Reuchlin and fell into a dispute with the redoubtable John Eck. Going to Wittenberg, he became at first an ardent follower of Luther, and then came under the influence of Marcus Stübner. We shall next meet him in Strassburg (Ch. 10.2).

We return at this point to the most renowned of the Zwickau converts.

To what extent Thomas Müntzer appropriated the ideas of the "prophets" during his sojourn in Zwickau can be learned primarily from his ironic *Propositiones probri viri domini Egrani,* ascribed to Erasmian Egranus as though directed against himself.[18] From this we learn that Müntzer, while in Zwickau,

---

[17] Of the later activities of the three original prophets, little is known. Storch and Stübner had separate conversations with Luther on infant baptism, which induced him to write on the subject and defend the view that through the work of the Holy Spirit a kind of faith is infused in the infant, and that the Christian life is in any event a continuous dying and rising with Christ. Storch was for a short time in Strassburg in 1524. The principal work on the Zwickau prophets is Paul Wappler, *Thomas Müntzer in Zwickau und die Zwickauer Propheten* (Zwickau, 1908), who clearly shows the difference between the baptismal theology of the men of Zwickau and of the Swiss Brethren of Zurich.

[18] Lohmann, *op. cit.,* 14, notes that Wappler in *Thomas Müntzer in Zwickau* tends to ascribe to the Zwickau period some of the more radical traits of the later Müntzer.

evidently continued to hold with Luther on the importance of the Lord's Supper and on the bondage of the will. Nevertheless, it is clear that under Storch's influence he had really broken with Luther's theology on two essential points, antipedobaptism and Spiritualist hermeneutics. Specifically, he was claimed by the Storchites, in the hearing before the town council, for his denial of the efficacy of the faith of the godparents in the baptism of a child, and he admittedly accepted the Storchite Spiritualist hermeneutics, according to which both the Old and the New Testaments are to be interpreted in the Spirit. This Spiritualism was accompanied by an intensification of the Lutheran sense of the difference between law and grace which will presently reappear metamorphosed as Müntzer's "bitter" and "sweet" Christ, although these distinctive terms were not yet employed. From Luther's faith alone in the historic work of Christ on the cross as the central redemptive principle, Müntzer had already moved on to the personal cross mysteriously assigned to each of the elect as preliminary tutelage before the visitation of the Holy Spirit.

Involved in the revolutionary Storchite movement, despite his own distinguishing views, Müntzer was obliged by the town council to leave on the night after his own hearing, 15 April 1521. He fled to Prague, and there he was received as a Lutheran(!), preaching Sunday, 23 June, in Latin in Corpus Christi and that afternoon in German in Bethlehem Chapel. Welcomed by the radical party among the Utraquists (Ch. 9.1), he was housed with the masters of the Caroline University. After four months it became clear that he was really much more radical than even the left wing of the Utraquists. He moved to the house of Lord Burian Sobek Konicy, who had translated several of Luther's works into Czech. Speaking through interpreters, Müntzer gave utterance to his more inflammatory convictions among Hussite radicals. Building upon the local Taborite expectations, he expressed his confidence in the imminent gathering of God's people. His Prague *Manifesto* appeared in several versions: a shorter German version of 1 November 1521,[19] and a longer German version of 25 November upon which, in turn, the Czech and Latin versions were based. The second German and the Czech versions were directed to the common people, and were gross and violent in language and tone.

[19] Reproduced by Brandt, *op. cit.* The basic work on Müntzer's seven months in Prague is Václav Husa, *Tomás Müntzer a Cechy*, Rozpravy Ceskoslovenské Akademie Ved, LXVII (1957), No. 11.

The poverty of the people was held up as occasion for repeated denunciation of their oppressors, both the learned and the priests. In the Latin version, along with many other modifications, Müntzer confined his rebuke to the priests. It is clear, therefore, from a comparison of the German and Latin texts that what Müntzer really had in mind was the spiritual impoverishment of all classes because of the treason of the clerics, the scholars and the priests.[20] It is they who had obscured or completely distorted the gospel. He cited Hegesippus as witness to the prostituting of the early church by the professionally religious. Restoration he foresaw in the common people, the long-suffering custodians of the truth they cannot theologically articulate. They should be given the power to elect their pastors, who in turn will deliberate in councils or synods responsible to the Christian laity. And the gospel, which the new pastors will proclaim with a new intensity, is that which Thomas Müntzer already adumbrated in the last days of his sojourn in Zwickau.

In the Prague *Manifesto,* Müntzer speaks of the bestowal of the sevenfold gift of the Spirit as the goal of redemption.[21] Among the gifts is the reception of direct instruction from the Holy Spirit in the form of vision, dream, ecstatic utterance, or inspired exegesis. Only the elect are vouchsafed this visitation, but before it comes, they must be awakened. This is the compelling task of the preacher. And Müntzer himself is no longer *magister,* but *nuntius Christi.* Before the elect are ready for the Spiritual visitation, however, they must undergo the harrowing of fear. Fear is the beginning of godliness. The work of Christ on the cross consisted in his having given the elect the example of a personal cross.[22] Although the cross is considered a divinely selected means of tutelage, the thought is nevertheless not far below the surface in Müntzer, and destined to become ever more prominent in his own life and teaching, that self-imposed discipline serves as a preparation for the predetermined "cross." Characteristic of the Prague *Manifesto* is the open espousal of the Storchite-Taborite chiliasm which justifies the violence of the elect.

[20] The several texts are admirably analyzed in their tendency by Lohmann, *op. cit.,* 18–30.

[21] These gifts are listed by Frederick Lewis Weiss, *The Life, Teachings, and Works of Johannes Denck* (Strasbourg, 1924), in connection with baptism, and see also below, Ch. 4 at n. 26.

[22] Heinrich Bornkamm calls this the "Theologie der Anfechtung," *Mystik, Spiritualismus und die Anfänge des Pietismus im Luthertum* (Giessen, 1926), 6.

When his preaching failed to call forth an uprising of the predestined saints, Müntzer withdrew from Bohemia in February 1522 and dropped for the time being the revolutionary theme. After wandering about somewhat obscurely, showing up once in Wittenberg to visit Luther,[23] Müntzer was accepted by the town council of Allstedt to become, on a trial basis, the pastor of the local St. John's Church. Here in a small Saxon town close to the border of the County of Mansfeld, Müntzer became provisionally the exponent of a magisterial reformation. Winning to his side John Zeyss, the electoral castellan, and hoping to win over even the elector's brother, Duke John, Müntzer carried out a twofold program. Radical though he was, even openly, he tried to maintain as good relations as possible with Wittenberg and the elector, publicly disavowing Storch.

Müntzer was uncommonly resourceful in his Germanizing of the liturgy, in *Das deutsche Kirchenamt* (1523) and *Deutsche evangelische Messe* (1524). The liturgical year was divided into four great seasons. To encourage popular participation, he contrived to have the major portion of the service sung, retaining the chants in German translation, and composing several hymns himself. He insisted on the whole of a psalm being sung instead of the opening words only, and the selections from the Scriptures were whole chapters. The Ten Commandments were carved in tablets and placed prominently in the church. Little of Müntzer's social radicalism came out in his liturgical work, except for such alterations as "Deliver us from the anti-Christian government of the godless" for the collect "Deliver us from the yoke of evil,"[24] and his insistence that the words of Eucharistic consecration be said by the whole congregation as a royal-priestly people. When criticized for allowing also merely nominal Christians thus to consecrate the Mass, he replied that Christ comes into the midst of the congregation only in answer to the petitions of the elect among them. He appears to have encouraged the postponement of baptism until children should be of sufficient age to understand the action, but he never proposed the rebaptism of adults. In Allstedt he took to wife a former nun.

Liturgiologist and family man, he was also all the while less openly engaged in working through his much more radical con-

[23] Therefore, Karl Holl, "Luther und die Schwärmer," *Gesammelte Aufsätze zur Kirchengeschichte*, I (1932), 420–467, postpones the dating of the final break with Luther to this stage, as against Lohmann, who sees in the *Manifesto* the definitive formulation of the new Thomas Müntzer.

[24] Oskar Mehl, *Thomas Müntzers Deutsche Messe* (Grimmen in Pommern, 1937), 4. Cf. Brandt, *op. cit.*, 113–125.

ception of reform and renewal. To this end he had organized a secret band who were destined to emerge as the executors of "the eternal covenant of God." He sent a threatening letter to the count of Mansfeld for refusing to allow his subjects to attend the new services in Allstedt. For this, Müntzer was obliged to apologize. His radical spirit soon found expression in the assault of his covenanters on the neighboring Mallerbach Chapel, 24 March 1524, destroying its miraculous image of the Virgin. The chapel belonged to the convent of Naundorf, to which the people of Allstedt had to pay feudal dues, all the more obnoxious for the reason that Müntzer and his followers were being execrated by the nuns as heretics. Confident in the support of the humbler members of society thus recruited[25] for the cause and not yet despairing of the endorsement of an eventually fully instructed magistracy—the town councilors and the castellan Zeyss might be considered prospective converts—Thomas Müntzer elaborated his more radical views in a series of important works which he was able to publish during his Allstedt pastorate.

Von dem gedichteten Glauben was composed before 2 December 1523. It contains fourteen points and a covering letter to John Zeyss in which, as we have noted, Müntzer acknowledges his indebtedness to Joachim of Flora.[26] In point 11 he gives his memorable wording to a distinction we have already met:

One should not climb in [to the church] by the window, nor have any other basis for faith than the whole of and not merely the half of Christ. He who does not wish to accept the bitter Christ will eat himself sick of honey.

First the elect must know spiritual misery and the abyss of despair, abandoning all pleasure in the world. He must have suffered the hell of unbelief. Thereupon follows the second stage of salvation, the bestowal of the personal cross, the gracious rod. And finally, with the bestowal of the Holy Spirit, the elect comes into possession (point 14) of the key of David, whereby he can unlock the book of seven seals, the Bible, and discern the spirits. Herein, Müntzer turns covertly upon Luther and the latter's insistence upon the outer and audible Word, as against

---

[25] Brandt, *op. cit.,* 63.
[26] Published 1534. Reprinted in Gottfried Arnold, *Kirchen- und Ketzerhistorie,* IV (Frankfurt a. M., 1700), 560; and in Brandt, *op. cit.,* on the basis of the original, 126–132. Page 132: *"Ihr sollt auch wissen, dass sie [die Wittenberger] diese Lehre dem Abt Joachim zuschreiben und heissen sie ein ewiges Evangelion in grossem Spott. Bei mir ist das Zeugnis Abbotis Joachim gross. Ich hab ihn [Pseudo-Joachim] allein über Jeremiam gelesen. Aber meine Lehre ist hoch droben."*

the inner Word, and excoriates the learned in religion ("scribes") in general, who have at best only "historic faith."

Müntzer turns openly on Luther in his *Protestation oder Entbietung . . . vom dem rechten Christenglauben und der Taufe* in twenty-two articles.[27] In the first seven, Müntzer gives full expression to his conception of baptism. He distinguishes between the inner and the outer baptism. The latter was surely not administered to children according to the New Testament, but neither was it administered to such saintly adults as Mary and the apostles. Therefore outer baptism is unnecessary for inclusion in the church of the faithful; inner baptism is.

Inner baptism is interpreted on the basis of the first six chapters of John, which contain a series of references to water. Water is interpreted as the movement of the Spirit, and movement is the convulsion (*erschütterung*) of the soul occasioned by the particular cross assigned by God to be borne. Müntzer interrelates John the Baptist's harsh preaching prior to the baptismal action of cleansing and renewal, Jesus' miracle of turning water into wine (interpreted as the blood of suffering), Jesus' parable of the living water at the Samaritan well which has God as its source, and Jesus' action with the water of the pool of Siloam moved by the angel (the symbol of the healing power of the individually borne cross). Baptism is seen by Müntzer on the basis of these four texts to be the symbol of the whole discipline of the God-bestowed cross which leads to the revelatory descent of the Holy Spirit. This conception of the baptismal action involving the whole redemptive process from the first movement of religious despair to possible martyrdom may well have been woven into the "martyr theology" of the evangelical Anabaptists.[28]

Another expression of Müntzer's martyr theology is an important letter written early in the Allstedt period to his followers

[27] Brandt, *op. cit.*, 133; December, 1523, published in 1524. The *Protestation* will be available in English translation by John Steely in the *Bulletin* of the Southeastern Baptist Theological Seminary, Wake Forest, N.C.

[28] One must study from this angle Ethelbert Stauffer's "Anabaptist Theology of Martyrdom," *MQR*, XIX (1945), 179. Lohmann, after noting that in contrast to the evangelical Anabaptists, Müntzer made little use of external baptism, goes on: "*Dennoch ist est möglich, dass Müntzer durch die Umdeutung des Kreuzes in den Taufgedanken bei der weiteren Verbreitung seiner Schriften die besondere Betonung der Taufe bei jenen verursacht hat, die dann ihrerseits für diese innere Taufe des Kreuzes ein äusseres Symbol suchten, das ihnen die Wiedertaufe bot.*" Lohmann, *op. cit.*, 49. She refers to George Haug in Müller, *Glaubenszeugnisse* (*QGT*, III), 7, and Emil Egli, *Die Züricher Wiedertäufer zur Reformationszeit* (Zurich, 1878), 19, but may be forcing a connection that the Holl-Böhmer school requires, i.e., that Müntzer is the originator of all Anabaptism.

in his birthplace, Stolberg.[29] Herein he warns them against premature or meaningless tumult. The reformed church of the future is to be made up of the divine elect. But these elect must first undergo, not only with patience, but also with yearning, the trials that God will place before them. The "lazy elect" are as good as lost. The "grace of *Anfechtung*" is bestowed only upon those who have demonstrated themselves worthy thereof by the discipline of self-imposed restraints.

The most extraordinary public utterance of Müntzer during his sojourn in Allstedt, indeed possibly the most remarkable sermon of the whole Reformation Era, was that delivered on 13 July 1524 at the castle, in the presence of Duke John (brother of Elector Frederick), his son, John Frederick, and selected town and electoral officials.[30] That so distinguished a company of magistrates listened without immediate protest to so inflammatory an appeal to Christian revolution requires an explanation that will place one back in the parlous and perplexing first years of the Reformation Era.

Ducal father and son were divided on the proper role of the Christian magistrate. The son sided with Luther and the conservative interpretation of the Reform. But the father, perplexed and thoughtful brother of the elector, stood under the influence of the radical court preacher of the ducal residence in Weimar, Wolfgang Stein, who was in turn under the influence of Carlstadt, already identified with radical changes in Orlamünde, and of Jacob Strauss in Eisenach. Basel-born Strauss had published two influential sermons, *Von der innerlichen und äusserlichen Taufe* and *Wider die simonische Taufe*, both in 1523. Herein he had come out for a simplified water baptism in German.[31]

[29] July, 1523; printed by Heinrich Böhmer and P. Kirn, *Thomas Müntzers Briefwechsel auf Grund der Handschriften und ältesten Vorlagen* (Leipzig, 1931), No. 41, p. 44; by Brandt, *op. cit.*, 62; commented on by Lohmann, *op. cit.*, 36 ff.

[30] It has been long supposed that the sermon was given before the two Ernestine dukes, John and Frederick the Wise, but it is certain that the elector was not present. See Carl Hinrichs, *Luther und Müntzer: Ihre Auseinandersetzung über Obrigkeit und Widerstandsrecht*, Arbeiten zur Kirchengeschichte, XXIX (Berlin, 1952), 5, n. 1. Also present were the electoral chancellor Dr. Gregory Brück (Pontanus), Dr. Hans von Grefendorf, the castellan John Zeyss, and the bailiff and council of Allstedt. *Ibid.*, 39.

[31] Barge, "Die gedruckten Schriften des evangelischen Predigers Jakob Strauss," *ARG*, XXXII (1935), 100 ff., 248 ff. In the second sermon mentioned, he wrote: "*In unser versammlung tauffen wir in form vnnd gestalt wie Christus gelert vnd geboten hat.*" On Strauss, see Barge, *Schriften des Vereins für Reformationsgeschichte*, No. 162 (Leipzig, 1937).

All these radical preachers were loyal to their prince, but held fiercely to the view that with the overturn of papal authority Mosaic law should obtain in evangelical lands. Up to this point, Müntzer was not markedly different from the other radical preachers who, Duke John thought, might well be right in their interpretation. Earnest about getting to the heart of the problem, curious about how things were going in Allstedt under Müntzer, and perhaps with the additional motivation of ascertaining whether he should ducally confirm the ministerial choice of the town council, John consented to hear Müntzer in the ducal castle in Allstedt. Müntzer had had more than a week to prepare for the momentous occasion. In his sermon he clearly enunciated his view of faith in contrast to that of Luther. He outlined his conception of history and of reform, and promulgated his doctrine of a godly magistracy.[32]

Appealing again, as in his Prague *Manifesto,* to Hegesippus' interpretation of the decline of the primitive church, Müntzer went on to reinterpret the Danielic theology of history. The multimetallic statue of the royal dream had throughout the Middle Ages been generally understood in Jerome's adaptation thereof. Accordingly, the fourth kingdom was construed as the Roman Empire, perpetuated in ever new permutations from Augustus, through Charlemagne, to the Holy Roman Empire of the German Nation. But Müntzer cunningly found in the iron-and-clay feet of the statue (which for Daniel had been but the extension of what he considered the fourth, the iron kingdom of Alexander the Great) the symbol of a fifth earthly kingdom, namely, feudal-papal Christendom, in which society was pulverized between church and state, in oppressive collusion. The Stone which in the royal dream broke these feet was, of course, Christ (Christ's people, the saints). Müntzer noted that this Stone increased in size, and it was his conviction that the royal priesthood of the common man was now in a position to break the last of the kingdoms of this world, the imperial-papal monarchy. But the present subaltern magistrates within the Roman Empire might well, as individuals, be among the elect and belong to this holy folk. It was therefore the basic thrust of Müntzer's sermon before the princes to awaken in them the awareness of their possibly predestined role and to induce them to join the covenanted people and to become indeed their spokesmen and their executives in punishing the godless reprobates under Antichrist.

[32] Critical edition by Carl Hinrichs, *Thomas Müntzer, Politische Schriften mit Kommentar,* Hallesche Monographien, XVII (Halle, 1950); translated by George H. Williams, *SAW,* 47–70.

Müntzer reinterpreted the politically conservative text of Rom., ch. 13, into a revolutionary passage in a way that must have seemed all the more cogent to Duke John for the reason that Luther had recurrently used it in support of magisterial authority.[33] In effect, Müntzer reversed the sequence of Rom. 13:1-4, construing vs. 1 f. as the sequel of vs. 3 f., and thus making the Ernestine princes, by hortatory anticipation, the executors of God's wrath against the godless and the protectors of the revolutionary saints. At the same time, Müntzer warned that if the princes should fail to identify themselves with the covenantal people, the sword would pass from them to the people.[34] Müntzer had no contract theory of government. Divine sovereignty resided in the godly people; the princes had the choice of joining the godly in their eschatological program or of suffering the consequences of righteous rebellion.[35] Only if they heeded God's will as interpreted by the new Daniel and replaced the Wittenberg scribe with a prophet who, besides knowing the Word, was also possessed of the Spirit, could the princes ever become worthy instruments of God!

It was the daring of Müntzer to think that Allstedt might become the focal point of radical reform, replacing Wittenberg. Müntzer was sustained in his expectation by his Spiritualist hermeneutics. He took the outpouring of the Spirit in himself and others as confirmation of the prophecy of Joel (chs. 2:27-32; 3:1-4) and the imminent formation of a covenant of miners and magistrates as the realization of the eschatological dream of equality of possessions. This was understood as the God-ordained imitation of the primitive church with the equalization of the saints in the common possession both of the gifts of the Spirit and the goods of life. In this confidence, he could brazenly call Luther "Brother Mastschwein," "Sanftleben," "Leisentritt," "Kolkrabe," "Meister Lügner," all of which appellations were

---

[33] Hinrichs has been especially discerning in showing the revolutionary permutation of Rom., ch. 13, in the hermeneutics of Müntzer.

[34] Müntzer had already given expression to this revolutionary but plausible reinterpretation of Rom., ch. 13, in two letters, one to the elector and meant also for sympathetic Duke John, 4 October 1523 (Brandt, *op. cit.,* 64), and one to the council and congregation of Allstedt, c. 7 June 1524.

[35] In another writing, Müntzer indicates that the princely representatives of the godly may enjoy certain minor privileges out of respect: princes, for example, may ride with eight horses, counts with four, lesser noblemen with two (Böhmer and Kirn, *op. cit.,* 162). Here one may detect clearly the influence of Eberlin of Günzberg, who made some such concession in the eleventh of his pamphlets entitled *Bundesgenossen*. Eberlin projected an equitable *Wolfaria* wherein each would be compensated according to his true contribution to the good of the whole. He also opposed men going beardless. *Flugschriften der Reformationszeit,* XI (1896).

more than billingsgate. With these descriptions he purported to descry in Luther a sign of the end of the age.

Of Duke John's reaction to the castle sermon we shall speak presently. On 24 July, Müntzer preached another sermon based on II Kings, ch. 22, appealing to the Josian reform and the royal renewal of the covenant as the pattern for the Ernestine princes.[36] But in his heart, Müntzer had undoubtedly abandoned something of his hope that the princes would in the end espouse the covenantal reform. For during these last two weeks of July, he completed his draft of what was later to be printed by John Hut as *Ausgedrückte Entblössung des falschen Glaubens*. It is in part a commentary on Luke, ch. 1, and is Müntzer's most vigorous and systematic defense of Spirit-possessed faith as opposed to the merely historic faith of the Wittenbergers, which he proceeds to expose as false. Müntzer shows how each in his or her turn among the great believers of the Bible at first opposed as impossible the promise of God: Abraham, Elizabeth, Mary. The Bible is not the source of faith, but its confirmation. Each soul must be crushed with doubt and suffering, and then emptied, before the overshadowing of the Holy Spirit conceives faith within the soul and thereby exposes the fatuousness of the imagined belief of the scribal Christian (Luther). Since this inner suffering can go on in the soul of every man, Müntzer is prepared to include even the nominal Christian, Turk, and pagan. He instances the centurion, who knew Christ afar off.

His doctrine, then, of Spirit-confirmed election had a programmatically ecumenical character. And although personal suffering was construed as the necessary prelude to salvation, Müntzer did not condone the iniquities of the social order as tolerable or even desirable because conducive to spirituality! With the other Reformers, he left the concept of disciplinary poverty to the Middle Ages and demanded community of possessions to meet at once human material necessities and deliverance from preoccupation with the things of the world: "In the face of usury, taxes, and rents no one can have faith."[37]

---

[36] This sermon has been lost. Müntzer refers to it in his letter to John Zeyss, 25 July 1524; Brandt, *op. cit.,* 68.

[37] *Entblössung, loc. cit.,* 48. The tract was printed in October, 1524, after Müntzer had established himself as an avowed revolutionary in Mühlhausen. But a draft thereof, adapted for the censor and still phrased in such a way as to admit the princes (in order to assure a legal transformation), was printed in Weimar. This is called by Hinrichs the *Gezeugnis,* and Müntzer himself refers to it as his "Auslegung des Evangelion Lucae" in his letter to Elector Frederick, 3 August 1524 (Brandt, *op. cit.,* 72). Here Müntzer also refers to a certain *"unterricht"* he had sent to the prince by Zeyss. Müntzer scholar-

As Duke John reflected on the radical character of Müntzer's reform, he summoned him for a hearing at the ducal residence in Weimar for 1 August. Duke John was by now alerted to the danger of disastrous revolution by Luther's vitriolic *Brief an die Fürsten zu Sachsen von dem aufrührischen Geist*.[38] Zeyss and two members of the town council accompanied Müntzer to the hearing in Weimar. There Müntzer acknowledged the existence of his secret band, which was thereupon ordered dissolved, but he denied that he had ever spoken out publicly against the Ernestine princes. Müntzer promised the authorities that he would refrain from incendiary activity and that he would not leave Allstedt on any revolutionary mission. His printer was banished. There was some discussion about the holding of a formal disputation with Jacob Strauss and the Weimar preacher Wolfgang Stein, who would mediate between Müntzer and Carlstadt of Orlamünde on the revolutionary left and Luther on the right, but the proposal broke down from its inherent weakness. Luther with his argumentation from the written Word and Müntzer with his argumentation out of the compulsion of the Spirit could never have debated from the same platform. Both sides instinctively shunned the proposed encounter.[39]

In his absence from Allstedt, Müntzer's ally Simon Haferitz had preached on 31 July, appealing to the congregation for further enlistment in the covenant. On his return from Weimar, the burning question for Müntzer was whether he could any longer hope to lead in a "legal" reform and, specifically, in view of the constraints imposed by the Weimar authorities, whether he could mount the pulpit on 7 August and not disappoint the expectations of his fervid followers. It was a trial of power. Feeling unequal to the test and fearing further circumscription of his activities, he broke his Weimar promise and left Allstedt on the night of 7/8 August 1524 to join the peasant revolt.

Besides the pacifistic sacramentarian Carlstadt and the belligerent priestly prophet of Allstedt, there was a third major

ship has regretted the loss of this document. It is the contribution of Hinrichs to have shown that the latter is none other than Müntzer's letter to Zeyss of 25 July (Brandt, *op. cit.*, 68). The significance of Hinrichs' work is to make clear that Müntzer was as late as the letter of 3 August, still hoping that the Ernestine princes might espouse covenantal reform, indeed as late as the night of his escape from Allstedt, 7/8 August 1524, and that even the enflamed, revolutionary *Entblössung* could be, during this critical transition, interpreted by Müntzer as a summons to a *legal* revolution with the prince on the side of the covenant, as was Josiah.

[38] Brandt, *op. cit.*, 202.

[39] Hinrichs, *Luther und Müntzer*, 90, 97; a further proposal was made after Müntzer's flight to Mühlhausen, *ibid.*, 139, 142.

spokesman of Spiritualism who likewise broke with Luther on social, ethical, and sacramental grounds. This was the evangelical Spiritualist and aristocratic Lutheran Reformer of Silesia, Caspar Schwenckfeld. But his role in the Radical Reformation can be best recounted in connection with the Swiss-Saxon Eucharistic Controversy (Ch. 5.3); however, we must first turn to the Great Peasants' War and the involvement of Carlstadt and Müntzer in it.

CHAPTER 4

THE GREAT PEASANTS' WAR, 1524–1525

Modern Christian historians in the Lutheran and Reformed traditions, as a consequence of their concern for civil, social, and ecclesiastical order and obedience—a legacy from Luther and his resolute stand against the revolutionary appropriation by the peasant insurgents of his good news concerning Christian freedom—have long perpetuated the customary burdening of evangelical Anabaptism with the charge of having arisen out of a combination of heresy and sedition, while historians standing in the Anabaptist tradition itself, because of their pacifism and aversion to both Marxism and secularism, have been primarily concerned to dissociate, so far as possible, the peasant unrest from the Anabaptist witness. Both groups of Christian historians have therefore largely left it to the Marxists, and others without confessional predisposition or inclination, to vindicate the evangelical ideals of the rebellious peasants. To work out a well-proportioned account of what was, in fact, the sixteenth-century interrelationship between the seditious peasant camps and secretive Anabaptist conventicles is not easy for anyone dissatisfied with the programmatic Protestant, the pious Mennonite, and the doctrinaire Marxist accounts.

Clear is the fact that in so far as Anabaptism is understood as the espousal of believers' baptism, it began *after* the outbreak of the Great Peasants' War in June 1524 (near Schaffhausen); for the first recorded evangelical rebaptism dates from January 1525 (Ch. 6.1), although there were, of course, Spiritualists, such as Müntzer and Carlstadt, who, actively, or passively involved in the uprising, were also concurrently opposed to the baptism of infants.

But if none of the participants in the peasant movement were at the time *ana*baptists, it is significant that they anticipated Anabaptism in three notable respects. The peasants, petty

59

burghers, and restless knights who banded together against the spiritual lords, both episcopal and abbatial, and against the violation of ancient local rights by the territorial princes (1) commonly called themselves covenanters *(Bundesgenossen)*, (2) universally demanded the elimination of tithes to absentee clerics, and (3) universally demanded the parochial or congregational election of their pastors.

Of the Anabaptists whose military or evangelistic careers in the peasant uprising are adequately documented, there are so few that a genetic or comprehensive account of the relationship between the Peasants' War and Anabaptism is difficult to establish.

As it happens, Balthasar Hubmaier, soon to become the first important theological spokesman of adult, or believers', baptism, who in the war bespoke the cause of the peasants and later organized the refugee Anabaptists in Nicolsburg in Moravia, was atypical even on becoming an Anabaptist, for he is perhaps unique among the South German Anabaptists in having to the end been willing to argue for the legitimacy of the sword in the hand of a Christian magistrate, be it of his Anabaptist patron in Moravia or of his Catholic executioner in Vienna. Thus, difficult though it is, by concentrating on the evangelical impulses in the war and its antecedents, we may rough in the background against which five or six selected Spiritualists and eventual Anabaptists may pass in review in the period up to the end of the Peasants' War in 1525.

In the perspective of the centuries, we can distinguish three phases of central European peasant revolt: (1) the medieval phase of sporadic outbursts, 1291–1517; (2) the Great Peasants' War, 1524–1525/6, universalized and religiously undergirt by an appeal to evangelical freedom; and (3) a decade later, the Münsterite uprising and synchronous revolts in Amsterdam and elsewhere and, in Moravia, the concurrent sublimation of the refugee peasants' yearning for evangelical social justice in the Hutterite communes, 1533–1535. The present chapter is limited to the first two phases.

1. MEDIEVAL PEASANT ASPIRATIONS TO 1517

Since the end of the Great Plague, there had been ferment and the turmoil of social readjustment among the German and Swiss peasants and bondsmen (serfs) comparable to that of the French and Flemish Jacquérie, the English Lollards, and the Bohemian Hussite Taborites. The spread of the peasant unrest

and uprisings and their variation from region to region can best
be understood in the light of the many regional differences in
the structure of the rural economy and the sociolegal institutions within the loose patchwork of principalities presided over
by the Holy Roman Emperor. These were a legacy from the different local developments in feudal times.

In general, the unrest occurred in areas where the peasants
had been prosperous and relatively free, but where a multitude
of petty civil and ecclesiastical lords were attempting to extend
and formalize their own jurisdiction at the expense of the peasants.

The struggle of the Germanic peasants to preserve the old
laws began in Switzerland. There the bailiffs and administrative
officials of the Hapsburgs had once tried to increase the original
exactions made on the peasants and to turn the difference to
their own profit. Thus the original Confederation (1291) was
directed against this administrative exploitation, and not directly
at the Hapsburg dynasts, although the uprising of the Alpine
yeomanry soon developed into a struggle for Swiss independence
from Austria. A second major peasant uprising in Switzerland—
the Swiss Peasants' War of 1513–1515—was directed against local
iniquities in the cantons where the burghers of the capitals were
encroaching upon the rights of the peasants in the outlying dependent villages, for example, in Solothurn, Lucerne, and Bern.

Elsewhere in the Empire in the southwest quadrant of Germania bordering on the German Swiss cantons, in the large angle
formed by the bend of the Rhine at Basel, and also in the Tyrol,
the uprisings were directed against a steady consolidation of increasing political absolutism, coupled with the introduction of
Roman law (the Code of Justinian), which threatened the accustomed freedom of the small farmers, especially in the rural
dependencies of the imperial cities and the smaller ecclesiastical
territories. The situation became even more hopeless where
monasteries, with their vast landed holdings, were directly dependent upon the docile service of their peasants and serfs and
were tightening their controls over them, heedless of the claims
of Christian charity.

The peasants combated the new trend by appealing, often in
Christian terms, to their traditional rights under Germanic
"common" law, a combination of feudal agreements and old
Germanic usages varying from place to place but characterized
everywhere by a high regard for the rights as well as the duties
of the common man.

The most significant late medieval movement in favor of the

old laws was that of "Poor Conrad" (*der arme Konrad*) in the duchy of Württemberg (most of Upper and Lower Swabia).[1] "Poor Conrad" was the name given to peasant sodalities formed mainly of the poor and disaffected, who attempted to forget their economic woes by means of fun and practical jokes. These groups were numerous and rather large, but without political significance until 1514, when Duke Ulrich of Württemberg attempted to increase his revenues by changing his system of weights. This aroused great antagonism among the peasants, who regarded, in Old Testament fashion, any tampering with the weights as an abomination. A certain Peter Gais threw some of the new weights into a river, in adaptation of the medieval trial by ordeal, saying that if God approved them, they would float! Calling himself Poor Conrad, he demonstrated the iniquity of the new taxation in several localities, and attracted a large number of followers. Another peasant, Gugel-Bastian of Bühl, began a semicomic flouting of authority under the same slogan, and put forward a number of serious social demands. His was not, however, an organized movement, and it was quickly dispersed. Although his most serious crime seems to have been poaching, Gugel-Bastian was arrested, tried, and executed on a variety of charges on 5 October 1514.[2]

Some groups appealed, partly under Hussite influence, to divine law, demanding a reordering of society on the basis of the gospel. By the beginning of the sixteenth century such agitation for reform, under the parole of either divine law or common rights, had come to involve ever larger areas. For the first time the different localities were beginning to align themselves on the basis of common interest. Peasants in Carinthia and Württemberg began to speak of divine law (*göttliches Recht*). Their slogan was taken over from a movement which had a long history among the German peasants. Unlike the other movements, which were largely conservative in nature and sought to protect or reassert old Germanic peasant rights, this new party envisaged a universal law, based on the will of God, i.e., on the Bible. As long as the peasants had been concerned with the old, "common" law, their movement remained fragmentary, since the laws, priv-

---

[1] The most important recent works on the war are Günther Franz, *Der deutsche Bauernkrieg* (Munich, 1935), and Adolf Waas, *Die grosse Wendung im deutschen Bauernkrieg* (Munich/Berlin, 1939). The latter is especially insistent on the religious and constructively constitutional character of the peasant movement.

[2] Cf. Heinrich Schreiber, *Der Bundschuh zu Lehen im Breisgau und der arme Konrad zu Bühl* (Freiburg im Br., 1824), 29 ff.

ileges, and abuses, far from being "common" were actually quite
disparate and varied from territory to territory. But the struggle
for divine, Biblical law, not limited by territorial boundaries,
could be pan-European.

Its espousal involved only a thoughtful, radical minority,
consciously devoted to the spreading of the movement and to
the planning of conspiracies. Combined religious and economic
motives often spread antagonism both toward the Jews as money-
lenders and later toward the bishops and abbots as exacting
landowners who demanded old and new levies of all kinds. The
symbol of the movement was the peasant's laced shoe, the
Bundschuh (as opposed to the nobleman's *Stiefel*). The organization itself came to be called by its symbol. Its program included
recognition of the Emperor and the pope but of no intermediate authorities, the reduction of taxes, the elimination of some
odd rents and exactions, in one organization (Alsace in 1493)
the extermination of the Jews, the abolition of clerical plurali-
ties, and (only in the 1493 platform) of aural confession, the
limitation of the power of the ecclesiastical courts, the control
of interest (not to exceed 5 per cent), and a universal peace
throughout Christendom. It was Joss Fritz who led the Bundschuh in 1493, 1502, and 1513, on both sides of the Rhine above
Hagenau. The most radical proposals of 1493, concerning the
Jews and the confessional, were not embodied in the more systematic program set out in 1513. The new program contained
a renewed promise of loyalty to the Emperor if he would accept
the demands of the peasants, accompanied, however, by the
threat of recourse to the virtually independent Swiss if he
would not.

A gradual shift of interest from the preservation of "common"
law to the establishment of divine law, the evolution of the
Bundschuh from a rabble combining grievance and prejudice
in 1493 to a responsible social movement with a balanced set
of political demands in 1517, had opened the peasant imagination
to the new evangelical impulses coming from Wittenberg and
Zurich. Influenced by the new ideas concerning ecclesiastical
reform, the peasants now began to demand, in addition to the
already current program of a return to feudal custom and the
institution of Biblical justice, the elimination of tithes and ad-
vowson and in their place the free election and voluntary support of their pastors.

In the fall of 1517 the peasants of the Bundschuh imagined
their demands sanctioned by Luther's appeal to evangelical freedom and to the Bible.

2. The Great Peasants' War, 1524–1525: Hubmaier, Carlstadt, Müntzer, Rinck, and Hut

In February 1524 all the planets were to meet in the sign of the Fish. A Tübingen mathematician had predicted this stellar configuration in 1499, and prophesied that a general flood would engulf the earth.[3] Many disagreed with him, since a new deluge would have violated the promise of God to Noah, but all agreed that some awesome evil impended. Prophetic slogans and pronouncements of various kinds, written for the most part in German, were widely read;[4] and an Alsatian peasant band were presently to excuse their conduct on the ground that their war had long been predicted and was therefore willed by God. Thus the year 1524 opened with great excitement and foreboding.

a. The Uprising in Stühlingen and Waldshut: The Role of Balthasar Hubmaier. Disturbances at Forschheim (Franconia) and St. Blasien (the Black Forest) on 23 and 30 May 1524 were more in the nature of raids on the monastery wine cellars than struggles for peasant rights. The serious war was set off on 23 June 1524, when the countess of Lüpfen-Stühlingen tried to send some of her peasants off to gather snails while they were intent on taking in their hay. The uproar, beginning in the vicinity of Schaffhausen, spread by December through Upper Swabia. The leader, Hans Müller,[5] sought outside support and came upon a possibility in the politically ambitious town of Waldshut, on an important ford of the Rhine not far from Schaffhausen. This town, far from the center of Austrian power, was ripe for evangelical leadership in that it sought, small though it was, some basis for becoming an imperial free city, or even freer still, like the neighboring Swiss cantons, and perhaps covenanted with them in the Confederation (like Appenzell a generation before). Since their Zwinglian pastor, Dr. Balthasar Hubmaier, was soon destined to emerge as a major figure of the Radical Reformation, we may appropriately interrupt our narrative of the war to glance back at the life of the controversial pastor of Waldshut up to the entry of the town into treaty with the insurgent peasants.

Balthasar Hubmaier (1481–1528), of Friedberg (near Augsburg), had studied at the University of Freiburg, where John

---

[3] Karl Schottenloher, *Zeittafel zur deutschen Geschichte* (Munich, 1939), Nos. 34472 and 34474.

[4] Old proverb: *"Wer im 1523 Jahr nicht stirbt* [uprising of the knights], *1524 nicht im Wasser verdirbt, und 1525 nicht wird erschlagen, der mag wohl von Wundern sagen."* Franz, *op. cit.,* 148.

[5] Franz, *op. cit.,* 165.

Eck, the opponent of Carlstadt and Luther at the Leipzig disputation, acquired powerful influence over him and encouraged him in his rapid progress in theology. Though a lack of funds had compelled him to accept a position as a teacher in Schaffhausen, he soon returned to the university and was ordained a priest. When Eck went to the University of Ingolstadt, Hubmaier followed and presently received the doctorate in theology, on the occasion of which Eck delivered the promotorial oration. He was presently made corector of the university and, in recognition of his eloquence as a preacher, was made chaplain in the cathedral in nearby Regensburg.

The populace of Regensburg was at the time involved in an anti-Semitic uprising in which Hubmaier took an ignoble part. It ended in the expulsion of the Jews and the tearing down of their synagogue, and the erection in its place of a chapel which soon became the goal of locally lucrative pilgrimages. In connection with them there were coarse abuses which so distressed Hubmaier that he willingly accepted a call as priest in Waldshut, where he preached his first sermon in the spring of 1521, still loyal, of course, to his Catholic faith. But in the course of the summer of 1522 he began to change, studying Luther's writings. After a careful study of and preaching from the major Pauline epistles, Hubmaier visited Erasmus in Basel. When a new call, from Regensburg, reached him, he accepted; but, when his new religious convictions became evident in his sermons, he was glad to be able to return to the still open position in Waldshut. He immediately engaged in correspondence with the Swiss Reformers, discussing with Zwingli the problem of baptism.[6] He involved himself in the Second Disputation in 1523 (Ch. 5.2.a) in Zurich, debating alongside Zwingli, and returned home to carry out, in his own Waldshut, reforms which they had only talked about in Zurich. He introduced the German service, abolished fasting regulations, and married. Here in Waldshut, far more than in Zurich, which was concerned to achieve the hegemony of the whole religiously mixed Confederation of peasant republics and city-states, it was possible for Hubmaier to combine creatively the local quest for civic liberty and the widespread urge for renewal of the church.

Thus it was that when the Great Peasants' War began in nearby Stühlingen and the peasants there rose against their lord

---

[6] He later wrote: "Then Zwingli agreed with me that children should not be baptized before they are instructed in the faith." *Ein gesprech Balthasar Hubemörs von Fridberg Doctors auff Mayster Vlrich Zwinglens zu Zürich Tauffbüechlen* (Nicolsburg, 1526), p. D III. *ML,* II, 354.

and converged on Waldshut, they found the town not only evan-
gelistically reformed under the leadership of its new pastor
Hubmaier but also on the point of resisting by arms the attempts of the Hither Austrian administration to suppress his
reformation.

Hubmaier's attitude in Zurich had undoubtedly disturbed the
Austrian government, which had been painfully watching the
swift progress of the great theological revolt. In the spirit of
Zwingli, Hubmaier had delivered his eighteen *Schlussreden* concerning the Christian life, which he hoped would win over the
clergy of Waldshut, the citizenry being already on his side. The
Catholic party in and about Waldshut in sharply worded letters
had demanded the removal of Hubmaier. The Austrian authorities were now insisting that he be turned over to the bishop of
Constance, but his Waldshut parishioners were protecting him.

The peasants of Stühlingen, striving to regain their old rights,
and the evangelical townspeople of Waldshut, supporting their
popular preacher, were differently motivated, but the common
foe was the Austrian archduke. Toward the end of July 1524,
a force of five hundred and fifty armed peasants visited Waldshut, and in the middle of August returned to make a treaty
with the town for mutual help and protection. The Austrian
authorities were not able to act decisively at first, but to protect
his reform, Hubmaier decided to seek temporary shelter in Swiss
Schaffhausen, where he had in student days been a teacher. He
left Waldshut on 1 September 1524.

Secure in their treaty with the town, the peasants moved out
from Waldshut in full armor to the parley with the lords. The
situation for the latter was difficult. They were tired of negotiating, but had no resources to take action. Several important
Austrian officials were thereupon invited to Radolfzell on 3 September to deal with the situation: Count Rudolf of Sulz, the
vicegerent of Upper Alsace, the representatives of Stuttgart, and
even the president of the imperial regiment in Esslingen,
Seneschal George of Waldburg. At this council of nobles and
officials it was decided to arm against the Swabian peasants, and
to raise twelve thousand foot and six hundred horse. But neither
the local nobility nor the Austrian government had the money,
and the resolutions remained on paper. But Count Rudolf had
been urged to seek a peaceable solution, and on 10 September
undertook to work out a compromise between Count Sigmund
of Stühlingen and his peasants.

Agreement was reached on essential points, but the peasants,
with their quite moderate demands, refused to surrender their

battle standard and to implore forgiveness in the open field; so the dealings were temporarily broken off. Thereupon Zurich sent one hundred and seventy volunteers to aid Waldshut and its peasant allies; and, as Austria did not choose to involve itself with the Swiss, it took no action against the town. Tension continued to grow toward the end of 1524.

In November and December, Thomas Müntzer was in the neighborhood of Waldshut, in Griessen, capital of the county of Stühlingen, and in the Hegau. His preaching does not seem to have been very successful in arousing the peasants, whom he sought to recruit in support of the Thuringian phase of the war. They refused to come except as mercenaries (and this Müntzer could not arrange). His ideas impressed Hubmaier, whom he does not, however, seem to have met in person.

It was about this time that Hubmaier returned from his temporary exile in Schaffhausen to resume his pastorate in Waldshut. In January he would be writing Oecolampadius about some advanced ideas he was developing about delaying the baptism of infants (Ch. 6.3).

The exiled Duke Ulrich of Württemberg took advantage of Austrian weakness to further his own plans to recover his duchy.[7] He had gathered a considerable army, and on 23 February 1525 he appeared before Stuttgart with six thousand foot and three hundred horse. It was the next day in distant Pavia that his patron Francis I of France was taken captive by the Emperor, by whom Ulrich had been deprived of his duchy. The Swiss recalled their mercenaries from Ulrich's service, leaving him desolate. The Austrians, released by their victory over France, were free to deal with Ulrich, while the forces which had been raised against Ulrich were also turned against the peasants.

On 1 March 1525, Sebastian Lotzer of Memmingen published the famous Twelve Articles, in the revision of which Hubmaier had a hand.[8] Their demands in summarized form were as follows: Every congregation should have the right to elect and to

[7] Born 1487, died 1550, duke 1498–1519, 1534–1550, Ulrich was driven out of his territory by the Swabian League in 1519 as a result of anger over his killing of Hans von Hutten, whom he charged with adultery with the duchess, and over his attempted seizure of the imperial town of Reutlingen. Espousing Protestantism, he was later restored to his patrimony by Philip of Hesse in 1534.

[8] He admitted this under torture at Vienna in 1528. Hubmaier was long considered the principal author of these controversial articles. Most scholars today, however, feel that Hubmaier's chief interest was for the freedom of the gospel, and that his association with the peasants was secondary. *ME*, II, 826–834, and the literature.

dismiss its own pastor (article i), and tithing for the support of the clergy should be limited to the "great tithe" (grain and produce), while the "small tithe" (livestock and dairy products) should be allowed to lapse (ii). Serfdom should be abrogated (iii), because Jesus Christ has redeemed or freed all men. Thus all men, not only the lords, have the right to hunt and fish (iv), and to gather wood from the common forest (v). Services are not to be exacted above what God's Word permits (vi), or what is customary (vii), and must be in proportion to the value of the land held (viii). Punishments must not exceed those provided by the customary law, whatever the provisions of the Roman law might have been (ix). Meadows and fields which have been common must be returned (x). The lords should not exact the customary death toll, depriving widows and orphans of their livelihood (xi). A final provision states that if any article can be shown to be contrary to the Word of God, it will be withdrawn (xii).[9]

In Memmingen, under Lotzer's leadership, a "Christian Union" (*Christliche Vereinigung*) of the peasant bands of the Allgäu, Lake Constance, and Baltringen was formed on 7 May 1525 on the basis of the Twelve Articles. They notified the Austrian-sponsored Swabian League of towns of their action and said that they had no intention of resorting to force. Under George Knopf, in the Allgäu, violence did break out, however, and the seneschal, George of Waldburg, struck back, annihilating a band of peasants at Leipheim near Ulm (4 April). The Leipheim Reformer Hans Jacob Wehe and five peasants were executed, and the towns of Leipheim and Günzberg were plundered. Alarmed and angered, the peasants of Upper Swabia assembled twelve thousand men. Seneschal George moved up with seven thousand troops, but hesitated to attack them. Because their demands were, after all, moderate, he signed the Weingarten Treaty, 17 April 1525, granting several of their points. The first phase of the war was at an end.

By the treaty the imperial seneschal gained freedom of action to deal with the other rebellious peasant groups, whose mood was fiercer and whose demands were more extensive than in the case of the Swabians.

b. The Franconian Phase: Carlstadt at Rothenburg. The hearths of the flaming movement outside Upper Swabia were Rothenburg, where the war broke out during March 1524, whence it spread through Franconia, and Mühlhausen, where Henry Pfeiffer's radical socioreligious reforms began in August

[9] Franz, *op. cit.*, 197–199.

1524 and then suddenly erupted in violence which swept through the whole of Thuringia in the last two weeks of April 1525. Another theater was Alsace. Two major spokesmen of the Radical Reformation were closely identified with the first two areas: Carlstadt with Rothenburg, in the role of ineffectual moderator of the excesses, and Müntzer with Mühlhausen, in the role of prophetic preacher. We shall limit ourselves in this section to the Franconian sector.

In Franconia, the peasants, together with the allied towns, generated proposals which were more radical than those in Upper Swabia, including the reorganization of the Empire with a peasants' parliament. The Franconian peasant army was characterized by a sort of Ironsides piety and sobriety, and was given considerable military discipline by three men drawn from the nobility—Florian Geyer, Wendel Hipler, and Götz of Berlichingen—who undertook the leadership of what had started out as a motley and disorganized force. Hipler had been formerly chancellor to the house of Hohenlohe and friend of the knight Götz (around whom Goethe was later to compose his play),[10] who led them in their march from Gundelsheim to Würzburg and back toward Heilbronn, deserting them at the last. Alone among the prominent figures, the knightly Florian Geyer stands out as a consecrated leader. Well-educated, moderately wealthy, he did not join the peasants' movement for opportunistic reasons but rather out of an inner conviction as to the need for reform and the legitimacy of the demands.

An account of the Franconian warfare may, for our purposes, begin with the entry of Carlstadt into the little imperial town of Rothenburg on the Tauber. Carlstadt, from whom we took leave in the previous chapter as he was turning down the covenantal overture from Müntzer in Allstedt well before the war, was an exile from Saxony, and by chance found himself at Rothenburg at the outbreak of the war. To be sure, there was reason for his stopping at Rothenburg en route to Basel. The Lutheran preacher there, Johann Teschlin, after passing through a bitterly anti-Semitic phase, had already developed a lay Christian puritanism very much like Carlstadt's own in Orlamünde. Accompanied by a crowd of followers, Carlstadt entered the diminutive imperial city toward the end of 1524. Because of his radicalism on the sacrament of the altar, and because of his having already been driven from Saxony under pressure from Luther, the town council, composed of patricians, drove him also from

[10] Götz's autobiography has recently been re-edited by H. S. M. Stuart (London, 1956).

Rothenburg by edict on 27 January 1525; but shortly thereafter he returned to take part, though somewhat incidentally, in the peasant uprising of which presently Rothenburg was to be a center.

During the fifteenth century the town had gone through periods of conflict in which gradually the artisans and also the peasants domiciled within Rothenburg's walls had gained some rights against the grudging patrician council. (Before this, the patricians had reserved for themselves the right of citizenship.) Although the Rothenburg peasant burghers were enfranchised, they still resented the patricians, and under pressure from the peasants outside the walls presently cast their lot with the insurgents.

The second phase in the second theater of the war began, without anyone's realizing it, 21 March 1525, when thirty peasants belonging to the militia of the dependent village of Ohrenbach entered the walls of Rothenburg, accompanied by pipes and drums, to make clear their grievances against the town council. When the patrician council turned them down they left in indignation. The other dependent villages recruited their armed strength, and the situation became immediately dangerous. The margrave, Casimir of Brandenburg, whose territory completely surrounded Rothenburg, offered his help, but the burghers and patricians were alike well aware that this could mean the crushing of their civil liberties by one who had long regarded the civic enclave as a thorn in his flesh. When, however, the council was about to secure the assent of the artisans in their guilds for support of what was, from the plebeian point of view, a reactionary policy, one Stephan of Menzingen arose and demanded that the artisans take counsel separately among themselves and pursue a policy more advantageous to themselves and also to the aggrieved peasants. Menzingen was himself a knight, who had once served under the margrave and had more recently become a bitter foe both of the margrave and of the town councilors.[11] Without deep religious or social convictions of his own, he had put himself at the head of the restive citizens of the town and moved rapidly toward gaining their support of the peasant uprising. He could see advantages for himself.

Through his efforts a committee of safety, or an emergency committee, was organized, which despite him was permeated by evangelical convictions, standing partly under the influence of the new social-sacramentarian preaching of Carlstadt. The more

[11] He had refused to pay dues on the castle, which he occupied on Rothenburg territory.

provocative actions of Stephan were at once mitigated or restrained by the former burgomaster Ehrenfried Kumpf, respected
by plebeians and patricians alike, who was able to argue with
the masses of his fellow townsmen for moderation, and with the
town fathers in the council for significant concessions to the
peasants in the dependent villages before it would be too late.
Presently, Kumpf brought forward the preacher Carlstadt, whom
the council had earlier driven from the town by edict, as an
appropriate arbiter in the current civil strife. Carlstadt himself
was reluctant to get into the social turmoil and resolved to confine himself to preaching social justice and counseling evangelical
moderation. In fact, the committee did not elect him as a representative in parleying with the peasants outside the walls. By
Easter, the townsmen had moved vigorously against the remnants of the Old Believers and their clerics in the small town.
On the Saturday before Easter, 15 April, a blind monk, completely under the influence of Carlstadt, arose to declare that
the sacrament of the altar was nothing more than a superstition
and heresy. On 17 April, Carlstadt himself mounted the pulpit
of the parish church and preached against both the Catholic
and the Lutheran views of the Sacrament, and with this unwitting encouragement the same kind of iconoclasm which had
broken out at Wittenberg in the absence of Luther now re-
sounded in Rothenburg. By this time the peasant uprising on
Rothenburg territory had fully coalesced with the larger Frankish uprising, and the situation was so desperate that the town
council seemed on the point of accepting the help of the hated
margrave. Thereupon it was possible for Stephan of Menzingen
to make clear to the artisans and local peasants that the liberties
of the townspeople were about to be curtailed, and he urged
them to accede to the ever-mounting demands of the enraged
Franconian peasants and specifically to join in "the brotherly
covenant," with a definite military target, namely, the strong-
hold of the bishop of Würzburg. The townspeople were not
unaware of the hazards of being allies of the peasant hordes, for
surely it would not be the most evangelical among them who
would make the deepest forays into the stores of wine in the
small town. Nevertheless, on 10 May 1525 the Rothenburgers
followed the towns of Heilbronn, Wimpfen, and Dinkelsbühl in
swearing allegiance to the peasant covenant by the solemn laying
on of hands.

It was the forthright and strong appeal of Florian Geyer which
finally brought the Rothenburgers around to the support of the
alliance. The old burgomaster Kumpf went along with the mili-

tary alliance in the hope that the peasant movement would be a means of spreading the gospel throughout the Empire. Carlstadt, who had undoubtedly heard the address of Florian Geyer in St. James's Church, felt that it was now his duty to go out with the belligerent citizens of Rothenburg, and to join the peasants as their chaplain, in order to keep the whole movement for social righteousness within bounds.

No sooner was Carlstadt out of the city than he experienced, to his amazement, the violence of the very peasants whose cause he had long espoused. The rumor had preceded him that for all his effort to identify himself with the cause of the peasants around Orlamünde and now in and around Rothenburg, he was no farmer but a university-educated scholar. Had it not been for the swift interception of the blow by a young councilor who, with Kumpf, belonged to the new military commission, a peasant mercenary would have succeeded in stabbing Carlstadt after a moment's rough interchange with him outside the town gates.

In a letter to the peasants in their encampment, Carlstadt recalled the example of Assyria and Moab and other peoples used by the Lord as the rod of his anger against his holy people. He reminded the peasants that though they were instruments of God's wrath, they too could in turn be punished because of their excesses.[12] This letter roused the peasants against him. It proved to be almost impossible for him to get any further hearing for his prophetically critical views of social justice.

Dejected and dismayed, he returned 16 May, and was scarcely readmitted at the gates of Rothenburg. Had it not been for the intervention this time of Menzingen, he would have been hanged by the very people who had once rallied to his sermons. On 18 May his opponents, the patricians in the council with a preference for Catholicism and the peasants and artisans who had never really understood what he was talking about in respect to the sacrament of the altar, insisted that the foreigner leave the town at once, and that Rothenburg be supplied with "true Christian preachers who preach and teach the holy gospel and God's word with forthrightness and clarity without any finespun glosses or human additions."[13] On the surface this looks like an evangelical appeal against a compromiser, but actually behind these tags taken from the new evangelical and Biblical terminology was a sacramental conception more conservative than Carlstadt's. For one of the other requirements of the same spokesman for the council and the peasants was the demand that laymen should be

---

[12] See below, Ch. 5, nn. 41 f.
[13] Barge, *Andreas Bodenstein*, II, 353.

enabled to receive the bread and the wine at least once a year, in order that "all Christian faithful men, according to the demand and requirement of our Lord Jesus Christ, receive under the form of bread and wine his blessed body and his rose-colored blood." The artisans who, with seeming appreciation and enthusiasm, had heard Carlstadt preach about the Sacrament as a sign pointing to the unique sacrifice of Christ on Calvary, had not fully understood him.

Carlstadt still persevered in his hope of mitigating the excesses of the peasant movement and joined the commission which represented Rothenburg at the meeting of the great Frankish *brüderschaft* at Schweinfurt on 1 and 2 June 1525. There had been an earlier meeting at Heilbronn to discuss the formation of a unified peasant front to become organized as an estate of the Empire, but the defeat at Zabern (17 May), which subdued the Alsatian sector, and especially the earlier defeat at Böblingen (12 May 1525) had momentarily caused the collapse of this constructive constitutional effort. Carlstadt's wife bravely accompanied him and endured with him the outrages that he had still to face in the midst of the peasants whom he as spiritual spokesman had sought to guide. The Schweinfurt Diet was a failure for want of adequate representation from different members of the alliance.[14]

Concurrently, the peasants were being put down at Königshofen (2 June) by the troops of George of Waldburg. Over the whole region, fields, orchards, and villages were in flames. Terror reigned at Würzburg. Completely demoralized, the remnants of the peasant army were defeated in battle near the villages of Sulzdorf and Ingolstadt on 4 June. Florian Geyer perished with a group of peasants he was leading at Schwäbisch-Hall, 9 July 1525.

Carlstadt broke his connection with Rothenburg, and we shall meet him next in Basel, where he will make an effort to concentrate on his Eucharistic theology and win for his views the Swiss and Strassburg theologians (Ch. 5).

While Carlstadt was becoming involved in the war at Rothenburg, his brother-in-law and former associate in Saxony, Dr. Westerburg, emerged in Frankfurt as the leader of both religious and social reform in giving assistance to the peasants who were seeking sympathy in the cities.

The peasant movement in the Rheingau, Mainz, and Frankfurt was constitutionally and religiously sound and momentarily successful. The peasants of the Rheingau, for example, allied with

[14] Franz, *op. cit.*, 332.

the knight Frederick of Greiffenklau and supported by Caspar
Hedio (Ch. 10.2–3) as evangelist, met in the Wacherholde, and
calling themselves *Bundesgenossen,* adopted the Rheingau articles, 23 April 1525, which renewed the rights contained in the
ancient charters and legal dicta, for example, the *Weistum* of
1524. New, however, was the demand for congregational election
of pastors and the closing of the locally oppressive monastery, and
the elimination of all tithes and dues for which the peasants,
knights, and townsmen were receiving no corresponding benefits.
The representative of the princely archbishopric acceded to the
demands without bloodshed.

Similar success temporarily attended Westerburg's efforts in
Frankfurt. The Forty-two Frankfurt Articles of April 1525 were
based on a brief draft of eleven prepared a week earlier by several
Christian brethren of Frankfurt and its dependency Sachsen-
hausen, led by Westerburg. They included religious, political,
and social demands and represented the desire of the artisans in
the town and the gardeners of its suburbs to improve their economic and political status in a manner comparable to the Twelve
Articles of Memmingen, in which Hubmaier had had a small
part.

Of special interest was the demand of the Westerburg group
that the pastors be elected conjointly by the parish and the town
council, and that they be obliged by specific regulations to observe their vows of chastity or otherwise openly marry. Among
the articles was the demand that the judicial procedure should
be democratized and that one of the two burgomasters be henceforth elected by the parish in order that the poor might be
heeded in the running of civic affairs.[15]

The articles were accepted by the Frankfurt council. They
were, in effect, the occasion for the revival of the reforming movement in Frankfurt, which had begun in 1522 and had been interrupted by the defeat of the imperial knights who had espoused
Luther's movement. Except for the Memmingen Twelve, the
Frankfurt articles were the only set printed,[16] and as a consequence became the model for similar statements as far north as
Münster and Osnabrück.

The swift destruction of the constitutional and religious gains
of the peasants and the petty burghers in the lower valley of the
Main from Frankfurt to Mainz was effected by the Swabian
League and the ruthless George of Waldburg even against the

---

[15] *Ibid.,* 374 ff.
[16] In Cologne and Mainz, but all that survives of them are the references
thereto in the records of the town council. Franz, *op. cit., Aktenband,* 378 ff.

restraining efforts of the electoral archbishop of Mainz (Cardinal Albert of Brandenburg) and his vicar, Bishop William of Strassburg. The latter, in whose city Hedio had by now settled as pastor, was somewhat sympathetic toward the peasants' complaint against tithes for no clerical service rendered. In vain did William seek to spare the Main and Rhine valley peasants from the harsh policy of the Swabian League. "Punishing the peasants" meant the repudiation of not only the most recent charters and treaties but also the more venerable *genossenschaftsrechte* of these yeomen and burghers.

As for the course of the peasant uprising closer to Bishop William's see, we shall have something further to say in connection with the peasant evangelist and consistent pacifist, Clement Ziegler, in Ch. 10.2.

As a result of the pressure of the territorial lords, Westerburg was banished from Frankfurt on the very day of the decisive Alsatian battle at Zabern. He thereupon returned to his native Cologne, and we shall see him next in connection with his doctrine of psychopannychism (Ch. 5.4) and as the leader of the Anabaptist movement in his native town.

c. Thuringia and Müntzer. We turn away from Franconia and back in time to pick up the narrative of the war in the Thuringian sector, where the leading roles were played by Henry Pfeiffer and, toward the end, by Thomas Müntzer. The region between the Harz Mountains on the north and the Erzgebirge on the south, settled by Lower Saxon and Rhenish colonists, had attracted settlers in the High Middle Ages with the promise of personal freedom and free tenure. Here any effort to restrict personal liberty in terms of the Roman law called forth bitter and determined opposition.

When Thomas Müntzer escaped from Allstedt, 7/8 August 1524 (Ch. 3.2) to join the Peasants' War, nearby Mühlhausen had already been a year in social, political, and religious turmoil. The revolutionary reformer was Henry Pfeiffer, who had come to the town as pastor in February 1523. His goal had been a larger representation of the humble citizens and the guilds in the town council, and the achievement of greater economic and social justice.[17] The notorious unrest excited Thomas Müntzer's eschatological expectations, and the political situation there suited his new mood. He at once set about having the revolutionary

---

[17] The main study here is by Otto Merx, *Thomas Müntzer und Heinrich Pfeiffer, 1523–1525: Ein Beitrag zur Geschichte des Bauernkrieges in Thüringen.* Only Part I was published: *Müntzer und Pfeiffer bis zum Ausbruch des Bauernkrieges* (Göttingen, 1889).

version of his *Entblössung* printed by John Hut.[18] Because of his greater fame as an antagonist of Luther and because of his writings, Müntzer has come to overshadow Henry Pfeiffer in the Mühlhausen uprising and the ensuing Peasants' War. The latter, lacking any other notable figure, has found in Thomas Müntzer its legendary hero or villain, depending upon the point of view. But Müntzer was active in the war at most for only three weeks, and the Mühlhausen *Chronicle*[19] is clear as to the major role of Pfeiffer.

Müntzer failed, to his great disappointment, to win the people of Mühlhausen for his own eschatological strategy. Availing himself of the revolutionary spirit, which betokened for him the fullness of time, Müntzer allied himself with Henry Pfeiffer for the realization of practical reform against the reactionary council. The people accepted him as a leader because he spoke their inflammatory language, but Pfeiffer's more practical aims were theirs. Müntzer tried to introduce his liturgy, which had been so popular in Allstedt, sending for his Mass books on August 15.[20] Although almost succeeding in their efforts, the two prophets were in a month (27 September 1524)[21] driven from the town by a combination of surrounding princes, town councils, and, significantly, also many peasants. Müntzer still regarded himself as a Biblical warrior-priest, signing his letters and otherwise referring to himself variously as "Thomas Müntzer with the sword of Gideon," "servant of God against the godless," "Thomas Müntzer with the hammer."

It was during his flight that Müntzer had printed in Nuremberg his *Hochverursachte Schutzrede* against "the Spiritless softliving flesh in Wittenberg," "Dr. Liar," "the Dragon," "the Archheathen," etc. Thus was he engaged in violent rebuttal of Luther's *Vom aufrührischen Geist.* Undoubtedly begun, if not actually completed, while still in Allstedt, this fierce tract makes no reference to Müntzer's new program in Mühlhausen. Breaking completely, however, with his Allstedt expectation that he might win the prince to his cause, Müntzer dedicates this tractate to Christ as Duke and King of Kings and to the Church of the poor, his Bride. This is one of the most significant of his writings. Herein the transition from concern for the impoverished in spirit (Prague *Manifesto*) to the poor in a frankly economic sense is completed.

[18] *Ibid.,* 135. On Hut, see below, Ch. 4.2.d.
[19] The relevant portions are reprinted in Brandt, *op. cit.,* 85 ff.
[20] Hinrichs, *op. cit.,* 134.
[21] Paul Wappler, *Die Täuferbewegung in Thüringen, von 1526–1584* (Jena, 1913); Austin P. Evans, *An Episode in the Struggle for Religious Freedom: The Sectaries of Nuremberg, 1524–1528* (New York, 1924).

Yet ambiguity remains because suffering, including a transitional state of poverty, is still thought of among the disciplines of redemption.

From Nuremberg, leaving Pfeiffer behind, Müntzer went on to Griessen, where we have already glimpsed him in the neighborhood of Waldshut.[22] While on flight from Mühlhausen, he preached the imminence of the Kingdom of God, sought support for the eschatological struggle, dined with Oecolampadius in Basel (October/December 1524), and received a letter (Ch. 5.2) from the Zurich patrician Conrad Grebel (September 1524), who had assumed the leadership of the radical and pacifistic Swiss Brethren and had recently read Müntzer's *Von dem gedichteten Glauben.*

In the meantime, Pfeiffer returned to the environs of Mühlhausen, and by the beginning of 1525, Müntzer was back himself. This time the two revolutionaries were more successful in their attack on the council and succeeded in replacing it with the so-called "eternal council" representative of the revolutionary classes.[23] Thomas Müntzer's *Aufruf an die Allstedter,* at the end of April 1525, among the most famous of his writings, appealing to his former parishioners, reflects the exuberant violence of this period. It surveys the glorious onset of saintly victory with uprisings everywhere in progress. "Let not the sword of the saint get cold," is his message;[24] "Throw the godless witches from the tower." The peasants' banners which Müntzer contrived were a white flag with a sword and a great white banner with a rainbow symbolic of the new covenant, for Müntzer had come to see in the peasant revolt the end of the fifth monarchy prophesied in Daniel and reprophesied in his own daring *Sermon Before the Princes* in Allstedt.

In this tense situation, Landgrave Philip of Hesse, quickly grasping the strategic problem, moved swiftly (14 May) against Müntzer's main group of peasants concentrated at Frankenhausen. After an initial skirmish in which the peasants maintained the advantage, the next day Philip offered them peace if they would surrender Müntzer. The peasants frittered away their

---

[22] For perhaps six months, according to Henry Bullinger. Ernst Staehelin, *Briefe und Akten zum Leben Oekolampads,* 2 vols. (Leipzig, 1927/1934), I, pp. 330 and 389–391, Nos. 227, 278.

[23] The idea of an eschatological council or synod crops up in the Radical Reformation and needs further investigation. It is discussed by Peter Kawerau, *Melchior Hoffman* (Haarlem, 1954), "Das Konzil der Endzeit," 85, 88.

It was a combination of a new apostolic council of (the New Jerusalem) and a new Pentecostal assembly of the upper room that was awaited.

[24] Brandt, *op.cit.,* 74.

initial advantage in discussion of this dishonorable proposal, for, while they were considering it, Philip's main force arrived and his artillery took up positions to fire on them. Too late they decided to fight, encouraged by Müntzer's appeals and the appearance of a rainbow over the Hessian troops. As soon as it became clear, however, that God was not protecting them, the peasants broke and fled, and were slaughtered like cattle.

Müntzer himself was not captured in the battle but overtaken in concealment. At the final hearing, Henry Pfeiffer proved to be more valiant than Müntzer, who recanted[25] and partook of the Communion after the Catholic manner. They were both beheaded. Mühlhausen was obliged to surrender territory to the surrounding princes and to pay indemnity for the destruction wrought by the armed bands which the town council had been unable to check without outside assistance.

d. *Three Minor Participants in the Thuringian-Franconian Phase of the War.* Besides Hubmaier at Waldshut, Carlstadt at Rothenburg, Westerburg at Frankfurt, and Pfeiffer and Müntzer at Mühlhausen as leading spokesmen of the civic rights of the peasants, mention can be made of the "military" careers of only a handful of others who, after the defeat of the peasants, were to become identified with Anabaptism and who are therefore of importance for our narrative. Some further biographical specificity about three of these—John Hut, George Haug, and Melchior Rinck—helps us to see the connection between the evangelical social idealism of the peasant unrest and Anabaptism.

While peddling his books between Wittenberg and Erfurt, John Hut, bookbinder and presently to become the apostle of Anabaptism in Upper Austria, went in the spring of 1525 to Frankenhausen, where Müntzer's army was stationed, hoping to earn money by selling books and pamphlets. He had already come to know Müntzer, who on his flight from Mühlhausen had spent a night and a day in his house and had given him to be printed the already mentioned exposition of Luke, ch. 1, *Die Entblössung.* He now heard Müntzer, at the acme of his prophetic career, preaching against the lords, and was deeply impressed. Müntzer echoed deep thoughts with which he had already become acquainted in John Denck (whom we shall meet in Ch. 7.1). Indeed, Hut had been driven from his home town for refusing, under Denck's influence, to have his child baptized. Not yet an Anabaptist, he was swayed by Müntzer's prophetic proclamation of the imminence of the advent of Christ. When the peasants marched to battle against Landgrave Philip, he went up the hill

25 Böhmer and Kirn. *Müntzers Briefwechsel,* 166 f.

with them, but because "the shooting was too thick," hastened back to the town, where he was seized by Philip's men. Fortunately, as a nonbelligerent, he was released. He now returned to Bibra, where he had formerly been a sexton in the service of the two local knights.

During the war, the peasants had burned down the knights' castle and had made one George Haug, a peasant from nearby Juchsen, the preacher of the village there. Haug had written a devotional tract bearing the title *Anfang eines christlichen Lebens,* 1524. Its motto was I Peter 3:15, a text which would later become programmatic for the Anabaptists; but the basic text was Isa. 11:2 f., with its strong eschatological and Spiritualist overtones. Appealing to the Isaianic sevenfold gift of the Spirit, as Müntzer did in his Prague *Manifesto,* Haug showed how a Christian life has to run through different stages of growth in order to arrive finally at the point of perfection where the mind becomes completely conformed to Christ. The gradual ascent to this goal is described by seven types of spirit, namely: the spirit of reverence, of wisdom, of understanding, of counsel, of strength, of patience, and of godliness. Alluding to the Messianic passage Isa. 11:1, "There shall come forth a shoot from the stump of Jesse, and a branch shall grow out of his roots," he goes on in poetic paraphrase of the two following verses to summarize his tract thus:

> To *fear* God from the heart is *wisdom;*
> To avoid evil is *understanding;*
> The understanding of divine love brings faithfulness
> (*Glauben*)
> And is good for them who do it.
> Not to let oneself be confused is *counsel;*
> To overcome self is *might,*
> And to judge all things and endure all is *knowledge*
> (*Kunst*);
> To become like Jesus Christ and of one mind with
> him is blessedness.
> In him (*da*) all rests and is the true Sabbath,
> Which God demands of us and which [or, whom] the
> whole world opposes.[26]

Haug invited Hut to preach on 31 May 1525. The former sexton and peddler preached on Baptism, Communion, idolatry, and the Mass. Though the peasants had been crushed a fortnight before at Frankenhausen, Hut still felt that he was living in the

---

[26] Müller, *Glaubenszeugnisse* (*QGT,* III), 10. *"Kunst"* here is similar to *"Gelassenheit."* The tract is close to Ruysbroeck and speaks of the abyss of the soul.

last days before the fulfillment of the promises, and he rebuked the holders of benefices and clerical beneficiaries of forced tithing, who served the gospel for the sake of their belly: "The Almighty God will punish them and all who oppose the truth; they will all perish in disgrace." He continues: "The subjects should murder all the authorities, for the opportune time has arrived: the power is in their hands."[27] This kind of utterance caused the authorities to class Hut as a disciple of Müntzer. It is on the connection between Müntzer and Hut that Henry Bullinger (and later historians)[28] have based their assertion that Müntzer was the father of the Anabaptist movement.

After the complete rout of the peasants in June, Hut, because of his Müntzerite pronouncements, was forced to flee to Augsburg, where he again encountered John Denck, himself recently banished from Nuremberg. (The meeting with Denck will produce a great change in Hut. He will accept rebaptism at Denck's hands on 26 May 1526, Ch. 7.4.)

It remains only to mention Melchior Rinck, presently to become the leader and martyr of Anabaptism in Hesse. Educated at Leipzig and Erfurt, and nicknamed "the Greek" in allusion to his mastery of the language, Rinck, after becoming a Lutheran pastor in Oberhausen (subsequently in Eckhardtshausen) near Eisenach, fell under the spell of Müntzer. He took part in the battle at Frankenhausen. After the collapse of the peasants' uprising and the execution of its prophet, Rinck tried to continue Müntzer's work by means of strong polemics against Luther's doctrine of justification, the proper fruits of which, he thought, were scarcer, the more closely one approached Wittenberg. We shall overtake him in the spring of 1527, when, with John Denck, Louis Haetzer, and Jacob Kautz, he will sign the seven articles for the important disputation with the Lutherans in Worms (Ch. 16.1).

e. Echoes and Reverberations. The final phase of the war arose simultaneously in Freiburg and far away in the counties of Tyrol

[27] Christian Meyer, "Zur Geschichte der Wiedertäufer in Oberschwaben," *Zeitschrift des historischen Vereins für Schwaben und Neuberg*, I (1874), 207–256, esp. 241, with a complete publication of the court records at Augsburg; Herbert Klassen, "The Life and Teachings of Hans Hut," *MQR*, XXXIII (1959), 171 ff., 267 ff. Hut explained at his trial that he had once thought the war was a sign that the last times had come, but he admitted to having clearly erred and said that he knew better now. He explained that he had never been a full adherent of Müntzer because "he did not understand him."

[28] Heinrich Böhmer, "Thomas Müntzer und das jüngste Deutschland," *Gesammelte Aufsätze* (Gotha, 1926), 221; Karl Holl, "Luther und die Schwärmer," *Gesammelte Aufsätze zur Kirchengeschichte*, I (Tübingen, 1923), 423 ff.

and of Salzburg after 30 April 1525, where the proud and hitherto free Tyrolese, under Michael Gaismair, sought to establish an Alpine peasant state like the earlier Swiss Confederation. Gaismair, a miner's son who became an episcopal secretary, was animated by a Christian spirit of charity and a desire to mitigate social evils. He believed that Christianity demanded equality among men. He had a vision of a peasant commonwealth, and was not concerned, as the other leaders were, about lesser rights and privileges. With all his enthusiasm for equality, Gaismair still left a place for the prince as head of the state, but lesser nobles and ecclesiastical princes and their domains were to be eliminated to make way for a peasants' republic on the crossroads of European trade.[29] It is of interest that the knightly physician Paracelsus (Ch. 8.4.b) sided with the peasants in their abortive Tyrolese revolution.

Archduke Ferdinand moved firmly but less cruelly than Seneschal George, and the last flames of revolt were stamped out in Salzburg in November 1525.

3. CONCLUSION

When the embers, quickened into a momentary flame a second time in Salzburg, were put out in 1526, the Great Peasants' War had come to an end. The peasants had been everywhere crushed because they had no universally recognized leader and only an improvised organization, and had to make do with the evangelical counsel of a few prophetic clerics and the military skills of a few disaffected knights. The latter themselves belonged to a politically doomed class. As for the clerics, a word in extenuation.

Carlstadt, who went out as chaplain from the imperial city of Rothenburg in league with Florian Geyer, and Müntzer, with his heraldic sign of a red cross and a naked sword, who was "a prophet in front of the army"[30] at Frankenhausen and was beheaded, are commonly disparaged as heretics and *Schwärmer*. In contrast, Ulrich Zwingli, who five years later will be drawn and quartered by the troops of the Catholic cantons on the battlefield of Cappel in 1531, is usually regarded as a hero and martyr of the Magisterial Reformation. Yet it was not an entirely different conception of the social implication of a reformed Christianity that separated the sacramentarian chaplain of Zurich from the Spiritualist chaplains of Allstedt-Mühlhausen and Orlamünde-Rothenburg.

We have glimpsed enough of the military action of the Great

[29] Franz, *op. cit.*, 264.
[30] Deuteronomy 20:2 (Vulgate text); see his *Sermon Before the Princes, SAW,* 64

Peasants' War; have characterized a sufficient number of its knightly, clerical, burgher, and peasant leaders; have overheard enough of the intermingled economic, social, and evangelical aspirations of artisans, miners, and petty burghers; and have inspected enough of their serious religio-constitutional program to conclude that we have indeed been witnessing the tragic unfolding of a civil war within the Empire, comparable to the upheaval in seventeenth-century England, where the same kind of religious, social, and constitutional factors reshaped the structure and character of English Christendom. But Germany's civil war was abortive.

The two turmoiled years (1524–1525) of the Great Peasants' War can also be compared as a civil war, except for its duration and magnitude, to the thirty years of the civil war of the dynasts (1618–1648) in their unrealized but inherently significant constitutional and religious potential. That more famous and longer war within the Empire, which finally ended by converting it into a sonorous shell, proved to be more important because it was fought out between the defenders of the Magisterial Reformation and the devout dynasts on the other side, sustained by the zeal of the Counter Reformation. But it was surely no more religiously motivated than the earlier civil war of the classes which we have just surveyed; and, had the misnamed Peasants' War— peasants as mercenaries or recruits have, after all, predominated in all wars since the end of the feudal age—succeeded in achieving its originally moderate constitutional and religious goals, the second and even more savage Thirty Years' War might never have come.

For not only was the economic and political situation of the peasants and the artisans worsened by their war, but also their enthusiasm for the Lutheran Reformation was destroyed.

At first, Luther had tried to promote peace in his *An Admonition to Peace: A Reply to the Twelve Articles of the Peasants in Swabia* (19 April 1525) ; but three weeks later, as soon as he became convinced that the peasants, especially outside Upper Swabia, were endangering his own heroic program for the recovery of the gospel from papal secularization by implicating it "selfishly in peasant sedition," he violently attacked them in *Against the Robbing and Murdering Hordes of Peasants*. Henceforth the Magisterial Reformation in Germany stood with the princes and the patricians. Lutheranism after 1525 lost something of its character as a pan-German people's movement.[31] The peas-

---

[31] On the survival of the popular character of Lutheranism after 1525, see Franz Lau, "Der Bauernkrieg und das angebliche Ende der lutherischen Reformation als Volksbewegung," *Luther-Jahrbuch,* 1959, 109–134.

ants for the most part acquiesced sullenly in the arrangements for the emergent territorial churches. Some of their theologically trained spokesmen, however, calling Protestantism the new indulgence system of salvation *sola fide,* in utter disillusionment led many from the Magisterial Reformation into the emergent Anabaptist movement, which, except for one effort, ever thereafter was to eschew military and political action and convert its constitutional energies and Biblical idealism into the formation of self-disciplined conventicles separated from the state.

Thereby Luther's own youthful vision of reformation was seriously impaired, for the principal victors in the civil war were the princes, who centralized, regardless of religious confession, their control in civil jurisdiction and religion, and with the slogan *cuius regio, eius religio* established either a Catholic or a Protestant Christianity in the spirit and with the precedent of Constantine, no longer, however, on the ecumenical basis of a universal empire but on the particularist basis of princely absolutism. The half-Catholic, half-Protestant reforming duke of Cleves was presently to say clearly what all German princes were assuming with but variations in style: *Dux Cleviae imperator est in ducatu suo.*[32]

No one has thus far identified as constitutive of a third phase in the history of central European peasant upheaval the establishment of the Hutterite communistic enclaves on a firm theological and economic footing in 1533 (Ch. 9.2) and the concurrent rise of the peasant-artisan, militantly Anabaptist Bibliocracy in Münster and its satellite towns in the fall of the same year (Ch. 13). By way of schematic anticipation we merely observe at this point that the truculence of the Münsterites, the joint Protestant-Catholic suppression of their movement, and the persecution of the pacifistic Hutterites are in part to be seen as extensions of the class conflict of the Peasants' War.

From 1524 to 1525 the peasants of Lower Germany and the Netherlands had been uninvolved, partly because of their more advantageous economic and juridical status. A decade later, Westphalia, the center of the region characterized socioeconomically by its relatively large proportion of yeomen *(meier)* holding sizable farms and enjoying stable rights and duties, would find itself suddenly the center of the eschatological and social aspirations of local and especially foreign artisans and peasants, sustained by the apocalyptic vision of Melchior Hofmann, who was, like Carlstadt, a nonviolent visionary.

---

[32] The duke received the *jus episcopale* from the pope in 1445. J. F. Knapp, *Regenten und Volksgeschichte der Länder Cleve, Mark, Jülich, Berg, und Ravensberg* (Crefeld, 1936), III, 120 ff.

Because the Münsterite uprising was to get out of hand and was to be stamped out, the only significant survival of the evangelically motivated social utopianism of the peasant uprisings in the opening third of the Reformation century was to be the sectarian socioeconomic colonization in Moravia by the Hutterites. Among them the theocratic ideals of both the Magisterial Reformers and the revolutionary Spiritualists would be sublimated in a new kind of conventicular commonwealth which was to merge congregation and community, family and manorial village, in the Biblically governed and communal *Bruderhof* or *Haushaben.*

Chapter 5

THE EUCHARISTIC CONTROVERSY DIVIDES THE REFORMATION, 1523–1526

With the Great Peasants' War behind us, we could step along a well-trodden path to examine the sprouting Anabaptist conventicles at the end of the great social harrowing. But the spread of the radical influence of the Netherlandish Sacramentists into Upper Germany and the Swiss cantons has still to be recounted.

Thus far, the Eucharistic Controversy has been seen primarily as a conflict between Carlstadt and Luther in Saxony, with echoes in Rothenburg, where exiled Carlstadt sojourned uneasily on his way to Basel. His brother-in-law, Dr. Westerburg, had already carried his Eucharistic tracts in manuscript thither, while Hinne Rode from Utrecht had, at about the same time, been introducing to the Swiss Reformers the Eucharistic theory of Cornelius Hoen. The influence of Carlstadt, Hoen, and also Erasmus, resident in Basel, was in the end effective in converting the whole of the Swiss Reformation to the sacramentarian position. Within the enclosing frame of the history of the classical Protestant or Magisterial Reformation, the conversion of the Swiss and, by contagion, many of the South German towns to the sacramentarian view has been seen by the Reformed and the Lutherans alike as a fateful division within the Protestant forces, and one with massive consequences alike for the development of German national history and the spread and confinement of Protestantism.

Within the even narrower framework of the present narrative, limited to the history of the Radical Reformation, the theological cleavage of Saxony and Switzerland has its own significance. Radical reaction to the sacramentally conservative Lutheran reform, which was seeking to preserve as much as possible of two or three of the seven medieval sacraments, tended to be Spiritualist with special reference to the sacrament of the Supper, drawing upon a Spiritualism inherent in the young Luther's own experience of salvation by faith alone. In contrast, radical or sectarian reaction to the Magisterial Reformation of the Swiss (which was itself, in being almost from the outset sacramentarian, already more radical than Luther's) involved alteration in the last sacrament remaining intact from the medieval church, namely, that of Baptism. Thus, while the radical form of Lutheranism was Spiritualism, the radical form of Zwinglianism was Anabaptism.

This generalization may be pinned down to names and dates. It was Conrad Grebel, the patrician companion of the peasant Reformer of Zurich, who first organized a sacramentarian anabaptist conventicle in January 1525. It was Caspar Schwenckfeld, the aristocratic Lutheran Reformer of Silesia, who in April 1526 first announced the radical Spiritualist principle of the general suspension of the external Eucharist. In effect, Schwenckfeld thereby interiorized the sacrament of the altar and limited the spiritual feeding to the regenerate. In an analogous way, Grebel reasserted the exclusively subjective and inward character of the sacrament of regeneration.

Although Anabaptism became fully articulate more than a year before radical evangelical Spiritualism, we shall postpone the discussion of it until the next chapter, because the radical thrust of sacramentarianism is as indispensable to an understanding of the emergence of Anabaptism as is the Peasants' War.

The first phase of the great Eucharistic Controversy within Protestantism as a whole extends, of course, to the Marburg colloquy in 1529. We shall, however, follow it stage by stage toward that fateful development only in so far as those now recognized as belonging to the Radical Reformation, both Spiritualists and proto-Anabaptists, participated in it transitionally.

1. HINNE RODE IN BASEL AND ZURICH
WITH OECOLAMPADIUS AND ZWINGLI

We took leave of Hinne Rode (Ch. 2.2) as he returned from Wittenberg to Utrecht, where he was deposed from the rectorship of the local school of the Brethren.

Leaving Utrecht, he journeyed with George Sagranus to Basel, staying in the house of the printer Andreas Cratander. There he dined with Oecolampadius, 22 January 1523.[1] He had with him the works of Gansfort, which he hoped could be published by Cratander, as they had been in part in Wittenberg. It is uncertain

---

[1] Oecolampadius to Hedio; Staehelin, *Briefe und Akten*, I, No. 142. Clemen, *loc. cit.*, says he came to Basel before September 1522.

whether Rode also shared Hoen's *Epistola* with Oecolampadius.[2] It is, however, quite probable. Rode may also have presented a copy of his own (or Hoen's) *Oeconomia christiana*. This was, in turn, read by the French refugee Evangelical from Meaux, William Farel, at the time sojourning in Basel, who translated it and had it printed by Thomas Wolff as *La somme de l'Écriture sainte et l'ordinaire des chrétiens enseignant la vraie foi* (Basel, 1523), the first evangelical book in French.[3] It is also possible that on this occasion Oecolampadius gave Rode a copy of *Das Testament Jesu Christi, das man bisher genannt hat die Messe*. This work was connected with Oecolampadius' earlier reform at Ebernburg, where, under the protection of the imperial knight Francis of Sickingen, he had evangelically reformed the Mass. It was presently to be translated by Rode into Dutch and published along with a Dutch version of the *Oeconomia christiana*.[4]

Before following Rode to Zurich at the suggestion of Oecolampadius, we shall do well to linger in the town and with its chief Reformer, alike important for the unfolding narrative of the Radical Reformation.

Basel, episcopal see, seat of a university, a publishing center, and the scene of the great reforming council 1431–1448, had in 1501 joined the Swiss Confederation. Despite his reforming zeal and humanistic patronage, Bishop Christopher of Utenheim (1502–1527) found himself gradually removed by the same civic drive that had already hollowed out city republics from the cores of many a prince-bishopric in the aging Empire. It was in 1521 that the citizens of Basel declared their full independence from their bishop in temporalities, eliminated their annual temporal oath to him, and named their own council and burgomaster. It would not be, however, until 1529 that Basel would become also spiritually independent. In the meantime, the leaven of humanism and of Lutheran solafideism was at work, and Oecolampadius (1482–1531) was at the center of the spiritual ferment.

As a student he had studied Roman law in Bologna and come under the reforming influence of Jacob Wimpfeling in Heidelberg and of John Reuchlin in Tübingen. On becoming cathedral preacher in Basel in 1515, he helped Erasmus with the preparation of the Greek New Testament. From 1518 to 1520 he held the

---

2 Ernst Staehelin, *Das theologische Lebenswerk Johannes Oekolampads*, Quellen und Forschungen zur Reformationsgeschichte, XXI (Leipzig, 1939), 269.
3 N. Weiss and Jean Meyerhoffer in the collective work *Guillaume Farel* (Neuchâtel/Paris, 1930), cxii, 118 ff.
4 On the complex question of authorship and versions, see Staehelin, *Briefe und Akten*, I, No. 142, n. 10.

same position of preacher in the cathedral in Augsburg. He began by championing Luther's solafideism, but then reacted against it, retiring to a monastery in April. In this contemplative mood he went through an evolution in his Eucharistic theology comparable to Gansfort's (Ch. 2.1), coming to recognize the Word of God as itself a kind of sacrament and the sacrament of the altar as a means whereby God reconciles himself with the faithful (and expressly not the nominal) Christians under the symbol of the bread and wine, and they become part of his mysterious body descending from heaven.[5] Almost exactly a year to the day before his dinner with Rode, Oecolampadius had escaped from his St. Bridget's cloister (23 January 1522), and, after passing by way of Mainz, Heidelberg, and Sickingen's Ebernburg, already well on his way to the sacramentarian conviction, he had returned in November to Basel, where by now the sacramentarian spirit was well advanced.

Here William Reublin, as people's priest in St. Alban's, destined to become an important Anabaptist leader, had, with audiences up to four thousand, been preaching against vigils, Masses for the dead, fastings, and other regulations and ceremonies, and against the bishop himself. The bishop had, of course, remonstrated in the city council. When, on 13 June, Reublin had gone so far as to replace a reliquary in the Corpus Christi procession with a Bible, declaring that the Word of God alone was the proper object of veneration, the support of the guildsmen was insufficient to prevent his banishment on 27 June. (We shall next meet Reublin in Ch. 6.3.)

Oecolampadius, in view of the popular support of Reublin, had only to be somewhat more circumspect to bring the whole town over to a sacramentarian reformation. We can well understand that after his dinner with Hinne Rode it was with much interest in the Dutch development that Oecolampadius encouraged his guest to go to Zurich to meet Zwingli.

This encounter of Rode and Zwingli, a major event in the development of Reformation thought on the Lord's Supper, took place in the summer of 1523. Zwingli found the *Epistola* of Hoen to be a revelation.[6] The idea of taking *est* to mean *significat* crystallized for Zwingli ideas that had been vague in Oecolampadius and Erasmus.[7]

---

[5] Staehelin, *Lebenswerk*, 151 ff., 268.
[6] So he later told Bugenhagen in a letter of October 1525. Zwingli, *Sämtliche Werke* (henceforth: *ZW*), IV (Leipzig, 1927), 564–576.
[7] Zwingli published the *Epistola* in 1525, omitting Hoen's name, evidently to protect him.

But before following the development of sacramentarianism in Zurich, we must return with Rode to the Netherlands. Rode was next with Martin Bucer at Strassburg in 1524, then in Deventer in 1525, and as a minister at Norden in East Frisia in 1527, where in 1530 he was to be dismissed because of "Zwinglianism" (!), disappearing thereafter from the records.[8] As for Hoen, he was arrested at his home in February 1523, *propter sectam Lutheranam,* put in chains, and taken to Geertruidenberg. The stadholder of the Netherlands (1507–1530), Margaret of Austria, soon had him brought back to The Hague for investigation of the complaint against him, for which he was allowed two doctors of theology to assist him. The inquisitor summarily sent Hoen to prison. The inquisitor was, however, dismissed the following October, and Margaret, in response to the pleas of the state council, returned Hoen to The Hague. He was released upon the bail of three thousand ducats, dying before April of 1524.[9]

2. THE EUCHARISTIC CONTROVERSY IN ZURICH: THE SECOND
   DISPUTATION, OCTOBER 1523: BALTHASAR HUBMAIER,
   CONRAD GREBEL, AND LOUIS HAETZER

To return to Switzerland, Rode had conferred with Zwingli in the summer of 1523. Then, in the early fall, there was an outbreak of iconoclasm that made Zwingli pull back. Up to this time, there was no real differentiation within the Zwinglian reform movement, for Zwingli himself shared pretty much the radical evangelical view on the Eucharist, images, and coercion in religion. On the latter issue, for example, he had declared as an Erasmian pacifist:

I believe that, as the church came into existence by blood, so it can be renewed only by blood [suffering witness], not otherwise. Never will the world be a friend to Christ. He sent his own as "sheep among wolves."[10]

But the willingness of the town council to go along with a cautious reform had led him to modify his stand and to reduce the demands made, in his early enthusiasm, in accommodation to the exigencies of local conditions. When, from 26 to 28 October 1523, magistrates of the greater and lesser councils and the leading divines, in the presence of more than five hundred priests, were engaged in the Second Zurich Disputation, in the council

---

[8] Lindeboom, *De Confessioneele Ontwikkeling,* 46.
[9] See also *ME,* II, 776.
[10] Letter to Myconius, 24 July 1520, *ZW,* VII, 341 f.

between the Old Believers and the Reformers, Zwingli was now the spokesman, among the latter, of conservative reform over against precipitate reform.

a. *The Second Zurich Disputation, October 1523*. The first two days were devoted primarily to the use of images, but the last day was entirely devoted to the problem of the Mass. Zwingli, for tactical reasons, preferred to gain time until the whole canton could be brought to espouse the Reform in theological depth and sociopolitical unanimity. Although with the spokesmen of the radical wing of the Zurich Reformation he had long been prepared to repudiate the *idea* of repetitive sacrifices on the altar, he was at least publicly disposed to hold that the Eucharist might well be a proper representation of Christ's unique, historic, and atoning sacrifice. Zwingli had thus moved all the way from an earlier confident expectation that the city council would abolish the Mass as an insult to God, through an avowal that he would preach and act regardless of what the council ordered, to his statement in the course of the Second Disputation that nothing should be done without express instructions from the magistracy, lest the canton be religiously divided as Bohemia was, following Hus. This was a fundamental shift from his earlier position on the relationship between church and state. Although he continued to defend the principle of the sole authority of Scripture, in practice he followed the wishes of the council, thus virtually committing the reformation of the church to the civil government. This was a grievous blow to many of Zwingli's friends, and it is at this point that we begin to see the definite indications of withdrawal of those interested in the immediate introduction of New Testament standards.

It was left to Ingolstadt-educated Dr. Balthasar Hubmaier, whom we have already met at the beginning of the Peasants' War in nearby Waldshut (Ch. 4.2.a), to give voice to the radical faction at the disputation:

I cannot announce it in any other way [Hubmaier proceeded diplomatically] than Zwingli and Leo [Jud] have done—by saying that the mass is no sacrifice, but rather a publishing of Christ's testament, in which is celebrated the memorial of his death, through which he no doubt offered himself once for all on the altar of the cross and cannot be offered again. . . . The reason that moves me to say this is . . . [that] Christ says, "This do," but not, "This offer." Whence it follows, first, that the mass, if it is held to be a sacrifice, profits neither living nor dead. For as I cannot believe for another, so it is not permitted me to celebrate mass for another, since truly this was instituted by Christ as a sign, in which the faith of believers is confirmed.

Secondly, since the body and blood of Christ are seals and tokens of Christ's words that it is customary to recite in the mass, priests ought to use and proclaim nothing but the pure and clear word of God, of which these are signs. . . .

Thirdly, he who does not proclaim the Word of God does not celebrate the mass. . . .

Fourthly, the mass should be read in Latin to the Latins, in French to the French, and in German to the Germans. For there can be no doubt but that Christ used a language at the Supper with his disciples that could be understood by all of them. . . .

Fifthly, he who undertakes to celebrate mass truly ought to feed not only himself, but also others hungering and thirsting in spirit, and that under both kinds. Christ taught this by both word and deed.[11]

Whether Hubmaier was in this speech dependent on Carlstadt is not certain. The most prominent associates of Hubmaier among the precipitate in the reforming party at the disputation were Louis Haetzer, Felix Mantz, and Conrad Grebel. Before picking up the unraveled threads of Eucharistic theology in Zurich, we should perhaps pause at this point to introduce these three other leading radical sacramentarians, unknowingly on the threshold of major careers in the rise of Anabaptism.

b. *Three Zurich Radicals: Haetzer, Mantz, and Grebel.* Among the three sacramentarian Radicals, Louis Haetzer was the most vigorous opponent of the use of images. Sacramentarianism and iconoclasm were inextricably interrelated in the Second Disputation in that the Radicals were coming to consider genuflection before the images of the saints and before the Eucharistic elements as equally idolatrous.

Haetzer, who was born in the district of Thurgau[12] about 1500 and had been educated locally for the priesthood before matriculation in Basel in 1517, had come to Zurich from his first charge as chaplain in nearby Wädenswil, attracted, no doubt, by the prospects of vigorous reformation in the cantonal capital and coming well prepared in the three classical languages of theology for participation in the great debates.

Leo Jud, Zwingli's successor at Einsiedeln and now pastor in St. Peter's, delivered an impassioned sermon 1 September 1523 against statues and paintings and demanded, perhaps for the first time in Zurich, their removal from the churches.

In the course of the consequent acts of iconoclasm and before the opening of the Second Disputation, Louis Haetzer published his first book, *The Judgment of God Our Spouse as to How One Should Hold Oneself Toward All Idols and Images.* Dependent

---

[11] *ZW*, II, 671–803; translated by Henry Vedder, *Balthasar Hübmaier: The Leader of the Anabaptists* (New York/London, 1905), 63 f.

[12] Now a canton, it was then subject to Zurich.

upon Carlstadt's earlier work (Ch. 3.1), this was a major link in the chain that was to lead to Zwingli's great treatise against images incorporated in the *Answer to Valentin Compar*[13] and therewith to the establishment of that hostility to the pictorial in religion which has characterized the sacramentarian Reformed tradition ever since, over against the consubstantiationist Lutheran development.

In the pamphlet, setting forth the arguments of Carlstadt more succinctly and cogently, Haetzer contended: (1) that God's commandment on idolatry was no less binding than the other nine; (2) that the pilgrimages to shrines was a clear indication that the images were in fact idols, since the saints, to say nothing of God himself, can be approached directly; (3) that far from being books for the illiterate, they have become substitutes for the Book; and (4) that instead of inducing worshipers to reverence and improvement, they in fact distract them from the Heavenly Father, who alone draws men unto him.

Felix Mantz, another Radical at the Second Disputation, was born in Zurich, c. 1498,[14] the son of either the Zurich canon *(Chorherr)* John Mantz, or the provost of the same name.[15] He applied in 1520 for one of the royal French scholarships for Swiss students in Paris. We first catch sight of him when, gripped by his great religious inspiration, he became a leader of the Radicals in Zurich. He was, together with Grebel, one of those who studied the ancient languages with Zwingli in 1522–1523, becoming proficient in Latin, Greek, and Hebrew.[16] Zwingli considered him for the post of instructor in Hebrew at the Great Minster School, which he proposed to reorganize (September 1523), but rejected him because of his radical theological tendencies. He became steadily more prominent in the growing cleavage between the Zwinglian conservatives and the hyper-Zwinglian Radicals.

With the destined leader of the Zurich Radicals, Conrad Grebel, we must linger longer. As a layman, he too took the floor

---

[13] The significance of Haetzer's iconoclasm and his dependence on Carlstadt have been demonstrated by Charles Garside, Jr., "Ludwig Haetzer's Pamphlet Against Images," *MQR*, XXXIV (1960), 3–19.

[14] Ekkehard Krajewski, *Leben und Sterben des Zürcher Täuferführers Felix Mantz* (Kassel, 1957), 18, says *"um 1500,"* citing *Aktensammlung zur Geschichte der Basler Reformation* (1921), I, 174:13–14, to refute the common tradition that Mantz was older than Zwingli, e.g., Paul Peachy, *Die soziale Herkunft der Schweizer Täufer in der Reformationszeit* (Karlsruhe, 1954), 27.

[15] One is attested in the records from 1494–1498, the other from 1494–1518.

[16] Krajewski, *op. cit.,* 24.

in the October disputation and spoke out against Zwingli's evasions on both images and the Mass.

Grebel,[17] a radical leader from a patrician family, was a humanist of refinement. Grebels had frequently been magistrates, and, for
several decades preceding the Reformation, there had been no
important political event in Zurich in which a Grebel did not
have a part. Conrad's father, Jacob Grebel, was the most influential and wealthy of the clan, with a successful career as an iron
merchant, magistrate, and representative of the canton in the
diet of the Confederation. Conrad, born in 1498, probably grew
up in the castle of Grüningen, where his father served two terms
as bailiff (*Vogt*) of the dependent territory. He attended the
Latin school, the Carolina in Zurich, which was doubtless like
other Latin schools of the day, rowdy in conduct and scholastic
in spirit. It nevertheless provided Conrad with the skills necessary to become a promising humanist scholar.

In the fall of 1514 he went to the university in Basel. The older
humanism which earlier characterized Basel had virtually disappeared with the departure of the famous Sebastian Brant in 1501;
and the new light of Erasmus had not yet begun to shine. Young
Grebel was fortunate, however, in becoming attached to the
bursa (collegiate society) of Henry Loriti, commonly called
Glarean (1488–1563). This promising scholar, only a few years
older than Grebel himself, seems to have been a source of inspiration to Grebel, who later complained that he had found no
teacher so good. After a term in Basel, Grebel obtained through
his father a scholarship in Vienna, where the great Swiss humanist Joachim von Watt, called Vadian (1484–1551), the future Reformer of St. Gall, was teaching and acting as a counselor and
patron to Swiss students who found their way to Austria. To
Vadian's first edition of a commentary on the ancient geographical treatises of Pomponius Mela, Grebel contributed a prefatory
poem, and to the second edition a new introduction. With the
aid of a royal scholarship (one of two granted annually to each
Swiss canton) from Francis I, also arranged by his father, Grebel
was able to study at Paris in 1518, whither his favorite teacher,
Glarean, had preceded him. In contrast to Basel and Vienna,
Paris was governed by the still medieval spirit of scholasticism.
Grebel came to know the Biblical scholar and translator LeFèvre
d'Étaples, who was at the College of Cardinal Lemoine (not, however, at the university). He enlarged his humanistic erudition by
contacts with William Budé also, and with William Cop, himself

---

[17] The basic work is that of Harold S. Bender, *Conrad Grebel, c. 1498–1526,
Founder of the Swiss Brethren, sometimes called Anabaptists* (Goshen, 1950).

a Swiss, but seemed to lose much of his enthusiasm for study and contemplated going to Italy.[18] Grebel's sojourn in Paris was overcast by a series of quarrels with Glarean (an eventual opponent of the Reformation), from whose *bursa* he withdrew after a stay of less than three months. His health seems to have been seriously impaired, perhaps by the riotous living of which his senatorial father accused him and on account of which his Viennese mentor, Vadian, sorrowed. His father held back six hundred of the eight hundred crowns of the royal pension. In a sober and somewhat melancholy state of mind, Grebel returned to Zurich in June 1520, his student days behind him.

At home, he found someone who had more to offer than the scholars of Paris. In October 1521, Grebel, together with Mantz and other Swiss students who had returned from abroad, intensified his study of Greek and Hebrew with Zwingli. Fellowship with old and new friends brought him much satisfaction. Through Zwingli, Grebel once again came into a more intimate contact with humanistic circles and even possibly with Erasmus. (He may have traveled to Basel with Vadian to meet him in 1522.) Unlike Erasmus, Grebel's Swiss humanistic friends, and Grebel himself, were chiefly interested in historical, geographical, and philological study, and only incidentally in moral and religious matters. Their Swiss patriotism was conspicuous. In religion, Grebel was still neutral, like Vadian and Glarean. He spoke easily of "gods," "goddesses," and "Fate."

In February 1522 he married a girl beneath his station and broke completely from his father. The assumption of domestic responsibility, the break with his family, the study of the Bible, together brought about an inner change or conversion in the spring of 1522. In his letters, after nine months' silence, we hear the words of an evangelical Christian. Instead of the self-pity moderated by a wan stoicism which had characterized his earlier laments to friends, an entirely new tone, moderate, simple, and objective, is evident. He gave to his children Biblical names. When his relatives remonstrated, he called their attitude "worldly." Grebel had passed from belletristic humanism to evangelical Christianity under the compulsion of Zwingli's moving exposition of the gospel from the Greek text. Zwingli recognized the value of the convert's support by having his vigorous ode hailing the Reformation presented in his own *Apologeticus Architeles*, August 1522. Grebel was a devoted Zwinglian from then until the

[18] Leonhard von Muralt, "Konrad Grebel als Student in Paris," *Zürcher Taschenbuch* (1936), maximizes the influence of these humanistic contacts; Bender, *op. cit.,* minimizes them.

iconoclastic outbursts in the fall of 1523, although he took no part
in the agitation with Leo Jud, Louis Haetzer, Pastor Simon
Stumpf of nearby Höngg, and others. Let us return now to the
disputation.

   c. *The Disputation Continued.* It was during the Second Disputation that Grebel saw Zwingli's evasions and also what Grebel
considered the intolerable subordination of the word of God in
the Bible to determination by the magistracy. (Leo Jud shared
this consternation.) Grebel urged that steps be taken at once
instructing the priests to cease perpetrating the idolatry of the
Mass, otherwise the disputation would be in vain. To this demand Zwingli responded: "My lords [of the council] will decide
whatever regulations are to be adopted in the future in regard
to the mass." At this tense moment it was not Grebel but the
iconoclast Stumpf who replied for the Radicals: "Master Ulrich,
you do not have the right to place the decision . . . in the hands
of my lords, for the decision has already been made: the Spirit
of God decides. . . . If my lords adopt and decide on some other
course that would be against the decision of God, I will ask
Christ for his spirit, and I will preach and act against it."[19]

   On the last day of the Second Disputation, Grebel's proposal
was under discussion and he was present, but without hope.
Pleading lack of fluency as a speaker, he encouraged Hubmaier
to take the floor, with whose speech on the Mass we began section 2. After Hubmaier's presentation, Grebel added, insisting
on fidelity to Biblical prescription, that the Lord's Supper could
be celebrated only in the evening, that ordinary bread should
be used, and that it should be taken by the communicant in his
own hands, rather than be placed upon the tongue by the
celebrant.

   During the Second Disputation on the Mass and images,
Haetzer had twice asked for the floor. At its close he was commissioned by the council to draw up, with the aid of another,
the Acts of the Disputation.[20] In the foreword, Haetzer praised
God in the majesty of his word as the arbiter of all theological
disputes and turned over for approbation his report to the Zurich
Council as a body exemplary of true Christian magistracy.

   d. *Conventicular Sacramentarians in Zurich, 1524.* The Radicals, including Haetzer, left the three-day disputation disillusioned with their former leader, and began to rally their forces.
Out of their study circles grew conventicles in which they
eventually dared to do among themselves what was not publicly

[19] The interchange is described by Bender, *op. cit.*, 98.
[20] Accessible in *ZW*, II, 671–803.

permitted in the Zurich churches until 1525.[21] Despairing of
Zwingli's precautionary conduct, Grebel wrote to Vadian that
"Zwingli, the herald of the Word, has cast down the Word, has
trodden it underfoot, and has brought it into captivity."[22] But
before their final break, Stumpf, Grebel, and Mantz at different
times individually submitted to Zwingli and to Leo Jud a plan
of reform, in general asking them to abandon entirely the previous organization of the church and to set up a new church of
faithful believers "according to evangelical truth and the Word
of God."[23] In this new church the Supper would be observed
as described by Paul and the Evangelists, and the disciplines of
the ancient church would be reinstituted. Pastors would no
longer live from tithes but from gifts, and "all things must be
in common," as in the apostolic church in Jerusalem. Out of this
new church (ecclesia) of the purified evangelical people (compare the proposals of the Forty-two Frankfurt Articles inspired
by Dr. Westerburg, Ch. 4.2.b), a truly Christian, i.e., noncoercive,
town council (senatus) would be "chosen by votes."[24] The Radicals were quite specific in their proposal for voluntary support,
offering Zwingli one hundred guilders annually if he would give
up his benefice on principle. At this point there was no question of postponing baptism, of rebaptism, or of the right of a
Christian to take part in the government. What Grebel sought
was the acceptance of the radical plan for a new community.
But between Zwingli's desire to compromise with the government and Grebel's demand for immediate regeneration there
was no mutually acceptable middle ground. The result of this
impasse was that the Radicals had to rethink their strategy, and
from the re-evaluation of the whole situation came the next step
in the development.

William Reublin, whom we last met in Basel (Ch. 5.1), was
now a preacher (since 1522) in two village dependencies of
Zurich: Wytikon and Zollikon. Having been the first Swiss priest
to marry (April 1523) and having preached iconoclasm, he began
early in 1524 to preach also against pedobaptism, on principle
separating church membership, betokened by baptism, from

[21] It was not until eighteen months later that the external changes in the
liturgy were permitted.
[22] 18 December 1523; Emil Arbenz, Die Vadianische Briefsammlung (henceforth: VB), III, 50.
[23] Bender, op. cit., 103.
[24] Zwingli, Elenchus, CR, XCIII, 33; ZW, III, 362; Bender, op. cit., 105 and
255, n. 29–31; The Latin Works and Correspondence of Huldreich Zwingli,
together with selections from his German works, edited by Samuel M. Jackson (New York, 1912–1929), 132.

citizenship, expressed in the annual oath of obedience to the state. By Easter 1524, as a consequence of his agitation, several parents in Zollikon declined to present their infants at the baptistery.

Another indication of the deep estrangement on the part of the Radicals from Zwingli, because of his determination to establish a prophetic theocracy of the whole people or civic Christianity, came from Haetzer, who published a German translation, with notes, of John Bugenhagen's exposition of Paul's epistles in June 1524.[25] In this book the whole Magisterial Reformation was criticized for not having applied the Word of God with all strictness and decisiveness. The book looks to a "second reformation" of fully committed members. Haetzer's notes indicate that he too was drawing close to the circle around Grebel and Mantz.

Although they had been rebuffed by Zwingli in their plan for a regenerate magistracy, the Radicals still hoped for the success of their idea of a complete restitution of New Testament Christianity somewhere through the establishment of a voluntarist association of kindred movements transcending territorial boundaries. In this expectation Grebel wrote ill-advisedly to Luther (from whom he received only an indirect reply), and then to Carlstadt and to Müntzer. Of these two foes of Luther's in the realm of both social practice and sacramental theology, it was Müntzer with whom the Zurich Radicals, led by Grebel, first sought to establish contact.

In a letter of 5 September 1524, with a substantial postscript[26] Grebel explained the admiration of his circle for both Carlstadt and Müntzer, and expressed their hope for mutual understanding. This letter to Müntzer, marking the emergence of the distinctively restitutional type of reform, is one of the principal religious writings of Conrad Grebel.[27] Carrying the corporate convictions and groping formulations of Grebel and his associates, including their charitable but firm critique of some alleged utterances and practices of Müntzer, it is especially valuable in that its topical coverage is sufficiently large to yield a fairly clear picture of the emerging faith and practice of the Swiss Brethren.

[25] *Eine kurze wohlgegründete Auslegung der zehn nachgehenden Episteln S. Pauli, ME,* II, 622.
[26] Critically edited by Böhmer and Kirn, *op. cit.,* 92–101; translated in *SAW,* 71–85.
[27] The clearest presentation of the two concepts, reform and restitution, in the Reformation Era is that of Franklin Littell, *The Anabaptist View of the Church* (2d edition, Boston, 1958).

Grebel is enheartened to find in Thomas Müntzer a kindred spirit, but in violation of the principle of *sola scriptura* he detects and deplores the following points observed in or reported perhaps falsely, he says, about Müntzer's reforming efforts: (1) Müntzer is chided for his retention of infant baptism as against the radical Swiss view that baptism is but a sign of the presence of repentance and the reception of grace, and that children, before they can distinguish between good and evil, are saved by Christ's blood quite apart from baptism, for Christ died to save not merely Christians but the whole world from original sin.[28] (2) The mere substitution of a German for a Latin Mass is not enough by way of restoring the commemorative Supper. (3) Müntzer fails to abide by the discipline of the ban according to Matt. 18:15–18. (4) Singing at worship Grebel holds to be contrary to the New Testament, as detracting from concentration on the Word and leading the better singers to vainglory and the poorer singers to embarrassment. (5) Müntzer's erection in the church of stone tablets of the Ten Commandments may lead to idolatry. (6) Müntzer should abolish clerical dependence upon benefices (with forced tithes and rents) and institute voluntary offerings. (7) Müntzer's reputed endorsement of the employment of fist and sword against the restraining lords is deplored. Characteristic of this still inchoate theology of the radical church is the fact that opposition to singing was taken up first in the letter. Of the seven points only one needs amplification in the present context.

Observe, in the following quotation, that Grebel, for all the simplicity of the service described, still, unlike Carlstadt and much like Oecolampadius, considers the bread in faith the body of Christ:

The Supper of fellowship Christ did institute and plant. . . . The server from out of the congregation should pronounce them [the consecrating words] from one of the Evangelists or from Paul. . . . An ordinary drinking-vessel, too, ought to be used. This would do away with the adoration and bring true understanding and appreciation of the Supper, since the bread is nought but bread. In faith, it is the body of Christ and the incorporation with Christ and the brethren. But one must eat and drink in the Spirit and love, as John shows in chapter 6. . . . Although it is simply bread, yet if faith and brotherly love precede it, it is to be received with joy, since, when it is used in the church, it is to show us that we are truly one bread and one body,

[28] I have made the point a little more explicit than Grebel at this conjuncture, anticipating later precision as clarified by Robert Friedmann, "Peter Riedemann—On Original Sin and the Way of Redemption," *MQR*, XXVI (1952), 210–215.

and that we are and wish to be true brethren with one another, etc. But if one is found who will not live the brotherly life, he eats unto condemnation, since he eats it without discerning, like any other meal, and dishonors love, which is the inner bond, and the bread, which is the outer bond. For also it does not call to his mind Christ's body and blood, the covenant of the cross, nor that he should be willing to live and suffer for the sake of Christ and the brethren, of the head and the members. Also, it ought not to be administered by thee [as an ordained priest, lest there be misunderstanding]. That was the beginning of the mass that only a few would partake.[29]

Since at the time of the letter (5 September 1524) no parish church in Zurich was observing an evangelical Communion, it looks as though Grebel and his associates must have been holding a service of Communion among themselves, according to the principles laid down in the letter:

Neither is it to be used in "temples" according to all Scripture and example, since that creates a false reverence. It should be used *much* and *often*. It should not be used without the rule of Christ in Matt. 18:15–18, for without that rule every man will run after the externals. The inner matter, love, is passed by, if brethren and false brethren approach or eat it [together]. . . . As for the time, we know that Christ gave it to the apostles at supper and that the Corinthians had the same usage. We fix no definite time with us.[30]

Apparently there was already in Zurich a circle where an evangelical-sacramentist *commemorative* Communion was being observed some months before adult rebaptism came to be considered a necessary condition for admission to the regenerate reformed Christian community.

It is important to note at this point that the pacifism of Grebel was not Erasmian-humanist in inspiration (as with Zwingli in his earlier phase), nor was it primarily based upon the Sermon on the Mount. It seemed, rather, to have been a consequence of Grebel's still more basic conviction as to the captaincy of Christ over the true *milites Christi,* recruited for service as a suffering church, making an ideal of absolute nonviolence and of suffering in Christ's name a confirmation of one's salvation.[31]

That Grebel wrote to revolutionary Müntzer surely does not warrant the allegation that the whole Swiss Brethren movement derived from Müntzer and the Zwickau prophets (cf. Ch. 23). There are, to be sure, phrases in Grebel's letter to Müntzer),

---

[29] See the whole letter, *SAW,* 71–85.
[30] *Ibid.,* 77.
[31] For further details, see Ethelbert Stauffer, "Anabaptist Theology of Martyrdom," *MQR,* XIX (1945), 179 f.

such as "the sweet Christ" (who may be experienced only after the believer has known "the bitter Christ" of suffering), which suggest the influence of the Allstedt Radical, but for the most part the Swiss Brethren represent a radicalization of Zwinglian rather than Lutheran doctrine and practice. By the time they came into contact with Müntzer, Grebel and Mantz had developed a theological position of sufficient depth and independence to allow them not only to hail Müntzer's spirit where it accorded with their idea of the gospel, but also to criticize him with conviction when he seemed to be at variance with it.[32]

As it fell out, revolutionary Müntzer never received the letter of pacifist Grebel. Grebel's effort to rally a far-flung co-ordinated evangelical reform failed.[33]

After the composition of this letter, the contents of which indicate that the Zurich Radicals (like the Dutch Sacramentists) were already pretty well organized as sacramentarians before they became Anabaptists, Carlstadt's brother-in-law, Dr. Gerhard Westerburg, came to Zurich with a view to establishing a common front against Luther and to publishing Carlstadt's sacramentarian tracts, composed in the Orlamünde period. We know that it was in the circle of Conrad Grebel, with whom Westerburg sojourned in Zurich, that the works were first read in manuscript form, for Grebel, in a letter to Vadian in St. Gall, 14 October 1524, referred to eight books by Carlstadt. He also knew about Luther's challenge to Carlstadt with the golden guilder, and observed: "A reasonable reader will judge from the Carlstadt books that Luther is retrogressing, and that he is an excellent procrastinator and a competent defender of his scandal."[34] The Zurich Radicals eagerly supported the printing of the Carlstadt books in Basel.

After the dispatch of Grebel's letters to Müntzer in September and to his brother-in-law Vadian in October, Carlstadt (from Orlamünde via Rothenburg) himself showed up, not in Zurich but in Basel, in November to pick up copies of his Eucharistic writings, which Westerburg had succeeded, in the meantime, in getting printed by Thomas Wolff and Johann Bebel. Oecolampadius had approved of their publication. Only the eighth, against infant baptism, did he eliminate. It is notable in this connection

---

[32] Krajewski, *Mantz*, 58 f.
[33] The autograph copy survives in the Vadian correspondence. It may be that with the arrival of Dr. Westerburg, Grebel was restrained from sending it on learning of Müntzer's belligerence.
[34] *VB*, III, 88.

that Felix Mantz, who had accompanied Westerburg from the Grebel circle in Zurich, sought on his own to get the baptismal tract published clandestinely.[35]

3. The Eucharistic Controversy Between the Swiss Sacramentarians and the Lutherans

We have already noted (Ch. 3.1) the earlier published works of Carlstadt, his introduction of the first Protestant Communion in Wittenberg, and his sacramentarian action in Rothenburg. It remains to summarize the Eucharistic theology of the Basel works, for it was their appearance at this time that marked the second stage of the intra-Protestant Eucharistic Controversy. In them he stressed the incongruity of imagining that at the Last Supper before the crucifixion the apostles, who had yet to grasp even the full significance of Jesus' words about approaching death, could have understood at all the alleged identification of the bread before them and the person presiding at the meal. Carlstadt declared that it was blasphemous idolatry to suppose that what was manifestly not true at the proto-Eucharist could be true at the first after Jesus' death. Appealing to the sequence of actions as preserved in Mark 14:23 f., he observed that the wine was first obediently drunk and "in the stomachs of the apostles" before Jesus spoke about blood, and that Jesus was referring to the bloody seal of the New Covenant, not to his own blood as wine. Similarly, Jesus pointed to his own body to be presently sacrificed on the cross, not to its presence or future presence under the appearance of bread. In the words of institution, *touto*, being neuter, refers to Jesus' body *(sōma)*, neuter, and not to the bread *(artos)*, masculine. Surely it was not bread but a body that was to suffer.

Thus it is not the sacrament which forgives sins but God in Christ on the cross who, having once forgiven them, has also once for all made it possible through the commemorative repetition of the Supper to recall with joy his unique action on Calvary. There are only two advents of Christ, the first in the Holy Land and the second yet to be. In the meantime, there is no provisional presence vouchsafed in the elements of the Christian Communion celebrated with regularity and expectancy till he come again. Paul knew "only Christ and him crucified." He

[35] Staehelin, *Briefe und Akten*, I, No. 226, and n. 10. On the chronology of Carlstadt's seven Eucharistic publications in Basel and their publishers, see E. Freys and Hermann Barge, "Verzeichnis der gedruckten Schriften des Andreas Bodenstein von Karlstadt," *Zentralblatt für Bibliothekswesen*, XXI (1904), 305–331.

did not say "Christ crucified on the cross and Christ distributed
in the bread and wine." Among all the numerous divine powers
bestowed upon the apostles, argues Carlstadt—namely, to heal
the sick, the lame, and the blind, to drive out the devil, to overcome the onslaughts of the devil, to baptize in the name of the
Triune God, etc.—the power to distribute the body and blood
of the Savior in sacramental form was not included. Carlstadt
does not hesitate to speak grossly of what he considers the Catholic and Lutheran idolatry of concentrating on the bread and
wine and thus turning one's glance from the unique historic
action on the cross and thereby misconceiving the uniqueness
of Christ's atonement.

The seven tracts in which Carlstadt expressed his matured
Eucharistic theology gained widespread attention when printed
in Basel in the fall of 1524. Felix Mantz secured a quantity of
them and distributed them in Zurich. When Carlstadt took
copies of his freshly printed works to Strassburg, the pastors
there were at once eager to get the judgment of the Reformers
of Wittenberg and Zurich. Luther replied, 15 December 1524,[36]
and Zwingli the following day. In his letter, Luther had for the
moment been willing to tolerate symbolical language, but
aroused to the seriousness and the scope of the challenge of the
Swiss and South German sacramentarians and "fanatics" and
spurred on by his old antagonist Carlstadt, Luther published
in January 1525 his *Wider die himmlischen Propheten,* followed
by a supplement.[37] He therein attacked Carlstadt's pastoral theology and practice at Orlamünde, his iconoclasm, his mysticism,
his acceptance of Old Testament statutes as binding along with
the Decalogue and natural law, and proceeded to stress his own
more conservative Eucharistic theology. Then, in March 1525,
Zwingli, having ever since Rode's appearance made up his mind
as to the basic theological issue, was emboldened to come out
publicly as a sacramentarian in a humanistic, symbolical interpretation in his *De vera et falsa religione.*

We have already taken note of Zwingli's enthusiastic reception of the theory of Hoen communicated by Rode and his recital
of his new-found conviction in the letter to Matthew Alber of
Reutlingen (of 16 November 1524).[38] This letter and his answer
to the Strassburgers he now published in the same month with

[36] *Ein Brief an die Christen zu Strassburg wider den Schwärmergeist [Carlstadt],*
  Werke, WA, XV, 391–397.
[37] *Werke, WA,* XVIII, 62–125, 134–214.
[38] *ZW,* III, 322–354.

De vera et falsa religione, and in August 1525, Hoen's *Epistola,*
without identification of the Dutch author.[39] Thereupon he became even more explicit in his espousal of the sacramentarian
position and avowed also his agreement with Carlstadt that the
body of Christ is seated at the right hand of God the Father
and cannot therefore in any sense be said to be present at the
church's commemoration of the Supper.

Luther in his sermon *Vom Sakrament des Leibes und Blutes
Christi wider die Schwarmgeister* of 29 March 1526[40] thereupon
made explicit his conception of the ubiquity of Christ, interpreting "the right hand of God" as symbolic of his omnipotence.
Defining his Eucharistic theology and his Christology over
against both Carlstadt and Zwingli, Luther distinguished three
sorts of bodily presence: the *esse circumscriptive* or *localiter* of
Christ at his first and second advent, the *ubicatio* as an aspect
of his omnipotence, and his *esse definitive* in respect to his supernatural yet localized presence in passing, for example, from
the tomb and in the Eucharistic consubstantiation. In the latter
action—the word itself was eschewed by Luther—Christ makes
himself uniquely available along with the elements of bread
and wine on Christian altars.

With this refutation, the sacramentarianism of Carlstadt and of
the Dutch and Swiss, abhorred alike by Luther, enters general
history as the main issue between the divergent wings within
the Magisterial Reformation. We shall henceforth be limited to
the Anabaptist appropriation of sacramentarianism. There remains only, at this juncture, to be mentioned the fact that Carlstadt, after vainly seeking out Westerburg in Frankfurt (whence
his brother-in-law had departed for Cologne), temporarily submitted to Luther;[41] and, disavowing any belligerent involvement
in the Peasants' War,[42] he was enabled to return to Saxony and
actually to live in Luther's house for a while, and elsewhere in
the environs of Wittenberg from 1525 to 1529.

---

[39] It is worthy of note that Hoen's marriage ring parable, going back to Tertullian (Ch. 2.2), reappears in Zwingli's Memorandum addressed to the
German princes at the diet of Augsburg in 1530.

[40] *Werke, WA,* XIX, 482–523.

[41] "Entschuldigung des falschen Namens des Aufruhrs," signed at Frankfurt,
24 June 1525, and published, with a magnanimous preface by Luther, in
Wittenberg, *Werke, WA,* XVIII, 430–445.

[42] His "Entschuldigung" is an honorable statement, disagreeing with Müntzer,
of whom he nevertheless speaks compassionately. Carlstadt shows how his
prophetic views of restraint were rejected by the peasants around Rothenburg.

4. Psychopannychism in Wittenberg and Zurich

We cannot take leave of the Spiritualist and sacramentarian Carlstadt without carrying a bit farther our earlier account of psychopannychism (Ch. 1.3.c), in which he also figures prominently. The discussion of soul sleep will seem less of an intrusion at this point in our narrative if we think of it as related to the analogous simplification and Biblicism represented in Eucharistic theology by the shift from the votive Mass to the commemorative Eucharist. But the correlation is not completely consistent; for, though Carlstadt was virtually one with Zwingli in Eucharistic theology, on the sleep of the soul, Carlstadt and Luther were, surprisingly, not far apart; and we take note, therefore, at the outset of this section of the interesting reversal of doctrinal affiliation. Luther was closer to the Catholic Mass than Zwingli, who held common ground with Carlstadt; but on the doctrine of the natural immortality of the soul, Zwingli stood with the Fifth Lateran Council (as later Calvin) over against Luther and Carlstadt and also such Anabaptists as Westerburg (Anabaptist after 1529), who held to the sleep of the soul.

Since psychopannychism is closely tied up with Biblical eschatology, it is clear why both Carlstadt and Luther could be drawn to this view, while humanist Zwingli, with much less of a sense of the imminence of the Kingdom of God, was satisfied with the traditional view.

In Luther, needless to say, the doctrine of psychopannychism bore no traces of Averroism. With his Biblical instinct and strong opposition to the whole penitential system of indulgences, Luther as early as 1520, in his defense of his propositions condemned in the bull of Leo, declared[43] that the doctrine of the soul as the substantial form of the human body is merely a papal opinion. In 1524 he declared in a sermon that the soul sleeps until God at the Last Judgment awakens both soul and body.[44]

For Carlstadt, in contrast to Luther, the Averroistic influence may have been operative. It will be recalled that Carlstadt had studied law at Siena (1516–1517), and it may have been on this

---

[43] In article 27.

[44] *Fastenpostille, Werke, WA,* XVII, 2, 235. In another sermon, in 1533, he declared: "We shall sleep until He comes, and knocks on the grave and says: 'Dr. Martinus, arise!'" *Werke, WA,* XXXVII, 151. Nevertheless, he occasionally lapsed into his inherited Catholic view of the afterlife, with the consequence that little by little within Lutheranism the doctrine of the sleep of the soul was replaced by the idea of a natural immortality. See Paul Althaus, *Die letzten Dinge: Lehrbuch der Eschatologie* (Gütersloh, 1956), 146 f.

occasion that he became acquainted with the widespread Paduan disavowal of immortality, a skepticism condemned by the Fifth Lateran Council. Westerburg had preceded Carlstadt to Italy, studying at Bologna (1515–1517). The Zwickau prophet Nicholas Storch, who stayed at Westerburg's home in Cologne in 1521, won him for the Lutheran Reformation. Storch's Taborite view of the sleep of the soul may well have been an additional factor in confirming Westerburg's psychopannychism.

The immediate situation out of which Carlstadt's book grew was his opposition to the indulgence system and particularly his impatience with the long hours he had to spend as a prebendary of All Saints' in saying votive Masses for the deceased members of the Saxon dynasty for whom the *Stift* in Wittenberg had been endowed in the fourteenth century. By dismantling the purgatorial theology he could justify spending his time in academic work! For Carlstadt, the doctrine of soul sleep was inextricably interrelated with his growing interest in Eucharistic theology and a radical reinterpretation of the Mass. It is also possible that the publication in Wittenberg of Gansfort's *Farrago* (1522), one part of which was a presentation of purgatory interpreted as spiritually purgative rather than as penal, intensified Carlstadt's convictions as to the problem of soul sleep. In any event, Carlstadt in 1523 published his *Vom Stand der christgläubigen Seelen, vom Abrahams Schoss und Fegfeuer der abgeschiedenen Seelen*.[45] In the same year, Westerburg published an eight-page pamphlet that earned for him the name "Dr. Purgatory." It was entitled *Vom Fegfeuer und Stand der verschiedenen Seelen: Eine christliche Meinung*.[46] Joined in a common cause in their denial of purgatory, their eschatologically grounded espousal of the temporary sleep of the soul, and their spiritualization of the sacraments of Baptism and the Eucharist, Carlstadt and Westerburg were exiled from Saxony in the autumn of 1524. While Carlstadt was still in Saxony, Westerburg left Frankfurt as his messenger for Zurich, conferring with Conrad Grebel, not only on the already discussed matter of the publication of Carlstadt's Eucharistic manuscripts, but also on the problem of the sleep of the soul; for in a letter to Vadian, 14 October 1525, Grebel writes that Westerburg had remained with them six days and

---

[45] His basic text was I Thess. 4:14 f.
[46] Fritz Blanke, depending upon Adolf Brecher, in a note in his edition of Zwingli's *Elenchus*, says that Westerburg derived his views from Carlstadt, but it could well have been the other way around. On Westerburg, see articles by Ernst Correll, *ME*, IV, 930 f., and by Brecher in *Allgemeine deutsche Biographie*, XLII, 182.

implies that he has read Westerburg's *"de sopore Animarum libellum."*[47]

There is no positive indication that Grebel's group adopted psychopannychism; but it is clear that Zwingli thought they did, for in an appendix to his *Elenchus* (Ch. 8.4.a) he, seeking to refute the position, will presently declare: "The Catabaptists teach that the dead sleep, both body and soul, until the day of judgment, because they do not know that the Hebrews used the word 'sleeping' for 'dying.'"[48]

Westerburg carried his sacramentarianism and psychopannychism back to Frankfurt, where we have already overtaken him as the drafter of the Forty-two Articles at the end of the Peasants' War, and whence he was obliged in May of 1525 to return to his native Cologne. There he was condemned in March 1526 for his teachings on purgatory and on soul sleep.[49]

Having looked for a moment at the first appearance of psychopannychism within the context of the Radical Reformation north of the Alps in connection with the Spiritualist sacramentarians Carlstadt and his brother-in-law, the latter on the point of becoming an Anabaptist, we may now return to the main theme of the chapter and take account of the Lutheran Reformer of Silesia turned Spiritualist on the question of the Eucharist.

5. Caspar Schwenckfeld and the Suspension of the Supper in 1526

Caspar Schwenckfeld (1489–1561) was a devout Silesian nobleman, an aristocratic evangelist among reformers largely of peasant and bourgeois origin.[50] A knight of the Teutonic Order, independent by virtue of his own landed properties, strategically located at the courts of the Duke of Silesia and two lesser princes, Schwenckfeld became a convert to Lutheranism in 1518 and, remaining true to the celibate vows of the military order, became a major exponent of the Lutheran reform in Silesia by

[47] *VB*, III, 88.
[48] *ZW*, VI, 188 f.
[49] The account of the hearing was published by Westerburg at Marburg in 1533. *ME*, IV, 931.
[50] The major biography is that of Selina Gerhard Schultz, *Caspar Schwenckfeld von Ossig (1489–1561): Spiritual Interpreter of Christianity, Apostle of the Middle Way, Pioneer of Modern Religious Thought* (Norristown, Pennsylvania, 1946). See also Wolfgang Knörrlich, *Kaspar Schwenckfeld und die Reformation in Schlesien* (Bonn, 1957). The numerous writings of Schwenckfeld and his associates are contained in the nineteen projected volumes of the *Corpus Schwenckfeldianorum* (henceforth: *CS*) (Leipzig, 1907–1961). For a brief biography and the literature, see *ME*, IV, 1120–1124.

1522.[51] A follower of Luther for eight years, 1518–1526, and thrice a visitor in Wittenberg, he was repeatedly and, in the end, crudely rebuffed by Luther on his peculiar view of the Lord's Supper. Thereupon, Schwenckfeld became the chief exponent of an irenic and evangelical Spiritualism, different from that of both sacramentarian Carlstadt and liturgical Müntzer, with a programmatic suspension of the outward Eucharist by 1526 and the enunciation of the doctrine of an inward feeding on the celestial flesh of Christ. In his interiorized eucharist, Schwenckfeld became the exponent of what he thought of as the middle or royal way, originally thought of as lying between Catholicism and Lutheranism, later as lying between the Magisterial and the Radical Reformation. He first used the term "royal" in *An Admonition to All the Brethren in Silesia,* 11 June 1524:

We are prone to swerve from the left hand to the right, contrary to the Lord's command: Turn not to the right hand nor to the left. We must walk on the royal road and seek to find the medium between the former hypocritical life and the present liberty. Otherwise all will be futile.[52]

By trusting solely in the sanctification of good works, the Catholics, he elsewhere humorously remarked, were "going on stilts," while the Lutherans were "trying to walk on their heads" in their programmatic insistence on forensic justification. The royal road was also for Schwenckfeld a narrow road which, though open to all, would be followed to the end by only a few. The Lutheran preachers, he once remarked, "wish to bring more people to heaven than God wants there."[53] Although Schwenckfeld once declared that he would return to the Catholic Church if only freedom of conscience were granted therein,[54] basically he considered himself a Protestant.[55]

He was an evangelical Spiritualist who, though he would gladly have conformed to any seriously reformed church, was

---

[51] The most recent study of the Reformation in Silesia, from the point of view of class factors, is that of Roman Heck, "Reformacja a problem walki klasowej chłopów śląskich w XVI wieku," *Odrodzenie i Reformacja w Polsce* (henceforth: *ORP*), VI (1961), 29–48.

[52] *CS*, II, 62; translated by Schultz, *op. cit.,* 104.

[53] *CS,* IV, 834; V, 132.

[54] *CS,* III, 106: quoted by Paul Maier, *Caspar Schwenckfeld on the Person and Work of Christ: A Study of Schwenckfeldian Theology at Its Core* (Assen, The Netherlands, 1959), upon which much of the following description depends. It is in English (cf. Ch. 31, n. 1) the best exposition of the structure of Schwenckfeld's thought as a whole and of his Christology in particular.

[55] See his thirty-six reasons for leaving the Catholic Church in *CS,* VII, 368 f., and the twenty points of doctrine which he held in common with the Lutherans, XII, 641.

insistent that the Spirit be free of all institutions, even in the established church, for he "spirits (*geistet* as a verb) where, when, and to what extent he wishes.[56] Schwenckfeld was therefore content to encourage prayer and study circles—*ecclesiolae*—awaiting the hand of God in any final decision as to the relative merits of the competing churches.

A major figure in the Radical Reformation, in contact with Spiritualists, Anabaptists, and Rationalists alike, Schwenckfeld was primarily concerned with what can be called a Eucharistic Christology; and it is therefore appropriate that he be introduced at this juncture in our narrative devoted to the sacrament of the altar. We shall here recount his life to that point in the Eucharistic Controversy when his life and thought join our general account.

Born in 1489 in Ossig in the principality of Liegnitz, Caspar Schwenckfeld, up to his conversion, followed the career of an aristocrat. He studied in Cologne, Frankfurt on the Oder, and apparently also in Erfurt; but, though widely read in canon law and the church fathers, including the Greeks, and familiar with the Rhenish mystics, he never submitted to the rigors of systematic theology, and never received a university degree. By 1511 he was active as courtier in Oels, then at Brieg, and at length at the ducal court at Liegnitz.

This town, capital of the little Silesian principality of the same name, lay in Lower Silesia, the almost entirely German part of the mixed German and Polish duchy. With the death of Louis of Bohemia at the battle of Mohács in 1526, the whole duchy came under the Hapsburg Ferdinand of Austria and Bohemia, and was ecclesiastically under the Polish archbishop of Gniezno. The Reformation had been introduced in Breslau, capital of Silesia, by Bishop John of Thurzo, a sober and devout churchman who in 1517 had anticipated Luther's attack on indulgences by his own action taken to eliminate a highly profitable but superstitious cult of Marian devotion in Breslau.[57] Breslau was deeply involved in the humanistic ferment of the early sixteenth century: it was Bishop John's adviser Dominic Schleupner who drew Luther's attention in 1520 to Lorenzo Valla's exposure of the Donation of Constantine as a forgery.[58] When John of Thurzo died on 2 August of that year, the Reformation in Breslau continued under the leadership of John Hess, formerly his

[56] *CS*, VII, 122.
[57] D. Erdmann, *Luther und seine Beziehungen zu Schlesien,* Schriften des Verein für Reformationsgeschichte, XVIII (Halle, 1887), 7.
[58] *Ibid.*

secretary, with the approval of the new bishop, James of Salza.

In the meantime, Schwenckfeld, who had taken up residence at the court at Liegnitz in 1518 and had been converted to Luther's reform at about the same time, was in the process of promoting the Reformation there. He had been turned to the evangelical understanding of Christianity by reading Luther's commentary on the penitential psalms. He soon became Duke Frederick II's chief adviser in ecclesiastical matters, and in 1522 prevailed upon him to espouse the reform in his territory.[59] The loyal Lutheran Hess soon found Caspar Schwenckfeld an uncongenial albeit courteous associate.

In the earlier phase of his reforming efforts, Schwenckfeld imagined that the old and the new could be harmonized. For example, in his epistolary counsel to the sisters in the convent of Naumburg (early 1523) he prescribed a feasible continuation of the cloistered life in an evangelical form.[60] On 1 January 1524, he and another nobleman addressed an open letter to the bishop of Breslau, urging him to exert his influence to bring about wholesale changes in the diocese. In this noble appeal, as in all his other writings, we note Schwenckfeld's characteristic respectfulness, refined feeling, evangelical fervor, and concern for the masses of people as well as for the religiously tutored, and also his moderation in his efforts to achieve these goals.[61]

It was from Luther, so the Silesian courtier thought, that he had learned that the sons of Adam, after they have by faith been incorporated into the Second Adam, are capable of exercising their free will to do good. In taking over Luther's doctrine of justification by faith in the historic work of Christ, whereby the faithful may be wrested from bondage to the world, Schwenckfeld characteristically chose to stress those utterances in Luther's new-found gospel which allowed him gradually to turn the doctrine of forensic justification into progressive sanctification. He only gradually came to realize how this perception of the Christian life differed from that of Luther, who had awakened these thoughts in him, and he long maintained that he taught only what the Austin friar himself had proclaimed before the molten experience of solafideism began to harden into a territorial-confessional system. Schwenckfeld held steadfastly to the end his Lutheran-Augustinian-Pauline conviction in the basic Protestant principle of justification by faith. But in his concern for the moral life and as a consequence of his peculiar interpretation

[59] After 1523 he withdrew from regular court attendance because of deafness.
[60] *CS*, I, 107 ff.
[61] *CS*, I, 284–304; reprinted in translation in Schultz, *op. cit.*, 33–53.

of the means of appropriating the work of Christ, he altered the emphasis, rendering it eventually in the characteristic formulation: "Justification derives from the knowledge (*Erkenntnis*) of Christ through faith."[62] And this knowledge of Christ was Eucharistically based, first in the observance of the Lord's Supper, as when the disciples at Emmaus recognized the resurrected Christ in the breaking of the bread, and finally, in the inward participation in the Supper as an inward feeding upon the divine nutriment, the bread from heaven. This spiritual nourishment was for him such that it enabled his will, hitherto bound, to be free. He was confident in the divine initiative in justificatory faith, but it was his experience from the beginning that incorporation in the Second Adam or the acquisition of membership (through faith) in the true church behind the visible church (the idea of an invisible church was derived from Luther) had enabled him to act freely, as had Adam in Paradise before the Fall:

Although it is impossible for the old corrupt man to keep the commandments of God, as loving God with thy whole heart and thy neighbor as thyself, which is the fulfilling of the law, it is not impossible for the new regenerated man, that is, for all Christians who believe in Christ, to keep them.[63]

With this conviction that the will of the regenerate man was able to achieve sanctification, Schwenckfeld greatly enlarged the original Lutheran concept and thereby came to insist that what had been for Luther a momentary experience of passing from law under grace might be likewise experiential and *prolonged* for all true believers. Therefore, against Luther, he would not tolerate the definition of the Christian as *simul justus et peccator*.

Indeed, it had been the palpable failure of Lutheranism to change the moral life of its proponents, especially among the simple parishioners, that had pushed Schwenckfeld, as a practical reformer, along the path that he called the royal way. But besides the ethical concern, there was also an experiential reality which compelled Schwenckfeld in the end to differentiate his position from that of Luther, and that was his conception of faith as a substantial, a physicospiritual, bond between the righteous celestial Christ and the formerly sinful, but now regenerated, believer.[64] It was this same conception of faith along with

---

[62] *CS*, X, 707.

[63] *CS*, XII, 901. This explicit formulation from *The Gospel of Christ and Its Misuse*, 1552, comes rather late in his career, but the idea was there from almost the beginning.

[64] Well analyzed by Frederick William Loetscher, *Schwenckfeld's Participation in the Eucharistic Controversy* (Philadelphia, 1906), 64, 72.

his high moral sense which impelled Schwenckfeld to dissociate himself from what he considered the philosophical makeshift and moral incongruity of Luther's doctrine of the Eucharist and which, because it was open to all, he pilloried as the "new indulgence." He earnestly asked the question whether Christ is in the bread or in the wine or in heaven. He was especially concerned about the problem of Judas at the Last Supper; and, confident that the answer to his questions lay in John, ch. 6, he sent out to Luther and certain colleagues in Silesia his *Duodecim Quaestiones oder Argumenta contra impanationem.*[65] His evangelical friend, Valentine Crautwald, was especially moved to meditate on the *Quaestiones* and in reaction thereto produced the distinctively "Schwenckfeldian" view of the Supper.

Crautwald, an alumnus of the University of Cracow, now canon and lector of theology at Liegnitz, concerned himself night and day in intensive prayer and study with the Eucharistic texts of the Greek New Testament and of the fathers, particularly Tertullian and Cyprian, until suddenly a great light seemed to break upon him, as he later described the experience. Here are his words in his letter to Schwenckfeld. They contain the substance of what at once became Schwenckfeld's Eucharistic theology:

In the morning as I awoke for the day and softly the [thought of the] eucharist returned to my heart, and behold after an interval there surged within me a tremendous force (as when a light suddenly appears in the darkness) which completely absorbed me and endowed with much wisdom led me to the understanding of the eucharist; for it went through the whole of my body but especially my head and opened up to me, as in the twinkling of the eye, all texts bearing upon the eucharist and the action at the Last Supper, speaking to me with a corporeal voice . . . and showed the proper order of the words of the Supper and that the standard thereof is the saying of Jesus in John 6, that the scripture at this point is harmoniously consistent [with the rest] and that *est* must be accented as meaning continuous *(perpetuum)* and not to be turned into *significat* [as with Hoen and Zwingli].[66]

This is but the second stage in what both Crautwald and Schwenckfeld regarded as a tripartite revelation. The third phase was the disclosure to Crautwald, after eighteen days of further study and prayer with two associates, that the institutional words had new meaning when so construed that *hoc* was understood

---

[65] July 1525; *CS*, II, 132–139.
[16] Latin letter of Crautwald to Schwenckfeld, translated into German by the latter, October 1525; *CS*, II, 198.

to point not to the seated body of Christ but to the bread at the Table as symbol of the enduring bread which is ever Christ himself:

That neither Luther has taught correctly about the sacrament nor Zwingli hit upon the right way in respect to the action of the sacrament of thanksgiving [is clear], for the words of the Dominical Supper must be weighed and compared with John 6 [:55]: My flesh *est* flesh indeed; and that the words This *est* my body are the same as: My flesh *est* food indeed [now and forever more].[67]

By finding in the words of institution as interpreted by John, ch. 6, a mystical flesh upon which only those who perceived Christ spiritually might feed, Crautwald, to whom the solution of the textual problem had come, and Schwenckfeld, who had initiated the prayerful inquiry and at once accepted Crautwald's illumination as God-given, were in a position at once to intensify the spiritually nutritional function of the Eucharist and withhold it from Judas and all others who follow Christ with their lips only. On the one hand, Schwenckfeld could now be so confident in the reality of saving faith that he no longer needed what he considered the carnality and grossness of Luther's doctrine of the ubiquity of Christ and impanation. On the other hand, by stressing the hyperphysical substance of faith, he could contend with conviction for the real presence while securing the Supper against defilement from Judas and all the merely nominal followers of Christ; for, he says, quoting Augustine, "only he who believes in him partakes."[68] The Christological, soteriological implications of this shift in Eucharistic theology are already clearly announced when Schwenckfeld writes:

Eating means . . . partaking of the nature (*natur*) of Christ through true faith. The bodily food is transferred into our nature, but the spiritual food changes us into itself, that is, the divine nature, so that we become partakers of it [II Peter 1:4].[69]

The Wittenbergers as a whole could see in Schwenckfeld's formulation nothing but sacramentarianism, when Schwenckfeld, on his first visit in the fall of 1525, turned from his ducal mission to confer more personally with Luther on Eucharistic theology. Luther, replying to the always eager and polite Silesian

[67] *Ibid.*, 205.
[68] Migne, *PL*, XXXV, col. 1607, quoted by Schwenckfeld, *CS*, III, 158. A later but substantially identical statement of Schwenckfeld's Eucharistic theology has been translated in *SAW*, 161 ff.
[69] *A General Epistle*, ? February 1527; *CS*, II, 574. Valid despite the date for the period *before* the *Stillstand* of 1526 (see below), because it presupposes both a sacramental and a spiritual eating.

courtier, said disparagingly: "Yes, Zwingli,"[70] and elsewhere called him "the third head," along with Zwingli and Carlstadt, of the sacramentarian sect.[71] Schwenckfeld himself recognized the kinship when he remarked to Luther that in trying to spiritualize the *Hoc est corpus* over against Luther's scholastic consubstantiation, some (like Zwingli) stressed the *est*, interpreting it as *significat*, others (like Oecolampadius) sought, rather, to make *corpus* the symbolic word in the institutional phrase, while he, like Carlstadt, spiritualized the demonstrative pronoun (*hoc*).[72] But unlike Carlstadt, Schwenckfeld interpreted the demonstrative pronoun as referring to that spiritual body of John, ch. 6, as the Biblical elaboration of the Eucharistic intention of Jesus. Schwenckfeld, in inverting the words of institution and construing the pronoun as a "spiritual demonstrative," secured Christ's presence at the Eucharist: "My body is this, namely, bread or true nourishment for the soul." Behind the Eucharistic elements, for the believing participant, was a spiritual bread identical with Christ's glorified humanity, or perhaps better, his celestial flesh (Ch. 11.3). Schwenckfeld could not accept Luther's doctrine of ubiquity. He understood Christ's session at the right hand of God in no localized sense. Indeed, he thought of Christ himself as "the right hand of God" and the Holy Spirit as "the finger of God."

Schwenckfeld made two more visits to Luther to share with him the inspired Silesian solution, wherein "the *hoc* remains *hoc*, the *est est*, and the *corpus corpus*."[73] On returning home from his last effort to come to some understanding with Luther on the Supper, Schwenckfeld received two harsh letters from Wittenberg (February and April 1526). Despairing of any immediate concord with Luther, Schwenckfeld experienced what he called a divine revelation, a "second awakening," from which he later dated his matured religious life.[74] Of the immediate consequence of this tremendous experience, *"das erschütterndste Ereignis,"* he later wrote, looking back: "Since the gracious visitation (*heimsuchunge*) by God I could not join with any party or church in the observance of the sacraments and in other

[70] During the colloquia in Wittenberg, 1 December 1525; recounted by Schultz, *op. cit.*, 74.
[71] *Luthers Werke, WA,* XIX, 123.
[72] Extract from the diary of Schwenckfeld, 1–4 December 1525; *CS,* II, 235 f.; interpreted systematically by Loetscher, *op. cit.,* 52.
[73] *CS,* III, 153.
[74] His various subsequent references to it are brought together by Schultz, *op. cit.,* 100–104.

respects, nor could I allow men to rule over my faith."[75] This and the earlier statement of how the Spirit "spirits" freely might be taken as the two basic propositions of Schwenckfeld's individualistic, evangelical Spiritualism. He first embodied his new conviction in the famous encyclical letter of 21 April 1526, signed by Valentine Crautwald himself, and the pastors and preachers of Liegnitz, wherein they announced the irenic strategy of *Stillstand*, the suspension of the Supper until all groups could be brought to some accord as to its proper meaning and practice, while in the meantime defending it from defilement:

We . . . confess and find ourselves in duty bound, and wholly trust no one will find reason to criticize this our Christian and just purpose, or to think ill of the fact that we admonish men in this critical time to suspend (*still stehen*) for a time the observance of the highly venerable sacrament, and first to concern themselves through the Word of God about the thing most needful . . . in order that we and other ministers of the Word will not be casting that which is holy unto the dogs.[76]

For the moment this proposed action did not look much different from the actual practice of sacramentarians, when on scholarly or diplomatic missions in Lutheran towns, of abstaining from Communion and vice versa. In justifying this provisional action, the Silesian Brethren went on to stress the ban as a means of protecting the Christian fellowship from merely nominal believers. The suspension was not a particular hardship for Schwenckfeld, who, like Gansfort (Ch. 2.1), had already come to think of an inward and an outward eating. The inner, contemplative action was in fact enhanced by the suspension of the external sacrament.

In the same letter the Silesians stressed the importance of a catechetical instruction before baptism. But here, too, it was possible to distinguish between an inner and a sacramental washing; and, although Schwenckfeld, in his opposition to infant baptism, eventually went as far as to say that the sacrament had not been administered correctly for a thousand years,[77] he never himself repudiated the external rite once it had been administered in infancy, and simply looked for a baptism by the Holy Spirit at some point in the unfolding of each Christian life, either conjointly with, prior to, or after water baptism.[78] But the inte-

[75] Letter to Landgrave Philip, after 18 May 1534; *CS*, V, 100.
[76] *CS*, II, Document XXVIII; translated in Schultz, *op. cit.*, 106 ff.
[77] *CS*, VII, 252; see Hans X. Urner, "Die Taufe bei Caspar Schwenckfeld," *Theologische Literaturzeitung*, VI (1948), 329–342.
[78] *CS*, VII, 450; XIII, 248.

riorization of the experience of Baptism, parallel to that of the Eucharist, was never developed by the Silesian Brethren; and baptismal metaphors were largely replaced by the Eucharistic terminology of the feeding upon the indwelling Christ in Schwenckfeld's description of the religious life.[79] Schwenckfeld, of course, stressed also the distinction between the inner and the outer Word; but he never depreciated the study of the written word, and the hearing of it in the divine service. He therefore acknowledged the preaching ministry. He later came to distinguish the true servants of the word commissioned of old, the present servants who still succeed in interpreting the Scriptures Christocentrically for their hearers, and the scribes (Schriftgelehrten) in whom the work of the Spirit seems suspended and who at best curb the populace and prevent tumult.[80]

The weekday conventicles of the Silesians or "brotherhoods" of "confessors of the glory of Christ" took form for study, prayer, preaching, admonition, and the answering of religious questions. They were in the later language of Pietism ecclesiolae in ecclesia.

The liturgy in use at Liegnitz has been reconstructed[81] in three parts, one for the morning service of prayers and meditations, with a spiritual communion based upon the reading and contemplation of John, ch. 6; one for vespers, with, among many others, a prayer for the magistracy; and a series of private and occasional devotions. Somewhat earlier, for his brotherhoods, Schwenckfeld had prepared what must be considered the first catechism for children of the Reformation Era.[82] Schwenckfeld did not conceive the prayer meetings as substitutes for an established church; and much later, when his following was to be widespread and numerous, he would seldom advise his Spiritualists against attending upon the stated services of the established churches.[83] He looked forward, however, to a church of the Spirit, characterized by the unity, purity, and gifts of the apostolic church.[84]

In order to encourage the irenic, "ecumenical" interchange among professors of Lutheranism, sacramentarianism, and the evangelical Spiritualism of the Silesian Brethren, Schwenckfeld inspired the short-lived University of Liegnitz, with twenty-four professors proposed (July 1526).[85] Silesian monasteries were, at

[79] Maier, op. cit., 25.
[80] CS, XII, 50; XIII, 359. Clarified by Maier, op. cit., 28.
[81] CS, II, Document XXXVII.
[82] Correspondenzblatt des Vereins für die evangelische Kirche Schlesiens, VII: 2, 155–158; to be printed in CS, XVII, as Document MCLXXV.
[83] CS, XII, 796.
[84] In conversation with Luther: Diary, 1525; CS, II, 280; IX, 905.
[85] CS, II, Document XXXIIII.

the same time, encouraged to reconstruct the disciplined life with fresh evangelical motivation.

The suspension of the Supper which Schwenckfeld urged upon his own brothers was originally provisional and irenic. But from being a temporary expedient, suspension evolved into a non-sacramental way of life. In an undated document[86] Schwenckfeld will advance a number of reasons for *Stillstand*, including his own sense of unworthiness and the unfeasibility of enforcing the ban. Still later, he will go on to say that the Supper has never been properly understood, that it is indeed "the sealed book of the Apocalypse, which has not yet been opened by the Spirit of God. Hence in good conscience we cannot commune with any party, but must stand still in this respect and guard ourselves against idolatry and misuse."[87]

As Schwenckfeld openly dissociated himself from Lutheranism and then by his radical Spiritualism made the extension of a true folk church ever less feasible, he gradually lost contact with the main forces of the ducal reform, the more so as the duke had to be circumspect in view of the hostility to all reform on the part of his new sovereign, Ferdinand, king of Bohemia and Hungary since 1526. The Breslau town councilmen had advised Ferdinand that he had better tolerate the Lutheran Reformation, for fear of driving the people into something worse, namely, Schwenck-feldian Spiritualism.[88] Ferdinand was determined to stamp out the Reformation; and, executing the Schwenckfeldian preacher of Striegau, John Reichel, as an example in 1527, he revealed his intention of using Schwenckfeldianism as a lever to pry out the whole Reformation movement. In a mandate of 1 August 1528, he declared the absolute annulment of evangelical reforms in Silesia, but the arrival of the Turks before Vienna in the spring of 1529 slowed up the implementation of the decree.

In the meantime, the Swiss sacramentarians Oecolampadius and Zwingli had published two of Schwenckfeld's works, approvingly but without his knowledge, *De cursu verbi Dei* and *The Ground and Cause of the Error and Controversy Concerning the Lord's Supper*. This indirect substantiation of the charge of sacramentarianism against Schwenckfeld alarmed the hard-pressed Duke Frederick II, who knew that he could salvage the reform in his lands only by dissociating himself from all such radical expressions. Schwenckfeld, for his part, in order to save what he could

---

[86] *CS*, III, Document LXXVIII (conjecturally dated December 1528); translated by Schultz, *op. cit.*, 111–112.
[87] *CS*, XVI, Document MCLXI.
[88] Erdmann, *op. cit.*, 58.

of the reform by his discreet withdrawal, went out of Silesia into voluntary exile (19 April 1529), preserving contact with his followers and estates by letter.

We shall next encounter him in Strassburg in Ch. 10 and pick up the history of the Radical Reformation in Silesia in Ch. 15.

CHAPTER 6

THE RISE OF THE SWISS BRETHREN
AS THE FIRST ANABAPTISTS

We took leave of the Zurich Radicals at a time when they were withdrawing from Zwingli because of his delay in carrying out his proclaimed reforms in deference to the town council and in the hope that thus the whole canton might be reformed in head and members. At first the differences between Zwingli and the Zwinglian Radicals had appeared to be merely a matter of emphasis—at most, differences over strategy and timing—but by 1524 it had become plain that the differences went deeper: the regular Zwinglians sought the gradual reformation of the whole of the Swiss commonwealth, while the Radicals were calling for the precipitate restoration of a righteous remnant. Zwingli's ideal was a cantonally reformed Alpine "Israel," still to be realized by the prophet's patient ecclesiastical diplomacy and patriotic grasp of the importance of swinging into line the other cantons of the Confederation. The ideal of the voluntarist Anabaptists was a mobile fellowship of conventicles, a righteous remnant assembling in Zurich and throughout its village dependencies and beyond, determined to put into immediate practice what their leaders had in breathless religious excitement learned from Zwingli himself in his appeal to Scripture as the ultimate authority. As we saw in the last chapter (Ch. 5.2.d), the moment the Bible-study groups had turned into sacramentarian conventicles preaching a reform of the parish churches, the change in the ecclesiological basis of the community as a congeries of conventicles—though they were at first, perhaps, considered temporary expedients—accelerated the alterations in theology in general. Just a few months earlier the radical party had employed the language of Zwingli in talking about faith alone in the unique action of Christ on Calvary. Now they had become specific about the relationship of faith to baptism and about election and inclusion in the covenant. The Radicals insisted that it was incongruous to regard the passivity of eight-day infants and the ecstasy of old men awakened to their sinfulness and rejoicing in the divine forgiveness as essentially the same baptismal action. They were certain that Zwingli was wrong in equating circumcision under the Old Covenant with baptism under the New.

The provisional sacramentarian conventicles became a new sect—that is, a true church of the remnant—the moment the Radicals, having defied the magistracy for its palpable failure to heed what they perceived to be the binding precepts of God through the New Covenant in Christ, came to regard even their baptismal birthright in the established or civic church as invalid and proceeded to dismantle the ecclesiastical structure of the centuries. They started all over, as if there had been no true Christians among them. Disillusioned with compromises in reformation, the Radicals were now bent upon a restitution. They began with the confession of guilt, proceeded to the washing away of sins in a new baptism, and covenanted together in the communion of mutually forgiven and forgiving saints—saints in the language of Acts, men and women set apart from the world in the acceptance of the resurrected Christ as the lord of their lives and sole arbiter through the apostles of the group disciplines and the divine assignments of the participants in the new life. The first true sect of the Reformation Era was formed when the sacramentarian Brethren separated from "the world," so defining it as to include not only the idolatrous realm (as both the sectaries and the Zwinglians saw it) of papal Christendom but also the comparably oppressive jurisdiction of a magisterially reformed cantonal republic. The first gathered church of sectarian "Protestantism" came into being precisely at that moment when a former priest in the home of a university-educated prophet of the new order received baptism on confession of sin from the hand of a layman, and when all present defended their action on the ground that the Christian conscience was no more beholden to the reforming magistrates and their divines than to priests and prelates.

The newly baptized convert on this momentous occasion had been baptized in his infancy, had been confirmed by a bishop, had taken quasi-monastic vows as a canon, had been ordained as a priest, and had undoubtedly many times been shriven in the quadripartite medieval sacramental action of penance, with its repentance, confession, satisfaction, and absolution. In a moment of anguish and exaltation all these actions of the medieval church were sloughed off as though they had never been; and, as a penitent in the sense of a disciple of John the Baptist, with a complete change of mind, *metanoia,* the clerical convert accepted believers' baptism as a truly ablutionary act of penance, as an affirmation of a new-found faith, and as a token of his membership in a new church taking form among the fifteen onlooking participants.

The scene of this event was the home of Felix Mantz in Zurich. The baptizer was the layman Conrad Grebel. The former priest thus rebaptized was George Blaurock.[1] The day was 21 January 1525, the birthday of Anabaptism.

In recounting the rise and the spread of this movement through German-speaking Switzerland and beyond, we must go back a month before this first rebaptism.

1. ZURICH AND ZOLLIKON: THE FIRST ANABAPTIST FELLOWSHIP

As late as December 1524, the separating Christians, who were already calling themselves Brethren in Christ, or simply Christians, and were soon to be called also Swiss Brethren, confessed their willingness to be persuaded by Scriptural argument, and made bold to petition the town council to ask Zwingli to debate with their representatives. To this end, Felix Mantz addressed to the Zurich council his eloquent *Petition of Protest and Defense* in December 1524.[2] In the middle of the month private conferences were secured at which Grebel, Mantz, and Haetzer opposed Zwingli and Leo Jud. The Brethren had felt themselves outmatched by Zwingli's debating skill, and had hence proposed a written exchange of opinions. The proposal was declined.

On two successive Tuesdays in January (10 and 17) 1525, Grebel, Mantz, Reublin, and Cajacob (Blaurock) faced Zwingli and Henry Bullinger. Each side claimed the victory in what goes down in history as the First Baptismal Disputation. At the end of the second session, Zwingli remarked "that it would be not only inadvisable but also dangerous to have further debate with them,"[3] because of the high state of public feeling occasioned by the disputation. It seems likely that Zwingli, who was originally a pedobaptist more out of expediency than principle, was unable

---

[1] John Allen Moore, *Der starke Jörg* (Cassel, 1955).
[2] *Quellen zur Geschichte der Täufer in der Schweiz,* edited by Leonhard von Muralt and Walter Schmid, I (Zurich, 1952), (henceforth: von Muralt, *Quellen*), No. 16; English translation in *Goshen College Record,* Supplement, XXVII (1926), 23–32 (incorrectly dated, and provisionally ascribed to Grebel). The basic study of all the disputations and the issues at stake between the Radical and the Magisterial Reformers in Switzerland is that of John Yoder, *Täufertum und Reformation in der Schweiz . . . 1523–1538* (Weierhof, 1959), but unavailable for the present study.
[3] *ZW,* IV, 207.

to present his arguments with sufficient conviction to create a compelling impression, while the passionate defenders of believers' baptism won many supporters by their straightforwardness and enthusiasm. But the Brethren were at a great disadvantage. The council, in fact, had already made up its mind, and Zwingli's debating skill was outstanding, particularly by contrast with people like Reublin, whom Zwingli characterized as simple of mind, foolishly bold, garrulous, and unwise. Thus it was no surprise that on the following day the town council reaffirmed its conservative stand on infant baptism, and decreed that all who should fail to have their infants baptized within eight days would be exiled. Three days later, on 21 January, Reublin, Haetzer, John Brötli, and Andrew Castelberger were expelled as foreigners, and Grebel and Mantz were forbidden to hold any more "schools" for "agitation."[4]

Brötli was a former priest who had left his parish to follow Zwingli, had married, and with his wife and child sojourned in Zollikon, where he lived from his own rural labor. He had won much local attention for his opposition to infant baptism particularly.

Castelberger was a bookseller nicknamed "on the crutches," in reference to his lameness. In his home in the Grisons (Graubünden) he had attracted numerous "confused people" at meetings which he held, preaching against usury, tithes, benefices, clerical pride, and war. He had come to Zurich, where he joined the new Anabaptist movement with enthusiasm, but swift expulsion prevented him from accomplishing anything in the town.

Blaurock, although also a foreigner, was not included in the expulsion order, because he was known to the authorities by only one statement made at the discussion on 17 January, where, as no one recognized him, he was referred to as "the one in the blue coat" (blauer Rock). A university-trained priest,[5] he and Castelberger are the first of the Rhaetians to make their appearance in our history.

The three Rhaetian leagues, of which Graubünden was the chief, constituted a tripartite confederation allied with the Swiss Confederation (and today its largest canton). Since this region played an important role as a refuge for German-speaking Anabaptists and Italian Evangelicals, it will be more fully treated in Ch. 22.1.

The "schools" condemned by the mandate of 21 January were

---

[4] Von Muralt, Quellen, No. 26.
[5] Blaurock matriculated at Leipzig in 1513; his first parish as priest was Trins in Graubünden.

evening gatherings in the homes of the pious for the purpose of listening to "readers" of the Bible and for discussion. Visiting readers kept these schools throughout the cantons in touch with each other. They represented, indeed, the first informal beginnings of the gathered churches of Anabaptism.[6] It seems likely, as we saw in Ch. 5.2.d, on the basis of the "much and often" of Grebel's letter to Müntzer, that some of them had been practicing a commemorative Communion service.

For many months the Brethren had prayed to God for guidance, to show them the moment when they should act. Now that it was clear that Zwingli and the authorities could not be won over to the program for the reconstitution of the primitive church it seemed that the time for restitution had come. It was on the very evening of the expulsion, 21 January, that the comrades assembled as a "school" meeting in the house of Felix Mantz. The Hutterite *Chronicle*[7] preserves Blaurock's reminiscences. It tells how first he sought out Grebel and Mantz:

With them he spoke and talked through matters of faith. They came to one mind in these things, and in the pure fear of God they recognized that a person must learn from the divine Word and preaching a true faith which manifests itself in love, and receive the true Christian baptism on the basis of the recognized and confessed faith, in the union with God of a good conscience, [prepared] henceforth to serve God in a holy Christian life with all godliness, also to be steadfast to the end in tribulation. And it came to pass that they were together until fear (*angst*) began to come over them, yea, they were oppressed (*gedrungen*) in their hearts. Thereupon, they began to bow their knees to the Most High God in heaven and called upon him as the knower of hearts, implored him to enable them to do his divine will and to manifest his mercy toward them. For flesh and blood and human forwardness did not drive them, since they well knew what they would have to bear and suffer on account of it. After the prayer, George Cajacob arose and asked Conrad to baptize him, for the sake of God, with the true Christian baptism upon his faith and knowledge. And when he knelt down with that request and desire, Conrad baptized him, since at that time there was no ordained minister (*diener*) to perform such work. After that was done the others similarly desired George to baptize them, which he also did upon their request. Thus they together gave themselves to the name of the Lord in the high fear of God. Each confirmed (*bestätet*) the other in the

---

[6] Fridolin Sicher, *Chronik*, edited by E. Götzinger, *Mitteilungen zur vaterländischen Geschichte*, XX (1885), 19.

[7] Preserved in a unique codex in South Dakota and critically edited by A. J. F. Zieglschmid, *Die älteste Chronik der Hutterischen Brüder* (Philadelphia, 1943). An excerpt, from which the selection is quoted, appears in *SAW*, 43 f.

service of the gospel, and they began to teach and keep the faith. Therewith began the separation from the world and its evil works.

The next day, at the well in Hirslanden (near Zurich), Brötli, under sentence of expulsion, was seen to baptize Fridli Schumacher by sprinkling him with water from the well. The apostolic simplicity of this scene at the well contrasts notably with the prevailing baptismal practice of the new liturgy of Leo Jud,[8] which included blowing upon the baptizand, exorcism, crossing, and the use of spittle and oil. In the course of the following week, Grebel, Blaurock, and Mantz reconvened the sacramentarian "school" or conventicle as an Anabaptist congregation at Zollikon, a prosperous village five miles out from the town of Zurich on the lake.[9] Some thirty-five converts rebaptized in Zollikon in the eventful week of January 22 to 29 were recruited from the class of small farmers, their wives, and hired help, rather than the wealthier farmers.[10] Here rebaptism in the simple form of affusion and the Lord's Supper with common bread and wine were re-enacted several times under the covering of momentous solemnity, and all in the simplest possible fashion, in imitation of the New Testament accounts. First, a New Testament story of the institution was read, following which there was a short address on the meaning of the sacrament, and finally the distribution of the bread and the wine. While in the reformed parishes of Zurich and in other dependent villages Mass was still being read in Latin by a vested pastor, and the people were receiving consecrated wafers and no wine, here in a Zollikon peasant house laymen were breaking plain bread and distributing it together with wine to all the participants, who were quite clear about the meaning of the ceremony, namely, that they from thence purposed to lead a godly life.[11] It is in this celebration of the Supper

[8] This baptismal service, in German, with its still Catholic features, was introduced in 1523. Not until the spring of 1525 was Zwingli's fully Protestant baptismal service introduced in Zurich.

[9] The week's activities have been vividly reconstructed by Fritz Blanke, "The First Anabaptist Congregation, Zollikon: 1525," *MQR*, XXVII (1953), 17, a translation from the German.

[10] Paul Guyer, *Die Bevölkerung Zollikons im Mittelalter und in der Neuzeit* (Zurich, 1946). But it was religious and not economic motivation, he clearly demonstrates, which enlisted these smaller farmers in the evangelical movement. See, however, the observations of Oskar Vasella, who suspects that the Anabaptists of Waldshut and the Grisons were socially more radical than those in Zurich. He distinguishes between rural parishes that were constitutionally independent and those that were benefices of abbeys or city churches. "Zur Geschichte der Täuferbewegung in der Schweiz," *Zeitschrift für Schweizerische Kirchengeschichte* (henceforth: *ZSKG*), XLVIII (1954), esp. 186.

[11] Von Muralt, *Quellen*, No. 32.

of the Lord that the congregation felt itself part of the communion of saints, united in one bond of love to God and to the brethren. There is early evidence that they took seriously their Communion as a token, also, of the community of goods, as in Acts, breaking the locks off their doors and cellars and sharing supplies.[12] Relief from the tremendous conviction of sin and the yearning for a purity of life prompted them to share all things.

In many ways, rebaptism had taken the place of the sacrament of penance, long debased by the indulgence traffic, while the Eucharistic elements were becoming the sacramental cement, giving coherence to the brotherhood of would-be saints. The initial call to believers' baptism stressed, over against pedobaptism, not the adult's capacity to believe but rather to repent. The revival at Zollikon involved the reconception of repentance. To the worn-out sacrament of Baptism had been restored the experiential significance of the now displaced sacrament of penance.[13]

Grebel, Mantz, Brötli, and Blaurock were preachers of repentance who were able to bring their hearers to a moving consciousness of sin and of their need for forgiveness. The court records of the hearings of the Anabaptists from the year 1525 repeatedly testify to the deepness of the conviction of sin and the anguished longing for forgiveness which characterized the early converts.[14] In contrast to the usual accounts of church history, which reveal the speculations and controversies of princes, theologians, and ecclesiastics, these transcripts of the Anabaptist hearings illuminate the spiritual struggles, fears, and joys of ordinary people.

Among the preachers of repentance, George Cajacob Blaurock stands out. The first to be rebaptized, he was zealous to the point of hardihood in his preaching and baptizing, and was soon styled "the new Paul." Nine days after his own rebaptism, he was emboldened to enter the village church of Zollikon, block the path of the pastor-priest, and ask him provocatively what he had come to do. The good Zwinglian answered, "I will preach God's Word." Blaurock answered, "Not thou, but I, have been called to preach."[15] The pastor, who was acting on the authority of the canons of the Zurich minster, ascended the pulpit and tried to preach, but Blaurock interrupted and disturbed him so much that

---

[12] John Kessler, *Sabbata* (c. 1533), edited by Emil Egli and Rudolf Schoch (St. Gall, 1902), 142.

[13] See Zwingli, *Of Baptism,* translated by G. W. Bromiley in *Zwingli and Bullinger, LCC,* XXIV (Philadelphia, 1953), 157.

[14] Cf. Fritz Blanke, *Brüder in Christo: Die Geschichte der ältesten Täufergemeinde* (Zurich, 1955), 35 ff.

[15] Von Muralt, *Quellen,* No. 29.

he stepped down again. Blaurock hoped, just as Grebel and Mantz had hoped earlier, that by getting the support of the people, he could persuade them to heed the Word of God and clear the temple of idolatry independently of the magistracy. The congregation was receptive and insisted that he continue, whereupon Blaurock began striking a board with a rod, saying, "It is written, My house shall be a house of prayer, but ye have made it a den of thieves." He created such a commotion that the magistrate intervened and threatened to put Blaurock in jail unless he desisted.

With this scene ended the eight days of relatively undisturbed Anabaptist revivalism in the Zurich region. Then the hand of the magistrate began to be felt, first mildly, then with increasing harshness, by all the leading representatives of Anabaptism. The mild Zwinglians were forced to turn with severity upon these ultra-Zwinglian brethren who made the Bible not merely the guiding authority but the imperious command of God. Brötli and others had already been expelled from the jurisdiction of Zurich.

On Monday, 30 January, Felix Mantz and George Blaurock, along with twenty-five others, were arrested in Zollikon and placed in the sequestered Austin monastery.[16] The prisoners denied that the council had competence in religion, and one of their number declared that he "had enrolled under the *Dux* Jesus Christ and would go with him to death."[17] The authorities sought to bring the earnest evangelicals around by disputation. Zwingli himself participated and argued that there was no second baptism in the Bible. Precisely that, they retorted, could be found in Acts 19:3–5, in which those who knew the baptism of John nevertheless received a second and a true Christian baptism from Paul.[18]

All except Mantz and Blaurock, who were "stiff-necked," were released on 8 February, on the condition that they would assemble only in groups of three or four and exclusively for Bible-reading and conversation, not for baptizing and preaching. Mantz, who was a Zuricher and obligated by oath to obey the authorities, refused to heed the council and insisted on written exchanges with Zwingli, both of them to argue solely from Scripture. Mantz was kept on in prison. In the course of further questioning he explained how the community of goods in Acts 2:42–47 was the consequences of a joyfully commemorative Communion in the

---

[16] *Ibid.*
[17] *Ibid.*, No. 33.
[18] *Ibid.*, No. 43.

benefits of the work of Christ in undoing the Fall.[19] Mantz's quiet steadfastness, his insistence on disputing by carefully written exegesis, and his refusal to renounce his baptismal theology, encouraged others like Brötli and Grebel, who were for the moment outside the jurisdiction of Zurich.[20]

Blaurock was released on 18 February. He immediately went out to Zollikon and began preaching to the conventicle in a private house, baptizing all who would repent.[21] In the meantime, a farmer, George Schad, had been recruiting, and on one day alone had baptized forty adults in the village church. Schad and Blaurock naturally aroused the authorities, who had released the Zollikon sectaries on their promise to abstain from precisely such behavior. The Anabaptists, for their part, had made this promise with a "mental reservation" to the effect that they would refrain unless God constrained them to do otherwise, and Blaurock had quickly persuaded them of their duty to obey God rather than men.

On 16 March the Radicals were again imprisoned.[22] During this time the Second Baptismal Disputation was held, in which Zwingli again participated.[23] Some of the debaters were held in prison for about two weeks, after which most of them yielded and paid their fines and costs (25 March); but Mantz and Blaurock remained in prison.

Soon, however, Blaurock and his wife were banished from Zurich and warned of severe punishment if they should ever return. They went to the Grisons. Mantz sometime after this escaped.[24] Seeking shelter, he came to Grebel's house in Zurich. The two men planned to go off together on a missionary trip outside the jurisdiction of Zurich, but Grebel's wife, who obviously did not share her husband's convictions, threatened to expose the escape of Mantz if he did not leave at once.[25]

Thereupon Mantz went to the Grisons (Ch. 22.1), following Blaurock. There he was arrested in July, turned over to the Zurich authorities, and would not be released until October 1526[26] (Ch. 6.4).

Grebel was in Schaffhausen for two months at the beginning

[19] *Ibid.,* No. 42a.
[20] *Ibid.,* No. 44.
[21] *Ibid.,* Nos. 48 and 50.
[22] Von Muralt, *Quellen,* No. 53.
[23] It was Krajewski who first clearly identified this second disputation, *op. cit.,* 93–97.
[24] For the detailed argumentation, see Krajewski, *op. cit.,* 99.
[25] Krajewski, *op. cit.,* 103.
[26] *Ibid.,* 111.

of 1525, seeking to convert the chief pastor of Schaffhausen, Dr. Sebastian Hofmeister, and his Schaffhausen colleague, Dr. Sebastian Meyer. Hofmeister had taken part in both the Zurich disputations of January and October 1523, serving, indeed, in the latter as its chairman. Grebel had reason to believe that Hofmeister could be won over to the new view on baptism. Hofmeister, for example, once wrote to him, saying that he had "openly declared before the council of Schaffhausen that Master Ulrich Zwingli erred in the matter of infant baptism" and that he himself had not wished to have his own child baptized.[27] But there is a great gap between antipedobaptism and anabaptism. In the end, Grebel's efforts while a guest in Hofmeister's home hardened the two Schaffhausen pastors against the Swiss Brethren. Grebel's main achievement in the town was his rebaptism of Wolfgang Ulimann from St. Gall, who insisted that Grebel immerse him completely naked in the icy Rhine.[28]

Though the first Anabaptist congregation of Zollikon had been scattered, the new movement was taking on form and direction. Basic was the conviction that upon all who had been experientially forgiven the Great Commission of Matt. 28:19–20[29] was laid to proclaim repentance and true baptism among all peoples in programmatic heedlessness of the territorial and prudential limitations imposed by the Magisterial Reformers.

2. ANABAPTISM IN ST. GALL, THE CANTON OF APPENZELL, AND RHEINTAL

The conditions under which the Swiss Brethren movement began in the town of St. Gall were different from those prevailing elsewhere, because at the outset it was tolerated by the authorities and its early progress was therefore rapid. The burgomaster (1526–1532) and town physician, Vadian, was married to Grebel's sister, and the two Biblical humanists had been for some time in correspondence. It was Grebel, indeed, who sent his former mentor of his Vienna student days the newly printed copies of the works of Tertullian, whom both admired for his rigorism. Little did Grebel realize that Vadian would one day turn all the

---

[27] Von Muralt, *Quellen,* 179; repeated by Hubmaier, *Der alten und der neuen Lehrer Urteil,* 1526. See further, C. A. Bächtold, "Die Schaffhäuser Wiedertäufer," *Beiträge zur vaterländischen Geschichte,* VII (1900), 87; Krajewski, *op. cit.,* 104–107.

[28] *Johannes Kesslers Sabbata,* edited by Emil Egli and Rudolf Schoch (St. Gall, 1902), 144.

[29] Cf. Franklin H. Littell, "The Anabaptist Theology of Missions," *MQR,* XXI (1947), 5–17.

arguments of Tertullian aimed at ancient heretics against the Swiss Brethren themselves.[30] Vadian saw no reason to suppress the movement at first and even sympathized with its disapproval of infant baptism.

The beginning of the evangelical movement in the town dates from the open-air preaching of Balthasar Hubmaier in May 1523.[31] In January 1524 the ever-enlarging circle of concerned evangelical brethren began meeting regularly of a Sunday evening for Bible study under John Kessler, a lay theological student recently returned from auditing courses in Wittenberg. Presently, Kessler would become a leading Zwinglian and the author of the important Reformation chronicle, *Sabbata*.[32] From a private home, the Bible-study group transferred its meetings first to the guildhall of the tailors, then to that of the weavers, and then to the second floor of the Metzge, which could accommodate a thousand people. At this point the magistrates placed St. Lawrence's at the disposal of the eager evangelicals.[33]

Then, in the early fall of 1524, one Lawrence Hochrütiner challenged the leader Kessler on the question of infant baptism. Hochrütiner, a native of St. Gall, had taken part in 1523 in destroying the crucifix at Stadelhofen near Zurich and distributing to the poor the chopped-up pieces as firewood. Obliged to leave the jurisdiction of Zurich, he had returned to St. Gall and become the most restless member of Kessler's study group. It was when Rom. 6:3, on baptism into the death of Jesus Christ, was under discussion that Hochrütiner spoke up saying: "I observe from your words that you mean one may baptize infants," and then proceeded to argue that only he who can believe may be baptized unto salvation.[34] Kessler was doing his best with a very obstreperous Bible class and simply indicated, in answer to Hochrütiner, that he "would not know for the moment what else to do" than to continue to baptize infants and then went on to observe that in making so much of believers' baptism the evangelical "Gallers"

---

[30] Conradin Bonorand, "Joachim Vadian und die Täufer," *Schweizer Beiträge zur Allgemeinen Geschichte*, XI (1953), 43–72.

[31] Kessler, *Sabbata*, 106.

[32] The most recent accounts of John Kessler (1502–1574) and of Anabaptism in his region are by John Horsch, "The Swiss Brethren in St. Gall and Appenzell," *MQR*, VII (1933), 205–226, and by Heinold Fast, "Die Sonderstellung der Täufer in St. Gallen und Appenzell," *Zwingliana*, XI (1960), 223–240.

[33] Kessler, *Sabbata*, 110.

[34] He was afterward among the fifteen in the house of Mantz in Zurich on the memorable occasion of Blaurock's rebaptism, where he was himself also rebaptized.

were actually becoming like Paul's reactionary Galatians in their stress on circumcision as essential to salvation![35] The government objected to Kessler's study group; and, despite his moderation, he was forbidden by the town council, on 15 September 1524, to carry on the work.

When he complied, his place was presently taken by the more radical Ulimann, returned from his rebaptism in the Rhine. Ulimann, whose father was a guild master in St. Gall and who had been a Premonstratensian in Chur (whence also Blaurock and Castelberger had come), proclaimed to a large company assembled in the weavers' guild hall that the Heavenly Father had revealed to him that he should avoid preaching in the church with its images, a place of lies, where the truth had never been proclaimed. Some of the Brethren regretted his move, pointing out that they had only recently been permitted to carry on their lections in a church.

At this point, two evangelical parties were forming within the shadow of the ancient abbey of St. Gall: the civic church, headed by Vadian, Grebel's old preceptor from Vienna days, his brother-in-law, and his faithful correspondent, and the gathered church of the radical followers of Ulimann, whom Grebel had immersed in the Rhine. When Grebel himself came to St. Gall for two weeks in April, he was outstandingly successful, and on the Palm Sunday of April 1525 he rebaptized great numbers at the riverbank.[36] At first the council put no obstacles in the way of the outdoor meetings of the Anabaptists. Grebel departed. Still cherishing the hope that its town council might adopt his doctrine and set the example to be followed by the other cantonal governments, in contrast to the reactionary policy of Zurich, Grebel later implored Vadian:

Become as a child, for otherwise you cannot enter into the Kingdom of God. If you are not willing to stand with the Brethren, at least do not resist them; do not give to other states the example of persecution.[37]

After Grebel departed, Hippolytus (Bolt) Eberli from the canton of Schwyz appeared. He belonged to the sacramentarian Brethren, and it was not until his arrival in St. Gall that he submitted to rebaptism and emerged as an eloquent field preacher of the rapidly growing Anabaptist movement. During the Easter holidays almost all the citizens and neighboring farmers as-

[35] Kessler, *Sabbata,* 143.
[36] *Ibid.,* 145.
[37] Letter to Vadian of 30 May 1525; *VB,* III, 116 ff.

sembled to hear the peasant preacher proclaim repentance and
the baptism of the reborn.[38]

In April 1525 the Brethren were summoned to the council to
answer for their teachings on baptism. Ulimann skillfully defended the Anabaptist position, saying that infant baptism was a
later institution of the church without Scriptural foundation;
that adult baptism implied the obligation to die to vices, live unto
Christ, and be obedient. The Dominical order to baptize believers
had been maintained for about two hundred years, he argued,
until the time of Cyprian. Ulimann reminded the conservatives
that baptism had anciently been performed only at Easter and
Pentecost with great solemnity and after the catechumens had
been fully instructed. Ulimann was at first requested "for the
sake of brotherly love to wait with the deed." When he refused,
the request was changed to a command with the threat of expulsion if he should not comply. Eberli, too, was asked to leave.
Shortly afterward Eberli was seized by the authorities in the
Catholic canton of Schwyz, and burned at the stake on 29 May
1525, the first martyr of the Swiss Brethren.

By now the exhortations of the Anabaptist revivalists every
evening and on holidays, in the mountains, woods, fields, and at
the gates of the city, had become so frequent and exciting that
the town churches were drained of their attendants, divided in
their counsel, and deprived of alms for the sustenance of the
poor. The town council thereupon reversed itself and demanded
that all preaching and disputing take place *in the churches,* and
that there be no more gatherings in or around the town.

Vadian prepared a refutation of Anabaptist doctrine for a disputation on 5 June 1525, but it was no easier, says Kessler, to
take from the conventicles their freedom in the fields than to
take a bone from a dog.[39] Their preachers contended that argumentation with scribes was useless, for the Heavenly Father had
hidden truths from the wise (Matt. 11:25). Nevertheless, a reply
to Vadian was drawn up. Ulimann was emboldened, in an evening sermon, to say that the magistrates who took counsel together
against the Lord and his anointed, were heathen; and, citing
Ps. 2, with its verse "Let us burst their bonds asunder, and cast
their cords from us," he aroused his followers to such a pitch that
a tumult might have ensued at any moment.[40]

To "imperiled" St. Gall, Zwingli dedicated his first literary
attack on the Anabaptists, his long-awaited disquisition *Of Bap-*

[38] Kessler, *Sabbata,* 146.
[39] *Ibid.,* 148.
[40] *Ibid.*

tism.[41] In the letter to Vadian accompanying it, Zwingli had written: "The issue is not baptism but revolt, faction, heresy."[42]

It is well that we interrupt the narrative of events in St. Gall to face squarely the arguments of Zwingli against the new movement that claimed his paternity despite his protestations.

Zwingli divided his book into four parts. In the first, on baptism and its New Testament sources, he distinguished four meanings for the word: immersion in water, baptism in the Spirit, baptismal instruction preceding the rite, and the baptismal faith. He felt that all these elements were important but did not need to be present in any one action; and, finding that the rite of water baptism was a covenantal sign rather than a strengthening of baptismal faith, he argued that it could be appropriately administered to children born in the covenant. In the second section he dealt with the institution of baptism and located it in John's action at the Jordan rather than in Christ's commission of Matt., ch. 28. This derivation of a sacrament from an action prior to the Passion indicates a considerable lowering of its redemptive significance. Zwingli based his assimilation of New Covenantal baptism and Old Covenantal circumcision on Tertullian and Lactantius. It was Henry Bullinger who first pointed out to Zwingli these patristic texts demonstrating the unity of the Old and New Covenants and consequently the equivalence of circumcision and baptism.[43] Zwingli refuted the objection that John did not baptize in the Triune name by saying that, without the words, he yet so intended. In the third and fourth sections he dealt with rebaptism and infant baptism. Dissociating it completely from its medieval accretions, he presented baptism as a covenant sign belonging to the family and community rather than to the individual. Declining to base infant baptism on the doctrine of original sin, and pointing to Col. 2:10–12 as proof that water baptism replaced circumcision as the covenant sign, he inconsistently surmised that John baptized (already circumcised) children at the Jordan. Zwingli argued against the Anabaptists that in administering baptism to the followers of John, the apostles did not actually rebaptize but simply baptized for the first time those who merely *knew* (but had not expressly hitherto received) baptism at the hands of John. He included with this treatise a copy of the sec-

---

[41] *Of Baptism, LCC,* XXIV, 129 ff.

[42] *VB,* III, 114.

[43] Letter to Zwingli preserved by Johann Jakob Simler, *Sammlung alter und neuer Urkunden,* II (Zurich, 1767), 100 ff. See further, though incidentally, Heinold Fast, "Research Notes," *MQR,* XXXI (1957), 294.

ond reformed order of Baptism, replacing the earlier Germanized but otherwise Catholic baptismal service worked out by Leo Jud.

The publication of Zwingli's book on 28 May was accompanied in St. Gall by an announcement from the pastor of the principal church that the book would be read that evening from the pulpit of St. Lawrence's. Anabaptist sympathizers were in more or less forced attendance. The church was packed. Ulimann arose and shouted: "Stop reading; tell us God's Word, not Zwingli's." When the pastor responded that the words were God's as explicated by Zwingli, the Anabaptists retorted that the congregation should then listen also to the explication of Conrad Grebel and to his letter addressed to the burgomaster. Thereupon, one of the burgo-masters (not Vadian) rebuked them for presuming to read a letter addressed in the first place to the magistrates of St. Gall. The Zwinglian chronicler of this heated exchange admits that Zwing-li's words were not felt to be cogent, that the audience as a whole felt that "the truth of God was on the side of the Ana-baptists."[44]

In June 1525 the Brethren were forbidden to hold any more meetings in or around town, fines were imposed for rebaptism, and a special militia of two hundred men was sworn in to cope with a possible revolt. Since Ulimann did not comply with the order to refrain from field preaching, he was sentenced to banish-ment on 17 July, but was later pardoned upon his oath. (He later led a group of Anabaptists to Moravia, and was with his second band proceeding from Appenzell to Moravia in 1528 when they were seized and put to death by Seneschal George of Waldburg.)[45]

Until the summer of 1525 the priests of St. Gall were com-pelled to continue saying Mass, and probably this is the reason why those seriously interested in a reform flocked to the Brethren, for they felt the inconsistency of denouncing the Mass as blas-phemy and still requiring its celebration. It was not to be abol-ished in St. Gall until 1528. The conservatism of the authorities in practice helped to incline the people to the uncompromising message of the Brethren. Vadian says, "None were more suscepti-ble to the doctrine of the Anabaptists than those who were in-clined to piety and uprightness of life.[46] Kessler describes the Anabaptists of St. Gall thus:

Their conversation and bearing shine forth as entirely pious, holy and unpunishable. They avoid ostentatious clothes, despise delicate

[44] Kessler, *Sabbata,* 149.
[45] He and ten other men were beheaded and their womenfolk drowned.
[46] Vadian, *Deutsche historische Schriften,* edited by Ernst Götzinger (St. Gall, 1875–1879), III, 408.

food and drink, clothe themselves with coarse cloth, decking their heads with broad felt hats, their way and conversation quite humble. They carried no weapon, neither sword nor dagger, except for a broken-off bread knife, saying that those were wolves' clothing which the sheep ought not to wear. They swore not, not even to the authorities, the civic oath. And if anyone transgressed among them, he was banned; for there was the practice of daily excommunication among them. In their talk and disputation they were grim and hardbitten and so unyielding that they would rather have died than have yielded a point.[47]

He goes on to raise the question whether they had received the Spirit through the preaching of the law or of faith.

But if a stubborn legalism characterized the majority of the St. Gall Anabaptists, a frenzied antinomianism took possession of enough of the others to give the whole movement notoriety. Over against the practice of daily excommunication and Biblical literalism, we see the swift degeneration of a section of the populace into a rank Spiritualism that did not stop at burning in the oven the very words of the New Testament which, only a few years before, had been the objective of heroic study in the face of magisterial opposition. The dictum that "the letter killeth"[48] induced these enthusiasts to destroy the written word and put their confidence in the vagaries of a Spiritualism no longer restrained by Paul's other dictum about discerning the spirits.

In reading Kessler, who, like Vadian, was originally well disposed toward the evangelical fervor of the Brethren, one gets the impression of excesses on the fringes comparable to those of later revivalism. Some simulated little children in preparation for the Kingdom, the imminent advent of which was discussed and calculated with enthusiasm. Group confession led to disclosures that alarmed spouses; children of seven and eight lay in a coma for hours, and there were other attempts at simulating death with Christ to the world. Glossalalia broke out. There was lewdness and unchastity and the extraordinary declaration of a deranged woman that she was predestined to give birth to the Antichrist, and there was a shocking fratricide by decapitation, perpetrated as God-willed by the killer and earnestly sought by the victim.

In this degeneration of the movement one seems to see beneath the lifted weight of centuries of ecclesiastical domination a squirming, spawning, nihilistic populace on its own, confused by the new theological terms of predestination, faith alone, *Gelassenheit*, and by the new Biblical texts seized upon with an almost maniacal glare. It is hard to find anything in common between

[47] Kessler, *Sabbata*, 147 f.
[48] II Cor. 3:6.

this phase of St. Gall Anabaptism and the sober fervor and evangelical zeal of Grebel, Mantz, and Blaurock.[49]

Because of the fantastic excesses of a few and especially because of the potentially revolutionary mood of the many, severed, as they thought, by right from the heathen magistrates and their ecclesiastical scribes, Grebel's vision of an intercantonal, evangelical church of committed believers faded into sectarianism. Vadian, despite the winsomeness of his brother-in-law, finally threw his weight against the Anabaptists under the pressure of the prophet-statesman-warrior of Zurich.

In the canton of Appenzell, closely associated with St. Gall in the reforming movement, and in the confederational condominium of Rheintal, the majority of the people in some villages were for a time Brethren, and even many of the Zwinglian preachers favored some of the Anabaptist measures. At the Rheintal synod at Rheineck, for example, the Zwinglian pastors reactivated the greater and the lesser ban as an integral part of evangelical parish life.[50] One of the Anabaptist leaders, John Krüssi, displaced the preacher at Teufen. He was later seized by night and burned in Catholic Lucerne in the late summer of 1525.

Thus far we have followed the impulses radiating from Zurich and Zollikon in the directions of Schaffhausen, St. Gall, and the canton of Appenzell. Returning to the original band and its dispersal after the eventful week in Mantz's house in Zurich and the activities in Zollikon, we follow another missionary, William Reublin, to Waldshut.

3. Reublin Baptizes Hubmaier in Waldshut

Although Waldshut was not a Swiss town, its relationship to the Zurich movement was so close that we must pause in our narrative of the phenomenal Swiss Brethren mission to recall the role of Waldshut in the Peasants' War (Ch. 4.2.a) and of Hubmaier in the sacramentarian controversy (Ch. 5.2.a) and to note the temporary conversion of the town to Anabaptism.

About a week before the decisive step into Anabaptism taken by the sacramentarian conventicle in Zurich, Hubmaier had

---

[49] John Horsch has sought to ascribe the excesses to Anabaptists who were coerced back into the Reformed state church and gave vent to their sense of constriction by turning Zwingli's doctrine of predestination into an excuse for libertinism. But he does not face the massiveness of the evidence laid out by Kessler, which, however much based on hearsay, looks authentic in the bulk if not in the details of every episode. Surely Horsch's distinction between *Wiedergetaufte* and *Wiedertäufer* does not hold up under scrutiny "An Inquiry Into the Truth of the Accusation of Fanaticism and Crime," *MQR,* VIII (1934), 18 ff.

[50] Bonorand, *loc. cit.,* 46, with the literature.

written 16 January 1525 from Waldshut to Oecolampadius in Basel, describing his local practice of the consecration of infants in the presence of the whole congregation and the postponement of the rite of Baptism for the purpose of bringing the sacrament of redemption into line with the Protestant principle of solafide-ism:

For we have publicly taught that children should not be baptized. Why do we baptize children? Baptism, say they [Zwingli and Leo], is a mere sign [of inclusion in the covenant]. Why do we strive so much over a sign? A sign and a symbol it certainly is, instituted by Christ with august words fraught with meaning: "In the name of the Father, the Son, and the Holy Spirit" [Matt. 28:19]. Whoever now attenuates or otherwise misuses it does violence to the words of Christ given at the institution of the symbolic action, in so far as the meaning of this sign and symbol is a pledge (*obstrictio*), whereby one pledges oneself to God because of faith in the hope of resurrection to a future life, an inward action which should be undertaken no less seriously than the outer sign. This meaning has nothing to do with babes; therefore infant baptism is without reality. In baptism there is the pledge (*obligatio*) to God, to which the Apostles' Creed today testifies, bearing the apostolic majesty before oneself and the renunciation of Satan and all his pomps unto water, i.e., unto death. In the Supper there is the pledge to one's neighbor to offer body and blood in his stead, as Christ for me. And so we have it in the laws and prophets. I believe, yea, I know, that it will not go well with Christendom until Baptism and the Supper are brought back to their original purity. . . .

Here, brother in Christ, you have my opinion; if I err, it is the brother's duty to call an ass back! For I wish nothing so much that I will not revoke it, yea, cut it off, when I am taught better from the word of God by you and yours. . . . Otherwise I abide by my opinion, for to that I am constrained by the command of Christ, the word, faith, truth, judgment, conscience. . . . Write me whether the promise [in Matt. 19:14], "Let the little children come to me," etc., especially belongs to infants. What prompts me to that is the word of Christ, "for of such is the kingdom of heaven," not "of them"; and also what the Strassburg brethren [Bucer and Capito] feel concerning it.[51]

Instead of baptism, I have the church come together, bring the infant in, explain in German the gospel, "They brought little children" [Matt. 19:13]. When a name is given it, the whole church prays for the child on bended knees, and commends it to Christ, that he will be gracious and intercede for it. But if the parents are still weak, and positively wish that the child be baptized, then I baptize it; and I am weak with the weak for the time being until they can be better instructed. As to the word, however, I do not yield to them in the least point.[52]

[51] A communication of November 1524.
[52] Staehelin, *Briefe und Akten,* I, No. 238.

Oecolampadius replied, disapproving of the substitution of consecration for infant baptism, contending with Augustine that the faith of the parents or the church suffices mysteriously for the child.

It was in vain that Hubmaier, 2 February 1525, offered to prove in public debate before the town authorities that infant baptism had no Scriptural warrant (*Öffentliche Erbietung*). Thus it was that when Reublin, formerly of St. Alban's in Basel and now an emissary of the Swiss Anabaptists, arrived in Waldshut and recounted what had been at length accomplished in Zurich and Zollikon, Hubmaier was favorably disposed to move in the same direction. Reublin first rebaptized a few of the ready ones in a village outside the town. He suggested postponing the main action until Easter, 16 April, and proposed to celebrate Jesus' institution of the Supper on Maundy Thursday with a whole lamb (apparently not carried out). On Easter, Hubmaier and sixty others accepted rebaptism at Reublin's hands.[53] Hubmaier, in the days following, rebaptized over three hundred, using a milk bucket with water from the fountain in the town square. On Easter Monday he observed the Lord's Supper among the rebaptized, following literally the New Testament pattern. With a towel in hand, the *doctor theologiae* washed the feet of his parishioners. A contemporary witness reports maliciously that after he was finished with the young women and came to the "old bucks," he complained of fatigue and suggested that someone else finish the task.[54]

Secure in his ecclesiastical position at Waldshut, and confident in his new practice of believers' baptism, concerned also to see this more consistent evangelistic position spread, Hubmaier wrote 10 July[55] to the Zurich council, begging Zwingli to debate the issue with him for the good of the Reformation cause, and requested a safe-conduct. Hubmaier was to persevere to the end in a conviction held in common with Zwingli, and in opposition to most of the Swiss Brethren, that the evangelical cause of a believers' church should be sanctioned and supported by an evangelical or regenerate magistracy. His position was, in this respect, identical with that held only *transitionally* by the pacifist Grebel. As he said in his letter to the Zurich council, he had hoped that

[53] Von Muralt, *Quellen*, No. 405.
[54] Heinrich Schreiber, *Taschenbuch für Geschichte und Altertum in Süddeutschland*, II (Freiburg im Br., 1840), 208 f. Schreiber here adduces unharmonized data from the chronicles of Freiburg and Laufenburg. Cf. W. Mau, *Balthasar Hubmaier*, Abhandlungen zur mittleren und neueren Geschichte, XL (1912), 86.
[55] Von Muralt, *Quellen*, No. 82.

if only the two Reformers could get together, their differences would be worked out satisfactorily.

The Zurich council apparently ignored the request, for Hubmaier was soon moved to refute Zwingli's *Of Baptism*, dedicated to St. Gall, in his own *Vom christlichen Taufen der Gläubigen*. It is humorous at points and well argued, as Zwingli was presently to acknowledge indirectly by his ill-tempered reply.

The development of a large Anabaptist congregation led by the town's chief pastor was cut short by the Austrian capture of Waldshut on 5 December 1525. Unable to count on Swiss military aid, as in the days when he was more moderate, Hubmaier took solemn leave of his Anabaptist parish. The next day the town yielded to the Austrians. The vicar-general (John Faber) of the bishop of Constance said Mass, and the town returned to Catholic allegiance. We shall next encounter the tattered refugee and his wife in Zurich.

4. The Anabaptist Missionaries Face the Magistrates in Zurich

In the meantime, Grebel had gone from St. Gall to Grüningen, his birthplace, where his father, Jacob Grebel, had been bailiff and where his evangelical preaching now met such favorable response that Mantz, fresh from prison, and Blaurock, from the Grisons, came to join him in the revival.

The religious revival in the bailiwick of Grüningen had grown out of social unrest and evangelical aspiration. The peasants of this district on the north shore of Lake Zurich, under a bailiff appointed in the cantonal capital, had for some time been restless under the domination of the abbot of Rüti and had sought relief from ancient abbatial exactions, at first with some encouragement from the Zurich authorities. The religious revolt, with the Anabaptist stress upon a free church without any tithes to the monastery, made an economic as well as a religious appeal.

On Sunday, 8 October 1525, at the village church of Hinwil, in the bailiwick of Grüningen, before the arrival of the local pastor, Blaurock entered the pulpit and opened his sermon with these words:

Whose is this place? If it is the house of God where God's Word is to be preached, I am here as an emissary of the Father to proclaim God's Word.[56]

The bailiff was summoned from the castle at Grüningen. Captured, Blaurock was seated on a horse, to be conducted to prison.

[56] *Ibid.*, No. 109.

From horseback he sang hymns and exhorted the sympathetic peasants, who followed in an ever-increasing throng, joined now by Mantz and Grebel. The bewildered bailiff scarcely knew what to do when the emboldened followers sought to arrange a preaching service en route! He managed to arrest Grebel. Mantz temporarily evaded capture. He had just been released from his second imprisonment (of three months) on condition that he cease baptizing. Owing to the widespread sympathy for them among the peasants of the bailiwick, Grebel and Blaurock were only reluctantly and with considerable negotiation turned over to the Zurich authorities. Only a free debate on the issues would, it was thought, appease the populace.

Thus, once again, Grebel and Mantz (soon thereafter also recaptured), along with Blaurock, faced in parlous debate their former teacher and once-admired friend, this time from 6 to 8 November 1525.

The discussions, held in the largest church in Zurich (the Grossmünster) because the town hall could not hold the crowd, constituted the Third Baptismal Disputation.[57] The disputation, extending into the evenings, was chaired by, among others, Vadian of St. Gall and Dr. Sebastian Hofmeister, who had been driven out of conservative Schaffhausen, where Grebel had been his guest, and who was now the pastor in the Fraumünster. The peasants of Grüningen had sent twelve neutral observers to judge whether the Brethren were given a full opportunity to unfold their thoughts without having Zwingli "strangle them inarticulate in their throats."[58] Besides the Grüningen delegation, there were Anabaptists on safe-conducts from St. Gall, Chur, and Zofingen. (Hubmaier in Waldshut had planned to attend the disputation, but he and his party were driven back by the Austrian forces.) Zwingli, Leo Jud, and Caspar Megander (Grossmann) were the three antagonists.[59]

Zwingli's charges[60] against the Swiss Brethren, some of them based on hearsay, were their alleged belief (1) that there should be no Christian magistracy, (2) that all things should be held in common, (3) that the saints are secure in not being able to sin after rebaptism, and (4) that they were prepared to resist by force. The fourth charge may have been based on a misquoted remark of Blaurock's and on his taking over in the village churches, first in

---

[57] So numbered, now that Krajewski has identified as the Second Disputation the *congressio* in March.
[58] Von Muralt, *Quellen,* No. 115.
[59] *Ibid.,* No. 129.
[60] Summarized thus by Bender, *op. cit.,* 157.

Zollikon and then in Hinwil, but it might also have been based on the extravagant assertions of Ulimann in St. Gall or the actions of Hubmaier in Waldshut.

The debate desired by the Anabaptist leaders really constituted a judicial hearing, after which they were arrested. Then followed a formal trial and imprisonment for life or until renunciation. It was the first incarceration for Grebel, the second for Blaurock, and the third for Mantz.[61]

From this point on, the legal repression of the three principal Zurich Anabaptist preachers becomes interlaced with the long-standing controversy between Dr. Hubmaier and Master Zwingli. With some financial means, Hubmaier and his wife made directly for Zurich, quixotically hoping that the radical cause could still be saved.[62] Arriving 7 December in Zurich, they spent the night with Henry Aberli, the following night at the inn of the widow Bluntschli. She and her daughter were presently fined for aiding an Anabaptist leader. When the council learned of Hubmaier's presence, they arrested him, 11 December, convinced that he "was hatching out some monstrosity . . . and that for this purpose he had crept secretly into the city."[63]

On 5 November 1525, Zwingli had completed his *Antwort*,[64] and Hubmaier was now perhaps glad to face his antagonist directly. The Zurich council, recalling Hubmaier's request (made in July from Waldshut) to discuss baptism with Zwingli, therefore accorded the sick refugee prisoner an opportunity to express himself. The colloquium took place on 12 December, the opposition represented not only by Zwingli but also by Leo Jud, Hofmeister, and Megander. The two principals have left divergent versions of the course of the discussion. Zwingli says that Hubmaier was left "mute as a fish."[65] Hubmaier was quite conscious of his own forensic superiority.[66] He made Zwingli recall that

---

[61] Earlier writers, based on *Heinrich Bullinger's Reformationsgeschichte,* edited by J. J. Hoffinger and H. H. Vogeli (Frauenfeld, 1838–1840), I, 296, say that the three leaders were released. The new view, based on von Muralt, *Quellen,* is represented by Bender, *op. cit.,* 159, and Krajewski, *op. cit.,* 121.

[62] Egli, *op. cit.,* 49, and Mau, *op. cit.,* 103, mention a stopover in Grüningen without, however, giving any source. I am following here the calendaring of von Muralt, *Quellen.*

[63] Zwingli to Peter Gynoraeus, 31 August 1526; *ZW,* VIII, No. 524.

[64] *Antwort über Balthasar Hübmaiers Taufbüchlein, ZW,* IV, 577.

[65] Zwingli discusses Hubmaier's reappearance in Zurich in two letters, the first, of 1 January 1526, to Capito, *ZW,* VIII, No. 434; the other, of 31 August 1526, to Peter Gynoraeus, *ZW,* VIII, No. 524; both translated by Samuel M. Jackson, *Huldreich Zwingli* (New York, 1901), 249 ff.

[66] He recounts the bitter story in his *Ein Gesprech,* published in Nicolsburg, 1521.

back in 1523 in "Graben street" he too had stressed the importance of instruction and had incorporated the idea in the eighteenth of his Sixty-seven Articles. Zwingli countered that the earlier conversation had revolved around the importance of Christian education in place of the old sacrament of confirmation, but had not presupposed the postponement of baptism. When Hubmaier acknowledged that this was after all the case, Zwingli commented that he was "charming." At length, fearful lest he be turned over to the Catholic Austrians,[67] Hubmaier consented to prepare in his own words a retraction, which he was to sign and turn over the next day to certain town councilors chosen for the purpose. Somewhere in the process Dr. Hubmaier was "thrust back into prison and tortured." Zwingli says that he "repeated the retraction three times when stretched on the rack (*ter extentus*)," bewailing his misery.[68] Somewhere in the dispute, now turned into a judicial hearing, Hubmaier protested that his recantation had been extracted by torture and appealed to what he hoped might be the appellate jurisdiction of a Confederal Swiss tribunal, since he was not a native of Zurich. Zwingli, at once patriotic, humane, and anti-Catholic, was a major factor in restraining the council from turning Hubmaier over to the Austrians; but he was indignant that Hubmaier himself would presume to carry his own case to a tribunal higher than that of Zurich—"in itself a capital offense," Zwingli remarked.[69]

The *Widerruf* (22 December)[70] is clear as to Hubmaier's retraction of his views on adult baptism; he says that he has been in part persuaded by the importance of charity in this action, lest all those Christians who for a thousand years (on Hubmaier's earlier reckoning) had unwittingly submitted to infant baptism be considered lost. The bulk of the piece is given over to an apology for his views on diverse matters, and he contends that he has been falsely charged with communism and with holding that "a Christian cannot sit in government," etc. The retraction reads in part as follows:

I, Balthasar Hubmaier, . . . confess openly with this my handwriting, that I have not otherwise known or understood all scriptures which speak of water-baptism than that one should first preach, after that believe, and thirdly be baptised, on which I have finally established

---

[67] The request for extradition, 14 December 1525, is given by von Muralt, *Quellen*, No. 402.

[68] Zwingli to Capito, *loc. cit.*, Nos. 434, 488.

[69] *Ibid.* The text at this point is, however, damaged and therefore uncertain.

[70] Von Muralt, *Quellen*, No. 147; Staehelin and Mau hold that this is the original form of the retraction, and not that later delivered in the churches, as Egli and Vedder maintain.

myself. But now Master Ulrich Zwingli has made known to me the covenant (*bund*) of God made with Abraham and his seed, also circumcision as a covenant sign (*bundzeichen*), which I could not disprove. Also it was put before me by others, as Master Leo [Jud], Doctor Sebastian [Hofmeister], and [Oswald] Myconius, how love should be a judge and judger in all scriptures, which has gone very much to my heart; and also I have thought much of love and have finally been moved to desist from my goal, namely, that one should not baptise children and that in rebaptism I have erred.[71]

A part of the agreement between the two parties was that Hubmaier would make his recantation public on a suitable occasion. In the meantime, he was put under the custody of the bailiff of Grüningen castle.[72] Sunday, 5 January 1526, was the date set. After the divine service, the formula of revocation was read from the pupit of the Fraumünster. Then Zwingli delivered a sermon and all seemed well. Hubmaier thereupon mounted the pulpit ostensibly to renounce his Anabaptism publicly. Perhaps he was counting on a popular uprising in his favor, for, instead of recanting, he seized the opportunity to harangue the congregation in favor of Anabaptism until Zwingli interrupted him.[73] The tumult subsided after Hubmaier was hurried off to the Water Tower. At first stunned and bewildered, he chose not to remember what he had done. But at length he rallied his strength to resist, and composed, in the squalor of the prison, his *XII Artikel christlichen Glaubens*. Then there was another hearing or two.[74] His case was now joined, 5 March, with that of the Zurich Anabaptists Mantz, Blaurock, and Grebel.[75] The Zurich triumvirate remained steadfast, but Hubmaier once again consented to recant publicly.

This he did in three churches on 13 and 15 April. In consideration thereof, the Zurich authorities, urged by Zwingli, allowed him to remain around for several weeks, that he might choose his own time to leave the town under the cover of secrecy, lest he be overtaken by his Austrian foes, or by the agents of the Catholic cantons. We shall meet him next in Augsburg en route to Moravia (Ch. 7.2). Meanwhile, we resume the account of the imprisoned Zurich Brethren.

The Third Baptismal Disputation in November and the three

---

[71] The last line, beginning with "goal," is crossed out and rewritten in the margin. The recantation bears no date, but appears to have been written 22 December 1525. Von Muralt, *Quellen,* No. 147; Vedder, *Hübmaier,* 138 ff.
[72] Von Muralt, *Quellen,* No. 144.
[73] Zwingli to Gynoraeus, *loc. cit.*
[74] Von Muralt, *Quellen,* 404, 170, and 179.
[75] *Ibid.,* No. 170.

months of their leaders' imprisonment only aroused the Anabaptist fervor in town and countryside. Local pressure and Zurich demands made "gray the head" of the Grüningen bailiff. The Zurich authorities resolved to be severe. A new mandate threatened with death all who should thereafter rebaptize anybody. The three principals of the Grüningen roundup and fourteen others, including Anna Mantz (the sister or mother of Felix) and five other women, were sentenced, 7 March 1526,[76] to the dungeon, there to remain on bread and water until rot or recantation released them from their wretchedness. Grebel managed to bring in a candle and a flint to enable the prisoners to read the Bible in the darkness.

Within two weeks,[77] Grebel, Mantz, Blaurock, and the others escaped, although the three conscientious leaders were at first loath to exploit a window carelessly left unlocked. The escapees went their separate, secret ways.

Mantz, a fortnight after his escape, rebaptized a woman in Embrach, in the northern part of the canton of Zurich. This particular rebaptism, preceded by instruction, was to come up at his last trial, and to give the legal basis for the severity of his punishment. From Embrach he went to the territory of Basel, where he conducted a service in the open field at night. He is described by a contemporary as reading part of the service (prayer or hymn) and Scriptures by candlelight. The government soon chased him out. He enjoyed great veneration among the Anabaptists. As a hostile contemporary wrote:

Wherever he went, he was accompanied on all sides by men and women, as though he were a visible divinity, and they hung on his lips as though in a trance and enchanted. He loved the fields and woods, the secure refuges of heresy. Whatever he said and commanded was held to be a divine oracle.[78]

Mantz was arrested in St. Gall, and released 18 October to perpetual banishment from that territory. From St. Gall, he returned to his native Zurich and to the very place in the canton where his preaching had been most successful, the bailiwick of Grüningen.

In the meantime another series of events had been unfolding, events destined to have considerable influence on the shaping of Zwingli's reform and his action toward the recalcitrant Anabaptists. Within the Zurich town council there was a party of

[76] *Ibid.*, Nos. 170 A and 172.
[77] 21 March 1526; von Muralt, *Quellen*, No. 178.
[78] John Gastius, *De anabaptismi exordio* (1544), 37–38; cited in Krajewski, *op. cit.*, 132.

patricians still sympathetic to the Old Believers, who survived in the canton and were still dominant in most of the other cantons of the Confederation. On one especially sore point they sided with the Catholic cantons: on the right to export surplus peasant sons as mercenaries. Fearful of the powerful Zwinglians, some of them, in order to hold off a consolidation of the reform, encouraged the anarchic effects of the pacifistic Anabaptists. Symbol of this resistance to Zwingli's program of total reform was Jacob Grebel, the father of Conrad. He was spokesman of the patrician party, which was opposed to the more democratic craft guilds on whom Zwingli depended for his power. His "treasonable" relations with Catholic cantons and the alarm of Zwinglians because of impending defeat in the Protestant-Catholic disputation in Baden in the canton of Aargau would presently seal the fate of the Zurich Anabaptists together with his own.

The Baden disputation, 18 May to 8 June 1526, three months after the escape of the Zurich Anabaptist leaders, was arranged to determine the future ecclesiastical policy of the Confederation as a whole, for the five Catholic core cantons (Schwyz, Uri, Unterwalden, Lucerne, and Zug) were as alarmed by the ravages of the Zwinglian Reformation in the confederated cantons of Bern, Zurich, Basel, Appenzell, and the city of St. Gall, as were the Zwinglians by the Anabaptist contagion within their own territory. In fact, as early as 11 July 1524, at the Confederal diet in Zug, the five Catholic cantons had threatened to exclude Zurich from the Confederation on the ground that the religious basis of the *Eidgenossenschaft* had been jeopardized by Zwingli. Bern, supported by Solothurn and Glarus, had forestalled this *démarche*.

Now at Baden, obese, irenic, and earnest Berchtold Haller of Bern and Oecolampadius of Basel faced the internationally famous Catholic theological pugilist, John Eck, supported by John Faber, the representative of the bishop of Constance. Zwingli, whose great cause was at stake, though granted a safe-conduct, declined to participate. Eck defended seven doctrinal points, including purgatory and the baptismal ablution of original sin, but the debate centered on Eucharistic theology, which Eck well knew divided even the Reformers among themselves.[79] Eck received eighty-two votes, Oecolampadius ten. Thereupon the cause of a total reform of the Confederation, Zwingli's dream, was shattered. Indeed, the Reform, even where it had progressed, was now seriously imperiled.

It was in this tense situation that Zwingli compassed the speedy

[79] Kessler, *Sabbata,* 212 f.

trial of Grebel's father as a treasonable recipient of foreign pensions, willing to recruit and export Swiss mercenaries in violation of the law of 1503 (suspended, however, in 1508 for the Confederation but not for Zurich), and at the same time moved sharply against the Anabaptists for imperiling the whole Confederation by their stand on the civic oaths and on war.

Conrad Grebel died of the plague in August, but his father remained a symbol of the lack of Reformed patriotism shown by both the Anabaptists and the Catholics. The town councilor most opposed to Zwingli's policies, a man "with a large, snowy beard and snowy hair," Grebel's father was beheaded at the fish market 30 October 1526. Therewith, Zwingli's confidence mounted as to the propriety and, indeed, urgency of further stern measures against the Anabaptists, whom Jacob Grebel and his faction had tended to protect, and whose anarchic tendency was destroying the cohesion of the Swiss Reformation as a whole.[80] "I believe the sword will be put to their [Anabaptist] necks," Zwingli had already written confidently.

On 19 November 1526 the Zurich council passed a new law, attaching the death penalty not only to acts of rebaptism (as in the mandate of 7 March) but also to attendance upon Anabaptist preaching. With the two principal Anabaptist preachers at large in his bailiwick, the graying Grüningen bailiff, George Berger, deliberately violated the council's explicit instructions that its decree be published, alleging as his excuse that he could the more cunningly apprehend the Anabaptists if they were not alerted. Indeed, he managed to catch four of them on 3 December, notably Mantz and Blaurock. On 14 December they were delivered up to Zurich.

The Zurich council proceeded now with all severity against the irrepressible sectarians. The charges leveled against Mantz were in effect a repetition of an earlier indictment (above at n. 60). He had set up a separate church, the members of which were supposed to be sinless; had taught that no Christian might bear the sword or occupy public office; had taught that all things should be held in common; and had violated his oath of 7 October 1525 and rebaptized again.[81]

Mantz was heard point by point, and answered each accusation manfully. He admitted his attempt to set up a separate church,

[80] This is the interpretation of John Horsch, "The Struggle," *MQR*, VII (1933), esp. 152–155. Walter Köhler reviews the whole case and finds the father truly culpable and no martyr of civil liberty. *ZW*, VIII, 780–782; VI (1938), 406–499, 537–544.

[81] Von Muralt, *Quellen*, No. 199; Krajewski, *op. cit.*, 138.

but said that the members did not claim to be without sin, only that they had resolved to obey the Word of God and to follow Christ, and that Heb. 6:4 restrained any church from reinstating a member who had once repented and sinned again. This for Mantz meant one who had repented and been (re)baptized.[82] He confessed his belief that no Christian could bear the sword or occupy public office, and added that the contrary could not be proved from Scripture. He denied having taught a comprehensive community of goods; he had only taught that Christians were obligated by the law of love to share their goods with their neighbors in want. As to whether he had rebaptized, he admitted the rebaptism of the woman in Embrach and went on to say that he would baptize anyone else who would accept instruction in the faith. When asked whether he was acquainted with the mandate of 7 March 1526, he answered that he was not, but that he did not dispute its formal validity. He denied that he had claimed to have had special revelations; he said only that on one or two occasions the letters of Paul had been suddenly "opened up" to him.

Blaurock was equally steadfast in his hearing, but he was not incriminated as Mantz was by having performed a witnessed rebaptism after his escape from prison.[83]

Finally, 5 January 1527, the verdict of the court was pronounced: for Mantz, execution by drowning; for Blaurock, since he was not a citizen of Zurich and had not demonstrably violated his oath in respect to rebaptizing, whipping through the town and perpetual banishment. The doctrines of Mantz were condemned in the verdict because they were contrary to Scripture, contrary to the entire Christian tradition, and furthermore caused nothing but uproar and disunity.[84] Zwingli was in agreement with the decision, and defended it in correspondence with Wolfgang Capito in Strassburg, who was disturbed by it.[85]

The execution of Mantz took place on the day he was condemned, 5 January 1527. He went to his death with courage. According to Bullinger, as he walked from the fish market (where shortly before Senator Grebel had been executed) to the river, he praised God while his mother and brother waited along the way to encourage him to remain steadfast. He was trussed, with a stick thrust between his roped, doubled-up legs and arms, and as he was being drawn into the icy water he sang, *"In manus tuas*

[82] Cf. Kessler, *Sabbata*, 148.
[83] In March of 1526.
[84] Krajewski, *op. cit.*, 144.
[85] *ZW*, IX, 8.

domine commendo spiritum meum."[86] He was then taken from the water and buried at St. James's, the first "Protestant" martyr at the hands of Protestants. The Anabaptist hymnal (*Ausbund*) preserves a hymn composed by him: "*Mit Lust so will ich singen.*"

An indication of the reluctance of the Zurich authorities to proceed against the Anabaptists en masse is the fact that although Mantz's family openly encouraged him as he went to his death, no action was taken against them. An hour after Mantz's execution, Blaurock, naked to the waist, was driven from the fish market to the town gate under a pelting of rods. At the gate, he swore against his will never to return, shook the dust of Zurich from his feet, and departed. Bullinger wrote: "He was no less fresh than Mantz."[87]

The first of the radical Zurich triumvirate, Conrad Grebel, as already remarked, had died before his father, a victim of the plague, about August 1526. He had left Zurich for Maienfeld in the Grisons, where his eldest sister lived, and where both Mantz and native Blaurock had a considerable following. Grebel had been able, during the six months' imprisonment, to compose in secret his third main surviving evangelical work, his *Taufbüchlein*. It was this and another document which Zwingli proceeded to refute in detail, addressing his former friend as a "shade," in mocking allusion to the doctrine of psychopannychism. This refutation is known as the *Elenchus* or *Refutation of the Tricks of the Anabaptists* (July 1527).[88] We shall return to it in Ch. 8.4.a.

5. THE SPREAD OF ANABAPTISM IN BASEL AND BERN

We were last in Basel with Oecolampadius and Hinne Rode (Ch. 5.1), and have taken note (Ch. 6.3) also of Hubmaier's raising the question of infant baptism with Oecolampadius, 16 January 1525, in the very month of the Zurich Anabaptist secession. Here suffice it to say that the field preaching of Felix Mantz in Basel territory (above, Ch. 6.4) only aggravated the situation there. Already, in August, Oecolampadius in Basel debated with the Anabaptist community, who met with the tailor Michael Schürer. Oecolampadius' account was published as *Gespräch etlicher Predikanten . . . gehalten mit etlichen Bekennern des*

---

[86] Bullinger, *Reformationsgeschichte*, I, 384.

[87] *Ibid.*, 382.

[88] The *Elenchus in Catabaptistarum strophas* is divided into three parts, the first directed against the *Taufbüchlein*, reassembled in translation as a fragmentary unit, by Bender, *op. cit.*, 294 ff.; the second against the seven articles of the Schleitheim Confession, on which more in Ch. 8.

Wiedertaufens. The Basel Anabaptists defended their missionary program on the basis of the Great Commission in Matthew, which sets preaching before baptism, and on the example of the Ethiopian baptized by Philip. Oecolampadius reminded them that they were founding a new sect which would end in separation and mob spirit. He argued, from Origen, Cyprian, and Augustine, that children had been anciently baptized with their parents in households and that the best way to reform the church was not through rebaptism but through the devout observance of the Lord's Supper and through the exercise of the ban.

On 10 October another disputation was to be held in the church of St. Martin's, in which Reublin had once served, and the struggle grew bitter.

Oecolampadius defended infant baptism in two additional works. The first, *Unterrichtung von dem Wiedertaufen, von der Obrigkeit und vom Eid*, was directed against Karl(in) Brennwald, who had been put in the dungeon of the Hexenturm after the Second Zurich Disputation. Brennwald had stated four articles of his faith in writing and had planned to defend them against Oecolampadius and the Catholic clergy before the council. This was not permitted. Oecolampadius attacked the Brethren with unusual acerbity, calling them Katabaptists (drowners), "for you murder the noble souls and good consciences in your baptism." Yet, citing the advice of Gregory of Nazianzus, he did suggest that it might be well to postpone baptism until a child's third year. As to the propriety of a Christian's serving as magistrate, Oecolampadius pointed out a statesman's many positive acts of service besides his judicial and military functions.

Oecolampadius' next book was directed against Hubmaier, *Wider der Predikanten Gespräch zu Basel von dem Kindertaufen* (August 1527). On 6 July 1527, Basel had already ordered corporal punishment and confiscation for adult baptism, postponement of infant baptism, and the sheltering of Anabaptists.

We now turn to Bern, the largest canton of the Confederation. The Anabaptist movement there emanated from Zurich, probably by way of the Aargau district (today a separate canton). A Waldensian residue in the Bernese population may well have made it receptive to the new evangel.[89]

Here the Reformation was not to be magisterially inaugurated until the mandate of 7 February 1528. The Anabaptist movement began as early as the fall of 1525 but proceeded slowly. The

---

[89] The arguments in favor of some survival of Waldensian influence are summarized by Delbert Gratz, *Bernese Anabaptists* (Scottdale, Pennsylvania, 1953), 1–5.

first notices are found in the correspondence between Berchtold
Haller of Bern with Zwingli and Oecolampadius and between
Bullinger and Henry Semler from the years 1525 and 1526.[90]
Haller announced that the council had already banished some
Anabaptists of the Aargau. The baker, John Pfistermeyer (Ch.
8.4), was exiled at the beginning of 1526, along with Jacob Gross
of Waldshut (Ch. 10.2). For a time the Brethren were quiet in
Bern, although they must have been secretly active in the Aargau
and the Emmental. Not until the spring of 1527 did Jacob Hochrütiner, John Hausmann, and six others come to Bern from Basel,
shortly after the execution of Mantz. They brought with them a
copy of the first Anabaptist synodal confession, which Haller sent
to Zwingli for refutation. (This was the Schleitheim Confession,
which with Zwingli's *Elenchus* will be dealt with in Ch. 8.)
Haller, sending on the Confession to Zwingli for refutation, was
himself loath to follow the severe example of Zwingli, imploring
him:

We know, of course, that the council is quite ready to banish the Anabaptists. But it is in our place to judge all things with the sword of
the Spirit, either from the pulpit or in conversation.[91]

[90] The upshot of extensive research is to be found in "Research Notes on the
  Beginnings of Bernese Anabaptism," *MQR*, XXXI (1957), 292–295.
[91] *ZW*, IX, 104.

CHAPTER 7

SOUTH GERMAN AND AUSTRIAN ANABAPTISM, 1525–1527

Distinct in origin and also distinguishable in ethos from the Swiss Brethren—but emerging concurrently with them—were the South German and Austrian Anabaptists, who found in John Denck their first spokesman.[1] It is an interesting coincidence that John Denck was banished from Nuremberg for his proto-Anabaptist faith on the very day, 21 January 1525, on which the first sacramentarian Anabaptist conventicle was gathered in Zurich.

In comparing the two Anabaptist movements, one sees as characteristic of the South German Brethren a greater dependence on medieval mystical and devotional literature than was the case among the Swiss Brethren, a greater openness to the eschatological summons in Thomas Müntzer's Spiritualism. Among the followers of Denck, the regnant principles were love and obedience, in contrast to the Swiss stress on the restoration of organized Christian life according to the precise prescriptions of the New Testament church. From the perspective of a later free-church tradition, one sees that while it was the circle around Grebel who contributed the principle of the separation of the voluntarist church from the state (over against Zwingli's covenantal theocracy), it was the circle around Denck who contributed the stress on the freedom of the will (over against Luther's bondage of the will in the realm of salvation).

1. John Denck's Banishment from Nuremberg

Denck (c. 1500–1527), variously called the bishop, the Apollo, the abbot, and the pope of the Anabaptists, followed a cycle not

---

[1] This basic distinction was first clearly drawn by Jan J. Kiwiet, *Pilgram Marpeck: Ein Führer in der Täuferbewegung der Reformationszeit* (Kassel, 1957), cap. 5.

uncommon in the left wing of the Reformation, moving from humanism through Lutheranism to Anabaptism and finally to evangelical Spiritualism. Denck passed from Catholicism to sectarianism by way of humanism and mysticism, without ever experiencing the intense conflict between law and grace which marked the conversion of Luther.

Born in Upper Bavaria in Heybach near Hugelfing of an educated burgher family, he studied at the University of Ingolstadt (1517–1519), mastering Latin, Greek, and Hebrew. After teaching languages in Regensburg, he went to Basel, attracted by the fame of Oecolampadius and Erasmus. Here he worked as a proofreader, editing the last three volumes of Theodore Gaza's Greek grammar. He mingled in the humanistic circle and attended in 1523 the university lectures of Oecolampadius on Isaiah.

Through a letter of commendation from Oecolampadius he received appointment as rector in Nuremberg of the school connected with St. Sebald's, one of the two main parishes, remaining there but a year and a half.[2] Here he came under the influence of the sacramentarian Spiritualism of Müntzer and Carlstadt.

At the beginning of 1524 he took a wife, who kept table for some of the pupils. He at first associated with Andrew Osiander, of the other main church, St. Lawrence's. Osiander, as chief ecclesiastical adviser in the town council, was cautiously leading into the Lutheran camp the great free city where the Catholic Imperial Council of Regency sat. The manufacturing town of Nuremberg, a center of Renaissance culture, with Willibald Pirkheimer and Albert Dürer as its illustrious exponents, had long been restive under the spiritual dominion of its bishop, whose see was in the less important city of Bamberg. Fearless, combative, opinionated, Osiander detected dangerous differences between himself and the spiritualizing humanist teacher, who began giving voice to aspirations more akin to medieval, mystical sectarian piety than to the new solafideism of Luther. Denck was, in fact, blending the humanistic piety, which he had encountered both in Basel and in Nuremberg, with the mystical piety of John Tauler as reinforced by the tracts of Müntzer.

Medieval sectarian dissent had survived in the populous, commercial center up to the eve of the Reformation. John Hus, fatefully en route to Constance, had been permitted to discuss his doctrines publicly in Nuremberg, and had won friends. Wal-

---

[2] The most recent work on this phase is by Georg Baring, "Hans Denck und Thomas Müntzer in Nürnberg 1524," *ARG*, L (1959), 145–181.

densian congregations gathered in and around the town. Diepold Peringer, the "peasant of Wöhrd," the illiterate revivalist whose sermons against images and the Mass and in defense of free will greatly impressed the chaplain of Elector Frederick the Wise, present at the diet of 1524, had a following in the city.[3]

In the course of the Peasants' War, Müntzer, on his flight south from Mühlhausen in 1524, remained in Nuremberg four weeks, presumably with Denck. He put Henry Pfeiffer and John Römer, the latter destined to be an Anabaptist leader in Thuringia, in charge of the printing of his two books, *Ausgedrückte Entblössung* and *Hochverursachte Schutzrede*. Looking back on his stay, Müntzer later wrote: "I could have played a pretty game with the people of Nuremberg had I cared to stir up sedition, an accusation brought against me by a lying world. Many people urged me to preach, but I replied that I was not there for that purpose, but rather to answer my enemies through the press."[4] We can imagine that the rector of St. Sebald's school was among those who urged him to preach. In October 1524, Osiander and the town authorities learned that Pfeiffer was in possession of Müntzer's inflammatory manuscripts and was trying to get them printed. In his refutation of the pamphlets, Osiander was incensed at Pfeiffer's use of the Mosaic law when arguing that false prophets should be put to death at the same time that he was blithely limiting himself to the New Testament or even the Spirit or inner Word with respect to contested points of doctrine. The town authorities, still nominally Catholic, although they had not enforced the recess of the diet held in Nuremberg itself on the suppression of Luther's writings, considered it advisable to be firm with what Osiander and Dominicus Schleupner of St. Sebald's identified as at once blasphemy and sedition. Since Müntzer had departed, action could be taken only against Pfeiffer, who was thereupon banished, and against the printer Jerome Höltzel and his helpers, who were temporarily arrested.[5] Denck was still unmolested.

The Spiritualist and sacramentarian Carlstadt was also an important figure in the eyes of the proto-Anabaptist sectaries of Nuremberg. Carlstadt, even before becoming a sacramentarian, had dedicated to Albert Dürer, as "his beloved patron," *Von Anbetung und Ehrenbietung der Zeichen des Neuen Testaments* (1519), in which he contended that the Dominical injunction

---

[3] On the sectarian impulses and the sources, see Evans, *Sectaries.*
[4] Johann K. Seidemann, *Thomas Müntzer* (Dresden, 1842), 48 f.
[5] Evans, *op. cit.,* 44 ff.

had been simply to eat and rejoice rather than to adore the bread and the wine.[6] Then, around November 1524, Carlstadt's fully sacramentarian *Von dem widerchristlichen Missbrauch des Herrn Brot und Kelch* was printed in Nuremberg by Jerome Höltzel, who had received the manuscript from the former Lutheran pastor of Jena, Martin Reinhart. Reinhart, a fellow exile of Carlstadt's, had in March published the articles presented by the Bohemian Brethren to the Council of Basel in 1430, and had even dedicated the leaflet to Pirkheimer and the whole Nuremberg council. His interest in the Bohemians has suggested a slight connection between the Nuremberg sectaries, now on the point of turning Anabaptist, and the "old Evangelicals."[7] Reinhart was somewhat surprised to find himself and his family ordered to leave the city in December. The publication of books by either Carlstadt or Müntzer was prohibited.

But the sacramentarian and Spiritualist views of Carlstadt and Müntzer echoed in the city especially in the artistic and humanistic circles. Denck was their spokesman.

He had come to believe that the solafideism of Luther jeopardized the moral life of the community, and he quietly fostered a Spiritualism which was pushed to an extreme at the hands of three so-called "godless painters."[8] They were ejected from the company of Albert Dürer, and as a result of their judicial hearing at the end of 1524 before the town council, Denck himself became implicated. The Biblical radicalism of the rector of St. Sebald's school jeopardized the Reform in Nuremberg and caused consternation lest he become the respected head of the anti-Lutheran party, with some support even from the more evangelical of the Old Believers. Denck was therefore brought before the town council at the instance of Osiander. To the council he addressed his Confession, in two installments, the first on 14 January 1525. The seven points at issue were the Bible, sin, the righteousness of God, law, gospel, Baptism, and the Supper. Denck at first paid little heed to the specific points at issue between himself and Osiander. In the Confession he gave expression to his conviction, reinforced by and to some extent palpably dependent on Müntzer, that the seeming contradictions or para-

---

[6] Barge, *op. cit.*, I, 328.

[7] This is Ludwig Keller's generic term for medieval mystical sectaries. See his *Johann von Staupitz, und die Anfänge der Reformation* (Leipzig, 1888), 202 ff.

[8] These painters were Sebald and Barthel Behaim and George Panz. They had read the tracts of Carlstadt. On the relationship, see Theodor Kolde, "Hans Denck und die gottlosen Maler in Nürnberg," *Beiträge zur Bayerischen Kirchengeschichte*, VIII (1902), 1 ff.

doxes of Scripture which had long puzzled him could be resolved by the harmonizing operation of the Holy Spirit bringing together the disparate Scriptural words in the reader's dynamic encounter with the inner Word.

The whole of the first installment[9] dealt with the general nature of faith. Starting with the Lutheran presupposition of salvation *sola fide,* as Grebel in Zurich started with the Zwinglian axiom of divine sanction *sola scriptura,* Denck tried to relate faith to grace in order in the end to relate faith to the two evangelical sacraments under dispute. Since it is faith that gives life or salvation, he declared that saving faith can never be the inherited belief, inculcated earnestly by one's parents. Otherwise, salvation would itself be hereditary. Therefore he had come reluctantly to admit that inherited faith is really a "false faith." He is sure that faith is a gift vouchsafed to "the blessed in the poverty of the Spirit," that is, in the utter emptying of oneself of self in the earnest scrutiny of Scripture, and that the power which "drives" Christ into one is the Christ already present, the inner Word which the Scriptures testify is also the Son of the Most High. Denck avows that unbelief is the great sin, which destroys the righteousness of God through legalism. He prays that God may help his unbelief. The Scriptures can be understood and bitter sectarianism avoided only if the Holy Spirit attends upon the living exegesis. And even then the incandescent Scripture is only a lantern in the darkness until the morning star is seen and the day breaks, and the sun of the righteous, Christ, shines in the heart.[10] Denck admits that this ultimate experience is not yet his. In reaching this goal, he knows that Christ as king working through the law is as important as the Christ with whom the believer must first die to rise again.

In the second installment,[11] Denck feels called upon to be more specific about the sacraments. Here again he stresses faith, not to the disparagement of the sacraments, but with a view to bringing faith and the Dominical ordinances into harmony. He distinguishes between an inner and an outer baptism and attaches importance to both actions. The first is the penetration of the hard ground (actually: *åbgrundt*) of human uncleanness by the omnipotent Word of God, as the dry earth is penetrated by good rain. The baptism of the believer with water is the "covenant of

---

[9] *Hans Denck Schriften,* edited by Georg Baring and Walter Fellmann, 2 parts (Gütersloh, 1955/1956) (henceforth: Baring and Fellmann, *Schriften* [*QGT,* VI]), part 2, 20–23.
[10] The same metaphor was used by John de Valdés.
[11] Baring and Fellmann, *Schriften (QGT,* VI:2), 23–26.

a good conscience with God." This, of course, is Luther's unique translation of I Peter 3:21 (RSV: "appeal to God for a clear conscience"), and Denck's employment of it here marks the moment in church history when a tremendous personal conviction is on the point of acquiring constitutional significance, for as soon as Denck's inward faith, to which he here bears testimony, will have been outwardly confirmed by believers' baptism at the hands of Hubmaier in Augsburg, the *covenantal* ecclesiology of the Anabaptist churches of South Germany will have taken form. But at this moment, Denck has gone no further than to say that the water covenant is desirable. He expressly says it "is *not necessary* to [personal] salvation." The inner baptism is what Mark intended in ch. 16:16: "Believe and be saved." And what Denck means by inward baptism is made clear when he observes that there is no point in washing carrots or cabbages while they are still growing in the dirt.

Taking up the meaning of the Supper, he uses the analogy of healing. The divine Physician has two ways of curing his patient, either by enjoining a fast or by bloodletting, that is, either by withdrawing the undigestible food of a false faith or by interposing an external suffering. Whether it is to be the one therapy or the other depends on the patient's need and temperament. In either case, the way is prepared by Christ the mediator for one's entry into the covenant with God through the redirection of the will. In this process the Lord's Supper has both an inward and an external significance, as does baptism. The living invisible bread strengthens one in the life of righteousness. And whoever is mindful of and drinks from the invisible chalice the wine mixed by God through his Son from the beginning of the world will be satisfied and think no longer of himself, but will become completely "divinized" through the love of God, and God will become "humanized" in him. That is the meaning of having eaten the body of Christ and drunk his blood, and he cites John, ch. 6.

Throughout the two installments of his Confession, Denck was markedly irenic in tone, and at the same time confident of the basic righteousness of the position taken. He had a copy of the Confession circulated.

The council found it unbearably "deceptive," and thus it was that the destined leader of South German Anabaptism was ordered to leave the town 21 January 1525, obliged to swear an oath not to return to Osiander's Nuremberg. He had to leave his wife and child, for whose support his property was confiscated. (Osiander himself will strangely reappear in our narrative in Ch. 25.3, himself charged with a heresy not unlike that of Denck.)

In the meantime having received an invitation from Müntzer, Denck taught during the spring in Mühlhausen, but was obliged to flee with Henry Pfeiffer and some four hundred others 19 May.[12] He thereupon sought work as a proofreader with his former Basel acquaintance Vadian, arriving in St. Gall in June 1525, at the flood of the Anabaptist tide in that relatively tolerant Swiss town. While staying in the home of an Anabaptist, though not himself as yet a convert, Denck is reported to have disturbed the local Anabaptists by his teaching on the universal salvation or the restitution of all (Acts 3:21), which appears prominently in several of his later works.

2. LOUIS HAETZER AND JOHN DENCK IN AUGSBURG

From September 1525 to October 1526, Denck resided in Augsburg. Here, midway between Zurich and Wittenberg, the city council was trying to find its place in the Reformation between Zwingli and Luther. Urbanus Rhegius was the powerful spokesman of Lutheranism.

The nucleus of the Augsburg Anabaptist community which Denck was destined to lead was the circle which Louis Haetzer for a while had directed. We last encountered Haetzer writing up the acts of the Second Zurich Disputation in October 1523 (Ch. 5.2). Protestant-minded members of the guilds had been gathering for evenings of religious discussion in various taverns, and the excitement engendered appears to have been spiritual in more than one sense. Haetzer, at the time a proofreader with the Augsburg press of Silvan Othmar, attended these sessions but soon criticized them for being more under the auspices of Bacchus than of Christ. Accordingly, he assumed the leadership of a gathering of more apostolical brethren, forerunner of the huge Anabaptist congregation in Augsburg. In this conventicle the sacramentarian Communion of Carlstadt and Zwingli was observed in defiance of the Lutheran majority among the city's Protestants. On 14 September 1525, Haetzer wrote to Zwingli, urging him to countervail the move of the local Lutherans to establish their view. Challenged by Urbanus Rhegius to a public debate, Haetzer failed to appear, and was banished "as the head of the sectarians, as an unclean, seditious person, hostile to the gospel." He went on, via Constance, to Basel (October). In this leaderless situation, the Augsburg conventicle undoubtedly welcomed Denck as an evangelical spokesman of learning comparable to Haetzer. He arrived from St. Gall in September 1525. Through

---

[12] Oecolampadius to Pirkheimer, 22 April 1525. Staehelin, *Briefe und Akten,* I, 365. Further evidence marshaled by Baring, "Nürnberg," *loc. cit.,* 178.

the autumn and winter, teaching the classical languages and giving spiritual counsel to the apostolic brethren, Denck was still a Spiritualist sacramentarian.

Then in April, Hubmaier, in flight from Zurich, where he had been pummeled and cajoled by Zwingli and Hofmeister and where he had recanted rebaptism and then reasserted it, arrived in Augsburg en route to Moravia. He found Denck and his conventicle ready to reconstitute themselves as the truly reformed church among whom the apostolic order would be fully restored by believers' baptism. It was probably at the beginning of May 1526 that Denck and others were rebaptized by Hubmaier. Hubmaier in turn learned from Denck to modify his Zwinglian view on predestination and free will.

On 26 May 1526 Denck in turn baptized fiery John Hut, fresh from Bibra. The two men had already become acquainted in Nuremberg in the midst of the Peasants' War (Ch. 4.2.d). They were of entirely different tempers. Our account of South German Anabaptism, with Augsburg as its center, now divides.

For the moment we shall continue to follow Denck, and then turn with Hut to Austria. About the same time that Denck rebaptized John Hut, he likewise converted John Bünderlin of Linz (1499–1533), a man much more like himself.[13] A spiritualizing proto-unitarian, much interested in eschatology, he will reappear as our story unfolds in Linz (Ch. 7.5), Strassburg (Ch. 10.3.a), and Prussia (Ch. 15.2).

The Lutheran pastor of Augsburg disparagingly called Denck "the abbot of the Anabaptists." To defend himself and the apostolic brethren, now fully Anabaptist, against Urbanus Rhegius, Denck proceeded to write three works, all in 1526: *Whether God Is the Cause of Evil,*[14] *Vom Gesetz Gottes,*[15] and *Wer die Wahrheit wahrlich lieb hat.*[16]

The first, in the form of a dialogue, deals with the problem of evil and free will and declares that God is not directly the author of evil. Though printed in Augsburg by Haetzer's publisher, Sil-

---

[13] Alexander Nicoladoni, *Johannes Bünderlin von Linz und die oberösterreichischen-Täufergemeinden in den Jahren 1525–1531* (Berlin, 1893). Nicoladoni did not know that Hans Fischer, the former secretary of Baron Bartholomäus von Stahremberg, was identical with Bünderlin. For the synthesis and the literature, see *ME,* I, 469 f.

[14] *Was geredet sei, dass die Schrift sagt,* Baring and Fellmann, *Schriften (QGT,* VI:2), 27–47; translated, *SAW,* 86 ff. Thor Hall shows the extent to which, for his doctrine of the freedom of the will, Denck reflected Erasmus, "Possibilities of Erasmian Influence on Denck and Hubmaier," *MQR,* XXXV (1961), 149–170.

[15] Baring and Fellmann, *Schriften (QGT,* VI:2), 48 ff.

[16] *Ibid.,* 67 ff.

van Othmar, it reflects Denck's involvement in the Nuremberg theological debate occasioned by a Sunday sermon on predestination preached by the peasant of Wöhrd. On the question of free will, Denck was far, not only from Luther, but also from Carlstadt (*Ob Gott eine Ursache sei des teuflischen Falls*, beginning of 1524), and was nearest Erasmus (*De libero arbitrio*, September 1524), to whom Luther had by now replied (*De servo arbitrio*, December 1525).

In his dialogue, Denck acknowledges that salvation is *in* man but not *of* him and notes the diverse disguises of selfishness impeding one's imitation of Christ through *Gelassenheit*, i.e., yieldedness to God's will in self-surrender. The mystical term suggests at once the *joyful abandonment* of the soul as bride to the heavenly Bridegroom (Canticles) and the call of the saints to a life of suffering and mortification as well as faith (Rev. 13:10). "Scripture speaks," he says, "of a tranquillity (*gelassenhait*), which is the means of coming to God; which is Christ himself, not to be regarded physically but rather spiritually." In a Neoplatonic sense, Denck thinks of evil as the absence of good and of sin as nothing; and then, to explain why God nevertheless chastizes his children for their sin, he answers thus:

For the same reason that a schoolmaster punishes his children for doing nothing. To do something is good. If we did *something,* to this extent we would have less need of punishment. But how sin [really] is nothing may be perceived by whoever gives himself over to God and becomes nothing, while at the same time he is created something by God. This each one will understand according to the measure of his resignation (*gelassenhait*).[17]

Elsewhere he writes of *Gelassenheit:* "If I run in the truth, that is, if I run sufferingly, then my running will not be in vain," and again, "There is no other way to blessedness than to lose one's self-will." *Gelassenheit* leads to progressive "divinization and inner lordship over all that is creaturely." Striking a universalistic note, Denck declares that God in his omnipotence has left it open as to who will reach the goal of blessedness. A hostile observer wrote to Zwingli in August 1526 reporting that for Denck "even the demons in the end will be saved."[18]

The second work of 1526 is the outcome of Denck's reflection on the problem of law, faith, and love as embodied in Romans and interpreted by Luther. Here we have Denck's first tract written existentially from within the Anabaptist fellowship of a

[17] Translated in *SAW*, 91.
[18] Peter Gynoraeus to Zwingli, 22 August 1526, *ZW*, VIII, No. 520, p. 689.

self-disciplined church. He deplores the moral miscarriage in Nuremberg and Augsburg of the Lutheran preoccupation with the sermonic proclamation of the Word, of forensic justification, to the neglect of parochial tutelage and discipline. At the same time, in his aversion to legalism, one detects also his Spiritualism. This is destined to become increasingly prominent in Denck, with his concern lest attention to apostolic injunctions, even in respect to baptism and the breaking of the bread, be converted into a new law.

The third Augsburg work of 1526, like the second printed by Philip Ulhart, assembles a series of apparent contradictions in the Bible. The first conflicting pair are Rom. 11:34 (Isa., ch. 40), "For who has known the mind of the Lord?" and Eph. 1:9, "For he has made known to us . . . the mystery of his will." The fortieth and last pair contrast God's hardening of Pharaoh's heart (Ex. 4:21) and Pharaoh's hardening his own heart (Ex. 8:15; 9:34). Many of these very contradictions had been pointed out by Erasmus in his *Ratio*[19] and would be picked up again by the Spiritualist Sebastian Franck (Ch. 18.3). Denck's purpose in assembling the seeming contradictions is made clear in his brief foreword. He wishes to show that reliance on proof texts inevitably divides Christians into bitter sectarian factions. Away with scribal and sectarian haggling over Scriptures! The Holy Spirit is the schoolmaster of the faithful, who alone can point out the inner Word behind the words. With a brief note to the reader, in allusion to the prophecy of Isa. 29:11f. that the Book of Life will be sealed to the literate and illiterate alike, Denck concludes that everyone should therefore be willing to give himself over to the Master, who leads even all the *doctores* to school and "who has the key to the book in which all the treasures of wisdom are contained," namely, the Holy Spirit.

In the course of the year 1526, in which Denck was writing and publishing his three tracts, he became involved in debate with Urbanus Rhegius. Of their debate we have knowledge only from the contradictory materials surviving from Urbanus himself.[20] Apparently, Denck's leadership of the Anabaptist community had escaped the notice of Urbanus for more than a year. He now acted swiftly, asked Denck about his views and his conduct, and found him evasive and then remorseful (*"hub . . . an zu weinen"*). The other Lutheran pastors were called in at one stage or another to warn and remonstrate. When a public disputation,

---

[19] *Ratio seu compendium verae theologiae* (Basel, 1519).
[20] Succinctly assembled and ordered by Baring and Fellmann in *Schriften* (*QGT*, VI:2), 12 f.

to which Denck at first agreed, began taking shape, he apparently
sensed that the preparations were all too reminiscent of the
"hearing" in Nuremberg, and he left.

3. DENCK IN STRASSBURG AND WORMS

Once again he sought a city of refuge, this time Strassburg,
"the city of hope" and "the refuge of righteousness," as the
Anabaptists called it. Because of its pre-eminent role in our
narrative, we shall postpone the fuller account of this strategic
crossroads of the Radical Reformation (Ch. 10) and take note only
of the activities of Denck while sojourning there from November
through December 1526.

On his arrival, Denck found an indigenous Spiritualist Anabaptist fellowship[21] centering in the home of the gardener-
preacher Clement Ziegler (Ch. 10.2) and a refuge community
of Swiss Brethren headed provisionally by one Michael Sattler[22]
(Ch. 8.1). He found, too, that the principal divines of the city
had, with the support of the magistrates, moved much farther
in the direction of sacramental reform than had those in Nuremberg and Augsburg. Denck found the indigenous, more Spiritualistic Anabaptists among the garden brethren most congenial.[23] Especially close was Denck's relation with Louis Haetzer,
at that time busy with his translation of Isaiah, and who also
entered the circle of Anabaptists meeting with Ziegler. Further,
some of the more substantial Strassburg burghers, repelled by
what they regarded as the failure of the municipal reformers to
bring about a moral change in their communities, were attracted
by Denck's piety. Moreover, there were many Catholic sympathizers in and out of the town council who were glad to indulge
the Anabaptist community for fear that sterner measures would
constitute a pattern for action against them whenever the town
should become officially Protestant. At least two somewhat
divergent Anabaptist circles in Strassburg constituted a threat to
the magisterial Protestant forces.

Thus it was not long before Denck was engaged in controversy
with the city's leading Reformers. As in Nuremberg and then in
Augsburg, so now in Strassburg, Denck was soon disowned by

[21] A. Hulshof, *Geschiedenis van de Doopsgezinden te Straatsburg van 1525 tot
1557* (Amsterdam, 1905), 33. The principal source collection is *Elsass, I:
Stadt Strassburg 1522–1532* (*QGT*, VII), edited by Manfred Krebs and Jean
Rott (Gütersloh, 1959). Nos. 60 to 66 deal with Denck.

[22] Hulshof, *op. cit.*, 33 and n. 2, says that the Sattler Baptists were much less
numerous than those of whom Denck was temporarily the spokesman.

[23] Camill Gerbert, *Geschichte der Strassburger Sectenbewegung zur Zeit der
Reformation 1524–1534* (Strassburg, 1889), 18, 152 ff.

those who had been at first receptive. In the first major recorded encounter, Capito but also and mainly Martin Cellarius discussed with Haetzer and Denck the problems of predestination and faith as worked out in Denck's *Was geredet sei*. For the most part the differences between the two sides were overcome in mutual respect and irenicism. It was Bucer who became Denck's principal antagonist, and a sharp encounter ensued in the disputation held in the presence of as many as four hundred burghers on 22 and 23 December 1526. Bucer, who in the end called him "the Anabaptist pope," much preferred Sattler. The disputation was based upon Denck's works, *Vom Gesetz Gottes* and *Von der Ordnung*, and concerned God's providence, human freedom, universal salvation, Christian magistracy, and the oath. Bucer insisted that Denck express himself fully and clearly. Denck said that he could not be any clearer than he was and asked the church to pray for him. Bucer convinced the tolerant council that Denck should be asked to leave.

Banished from Strassburg as an underminer of magisterial authority, Denck stopped briefly at Bergzabern and then at Landau. In the former he angrily "vociferated" with the local Jews concerning the law.[24] In Landau, where there was already an Anabaptist community, he and Melchior Rinck (Ch. 4.2.d) debated on adult baptism with the evangelical pastor John Bader[25] (who later drew close to Schwenckfeld), 20 January 1527. The effect was to increase the local Anabaptist following.

Denck's destination was the imperial city of Worms, where the local reform was about to be pushed rapidly in the direction of Anabaptism and then suddenly checked. Rinck, Haetzer, and Denck were able to bring two of the younger Lutheran preachers of the town, Jacob Kautz and his copreacher Hilarius, into the Anabaptist circle.

In this favorable environment, Denck produced, alone or in collaboration, three important works. The first was his beautiful and long influential *Von der wahren Liebe*, 1527,[26] divided into two quite distinct parts, the first warmly mystical and devotional, the second practical. It was in this work, published in Worms,

---

[24] So reported the local pastor Nicholas Thomä Sigelspach. This impression must be thought of as applicable to the specific occasion and not to Denck's usual manner.

[25] Two accounts of the debate are preserved, that of Capito to Zwingli, *ZW*, VIII, 819 f., and that of Bucer, *ZW*, IX, 184 f. Hulshof devotes a chapter to the antagonism of the two, *op. cit.*, iii. Recently Rinck's refutation of Bader has come to light. Gerhard J. Neumann, "A Newly Discovered Manuscript," *MQR*, XXXV (1961), 197–217.

[26] Baring and Fellmann, *Schriften* (*QGT*, VI:1), 35 f. and part 2, 75 f.

that Denck made explicit what was implicit in his Nuremberg Confession with respect to the interrelationship of the inner and the outer or covenantal baptism of the good conscience:

Therefore also the sign of the covenant (*bundzeychen*), baptism, should be administered to those only, and not withheld from them, who, invited thereto by the power of God through the awareness of true love, desire it and pledge themselves to imitate it [that love]. And yet they should nevertheless remain uncoerced by the brethren of the covenant (*bundsgnossen*) and kindred [in Christ] in the pursuit of love, for as the Psalter says: 110:3: "Thy people will offer themselves freely [in the day of thy power!]."[27]

Bundesgenossen (Dutch: *bondgenoten*) is a major constitutional-eschatological term, fraught with significance for the whole Anabaptist movement. Although there can never be certainty on this point, it would appear that we have in Denck's *Liebe* the cradle of the term.[28]

The second Worms tract was *Ordnung Gottes*,[29] a reworking of his *Was geredet sei*, stimulated by the Strassburg disputation.

The third Worms publication was primarily the work of Haetzer, who with Denck's help pushed to completion the translation of all the prophets from Hebrew into German. From its appearance in 1527, until the completion of Luther's translation in 1532, *Alle Propheten verdeutscht* was widely read and went through numerous editions.

Evangelical Anabaptism was on the point of prevailing in Worms when Denck's follower Kautz tacked up seven Anabaptist theses on the door of the Dominican Church on Pentecost, 9 June 1527.[30] Denck was probably the father of Kautz's theses. The most important of these challenges to the divines of the Worms parishes were the theses that infant baptism is against God, that neither external word nor sacrament has any significance unless inwardly echoed or appropriated, that neither the sin of Adam nor the suffering of Christ is meaningful unless inwardly acknowledged, and that Christ in effect saves only in the measure

---

[27] *Ibid.*, 80 f.

[28] So *ibid.*, 81, n. 2. Denck may well have discussed the concept in Strassburg before he put it in print. We find that in the hearing of August 1526 the furrier Jacob Gross from Waldshut appealed to Luther's translation in claiming that baptism is a covenant of the good conscience. Hulshof, *op. cit.*, 19 f. Another view is that of Cornelius Krahn, *Der Gemeindebegriff des Menno Simons im Rahmen seines Lebens und seiner Theologie* (Karlsruhe, 1936), 23, n. 53, where a connection is made between Kautz, Reublin, and Hofmann in Strassburg in 1529.

[29] Baring and Fellmann, *Schriften* (*QGT*, VI:2), 87 ff.

[30] Manfred Krebs, *Baden und Pfalz* (henceforth: *Baden und Pfalz* [*QGT*, IV]) (Gütersloh, 1951), No. 129.

that one faithfully follows in his steps and obeys the eternal will of God. The disputation failed to take place because the Lutheran pastors were not inclined to participate.

On 13 June, Kautz and others gave a free testimony and broad explanation of their Anabaptist views to a large audience. The Catholics denounced the theses to the elector palatine, saying that Kautz's ideas concerning Baptism and Communion were a horror to all true Christians, and the Lutheran preachers replied to Kautz's theses with seven articles.

On 1 July the city council banished Kautz and Hilarius. The next day Bucer in Strassburg, who had anxiously followed developments at Worms, published against Kautz and Denck the *Getreue Warnung*,[31] in which he refuted the articles point by point and expressed his distress at the vanity of Kautz in challenging the Worms preachers and his alarm at the Anabaptist reduction of the atoning role of Christ to that of exemplar.

About this time, Denck and Haetzer left Worms. Rinck, already banished, will crop up in Hesse (Ch. 17.1). Anabaptism in Worms immediately declined.

From Worms, Denck planned to return to Augsburg, there to rally the Anabaptist forces in a great conclave. But before returning with him there, we do well at this point to pick up the story of his great convert from revolutionary Spiritualism to evangelical Anabaptism, John Hut.

4. John Hut

From the day of his rebaptism in Augsburg at Pentecost, 26 May 1526, Hut was an impassioned missionary of the gospel of baptismal rebirth. He is described by the council of Nuremberg thus:

Of the brotherhoods the chief instigator, patron, and standard-bearer is John Hut, a clever fellow, rather tall, a peasant with light brown cropped hair and a blond moustache. He is dressed in a grey, sometimes a black, riding coat, a broad black or grey hat, and grey pants.[32]

Baptizing almost on the run, he used as a standard formula the Great Commission of Matt., ch. 28. We have the court record of his brief description of his own theology of baptism and his theology of preaching:

The word which stands in Mark 16:15 had moved him [Hut] to preach, namely, that preaching was first, afterwards faith, and thirdly

[31] Krebs and Rott, *Elsass*, I (*QGT*, VII), No. 86

[32] Karl Schornbaum, *Bayern*, II (henceforth: *Bayern*, II [*QGT*, V]) (Gütersloh, 1951), 8. See further, Herbert Klassen, "The Life and Teachings of Hans Hut," *MQR*, XXXIII (1959), 171–205, 267–304.

baptism. And man must let the word of the Lord stand. [He is] not to do anything apart from it, [and] also shall depart neither to the right nor the left, according to the last of Matthew [ch. 28:19–20], that one shall first teach and afterwards baptize.[33]

Hut wrote formally on baptism in *Vom Geheimnis der Taufe*.[34] Like his teacher Denck, Hut distinguished three kinds of baptism, based upon I John 5:6–8, namely, baptism by Spirit, by water, and in blood or anguish. The first is the inward covenant between man, the believer, and God through the action of the Holy Spirit. This is the baptism in "the water of all affliction" by which "man sinks into the death of Christ." Yet this inward baptism antedated Jesus: "This baptism was not introduced for the first time in the days of Christ, but all the elect friends of God from Abraham on have been baptized therein, as Paul [I Cor. 10:1 f.] indicates." The second kind of baptism is the external covenant, whereby the believer testifies that he will live in true obedience toward God and his fellow Christians, and that he is, like them, subject to the ban, and the discipline of the church in love. The third baptism, in blood, is something that Hut emphasizes more than Denck. It is the baptism with which Christ himself was finally baptized. It is repeated wherever in the world his saints' blood is shed: "Baptism is nothing other than a struggle with sin for the whole of life." Hut, the former follower of Müntzer with an inner baptism of the cross, had found in Denck's covenantal baptism the external symbol of that inner baptism and the consummation thereof in prospective martyrdom.

As part of the legacy from Müntzer, Hut continued to proclaim the imminence of Christ's advent. In his fiery sermons he stressed the judgment upon the house of God and upon the world, and looked forward to the resurrection of the righteous. He construed the Turkish inroads into Christendom as a sign of Christ's imminent return. Appealing to Rev., ch. 13, and Dan., ch. 12, he interpreted the traditional figure of three and one half to mean that three and one half years—either from the recent restitution of believers' baptism or from the outbreak of the Peasants' War—had been given by the Lord during which the good news of a saving repentance could still be proclaimed. According to one reliable testimony, he foresaw the advent of Christ during Pentecost in 1528. A medieval prophecy of one Albert Gleicheisen of Erfurt (1372) was another source for Hut's conjecture.[35]

---

[33] Deposition of 16 September 1527, quoted by Christian Meyer, "Zur Geschichte der Wiedertäufer in Oberschwaben," *Zeitschrift des Historischen Vereins für Schwaben und Neuburg*, I, 223.

[34] Müller, *Glaubenszeugnisse* (*QGT*, III), 12–28. Cf. Ch. 31, n. 31.

[35] Gleicheisen's prophecy is preserved in the *Kunstbuch* (Ch. 31.1). See Ch. 9.2

For Hut, baptismal repentance did not safeguard the believer from suffering and persecution (II Tim. 3:12), but he was convinced that those who repented in the last days would certainly survive to join with Christ in the rule of the earth (I Cor., ch. 15).

Although Hut regarded himself as an apostle sent, he did not believe himself to be a special prophet. One of his leading Austrian disciples, however, even in the uncongenial setting of a judicial hearing, made bold to call him "a prophet sent of God [to the nations]," citing Jer. 1:5.[36] Hut was interested in visions and dreams, and distinguished three kinds: those which come from the flesh, and are worthless; those which are inspired by the devil; and those occasional visions in which God is revealing himself through certain signs and words (Num. 12:5).[37] Hut's interest in dreams as the vehicles of divine revelation reappears among the *Träumer* of Hesse (Ch. 20.2).

Certain of his own commission from on high, Hut set forth from Augsburg, and probably went first into Franconia. At Königsberg (in Franconia) he declared that he could now see how the peasants had been in error, seeking their own glory and not God's.[38] In his native town of Bibra, he won the cooper George Volk Kolerlin of Haina; in Gross-Walbern, Kilian Volckhaimer; in Coburg, Eucharius Kellermann Binder. The last two accompanied him on most of his missions.

It was in the fall of 1526 that Hut preached his sermon in condemnation of the peasants for prematurely resorting to the sword in their uprising. In God's time, which Hut thought he could calculate with some precision, the righteous would be given the authority to rule and the ungodly would be overthrown. The Christians in the meantime should flee to Mühlhausen, Nuremberg, and Hungary, awaiting the judgment of God on Christendom through the Turks as the rod of his anger. Volk was left in charge of the Königsberg Anabaptist congregation.

Near Erlangen, Hut converted George Nadler and gathered altogether a congregation of some thirty. The group was broken up by the authorities from Nuremberg. Several of his followers were seized but soon released and expelled from the city.

Thereafter, Augsburg became his principal base. Here Hut reorganized the stricken Anabaptist community. For perhaps ten days he lived in the home of the patrician Eitelhans Langen-

---

[36] Ambrose Spittelmaier, hearing of 25 October 1527; Karl Schornbaum, *Quellen zur Geschichte der Wiedertäufer, Bayern,* I (Leipzig, 1934) (henceforth: Schornbaum, *Bayern,* I [*QGT,* II], 50.
[37] Meyer, "Zur Geschichte der Wiedertäufer," *loc. cit.,* 232.
[38] *Ibid.,* 241.

mantel. In March 1527, Langenmantel accepted rebaptism in his own home at the hands of Hut.

Langenmantel, brother of the gallant George who had fallen as leader of the Black Knights on the French side at the battle of Pavia, had long favored the Reformation, and he was early attached to its more apostolical and sacramentarian form as represented by Louis Haetzer. From Langenmantel there survive at least seven tracts, written between 1526 and 1527, mostly on the Lord's Supper.

At this time, Hut converted Jacob Dachser, a priest who had served as a teacher in Munich, and also the former Franciscan friar, Sigmund Salminger. While the pre-Lenten carnival was raging in the streets and inns, Hut gathered the Anabaptists of the city together for the election of a directorate. The lot fell upon Salminger as the leader and Dachser as his assistant. Poor relief was organized among the Brethren, and the lacemaker Conrad Huber and the weaver Gall Vischer were made stewards for the poor. The Anabaptist community, thus reorganized for mutual aid, grew rapidly, augmented by immigrants from other places. Their frequent services were usually held at night or in the early morning in order to escape observation by the authorities, and perhaps also in order to lose the least possible amount of working time.

From Augsburg, Hut went to Passau and converted a group around George Nespitzer, the brother-in-law of Eucharius. From Passau a major missionary journey was taken into Moravia, where at Nicolsburg, Hut met Balthasar Hubmaier, and engaged him in a memorable disputation (to which we shall return in Ch. 9.2.b). Because of his eschatologically oriented pacifism, he was imprisoned by the otherwise benevolent patron of the local Anabaptist colony; but he escaped with Oswald Glait, one of the Nicolsburg Anabaptist pastors who agreed with him against Hubmaier. Hut and Glait made their way to Vienna, where some fifty converts were rebaptized.

At this point in our narrative of the life of Hut, called "the apostle of Austria," it is important to say something about the region as a whole.

5. Austrian Anabaptism

"Austrian," which has at least five different meanings, depending upon the time and the context, is here used primarily in reference to the two ancient Hapsburg archduchies of Upper and Lower Austria (with Linz and Vienna, respectively, as the capitals), from which Archduke Ferdinand took his title, and the related provinces of Tyrol, Carinthia, Styria, and the temporal archbishopric of Salzburg. The extent of the Radical Reformation in these Austrian areas has been obscured for a long time[39] because of the very great success of Archduke Ferdinand and later the Counter Reformation in scouring clean of all religio-social heterodoxy the mining valleys that once teemed with Anabaptists.

The importation of foreign miners in the newly worked Fugger holdings in the valleys, the consequent breakup of customary social securities, and the distention and consequent understaffing of the old medieval parishes inundated with immigrants constitute the social and economic matrix of Austrian, and particularly Tyrolese, Anabaptism, and before that of the peasants' uprisings in the same areas (Ch. 4.2.e). Anabaptism was, in fact, "the core of the Protestant revolution in Tyrol."[40] Revolt and Anabaptist evangelicalism seem to have been successive solutions or responses to the same social disturbance in the congested valleys, but once converted to Anabaptism, the Austrians were nonresistant to the point of being almost eager for martyrdom. Austrian Anabaptists appear to have been recruited from among all classes.[41] Artisans and miners were much more numerous in relation to peasants than in the other sections of the Empire.

Although ruthlessly wiped out, Austrian Anabaptism constitutes an essential link in the diffusion of radical evangelicalism from Switzerland[42] (George Blaurock) and South Germany (John Hut) into Moravia and also into Venetia. Because of continuous terror under Ferdinand and his officially appointed constable for

---

[39] The most recent work dealing with the subject is Grete Mecenseffy, *Geschichte des Protestantismus in Österreich* (Graz/Cologne, 1956), ch. vi, "Das österreichische Täufertum." The earlier work by Georg Loesche, *Geschichte des Protestantismus im vormaligen und im neuen Österreich* (Vienna/Leipzig, 1930), has no special section on the Anabaptists but deals with them proportionately throughout the early part of the book. The articles on the two Austrian duchies in *Mennonitisches Lexikon* are fuller than the condensation under the heading "Austria" in *ME*, I, 193–199. Articles containing useful material are Robert Friedmann, "The Epistles of the Hutterian Brethren," *MQR*, XX (1946), 147; Johann Loserth, "Anabaptists in Carinthia in the Sixteenth Century," *MQR*, XXI (1947), 235.

[40] Ernst H. Correll, "Anabaptism in the Tyrol," *MQR*, I (1927), 52.

[41] Paul Dedic carefully assessed the proportion of clergy, nobility, freemen, peasants, artisans, and workers among the Anabaptist recruits in "The Social Background of the Austrian Anabaptists," *MQR*, XIII (1939), 5–20.

[42] Correll, "Anabaptism in the Tyrol," *loc. cit.*, 53, indicates that further investigation might bring surprises and open to question the claim of Zurich to be the cradle of Anabaptism.

Anabaptists, and the necessity of mutual aid among the refugees, Austrian Anabaptism came very soon to be differentiated from that of the Swiss Brethren, and even that of the South German Brethren not under Hapsburg jurisdiction, in its communitarian emphasis, which eventuated in the collective farms of relatively tolerant Moravia (Ch. 9.2.d).

It was into this area, midway between the Swiss Confederation and the margraviate of Moravia, destined to be the principal asylum of Austrian Anabaptists, that Hut came in his escape from Nicolsburg after the disputation with Hubmaier.

Leaving Oswald Glait in charge of the new Viennese congregation, roving John Hut moved into Upper Austria, with two companions, the former monk Jerome Hermann of Mansee and Eucharius Binder. The center of his Upper Austrian mission was the town of Steyr, with its iron foundries, where a Waldensian conventicle may have survived into the century.[43] When his meetings came to the attention of the authorities, Hut escaped, but his patrons and the converts whom he had baptized were arrested, tried, and several of them executed. He next moved down the Enns River to Linz, the archducal capital, where John Bünderlin (1499–1533)[44] was in charge of the local congregation. He had been converted and rebaptized by Hut in Augsburg in 1526 (Ch. 7.2) and commissioned as apostle, with his native Linz as his base, while serving at the same time as humanistic secretary to the Baron von Stahremberg. Bünderlin about this time was obliged to leave Linz, and his work was continued by Leonard Freisleben (Eleutherobios), who may have been baptized by Hut.[45] From Linz, Hut moved on to Freistadt, close to the Bohemian border, to strengthen the local Anabaptist conventicle. From there he moved into the temporal bishopric and archbishopric, respectively, of Passau and Salzburg.

Before returning with Hut from his intensive missionary activity in the Austrias to the great synod in Augsburg, we might pause to become acquainted with three of his most important Austrian converts and apostles.

Leonard Schiemer, John Schlaffer, and Ambrose Spittelmaier, all of them belonging to Hut's Austrian circle of converts, all of them suffering martyrdom within a month or two of Hut himself,

---

[43] This is the view of Nicoladoni, *op. cit.*

[44] Nicoladoni, *op. cit.; ME*, I, 469–470, which is important in annexing to the biography that of Hans Fischer, secretary of Baron Bartholomäus von Stahremberg, now known to have been Bünderlin.

[45] After Freisleben, Wolfgang Brandhuber, a major leader of Austrian Anabaptism, was based in Linz.

may be introduced at this point as representative spokesmen of Austrian Anabaptism.[46] Common to all of them was a much greater stress upon the imminence of Christ's second coming than among the Swiss Brethren, a much greater stress upon personal suffering as a confirmation of their conforming to the way of Christ in this world, and a greater stress also on the sharing of goods, a trait destined to be fully developed in the Christian communism of the Austrian refugees in Moravia, the Hutterites. Two of these leaders had been Catholic clerics, Schiemer a Franciscan friar and Schlaffer a priest, while Spittelmaier stood apart from the mass of Austrian Anabaptists in having been university-trained.

Leonard Schiemer spent six years as a Franciscan friar and six months as an Anabaptist apostle. Finding nothing but strife and hypocrisy in his convent at Judenburg (Styria), he escaped (c. 1526–1527) and made his way first to Nuremberg, where he must have met some of the leading Anabaptists. From there he went to Nicolsburg, finding Hubmaier, who taught him much about the new concept of Christianity, but with whom he differed on the question of the sword. He went on to his childhood home of Vienna, where Hut and Glait were active. Converted by Hut, he was baptized by Glait, and sent to the industrial city of Steyr in Upper Austria. There he was elected preacher (*Leermeister*) and commissioned to spread the new message in Bavaria, Salzburg, and the Tyrol.

His influence was tremendous. After only a day in Rattenburg, in the Inn Valley, he considered himself the bishop of the congregation there. After a ministry of scarcely six months, he was captured in Rattenburg on 25 November 1527. Held somewhat loosely in prison by a benevolent magistrate, he continued to lead the Rattenburg congregation. An attempt to escape brought on severer imprisonment.

Pending his trial, Schiemer was given the opportunity and means of writing down his Anabaptist convictions. There are at least seven or eight extant tracts of his, one of them a twelve-point church order later adopted by the proto-Hutterites in Moravia (Ch. 9.2.d) and another a twelve-point exposition of the Apostles' Creed in an Anabaptist sense.[47] Another, *Vom Fläschl*,[48] is a profound and touching allegory of the importance of suffering on the

[46] Cf. Robert Friedmann, "Leonhard Schiemer and Hans Schlaffer: Two Anabaptist Martyr-Apostles of 1528," *MQR*, XXXIII (1959), 31–41.

[47] These tracts and his life are more fully treated by Robert Friedmann, *ME*, IV, 452–454, and in "Leonhard Schiemer and Hans Schlaffer," *loc. cit.*; the tracts are printed in part in Müller, *Glaubenszeugnisse* (*QGT*, III).

[48] Müller, *Glaubenszeugnisse* (*QGT*, III), 72–74.

road to Christ. Schiemer, seizing upon a charge commonly made against the Anabaptists, that they were a godless lot of witches who drank in their covens from a potent flask carried by Hut, likened the Anabaptist way to the narrow neck of a bottle. Once one has passed through the strait place of tribulation, one goes on and comes into the wideness of God's mercy and Christ's consolation. In this work, Schiemer is close to the spirit of the great medieval mystics.[49]

The brief career of John Schlaffer resembles that of Schiemer at many points. A priest since 1511, he laid down his office in 1526, under the influence of Luther, decrying his former office as that of a "false prophet." For a while (1526–1527), he stayed with the Protestant Lord Zelkin at his castle Weinberg near Freistadt. The details and exact sequence of his conversion, probably induced by Hut, and of his mission are not known; but he, like Schiemer, apparently visited Nicolsburg and sided with Hut in the debate with Hubmaier. He returned to Freistadt to gather an Anabaptist conventicle, and went west, probably to participate with Hut in the Martyrs' Synod in Augsburg. From there he went to Nuremberg and Regensburg, finally heading back to Rattenburg in the late fall. On his way from Rattenburg to Hall, he was captured on 5 December 1527 at an Anabaptist meeting at Schwatz on the Inn River.

Nine tracts, eight of them written in prison shortly before Schlaffer was beheaded, survive in the Hutterite codices.[50] One of them is a long prayer written the night before his execution, in which he reviews his whole life and thought in direct address to God. His talent lay indeed in his gift of prayer.[51]

The last of the Austrian triumvirate who remains to be characterized, before we look at their theology as a whole, is Spittelmaier. A native of Linz, he had some university training and thus a good command of Latin. He was rebaptized by Hut and commissioned to preach widely in Austria and Bavaria. The five extant records of his clear answers to questions under torture before he was beheaded at Cadolzburg give a good picture of the itinerant evangelist of the Anabaptist gospel, while his version of the "seven decrees of God" clarifies the eschatology of the Hut movement as a whole.[52]

---

[49] Friedmann, "Leonhard Schiemer," loc. cit., 33, 35.
[50] Some of them have been printed by Müller, Glaubenzeugnisse (QGT, III). They are briefly characterized in connection with his life by Robert Friedmann, ME, IV, 457–459.
[51] Friedmann, "Leonhard Schiemer," loc. cit., 38.
[52] Printed in Schornbaum, Bayern, I (QGT, II), 32–39. His life is given by Herbert Klassen, ME, IV, 599–601.

A composite of the recorded views and actions of Hut's Austrian disciples Schiemer, Schlaffer, and Spittelmaier is worth formulating at this point for the light it will throw on the eventual conversion of refugee or transplanted Austrian Anabaptism into Hutterite communism (Ch. 9.2), and its consequent differentiation from South German Anabaptism, just as the latter was marked off from the movement of the Swiss Brethren.

We may begin with their doctrine of grace, a topic on which Anabaptists did not ordinarily express themselves explicitly. Schiemer, in a letter from prison to his congregation in Rattenburg, interestingly distinguished three kinds of grace.[53] He says that the Lutherans and the Catholics talk learnedly, employing a variety of Latin terms (of which he gives a perhaps intentionally garbled selection) about faith and all kinds of grace, but neither of them, he points out, seems to know from personal experience what the authentically Scriptural kinds of grace are.

The first grace is the Light which was intended to shine in all men. Schiemer does not know from observation about Turks and heathen, but he assumes that the Light is accessible to them also, while Schlaffer expressly includes Jews, Turks, and pagans.[54] Moses with the law represented the external manifestation of the Light, the distinctive function of which is to enable the enlightened one to distinguish between good and evil and hence to become aware of his sinfulness. Schiemer stresses, over against Luther, that the divine is *in* the believer, not simply *among* men; but he goes on to show that whether the Light is external, as in the Old Covenant (a "taskmaster"), or internal, as in the New, there is only one group among three kinds of people for whom the internal Light proves efficacious in helping them to go on to the second grace. A very large number of people simply put out the Light as fast as they can and revel in their darkness. Others are lazy and numb, and fail to see very much. The third group are those who are very eager in their devotional practices and in their daily discipline under the illumination of the Light, and who yet over and over again succumb to temptation.

But this group are at least contrite, and it is this very contrition, combined with divine chastisement, that leads them on to the reception of the second grace, which is a constant righteousness. Physical and spiritual chastisement or anguish involves the ready assumption of a personal cross, which at length enables the be-

---

[53] Müller, *Glaubenszeugnisse* (*QGT*, III), 58–71. Alvin J. Beachy is currently at work on a Harvard Th.D. thesis, "The Concept of Grace in the Radical Reformation."

[54] Müller, *Glaubenszeugnisse* (*QGT*, III), 96.

liever to pass penitently and, one can say in the original Catholic context, penitentially, to that constant righteousness. It is in this state of chastisement where the believer is following in the footsteps of Christ to his cross, that he no longer is in sin and subject to the lusts of the flesh, which are macerated in the anguish of the personal cross and replaced by the willing of the divine will.[55] But instead of the priestly church imposing penitential acts, it is Christ himself who, just as a physician and surgeon does, imposes harsh medicines, bleedings, and the like, to bring about a cure; or again, it is Christ who hews down the tree, saws it up, and planes the wood for the construction of a house; or again, Christ who directly tries the gold and silver ore "in the smelter of *Gelassenheit.*"[56] This is the gospel *of* all creation *(aller Kreatur)* based on the Dominical injunction in Mark 16:15, but with the original dative converted into a genitive! Suffering, as their teacher Hut had declared, is the way of all flesh.

The Christian should pray for this particular cross and be glad when it comes, for amidst tribulation comes the third grace, which is the oil of the Holy Spirit, the healing grace that makes even judicial torture and martyrdom an occasion for joy and divine benediction. This is the true holy oil of which James (ch. 5:14) wrote. It "is not the olive oil of Italy" in the sacrament of extreme unction, but the oil of gladness and benediction, by which the true pilgrim prepares to enter, not Canaan, but the heavenly Jerusalem.

Thus the three Catholic sacraments of Baptism, penance, and extreme unction have, in a way, been transformed into the three actions of grace, consisting of adult repentance in the light of the Anabaptist gospel, a life of contrition and penitential suffering, and the benediction of martyrdom or its equivalent in steadfastness. But all three moments are also called baptisms by the Anabaptists (Schiemer: *Von dreierlei Taufe*[57]). They are the baptism of the Holy Spirit (inward repentance and a change of heart), that of water (external covenant, believers' baptism), and that of martyrdom, or blood.

Under no debt to Schiemer for his terminology, Schlaffer, no doubt drawing upon medieval mysticism, describes the same spiritual and physical experience of the cross, but in such phrases as "death," "deep," "descent into hell," and "lowliness" *(Niedrig-*

---

[55] *Ibid.,* 89.
[56] Ecclesiasticus 2:5 and its New Testament echoes, which Luther renders the *"Feuer der Trübsal,"* the followers of Hut turn into *"Schmelzofen der Gelassenheit."*
[57] Müller, *Glaubenszeugnisse (QGT,* III), 77–79.

keit). Christ, "the lamb slain from the beginning of the world," is[58] the exemplar of all the faithful, from Abel slain by Cain to the Anabaptists slaughtered by the new Caesar. For suffering is ever the mark of his chosen ones: "Here I stand as a lamb which does not open its mouth as it is being slaughtered, to whom may Christ grant strength and help."[59] The *descensus Christi* in the Apostles' Creed refers as much to the daily humiliation (*Niedrigkeit*) of Christ among his own now as to the descent aforetime into Hades to rescue the saints of the Old Covenant:

The deep (*tüefe*) of Christ is the lowliness and abandonment (*gelassenhait*) into which everyman is led; and it is called hell, where one feels, in fact, abandoned not only by all creatures but even also by God. . . . Into this deep must go all who would in Christ be blessed. For whoever will not be condemned with Christ by the world and enter this hell, must afterwards be thrust into the other hell. Whoever with Christ, that is, in Christ, enters this hell will be brought out again by God, for he will not suffer his members to remain in hell.[60]

Concerning the state that Schlaffer described as the "deep" and Schiemer as the "second grace" of suffering, Spittelmaier used the term "living soul carried by a dead body," in contrast to the lively body with a dead soul so common among nominal Christians.[61] For other interpretations of the *descensus* in the Radical Reformation, see Ch. 32.2.c.[62]

Eschatological urgency characterized the proclamation of all the disciples of Hut. It was Spittelmaier who most clearly expressed their distinctive views in a series of what he called "the Seven Decrees of Scripture,"[63] which will come under debate at both Nicolsburg (Ch. 9.2) with Hubmaier and at the Augsburg synod with Denck (Ch. 7.6).

The first decree is the covenant of God in the already discussed threefold baptism of Spirit, water, and blood (anticipated at each Communion by the chalice), whereby God accepts his creatures as his own children, promising to be with them in all their tribulations but not sparing them chastisement any more than he had his only-begotten Son. God's re-creation of sinful men and women into dutiful children is no less a miracle than the original creation from the dust. But it is not for children who have yet to

[58] *Ibid.,* 88.
[59] *Ibid.,* 96.
[60] *Ibid.*
[61] Schornbaum, *Bayern,* I (*QGT,* II), 49.
[62] Cf. *ARG,* XXXVIII (1941).
[63] Included under item 10 of Spittelmaier's statement of 25 October 1527; Schornbaum, *Bayern,* I (*QGT,* II), 49 f.

come to know good from evil. Water baptism, with its eschatological intention, is a seal, says Schiemer. A child should not be baptized any more than an envelope should be sealed in which there is no communication. Until a child is brought through the Light to know good and evil, the child is accounted among the good, for "of such is the kingdom of heaven."

The Austrian Anabaptist formula of Baptism is described by Spittelmaier: "I baptize in the name of the Father, Son, and the Holy Spirit, and take water from a pitcher or pail, and dipping two fingers in it, make a little sign of the cross on the forehead."[64] Schlaffer, like Schiemer, stressed the thirtieth year in imitation of Christ, arguing that the Christian life is not child's play (Kinderspiel), for after baptism come the great temptations:

> Christ himself received it only in his thirtieth year from John the Baptist and was from that moment on led by the Spirit into the wilderness and tempted by Satan . . . for the Christian life is not child's play; but bitter earnestness, truth, courage, and saintliness must be there.[65]

The second decree is the establishment of the Kingdom of God for those who are poor in spirit. Combining both the Matthaean and Lucan versions of this part of the Dominical sermon, Spittelmaier interprets poverty of the spirit in the sense of clutching at nothing, with the consequence that the loving sharing of goods prepares for the Kingdom.

> Nobody can inherit the kingdom unless he is here poor with Christ, for a Christian has nothing of his own: no place where he can lay his head. A real Christian should not even have enough property on earth to be able to stand on it with one foot. This does not mean that he should go and lie down in the woods and not have a trade, or that he should not work, but only that he might not think they are for his own use, and be tempted to say: This house is mine, this field is mine, this money is mine, but rather ours, even as we pray: Our Father. In brief, a Christian should not have anything of his own, but should have all things in common with his brother, not allow him to suffer need. In other words, I do not work that my house may be filled, that my larder be supplied with meat, but rather I see to it that my brother has enough, for a Christian looks more to his neighbor than to himself (I Cor., ch. 13). Whoever desires to be rich in this world, who is concerned that he miss nothing when it comes to his person and property, who is honored by men and feared by them, who refuses to prostrate himself at the feet of his Lord like Magdalene, . . . will be humbled.[66]

[64] Müller, Glaubenszeugnisse (QGT, III), 26.
[65] Ibid., 92 f.
[66] Schornbaum, Bayern, I (QGT, II), 49.

Spittelmaier stresses the fact that in work—he mentions specifically the housewife at her spinning wheel—the Christian, like Jesus himself in the carpentry shop of his father, can daily learn the will of God, invisible in his visible creatures.[67] Communal life in the context of the Kingdom is opposed to every form of idolatry. The Christian refuses to accept the magistrate in the place of God, and guards against the subtler and more rationalized forms of idolatry: of self, possessions, wife and family.[68] A true believer may even leave kith and kin to follow Christ if his or her spouse fails to follow Him. Christians, Spittelmaier says, should not buy or sell among themselves, but share whenever the need is clear.[69]

The community of goods is founded in the oneness of Christ with the Father and the oneness of Christ's followers in him, their head.[70] The third decree is, in fact, the complete interdependence of the loyal members of the one body of Christ and mutual obedience in forthright admonition one of the other in the face of the whole congregation. Since true Christians belong to the Kingdom and the community of mutual aid, they have no need of the organs of the state, which are ordained of God for the punishment of the wicked (and the testing of the faith of the righteous).

The fourth decree concerns the end of the world, purged by fire, earthquake, lightning, and thunder until all the wisdom of the wise and the wealth of the mighty is melted up and the way prepared for the descent of the Kingdom from heaven.

All three of our Austrian apostles, confident in the imminence of Christ's second advent, avow their belief in the sleep of the soul pending the resurrection and the last judgment.[71] With the fires of the last judgment approaching, Spittelmaier insists that the only purgatory is that through which the true believers are themselves being purged and cleansed by water and fire and blood.[72]

The fifth decree concerns the Last Judgment and the conviction that the true believers who have suffered the cross, hell, and purgatory in witnessing to Christ will be spared the same torments at that time, while the others will suffer their due.

The sixth decree concerns the resurrection, and the seventh the eternal punishment of the wicked.

Before the Austrian evangelists baptized, they preached this

[67] *Ibid.*, item 9.
[68] Schlaffer, Schiemer, and Spittelmaier.
[69] Schornbaum, *Bayern,* I (*QGT,* II), 64.
[70] Peter Riedemann, *Confession of Faith* (London, 1950), 88, always cited in the text as *Account.*
[71] Spittelmaier, *loc. cit.,* 37, item 25; Schiemer, *loc. cit.,* 67.
[72] *Loc. cit.,* 55.

fiery, seven-point message of the latter days. All Hut's apostles were irrepressible. In one instance, given the opportunity to escape by promising not to preach within a radius of thirty miles, the apostle refused the offer on the swiftly marshaled Scriptural grounds that he who is called an evangelist is no longer free for prudential reasons to withhold the message.[73]

The consciousness of being prophets or apostles was keenly developed among them. One evangelist spoke of Christ himself as a prophet like any other, saying that not until he was received by the Holy Spirit (at the Jordan) was he (adopted) as "a true God ... like unto his Heavenly Father."[74] This same evangelist drew attention to the fact that he was baptized by John Hut at precisely the same age that Jesus was baptized by John at the Jordan.[75]

Spittelmaier gave a vivid account of how he and his fellow evangelists proclaimed their gospel of repentance, suffering, and imminent[76] vindication. When he came into a town he would go to the inn, ask about the local preacher, whether or not he preached the gospel, what the gospel was, and then ask the same person whether he was himself a true Christian. When he found some of the Brethren, or friends close to them, he would suggest that they have a boy or little girl go around and quietly tell others where a meeting would take place—in a house, garden, field, or wood— and then our evangelist would pay the innkeeper for his food and drink, and leave.[77]

All three of these Austrian evangelists are harsh and even sardonic in caricaturing the nominal Christians. Schiemer disfigures, even though he enlivens, his letter on the three states of grace by his description, petition by petition, of what the Lord's Prayer really means to the nominal Christians—Catholics, Lutherans, and Zwinglians alike—who are, he says, much relieved that God is indeed "in heaven" and not too close, who pray for "our daily bread," but as soon as they get it, turn it into "my" bread, and, dissatisfied with temporal provisions for a day, strain to pile up possessions for days and years ahead. Never ask a nominal Christian to pray for you, Schiemer concludes. But over against this is the long, beautiful prayer of Schlaffer, composed the night before his execution; and all three displayed magnanimity in

---

[73] Answer of Spittelmaier, *loc. cit.*, 63.
[74] Spittelmaier, *loc. cit.*, 63 f.
[75] Spittelmaier, *loc. cit.*, 50.
[76] Cf. Schiemer, *Twelve Articles;* Müller, *Glaubenszeugnisse (QGT,* III), 55.
[77] Combining his answers in judicial hearings, as given in Schornbaum, *Bayern,* I (*QGT,* II), 27 and 36.

holding open the redeeming power of the Light of the World to those outside the Christian dispensation.[78] They reserved their harshness for the Christian scribes, who should know better, and proclaimed the gospel in all its fullness.

From the proclamation of Hut's three Austrian disciples, we return to Hut himself and with him to Augsburg.

6. The Martyrs' Synod in Augsburg, August 1527

Both Hut from Austria and Denck from Worms via Switzerland converged upon Augsburg to participate in the synod of August 1527. There were possibly three sessions: the first in the house of the steward for the poor, Gall Vischer; the second and principal session on Saint Bartholomew's Day in the house of the butcher Matthew Finder, 24 August, with some sixty present; and the last in the house of another steward for the poor, Conrad Huber, where Hut was domiciled. This last, Denck did not attend.[79] It was specifically called by Hut a *concilium*.[80] In some still obscure way the Anabaptists[81] thought of the calling of a council, synod, or great disputation as one of the foreseen signs of the last times (cf. Rev. 16:6; 19:19). As once in the upper room in Jerusalem the first apostolic council had convened and the flames of the Spirit had descended upon the participants, so in the fullness of the dispensations, the Spirit would come again in power, anointing the new apostles for the last days before the millennium.

Among the principal issues under discussion were the Seven Decrees already noted above, especially those concerning the Kingdom, the manner and expected moment of its approach (Pentecost, 1528), the role of the Anabaptists in preparation for it, and the place of the magistracy in the interim. On these matters, Denck was much more cautious than Hut. A second work of the synod was the ordination of more apostles to proclaim the Anabaptist evangel and to organize what both of them and their company believed to be the "third" and final reformation.

The presence in the city of such a vast number of Anabaptists alarmed the city fathers. The city's principal divine, Urbanus Rhegius, crowned imperial orator and poet laureate by Emperor

---

[78] Described by Robert Friedmann in his article, *ME*, IV, 458.

[79] The bare facts in sober presentation are admirably compressed into Fellmann's brief sketch of Denck, *Schriften* (*QGT*, VI:2), 17 f.

[80] Christian Meyer, "Zur Geschichte der Wiedertäufer," *loc. cit.*, 242.

[81] Peter Kawerau, *Melchior Hoffman als religiöser Denker* (Haarlem, 1954), 85, 88, mentions the eschatological council but does not solve the problem of a council of the righteous.

Maximilian, had for some time been devoting his rhetorical skill and theological cunning to Anabaptist research and refutation. The first in a long series of publications was his *Wider den neuen Tauforden,* 1527, in reply to a pamphlet by the local Augsburg Anabaptist deacon Jacob Dachser. But more important than this was his drawing up a series of articles summarizing Anabaptist doctrine and practice as derived from judicial hearings, confessions, and Anabaptist tracts. In numerous versions these articles, numbering from seven to more than a score, were usually referred to as "the articles of Nicolsburg" and were falsely ascribed to Hubmaier.[82] The foes of the Anabaptists regarded these articles as containing the essence of the Anabaptist heresy and sedition and as the actual agenda of the disputation at Nicolsburg in May 1527 (Ch. 9.2.b).

To dissociate these articles from Nicolsburg, we shall quote a version antedating the famous Moravian disputation. At the same time, we adduce them here not only as a hostile interpretation which goes far to explain the alarm of the Protestant divines and magistrates but also as a useful guide to undoubted excesses of Hut's movement as pointed up by the discerning, albeit intemperate, and hostile observer. The version is that which appears in a communication of the council of Nuremberg to the council of Strassburg as early as 21 March 1527, with special reference to Hut (before the Nicolsburg disputation in May):[83]

For out of the [initial] error of the Anabaptists stem even worse aberrations, namely, (1) that Christ was only a man and not God, (2) that he was conceived in sin, (3) that he has not done satisfaction for the sins of man, (4) that magistrates cannot be Christians, (5) that God will descend again to earth and a physical kingdom will be established, (6) that all governments will be wiped out and will not be endured, and (7) that all things should be in common.

To this group of seven points there would soon be added the Anabaptist insistence that the new gospel be preached only secretly in houses and in the woods, and the Anabaptist reliance on visions, dreams, and inspiration, while the first point would be made more specific in the allegation that the Anabaptists be-

---

[82] The best account of the articles and their variants is that of Wilhelm Wiswedel, *ME,* III, 886–888. The account does not give sufficient weight, however, to the fact that though in their present form the articles stem from enemies, many Anabaptists confessed to all or some of the articles both freely in their tracts and under duress in judicial hearings. Three Strassburg versions are printed by Krebs and Rott, *Elsass,* I (*QGT,* VII), No. 116, along with a survey of all the other versions more recent than Wiswedel.

[83] Krebs and Rott, *Elsass,* I (*QGT,* VII), No. 79; cf. Nuremberg to Regensburg, 18 March 1527; Schornbaum, *Bayern,* II (*QGT,* V), 8.

lieved that Jesus was only a prophet; the second, that Mary was not the mother of God but only of Jesus and that the angels assumed flesh at the same time as the Word; the fourth, that there should be among Christians neither violence nor government; and the fifth, that the descent of God or Christ would come about in precisely two years. This last variant would suggest that the "Nicolsburg articles" were drawn up in the spring of 1526, when the Hut movement would have considered the *eschaton* as just two years ahead.

In any event these were the views which Urbanus Rhegius in Augsburg and which the magistrates in Nuremberg ascribed to the large group of Anabaptists now foregathered in synod. They were thought of as connected "by secret passwords" and other "tokens" with a whole network of traitorous conventicles undermining the Empire.

The patrician Langenmantel was arrested 15 September 1527. After a disputation he temporarily withdrew from the Anabaptists and even conformed on the matter of infant baptism, but was nevertheless banished. With the arrest of a patrician, the execution of the revolutionary book peddler and principal missionary of the South German and Austrian Anabaptists was not far off. Hut was likewise seized on 15 September 1527.

He submitted to a series of hearings, on 16 September and notably on 4 November, when he admitted to all the "Nicolsburg articles."[84] Earlier, Spittelmaier had confessed that Christ was a prophet, that Mary was the mother of Jesus and not the mother of God, and that Christ had not rendered satisfaction for the sins of the whole world, in the sense that to be saved, the Christian had still to undergo the same suffering to which Christ pointed the way. This was indeed the same point made also by Kautz and Hut's baptizer, Denck, in the terminology of the seven theses of Worms of June 1527 (Ch. 7.3). Another early convert of Hut, Gall Vischer, would also presently confess to all these points and become quite specific about dreams and visions (Ch. 8.3). Moreover, many of the more Spiritualist articles reappear in Hut's convert Bünderlin, who removed to Strassburg, and in others of the "garden sect" who seemed quite prepared to adopt the spurious "Nicolsburg articles" as their own (Ch. 10.2).

It is from Hut's admissions, made under torture, that we gain exact information about such things as his life in Bibra, his part in the Peasants' War, his association with Müntzer and Denck, and his Anabaptist mission from Franconia to Moravia.

His son, Philip, recorded in the Hutterite *Chronicle* that his

[84] Wiswedel, "Articles," *loc. cit.,* 887.

father had been racked in the tower and then released, and that he lay as one dead, when a candle left by the guard in his cell was tipped over and Hut was burned to death by the inflamed pallet.[85] He perished 6 December 1527, before the trial was over, but his body was tied to a chair in court and formally condemned to be burned at the stake on the following day.

At the close of the synod, Denck, for his part, in the company of several others, left Augsburg, showing up in Ulm and even in Nuremberg. Denck no longer regarded his former oath not to re-enter that city as binding. Soon the news came of the disastrous arrest of the brethren who had tarried in or around Augsburg. With this sudden crumbling of the great design of the Augsburg synod, Denck became disheartened, convinced that by a succession of setbacks, beginning with his exile from Nuremberg, God had intended to show his disfavor with the Anabaptist cause. Moreover, Denck had become painfully aware of the divisive and sectarian character of the movement which he had headed. In remorse, he repaired to his beloved Basel.

From within the city he directed a letter to his former teacher and patron, Oecolampadius, expressing his disillusion with the excesses of Anabaptism and his sad surmise that its radicalism was not the will of God after all. He sought the understanding and the protection of the Reformer. Succor was granted, and Denck prepared a kind of *apologia pro vita sua,* which was somewhat tendentiously edited by the Basel Reformer as a recantation.[86] Herein, Denck moderated his view on baptism. He avowed that it was the means of being inscribed in the church, and that to extend this privilege to children was a human but tolerable commandment, and he would no longer protest against it. He would not repudiate his rebaptizings. He was content to let matters stand as long as he had no further clear instruction from the Lord. It was now his view that though "the spiritual man judges all things" and is not bound by any form, nevertheless, out of Christian charity, he submits to prevailing Christian usage. Thus, as a matured Spiritualist he despaired of divisive sectarianism, but it was only as an act either of prudence or of charity that he conformed to the established church of Basel. Even in Augsburg at the end of the synod, Denck had shown how closely he verged on

---

[85] There is a different account of his death. According to it, Hut had a premonition of his death by violence, and decided to escape by a ruse. He managed to make a light and by means of rags produced smoke which he thought would bring the guard in haste, from whom, in the confusion, he planned to take the keys and escape. But he was asphyxiated.

[86] Baring and Fellmann, *Schriften (QGT,* VI:2), 104–110.

the point where Anabaptism goes over into contemplative Spiritualism. In Basel he recrossed the border. The Catholic humanist of 1520 had become the conforming Protestant Spiritualist of 1527.

Gentle, indisposed to controversy, ill-cast even as the temporary leader of South German Anabaptism, he knew no abiding place. Not yet thirty-two, he died of the plague soon after his apologia.

CHAPTER 8

THE SCHLEITHEIM CONFESSION OF 1527: SWISS AND SOUTH GERMAN DEVELOPMENTS TO 1531

The fateful synod in August in Augsburg of South German and Austrian Anabaptists under the leadership of John Hut and John Denck was preceded by the synod in February in Schleitheim of the Swiss Brethren under the leadership of Michael Sattler and possibly William Reublin. Although each assembly was considered by its respective participants as a major event affecting a wide circle of Anabaptists, the personnel and the problems of the two synods differed markedly. On the agenda of the Augsburg synod were Hut's seven divine decrees (best known in Spittelmaier's version), relating to the end of the age. On the agenda of the Schleitheim synod in the canton of Schaffhausen were seven articles commonly called the Schleitheim Confession of Faith, relating to the organization and self-disciplining of a free-church movement, which was now obliged to cope with antinomian and Spiritualist excesses on its fringes.[1]

It was a copy of this Confession of Faith which certain participants brought to Bern and which Haller forwarded (Ch. 6.5) to Zwingli for refutation in his *Elenchus* (Ch. 8.4.a). Subsequently Calvin too will refute it, article by article, in his *Brière instruction* (Ch. 23.2).

It is quite probable that Sattler, the leader of the Schleitheim synod, who had been associated with Denck, against whom he had argued when they were together in Strassburg in 1526, now sought to differentiate the literalistic, Biblical Swiss Breth-

---

[1] The Confession has been several times printed and translated. The best translation is that of John C. Wenger, "The Schleitheim Confession of Faith," *MQR*, XIX (1945), 243–253; the critically edited German text, with the most recent interpretation of its genesis and significance, is the work of Beatrice Jenny, "Das Schleitheimer Täuferbekenntnis, 1527," *Schaffhauser Beiträge zur vaterländischen Geschichte*, XXVIII (1951), 5–81.

ren from the spiritualistic South German Brethren such as Denck and Hut. In any event, the mood at the synod of Schleitheim exhibited a sobriety which was in marked contrast to the eschatological tension of the disputation of Nicolsburg (yet to be fully recounted in Ch. 9.2) and the eschatological-missionary fervor of the Martyrs' Synod of Augsburg, which met respectively in May and August of 1527.

1. "THE BROTHERLY UNION OF A NUMBER OF CHILDREN OF GOD
   CONCERNING SEVEN ARTICLES," SCHLEITHEIM, 24 FEBRUARY
   1527

The Schleitheim Confession, entitled originally *The Brotherly Union* (*Brüderliche Vereinigung*), addressed to "the children of light . . . scattered everywhere," is directed not primarily against the Magisterial Reformation[2] but rather against "certain false brethren among us . . . in the way they intend to practice and observe the freedom of the Spirit and of Christ."

[These false brethren and sisters] have missed the truth and to their condemnation are given over to the lasciviousness and self-indulgence of the flesh. They think faith and love may do and permit everything, and that nothing will harm them or condemn them, since they are believers.[3]

The antinomian excesses which Kessler reported on the fringes of the Anabaptist revival in St. Gall (Ch. 6.2) were now being firmly reproved by the leaders of the movement.

The first article on baptism is not notable, except perhaps for specifying, in addition to repentance and the resolution to amend one's life found in earlier accounts (Ch. 6.1), the concurrent intention "to be buried" with Christ in order "to be resurrected with him." In the second article, excommunication (the ban), which appeared among the Swiss Brethren at least as early as Grebel's letter to Müntzer (Ch. 5.2), is given renewed importance as the Dominically instituted means of purifying the brotherhood *before* the administration of the Supper. According to this second article:

The ban shall be employed with all those who have given themselves to the Lord, to walk in His commandments and with all those who are baptized into the one body of Christ and who permit themselves to be called brethren or sisters, and yet who slip sometimes and fall

---

[2] This is the older view which Jenny, *op. cit.*, has refuted, building on Fritz Blanke, "Beobachtungen zum ältesten Täuferbekenntnis," *ARG*, XXXVII (1940), 246 ff.

[3] Wenger translation, *loc. cit.*, 247 f.

into error and sin, being inadvertently overtaken. The same shall be admonished twice in secret and the third time openly disciplined or banned according to the command of Christ [Matt., ch. 18]. But this shall be done according to the regulation of the Spirit before the breaking of bread, so that we may break and eat one bread, with one mind and in one love, and may drink of one cup.

In safeguarding the purity of the communion fellowship by means of committing themselves to the discipline of the pre-communion ban, the Schleitheim brethren were clearly breaking away from the Zwinglian view that the saints or the elect are known only to God and that the true church is invisible. The third article reads in part:

Whoever has not been called by one God to one faith, to one baptism, to one Spirit, to one body, with all the children of God's church, cannot be made [into] one bread with them, as indeed must be done if one is truly to break bread according to the command of Christ.

The fourth article differentiates the baptismal community, continuously purified by the ban and solidified as one body and one loaf in Communion. In this article on separation (*absünderung*), what the predestinarian doctrine of the Magisterial Reformation at least keeps invisible the free-will perfectionism of the "free church" makes boldly visible and mordantly moral:

For truly all creatures are in but two classes, good and bad, believing and unbelieving, darkness and light, the world and those who are out of the world, God's temple and idols, Christ and Belial; and none can have part with the other.[4]

The Confession makes specific the habitat, conduct, and institutions of Belial:

By this is meant all popish and antipopish [Protestant] works and church services, meetings, and church attendance, drinking houses, pledges and commitments [made in] unbelief and other things of that kind, which are highly regarded by the world and yet are carried on in flat contradiction to the command of God, in accordance with all the unrighteousness which is in the world. . . .
Therefore there will also unquestionably fall from us the unchristian, devilish weapons of force—such as sword, armor and the like, and all their use [either] for friends or against one's enemies—by virtue of the word of Christ, Resist not [him that is] evil.

The phrase translated "pledges and commitments" is obscure in German *(burgschaften und verpflichten des unglaubens)* and

4 *Ibid.*, 249, with a slight change.

was construed by Zwingli as *foedera infidelitatis*. It could mean vows made when the Brethren were Catholic or oaths sworn when they were still Zwinglians, but more likely it means all associations with unbelievers, including unregenerate spouses.[5]

Since marriage is nowhere mentioned in the Confession, although "sisters" are referred to as being on the same level as the brethren, and since also women were very prominent in the whole Anabaptist movement (as in the primitive church), it may be appropriate to observe here that a covenantal conception of marriage was replacing the sacramental view. Divorce and remarriage within the community of explicit faith, with sporadic outcroppings of libertinism, was a concomitant of Anabaptism during the transition from the medieval to the sectarian conception of wedlock (see further, Ch. 20).

The fifth article is of interest because it shows that, within less than three years after the layman Grebel rebaptized the priest Blaurock in Zurich (Ch. 6.1), the office of the pastor (*hirt*) among the Swiss Brethren has been clearly defined. His task is, first of all, to read the Scriptures and to admonish, teach, and warn in the light of the text. In this pre-eminence of Bible-reading and instruction the gathered church preserves the character of the original Bible-study groups out of which Swiss Anabaptism emerged. The pastor "leads out in prayer," undoubtedly to be followed by various inspired members of the congregation. He breaks the bread and in this connection disciplines and bans "in the name of the church." Provision is also made for the disciplining of the pastor by the congregation. If he is banished or martyred, another should be ordained (*erwelt; verordnet*) "in the same hour in order that God's remnant and little folk (*völckle*: little people) may not be scattered."

The pastor here described, "supported by the church . . .," that he who serves the gospel may live of the gospel," is no longer the itinerant evangelist or swiftly roving apostle of the first year of the movement, but is already a settled minister.

The sixth and largest article deals with the sword, which is acknowledged to be "ordained of God outside the perfection of Christ":

It punishes and puts to death the wicked, and guards and protects the good. . . . In the perfection [of the church] of Christ [Matt. 5:48], however, only the ban is used for a warning.

The contrast is drawn in connection with the woman taken in adultery between what "the Father" ordained in the Old Cove-

[5] This is the view of Jenny, *op. cit.*, 61.

nant, namely, that she be stoned to death, and what Christ set as an example for discipline under the New Covenant. Here the Schleitheim synod is defining its conviction over against Zwingli on the one side and perhaps on the other those Anabaptists like Hubmaier who, though separating the church from the state, found a place for a Christian magistracy (Ch. 9.2.b) and also those Anabaptists like Hut who, while restraining the saints for the present, foresaw a great struggle at the imminent end of the age and the rule of the saints with Christ. By implication the synod claims for the covenantal conventicle the divine righteousness which Zwingli had distinguished from God-willed human righteousness.[6] As Christ refused to act the part of a judge (Luke 12:13), so must his follower. As Christ refused to be made a king (John 6:15), so must his follower refuse to take part in all forms of earthly government. Quoting I Peter 2:21, the synod declared that in suffering, and not in ruling, Christ left an example for true Christians following in his steps, and concluded that "the regime of magistracy is according to the flesh but that of Christians according to the Spirit."

The seventh article concerns the oath. A religious duty in the Old Testament, it was solemnly superseded in the injunction of Jesus (Matt. 5:33–37) and of James 5:12. We need not enlarge upon the disastrous civic consequences of the Anabaptist refusal to take the annual oath to uphold the constitutions of the city republics of the southwest quadrant of the Empire. It is of interest that in the imperial city of Strassburg the very next year, *all* the local Anabaptists were prevailed upon to take the civic oath.[7]

The Schleitheim Confession was far from being a balanced testimony of the faith and practice of the Swiss Brethren. It was, rather, like most synodal utterances, shaped by the immediate concerns of the movement to disavow excesses and aberrations from within and to resist challenges from without.

2. THE TRIAL AND MARTYRDOM OF MICHAEL SATTLER

Michael Sattler, despite Capito's offer to let him remain in Strassburg after the expulsion of John Denck (Ch. 10.2), had gone at the invitation of William Reublin to Horb on the Neckar. It was from this center that the Hohenberg region was being missionized.

---

[6] *Von der göttlichen und menschlichen Gerechtigkeit* (1523), ZW, II, 458–525.

[7] So Bucer reported to Ambrose Blaurer, 8 February 1528; *Briefwechsel der Brüder Ambrosius und Thomas Blaurer,* edited by Traugott Schiess, I (Freiburg im Breisgau, 1908), 146.

While Sattler was in Schleitheim, presiding at the foregoing synod, the authorities discovered his Anabaptist groups in Horb and Rottenburg, and were in a position to apprehend Sattler and his wife, Matthew Hiller of St. Gall (baptized by Jacob Gross in Strassburg), and others on their return from Schleitheim. After numerous delays because of widespread popular sympathy with the defendants, and in spite of Archduke Ferdinand's suggestion of an immediate "third baptism" (drowning), the captives were brought to trial in Rottenburg on 15 May 1527. The proceedings of the trial have been recorded in four accounts which are notable for the picture they give of the provocative sense of divine commission on the part of the martyrs and the mingling of fairness, fierceness, and frustration in the efforts of the Catholic tribunal[8] in a Hither Austrian territory.

Sattler refused the services of counsel, stating that in questions of religion the resort to law was forbidden to them by God's Word, although he did recognize the judges as servants of God on other questions. There were nine civil and religious charges against Sattler and his followers. In general they were accurate. Sattler could substantiate his views with Scriptural texts and with careful argument, but he could not exculpate himself in the eyes of the judges. He was unwilling to deny the charges or retract the views attributed to him. On the question of the veneration of the Virgin and the saints, he explained that they could not be intercessors because, like the rest of the faithful, they were sleeping (psychopannychism) and awaiting the judgment. Questioned about the use of the sword, he disavowed armed resistance, but said that if war were right, he would rather fight against "the spiritual Turks," the so-called Christians who persecute, capture, and kill God's people, than against the Turks in the flesh, who make no pretense of following Christ. One exasperated court official retorted: "The hangman shall and will dispute with you."

The verdict, which was death by burning, preceded by various grisly tortures, was carried out on 21 May 1527. Throughout the fiendish abuse to which his executioners subjected him, Sattler continued to remain steadfast, and one version of the martyrdom attributes the following words to him immediately before his

---

[8] An account of the famous trial and the martyrdom is printed in *SAW*, 136–144. For the legal theory and practice seen comprehensively, consult Horst Schraepler, *Die rechtliche Behandlung der Täufer in der deutschen Schweiz, Südwestdeutschland und Hessen 1525–1618* (Weierhof, 1957).

death: "Almighty, eternal God, thou art the way and the truth; because I have not been shown to be in error, I will with thy help this day testify to the truth and seal it with my blood."[9]

Both Capito and Bucer, who had opposed Sattler in Strassburg, were dismayed at his death and wrote in favor of him and his followers. Capito, although uneasy about what he called "the new monkery" of the Anabaptists, intervened with the Catholic authorities for the sake of the survivors still held after the unusually cruel death meted out to Sattler. Bucer, in another connection, wrote at the same time: "We do not doubt that Michael Sattler, who was burned at Rottenburg, was a dear friend of God, although he was a leader of the Anabaptists, but much more skilled and honorable than some."[10] He pointed out that even though Tertullian erred as a Montanist Spiritualist, and Cyprian as an anabaptist, they were rightly revered as true martyrs of the church. Bucer expressly distinguished Sattler favorably from Denck, for example, on the crucial issue of the atonement.

The impression which Sattler's martyrdom made in Rottenburg was profound, and led in Württemberg and the Hither Austrian jurisdictions to more earnest efforts to convert, rather than exterminate, the Anabaptists. After Sattler's execution, the authorities at Horb elaborated the medieval practice of public penitential discipline, with special reference to Anabaptists who could be induced to purge themselves of their errors. The pattern is typical. Twenty-four men and women who had been induced to recant were led to the market place, where they had to swear before a notary and several trustworthy witnesses that they would abandon their error and zealously adhere to the Holy Catholic Church and its regulations to the end of their days. On the next seven Sundays they were to gather at the altar for early Mass, with bare heads and feet, and loose hair, in gray robes on which a representation of the baptismal font was painted in white, and to make a procession around the church behind the cross. As a sign of penitence each had to carry in his left hand a rod, in his right, a lighted candle, and after the procession to kneel before the altar. The priest would thereupon strike them three times, give them absolution, and bid them stay on their knees for the remainder of the service. They had to wear the gray garb for a year and a day, and on specified occasions go to confession and to Communion. For the rest of their lives

[9] *SAW*, 143.
[10] *Getrewe Warnung* (July, 1527); Krebs and Rott, *Elsass*, I (*QGT*, VII), 110; for Capito's letters, *ibid.*, Nos. 83 f.

they had to avoid all other public and private gatherings in or out of doors, and could carry no weapon except a blunted bread knife. Finally, they were not to leave Horb without permission for the rest of their lives.[11] Many valiant Anabaptists, refusing to repent, escaped from Horb and surrounding centers to Strassburg.

3. ANABAPTISM ELSEWHERE IN SOUTH GERMANY, EAST OF THE RHINE, FROM 1527 TO 1531

The trial and execution of Sattler and the recantation of several other Anabaptist captives at Horb has been adduced as a famous and representative episode in the annals of the Radical Reformation in South Germany. Members of Sattler's company were recruited from many places in Switzerland and South Germany. In recounting other episodes and trends in this area after the close of the Martyrs' Synod in August 1527, we shall bear in mind that the sober strain of Anabaptism associated with Grebel and Sattler intermingled at many points with the spiritualist strain associated with Denck and Hut.

When the Augsburg conventicle was seized 15 September 1527, several of the leaders and members recanted. Some were banished rather than put to trial, as Hut was. Among the banished was the patrician Langenmantel, who removed to a house in Leutershofen, where a new conventicle was assembled under his protection. But on the night of 11 March 1528, Langenmantel was seized by the captain of the Swabian League and beheaded. Another member of the smashed Augsburg conventicle who recanted, though his wife remained steadfast, was Augustine Bader, who had a strange prophetic career still ahead of him.

Bader returned to the remnant of the Augsburg conventicle and was, strangely enough, elected bishop (*Vorsteher*). He preached and baptized in the environs, and in February visited Kaufbeuren, accompanied by Hut's early convert, Gall Vischer. After its reorganization, the church of Kaufbeuren was ruthlessly stamped out in June of 1528. The leaders were all beheaded, and the remaining thirty members were burned through the cheeks, beaten, and driven out of town.

Stirred to apocalyptic indignation by this cruel blow, Bader developed messianic pretensions. His fantastic ideas were not acceptable to the majority of some one hundred Swiss and South German Anabaptists convened in council, whom he tried to win

[11] *ML,* II, 347.

over in Teufen near St. Gall at Christmastide 1528.[12] Rejected
by the synod of Teufen and by his own congregation at Augsburg, Bader revived and amended Hut's prophecies and proclaimed that a great judgment would break in upon the world at
Easter 1530. He held that the Turk would be the instrument
of ushering in the Kingdom and punishing the godless. At the
same time he hoped that the crushing of pretentious and morally
derelict Christendom would be the means of bringing about the
final conversion of Turks and Jews. His eschatology included
the elimination of all sacraments offensive to Jews and Moslems
and the espousal of the doctrine of the sleep of the souls of
the godly prior to the general resurrection and the Last
Judgment.

Bader and his small following, including the ever-loyal Gall
Vischer, rented a shed at Lautern near Ulm, where they and
their families set up a common fund and awaited further
revelation.

Gall Vischer and another follower, John Köller, a young tailor,
describe how Bader had visions of Christ and Moses.[13] Particularly interesting is the apparition of Moses. When Bader was on
his secret way back to Augsburg, Moses purportedly appeared
to him in a vision and led him and his companions under the
cover of darkness onto a moor. There, taking each other by the
hands, Bader and his group danced in a circle while Moses was
heard to sing his song addressed to the Creator of the heavens
and the earth in celebration of the escape through the Red Sea
(Ex. 15:1–18, Rev. 15:3 f.). As the prophet proceeded to enter
the waters of a creek up to his knees, he slipped on two stones
and was completely immersed, a slip that was apparently construed as a redemptive omen.

Bader's group, encouraged by Oswald Leber (one of their
number and formerly pastor in Herbolzheim), sought out Jewish
communities, tried to learn Hebrew, and interpreted the Old
Testament and the Apocrypha with the help of rabbis.

The core of Bader's apocalyptic conviction and that of the
small company who clung to him was that his own infant was
the proclaimed messiah in bold assimilation of Nathan's proph-

---

[12] Josef Beck, editor, *Die Geschichts-Bücher der Wiedertäufer in Österreich-Ungarn*, Fontes Rerum Austriacarum XLIII (Vienna, 1883), 64.

[13] Bossert, *Württemberg (QGT*, I), 953 ff. The fullest account of the Bader episode is by G. Bossert, "Augustin Bader von Augsburg, der Prophet und König, und seine Genossen," *ARG*, X (1912), 117–165, 208–241, 295–349; XI (1913), 19–72, 103–133, 176–199.

ecy for David (II Sam. 7:12: "I will raise up your son after you, who shall come forth from your body, and I will establish his kingdom"). In confirmation of Bader's role as regent of the prospective messiah, the aged Gall Vischer was possessed of a vision in the shed one evening, of a golden crown, scepter, and other royal insignia descending in front of the prophet. The group was prompted to turn these visionary emblems into tangible regalia, and the tailor Köller proceeded with the task.

Suspicion was aroused, and on the night of 15 January 1530 the entire company was seized—five men, three women, and eight children. The hearings were drawn out and carried on in several cities because of the widespread fear among officials and divines that "the Anabaptist king" was conspiring with the deposed duke, Ulrich of Württemberg, to unseat Hapsburg rule in Hither Austria. The unusually cruel manner in which Bader was executed on 30 March 1530 aroused sympathy for him. The more moderate Anabaptists were everywhere unfairly implicated in Bader's excesses. Even the diet of Augsburg dealt with the supposed threat, and the Augsburg Confession makes an unmistakable reference to Bader (article xviii).

In view of the Bader episode, it is notable that several South German towns—Ulm, Memmingen, Biberach, Isny, Lindau, and Constance[14]—before joining the newly formed Smalcaldian League rejected the use of force in dealing with the Anabaptists, as countenanced by the Lutherans at Speyer in 1529, and went even farther, declaring, "in order that the accusations of the Anabaptists might be somewhat moderated and their mouths closed," that infant baptism need not be compulsory. Even after the failure of repeated efforts to win them over to the support of the Christian commonwealth by oath and military service, the only punishment was to be banishment. The so-called Memmingen Resolutions of March 1531 go on to declare:

On account of the Anabaptists we wish very sincerely that they be treated as tolerantly as possible, so that our gospel be not blamed or impugned on their account. For we have hitherto seen very clearly that the much too severe and tyrannical treatment exercised toward them in some places contributes much more toward spreading them than toward checking their error, because many of them, some out of stubbornness of spirit and some out of pious, simple steadfastness, endured all dangers, even death itself, and suffered with such patience that not only were their adherents strengthened, but also many of ours were moved to regard their cause as good and just.

[14] Reutlingen could not be present because of the local plague. For the whole story, see *ME*, III, 568 f.

Thus it is contrary to the right of Christian government to force faith upon the world with the sword and other violent compulsion and to uproot evil therein, which should be resisted alone through the mighty Word of God, and the person erring in faith shall not be suddenly knocked down, but should be tolerated in all Christian love as a harmless person.[15]

The drafter of the Memmingen Resolutions was Ambrose Blaurer. In September 1531, Blaurer was invited to Esslingen, where he sought to cope with the local Anabaptists. The Anabaptists had, in a sense, prepared the way for the Magisterial Reformation when the town council of Esslingen, exasperated by these sectaries, invited Blaurer to come and to reform the town according to the best magisterial standards. A glance at this representative community will tell the story of many another South German city between 1527 and 1531.

The imperial city of Esslingen was situated down the Neckar from Horb and Rottenburg. In the year that Sattler was executed up the river, there was in Esslingen an Anabaptist conventicle. In November of that year several members were rounded up. Under torture certain ones apparently expressed quite radical Müntzerite ideas, saying that all who refused the rebaptism of the covenant should be killed as heathen, and that they were awaiting help from the Anabaptists in Moravia.[16] They had a common treasury for the help of indigents and refugees. Some averred that Christ was only a prophet and was a son of God only in the sense that they, too, strove to become sons of God. They adhered also to the doctrine of the sleep of the soul.[17] The Esslingen chronicler observed, however, that despite their departure from Catholic norms, they "are still the best and most pious; they do not swear, they do not practice usury, they do not drink to excess."[18]

On his arrival in September 1531 the author of the humane Memmingen Resolutions must have commended himself at once to the locally persecuted Anabaptists. He stressed preaching and moral purity, and introduced church discipline, withholding the sacraments from the unworthy. He was presently able to write Martin Bucer of his success:

I treat the Anabaptists in such a way that they love me and attend my sermons regularly and attentively. Most of them have desisted

---

[15] Translated in *ME*, III, 508 f.
[16] K. Pfaff, *Geschichte der Stadt Esslingen* (Esslingen, 1840), 473; *ML*, I, 610.
[17] Pfaff, *op. cit.*, 47.
[18] Quoted by Pfaff, *op. cit.*, 97.

from their error and have joined us. The rest, of whom there are very few, will, I hope, do the same.[19]

Soon after writing this note, Blaurer, with his winsome ways, returned to Constance, and the Anabaptists were immediately disaffected.

We cannot mention Constance at this point without due reference to Louis Haetzer, who had been beheaded there on a charge of adultery, 4 February 1529, on the site of Hus's execution. Although he was clearly guilty of the charge, the extremity of the punishment can best be accounted for by the charge of anti-Trinitarianism. We were last with Haetzer in Worms in 1527, when he was engaged with Denck in translating the prophets (Ch. 7.3).

In the meantime, Haetzer returned to Augsburg (he did not, however, participate in the Martyrs' Synod), met Schwenckfeld, went forth briefly to Nuremberg, and to Regensburg, baptizing four converts in the latter town. His Augsburg base was the household of one George Regel. Here he continued his translation, turning now to the Apocrypha, and in the preface to Baruch he attacked the Magisterial Reformation for disparaging the apocryphal books on the insufficient grounds that they were known only in Greek and Vulgate versions or that they were too apocalyptic and visionary. The fact is that they suited his own growing Spiritualism, and he defended them. He also edited *Theologia Germanica,* as would appear from the presence of his motto at the end of the edition: "O God, redeem the prisoners." He wrote two manuscripts, now lost, "Booklet concerning Schoolteachers" and "Booklet concerning Christ," which featured in his trial at Constance.[20] The first was apparently directed against the "scribes" of the Magisterial Reformation, who missed the Spirit behind the letter, and the second may well have developed further the ideas contained in both the Worms and the "Nicolsburg articles" about Christ as Prophet, hints of which may be overheard in some of Haetzer's early works, especially in his translations from the Scriptures. The clearest evidence of Haetzer's final anti-Trinitarian Spiritualism is a stanza from one of the many hymns that he composed (and which were cherished especially in the Hutterite tradition). From the other-

---

[19] Schiess, *Briefwechsel: Blaurer,* 292.

[20] J. F. G. Goeters, *Ludwig Hätzer,* Quellen und Forschungen zur Reformationsgeschichte, XXV, 139–147, extensively covers the sparse evidence as to their contents. For the Regels in Augsburg and for the religio-political policy of the alertly Catholic duchy of Bavaria, see Gerald Strauss, "The Religious Policies of Dukes Wilhelm and Ludwig of Bavaria in the First Decade of the Protestant Era," *CH,* XXVIII (1959), 1–24.

wise lost *Rhymes or Songs under the Cross,* there survives the following explicitly anti-Trinitarian utterance, placed in the mouth of God:

> I am He who created all things through His own might.
> Thou askest, how many persons am I?
> I am one!
> I am not three persons, but I am one!
> And I cannot be three persons, for I am one!
> I know nothing of persons: I alone am the source of all life.
> Him who does not know me, I know not;
> I alone am![21]

So much for what appears to be the first explicit expression of unitarianism within the German-speaking realm of the Radical Reformation.

While working through the last phase of his theology, Haetzer was exposed in the house of George Regel to his besetting temptation, for which he earlier had been asked to leave Basel. This time, however, it was adultery with the mistress herself of the little Anabaptist maid he had earlier taken to wife. Madame Regel had given him a ring and financial help. It was technically on this count that he was apprehended in his native Bischofszell at the request of the town council of Augsburg and stood trial at nearby Constance. Ambrose Blaurer's brother Thomas, a Wittenberg-trained jurist, was chief prosecutor.

With Ambrose, his brother Thomas Blaurer, and ill-starred Haetzer, we have returned to the border of the Swiss Confederation. We leave Constance for Zurich, where Haetzer had once been a minor ally of Zwingli (Ch. 5.2).

4. SWISS DEVELOPMENTS BETWEEN ZWINGLI'S REFUTATION OF THE CONFESSION IN 1527 AND HENRY BULLINGER'S ATTACK IN 1531

a. Zwingli's "Elenchus." We were last in Zurich in January 1527 at the execution of Felix Mantz (Ch. 6.4). We saw how Zwingli had come to look upon the withholding of children from baptism and the rebaptism of adults as tantamount to subversion of church and state. The irresponsible radical evangelicals were jeopardizing the complete conversion of the canton from Catholicism to Protestantism, and that of the Confederation as a whole,

---

21 The stanza is preserved by Sebastian Franck in his *Chronicle.* It is reprinted in Goeters, *op. cit.,* 138, and Frederick L. Weis, *The Life and Teachings of Ludwig Hetzer, a Leader and Martyr of the Anabaptists: 1500–1529* (Dorchester, Massachusetts, 1930), 214 f., from which the translation is taken.

by moving ahead of the magistracy, defying the magistracy, indeed dechristianizing the office of the magistrate. To Zwingli, this unilateral and reckless action betrayed a want of charity and humility and Christian realism. Thus, in his concern for total reform, Zwingli had come around to construe baptism as the Christian equivalent of circumcision, and hence as the covenantal seal of civic-religious membership in the new Alpine Israel, the Swiss Confederation, of which Zurich might be considered the foremost tribe. Any radical dissociation of citizenship from church membership was linked in his mind with the social restiveness of the peasants, and with the insubordination of the tribute villages claiming autonomy in the spurious name of Christian freedom, while any talk of toleration smacked of treason and reaction in favor of the patricians and the Old Believers.

Zwingli had already written against the Anabaptists four times (cf. Ch. 6.2) when he took up the task again in 1527 in his *Elenchus in Catabaptistarum strophas.*[22] We will here examine his objections to Anabaptism as expressed in the *Elenchus.*

Zwingli contended that antipedobaptism leads to anabaptism, which is at once uncharitable and heretical in that it repudiates the rite submitted to by countless generations of faithful believers and therefore is tantamount to crucifying Christ a second time, and is treasonable, since it dissolves the sacred ties of the Christian commonwealth. In emphasizing works as the effective means of salvation rather than simple faith, Zwingli feels that Anabaptism undoes the significance of Christ's atoning role and unwittingly reproduces in allegedly evangelical form the pride and exclusiveness of the monks. It severs the Old Testament from the New, disparages the Old, and in effect construes the promise to Abraham as more inclusive than the promise through Christ, since circumcision was for the children of the faithful, baptism allegedly for adults only.

The postulates of Anabaptism have serious political and moral consequences. The concentration on the New Testament leads to a disproportionate emphasis upon Christ in his human nature and his humble role on earth, and neglects his resurrection and ascension to the right hand of God, whence in judicial glory he rules the world.[23] Moreover, the repudiation of the oath, which in any event follows from a misconstruction of Scripture,

[22] Translated as *Refutation of the Tricks of the Anabaptists,* Zwingli, *Works,* III, 357–437.

[23] The most recent interpretation of Zwingli's religio-political concerns is that of Heinrich Schmid, *Zwinglis Lehre von der göttlichen und menschlichen Gerechtigkeit,* Studien zur Dogmengeschichte und systematischen Theologie, No. 12 (Zurich, 1959).

dissolves the civil compact. Jesus' injunction about the simple yea and nay was concerned with private affairs. He expressly enjoined obeying Caesar in public affairs and he considered the oath a proper requirement of Caesar. As to the fatuous distinction between the temporal and spiritual made by the Anabaptists, it is clear that it takes more spiritual power to discriminate and act justly as a magistrate than simply to evade the duties of organized society. As to the moral life, Zwingli holds that Anabaptists are, by and large, as much subject as others, probably more, to sinful proclivity, and in denying it, indulge in the two worst spiritual evils, namely, pride and hypocrisy. They condemn all joy in moderation, and "he who takes it away from the pious will have to restore it with interest." Anabaptist communism leads to all kinds of grave economic and moral excesses in the name of charity, and Anabaptist spiritualism leads to irresponsible ecstasy akin to epilepsy, babbling, raving, deceit, and imposture, all in the name of inspiration.

The *Elenchus* was Zwingli's last literary attack upon the Anabaptists.

In 1529 compulsory attendance at the established church service was instituted, while the criticism of the low moral state of the civic clergy as well as the population in general was met by sharp regulations against the most common vices and an elevation of requirements for the clergy. All these measures were combined and intensified in the sharp and comprehensive Moral Code of 26 March 1530 (*Das grosse Sittenmandat*), which in paragraph ix forbade help or housing for Anabaptists on pain of heavy penalties. This article was designed to refute the charge of the Catholic cantons that Zurich was tolerating the "vicious sect," and to meet the threat of a movement which rejected the oath and all military service, thereby impairing the military potential of the Protestants in their struggle with the Catholic cantons.

Zwingli's concern with the Anabaptist problem and his leadership of the Reformed cantons was abruptly broken off in the midst of war against the Catholic cantons. The quartering and burning of his body on the battlefield in 1531 was followed by the second Peace of Cappel, which put a halt to the spread of Protestantism within the Confederation. Oecolampadius died in Basel. Within a month the Swiss Reformation was bereft of its two outstanding leaders.

b. *Basel: Three Radical Physicians—Paracelsus, Servetus, and Otto Brunfels*. We may pause here to pick up the thread of our narrative in Basel up to the death of Oecolampadius. We were

last in Basel on 6 July 1527, when the town council, after several
disputations, resorted to a strict but not yet severe mandate
against the Anabaptists (Ch. 6.5). In the four years following,
the main developments in Basel for the history of the Reformation Era as a whole and for the Radical Reformation in particular happen to center, not in the Anabaptists, but rather in the
call of Paracelsus as professor of medicine at the university in
the spring of 1527; in the magisterial abolition of the Mass on
9 February 1529, accompanied by the slashing, hacking, and
burning of the images by the impatient populace; in the resolute departure of Erasmus for still Catholic Freiburg (Breisgau),
to the utter dismay of Oecolampadius, who implored him to
remain; and in the arrival, in the summer of 1530, of Michael
Servetus, full of hope that his Trinitarian speculations would be
eagerly attended to by the northern evangelicals.

Philip von Hohenheim, later called Theophrastus Paracelsus,
was born the son of a physician in Einsiedeln in 1493. With the
counsel of Vadian, he had studied widely in several German
universities (1507–1512). In Ferrara he had acquired his doctorate in medicine and had adopted his programmatic name, announcing cryptically his intention of going beyond even the
comprehensive and experimental conception of medicine held
by the recently rediscovered Roman, Cornelius Celsius. From
Ferrara he set out upon his great peregrination (1512–1524) as
camp and ship doctor and surgeon ("a physician should be a
wayfarer"), that led him down the peninsula over to Spain and,
clockwise, around the whole of Christendom and the Middle
East from Lapland to Nubia. He returned to his father's home
in Carinthian Villach in time to become involved on the side
of the revolting miners and peasants (Ch. 4.2.e). Arriving in
Basel by way of Strassburg, he took up his duties on the medical
faculty in time to have conferred with Denck, who died in Basel
of the plague in mid-November of that year. Paracelsus, who
attended medically upon the impoverished and the wealthy alike,
may indeed have called upon Denck in his extremity.

His physics and physiology were posited on a doctrine of the
general animation of nature. As a writer on medicine, botany,
and natural philosophy, Paracelsus was amazingly prolific.[24]

Paracelsus never became an Anabaptist, nor an anti-Trini-

[24] The *Gesammelte Werke* of Paracelsus, edited by Karl Sudhoff and Wilhelm
    Matthiessen (Munich, 1922–1923), include fourteen volumes of the medical,
    scientific, and philosophical writings in the first division. Of the second
    division, the theological and religious-philosophical works, three volumes
    have been published. There is a comprehensive guide to all his printed
    works: Karl Sudhoff, *Bibliographia Paracelsica* (Berlin, 1894; Graz, 1958),
    and a journal devoted to him, *Nova Acta Paracelsica,* I (1944–   ).

tarian, but he belongs to our history[25] because of his sympathetic involvement in the Peasants' War, because of his abiding interest in the amelioration of the condition of the downtrodden and neglected,[26] because of his espousal of peace and toleration,[27] because of his numerous theological writings on Baptism, the Lord's Supper, and eschatology, and, in the end, because of his travels as an itinerant preacher and healer, many of whose sermons survive. He took a very strict view of the Sabbath, saying that it should be used for absolutely nothing but worship, not out of a spirit of legalism but because of the innate congruity between man and God and the need to align them in the spirit.[28] Paracelsus retained a high concern for the immaculate conception of Mary and her virginity *post partum*. Of his Bible commentaries, the one on the Psalter[29] should be mentioned, and of the dogmatic writings, the one on Communion addressed to Pope Clement VII. In this book, Paracelsus, like Sebastian Franck (Ch. 10.3.d), denied the claim alike of the Catholics, Lutherans, Zwinglians, and Anabaptists that they were the possessors of the Holy Spirit.

Franck and Paracelsus met at least twice. There were meetings, also, with Caspar Schwenckfeld. But the Silesian and the Swabian, the one a pious seeker, the other an impetuous physician acquainted with disease, grief, and squalor, had little in common, though both were knights, except their prolific literary productivity and their evangelical zeal.

Paracelsus was to die a nominal Catholic, hoping for the restoration of the church by the pope: "In the pope there will be a blessed spirit, and thus a blessed spirit in the sheep." Paracelsus was, however, like Schwenckfeld, essentially a Spiritualist, in his conception of the inward feeding upon the celestial flesh of Christ in the Lord's Supper, and like Franck in his nonconfessional motto: "Let a man belong to no one else, if he is able to belong to himself."[30]

[25] The best brief account of his theology in the light of the recent critical literature is that of Kurt Goldammer, *Paracelsus: Natur und Offenbarung* (Hanover, 1953).

[26] His social writings have been selectively edited and interpreted by Kurt Goldammer, *Paracelsus: Sozialethische und sozialpolitische Schriften* (Tübingen, 1952).

[27] See Kurt Goldammer, "Friedensidee und Toleranzgedanke bei Paracelsus und den Spiritualisten, I: Paracelsus," *ARG*, XLVI (1955), 20–46.

[28] Goldammer, *Schriften*, 24 f.

[29] Edited by Goldammer in two volumes, series cited, Abt. II, Vols. IV and V (1955, 1957).

[30] Goldammer, *Paracelsus: Schriften*, 90. The medical, psychological, and religious literature on Paracelsus is extensive. The most recent biographies are those of Ludwig Englert, *Paracelsus, Mensch und Arzt* (Berlin, 1941); Fried-

Paracelsus was driven from Basel in February 1528. The immediate issue was the failure of a canon of patrician wealth to pay the high honorarium for medical services which Paracelsus, who ministered gratis to the numerous poor, asked in payment for his great success in what was widely regarded as a medically impossible assignment. The altercation came before the town tribunal. Paracelsus, envied by the other doctors, feared by the local druggists, whom he had ridiculed and rebuked for their malpractices, and distrusted by the patrician divines as sympathetic to the lower classes, lost his case. We cannot follow him to Colmar, Esslingen, Nuremberg, possibly Strassburg again in 1531, St. Gall (with Dr. Vadian), Innsbruck, Augsburg, Munich, Moravia, Vienna, and finally to Salzburg. We shall, however, have occasion later to consider his teaching concerning baptism (Ch. 11.1.e) and marriage (Ch. 20.1).

We turn now to a doctor yet to be, Michael Servetus.

We last encountered Servetus when his studies in law and Scripture at Toulouse and his despair at the unholy reconciliation of Emperor and pope at the coronation in Bologna (Ch. 1.2.c) had matured in him the conviction that the church fell when it entered into an alliance with the Empire under Constantine and specifically when the Biblical view of Jesus Christ and his relationship to God the Father underwent serious distortion in the Constantinian-Nicene formulation of the Godhead, so offensive to Jews and Moslems, so bewildering to simple Christians.

For a while, Servetus was the guest of Oecolampadius, and probably earned his board by correcting proof. The works of Irenaeus and Tertullian, upon whom rested so much of his patristic argument against the Nicene formulation of the doctrine of the Trinity, had recently been issued from the Basel presses. The editor of Tertullian, Beatus Rhenanus, had felt called upon, in a section of the appendix, to deal with Tertullian's seeming divergency from the Nicene formulation. With the stimulation of this new patristic material, Servetus worked at a modalistic doctrine of the Trinity, which would make it possible for him to picture Christ delivering up the Kingdom to the Father, "just as the general of the whole army offers the Emperor the palm

rich Jäger, *Theophrastus Paracelsus, 1493–1541* (Salzburg, 1941); W. E. Peuckert, *Theophrastus Paracelsus* (2d edition, Stuttgart, 1943); Georg Sticker, *Paracelsus, ein Lebensbild* (Halle, 1941); Ildefons Betschart, *Theophrastus Paracelsus, der Mensch an der Zeitenwende* (2d edition, Einsiedeln, 1942); Basilio de Telepnef, *Paracelsus: A Genius Amidst a Troubled World* (St. Gall, 1945); Henry Pachter, *Paracelsus* (New York, 1951).

of victory; and the dispensation of the Trinity will then cease."[31]

Oecolampadius at first was open-minded and perhaps even prepared to make terminological concessions, but he finally lost his patience, irritated no doubt also by Servetus' youthful eagerness to instruct the older man. Servetus, feeling that he had been harshly treated, wrote out a confession of faith,[32] to which Oecolampadius replied:

You accord more honor to Tertullian than you do the whole Church. You deny the one person in two natures. By denying that the Son is eternal you deny of necessity also that the Father is eternal. . . . I will be patient in other matters, but when Christ is blasphemed, No![33]

Oecolampadius, at a conference in Zurich with Zwingli and Henry Bullinger, Capito and Bucer,[34] expressed his alarm at the effect Servetus might have upon their relations with the Catholic cantons, a prospect all the more disturbing since Servetus would presently make bold to write to Erasmus in an effort to gain his support for the allegedly more evangelical Trinitarian views.[35]

Ever since the abolition of the Mass in Basel, the mandates against the Anabaptists grew sterner, for Basel was becoming a center of refugee conventicles. The first execution in Basel was in 1528, the next in January 1530. About a month after Servetus arrived in Basel, one Conrad in der Gassen was brought to trial for denying the divinity of Christ, and executed 11 August 1530.[36]

We shall next encounter Servetus in Strassburg (Ch. 10.3.f).

Before going on to the developments in Bern, we can fit briefly into our narrative at this point another radical physician who may be grouped with Paracelsus and Servetus, Otto Brunfels (c. 1488–1534), a Carthusian in Strassburg, a Protestant preacher under the protection of the imperial knights Ulrich of Hutten and Francis of Sickingen, then back in Strassburg as teacher, theological writer, botanist, and physician (1524–1533). He was a proponent of the sleep of the soul at death, revelatory dreams, and the doctrine of the priesthood of all believers, but held the number of the elect to be very few; he opposed the payment of tithes and other feudal dues unless used for the poor or for education, defended the Anabaptists against coercion, agreed with

---

[31] On the Errors of the Trinity, translated by Earl M. Wilbur, Harvard Theological Studies, XVI, 26.

[32] Not extant.

[33] Staehelin, Briefe und Akten, No. 765; translated in Bainton, Hunted Heretic, 52; Oecolampadius wrote a sterner letter, No. 766.

[34] The conference was reported by Bullinger, Calvin, Opera, VIII, 744:1.

[35] Wilbur, Unitarianism, 58, n.32.

[36] Staehelin, Lebenswerk, 535.

them to the extent of opposing on principle the entry of the magistracy into the affairs of church and conscience;[37] and he found time to become (according to Carl Linnaeus) "the father of modern botany." He ended his days as city physician in Bern.

c. Bern. We turn from Basel, temporary residence of Servetus and Paracelsus, to the canton of Bern. Here, prudence and proximity to the Catholic cantons had for some time dictated a policy fateful to Zwingli's military effort at Cappel.

It will be recalled that it was from Haller in Bern that Zwingli received the copy of the Schleitheim Confession for refutation. In the great disputation from 7 to 26 January 1528, Haller, with Wolfgang Capito and Martin Bucer from Strassburg, successively overcame the Catholic debaters, and the Bern council voted for reformation, officially suspending the Roman rites by the mandate of 7 February. In the disputation, eight representatives of the growing body of Anabaptists were heard by the Zwinglians on 22 January,[38] these Radicals including George Blaurock, John Hausmann (called Sickler) from Basel, and John Pfistermeyer. The latter, apparently converted by Jacob Gross of Waldshut, the evangelist of the Aargau and cofounder of the Strassburg Anabaptist community, had swiftly emerged as the principal spokesman of Bernese Anabaptism. The interview during the recess in the Zwinglian-Catholic disputation turned out to be a judicial hearing, following which the Anabaptists were warned not to be caught in Bernese territory or they be drowned. Between 8 and 15 July 1529 the first death sentences were executed.

After the arrest of Pfistermeyer, who persisted in returning to preach in the capital of Bern, a formal debate, 19 April 1531,[39] was arranged between him and several Reformed church divines, including not only Haller of Bern but also Megander and Hofmeister, both of Zurich. The question of taking interest played a considerable role in the debate. Also figuring largely was the impediment, as it was argued, which the traditional system of tithes and prebends placed in the way of the divine commission of ministers to preach to the nations. In addition, there were the usual articles on military service, capital punishment, the

---

[37] His Pandectarum veteris et novi Testamenti libri xii of 1528 ff. is excerpted in Krebs and Rott, Elsass, I (QGT, VII), No. 77.

[38] Leonhard von Muralt, "Das Gespräch mit den Wiedertäufern am 22. Januar 1528 zu Bern," Zwingliana, V (1933), 409.

[39] Ein christenlich gespräch gehallten zu Bernn zwüschen den Predicanten und Hansen Pfyster Meyer von Arouw den Widertauff, Eyd, Oberkeyt und andere Widertöufferische Artickel betreffende. Copy in Goshen College Library.

oath, and the relationship between circumcision and baptism. On
the last issue, the Magisterial Reformers argued that just as children enjoy the benefit of civil society before they can understand it or take their part in supporting it, so infants may begin
to participate in the benefits of the community of saints without
being at first able to understand them.

At length, Pfistermeyer, given further opportunity to study
and reflect, admitted that he could find no more Scriptural texts
to oppose the magisterial divines, and submitted. In fact, he
later (somewhat perfunctorily) sought to win back those whom
he had led (Ch. 23.2).

d. Bullinger's "Von dem unverschämten Frevel." It was
against Pfistermeyer and his following that Henry Bullinger
(1504–1575), successor of Zwingli at Zurich, directed the first of
his attacks on Anabaptism. Formerly priest in his home parish
of Bremgarten (Aargau), Bullinger is introduced at this point in
our narrative as a major historian of the Reformation in Switzerland and as a tendentious chronicler and lifetime opponent of
Anabaptism.

Even before his call to Zurich, he had been moved by the
activity of Pfistermeyer in the free territory between the towns
of Zurich and Aargau (the present canton of Aargau) to take up
the task of refuting the Anabaptists. Pfistermeyer's preaching had
drawn large crowds. His views on tithes and interest had caused
the official ministers much discomfort. They appealed to Bullinger for a refutation of the Anabaptist position. Bullinger
began his book Von dem unverschämten Frevel in April 1530
and finished it toward the end of the year. It was printed the
next year in Zurich.

The book has four sections (books), in the form of dialogues
between an Anabaptist sympathizer, Simon, and the defender
of orthodoxy, Jojada. Two appendixes complete the work. In
the course of the discussion, Jojada convinces Simon of the cor-
rectness of the established doctrine. The argument is a popu-
larization of the problems and the orthodox solution to them.
Although not particularly fair in representing Anabaptist views,
it is moderate in tone. Bullinger deals with the problem of spirit
and letter, the nature of the ministry, the need for education
and a regular call, justification and sanctification, the possibility
of a sinless congregation and the dangerous assumptions involved
in it, the sleep of the soul, rebaptism, baptism of children, the
Christian and the magistracy—the oath, tithes, interest, usury,
and war; in short, with the whole catalogue of points of conflict
between the Anabaptists and the magisterial churchmen, espe-

cially as those points would stand out in the mind of a plain man trying to lead a sincere Christian life. Bullinger does not deny the more moderate Anabaptists a certain piety and sanctity of life, but denies "that this devotion of theirs is without blame, or is sincere and pure," for "they divide the church, where there is no need,"[40] and "stir up sedition and tumult, and do make every rascal knave minister of God's word."[41] His main charge against them is that they disrupt the church and offend the institution of Christ as well as all the martyrs and confessors of history. Thus the substance of his refutation is essentially moderate; and, although it is not his chief objection to them, he (like Kessler in the *Sabbata* [Ch. 6.2]) vividly describes the excesses of his opponents:

And whereas they be wholly given to such foul and detestable sensuality, they do interpret it to be the commandment of the Heavenly Father, persuading women and honest matrons that it is impossible for them to be partakers of the Kingdom of Heaven unless they do abominably prostitute and make common their own bodies to all men, since it is written, we must forsake and renounce all things that we love best, and that we ought to suffer all kinds of infamy or reproach for Christ's sake, besides that the publicans and harlots shall be preferred to the righteous in the Kingdom of Heaven.[42]

One of their doctrines is particularly obnoxious to Bullinger, namely,

That Christ did take away only original sin, affirming that they, who do fall again, after that they be once purified, and cleansed by the water of regeneration, shall not obtain daily remission of their sins.[43]

Somewhat inconsistently he accuses them also of the doctrine of the restoration (*apokatastasis*) of all men and of the demons as well, and mentions—

Anabaptists in Augsburg, in Basel, and in Moravia [an allusion to the spurious Nicolsburg articles], which did affirm that Christ was but a prophet, saying that the ungodly persons, which for their ungodliness were damned, and the devils also, should enjoy the heavenly bliss.[44]

Bullinger is especially concerned with their psychopannychism:

They say that the souls, after the death of the body (if they do depart

---

[40] From the English translation, *An Holesome Antidotus or Counter-Poysen against the pestylent heresye and secte of the Anabaptistes. . .*, translated by John Veron (London, 1548), 35, spelling modernized.
[41] *Ibid.*, 42.
[42] *Ibid.*, 25 f.
[43] *Ibid.*, 48–49.
[44] *Ibid.*, 24.

in faith), sleep in the bosom of Abraham, till the day of judgment, and that then, they enter into everlasting life.[45]

Considerable space is devoted to a refutation of the sleep of the soul, based in part upon Scriptural interpretations ("Christ proved that there was an everlasting life by his rising again"), but largely on Bullinger's philosophical view of the nature of the soul. Like Zwingli and the Fifth Lateran Council (Ch. 1.3.a), he holds that the soul as a spirit is liable to no bodily infirmities, neither to death, nor fatigue, nor sleep.[46]

The picture which Bullinger drew has strongly influenced the historian's idea of Anabaptism and the long traditional tendency to see in the Swiss Brethren the descendants of Thomas Müntzer and the Zwickau prophets.[47] The esteem which Bullinger enjoyed in England led to three translations of large sections of this work.[48] Sebastian Franck (Ch. 10.3.d) included extracts from it in his *Chronicle,* which appeared in September of 1531.

With Bullinger's literary consolidation of the Swiss Reformed opposition to Anabaptism, with the deaths of both Zwingli and Oecolampadius, and incidentally with the departures of Paracelsus and Servetus for Alsace, we have come to a natural halting point in the history of Anabaptism in its homeland.

We must now pursue its development transplanted from the Confederation, South Germany, and the Austrias, to Moravia.

---

[45] *Ibid.,* 199.

[46] *Ibid.,* 197 ff.

[47] Significantly, Bullinger himself did not suggest this origin for the Swiss Anabaptists until his later work, *Der Wiedertoufferen Ursprung,* 1560. This view had been frequently repeated, on Bullinger's authority, by subsequent historians. Cf. Harold S. Bender, "The Zwickau Prophets, Thomas Müntzer and the Anabaptists," *MQR,* XXVII (1953), 3–16 and below, Ch. 33.

[48] (1) The work cited above in n. 40; (2) *A most necessary and fruteful Dialogue, betweene ye seditious Libertin or rebel Anabaptist, and the true Christian . . .* (Worcester, 1551); (3) *A most sure and strong defence of the baptisme of children, against ye pestiferous secte of the Anabaptystes* (Worcester, 1551).

CHAPTER 9

RADICAL CHRISTIANITY IN THE KINGDOM OF BOHEMIA AND THE MARGRAVIATE OF MORAVIA, 1526–1529

The Slavic kingdom of Bohemia and the margraviate of Moravia had already undergone a national reformation in the fifteenth century accompanied by the full range of sectarian and spiritualizing tendencies.[1] The Unity of the Brethren (*Unitas Fratrum*), which had channeled the communitarian, pacifist impulses of rural and proletarian Hussitism since 1467, had itself, by 1500, polarized into a major and a minor party along discernible class lines. Thus when Swiss, South German, and Austrian Anabaptists penetrated the region as refugees, they found a religiously and ethnically checkered landscape opening before them.

Although the nobility and the majority of the population were Czechs, in the mountainous crescent that formed the borders with Silesia, Saxony, and Bavaria, traders, miners, and peasants of German speech preponderated. Several towns were largely built up by Germans, and there were various enclaves of German settlers throughout both the kingdom and the margraviate.

In the fifteenth century, the German-speaking population had remained unaffected by the enthusiasm of the Czechs for the Hussite reforms. Conversely, in the sixteenth century, it was primarily the indigenous Germans who responded to Lutheranism. Thus the outbreak of the Reformation in neighboring Saxony, beginning in 1517, and the immigration of Anabaptist refugees, beginning in 1526, threatened to upset the perilous religious equilibrium obtained at great cost after the ravages of the Hussite wars.

Indicative of the extraordinary fluidity of the religious situ-

---

[1] The most recent survey of Czech church history for our period is that of Rudolf Říčan, *Das Reich Gottes in den böhmischen Ländern*, translated from the Czech (Stuttgart, 1957), with a map. See also R. R. Betts, "The Social Revolution in Bohemia and Moravia in the Later Middle Ages," *Past and Present*, No. 2 (November, 1952), 24–31.

ation in the region was the synod convened in March 1526 by the Utraquist nobleman John Dubčanský. At his Moravian estate near Habrovany,[2] he was organizing a center of Protestant reform and was at that early date in possession of both Lutheran and Zwinglian works. He called the synod at Austerlitz (Slavkov) to unite the evangelical parties of Moravia and Bohemia, namely, the Utraquists, the two parties of the Unity, and the Lutherans. Among the Lutherans present was Oswald Glait of Nicolsburg (Mikulov), whose printed report in a sole surviving copy contains several articles agreed upon.[3] At the time of the synod, Glait was assistant minister of the newly organized Lutheran congregation (1524) under the protection of Leonard, Lord of Liechtenstein.[4] Glait's senior colleague was the Bavarian John Spittelmaier, assisted by the former provost of Olmütz (Olomouc), Martin Göschel, who had been driven from the cathedral there because of his evangelical sentiments.

In July of 1526, Balthasar Hubmaier arrived in Nicolsburg and converted both Pastor Glait and Lord Liechtenstein to Anabaptism. The town was well on its way to becoming a major center of the Radical Reformation. Henceforth, refugee Anabaptism, soon to divide into several factions; indigenous Hussitism, already divided into several churches and parties; Lutheranism and Catholicism, all formed a complicated patchwork of confessions as colorful and variegated as the manorial fields and meadows and the peasant plots of feudal Moravia itself.

Although many of the Anabaptist refugee colonists, such as Hubmaier and Glait, came from South Germany and Switzerland, most of the immigrants streamed in from Upper Austria and the Tyrol, the dark valleys of death and heroic deeds (Ch. 7.5). They were following the familiar roads and rivers that carried salt from Salzburg into Bohemia.

The opportunity for the spread of Anabaptism was much greater in the margraviate of Moravia than in the kingdom of Bohemia because the local nobility were much less amenable to control from Prague or Vienna. The provincial estates, jealous

---

[2] The main account of these Brethren is that of Otakar Odložilík, "Jednota bratří Habrovanských," *Český Časopis Historický*, XXIX (1923), 1–70, 201–364.

[3] *Handlung yetz den XIV tag Marcij dis XXVI jars, so zu Osterlitz in Merhern durch erforderte versammlung viler pfarrer und priesterschaften, auch etlicher des Adels und anderer, in Christlicher lieb und ainigkeyt besechehen und in syben artickeln beschlossen, mit sambt derselben artickel erklärung. I Cor. I.* The only known copy is in the National Library in Vienna. *ME*, II, 522.

[4] Jakob von Falke, *Geschichte der fürstlichen Häuser Liechtenstein* (Vienna, 1877), II, 43.

of their local autonomy and resentful of any aggressive interference from the outside, elected their own governor. There
were three main royal cities—Olmütz, the seat of the bishop of
Moravia; Brünn (Brno); and Znaim (Znojmo). Most of the
smaller towns, such as Nicolsburg, were centers of the large
manorial estates, where the local lords could act more or less
as they pleased. The lords, eager for diligent cultivation of their
estates and for industrious artisans in their hamlets, were responsible for the high degree of religious toleration in Moravia.

After the death of King Louis II of Bohemia and Hungary
in the battle of Mohács against the Turks in 1526, the new margrave of Moravia and king of Bohemia and of Hungary was the
Emperor's brother, Ferdinand (1503–1564), archduke of Austria
and resident in Vienna from 1521 on.

Ferdinand had been born in Alcalá, famous as the site of
Ximenes' brilliant humanistic university, and had been educated
in Flanders in the circle around Erasmus. He now had ample
opportunity in the government of his new kingdoms to show
that he had assimilated the sterner rather than the more humane
traits of Ximenes' tutelage, and that he was not favorable to
Erasmian moderation. Before his accession to the royal dignity,
he had already been vigorously and personally engaged in cleansing his Hapsburg archduchies of Upper and Lower Austria,
Tyrol, Styria, and Carinthia of all evangelical traits. He was well
acquainted with Hubmaier's activities in Waldshut in Hither
Austria. As king on the frontier of Christendom, concerned to
carry out his brother's imperial instructions, Ferdinand faced
the double challenge of warding off the infidel from the gates of
Vienna and of repressing the triple-headed monster of heresy
within his realms without so offending the Protestant princes of
the Empire that they would withhold their support from the defense of Vienna. He could channel his devout energies by spe-
cializing in the persecution of the Anabaptists, whom Lutherans,
Zwinglians, and Catholics alike regarded as subversive. He appointed a special commissioner (*Provos*) to hunt down Anabaptists throughout the Hapsburg realms (especially in Lower
Austria), the nobleman Dietrich von Hartitsch.

The Anabaptists of Moravia were not entirely beyond the
commissioner's reach, but Ferdinand often preferred to bypass
both the *Provos* and the *Landeshauptmann* and have his orders
carried through by the bishop of Olmütz. Before recounting the
story, however, we should look at the earlier dissenters from
Catholicism in Ferdinand's Slavic kingdom and margraviate.

A glance back at the Hussite schism and related sects is necessary for any complete coverage of the Radical Reformation.

The very existence alongside the Roman Church in 1526 of three Czech communions deriving directly or indirectly from John Hus facilitated the extension of the patterns of toleration to the more radical German-speaking Anabaptist and Italian anti-Trinitarian refugees in the same area. Moreover, there could not fail to be some interchange and mutual influence, despite the language barrier and ethnic antagonism between the Czechs and the German colonists of medieval and more recent times.

1. Utraquists and the Two Parties of the Unity of the Bohemian Brethren to 1526[5]

Communion in both kinds,[6] begun by Jacobellus of Stříbro in 1414, approved by John Hus at Constance in 1415, was in 1417 by the nationalized Czech University of Prague declared to be indispensable for salvation. The Czech national reform movement, it will be recalled, soon divided into two main parties.

The moderate Utraquists took their name from their stress upon Communion distributed to the laity as to the clergy *"sub utraque specie."* They recruited their strength among the nobility, the higher nationalist clergy (cf. Gallicanism), and the burghers of Prague, and were led by John Rokycana[7] (c. 1390–1471). The Radicals, the chiliastic and communistic Taborites, composed of peasants and lesser gentry, were led by the revolutionary Utraquist priest John Želivský. They looked forward to Christ's second coming in 1420. In that year they broke with the tradition of apostolic succession and elected their own bishop. With the failure of the expected parousia, like the Maccabeans long before them and like the Münsterites to come (Ch. 13), they became fighting saints. They supplemented their utraquist convictions with a complete religious and social program eschatologically grounded, taking their name from the hilltop encampment called Tabor (Judg. 4:6), where the forces of Issachar and Zebulon had once assembled preparatory to fighting the Canaanite commander Sisera. The Taborites were led in battle by the one-eyed squire John Žiška.[8]

Utraquists and Taborites had jointly signed in 1419 the Four

---

[5] For the late fifteenth-century development and for the early years of the Reformation Era, the most useful study of the radical trends is that of Peter Brock, *The Political and Social Doctrines of the Unity of the Czech Brethren* (The Hague, 1957). See also the biographical study of Otakar Odložilík, "Two Reformation Leaders of the Unitas Fratrum," *CH*, IX (1940).

[6] First served in St. Martin's in the Wall, Prague.

[7] Frederick G. Heymann, "John Rokycana—Church Reformer Between Hus and Luther," *CH*, XXVIII (1959), 3–43.

[8] Frederick G. Heymann, *John Ziska and the Hussite Revolution* (Princeton, 1956).

Articles of Prague (so designated by 1420), which demanded free preaching, Communion in both kinds, the cessation of temporal rule by the clergy, and the punishment of mortal sins committed by the clergy. Together the two Hussite parties fought fiercely against the Catholic crusaders headed by the Emperor Sigismund, who, after his coronation in Prague as king of Bohemia in 1420, was forced by Žiška to withdraw. The united Hussites, with their battle hymn, "Ye Warriors of God," were a terror to the crusaders. Poorly equipped peasants, armed with staves and flails, were ordinarily no match for cavalry; but Žiška developed the device of a mobile fortress by using wagons mounted with howitzers.

Within the radical Taborite community, two extremist religious spokesmen emerged. In 1420 the Picard (Beghard) priest[9] Martin Houska carried the Eucharistic theology of Jacobellus into sacramentarianism. Houska held that a Taborite priest should not put the wafer into the mouth of the communicant but should give a whole loaf to the congregation, asking the members to break and divide it among themselves. This alteration of the significance of the very elements for which the Hussites had been fighting was as repugnant to Žiška as to the still more conservative Utraquists; and he persecuted the "Picards" for undermining the Eucharistic basis of Hussite militancy.

Žiška was still more severe on the Adamites, a libertine sect led by Peter Kániš, who considered themselves free to behave as in Paradise before the Fall. Fifty of some three hundred Adamites banished from Tabor were burned at his command in 1421.

The fiercely puritanical Taborites, thus purified of libertinism and sacramentarianism, were still at odds with the Utraquists, whom Žiška besieged in Prague. It was John Rokycana, representing both the prince regent (Korybut of Lithuania) and the Utraquist masters of the Caroline University, who negotiated, under a flag of truce, a reconciliation with Žiška in 1424. That year Žiška died of the plague, whereupon his followers took as their name "the Orphaned."

In 1433 at the Council of Basel, Rokycana, as spokesman of moderate Czech religious nationalism, negotiated the conciliar approval of the Prague articles, revised as the Prague *Compactata*. Solemnly ratified in Bohemia and accepted by Emperor Sigismund, the *Compactata* were thenceforth the legal basis for the

---

[9] "Picard" is a deformation of the term "Beghard." F. M. Bartoš, "Picards et 'Picarti,'" *Bulletin de la Société d'histoire du Protestantisme français,* LXXX (1931), 465–486; LXXXI (1932), 8–28.

existence of a semiautonomous national church of the Czech people alongside the fully Roman minority, the principal mark of the national church being the use of the chalice in the Communion of the laity. The dissatisfied Orphaned Taborites, who had fallen out again with the Utraquists, were decisively defeated at Lipany (Böhmischbrod) in 1434.

Out of the disintegration of the Taborites as a military power, a new radical movement began to clarify its religious convictions and reconceive its role. The transformation of the defeated Taborites was directed by three leaders. The first was Wenceslas Koranda the Elder, initially close to Žiška in the belligerent chiliasm of the early period. The second was Nicholas of Pelhřimov, called the "little bishop" *(Biskupec)* because of his election as head of the Taborite clergy in 1420 in recognition of his great erudition and his important apologia for the movement. The third was Peter Payne, master of Oxford, sole survivor of the older Wycliffism in Bohemia, a capable diplomat who had represented the Orphaned Taborites at the Council of Basel.

A notable event in the development of the altered relations of the Utraquists and the chastened Taborites was the theological disputation, concerning the Eucharist, held at the synod of Kutná Hora (Kuttenberg) in 1443. The conservative Utraquists, led by Rokycana, maintained that Christ was *essentialiter* and *naturaliter*, that is, by substance and by nature in the Eucharistic elements. The Taborites, intent upon the anticlerical significance of lay Communion with the chalice, denied a physical presence of Christ in the Sacrament and spoke rather of a sacramental mode of his presence.

In his philosophical Eucharistic realism, Rokycana went, interestingly, much farther than the Romanists. He argued for the substantial or physical presence of Christ, first in the wine and then the bread, with two distinct intentions. As with the Romanists, Christ was present in his entirety in each element. But Rokycana argued also that Jesus would never have instituted the double action without a double purpose. Accordingly, Christ is substantially (1) in the wine, as blood washing away sin, and (2) in the bread, as a body enabling the believer to be united with him.[10] Rokycana, representing the aspirations of the conservative nationalists, the Czech lords, knights, and squires, and the burghers of Prague, had been elected archbishop of Prague by a special committee of the Bohemian diet, but because of his aberrant Eucharistic theology and his irregular election, his position was never confirmed by the pope. Hence he was never able to

[10] Heymann, "Rokycana," 23 f.

occupy the cathedral, on the castle side of the Moldau, which remained throughout that century and the next in the hands of the Romanist canons. Rokycana's procathedral was on the right bank in the old city, the famous chapel opposite the Týn, which was the great court of the merchants. Under his preaching, in which he drew upon the evangelical ideals of the earliest associates and forerunners of Hus, a loose fellowship of his "hearers" sprang up in and outside of Prague.

We cannot here rehearse the story of the Hussite civil wars during the ineffectual reigns of Albert of Austria (1437–1439) and his son Ladislas Posthumus (1439–1457), except to note the rise of the young nobleman George Poděbrady, who seized Prague in 1448, devoted himself to reconciling the Catholics and Utraquist squire Peter Chelčický (1379/1381–c. 1467). In his of Tabor in 1452. Thereupon he was generally regarded as the lawful administrator of the kingdom.[11]

Although he succeeded in bringing back Ladislas into Prague, the king died; and George himself was elected king (1459–1471). Since the Catholic liturgical order of coronation, dating from Charles IV, included the traditional privilege of the royal Communion in both kinds, Utraquists were content to regard their somewhat compromised ruler as a true Hussite, even though the coronation Mass was entirely in the hands of Romanists.

In this new situation with a Hussite king consecrated by Romanist clerics, with the Utraquist archbishop-elect still unable to occupy the cathedral within the shadow of the castle, and with the radical Taborites twice crushed, a new form of popular Hussitism was on the point of emerging, this time socially egalitarian, and utterly pacifistic. Waldensians, evangelical Taborites, fellowships made up of Rokycana's "hearers," and other brotherhoods were to be drawn into this inchoate Unity of the Brethren.

The spiritual father of the *Unitas Fratrum*[12] was the pacifistic Utraquist squire Peter Chelčický (1379/1381–c. 1467). In his *Net of Faith*, he deplored the excesses of the Emperor, of the pope, and, by implication, of even a Hussite king, who were like whales in their huge and unrestrained power, tearing the simple net of Peter the Fisherman and permitting the little people of Bohemia and other lands to escape salvation. His radical recon-

---

[11] See the forthcoming book of Otakar Odložilík, "The Hussite King."

[12] Erhard Peschke, *Die Theologie der Böhmischen Brüder in Ihrer Frühzeit,* I (Stuttgart, 1935); Matthew Spinka, "Peter Chelčický, The Spiritual Father of the Unitas Fratrum," *CH,* XII (1943), 1 ff.; Joseph T. Müller, *Geschichte der Böhmischen Brüder,* I (Herrnhut, 1922).

ception of Hussitism as an apostolic restitution attracted the favorable attention of John Rokycana, who in turn recommended Peter to a group of his devout followers, led by his nephew Gregory (d. 1474). It was, in fact, Rokycana who enabled them, when they came to form a religious community, to settle in Kunvald in 1458 on an estate of the Utraquist King George of Poděbrady. Calling themselves at first Brethren of Christ's Gospel, they drew together by visitation and correspondence several other similar brotherhoods. They negotiated for a merger with the Waldensians but were restrained from union with them because of their disappointment at the extent to which the apostolic ideal of poverty and the community of goods seemed to have been allowed to lapse among many of the Waldensian leaders.

By 1467 the brotherhood of Kunvald Brethren, under Brother Gregory's leadership, took their decisive step in their radical reconception of the Christian life, and at a synod at Lhotka (near Rychnov) organized as a church separate from the Utraquists (the majority of the Czech people) and the Romanists (both Czechs and Germans), calling themselves now the *Unitas (Jednota) Fratrum.* Selecting by lots three of their number to be priests, and choosing one of them, Matthew, as their bishop, they secured ordination from a local but unnamed Waldensian elder, who reordained the local priest Michael of Kunvald, sympathetic to the Brethren. The latter, with both a Roman and a Waldensian ordination, now consecrated Matthew bishop. Matthew, in turn, consecrated the two brethren already chosen for the new priesthood and reconsecrated Michael, now a priest of the Unity.

As we have already anticipated, this pious, pacifistic Unity went so far in their sectarian exclusiveness as to practice the rebaptism of all converts, not only from Roman Catholicism but also from Utraquism. In 1478[13] they defended their views before the Utraquist masters of the Caroline University. The Unity of the Brethren, completely separated from the state and the world, began on the threshold of the Reformation to break up into a burgher party disposed to make some accommodations to civic life, in order to be spared molestation and persecution from the Utraquists and Catholics and a rural party still strictly adherent to the ideals of Peter Chelčický and Brother Gregory.

By the edict of the synod of Brandýs in 1490 the inner council of the Unity, seeking to mitigate the pacifistic anarchism and community of goods of the earlier days, permitted members to remain in good standing even though they accepted civic offices

[13] Husa, *op. cit.,* 77, n. 242.

and in other ways responded to the demands of the state and town life. The rural rigorists, led by Brother Jacob Štěkenský and Brother Amos, resisted the edict, holding that for all its pious hedging it effectually nullified the testimony and the sacrifices of all the faithful in the years gone by. Bishop Matthew, siding somewhat reluctantly with the party of accommodation, was the target of their attacks as the betrayer of the tradition of which he should have been the most courageous custodian. Although the conservatives temporarily regained control of the inner council, at a synod in Rychnov in 1495 the concessions to life in civil society were reaffirmed.

In protest, Brother Jacob declared in an encyclical letter against Bishop Matthew and Brother John Klenovský, a prime mover in the Major (burgher) Party:

But now the Brethren say: Let us, therefore, open the gates of the fold in order to gather in more sheep. And when they have opened up the fold, the sheep that are already there run out and the wolves tear them to pieces. . . . The gates are God's commandments and the prohibitions of Christ the strait path and the narrow doorway. And whoever broadens these, . . . saying that a Brother may become an alderman and a judge, and takes oaths, is like unto a rogue and a thief who comes not in by the door.[14]

Jacob also complained that the leaders of the Unity no longer went about preaching the gospel as the apostles had, but "have settled in one place and concern themselves with their parsonages . . ., leading a peaceful existence."[15]

Despite a notably irenic parley between the spokesmen of the two sides at Chlumec on the river Cidlina, 23 May 1496, the two parties were well on their way to becoming two separate communions. The schism was consummated in 1500, when Jacob wavered and the remaining chief of the Minor Party, Amos, boldly proceeded to the ordination of a separate priesthood for his "Amosites." At the same time the Major Party was reconstituted by the election of a collegiate episcopacy of four elders to succeed Bishop Matthew. As an indication of the accumulated bitterness one must note with sorrow that the Amosites wrote in 1503 to King Ladislas II (1471–1516), suggesting that the recent constitutional changes within the Unity were seditious in intent. As a result of this denunciation of Brethren by Brethren the angered and alarmed Jagellon king was moved to persecute the Unity with renewed vigor, and several of the conservatives were burned.

[14] Brock, op. cit., 153.
[15] Ibid., 154.

For the rural dissenters the melancholy schism had come about because the townsmen among the Brethren would no longer accept all the precepts of Christ as renewed by Chelčický and Brother Gregory. For the main body of the Unity the issue was rather a matter of discipline and love. The Major Party would always have upheld the rural Brethren in their conscientious adherence to the rigorous standards of Chelčický and Brother Gregory, but they deplored the intolerance exhibited by the dissenters in their vilification of those members of the Unity who had acquired property and social responsibilities or been converted to the fellowship from the ranks of the gentry and lower nobility.

Although it was the rigoristic Amosites who were most like the Anabaptists and would in due course make overtures to them, we shall first round out our account by describing more fully the position of the main body of the Unity under their chief spokesman in the first quarter of the Reformation Era. Brother Luke (c. 1458–1528)[16] was a former Utraquist of Prague, a vigorous spokesman, who joined the Unity in 1482, before the schism. He reintroduced certain principles of sacramental theology derived from the thought of John Rokycana. In 1491 he and several others entered into contact with the Eastern Church, and in 1498 they visited Italian Waldensians (Ch. 21.1), ever seeking the ideal apostolic church.

In 1511 Brother Luke prepared a Latin defense of the position of the Unity for the king. It was published in Nuremberg and refuted in a Leipzig *Confutatio* by Jerome Dungersheim in 1514.

At first Luther's attitude toward the Brethren (*Pighardi*), whom he failed adequately to distinguish from the Waldensians, was hostile, like that of all orthodox Saxons, who on principle hated Czech heretics whether "marauding and bellicose" or pacifistic. He first referred to the Unity in his lectures on The Psalms in 1513, then again in his lectures on Romans in 1516, where he was arguing directly against Brother Luke.[17] Before noting Luther's change of attitude after the Leipzig disputation with Eck in 1519, we should form a picture of the thought of the Major Unity as an important formulation of sectarian theology

---

[16] The most recent study is that of Amadeo Molnár, "Bratr Lukáš," *Theologia Evangelica*, I (Prague, 1948). There is a good deal of fresh material by the same author in "Luc de Prague et les Vaudois d'Italie," *Bollettino della Società di Studi Valdesi*, LXX, No. 90 (1949), 40–64.

[17] S. Harrison Thompson, "Luther and Bohemia," *ARG*, XLIV (1953), 160–181.

in the Reformation Era and properly falling within the purview
of our account of the Radical Reformation.

It is noteworthy that in reacting against the tenacious Biblicism
and traditionalism of the Minor Unity, Luke heard the voice of
God, not in the written word, but in the life and order of the ongoing community as the bearer of the word. Luke stressed the
collective nature of the Christian search and answer: "Christ is
to be sought among the living, and not among the dead . . . or
on a dead page."[18] The faith of the church was for him the key
to the Scriptures, actualized in the communion of saints and
above the Scriptures. The church was nevertheless understood as
limited in its teachings by the Bible: "Christ has deposited the
entire truth in the . . . Holy Scripture, and confined the church
to it."[19] Thus, there were no doctrines or precepts stemming from
Chelčický or any other revered forebear which could not be
altered from time to time if a better understanding of Scripture
should so dictate. Luke's broad understanding of Christian
righteousness and the Christian responsibility in the world did
not, however, mean a relaxation of church discipline.

In Luke's scheme, the Word of God was God's substantial work
in Christ alone; but by extension it was also the word of Scripture, as the echo and the sign of the revelatory action. Christ was
present in the Bible "declaratively," but not "ministerially," or
in a "substantial" way; for Luke insisted against literalists near
and far on distinguishing "between the outer letter of the law . . .
and the inner truth which is comprised in it."[20] Moreover, since
faith comes from hearing, not from reading, in Luke's view, it
was only in the preaching of the church ministerially that the
Biblical Word assumed actuality. Preaching was not automatically
redemptive, however, for its success depended on the free activity of the Holy Spirit. Luke suspected that Luther's confidence
in the power of the preached word was close to magic.

The basic themes of Luke's Christology are given in his
unusual teaching about the *modi essendi Christi*,[21] which also
helps explain his doctrine of the Eucharist. The scheme goes
back to the three great Taborite theologians, whose Christology
he elaborated and perfected. According to Luke, Christ (1) was
"corporally" on earth and is glorified in heaven, (2) is omni-
present "virtually" in the government of the world, (3) is

---

[18] Molnár, "Lukáš," 11.
[19] *Ibid.*, 113.
[20] *Ibid.*, 82.
[21] *Ibid.*, 48.

"spiritually" present in the church of the faithful by his grace and the gift of the Spirit, and (4) is present in all the sacraments.

The Major Unity retained the seven medieval sacraments under the leadership of Luke, who could not agree with Luther that the sacraments, to be true, had to be *directly* instituted by Jesus Christ. Although the Brethren agreed with Rome as to the number of the sacraments, they differed in their interpretation. It was the redemptive act of Christ, not the ministerial sacrament of the church, which was "substantial." A sacrament as "ministerial" might not always be valid.

Luke, for example, defended anew in a book published in 1521 the practice of rebaptizing converts from Catholicism and the Utraquist Church. Baptism, for Luke, had a twofold purpose: (1) to testify to the new birth, and (2) to bring the candidate into the spiritual body of the church. As to infant baptism, he said that the children of the Brethren were being baptized only with a view to their future faith, which would be professed in the sacrament of confirmation.

As for the Eucharist, in Luke's sacramental theology the bread was Christ's natural and spiritual body in a spiritual manner. Luke separated the body from the rest of the person of Christ, insisting that since Scripture spoke only of the body, there was no question of the whole Christ being present, and, therefore, he rejected adoration of the elements. Luke did not explain how Christ's body, by itself, could be of salutary significance.

Luke preserved the traditional Unity view of a special sacerdotal order in the church, which, however, presupposed both the unique priesthood of Christ and the spiritual priesthood of all believers.

In his conception of penance, Luke made a distinction between penance and penitence, and stressed that the latter could not be reduced to specific moments in life, but was rather the posture of a Christian throughout his entire life. Sacramental penance was but a natural consequence of penitence. Although a Christian could find forgiveness without sacramental absolution in case of necessity, he should ordinarily make his confession before a priest as to an ambassador of Christ. The priest's power to "bind" and to "loose" was a part of the power of the keys, which to the Brethren was a cardinal possession of the church, by means of which the body of Christ was continually being purged and healed.

We have already anticipated Luther's sudden change of opinion toward the Major Unity. At the Leipzig disputation in 1519, where Luther had insisted that Christ and not the pope is the sole head of the communion of saints, Eck taunted him with being a Hussite, and on 5 July, Luther returned from the dinner recess, having read the minutes of the Council of Constance concerning Hus, and boldly declared that that council had erred. By 1520 he had read Hus's *De ecclesia* and presently had it printed, avowing his complete change of mind concerning the hated Hussites:

Without being aware of it, I have till now taught and held the whole doctrine of John Hus, and John Staupitz has taught the same things in ignorance. In short, we are all Hussites without knowing it, and therefore Paul and Augustine are literally Hussites.[22]

By now Luther was able to distinguish between the Utraquists, with whom he felt more affinity, and the Unity. Luther was still disconcerted by the practice of anabaptism among the Unity and by their apparent sacramentarianism in refusing to kneel before the Eucharistic element. His *Vom Anbeten des Sakraments des heiligen Leichnams Christi* (1523)[23] dealt with their interpretation of the divine presence in the sacrament of the altar, and he insisted, in connection with baptism, that it was the present faith of the church and not the intended resolution of the child at confirmation which made infant baptism valid.

Despite outstanding differences with the Magisterial Reformers (Luther and Zwingli), the Utraquists and the main body of the Unity were being considered by Luther in 1520 as essentially evangelical, i.e., solafideist, just as by 1530 the Swiss Reformers would so consider the Italian Waldensians (Ch. 21.1). After the death of Brother Luke, the Major Party would even abandon the practice of rebaptizing converts, lest they be confused with the Anabaptists.

Such, however, was not the attitude of the Minor Unity, the Amosites. These rigorists under Brother Amos, and after his death in 1522 under his successor, Brother John Kalenec, until the middle of the century, were quite favorably disposed toward the German communitarian Anabaptists settling among them; and, had they been more generally known, would not have been considered by either Luther or Zwingli as true Protestants.

The leading principles of the Amosites after the schism had been the virtues of suffering and poverty, obedience to the laws of Christ upon the Mount and to the precepts of Chelčický, and grateful acceptance of smallness as ever the mark of God's

---

[22] *Dr. Martin Luther's Briefwechsel,* edited by Ernst Enders (Calw/Stuttgart, 1887), II, 345.
[23] *WA,* XI, 431–456.

righteous remnant. Besides their pacifism and their refusal to take the civic oath or assume any magisterial office, the Amosites were also anti-Trinitarian under the continuing influence of Brother Matouš, the weaver, who as early as 1488[24] had been expelled from the Unity for denying the divinity of Christ and who had become closely associated with Jacob and Amos in the formative years of the Minor Party.

Kalenec, the successor of Amos in 1522, was a born Utraquist who had early come under the influence of Lutheranism and of a sectarian preacher, one Cvilda, a furrier. Kalenec himself was a cutler by trade, living outside the walls of Prague. When he became an Amosite, the Minor Unity took on, locally, new life. The Brethren met in his house in the Újezd district. Here he re-baptized and administered the Communion wine from a wooden chalice. Here his followers were relatively safe from probing constables under the control of the Utraquists.

At this time about three quarters of Prague was Utraquist, that is, most of "the old town" and "the new town" outside the old walls, situated on the right bank opposite the complex of convents, houses, the cathedral, and the castle on the high left bank, which always remained Romanist. Under the dissolute King Louis II (1516–1526) there had emerged a radical Utraquist party disgusted with this corrupt Catholic youth and much attracted by the prospects of a more thorough national reform under the Lutheran auspices. It was this party among the Utraquists (destined to be known as Neo-Utraquists) who had solemnly welcomed Thomas Müntzer as a Lutheran (Ch. 3.2) in June 1521 and opened to him the foremost preaching stations in the old and the new towns and lodged him for four months with the masters in the Collegium Carolinum in the old town.

When Müntzer left the masters to proclaim more boldly his radical eschatological and social convictions, he was not so likely to have found a hearing among the Brethren of the Major Unity, whose leaders, in any event, were not in Prague, as among the humble followers of Kalenec outside the walls with his associate John Roh.[25] Roh had been in Wittenberg and of course knew German. Müntzer's Prague Manifesto of November 1521 would surely have been heard by, or at least well known to, the Amosites in and around Prague, and it would have awakened in them the memory of the chiliastic Taborite eschatology of the heroic days. And, although as an ardent pacifist Kalenec would have understood the eschatological role of his followers, the righteous rem-

---

[24] Brock, *op. cit.*, 136.
[25] Husa, *op. cit.*, 77.

nant of a remnant in the latter days, somewhat as did John Hut after his conversion to pacifistic Anabaptism, still he would have been stirred by the trumpetings and the garish hues of Müntzer's apocalyptic vision and Manifesto. Kalenec soon sought to revive the revolutionary social ideals of Chelčický and Brother Gregory and even perhaps of the older Czech evangelical theologians before them.

When the conservative party among the Utraquists regained control of the city council, the sectaries suffered; and, along with an unnamed German-speaking journeyman painter, in December 1524, Kalenec was arrested, branded, and driven from the capital.

He established himself in Letovice in Moravia, where he gathered a congregation about him. It was apparently under his leadership that the Minor Unity adopted the wooden sword or staff as the symbol of their pacifism. As early as 1523, Brother Luke wrote contemptuously of their "angrily and poisonously condemning other people" by taking up the way of nonviolence so ostentatiously: "I highly disapprove of these vain Pharisees wandering around with staffs, who display their righteousness."[26]

In Moravia, Kalenec sought contacts with other sectaries such as the fifteenth-century Spiritualizers, the Nicholites; and, when the Anabaptists began to settle in Moravia, Kalenec wrote to them at once as follows: "We rejoice at the fact that you have condemned infant baptism, baptizing a second time in faith, and also that you have attained the equality of the First Kingdom, that is, of the Church, where none may say: This is mine."[27]

We now turn from the Minor and the Major Unity of the Brethren to these radical immigrants in Moravia, the Anabaptists from Switzerland, South Germany, and Austria.

2. Anabaptist Refugee Colonies in Moravia

a. Hubmaier, Anabaptist Patriarch of Nicolsburg. In some way word of the progress of the gospel in Moravia reached Balthasar Hubmaier in Zurich, because when he left in May of 1526, he turned his steps toward Nicolsburg, pausing briefly, as we saw (Ch. 7.2), in Augsburg. He was encouraged by an invitation from Lord Leonard of Liechtenstein himself.

There was, we remember, in Nicolsburg a German-speaking Lutheran parish. Hubmaier set out to transform it into an

---

[26] Brock, *op. cit.*, 253.
[27] *Ibid.*, 252. Brock is here translating from material supplied by Odložilík, "Habrovanských," *loc. cit.*, 357, where it is dated inferentially as of 1524. But it is undoubtedly after 1526. The reference is to Anabaptists who have come from "above," i.e., no doubt from the Alps or up the Danube.

Anabaptist congregation, as he had temporarily likewise converted to Anabaptism his Zwinglian parish in Waldshut. Hubmaier stayed in the home of Oswald Glait, who had returned from Dubčanský's Austerlitz synod (March), and in Glait's home finished the baptismal tract *Der uralten und neuen Lehrer Urteil, dass man die jungen Kinder nicht taufen soll* (July 1526). Hubmaier was accompanied by the Basel publisher Simprecht Sorg (Froschauer), who established himself there and printed Hubmaier's tracts.

To his new patron, Hubmaier dedicated two of his publications, playing on the name with Light of the world (*Liecht*) and Rock (*Stein*) upon which the true church was being built. Liechtenstein's town of Nicolsburg was by learned punning transformed into Nicopolis, which thus became not only the city of Christian victory but also "Emmaus" (Luke 24:13), the very place where the resurrected Christ first appeared to his disciples in the breaking of the Communion bread. (The identification of Emmaus and Nicopolis goes back to Josephus.)

In Nicolsburg, where most of his works were published, Hubmaier rounded out his Anabaptist theology, so different from that of other evangelical Anabaptists in respect to anthropology and the use of the sword that we should pause at this point to see it as a whole.

Hubmaier postulated a trichotomous man. He supposed his view Biblical, but it was actually Platonic, and it imparted a distinctive character to the whole of his theology as we assemble it from his numerous works. The Biblical starting point was I Thess. 5:23: "And I pray God your whole *spirit* and *soul* and *body* be preserved blameless unto the coming of our Lord Jesus Christ." Here and elsewhere Hubmaier found confirmation for his anthropology. More important still, by exploiting the Vulgate text for his purpose he insisted that the *spiritus* had, even after the Fall, remained *integer* (whole). Hubmaier could not be swerved from his doctrine of a tripartite man by the fact that in the Greek and even in the Vulgate (alternatively construed) the key word is *adverbially* applicable alike to soul, body, and spirit, instead of adjectively alone to *spiritus*. He further substantiated his view that man's highest faculty remained intact by pointing to I Cor. 2:15: "But he that is spiritual judgeth all things, yet he himself is judged of no man." On these two texts Hubmaier built up his peculiar doctrine of man and the Fall.

Each of the three levels of man's being has its own will. The spirit-will was nonparticipant in the primordial defection. The soul-will, symbolized by Adam, assented, to be sure, to the temptation of the flesh, symbolized by Eve (taken as a rib from the flesh of Adam), and the soul lost thereafter the capacity to distinguish between good and evil. The body, completely corrupted by the Fall, thereafter carried the morally witless soul about as a hapless prisoner and forced accomplice of its deeds.

Salvation from this plight consists in the restoration to the soul of the capacity to distinguish good from evil in order that the soul, thus empowered, can throw its weight with the spirit against the body. The saving word is the gospel of Christ, which restores the believer to the condition of Paradise before the Fall within the disciplined community of grace, the gathered church of the regenerate:

Enlightened by the Holy Spirit (the soul) now again comes to know what is good and evil. It has recovered its lost freedom. It can now freely and willingly be obedient to the spirit and can will and choose the good, just as well as though it were in Paradise, and it can reject and flee from evil. So now, the soul, after restoration, is whole, through the sent Word, and is truly made free. Now it can choose and do good . . . since it can command the flesh, tame it, dominate it, to such an extent that it must make it go against its own nature even into the fire with the spirit and the soul, for the sake of the name of Christ.[28]

Hubmaier held that regenerate man had a capacity which Adam did not have before the eating of the apple, namely, through Christ the knowledge of good and evil. To be of the church was in this respect better than to have been in Paradise. Hubmaier, emphasizing the incarnation of the Son of God as the Second Adam,[29] defined faith as the saving assent to this good news.

Hubmaier not only placed the cause of the original defection of man in his will rather than in the flesh,[30] but he also sharply distinguished in God himself between the absolute will (*voluntas* or *potestas absoluta*) and the revealed will (*revelata* or *ordinata*).[31] The former being inscrutable, Hubmaier found security in the revealed will, as caught (*gefangen*) and bound (*gebunden*) and upon which a system of salvation could be confidently erected; for Christ, the revealed will of God, possessed the two keys whereby the believer is admitted to the church of the redeemed

---

[28] *On Free Will,* translated in *SAW,* 126.

[29] Only once does Hubmaier mention the atonement. This is confirmed by Carl Sachsse, *Balthasar Hubmaier als Theologe,* Neue Studien zur Geschichte der Theologie und der Kirche, XX (1914), 173.

[30] Sachsse, *op. cit.,* 179.

[31] *Ibid.,* 132

by baptism and locked out by the ban. Christ bestowed them upon the apostles and thence upon the whole church,[32] outside of which there is no salvation:

Again, whomever the Church binds and casts out of her assembly on earth, he is bound before God in heaven and excluded from the catholic Christian Church (out of which is no salvation), since Christ himself while he was yet on earth, hung both keys at her side, giving them to her alone, his spouse and beloved bride.[33]

Entry into the church is effected through the portal unlocked by baptism, through which the believer gains admittance to Noah's ark above the floods of this world's sin.[34] In *Eine Form zu taufen in Wasser die im Glauben Unterrichteten*, 1527, dedicated to the same lord, John Dubčanský, who convened the inter-confessional evangelical synod in Austerlitz, Hubmaier describes the actual practice in Nicolsburg with instruction in the law, the gospel, doctrine, and the exercise of prayer, which in due course is followed by the baptismal vows, baptism, the laying on of hands, and reception into membership. Believers' baptism is Christ's baptism, as distinguished from that of John, which was unto repentance only. Christ's baptism ensures forgiveness, for by it one is admitted to the fellowship of his church, vows obedience to his commandments, and submits ever thereafter to the discipline of the brethren:

Hereby also the recipient of baptism is externally marked, inscribed, and incorporated into the fellowship of the Church, according to the ordinance of Christ. Publicly and orally he vows to God, by the strength of God the Father, Son, and Holy Spirit, that he will hence-forth believe and live according to the divine word, and in case he should be negligent, that he will receive brotherly admonition, according to the order of Christ in Matt., ch. 18. Such are the genuine baptismal vows, which we have lost for a thousand years, Satan meanwhile crowding in with his monastic and priestly vows, and putting them in place of the holy.[35]

The discipline of the ban, the second key, is the power to banish from the new Paradise. Hubmaier wrote about this first in Waldshut and reprinted the work in Nicolsburg, *Von der brüderlichen Strafe*, 1527, wherein he distinguished the administration of churchly discipline for gross and for inward sins.

---

[32] Christ will use the keys again himself at the Last Judgment and give them back to God. Sachsse, *op. cit.*, 190.

[33] Article X, *Twelve Articles:* Vedder, *op. cit.*, 135.

[34] *Ground and Reason:* Vedder, *op. cit.*, 206.

[35] *Table of Christian Doctrine*, No. 11: Vedder, *op. cit.*, 202. *Vom Touff*, cap. 2; Mau, *op. cit.*, 95.

He carried his thinking on the ban farther in *Vom christlichen Bann,* 1527, stressing the fact that shunning the excommunicated should be prompted not by hatred but by love and the ardent hope that by public repentance the banned might be readmitted to the fellowship. Mutual fortification of the brethren was secured, not only through brotherly surveillance, but also through the Lord's Supper.

Ever distinguishing his view from that of Zwingli,[36] Hubmaier had early stated that, as believers' baptism is a pledge to Christ, so the Supper is a mutual pledge, one to another: "In baptism one pledges himself to God, in the Supper to his neighbor, to offer body and blood in his stead, as Christ for us."[37] In contrasting the roles of the two sacraments as co-ordinate bonds or covenants, Baptism was deepened to embrace the appropriation of Christ's redeeming work through death and resurrection with him to a new life, and the Supper was freed to become the rite of Communion of like believers, one with another, which it could not so readily become in the pedobaptist reforms.

From his base in Nicolsburg, Hubmaier felt commissioned to weld together the large but disparate congregation of indigenous former Lutherans and of Anabaptist refugees. And with the hope too of winning over the local Utraquists and Brethren of the Unity, Hubmaier developed a somewhat elaborate Communion service. In two booklets, *Ein einfältiger Unterricht* (1526) and *Form for the Celebration of the Lord's Supper* (1527),[38] he restated his Eucharistic theology and described the institution as observed in Nicolsburg. It is of interest that he dedicated the latter to Lord Burian of Konice, in whose house Müntzer presumably stayed during his last three months in Prague.

In the first work Hubmaier reproached Zwingli for accepting Hoen's tropological interpretation of *est* as *significat,* giving his own special sense of *est* as a reference to the crucified body. "This is my body," must be taken to mean, "This bread is the body of Christ that was crucified." But, of course, it was not bread which was crucified. Therefore the "bread" referred to must be the body of Christ not in reality but in remembrance; and indeed the words "in remembrance of me" do qualify all the preceding words. Hence the breaking, distributing, and eating of the bread

---

[36] Vedder, *op. cit.,* 209 f., says that Hubmaier, out of rivalry, is making distinctions without a difference, but there seems to be much more than scholastic vanity involved.

[37] Hubmaier to Oecolampadius, 16 January 1525; *ZW,* II, i, 338; Vedder, *op. cit.,* 108. We have already quoted from the baptismal section of this letter in Ch. 6.3 at n. 52.

[38] Translated by W. J. Mc Glothlin. See *SAW,* 287.

is not an action in relation to the body of Christ, but a remembrance of his Passion, an eating together in the faith that he who is now in heaven seated at the Father's right hand died for his followers. Hubmaier describes perhaps ideally what the observance was like in Nicolsburg after the purification of the congregation by exhortation and the occasional exercise of the ban.

It is not at this stage clear whether we should look upon Hubmaier's Eucharistic theology as a distinctive variant within the Radical Reformation or as simply an appropriation of the views of Carlstadt.

Although the New Testament church was constituted, according to Hubmaier, by believers' baptism, Hubmaier was not prepared either to claim that his Anabaptist conventicles were sinless, or that the pedobaptist churches were wholly false. He even recognized some validity in the Church of Rome. Like Zwingli, upon whom he was here dependent, but whose ecclesiastical dichotomy he revised, Hubmaier distinguished between the local church which might indeed err (even presumably when exercising the ban) and the universal church which could not err. Hence, especially in his final *Rechenschaft seines Glaubens* in twenty-four articles, he expressed a willingness to submit to a truly universal council. Nor was this mere expediency. It was in keeping with his conviction that the universally operative Holy Spirit, the divine which, according to his trichotomous scheme, moved freely in each redeemed person, would operate most effectively in a universal conclave where the divisiveness and partiality of fleshly wills could be offset by the dynamic presence of the Spirit of God in force.

Hubmaier's trichotomous anthropology was likewise instrumental in shaping his doctrine of the state, wherein he differed from most other Anabaptists, approaching Luther and Zwingli in his *On the Sword* (1527).[39] Since the Spirit- and Word-strengthened soul must still operate through the body and since, moreover, there are many merely nominal Christians or outright pagans who have not even this in their favor, the state is a necessary instrument, ordained indeed by God, a coercive force in the secular or unredeemed realm comparable to the ban in the punishment permitted in the Paradise restored, the covenantal church.

Moreover (and here he goes beyond Luther, agreeing more with Zwingli), Hubmaier asserts that the true Christian must support the state for his own good and for the good of others.

[39] The whole of his treatise, *Von dem Schwert*, 1527, is translated by Vedder, *op. cit.*, 275–310.

Hubmaier at Waldshut had been quite forward in taking his part in defense of the town. The magistrate, Hubmaier held, may be expressly Christian precisely in the manner of his discharging his office. If, for example, the magistrate puts to death justly without any hate or vindictiveness in his own heart, he is more than a magistrate: he is a *Christian* magistrate, fulfilling his God-ordained duty in this world, which must never, however, be identified with the Kingdom. Otherwise, Hubmaier remarks, a Christian would not pray that it come, in repeating the Lord's Prayer. That Hubmaier's countenancing of a just war and capital punishment was not an expedient accommodation to the advantageous position occupied by the Nicolsburg colony under the protection of the lords of Liechtenstein is evident from his conduct and pronouncements from the beginning of his career. For example, in *Von Ketzern und ihren Verbrennern* (Waldshut, 1525), he wrote: "The secular power rightly and properly puts to death the criminals who injure the bodies of the defenseless (Rom. 13:3 f.)."[40] He was, however, quite clear that church and state were two separate realms and deplored the confusion of them and the encroachment of the instruments of the one on the other, warning against the use of coercion in religion: "A Turk or heretic is not convinced by our act, either with the sword or with fire but only with patience and prayer; and so we should await with patience the judgment of God."[41]

It was in a series of discussions and disputations in Nicolsburg in the spring of 1527 that Hubmaier expressed himself most memorably on the rights and duties of the Christian magistrate and the Christian subject.

b. *The Nicolsburg Disputation of May 1527.* A major event in the history of Anabaptism was the arrival in Nicolsburg of the fiery apostle, John Hut. All of his career has been recounted in Ch. 7 except for this important episode.

Even before Hut's advent, the large, disparate community of Anabaptist refugee colonists under the protection of the lords of Liechtenstein was being divided into two camps on such issues as eschatology, the community of goods, and the role of the magistrates. In the conservative camp stood one rebaptized magistrate, the lord of Liechtenstein himself, and the two divines, J. Spittelmaier and Hubmaier. Outside the walled town with its castle, in the neighboring village of Bergen, was the camp of the radicals led by the one-eyed Swabian, Jacob Wiedemann, and Philip Jäger.

40 Vedder, *op. cit.,* 86.
41 *Von Ketzern,* 16: Vedder, *op. cit.,* 86.

The arrival of Hut completed the polarization of the refugee community in that he placed in an intensely eschatological framework the expendable role of the magistrate and the pre-eminence of agapetic communism in imitation of the Pentecostal community in Acts. He had been anticipating Christ's second advent three and one half years from the outbreak of the Peasants' War, namely, at the approaching Pentecost of 1528.[42] We have already dealt with Hut's eschatological Seven Articles, or Judgments, as they were developed by his Austrian disciples and as they constituted part of the agenda of the Martyrs' Synod of August 1527 (Ch. 7.6). We have also seen how other articles, tendentiously drawn up by opponents and ascribed either to him or to Hubmaier and called the "Nicolsburg articles," were used in the Augsburg trial against Hut (Ch. 7.6). Belatedly, we are now coming to the original Nicolsburg disputation itself and the momentous emergence of proto-Hutterite pacifistic communism as a consequence of these and associated disputes.

The collation of several chronicles and disparate court records yields a fairly coherent picture of what happened.[43]

When Hut arrived he found the Radicals under Wiedemann in Bergen congenial and supported them in the churchyard disputation on (war) taxes and the community of goods. The Bergen Radicals and their sympathizers in Nicolsburg, confirmed in their eschatological and communitarian leanings by the presence of Hut, brought it about that a major disputation was arranged, possibly in the presence of Lord Leonard of Liechtenstein, in the castle of Nicolsburg, with Glait, Spittelmaier, and Hubmaier on the conservative side.

One disagreement between Hubmaier and Hut related to the somewhat contradictory charge of the Radicals that Hubmaier baptized large numbers at their simple request, without individual examination, and on the other hand that he and the lords did not house and care for the refugees with true Christian magnanimity by adopting the principle of Christian sharing of all goods. But the main disagreement related to the use of the sword, the propriety of paying taxes for military purposes in defense of Christendom, and the role of a benevolent and even regenerate magistracy (such as was embodied in the lords of Liechtenstein)

---

[42] This is, for example, the assertion of George Nespitz, Schornbaum, *Bayern*, I (*QGT*, II), 188.

[43] Josef Beck, editor, *Die Geschichts-Bücher der Wiedertäufer in Oesterreich-Ungarn*, 49 ff., 70 ff. Hutterite *Chronicle*, edited by Zieglschmid, p. 49; the confessions of John Nadler, George Nespitz, *et al.*, Schornbaum, *Bayern*, I (*QGT*, II), 153, 184, etc.

with respect to the ushering in of the Last Judgment, the end of the world, Christ's second advent, and the setting up of his Kingdom.[44]

Hut pressed his pacifistic views with his wonted passion and as a consequence sounded to Hubmaier and the magistrates present alarmingly seditious in view of the asylum provided the Anabaptists by the rebaptized or at least devoutly evangelical lords and in view of the pressure from King Ferdinand on the Liechtensteins and other noblemen for financial and direct military support against the Turks.

In explaining Hut's pacifism, one is helped at this point by distinguishing at least four kinds of opposition to warfare in the Radical Reformation as a whole. There was the Erasmian prudential pacifism, which saw war as wanton and futile, with a truly just war as very rare and even then usually avoidable (Ch. 1.2.a). Of this view, Hubmaier was with modifications a spokesman at Nicolsburg. There was, secondly, the evangelical pacifism of conventicular separatism (Grebel) based upon Dominical counsels in the Gospels. Thirdly, there was the suffering pacifism which sought out in persecution and martyrdom from "worldly Christians" a confirmation of their elect faith. And, finally, there was the closely related provisional and suffering pacifism which, while accepting the daily cross including even death, stressed the eventual compensation or vindication in the quite bloody eschatological warfare of the saints as foreseen by the seer of The Revelation and other apocalyptists ancient and medieval.[45] It is not clear at this distance whether Hut represented at Nicolsburg the third or the fourth stress.

In either case Lord Liechtenstein, alarmed at what he heard or what was at once reported to him, forcibly detained Hut in the castle. Under the cover of darkness, from the window of the room where he was locked up, Hut was lowered by a friend over the tower wall in a net for snaring hares, and he escaped to meet his fate in Augsburg (Ch. 7.6).

The news that the great apostle had been imprisoned by the

[44] The so-called *Articles of Nicolsburg,* purporting to transcribe the substance of the disputation and incorporating a number of doctrinal items obnoxious to most Anabaptists, has proved to be a forgery originating perhaps in Augsburg in connection with the trial of Hut. See *ME,* III, 886–888, also Ch. 7 at n. 82.

[45] It very often happens, in the history of the Biblical people, from the Qumrân caves to the kingdom halls of Jehovah's Witnesses, that provisional pacifism becomes a settled way of life perpetuated through the generations, while the originally fiery hopes of a compensatory and divinely sanctioned belligerence die down and become sublimated.

princely members of the Anabaptist community aroused the people in an uproar against Lord Liechtenstein and Pastor Hubmaier. A great disputation was arranged in the *Spital* church next to the castle, and Hubmaier addressed a large and excited congregation on the propriety of a magistrate's using coercion and power under the restraints of a Christian conscience; and, as to the imminence of the Kingdom, he argued that Jesus himself had refused to countenance all attempts to reckon the times and seasons.

The Radicals were dissatisfied and presumably conferred once again in Bergen and bided their time. Moravian Anabaptism was on the point of its definitive schism. Before following the exodus of the secessionist communists to Austerlitz under Wiedemann, we must accompany Hubmaier to his martyrdom in Vienna.

c. The Martyrdom of Hubmaier. On 10 March 1528, less than nine months after Hubmaier signed the foreword of his book on the sword, growing out of the Nicolsburg disputation, he was put to death by the authority of Ferdinand in Vienna.

The surviving records of his arrest are contradictory.[46] Ferdinand had been elected margrave of Moravia in October 1526 and by July 1527 he had reached out to the new center of Anabaptist propaganda and demanded the arrest of Lord Liechtenstein's chaplain on the ground of his earlier sedition in Waldshut. Anabaptist Lord Liechtenstein may well have been surprised to learn that his ardent defender of the magisterial sword in the Nicolsburg disputation had once sought to attach Waldshut, through the instrumentality of the revolting peasantry, to the Swiss Confederation. Yet it is hard to imagine the rebaptized patron acquiescing in the learned chaplain's arrest. One account has Hubmaier actually forged to a wagon for the trip to Vienna to stand trial as a fugitive from Austrian justice. It is possible that for all his valor in defending the sword, he had actually made more concessions to the Radicals than Liechtenstein himself could countenance. Hubmaier's loyal and brave wife accompanied him.

At the first hearing in the prison in Vienna, his alleged treason at Waldshut bulked large.[47] He was then placed in Kreuzenstein castle while materials for his trial on his Waldshut activities were being assembled in the capital of Hither Austria (Ensisheim).

Though perhaps not originally specified in Ferdinand's demand to Lord Liechtenstein for the extradition of Hubmaier,

---

[46] Josef Beck, editor, *Die Geschichts-Bücher der Wiedertäufer,* 52 f.
[47] Ferdinand's letter of 22 July 1527, referring to the first hearing, is given in translation in Vedder, *op. cit.,* 222 f.

surely the charge of heresy played as important a role as that of sedition. In any event it occurred to Hubmaier that he might mitigate the wretchedness of his imprisonment by appealing to his old schoolmate, Dr. John Faber, vicar-general of the bishop of Constance, for a theological colloquium. Faber hastened to the castle, prepared to argue from the Scriptures alone (*sola scriptura*), and brought with him two other Catholics, one of them being at the time rector of the University of Vienna. The ensuing conversations were animated and protracted. One of the debates ended at two in the morning and was resumed at six! On many points, Hubmaier in his extremity could more easily make concessions to Catholic Faber than earlier in similar circumstances to Protestant Zwingli, for example, on the freedom of the will and the importance of good works. Other items, such as Mary's motherhood of God, the invocation of saints, the utility of fasts, all of which Hubmaier granted, suggest the kind of accommodation he could make in a Catholic context freed from the severities imposed by the formal Protestant principle of justification by faith alone. But on what he considered the essential Anabaptist points he stood firm, namely, on believers' baptism and the commemorative character of the Eucharist, although in respect to both he insisted on his being as far asunder from Hut "as heaven and hell." He of course stressed also his disagreement with Hut on the legitimacy of Christian government. On Baptism and the Eucharist, he expressed his readiness to defer to the next general council of the church.

Hubmaier then drew up on 3 January 1528 twenty-seven articles for the scrutiny of Ferdinand, *Eine Rechenschaft seines Glaubens*.[48] It was, of course, regarded by the Viennese authorities as an insufficient recantation. He was asked to work further on Baptism and the Mass.

At the final trial, treason at Waldshut and heresy at Nicolsburg were equally prominent. Although he confessed under torture to treasonable conduct in the Waldshut uprising, he did not abandon his principal evangelical convictions. As he was led forth for execution, his long-suffering wife, of whom it is recorded that "she was hardened in the same heresy, more constant than her husband," exhorted him to be courageous. Accompanied by troops and a large crowd, he kept up his spirits by repeating Biblical passages to himself. At the pile of fagots he cried out in the Swiss dialect:

---

[48] Printed by Johann Loserth, *Doctor Balthasar Hubmaier und die Anfänge der Wiedertäufer in Mähren* (Brünn, 1893) 176–180; translated in Vedder, *op. cit.*, 230–235.

O gracious God, forgive my sins in my great torment. O Father, I give thee thanks that thou wilt take me out of this vale of tears. With joy I desire to die and come to thee, O Lamb, that takest away the sins of the world!

As his clothes were stripped from him, he declared he would gladly leave them with his body as, mindful in this anguished moment of his own theory of the wills of the body, of the soul, and of the spirit, he repeated in Latin the words of Jesus: *"In manus tuas, Domine, commendo spiritum meum."*[49] When sulphur and gunpowder were rubbed into his hair and long beard, he imploringly cried: "Oh, salt me well, salt me well!" As they took flame, his last word was the ejaculation: "O Jesus, Jesus!"[50] His wife, a few days later, was thrown into the Danube with a stone tied about her neck. By fellow believers they were, of course, regarded as martyrs. To defend the judicial action taken against them, Dr. Faber published at once his explanatory *Ursache, warum der Wiedertäufer Patron und erster Anfänger . . . verbrennt sei.*

One month after Hubmaier's execution in Vienna, Ferdinand ordered the burning, 10 April 1528, of three Anabaptists in Brünn, of whom one was, significantly, a Slav, John Čižek (possibly a convert from the Minor Unity).

In Nicolsburg itself, the stricken Anabaptist community could not rally from the loss of its pastor-theologian, the failure of Lord Liechtenstein to protect him, and the concurrent defection of those who in the great disputation on the sword had opposed Hubmaier and Lord Liechtenstein. Remnants of the Nicolsburgers were absorbed by the later Sabbatarians. We turn to those whom Hubmaier's pastoral colleague John Spittelmaier had dubbed the *Stäbler* (men of the staff) in allusion, no doubt, to their having adopted as their symbol the staves carried by the Brethren of the Minor Unity.[51]

d. *The First Anabaptist Communitarians: Austerlitz 1528.* Some time before the Nicolsburg disputation between Hubmaier and Hut, the determined group of whom Hut was only temporarily the spokesman, led by Jacob Wiedemann and Philip Jäger (also called Weber), had in and around Nicolsburg withdrawn from the pastoral oversight of Hubmaier and Spittelmaier to form their own separatist congregation, completely pacifistic

---

[49] These were the same words used by the first Zurich martyr, Felix Mantz. On the trichotomous anthropology of Hubmaier, see above at n. 28.
[50] The final scene is somewhat more fully recounted in Vedder, *op. cit.*, 242–244.
[51] Brock, *op. cit.*, 253. For Čižek, see Ch. 10, n. 76.

and communitarian. At least once after the arrest and departure of Hubmaier there was a formal disputation between Spittelmaier and the two more radical leaders. It is possible that they differed also from Spittelmaier (and Hubmaier) on the theology and practice of baptism, as well as on eschatology, communism, and the sword.[52] Their emergent communism on the pattern of Acts seems, in fact, to have grown out of the conception of baptism as a life of suffering as well as to have been at first eschatologically motivated. The exigencies of the situation also obviously called for mutual aid.

Lord Liechtenstein, desiring uniformity of religion on the estates under his control and unwilling to countenance a completely pacifistic program in the church of which he himself was a baptized member, reluctantly asked the dissidents to leave, after talking through the whole problem of faith and social order with them and permitting them to remain on until the worst of the winter was over. The Hutterite *Chronicle* describes the sequel of the last parley, in effect the beginnings of Anabaptist communism:

Therefore they sought to sell their possessions. Some did sell, but the others left them standing so, and they departed with one another from thence. Whatever remained of theirs the lords of Liechtenstein did send after them. And so from Nicolsburg, Bergen, and thereabouts there gathered about two hundred persons without [counting] the children before the town [Nicolsburg]. Certain persons came out . . . and wept from great compassion with them, but others argued. . . . Then they got themselves up, and went out and pitched . . . in a desolate village[53] and abode there one day and one night, taking counsel together in the Lord concerning their present necessity, and ordained (*geordnet*) ministers for their temporal necessities (*dienner in der Zeitlichenn Notdurfft*). . . . At that time these men spread out a cloak before the people, and every man did lay his substance down upon it, with a willing heart and without constraint, for the sustenance of those in necessity, according to the doctrine of the prophets and apostles [Isa. 23:18; Acts, chs. 2; 4; 5].[54]

The sanction here of Isaiah is all the more interesting for its persistence in the record well after the original eschatological ardor prompting the exodus had cooled. The reference is to the destruction of Tyre "after seventy years of harlotry" and the sharing of her stores among "those who dwell before the Lord."

---

[52] See Hubmaier's *Rechenschaft,* articles 14 and 25: Loserth, *Hubmaier,* 177, 179; Vedder, *op. cit.,* 232 f.
[53] In Bogenitz (Purmanice), which had been desolate since 1450.
[54] Zieglschmid, *Chronik,* 86 f.

John Hut, their fiery spokesman against the *Schwertler* (men of the sword) at the Nicolsburg disputation, had apparently preached that Christ would usher in his Kingdom during the approaching Pentecost that spring and had in this pitch of eschatological excitement exhorted them "to sell house and goods."[55]

In the meantime Lord Liechtenstein had become remorseful about his decision and rode after them with several of his retainers and spoke to them, asking why they had departed, and insisting that they might after all have remained in Nicolsburg. Thereupon they asked why he had not let them remain. They restated their pacifist convictions, the *Chronicle* reports, declaring that they "had not done it of rashness, but alone out of the fear of God, yea for the sake of their hearts and consciences, which did testify against his brethren (the *Schwertler*) and against his preachers' doctrine and life," and specifying that they objected to the way Lord Liechtenstein "and his brethren" had resisted by force Ferdinand's special commissioner against Anabaptists (*Provos*), a defensive action, "to which his preachers had spurred him."

As they departed, Lord Liechtenstein rode with them a way as escort, giving them drink and freeing them of tolls. They spent the following night by a hermit's hut until the breakfast hour, seeking carts so that their sick and the children might be carried. They sent four men to Austerlitz, and besought the local lords, four brothers of Kaunitz, who already had a *Unitas* colony on their estates, to receive them and "to leave their conscience free and unhindered." They set forth certain articles, concerning war and war taxes. To all this the lords were willing to accede, adding enthusiastically "that even if their number were a thousand, they would yet receive them all." The noble brothers sent three wagons to them to help. When the company arrived in Austerlitz, the lords also gave them a desolate, burned-out courtyard as temporary shelter. By that time they had been three weeks under the open sky. The lords and townspeople, welcoming these sturdy colonists, showed them many favors, offering even to help them build houses on the Hare Market, giving them wood as necessity required, and pronouncing them free of all services, usury, taxes, etc., for six years.

In the course of the year, the colony received Tyrolese and other refugees, who rejoiced with them in the hope that the

---

[55] Hubmaier, *Rechenschaft,* article 14. Hubmaier adds: "Leave wife and child," but his reference was to Hut's general theme as an itinerant evangelist, himself paraphrasing Jesus in Matthew.

wastelands of Moravia would blossom like the rose (Isa. 35:1), that the woman (the true church) fleeing into the wilderness to escape the clutches of the dragon (Rev. 12:6) would soon be vindicated in the providence of God. The newcomers apparently brought with them a communal order which had been worked out for the Rattenberg Anabaptists by one of two priestly converts active in the Inn Valley, either John Schlaffer or, more probably, Leonard Schiemer (Ch. 7.5).[56]

Seven- or twelve-point church orders were common, as were also twelve-point commentaries on the Apostles' Creed, for example, the Twelve Articles of Hubmaier, the Twelve Articles of Schiemer himself, and later the Account (*Rechenschaft*) of Peter Riedemann. One version of the Rattenberg order of 1527 is copied out in the Hutterite *Chronicle* with the indication that it had become the constitution of the Austerlitz community in 1529.

The adopted twelve-point program may be called the primitive constitution of the proto-Hutterites. The communal order of 1529 brings out the unique feature of the Austrian Brethren who, under the impact of Hut's eschatology, stressed sharing of temporal goods somewhat more than did the Swiss Brethren. Article iv reads:

Every brother and sister should utterly devote himself to the community (*Gemain*), body and soul (*Leben*) in God, receive all gifts from God, [and] hold them in common (*gemain*) according to the practice of the first apostolic church (*Kirchen*) and community of Christ in order that the needy in the community might be sustained like the Christians in the time of the apostles.[57]

In the following article, communism is structured on the basis of a year's experience by the provision that the sharing is to be administered diligently by the elected *Diener der Notdurft*, and not individually. From the other articles of the primitive constitution one sees a group gathering often for worship "at least four or five times a week" (article ii), with two or three standing

[56] Robert Friedmann first identified the order in the *Chronicle* as Austrian in provenance, and in printing a translation of a fuller text than that available in the *Chronicle* as edited by Zieglschmid, assigned it to Schlaffer and dated it 1527; "The Oldest Church Discipline of the Anabaptists," *MQR* XXIX (1955), 162–166. Then, in his major article on Schiemer in *ME*, IV, 252–254, he reassigned it provisionally to Schiemer. The present writer, accepting the Austrian origin of the order, feels that its inclusion in the *Chronicle* would indicate also its status among the proto-Hutterites, who may indeed have adopted it from the more recent Tyrolese immigrants in 1529, as the chronicler Braitmichel says.

[57] Zieglschmid, *Chronik,* 84.

up in meeting to speak at once (discouraged therefrom in article vii), ever watching for the imminent advent of the Lord (article xii), confident that in the divine service God would "open to them his will" (article i), and prepared for his loving chastisements (article xi). It is clear also that, as with the apostolic Corinthians, the meals together might become unseemly (article x).

We shall next visit Wiedemann's communist colony at Austerlitz when we come in 1529 from the Tyrol in the company of Jacob Hutter, destined to reorganize the Austrian refugees and seceders from Nicolsburg on so firm a foundation that they would ever thereafter bear his name (Ch. 16). In the meantime we must take note of very important regional developments elsewhere in the Empire.

CHAPTER 10

SPEYER AND STRASSBURG, 1529: THE MAGISTERIAL
AND THE RADICAL REFORMATION IN A
REPRESENTATIVE URBAN REPUBLIC

We have now several times in our complicated narrative reached
the year 1529. It was in this year that John de Valdés left Spain
for Italy (Ch. 1.2.c) and that Caspar Schwenckfeld withdrew from
Silesia for Strassburg (Ch. 5.5). It was in this year that the last of
the original Zurich triumvirate, George Blaurock, was martyred
in the Tyrol. In the preceding chapter we followed the developments in Moravia to the same year, when Jacob Hutter, a kind
of heir of the Tyrolese mission of Blaurock, was on the point of
leading to Moravia his first band of Austrian-Tyrolese refugees.
In this same year Suleiman the Magnificent, victorious at Mohács
three years earlier, was besieging the Hapsburg capital of Vienna.
In this year also, the Magisterial Reformers, trying to find a
theological basis for a united Protestant front, convened in colloquy at Marburg, a crucial episode in the long and bitter
Eucharistic Controversy between the partisans of Luther and the
partisans of Zwingli.

In the present chapter, the year 1529 is important for the fact
that the Lutheran princes and municipal representatives, at the
very diet wherein they for the first time received the abiding
designation *Protestantes,* agreed with the Catholics, in the face of
the Turkish threat, to turn unitedly upon the eschatologically
pacifistic and anarchic Anabaptists. Old Believers and Lutherans,
activating a section of the Code of Justinian, together reinforced
earlier mandates to prosecute the Radical Reformers as at once
heretical and seditious.

In this same year, 1529, the magistrates of the imperial city
of Strassburg, by abolishing the Mass, officially joined the Reformation movement. For some time before this, the tolerant
town had been the asylum of the sorely persecuted Anabaptists,

Spiritualists, and Rationalists, "the city of hope"—to the great embarrassment of the principal municipal Reformer, Martin Bucer.

The bulk of the present chapter will be devoted to the sectarian history of this extraordinary urban republic to which, because of its irradiating power, we have already been obliged to make a number of anticipatory references. In bringing together in the same chapter the sectarian history of a representative imperial city and the religio-political deliberations of an imperial diet, and in dealing in the former somewhat more than elsewhere in our narrative with the niceties of the problems raised by the Radicals in the minds of the magistrates and the divines of that urban republic, we hope also to make clearer than hitherto what, on the level of local politics and ecclesiastical strategy, was in fact involved in the gradual differentiation between the Radical and the Magisterial Reformation.

As for the latter term, it will be recalled that for all their temperamental, theological, and environmental differences, Luther and Zwingli, as later Cranmer and Calvin, agreed in assigning to the evangelical magistrate, that is, to the king, the prince, or the town councilor, a distinctively Christian vocation. Although these four Magisterial Reformers and their allies and counterparts in other territories, like Bucer and the other parish preachers of Strassburg, in most cases altered their formulations in the course of their Reformation careers, and in any event differed among themselves, they were always at least firmly set against the radical program of the separatists; for the separatists on principle broke with that ancient and medieval conception of the *corpus christianum,* which, going back to Constantine, Theodosius, and Justinian, understood the church and the civil community as virtually coterminous and which hence construed schism as tantamount to sedition. Although the Magisterial Reformers, as we have said, varied in their pronouncements and in their actions from the bare insistence that the magistrate had the duty to defend the true faith all the way to a parliamentary (quasi-conciliar) enactment of the royal headship of a national church, they all held a common ground over against the bulk of the Radical Reformers in their double asseveration that a Christian might in good conscience discharge any of the necessary functions of the body politic, from tax collector to hangman, and that, correspondingly, the state thus manned had a duty to serve true religion. The Magisterial Reformers, to be sure, could not always agree where the exercise of magisterial authority should stop, whether at the drawbridge of ecclesiastical discipline, at the portal of doctrine, or merely at the threshold of conscience; but both they and also the magistrates themselves (who either pressed for such sanctions or who in other cases hesitatingly fulfilled the grave duties imposed upon them by the Protestant theory) were united in refusing either to strip the reforming states of their Christian sanctions or to deprive the Reformed churches of civic support.

It should be added that the classical Protestant (anticlerical) principle of solafideism and the correlative doctrine of the priesthood of all believers had given the evangelical layman a place alongside the partially declericalized divine, but that within the context of the Magisterial Reformation this doctrine of the lay priesthood had tended so to reinforce a late medieval laicism everywhere that it gave considerable theological color to the preeminence of civic magistrates as the principal laymen of the Reformed churches. In contrast, in the context of the Radical Reformation, such an assimilation of sociopolitical rank and function to correspondingly important roles in the community of faith was inadmissible in large measure because in almost all forms of separatist Christianity in the Reformation Era the Christian vocation of all civil functions that required the use of the sword either in penal coercion or in the maintenance of peace was denied on principle.

Nevertheless, despite the basic difference of orientation in respect to the state as between Reformers and Restitutionists, the line between the Radical and the Magisterial Reformation was seldom drawn with a single stroke. In Strassburg, perhaps more than in any other center, transitional figures abounded and in-between positions were long defended among divines and magistrates, independent burghers, and avowed separatists. We shall have occasion in Strassburg, as a kind of case history, to observe how the regent principle of Protestantism, namely, solafideism, for some time retarded the decisive implementation of the countervailing principle of ecclesiastico-political conformism, and how the Protestant stress on faith over works returned again and again to unsettle both the divines and the magistrates as, with an uneasy theological conscience, they tried to accommodate themselves to the tactics imposed upon them by circumstances. At the same time, we shall observe on the other side the intense eschatological expectancy of some of the Radicals. Among some there was a swiftly emerging neoapostolic authoritarianism in the growing stress on the government (provisional or eschatological) of the saints. These circumstances tended to give to the teeming and vociferous Strassburg community of Radicals the appearance of a veritable *imperium in imperio;* and, as such, it seemed to present a threat to an orderly urban republic.

With the puissant meekness of saints, the Radicals in Strassburg, as elsewhere in the Empire, with their fraternal solidarity and their extraordinary mobility and interrelatedness, seemed to embrace dissidents far beyond the local jurisdictions in an international movement of frightening momentum. Their *élan* unnerved the local magistracy even more than the irrational insouciance of martyr-Christians had affected a humane and dutiful governor of ancient Bithynia; for unlike Pliny the Younger, the Strassburg *Stettmeister* accepted the same Scriptures as the would-be martyrs and was as sensible as his critics to the possibility of divine, no less than imperial, chastisement for the dereliction of his Christian duty as he understood it.

By our placing in the context of the Magisterial Reformation in Strassburg the extraordinary number of personalities of the Radical Reformation who crowded into the same territory, notably in the year 1529, we shall here be able to take note of enough of the thought and the institutions of the magistrates and the divines to show the strains inherent in and between the two reformations which we have, for the purpose of our study, characterized as "magisterial" and "radical."

Accordingly, after discussing the patristic and imperial background of the Protestant consent to the decisive mandate against the separatists at the diet of Speyer (Ch. 10.1), we shall proceed to our account of the relations between the divines and the separatists in Strassburg to 1529 (Ch. 10.2), then to a biographical introduction of seven or eight major spokesmen of the Radical Reformation who converged on Strassburg, especially in the years 1529 and 1531 (Ch. 10.3), and finally, to the territorial synod of 1533 and the somewhat reluctant imposition of a magisterially enforced confession of faith and ecclesiastical ordinance upon the instinctively tolerant urban republic (Ch. 10.4).

1. The Diet of Speyer, 1529: The Magisterial vs. the Radical Reformation, 1522–1529

When the imperial diet convened in Speyer in the spring of 1529, the Catholic and imperial forces considered their strength sufficient to rescind the agreement reached at the diet in the same city in 1526, which had made provisional arrangements for the partisans of Luther, pending the decision of an ecumenical council. To this repudiation of an earlier accord, six evangelical princes and the representatives of fourteen South German cities protested on 19 April 1529, thereafter to be designated the "Protestants." For the moment, only Lutherans were involved, for they were willing to hold the sacramentarians in check (Ch. 5.3). Both Lutheran Protestants and Catholics could agree in making even more explicit than before the death penalty for the crime and heresy of rebaptizing.

Though there had been earlier local mandates, and in 1528 an imperial mandate, against the Anabaptists, that of the "Protestant" diet of Speyer is the most important; and in the tense religio-political context of this diet, its approbation by the Lutherans makes palpably clear the great difference between the Baptist and the Protestant traditions, though today their descendants often claim a common origin.

Charles's mandate of 23 April 1529 reads in part as follows:

Whereas it is ordered and provided in *common* [i.e., canon] *law* that no man, having once been baptized according to Christian order, shall let himself be baptized again or for the second time, nor shall he baptize any such, and especially is it forbidden in the *imperial law* to do such on pain of death; whereupon We therefore at the beginning of 1528 . . . earnestly entreated you altogether and especially as Roman Emperor, supreme advocate and guardian of our holy Christian faith, by Our public mandate, to exhort, to restrain, and to warn your subjects, relatives, and those who belong to you against the recently arisen, new error and sect of anabaptism and its capricious, seductive, and insurrectionary adherents by your [direct] command, by your learned Christian preachers from the pulpits and otherwise, also to remind them faithfully and earnestly of the penalty of the law in such a case, and especially of the great punishment of God . . . and to proceed against those who are discovered in such a vice and error, and not to be tardy therein: to the end that such evil be punished and that further nonsense and any extension thereof be prevented and warded off. Notwithstanding, we find daily that despite the cited common law and also Our mandate . . . , this old sect of anabaptism, condemned and forbidden many centuries ago, day by day makes greater inroads and is getting the upper hand. In order to prevent such evil and what may proceed from it, to preserve the peace and unity of the Holy Empire, as well as to dispel all dispute and doubt about the punishment for rebaptism . . . , We therefore renew the previous imperial law, as well as Our above-named imperial mandate, . . . that . . . every anabaptist and rebaptized man and woman of the age of reason shall be condemned and brought from natural life into death by fire, sword, and the like, according to the person, without proceeding by the inquisition of the spiritual judges; and let the same pseudo-preachers, instigators, vagabonds, and tumultuous inciters of the said vice of anabaptism, also whoever remains in it, and those who fall a second time, let them all by no means be shown mercy, but instead be dealt with on the power of this constitution and edict earnestly with punishment.[1]

The opposition to more than one baptism goes back, of course, to the ancient church with its formulation, "One Lord, one faith, one baptism" (Eph. 4:5). But in North Africa, Cyprian, whom the sixteenth-century Anabaptists readily cited, held that the baptismal action of schismatics or heretics was not a true baptism, not being an initiation into the true church; and he therefore defended what could be called rebaptism. The bishop of Rome opposed this view, holding that the validity of the baptismal action depended solely on the proper formula and intention; and his view of the sacrament as operative *ex opere operato* became standard. Cyprian's more sectarian view persisted, however, into the following century among the Donatists of North Africa, who, claiming to constitute the true catholic church, rebaptized all recruits from the imperially preferred or established church. It was against the recalcitrant Donatists that the emperors Honorius and Theodosius directed their rescript of 21 March 413, embodied thus in the Theodosian Code:

We trust that from fear of a most severe threat no person whatever has committed a crime from the time it was interdicted,[2] nevertheless, in order that men of depraved minds may abstain from unlawful acts even under duress, it is Our will that the regulation shall be renewed that, if after the time that the law was issued any person should be discovered to have rebaptized anyone who had been initiated into the mysteries of the Catholic sect, he shall suffer the penalty (*supplicium*) of the former statute (*statuti prioris*),[3] along with the person rebaptized, because he has committed a crime that must be expiated, provided, however, that the person so persuaded is capable of crime by reason of his age.[4]

The Theodosian Code,[5] although determining severe penalties for heresies, including confiscation of property, exile, deprivation of heirs, and corporal punishment, did not specify capital punishment for Donatist rebaptism.[6]

[1] Text translated from that in Bossert, *Württemberg* (*QGT*, I), 3 f. It was in the earlier mandate of 1528 that Charles identified common law with spiritual or canon law.

[2] Ancient reference uncertain.

[3] Ancient reference uncertain.

[4] "Ne Sanctum Baptisma Iteretur"; *The Theodosian Code, lib.* XVI, *tit.* vi, 6, translated by Clyde Pharr, *The Corpus of Roman Law*, I (Princeton, 1952).

[5] *Lib.* XVI, *tit.* v.

[6] G. G. Willis, *St. Augustine and the Donatist Controversy* (London, 1950), 129 f., agrees that the penalties against the Donatists, although severe, were not capital. Nor does William H. C. Frend, *The Donatist Church* (Oxford, 1952), 233–249, mention the death penalty for rebaptism.

The Justinianian Code, in reproducing the Theodosian rescript,[7] replaced the indefinite *supplicium statuti prioris* with the deadly but still equivocal *ultimum supplicium*. It was primarily against the dualistic Manichaeans, in part identified ideologically with the hostile Persian Empire, that the Roman codes insisted on the death penalty (*summum supplicium*). In the course of the Middle Ages, what was limited to the Manichaeans was extended by way of the Cathars to all heretics (*Cathari, Ketzer*).

Thus in the fullness of the Christian dispensation, Justinian, who was more severe than Theodosius, was in turn exceeded in hardness by Charles V, inured to Inquisition (Ch. 1.1)

From April 1529 the Anabaptists lived the life of the hunted; and even Christians who were not of their view could be conveniently labeled Anabaptists and thereby made subject to the mandate and its innumerable imperial and local sequels.[8] It is an anomaly of the Reformation Era that precisely the Protestants— who in the most important respects (except for their theological devotion to Augustine) were much more like the "nationalist," "puritan," and often bellicose schismatics of North Africa than were the pacifistic Anabaptists—turned out to be almost as zealous as the Catholics in applying the anti-Donatist laws against the Radical Reformation.

There were, to be sure, personal and regional differences in the implementation of the imperial mandate. In fact, there were Protestant and Catholic magistrates on almost every level of officialdom whose conscientious mitigation or even evasion of the stern orders of the state and the established churches ought to be considered as integral a part of the narrative of the Radical Reformation as the testimony of the baptist martyrs themselves. These exceptional divines and magistrates were all the more courageous in their humanity in that they shared neither the fierceness of the persecutors nor the pathetic folly (as they would have considered it) of the victims.

Many of the Magisterial Reformers indeed suffered on the rack of conscience. Theirs was a painful ecclesiastico-political dilemma. Despite their protestation of the principle of *sola scriptura*, in their stripping away of the scholastic accretions to the faith, they adhered uncritically to the creedal formulations of ancient *imperial* Christianity. Despite their enunciation of the principle of *sola fide*, they clutched all the more tenaciously at infant baptism in their effort to salvage from the decaying morass

[7] *Lib.* I, *tit.*, vi, 2.
[8] *ME*, III, 446–451, conveniently lists and dates all the mandates from 1525 to 1761.

of late medieval Catholicism those institutions and practices which they could regard as validly Catholic. In their attempt to reassemble from long papal neglect and exploitation the bewildered Christian flock, they naturally turned in their desperation to princely shepherds (*Notbischöfe*). To these magistrates the Reformation could be most readily commended if it purported to be at once Catholic and obedient to those placed by God in civil authority.

Of the Magisterial Reformers, John Brenz of the imperial city of Schwäbisch-Hall and Ambrose Blaurer (already encountered in Ch. 8.3) stand out as representative early critics of the imperial restoration of the death penalty against Anabaptism. It was specifically against the mandate of 1528 that Brenz published his widely reprinted and translated *Ob eine weltliche Obrigkeit mit göttlichem und billigem Rechte möge die Wiedertäufer durch Feuer oder Schwert vom Leben zu Tode richten*. It was directed to Melanchthon and argued that Theodosius had originally consented to threaten anabaptists with the death penalty only in his desperation to secure the support of the patriarch of Constantinople in the struggle against the Persians. Brenz urged prudential moderation and cleverly showed how the mandate could be used against monks for practicing the community of goods and against the Catholic clergy in general for not taking the civic oath and refusing to bear arms.[9]

If Brenz and a few other tolerant divines in the Magisterial Reformation stand out as literary opponents of the death penalty for heresy, and if the eight Swabian towns from Constance to Hall under the influence of Blaurer (Ch. 8.3) are notable for their rejection of the imperial mandate of Speyer, it is nevertheless the Alsatian city of Strassburg which was most unusual in fending off the application of the imperial mandate.

2. STRASSBURG, 1522–1529

Strassburg, with its creaking timber bridge, the only one across the Rhine, was a crossroads city of politics as it was of commerce and religion. A patrician revolt in the thirteenth century, followed by a revolt of the commoners in the fourteenth century, had completely wrested the control of the city from its prince-bishop, who was obliged to content himself with the fringes of his temporal bishopric. The core thereof had emerged as a pros-

---

[9] Brenz later became harsher in his judgment of the Anabaptists. His relationship to the Radical Reformation is substantially brought together with the literature in *ME*, I, 418-420.

perous and powerful urban republic, whose nobles and guildsmen
by 1482 (the adoption of the *Schwörbrief*) had hammered out a
constitution renowned for its efficiency despite the elaborate
precautions for checking and balancing the competing interests
of the various classes of society. The city, answerable to the
Emperor alone, had a reputation for judicial and penal moderation, summed up in the current saying: "He who would be
hanged anywhere else is simply driven from Strassburg by flogging." Strassburg also had, even in the Middle Ages, a reputation
for religious vitality, variety, and toleration, a trait which persisted into the Era of Reformation.

In recounting the sectarian history of this urban republic we
can be somewhat more attentive here than elsewhere to the role
of the magistrates and the established Reformers in order, in this
one selected area of the Empire, to have before us that kind of
institutional detail which will give sixteenth-century specificity
to the secondary theme of this chapter, the relationship between
church and state in the Radical Reformation. Although we shall
not overburden the sectarian narrative with constitutional details, content to refer in a general way to "the magistrates," we
should at least have before us at the outset an outline of what
constituted the magistracy (*Magistrat*) of Strassburg.[10]

The vital organs of the body politic of Strassburg were the
twenty guilds. These guilds or lodges were largely vocational,
as elsewhere, but more than in most other towns they were in
Strassburg fraternal and social in character, and were as often
named after the tavern where they habitually convened as after
the crafts and trades grouped in them. These twenty corporations
were directly represented by elected life members in the assembly
of the three hundred. The nobles, made up of the descendants
of medieval episcopal functionaries and castellans with town
houses and the right of citizenship, likewise convened in clubs,
eventually reduced to two quasi-political organizations roughly
comparable to the corporations. In the course of the Reformation even the weekly convocation of the parish clergy took on the
socio-political character of the corporations.

Annually the guildsmen elected twenty members of the city
council (*Rat*, senate); the nobles, ten. Besides the guildsmen's assembly of three hundred and the mixed council of thirty, there
were several lesser chambers, committees, or commissions, notably

---

[10] For the civil constitution of the city, Franklin Ford gives the best brief
rounded account, *Strasbourg in Transition* (Cambridge, 1958), ch. i. See also
Robert Kreider, "The Anabaptists and the Civil Authorities of Strasbourg,
1525–1555," *CH*, XXIV (1955), 99 f.

"the thirteen" and "the fifteen," and the combination of these two, which constituted the "twenty-one." The last was the most powerful of the subordinate commissions and also the largest. Through the addition of several specially designated commissioners, it actually had a dozen more members than its name warranted.

Above the popular assembly and the mixed council with its several subordinate but sometimes rival and countervailing commissions, there were two kinds of headship of the urban republic, again a constitutionalized transmutation of the basic conflict and compromise between nobles and commoners. The highest office was that of *Stettmeister,* held by four noblemen designated by their peers. Each ruled in turn for three months out of the year of office. Below this rotating, collegiate mayoralty was the city manager, the *Ammeister,* who was elected for a solid year by fellow guildsmen in the council. Since the single commoner *Ammeister* was closer to the city's internal affairs than the four noble *Stettmeisters,* who were quarterly taken up by ceremonial and diplomatic duties, he was the pivot of city politics; but he also had always to heed five other retired *Ammeisters,* who preserved the title as an honorific and merely awaited the expiration of the five years required by the constitution to be re-elected. In effect the office of *Ammeister* was also, over the years, tightly corporate.

Such was the complicated magistracy of Strassburg when, in February 1529, the city state officially declared itself for the Magisterial Reformation by abolishing the Mass.

The beginnings of Protestantism in Strassburg antedate this action by a decade. Matthew Zell (1477–1548) came from the rectorship of the University of Freiburg in 1518 to serve as pastor of the cathedral parish. He was won for the Reformation cause. He authorized the optional use of German in baptism and encouraged his assistant, Diebold Schwarz, to conduct the Mass in German and to administer Communion in both kinds for the first time in Strassburg in a semi-crypt of the cathedral, 16 February 1524. In the same year Zell married and was excommunicated by the bishop, who, from his palace at Saverne (Zabern), for the most part sustained friendlier relations with "his" city clergy than in any comparable situation elsewhere in the Empire. It was the magistracy which kept Zell in his position. The city was indeed in effect a partisan of the Magisterial Reformation when, on 24 August 1524, the magistrates took over the entire responsibility for the nomination, installation, and remuneration of the pastors of all seven of the city parishes.

As we shall see, Zell was open to some of the claims of the Radicals by reason of his natural humaneness, supported by his courageous and intuitive wife. The openness of his colleague Wolfgang Capito was, in contrast, fully as much theological as it was temperamental. Born in Hagenau, Capito (1478–1541) studied successively at the Universities of Pforzheim, Ingolstadt, and Freiburg to become a doctor in medicine, law, and theólogy. For a while he served as preacher in the cathedral in Basel and lecturer in Hebrew at the university, becoming an acquaintance of Erasmus and a lifelong proponent of irenicism in theology and pacificism in politics. Though while in Basel he had contact with the ideas of Zwingli and Luther, it was not until after serving as chancellor under Archbishop Albert of Mainz that, in 1523, he visited Wittenberg and openly espoused the evangelical cause. In Strassburg he became that very year provost of the collegiate church of St. Thomas, and subsequently he removed to New St. Peter's as chief pastor. Capito's house until the death of his first wife in 1531 was the rendezvous of all kinds of dissenters. His wife's renowned table, along with his hospitality to people of varying religious convictions, made of their home a theological salon.

Martin Bucer (1491–1551), a former Dominican who had been tremendously impressed by Luther at Worms, came to St. Aurelia's in Strassburg from Weissenburg (present-day Wissembourg), where he had founded a Lutheran congregation. He arrived in the same year as Capito (1523). Soon, by virtue of his great natural endowments and energy, he emerged from his new assignment at St. Thomas' as the leader and spokesman of the reforming clergy of the whole city.

We shall meet the other municipal reformers of Strassburg in the course of our narrative. We look now to the radicals, refugees and natives, crammed in the city and its outlying villages.[11]

The history of the Radical Reformation in Strassburg begins with the physician and lay preacher Karsthans Maurer[12] during the summer of 1522 when, in the alleys and among the booths

[11] For the history of Strassburg radicalism, see Gerbert, op. cit., Hulshof, op. cit., and Timotheus W. Roehrich, "Zur Geschichte der strassburgischen Wiedertäufer in den Jahren 1527 bis 1543," Zeitschrift für die historische Theologie, XXX (1860), 3–121. Of the projected three volumes of Alsatian Täufer-Akten, I have been able to use Elsass, I: Stadt Strassburg 1522–1532, edited by Manfred Krebs and Jean Rott (henceforth: Elsass, I [QGT, VII]), and Elsass, II: Stadt Strassburg 1533–1535 (henceforth: Elsass, II [QGT, VIII]) (Gütersloh, 1959 and 1960).

[12] Krebs and Rott, Elsass, I (QGT, VII), Nos. 1–4, and for his life, p. 1, n. 3.

and small shops at the base of the cathedral, he spoke out against the sacraments, the hierarchy, and the magistrates, and in favor of the ideals of the Bundschuh.[13]

The most unusual and distinctive figure in the Radical Reformation in Alsace was the lay preacher and peasant leader Clement Ziegler.[14] Ziegler was a member of the guild of gardeners, which included also the shepherds and day laborers. The largest corporation, with six hundred members, and the most proletarian, it met in three sections.

During the great flood of 1524, Ziegler was miraculously saved from drowning, and, in allusion to Ps. 18:16, he considered himself drawn "out of many waters" to proclaim publicly the gospel as he had been coming to express it among "the Brethren" in the Bible-study meetings of his guild.

His first published tract was on idolatry, *Ein kurzes Register*,[15] published in June 1524. Bringing together the Biblical passages against images, he went beyond Carlstadt (Ch. 3.1) and Haetzer (Ch. 5.2.b) in closely interrelating iconoclasm and sacramentarianism in an eschatological setting. Pointing out that the observation of the Supper, according to Paul (I Cor. 11:26), was a proclamation of Christ's death till he come again, Ziegler argued that in the canon of the Mass the priest, contrariwise, was addressing himself to Christ or the exacting Father of Jesus Christ, and even then in a tongue foreign to the people to whom he turned his back in the officiation. Ziegler expressly linked the elimination of Eucharistic and iconographic idolatry with the reactivation of the world mission of the church to the heathen, and particularly to the Jews of the Latter Days, quoting Mal. 4:5 f.

The combined influence of the two Spiritualist sacramentarians, Ziegler and Carlstadt, brought about sporadic iconoclasm in late August and September 1524. Thereupon the magistrates, while condemning violence and private acts of vandalism, proceeded to the orderly removal of the more revered pictures and reliquaries from the cathedral and St. Aurelia's.[16]

Already by the summer of that year, 1524, Ziegler had given expression to the underlying Christological convictions that had prompted him to denounce iconographic and Eucharistic idola-

[13] *Ibid.*, No. 5.
[14] Rodolphe Peter, "Le maraîcher Clément Ziegler," *Revue d'Histoire et de Philosophie Religieuses*, XXXIV (1954), 255–282; Krebs and Rott, *Elsass*, I (*QGT*, VII), Nos. 6–8.
[15] *Elsass*, I, No. 6.
[16] *Ibid.*, p. 8, n. 3.

try in *Von der Vermählung Mariä und Josephs* and *Von der wahren Geniessung beider Leibs und Bluts Christi und von der Taufe*. These were followed at the end of the year and at the beginning of 1525 by a third sacramentarian tract, *Ein fast schönes Büchlein . . . von dem Leib und Blut Christi*.[17] In brief, Ziegler held that Christ was the first-born of Mary in the sense that the miraculously begotten of the Father "within the Trinity," having a body "before the foundations of the world," acquired also visible human flesh at the incarnation. It is the celestial body, said he, which should be stressed in the mission to "the Turks, Tartars, Greeks, Jews, and heathen," for the non-Christians always have direct access "through faith" to the heavenly Christ in his glorious body but may well be offended by the Catholic preoccupation with the Eucharistic flesh and the accompanying idolatries.[18] We shall have several occasions in this chapter to note the permeation of Ziegler's doctrine of the heavenly body of Christ through a large section of the radical community of Strassburg.

Ziegler also attacked the practice of infant baptism and the use of oil and chrism, possibly under the influence of Jacob Strauss of Eisenach, whose tract *Wider die simonische Taufe* of 1523 (Ch. 3.2) was reprinted in Strassburg in 1524.[19] Thus it was that in the spring or summer of 1524, Ziegler stressed the Marcan injunction (Mark 16:15) to preach the gospel to all creatures; and, appealing also to the liturgical sequence for Whitsuntide, *Veni sancte Spiritus*,[20] he set forth his deep conviction that proclamation should come first, then fire in the sense of love and the Holy Spirit, and only at the last the water as an outward sign of faith. As for children, he appealed to the Dominical injunction that the little ones should come unto him without baptism, for of such is the Kingdom. He pointed out the inconsistency of going against Jesus' words in two respects, namely, supposing that infants were damned without baptism and of baptizing without explicit faith and love in the baptizand.[21] Although Ziegler did not suggest rebaptism, he vigorously agitated for the elimination of oil, salt, the stone baptistery, and godparents.

---

[17] *Ibid.*, Nos. 7, 8, and 24.

[18] *Ibid.*, No. 24, p. 35.

[19] See extracts in *Elsass*, I, p. 18. For the general importance of Strauss, see Joachim Rogge, *Der Beitrag des Jacob Strauss zur frühen Reformationsgeschichte* (Berlin, 1957).

[20] Krebs and Rott, *Elsass*, I (*QGT*, VII), p. 15, line 20.

[21] *Ibid.*, p. 16, lines 7–20.

Besides his radical convictions in respect to images, the Mass, and baptism, Ziegler shared the evangelical aspirations of the peasants in the realm of social justice. Although remaining a convinced pacifist, he moved out of Strassburg and joined the peasant revolt.

Strassburg had been the focal point of the Upper Rhenish Bundschuh coming to its climax in 1517 (Ch. 4.1). The first protests in Alsace leading to the Great Peasants' War proper took place in the second half of April 1525. It was natural that the leading lay preacher of the gardeners' guild of Strassburg should take a prominent part in the demands for evangelical justice. It was under the immediate influence of a pamphlet by the Strassburg teacher and physician Otto Brunfels (Ch. 8.4.b), *Von dem Pfaffenzehnten CXLII Schlussreden* (1524), that Ziegler also preached against tithes and rents to the clerical holders of landed properties, appealing to Matt. 23:23, wherein Jesus rebuked the scribes and Pharisees for tithing mint, dill, and cummin and neglecting the weightier matters of the law.[22]

Filled with evangelical fervor and with concern for the realization of the social program of the uprisen peasants, Ziegler, in his *Eine fast schöne Auslegung des Vaterunser,* declared that just as Luther was considered "an instrument of God and a prophet," so Christ himself in these days would have enrolled as a Bundschuher.[23] That Ziegler was at the same time opposed to violence in the vindication of the rights of the peasants is shown in his commentary on "our daily bread" and "deliver us from evil," where he interpreted the sword in the building up of Jerusalem in the latter days as the sword of the spirit construed as the discernment of the Scriptures.

It was from February to April 1525 that Ziegler preached in various communities, urging the peasants to read the New Testament, and pointing out that Jesus was the friend and associate of the poor and the humble. When his gatherings were several times disbanded by force of arms, and when the peasants (including fellow members of the gardeners' guild of Strassburg) for their part also resorted to arms in the Alsatian phase of the Great Peasants' War, Ziegler himself withdrew. His last recorded sermon to the peasants was in April in a churchyard in the neighborhood of Schlettstadt (Sélestat).[24] His name and ideal lived on until the termination of the war in the Alsatian sector

[22] *Ibid.,* p. 32.
[23] *Ibid.,* No. 25, p. 36.
[24] *Ibid.,* No. 32; April 2.

in the peasant parole: "For the gospel, Christ, and Clement Ziegler!"[25]

A third Alsatian agitator of note was the obstreperous and eccentric weaver John Wolff, from nearby Benfeld, who predicted that the millennium would come at the stroke of midnight on Ascension Day, 1533. He espoused the prophetically social convictions of Ziegler and Karsthans but in a somewhat different accent. He excoriated the magisterial divines for turning the populace destructively and excitedly against mere externalities, i.e., in the abolition of the Mass, the removal of images, and the dissolution of cloisters, while all the time they for their part battened rich and strong, ate well, wore fine shoes, and insisted on being called doctor and master and did nothing to rid their cities and cantons of such gross wickedness as adultery, prostitution, usury, and unjust land rents and tithes. On 17 June 1526, Wolff in the cathedral raised his voice against the preacher Matthew Zell, charged him with spiritual lying, and demanded that he descend from the pulpit and cede his place that the Holy Spirit might be truly heard on the text before them.[26] Wolff, like Ziegler and Karsthans, was a vigorous antipedobaptist in his denunciation of the magisterial divines for perpetuating infant baptism and against God's word imposing on little children an engagement of which they were not capable.

The three antipedobaptists scanned the whole Reformation horizon in their denunciation. In Strassburg itself, as a matter of fact, several of the principal parish pastors were themselves theologically uneasy about infant baptism, particularly Capito and the Zells, Catherine as much as Matthew.

Tolerant and hospitable, Matthew Zell once declared, "He who accepts Christ as his Lord and Savior shall have a place at my table, and I will have a place with him in heaven." He was several times to declaim from the pulpit that he was not in agreement with the proposals gradually made by Bucer and others to control Anabaptism, for he was in favor of the Anabaptist and Spiritualist view that the government should not by coercion enforce its will in matters of faith.

Zell had found a faithful supporter of his benevolent ideals in his wife, Catherine. She made their home a haven for all those persecuted in the name of orthodoxy, concerning herself not at all with the particulars in which they differed from the local, reformed parishes. Waldensians, Spiritualists, and Ana-

[25] Pointed out in context by Peter in his section "L'Agitation dans la Guerre des Paysans," *loc. cit.*, 270–274.
[26] Krebs and Rott, *Elsass*, I (*QGT*, VII), Nos. 47, 53, 85.

baptists were welcome; for, as she said, "it is our duty to show love, service, and mercy to everyone; Christ our teacher taught us that." She was to survive her husband by a good many years, and to continue her merciful work after his death in accordance with his wish. Much later she would write a letter defending the Anabaptists:

Now as to the poor Anabaptists, . . . the authorities everywhere chase them as a hunter urges his dogs upon a wild boar or a rabbit. They, after all, confess Christ with us on the main things in which we differ from the Papacy. . . . Shall one then persecute them and Christ in them whom they confess with zeal, and many of them have confessed unto misery, prison, fire, and water? Rather give yourselves the blame that we in our life and teaching are the cause of their separating. . . . He who does evil, him shall the government punish, but it shall not compel and govern faith. It belongs to the heart and the conscience and not to the external man.[27]

Catherine Zell was a resourceful and courageous woman, with a deep sense of her Christian mission to be charitable in the realm of conflicting convictions.

Capito, of all the major Strassburg divines, was the closest in theology to the Spiritualists, the moderate Anabaptists, and the opponents of the Nicene formulation of the Trinity. In his *Kinderbericht* of 1527 he would be openly expressing his theological dissatisfaction with pedobaptism, reluctantly accepting it as a practical measure, neither proved nor forbidden by Scripture.

The simplification of the rite of Baptism had so far proceeded in Strassburg that it was everywhere conducted in German and denuded of its liturgical incrustations, and performed at the altar rather than at the baptistery while increased attention was being given to the need of preparing the infant for instruction in the covenant.[28]

After Zell and Capito, it was Bucer who was leading the way toward the evangelical reconception of baptism. Under the impact of the agitation of the lay preachers and with pressure from his two troubled colleagues, Bucer had been prompted by his own concern for the primacy of faith (solafideism) to speak forth in the name of the Strassburg divines in favor of modifications in respect to both baptism and the ban in *Grund und Ursache aus göttlicher Schrift*, published early in 1525.[29] Herein he maintained that pre-eminent in the Reformation in Strassburg was the recovery of the importance of faith and therewith the simplifi-

---

[27] Gerbert, *op. cit.*; cited in *ME*, IV, 1023.
[28] *Elsass,* I (*QGT*, VII), Nos. 26 and 34.
[29] *Ibid.,* No. 22; the preface is dated 26 December 1524.

cation of the baptismal rite. At the same time, precisely because water baptism was an outward form, he argued that it should be administered to children at a convenient time and accompanied by the parental promise to provide Christian nurture for the child and by the general disavowal of any redemptive efficacy in the rite alone. He was even prepared to let parents who, for conscience' sake, demurred postpone the rite for their children so long as they manifested love and a sense of solidarity with the Christian community at large. But Bucer was, of course, firmly set against separatism and rebaptism, precisely, he said, because a renewed baptism placed too high a value on an outward sign and because it implicitly disparaged the birthright membership of the majority. He pointed out, moreover, that the postponement of baptism would encourage boys and girls to grow up without counting themselves Christian, and justify any unseemly conduct on their part until such a time as they should choose to become pious and submit to baptism. As for the confession of sin which Ziegler and others had come to connect with believers' baptism, Bucer saw that the confession of one's sins should be the initial act at every divine service.

As for the ban, the other portal of the separatist conventicle, Bucer was beset by a consideration of which the sectaries could remain oblivious. For the Magisterial Reformers there was nothing inherently wrong in restoring the right of the major and the minor ban or excommunication to the whole church or parish. This was indeed the logic of the Protestant principle of the priesthood of all believers. But the evangelical magistrates themselves, after being liberated from the menace of the papal ban, were not disposed to encourage a new and locally more powerful clericalism or ecclesiaticism in their midst. Not on principle averse to the practice of moral self-discipline among the artisans in their sodalities, the magistrates were on the defensive whenever the Reformers, under pressure from the sectaries, proposed measures that would involve all classes in the exercise of ecclesiastical discipline.

As for the magisterial exercise of the ban in grievous cases, Bucer was not satisfied with the theory that would make of the magistrates the principal laymen of the church and as such qualified to discharge for the royal-priestly laity the more important disciplinary functions. A little bit later Bucer would take over from Oecolampadius the idea of church wardens (*Kirchenpfleger*) whom he thought he could assimilate to the elders of the apostolic church and charge with the discipline of the parish, including the ministers. According to this plan there would be three in each parish: two drawn from one of the magistracies, and one an elected private member of the local church. Although we are getting ahead in our narrative, by adding that three church wardens from each of the city's seven parishes would in due course constitute a powerful disciplinary board of twenty-one (1531), much more magisterial than ecclesiastical, we do so to indicate that even Bucer was at one time sensitive to the moderate Radicals on such matters as pedobaptism, moral reform, and the separation of the two swords.

It was, then, into a community where such moderate or open-hearted Reformers as Zell, Capito, and Bucer had the confidence of the magistrates, and where such spokesmen of radical reform as Ziegler and Wolff had eschewed force in the implementation of social and sacramental ideals, that radical evangelicals from other parts of the Empire came streaming.

Carlstadt was in Strassburg for a few days in October 1524. Hubmaier perhaps sojourned briefly in Strassburg and in any event had printed there his reply to Zwingli on baptism, *Von der christlichen Taufe der Gläubigen*,[30] in July 1525. Martin Cellarius, temporarily converted to the views of the Zwickau prophets, arrived in 1526. Though he never became an Anabaptist, he was sympathetic, and the following year he would be publishing his *De operibus Dei*, which departed from traditional Nicene language. William Reublin, Louis Haetzer, John Denck, Jacob Gross, and Michael Sattler all arrived in quick succession toward the end of 1526.

Denck, fleeing Augsburg (Ch. 7.3), was associated with Haetzer, who was staying with Capito—Hebraists all. Denck was associated also with Clement Ziegler. After a series of discussions and disputations, it will be recalled, Denck and Haetzer were expelled from Strassburg, and joined Jacob Kautz in Worms.

Michael Sattler's presence in Strassburg is notable for the relatively favorable impression he made on Capito and Bucer (Ch. 8.2) and for twenty theological principles he enunciated in a letter to these two divines, explaining why he could not longer remain in Strassburg.[31]

A large band of refugees came from St. Gall and Waldshut, headed by Jacob Gross, who also associated himself with Ziegler. Gross had been converted by Grebel and baptized by Hubmaier. Gross stood out against entering into military service with the peasants in league with his native Waldshut. He subsequently evangelized in several districts in Grüningen and Bern, convert-

[30] *Ibid.*, No. 3.
[31] *Ibid.*, No. 70.

ing John Pfistermeyer (Ch. 6.5). In his Strassburg hearing at the end of 1526 he stressed his Christian pacifism and the community of goods; and, although he acknowledged the local authority and declared himself ready to "stand watch, wear armor, and hold a pike in his hands," he would never use it to kill a fellow man.[32] He was later to leave for Augsburg, where he was seized with John Hut.

The first explicitly anti-Trinitarian speculation among the Radicals of Strassburg is documented in a letter written to Luther, 2 April 1527.[33] Shortly thereafter, Bucer warned Denck, Haetzer, and Kautz now active in Worms (Ch. 7.3) about their Anabaptist tenets, and he showed extended consternation with their explicit repudiation of the traditional doctrine of the atonement in their preoccupation with a suffering imitation of Christ and in their formulation of a doctrine of universal salvation to include the devil and his hosts.[34]

The fact that the "Nicolsburg articles" were known in Strassburg, possibly as early as the summer of 1527, in several versions, and ascribed to the "new sect of the garden preachers,"[35] shows that such tenets as the limited role of Christ as prophet and exemplar only, the universal salvation of even the devils, and the community of goods, were plausibly ascribed to some of the local Anabaptists. The first Strassburg anti-Trinitarians known by name—the sheathmaker Thomas Saltzmann and the cobbler Conrad Hess—were brought in for a hearing, c. 27 November 1527.[36] Although these Judaizers claimed to have some sympathy with the Anabaptists, they seem to have had no contact with either the circle around Ziegler, Denck, and Haetzer, or the group led provisionally by Gross and Sattler. The Judaizers would accept only the Pentateuch as divinely binding, denied the Trinity, insisted that there was but one God, and considered Jesus a false prophet who was rightly put to death. For this, Saltzmann was decapitated shortly before Christmas 1527.[37]

Already in July of this year, the first Strassburg mandate against Anabaptists had been formulated in exacerbation by the *Stettmeister*, Jacob Sturm.[38]

In September 1528, Pilgram Marpeck, destined to become a

[32] *Ibid.*, No. 67.
[33] *Ibid.*, No. 81.
[34] *Ibid.*, No. 86 (esp. pp. 105 ff.); No. 91, p. 121; No. 99, p. 127; etc.
[35] *Ibid.*, No. 116.
[36] *Ibid.*, Nos. 110, 111, 113, 114.
[37] *Ibid.*, No. 114.
[38] *Ibid.*, No. 92.

major spokesman of South German Anabaptism, arrived in Strassburg, where he acquired citizenship by joining the gardeners' guild.[39] Born in the Tyrol, in the mining town of Rattenberg, around 1495, educated in the Latin school, he was made a town councilor and municipal engineer. He had become interested in Lutheranism and had then fallen in with the Anabaptists. It will be recalled that both Schiemer and Schlaffer (Ch. 7.5) preached in or near Rattenberg. Driven out for his refusal to co-operate with the magistrates in "investigating" the miners, i.e., catching Anabaptists, Marpeck left behind a substantial estate, which was confiscated.

When he arrived in Strassburg, Marpeck made contact with the local Anabaptists, who were meeting in private homes, belonging variously to Fridolin Meyger, to Luke Hackfurt, steward of the city's relief program and sympathetic to the moderate brethren, and to the boatman Nicholas Bruch. Fridolin Meyger (Meier), an alumnus of Basel, was a notary of contracts in the episcopal chancery. He had been converted and baptized by Kautz. He had come to think of Anabaptism "as a middle way between the papacy and Lutheranism." His evangelical radicalism was socially oriented. In the line of Brunfels he protested against the social injustices of usury.[40] Marpeck had to absent himself from the meetings of this circle when he became engaged in timbering operations in the valley of the Kinzig in the Black Forest across the Rhine from Strassburg. In his home there, he and his wife sponsored a local Anabaptist meeting. It is of interest as an indication of the mounting radical tide that at about this time the parish of Robertsau (formerly Ruprechtsau), a village annexed to Strassburg, made bold to beseech the council to approve the election of Clement Ziegler as their lawful preacher on the death of the incumbent, but the council refused.[41]

When Marpeck again moved into the city itself, he gained many friends and followers, and was even well received by several of the leading preachers. But before long the latter became uneasy about his presence.

In October 1528, just a year after his arrival in Strassburg territory, Marpeck and his associates, Fridolin, Reublin, and Kautz (who had returned secretly from Worms despite Bucer's warn-

---

[39] *Ibid.*, No. 153, n. 4. For the extensive literature on Marpeck, see article in *ME*. "Pilgerholz" long survived as the designation for wood taken from the forests in Pilgram's manner.

[40] For Fridolin's conception of Anabaptism as a middle way, see *Elsass*, I, No. 182, p. 236; for his opposition to interest, No. 172; for his baptism by Kautz, No. 179.

[41] *Elsass*, I, Nos. 118 f.

ing), were summoned for a judicial hearing. They asked for a public disputation.[42] After a long delay, Zell, Caspar Hedio (special preacher at the cathedral), Capito, and Bucer joined in requesting of the council a public disputation.[43] After eighty-six days in prison, Kautz and Reublin, well recognized by the divines and the magistrates as leaders of renown among the Anabaptists far beyond the local community, prepared a written confession of faith.

This confession is a moving document in its straightforward recollection of the sinful life of these two clerics before they heard the Anabaptist gospel of repentance and rebaptism in the covenant of a good conscience with God, and the incorporation, in self-emptying *Gelassenheit,* into the body of which Christ alone is head. Both writers stress, in a somewhat Lutheran fashion, the difference between the invisible and the visible church, the latter separated from the world in its possession of believers' baptism, the breaking of the bread, and the ban. Reublin and Kautz then describe how, as a ship is driven before the wind, they have been driven by the cross, to proclaim the gospel to all people who will first believe and then be baptized.[44] To this apologia the municipal divines responded at length.[45] After more disputation and threats, Reublin was to get away to Moravia. Kautz abandoned his extreme position. Meyger, defended by the bishop from his seat at Saverne, conformed. Marpeck alone managed to hold his own in Strassburg to emerge as the chief spokesman of normative Anabaptism (Ch. 10.3.h).

Such in brief was the sectarian history of Strassburg when, on 20 February 1529, the town council officially abolished the Mass. Brought up to that point in our general narrative from which we reached back to carry forward the story in Strassburg, we are now ready for an even more eventful period, from February 1529 to June 1533.

3. STRASSBURG, 1529–1533

The period in Strassburg history between the abolition of the Mass in February 1529 and the convocation of the first territorial synod in June 1533 is characterized on the radical side by the

[42] *Ibid.,* Nos. 155 f.
[43] *Ibid.,* No. 167.
[44] 15 January 1529; *Elsass,* I, No. 168. On the invisible church we are indirectly informed by the long refutation, No. 171.
[45] 23 January 1529; *Elsass,* I, No. 171.

arrival of an extraordinary number of major figures of the
Radical Reformation. Many of them arrived in the year 1529,
prophets, apostles, and speculative seekers from as far away as
the Netherlands and Moravia, Italy and Spain.

a. John Bünderlin and Johannes Baptista Italus, 1529. At the
beginning of 1529, John Bünderlin, disciple of Denck and Hut
and sometime leader of the Anabaptist community in Linz (Ch.
7.5), sought asylum in Strassburg. He was twice arrested,[46] the
second time while in the house of the aforementioned boatman,
Nicholas Bruch, where, as visiting apostle, he was reading aloud
to the assembled brethren a portion of a booklet he had written.

He had managed to get two books published in Strassburg in
1529: the one, *Eine gemeine Berechnung über der Heiligen
Schrift Inhalt,* in which he sought by natural reason to clarify a
number of disputed points, holding fast to that which was good;
the other, on the incarnation and the atonement, *Aus welcher
Ursache Gott sich niedergelassen hat und in Christo Mensch
geworden ist.* In 1529, Bünderlin left Strassburg for Constance.

Soon thereafter there arrived a stray prophet of penance from
Italy, called Venturius, or Johannes Baptista Italus. He stayed in
Capito's home and through an interpreter told his life's story as a
visitor in Turkey, where he beheld in a vision the conversion of
Turks and Jews to Christ. On his return to Italy he lived the life
of a prophetic hermit, frequently imprisoned for his fiery de-
nunciations in the tradition of Savonarola. He had openly
preached that the sack of the Eternal City in 1527 was condign
punishment of the pope. He was now in Germany to summon
Luther and King Ferdinand likewise to repentance. Perhaps a
little hazy on the imperial constitution or on German geography,
he demanded that the Strassburg council cite the great Reformer.
The Strassburg authorities seemed to have been largely amused
at the prophet's sudden enlargement of their jurisdiction.[47] It is
of marginal interest that as early as 1527, the very day of the first
Strassburg mandate against Anabaptists, Bucer had taken occasion to warn the Italian Evangelicals against the Anabaptists.[48]

b. Caspar Schwenckfeld, 1529. Schwenckfeld, no doubt, left
Silesia with the hope that the mediating theologians of Strassburg would adopt his Eucharistic theology and be won over also
to his theory of an external and an internal baptism which he
and Crautwald had worked out. Schwenckfeld had already been

[46] Nicoladoni, *op. cit.,* 118.
[47] Krebs and Rott, *Elsass,* I (*QGT,* VII), Nos. 205, 206a.
[48] *Ibid.,* No. 91.

in correspondence with Bucer on this matter. His view on the Lord's Supper had, in fact, been warmly received, although perhaps not well understood.

When the Silesian nobleman entered the city in early May 1529, he lived in hospitable Capito's home and formed a close friendship with the Zells. Schwenckfeld regularly attended divine service in the cathedral and elsewhere, standing with cupped ear right under the pulpit because of his deafness, to get every word from the lips of Matthew Zell. He also preached himself, though as a layman no doubt only in private assemblies, but he was for a while regarded as a kind of assistant or consultant to the cathedral clergy.

Schwenckfeld was scarcely established in his new abode when the plans for the Marburg colloquy, to be convened by Philip of Hesse, were noised about. In June, Schwenckfeld busied himself with his first *Apology* to Frederick II of Liegnitz, who was now restoring the Communion which, under Schwenckfeld's influence, had been suspended. For this book, Capito wrote a commendatory preface, calling its author his "dear brother."[49] To the book was appended a section on the ascension and session of Christ at the right hand of God which bore negatively on Luther's doctrine of the Eucharistic ubiquity of Christ and impanation. Presently the Swiss party, including Zwingli and Oecolampadius, stopped off at Strassburg en route to Marburg, and Schwenckfeld had the opportunity of sharing his Eucharistic views in conversation with the Swiss Reformers and explaining to them that for all their (unauthorized) support of his Eucharistic theology (Ch. 5.3 and 5), they had in fact seriously misunderstood his intention. He was therefore eager to be included in the great Eucharistic colloquy to explain more fully and widely his doctrine of the inward feeding on the celestial flesh of Christ. His request was in vain.

At Marburg, Zwingli learned how deeply Luther disliked and distrusted Schwenckfeld. On their return from hearing Luther's vituperations, most of the Swiss and Strassburg divines became very cool toward Schwenckfeld in the interest of Protestant summit harmony. But Schwenckfeld continued to live with Capito. He visited Kautz in prison, brought him some of his own writings and those of others, and on 9 October 1529 he and Capito together secured permission from the town council to take Kautz home with them for four weeks with a view to converting him.[50]

New developments conspired to estrange Capito from

[49] *CS*, III, 394.
[50] *Elsass*, I (*QGT*, VII), Nos. 193 and 195.

Schwenckfeld and the Anabaptists. Capito's young wife died in November 1531. Capito interpreted her being taken from him as divine chastisement for his toleration of the Radicals. His patience with the Anabaptists burst into indignation when shortly after his wife's death, at the request of Lord Liechtenstein of Nicolsburg, he took up the task of refuting the seventh-day adventism (Sabbatarianism) espoused by Hut's disciple Oswald Glait.[51]

Capito, with some managing by Bucer in order to stabilize his stricken and always wayward colleague, married the widow of Oecolampadius. Schwenckfeld, already pushed well to the margins of Strassburg theological society, thereupon moved to the home of Jacob Engelmann, where religious assemblies were regularly convened. Schwenckfeld did convert to his views a city almoner, Alexander Berner. Now that the theological and ecclesiastical tension between Capito and Bucer had been overcome by a second marriage and maturer reflection on Capito's part, Schwenckfeld in his isolation became all the more irritating to the principal Reformers, and he drew closer to the sectaries.

The city Reformers insisted that Schwenckfeld identify himself with an established parish, whereupon he replied as spokesman of the invisible church:

To my mind, I am one with all churches in that I pray for them, in that I despise none, because I know that Christ the Lord has his own everywhere, be they ever so few.[52]

He reminded his antagonists that a score of years before, they and their fathers had been in another church. Surely one could not deny that some among those so dear and close to them as their own parents had been saved even from within the now abominated Roman Church. He chided them for the divisiveness and acrimony attending the reformation and dismantling of the old order and the undue emphasis on conformity enforced by the magistrate. When they asked him to produce something better or become ecclesiastically more brotherly, rather than so standoffish, provisional, and uncommitted, he replied with extraordinary confidence—to them it looked like the conceit of a nobleman who purported to be a divine—saying that he could join with none in whom *the Christ within him*, the true Christ of experience, was not congruent:

The opinion which I have, I have for myself. If it pleases anyone, he may accept it. I hope that opinion is the mind of Christ and the right foundation. If it does not please anyone, I commend him to God.

[51] *Ibid.*, No. 290a.
[52] *CS*, IV, 830 f.; translated by Schultz, *op. cit.*, 212.

But I cannot be one in faith with either the Pope or Luther, because they condemn me and my faith, that is, they hate *my Christ in me.* To have the real Christ according to the spirit is very important. Christ does not condemn himself. He does not persecute himself.[53]

Seeking souls for Christ and with no intention of building up "any Crautwaldian or Schwenckfeldian church"[54] to add to the confusion of competing churches, Schwenckfeld wrote, edited, disputed, or, as he would say, conversed, corresponded, and traveled, as a lay evangelist. With Strassburg as his base, he moved about Landau (where he finally converted the local Zwinglian Reformer, John Bader, to his view), Hagenau, Speyer, and Rappoltsweiler (Ribeauvillé).

While based in Strassburg, Schwenckfeld published an anthology of the *Corpus juris canonici,* selecting canons and decretals consonant with the New Testament and freedom of conscience.[55] He also composed two catechisms and promoted a new German version of the *Imitatio Christi,* published by his printer, Philip Ulhart, in Augsburg in 1531. The edition is notable in leaving out book four on the sacrament of the altar. The edition was obviously intended as a devotional work for all parties, theologically divided at the diet of Augsburg the year before.

Though Schwenckfeld was an antipedobaptist and moved in Anabaptist circles, his own view of Christ's baptism as being inward, like the Eucharist, meant that he could not accept the outward rite, even believers' baptism, as either redemptive or constitutional. He steadfastly refused to accept the covenantal implications of Luther's peculiar translation of I Peter 3:21 *as interpreted ecclesiologically by the Anabaptists.* He persisted instead in keeping to the Greek and Vulgate versions.[56]

His impression of the Strassburg Anabaptists of this period is of interest. His description of them as a whole should be put before the reader. In his *Judicium de Anabaptistis,* c. July 1530, apparently requested by the Strassburg authorities, Schwenckfeld says that he does not wish to judge them without knowing them better, but then gives his impression. He says that they

---

[53] *CS,* IV, 832; Schultz, *op. cit.,* 212.
[54] *Ibid.*
[55] *CS,* III, Document CI, c. June 1530.
[56] In his anthology of Canon Law, *CS,* III, 795, Schwenckfeld took over from a Lutheran predecessor in this effort Luther's translation of *interrogatio* in I Peter 3:21 as *Bund;* but elsewhere Schwenckfeld always avoided the term "covenant" here, and like Michael Servetus (Ch. 11.1), kept to the Greek original.

seem to lack the true knowledge of Christ and that there is no palpable evidence of their being any more regenerate than the solafideists, or better endowed with the gifts of the Spirit. He observes further:

It were well if they would put more stress on catechetical instruction in the Christian faith rather than on taking everyone into their congregation and appointing him to be a pastor *(Vorsteher)*. . . . It appears that they consider all who are not of their group as godless, and will have nothing to do with them, refusing to take in all who are weak in faith.[57]

Schwenckfeld deplores their undue emphasis on outward baptism, stressing the letter more than the spirit. He takes issue with them on their radical eschatology, chides them for being so preoccupied about events even before the beginning and after the end of the world, and expresses the wish that they might spend less time discussing how things are in the presence of God. Tolerant of them and desirous of interceding for them with the authorities, he wishes that they themselves would testify more openly and irenically.

In the end, ironically, Schwenckfeld will be placed alongside the millennialist Melchior Hofmann in the synodal disputation in 1533 (Ch. 10.4).

c. Melchior Hofmann, 1529. In June 1529, a month after Schwenckfeld, Hofmann arrived in Strassburg, where he was received as a champion of the symbolical view of the Communion.[58] He had, on 8 April 1529, engaged in a disputation at Flensburg in Denmark in the presence of the king, where, as one but recently converted from the Lutheran to the Zwinglian view of the Eucharist, he fought vigorously against the Lutheran disputants.

Because of his impending pre-eminence in the Anabaptist movement and its extension into the region of the Lower Rhine and the Netherlands, we pause at this point in our narrative to recount his life briefly before his arrival and his conversion to Anabaptism while sojourning in Strassburg.

Swabian by birth and a furrier by trade, Melchior Hofmann[59] (c. 1495–1543 or 1544) had been won over to the Lutheran cause by 1522 and had become an itinerant evangelist. His trade took

---

[57] *CS*, III, 832 f.

[58] Krebs and Rott, *Elsass*, I *(QGT*, VII), No. 188.

[59] The principal modern works are W. I. Leendertz, *Melchior Hofmann* (Haarlem, 1883), Friedrich Otto zur Linden, *Melchior Hofmann: ein Prophet der Wiedertäufer* (Haarlem, 1885), and Peter Kawerau, *Melchior Hoffman als religiöser Denker* (Haarlem, 1954). The first two works named contain certain of Hofmann's documents.

him into the fur country of the Teutonic Order.[60] A gifted tradesman and a popular preacher, he found a text admirably suited to his needs in Gen. 3:21 when he declared that as God had prepared animal skins for the protection of fallen Adam and Eve, so had he for all sinners, the *Lämmlein* Christ, to be put on in faith (Gal. 3:27).

In 1523 he was in Wolmar, where he was welcomed as Luther's fiery apostle to Livonia. In the fall of 1524 he was established in Dorpat, where he preached against the use of images and the practice of auricular confession as a prerequisite for the receiving of Communion. He did not himself participate in the iconoclastic outburst which took place 10 January 1525. Popular support prevented the Catholic authorities from arresting him, but even the pro-Lutheran clergy could not fully accept so untutored a preacher. They noted with uneasiness the strong eschatological accent in his proclamation of Luther's gospel and his encouragement of conventicular dissent. At the behest of the town council of Dorpat, he went to Riga, to secure the approval of evangelical preachers there, and then to Wittenberg, to obtain from Luther himself a confirmation of his doctrinal soundness. He wrote back to his Dorpat community from Wittenberg in the spring.

He did not meet Carlstadt at this time, but he became acquainted with Carlstadt's writings. On his return to the Baltic, he resettled in Dorpat and prudently dissociated himself from Thomas Müntzer. He still thought of himself as loyally carrying out the Lutheran reform. Luther's support had inflated his self-esteem; and this swagger, together with his not entirely unwarranted censure of their conduct, alienated the local pro-Lutheran pastors from him. He considered himself a prophet, and referred frequently to Enoch and Elijah, feeling that he was perhaps preordained to fulfill the eschatological role of the one or the other.

Violently opposed in Dorpat, Hofmann went to Reval (Tartu) in the fall of 1525. As the preaching offices were filled, he became the "servant of the sick," supporting himself by his trade and by exhorting. Here, too, he antagonized the settled clergy because

---

[60] For Hofmann in a larger perspective, see Leonid Arbusow, *Die Einführung der Reformation in Liv-, Est- und Kurland*, QFRG, III, Leipzig, 1921). Riga was the archiepiscopal center of the Teutonic Baltic coast. Hanseatic merchants were firmly established there and in Dorpat and Reval to the north, roughly coincident with the territory of the *Herrmeister* of the Teutonic Order for Livonia (Wolter von Plettenberg, 1493–1535). For the southern part of the archdiocese and for the *Hochmeister* Albert (1511–1525), thereafter Lutheran Duke of Prussia (1525–1568), see Ch. 15.1.

of his emphasis on a holy life in addition to faith and because of his views on the Eucharist. Professional pride on the part of even the pro-Lutheran clergy, combined with theological and social alarm, now brought about his expulsion from the Baltic altogether. The prospect of success took him to Stockholm, a center of the fur trade. Early in 1526 he was there as preacher to the large German-Lutheran community.

From Stockholm in 1526, Hofmann directed two pamphlets in Low German to the Livonians, his indignant *Formaninghe*[61] and his *Exposition of the XIIth Chapter of Daniel*,[62] wherein he said that the end of the world could be expected in 1533 ("the seventh year after 1526"). Still precariously Lutheran, he continued to follow Luther on auricular confession, but revealed an increasingly mystical and spiritualist view of the Lord's Supper, and a tendency to mitigate Luther's predestinarianism. In his teaching on the Supper, the influence of Carlstadt was now apparent. Hofmann suggested that while the serpent caused the first Adam to eat of the apple, the Second Adam "eats the faithful unto himself." In Stockholm he married and a son was born. Perhaps he intended to remain, but King Gustav Vasa feared the evangelist's temperament would cause disturbances, and he requested him to resign.[63]

From Sweden, Hofmann returned to Germany, first to Lübeck, where the city council took action against him. Only a hasty flight saved his life. Early in 1527 he arrived in the duchy of Holstein, which, with that of Slesvig, was under the royal Danish crown. In May he made a brief and disappointing visit to Wittenberg. On his return, King Frederick I (1523–1533) permitted him to preach in Kiel. Hofmann had difficulties with the local pastor, who appealed to Luther. Luther at first supported Hofmann, but the favorable opinion was of short duration. Hofmann engaged in controversy with Nicholas Amsdorf in Magdeburg. Luther finally wrote to strongly Lutheranizing Duke Christian, urging that Hofmann be restrained from further preaching until he should be better informed.

Hofmann, in passing from his Lutheran into his explicitly sacramentarian phase, published in 1528 at least three now lost works dealing with the subject. As a consequence he came into

---

[61] *An de gelöfigen vorsamblung inn Liflant ein korte formaninghe,* edited by August Buchholz, *Festschrift Oberpfarrer Taube zu Riga* (Riga, 1856).

[62] *Das XII Capitel des propheten Danielis ausgelegt,* printed by Barthold Krohn, *Geschichte der fanatischen und enthusiastischen Wiedertäufer vornehmlich in Niederdeutschland: Melchior Hofmann und die Secte der Hofmannianer* (Leipzig, 1758).

[63] Letter of 13 January 1527; *ME,* II, 779.

serious conflict with the Lutheran clergy of Holstein concerning
the Communion. The already mentioned disputation was arranged at Flensburg for the spring of 1529, with a stately audience
of four hundred, including the nobility and clergy. John Bugenhagen served as referee. Hofmann was supported by John van
Campen, Jacob Hegge of Danzig, and John Barse, each speaking in his turn. Hofmann boldly upbraided the duke, and the
result of the disputation was Hofmann's condemnation and expulsion from Denmark[64] and the duchy.

From Holstein, Hofmann went to East Frisia, meeting Carlstadt
en route. He had called Carlstadt to support him against the
Lutherans, but Carlstadt was not able to secure a safe-conduct.
While Carlstadt actively opposed the plan of Count Enno II in
Emden to reinstate Lutheranism in place of the Reformed faith,
Hofmann remained quiet, at work on his notes on the Flensburg
disputation. With his manuscript, Hofmann came to Strassburg.

On his arrival he kept quiet, staying in the house of Andrew
and Catharine Klaiber. He immediately published his account
of the Flensburg disputation, *Dialogus und gründliche Berich-
tung*. He exchanged views with Schwenckfeld on the Lord's
Supper and Christology. Going his solitary way, he was inwardly
constructing, from his allegorical, spiritualizing interpretation of
the Bible, with a special fondness for the Apocrypha, an elaborate
eschatological theology. The established Reformers of Strassburg
advised him to return to his furrier's trade; but Hofmann was
certain that the Holy Spirit fully compensated for any lack of
education. Indeed, he was convinced that university training
could be a hindrance rather than a help to an evangelist. He devoted himself to the publication of several booklets, which appeared early in 1530: *Weissagung aus heiliger göttlicher Schrift,
Prophezei oder Weissagung,* and *Auslegung der heimlichen Offenbarung Johannis.*

This last tract, dedicated to the king of Denmark, whose son
had driven him from Flensburg (!), was one of his most significant works, with its glowing description of the return of Christ.
Hofmann declared that Paul was the angel who had bound Satan
for a thousand years (Rev. 20:2). After the expiration of this
period, Christianity had fallen into its current deplorable state,

---

[64] Duke Christian, Frederick's eldest son, was destined to succeed him only after
an interregnum during which the popular forces allied themselves with
Jürgen Wullenweber of Lübeck against episcopal and feudal reaction. As
king of Denmark (1536–1559), Christian III established Lutheranism as the
state religion. Beginning in 1554, he started issuing warnings against Anabaptists in his realm, most of them refugees from the Netherlands. *ME*, 35 f.

now soon to be repaired. Many came to consider Hofmann himself as the returned Elijah, one of the two witnesses of Rev. 11:3.

Hofmann declared that just as Rome was interpreted as the spiritual Babylon, so Strassburg was the spiritual Jerusalem.[65] He stated that Strassburg would be the center for the eventual one hundred and forty-four thousand heralds of world regeneration (Rev. 14:1). After a bloody siege of the elect city, the royal priesthood, the priestly kingdom of the persevering saints, would rally under their chosen, righteous pastors. That would be the breakthrough. In this apocalyptic mood Hofmann found IV Esdras especially useful. It was no doubt the combination of his exegetical fervor and his observation of the extraordinary role the city was already playing in the Radical Reformation that convinced him that Strassburg was the elect city. It was in his concentration on prophecy and millennialism that Hofmann became associated with Leonard and Ursula Jost, both of whom were receiving visions and revelations interpretive of his mission. Another prophetess was Barbara Rebstock. Hofmann considered their oracles comparable to those of the Old Testament, and in two books he published and interpreted them. The first was devoted to Ursula's vision, *Prophetische Geschichte und Offenbarung*, 1530. The second, containing the prophecies of her husband, has been lost. These two collections of contemporary prophecy made a deep impression, in the middle Rhine and especially in the Netherlands.

Hofmann had not actually joined the Anabaptists when he boldly and confidently presented a petition to the Strassburg council in April 1530, demanding that a church edifice be assigned to the Anabaptist community.[66] With the Mass but recently abolished, he demanded equal rights for the Anabaptists alongside the established church. Hofmann now took the formal step of joining the brotherhood by submitting to rebaptism. With this further break from his earlier Lutheranism went the transformation of his views on predestination, drawn up in his *Verkläring*, in which Hofmann presented the view, akin to that of Schwenckfeld, that after regeneration the will is freed and therewith responsible for its decisions, and hence that after adult or believers' baptism all sin committed is against faith, the gift of the Holy Spirit, and therefore unforgivable.[67] Despite his eschato-

---

[65] The Scriptural basis for the doctrine is John 1:17; 3:13; I Cor. 15:47. For his own claim to be Elijah, see Krebs and Rott, *Elsass*, II (*QGT*, VIII), No. 368, p. 18.

[66] *Elsass*, II, No. 211.

[67] Well analyzed by Kawerau, *op. cit.*, 58 ff.

logical intensity, Hofmann continued to counsel obedience to what he considered the provisionally authorized magistracy.

The city council of Strassburg ordered the arrest of Hofmann, both because of his petition and because of the seditionary implications in his exposition of Revelation. On 23 April 1530 he escaped from the city in haste and headed for Emden, where he fathered an Anabaptist congregation and thereby introduced the potent seed of Hofmannite (Melchiorite) Anabaptism into the moist soil of the Lowlands, long harrowed and tilled by sacramentarian heresy and persecution (Ch. 12). He was back in Strassburg, however, the same year, this time in complete concealment, and the magistrates were not aware of his presence. At the end of 1530, he again departed.

d. Sebastian Franck, 1529. In the fall of 1529, Sebastian Franck joined the variegated company of sectaries and seekers in Strassburg. Several generations of modern scholars have so concentrated on Franck that he has now emerged as the basic figure about whom the "Spiritualist" has been defined and developed as a type in the sociology of religion.[68] Before recounting his Strassburg career, we must look to his earlier life.[69]

Born at Donauwörth in 1499, Franck had studied at Ingolstadt from 1515 to 1517, a student of Agricola for his Greek and of Jacob Locher and Urbanus Rhegius (Ch. 7.2) for rhetoric and poetry. Franck wrote Latin, understood Greek, but was ignorant of Hebrew. At the beginning of 1518 he had gone to Heidelberg to study theology with the Dominicans, and in April he, like Bucer, attended the famous disputation in which Luther defended his position. From these years of study, Franck preserved a passionate love for the history of Germany, having undergone the influence of Jacob Wimpfeling, the author of *Germania* (1501).

Ordained as priest, Franck became Lutheran preacher in Ansbach-Bayreuth in 1526, thereafter chaplain in Gustenfelden under the patronage of Nuremberg in the same margraviate. He married Ottilie Behaim, sister of the famous "godless painters" Bartholemew and Sebald Behaim (Ch. 7.1), known to John Denck.

While still a Lutheran at Gustenfelden he mildly opposed Denck. Franck was, even as a Lutheran, incipiently sympathetic toward Denck's view; but he began his literary career by trans-

---

[68] *SAW*, Introduction, 27.
[69] The most recent studies of Franck, with the literature, are Eberhard Teufel, "Landräumig," *Sebastian Franck, ein Wanderer an Donau, Rhein, und Neckar* (Neustadt an der Aisch, 1954); *ME*, II, 363–367; Doris Rieber, "Sébastien Franck," *BHR*, XXI (1959), 190–201.

lating into German for the benefit of the people Andrew Althamer's Latin *Diallage* directed against Denck. In passing, at
least, he also attacked the abuses of the Lutheran doctrine of
justification by faith alone, insisting that the fruits of justification
had been neglected. He opposed the abuses of the Scriptures,
having in mind not only the Anabaptists and Spiritualists, but
also some of the Lutheran theologians. Franck was quite serious
in his espousal of Althamer against the Anabaptists and Spiritualists; at the same time, where Althamer insisted on the literal
Biblical word, Franck reminded the reader of the Spirit behind
the word. In effect, his emended translation represented his last
work as a Lutheran and his first work as a Spiritualist.

In 1528, Franck published a booklet against drunkenness,
based on Biblical passages.[70] In this book he urged the clerical
excommunication of open sinners, with the support of the magistrate. Osiander, pastor at Nuremberg, supported him, but the
magistracy of the town opposed the effort. In revulsion from the
solafideist, magisterial reform, Franck left the ministry.

He thereupon established himself briefly in Nuremberg as a
printer. Here he published his *Türkenchronik*, a German translation from the Latin of an unknown author who was a Transylvanian Saxon, held prisoner by the Turks for twenty-two years.
Franck makes of the preface an occasion to contrast the simplicity
of the life and worship of the Turks with the impure life, the
divisions, and the complicated rituals of Christians. He speaks
of a dozen sects of Christianity, to which now, he says, three new
ones have been added, namely, the Lutheran, the Zwinglian, and
the Anabaptist. A fourth new one is in the process of formation,
the Spiritualist, which will eliminate all audible prayer, preaching, all ceremonies, sacraments, and ordinances such as excommunication, and also the ministry. Spiritualists, he writes approvingly, will be content with an invisible church without exterior means.

It was then, as a programmatic Spiritualist, that Franck moved
to Strassburg in 1529. He was naturally attracted to Schwenckfeld. The two must also have discussed a common interest in
the celestial flesh of Christ, which Ziegler, Hofmann, Servetus,
and Paracelsus also held in one form or another (Ch. 11.3). He
may have met Bünderlin before the latter's departure in 1529.
He would later have contact with John Campanus and Servetus.
It was in his letter to Campanus, written from Strassburg in 1531
(Ch. 18.3),[71] that he elaborated and made programmatically his

[70] *Von dem greulichen Laster der Trunkenheit*, which was reprinted in 1531.
[71] Translated in *SAW*, 147–162.

own the fourth sect which he had earlier mentioned in the preface to the *Türkenchronik*.

In the middle of 1531, Franck was at Strassburg and turned over to Balthasar Beck the printing of his *Chronica, Zeitbuch und Geschichtsbibel,* which appeared 5 September 1531, and which throws light on the contemporary history of the Radical Reformation. In the *Chronica,* Franck borrowed considerably from earlier chronicles.[72]

The first part of his *Chronica* extends from the creation of the world to Christ, the second recounts the history of the emperors from Augustus to Charles V. The preface of this part pictures an eagle as a voracious and bloody creature which thereby commends itself for the ornamentation of the escutcheon of the Emperor. On the Peasants' War, Franck adopts the view of Luther, namely, that every form of resistance against the order established by God is an insurrection, and that the gospel instructs Christians to endure injustice rather than to commit it. As a humanist Spiritualist he is sometimes given to rather harsh statements about the *canaille.* The third part of the *Chronica* is itself divided into three parts, the first being the chronicle of the popes from Peter to Clement VII. Here, Franck opposes the Catholic claims, denies the Roman pontificate of Peter, and treats as fraudulent the Donation of Constantine. The second part deals with the councils and the third with heretics (as seen from the Roman point of view), including Wyclif, Hus, and Gansfort. This is the most original and valuable portion of the whole *Chronica,* for Franck characterizes the Anabaptists of his own time, many of whom he knew personally. For this chronicle of heresies, Franck utilized the catalogue of heretics prepared by the Dominican Prior Bernard of Luxemburg (Cologne, 1522). Franck in his work shows great familiarity with the works of Luther and pays tribute to him for his struggle against the abuses of the papacy and for his achievement in translating the Bible. Franck includes Erasmus among the heretics, to the great humanist's indignation. Erasmus would soon demand that Bucer investigate the book and its author.[73]

Because of the opposition of diverse groups led by Bucer, the *Chronica* was confiscated and Franck was arrested. When re-

---

[72] Franck himself indicated, on the verso of the title page, 111 sources which he had read or found cited by others. Bucer later, 1535, accused him of having fraudulently obtained permission to print this work by representing it as consisting solely of extracts from history without significant or tendentious comment.

[73] Krebs and Rott, *Elsass,* I (*QGT,* VII), Nos. 262, 286, and 315a.

leased, he was expelled from Strassburg, 30 December 1531, and the sale of his books was forbidden.[74] We shall pick up his trail again (Ch. 18.3).

e. *Christian Entfelder, 1529.* Among the many Radical Re- formers who appeared in Strassburg in 1529, Christian Entfeldei has yet to be mentioned, a disciple of John Denck and friend ol Balthasar Hubmaier. Little is known of Entfelder's career and thought.[75] During 1526–1527, he had served as the preacher of an Anabaptist congregation in Eibenschitz (Evancice)[76] in Moravia. The Swiss and Austrian Brethren, to whom Entfelder no doubt ministered, had their meetinghouse in a lane in a suburb. There were also some Schwenckfeldians who came from Silesia in 1527. Having left Moravia, perhaps because of Ferdinand's burning of three Anabaptists in his district (Ch. 9.2.c), Entfelder removed to Strassburg, where he was briefly associated with Bünderlin. During his sojourn in Strassburg, Entfelder produced three books.[77]

The first book, *Von den mannigfaltigen im Glauben Zer- spaltungen* (24 January 1530), dealt with the Spiritual basis of religious divisions, treating the problem of faith and sanctifica- tion and the disputes over Baptism and the Supper. Scripture by itself, Entfelder declared, was like a razor, inflicting wounds if not properly handled.[78] Moreover, to seek to extract holiness from the Bible as it stands is like trying to draw water from a dry well. It is out of God's living Word (inner grace) that holiness proceeds. Entfelder was not entirely individualistic about the quest for holiness. He yearned for the company of like-minded seekers and saints, defining the church in this book as "a chosen, saved, purified, sanctified group in whom God dwells, upon whom the Holy Spirit has poured out his gifts, and with whom Christ the Lord shares his offices and his mission."[79] It was out of his concern to distinguish the inner Word of personal ex-

---

[74] *Ibid.,* No. 294.

[75] The fullest account is in Rufus M. Jones, *Spiritual Reformers in the Six- teenth and Seventeenth Centuries* (London, 1914), 39–43.

[76] Evancice was in the Brno district of Moravia (formerly a seat of Hussite strength) where on 10 April 1528 Thomann Waldhauser, John Čižek, and one other Anabaptist were burned. *Elsass,* I, No. 131, p. 159.

[77] Printed at Strassburg and at Augsburg. They are rare. They have been excerpted with special reference to the doctrine of the Trinity by Stanislas von Dunin-Borkowski, "Quellenstudien zur Vorgeschichte der Unitarier des 16. Jahrhunderts," *75 Jahre Stella Matutina, Festschrift,* I (Feldkirch, 1931), 107–109.

[78] A similar reservation in John de Valdés, Ch. 1.2.c.

[79] Quoted by Jones, *op. cit.,* from the end of Entfelder's book, where he addresses himself to the Brethren.

perience, the outer Word (the historic Christ, the Bible, and the communion of the saints), and the eternal Word that Entfelder developed his mystical doctrine of the Trinity (Ch. 11.2).

A second work, systematically dealing with the Persons as powers, was entitled *Von Gottes und Christi Jesu unseres Herrn Erkenntnis* (1533). A third work of only seventeen pages, *Von wahrer Gottseligkeit* (1530), considered the six stages through which Christ is mystically formed in the believer in the process of his being reborn:

It is desirable [he says] to know that divine blessedness is nothing other than a peace (*ruow*) which the Spirit of God effects in a person through Christ to the end that one is at leisure from all that is creaturely, including self. All one's senses, emotion, and thought, drawn away from the beautiful and luscious apple of this world, bids farewell to father, mother, sister, brother, wife, child, house, barn, meadows, fields, goods and gold, body and business (*leib und leben*). . . . And though the world cries out and complains against and becomes indignant at such a person for disparaging its activities and will not be compared with it, he stands fast in his *gelassenheyt*, remains quiet, and leaves it to his Lover to answer for him in His own time, who will know how to deal justly with him.[80]

In such a passage flow currents common to the Rhenish mystics, the more contemplative Anabaptists like Denck, and the more apocalyptic Austrian converts of Hut (Ch. 7.5).

In pursuing the sectarian history of Strassburg, we have been struck by the number of major spokesmen of the Radical Reformation who found their way there all in the year 1529. As we proceed biographically, we now introduce three more figures. By chance all three of these revolutionaries converged on Strassburg in 1531: Bernard Rothmann, destined for a leading role in the rise of the polygamous theocracy of Münster,[81] and two leading revolutionaries in respect to the doctrine of the Trinity—the proto-Unitarian Michael Servetus and the binitarian John Campanus. (We shall postpone the full treatment of Rothmann to Ch. 13.1.)

The assumption that these three visitors had theological contact with one another and with the indigenous separatists is based on the references made to the others in the surviving documentation, and to Bünderlin, Franck, Hofmann, or

---

[80] Translated from the excerpt reprinted by Dunin-Borkowski, "Quellenstudien," 109.

[81] The surmise that Rothmann was in Strassburg in the spring of 1531 is based on his own letter in which he avowed his intentions to visit the city, Krebs and Rott, *Elsass*, I (*QGT*, VII), No. 249.

Schwenckfeld. We know very little about the sojourn of the three visitors of 1531, but since all three adhered in one form or another to the doctrine of the celestial flesh, we can conjecture that they visited the home of the Melchiorite goldsmith, Valtin Duft, and perhaps that of Clement Ziegler in the Robertsau. That Schwenckfeld and Servetus were in contact is documented.[82]

f. Michael Servetus, 1531. It was in May 1531 that Servetus arrived in Strassburg. We were last with him, Brunfels, and Paracelsus in Basel (Ch. 8.4.b), where Servetus, despite some initial success, was dejected by his failure to win Oecolampadius to his views. He went to Strassburg with a double purpose: to get his book on the Trinity printed in nearby Hagenau and "to confer concerning Holy Scripture with Martin Bucer and Capito."[83] As early as 1530 he had joined Bucer, whose commentary on the Synoptic Gospels (1527) he greatly admired, in a visit to Luther in Coburg at the time of the Augsburg diet. Once in the crossroads city, Servetus stayed in the home of Capito along with that other distinguished house guest, Schwenckfeld.[84] It was at the suggestion either of Capito in correspondence or of a Basel printer that Servetus arranged in Hagenau to have John Setzer publish *On the Errors of the Trinity* (June, 1531). The Hagenau printer stood on the Lutheran side in the Eucharistic controversy, against the Swiss, and may have accepted the printing job to irritate them and to embarrass them for having domiciled Servetus in Basel. In any case, Setzer concealed himself and his press: Servetus confidently had his name appear on the title page.

The work consists of seven books, in the first of which Servetus propounded his modalism and his conception of Christ as the natural Son of God, begotten, not eternally, but in a mysterious way through the operation of the Holy Spirit. The Spirit was here thought of as the seed of God rather than as a distinct Person. The remaining six books elaborate the theme and attack

[82] See *Elsass*, I, No. 241, n. 4, and Document MCLXXXV in *CS*, XVII.

[83] The statements of Servetus concerning his relations with Bucer and Capito are printed in Calvin, *Opera*, VIII, coll. 764 ff. Capito's relations with Servetus and other Radicals are discussed with considerable documentation, some of it not elsewhere printed, by Otto Strasser, *Capitos Beziehungen zu Bern,* Quellen und Abhandlungen zur Schweizerischen Reformationsgeschichte, IV (Leipzig, 1928), 67 ff. The visit to Coburg as worked out by H. Tollin, *Michel Servet und Martin Butzer* (Berlin, 1880), ch. iv, is not accepted by all scholars.

[84] It is assumed that Schwenckfeld was still living at Capito's until the death in November of the mistress of the house. Cf. also Haller's letter to Bucer, 4 October 1531, wherein the two guests are linked with Capito: Krebs and Rott, *Elsass*, I (*QGT*, VII), No. 269.

Luther on justification by faith in the strong language of contemporary theological debate.

Some Strassburgers were receptive, though amply warned against Servetus and his work, notably by Berthold Haller in Bern, who also drew attention to the chiliastic context of Servetus' anti-Nicene views.[85] "By certain Strassburgers the book . . . was lauded."[86] Capito, for example, was at first impressed by the bold reconception of the Trinity and Servetus' appeal to the Hebrew texts in support thereof.[87]

Bucer, however, sought to refute some of Servetus' points as early as December 1531 in his lectures. Bucer felt the sting of some of Servetus' assertions (in a no longer extant letter) about the Strassburger's conception of the Lord's Supper and the mediatorial role of Christ. Addressing Servetus as "beloved in Christ," Bucer contended that while he did indeed oppose the idea of impanation or carnal manducation, he nevertheless believed with Servetus in some kind of real, efficacious presence. As to Servetus' conception of redemption—that Sonship was possible only after the incarnation and that Christ descended into hell to save the Old Testament worthies—Bucer reasserted the conviction that the Israelites before the advent of Christ, by election and by their faith in the incarnation ahead, were rightly called in the Old Testament "sons of God"; and against Servetus, Schwenckfeld, and Marpeck alike, Bucer said that the descent into hell in the Apostles' Creed meant only that Christ was buried and underwent what all who die experience.[88]

In Basel, Oecolampadius, on procuring a copy of *The Errors,* denounced it as blasphemous, wrote to Bucer that the book was malevolently favored by those who hated their church, and urged him to write a full refutation of Servetus, lest the Swiss and Alsatian churches be thought the originators of the blasphemy.[89] Bucer, after much outside pressure, refuted the work publicly.[90] The town council ordered Servetus to avoid Strassburg on pain of punishment.[91]

Servetus returned to Basel, still counting unrealistically on support from Oecolampadius. Just before his death late the same year, Oecolampadius rendered an opinion to the city council of Basel in which he urged that, despite certain good points in the

[85] Cf. *Elsass,* I, No. 319.
[86] Oecolampadius to Zwingli, Strasser, *op. cit.,* 70, n. 7.
[87] Krebs and Rott, *Elsass,* I (*QGT,* VII), No. 319.
[88] *Ibid.,* No. 292a, p. 592.
[89] Staehelin, *Briefe,* II, Nos. 895, 897, 904, 914.
[90] Krebs and Rott, *Elsass,* I (*QGT,* VII), No. 331.
[91] 11 December 1531, *ibid.,* No. 280.

book, Servetus should retract his errors in writing. This counsel, and the unexpected hostility all through the Upper Rhine which the work had provoked, was undoubtedly the reason for Servetus' putting his view in conciliatory form in his smaller *Dialogues on the Trinity*,[92] from the same press in Hagenau at the beginning of 1532. In the uproar over his first work, said Servetus by way of introduction, there had been two main objections. In response to the first, his alleged violence toward Luther, he could soften considerably his statements about justification without undermining his own great concern for sanctification. On the main objection, modalism, he was now prepared to go rather far in an effort to use traditional language about the three Persons; and he was on his way to recognizing what he would make more explicit in his *Restitutio Christianismi* of 1553, that once the natural divine Sonship of Christ is acknowledged as the revelatory point of departure, and the abstractions of scholastic and patristic theology are understood to mean a miraculous physiological procreation, then one could by extension speak of the Son and even of Christ as eternal and divine with respect to God's *intention*. The Strassburg divines finally put in their own words what they thought Servetus had said, namely, "that the eternal Logos of God was [before the mundane generation] nothing but a pattern (*vor* or *verbildung*) and shadow of the Man, our Lord Jesus Christ [shadowed forth] in all creation in God's diverse epiphanies, and in the coming and going of his angels."[93]

Distressed by the failure of all groups to be tolerant of fresh theological construction, despite their claim to be reformers, Servetus expressed the hope that the "Lord destroy all the tyrants of the church." Condemned in Strassburg and Basel, excoriated in Wittenberg, plotted against in Spain (with a diabolical plan to use his own brother to ensnare him), Servetus later recalls his desperation at the age of twenty, when, "taught of no man," he felt a certain divine impulse "to make known to the world his theological insights":

When I began, such was the blindness of the world that I was sought up and down to be snatched to my death. Terrified on this account and fleeing into exile, for many years I lurked among strangers in sore grief of mind. Knowing that I was young, powerless and without polish of style, I almost gave up the whole cause, for I was not yet sufficiently trained. . . . O most clement Jesus, I invoke thee again as divine witness that on this account I delayed and also because of the

[92] Translated by Wilbur with the *Errors, loc. cit.,* 185–264.
[93] The phrasing of article i of the Strassburg synod of 1533 (Ch. 10.4), Krebs and Rott, *Elsass,* II (*QGT,* VIII), No. 25.

imminent persecution, so that with Jonah I longed rather to flee to the sea or to one of the New Isles.[94]

The reference may well be to the possibility of joining the Welser colonizing expedition to Little Venice, Venezuela. But instead of to the New World, Servetus went to France. We shall later take up in further detail his Trinitarian, Christological, and baptismal views (Ch. 11) and meet him again in dispute with Calvin (Ch. 23.4).

g. *John Campanus.* John Campanus (1500 – c. 1575)[95] showed up in Strasbourg late in 1531.[96] Although his primary sphere of influence was the duchy of Jülich, we introduce him at this point as one of the earliest anti-Nicene theologians of the Reformation Era and as an acquaintance of Servetus and Schwenckfeld. Born in Maeseyck or Kampen in the princely bishopric of Liège and educated at Düsseldorf and Cologne, he went to Wittenberg, studying there between 1527 and 1530, and leaving from time to time on diverse theological errands, notably to attend but not to participate in the Marburg colloquy in 1529. At the time he was Lutheran, but he broke with Luther over the questions of the correct understanding of the Lord's Supper and of the doctrine of the Trinity. In March 1530 he went to the elector's court at Torgau and so alienated the Wittenbergers that Melanchthon thereafter had him very much in mind and immortalized him in the condemnation of the "neo-Samosatenes" of the Augsburg Confession (article i).

The main extant record of Campanus' thought is his *Restitution göttlicher Schrift* (1532). Written in German, it is based on three slightly earlier and allegedly more scholarly Latin works, chief of which was his *Artikel-Buch,* presumably the same as his *Contra totum post apostolos mundum* (c. 1530). The German ver-

---

[94] From a unique portion of the text in the Edinburgh MS. of the *Restitutio,* published in *Journal of Modern History,* IV (1939), 89, and again in Bainton, *Hunted Heretic,* 73 f.

[95] The chief work on Campanus has long been Karl Rembert, *Die "Wiedertäufer" im Herzogtum Jülich* (Berlin, 1889). The most recent work is the unpublished Harvard Ph.D. thesis, "The *Restitution* of John Campanus," by Chalmers McCormick. See also *ME,* I, 499 f.

[96] The main supports for this surmise are the following: (1) Bucer's reference to the recent arrival of "a Dane who wrote *Contra totum post apostolos mundum*" in a letter to Ambrose Blaurer, 29 December 1531, *Briefwechsel,* No. 250, p. 308; (2) the numerous references in Strasbourg to his books; (3) Melanchthon's statement in *CR,* II, 34; and (4) the fact that Franck, who wrote him in February 1531, addresses him as one whose acquaintance he has recently made. For an interesting group of largely Melchiorite books sent to Strasbourg from Speyer in 1537, including a *Restitution,* see Krebs, *Baden und Pfalz* (*QGT,* IV), No. 411.

sion thereof, the *Restitution* in thirty chapters, is primarily an indictment of Luther and Melanchthon. Campanus accuses Luther of having deprived the Christian laity of their right to sit in judgment (I Cor. 14:23 ff.) when Scripture is being interpreted (*Sitzerrecht*). Within this framework, he disparages his opponents for multifarious minor and major errors. Among the lesser matters are the inviolability of a widow's oath, the difference between the leviathan and a whale, the signs of the Last Judgment, and the impropriety of a Christian's engaging in legal suits on his own behalf. The greater portion of the *Restitution*, however, focuses on the "fundamental articles," in which Campanus presents his conceptions of God and of the sacraments. Basing his conception of God on Gen. 1:26 f., he argues that God the Father and Christ the pre-existent Son are two persons of one essence, just as man and wife are two persons but one flesh. The Holy Spirit is not a person, but rather the mutual bond of love between the Father and the Son. We shall have occasion to go more fully into his binitarianism and baptismal theology (Ch. 11).

Now that we have rehearsed the sectarian history of Strassburg from 1522 to 1529 (Ch. 10.2) and have introduced some seven or eight of the radical leaders who arrived in 1529 and 1531, we are in a position to recount the sectarian history of Strassburg as a whole up to the first territorial synod of the reformed city-state, convened in 1533 to draw up a territorial confession of faith and order and to put an end to all forms of separatism.

h. Strassburg Sectarians, 1531–1533. Between the arrival in 1531 of Rothmann, Servetus, and Campanus and the synodal hearings of Ziegler, Schwenckfeld, and Hofmann in June 1533, the most significant development lay not on the theological fringes of sectarianism, but at its center. This was the emergence of Pilgram Marpeck as the major spokesman and theorist of responsible, pacifistic, evangelical Anabaptism unencumbered by any marked aberrations from Protestant orthodoxy with respect to the Trinity, Christology, and eschatology. After the arrest, defection, or flight in 1529 of such leaders as Bünderlin, Reublin, Kautz, and Fridolin Meyger, it was Marpeck who remained the strategic figure in the consolidation of evangelical Anabaptism in his effort to hold the ground between the Spiritualism of Schwenckfeld and the potentially bellicose eschatology of Hofmann.

It was a tribute to Marpeck as the master craftsman of a toughly woven sectarianism that Bucer, between December 1531 and January 1532, in numerous oral and written exchanges, felt obliged to come to terms with Marpeckian Anabaptism point by point in order to vindicate the magisterial Protestantism of the civic territory and thus check the numerous defections to sectarianism.[97] In the exchange, Marpeck was enabled to sharpen up his own position and become as a consequence the chief formulator and organizer of normative (noncommunistic) Anabaptism for the whole of the High German zone from Metz to Austerlitz (Slavkov) in the course of the twenty-five years between the opening of these major debates with Bucer and his death in 1556. His Strassburg career cannot, of course, be told apart from his relationship to the extremists among whom he lived.

In a city where Bünderlin and Entfelder were widely read, where Hofmann was stirring up eschatological excitement, and where Schwenckfeld was giving contemplative separatism the tremendous support of his noble bearing and his literary productivity, a major parting of the ways of radical reform was taking place. Marpeck had taken the initiative in attempting to formulate an Anabaptist church order for the distraught moderate evangelical separatists. He wrote two works against Bünderlin in the first half of 1531.[98] He did not at the time engage in controversy with either Schwenckfeld or Hofmann. Instead, he directed his principal assault at Bucer.[99]

Marpeck's forthrightness and sobriety in expressing his separatism constituted a major challenge for the municipal clergy because a theologically orthodox, moralistic sectarianism was in its cohesiveness and attractiveness more of a threat to the realization of a unified territorial reformation than speculative spiritualism or fevered millennialism. Bucer, admitting that Marpeck and his loyal wife were otherwise of unblamable conduct,[100] accused the sinewy theologian of being an obstinate, stiff-necked heretic, lacking in love and overconfident in his own supposed knowledge.

At issue with Bucer was Marpeck's insistence that the freedom

---

[97] As an indication of the importance of Marpeck, we may adduce the fact that most of the documents in Krebs and Rott, Elsass, I (QGT, VII), between pp. 359 and 534 are almost exclusively taken up with the Marpeck-Bucer interchange and that Marpeck appears frequently at other points.

[98] Discovered and edited by William Klassen, "Pilgram Marpeck's Two Books of 1531," MQR, XXXII (1959), 18–31.

[99] 19 August 1531; Krebs and Rott, Elsass, I (QGT, VII), No. 258.

[100] At this point in the religious history of Strassburg, two works become especially important: Hastings Eells, Martin Bucer (London, 1931) and François Wendel, L'Eglise de Strasbourg: sa constitution et son organisation, 1532–1535 (Paris, 1942), Études d'Histoire et de Philosophie Religieuses, No. 38.

of the gospel should never be thrust upon the whole population, indeed that the untutored masses in so far as they were incapable of self-discipline should remain under the yoke of the law of the Old Covenant. Marpeck sought for the true, self-disciplining evangelicals (the Anabaptists) the public authorization of their use of at least one of the church edifices of the city.

Constitutive for such an evangelical or truly New Covenantal church living under the gospel rather than under the law was the acknowledgment of personal sin, the entry into the New Covenant by believers' baptism, and the observance of the evangelical law. This meant expressly the separation from the world, including the whole sphere of the law and its *legitimate but subchristian* institutions such as the state. Marpeck thought of Bucer's territorial reformation as the replacement of Catholic legalism by Jewish legalism. He felt that Bucer and the Swiss Reformers, far more than Luther, were unwittingly organizing a church of the law in succession to the people of the law by construing baptism as the equivalent of circumcision and by sanctioning a territorially or socially diffused *implicit* faith in their appeal to an inscrutable and hence unverifiable predestination in opposition to the *explicit* faith of resolute members of self-disciplined conventicles.

At the beginning of December 1531, Marpeck requested the council to permit him to debate publicly with the municipal clergy, but he was granted only a colloquium before the assembled council, the committee of twenty-one and the pastors. The public was to be excluded. The colloquium took place on 9 December 1531.[101] Thereafter the council ordered that Marpeck "keep his mouth shut."[102] On the following day, Marpeck had another discussion with Bucer.[103] Thereupon the municipal preachers themselves appealed to the council for both a fully public disputation and an improvement of moral conditions in the town.[104] Then in twenty-nine articles Marpeck presented his Confession of Faith (*Bekenntniss:* discussed further Ch. 18.5), defending adult baptism, and arguing that as of that day there was still no Christian order in Strassburg.[105] Bucer set out to refute him, article by article, repeating the view that infant baptism, like circumcision, was the symbol of initiation into the community of faith.

[101] Krebs and Rott, *Elsass*, I (*QGT*, VII), No. 277.
[102] *Ibid.*, No. 281.
[103] *Ibid.*, No. 283.
[104] *Ibid.*, No. 284.
[105] The *Bekenntnis* of Marpeck is edited by John Wenger, "Pilgram Marpeck's Confession of Faith," *MQR*, XII (1938), 167–202. See also Krebs and Rott, *Elsass,* I (*QGT*, VII), No. 302, and Bucer's refutation, No. 303.

Marpeck was ordered by the council, 18 December 1531, to desist from his effort to overthrow infant baptism and to set up a separatist church, or else leave the city and region.[106] Two days later, Marpeck notified the council that he would leave, but said that if the Spirit of God should impel him to return, he could accede to God's will.[107] He asked for a period of grace. He was granted two weeks to prepare for his departure. There was at least one more disputation, however, sometime before 12 January 1532;[108] but the earlier verdict stood. (We shall next encounter Marpeck in extended debate with Schwenckfeld, Ch. 18.)

While Marpeck and Bucer were engaged in increasingly tense exchanges, Hofmann entered Strassburg for his sojourn. On returning to his base from his Dutch mission, he sustained a tremendous blow to the cause, the recantation and decapitation of his Dutch deputy (Ch. 12.3) and nine others in The Hague. Because of this ferocity in Catholic terrain, so different from Hofmann's experience in Protestant territory, he ordered the suspension of the ordinance of believers' baptism for two years, appealing for Biblical sanction to Ezra 4:24. The emergence (*Durchbruch*) or the descent of the New Jerusalem (Rev. 21:10) was being temporarily interrupted, he inferred, as the reconstruction of the ancient Temple had been held up because of the hostility of the Samaritans. Hofmann was thus returning to Strassburg as a proponent of the provisional suspension (*Stillstand*) of (re-)baptism as Schwenckfeld was a proponent of the suspension of the Eucharist. Since Hofmann, of course, still opposed infant baptism as did Schwenckfeld, and since Hofmann was closer to Schwenckfeld on Christology (celestial flesh) than to Marpeck, it is understandable that the divines and magistrates of Strassburg more and more linked the furrier and the nobleman, as did likewise some of the Melchiorites themselves who were conjecturing that Schwenckfeld might be the hidden Enoch and as such the eschatological counterpart of Hofmann, the new Elijah.

Hofmann occupied himself with the writing and printing of three new works. One of them, *Von der wahrhaftigen Menschwerdung des ewigen Worts*,[109] departed from traditional Nicene and Chalcedonian language. Thereupon the Strassburg authorities ordered Hofmann's arrest, 11 December 1531.[110] He was able,

---

[106] *Elsass,* I, No. 287.
[107] *Ibid.,* No. 290.
[108] Cf. *ibid.,* No. 306, and the preceding pp. 426–529.
[109] *Ibid.,* Nos., 279, 298.
[110] *Ibid.,* No. 280.

however, to get the two other works printed, either in Strassburg or Hagenau, at the beginning of 1532. With a renewed order for his arrest, Hofmann withdrew from the city.

He traveled through Hesse, where the landgrave Philip heard him preach,[111] presumably on his way to his mission field in the Netherlands. There he published an exposition of the epistle to the Romans. He was now surer than ever that the new age was dawning and that he was the Elijah presaging the second advent of Christ.

To Strassburg he returned in the spring of 1533, his fourth visit, and proceeded to write or publish four or five more tracts of an intensely eschatological character. For two months his writing and preaching in the house of the goldsmith, Valtin Duft, was tolerated by the Strassburg magistrates until at length Hofmann himself courted arrest by sending a provocative letter to the council in May, along with one of his tracts on the sword, where he again described the strategic role of Strassburg at the impending second advent. From his behavior in Strassburg and from his writings to date, notably from the commentary on the thirteenth chapter of Romans, it is clear that Hofmann still adhered to a peaceful attitude toward all magistrates as provisionally ordained of God. He did not countenance a resort to violence to advance the cosmic calendar nor social revolution to accelerate the divine "break-through." He chose to go bareheaded and barefooted in testimony of his confidence in the proximity of the Kingdom and he ate only bread. Not wishing to give occasion for purely social and political demonstrations, Hofmann made a practice of taking long walks on holidays to avoid being sought out by the idle and restless elements in the population.[112] In May he underwent two judicial hearings[113] and was put under mild arrest. He was permitted to write and to receive the brethren and to counsel with them, pending the territorial synod of the reformed church of Strassburg, which was in preparation.

On this note of expectancy in Strassburg sectarianism, we may turn to the synod of Strassburg and the new resolve of the magisterial divines to come to terms once for all with the leaders of sectarianism, notably Hofmann, Schwenckfeld, and the followers of Kautz or of Marpeck, and, having worsted them in the eyes of the citizenry, to construct an ecclesiastical order and a confession of faith for the unified church of their urban republic.

---

111 *Elsass*, II, No. 407.
112 *Ibid.*, No. 368, p. 17. For a follower's description of the "break-through" (*Durchbruch*), see Polderman, *ibid.*, No. 610, p. 388.
113 *Ibid.*, Nos. 364, 368.

4. THE SYNOD OF STRASSBURG AND ITS CONSEQUENCES, 1533–1535

A major event in the history of the Reformation of the imperial city-state of Strassburg was the extended synod of June 1533. Groping for an ecclesiastical consensus that would demarcate the theological position of the free city over against the sectaries and the local partisans of the bishop, Bucer was under the practical necessity of so formulating it that Strassburg would continue to qualify for its important role in the (Lutheran) Smalcald League without offending the sympathizers in Strassburg of the more sacramentarian Swiss formulations. At the same time, the divines of the city's seven parishes and the magistrates could no longer conceal the fact that a few of their number were, in varying degrees, receptive to some of the theological, moral, and religio-political criticism coming from the Radicals. Thus, as in perhaps no other region, was the formulation of the Magisterial Reformation so explicitly drawn up in refutation of the Radical Reformation as in the synod of Strassburg in 1533. The synod reflects, indeed, a desperate struggle for ecclesiastical order against chaos, of law against religious anarchy. Bucer was later to interpret the crisis, with excessive remorse, as due to "the long-standing and impious clemency" shown toward the separatists by himself and the Strassburg divines.[114]

Although the first mandate against the Anabaptists had been issued by the city council back in July 1527, private citizens and innkeepers had obviously not been refusing to feed and lodge the immigrant sectarians. By the end of 1532 so many Radicals had streamed into the city and so many of the immigrant and the indigenous separatists were agitating and recruiting that Bucer and his colleagues were alarmed for the safety of their reformation. Jacob Kautz, for example, was back in the fall of 1532, demanding to defend Anabaptism in public debate.

On 29 November 1532 (almost a year after the banishment of Marpeck), Capito, Hedio, Bucer, and Zell, in the name of the municipal preachers and the board of twenty-one churchwardens, requested the city council to comply with Kautz's request in the hope that the whole Anabaptist cause could be in his person publicly repudiated; and in the same supplication they submitted a three-point recommendation for the further strengthening of the territorial church: that an annual church visitation be instituted, the operative ecclesiastical traditions and new ordinances be codified, and a territorial synod be convened semiannually.

[114] *Ibid.,* No. 362.

Before this proposed synod could materialize in June, a complex, interrelated series of judicial hearings and lesser synods and ecclesiastical deliberations took place, the most important of which were the following: the magisterial hearings in May of the Anabaptist bigamist, Nicholas Frey, and of the Anabaptist apocalyptist, Melchior Hofmann. Concurrently there was a committee at work drafting a composite confession of faith and order, based on the *Tetrapolitana,* and the twenty-two articles suggested by Bucer in his letter[115] written to the principal Strassburg divines from Basel where Bucer was to attend the cantonal synod. Thirdly, there was a preliminary municipal synod (*Stadt-Synode, Vorsynode*) sitting from 3 to 6 June. Fourthly, there was the territorial synod itself (*Land-Synode, Hauptsynode*), sitting from 10 to 14 June. Then, after the territorial synod, there were, fifthly, two lines of action, the deliberations of the magistrates in fixing the various penalties for the heretics and schismatics heard by the synod and the deliberations of the divines in drawing up ordinances agreed to by the synod. Some of these activities led to what may be called, sixthly, a postsynod, actually the autumnal or second semiannual synod, foreseen by the planners.

As for the preliminary judicial hearings of Frey and Hofmann, we have already discussed the appearances of the latter (Ch. 10.3.h) and we shall refer to the former in connection with the territorial synod. We are therefore free to concentrate on the second and third episodes, leading up to the territorial synod.

a. Preparations for the Territorial Synod. The commission set up by the council to draft the confession of faith and order and to prepare the agenda for the territorial synod was made up of four preachers (Bucer, Capito, Hedio, and Melchior Cumanus of St. Aurelia's) and four of the city's twenty-one lay wardens (*Kirchenpfleger*). It will be recalled (Ch. 10.2) that when Bucer originally proposed the organization of this board, he thought of the wardens as "apostolic elders" and, as such, quasi-ministerial, but by now their pre-eminently magisterial character was clear.[116]

The draft confession produced by the joint commission consisted of sixteen articles.[117] They were notable for their defense of the Trinity expressly against the recent formulations of Servetus (article i),[118] their defense of Chalcedonian Christology against Hofmann (article iv), their repudiation of the sacrificial interpre-

115 *Ibid.,* No. 358.
116 Wendel, *op. cit.,* 45 f.
117 Krebs and Rott, *Elsass,* II (*QGT,* VIII), No. 371.
118 Quoted in part above at n. 93, Ch. 10.

tation of the Eucharist against the Catholics (article ix), their stress on the importance of an inclusive and visible Communion against Schwenckfeld (article x), and their defense of infant baptism against all the Anabaptists and Spiritualists (articles vii, viii). Bucer himself, it may be remarked, was now on the point of considering infants as belonging more to the commonwealth than to their parents.[119]

Especially important were the last three articles, dealing at some length with the Biblical and theological justification for the positive role of the magistrates in the reform and in the maintenance of the church. These three articles were elaborated not only against the Anabaptists but also against one of the official Strassburg divines, Dr. Anthony Engelbrecht, and his sympathizers among the city clergy and burghers. The commission justified a mixed synod of divines and magistrates by appealing to the precedent of the council of Jerusalem with apostles and elders and the councils presided over anciently by Constantine and his successors.

It was the committee for drawing up the sixteen articles and the agenda which also suggested the convocation of a preliminary synod confined to the city clergy before involving the rural clergy prematurely in the problems not yet wholly solved by their more sophisticated city brethren. Accordingly, a municipal synod gathered on 3 June in St. Magdelene's,[120] especially fitted out for the occasion. Present were the pastors and their associates of the city parishes, the twenty-one churchwardens, and the masters of arts and all other teachers. Four delegates from each of the city's guilds were also present as witnesses. The synod convened under the collegial presidency of four members of the council, of whom the most distinguished was Stettmeister Jacob Sturm. Capito, who had once taken a leading part in the cantonal synods of Bern in 1528 and 1532 (Ch. 23.2), delivered the opening sermon.

The choice of Capito was technically dictated by the order of precedence among the established preachers and also out of recognition of his important role in the recent Bern synod; but Bucer, who had also played a part in the recent synod of Basel, will have had good strategic reasons for urging Capito to become conspicuously identified with the work of the Strassburg synod. Even after his second marriage and his resolution to be more severe with the sectaries, Capito would once in a while return musingly to some of his older positions. In explaining the sixteen

---

[119] *Bericht aus heiliger Schrift* (1534), fo. 92b; cited by Wendel, *op. cit.*, 118.
[120] Wendel, *op. cit.*, 69 ff.

articles to the congregation in St. Magdelene's convent church of the penitents, Capito will surely have recalled in his mind's eye many a winsome visitor or house guest whose views he was now exhorting the synod to condemn. In condemning, for example, "a certain Spaniard" in the first article, he will have remembered that he himself had not always been so clear about Servetus' error and that when he and Bucer were toiling over the text of the *Tetrapolitana* he had himself for some reason substituted *Trias* for *Trinitas* and *discrimen* for *distinctio person-arum*.[121]

After Capito's inaugural disquisition, the proposed articles of faith and order were formally reread in their entirety and then taken up one by one, while each of the pastors and assistants was invited to consent or comment.[122] There were some important differences of conviction expressed, especially with respect to the Eucharist, but the most lively discussion centered in the last three articles, which were opposed by Anthony Engelbrecht and by several others with less insistence, on the ground that, on the one hand, the magistrates were thereby being allowed impertinent access to the realm of conviction and conscience and that, on the other, the divines themselves through the synodal system were on the point of converting the Reformed church into a "new papistry," the more powerful because local.

It may be worth-while to permit the figure of Dr. Engelbrecht to stand out in synod, because he makes once again specific and plausible the generalization that there were, particularly in Strassburg territory, many mixed or transitional types between the Magisterial and the Radical Reformers. Bucer and Capito thought of him as the spokesman of the "Epicurean" party or "sect"[123] among the burghers and divines who, like the Spiritual Libertines elsewhere (Chs. 12.2; 23.3), espoused fraternal freedom of inquiry and discussion as a safeguard against a Protestant "popery."

These Epicureans had much in common with Franck, Entfelder, Bünderlin, and Schwenckfeld. All of them humanists, they found a favorable hearing among some of the patricians who were none too eager to come under any continuous or impertinent ecclesiastical supervision. One may here generalize in pointing

---

[121] Strasser, *op. cit.*, 71.

[122] *Elsass*, II, No. 373.

[123] Besides Engelbrecht and Schultheiss, the principal members of the party were Jacob Ziegler, John Sapidus (Witz), the teacher of the second Latin school, and the teacher and botanist Otto Brunfels, whom we have already treated outside his Strassburg setting—namely, in Basel with Servetus—who was also called by some an Epicurean. *Elsass*, II, No. 406a; also, Nos. 353, 402, p. 112; No. 492, p. 263. See on the Epicureans, Wendel, *op. cit.*, 38 ff.

out that some of the liberal patricians (prosperous commoners are here included with the nobles), "the Epicurean prelates" (another of Bucer's terms), and the Anabaptists of all persuasions were tactically or instinctively in league in opposing the use of magisterial coercion in support of ecclesiastical (synodal) doctrine and discipline; but, of course, they acted from different motives, not always even entirely clarified in their own minds.

The liberal nobles and the humanistic burghers, for example, could openly or covertly side with both the Epicurean Libertines, the other Spiritualists, and the Anabaptists in the hope of preventing their own established clergy from imposing too rigorously the disciplines of Protestant salvation upon them and their pleasant city.

The tightly sectarian Anabaptists, in contrast, certain of their Biblical faith and discipline, wished to be separated from the prudential or coercive magistrates in order to be freer and swifter in the exercise of the ban and the other disciplines of a self-contained sect.

The Epicurean clerics themselves appear to have been earnestly concerned for the open quest of truth and were ever ready to keep free the channels of communication and fresh revelation in order that "the gifts of the Spirit might pour out alike over the great and the humble."[124]

During the synodal discussions, after Engelbrecht, the second most important Epicurean was the pastor of Schiltigheim,[125] Wolfgang Schultheiss, from whom we have just quoted. In a long poem, *Ermahnung zum geistlichen Urteil*, in 1530, he had appealed to I Cor. 14:29 f. in an effort to encourage the free flow of the Spirit and to restore an irenic manner in the discussion of things spiritual, the Bible, new interpretations of old passages, all with the possibility of contemporary fresh inspiration. Schultheiss in his defense of the right of the whole congregation to judge Scripture, lest a "new tyranny" replace the old, was insisting on what Campanus in connection with the same passage in Corinthians had called the *Sitzerrecht* (Ch. 10.3.g).

Dr. Engelbrecht no doubt owed some of the ideas he expressed in synod to Schultheiss. Formerly the suffragan bishop of Speyer, Engelbrecht had been the very one to release Bucer from his Dominican vows. When Engelbrecht in his turn came to Strassburg as an evangelical, he was made pastor of St. Stephen's. A man of considerable educational attainment and administrative experience behind him, Engelbrecht displayed in the Strassburg

[124] *Elsass,* II, p. 293, line 2 f.
[125] *Ibid.,* No. 236a.

municipal synod and elsewhere something of the mentality and
the manner of the Spiritualists and the separatists, and he would
presently be vilified by the majority of the municipal clergy as
both an Epicurean and as a consorter with ragamuffins and alley
evangelists. In synod he defended the principle of the separation
of the two kingdoms and the distinction between the two swords,
appealing expressly to the early Luther. Accordingly, he argued
for a clean separation in Strassburg territory between religion and
politics. He did not deny that government was of God and that
the magistrate might well have a Christian vocation, but he
pointed out what he considered the inconsistency of the Magisterial Reformers who, having once called for the free proclamation of the gospel, were now formulating it in synodal decisions
and, appealing to the precedent of Constantine and especially of
Justinian, were using the authority of the state to enforce these
decisions against conscientious dissidents. Engelbrecht was convinced, he said, that there was no place for coercion in the realm
of doctrine and conscience, for only God can legitimately and
efficaciously penetrate this realm. He held not only that the
magistrates should refrain from dictating doctrine but also that
the divines for their part should refrain from meddling in government, whether for the sake of protecting themselves and their
doctrine or for the amelioration of government. In the case of
a religiously indifferent or hostile magistracy, the divines should
be content to prepare themselves and their flocks to suffer for
their faith in holy patience (Rev. 13:10). In deploring the
emergence of the mixed synod as the beginning of a "new
papistry," interposing itself between God and the believer,
Engelbrecht cited Erasmus on Hilary of Poitiers to prove that
synods and councils historically had led to the emergence of the
papacy. Engelbrecht angered the synod by insisting that coercion
of conscience, like that shown by the Jews, the Mohammedans,
or the Catholics, was no better for being called Lutheran, Zwinglian, or Anabaptist (a prophetic glance, perhaps, toward
Münster).[126]

On the last day of the municipal synod, the discussion of faith
and order was interrupted by a novel procedure which had been
recommended by the original planning commission. This was
the mutual censuring of the preachers. The four synodal presi-
dents, along with the churchwardens (*Kirchenpfleger*) who had
been charged with the surveillance of the ministers since 1531,
now retired to a private room, where the preachers were severally
interviewed. Each was allowed in his turn to make any observa-

[126] *Ibid.*, No. 373, supplemented by Engelbrecht's enlarged statement, No. 374.

tions he cared to about the behavior and thinking of his colleagues. Nerves exacerbated by synodal debate were assuaged by
the opportunity thus afforded in secret. It is not surprising that
Dr. Anthony Engelbrecht[127] was most frequently mentioned as
censurable, specifically for absenting himself frequently from the
weekly convocations of the municipal clergy, for frequenting
taverns and promenading, for having "bad company at table,"
for baptizing in houses, for not taking his sermon preparation
seriously, and for allowing his maid and his serving boy to go
unkempt in the alleys.[128]

The censuring of the clergy completed, the municipal synod
resumed the discussion of the sixteen articles and turned to the
ecclesiastical ordinances which were to be put in final shape.

b. The Territorial Synod, June 1533. Four days after the close
of the municipal synod the territorial synod convened on 10 June.
The first day was given over to the comment on, and assent to,
the sixteen articles on the part of the representatives of twenty-
three annexed or dependent villages and bailiwicks,[129] ranging
from Kehl on the opposite bank of the Rhine to Detweiler (near
present-day Saverne), and Wasselnheim (present-day Wasselonne).
Then during the next four days the synod occupied itself with
examining several radical leaders and otherwise prominent personalities, two of whom—Hofmann and Frey—had already been
examined several times by the magistrates.

The first to be questioned was the gardener-preacher Clement
Ziegler, in whose house in the annexed village of the Robertsau
many Anabaptists had been meeting. Ziegler reasserted his opposition to civil punishment for religious beliefs. Holding to universal salvation, he did not now, as he had earlier (Ch. 10.2),
condemn infant baptism.[130] Bucer, who conducted most of the
examinations, was satisfied that Ziegler's heresy was relatively
harmless, and he was dismissed.

After the brief investigation of Martin Storen (Stoer), a follower of Ziegler,[131] who was, however, indisposed to go at length

[127] *Ibid.,* No. 373 (D), where Dr. Anthony (Engelbrecht) is to be distinguished
from Master Anthony (Firn).
[128] The charge concerning baptism is also borne out in No. 358, p. 5. The
convocation from which he so frequently absented himself because of his
"anticlericalism" was, in effect, the clerical guild, the corps of pastors functioning in a way analogous to the twenty-one other corporations. Wendel,
op. cit., 46 f., esp. n. 62.
[129] For a list of dependencies with their various relations to the city chapters,
see Wendel, *op. cit.,* 67, n. 30. For the replies of the representatives, see
Krebs and Rott, *Elsass,* II (*QGT,* VIII), No. 384 (A).
[130] Krebs and Rott, *Elsass,* II (*QGT,* VIII), pp. 76 f.
[131] On Storen as a follower of Ziegler, see *Elsass,* II, No. 504, p. 275.

into his own convictions and speculations, Melchior Hofmann appeared before the synod. In the course of his first and subsequent appearances he advanced his views with passion and later summarized them under five headings.[132] In Bucer's later summary[133] and refutation the propositions were reduced to four. Hofmann rephrased his doctrine of the single celestial nature of Christ against the version of Schwenckfeld (according to whom there were two natures, both of which in effect were celestial) and against the traditional (Chalcedonian) doctrine of a divine nature and a human nature complete with human flesh. While insisting on the full deity of Christ, Hofmann opposed addressing the Son or the Holy Spirit in prayer.[134] With respect to his Christology, more than with any other of his points, Hofmann conducted himself before the synod more as an impassioned evangelistical theologian than as a visionary heretic under inquisitorial scrutiny. He brought forward his other four points also with great conviction in the course of several sessions, namely, that the Second Adam died for the salvation of all mankind, since in the first Adam all mankind has suffered the punishment of eternal death; that divine illumination in the presence of Scripture could restore to every man the freedom of the will once possessed in Paradise; that infant baptism was of the devil and that believers' baptism was the only valid public testimony of a renewed mind and will; and that there was no pardon for intentional sin, that is, for sin committed after the illumination of baptism. On this last point Hofmann was particularly emphatic, citing Scripture with great cogency (Lev. 15:30, and Heb. 10:26). He also brought this same text of Hebrews into relation with another in Leviticus (ch. 4:13 ff.) to substantiate his point that the atoning sacrifice of Christ, the eternal High Priest, was for the *unknown* sins of the community and of the individual, namely, original sin and prebaptismal sins committed before the believer's Scriptural and spiritual illumination as to right and wrong. Citing IV Esdras 7:5, 9; Rev. 21:8; and II Peter 2:21, Hofmann pictured the Christian life after entry into the covenant of a renewed will and conscience as a great struggle against falling from (the second) Paradise (the church of the reborn) for a second time, now into the harrowing death of fire and brimstone. This "second death" was worse in its consequences than if one had never come to know the way of righteousness and to turn from it.

On 12 June, Caspar Schwenckfeld, who had submitted five of

---

[132] *Ibid.*, No. 398.
[133] *Ibid.*, Nos. 402, 444.
[134] *Ibid.*, No. 384, p. 83

his books for scrutiny, was examined. He asked that one of these, in particular, the *Protest*,[135] be read before the synod to clear him of the charge of being a disrupter of the duly reformed territorial church. To the municipal reformers the *Protest* seemed to be an ingenious attempt to say contradictory things by alternate affirmation and qualification,[136] especially with reference to the observance and the meaning of the Supper. On Christology and the atonement, Schwenckfeld insisted over against Bucer and the whole tradition of the West that Christ, "undivided," suffered as one Person in his divine nature also and not only in his human flesh and nature.[137] Schwenckfeld loftily offered to instruct Hofmann privately on the matter of the celestial flesh and for the moment contented himself with reiterating his defense of prayers addressed to Christ, as to the Father. Schwenckfeld, suddenly taken ill, was unable to return to the examination after the midday repast.

Hofmann was therefore recalled. The discussion with him lasted well into the next day. He had, at an earlier judicial hearing,[138] declared that he had been in dispute with Schwenckfeld on the matter of the celestial flesh of Christ ever since the beginning of 1529 and took this occasion to explain to the synod, as we have already noted, how he differed from Schwenckfeld, notwithstanding his great esteem for the pious Silesian.

After the second appearance of Hofmann, the synod summoned Nicholas Frey with a view to establishing a connection between his notorious bigamy and his espousal of Anabaptism. The case, one of the best documented of its kind,[139] is at once typical of the desertions for cause of the covenant which we find occasionally throughout the Radical Reformation and at the same time

---

[135] The *Protest* is published in *CS*, IV, 788–790. See also *The Articles Necessary for Consideration at a Synod*, *CS*, III, 112–116. Eells, *op. cit.*, 148, holds that Schwenckfeld submitted his books, including the *Protest*, with the hope of getting synodal endorsement. Schultz, *op. cit.*, 214 f., is clear that Schwenckfeld, whatever hopes he may have entertained, knew very well that he had been cited before the synod on a standing superior to that of Frey and Hofmann only in the fact that he had, of course, never been called before the magisterial court for actions or thoughts coming primarily within their jurisdiction. The synodal commission for scrutinizing the writing of Hofmann and Schwenckfeld reported on the two men together. *Elsass*, II, Nos. 441, p. 178; 444.

[136] Cf. Schultz, *op. cit.*, 215; Eells, *op. cit.*, 148.

[137] Krebs and Rott, *Elsass*, I (*QGT*, VIII), No. 381, p. 81.

[138] *Ibid.*, No. 368, p. 19.

[139] The more important documents upon which the following account is based are *Elsass*, I, Nos. 361, 369, 384, p. 83; Nos. 388, 410, 456, and esp. 464 (Capito's account). François Wendel does not deal with Frey but he does deal

poignantly personal, and it is therefore socioreligiously of exceptional interest. We are helped to see Frey and his devout and duped second spouse in a larger context (cf. Ch. 20) if we but remind ourselves that most of the clerics who were sitting in synod in judgment upon him had themselves repudiated their sacramental vows of celibacy to marry, becoming Protestants, and that the principal divine among them would, a few years later, be finding Biblical reasons for justifying the notorious bigamy of a leading Protestant prince.[140] The divines and magistrates in synod were judging (according to common law rather than according to the Bible) an admittedly fantastic layman who, too, had repudiated his sacramental vows, in his case of marriage, to marry a second time "within the covenant" on becoming an Anabaptist and after his first spouse had refused to follow him into the baptismal covenant. To be sure, in having eventually gone beyond covenantal (re-)marriage to propound a rather elaborate theology of spiritual marriage as itself the means of redemption, Frey presented the magistrates and divines of Strassburg with a particularly vexing problem; and, in view of his messianic pretensions, it is indeed extraordinary that they allowed him to express himself so fully and delayed action against him for so long.

A furrier by trade and a brother of a Rottenburg town councilor, Frey, who had earlier taken part in the Peasants' War, was baptized by an emissary from Zurich, and became a member of the Anabaptist conventicle (Ch. 8.2) gathered in Windsheim. He was imprisoned and then released after abjuring his separatism, but in his heart he belonged to the new movement and lay tormented in his home, discussing his faith with his wife. Fearing persecution, he prudently left for Nuremberg, whither his wife forwarded one hundred fifty gold guilders to aid him in exile. From his relative security, he wrote appealing to her to join the covenant, sell the house, and come to him with their seven or eight children. After some hesitation, no doubt both religious and practical, she refused to follow him; and for dereliction of domestic duty and for increasing evidence of his being given to

with adjustments in the conception and practice of marriage in Strassburg in *Le mariage à Strasbourg à l'époque de la Réforme, 1520–1692* (Strasbourg, 1928). The article on Frey in the *ME* indicates that he was baptized as early as 1525, but in view of the known activity of his Swiss baptizer, Julius Lober, it would appear that the baptism of Frey is to be dated from 1531 or at the earliest, 1530.

[140] For Bucer on the bigamy of Philip of Hesse, on divorce, and marriage in general, see Wendel, *Mariage*.

religious vagaries, the Rottenburg-Windsheim Anabaptist community excommunicated him.

At the residence near Bamberg of Baron George Pfersfelder, who was favorably disposed toward Anabaptism and Spiritualist speculation, Frey made the acquaintance of the baron's widowed sister. It was perhaps at this juncture that Frey's interpretation of his mission with special reference to marriage underwent an extraordinary transformation that reminds us of the cosmic and redemptive androgynous messianism of William Postel and Paracelsus (Ch. 20).

The receptive widow, Elizabeth, encouraged by a nocturnal vision, yielded herself in *Gelassenheit,* spirit and body, to the charismatic visionary. Frey came to regard their spiritual union as redemptive for all who would heed their message. In some obscure way he related Elizabeth (as the new Mary and the new Eve) and himself (as an epiphany of Christ and the visible head of the church invisible) to the Trinity, and he spoke of his visions and oracles as received "in the Trinity." He declared somewhat incoherently that Elizabeth was "a virgin before her birth, during her birth, and after her birth" and as such "the mother of all believers" and "the foundress of true Christian faith." In likening her to Eve and to Mary, Frey went so far that, when Catherine, his first wife, came to Nuremberg to search him out and the jealous Elizabeth struck her rival on the head, he interpreted the blow as that delivered by the new Eve against Satan and his wiles; and he cited the words of Jesus (Luke 14:26) about leaving wife and child as the sanction for his entry into "the covenant of God," betokened now by spiritual marriage rather than by baptism.

It was with this conviction that the couple had removed to Strassburg and had associated themselves with Hofmann and other speculative separatists who foregathered in the house of the goldsmith Valtin Duft. When, however, Hofmann fully grasped what Frey meant by his "spiritual sister," he condemned him with indignation, and the couple had to find new lodgings. Hofmann's own theology abounded in nuptial terminology (Ch. 11.3), but he was shocked to find out that Frey was using this patriarchal-mystical language in a sense that seemed to him common adultery decked out with ostrich plumes plucked from Scripture. The two Radicals were henceforth determined enemies. Hofmann was particularly grieved to be now associated with his enemy during the synodal hearing.

Under questioning before the synod, Frey continued to assert that Elizabeth Pfersfelder was his only true wife; but, no doubt to the great relief of both the Melchiorites and the Marpeckians, he no longer considered himself of their number, maintaining instead that neither the baptism of the synodal divines nor that of the Anabaptists was the true one and that the only true church, of which he considered himself the visible head, was essentially inward and free of all externalities except for the covenant of spiritual marriage which it was his evangelical mission to proclaim.

Despite his abjuring Anabaptism, the divines of the synod were able to associate his original bigamy with Anabaptism and the vagaries growing out of it with Spiritualism, respectively with Hofmann and Schwenckfeld, and thereby to point up their claim that the self-styled puritans were not free from that misconduct and worse which had been their original justification for separating from the church of the multitude.

Meanwhile, Schwenckfeld had sufficiently recovered to make his second appearance before the synod on the afternoon of 13 June. With Bucer he exchanged views of the sacraments and justified his view, based on Rom. 4:11 ff., that before the introduction of circumcision, Abraham and the saints lived by faith and without the need of any visible signs, which Schwenckfeld considered a provisional concession to the Jews. Abraham was thus in terms of Schwenckfeld's inner Christianity expressly a Christian before he was a Jew (Ch. 18.5). For his theory that there were Christians before there were Jews, Schwenckfeld could have appealed to Eusebius (*Ecclesiastical History,* I. iv. 6), who in his turn had drawn upon a favorite theme of the Apologists (Tertullian: *anima naturaliter christiana,* and Justin Martyr: I *Apologia,* xlvi). Schwenckfeld's restorationism, more radical than that of the Anabaptists who were usually content with the restoration of apostolic Christianity, was more than Bucer could suffer. To be sure, Schwenckfeld was now willing to allow the principal visible Christian rite, infant baptism, to be continued so long as it was not called "the baptism of Christ." Schwenckfeld wished to reserve the latter term for the inward baptism of fire (illumination) and the Spirit. In the course of the discussion, Schwenckfeld unwittingly associated himself with Engelbrecht and the other "Epicureans" on church and state. While admitting that the magistrate might well take care for the furtherance of divine worship, the pastors themselves, he said, should never appeal to the magistrates to protect them personally from criticism or persecution. At about this point it was decided to continue the controversy with Schwenckfeld in writing.

After the midday repast Martin Storen was re-examined. Still

reluctant to air his beliefs, he accepted all the sixteen articles
save those on the Supper and Baptism, where he followed Ziegler
and Schwenckfeld, and on the incarnation, where he chose to
await further light. With this partial submission of Storen, the
territorial synod came to an end. A commission was set up to put
the record in final form and to formulate the ecclesiastical
ordinances.

c. *The Consequences of the Synod, 1533–1535.* Bucer emerged
from the synod as, in the eyes of the other preachers, *"nostrae
ecclesiae episcopus."*[141] A post-synod or autumnal synod in October[142] took up the unfinished business; and the magistrates,
under increasing pressure from the new *episcopus,* moved somewhat reluctantly toward the consolidation of the Magisterial
Reformation. It was magisterial in the sense that the instinctive
disposition of all magistrates to have a hand in the control of the
externals of the church had not only received theological endorsement in the Protestant principle of the priesthood of all believers
but was also being enlarged to include doctrine and discipline,
and acquiring further justification in the effort of the Magisterial
Reformers to consider the magistrates as the effectual successors of
the apostolic elders and corporately as the local equivalent of the
ancient Christian emperors in council. Moreover, the involvement of the magistrates in the internal affairs of the territorial
church of which they were members was now being urged upon
them by the Magisterial Reformers, in their near desperation
with the separatists, not merely as a right of patronage but as a
duty, not as a concession but as an imperious vocation.

Acting upon the recommendations of the October synod, the
magistrates accordingly demanded the expulsion of the Hofmannites, designated certain councilmen as *Täuferherren* (constables)[143] to deal with the obstinate, took note of the departure of
certain Epicureans such as Otto Brunfels and Jacob Ziegler, and
proceeded to authorize the redaction of a set of disciplinary
ordinances or blue laws corresponding to, and supplementing,
the theologically more amplified ecclesiastical ordinances of the
synod.

The punishment of the several separatists heard by the territorial synod was diverse. Though Clement Ziegler and Storen
were formally banished, they were allowed to stay in Strassburg

---

[141] Letter of Capito to Grynaeus, 13 September 1534; cited by Wendel, *Constitution,* 95
[142] Wendel, *Constitution,* 101, discusses the two ways of interpreting the synodal
session of October 1533.
[143] Wendel, *Constitution,* p. 107.

territory so long as Ziegler desisted from preaching. Storen had shown no disposition to propagate Ziegler's ideas. Eventually, Ziegler was given to further visions, which he published and reported to the magistrates.[144]

As for the Epicureans, Engelbrecht, although he was not formally summoned before the council, being himself a member of convocation, was under censure and was in due course removed from St. Stephen's.[145] The other Epicurean, Wolfgang Schultheiss, was threatened with suspension.[146] Jacob Ziegler had by now left the city. He wrote *Synodus*,[147] a largely Biblical refutation of the religio-political presuppositions of the recent territorial synod. Written in mordant Latin, it differed from many an Anabaptist tract on the same theme in citing a relatively large number of Old Testament texts warning against the placing of sacerdotal authority and political dominion in the hands of the same person or class. The work was refuted by Bucer.[148] We shall meet J. Ziegler briefly as an emissary of several German houses in Venice, an abiding friend of Schwenckfeld (Ch. 21.4).

As for Schwenckfeld, the Strassburg synod was tired of his endless, repetitious, soft-spoken practical separatism, but it was reluctant to treat the Silesian nobleman with harshness, the more so for the reason that Matthew and Catherine Zell at the cathedral parish were still disposed to favor certain of his views. At the synod, the books which Schwenckfeld had submitted for scrutiny had not been carefully read, and he insisted that Bucer at greater leisure specify their failings. In return Bucer asked Schwenckfeld for a statement to the effect that, despite all the qualifications he might wish to make, the church of Strassburg was after all proclaiming the gospel and deserved to be heeded by the whole population. Schwenckfeld promised to produce such a statement "as the Lord might direct," and reiterated his plea for Bucer's book review. Shortly afterward Bucer sent it to him. Schwenckfeld composed a reply, read it to Capito and Hedio, and then pressed Hedio to appease Bucer.

In September, Schwenckfeld left Strassburg for Augsburg, arriving there on 3 October. Here he complained that he had been condemned in Strassburg for attacking the view once defended by none other than Luther, on the separation of the two

---

[144] Krebs and Rott, *Elsass*, II (*QGT*, VIII), Nos. 453, 486.
[145] 3 March 1534; on Engelbrecht's views after the synod, see *Elsass*, II, Nos. 472, 488, 501, 515, 516, etc.
[146] Cf. *ibid.*, No. 499, p. 269.
[147] On Jacob Ziegler's views, see *ibid.*, esp. Nos. 478, 530.
[148] *Ibid.*, No. 509.

kingdoms. Bucer read before the Strassburg city council his catalogue of Schwenckfeld's faults but unfairly withheld Schwenckfeld's rejoinder. More fairly, Bucer, when he came to send his catalogue to the preachers in Augsburg, in requesting them to hand it over to Schwenckfeld, added that they should receive him charitably. There can be little doubt but that the intense and extended concern of Bucer to refute Schwenckfeld in the eyes of the liberal and receptive magistrates of Augsburg and elsewhere was to check the "Epicurean" spirit from inhibiting the humanistic patricians of the South German towns in supporting the Magisterial Reformation with requisite energy. Schwenckfeld returned to Strassburg, but this time the council was prevailed upon to ask him to leave for the peace of the territorial church (22 July 1534).[149] We shall follow Schwenckfeld's subsequent career in due course (Ch. 18).

The fate of Nicholas Frey was death by drowning, but not until after a number of dramatic and patient efforts had been made to reconcile him with his first wife. She was brought from Windsheim. She visited him several times in prison, throwing her arms about him in her importuning. She had brought with her two of his children to facilitate the reconciliation if possible, but he obdurately refused to have anything to do with them. When finally the council resolved to drown him for bigamy and sent a red-bearded servant to announce the sentence to him, he spoke of the messenger as a Judas, although this did not prevent him from calling the messenger also a brother. Confident to the end that he was the stone that the builders of Strassburg had rejected, and increasingly insolent toward even his sympathizers, Frey went to the council chamber and from there to the bridge over the Ill (at present: Corbeau) for the drowning, utterly certain of the ultimate consummation of his mission. Both he and Elizabeth expected miracles to follow his execution.

Elizabeth originally besought the council to be permitted to die with her spouse, but after the evident failure of his mission and the want of miracles, she implored the church of Strassburg that she be forgiven for her folly and for her adultery. But even this repudiation seemed insufficient to Capito, who, noting the impression of Frey's steadfastness in his asseverations at his numerous hearings and at the execution, wrote a booklet on true and false martyrdom, incidentally supplying considerable detail on the erroneous views of Frey.

The fate of Melchior Hofmann was life imprisonment. But

149 *Ibid.,* No. 588

neither the magistrates nor the divines could entirely forget him, partly because the restless prophet called frequent attention to himself by his fasts and his fulminations, his ailments and his literary attacks; partly because some among the magistrates could not entirely rid themselves of the haunting thought that he might after all be, as he persisted in styling himself,[150] the new Elijah and a portent of the role their city might play at the Second Advent; and partly because both the magistrates and the divines of Strassburg were humane and lenient, the more so in Hofmann's case because he often seemed to them more demented than heretical.

Though within a few days of the territorial synod the city council made the terms of his imprisonment more severe, Hofmann managed with the help of his Dutch disciple, Cornelius Polderman of Middelburg, to have two tracts published and an account of the recent territorial synod.[151] In Hofmann's account it would be quite evident to his Netherlandish followers that he was the victor over Bucer. For this reason, Bucer himself felt obliged to retell the whole story for the benefit of those in the Netherlands disposed toward moderation,[152] while the commission appointed by the territorial synod, for its part, later made available its judgment on the books of both Hofmann and Schwenckfeld which had been laid before the synod.[153]

Polderman, as Hofmann's deputy, was now recognized by many Melchiorites as the new Enoch. As to this, the second most important eschatological title or role, it will be recalled that some of the Melchiorites in Strassburg at first thought of Schwenckfeld as Enoch. The distant Netherlanders were, for their part, by now divided in their views as between Polderman and John Mathijs, the third claimant to the title (Ch. 12.3). Polderman was called several times before the Strassburg magistrates.[154] In his first request [155] to the city council to be permitted to visit the prisoner, he roundly denounced the council and the divines of Strassburg for calling Leonard and Ursula Jost and Melchior Hofmann fools instead of heeding their prophecies as had the Netherlanders, who for their part had no doubt but that Strassburg was the revealed city of hope. In his request, Polderman incidentally mentioned his intention of giving the prisoner a

[150] *Ibid.*, No. 607.
[151] *Ibid.*, Nos. 398, 399.
[152] *Ibid.*, No. 402; Bucer's report in Dutch translation, *BRN*, V, 199 ff.
[153] Krebs and Rott, *Elsass*, II (*QGT*, VIII), No. 444.
[154] *Ibid.*, Nos., 461, 466.
[155] *Ibid.*, No. 461.

copy of the work of an ancient Christian prophet, the *Shepherd of Hermas,* circulated by Waldensians, printed by Lefèvre, 1513.

The strange claims of the prisoner seemed indirectly substantiated by the numerous communications received by the Strassburg authorities from all quarters and especially from the Netherlands. These indicated the veneration in which Hofmann was held by his devotees. The Strassburg magistrates were also made aware of the importance of their prisoner in the eyes of the religious insurgents of Münster (Ch. 13). In December 1533, Bucer wrote to Bernard Rothmann in Münster, warning him against the fearful social consequences of abandoning infant baptism in following Hofmann. This was Bucer's major work on the subject, *Quid de baptismate . . . sentiendum.*[156]

In the meantime, Hofmann had become sick, partly because he refused the daily hot meal placed before him. Hedio and Zell visited him in his hole and found that he would abandon neither his fast of bread and water nor his five-point theology. After their visit they intervened with the magistrates to have his wretchedness alleviated to the extent of his being given a larger room with a window, where he could keep himself clean and tend to his sores and repose on a pallet.[157] Somewhat later he was heard chanting a psalm after which he shouted thrice from his window: "Woe, ye godless scribes of Strassburg!" All around people crowded to their windows to hear his imprecations.[158] In August, Hedio and Zell returned, this time in the company of Bucer, the president of the synod, and the chief constable for separatists. They all argued with him in vain.[159] In November at a special hearing, Hofmann repeated all his arguments and insisted, despite the extraordinary turn of events among his followers in Münster, that it was Strassburg which would be the scene of the Great Assize; and he appealed to the precedent of Jonah warning Nineveh to explain his mission.[160]

Hofmann's following in Strassburg was still centered in the home of Valtin Duft, the goldsmith from Heidelberg. One meeting of the group was held in a nearby tavern, which Dr. Gerhard Westerburg, who was staying at Capito's house, attended.[161] About this time Duft was expelled from Strassburg as a fomenter of Melchiorite Anabaptism.[162]

[156] 18 December 1533; selections therefrom, *ibid.,* No. 471.
[157] *Ibid.,* Nos. 451, 467, 485.
[158] 28 April 1534; *ibid.,* No. 546.
[159] *Ibid.,* No. 594.
[160] *Ibid.,* No. 617.
[161] *Ibid.,* No. 533.
[162] *Ibid.,* Nos. 497, 520.

While Hofmann from prison continued to inspire a loyal following in the city and in other Middle German towns such as Speyer as well as the whole of the lower Rhine, other Radicals in Strassburg, not always clearly distinguished from the Melchiorites, persevered in their more moderate course. It will be recalled that Kautz returned briefly after the departure of Marpeck to demand the public disputation which in part occasioned the great synod; but it was now Leonard Scharnschlager who was emerging in the period after the synod as the local spokesman of the Marpeckian circle in the polarization of the Strassburg Anabaptists into Marpeckians and Melchiorites.

The Tyrolese soapmaker had come to Strassburg about 1530. He distinguished himself as a moderate in opposition to Hofmann.[163] It is possible, however, that Scharnschlager's acquiescence in a temporary suspension of baptism reflects Melchior's policy. In any event, after Marpeck's departure for Moravia in January 1532, Scharnschlager at some point began to implement Marpeck's instructions not to undertake any more baptisms for a while. The alleged reason was that schism might arise or that unprepared and overzealous recruiting might, like bad leaven, contaminate the Anabaptist community. A correspondent of Scharnschlager testified to this effect in Speyer, which would indicate that Marpeck's instructions, in harmony at this point with Hofmann's, were being observed in a wide circle. It is of further interest that there was at this time some discussion by Scharnschlager as to whether the covenant of a good conscience could be entered into without water baptism. Scharnschlager said that a covenant without water was no more valid than the water without a true covenant as in pedobaptism.[164] Scharnschlager first appeared publicly with a group of Anabaptists, including the printer of Polderman's commentary,[165] in a judicial hearing 2 May 1534.[166] He soon thereafter prepared a notable statement on the freedom of religious conscience, which he laid before the magistrates in June.[167]

Herein, Scharnschlager respectfully drew the attention of the magistrates to the intolerable inconsistency of their demanding from the separatists conformity in religion while at the same time, as the magistrates of an imperial city, they themselves

---

[163] *Ibid.*, No. 368, p. 19.
[164] Letter of Scharnschlager in December 1532 to one Michael Leubel in Speyer and the hearing of the latter and others in Speyer. Krebs, *Baden und Pfalz* (*QGT*, IV), Nos. 409 f., esp. pp. 420, line 27; 424, line 12.
[165] Krebs and Rott, *Elsass*, II (*QGT*, VIII), No. 491.
[166] *Ibid.*, No. 550.
[167] *Ibid.*, No. 576.

declined to conform to the express command of their immediate superior, the Emperor. Scharnschlager, not unlike Engelbrecht and Schwenckfeld, pointed out, moreover, that both Luther and Zwingli in the flush of reformation had clearly distinguished the two kingdoms and the two swords, and that, although they had now abandoned the principle, the one fatefully at Smalcald, the other fatally at Cappel, the principle was still valid. In any event, the evangelical separatists should not be pilloried for pursuing a policy that was clearly enunciated in the New Testament; and he proceeded therewith to range cogently one over against the other the New Testament texts on the worldly and the spiritual sword.

Anti-Trinitarianism was newly represented in Strassburg in passing: by a Strassburg citizen, the Alsatian knight Eckhardt zum Drübel, who published in August *Von dem einigen Gott;*[168] and by a visitor, Claude of Savoy, called a "Trinitarian" (*Trinitarius*) in a sense just contrary to that which the designation will soon acquire in the course of our narrative, and who was obliged to leave Strassburg in the fall of 1534.[169]

During all this time, Bucer was still in dispute at long range with Schwenckfeld, Engelbrecht, and Jacob Ziegler on the invisible church, and on the separation of church and state, and locally with Matthew and Catherine Zell, who threatened to divide the established church of the territory of Strassburg in their opposition to what they considered the theologically offensive fiction of godparents, a position they took in partial sympathy with the views of Schwenckfeld and the Anabaptists.[170]

On 13 April 1534 the council decided to take stern measures. Having adopted the *Tetrapolitana,* the XVI Articles of the territorial synod, the associated ecclesiastical ordinances, and Bucer's Greater Catechism as binding on the city, the council decreed[171] that stubborn and obnoxious Anabaptists should leave the territory.

Against this move and other similar actions, an otherwise largely unknown, apparently well-educated Anabaptist in Austerlitz, Kilian Auerbacher, wrote to Bucer in anguished protest,[172] reporting in his long letter that the far-flung evangelical community had come to think of Strassburg as the one city of the German

[168] *Ibid.,* No. 604.
[169] *Ibid.,* Nos. 603, 608, 614, 632.
[170] *Ibid.,* Nos. 455, 622.
[171] 4 March 1534 the city council decided to abide by the two confessions, *ibid.,* No. 518. For the Greater Catechism, see No. 533.
[172] *Ibid.,* No. 625. Auerbacher is known as an ally of Jacob Wiedemann in the altercation with Reublin over communism, No. 240 (see also Ch. 9.2.d).

nation where the gospel might be proclaimed freely and where refugees for reason of conscience might be sure to find understanding and protection, a city where Bucer himself, as in his commentary on the Synoptic Gospels (1527), had on principle shown that Christians should eschew the use of magisterial coercion, but that now since the territorial synod, the whole evangelical community was lamenting Bucer's change in spirit. They were observing with consternation, said Auerbacher, that now even the Strassburg divines were becoming like the surly sheep elsewhere that nip and butt at each other and push other sheep from their places in the sheepfold of the Good Shepherd. Had Bucer replied to the Moravian, he would surely have referred to the sheep turned into wolves and lions under the inspiration of Hofmann in Münster.

While the Münsterite upheaval (Ch. 13) grew each day more serious for the whole of the Reformation movement, Strassburg was several times importuned to participate with money and troops. It was at length warned that fanatic emissaries, indirectly inspired by Hofmann, were on their way up the Rhine with considerable funds to recruit "comrades of the covenant" in Strassburg territory.[173] The Strassburg authorities, however, limited their contribution for the joint Protestant-Catholic reconquest of Anabaptist Münster to sending an embassy thither and to holding the prophet of the movement in prison.[174]

When in February and March 1535 the city council of Strassburg finally ordered that the infants of all citizens be baptized within six weeks of their birth and that the civil oath be exacted from all separatists on pain of exile,[175] the period of magisterial magnanimity had come to a full stop. With the tragedy of Münster before them, the Strassburg magistrates and divines had had to abandon a policy which for the age had been one of conspicuous moderation. Bucer wrote to his Zurich friends, Henry Bullinger and Leo Jud,[176] expressing alarm and chagrin that they had ever given credence to the idea that Strassburg might indeed become "a second Münster." It should be remarked that Leo Jud, at least, had once been quite taken by some of Schwenckfeld's ideas on tolerance and some of the democratic principles of the Anabaptists.[177] The Strassburg divines and magistrates, so long embarrassed by the effects of their extended

[173] *Ibid.*, No. 631.
[174] *Ibid.*, Nos. 519, 652.
[175] *Ibid.*, Nos. 638, 647.
[176] *Ibid.*, No. 671.
[177] Cf. *ibid.*, No. 463, and frequent earlier references to Leo Jud.

toleration (1522–1535), were no doubt secretly relieved that the full force of the Hofmannite hurricane had swerved from Strassburg in another direction.

As for Hofmann himself, in his Strassburg confinement, he repudiated the belligerence of his followers in Münster and by April 1535[178] interpreted the grisly development there as a fulfillment of his own prophecy of some dreadful carnage presaging, sometime within the third year of his preordained imprisonment, the advent of Christ in Strassburg, whence the banner of God's righteousness was yet to be carried to the ends of the world.

Before carrying our narrative to Münster and the Netherlands to trace the extraordinary expansion and displacement of emphasis in the Anabaptist movement in this region, we must linger in Strassburg and re-examine systematically and comparatively some of the regent principles of the Radical Reformers whose Strassburg careers we have found interwoven with the Reformation history of the most tolerant of the Reformation cities.

[178] *Ibid.*, No. 654. On the casualness of the captured leaders of Münster toward Hofmann, see the Strassburg envoy's report of his interview, No. 700.

CHAPTER 11

UNUSUAL DOCTRINES AND INSTITU-
TIONS OF THE RADICAL REFORMATION

At this point in our narrative, keeping in mind the various representatives of Anabaptism, Spiritualism, and Evangelical Rationalism congregated in Strassburg, we do well to take further account of the doctrines and practices which set them and their associates apart from the proponents of the Magisterial Reformation. We have already given considerable attention to the sacramentarian view of the Eucharist, which much of the Radical Reformation held in common with the Magisterial Reformation as it took shape in Switzerland and elsewhere in the southwest quadrant of the Empire (Chs. 2, 3, and 5). We have also dealt with the doctrine of the sleep of the soul, which much of the Radical Reformation held in common with the young Luther over against both the Catholic and the Reformed churches (Chs. 1.3.c and 5.4). Other doctrines and institutions have been discussed in connection with certain seminal thinkers such as Denck, and with certain events such as the Nicolsburg disputation and the Schleitheim synod, but a systematic coverage of several of the other doctrinal peculiarities of the Radical Reformation is overdue.

We may begin by analyzing further the theology and practice of baptism in the several currents of reform and restitution. From this we shall pass to a consideration of implicit and explicit alterations in the doctrine of the Trinity and in Christology, in close connection with the thought of several of the figures introduced into the Strassburg story. The consideration of a number of other doctrines and convictions closely related, such as the competing conceptions of the atonement and the various theories of restitution and restoration, will be postponed until certain events and new personalities have been introduced into the general and regional narrative.

299

1. Baptismal Theologies in the Radical Reformation

As we have seen, the Anabaptists were not without immediate precedent in their restoration or institution of believers' baptism. The Unity of the Brethren rebaptized converts well into the Reformation Era (Ch. 9.1), and the Waldensians, as we shall presently see (Ch. 21.1), were on principle antipedobaptists. Moreover, the Magisterial Reformers themselves, in their initial emphasis on salvation by faith alone, had to grope for a while before coming down firmly in defense of the traditional practice of infant baptism, either by stressing the entirety of the Christian life from birth to death as metaphorically a baptismal dying and rising with Christ (Luther), or by insisting on birthright baptism as the New Covenantal equivalent of circumcision (Zwingli and Bucer).

We have also observed that the Swiss Brethren, with their more radical implementation of the doctrine of repentance and salvation by faith alone in the unique redemptive work of Christ, were very clearly putting contritional believers' baptism into that experiential void in adult life left by the neglect or programmatic rejection of sacramental penance so long encumbered by the indulgence traffic (Ch. 6.1). Zwingli saw this very clearly when, after pointing out that "one of the good results of the [baptismal] controversy has been to teach us that baptism cannot save or [permanently] purify," he compared the sense of temporary relief experienced by the Anabaptist at his baptism and the Old Believer immediately after his confession. Zwingli was reporting recent encounters with Anabaptists in a disputation:

But in the [recent] disputation there were some [Anabaptists] who . . . had experienced a great release at the moment of baptism. To this Myconius answered: "Did you not come to baptism with considerable apprehension?" One of them replied: "Yes"—for they claim that no one should let himself be baptized unless he knows that he can live without sin. Then said Myconius: "The release which you experienced in baptism was simply a cessation of that apprehension which you yourself had created." They affirmed, however, that God had done something quite new towards them—the very experience which at one time we had in penance. For there, too, we were in great fear and distress before we made our confession, but the moment we had made it we said: "God be praised, I feel a great joy and refreshing." And all that we really felt was a relaxation of the previous tension. Yet the penitent could easily claim that in penance or papal absolution he experienced within himself a great renewal the moment he made his confession. And it was simply the removal of his apprehension. This is proved by the fact that our lives did not undergo any great change in consequence. Now those who allow themselves to be rebaptized make much of a similar experience.[1]

The Anabaptists claimed, of course, over against Zwingli and Bucer and other critics that the once-for-all removal of apprehension was also the occasion for entering into a covenant with God in a renewed conscience and with renewed determination to lead a godly life.

In our further effort to become systematic about what baptism meant to the spokesmen of the Radical Reformation, besides recognizing that they themselves were not always explicit about their convictions and that their emphases changed, we do well to pull apart from the knotty problem the three strands of argumentation and usage that are tangled together in the documentation before us.

One problem, namely, the manner of baptism, whether by immersion or by pouring, we can put to one side in this chapter, not because it is a trifling matter, but rather because we have not yet reached the point in our narrative where the Italian, Netherlandish, Polish, and Hungarian variations can be adduced and systematically interpreted. Suffice it to say that up to this point in our narrative most of the rebaptisms have been pourings, both by necessity and by preference, outside the church edifices, occasionally at riverbanks, often in houses, and even at town pumps, with the water poured from common containers.

A second matter about which there need be no confusion are the Biblical texts under discussion. Magisterial and Radical Reformer alike went at once to the Bible, since in the case of baptism there were no major conciliar formulations, as there were with Christology and the doctrine of the Trinity, through which the Catholic Magisterial Reformers would have been constrained to inspect the Biblical evidence. It was plain for all sides to see that there were two water baptisms in the New Testament, that of John to which Jesus submitted and that of Jesus himself *after the resurrection,* when he commissioned the apostles to baptize in the name of the Father, the Son, and the Holy Spirit (Matt. 28:19). Since the apostolic church itself made a sharp distinction between the baptism of John and the baptism of Christ (Acts 19:5), it was natural for the sixteenth-century discussions to turn on their relationship to each other and on the question of whether the efficacy or significance of Christian baptism depended solely upon the atoning work of Christ, in which

---

[1] *Of Baptism, LCC,* XXIV, 156 f. A recent collection and analysis of baptismal loci is that of Gerhard J. Neumann, "The Anabaptist Position on Baptism and the Lord's Supper," *MQR,* XXXV (1961), 140–148.

case John's penitential and ablutionary baptism would have no point at all and would belong, like circumcision, to the Old Dispensation prior to the vindication or authentication of Christ's sacrifice in his resurrection. Then, besides the two water baptisms, there were the metaphorical baptisms by the Spirit, by fire, and by blood.

The third problem was the relationship of Christian baptism to Jewish circumcision, and concurrently the relationship between saving faith in Christ and eternal predestination to salvation, confirmed either by circumcision or by water baptism. Old Covenantal circumcision could be regarded by one side as the equivalent of infant baptism in water, by the other as transcended by the new covenant written in the heart, an essentially adult experience and transaction. In the rival interpretations of the expressly baptismal loci of the Bible and the related texts on water and circumcision in the Old Testament, and also the Dominical references to children in the New Testament, the Magisterial Reformers were virtually agreed over against both the medieval church and the Radical Reformers that it was possible by means of the Jewish-Christian doctrine of predestination (brought into relation with the specifically Christian formula of one God, one faith, one baptism) to equate Old Testament circumcision, John's penitential baptism, and Christ's (postresurrectional) pistic baptism (applicable to an infant on the eighth day in analogy to circumcision and by virtue of the pledge of the parents and the church to nurture it in faith). In contrast to the relative homogeneity of a theology of baptism on the side of the Magisterial Reformers, there was considerable variation of conviction on the side of the Radical Reformers. Between the two sides the recurrent debates centered in three issues.

There was (a) the issue as to whether infants were in fact baptized according to the records of the New Covenant. There was (b) the issue whether the covenantal sign and action (circumcision and baptism) should be thought of as less inclusive under the New than under the Old Dispensation. On this turned the third issue, (c), as to whether baptism should be thought of as purely testimonial, or as personally redemptive, or as ecclesiologically constitutive (or as a combination of two or three of these principles).

On the first issue, the whole of the Radical Reformation was united in being at least antipedobaptist. Modern scholarship, of course, having at its disposal more texts and a much greater refinement in their analysis than obtained on either side of the great controversy in the sixteenth century, is able to be more confident and specific than the Magisterial Reformers as to the occurrence of child (though not infant) baptism in the ancient church;[2] for Luther, Zwingli, and Bucer were indeed very hard put to it, except with the analogy of circumcision and the New Testament reference to the baptism of whole households, along with Jesus' several approving references to little children, to document their claim for infant baptism in the New Testament. But if the antipedobaptists were of one mind about the first issue and the Biblical foundation of their unswerving conviction, on the second and third issue there were deep differences, not only within the Radical Reformation as a whole, but also within Anabaptism itself. These differences centered in the interpretation of John's baptism.

All participants in the Radical Reformation stressed the imitation of Christ in a way which the Magisterial Reformers, with their Augustinian stress on original sin and their Pauline stress on salvation by faith alone, regarded as at once presumptuous and, in any event, futile. Now in imitating Christ a group already committed to the principle of believers' baptism could not help finding in Jesus' baptism at the hands of John the prototype of their own experience. Indeed, since Jesus was thought to have been exactly thirty years old when the Holy Spirit descended upon him and God the Father from heaven declared that in that moment Jesus was spiritually begotten as the divine emissary into the wilderness of this world, several evangelists within the Radical Reformation attached importance to the year thirty itself; for example, Schiemer, Schlaffer (Ch. 7.5), and Servetus; and, in any event, all the antipedobaptists were confident that they were imitating Christ in their penitential submission to believers' baptism, which thereupon exposed them at once to the temptations of the wilderness of a conformist Christendom.

But in imitating Christ at this point they were also enhancing the baptism of John, that is, they were, despite themselves, making the penitential baptism of John more important than the postresurrectional baptism commanded by Christ. Thus they felt it incumbent on themselves to stress Christ's *distinctive* injunction to proclaim the gospel to all nations (Matt. 28:19). The inner tension between baptismal regeneration in imitation of the only-begotten Son of God at Jordan, that is, *John's* baptism, and the obligation to administer Christ's baptism was, in fact, the mainspring of the tremendous and almost compulsive missionary mobility of the first generation of converts. At the same time their virtual conversion of Christ's baptism into innumerable re-enact-

[2] See, for example, Joachim Jeremias, *Die Kindertaufe in den ersten vier Jahrhunderten* (Göttingen, 1958).

ments of John's baptism, at once penitential and regenerative and epiphanal (or testimonial), brought about both a displacement in emphasis in the interpretation of the gospel and of discipleship and therewith also an alteration in the doctrines of justification, sanctification, and especially the atonement.

Thus far we have sorted out from the tangled skein of baptismal theology the mode of baptism, the problem of two Scriptural water baptisms and two covenants, and the conflict between the motifs of imitation and obedience in respect to the two water baptisms, which, as we have just seen, imply competing conceptions of what constitutes salvation.

At this point we can begin to differentiate some six variant baptismal theologies, implicit or explicit, in the Radical Reformation: namely, (1) the baptismal theology of the two dispensations (Grebel, Hubmaier, Marpeck); (2) the baptismal theology of three levels or intensities (Denck, Hut, Schiemer); (3) the covenantal-betrothal concept (Campanus, Hofmann); (4) the deificatory theory of believers' baptism (Servetus); (5) the humane-magical defense of baptism for infants and the insane (Paracelsus); and (6) the interiorization or spiritualization of baptism to the point where it is replaced by an all-embracing Eucharistic theology or predestinarian regeneration (Schwenckfeld, Camillo Renato, Faustus Socinus).

a. The Baptismal Theology of the Swiss and the South German Anabaptists. The Swiss Brethren, both in their first actions and utterances in Zollikon and Zurich and in their more mature formulation in the Schleitheim Confession, distinguished sharply between the Old Covenant and the New, between the covenantal community of the law and the covenantal community of love, and hence also between circumcision and (adult) baptism. The South German and Austrian Brethren in contrast, from Denck through Hut and beyond, stressed, instead of the *two dispensations,* the *three levels* of baptism which, to a certain extent, could be documented in the lives of the Old Covenantal saints as well as in Christians. For here the stress was experiential and eschatological, rather than ethical and Biblically restitutional. The difference between the two circles was undoubtedly due to the fact that medieval German mysticism and the Müntzerite theology assumed greater influence in shaping the convictions of the South Germans than of the Swiss Brethren.

For the Swiss Brethren, to be sure, and for Hubmaier and those whom he influenced, the baptismal act was, from the beginning, at once penitential and covenantal; and the only change that can be noted in the history of baptism in this tradition is an increasing stress, in the first generation of Covenanters, upon baptism as covenantal and ecclesiologically constitutive. The atoning work of Christ is affirmed, for example, in the preamble to the Schleitheim Confession, which specifies the blood atonement.[3] But in the circle of Denck and Hut and in the even wider circle under the influence of Hofmann, distinct phases in the development of their baptismal theology and conception of salvation can be detected. In the baptismal theology of Denck, Hut, and eventually the Hutterites, the mystical "gospel of all creatures" is prominent, referring to suffering, which is the way of all creatures in their kingdom of blood.

The dative of Mark 16:15, the commission to preach *to* all creatures, is here converted into the genitive *"aller Kreatur,"* of all creatures. In the whole of the Radical Reformation, in so far as it was influenced by Müntzer, Denck, and Hut, the gospel *of* creation was (psychologically, and in respect to the morphology of religion) at once the counterpart of natural theology in Catholicism and the doctrine of corporate or original sin and fallen nature in both Catholicism and the Magisterial Reformation, particularly the latter. (On original sin, see further Ch. 31.2.) But far from being either a matter of rational observation unaided by revelation or a matter of written revelation and creedal formulation, "the gospel of all creation" was for the South German Anabaptists an inspired vision and propaedeutic insight into the nature of the world as it is. The believer who knows and then accepts "the bitter Christ" (Müntzer, Ch. 3.2) in creatureliness is one in whom has already been awakened the gospel of suffering and to whom can be vouchsafed the redeeming word that suffering is the way of all, even of the Son of God.

Out of this inward baptism comes the willingness to join with kindred souls whom the Lord chastens out of love in a covenant of the good conscience with God by means of water baptism as a *Bundesgenosse* (Covenanter). Up to this point the Denckian Anabaptist was talking the language of the mystics, but, when he constitutionalized the experience, so to speak, ecclesiologically, something new or at least different from Waldensian and Grebelian adult baptism had entered the field. From the inner or spiritual baptism and the water covenant, Denck himself looked to a third baptism; but this he did not stress and did not himself undergo.

In his disciples Hut, Spittelmaier, Schiemer, and Schlaffer (Ch. 7.5), we saw how the spiritual baptism was reduced from perhaps a lifetime of meditative suffering (*Gelassenheit*) to a briefer season, perhaps an hour, of perceptive anguish in the presence of a revivalistic apostle, whereupon the stress was shifted

[3] *Loc. cit.,* 247. See Ch. 8, n. 1.

from the inner baptism and even the covenantal baptism of water to the preparation for the personal testimony, which would surely involve blood, either the blood of the martyr or the blood of the wicked in the eschatological conflict which Hut and his followers regarded with profound agitation as imminent. More and more the stress fell away from anguished repentance and public testimony of a reordered will and new-found being in Christ to a stress upon outward suffering or being buried or mortified with Christ in the world in order to be spared the more powerful purgation and greater hell awaiting those who should fail to accept "the gospel of all creatures."

A third stage in the altering morphology of baptism in the line of Denck and Hut lies ahead of us in the general chrono-logical narrative, but we may anticipate it here. This change would come when the first-generation Anabaptists were suffi-ciently established in conventicles or colonies, as, for example, the Hutterites in Moravia, to have an appreciably large and finally predominantly "birthright" membership. This alteration in the basic type of membership will coincide with the sub-sidence of the eschatological mood and the preoccupation of the community with itself as a church. Children born within the community of the New Covenant will seldom be able to traverse the same experiential ground as their come-outer parents. In consequence, few prior to their baptism on coming of age will go through the long inward contemplative suffering of Denck or Hut. Thus, for the birthright members, the three levels of the original schema will become equalized and concentrated in the three-day baptismal liturgy with its three *Taufreden* and corre-sponding prayers and sermons from a Friday evening to Sunday morning.

By this covenantal action one will become a member of the righteous remnant, the true church, outside of which there is no salvation. Here the legacy of Hubmaier will be felt, for in his covenantal view, it was the divinely gathered church which through its administration of true baptism and the ban held the two keys to the Kingdom (Ch. 9.2). Among the Hutterites, it will be soon asserted, moreover, that the mark of the true apostolic church is the community of goods; and, in a paraphrase of Cyprian, that "where there is ownership . . . one is outside of Christ and his communion (*gmain*) and thus has no Father in heaven."[4] Thus, where for Denck it was the long inner suffer-

---

[4] This communistic appropriation of the Cyprianic *extra ecclesiam* and *nisi matrem* is found in Ulrich Stadler; Müller, *Glaubenszeugnisse* (*QGT*, III), 22. For the *Taufreden*, see *ME*, IV, 686 f.

ing prior to water baptism which was the most important of the "three baptisms" and for Hut the baptism in blood, for the Hutterites it will be precisely the constitutive water baptism that is stressed. The baptism of blood is now understood *corporately* more than individually, the suffering of the righteous remnant under the buffets of the worldly. Water baptism in the midst of the wilderness of the world is identified with that of John in the wilderness of Jordan; and the baptismal community itself, instead of looking fixedly upon the signs of the end of the age, now turns its glance back into the Old Testament, seeing itself continuous with God's ongoing righteous remnant, of whom Noah's company amidst the flood was a prototype. The *Chronicle* of the Hutterites, from which we have several times quoted, carries their story from Paradise to Moravia.[5] So strong is the covenantal baptism among them (as later among the various factions within Anabaptism in the Netherlands) that we shall presently be reporting frequent instances of Anabaptist rebaptisms.

The confluence of Hutterite, Renatian (Italian, Ch. 22.1), and Servetian baptismal theology in Polish Anabaptism lies well ahead in our narrative (Ch. 27.2). The special views of Marpeck are reserved for later treatment (Ch. 18.4), but we can conveniently take up the betrothal-covenantal type as represented by Melchior Hofmann.

b. Hofmann's Nuptial Theology of Baptism. Soon after his conversion to Anabaptism in Strassburg, Hofmann wrote *The Ordinance of God*, 1530,[6] destined to be very influential both in the Netherlands (Ch. 12.3) and in Münster (Ch. 13). If in the baptismal theology of the Swiss Brethren the covenant of baptism was interpreted in the first generation with the emotion and in the language of the otherwise discarded sacrament of penance, we may say of baptism among the Hofmannites that it was interpreted with the emotion and in the nuptial language of the sacrament of marriage. Paul, in II Cor. 11:2, wrote of betrothing his converts to Christ and presenting them as a pure bride to her one husband. Hofmann on the basis of this text and the nuptial language not only of Canticles but also of much of the prophetic literature likened the baptismal covenanting with Christ and his church to betrothal. He thought of the Anabaptists as collectively the bride (God's elect) following him in the

---

[5] This description and analysis of the baptismal theology of the Hutterites is based in part on what Schwenckfeld wrote at length against one Hans Klöpfer von Feuerbach, a convert to the Hutterite form of Anabaptism from non-communitarian Anabaptism. *CS*, XII, Document DCCCX (1552).

[6] Translated in *SAW*, 182–203.

wilderness, in a land not sown (Jer. 2:2), and as the woman of Rev. 12:6, who, having fled into the wilderness, awaits her vindication after twelve hundred and sixty years in hiding from persecution. For Hofmann, the mystical experience of the wilderness, corresponding to the experience of spiritual suffering or mortification in Denck, both preceded and followed the betrothal covenanting in water baptism. Just as the elect of the Old Covenant, after "baptism" in the Red Sea, wandered forty years in the desert in order to be tempted, tested, and tutored by the law, so Jesus, after his baptism, setting hereby a pattern for his true followers, was driven by the same Spirit (whereby he had that very day been begotten as the adoptive Son of God) into the wilderness to be tempted for forty days. The wilderness motif is mingled with the nuptial and baptismal language when Hofmann enjoins those "who have surrendered themselves to the Lord" to "lead themselves out of the realm of Satan . . . into the spiritual wilderness and also wed and bind themselves to the Lord Jesus Christ, publicly, through the true sign of the Covenant, the water bath and baptism."[7]

As with Hut, the sense of the imminence of the advent of Christ was intense:

And now in this final age the true apostolic emissaries of the Lord Jesus Christ will gather the elect flock and call it through the gospel and lead the Bride of the Lord into the spiritual wilderness, betroth, and covenant her through baptism to the Lord.[8]

When he writes of the bride he has in mind interchangeably the individual soul in the tradition of the Rhenish mystics and the collectivity of the redeemed in the language of the seer of The Revelation. Apparently much more than with the baptismal theology in the line of Denck and Hut, with Hofmann the Lord's Supper is thought of as the direct consummation of the redemptive experience of baptismal betrothal.

When . . . the bride of the Lord Jesus Christ has given herself over to the Bridegroom in baptism, which is the sign of the covenant, and has betrothed herself and yielded herself to him of her own free will . . . thereupon the Bridegroom and exalted Lord Jesus Christ comes and by his hand—the apostolic emissaries are the hand—takes bread (just as a bridegroom takes a ring or a piece of gold) and gives himself to his bride with the bread . . . and takes also the chalice with the wine and gives to his bride with the same his true bodily blood . . . in such a way that the Bridegroom and the outpouring of his blood is

---

[7] *The Ordinance of God, SAW,* 186 f.
[8] *Ibid.,* 188.

[one] with hers. . . . She [is] in him and, again, he is in her, and they together are thus one body, one flesh, one spirit, and one passion, as bridegroom and bride![9]

Hofmann's baptismal theology was undoubtedly well advanced before he assimilated to it the public covenantal act of water baptism insisted upon by the Strassburg Anabaptists whom he had joined. Meditation on the inner baptism of the Spirit in the mystical tradition had, in Hofmann as in Hut (under the influence of the same mystical tradition mediated and made more specific in Müntzer and then in Denck), found its outward symbol in public baptismal espousal.

After the execution of some of Hofmann's first Anabaptist converts in the Netherlands in 1531, he programmatically suspended rebaptism among his followers for two years, appealing, it will be recalled, to Ezra 4:24 and the suspension of the construction of the Temple in Jerusalem. He later, when imprisoned in Strassburg, though steadfastly persevering in the main tenets of his theology, was willing to admit the legitimacy of infant baptism (having nothing to do with his betrothal concept) since it was vouched for in Irenaeus, Origen, and Pseudo-Dionysius (whom Hofmann, of course, thought of as apostolic) and especially since Paul was even willing to sanction baptism for the dead (I Cor. 15:29). The suspension and later concession together show that the *inner baptism and betrothal* in the course of one's sojourn in the wilderness of life was to Hofmann the essential part of this system.[10]

We cannot pursue at this point the development of Hofmannite baptismal theology in Mennonite and Münsterite formulations, where the external covenant acquired much more importance than it had for him.

c. Campanus. We may, however, touch briefly upon the nuptial baptism of Campanus. This was most fully stated in his *Restitution* of 1532,[11] and, like Hofmann's baptismal *Ordinance* of 1530, had considerable influence among the Lowlanders, particularly the Münsterites. It is not, however, certain that Campanus opposed infant baptism. He was never accused of Anabaptism by Luther and Melanchthon, who on other matters (i.e., the Trinity) vigorously assailed him. It is possible that, like Luther, he thought of the Christian life as a continuous baptism, the more plausibly for the reason that Campanus likened baptism

[9] *Ibid.,* 194.
[10] The confession of 1539 is printed by Hulshof, *op. cit.,* 180 f.
[11] The German text is available in typescript in MacCormick, *op. cit.,* 220–242.

to marriage. In any event his elevated analysis of it ill comports with any perfunctory practice of pedobaptism. In his mystical nuptial language, which is closely related to his marital conception of the relation between the Persons of the Godhead and of the interdependence of man and woman (Ch. 11.2), Campanus does not draw back from speaking of the divine transaction at baptism as a cohabitation (*Beischlaff*).[12] In brief, his baptismal theology combines elements of Luther (duration), of Hofmann (betrothal), and of Paracelsus and Servetus (physical alteration).

Campanus closes his rather long treatise on baptism in his *Restitution* with the fanciful reference to himself now "hanging up his harp," after doing his best in minstrel praise of God's wonderful goodness in the institution of baptism.[13] It is wonderful because in baptism one is baptized into the name of Christ, which means that one becomes, like Christ, a son of God. He is the paradigmatic Son by nature, and the baptizand becomes by grace participant in his filial, i.e., divine, nature.[14] And in becoming a son, one ceases to be a servant and can therefore, no matter how wayward temporarily, never be extruded from the household of the Heavenly Father, nor from the community of faith. But one becomes more than a child, protected and perhaps chastised by God: one becomes, also, for life a bride of the heavenly bridegroom, who "talks lovingly to, plays, and sleeps with" his spouse, but who is also a jealous lover and may chasten, withhold himself, rebuke, and otherwise keep the baptized and therefore betrothed Christian from ever so loving the world that he forgets the divine love. For "the life of a Christian with God is not other than the life of bride and bridegroom."[15] In baptism there is at once a dying to the world and a resurrection, but this seems to be a minor motif in the baptismal theology of Campanus; and there is no suggestion of a wilderness temptation connected with the once-for-allness of the adult baptismal betrothal in Hofmann's scheme. Like Paracelsus (Ch. 11. 1.e), Campanus sees in the naming and blessing of Christ (he does not mention chrismation) the rite of becoming not only sons of the Father and brothers of Christ but, by that fact also, both "spiritual kings" and priests, "alike for ourselves and for

---

[12] *Ibid.*, 238: "*So fern wir glauben, sag ich, dann Got Christus, daz wort, der geist desz glaubens, dise vier stück gehören zu disem beischlaff und handel der widergeburt.*"

[13] *Ibid.*, 242.

[14] His words are "*seiner sonheyt mitteylhafftig.*" Campanus is not entirely clear in distinguishing, as promised, *loc. cit.*, 224, between the benefit from baptism that derives, respectively, from Christ's deity and from his humanity.

[15] Campanus, *loc. cit.*, 227 ff.

our spiritual brethren."[16] It is by virtue of this latter office, conferred by royal baptism, that the Christian is authorized to pray for himself and for others effectively in intercession before the throne of grace. The treatise on baptism in the *Restitution* leads directly to the section on prayer.

d. Servetus. In a quite different baptismal theology, that of Michael Servetus, we encounter both the strict separation between the two dispensations characteristic of the Swiss Brethren and the eschatological and experiential intensity of the South German and Austrian Anabaptists in the line of Denck and Hut. In addition, much is made of the physical transformation wrought in adult immersion and regeneration, which is deificatory in intention. A discussion, at this point, of the deificatory baptismal theology of Servetus may seem out of place. It is true that his extant Alsatian works were devoted to the doctrine of the Trinity, but it was in Strassburg that he became acquainted with the tremendous upsurge of interest in believers' baptism and he made it his own; and we know that he wrote to Bucer in 1532 a no longer extant letter on baptism and the Supper.[17] In any event he wrote on the subject of baptism in *Declarationis Jesu Christi filii Dei libri V*, c. 1540.[18] His still later *Restitutio Christianismi* of 1553 could be described, indeed, as a comprehensive baptismal theology beginning with the man Jesus Christ, the Son of God, baptized by John. In any event Servetus was to be put to death on two capital offenses according to the Code of Justinian, anabaptism and the rejection of the Nicene doctrine of the Trinity. It is, therefore, quite appropriate to bring in his conception in this systematic coverage of baptism, even though we must reach forward to the work of 1553 for some of the materials.

Servetus distinguished emphatically between the baptism of John and that of Christ, holding "that the entire efficacy of baptism depends upon the power of the resurrection of Christ" and "that the baptism of John has disappeared with the Law,"[19] citing in proof the rebaptism of John's disciples in Acts 19:5.

[16] *Ibid.*, 241 f.

[17] Krebs and Rott, *Elsass*, I (*QGT*, VII), No. 329.

[18] The book has just recently been identified by Stanislas Kot as the work of Servetus. The headings of the work, yet to be edited, including the section "De baptismo aquae et spiritu," are given by Kot in *Autour de Michel Servet et de Sébastian Castellion*, edited by Bruno Becker (Haarlem, 1953), 113.

[19] *Restitutio Christianismi*, 1553 (as reprinted at Nuremberg, 1790), 492; German translation by B. Spiess, *Wiederherstellung des Christentums* (2d edition, 3 volumes in 1; Wiesbaden, 1895–1896), II, 214. Hereafter the references will be to both versions, each of which is rare.

Even the apostles, before the death and resurrection of Christ, were like catechumens, as are indeed all present-day pedobaptists, who have only the ceremonial washing and not the healing, nor the illumination, nor the experiential regeneration of believers' *immersion* with Christ and *emersion* with Christ. Servetus derived redemptive, that is, deificatory, baptism from Acts 13:33 when the Messianic (royal) Sonship of Christ was pronounced at the moment of his ascension, as his mediatorial (priestly) Sonship had been announced at his baptism at Jordan.

At the same time, Servetus found the baptism of Christ by John as exemplary and the starting point for his conviction that what happened to Jesus Christ the Son of God by nature at Jordan became possible for all believers in Christ after his resurrection, namely, through his instituting believers' baptism by immersion, that all might follow him and become sons of God by adoption, and indeed gods. For this basic element in his theology, Servetus quotes, among others, Clement of Alexandria: "Being baptized [as Christ was at Jordan], we are illuminated . . . and adopted as sons; perfected, we are redeemed as immortal, made gods, and all sons of the Most High."[20]

In stressing the physical process (immersion) even more than the public testimony connected with adult baptism, Servetus vigorously opposed all those who stressed faith and tended to slight the physical action. He insisted that baptism is not a mere sign or an external washing but an inner gift; and when opponents cried that God was thereby being bound to externals, Servetus retorted by supplying many examples from the Old and New Testaments of faith's being linked with an action. Noah was saved, not by faith alone, but by getting into the ark as directed. The Syrian Naaman was not saved from leprosy by faith alone but by going (seven times) into the Jordan (II Kings 5:10). Moreover, it was also precisely at his baptism at the Jordan that the Spirit descended on Christ himself.[21]

Baptism is the ordained Christian ark, "rescuing man from the abyss of perdition," a spiritual-physical transaction typologically represented not only in the ark and the Flood but also in the passage of Moses through the Red Sea; in the passage of Joshua and the Children of Israel through the Jordan into the Promised

[20] Clement, *Paedagogue*, I, 6: *Restitutio*, 488/II, 212. He also quotes the *Recognitions* of Pseudo-Clement (I, 55) "that whosoever shall not obtain the baptism of Jesus shall not only be deprived of the kingdom of heaven, but shall not be without peril at the resurrection of the dead."

[21] *Restitutio*, 484/II, 209; "*This day* have I begotten thee." Servetus does not attempt to reconcile the baptismal and the ascensionist generations of the Gospels and the Acts respectively.

Land "as victors" (Deut. 1:31; 31:13; 32:47; Josh., chs. 4 and 5); in the watery vision of Ezekiel and the guiding angel (Ezek., ch. 47); in the vision of Isa. 33:21 about "those most pleasant rivers of Paradise which the [proud] galley of the Papal Church cannot navigate" and again in the vision, Isa. 43:2–14, where the Lord, "having brought down Babylon," permits his own to "pass through the waters"; and in the healing waters of Siloam (John, ch. 9) and Bethesda (John, ch. 5). In the latter with its five porticoes, Servetus saw symbolized the body and its five senses stirred or awakened by the Spirit, and in the age of over thirty years of the man waiting at the pool he saw the Dominical authorization for the delay of redemptive immersion until such a time as the believer might truly appropriate the benefits of its healing waters. Servetus specified that the baptizand "should go down into the water and then have water poured upon his head." He argued that the significance of baptism can be understood, and its regenerative experience appropriated, only in spiritual maturity, and that Jesus himself set the proper pattern in being himself baptized at the age of thirty:

These things can be understood by no one fully in the first adolescence, because at this stage that spirit of divinity is submerged in the storms of youth and that hidden fire [the Spirit] is unable to be felt amidst the flowing saps (*humor*) of maturing flesh. Just as an adolescent is not really fitted to grasp ethical teachings, so also he is not fitted to understand the gospel, however much he may be instructed at this time. Therefore Christ after the earlier period of instruction set forth as the proper age for baptism that of thirty years.[22]

In stressing faith and minimizing the physical, the solafideist pedobaptists failed, Servetus said, to make the distinction well known to the ancient church between catechumens and neophytes. The catechumens knew *about* salvation; the neophytes rejoiced *in* their salvation. But the pedobaptists have entirely lost the ancient experience and hence the conception of baptismal regeneration, and concentrate on Christ's presence solely in respect to the sacrament of the altar:

You are [, however,] not able to eat because you *have not been born!* Are you not stupid, you who will that Christ's body be present at the Supper, but do not will that his spirit be present in baptism?[23]

His baptismal theology was much more closely linked with a doctrine of the fall of man from Paradise than was that of the Swiss Brethren and the South German Anabaptists. In fact, it

[22] *Restitutio*, 372/II, 90.
[23] *Ibid.*, 487/II, 211.

was the very physical sense of original sin and the pervasiveness of demonical temptation that for him made baptismal reparation such a relief and remedy for the assaults of wickedness from within and without. "Continuously," he wrote, "we have in us two princes (*principes*) in combat, God in the spirit and the serpent in the flesh."[24] Servetus thought even of the highest science as "serpentine" when not baptized in Christ.

He visualized the two trees in Paradise, the tree of life and the tree of the knowledge of good and evil, and considered them both as representing Christ. The latter, no less than the former, "was good . . . because in the Paradise of God no evil tree could grow up."[25] Adam's fall was occasioned by his eating *prematurely* of "the unripe fruit" of the second tree, and thereby he was deprived of the fruit of both trees and became subject to death and liable to even greater delinquency: "It [the fruit of the second tree] was at the time forbidden to Adam and reserved for Christ alone, in order that we, when we should have acquired *through him* knowledge without deceit, would become like gods." For even if Adam had not sinned, "Christ who was as Word with God would have ultimately shared that knowledge with the world," making the state of the reborn in Christ superior to that of Adam before the Fall. (The concept of *felix culpa* was seldom so stressed in the whole Reformation Era as by Servetus. Compare, however, Hubmaier's conception of the baptismal empowering of the believer to distinguish between good and evil [Ch. 9.2]). Thus God, who had intended that man should have life and someday also the knowledge of good and evil, established in his program of redemption first the law. From fallen Adam to the establishment of the law under Moses, unmitigated death reigned (Rom. 5:14), but with the law the elect people were enabled to distinguish between good and evil and prepare themselves for an eventual salvation. Provisionally they were encouraged in a temporal way by the promise of entry into a land flowing with milk and honey. Canaan in Servetus' speculations was, in fact, a small portion of what had once been Paradise, now blasted by man's sin and only partly and precariously restored with but two of the original four rivers still flowing, and even these at too great a distance to produce verdure in Canaan.

The identification of Eden and Canaan was very important in Servetus' baptismal theology. It was grounded textually in Isa. 51:3; 58:11; Ezek. 36:35; and Joel 2:3, where Zion, like a

24 *Ibid.*, 366/II, 84.
25 *Ibid.*, 370/II, 88.

desert, is variously described as becoming like Paradise, with the spiritual verdure made possible by the flowing of waters interpreted by Servetus as anticipatory of the life-giving waters of baptism.[26] Servetus made the whole of his Paradise-wilderness theology baptismally specific in appealing to Christ's word in John 7:38: "He who believes in me, as the scripture [Isa. 44:3; 55:1; 58:11] has said, 'Out of his heart shall flow [the four] rivers of living water.'" Servetus, seizing upon this text, in which the Evangelist specifically refers to the gift of the Holy Spirit and says it cannot be imparted until Christ himself is glorified, developed the great conviction about the restoration of Paradise made possible by Christ's death, resurrection, and glorification and by his institution of believers' baptism ("believes in me"). Redemptive rebirth is from above in water and the Spirit (citing Col. 1:13 and Eph. 2:6), whereby the believer is delivered from the dominion of death and serpentine darkness and transferred to the Kingdom of the Son.

Salvation for Servetus was very rich in meaning, involving the body, mind, and heart, namely, salvation from physical death (ultimately at the resurrection), salvation from distorted (serpentine) science, and salvation from all manifestation of hate. Servetus, harking back to the original cause of the Fall, stressed the ubiquity of "serpentine knowledge from the coils of which the believer can be released only in dying with Christ in baptism":

Serpentine knowledge *(serpentina sapientia)*, when we begin to taste it, drives us into sin and hurls us into a kind of abyss *(barathrum)* of death, so that a new kind of death requires a new kind of life through Christ, a spiritual death, a spiritual life. There follows here by a certain antithesis a true measure *(commoditas)* of penitence, faith, and baptism. . . . In this mystery, our sins having been forgiven, Christ again, through the Holy Spirit, endows us with the knowledge of good and evil and deifies us with a new deity *(deitate)*, freeing us from the serpentine deity, which is the wisdom of the world.[27]

Those who from Moses to Christ had lived at least by faith were relieved in hell by the assurance of eventual resurrection. To this end, Christ harrowed hell for three days. The *descensus* was a very prominent feature also in other baptismal systems (Ch. 32.2).

---

[26] *Ibid.*, 374/II, 92. On the whole development of this motif, see my article "The Wilderness and Paradise in the History of the Church," *CH*, XXVIII (1959), 3 ff., and my book *Wilderness and Paradise in Christian Thought* (Harper & Brothers, 1962).

[27] *Restitutio*, 367/II, 85.

Hence the importance attached in radical circles to the Gospel of Nicodemus (Ch. 32.1).

Moreover, with the institution of believers' baptism, whereby one becomes reborn as the adoptive son of God by grace, that second death, which is the death of the spirit, has been overcome. But both the relieved saints in hell and those properly rebaptized must await the final victory over the first death, when, at the resurrection, hell gives up the dead, "the great and small," that is, not only the righteous and the wicked, but among the righteous those who have not been baptized, including the saints of the Old Testament and children under the New Dispensation. Christ will save the little ones directly: "Those who perished solely because of the deed of Adam, solely also through the deed of Christ will be helped without pedobaptism."[28]

At this point we may turn to Servetus' reasons for opposing infant baptism, only some of which have been thus far suggested.

Servetus holds that children, though implicated in the Fall and therefore under the condemnation of the first death, have not yet become infested with serpentine knowledge and are not direly in need of Christ's redemptive baptism, which, in any event, can do them no good until the serpent is fully uncoiled within them: "Whoever has not yet the deity of the knowledge of the serpent is not capable of the new deity of Christ."[29] Servetus lists twenty-five reasons against pedobaptism and concludes:

Baptism is, having heard the word of the gospel, in the unity of faith, to be cleansed by the laver of water into the unity and fellowship of the spotless heavenly Church [Eph. 4:4 ff.; 5:26 f.]. In infant baptism no spiritual church is assembled, but a Babylonian chaos.

One can hear the familiar cries of baptized babies in church!

One of the least developed parts of Servetus' baptismal theology is the relationship of baptism to the church. In antipedobaptist proposition number twelve, he quotes I Peter 3:21, which for Denck, on the basis of Luther's translation, had become determinative for the conception of the baptized *Bundesgenosse*. Servetus gives the Greek behind German *Bund* and the Latin *stipulatio*, and betrays no awareness of its constitutive, ecclesiological significance for most of the German, and later the Dutch, Anabaptists. Servetus, indeed, seems for a long time to have been the only member of his church.

[28] *Ibid.*, 368/II, 86.
[29] *Ibid.*, 368/II, 86.

We may pause to mention the possible origin of Servetus' baptismal theology. We have already surmised that he shared the concern of many a Spaniard about the inefficacy of baptismal affusion in the case of the Marranos forced as adults to change religion (Ch. 1.2.c). Here we limit our observations to the possibility of Paulician influence on Servetus and on Anabaptism in general.

Analogically if not genetically, the relationship between Greek (and Armenian) Paulicianism and Anabaptism is astonishingly close, except on the question of pacifism. But even here, the Paulician stress on the cross of personal suffering and prospective martyrdom in connection with believers' baptism suggests the Anabaptists. The Paulicians stressed the age of thirty for baptism and in the manner urged by Servetus. Repudiating the baptism of the Orthodox Church, the devotees of this ancient Eastern sect, which has survived into modern times,[30] likewise practiced rebaptism. Their whole theology centered in the baptism at Jordan. The latter was basic in their Adoptionist Christology[31] and in their insistence upon believers' baptism.

Whether the Anabaptists of Austria by way of the Danube or the Venetian Anabaptists (Ch. 22.2) by way of their Greek colonial outposts came into direct contact with the Paulicians during the formative period of Anabaptism is not certain. But we know that some of the Venetian Anabaptists sought refuge among a kindred group in Thessalonica and Larissa (Ch. 22.4) and that later three Paulician Baptists visited Moravia and were well received (Ch. 26.2). It is of interest also that the eleventh-century archbishop of Ochrida, Theophylact, who was familiar with Paulicians in the Balkans (calling them incorrectly Manichaeans), wrote extensive Biblical commentaries. These were published by Oecolampadius in Basel in 1524, 1525, 1527, and were well known to several leaders of the Radical Reformation, for example, to Grebel, Crautwald, the Münsterites, and Hubmaier. (The latter faultily cites Theophylact as patristic along with Cyprian in favor of believers' baptism.)[32] It is of special interest, therefore, that Theophylact, like Servetus, Schlaffer, and Schiemer, speaks of the exemplary thirty years of Christ at his

---

[30] The most accessible version of their baptismal theology is *The Key of Truth: A Manual of the Paulician Church in Armenia* (Oxford, 1898).

[31] There is even some indication that Christ is fully Son only after his ascension. Cf. Servetus, Ch. 11.3.c.

[32] Several references are brought together in *SAW*, 80, n. 25. Theophylact is sometimes called Vulgarius. See Krebs and Rott, *Elsass*, I (*QGT*, VIII), p. 172, n. 16. Ochrida or Okrid is in Southern Yugoslavia.

baptism and of the dove and the olive branch (symbolic of salvation in the ark above the floods) in his commentary on Matthew.[33]

e. Paracelsus. By the time Servetus came to write extensively about baptism, he was a physician. He shared with another physician, Paracelsus (Ch. 8.4.b), a physical, almost a magical, view of baptism. But whereas Servetus stressed as an Anabaptist the postponement of the rite, if feasible, to the Dominical year thirty, when it might exercise its potency to the full, Paracelsus supplied fresh arguments for the baptism of infants.

He wrote about baptism in two treatises, *Vom Taufen der Christen*[34] and *Libellus de baptismate christiano.* He first of all stressed the indelible character of baptism, drawing attention to the chrism as well as the water whereby each baptizand becomes an anointed *christus* or king. He compared the sign of baptism to military insignia for identification in spiritual warfare, to the cassock of the priest, which makes him inviolable, to the cowl of the monk or friar, which betokens his being partly withdrawn from the world, and even to circumcision, which is an ineffaceable mark to be heeded by the world and the devil.

But much more distinctive than Paracelsus' arguments for the indelibility of the sacrament are his arguments against the Anabaptists, who in stressing explicit, testimonial faith not only postpone the rite unnecessarily in respect to infants but, by implication, condemn to perdition the large number of the illiterate, the deaf and dumb, the feeble-minded, and the insane, of whom, as a humane physician, Paracelsus had reason to be especially conscious. Concerned for their salvation, he pointed out that Jesus himself had been especially cognizant of the needs of the sick and the insane and ordained baptism in the name of the Triune Godhead as the means of saving the many who would be lost if there were only the Johannine baptism on confession of sin and avowal of faith:

For, as long as it is faith which makes one blessed through Christ, the little ones, namely, infants, fools, the deaf and dumb, the insane, and otherwise simple people who are neither conscious of, nor capable of, overcoming sin, are robbed of salvation without even knowing it, for [according to this view] they are damned [at least, the adults]. But Christ is merciful. . . . He redeemed them [also] on the cross and instituted baptism in order that they might be blessed and, remaining thus, enter into the kingdom of God. . . . As soon as they are baptized they are blessed and redeemed without [the need of explicit] faith,

---

[33] Migne, *PG,* CXXIII, col. 178.
[34] Available in *Gesammelte Werke,* Abt. II, Vol. I, 317–359.

love, or hope. . . . Once baptism is there, it protects the soul of the captive. Thus all they are blessed who are deprived of [the capacity] for faith; and the devil may thereafter do no harm to the soul, neither that of children nor that of the crazy, the imbecile, or the possessed. . . . For why otherwise did Christ improve upon the baptism of John with his word and blessing of the Trinity, if it was not to protect those deprived of their reason?[35]

Paracelsus, who stood with the peasants in their uprising in the Tyrol, who consorted with Anabaptists and Spiritualists, cogently reminded his intellectual and martyr-minded associates that Christ came to exalt those also of such low degree that they could never aspire to all the disciplines of the spirit.

Of the Spiritualist and Rationalist theologies of baptism we shall speak in connection with Schwenckfeld's associate Crautwald in Silesia, Ch. 15.3, Camillo Renato in Ch. 22.1, and Faustus Socinus in Ch. 29.8.

2. ALTERATIONS IN THE DOCTRINE OF THE TRINITY

The term "anti-Trinitarian" has been commonly used for some time to designate the opponents in the sixteenth century of the Nicene formulation of the doctrine of the Trinity. The term, with or without hyphen, has been variously capitalized, thereby giving a detectable typographic correlation with the writer's sympathies, as between the "Antis" and the "Trinitarians"! Even the "purely objective" historian cannot extricate himself from partisanship by capitalizing both parts or leaving them both in lower case. His most obvious recourse, namely, to replace "anti-Trinitarian" with one or another ancient appellation for heresy, merely compounds the confusion, because "Arian," "Sabellian," and "Photinian," which were revived polemically in the sixteenth century, are imprecise and in many instances utterly inappropriate.

Therefore, in the interest of greater precision, the standard generic term for all those commonly called anti-Trinitarian in modern scholarly literature will hereafter, in this narrative, be "anti-Nicene";[36] for common to all sixteenth-century opponents of the Nicene-Constantinopolitan formulation of the doctrine of the Trinity as three Persons in one Substance was their objection to the ultimately Greek philosophical terminology enforced by the authority of the Roman Empire and Constantine.

---

[35] Paracelsus, *Vom Taufen der Christen, loc. cit.,* 324 ff.
[36] This does not mean that the discarded term will not appear from time to time for specific purposes.

The basic opposition of the whole of the Radical Reformation to the intrusion of the state into the realms of conscience found doctrinal expression also in the opposition of the anti-Nicenes to conciliar decisions enforced by the Roman Empire, just as the Anabaptists protested what they considered the improper transformation of baptism as an ordinance of the community of rebirth into a regulation for the community of birth (civil society).

The anti-Nicenes, however, were more willing than were most Anabaptists to supplement the Bible with ante-Nicene (that is, pre-Nicene) patristic sources.

But even the Anabaptists, and for that matter many of the Magisterial and Counter Reformers, would have to be put down as anti-Nicene in a sense which, despite wide reading in the fathers, they would only slowly have acknowledged.

Most of the fathers of Nicaea in 325, in arguing for the consubstantiality of the Father and of the Son (and at Constantinople, 381, of the Holy Spirit) were philosophically much more sophisticated than were either the Magisterial or the Radical Reformers in the sixteenth century. The fourth-century Greek divines were engaged in a tremendously creative effort in constructive theology, fusing Greek philosophical and Biblical terms and categories. But as Christians their God, in contrast to the gods many and lords many of the Greco-Roman world, was essentially invisible. The artists of their age, in mosaic and fresco, never presumed to go beyond the convictions of the theologians. They pictured Christ as the Good Shepherd, as Suffering Servant, and as Pantocrator, but they did not seek to picture the Godhead or God the Father invisible. And when the Nicene divines agreed, after identifying the Son of God with the philosophical Logos (by way of John's Prologue), to speak of the relationship of that Logos as Son to God the Father as one of eternal generation rather than of eternal prolation or of contemplation—there were several other likewise rejected metaphorical equivalents—they were even then moving in the realm of philosophical abstraction. Precisely in their rejoicing in Jesus Christ as God visible, the Nicene fathers were philosophically and also liturgically remote from the anthropomorphism which in the course of the Christian centuries came to make it possible for Western medieval artists and theologians alike to picture God the Father as anthropomorphically as the church fathers of antiquity had pictured and glorified Christ. In fact, in late medieval popular piety and iconography in the West, God the Father was augustly paternal, while the Son, though often pictured as almost identical in appearance *in his glory*, was more commonly thought of or experienced in his incarnational infancy, *in his humiliation* on the cross, and in the Eucharistic sacrifice. At the same time, late medieval scholasticism was familiar with the sophisticated assertion that God the Father, in his *potestas absoluta,* could have willed to be present for man's redemption not only in the man Jesus but in an ass or a stone.

Thus, when the whole of traditional Christian doctrine became subject to both learned and popular scrutiny in the light of the Scriptural and solafideist and antischolastic, but still "catholic," stress of the Magisterial Reformation, it was inevitable that within the Radical Reformation there would be diverse attempts to return to what could be considered a more Biblical interpretation of the doctrine of the Trinity.

Christian Entfelder's *Von Gottes und Christi . . . Erkenntnis* of 1530 was the first attempt in the Reformation Era to dissolve the dogma of the Trinity into a purely philosophical speculation while preserving its mystery and redemptive significance. In this respect, Entfelder was closer to the Nicene fathers than many of the Magisterial Reformers and was in any case much more sophisticated than most of the other Radical Reformers who tended to take quite literally the paternity of God the Father. Entfelder shows how the undivided Godhead (of the Rhenish mystics) out of his love has revealed himself in threefold power (*mit dreifaltiger Krafft*). Traditionally these three powers have been known as the three Persons. The first is essence (*Wesen*), as the self-sufficient power underlying all things; metaphorically, the Father. The second power is reality or activity (*wirklichait*), arising "essentially from the essence" but inseparable from it and eternal. This activity is the Word or Son, as the power manifested in creation, seeking to be the place of peace (*ruostat*) for all the children of God but ever without coercion and always with respect for the free will of man:

Leaf, grass, and all the animals on the earth, in the sky, and the water, yea, everything that a person eats, drinks, works, and does, gives testimony to this activity, that would gladly lead us at the right [hand] unto the garden of delights of the goodness of the divine essence, nevertheless without coercion (*bezwengnusz*), as also God himself and all creatures according to their kind offer their goods freely and let them ripen in their own season. Thus, also, the divine activity awaits patiently upon man's will to the end that it, wanting not in the same action with which other creatures are endowed, will freely testify to this [divine] activity and yet, if it chooses the left . . . will not have reason to complain.[37]

This "pantheistic" description of the pervasiveness of God reappears in much the same phrasing in Servetus (Ch. 23.4). After the goodness of the essentiating Father, through the love of the all-activating Son, pervaded all creation and sought to make love available, this goodness could then be called "Spirit or wind, holy in fact, fruitful, and pure, because it alone, from an immortal, holy essence, through the living, pure activity bloweth where it listeth." Here, in language no longer Nicene or traditional, Entfelder, still without reference to the incarnation and using "power" in preference to "person," nevertheless restates in the vernacular of mystical speculation the patristic concern for an internal, as distinguished from the purely economic or dispensational, Trinity.

After describing how human beings are variously reminded of the revealed knowledge of God by means of manifold causes and oppositions in creation, Entfelder writes concerning the knowledge of the true Mediator, who is not merely a divinized man, but actually a man from heaven:

Although the paternal essence, God as God declares himself to be such in the highest, . . . the [divine] activity, itself God, allowed itself to be seen in the deep (*in der tieff* [of the incarnation]) as man and Son, to be heard, grasped, and to be felt in flesh but without sin. . . .[38]

This Christological passage may sufficiently bring Entfelder's Trinitarian speculation down to earth, suggesting that in his Christology of the heavenly man he was like so many others in the Strassburg circle, a proponent of some form of the doctrine of the celestial flesh of Christ (Ch. 11.3).

Servetus, the most articulate anti-Nicene, did not in 1531 propose to reject the doctrine of the Trinity but rather to correct the errors of the scholastic and Nicene formulations. He would replace the philosophical argument undergirding the Trinity, which identified the substance of the three Persons (consubstantiality) with the more primitive, Biblically defensible argument of the unity of rule (the monarchianism of the Father and the Son and the Holy Spirit), an argument which never, even in the fourth and fifth centuries, completely disappeared as a subsidiary

---

[37] Entfelder in Dunin-Borkowski, "Quellenstudien," *loc. cit.,* 108. For the medieval mystical and scholastic background, see Karl Ruh, "Die trinitarishe Spekulation in deutscher Mystik und Scholastik," *Zeitschrift für deutsche Philologie,* LXXII (1953), 24–53; Roland Bainton, "Michael Servetus and the Trinitarian Speculation of the Middle Ages," *Autour de Servet et Castellion,* 29–46.
[38] *Loc. cit.,* 108.

orthodox defense of the unity of the Godhead.[39] Servetus never
felt free to disregard the testimony of the pre-Nicene fathers and
concentrate solely on Biblical texts. For him the fall of the
church dated specifically from the intrusion of Constantine into
the formulation of Christian doctrine at the Council of Nicaea.
Servetus, of all the anti-Trinitarians, therefore would have been
most pleased with our designation "anti-Nicene." Servetus was
particularly indignant at what he considered blasphemous scholastic sophists who, in their abstraction, would deny the essentially
paternal character of God the Father and speculate on the possibility of redemption through the Logos as immanent in an ass or
stone. Later on, Calvin would misunderstand him and accuse
him of a pantheism in which God could be thought of as well
in a stone as in a man (Ch. 23.4).

Accepting the man Jesus as messianic Son and as such the foundation of a reconstructed Christian theology[40] and picturing God
the Father in the manner of late medieval piety, very much as the
Nicene and Chalcedonian theologians did *Christos Pantokrator,*
and finally taking quite literally the evangelical accounts of the
conception of Jesus, Servetus declared that Jesus Christ was born
of Mary as the natural and unique Son of God; and he thereupon
repudiated as a philosophical sophistication the claim of the
"Trinitarians"[41] that the mundane generation of the God-Man
had been preceded by an eternal generation of the Logos-Son.
But, Servetus declared, to the natural Son of God and Mary, God
the Father gave all power on heaven and earth; and Christ
could be therefore properly called God likewise, "the mighty
God," prophesied by Isaiah (ch. 9:6). For Servetus, the Holy Spirit
was a power and not a Person of the Godhead. In the *Dialogues*
and the earlier *Errors of the Trinity,* Servetus was unprepared
to say of the Word of God that it was generated of the Father
or that the Word was the Son of the Father before the earthly
incarnation.

But in the *Declaratio* of c. 1540 and in the matured work, the
Restitutio of 1553, Servetus will be prepared to identify and use
interchangeably what originally he had distinguished, namely,
the prolation of the Word and the generation, or filiation, of the
Son (Ch. 23.4).

---

[39] The monarchian argument was stated earlier in Tertullian's analogy of the
unity of imperial rule, despite the frequent plurality of imperial vicegerents.

[40] Servetus is much clearer about this in his *Restitutio* of 1553 than in *On the
Errors of the Trinity* in 1531.

[41] The term *"trinitarii"* for his opponents appears in *Errors* and again in *Restitutio,* 72. See Ch. 23.4.

If in Entfelder in 1530 we have a mystical trinitarianism with progression from abysmal unity to trinity within the eternal Godhead before creation, and if in Servetus in 1531 we have a modalistic trinitarianism and personal Son only with the birth of Mary's child, in Campanus in 1532 (Restitution) we have a clearly enunciated binitarianism which, in denying personality to the Holy Spirit, as in the case of Servetus, nevertheless postulates an eternal binity of persons, God the Father and God the Son in one essence and one nature, just as man and wife are two persons but one flesh. Campanus' Scriptural point of departure was Gen. 1:26 ff.: "Let us make man in our image, after our likeness; . . . male and female he created them."[42] Campanus saw in the "birth" of Eve from the side of Adam, which he construed as concurrent with the creation of Adam himself, and in the nuptial-generative union of a husband and wife as one loving flesh in marriage and procreation, the moment and the action in which creation mirrors the divine. Not in his being androgynous, not in his being bisexual or sexual as other animals, but in his essentially nuptial nature, man, of all God's creatures, was created in the image and likeness of the Godhead. But as the wife is subject to the husband in that relationship, so the Son is subject to the Father (I Cor. 11:3), for, though the Father and the Son are one, the one in the other (John 10:30 and 14:11), yet the Father is greater than the Son (John 14:8). This pre-eminence and priority of the Father, however, is a precedence *within eternity before the creation of the world,* which was accomplished by (von) the Father through (durch) the Son. This nuptial conception of the Godhead does not make of the Son a spouse. One may compare here the baptismal-nuptial theology of Hofmann (Ch. 11.1.b). But it explains how Christ, though eternal, is not coeternal with the Father, how Christ is subordinate in authority to the Father; and especially how the Holy Spirit is not a person in the Godhead, but rather the common bond between the Father and the Son. Campanus was convinced that the loss of this originally apostolic and Biblical understanding of God and man accounted for the fall of the church, and it was this conviction that prompted Campanus to write his now lost *Contra totum post apostolos mundum*[43] and his German abridgment of this earlier work, the *Restitution,* 1532.

Campanus regarded himself as orthodox in the sense of his being apostolic and in a later letter he acknowledged that,

[42] Supplemented by Gen. 5:1 f.
[43] In manuscript or in print by July 1531; possibly identical with an allegedly Latin "Artickel-Buch."

whereas he had sought truth "among the sects and all the heretics, he was committed to a 'Catholic restitution.' "[44]

3. ALTERATIONS TO CHRISTOLOGY

Common to certain spokesmen in all three groupings of the Radical Reformation were: (1) a distinctive Christology (the celestial flesh or body of Christ); (2) a corresponding deificatory, as distinguished from a forensic, view of salvation; (3) also in most cases an espousal of the freedom of the will in striving for sanctification made possible by the incarnation or the example of Christ; (4) a mystical-physical view of the Lord's Supper; (5) a perfectionist view of the church; and (6) a covenantal view of marriage (Ch. 20). We shall be limited in the remainder of this chapter to the aberrations from orthodoxy in respect to the natures of Christ (Christology) and deal only incidentally with the corresponding variations in the concept of the work of Christ (soteriology), and only with two examples of the mystical-physical view of the Lord's Supper (Ch. 11.4).

The Christological aberrations of the Radical Reformation ranged all the way from an insistence on the exclusively divine nature of Christ to the exclusively human nature of Christ as prophet or adoptive Son of God. Within this wide range of views a clustering of unusual formulations is commonly designated the doctrine of the celestial flesh of Christ. Actually this is not an accurate label. Some of the proponents held to the orthodox (Chalcedonian) formulation that Christ was indeed a Person in two natures, but then insisted that the divine nature was a divine flesh or even a divine body brought down from heaven. Others insisted that Christ's nature was single and divine, a celestial flesh.

The two main versions of the doctrine of the celestial flesh of Christ—namely: (1) that Christ brought his own body or flesh with him from heaven and was from the beginning, in effect, one Person in one nature, become visible or corporal in Mary; and (2) that Christ was spiritual, procreated at a moment in time

---

[44] Letter to Peter Tasch in 1546; Rembert, *op. cit.*, 270. It is not likely that Campanus' Binitarianism was influenced by the hierogamy of the Cabbalists, although he knew Hebrew. Cf. Ernst Benz, *Adam: der Mythus vom Urmenschen* (Munich, 1955), 39 f., and William J. Bouwsma, *Concordia Mundi: The Career and Thought of Guillaume Postel (1570–1581)* (Cambridge, 1957). For the possibility of Cathar influence on the theology, anthropology, and sacramental theology of speculators such as Campanus, Servetus, and Paracelsus, see S. Hannedouche, "La Cène du Seigneur de Paracelse et le Rituel Cathare," *Cahiers d'Études Cathares*, V (1954), 3–15.

(begotten and not created) and had thus a human nature from Mary as well as a divine nature—can be correlated with two divergent views as to the relative importance of the male and female in ordinary procreation.

According to the Aristotelian-Thomist view, the male seed was alone formative. According to modern biology and in what is traditionally called the Lucretian-Hippocratic view, the male and female are, of course, equally contributive in the generation of progeny.[45] Both of these philosophical-biological presuppositions are represented among the proponents of celestial flesh Christology. Although they variously expressed their views and made claims and counterclaims about their relationship to each other, it seems fairly clear that there were in fact three main lines of development, namely: (1) that connected with the Silesian Schwenckfeld, who indeed claimed to be the purest exponent of the doctrine in the Reformation Era; (2) that of Ziegler and Hofmann, extending from the latter through Menno Simons and Dietrich Philips into the whole of Netherlandish and North German Anabaptism; and (3) that of Servetus, with faint traces in Poland and elsewhere. To characterize their positions in a word: Clement Ziegler, the gardener-preacher of Strassburg, believed that Christ brought his translucent body with him from heaven and acquired visibility from the flesh born of Mary. Hofmann postulated a single divine nature from heaven but called it celestial *flesh,* identical with manna. Servetus, though he originally distinguished between the prolation of the Word and the generation of the Son, came to speak of three phases of generation and granted that a Christ of two natures took one of them from Mary, who was therefore truly *Theotokos* (Mother of God). Schwenckfeld postulated two natures, the one celestial and the other human but "uncreaturely," and he therefore thought that he could expressly refute the charge of Eutychianism or Monophysitism.

The doctrine of the celestial flesh of Christ among the Radical Reformers has been generally understood both by their contemporary foes and their modern interpreters as a revival of ancient Gnostic and Monophysite Christology, and as an abortive effort within radical evangelical circles, dissatisfied with the strictly Chalcedonian Christology (despoiled by the Protestant Reformers of the associated, scholastic doctrine of the immaculate

---

[45] William Keeney has brought this out clearly in his Hartford doctoral thesis, "The Development of Dutch Anabaptist Thought" (1959).

conception of Mary) to account for the postulated sinlessness of Christ and also his divine incapability of sinning. The ancient heretical Christology, originally developed by Valentinus and assimilated by Apollinarius (surviving as Pseudo-Athanasius) and by Hilary of Poitiers, was variously communicated to the sixteenth-century Radicals in these texts, or by misinterpretation, perhaps, in the texts of the anti-Gnostic writers such as Irenaeus and Tertullian;[46] and in part, indirectly, by the perpetration of the celestial flesh heresy in Bogomile and Cathar circles.[47]

It is just as likely, however, that medieval mystical and Eucharistic language and lore explain some of the peculiarities of the doctrine in its sixteenth-century formulation. In fact, in the absence of clear documentation of patristic-heretical or medieval sectarian influence, it seems more plausible to account for the widespread and variegated outcropping of the celestial-flesh doctrine in the sixteenth century as an effort to restate the Christological problem in the language of Eucharistic piety, experientially much more real than the philosophical terms employed a millennium or more earlier, when the church was concerned to safeguard for philosophical (not Biblical) reasons the impassibility of God and for soteriological reasons to vindicate the full humanity of Christ.

At Chalcedon in 451 (as at Nicaea in 325) the fathers had in mind that God became man in order that man, redeemed from the world through baptismal death to the world, might become divine through the death and resurrection of the one Person in two natures. But already in the eleventh century in the West the sacrament of the altar had become even more important than baptism as the effective rite of redemption.[48]

The flesh of Christ born of Mary and the Eucharistic body had long been identified in pious practice and theological clarification. The familiar twelfth-century motet addressed to the Host, *Ave Verum corpus natum* besings the oneness of the body of the Son of Mary and that body on every Christian altar. In the course of the Second Eucharistic Controversy in the Middle Ages there had been a programmatic diversion of the Pauline term for the Eucharistic body, *corpus mysticum,* as a designation of the body

[46] Specifically, *Adversus Valentinianos* and *De carne Christi.*
[47] Hans Schoeps, who has written the only monograph on the subject *Vom himmlischen Fleisch Christi* (Tübingen, 1951), gives here two explanations and points to the familiarity of both Schwenckfeld and Servetus with the patristic texts.
[48] See my *Anselm: Communion and Atonement* (St. Louis, 1959).

of the faithful and the concurrent substitution of the unequivocal *corpus Christi* for the sacramental presence.[49] With the festal
elevation of this *corpus Christi* enshrined in a monstrance to be
carried into the streets once a year,[50] it was natural that devout
and theologically serious Christians should resort to Eucharistic
terms in interpreting the original incarnation (Ch. 2.1) and that
in the breaking-up of Christendom in the sixteenth century the
Radicals should follow the medieval scholastics and mystics in
trying to restate in a meaningful way the problem of the two
natures of Christ—a celestial flesh (or nature) that was like manna
from heaven and might be tasted again by the devout as the *substantia* of the Host terrestrial, and a flesh (or nature or appearance), its historic and now liturgical *accidentiae*. The Radical Reformers were freer than the Magisterial Reformers to appropriate
the terminology of impanation in discussing the historic incarnation because they were not bound to the creeds and formularies
of the ancient church and could, with their Eucharistic presuppositions, find in the Bible itself a number of texts which they
could easily turn to advantage in their arguments with the Magisterial Protestants, who were always self-conscious about their conciliar orthodoxy.

For the details, we turn now, first, to Clement Ziegler, of
Strassburg, the earliest exponent of the doctrine, and to its
most extreme proponent, Melchior Hofmann, converted to Anabaptism while a sojourner in Strassburg.

a. Clement Ziegler and Melchior Hofmann. Although the doctrine of the celestial flesh of Christ seeped into the Radical Reformation through the innumerable fissures in the late medieval
corpus christianum, one is moved to assign a prominent role as
formulator and mediator to Clement Ziegler, who must have
played host to more than one of the radical sojourners in
Strassburg.

Ziegler did not disavow a corporal materialization in Christ's
becoming man through Mary, virgin *post partum;* but, as early
as 1524, he stressed the doctrinal tenet that the Son was born
of the Father within the Trinity before the foundations of the
world were laid,[51] and that "the body which Christ had before
the foundations of the world were laid is the communion in the

[49] The liturgical and theological shift in terminology as a consequence of the
Second Eucharistic Controversy is traced by Henri de Lubac in *Corpus
mysticum* (Paris, 1949).
[50] Beginning in 1264.
[51] Krebs and Rott, *Elsass,* I (*QGT,* VII), No. 7.

body of Christ in the flesh, which communion we enjoy in spirit under the bread of the altar . . ."[52] He continues:

> If the splendor (*clarheit*) of the first body were not there in the second body of Christ, which he took upon himself from the Virgin Mary, the fleshly body of Christ would have been mortal and would not have been resurrected; but precisely the first body with its splendor . . . is the eternal Word. . . . Why therefore do we take the body of Christ not according to its divinity instead of according to humanity of the flesh?[53]

Hofmann went farther than Ziegler and denied a human body or flesh of Christ.

Although Hofmann's views on the incarnation were essentially Valentinian, there is scarcely any possibility that he had ever encountered ancient Gnostic or even anti-Gnostic texts on his own. But, like Valentinus, he held that Christ brought his body with him from heaven, taking nothing of the substance of Mary, passing through her "as water through a pipe." In his biological presupposition Hofmann stood, no doubt quite unconsciously, in the Aristotelian-Thomist line. (Aquinas himself had not extended the principle from anthropology to Christology.) But Hofmann could have seen about him iconographic representations of what he himself was prepared to make doctrinally explicit.

A roughly contemporaneous woodcut shows the crowned head and upper half of God the Father, while what would be the lower half is taken up by a cloud-enclosed space containing a naked infant bearing a cross and preceded by the Dove, effecting the descent of the body of the Son of God into the womb of Mary. A matching woodcut shows the same infant body preceded by the Dove descending upon the altar at the elevation of the Host after the priest[54] has pronounced the words: *Hoc est corpus meum.*[55]

The close connection between Christology and the Eucharist

---

[52] *Ibid.,* No. 24, p. 33.

[53] *Ibid.,* p. 34.

[54] In this particular illustration, the celebrant is a bishop.

[55] The two woodcuts referred to were published by George Blandrata and Francis Dávid in *De falsa et vera unius Dei Patris, Filii, et Spiritus Sancti cognitione* (1567). They represent pictures (the liturgical garments clearly belong to the very late Middle Ages) from the papal residence in Rome and elsewhere. They are reproduced more accessibly by Konrad Górski, *Grzegorz Paweł Brzezin* (Cracow, 1929), 207 and 204, figures 7 and 4. See further, Wilbur, *Unitarianism,* 35, n. 22.

was in Hofmann reinforced by the nuptial imagery of medieval mysticism and specifically by the symbolism of the pearl.

Medieval natural history supposed that pearls were formed by dew descending from heaven and crystallizing in the oyster, a solid form of celestial water. This fanciful analogy proved useful to Hofmann in explaining how the heavenly flesh of Christ came to earth and was solidified in the womb of Mary: "The Eternal Word, which was true heavenly dew, in an unsensual and incomprehensible way but through the Holy Spirit, fell from the mouth of God into the wild mussel of the Virgin Mary, and in her became a bodily Word and spiritual pearl."[56] Appealing to Ecclus. 43:20, he says that as water becomes ice from the blowing of the cold north wind, so the Eternal Word of God became "a tangible water" or ice or crystal through the wind of the divine Spirit.[57] In Eucharistic piety, the heavenly dew could also be compared to the heavenly manna, which descended upon the desert for the nutriment of the chosen people. Thus the dew-pearl-manna, treated as one substance in diverse modes, could be used to refer to Christ in his several roles. The dew could represent him in his heavenly essence, the pearl in his human existence, and the manna as he presents himself in Communion. Before Hofmann, John Ruysbroeck had made the same combination, speaking of "the sparkling stone," smooth, round, and even, which is Jesus Christ; the "hidden manna, which shall give us eternal life."[58]

The pearl as a synonym for the manna and for Christ's body in the Eucharist is a usage dating back to Rabanus Maurus in the ninth century.[59] Its usage in both romantic and ecclesiastical allegory shows that it was widespread. The nuptial language is very bold in Hofmann.[60]

Hofmann was quite specific "that the Eternal Word of God did not take our nature and flesh from the Virgin Mary but himself

---

[56] "Die . . . sendebrief . . . to den Römeren," *BRN,* V, 311.

[57] *Ibid,* 312.

[58] "The Sparkling Stone," in *Late Medieval Mysticism, LCC,* XIII (Philadelphia, 1957), 315. This imagery was well supported by Scripture, e.g., John 6:49–51; Rev. 2:17.

[59] S. K. Heninger, Jr., "The Margarite-Pearl Allegory in Thomas Usk's *Testament of Love,*" *Speculum,* XXXII (1957), 92–98. The analogy in the late Middle Ages was used also in the poetry of courtly love.

[60] W. J. Kühler in *Geschiedenis der Nederlandsche Doopsgezinden in de Zestiende Eeuw* (Haarlem, 1932), I, 56 f., suggests that Hofmann's idea came from the circle of the *Devotio Moderna* and Alain de la Roche (van der Klip) who died in Zwolle in 1475. See Johan Huizinga, *Herfsttij der middeleuwen* (London, 2d edition 1921), who also suggests the possible influence of Alain de la Roche. See also *Studia Eucharistica* (Antwerp, 1946), 348, 363.

became flesh (John 1:14), that is, our Lord Christ has not two but only *one nature*."[61] In the second article, he argues that if Jesus had taken on the flesh of Mary, he would have had Adamic flesh, which could neither "save us" nor "serve us as food for eternal life." It is not entirely clear what distinction he might have in mind between salvation and eternal life, but it is clear that he connects believers' baptism and Communion, the historic redemptive action of cross and resurrection and the experiential appropriation of that work. In the third article, Hofmann appeals to I Cor. 15:47 in contending for the heavenly origin of the Second Adam, and, in the fourth, he strengthens his argument that Mary no more than Joseph was a true parent of the Father-begotten Son in characterizing Christ as the true Melchizedek without earthly father or mother (Heb. 5:10; 6:20; ch. 7).

Hofmann had a thoroughgoing doctrine of the sinfulness of man, holding that all men are cursed on account of Adam's sin. All of Adam's seed belong to Satan. Adam has brought universal death into the world.[62] Consequently, if Christ were of the seed and flesh of Adam, he would have had to die for his own sins, he would have deserved damnation, and he would have belonged to Satan with the rest of mankind. Had he taken from Adamic Mary "the outer tabernacle of his being" (flesh), he "would not have suffered for us, but only the tabernacle would have suffered, and Mary's flesh."[63] He could not then be Redeemer. Therefore the eternal Son came from heaven, and was the Second Adam. He redeemed men from death and removed all sin. Just as all the descendants of Adam and Eve are cursed, so all the descendants of the Second Adam (Christ) and the "spiritual Eve" or "the Bride of the Lord Jesus Christ" (the church) are redeemed. It is not essential that he be identical with mankind, for salvation is a matter between God and Satan.[64] To put, Hofmann argued, the stress on the *death* of what orthodox theologians would insist was the Adamic human nature of the one Person in

---

[61] Zur Linden, *op. cit.*, 329. At this point Zur Linden's modernized German reads *"Vater"* instead of *"Natur."* Schoeps, *op. cit.*, corrects this. Schoeps can be further substantiated in this crucial reading by Zur Linden's own *Beilage*, V, *op. cit.*, 451, wherein Schwenckfeld is opposing Hofmann's first article and indicates his own divergence from Hofmann in holding to two natures in the one Person. The Dutch version of the *Handelinge* given at this point also indicates that Hofmann had contended for one nature. *BRN*, V, 227.

[62] Kawerau, *op. cit.*, 46 ff. Cf. *Wahrhaftige Zeucknis gegen die Nachttoechter und Sternen . . .*, reprinted by Leendertz, *op. cit.*, 386–392.

[63] *Auszlegung der Offenbarung Joannis* (1530); Krebs and Rott, *Elsass*, I (*QGT*, VII), No. 210.

[64] Kawerau, *op. cit.*, 47.

two natures and to find satisfaction in the death of the human nature in isolation was to deprive precisely the *resurrection* or the *ascension* of its redemptive significance.

b. *Schwenckfeld*. Schwenckfeld, who wrote the most on the subject, who was the most nearly orthodox, and who declared that both Hofmann and Franck took "their errors from our truth, like spiders who suck poison out of a beautiful flower,"[65] and that Servetus for his part too had gone astray,[66] clarified his position over against Hofmann in holding emphatically to two natures in Christ; but he differed from the traditional Chalcedonian formulation of Catholics and Protestants alike in his appropriation of patristic and particularly Greek texts. It is probable that Schwenckfeld's doctrine of Christ, salvation, and the Eucharist derive from his study of Ignatius, Irenaeus, Athanasius, Cyril of Alexandria, and especially Hilary of Poitiers, all of whom he cites and quotes.[67] Augustine's distinction between "the bread of the Lord" and "the bread which is the Lord," based primarily on John, enabled Schwenckfeld to represent the human nature as "uncreaturely" and hence as scarcely distinguishable from the divine nature in Christ. Christ was the unique, natural Son of God and Mary, procreated, not created. Schwenckfeld applied the Nicene "begotten, not made" to the whole Christ and not merely to his divine nature or eternal Logos.

Schwenckfeld, though standing as Hofmann did in the Aristotelian-Thomist tradition on the biological point, did not deny that Mary was the true mother of Jesus Christ, or that Christ had received "the flesh and the tabernacle of his body from Mary, the virgin,"[68] by the mysterious power of the Holy Spirit. But he insisted that Sonship is not creatureliness, for the Almighty God has the power to bring pure, uncreaturely flesh out of a holy virgin. He who cursed all Adam's flesh can also circumvent that curse by his almighty power.

This is one of the two *nova* in Schwenckfeld's Christology, and

---

[65] *CS*, V, 522–523. Franck, who is here linked disparagingly with Hofmann, expressly attacked, in 1534, Hofmann's doctrine of the incarnation in *Paradoxa* (No. 145).

[66] See the addendum to his *Vom Ursprung des Fleisches Christi*, 1555; *CS*, XIV, 307–348.

[67] Especially interesting is Hilary's *De Trinitate* x, 18, where Christ is said to have a *coeleste corpus;* cited by Schwenckfeld in *CS*, VI, 85, 235 f., 238; VII, 286, 313 f.; 27, 325, 339; and especially Document MCXLIV, *Proof from the Scriptures and the Fathers, CS*, XVI, and Document MCCXXIV, *Opinions of Hilarius, CS*, XVII.

[68] *CS*, VII, 304.

the other is the progressive deification of this uncreaturely humanity from the uniqueness of its conception, through such episodes as the momentary transfiguration, to the resurrection, ascension, and glorification. Originally, Schwenckfeld had reluctantly acknowledged that the human nature of Christ was creaturely: "Besides the union of the Word of God with the flesh, there can be no other essential union of God and the creatures."[69] But he recoiled from admitting even this, and just as he had been able to dissociate the inner Eucharist from the external and suspend the latter (Ch. 5.5), so also he soon eliminated the creaturely in the incarnation, preferring to think of the humiliated humanity as being "the new creature"[70] or as belonging to the "new order of re-creation or rebirth."[71] Instead of contrasting divine and human natures in the one Person, Schwenckfeld spoke rather of the two states of the humiliated and the glorified noncreaturely humanity. Besides these two stages in the "human," "noncreaturely" nature, he formally held to the existence of a second nature. In both the earthly and in the risen Christ, he insisted on the two natures, the one from heaven, the other derived from Mary but virtually identical with the other after the resurrection and glorification. Schwenckfeld never made entirely clear what the divine in Christ was, apart from his "uncreaturely" human nature. Under pressure he came to distinguish between the crucified and the glorified body of Christ, but even then he so insisted on the unity of Christ that he would never have spoken of him at any time as a man like other men:

I recognize nothing of creation or creatureliness in Christ but rather a new divine birth and natural progeny (*kindtschafft*) of God. Wherefore I cannot consider the Man Christ with his body and blood to be a creation or a creature. Rather, I believe and confess with Scripture that he is wholly God's only-begotten Son and that Christ, the Son of God, his Heavenly Father, the whole Person indivisibly (*unzertailig*) God and Man, was born in time of the Virgin Mary; also that he suffered and died for us upon the cross in personal unity and wholeness, and as such rose again and ascended into heaven, that he sits at the right hand of God and rules also in his human nature wholly with God his Father in divine glory, unity, and essence, from which he will come to judge, etc.[72]

Schwenckfeld held further that God had foreordained Christ from eternity, having foreseen prior even to creation that man-

---

[69] *CS*, II, 481.
[70] *CS*, V, 793.
[71] *CS*, VI, 136.
[72] *An Answer to Luther's Malediction*, translated in *SAW*, 180 f.

kind would fall, and that therefore even his uncreaturely human nature (flesh) existed in the prescience of God. The patriarchs believed in Christ and were truly nourished by this celestial flesh.[73]

Charged by Luther as a Eutychian, Schwenckfeld replied with firmness, vexed that he had been chronically and even maliciously misunderstood:

Since my whole activity and altercation has had to do exclusively with the humanity of Christ, with his true body, blood, and flesh, and their properties, status, essence, and majesty in glory against those who want to rob his humanity of this splendor—how can I, then, deny the humanity of Christ and blood and flesh, or maintain only one nature, namely, only the Word in Christ, and make out of the human nature a divine nature, as they allege? This has never in my whole life come into my mind, that is, that I should not hold and confess Christ as a hero (heldt) with two natures to be true God and true man.[74]

This same hero, however, who was fully God as God's Son, was not only born with passible flesh, but he also died as God; for, if "The eternal God can be born, undoubtedly he can also suffer,"[75] and thus the "suffering and death of Christ pertained not only to his humanity . . . but . . . to the entire Son of God in the united person who hung on the cross and died."[76] At his death, Christ, who "was killed in the flesh and made alive in the spirit,"[77]

. . . descended in the spirit to the prison [hell] and preached to [the patriarchs] in the spirit, proclaiming to them the salvation for which they had been expectantly waiting and the gospel of grace; yea, he held spiritual conversation with them concerning all the secrets of his death, kingdom, and judgment, just as Christ preached the eternal gospel to our souls and consciences and taught his disciples. There he illumined them with divine wisdom, enriched them with joy and endowed them with blessedness, and took all their souls out of the dungeon of the prison and led them with him into his heavenly kingdom and prepared place, and made the outer court of hell empty, so that the place is now different from what it was before the ascension of Christ.[78]

The process of vivification of the souls of the patriarchs in the forecourt of hell ("The lord kills and gives life; he leads into hell

[73] CS, IV, 27; VIII, 855.
[74] An Answer to Luther's Malediction, SAW, 179 f.
[75] CS, V, 752.
[76] CS, V, 648.
[77] CS, X, 364; Postil on Luke, ch. 16.
[78] Ibid.

and out again")[79] was as a "spiritual conversation," a kind of Schwenckfeldian communion. At his death the Son of God entered hell as *Christus victor* and Schwenckfeld suggests that he shared his uncreaturely flesh with the departed dead in a kind of Eucharistic *descensus* that recalls Rupert of Deutz.[80]

After the resurrection, the Logos and glorified flesh (the uncreaturely human nature) together constitute the Second Person of the Trinity.[81] More than Schwenckfeld realized, however, that glorified flesh discharged in his system the function of the Third Person in traditional Pneumatology.[82]

Schwenckfeld quoted the Greek fathers on the purpose of the incarnation as making it possible for man to become what God is.[83] Specifically, Christ became a new man that he might feed the believer with his mystical flesh and nourish him unto a new life.[84] Man was entirely corrupt after the fall of Adam, but now the pure and holy man, the new Adam, can nourish those reborn in him to a new life. Since the human nature of Christ is uncreaturely, the believer, in receiving this celestial or mystical flesh. is enabled to progress toward deification. Christ, not partaking of Adam's sinful flesh, was born of woman to become the founder of a new order of being. All who through faith are born again in Christ stand no more on the side of the creature, but gradually "participate abundantly in the divine essence, life, spirit, and nature already here on earth." He cites II Peter 1:4.[85] In Schwenckfeld's soteriology, the *Christus incordatus,* referred to as the mystical *Christus impanatus,* has taken the place of *Christus incarnatus.*[86] In place of Luther's forensic justification has come a deificatory sanctification, similar to that of Servetus.

c. Servetus. Servetus developed still a third variant in the doctrine of the celestial flesh of Christ; but as an anabaptist he connected deificatory sanctification pre-eminently with believers' immersion. In the *Dialogues on the Trinity*[87] he says of Christ's celestial body the following:

---

[79] *Ibid.,* 361.
[80] *CS,* IV, 525 ff.; V, 421; VII, 519 ff.; X, 363 ff.; see my *Anselm,* 59, and Maier, *op. cit.,* 51, who, however, does not bring out the Eucharistic-redemptive role of the *descensus.*
[81] Maier, *op. cit.,* 74 and n. 2, for the places.
[82] Noted by Maier, *op. cit.,* 106, with the references.
[83] *CS,* VI, 81.
[84] *CS,* V, Document CCXXI, 519–526.
[85] *CS,* VI, 636.
[86] Schoeps, *op. cit.,* 31.
[87] I, 7; Wilbur edition, 197.

Indeed the body of Christ is itself the body of the Godhead; so that deity is plainly said to be in him bodily. The body of Christ its very self is divine and of the substance of deity. . . . The whole fulness of God, the whole of God the Father together with all the fulness of his properties, whatever God had, this dwells fully in this man. Indeed, if you note more carefully how great a thing it is for Christ to be the bodily and express image of the Godhead, you will clearly see that there is substantial Godhead in the body of Christ, and that he is himself really of the same essence, and consubstantial with the Father. The bodily Godhead in the substance of Christ is such that it was seen and touched by John with the bodily eye and the bodily hand.

Servetus continues in his demonstration, contending that the Word which, according to John 1:14, became flesh actually brought this flesh down from heaven:

For these are words of Christ which can by no means be misinterpreted, in which he declares that he and his flesh came down from heaven; for he says that the bread which came down from heaven is his own flesh [John 6:51]. Again the type of the manna given from heaven clearly proves this very thing; for the falling of the manna is to be ascribed to the flesh of Christ, since it is the food represented by that food. Again, the second man, Christ, came from heaven as a heavenly being [I Cor. 15:47].[88]

Servetus even appeals to Ex. 4:3, the memorable episode of Aaron's rod which, flung upon the earth, was turned into a snake, as an allegory of the incarnation of the Word made flesh.[89]

Thus the doctrine of the celestial flesh of Christ finds expression in four phases. There is, firstly, the flesh derived from the substance of Mary; secondly, the flesh by which Servetus means the substantial Word of God distinguishable from God's Spirit; thirdly, the idea of the man Jesus Christ in the mind of God from all eternity; and fourthly, the flesh of the resurrected and exalted Jesus Christ. Servetus the experimental physician did not begin his theological exploration with a postulated God-man before all ages, but with the historic Jesus recorded in the Gospels. Here, taking the words literally, and in so far as possible anatomically, he understood that God the Father sent the Word forth from his mouth, a seed which like a cloud of dew (ros) contained the elements of fire, water, and air and, passing through the nostrils of the Virgin, had the power to bring forth a man-child in her womb. God and his Word, replacing a man and his seed, procreated a natural son who was different from all

---

[88] Dialogues, I, 9; Wilbur edition, 200.
[89] Dialogues, I, 9; Wilbur edition, 199.

the other sons of woman in being of the same substance as the Creator rather than of the same substance as the creatures. In thus bearing the Son of God, Mary was *Theotokos* (*Deum generans seu Dei genitrix*).

Servetus' later discovery of the pulmonary circulation of the blood and the process of oxygenation[90] was motivated in part by his desire as a physician to show (like another physician, Paracelsus) that the Spirit, entering the blood system by the nostrils, makes physiologically plausible the doctrine of the virgin birth of Christ.

4. The Lord's Supper in the Theology of Ziegler and Servetus

We began in this chapter with a systematic treatment of the sacrament of Baptism (Ch. 11.1). After discussing alterations in the doctrine of the Trinity and Christology (Ch. 11.2 and 3), we might well bring the chapter symmetrically to a close with a general coverage of the sacrament of the Eucharist. But we have already devoted considerable attention to Eucharistic and sacramentarian thinking in earlier chapters, and there remains little to be said further at this point except to underscore the fact that in Schwenckfeld the Eucharist, even though primarily an inner feeding, virtually replaced baptism as the action whereby the believer is initiated into the community of the redeemed. There was something of this also in Paracelsus and the young Luther.[91] In fact, the sacrament of the altar had gone far, in the Middle Ages, to replace baptism as the essentially redemptive sacrament; and in their emphasis on the redemptive role of the Eucharist, Schwenckfeld, Crautwald, and other Spiritualists whose Eucharistic language had disappeared beneath more general mystical terms, were on sacramental theology even further from the Anabaptists than they were able to explain.

Let Ziegler speak for all these Spiritualists. It was well before Schwenckfeld that this Strassburg gardener declared at the end of 1524:

I say therefore, if thou art a believer in Christ and art mindful in thine heart of Almighty God, that he is thy gracious Father . . . and art mindful of Jesus Christ's becoming man and of his bitter suffering . . . and believest that all such has happened for thine own good unto the resurrection and eternal life . . . whenever that takes place in the heart of anybody, regardless of where that person is— hewing timber or cleaning a stall, washing dishes or sweeping the

[90] Announced for the first time in the *Restitutio*.
[91] See Goldammer, *Paracelsus: Offenbarung*, 84 and n. 55.

house, ploughing the field or mowing the meadow, yea, tending the cattle in the pasture—when such thoughts are opened up within, that person with certainty tastes the body and the blood of Christ, and he does so although there be no priest, no altar, and no outward sign.[92]

Spiritualism was clearly indigenous to Strassburg and may well have influenced in that direction such Anabaptist refugees as Entfelder and Bünderlin.

In contrast to the Spiritualists and the sacramentarians (both Magisterial and Radical) stood Servetus, who, it will be recalled, criticized Bucer in 1532 for not having an adequate doctrine of the real presence of Christ with the elements of the Supper. Servetus, to be sure, in his writings on the doctrine of the Trinity, 1531 and 1532, evidenced little interest in the Lord's Supper, but it became a major concern in the *Restitutio Christianismi* of 1553.

In brief, his views are as follows: Just as the inward man cannot be born without faith and baptism, so he cannot remain alive without love and the sacrament of the Lord's Supper. The adoptive child of God, that is, one who has been born again in baptism, must find regular nourishment if he is not to perish. Servetus quoted Irenaeus, *Adversus haereses,* on how, as a liquid is necessary to make dry flour into a loaf of bread, so the immersion of believers is necessary to make of them the new body of Christ. As by food from the tree of life the old man (Adam) died, so by the new food from the tree of Calvary on which the New Adam died, every renewed man is sustained and thereby enabled to persevere unto immortality, when Paradise is regained.

The baptized Christian may not, however, approach the Table of the Lord unprepared. What repentance was for the catechumens before their baptism, spiritual preparation is for those who communicate in the Lord's Supper. Whosoever remains in his guilt, for example, by refusing to be reconciled with his fellow believer must remain excluded from the Communion so long as he persists in his unrepentance. A good preparation for Communion, besides repentance, fasting, and prayer, is the presentation of quantities of bread and wine for distribution to the poor brethren. A proof of the love and the thankfulness of the believer for his salvation in Christ is the oblation in kind which has been in usage ever since the time of the apostles. A voluntary community of goods, to the extent to which it seems good to each one, even including voluntary poverty, is a sign of the health of the whole body of Christ. Where there is not that love which eliminates all difference of class, it is impossible to have a love feast (*agapē*)

[92] Krebs and Rott, *Elsass,* I (*QGT,* VII), No. 24, pp. 33 f.

in the way Jesus and his followers observed it. For this reason the congregation should not divide itself during the Lord's Supper into different divisions which communicate privately among themselves, but exactly as the many grains make one loaf of bread, so all the communicants should make a single, undamaged, unbroken body.

The most obnoxious thing of all would be for someone to say that from this body the Head is absent, that the body is on earth and the Head in heaven. If Christ were not present at baptism with his Spirit and in the sacrament of the Eucharist with his body, these actions would not have been so solemnly enjoined. The Supper is the necessary complement of baptism. By the feeding with the bread, Christ allows believers to partake of himself, for truly he said of that celestial bread, "This is my body."

Such different things as bread and a body the Bible has not elsewhere associated. At the Last Supper there was a secret and mystical relationship established between them. The body of Christ is truly bread, as he is truly the daily bread for the inner man. The bread is truly Christ's body, because the breaking of this bread effects the partaking of the celestial flesh. The digestive mechanism of the inner man is faith and love. In the sacrament he prays to Christ, constantly mindful of his immeasurable deeds and benefits. Servetus rejects the teaching of the Catholics and Lutherans alike, who think that one chews the body of Christ with teeth and swallows it. He rejects the mindless magic of the transubstantiationist, who makes of bread a nonbread, prays to the bread, and allows that the flesh of Christ could be, by accident, eaten by dogs. It is, instead, a celestial food, whereby the faithful soul grows together to become one substance with the heavenly body of Christ.

He rejects also the cold, sophistical symbol of the sacramentarians, including Bucer. For the bread is an outward sign of an *interior* event or action. The expletive *hoc* would be meaningless if it did not point to something which is present. Servetus with his doctrine of the celestial flesh of Christ (Ch. 11.3.c) holds fast to the allegedly apostolic pattern, according to which the inner man has more community with the substance of the body of Christ than Christ himself did with his mother when she carried him under her heart according to the flesh.[93]

Just as the believer becomes in the sacrament one with Christ, so he becomes one with his fellow communicant, whom he loves as Christ. Whoever fails to make use of the sacrament as the Lord

[93] H. Tollin, "Servet über Predigt, Taufe und Abendmahl," *Theologische Studien und Kritiken*, 1881, 296 f.

enjoined cannot know his own innermost substance, cannot know to what a celestial and eternal being he as believer is called through the resurrection of Christ. The apostolic Supper contains in itself, in its mystery, all the ancient offerings, both the expiatory and the thank-offerings. Yet the truly apostolic observation of the Supper does not consist in aping the original in pedantic detail. Christ used the bread and wine to simplify, not to complicate, the observance of the sacrament. If Christians live in a place where there is no wine, any other drink will serve the purpose equally well.

Servetus was not a transubstantiationist, consubstantiationist, or sacramentarian. He was closest to the Spiritualist Schwenckfeld. The sources of the Eucharistic piety of both men were medieval far more than patristic or Gnostic.

Very near the beginning of our narrative we suggested (Ch. 2.1) that the intense Eucharistic piety of a Wessel Gansfort, with its long abstentions from actual communication out of awe, could have contributed in the end to the rejection of the bread altogether by the Sacramentists in the Netherlands.

In any event, we are coming almost full circle in our narrative as we return to the Netherlandish Sacramentists on the point of their becoming Anabaptists.

CHAPTER 12

THE SPREAD OF HOFMANNITE ANABAPTISM TO THE
NETHERLANDS AND NORTH GERMANY TO 1534

A regional approach to the history of the Radical Reformation
does not commend itself in a period when the Holy Roman Empire counted as many autonomous political units as the United
States counts denominations. Moreover, the extraordinary mobility of the Radical Reformers in flight and on missions further
complicates any account based primarily on locality. Nevertheless, there are regional differentiations sufficiently distinctive to
warrant specialized treatment. The Netherlands and North
Germany constitute such a unit. Linguistically, this area of Low
German speech was divided from the rest of the Empire by a line
running roughly from Aachen (Aken) to Magdeburg (Maagden-
burg) and eastward.

The differences between Low and High German at their extremes, Flanders and Switzerland, were such that the preaching
of the Radical Reformation, which in its Anabaptist phase was
primarily a movement of the common people, could be carried on
between the two speech areas only by means of translations,
interpreters, and bilingual missionaries.

Within the Low German area there were, as elsewhere, numerous local dialects, some of them already well established as literary languages, notably that which is called interchangeably
"Flemish" in modern Belgium and "Dutch" in the Netherlands,
and which was already, in the sixteenth century, comparable in
standardization as a literary language to the High German of
the Saxon court and the South German printers.

Further differentiation of the area under consideration must
be made along political lines. The Netherlands, or Low Countries, for the purpose of our narrative, extend from the County
of Flanders to the County of East Frisia; and, except for the
latter and the princely bishopric of Liège, were largely in

341

Hapsburg possession or the threat thereof; and the whole area was largely Flemish/Dutch in speech.[1]

An ecclesiastical peculiarity of the populous area, constituting, roughly, modern Belgium and Holland, was the fact that, until the Catholic organizational reforms demanded by Philip II, all of it was under the jurisdiction of bishops and archbishops outside the region, except for the ancient princely bishopric of Utrecht, which was already on its way to secularization (1528)[2] by the opening of the Reformation Era. The absence of native bishops caused the serious loosening up of diocesan and parochial religious nurture and supervision, with the responsibility for checking heresy lodged largely in the hands of the Spanish vicegerents and the provincial courts. In patriotic self-defense the native magistrates, especially in the larger towns, often defended religious aberrations in the name of local autonomy. Especially was this true in the northern provinces.

Another feature of the Netherlands at this time was the involvement of the maritime towns in wars with Denmark and Lübeck over fishing rights and competitive commercial activities, resulting in economic and social disturbances in the ports.

Already at the opening of the sixteenth century, and long before the Calvinist wars of freedom which would finally win for the northern provinces of the Netherlands their independence from the Hapsburgs, the northern and southern Netherlands were culturally and, to a certain extent, religiously distinguishable. Modern Dutch historiography, Mennonite and Reformed alike, has tended to neglect the developments in the southern provinces.

"North Germany," for the purpose of the present narrative, includes East Frisia (Emden), linguistically and culturally linked with West Frisia, and all the principalities north of the aforementioned speech boundary from Aachen east to the borders of the kingdom of Poland (which up to its tripartition, 1772–1795, included both royal and ducal Prussia, Ch. 15). Within North Germany thus circumscribed, our narrative (here and in Ch. 13) is focused on the solid cluster of princely bishoprics (Münster, Osnabrück, Minden, and Paderborn), contiguous to a second cluster of four dynastically consolidated principalities on either side of the Rhine (Cleves, Jülich, Berg, and Mark), at the center

---

[1] The area coincides roughly with the imperial judicial circle (1512) of Burgundy (less Luxemburg, but including Liège).

[2] A. F. Mellink, *De Wederdoopers in de Noordelijke Nederlanden, 1531–1544* (Groningen, 1953), 335.

of which towered the imperial city of Cologne, surrounded by the relatively small temporality of the electoral archbishopric.[3]

Socioeconomically, this region was characterized by the large percentage of yeomen (*maiers*) with sizable farms or peasants long freed of onerous feudal services, a condition which had immunized the region from the contagion of the Great Peasants' War, 1524–1525. But their turn was approaching as Melchior Hofmann from Strassburg evangelized the whole region, directly and with the help of his apostles, proclaiming the imminence of Christ's second advent. (We shall reserve for Ch. 13 our detailed account of Anabaptism in the Münster region.)

There is thus the very important theological differentiation to be noted between the Anabaptism that took its rise in Switzerland and that which spread like wildfire through the Netherlands and Northwestern Germany. Under the impulsion of its first apostle, Anabaptism in this region was for a season intensely eschatological; and even after it subsided and, for the most part, came to renounce the Maccabean belligerence of Münster and other centers of aberration, it continued to bear the distinctive theological marks of its greatest apostle, notably his Christology and hermeneutics.

But there is one further differentiating feature of the Anabaptism of this region, at once religious and sociopsychological in character. Anabaptism in the Netherlands found its first recruits among the indigenous Sacramentists and thereby fell heir to a late medieval tradition of popular piety or iconoclasm, depending upon the point of view. Anabaptism in the Low Countries was thus the earliest bearer of religiously oriented Dutch-Flemish national self-consciousness. In most other areas we have considered, Anabaptism arose out of dissatisfaction with the Magisterial Reformation and was therefore in its basic posture anti-Protestant, whereas in the Netherlands, Anabaptism was the first major onslaught of organized reformation. It preceded revolutionary-nationalist Calvinism by more than a generation.

Because of the importance of the Sacramentists and the "national-reformed" impulse in the Netherlands, we must, before going on to the Hofmannite mission in detail, pick up the story of the Netherlandish Sacramentists where we left them at the death of Cornelius Hoen in 1524 and carry it forward to the dismissal of Hinne Rode in 1530, and introduce also the Netherlandish Libertines.

---

[3] The area coincides roughly with the imperial judicial circle (1512) of the Lower Rhine and Westphalia.

1. The Netherlandish Sacramentists, 1524–1530

What in Switzerland was "a pearl of great value" (Zwingli) was in the Catholic Low Countries a pernicious doctrine, though stoutly adhered to by a large number of people of position, education, and local authority, as well as by the common people. We have already traced to 1525 the long tradition of a violent popular opposition to the Catholic sacrament of the altar running alongside the devoutly contemplative, Biblicohumanistic assimilation (in Gansfort and Erasmus) of *credere* and *edere* (Ch. 2). In the five years leading to the emergence of Melchiorite Anabaptism, these two sacramentarian currents mingled. Moreover, the local magistrates, being in any event frequently sympathetic toward the humanistic form of sacramentarianism, commonly protected the perpetrators of popular, iconoclastic sacramentarianism in their patriotic zeal to resist every Hapsburg attempt at administrative centralization and curtailment of the ancient rights of the provincial estates and town councils.

By 1525 it was therefore possible for Erasmus to write that the greatest part of the people in the provinces of Holland, Zealand, and Flanders had been won for the Reformation,[4] by which, of course, he meant that the greatest part of the *city* population had been won for the national (anti-Hapsburg) sacramentarian ideal. In the same year, Bucer, with more relish than Erasmus, but with greater precision as to the tenet, even if with exaggeration as to the number of those holding it, wrote that "the whole of [the provinces of] Holland and Frisia, now through Rode and certain others," know the truth about the sacrament of the Supper.[5]

One of the victims of the Inquisition in the Low Countries was the Sacramentist John Pistorius (Jan Jans de Bakker) of Woerden. A former priest, he had rejected the Mass, visited Luther, married, and become a baker. He was arrested in May 1525 and imprisoned at The Hague. From 11 July to 7 September 1525 he was interrogated by the inquisitor and sentenced as a "Lutheran"! He may have been Lutheran in calling the papacy "the church of the malignants," from which he was glad to be banned. But he was surely not Lutheran when he declared: "Wherever and in whatever manner the Word of God is instilled in believing Christians, there is the true celebration of the sacrament."[6] He was burned at the stake at The Hague on 15 September 1525.

---

[4] *Epistolae*, edited by Allen, VI, 155; Mellink, *op. cit.*, 337, 338.
[5] Quoted by De Hoop Scheffer, *op. cit.*, 548.
[6] Noted by J. Alton Templin in his projected Harvard Ph.D. thesis, "The Sacramentists in the Netherlands, 1500–1566."

From 1525 to 1530 the Sacramentist movement steadily gained adherents. As in Switzerland, the attack on transubstantiation prepared the way for the covenantal conception of baptism.[7] Whereas the first leaders of Sacramentism were commonly priests, monks, and friars, from 1525 on the leadership of the Sacramentist conventicles was increasingly in the hands of devotees without formal theological training.

The earliest martyrdom of a woman to be preserved in the Anabaptist *Martyrs' Mirror* (1570)[8] is that of the spirited Sacramentist Wendelmoet Claesdochter, young widow of Monninkendam in 1527.[9] The account of her trial and execution pictures a confident, if not presumptuous, woman who suffered death for her Sacramentist faith, in the popular tradition, perhaps, of Tanchelm rather than in the more devout line of Gansfort.

On 15 November 1527, Wendelmoet was brought from the castle of Woerden to The Hague to stand trial for heresy. Three days later she was arraigned before the stadholder, the count of Hooghstraten, and the full council of Holland. She stood firm in her faith. When asked what she thought concerning the sacrament of the altar, she replied: "I hold your sacrament to be bread and flour, and if you hold it as God, I say that it is your devil." Concerning the extreme unction, she answered: "Oil is good for salad or to oil your shoes with." When two Dominican friars came to her, one as confessor, and showed her a wooden crucifix, saying, "See, here is your Lord and your God," she answered:

This is not my God; the cross by which I am redeemed is a different one. This is a wooden god; throw him into the fire, and warm yourselves with him.

The dean of Naeldwijck, subcommissioner and inquisitor, then proceeded to read aloud the sentence, first in Latin and then in Dutch. She was delivered to the secular arm, and the chancellor declared that she was to be burned at the stake. At this point she was led out for the execution. She was again offered a cruci-

---

[7] Mellink, *De Wederdoopers,* cap. iv, brings together the older and most recent monographic and regional studies and sources to show conclusively that the way for Anabaptism was prepared by Sacramentism.

[8] Thielman van Braght, *The Bloody Theater or Martyrs' Mirror,* translated by Joseph F. Sohm (Scottdale, Pennsylvania, 1951), 422 f.

[9] Also called Weynken Claes; *ME,* IV, 938. J. C. van Slee, in "Wendelmoet Claesdochter van Monninkendam," *Nederlandsch Archief vóor Kerkgeschiednis* (henceforth: *NAK*), XX (1927), 121–156. She was not listed in the first three editions of the forerunner of the *Mirror,* namely, the *Offer des Heeren,* but was inserted into the appendix of the edition of 1570.

fix, but she refused to kiss it, and would not call on the Virgin Mary, insisting that she had Christ at the right hand of God interceding for her. In the next breath, however, she also declared, in turning away from the crucifix: "This is not my Lord and my God; my Lord God is in me, and I in him."

When she had reached the scaffold to be strangled and then burned, it was suggested to her that she ask forgiveness of all present for any offenses she had committed against them. This she did. A friar urged her to recant, but she obstinately refused. She went to the bench and seated herself at the stake. After the rope was in place around her neck, the friar asked her: "Mother Weynken, will you gladly die as a Christian?" "Yes, I will," she replied. "Do you renounce all heresy?" "I do." The friar took heart and said: "This is well. Are you also sorry that you have erred?" She replied: "I formerly did err, and for that I am sorry; this, however, is no error, but the true way, and I adhere to God." With this unexpected twist on "error," the executioner began to strangle her. She lowered her eyes and closed them as though asleep. (By 1534 the town of her birth was predominantly Anabaptist, and later a large Mennonite congregation centered there.)

Among the Sacramentists whose names are preserved in the hearings and who after 1530 became prominent in Melchiorite Anabaptism were the burgomaster of Deventer, Jacob van Wynssem, whom Rode called on in 1525,[10] the priest Hadrian Cordatus of Ypres, summoned in Middelberg for a hearing in 1527,[11] and the goldsmith Dominicus Abels of Utrecht, apprehended in 1528.[12] The glass painter David Joris (Ch. 13.5), the leader of the Delft conventicle after the departure of Wouter, climaxing his iconoclastic disturbances, attacked the image of Mary in the Assumption Day procession in 1528. He was condemned to scourging, the boring of his tongue, and three years' banishment. In the same year on Corpus Christi Day in Leiden, where there had for some time been hedge and alley preaching in the manner of the later Calvinists (but without hymn-singing),[13] the Delft tailor Gijsbrecht Albrechts tacked his Sacramentist proclamation to the church door and threw another copy into the pulpit during the sermon. In the same year, also, in Haarlem, the baker John Mathijs (Ch. 13.1) suffered the same punishment as Joris for Sacramentist iconoclasm.[14]

---

[10] Mellink, *op. cit.*, 336.
[11] *Ibid.*, 338.
[12] *Ibid.*, 336.
[13] L. Knappert, *Het Onstaan*, 111 f., 137, 142.
[14] Kühler, *op. cit.*, 48; Mellink, *op. cit.*, 342.

Perhaps the most representative humanistic Sacramentists destined to turn Anabaptists would be Henry Schlachtschap (Slachtscaep) of Maastricht and Henry Rol of Grave in the province of Brabant. Both of them, the former a priest and the latter a Carmelite friar, became in the end, like Mathijs, identified with the Anabaptist theocracy of Münster, but neither should be associated with its excesses. We may take Rol as our example of the transition from indigenous Netherlandish Sacramentism to Melchiorite Anabaptism and look briefly at his view of the sacrament of the altar.

It was in Haarlem, where there were "divers conventicles, where clandestine sermons and disputations were held of an evening and attended by many persons,"[15] that Rol, as a Carmelite, may well have become acquainted with Sacramentism. In any event, he was well on his way to the sacramentarian view when he was engaged as house chaplain, in 1530, to the bailiff Gijsbrecht van Baack, who locally represented the stadholder of Holland, and was himself an independent thinker.

Rol was sent by the bailiff to the diet in Augsburg, and perhaps it was on a long trip back that Rol, with Bernard Rothmann (Ch. 13), stayed around May 1531 in the home of Capito (Ch. 10.3.e) in Strassburg.[16]

Rol's Sacramentist views are found in his two tracts, *Die Slotel* (*The Key of the Mystery of the Supper*), written in East Frisian before 1532,[17] and *Eyne ware Bedinjnckijnge* (*A True Consideration How the Blessed Body of Christ is Different from our Unworthy Body*).[18] Rol, like Hofmann, appeals to the image of the Passover lamb, but he does not make use of the manna image, perhaps because he eschews the doctrine of the celestial flesh of Christ, with which it was linked, and has no place for Hoen and Hofmann's bridal imagery with its ring, the analogue of the bread. It was not the eating of the paschal lamb that saved the Hebrews and it is not the eating of the bread in the Communion service that redeems Christians is his view.

Rol deals with the question of who should be called to the Communion service. In Israel, only they participated in the Communion of the Passover lamb who also bore the token of circumcision. Correspondingly, only those Christians should approach the Communion who are "inwardly circumcised, i.e., who believe

[15] De Hoop Scheffer, *op. cit.*, 560; Mellink, *op. cit.*, 342.

[16] Christian Sepp, *Kerkhistorische Studiën* (Leiden, 1885), 26; Mellink, *op. cit.*, 346, 2; Krebs and Rott, *Elsass*, I (*QGT*, VII), No. 249.

[17] *BRN*, V, 1–123; discussed in *ME*, IV, 544, and Rol himself in *ME*, II, 704; also in W. Bax, *Het Protestantisme in het Bisdom Luik en vooral te Maastricht, 1505–1557*, I (The Hague, 1937), 95–96, 101–102.

[18] *BRN*, V, 95–123.

in Christ and who are baptized." Whether Rol meant here baptism by water or by the Holy Spirit is not clear. Those who wish to take part in the Communion must be "alive" (i.e., faithful), not "sick" (i.e., doubting the grace of God), "hungry" to proclaim the glory of God and "thirsty" for salvation.

Rol relates the atonement to the Lord's Supper in an unusual way.[19] He moves from Israel in bondage to Egypt being fed by God upon the paschal lamb, to mankind in bondage to the devil being fed, while still in prison, by the food from God's Table. With the help of an allegory, he makes God the Father the giver of the bread and wine. The Father is likened to a judge who has put a man in prison to await execution. The son of the judge implores him to be permitted to take the sentenced man's place. To this the father-judge (unaccountably) assents and sends to the prison food from his own table. As soon as arrangements can be completed, the condemned man will go free; meantime he can partake of the goodly nourishment in the glad prospect of liberation, whereas before he would scarcely touch his wretched provender. The Eucharistic bread and wine are, indeed, no different from any other food and drink, but coming from the Table of the Lord himself, they are an earnest of more to come and induce joy, for they are tokens of the promised release from bondage. The relation in Rol's parable is thus between an adoptive son (substituted for the redeeming Son) and the Heavenly Father, whereas for Hoen, as for Hofmann, the Eucharistic relation is that between a believing bride and Christ the loving Bridegroom.

In 1531, Rol went to Wassenburg in Cleves (Ch. 12.4) and in the summer of 1532 was drawn to Münster, where he became preacher in St. Giles's and in 1533 preached against infant baptism. In October he signed, with Bernard Rothmann, the principal Radical Reformer in Münster, the confession called *Bekenntnisse van beyden sacramenten Doepe unde Nachtmael*. On 6 November 1533 he was banished by the conservative faction and visited the provinces of Holland and Frisia, but on 1 January 1534 he returned to Münster to preach, and was rebaptized on 5 January 1534[20] by an emissary in Münster of the former Haarlem baker and Sacramentist, John Mathijs. Already the biography of the former Carmelite of Haarlem has merged with the yet to be recounted history of Münster. But since he has been introduced as a representative Sacramentist, we may tell his tale here to the finish.

---

[19] *Die Slotel, BRN*, V, 56 f.
[20] By either Bartholomew Boeckbinder or William Kuyper.

In the house of Bernard Knipperdolling, soon to be the radical mayor of Münster, Rol rebaptized that same January Dr. Gerhard Westerburg (Ch. 4.2), brother-in-law and purveyor of the Eucharistic theology of Carlstadt. On 21 February 1534, Rol left Münster to win recruits for the "New Jerusalem." He went first to Wesel, where he rebaptized a number of converts, and on 2 August 1534 he arrived at Maastricht, where he found a group of Sacramentists formerly under the leadership of Henry Schlachtschap meeting in the house of the cobbler John van Genck. Rol taught them Melchiorite principles. It was while guiding the conventicle that he was arrested on the evening of 2 September 1534 and soon thereafter executed.

In following one representative Sacramentist into Anabaptism, we have not only gone beyond the chronological frame of the present section, but we have put to one side the large number of Sacramentists who were never caught up in the Anabaptist apocalyptic revolution.

Notable Dutch Sacramentists in the devout and humanistic tradition of Hoen, and destined never to become Anabaptists, were John Snijder (Sartorius), William Gnapheus, and Gellius Faber. In fact, they came, in time, to count themselves "Zwinglians." Faber, indeed, was to become a major opponent of Menno Simons.

Sartorius (c. 1500–1570), from Amsterdam, was influenced by the already mentioned former Dominican, Wouter, in Delft (Ch. 2.2). As early as 1525, severely critical of the doctrines and practices of the Catholic Church, Sartorius preached salvation by faith, and published a Latin treatise on the Lord's Supper in which he rejected the Catholic doctrine of transubstantiation. In the same year he was imprisoned at The Hague, charged with heresy, but recanted and was set free. He continued his evangelical preaching and was a Latin teacher in Amsterdam until 1535, under the protection of its tolerant magistrates. Thereupon he became head of the Latin school at Noordwijk near Leiden, influencing and stimulating the evangelical-minded of Leiden and Haarlem. He later ministered at Zutphen, visited Basel, and then became the leader of the evangelical group in Delft after the successive departures of Wouter and Joris.

William Gnapheus de Volder (1493–1568), who was rector of the Latin school at The Hague in 1522, was in 1523 forced to leave because of anti-Catholic ideas, and imprisoned. He was a cellmate of Pistorius, who dictated to him the questions of the inquisitors. Gnapheus wrote a circumstantial account of the cross-examination of himself and Pistorius. He settled, after much wandering, at Elbing in royal Prussia, in 1531, where he wrote an evangelical treatise for the sick and suffering, *Een troost ende spiegel der siecken ende derghenen die in lijdn zijn* (showing the influence of Hoen) and became rector of the Latin school. We shall next meet him briefly in Ch. 15.

Gnapheus and Sartorius, unlike Wendelmoet, as Sacramentists were virtually the same kind of Reformed Christians as those who, in Switzerland, endorsed the Magisterial Reformation of the cantons and adhered, as against Luther, to the sacramentarian view of the Supper.

They therefore readily thought of themselves as "Zwinglians," overlooking, in their eagerness for a respectable label, the local origin of the kind of Eucharistic theology which Zwingli had come to espouse. They differed also in one very important respect from the Swiss Zwinglians in not having a political assignment. The Netherlandish Sacramentists of the humanistic type, like the Italian Waldensians who were likewise to be won over to the side of the Magisterial Reformers, retained their earlier views against war. Only on the sacrament of the altar were they "Zwinglian." Culturally, temperamentally, or sociologically, they were, in their oppressively Catholic environment, at least as much akin to the pacifistic Grebelians before their espousal of believers' baptism as to the Zwinglians. The irenic, Erasmian Sacramentists represent a much more widespread manifestation of the national-reformed consciousness in the Netherlands than the few names here adduced would indicate. For their place was soon to be taken by, and many of their members were to be recruited for, the more aggressively sectarian and eschatologically oriented Anabaptists; and the memory of their testimony was to be further faded by the more truly "Zwinglian" freedom fighters under William of Orange, who, though appealing to John Calvin as their mentor, were actually closer to Zwingli and his conception of spiritual warfare.

The Reformation in the Netherlands has been seen as passing through three main phases—Sacramentist, Anabaptist, and Calvinist. "Lutheranism" in the Netherlands generally meant Protestantism or anti-Catholicism, and seldom implied the peculiar tenets of Luther, for example, his view of the sacraments. But there was one other religious movement in the Netherlands which cannot be subsumed under any of these headings: Libertinism, akin to Sacramentism, though predestinarian and more speculative. When Wendelmoet Claesdochter, for example, said that God was in her and she in him, she was a Sacramentist echoing the Fourth Gospel in a Libertine key.

2. LIBERTINES OR SPIRITUALIZERS

Only fragmentary biographical and theological documentation survives of the Netherlandish movement to which the hostile gave the name Libertinism in reference to Acts 6:9, the *synagoga Libertinorum* overcome by Stephen. The Libertines preferred the name Spirituals[21] or called themselves after one or another of their current leaders (Loists; later: Quintinists, Jorists).

Several of these groups have been recently brought typologically together as Libertines, co-ordinate in significance with four other Continental groupings in the mid-sixteenth century, the militant Catholics, the Lutherans, the Reformed, and the Anabaptists.[22] But this classification is typologically and even geographically partial, and it seems best to designate the Libertines as they have been most recently documented, described, and analyzed as "Spiritualizers"[23] and, as such, one of the subgroupings of our Spiritualists.

The Netherlandish Spiritualizers, then (Libertines, Loists, Familists, Spirituals, and to a certain extent the Sacramentists),[24] were a loosely interrelated antinomian movement of the sixteenth century, compounding variously the self-deification of Rhenish mysticism, the libertarianism of the medieval Brethren of the Free Spirit and other groups, the ecclesiastical indifferentism of Erasmus, and the Christian antinomianism of Luther, and in some places, at least, the Averroism of Padua. They were alike in attaching little or no importance to external sacraments.

The Loists took their name from Eligius (Loy) Pruystinck, a slater (*schaliedekker*) of Antwerp. In the middle of March 1524 Loy set out, as at an earlier date Hinne Rode had, for Wittenberg to see what Luther would make of his doctrine. A disputation took place in Luther's house between Loy with several

---

[21] Calvin, *Contre la secte phantastique et furieuse des Libertins qui se nomment Spirituelz*, 1545, *Opera*, VII, 226. See Ch. 23.3.

[22] See H. de la Verwey, "Trois hérésiarques dans les Pays-Bas du XVIe siècle," *BHR*, XVI (1954), 312–330. See also the characterization of the use of the terms "Libertine" and "Esprit fort," especially in the seventeenth century, in Henri Busson, *La Pensée réligieuse française de Charron à Pascal* (Paris, 1933), 1–15. The literature of the spiritual Libertines has been sorted out and discussed by Busson in *Les sources et le développement du rationalisme* (Paris, 1922), 314–345, revised as *La Rationalisme dans la littérature française de la Renaissance (1533–1601)* (Paris, 1957), 296–317.

[23] The useful English term is Franklin Littell's adaptation of the term "Spiritual," popularized by Ernst Troeltsch. See Littell's *The Free Church* (Boston, 1957), 31 f.

[24] They have some affinities with the Illuminists of Spain (Ch. 1.1), the evangelical Spiritualists of Germany, and the later Nicodemites of Italy (Ch. 22.5).

companions and Melanchthon. Afterward Luther directed a letter to his own adherents at Antwerp (April 1525), warning against the dangerous "poltergeists,"[25] and "the new prophets" from Antwerp, who identify the reason of man with the Holy Spirit.[26] Luther's letter arraigns Loy as heretical, on eight briefly stated charges. They are Luther's intolerant transcript, colored, perhaps, by his recent encounter with the Zwickau prophets (Ch. 3.2) mentioned in the same letter. According to Luther, the Loists held (1) that every man has the Holy Spirit, (2) that the Holy Spirit is none other than man's own reason and understanding, (3) that everyone believes, (4) that this belief is to wish for one's neighbor what one wishes for oneself,[27] (5) that there is no hell or condemnation except for the flesh, (6) that all souls will enjoy eternal life, (7) that sin is not committed so long as one does not so intend, and (8) that whoever has not the Holy Spirit (likewise) has no sin, for he has no reason.[28]

Loy, adopting what looks like an Averroist view (Ch. 1.3.c) of the universal Intellect (*spiritus*), held that man's intellectual nature is a spiritual substance and that everyone who is reborn possesses the Holy Spirit. (In 1502, for comparison, the heretic Herman of Rijswijk, in or near The Hague, condemned by the Inquisition to life imprisonment, had declared that there is no personal immortality, had denied God's creation out of nothing, had called Christ a "fool and an innocent phantast," and had specifically acknowledged his debt to Averroes, however much he simplified the philosophy of the latter.[29]) Since man's flesh and spirit are thoroughly independent, and with no influence upon each other, the (renewed) spirit of man, according to Loy as interpreted by Luther and confirmed in part by the extant Loist *Summa doctrinae*,[30] incurs no responsibility for the weakness of the flesh. His spirit, as such, is sinless. The final goal of man is to vanish into the divine being. Loy based the radical dualism

---

[25] *Briefe*, XVIII, *WA*, 541–550.

[26] In a letter to George Spalatin, 27 March 1525, Luther mentions the presence of a "*novum genus ex Antwerpia . . . asserentium, Spiritum sanctum nihil aliud esse quam ingenium et rationem naturalem.*"

[27] To improve the order, I have placed Luther's sixth article in the fourth place.

[28] *Briefe*, XVIII, *WA*, 548 f.

[29] Johannes Lindeboom, *Stiefkinderen van het Christendom* (The Hague, 1929), 156; *Corpus documentorum inquisitionis Neerlandicae*, edited by Paul Frédéricq, I, 494, 502. Lindeboom puts the Free Spirits and the Loists in the same chapter.

[30] The *Summa* is printed by Ignatius Döllinger, *Beiträge zur Sektengeschichte des Mittelalters*, II (Munich, 1890), 664–668.

of what he called the two *homines* upon a forced exegesis of the Bible, and particularly of Paul. For example, he brought into contrast I John 3:9: "No one born of God commits sin" and I John 1:6, tendentiously singularized: "Whoever says he has no sin is a liar," and then proceeded to apply the first dictum to the spiritual man and the second to the carnal man.[31] We may compare this radically dualist solution to seeming contradictions in Scripture with the Spiritualist Anabaptist synthesis in, for example, John Denck (Ch. 7.1).

Loy and his followers certainly had much in common with such diverse forms of piety and libertarianism as that of the Beghards and the Brethren of the Free Spirit, though it is difficult to establish the relation between the Loists and any sects antedating the Reformation Era.

On his return to Antwerp, Loy and nine of his followers, people of humble origin like himself (two of them women), were subjected to an examination by the Inquisition, 26 February 1526. They recanted and were cleared with the sentence of public ecclesiastical penance and the burning of their books. Loy was specifically required to wear a crucifix.

Loy's doctrine in the following decades continued to spread not only among the humbler classes but also among the rich burghers, especially after a severe outbreak of the plague in 1530, and not only in Antwerp but also in Flanders generally, in Brabant, and in the districts about Cologne. The poor were wont to drop on their knees at his approach, reminding us of Tanchelm centuries before (Ch. 2.1). Symbolizing his vocation of poverty and his claim to prophetic authority, Loy dressed in robes torn and then patched with jewels.[32] Loy circulated Libertine works edited for him by Dominic van Oucle and printed in Germany.[33] Another Loist, the former Lutheran Christopher Hérault, a watchmaker of Paris, was executed at Antwerp on delation. Loy himself was also arrested in Antwerp and then sent to Vilvorde to face examination along with other followers, condemned 24 October 1544, and burned alive the next day before the gates of the city. On 28 February 1545, three of the principal remaining Loists were decapitated, and the sect came to an end in the Netherlands. Some Loists fled to England. The

---

[31] *Summa, loc. cit.,* 666 f.

[32] Norman Cohn, *The Pursuit of the Millennium* (London, 1957), 178.

[33] Van Oucle was later arrested at Rozendaal (Holland) and carried to Antwerp for a hearing, where he (14 September 1544) strangled himself in prison. J. Frederichs, article, *Biographie Nationale de Belgique,* XVI (1901), cols. 781 f.

execution of the last of the Loists in Antwerp in 1545 may have contributed to Calvin's decision to write a major refutation of all the Libertines in that very year (Ch. 23.3).

The exact relationship between the Loists and the Libertines pilloried by Calvin cannot be worked out at this distance. In Calvin's polemic, the Loists are not actually mentioned and another Flemish progenitor of Libertinism is referred to, namely, one Coppin.

The Fleming Coppin, of whom little more is known except that he preached at Lille about 1529, saw his teaching carried into the French-speaking part of the Netherlands and into France by two tailors, Quintin of Hainaut, and Bertrand of Moulins, and also by Claude Perceval and the former priest, Anthony Pocquet. Pocquet (also, contemporaneously, Pocque), born in Enghien around 1500, became a doctor in canon law.[34] We have a pretty clear picture of Pocquet's system, though from his own hand we have only his Communication to his followers, reproduced in sections for refutation seriatim by Calvin, and presumably complete.[35]

Pocquet had an interesting theology of history. In the traditional Tychonian-Augustinian rather than the Joachimite periodization of history, Pocquet outlined the seven ages of the world, the seventh corresponding to the first, that is, paradisic.[36] The Holy Spirit and Christ alike belong to the last age. Regenerate man belongs both to the old and the New Adam. There is still enmity between man and the devil in the world, the hardness of the law, self-fullness, willfulness, and death. But regenerate man is already a new creature in Christ, the Second Adam, reconciled with God, justified, illuminated, and mortified in the believer's assumption of his own cross. Pocquet belongs to the mystical tradition in his view of the atonement in that for him, instead of Christ's taking the place of the sinner on the cross, he weds himself to the believer. As the rib was taken from the first Adam to form Eve, so on the cross the side of the Second Adam was pierced to bring forth his "sister and spouse"

---

[34] Charles Rahlenboeck, article, *Biographie Nationale de Belgique,* XVII (1903), cols. 843 f.

[35] See Calvin's *Contre la secte phantastique, Opera,* VII, cols. 226–241. Summarized and analyzed by Karl Müller, "Calvin und die Libertiners," *ZKG,* XL (1922), 90–98. In addition, Calvin mentions four manuscripts that a friend of his procured for him while Pocquet was in Montpellier in the suite of Queen Margaret and an exegesis of Luke (mentioned in *Opera,* XIII, 27, 1060), none of the five extant today.

[36] Calvin, *Contre la secte phantastique, Opera,* VII, col. 237, where the seven times of the Apocalypse are referred to.

(Canticles), the church.[37] Justification is the bestowal of the Spirit experienced by the believer. Pocquet attaches importance to the double portion of the Spirit (II Kings 2:9) poured out on Elisha, a symbol of the end of the age. On the cross the church was founded, which is the extension of Christ's human nature. Yet the believer must die. Pocquet held to the doctrine of the sleep of the soul, to be awakened to the life of the redeemed at the end of the seventh age.

Several ill-assorted ethical and practical consequences, drawn from Pocquet's injunction to be utterly obedient to and trustful of God, were brought under three heads: (1) the abandonment of medicaments, (2) the elimination of the power and authority of the state in spiritual matters, and (3) the formation of a truly spiritual community wherein love of neighbor and enemy exceeds love of self and kin, as a replacement of the institutions of unregenerate society (not only the state but even the family, and of course the worldly church).

We shall next meet Pocquet and his followers at the court of Queen Margaret of Navarre (Ch. 23.3). It is still uncertain what may have been the relationship of the Loists and Libertines to the Sacramentists and to the Anabaptists, who in the Netherlands were at first called Melchiorites.[38]

3. The Melchiorites (Hofmannites) and Obbenites

Sacramentist (sacramentarian), eschatologically oriented Anabaptism suddenly arose in the Netherlands in May 1530 under the apostolate of Melchior Hofmann just about five years after the emergence of sacramentarian, pacifistic Anabaptism in Zurich and Zollikon under Conrad Grebel (Ch. 6.1). It would be an oversimplification to ascribe all the differences between the Swiss Brethren and the Netherlandish Melchiorites to the differences in temperament, education, and theology between patrician Conrad Grebel and furrier Melchior Hofmann.

As different as are the Alpine streams and headwaters of the Rhine from the canals and marshes of its estuary, so also were the religious currents in the Swiss Confederation of cantons,

---

[37] *Ibid.*, col. 237.

[38] A valuable collection of sources and the history of the sect is given in Julius Frederichs, *De secte der Löisten of Antwerpesche libertijnen 1525/1545* (Ghent, 1891); "Un lutherien français devenu libertin spirituel," *Bulletin historique et littéraire de la société de l'histoire du protestantisme français*, XLI (1892), 250–269; "La Moralité des libertins spirituels," *ibid.*, 502–504; A. Jundt, *Histoire du panthéisme populaire au moyen âge* (Paris, 1875), 122 ff.

which had long before wrested independence from the Hapsburg, and the religious currents in the Netherlands, now restive
under or threatened by the Spanish branch of the same house of
Hapsburg. The "Zurich" of Netherlandish Anabaptism lay outside Hapsburg jurisdiction. It was Emden in East Frisia. To
Emden a large number of Dutch Sacramentists had been fleeing. Hofmann (himself but recently rebaptized in Strassburg, Ch.
10.3.c) rebaptized nearly three hundred of them[39] in June 1530
in the vestibule of the Grosse Kirche and united them in a
covenanted congregation. In this mood Hofmann published his
Ordinance of God, 1530 (Ch. 11.1.b),[40] in which he for the first
time in his ministry made rebaptism programmatic. The divine
ordinance was, of course, the baptismal injunction of Matthew
28:19.

Hofmann's principal Anabaptist convert in Emden and deputy for the Netherlandish mission was John Volkerts (called
Trijpmaker), by some styled "the new Enoch." Volkerts was
soon banished from East Frisia under pressure from the local
Zwinglian preachers. He moved to Amsterdam and founded the
Anabaptist conventicle there. He was apprehended in the fall
of 1531, despite the efforts of the burgomaster to save him. During his trial, Trijpmaker recanted and yielded the names of more
than fifty converts in Amsterdam. Nine of them were apprehended[41] and with him beheaded at The Hague, 5 December 1531.
Among those who witnessed the grisly scene was David Joris.[42]

Stunned, Hofmann wavered momentarily in his eschatological
faith; he had by then returned to Strassburg (Ch. 10.3.h) for a
third sojourn. Revising his eschatological calendar, he prudently
counseled "standing still" for two years pending the return of a
favorable conjuncture of events.[43] This counsel of strategic delay
(*Stillstand*) in the construction of the spiritual temple was based
upon the prophetically enjoined interruption in the work on
the "Temple" in "Jerusalem" (Ezra 4:24) until a new "Darius"
should make possible resumption of the spiritual construction.

In the meantime, his followers, called Melchiorites, had spread
widely in the Netherlands. Plague, flood, and famine caused by
war and blockades intensified the eschatological mood between
1528 and 1536, dominating all other subjects in the pamphlet

[39] Obbe Philips, *Confession, SAW*, 204.
[40] Written in Low German, it survives in Dutch translation; translated in
SAW, 182–203.
[41] Philips, *Confession, SAW*, 210.
[42] Roland Bainton, *David Joris: Wiedertäufer und Kämpfer für Toleranz im
16. Jahrhundert, ARG*, Ergänzungsband VI (Leipzig, 1937), 5.
[43] Philips, *Confession, SAW*, 211. Cf. above, pp. 276, 309.

literature. Hofmann and his evangelists were reaping where the Sacramentists had sown.

His two most important converts, after Trijpmaker, were in West Frisia the barber-surgeon Obbe Philips of Leeuwarden, and the Haarlem baker John Mathijs. In these two converts the extremes within Netherlandish Anabaptism are to become apparent. Obbe Philips will eventually withdraw as a Spiritualist; John Mathijs, assuming the mantle of Trijpmaker, will end up as a Münsterite revolutionary (Ch. 13.1).

Obbe Philips (c. 1500–1568) had been eyewitness to the execution in Leeuwarden of the first Anabaptist martyr in the Netherlands, the Melchiorite Sicke Freercks, 20 March 1531. This execution was memorable, for it was a turning point, also, in the spiritual evolution of Menno Simons (Ch. 14.1). Sicke had been converted by Hofmann and rebaptized by Trijpmaker in Emden the previous November, and thereupon was sent to Leeuwarden, where he had won over the local Sacramentist conventicle to Anabaptism. At the beheading, a drummer among the soldiers' ranks and a friend of Sicke's interrupted the solemnity of muffled drums with a tirade against Catholicism and escaped in the midst of a benignant throng.

Obbe and his brother Dietrich (Ch. 19.2.b), a Franciscan friar, sons of the local priest who had lived in concubinage, inwardly espoused the martyr's cause. The two brothers had for some time been reading Lutheran tracts,[44] and had drawn apart from the local parish, with a number of other evangelical Sacramentists, to "worship God quietly in the manner of the fathers and the patriarchs" so that "each one could seek God from his heart, and serve and follow Him without a preacher, teacher, or any other outward meeting."[45]

When Hofmann returned to the Netherlands 1532–1533, he met resistance among his own followers—notably Mathijs—on the policy of prudential suspension of the ordinance of baptism. Mathijs declared himself to be a prophet sent by the Holy Spirit, an envoy of God. Putting aside his incredulous wife and taking a "pretty young slip of a girl" who "had great knowledge of the gospel,"[46] he came clandestinely to Amsterdam. The contemporary account continues:

Now when he came there, he professed to have been greatly driven by the Spirit and [told] how God had revealed great things to him which he could tell to no one, that he was the other witness, Enoch

[44] This is evidenced by his *Enchiridion; BRN,* X.
[45] Philips, *Confession, SAW.*
[46] *Ibid.,* 214.

[Hofmann being generally recognized as Elijah]. Now when the friends or brethren heard of this, they became apprehensive and knew not what they should best do. . . . They had also heard that Cornelius Polterman [or perhaps Caspar Schwenckfeld][47] was Enoch. When John Mathijs learned of this, he carried on with much emotion and terrifying alarm, and with great and desperate curses cast all into hell and to the devils for eternity who would not hear his voice and who would not recognize and accept him as the true Enoch. Because of this, some went into a room without food and drink, in fasting and prayer, and were almost all as disconsolate over such threats as if they lay in hell. For we were at that time all unsuspecting and no one knew that such false prophets could arise in the midst of the brethren. . . . Then they again came to themselves and the fearful anxiety subsided among them. And therewith and after much negotiation they attached themselves to John Mathijs and became obedient.[48]

Mathijs persisted (over against Hofmann's counsel) in public rebaptism to rally recruits and proceeded to ordain twelve apostles, among them John Beuckels of Leiden.[49] In the meantime, it had been predicted that Hofmann himself would be imprisoned for six months before the expiration of the Biblically suggested delay. We have already heard him on trial in Strassburg.

While Hofmann was eagerly sending out bulletins and instructions from his cell, it was Obbe Philips who sought to implement his policy of passive preparations for the impending advent of Christ. Already in Leeuwarden the more militant version of the Melchiorite gospel as represented by Mathijs was gathering recruits. During Obbe's absence on a preaching mission, Peter Houtzagher, one of the apostles of Mathijs, proclaimed "the imminent destruction of all tyrants." The danger of an uproar was so great that Obbe, on his return at midday, found the city gates closed and only with difficulty gained entry. Soon his own name appeared in the placards of the stadholder as one of "the seducers and deceivers who wander about the country, and rebaptize people." Condemned as an insurrectionist 23 February 1534, Obbe fled to Amsterdam. There, in the very month when fellow Melchiorites were taking over in Münster, the men who had ordained Obbe marched through Amsterdam 21 March 1534, bearing swords and proclaiming that "the new [part of the] city is given to the children of God!" On 26 March these "children of God" were executed, and Obbe at this spectacle turned in revulsion from the violent form into which Melchior's Dutch followers had converted the movement.

[47] *Ibid.*, 212.
[48] *Ibid.*, 214.
[49] *Ibid.*, 215.

Surely disillusion followed upon the protracted imprisonment of the prophet in Strassburg and Melchior's recognition of another Enoch instead of presumptuous Mathijs, namely, Cornelius Polterman of Middelburg. Thereupon the Amsterdam Melchiorites, formerly under Trijpmaker, now under Obbe's leadership, renewed their study of the Bible and became known as Obbenite Melchiorites. The more frenzied Melchiorites, lured by Mathijs and the new developments in Münster, left the Netherlands in high expectations. Enough of this expectant mood survived in Amsterdam, however, to make it possible for the Anabaptist leader of Münster to name Jacob van Campen putative bishop of the "new Zion in Amsterdam."[50] Obbe opposed this faction and dissociated his group from the seven enthusiasts, men and women, who walked naked and unarmed, 10 February 1535, to proclaim the "naked truth" of the new Eden. They were beheaded.

When that spring Obbe withheld support from the forty insurrectionists who on the night of 10 May 1535 sought to storm the town hall, the separation of the two branches of Melchiorism was complete. By the eve of the Münster tragedy most of the Amsterdam Melchiorites had come to an evangelical position very much like that of the Swiss Brethren, rejecting violence.

During the rule of the two Johns (Mathijs and Leiden) in Münster, Obbe nevertheless received the "books, writings, and letters which they daily sent us." But the revolutionary Melchiorite debacle both in Münster and in Amsterdam brought him to confess with mounting anguish that "we [were] poor people [who] could not yet open our eyes while it all happened so crudely that one was not able to grasp the lies and obscurity." Deception by false prophets destroyed not only Obbe's hope for a restitution of the apostolic church but also confidence in his own apostolate, for he had been indirectly ordained by Mathijs. Thus Obbe doubted also the validity of those whom he had in turn ordained, namely, his brother Dietrich Philips, Menno Simons, and Davis Joris.

Obbe Philips withdrew or, rather, was forced, from his own brotherhood (1539/1540). As a Spiritualist, he was roughly the Dutch counterpart of John Denck, who "retracted" at the end (Ch. 7.6). The account of his Melchiorite conversion and his subsequent disillusionment is contained in his *Confession,* on which so much of the foregoing account depends.[51] In despair he

[50] Johannes ter Gouw, *Geschiedenis van Amsterdam*, IV (Amsterdam, 1884), 263–284.
[51] The *Confession* was written shortly before 1560.

will open his *Confession,* quoting Rom. 10:15: "And how can men preach unless they are sent?"

We have scarcely been able to recount the story of Netherlandish Anabaptism in isolation from what was concurrently happening in Münster; for in the feverish pitch of excitement the Dutch and Flemish devotees of Melchior Hofmann were being spiritually racked by their desire to be loyal to the pathetic imprisoned prophet in Strassburg (which had been heralded as the new Zion), and by their overwhelming fascination for the proud prophet in Münster, where a "regenerate" magistracy was in fact building up the Zion of their dreams.

Nevertheless, before this story can be told in its entirety, we must take heed of another regional development essential to an understanding of the extraordinary combination of forces that brought about the Münsterite theocracy.

4. The Evangelical Catholic Reform in the Duchies of Cleves and Jülich and Related Principalities

Cleves and Jülich were the principal territories in that consolidated cluster of four principalities encircling Cologne and contiguous with the Netherlands to the east and north. Here the medieval piety of the Rhenish mystics, the *Devotio Moderna,* and the conventicular organization of the Waldensians survived into the Reformation Era and blended readily into the new Anabaptism without any abrupt transition. Here, Duke John III (1521–1539), whose ducal predecessors had already liberated the region from the ecclesiastical jurisdiction of Cologne, pursued an independent course in his attitude toward the Reformation, and while trying to preserve the unity of the medieval church within his territories, made certain local accommodations in his *Kirchenordnung* of 1532. Here on the lower Rhine from the archiepiscopal cathedral, Herman of Wied (since his elevation as archbishop-elector in 1515 until his deposition in 1546 as a Lutheran) took strong measures against the Anabaptists, but pursued a policy that unwittingly contributed to an extraordinary diversification of religious life throughout the princely archbishopric and beyond.

Besides the imperial city of Cologne, administratively separated from the electoral archdiocese, there were two towns within the jurisdiction of Duke John which stand out in the early history of the Radical Reformation on the lower Rhine, namely, Wesel in the duchy of Cleves and Wassenberg in the duchy of Jülich.

In Wesel the second master of the municipal Latin school was Adolf Clarenbach, who may be taken as a representative figure in the transition from late medieval to Reformation piety. He had studied in Münster, presumably at the school of the Brethren of the Common Life, and acquired the master's degree at the University of Cologne. After teaching in Wesel he was expelled for his Lutheran sympathies 11 September 1525 and established himself at Osnabrück as a Latin teacher and lay leader of an evangelical circle. To them he lectured on several books of the New Testament and for them he wrote a book on faith, hope, and charity against the legalism of the medieval church. He was expelled in 1527 and stayed with John Klopreis in the latter's parish near Wesel. When Klopreis was summoned to Cologne for heresy, Clarenbach accompanied him to encourage and defend him. He and his associate, Peter Fliesteden, after sustaining unspeakable torture, were put to death in September 1529, while Klopreis, destined to become an important Anabaptist leader, was merely imprisoned. Clarenbach was not an Anabaptist, but, in his rejection of the oath, his conception of the Supper, his close association with several proto-Anabaptists, such as John Klopreis and Dr. Gerard Westerburg, he was very closely related to them.

Klopreis escaped from Cologne New Year's night and found refuge in Wassenberg under the tolerant bailiff Werner von Pallant, who worked zealously for the Reformation but denied the right of the magistrate, in this case his superior, Duke John III, to control religious developments. Here religious leaders known collectively as the Wassenberg Preachers had been foregathering since 1528. They were, besides Klopreis and Dionysius Vinne, the already mentioned Henry Schlachtschap of Tongres and Maastricht, Henry Rol, and John Campanus. They were antipedobaptists and in the end most of them became spokesmen of Anabaptism, but they differed among themselves and were unified largely in their opposition to Duke John's evangelical Catholic reform imposed from above.

We have already met Campanus in Strassburg, where we had occasion to examine his sacramental theology and binitarianism (Chs. 10.3.g and 11.2). He was in Jülich again in 1531, where Duke John ordered his arrest, but he was able to enjoy his freedom in Wassenberg. When Werner von Pallant was threatened with the loss of his position as bailiff in 1533, his protégés who had not already been lured there fled to Münster.

CHAPTER 13

MÜNSTER

In an earlier chapter (Ch. 4) we have seen how peasant economic unrest, accumulating over several centuries and changing governmental and legal structures, combined with a new sense of the freedom promised by the gospel and a sensitivity to its demand for a holy life, led to the brief but bloody Peasants' War of 1524–1525. We now turn to the North German area, where a decade later the same basic factors, recombined with unusual local conditions and religious expectations, brought about a much more radical society, centered in the bellicose and polygamous commonwealth of Münster, putative capital of a kingdom embracing the religio-social aspirations and commanding the allegiance of thousands of Melchiorites from Brussels to Emden, from Wassenberg to Waterland. Whereas the earlier movement had started out as a social protest, and had become evangelically sublimated in pacifistic conventicles, the Münsterite-Netherlandish episode of 1533–1535 started out with a powerful sense of evangelical, eschatological expectancy, and became socially revolutionary and massively oppressive.

As in the Peasants' War, so in the Münsterite-Netherlandish upheaval, evangelical and social factors combined. Distinctive, however, was the fact that the northern movement was constitutionally and eschatologically Anabaptist, or more specifically, Melchiorite. Baptism, from being the seal of conventicular membership, became the badge of loyalty to the provisional kingdom of a Maccabean apostle-prophet-king and acquired civic, as distinguished from purely ecclesiastical, significance. Indeed, in the Münsterite upheaval, the conventicular church was transformed into a militant commonwealth, and in contrast to Anabaptism in the South and East, Münsterite Anabaptism programmatically used the Old Testament as model and sanction. For in

362

the Münsterite conception of restoration, it was far more the Children of the Covenant in exodus from Egypt than the primitive church in Jerusalem under the Roman Empire which they were intent upon imitating. Their vision of Christ's second advent, drawn from the seer of The Revelation and sharpened further by the prophecies of imprisoned Melchior Hofmann, embraced a kingdom of righteousness that was fiercely intolerant of all who failed to respond to the rigors and delights of the anabaptist Valhalla, realized in the midst of a prince-bishop's see.

The allusion to the mythological is as much an allusion to the operatic or dramatic. We cannot grasp the extraordinary strutting and posturing in the cathedral square of Münster, first under the prophet John Mathijs and then under his successor king, John Beukels of Leiden and his harem,[1] without recognizing the extent to which the whole of the Münsterite action was a comic-tragic morality play, brought out into the open from the chambers of rhetoric.[2] Several of the chief actors had, in fact, been members of such chambers in the various Netherlandish towns whence they came. Theirs was now an increasingly grim morality play of the good against the bad, enacted with stage properties sacked from the homes of the wealthy and the treasure room of the prince-bishop, with a plot drawn eclectically from the Old and the New Testaments and the lives of kings and emperors, and with characters impersonated by an extraordinary company of figures, all of whom almost to the end remained confident that they were playing preordained and well-nigh cosmic roles under the director of the world theater.

The tragedy of Münster revolves not only around the aspirations and perversions of two Johns from the Netherlands but also around the aspirations and the vagaries of two Bernards from within Münster itself, Bernard Rothmann, the local Lutheran priest, in league with the cloth merchant Bernard Knipperdolling, spokesman in the two city councils of the seventeen powerful guilds. Indeed, we cannot understand the Münsterite-Netherlandish upheaval unless we also recognize in it the confluence of two originally distinct movements, namely: (1) the local city reformation, complicated as elsewhere by the standard pattern of class conflict between patricians and artisans and between burghers as a class against the cathedral and local monastic

---

[1] C. A. Cornelius, *Das münsterische Wiedertäuferreich* (Münster, 1853), *Geschichtsquellen*, II, 60.

[2] Leonard Verduin, "The Chambers of Rhetoric and Anabaptist Origins in the Low Countries," *MQR*, XXXIV (1960), 192–196.

clergy,[3] and (2) the Melchiorite movement in the Netherlands, which suddenly turned toward Münster as the very place where, because of the extraordinary beginnings of the Reformation there, the millennium prophesied by Melchior Hofmann seemed on the point of being realized.

1. Pastor Bernard Rothmann and Mayor Bernard Knipperdolling and the Beginnings of the Reformation in Münster in July 1531

Münster, at the outset of the frenzy, had a population of about fifteen thousand. It was the chief city of a large princely bishopric. It differed from nearby Cologne in the relatively greater political power of its craft and merchant guilds, which were fully represented in the councils of the city. This fact, and the fact that the prince-bishop resided outside the walls, made radical changes possible at any time.[4]

Bernard Rothmann (c. 1495–c. 1535), born in the princely bishopric, had served as a teacher in Warendorf and then briefly in 1529 as preacher in the cathedral of St. Maurice in Münster, when the canons, recognizing his great abilities, collected money to enable him to study further at the University of Cologne. The guildsmen among whom he was popular also gave him money, secretly, to study in Wittenberg. He left in 1529 for an extended tour of the great centers of the Reformation, becoming a friend of Melanchthon in Wittenberg and apparently also of Capito in Strassburg, where he may also have made the acquaintance of Schwenckfeld.

On his return to Münster at the beginning of July 1531, his quickening sermons made him very much heeded in the town. Thereupon the bishop, partly under direct pressure from Charles V, removed him from the cathedral and outlawed him, but the guildsmen protected him.

[3] During the Peasants' War, some forty citizens had presented the town council XXXVI Articles, largely directed against the economic abuses of the untaxed clergy.

[4] Recent works are: John Horsch, "The Rise and Fall of the Anabaptists of Münster," *MQR,* IX (1935), 92 ff., 129 ff.; Fritz Blanke, "Das Reich der Wiedertäufer zu Münster 1534–1535: I, Die äusseren Vorgänge," *ARG,* XXXVII (1940), 13–37; A. F. Mellink, "The Mutual Relations Between the Münster Anabaptists and the Netherlands," *ARG,* L (1959), 16–33; Friedrich Brune, *Der Kampf um eine evangelische Kirche im Münsterland 1520–1802* (Witten, 1953). A major source is Hermann von Kerssenbroeck, *Geschichte der Wiedertäufer zu Münster,* translated from the Latin MS. (Münster, 1771); reprinted by Heinrich Detmer in *Geschichtsquellen des Bisthums Münster,* VI:2 (Münster, 1889), citations to the latter.

On 23 January 1532 Rothmann published his creed in thirty articles.[5] It was largely Lutheran except perhaps for the article on the sacrament of the altar, which he considered as a recurrent assurance of salvation and which he made bold to compare with the fleece of Gideon (Judg. 6:36–40). It will be recalled that this fleece when placed upon the ground drew unto itself dew sufficient to be wrung out while the ground around it remained dry; and this was taken by the warrior of God as a sign of certain victory, but also the contrary phenomenon, when the fleece repelled the dew that settled elsewhere. Rothmann's bellicose theology was already adumbrated in his choice of a Eucharistic text!

On 18 February, Rothmann preached the first unequivocally Protestant sermon in the churchyard of St. Lambert's just outside the cathedral square. Despite the efforts of the new bishop, the town council, which had traditionally the right to nominate the pastors of all six parishes of the town, appointed the popular Reformer as pastor of St. Lambert's. On 10 April it drove the priests of the other five out and replaced them likewise with evangelical preachers, among them Henry Rol at St. Giles's.

During the same month a number of preachers from Wassenberg, whom we have already met in Ch. 12.4, entered the town and reinforced the decision of the council. They were, besides Rol, John Klopreis and Dionysius Vinne, who had been expelled by Duke John of Cleves–Jülich because they would not accept his solution for the Catholic-evangelical problem. By then only the cathedral and the monastic churches in Münster held out as Catholic.

Rothmann and the other evangelical preachers now published a notice containing sixteen articles against the Catholic Church.[6] They are still moderately "Lutheran" in tone, denying the sacrifice of the Mass, stressing, however, the real presence. Three articles stress the importance of conducting the services in the language of the people. Infant baptism is retained but must be carried out in the vernacular.

A reformation in this sense was authorized by acts of the city council in August 1532; but the newly elected Bishop Franz von Waldeck, immediately upon his assumption of temporal jurisdiction over the prince-bishopric, set about stemming the reformation tide. His concerted plans were abruptly thwarted when a thousand armed citizens surprised his reveling canons on 26 De-

---

[5] Preserved by von Kerssenbroeck, *Geschichte der Wiedertäufer,* 167–182; Detmer, *Geschichtsquellen,* VI:2, 178 ff.

[6] 15 August 1532; Detmer, *Geschichtsquellen,* VI:2, 238 ff.

cember in nearby Telgt and led them into Münster as hostages. When the bishop responded with an immediate levee of troops, Philip of Hesse, to whom Franz was indebted for political favors, sought to prevent armed conflict.

The religious division of the town was confirmed in a treaty, 14 February 1533, between the bishop and the city council through the mediation of Landgrave Philip of Hesse and by appeal for sanction to the recently concluded Religious Peace of Augsburg. The municipal elections in March confirmed the position of the evangelical party and the supporting guilds. The adoption of an evangelical church order[7] officially introduced the Lutheran Reformation in Münster. An evangelical school was established. The stage was now set for Rothmann's radical Zwinglian phase.

By May, Rothmann, under pressure from the Wassenbergers, who were now augmented by the arrival of Herman Staprade and others, became outspoken in his opposition to infant baptism and wrote to Bucer, assured that he could get support on this from Strassburg. Rothmann, of course, had miscalculated.

In the summer of 1533, Rothmann boldly officiated at a Lord's Supper outside St. Lambert's, using ordinary bread sprinkled with wine, an innovation which at once earned for him the nickname "Bread Bernard" (*Stutenbernt; Stuten*=bread).

From this point on the evangelical movement in Münster divided into the conservative Lutherans, led by the syndic John von der Wieck, who looked to the Smalcald League for support, and the increasingly radical evangelicals, led by Rothmann.

A disputation between the Catholic and the conservative Lutheran parties was held 7 and 8 August 1533, with a view to reducing the differences between them and to checking the Rothmannites, whom they agreed somewhat prematurely to call Anabaptists. The Rothmannites, defending believers' baptism (but not re-baptism), were victorious[8] in the eyes of the council, who by October were forced to reinstate Rothmann and his group on the condition that Rothmann not discuss either sacrament further. Thereupon, Rothmann and the Wassenbergers, among them Henry Rol, composed the already characterized (Ch. 12.1) *Bekenntnisse,* published in Rothmann's own print shop on 8 November 1533. The booklet announced that baptism "is a

---

[7] No longer extant.
[8] Heinrich Detmer, "Das Religionsgespräch zu Münster am 7. und 8. August 1533," *Monatshefte der Comenius-Gesellschaft,* IX (1900), 273–300.

dipping into water, which the candidate desires and receives as a true sign that he has died to sin, been buried with Christ, and arises in a new life, henceforth to walk not in the lusts of the flesh, but obediently according to the will of God."

Rothmann's intractable policy in continuing to condemn infant baptism now caused von der Wieck to make common cause with the Catholics against him, and on 4 November the council decreed that Rothmann and his sympathizers should leave the city on the next day. To ensure compliance with the order, Rothmann's armed opponents assembled in the market place. Rothmann's friends also made preparations to fight. The Catholics thereupon demanded that not only Rothmann but also all those who had helped him in his rise to power be expelled, including the Lutherans, who had only recently come out against him. Alarmed by this, von der Wieck changed sides at the crucial moment, and Rothmann was allowed to remain again on the condition that he refrain from preaching.

The conservative Lutherans consolidated their position by December 1533 and recovered the charge of all the parish churches. But the city contained such large numbers of Sacramentists and by now also some Melchiorite Anabaptists that Rothmann continued to enjoy freedom. On 15 November he met with the two Lutheran theologians sent from Marburg by Landgrave Philip to smooth matters over. The Marburgers found that there was little difference among themselves and Rothmann, except on the question of the proper age for baptism. The Marburgers obviously inclined toward Zwinglian views on the Supper. Their indirect support made Rothmann more aggressive, and on 8 December one of his followers preached in the courtyard of St. Lambert's. This action convinced the town council that they would have no peace on the baptismal issue so long as Rothmann remained in the city, and on 11 December they again determined to exile him. But he again defied them, supported by the guilds, and preached openly. People flocked to his support. The magistrates were powerless. By January 1534 it was he who controlled the situation at Münster, having charge of every church except the cathedral and St. Lambert's, where one of the two Marburg theologians, Dietrich Fabritius, was preaching.

As the movement in the town, with the flouting of the city council, became political as well as religious in its appeal, many underprivileged and potentially disorderly elements began arriving from the surrounding region. In the previous summer Rothmann had already begun to emphasize Christian stewardship and the duty of the Christian to use his possessions for the common good. This message had fallen on responsive ears in the adjoining territories, for crops had been poor and food was dear.

In the meantime, the Melchiorite leader John Beukels of Leiden (destined to be the Anabaptist king of the impending revolutionary theocracy) visited Münster in the late fall of 1533, and, having found Bernard Rothmann, the leading preacher openly teaching that infant baptism was unscriptural, returned to Holland with the good news that the extraordinary development in Münster seemed to coincide with the prediction of Melchior Hofmann and to presage the end of the old order. Back in Holland, John Beukels fired the imagination of John Mathijs, who, as we have already noted (Ch. 12.3), now presumed to challenge Hofmann's injunction to suspend the ordinance of rebaptism for two years, pending an end to the persecution. On the ground of the extraordinary toleration already obtaining in Münster, Mathijs justified, as by divine warrant, the resumption of believers' baptism for the recruitment of the people of the New Covenant (*Bundesgenossen, bondgenooten*) and for this purpose ordained apostles, among them John Beukels himself. We have already seen John Mathijs in Amsterdam in November making this announcement. Many Melchiorites, despite Obbe Philips' opposition, by now accepted the revisionist message, and all who had hitherto hesitated, either out of fear or out of respect toward imprisoned Hofmann, agreed that the cosmic schedule and road signs had been miscalculated and misread, and now turned to Münster as the city of hope, the dwelling place of God's righteousness.

With a new prophetic community, with apostles (*sendboten*) from John Mathijs fanning out with the good news, and with a fully articulate antipedobaptist confession on the part of the radical evangelical party in Münster, the moment was ripe for the conversion of the two Münsterite Bernards at the hands of the emissaries of Melchiorite John Mathijs, of Haarlem, as the new Enoch, seconded by John Beukels, of Leiden.

2. THE ARRIVAL OF THE MELCHIORITE-JOHANNITE EMISSARIES IN MÜNSTER

On the eve of Epiphany 1534, two of the twenty-seven apostles ordained by John Mathijs appeared in Münster, Bartholomew Boekbinder and William de Kuiper. They at once rebaptized Rothmann and Rol, the latter living in the home of the patrician Bernard Knipperdolling. Within eight days Rothmann and his helpers went on to baptize fourteen hundred citizens, not in the churches but in private houses. More Anabaptists arrived from the Netherlands, including both John Mathijs himself and John Beukels, who were furious at the persecution of their followers throughout the Netherlands and were beginning to talk about the right of the true believers to destroy those who would not accept the message of rebirth and restitution. Mathijs informed Rothmann that the time for a clear break with the old customs had come.

Alarmed by this trend, the town council tried again to check the insurgents. The bishop had in the meantime collected an armed force near the city and offered to assist the council. But the citizens rallied to Rothmann, intimidating the burgomaster, and a compromise was reached allowing toleration for all. Henry Rol and others were sent out as emissaries to rally soldiers (*conscribendi milites*) for the new Jerusalem. Catholics and Lutherans began to leave unobtrusively. When the new elections to the town council took place on 23 February, Rothmann's supporter Bernard Knipperdolling was elected burgomaster.

The city was in reality no longer ruled by the council, however, but by John Mathijs. Not satisfied with simply expelling the conservative burghers, Mathijs announced 25 February his intention of killing all the "godless," i.e., all those who refused to join the rebaptismal covenant. It is significant for the swift evolution of baptism as a covenantal sign that occasionally outside Münster new recruits were made fellows of the covenant simply by the laying on of hands, without the affusion of water, and with the simple benediction: "Grace and peace from God our Father be unto all of them of good will."[9]

Knipperdolling persuaded Mathijs to let the burghers of Münster have until 2 March to enjoy the peace of Zion or leave town. In order to retain the initiative, Mathijs announced that he had received divine instructions postponing in fact the date of their expulsion. By the appointed time all of the Lutherans and Catholics had left. A blacksmith, Hubert Ruescher, who dared to call Mathijs a deceiver, was slain on the spot by the prophet himself. The expulsion of non-Anabaptists induced the bishop to intensify his preparations to invest the city and to seek assistance from Hesse, Cologne, and Cleves. On 25 February the citizens acted to avert the impending siege and destroyed a few outlying points which could have served a besieging army, but three days

---

[9] G. Grosheide, "Verhooren en vonnissen der Wederdoopers, betrokken bij de aanslagen op Amsterdam en 1534 en 1535," *Bijdragen en Mededelingen van het Historisch Genootschap,* XLI (Amsterdam, 1920), 16, 24, 172 f.

later the soldiers of the prince-bishop had begun to throw up earthworks around the city and to seal it off. Presently, the imperial stadholder of Frisia and Overijssel appeared in the bishop's camp to give military assistance. The townspeople valiantly strengthened the defensive works of the already heavily fortified city. The entire population, including the women, helped. All men of military age were divided into military units, and boys were taught to shoot.

To strengthen the city militarily but above all spiritually, John Beukels, with the authorization of John Mathijs, sent out another call to the Covenanters in the Netherlands, inciting them to speed to the "holy city of Münster" and thereby escape the impending judgment of the Lord. The first uprising in Amsterdam had failed 21 March (Ch. 12.3). Urging the refugees to come swiftly and hence unencumbered, "for there is plenty enough for the saints," Mathijs set the Bergklooster near Hasselt in Overijssel as the assembly point for the march and noon, 24 March, as the time.[10] Although five ships bearing Covenanters were stopped at Haarlem and six others were confiscated in Amsterdam, about thirty ships were able to leave Monnikendam to cross the Zuyder Zee, some three thousand men, women, and children arriving on the east shore with their spears, harquebuses, broadswords, and halberds. Others by land were converging on Hasselt. Both groups were captured and obliged to turn back. Few captives were executed because of the danger of depopulating the country.

Although Mathijs had only six weeks of rule in Münster, he was able to accomplish many things, among them the introduction of communism. The monasteries had already been plundered, and to prevent the same thing from happening to the houses of the exiles, he announced the confiscation of their property and collected all privately owned money. Food was made public property, but the individual households were not broken up and consolidated. Real property was also declared to be common, although the householders were allowed to continue using what had been theirs. Evidence of the change was given by the regulation that the doors of the houses had to be kept open day and night; only a small grating was allowed to keep out pigs and fowls.

Politically supervised communism in Münster may be said to have been an outgrowth of military exigency reinforcing a desire inherent in Anabaptism everywhere to restore the communal life of the primitive church as recorded in Acts and the Pseudo-Clementine Epistle IV (on which more in Ch. 16.3).

[10] Mellink, "Münster Anabaptists," *loc. cit.,* 19.

In order to show their bravery, the men of the city staged occasional sorties against the beleaguerers. On such a sally, on Easter Sunday, 4 April 1534, John Mathijs lost his life. There seems to be some indication that he thought God would help him, almost singlehanded, to overcome the episcopal troops, and that John Beukels may have encouraged him in this fatuous expectation.

John Beukels immediately took over the control of Münster, and dissolved the council which had been elected in February, on the ground that it had been chosen by men. He, as the voice of the Lord, chose twelve whom he called the Elders or Judges of the Tribes of Israel, to control public and private, worldly and spiritual, affairs. The twelve published a new code of moral law,[11] which enjoined a stricter communism of goods, required certain handworkers, previously employed for money, to continue in their trades without pay as servants of the community, and provided a strict military organization. Unlike the Swiss and South German Anabaptists, who believed in the separation of church and state, for the Münsterites, church, state, and community were now coterminous. Since the regenerate church could contain only the righteous (following Hofmann), the twelve judges under John Beukels took a very harsh view of any sins committed after (re-)baptism. This meant that all citizens were to be subjected to extremely strict laws:

If we are sons of God and have been baptized in Christ, then all evil must disappear from our midst. The authorities can do the most to bring this about, as Romans 13 says. . . . If you do not wish to fear the authorities, then do good and you will receive praise. If, however, you do evil, then beware! They wield the sword not in vain; they are God's servants, his avengers to punish the evildoer. . . . "All the sinners of my people shall die by the sword" [Amos 9:10].[12]

To resist John Beukels meant to resist the divine order. Sins punishable by death included blasphemy, seditious language, scolding one's parents, disobeying one's master in a household, adultery, lewd conduct, backbiting, spreading scandal, and complaining![13] It is clear that this was a code of martial law for the Lord's army under siege, where even a minor breach of discipline

[11] *Ordnung des weltlichen Regiments.*
[12] *Die Wiedertäufer zu Münster 1534–1535: Berichte, Aussagen, und Aktenstücke von Augenzeugen und Zeitgenossen,* edited by Klemens Löffler (Jena, 1923), 81.
[13] *Ibid.,* 81 ff.

might cause disaster. In this *Ordnung* the citizens in covenant were referred to as "Israelites."

John Beukels also published a confession of faith[14] which was sent to Philip of Hesse. An active Anabaptist propaganda was carried on everywhere. The writings of Rothmann and others were thrown from the walls or fired in cannisters into the enemy camp.

The most controversial innovation of the Münsterites was polygamy.

Polygamy (on which see further, Ch. 20.2) was introduced partly because of a desire to emulate the Old Testament patriarchs, in accommodation to the continuous attrition of the male population. John Beukels seems to have been solely responsible for the practice. He chose an appropriate psychological moment to introduce this radical measure. It was immediately after a full-scale attempt to storm the town had been repulsed with great loss to the attackers (25 May) and when the feelings of triumph and the confidence in being God's chosen people ran high. Although most of the preachers in Münster were against it, John, perhaps with the counsel of the Wassenberger Henry Schlachtschap, established polygamy on his own authority by announcing that all who resisted it were to be considered reprobates (and therefore in danger of execution).[15]

Rothmann, thus persuaded, preached for three days in the market place, endeavoring to show that plural marriage was appointed by God for the New Israel which he had restored in Münster. All persons of marriageable age were ordered to marry. Unmarried women had to accept as husband the first man to ask them. This led to disorder in the competition to see who could gather the most wives, and the regulation was finally moderated to allow women to refuse unwelcome suitors.

Alone among John's measures, polygamy called forth intense resistance; and, when complaints availed nothing, a group of citizens led by Henry Mollenhecke surprised and imprisoned John on 29 July, in an effort to force him to abandon polygamy. He refused. They decided sorrowfully that their New Israel had gone into captivity, and considered turning the town back to the bishop. While they were deliberating, townspeople loyal to John freed him and imprisoned them. Mollenhecke, with forty-eight others, was cruelly put to death. A few more executions followed, and eventually no one dared to oppose John on this or

---

[14] *Bekentones des globens und lebens der gemein Christi zu Monster.*
[15] Horsch, "Münster," *loc. cit.,* 137.

any other point. Bernard Rothmann followed John's polygamous example, and eventually acquired nine wives.

Meanwhile, sorties from the town incessantly harassed and embittered the besiegers. Although the Münsterites were able to capture some weapons and supplies from the enemy, they could accomplish no real relief in the face of the complete blockade. Hille Feyken, a girl of Münster, hearing at worship the story of Judith and Holofernes, decided to assassinate the warrior bishop. With a poisoned shirt to present to the bishop, she left the city 16 June 1534 and proceeded to the enemy lines, expecting to be let through. She was arrested instead. Pretending, then, that she had wished to betray the city, she reached one of the besiegers' camps; but before she could compass her mission she was exposed and vengefully beheaded.

In addition to the hoped-for reinforcements of believers in the messianic kingdom, there was also some hope of securing assistance for the radical Münsterite Anabaptists from Emperor Charles V! Wanting to include the prince-bishopric of Münster in his hereditary lands, as he had done with Utrecht, Charles began negotiations with Bishop Franz von Waldeck in order to get him to become his vassal. When the bishop refused, Charles approached the Münsterites. In July 1534 an imperial agent was in Münster negotiating with Rothmann.

On 31 August, after another severe bombardment, the bishop's troops again attempted to storm the town, and were beaten back with heavy casualties. John had commanded the defenders to let the bishop's men gain the first ring of fortifications before opening fire. Once within the exposed area between the outer breastworks and the main wall, they were caught in a fierce fire from muskets and cannon, as well as a shower of arrows, rocks, burning pitch-soaked wreaths, and boiling lime from the women. The besieging army, consisting chiefly of workmanlike mercenaries, resented this fanatical unreasonableness in battle.

Strengthened by his new victory, John Beukels had himself anointed and crowned by the "limping prophet" John Dusentschuer as "a king of righteousness over all" early in September. The twelve ruling elders were first asked for the sword which they had earlier received as a token of their authority, and it was handed to John, who was thereupon anointed by Dusentschuer with these words: "Upon the command of the Father, I anoint thee to be King of the people of God in the New Temple; and in the presence of all the people I proclaim thee to be ruler of the new Zion." The former tailor of Leiden had clerical vestments converted into royal robes; he held a golden apple in his hands, representing universal rule. This reproduction of the *Reichsapfel,* symbolic of global sway, was penetrated by two swords, girded by a horizontal band supporting a cross, and surmounted by a crown. The organization of the royal anabaptist court, with its four councilors, shows the Dutch influence. Henry Krechting, a former priest, became in due course chancellor. King John appeared three times a week in the market place before courtiers and subjects who bowed and prostrated themselves as he proceeded.

The people did not show any great enthusiasm at this development. In fact, Knipperdolling made an attempt to displace John Beukels, acting on the strength of a new revelation, which told him that while John was king according to the flesh, he (Knipperdolling) was called to be a spiritual king. But he learned that independent revelations were not permitted in Zion. On this one occasion, John Beukels showed clemency, for Knipperdolling was not executed. After a few days' imprisonment he was even restored to his office, as John's second in command (*Schwertträger*).

This threat to his power ended, John proceeded to a great messianic exercise. On 13 October he caused the whole population to assemble in the cathedral square at the sound of a trumpet. He let it be known that he was going to lead an exodus from Münster to welcome the Covenanters from the Netherlands marching to the relief of the city. After a military display of cavalry and infantry, King John surprised the people with the announcement that all this was just a test of their loyalty to the Heavenly Father. Thereupon, the whole population sat down at tables erected in the square. It was an amazing sight, a merry populace at long tables, joking and singing psalms, while the king and queen personally served them. Then followed a solemn Communion, at which John, Queen Divara, and the chief councilors distributed the bread and wine. This unique combination of a military exercise and a royal feast must have been thought of as the messianic banquet on the Mount of Zion.[16]

Then the king announced that God had deposed him from the kingship; but the "limping prophet" told him that God forbade this and crowned him king again. The people formally assented to the recognition of John's sovereignty.

John realized that Münster, although he had successfully thrown back two attempts to storm the walls, could be saved only by outside help. In consequence he sent out twenty-seven apostles in the direction of the four winds to spread the message of the

[16] The paradisic-messianic motif comes out expressly in *Eyne ware Bedijnckijnge* where Rol wrote of "the Paradise of the Body of Christ." *BRN,* V, 106.

new Zion. Among the messengers were such prominent ministers as the prophet Dusentschuer, Schlachtschap, Vinne, Klopreis, and Henry Graess van Borken (destined to turn traitor). They set out for the four Westphalian towns of Soest, Koesfeld, Warendorf, and Osnabrück. All except Graess were executed. Of the original ministers in the upheaval, Rothmann alone survived, having remained in Münster as royal spokesman.

It was at this parlous moment in the frenzied rise of John "Koninck der Wederdoper to Monster"[17] that Rothmann was working on his *Restitution*, published in October 1534.

3. ROTHMANN'S "RESTITUTION"

The *Restitution* of Rothmann belongs to a group of several works composed in the Reformation Era bearing the title or embodying the conception of a restitution or restoration of the primitive church. We have already drawn upon that of Campanus, 1532 (Ch. 11.3), who stressed the restoration of the allegedly primitive, nuptially conceived binitarianism of apostolic Christianity. The fourth part of *'T Wonderboek* (1542) of David Joris is also entitled "Restitutio oder wederbrenginghe Christi" (Ch. 19.1). Dietrich Philips will write, in opposition to Rothmann and the Münsterite aberration, his own *Van de geestelijcke restitution* (Ch. 19.2.b). William Postel will publish his *Restitutio rerum omnium* (Paris, 1552). We have already made use (Ch. 11) of Servetus' *Restitutio Christianismi* (1553).

So widespread was restorationism (restitutionism) as the sixteenth-century version of primitivism that it may be said to be one of the marks of the Radical Reformation,[18] over against the (institutional, ethical, and partly dogmatic) Reformation on the Magisterial side. To be sure, there were even in the Magisterial Reformation certain restorationist, as there were also certain Renaissance, impulses. Of none of the major Protestant Reformers was this more true than of Calvin[19] (who, incidentally, in other respects, too, revealed himself to be frequently close to the radical spirit, for example, with respect to the independence of the church and the ecclesiastical use of the ban). But, just as all the Magisterial Reformers shared with the Renaissance humanists the drive to return *ad fontes* and yet differed from them pro-

[17] Such is the legend on his coins.
[18] The basic work here is that of Littell, *Anabaptist View of the Church*, Chs. 2 and 3. Frank J. Wray, "The Anabaptist Doctrine of the Restitution of the Church," *MQR*, XXVIII (1954), 186–196, a portion of his forthcoming book; and Leonard Verduin's forthcoming "The Restitutionist Movement."
[19] See, for example, his Commentary on Isaiah 51:16; 55:5; 60:4; *CR*, LXV, coll. 237, 286, 357.

foundly, so the restorationists differed from the Protestant Reformers profoundly despite their common drive away from a scholasticized, commercialized, and politicized Catholicism. The Magisterial Reformers for their part were content to restore classical Christianity, that is, Biblical, patristic, and conciliar doctrine and usage. The programmatic restorationists, however, were much more selective. They thought specifically of the saints of Jerusalem, of "the Christians" before Abraham and including Abraham "before he became a Jew" by circumcision and other externalities, and of the denizens of Paradise before the Fall. In the last instance, restorationism implied the salvation not only of all the descendants of Adam but also of all the fallen spirits, including Satan himself. Against such universalism and primitivism common among the Radicals (Ch. 32.2) classical Protestantism was on its guard with the aid of such doctrines as predestination and the bondage of the will.

The *locus biblicus* of radical restorationism is Acts 3:21, which speaks (in the Vulgate) of the eschatological *"tempora restitutionis omnium."* The messianic Anabaptist visionary Augustine Bader (Ch. 8.3) had already appealed to this passage during Lent, 1530, when he made bold to combine the prophetic (Isaianic, Jeremian) and apostolic conceptions of the Restoration of the unencumbered life of the true saints and the righteous remnant, declaring that "the time of the restoration of all things was about to be realized in the needed elimination of external sacraments and ceremonies."[20] Rothmann himself, in addition to Acts 3:21, in order to explain what he interpreted as the birthpangs of the Restoration, cited also Matt. 23:34–39 in support of his view that the new apostles sent by Christ in the fullness of time should expect persecution: "Therefore I send you prophets and wise men and scribes, some of whom you will crucify . . . and persecute from town to town. . . . For I tell you, you will not see me again, until you say, 'Blessed be he who comes in the name of the Lord.'"

The restorationists differed among themselves largely as to whether their stress came down on the ancient church, on which some were trying literally to model their efforts (as were most evangelical Anabaptists), or whether their stress was upon the future action of Christ himself in his impending advent (the Spiritualists). Some of the latter had felt, as Müntzer did, that their own action would shape the future; others like Schwenckfeld simply awaited the divine dispensation.

The Anabaptists were similarly divided. The Swiss, South

[20] Krebs and Rott, *Elsass,* I (*QGT,* VII), No. 215a.

German, and the Austrian-Moravian restorationists were, for the most part, content to model their conventicles on the pattern provided by the records of the primitive church and to await in the loving patience of a disciplined community the advent of Christ and his reordering of the world. But the Münsterite restorationists, looking back upon a succession of falls and restitutions, found specific guidance for the task ahead and abundant sanction for their vigorous, even ruthless, shaping of events.

Rothmann no doubt had read Campanus' *Restitution* (1532), when in 1533 he printed his *Bekenntnisse,* devoted to the restoration of the two sacraments of Baptism and the Supper.

The restorationism of his own *Restitution* of 1534 extended the scope of his task and placed it in a fuller eschatological setting. Rothmann saw, besides the fall of man from Paradise and the restoration in Christ, a series of falls and restorations, namely, the fall into bondage to Egypt and return to Canaan, the exile in Babylon and the restoration, another fall, this time of the New Covenantal people in the second century, and a final restoration, begun by Erasmus and Luther and climaxing in John Beukels:

Then behold how through Erasmus, Luther, and Zwingli the [new] beginning was made, but only in Melchior [Hofmann], John Mathijs and here in our brother, John of Leiden, has the truth been gloriously established.[21]

In Rothmann's restorationism, Paradise and Old Israel, as well as the apostolic church, were at once paradigmatic and anticipatory of what would be valid in the new commonwealth, in preparation for the direct and universal rule of Christ in the millennium. There was therefore no disposition, as with other Anabaptists, to allegorize or otherwise gloss the Old Testament injunctions. Rothmann felt that he was the theological spokesman of the "children of Jacob" helping God punish and annihilate the "children of Esau."

Rothmann held that the two Testaments were one, just as God himself is one, and that the proper understanding of the Scriptures had been restored by God to the Münsterites. Among these correct Scriptural formulations was the Melchiorite proposition that the Word of God became flesh in, not that he took flesh from, the Virgin. The ideological or religio-political significance of the Melchiorite doctrine of the celestial flesh of Christ (Ch. 11.3) is evident in the fact that medals and other tokens were stamped with the slogan: "The Word has become flesh and dwells in us: one God, one faith, one baptism." The divine was

<hr>

[21] *Restitution,* edited by Knaabe, *loc. cit.,* 17.

with them, so they believed, and their conflation of church and state in one holy, communal, polygamous commonwealth found sanction in the oneness of Christ's nature.

Rothmann, following Hofmann, also asserted further that God had restored the power to will either good or evil, and that salvation consisted in choosing to be baptized into the disciplined church of Christ. By means of freely willing, anyone might appropriate the gift of God, submit to baptism, and become truly a member of Christ's church and be saved. The community of goods was the mark of membership in the redeemed communion of saints. If believers' baptism was the ordinance of admission to the people of the Covenant, the Supper was the ordinance of holding them prayerfully together in recollection of Christ's redeeming work and in supplication "for all the dear brothers and sisters who are still subject to the dragon."

Rothmann defended polygamy as another divinely sanctioned restitution. Since the only legitimate purpose of marriage was to be fruitful and multiply, a husband should not be held back from fructification by the sterility or pregnancy or indisposition of one wife. Moreover, if a man is dependent sexually upon one wife, she leads him about "like a bear on a rope." It was about time that women, "who everywhere have been getting the upper hand," should submit to men as man to Christ, and Christ to God. The Old Testament provision for plurality of wives was never divinely suspended or superseded. The very fact that the apostles insisted that a bishop be a man of one wife (I Tim. 3:2) showed that the other Christians in the primitive church practiced polygamy!

Another important restitution was government by saints. The sword of David and the throne of peace-loving Solomon had been restored by the hand of God in Münster. The miracles of the new order abounded, and should be proclaimed everywhere and, better still, the city thus governed and motivated should be visited and dwelt in to be believed and wondered at directly.

In December, Rothmann made even more explicit his teaching on government by saints in the latter days,[22] an appeal to "all true Israelites and covenanters of Christ" to take up arms in revenge (*wrake*) and in defense of the theocracy.

4. RESTITUTION AND REVENGE

Rothmann's two books at the end of 1534 ironically suggested by their titles the reversal of the fortunes of the Anabaptist theocracy, for within a year the bishop would be reinstated in

---

[22] "*Eyn gantz troestlick bericht van der Wrake unde straffe des Babilonischen gruwels.*"

Münster and the combined Protestant and Catholic forces would wreak revenge upon the ephemeral kingdom.

Toward the end of November 1534, a new company of messengers went out, to Frisia, Holland, Brabant, Cleves, Jülich, and Liège, supplied with money to buy food for Münster, and with copper identification tokens ("Word becomes flesh") and many pieces of polemical literature, including Rothmann's *Restitution*, which had just appeared. The greater number returned to Münster by Christmas, apparently bringing considerable food with them.

On Christmas Eve a new mission left the town, John van Geelen to Wesel and Henry Cramer to Deventer, acting on the advice of Henry Graess and carrying Rothmann's new book *Van der Wrake*. Graess, who was now acting as an agent for the bishop, pretended that he had miraculously escaped from imprisonment, which greatly increased the respect he commanded. His declaration that rescue would soon be forthcoming from the outside, particularly from Wesel, Deventer, and Amsterdam, encouraged the citizens and caused King John to take him further into his confidence. But fearing that his treacherous mission would come to light, Graess cut short his stay at Münster on 2 January and set out after the emissaries of Christmas Eve, ostensibly to raise four white banners of righteousness in the Netherlands, to proclaim the coming of the king of Zion, and to lead the Covenanters to march to Münster. Assembly places were to be Deventer, Ysenbroeck, and Limburg. The four banners were to be unfurled, one in Jülich, one somewhere in Holland or Waterland, one somewhere in the region of Limberg between Maastricht and Aachen, and one in Frisia near Groningen.[23] At Appingedam, near Groningen, a thousand people gathered under the leadership of the ecstatic prophet Herman Schoenmaker, who had messianic pretensions and wanted to kill all monks, priests, and civil officials. But Schoenmaker was too rabid and wrecked his own particularist movement. In the desperate situation, King John promised salvation (*erlösung*) and vindication at Easter, and the people took heart.

In the meantime, however, the treachery of Graess had been exposed. In Amsterdam, John van Geelen tried to repair the damage, but not before several brethren had been executed in Wesel. In January, too, the episcopal forces finally completed their investment of Münster, where King John had been preparing five companies to sally forth to meet the rescuing bands. But all efforts to

---

[23] Grosheide, "Verhooren en vonnissen," *loc. cit.*, 16.

produce relief failed. Many were arrested in Deventer, Kampen, and Zwolle, and the failure to secure public support in Amsterdam was signalized by the desperate behavior of the *naaktloopers* 10 February 1535 (Ch. 12.3).

On 23 March eight more envoys succeeded in escaping the now completely beleaguered city, including van Geelen, in the final attempt to rally the Dutch Anabaptists to the rescue. These new messengers gathered a gang of three hundred and made a successful assault on the Old Cloister[24] near Bolsward, a fortified Cistercian abbey. It was in turn besieged by the imperial stadholder Schenck van Tautenburg, who brought up heavy guns and finally, after much fighting, captured it on 7 April. Peter Simons (possibly a brother to Menno) perished in this battle. The senseless carnage forced Menno to bestir himself on behalf of the poor, misled Anabaptists (Ch. 14.1).

Within beleaguered Münster, John, to prevent surprise and defection, established in May twelve "dukes" to guard the gates, and, in order to avoid strife among them after the victorious outcome of the battle, he went on to assign to them their future duchies in the enlarged kingdom. John maintained discipline by the severest measures. In his mingled shyness and ruthlessness, religious fanaticism and maniacal wickedness, he made life wretched for his subjects, and also for his wives. One of the most spirited among them was beheaded by him in the market place for her saucy criticism of his rule, and he trampled on her body while the rest of his harem looked on.

John attempted to keep the people's spirits up by means of dancing and spectacles. But all of these props availed nothing. Increasing famine caused John to send the women, children, and aged men out of the city in June 1535. Many of these people were killed by the besieging army after shameful atrocities. In spite of everything John did, the continuing siege and famine sapped the morale. The besiegers too were growing discouraged at the stubbornness of the town and were moodily preparing for a long wait when an unexpected event suddenly settled the affair. Two men, Hans Eck and Henry Gresbeck,[25] deserted and betrayed one of the gates of the town to the bishop. After a fearful battle the city was taken on 25 June, and almost all of the inhabitants slaughtered.

Chancellor Henry Krechting was, of all the leaders, alone able

[24] Oldeklooster, Oudeklooster.
[25] His *Bericht von der Wiedertaufe in Münster* is published by Cornelius, *Berichte des Augenzeugen, Geschichtsquellen des Bisthums Münster*, II (Münster, 1853).

to escape. Rothmann apparently died in the fighting. King John, Bernard Knipperdolling, and the chancellor's brother, Bernard Krechting, were captured and exhibited throughout Northern Germany. Knipperdolling and Krechting remained loyal to their Anabaptist faith, but John Beukels made a partial recantation before his death, and even offered, if his life were spared, to persuade the remaining Anabaptists to give up all thoughts of violence and to remain faithful to the new government. The three surviving principals were condemned and tortured with red-hot tongs on a platform for all to see in Münster on 22 January 1536. Their seared bodies were placed in iron cages and suspended from the tower of St. Lambert's Church.

5. David Joris and the Batenburgers at Bocholt, 1536

After the fall of the Anabaptist Bibliocracy in Münster in June 1535, and the execution of King John in January 1536, a group of radical Anabaptists from as far away as England met in August 1536 at the still tolerant town of Bocholt near Wesel to attempt to come to some mutual understanding and to unify the shattered and scattered Melchiorite forces. The meeting was attended by followers of David Joris, of John of Batenburg, and by a group of former Münsterites.[26]

We last met Joris in banishment from Delft as a Sacramentist leader (Ch. 12.1). He had returned to Delft and then joined the Melchiorites, receiving baptism from Obbe Philips in September 1534. As an outward sign of his rebirth, he had resumed the name David, which had been given him by his father (who was, at the time of the infant's birth, playing the part of King David in a *rederijker* play), and abandoned the name of John, which had been given him by the consecrating bishop at the time of his confirmation. Presently his own followers called themselves, after him, Davidjorists.

John of Batenburg, illegitimate son of the noble house of that name in Gelderland, had been mayor of Steenwijk in Overijssel before he joined the Anabaptists. He was now the leader of the faction among the Münsterites who still adhered to the Maccabean principles of the two Johns and were therefore called *"Zwaardgeesten"* (sword-minded) or, after him, Batenburgers. Batenburg was one of the instigators of the Münsterite assault of the Oude Klooster of Bolsward in 1535. The Batenburgers,

[26] For Anabaptism in the region after the debacle, see Cornelius Krahn, "Anabaptism in Westphalia," *MQR*, XXXV (1961), 282–285.

even more radical than the Münsterites at the zenith of their excesses, believed that all who did not join with them had to be killed. They sanctioned the plunder of churches, and divorce was obligatory for anyone whose spouse refused to join the group. They continued to practice polygamy and held goods in common. With Batenburg as their new Elijah, they clandestinely waited for the belligerent second advent of the Lord. In the meantime, they allowed adult baptism to lapse, and attended Catholic services in order to escape detection and persecution.

Batenburg did not himself attend the meeting at Bocholt. Joris was mediator between the belligerent Batenburgers and those Obbenites and others who insisted on pacifism and the rejection of capital punishment, on believers' baptism, discipline, and sober behavior. By spiritualizing and allegorizing the beliefs and programs of the parties concerned, however, Joris was able to bring them to an ephemeral compromise at Bocholt. Rebaptism was abandoned, the use of the sword by the saints was declared justifiable but inexpedient, since the millennium was clearly not yet at hand.

There survive from Joris' hand, skilled at both painting and poesy, several hymns written before and perhaps also after the fall of Münster, one of which especially conveys the characteristic mingling of belligerent expectancy and the preparedness for present suffering:

> All the godly must drink
> From the chalice of bitterness, "pure red wine,"
> But the dregs shall God give to the godless to drain.
> They shall spew and shall belch and fall into death
>   without end.
> Understand, "dear Christian.
> Hold fast, God's honor spread.
> Be ready ever to die."[27]

Joris himself stood much closer to the Obbenites, especially on the issue of the sword. According to the teaching of Christ, the saints must suffer and offer no resistance. He rejected polygamy. In doing so he showed familiarity with the schema of Joachim of Flora, according to whom the believers were still living in the age of the Son, characterized by monogamy, as the age of the Father had been marked by patriarchal polygamy, and as the

---

[27] From Joris, *Een Geestelijck Liedt-Boecxken,* 1529–1536, printed in *Liederen van Groot-Nederland,* edited by F. R. Coers (Utrecht, 1930); the selection is printed by Bainton, *Joris,* 18, and Bainton, *The Travail of Religious Liberty: Nine Biographical Studies* (Philadelphia, 1951), 127.

future coming age of the Spirit would be marked by celibacy. On the Bocholt issue of Adamism, Joris said that he himself had no inspiration to go about naked, either as a sign, like Isaiah, or as a mark of the return of paradisic perfection, but that this recurrent phenomenon in religion was permissible if one were impelled thereto by God. He was in agreement with the Radicals in his expectation of the imminent coming of the Lord.

Batenburg lived only a short time after the colloquy at Bocholt. Traveling to the southern Netherlands, he was captured at Vilvoorde near Brussels and imprisoned in December 1537. He tried to present himself as a constant opponent of plunder and destruction, and revealed the names of many Anabaptists. The magistrates remained unconvinced of the sincerity of his protestations, and Batenburg was executed in 1538. The belligerent fellowship survived his execution. With the extermination of their later leaders, one Appelman in Leiden and Peter van Orck in Münster, both in 1544 (the same year as Loy near Antwerp, Ch. 12.2), the sect seems to have been greatly reduced.[28]

Shortly after the colloquy at Bocholt, Joris received a letter[29] from one Anneken Jansdochter, who acclaimed him as a prophet of God, the "fan" in the hand of the Lord to winnow and "prepare for him an acceptable people that he may speedily come to his temple." Joris, as he himself described it, remained in a kind of ecstasy for more than a week after reading the letter; and, when he came to himself, began to think of himself as the third David, the first being David the king and the second, Christ, his descendant. He claimed belief and loyalty from his followers. To their stress on the written Word he opposed the inward Word. He proclaimed the inwardness of the resurrection in spirit and the victory over evil, death, and darkness. In the same manner, he said, the trumpeting of the Last Day, death, and damnation all take place within a man. He preached humility, self-denial, and asceticism.

A group of followers, quickly increasing, gathered about him in Delft. A price was put on their leader's head in 1538, and by 1539 the authorities found it necessary to take even more vigorous action against them. His well-to-do sponsor, Anneken Jans, who with her husband had sought asylum in England, was, on a return trip to Delft, apprehended in Rotterdam, having fallen under suspicion for singing a hymn with her traveling companion,

[28] Yet as late as 1552 in Leiden there was fear of a Batenburger attack, as also in 1553 in Courtrai in Flanders. *ME*, I, 247 f.
[29] Quoted in Bainton, *Travail*, 130.

Christina Barents of Louvain. They were immediately tried and convicted of heresy.

Anneken addressed a petition to the crowd on the way to her execution, requesting that someone adopt her infant, Isaiah, for whose benefactor she at the same time provided a substantial purse. The son was to grow up to be a brewer and mayor of Rotterdam and marry the daughter of the Arminian statesman and martyr, John Oldenbarnevelt.[30] Anneken could not have foreseen, in her extremity, that her son would choose on maturity to dissociate himself from the faith of his mother.

She had already written out a beautiful will and testament addressed to him, many times reprinted. It may be here quoted at length, as its phrasing captures the spirit of the Melchiorite Anabaptist way of life. Though the Münsterite cause had collapsed, we overhear in Anneken's testament something of the eschatological fervor of the first generation before the hope for the idea of the imminent Kingdom of Christ and for the corule of the saints had subsided. In putting the testament in the little boy's hands, Anneken expressed the full range of New Testament convictions, from the Sermon on the Mount through the Johannine epistles to the book of the Revelation:

My son, hear the instruction of your mother. . . . Behold, I go today the way of the prophets, apostles, and martyrs, and drink of the cup of which they all have drunk. I go . . . the way which Christ Jesus, the eternal Word of the Father, full of grace and truth, the Shepherd of the sheep, who is the Life, Himself went, and who . . . had to drink of this cup, even as He said [cf. Mark 10:38 ff.]: "I have a cup to drink of, and a baptism to be baptized with. . . ." Having passed through, He calls His sheep, and His sheep hear His voice, and follow Him whithersoever He goes; for this is the way to the true fountain. This way was traveled by the royal priests who came from the rising of the sun, as we read in Revelation, and entered into the ages of eternity [I Peter 2:9].

This way was trodden by the dead under the altar, who cry, saying [Rev. 6:9–11]: "Lord Almighty God, when wilt Thou avenge the blood that has been shed?" . . . These also drank of the cup, and are gone above to keep the eternal, holy Sabbath of the Lord. This is the way in which walked the twenty-four elders, who stand before the throne of God, and cast their crowns and harps before the throne of the Lamb, falling down upon their faces, and saying [Rev. 4:8, 10]: "Lord, unto Thee alone be praise, glory, power, and strength, who shalt avenge the blood of Thy servants and ministers, and shalt through Thyself gain the victory. . . . "Behold, all these had to drink of the cup

[30] The relationship between freewill Anabaptism and Arminianism in Holland needs to be investigated.

of bitterness, as will also all those have to do who are still wanting to complete the number and fulfillment of Zion, the bride of the Lamb, which is the new Jerusalem coming down out of heaven [Rev. 21:2], the city and throne of God, in which the glory of the great King shall be seen. . . .

Behold, all these could not attain to this, without first suffering judgment and chastisement in their flesh; for Christ Jesus, the eternal truth, was the first, when it is written [Rev. 13:8]: "The Lamb slain from the foundation of the world." So Paul says [Rom. 8:29 f.]: "Thus it pleased the Father, that all whom He predestinated from eternity, He called, elected, justified, and made to be conformed to the image of His Son." Our blessed Saviour also says: "The servant is not above his Lord; but it is sufficient for him, that he be like his Lord and Master." Also Peter says [I Peter 4:17 f.]: ". . . If the righteous scarcely be saved, where shall the ungodly and the sinner appear?" See, my son, here you can hear that no one can come unto life, except through this way. Therefore enter in through the strait gate, receive the chastisement and instruction of the Lord, bow your shoulders under His yoke, and cheerfully bear it from your youth, with thanksgiving, rejoicing and honor; for He accepts or receives no son, whom He does not chasten. . . .

Therefore, my child, do not regard the great number, nor walk in their ways. Remove thy foot far from their paths, for they go to hell, as sheep unto death. . . . But where you hear of a poor, simple, cast-off little flock [Luke 12:32] which is despised and rejected by the world, join them; for where you hear of the cross, there is Christ. . . . Flee the shadow of this world; become united with God; fear Him alone, keep His commandments, observe all His words, to do them; write them upon the table of your heart, bind them upon your forehead, speak day and night of His law. . . . Take the fear of the Lord to be your father, and wisdom shall be the mother of your understanding. . . . Be not ashamed to confess Him before men; do not fear men; rather give up your life, than to depart from the truth. If you lose your body, which is earthly, the Lord your God has prepared you a better one in heaven [II Cor. 5:1].

Therefore, my child, strive for righteousness unto death, and arm yourself with the armor of God. Be a pious Israelite, trample under foot all unrighteousness, the world and all that is in it, and love only that which is above. Remember that you are not of this world, even as your Lord and Master was not. Be a faithful disciple of Christ; for none is fit to pray, unless he has become His disciple, and not before. Those who said: "We have left all," also said: "Teach us to pray" [Luke 18:28; 11:1]. They were those for whom the Lord prayed, and not the world [John 17:9]; for when the world prays, they call upon their father, the devil. . . . Therefore, my son, do not become like them, but shun and flee them, and have neither part nor fellowship with them. . . . Whatever you do, do it all to the praise of His name.

Honor the Lord in the works of your hands, and let the light of the Gospel shine through you. Love your neighbor. Deal with an open, warm heart thy bread to the hungry, clothe the naked, and suffer not to have anything twofold; for there are always some who lack. Whatever the Lord grants you from the sweat of your face, above what you need, communicate to those of whom you know that they love the Lord; and suffer nothing to remain in your possession until the morrow, and the Lord shall bless the work of your hands, and give you His blessing for an inheritance. O my son, let your life be conformed to the Gospel, and may the God of peace, sanctify your soul and body, to His praise.

O holy Father, sanctify the son of Thy handmaiden in Thy truth, and keep him from the evil one, for Thy name's sake, O Lord.[31]

Here is the testament of a Dutch woman of means, a follower of Melchior Hofmann, still unshaken by the aberrations and destruction of Melchiorism in its Münsterite form, now inclined, however, toward David Joris' more spiritual interpretation of Scriptures. Here we have an extraordinary specimen of the martyr theology akin to that of the South German Anabaptists, but with a much stronger accent on the imminent vindication of God's "Israelites" in a vision of future righteousness that does not draw back from the gory prospect of the divine wrath inflicted on the uncircumcised in spirit.

With Anneken's testament we hear the last echoes of the original Melchiorite gospel. We have noted the breakup of the movement into three distinct currents: (1) belligerent Batenburger libertinism, (2) mystical Davidjorist Spiritualism, and (3) disciplined evangelical Anabaptism, increasingly preoccupied with sectarian organization and the codification of orthodoxy under Menno Simons.

[31] Reprinted in van Braght, *Martyrs' Mirror*, 453 f. It is here given in slightly reduced form, and with some of the Scriptural references which appear in the original omitted without indication.

CHAPTER 14

THE REGROUPING OF FORCES AFTER THE DEBACLE IN MÜNSTER: MENNONITISM

1. MENNO SIMONS, HIS EARLY CAREER AND CONVERSION

Before I had ever heard of the existence of the brethren, . . . a God-fearing, pious hero named Sicke [Freerks] Snijder was beheaded at Leeuwarden for being rebaptized. It sounded very strange to me to hear of a second baptism. I examined the Scriptures diligently and pondered them earnestly, but could find no report of infant baptism.[1]

With these words, Menno Simons, a Roman priest for seven years, described his first contact with the idea of believers' baptism. Yet this man who did not even know what kind of faith it was for which Sicke Freerks had been willing to die later gave his name to the whole movement of which Sicke had been the first martyr in the Netherlands (Ch. 12.3).

It has occasionally happened that a movement is named for a man not its founder. Menno Simons did not join the Anabaptists in the Low Countries until after they had experienced initial successes, felt the fangs of persecution, and been shaken to the core by the great debacle of Münster in 1534–1535. Yet in some way the influence of this relative latecomer, who was a pastor more than a theologian, was such that his name caught the imagination of many and has come to be applied, not only to the Dutch Anabaptists, but also to the Swiss and South German Brethren as well.[2]

Menno was born in 1496 in the village of Witmarsum in West

[1] Menno Simons, *The Complete Writings*, translated by Leonard Verduin, edited by John C. Wenger (Scottdale, Pennsylvania, 1956), 668.

[2] For the periodization and biography I am following Harold Bender, "A Brief Biography," included in *The Complete Writings;* Karel Vos, *Menno Simons, 1496–1561: Zijn leven en werken en zijne reformatorische denkbeelden* (Leyden, 1914); Cornelius Krahn, *Menno Simons (1496–1561): Ein Beitrag zur Geschichte und Theologie der Taufgesinnten* (Karlsruhe, 1936). A major source for the biography is Menno's own reminiscence in his *Reply to Gellius Faber, Writings,* 623 ff.

387

Frisia, the son of a dairy farmer named Simon (hence Simonsz, i.e., Simonszoon). Before entering the Roman priesthood, he studied in a monastery, possibly at Bolsward. He learned to read and write Latin and to read some Greek. He gained familiarity with some of the church fathers, such as Tertullian, Cyprian, and Eusebius. Although he was not systematically trained in the Bible, he would have come to know large portions of it through the Roman liturgy.

Menno's ordination to the priesthood took place in March 1524, when he was twenty-eight years old. He was first assigned as vicar to the parish of Pingjum near Witmarsum, where he served for seven years, the second in rank of three priests. From his own later account he spent his time in the perfunctory performance of the usual duties of a country priest, utilizing his free hours for playing cards, drinking, and "frivolities of all sorts." But early in his sacerdotal career, doubts began to disturb this outwardly harmonious life. In 1525, the same year in which the Swiss Brethren, who were later to be called by his name, were organizing their restored New Testament church in Zurich, Menno was beginning to doubt the doctrine of transubstantiation:

It occurred to me, as often as I handled the bread and wine in the Mass, that they were not the flesh and blood of the Lord. I thought that the devil was suggesting this, that he might separate me from my faith. I confessed it often, sighed and prayed; yet I could not come clear of the idea.[3]

In his pondering, it may be that Menno knew about the ideas of Cornelius Hoen espoused by the Sacramentists in nearby Leeuwarden (Ch. 12.1). He was unable to get satisfaction from his fellow priests in Pingjum on the question, and he felt impelled to search out the New Testament for substantiation or assuagement of his suspicions. "I was in so far helped by Luther . . .," he wrote, "that human injunctions cannot bind unto eternal death."[4] From this time on, he made progress in the study of the Scriptures, and came to be considered by some (incorrectly, he says) an "evangelical" preacher. Although he attributed to Luther his confidence in the right to depart from the teachings of men on the Eucharist and to return to the testimony of Scripture, he did not accept Luther's specific view of the sacrament of the altar.

It was not his developed sacramentarianism which finally moved him to transfer his allegiance from the Roman Church, for he continued to celebrate Mass for several years after he had

---

[3] Menno, *Writings*, 668.
[4] *Ibid.*

become convinced that it was theologically untenable. It was rather the problem of baptism. He became acquainted with Cyprian's approval of adult baptism, around 1529, when he read about it in the writings of Theobald Billicanus of Nördlingen.[5] Then, in 1531, he learned of the heroic death of Sicke Freerks in nearby Leeuwarden, the same Anabaptist martyr who had moved the brothers Philips to join the Melchiorite Covenanters. Although the cause for which Sicke died, rebaptism, seemed very strange,[6] Menno was deeply impressed by the high seriousness of the new movement and was dismayed to find no support for infant baptism in the New Testament. Whereupon he turned to the fathers:

They taught me [he writes] that children are by baptism cleansed from their original sin. I compared this idea with the Scriptures and found that it did violence to the blood of Christ.[7]

From now on this distinction was determinative for Menno. Calvary frees the whole world from original sin. The slate is wiped clean for all mankind, for Christ came to take away the sins of the whole world. This is the good news for them to whom it is disclosed, but its effect is operative whether it is known or not. To this extent, Menno, like Denck in the South, had recognized a basis for universal salvation. Baptism becomes, in consequence, the means of liberating the Christian believer from personal sins. Menno found confirmation of his growing convictions about adult baptism when he turned to the Protestant Reformers to find them mutually contradictory as to the propriety of infant baptism, Luther holding stubbornly that in some sense infants do have faith by godparental proxy, Bucer holding that it is a pledge of Christian nurture, Zwingli and Bullinger holding that it is the New Covenantal equivalent of circumcision.

In spite of Menno's conviction on the question of infant bap-

---

[5] In his *Foundation Book* of 1539, Menno wrote that more than ten years before, that is, around 1529, he had read in the works of the "Nördlingen preachers" about Cyprian. That would have been Billicanus, *Renovatio ecclesiae nordlingiacensis . . . per diaconos ibidem* (1525).

[6] In recalling the Leeuwarden martyrdom of 1531, Menno says that he found second baptism "strange," in seeming contradiction to his statement about Cyprian. This discrepancy, first pointed out by S. Cramer, *Doopsgezinde Bijdragen* (1912), 1, could be explained by a lapse of memory. Krahn, however, preserves the reliability of both accounts by pointing out the difference between Cyprian's stress (in Billicanus) on adult baptism rather than on rebaptism. However, Cyprian was an advocate of the rebaptism of the lapsed and of heretics (Ch. 10.1), and Krahn's solution may not stand. *Beitrag*, 24.

[7] *Writings*, 669.

tism, it was still several years before he was moved to action. He did not associate himself with the small groups of Melchiorites in the vicinity, but on the contrary accepted Roman ecclesiastical promotion to the post of pastor in his home church at Witmarsum, "led thither," he said, "by covetousness and the desire to obtain a great name":

There I spoke much concerning the Word of the Lord, without spirituality or love, as all hypocrites do, and by this means I made disciples of my own kind, vain boasters and frivolous babblers, who, alas, like myself did not take these matters too seriously.[8]

Although he was outwardly moral and was admired, he was not satisfied with his spiritual state. His conscience was continually troubled by the contradiction between his beliefs and his conformity to the old order. Nevertheless, Menno remained within the Catholic Church. The excesses of Münsterite Anabaptism elicited from him indeed a tract against John Beukels of Leiden (April/June 1535), the first of his surviving works. He stood, at this point, vacillating between Catholicism and Anabaptism, turmoiled by both.

By a strange twist, it was not Menno's own sacramentarian and anabaptist convictions which brought him to break with Rome but a horror of the fanatical blasphemies of Münster. It was the very excess of the Anabaptist movement that in the end contrived to pull him from his rectory to lead the bewildered flock of misguided Melchiorites.

Some three hundred of these radical Anabaptists, en route to Münster under John van Geelen, entrenched themselves in the Old Cloister at Bolsward and were besieged and overwhelmed 7 April 1535. Among the slain was Peter Simons, gatekeeper of the Münsterite queen (Ch. 13.4). Though Menno was expressly opposed to their show of force and to their insufficiency of Biblical doctrine, he felt that he should lead these shepherdless sheep to the valid goal of their deepest aspirations, with which he had come to sympathize. With trembling heart, Menno asked God to forgive him his prudential delay. He writes movingly of his final spiritual struggles:

Afterwards the poor straying sheep who wandered as sheep without a proper shepherd, after many cruel edicts, garrotings, and slaughters, assembled at a place near my place of residence called Oude Klooster. And, alas! through the ungodly doctrines of Münster, and in opposition to the Spirit, Word, and example of Christ, they drew the sword

[8] Ibid.

to defend themselves, the sword which the Lord commanded Peter to put up in its sheath.

After this had transpired, the blood of these people, although misled, fell so hot on my heart that I could not stand it, nor find rest in my soul. I reflected upon my unclean, carnal life, also the hypocritical doctrine and idolatry which I still practiced daily in appearance of godliness, but without relish. I saw that these zealous children, although in error, willingly gave their lives and their estates for their doctrine and faith. And I was one of those who had disclosed to them the abominations of the papal system. But I myself continued in my comfortable life and acknowledged abominations simply in order that I might enjoy physical comfort and escape the cross of Christ.

Pondering these things my conscience tormented me so that I could no longer endure it. . . .

I began in the name of the Lord to preach publicly from the pulpit the word of true repentance, to point the people to the narrow path, and in the power of the Scripture openly to reprove all sin and wickedness, all idolatry and false worship, and to present the true worship; also the true baptism and the Lord's Supper, according to the doctrine of Christ, to the extent that I had at that time received from God the grace. . . .

Then I, without constraint, of a sudden, renounced all my worldly reputation, name and fame, my unchristian abominations, my masses, infant baptism, and my easy life, and I willingly submitted to distress and poverty under the heavy cross of Christ.[9]

For nine months Menno endeavored to use his Witmarsum pulpit as the base from which to effect an evangelical reform. Then, in the very month that King John Beukels was tortured to death at Münster, Menno bravely laid down his priestly office, 30 January 1536, and vanished from the public eye. He had decided that he could no longer continue even a purely external connection with the Roman "Babel." Menno made the break directly from the security of a Catholic rectory to the peril of the open roads in a land which remained Catholic and where the edict against Anabaptism was ruthlessly enforced. And he made the break at precisely that moment when revolutionary Anabaptism was most hated by the authorities and most discredited by its devotees. The fact that he had no fellowship with the Anabaptists around him before the Münsterite debacle, and that from the outset he opposed the ideas being spread by the Münsterite missionaries, gives credibility to his frequent assertion that his new faith came to him "through much reading and pondering of the Scriptures, and by the gracious favor and gift of God, and

9 *Ibid.*, 670 f.

not by the instrumentality of the erring sects as it is reported of me."[10]

Determinative in this break was the experience of "spiritual resurrection."[11] At first he sought seclusion. It is quite probable that he looked for refuge on the estate of Ulrich van Dornum, at his castle at Oldersum on the Ems, south of Emden, which had earlier protected Carlstadt and Hofmann in 1529. (It was with Ulrich's support that Hofmann, who had become an Anabaptist in 1530, had carried on his extraordinarily successful mission in Emden.) It may have been true that Menno received instruction from Obbe Philips, who rebaptized him. Toward the end of the year of retirement which followed his public break with the Roman Church, after apparently having moved back and forth between Witmarsum, Leeuwarden, Groningen, and Oldersum, he seems to have settled down in or near Groningen. A small group of evangelical Anabaptists sought him out and implored him to take pastoral charge over the ruined vineyard of the Lord.

He saw the perils to which he would be subject in undertaking an Anabaptist ministry, but the feeling of pastoral obligation toward the "sheep which have no shepherd" compelled him to overcome his apprehensions and to plunge into the work to which he heard the Lord calling him. His explanation of the pastoral vocation is indicative of the important place which the church as the instrument of God in the calling and establishment of a pastor played in his thinking.

There are two ways, he was soon to write, in which Christian preachers are called: some by God alone, without any human agent, others by means of the pious, as in Acts 1:23–26.[12] Further: "All who rightly preach Christ and His Word, and with it bring forth children to the Lord, must have been called by one of the aforementioned methods."[13] Without a proper vocation, no one can rightly preach the gospel; for "as Paul says [Rom. 10:15], 'How shall they preach except they be sent?' "[14] Thus it is clear why for Menno, in contrast to the Magisterial Reformers, the Roman ordination to the priesthood was no longer valid, and why he insisted upon a new calling and valid ordination according to the true divine institution. Menno, like many another former priest or friar, was not only an *ana*baptist but also a

[10] *Ibid.*, 669.
[11] This is the title of one of his first writings, *Van de geestelijke verrijenisse* (c. 1535).
[12] *Foundation Book*, 1540; *Writings*, 159.
[13] *Ibid.*, 160.
[14] *Ibid.*, 161

*re*ordinationist. His second ordination took place early in 1537[15] and was almost certainly performed by Obbe Philips.

Menno's acceptance of leadership came at a crucial time for the brethren who had remained faithful to Scriptural, evangelical, peaceful Anabaptism and had not yielded to the fanatical ideas of John Mathijs and John Beukels. They were dispersed and discouraged. Constantly dogged by the authorities, Menno led a wanderer's existence, visiting the scattered brethren, preaching, baptizing, catechizing, and endeavoring to build up the churches wherever he went. Although he married in 1536 or 1537, he had no fixed abode.[16]

At the same time, he busied himself with the writing of numerous tracts, including *The Spiritual Resurrection*, c. 1536, *Meditation on the Twenty-fifth Psalm*, c. 1537 (an autobiographical interpretation), *The New Birth*, c. 1537, *Christian Baptism*, 1539, *Foundation of Christian Doctrine*, 1540, which helped consolidate his position of ever-increasing authority over the brotherhood stretching along the Hanseatic Coast and up the Rhine as far as Bonn.

A field ripe for harvest had been in danger of being ruined by the unruly, or dreamy, or fatigued laborers. Menno Simons rallied the constructive forces in Netherlandish Anabaptism. It was due to his sober, unremitting, and evangelically inspired leadership that the Netherlandish and North German movement was preserved from disintegration and fanatical aberration. By 1542 Menno was so manifestly a major sectarian leader that at Leeuwarden a price of five hundred gold guilders was put on his head. There was full warrant for the historical chance which has attached Menno's name to almost the whole surviving Anabaptist movement. Anabaptists were first referred to as "Mennonites" (*Mennisten*) in 1545 in a decree of Countess Anna of Oldenburg, regent of East Frisia.

Representative of the courage of the Anabaptists who rallied around the new leader and their determination to endure anything rather than inform on fellow-believers is the testimony of Elisabeth Dirks, a woman brought up in a convent and reputed to be the first Mennonite deaconess. Apprehended at Leeuwarden, she was mistakenly identified as Menno's wife, and was subjected to examination by torture to secure information concerning him and other Anabaptist leaders. In spite of thumb screws and the Spanish boot, she would not reveal a single name. It was her brave contention that she was heeding God's commandment to

[15] Approximate date supplied by Bender, "Brief Life," *Writings*, 23.
[16] Cf. *ibid.*, 25 f.

honor one's "parents," and in Christ all her associates were kith and kin upon whom she was not free to inform. The refusal to give names under torture is one of the recurrent themes in all the Anabaptist martyrologies which linked the sixteenth-century Radicals self-consciously with the early Christians who likewise refused to be *delatores* and *traditores*.[17]

2. "THE FOUNDATION," 1540: CHRISTOLOGY AND THE BAN

The Foundation of Christian Doctrine,[18] written in Dutch with a strong coloring from Low German (Oosters),[19] took as its text I Cor. 3:11: "For no other foundation can anyone lay than that which is laid, which is Jesus Christ." Commonly called *The Foundation Book*,[20] it has become the foundation of Mennonitism and is therefore entitled to special attention at this point, along with Menno's other writings.

In the first edition[21] of the *Foundation,* Menno was concerned in part to redirect the misled radical Anabaptists into peaceful associations and in part to legitimize the movement in the eyes of the magistrates. To this end he stressed its orthodoxy and its orderliness wherever possible.

Yet he persisted in retaining the peculiar Melchiorite view of the incarnation communicated to him by Obbe Philips.[22] In modified form it was inextricably bound up, it would appear, not only with his experience and conceptualization of rebirth but also with his view of the church as the community without spot or wrinkle.[23] In *True Christian Faith,* Menno wrote:

For all who are in Christ are new creatures, flesh of His [celestial] flesh, bone of his bone [an allusion with Paul to the first Adam], and members of His body.[24]

[17] Elisabeth was drowned 27 May 1549. Van Braght, *Martyrs' Mirror,* 481 ff., 546 f. I have placed the Anabaptists in the long history of conscientious objection to delation in my "Reluctance to Inform," *Theology Today,* XIV (1957), 229–255, esp. 253.

[18] Its title page bears the date 1539 and its last page the date 1540.

[19] See article "Oosters" in *Mennonite Encyclopedia.*

[20] *Fundament-Boek: Writings,* 103–226.

[21] The second edition of 1554, probably in Lübeck, withdrew some of the material considered by the erring brethren as perhaps no longer pertinent. A further revision appeared in 1558.

[22] See Irvin E. Burkhart, "Menno Simons on the Incarnation," *MQR,* IV (1930), 113; 178; VI (1932), 122, which minimizes the doctrine, and J. A. Oosterbaan, "The Theology of Menno Simons," *MQR,* XXXV (1961), 187–196, which brings Menno and Karl Barth into line!

[23] Krahn, *Menno,* Excursus III, "Der Gemeindebegriff Mennos im Zusammenhang mit seiner Lehre von der Menschwerdung Christi," 155.

[24] *Writings,* 402.

We have dealt elsewhere (Ch. 11.3) at great length with variations in this doctrine among the Radical Reformers, and we could perhaps let that suffice, but since, by way of Menno, Melchior Hofmann's doctrine has survived into modern times, we must give specific attention to Menno's version.

Menno was not really happy with Hofmann's solution. He modified it to the extent that he was willing to grant that Christ drew nourishment from the body of Mary while in the womb. He said that he would rather not speak on the subject at all, but was compelled to do so by his opponents.[25] Like Hofmann and Obbe, he felt that the orthodox theologians did away with the redemptive suffering of God and also posited a Christ capable of sin by reason of his Adamic humanity. Menno emphasized that all of Adam's flesh are justly condemned, that Christ is not divided into two natures, but is one whole Christ. He stressed that the Word *became* flesh, but did not *take* flesh:[26] "I have shown and confessed to you our firm position on the incarnation of the Lord, that He did not become flesh *of* Mary, but *in* Mary." Menno might have expanded his prepositional distinctions and said that Christ was conceived in (*in*), through (*door, durch, per*), or from (*van, von, de*), but was born out of (*uit, aus, ex*) Mary.[27] He goes on to affirm that the entire Christ has been sent forth from the Father:

For Christ Jesus, as to his origin, is no earthly man, that is, a fruit of the flesh and blood of Adam. He is a heavenly fruit or man. For his beginning or origin is of the Father [John 16:28] like unto the first Adam, sin excepted.[28]

Menno cited the now familiar passages, particularly John 1:14 and 6:32, to explain the doctrine of the heavenly flesh with respect to the Eucharist. Since his followers were partaking of the heavenly flesh of Christ in Communion, they had to exclude all impure and unworthy persons. Thus the Mennonite doctrine of the incarnation, bound up with the doctrine of the church as a disciplined and ordered body, led to a sharp distinction between the true congregation of the kin of Christ and the surrounding society of the unregenerate tethered to the first Adam. Christ, as the Second and Heavenly Adam, stands at the head of a new

[25] Cf. *Brief and Clear Confession*, 1544; *Writings*, 419 ff.
[26] *Brief and Clear Confession, Incarnation of Our Lord*, in *Writings*, 419 f., 783 f.
[27] The terminology has been admirably clarified for Menno and the Dutch Anabaptists generally by William Keeney, "Calvin's Treatment of the Anabaptists," summarizing his results on 136.
[28] *Brief and Clear Confession; Writings*, 437.

creation, and thus the reborn members of his church constitute a wholly new society.

To sum up the development from Hofmann through Menno: For Hofmann, the doctrine of the heavenly flesh was the sanction of a new order, the Kingdom, which he conceived experientially and eschatologically. For Menno, the new order was seen primarily in the church of the regenerate, faithfully nourished by a heavenly bread, a spotless community in the wilderness of evil.

Thus, especially important for Menno's realization of the brotherhood of saints was the discipline of the ban. One may pause here for a helpful generalization about baptism, the bond (covenant), and the ban. The first Anabaptists in Zurich, 1525, were naturally preoccupied with believers' baptism. Hofmann, converted to Anabaptism in 1530, stressed believers' baptism as the bond which constituted the believers members of the covenantal community of the saints, *bondgenooten*. By 1540, though baptism and bond remained important constitutive elements, the inner discipline of the fellowship based upon the ban was now receiving major attention. Once the ecclesiological as well as ethical significance of group discipline is granted, one need not feel that it is to disparage Menno to characterize him as the theologian of the ban. "In my opinion," he wrote, "it is a leading characteristic, an honor, and a means of prosperity for a true church."[29]

The ban, as we know from the Schleitheim Confession (Ch. 8.1), is based on Matt. 18:15–18, and avoidance, or shunning, on I Cor. 5:11. The former is common to all Anabaptists, although they have differed as to whether the authority to exercise it rests with the whole congregation or with the elders. Shunning was especially developed by the Mennonites.

Menno placed the ban and avoidance under the Christian imperative to love. By love he meant the intent to save the purity of doctrine and of the fellowship, and to secure the eventual salvation of the wayward brother. Hence, the concern that the three stages of admonition enjoined by Matt., ch. 18, before the final exclusion, be fully observed. Menno elsewhere was at pains to show that the formal ban is but a social confirmation of what has already taken place since the banned is by sin severed from Christ in his heart:

No one is excommunicated [the ban] or expelled by us from the communion of the brethren [shunning] but those who have already separated and expelled themselves from Christ's communion either by

[29] *Instruction on Excommunication; Writings*, 962. One of Menno's disquisitions on the ban is printed in *SAW*, 261 ff.

false doctrine or by improper conduct. For we do not want to expel any, but rather to receive; not to amputate, but rather to heal; not to discard, but rather to win back; not to grieve, but rather to comfort; not to condemn, but rather to save.[30]

Menno was convinced that true regeneration would produce the works of faith, but he lamented the fact that many Anabaptists who professed Christ did not always live unto him:

O brethren, how far some of us, alas, are still distant from the evangelical life which is of God! Notwithstanding that they stay out of the [state] churches and are outwardly baptized with water, yet they are earthly and carnally minded in all things, thinking perhaps that Christianity consists in external baptisms and in staying away from the [established] churches.[31]

His advice on how to deal with the earthly and carnally minded was not only animated by Christian charity but was also characterized by subtle insight into the situation of the righteous critics:

When you shun them as children of darkness and of death, see to it that you yourselves may be children of the light and of eternal life . . . lest you who shun others on account of their evildoing secretly commit worse things in the sight of God.[32]

The ban, accompanied by shunning and the solemn readmission of a wayward member, in some cases many times in the course of his life, was clearly taking over the function of the medieval sacrament of penance, which Menno had known and employed as a priest and now reinstated in what he considered apostolic form:

You see, brethren, I will let every apostate brother determine . . . with what intention this excommunication or ban was so diligently practiced, first by Christ Jesus and His apostles, and afterward by us, who are intent upon recovering again Christian doctrine and practice as may be learned from . . . scriptures.[33]

Among the Netherlandish Anabaptists, despite Menno's charitable construction of the uses of the ban, innumerable schisms would eventually be formed in terms of relative "hard" and "mild" banning and shunning. Scripturally, the Pauline injunction "not to eat with" (I Cor. 5:11) could be interpreted as limited to the Supper or it could be extended to exclude all social intercourse with the banned. The ban in terms, also, of "bed

[30] *Admonition on Church Discipline,* 1541; *Writings,* 413.
[31] *Ibid.,* 410.
[32] *Ibid.,* 415.
[33] *Ibid.*

and board" would become a particularly difficult problem for Mennonite spouses. Menno himself will not always be as charitable as in these early works on the subject.

3. THE SPREAD OF ANABAPTISM IN THE SOUTHERN NETHERLANDS (BELGIUM)

As in the northern provinces of the Netherlands, so in the southern (roughly, modern Belgium), Anabaptism was preceded by teeming late medieval heresy and conventicular life, with Sacramentism prominent. In contrast, however, to the north, there were a number of authentic followers of Luther, notably in Antwerp. Here there were many printing presses to spread the new ideas. Jacob Praepositus, prior of the Augustinian convent, and Cornelius Grafaeus, the town secretary, had promulgated Lutheran doctrine as early as 1519. Two Augustinian friars, Henry Vos and John van Essen, were burned as martyrs in Brussels on 1 July 1523, in whose memory Luther composed a hymn.

With the emergence of Netherlandish Anabaptism in 1530, the recruits in the southern provinces seem to have been drawn as commonly from the Waldensian and Libertine circles as from the Sacramentists; and, although the Melchiorite vision of Anabaptism, with its distinctive marks (celestial flesh and eschatological intensity), spread widely, there must have been other strands.

The organization and discipline of the southern Anabaptists differed from those of the north, though the growing influence of Menno Simons was felt in the south as well. In Frisia and elsewhere in the North, the conventicular center of authority lay in the small circle of the elders, who alone might baptize, whereas in Flanders the authority lay with the brotherhood as a whole. Baptisms were frequently performed by men who had not received ordination. In the application of the ban and avoidance in marriage, the south was more moderate in spirit (*Lieffelijcke Vermaninge*), and the ban remained in the hands of the brotherhood as a whole, instead of being handled by the elders.[34] As to the social backgrounds, the southern Anabaptists were more com-

---

[34] This regional differentiation was originally a matter of sheer circumstances. It was hazardous for a Mennonite overseer (elder) to circulate in Flanders outside thronged Antwerp. As late as 1545, the first recorded synod (presumably in Ghent) of Flemish ministers (deacons), led by Adrian van Kortrijk, petitioned (without immediate results) the church in Antwerp to appoint "a man *living in Flanders* whom we with the consent of the congregations and your counsel could have put to the test, letting him have in all of Flanders the oversight..., that we might also have an oversight over his behavior."

monly recruited from among weavers and small merchants than in the north where peasants, fishers, sailors, and their womenfolk predominated. Most of the converts were Flemish-speaking.

In the first phase of "Belgian" Anabaptism, 1530–1550,[35] the movement spread to most of the large centers of Flanders, Brabant, and the princely bishopric of Liège.

Aachen, Maastricht, and Liège were closely interrelated. William Stupman (Mottencop) of Aachen was the organizer of conventicles in these three towns. The members at first called themselves simply "Christian Brethren."[36]

In Maastricht (now in the Dutch province of Limburg) the soil had been well prepared by the Beghards and Beguines, for whom the city had been a late medieval center, and by the Sacramentists. By 1527 there was a Sacramentist brotherhood there perhaps identical with the "Christian Brethren" above. Accused of "Lutheran heresy," the Brethren had a strong following among the guilds. By 1530 they were visited by several Anabaptist leaders from abroad, including William Stupman, Henry of Tongres, and the Wassenberg preacher Gisbert von Ratheim. By 1533 there were over a hundred Anabaptists in Maastricht. Especially significant was the already mentioned visit of Henry Rol (Ch. 12.1), who arrived in August 1534. After his being burned at the stake in September 1534, there followed, in January 1535, a severe persecution, and the congregation was extinguished.

There were also Sacramentist radicals in Liège who may have participated in the insurrection against the episcopal government in 1531. Anabaptism was organized in Liège in this circle by William Stupman of Aachen in 1533.

Between 1534 and 1535 a large number of Anabaptists from Liège and Maastricht took refuge in Antwerp destined to become the ganglion of the network in the southern provinces. John van Geelen as an emissary of John Beukels preached Münsterite doctrine in Antwerp and recruited followers there in 1534. He lived in the home of a certain Jacob. Münsterite followers in the southern provinces were, however, rather few by

---

[35] The second period is from 1550 to 1576, Ch. 30.1. This periodization depends upon A. L. E. Verheyden, *Anabaptism in Flanders, 1530–1650* (Scottdale, Pennsylvania, 1961); cf. *MQR*, XXVIII (1947), 41–63; another briefer survey is that of Léon-E. Halkin, *La Réforme en Belgique sous Charles-Quint* (Brussels, 1957), cap. iii, not entirely accurate but with a bibliography to date. The Anabaptists of the southern Netherlands may be seen in a larger setting in Robert Collinet, *La Réformation en Belgique au XVIᵉ Siècle* (2d ed., Brussels, 1958).

[36] It is possible that this was an Anabaptist group resembling the Swiss Brethren in doctrine.

comparison with those who were won over in the northern provinces, and there were not many who were willing to heed the call to violent action. Five Anabaptists were summoned for a hearing in Antwerp on 12 February 1535, when the disturbances in Münster were at their height, and the civil authorities were inclined to see in every Anabaptist a revolutionary. Jerome Pael was beheaded as the first martyr 17 February. Native and immigrant Anabaptists were threatened with the severest penalties, even for holding meetings.

The first Anabaptist victims in Ghent were William Mulaer, beheaded 15 July 1535, Arendt de Jagher, and John van Gentbrugge, who were beheaded four days later. Ghent presents a long list of martyrs, Anabaptists and, later, Calvinists. Some 252 were to die there in two generations, of whom by far the larger number were Anabaptists. In its early days a certain revolutionary spirit can be detected in the Ghent conventicle, e.g., in Matthew Waghens, "archdeacon" burned 1538. The congregation seems to have consisted mostly of refugees seeking shelter.

The numerous Anabaptists of Bruges (the inquisitor Cornelius Adrians attests seven hundred living there) were not affected by the fanaticism of Münster. Bruges eventually produced at least forty-seven martyrs, of whom two died in prison, two were buried alive, and forty-three were burned at the stake.

Anabaptism spread in Flanders as far as Oostende and Cassel (today in French Flanders). In Lille (Rijssel), which belonged to Flanders in the sixteenth century, there was also a group of Anabaptists. A barber-surgeon of the town was drowned in the Moselle at Metz on the specific charge of having held the doctrine of the sleep of the soul. Anabaptists are recorded in Courtrai (Kortrijk) as early as 1533. The Brussels Anabaptists were not so numerous. John van der Mase, from Brussels, who had been at Münster, preached in Courtrai. The fall of Münster cured him of his radical sentiment. Through his preaching and that of Peter van Gelder the local congregation of Anabaptists flourished, and somewhat later (1553) Courtrai was said to be the most Anabaptist town of Flanders.

Giles of Aachen was a widely known Anabaptist in the southern Netherlands, and may be taken as representative of the itinerant preachers, who addressed small gatherings in concealed places or larger groups in remote areas, or even, as the medieval preaching friars did, in the streets and marts. Born about 1500 in or near the town of Susteren in Jülich, he had been a priest. "Pale, of average height, with a pointed brown beard and large eyes," he was ordained an elder in 1542 by Menno. Baptizing widely in Flanders, he was suspended from office for adultery in 1552. Reinstated after due penitence in 1554, he was captured; and, although he recanted—to the great shame of the brethren—he was beheaded in 1557 in Antwerp as *"Anabaptistarum Episcopus."*

4. ENGLISH ANABAPTISM TO 1540

It will be recalled in the account of the colloquy at Bocholt (Ch. 13.5) that the expenses were borne by a certain English Anabaptist known only by his Christian name. Although precise information is lacking, it is certain that Anabaptists of Dutch and Flemish origin were present in some strength in England prior to 1536. They found in Lollardy a well-fertilized English soil for the sprouting of the Anabaptist seed. The "new Anabaptist was but old Lollard writ Dutch."[37] The brisk wool and textile trade in ships plying the North Sea provided opportune ways to the havens of England. The Anabaptists who made the voyage settled in London, Hull, and other eastern port towns, to live there to themselves and to remain in their belief largely unmolested, until the news of Münster also crossed the sea.

As early as 1528, the year before he became Lord Chancellor, Thomas More had begun correspondence with Erasmus concerning the *Anabaptistarum haeresis*. In 1533, in his *Confutation*, More charged the Biblical scholar and translator William Tyndale with holding certain heretical beliefs common to the Anabaptists. Nor was More completely wrong; for, although Tyndale did not agree with the Radicals on the matter of baptism, he did share with them belief in the doctrine of the sleep of the soul,[38] and was soon put to death (1536) with Henry's approval at Vilvoorde, the scene of many Flemish martyrdoms. His last words were: "Lord, open the King of England's eyes." He had for some time anticipated a fiery death and had written: "There is none other way into the kingdom of life than through persecution and suffering of pain and of every death after the example of Christ. For Christ also suffered for us, leaving us an example that we should follow his steps, who did no sin." After his death, "the Christian Brethren" and "Known Men" (I Cor. 14:9) circulated his Bible. Lollard Sacramentists, these knowers of Holy Writ and daring colporteurs, resembled proto-Baptist Brethren elsewhere.

English authorities were well aware of a number of Anabaptist beliefs and practices, not only by news from the Continent, but through the description of this "third faccyon" of the Reforma-

[37] The most recent account of English Anabaptism is that of Irvin B. Horst, *ME*, II, 214–221. His doctoral dissertation is soon to be published.
[38] Tyndale's *Works*, edited by John Foxe (London, 1573), 324.

tion published by William Barlow in his *Lutheran Faccyons* (1531). Sometime during the years 1532–1534, six English-speaking and two Flemish Anabaptists were arrested in connection with the importing and distributing of "the booke of the Anabaptist confession." Investigation elicited the information that they met in London (at the house of one of them, John Raulinges) under the leadership of one Sebastian, "the bishop & reder of the Anabaptists." During the fall or winter of 1534, Anabaptist *leraers* from England were present in Amsterdam. A number of Anabaptists fled to England after the seditious uprising at Amsterdam of 10 May 1535. It may be that the twenty-five Dutch Anabaptists arrested and tried at St. Paul's on 25 May of that year (fourteen of whom were condemned and burned in London and other English towns on 4 June) were participants in that flight. In June of 1535, David Joris set sail for London. However, when he learned of the persecution there, he changed his plans and returned to his port of embarkation, Flushing in Holland. The Rotterdam heiress Anneken Jans, who wrote ecstatically of David Joris (Ch. 13.5), together with her husband Arent, fled from Den Briel in Holland to England in the summer of 1536.

In July of 1535, Henry VIII's chief ecclesiastical adviser and instrument, Vicar-General Thomas Cromwell, received word from his agents on the Continent that many an Anabaptist, harried by the reaction that followed the collapse of Münster, was taking the North Sea route to the comparative safety of England. Among those escaping to English shores at this time was John Mathijs of Middelburg, whom we have already met representing the English Anabaptists at the Bocholt conference. The Anabaptists are mentioned (and their ideas on baptism opposed) in the Ten Articles of 1536 and *The Bishop's Book* of 1537.[39]

Sometime in 1538, Philip Melanchthon came into possession of a letter written to an imprisoned Anabaptist by the Hessian Peter Tasch (Ch. 17.2). It indicated, in passing, the existence of close and frequent communication between the German Radicals and their English brethren:

> In England truth advances powerfully in stillness, the Lord alone knows for how much longer. The brethren have openly published a book on the [Melchiorite view of the] incarnation of Christ: I [Peter Tasch] have myself read it. . . . I feel certain the Lord is with them, and I would have journeyed also in England, if I had not felt in my conscience obligated to be elsewhere.[40]

[39] Also in *The King's Book* of 1543.
[40] Günther Franz, *Wiedertäuferakten 1527–1626*, Urkundliche Quellen zur hessischen Reformationsgeschichte, IV (Marburg, 1951), No. 62, pp. 160 f.

Apprised by this letter of the scope of the movement, Philip of Hesse and John Frederick of Saxony sent a warning, composed by Melanchthon, to Henry VIII (September 1538), advising the English monarch to beware of the "Anabaptist pest." It cannot be merely coincidental that, on 1 October 1538, Henry ordered Archbishop Thomas Cranmer "to search for and examine Anabaptists . . . and destroy all books of that detestable sect." The month following, two proclamations to strengthen the realm against these heretics were issued. The first prohibited the printing, importing, and possessing of Anabaptist books, the second ordered all rebaptized persons immediately to leave England. Among the Anabaptists apprehended at this time, a number recanted and were therefore released. Three, however, died for their faith. On 29 November 1538, the already mentioned John Mathijs of Middelburg suffered at the stake at Smithfield, together with the wife of the Fleming Peter Franke. Franke himself was burned the same day at Colchester. He impressed many of the local burghers by his character and piety. We have already mentioned (Ch. 13.5) Anneken Jans and Christina Barents, en route from England to Delft in December 1538 to be apprehended at Rotterdam.

The attention drawn to the Anabaptists by public executions induced native-born Englishmen to espouse their cause. On 26 February 1539, Henry felt moved to pardon all English heretics, but he expressly excluded from his clemency those of foreign birth. The general pardon was repeated in July of 1540. This time Anabaptists were specifically excepted and the chief tenets of their faith were described, namely, their practice of adult baptism, their refusal to "beare office or rule in the Commen Welth" and to swear oaths, their doctrine of the celestial flesh of Christ, and their insistence that "all things be common." Henry's Six Articles Act of 1539, the "Whip with Six Strings," resulted in the execution of over a score of persons during the years 1540–1546. Not all the victims were Anabaptists. One Maundevald, "a French groom of the Queen," and an Englishman named Collins were burned as Anabaptists in the spring of 1540. On 10 April a follower of Menno named Barnes was committed to the Tower of London, together with two "accomplices," and, as the account runs, "accompanied by 10 or 12 burgesses of this town and 15 or 20 (?) strangers, mostly from Flanders and all Anabaptists." Two Flemish Anabaptists were executed in June of 1540.

We shall pick up the story of English Anabaptism in Ch. 30.3.

CHAPTER 15

NETHERLANDISH SACRAMENTISTS AND ANABAPTISTS IN POLAND AND LITHUANIA: SILESIAN RADICALISM, 1528–1548

The Netherlandish Anabaptists extensively colonized the marshy delta of the Vistula and surrounding territory in Poland, where in a war-devastated area they were welcomed because of their experience with dikes, canals, and the cultivation of swampy ground. The region from Danzig and Elbing at the extreme of the delta to Toruń (Thorn), where the Vistula takes a sharp turn to the north, may be considered the asylum for Netherlandish religious refugees comparable to Moravia for the Anabaptists from the Alpine territories of the Hapsburgs. The economic motivation in extending toleration to dissenters is clearest in these two areas. In Poland even the bishop of Culm seems to have winked at the concessions in the interest of the common welfare.

1. THE KINGDOM OF POLAND AND THE GRAND DUCHY OF LITHUANIA: GENERAL ORIENTATION

The kingdom of Poland under Sigismund I (1506–1548) was composed of four geographical divisions: Great Poland (to the west), Little Poland (to the southeast), and the two Prussias. Prussia, ruled as the temporal domain of the Teutonic Knights, had been added to Poland in 1454[1] under the Jagellon dynasty (1386–1572) in a conflict with this powerful missionary-military order. When in 1525 the grand master of the Order, Albert, became the first avowedly Lutheran prince, he received a portion of the secularized lands as a fief of the Polish king. Henceforth, his domain, with Königsberg as the ducal seat, was commonly called ducal (subsequently, East) Prussia. The remainder, royal Prussia, consisted of the lower Vistula valley from Danzig to Chełmno (Culm).

---

[1] By royal decree in 1454; after conflict, by treaty in 1466, whereby the grand master became a vassal. Cf. Ch. 10, n. 60.

The kingdom of Poland and the vast grand duchy of Lithuania were dynastically linked, and in 1569, by the Union of Lublin, they would become federally united as a common royal republic. Within Poland there were three semiautonomous municipal territories, corresponding to the city cantons of Switzerland and the imperial free cities of the Empire, each with a partly or largely Germanic citizenry, with the Poles predominating in the dependent villages. These territorial towns were Danzig, Elbing (Elbląg), and Toruń. The whole of Poland and Lithuania, in so far as the population was Catholic, had for some time stood ecclesiastically under the archbishop of Gniezno (Gnesen), except for the coastal lands held by the Teutonic Order. The bishops here were either directly under the pope or, to the north, under the archbishop of Riga. The archdiocese of Gniezno included also Silesia, which was politically a duchy of the kingdom of Bohemia. In the whole of Poland there was only one princely bishopric, that of Ermland, destined to remain a substantial Catholic enclave within Lutheran ducal Prussia.

For the rest, the two Polands and Lithuania were divided into thirty palatinates, each administered by an appointive palatine (voivode). The palatinates were in turn divided into over eighty castellanies. This feudal society was a limited constitutional monarchy of mixed character. The state was administered as a federation of palatinates with a king (elective after 1572) at the head of all. The senate, consulted by the king in all vital matters, had considerable advisory power. Its one hundred and thirty-nine members, appointed for life by the king, were led by the archbishop of Gniezno and included fifteen members of the higher clergy. The diet (*sejm*) was composed of some two hundred members of the lesser nobility, elected by provincial diets to represent the palatinates. At the end of each annual session of the diet, it met jointly with the senate to consult on the laws passed, which, when agreed and subscribed to, became, collectively, the "constitution."

Reform movements gravitated toward Poland with a sure instinct for survival. The influence of Wyclif had come to Poland by way of Bohemia, through the masters of the University of Prague, who reorganized the university at Cracow at the royal request. In no other land outside Bohemia did Hussitism gain such widespread support as in Poland and Lithuania. Hussite preachers were constant visitors to Poland, and Hussite convictions, at once antipapal, anti-German, and pro-Slavic, won considerable support especially in Lithuania, where a leading prince palatine was for a time an ardent Hussite. In 1500, the nobles of

Great Poland had under Utraquist influence insisted upon their right to the cup at Communion.

In the regions under review in this chapter the Reformation began in 1518, when a monk and preacher of Danzig, James Knade, renounced his monastic vows, married, and set forth Luther's views publicly, calling for reform. Imprisoned by the bishop of Kujawy, he was eventually released and allowed to remove to Toruń, where he continued his activities. By 1522 Danzig had two reform parties, and in 1525 the iconoclastic wing established a popular city government. King Sigismund crushed this movement, executing a large number of its participants in 1526 and restoring the municipal rule of the patricians and Catholic worship. By 1543, Danzig was to become relatively secure for mutually tolerant Lutherans, Sacramentists, and Anabaptists.

Duke Albert's success, beginning in 1525 in Lutheranizing his German-speaking territory, opened the door for the Protestantization of Lithuania, especially because Albert sought to spread Lutheranism in Polish and Lithuanian. Despite the determination of the king and the hierarchy to stem the Reformation tide, "Lutheranism" in royal Prussia, grand-ducal Lithuania, and Great Poland broke the cultural barrier between the German burghers and the Slavic serfs outside their urban colonies and temporarily affected large sectors of the Polish gentry. The *Unitas Fratrum* (especially after the expulsion from Moravia in 1547 enlisted Polish-speaking followers, notably in Great Poland. Presently from 1550 on, the Helvetis[2] version of Protestantism, particularly Calvinism, would commend itself to the magistrates of Lithuania, Samogitia, and almost the entire gentry of Little Poland, who preferred it to Lutheranism because of its partly non-Germanic origin, because of its recognition of the parity of laymen and clergy in church synods, and because of its being considered especially appropriate for a free republic.[3]

The Dutch and German Anabaptism in royal and ducal Prussia and on the Silesian and Moravian borders of the kingdom and especially the Polish-speaking Anabaptism eventually to emerge

[2] The term "Helvetic" is used here and later in preference to "Calvinist" (which has become the useful alternative to the imprecise "Reformed") because throughout the whole course of our narrative Basel and Zurich, though also Germanic, were almost as influential in Polish circles as Geneva. "Helvetic" is used in preference to "Swiss" in suggesting a spiritual abstraction.

[3] Details on the progress of the Magisterial Reformation in Poland may be found in Paul Fox, *The Reformation in Poland* (Baltimore, 1924). The most recent work is that of Bernhard Stasiewski, *Reformation und Gegenreformation in Polen* (Münster, 1960).

within the context of the Reformed Church of Poland and
Lithuania were, both by analogy and by genetic succession, a
regional variant of the same general movement which swept
Central Europe in the sixteenth century.[4]

The same social, temperamental, and theological forces would
soon be at work within the Helvetic church of Poland and Lithuania, producing the radical Polish Brethren, which operated in the
Zurich Reformation to produce the Swiss Brethren. Delay by
a quarter of a century in the appearance of Anabaptist characteristics *in Polish garb* is one with the fact that the Reformation
as a whole came somewhat later to this Slavic region. There is
evidence, however, that from the very beginning the radical impulses of the people's reformation which were unwittingly released by the Magisterial Reformation in Germany penetrated
the language barrier and very early gave the Reformation there
a gathered or conventicular character, i.e., sociologically a sectarian stamp.

The radicalization of the Helvetic Reformed Church of Little
Poland and Lithuania in the direction of anabaptist unitarianism
(the Minor Church or Polish Brethren) lies far ahead in our
narrative (Ch. 25). At this juncture we shall limit ourselves to an
account of the colonization and penetration of Poland by Netherlandish, Silesian, and Moravian Anabaptists and Spiritualists to
the end of the reign of King Sigismund in 1548.

2. SACRAMENTARIANS, SPIRITUALISTS, AND ANABAPTISTS IN THE PRUSSIAS TO 1535

Spiritualist and Anabaptist tendencies in the Germanic areas
came earlier to the fore in royal and in ducal Prussia, in fact
within a few years of the conclusion of peace in 1525 between
the king of Poland and the grand master of the Teutonic Order.
Devastated by four years of war and in September 1525 turmoiled
by a divine-rights peasant uprising, the religiously and economically disordered region was open to colonization. The first Dutch
settlers were Sacramentist refugees, arriving in Bardehnen (ducal
Prussia) in 1527. In and around Elbing (royal Prussia) they were
so numerous by 1531 that the Catholic bishop of Ermland besought the town and then the king to expel them.[5]

Silesian and other Spiritualists of the circle of Caspar Schwenck-

---

[4] The following is an abridgment and adaptation of the author's "Anabaptism and Spiritualism in the Kingdom of Poland and the Grand Duchy of
Lithuania: An Obscure Phase of the Pre-History of Socinianism," *Studia
nad Arianizmem*, edited by Ludwik Chmaj (Warsaw, 1959), 215–262.

[5] Felicia Szper (born in Warsaw), *Nederlandsche Nederzettingen in West
Pruisen gedurende den Poolschen Tijd* (Enkhuizen, 1913); other studies,

feld and a number of spiritualizing Anabaptist leaders were also strangely prominent in the early phase of Duke Albert's effort to supply his newly reformed duchy with evangelical clergy. Albert and Schwenckfeld's erstwhile protector, Frederick II of Liegnitz (Ch. 5.5), were kindred spirits in respect to the Reform and were closely related by marriage.[6] Paul Speratus, Lutheran bishop of Pomesania (one of the two episcopal sees within ducal Prussia), and Duke Albert had been in epistolary contact with Schwenckfeld since 1525. Schwenckfeld was guest of Albert briefly in 1528 and wrote him subsequently on the Eucharist against the views of Luther, Zwingli, and Calvin.[7] Albert, in his turn, described the dearth of evangelical pastors and dispatched his chief counselor, the powerful Baron Frederick of Heydeck, himself markedly favorable to the more Spiritualistic interpretation of the Reformation, to Silesia in order to recruit ministers of the Schwenckfeldian type for ducal Prussia.

By 1531 the conflict in ducal Prussia between normative Lutheranism, as represented by Paul Speratus, and the spiritualizers became so intense as to necessitate the convening of a synod in Rastenburg, 5 June 1531, and a subsequent colloquy, 29 and 30 December 1531, in the presence of Albert with Speratus and the other Lutheran Bishop, George Polentz, for the conservative Lutheran side, and on the Schwenckfeldian side, Heydeck, Peter Zenker, and Fabian Eckel of Liegnitz. At least three Anabaptists of a spiritualizing tendency also participated.

The first of these was John Bünderlin of Linz, whom we last met in Strassburg (Ch. 10.3.a). The second was John Spittelmaier, who had stood with Hubmaier in the Nicolsburg disputation on the use of the sword by Christians and the propriety of paying war taxes, and who had succeeded Hubmaier. It was under his pastorate that the first communitarians had withdrawn as "staff men" to Austerlitz (Ch. 9.2.d). The third was Oswald Glait, who

more exclusively demographic, but indispensable for an indication of the great scope and intensity of the Dutch colonization, are the following: B. Schumacher, *Niederländische Ansiedlungen in Preussen* (Leipzig, 1903); Horst Penner, *Ansiedlung mennonitischer Niederländer im Weichselmündungsgebiet von der Mitte des 16. Jahrhunderts bis zum Beginn der preussischen Zeit* (Karlsruhe, 1940); Benjamin H. Unruh, *Die niederländischniederdeutschen Hintergründe der mennonitischen Ostwanderungen im 16., 18. und 19. Jahrhundert (ibid.,* 1955); E. Hassinger, "Wirtschaftliche Motive und Argumente für religiöse Duldsamkeit," *ARG,* XLIX (1958), 228. On the evangelical German-Slavic peasant revolt in Prussia, see Henryk Zins, *Powstanie chłopskie* (Warsaw, 1953).
[6] *CS,* II, 109, *passim.*
[7] *CS,* III, 341, *passim.*

had preceded Hubmaier at Nicolsburg, accompanied him to his martyrdom in Vienna, and then turned Sabbatarian (Ch. 15.3).

After the Rastenburg colloquy, Albert decided in favor of the more conservative Lutheran view and also expelled the three aforementioned spiritualizing Anabaptists, 16 August 1532. His lingering Spiritualist sympathies were indicated, however, by the fact that both Baron Heydeck and the Anabaptist-Spiritualist Christian Entfelder (Ch. 10.3.e) were long prominent among his advisers. The latter, ducal counselor from 1536 to 1546, was especially qualified for working out the contracts for the ever-increasing number of Netherlandish Anabaptist colonists.

Not content with the banishment of the most radical of the Spiritualists and Anabaptists, and alarmed lest the heavy immigration from the Netherlands imperil Lutheranism in ducal Prussia, Speratus addressed a (now lost) letter of warning, *Ad Bataves vagantes* (1534), to which the group centered in Elbing responded in (the also lost) *Apologetica responsio Hollandorum* (1536), perhaps written by the Sacramentist William Gnapheus (Ch. 12.1).[8]

In the same year that Lutheran Bishop Speratus wrote his letter, Catholic Bishop Mauritius Ferber of Ermland directed his efforts toward Danzig and besought the magistrates to prevail upon the town councils of the Netherlandish ports of Amsterdam, Antwerp, Veere, and Enkhuizen to hold back the fleeing heretics from taking ship. The Netherlandish authorities, however, were all too glad to be rid of them while confiscating their meager baggage; and Ferber had to rely solely on action within Danzig itself and succeeded (partly because of the hostility of the guildsmen who regarded the refugee artisans as competitors) in having the heretical Netherlanders driven into Schottland on the Vistula just outside the boundaries of greater Danzig in territory under the spiritual jurisdiction of the bishop of Kujawy. By the middle of the sixteenth century the Dutch Anabaptists had thickly settled selected lowlands on either side of the Vistula up to the walls of Toruń.[9]

After 1535 the Netherlandish colonists were predominantly Anabaptist. Whether they were in 1535 of the revolutionary type or the evangelical type is difficult to determine. (The actual designation "Mennonite" first appears in 1572.)[10] The fact that the Netherlandish colonists were generally concerned, in the

---

[8] Szper, *op. cit.*, 192. See Theodor Wotschke, "Herzog Albrecht von Preussen und Wilhelm Gnapheus," *ARG*, XXX (1930), 122–131.

[9] Szper, *op. cit.*, 22, 196.

[10] *Ibid.*, 200 f.

drawing up of their compacts, not to take the oath, nor to bear arms, would indicate their predominantly pacifistic inclination. Compulsory state labor and military service were not required of them in the ducal compacts worked out for them by Christian Entfelder.[11]

Before following the Polish and Prussian developments further we should pick up the closely related Silesian story.

3. Silesian Spiritualism and Anabaptism, 1527–1548

We were last in Silesia as Caspar Schwenckfeld was taking leave in voluntary exile (Ch. 5.5) to begin his eventful sojourn in Strassburg in 1529 (Ch. 10.3.b). We have not hitherto dealt with Silesian Anabaptism.[12]

Prior to his departure, Schwenckfeld had engaged in a debate on the Sabbath with Oswald Glait (Ch. 15.2). Formerly the associate of Hubmaier[13] at Nicolsburg, then a partisan of Hut, and now a propagator of Sabbatarian Anabaptism, Glait, beginning in 1528 with his fellow worker, Andrew Fischer[14] (Ch. 15.4), successfully propagated his Sabbatarian, anti-Trinitarian Anabaptism among the more prosperous peasants around Liegnitz in Silesia.[15] After his removal to Strassburg, Schwenckfeld was requested by Lord Leonard of Liechtenstein in Nicolsburg to refute Glait on his Sabbatarianism. This Schwenckfeld did while still in Strassburg in his *Against the Ancient and the New Ebionite Error of Those Who Confuse Moses with Christ, the Law with the Gospel*.[16] Valentine Crautwald also wrote against the Silesian Sabbatarian Anabaptists, as did Capito in Strassburg[17] and Luther.[18]

Much of the mood of the Silesian Reformation at this time is preserved in the correspondence between Strassburg and Liegnitz,[19] particularly the two letters of Valentine Crautwald to Capito and Bucer in June and July before Schwenckfeld's exile. Notable, for example, is Crautwald's warning to the Strassburgers

[11] *ML*, II, 323.
[12] The most recent work is that of Eva Maleczyńska, "Gabrielowcy sląscy," *ORP*, VI (1961), 17–28.
[13] For the most recent evaluation, see Wilhelm Schulze, "Neuere Forschungen über Balthasar Hubmaier," *Alemannisches Jahrbuch*, 1957, 224–272.
[14] The fullest treatment of Fischer is that of Petr Ratkoš, "Die Anfänge des Wiedertäufertums in der Slowakei," *Aus 500 Jahren deutsch-tschechoslowakischer Geschichte*, edited by Karl Obermann and Josef Polišenský (Berlin, 1958), 41–59.
[15] *CS*, IV, 450.
[16] *Ibid.*, 444–518.
[17] Krebs and Rott, *Elsass*, I (*QGT*, VII), Nos. 290a and 290b.
[18] *Brief wider die Sabbather*, *WA*, I, 309 ff.
[19] Krebs and Rott, *Elsass*, I (*QGT*, VII), Nos. 99, 141, 143 f., 182a.

and other proponents of the Magisterial Reformation, prompted in part by the Judaizing trend among the local Anabaptists, that Christians should rely more on the ever-present Spirit of Christ than on any rabbi who might instruct them on fine philological points in Hebrew: "Scholastic and sophistic foolishness has been exploded; there follows now, unless the Lord provide otherwise, rabbinical and Jewish perfidy." This bitter generalization in respect to the trend of Protestantism outside Silesia is connected particularly in Crautwald's mind with the Protestant identification of circumcision and baptism, the Protestant willingness to use the coercive power of the state in the realm of conscience, and the specifically Lutheran Eucharistic Christology, which he disparagingly compares to the three-bodied monster, Geryon, slain by Hercules.

We have already dealt with Crautwald's Eucharistic theology adopted by Schwenckfeld. Of interest now is his (and Schwenckfeld's) view of baptism, which is, like the Eucharist, essentially an inward transaction. As for the outward form, Crautwald appeals to John 13:10 and by implication to the fact that the institution of an external baptism is not described in the Fourth Gospel. At the same time Crautwald gives evidence that he was familiar in Silesia with the practice of a "second" baptism among the Catholics in Poland to regularize or effectuate baptisms performed in the language of the people, and of a "third" baptism among some Silesian Anabaptists who insisted on confessing their believers' baptism by full immersion.[20]

With the departure of Schwenckfeld, Crautwald's position was weakened. Duke Frederick moved to reinstitute the observance of Communion, and asked Duke Albert in Königsberg to send him the influential Baron Frederick of Heydeck to help in reforming Silesia. Heydeck, inclined, as we have noted, to Spiritualism, shortly after his arrival in Liegnitz fully succumbed to Schwenckfeldian ideas. The embarrassed Duke Frederick then appealed to John Hess in Breslau to help Heydeck draw up a mutually satisfactory order for the Lord's Supper. Hess, however, was unwilling to discuss any compromise formula. In the meantime, the conflict in ducal Prussia between normative Lutheranism and the spiritualizers had broken out, and Frederick hoped to benefit from the Rastenburg colloquy of 1531 (Ch. 15.2). But this colloquy did not solve the problem either for Duke Albert in Königsberg or for Duke Frederick in Liegnitz.

Frederick continued to work at an acceptable order for the

---

[20] Krebs and Rott, *Elsass,* I (*QGT,* VII), No. 141, p. 168.

Communion. His lack of success left Liegnitz in relative isolation, with Valentine Crautwald and John S. Werner continuing to give Schwenckfeldian leadership there and in Brieg. Then, when the Wittenberg Concordia of 1536 brought a measure of harmony to the German Protestants, Duke Frederick felt obliged to fall into line; and, failing to persuade Werner of the urgency of doing so, he dismissed him in 1540.[21]

Werner's dismissal caused consternation among his congregation, and attendance at services conducted by the orthodox Lutherans declined. Many of the most devout found their spiritual nurture in Schwenckfeldian conventicles.[22] The Duke eventually undertook a number of measures to suppress Schwenckfeldianism. Eckel and Werner emigrated to Glatz. When Glatz came under Bavarian Catholic control in 1548, the movement suffered severely.

Silesia was also the scene of much of the activity of the Nuremberg furrier Gabriel Ascherham,[23] a man of uncertain talents whose name is associated with divisiveness among the Anabaptists of Moravia and who may be characterized *in the end* as a Spiritualist (like Entfelder and Bünderlin). He had practiced his trade in Schärding in Bavaria before his conversion to Anabaptism. From Bavaria, missionary activity took him to Silesia, probably in the company of John Hut. They moved about in the vicinity of Breslau, Glogau, and Glatz, and found considerable Anabaptist activity in progress. Hostile contemporary accounts[24] describe him in unflattering language, as "lukewarm and limp," and "following the wind."[25] In spite of his alleged vacillations he established a number of strong Anabaptist communities in Silesia. But the royal edict of 1 August 1528 put a stop to their growth and forced many to emigrate to Moravia. Ascherham led one group of two thousand into Moravia, having collected seven thousand guilders for the trip. Probably this numerical superiority of his following was responsible for his selection as bishop of the Rossitz-Auspitz congregations in Moravia when they combined at Jacob Hutter's suggestion in 1531. The story of Ascherham in Moravia will be told in Ch. 16.1.

When the persecution began in Moravia in 1535, Ascherham and his followers returned to Silesia (especially the towns of

[21] Letter to Schwenckfeld, *CS*, VII, Document CCCXVIII.
[22] Schultz, *Caspar Schwenckfeld*, 166.
[23] Wilhelm Wiswedel, "Gabriel Ascherham und die nach ihm genannte Bewegung," *ARG*, XXXIV (1937), 1–35; 235–262.
[24] E.g., the Hutterite *Chronicle*, and *Wiedertäuferischen Gesindleins in Mähren und Schlesien seltene Beschaffenheit* (n. p., 1535).
[25] *Gesindleins;* cited in Wiswedel, "Ascherham," *loc. cit.*, 2.

Schweidnitz, Guhrau, Jauer, and Habelschwerdt). In Habel-schwerdt in the County of Glatz the population was divided be-tween Schwenckfeldians and Anabaptists. By 1538 the Catholic pastor Peter Eiserer locked up the church, gave the keys to the town council, and left. It was at Habelschwerdt, on the Neisse and Weistritz Rivers, that adult baptism by immersion, already al-luded to by Crautwald as early as 1528, was first practiced for large numbers.

By 1545 the Habelschwerdt Anabaptists, the "unity of the pious" (*Verein der Frommen*), had won over almost the whole population. In addition to immersion, they also taught com-munity of goods, apparently more in the sense of fraternal shar-ing than common ownership. In 1546 the Habelschwerdt Gabrielites let the Schwenckfeldian pastor of nearby Arnsdorf use the local church edifice, since "for them the whole town was a temple."

They held their meetings in citizens' houses, offered their common prayers, and chose preachers and teachers from among themselves to expound the scriptures according to their understanding. The Neisse and Weistritz were the great and general baptismal bath (*Taufbad*) in which adults were immersed and made members of their covenant (*Bund*).[26]

In 1545, Gabriel Ascherham died at the Gabrielite colony in Wschowa, just over the border in Poland.

Beginning in 1548, the Gabrielites of Habelschwerdt were persecuted. Many fled to ducal Prussia, where Frederick of Hey-deck secured asylum for them, and others sought sanctuary in Poland, where their practice of immersion was to become cus-tomary among the Polish Brethren (Ch. 25.2). Most of the Silesian Gabrielites eventually joined either the Hutterites or the Schwenckfeldians. But as late as 1558 a commission found that there were still Anabaptists active in the County of Glatz; and a new decree was issued by the Emperor and the duke of Silesia, banishing them from all the lands of the Bohemian crown. The same commission also reported that of the pastors active in the county, thirteen were Roman (five absent from their charges and the majority married),[27] eleven were Lutherans, five were Schwenckfeldians, and eight half Schwenckfeldian, half Lutheran. (Fifteen pastors were removed, and five conformed to the Roman Church.)

---

[26] Aloys Bach, *Urkundliche Kirchen-Geschichte der Grafschaft Glatz* (Breslau, 1841), 98 ff., 107.
[27] *Ibid.*, 111 f.

4. ANABAPTISM IN POLAND

Anabaptism penetrated Polish-speaking territory not only from the Dutch-settled delta of the Vistula but also from Silesia and from Slovakia.[28]

In Zip (Slovakian: Spiš; Polish: Spisz), in the region of the High and Low Tatras, there were over a dozen Saxon towns, notably Schwedler, Käsemark, Leutschau, and Spitzer Neudorf (Spišska Nová Ves), that, beginning in 1529, constituted an important hearth of communitarian, anti-Trinitarian Anabaptism. Nominally controlled by Hungary during this period, Zip was governed as a Polish protectorate.

The leader of this radical "Lutheran" movement was the university-trained Andrew Fischer (c. 1480–c. 1540), restlessly at work in Silesia (Ch. 15.3), Moravia, Zip, and Little Poland. His principal following was among artisans, miners, and yeomen, though not without here and there the protection of a sympathizing knight or town councilor. Originally, Fischer, like other evangelical Anabaptists, opposed oaths and the use of the sword. Later, when he came to enjoy the friendship of Leonard of Liechtenstein, he, like Balthasar Hubmaier, revised his position on the legitimacy of the use of the sword by a Christian magistrate. Indeed, his eventual espousal of Sabbatarianism, consonant with his later Judaizing tendency in sacramental theology and Christology, seems also to have betokened an Old Testament concern for the law and the state in a covenantal context. As for the doctrine of the Trinity, it is of interest that Fischer's subordination of the purely human, suffering Son to the stern Father was already a folk belief in the High Tatras region, as can be seen from the popular iconography.[29] The community of goods was espoused and practiced by the Zip Anabaptists, and there is evidence that along with their readiness to divorce in order to remarry within the covenant, some of them also believed and practiced the community of wives. Fischer—widowed by the brave martyrdom of his second wife while he was himself miraculously escaping the hangman's noose—was several times married. One of Fischer's most articulate converts was John Reyss (Russe). The name suggests that he had been a member of the Orthodox Church. From Reyss, who was captured while Fischer escaped over the border into Poland, we learn that the Zip Anabaptists attached importance to baptism or rebaptism at the age of thirty or thereafter.

It was in the winter of 1529/1530 that Fischer escaped into Polish territory and stayed in Cracow, before going to Moravia,

[28] Ratkoš, op. cit.
[29] Gothic Museum, section on folk art, Cracow.

"where a large number of the heretical brethren" were to congregate for the purpose of organizing their mission on a large scale.[30]

When the notoriety of the Münsterite Anabaptists prompted King Ferdinand to drive out his Moravian Anabaptists, they took refuge not only in Silesia and Slovakia but also in Poland. Some settled at Międzyrzecz (Meseritz).[31] Ascherham founded several Gabrielite colonies not only in Silesia (Ch. 15.3) but also on the Vistula near Chełmno, Swiecie (Schwetz), and Grudziądz (Graudentz), settling himself near Wschowa (Fraustadt).[32] Other Anabaptist refugees found protection from the gentry around Poznań (Posen) in 1537.[33] A company of some two hundred Anabaptists, mostly Silesians, were reported on a trek through Toruń and Grudziądz to Marienwerder (Kwidzyń) on the Vistula, just over the border into ducal Prussia.[34] Pursued by the same edict of Ferdinand, other groups of communitarian Anabaptists from Moravia under the leadership of Ulrich Stadler (Ch. 16.1) settled around Kraśnik near Włodzimierz on the estates of the Teczyński family. It is quite possible that this settlement was negotiated by Jerome Łaski, the brother of the Reformer John.[35] These Hutterites were very eloquent in their exclusive devotion to Christ as their only King and Lord.

Little wonder that King Sigismund I, alarmed at the infiltration of his Catholic kingdom by the most radical of heretics from the Hapsburg domains of the Netherlands, Moravia and Silesia, published an edict, 27 September 1535, warning his subjects, and especially the prefects of the border towns and townships, to refuse "water and fire" to the "godless race" and to take measures lest they "enter into relations" with loyal Polish subjects.[36]

In ducal Prussia, meanwhile, the Sacramentist Gnapheus (Ch.

---

[30] Ratkoš, op. cit., p. 52, n. 45.
[31] Theodor Wotschke, "Die unitarische Gemeinde in Meseritz-Bobelwitz," Zeitschrift der historischen Gesellschaft für die Provinz Posen (1911), 163.
[32] Unruh, op. cit., 104.
[33] Stanislas Kot, Socinianism in Poland: The Social and Political Ideas of the Polish Antitrinitarians in the 16th and 17th Centuries (Boston, 1957), 13, n. 10. But Kot's source reference should be corrected to read: Acta historica, Vol. XII, No. 95.
[34] Schumacher, op. cit., 154 ff.
[35] Müller, Glaubenszeugnisse (QGT, III), 211–236; Eduard Kupsch, "Der Polnische Unitarismus," Jahrbücher für Geschichte Osteuropas, V (1957), 401–440; Eva Maleczyńska, "Ulryk Stadler na tle losów anabaptystów w pierwszej połowie xvi wieku," Przegląd Historyczny, I (Warsaw, 1959), 473–485.
[36] Andrew Frycz Modrzewski refers to measures being taken in regard to Anabaptists in his letter to John Łaski, 20 June 1536, apud S. A. Gabbema, Illustrium virorum epistolae (Harlingen, 1669).

15.2) had left Elbing to become ducal counselor at Königsberg, and lectured at the *paedagogium* (converted into a university in 1545). In 1542, the Anabaptist Dr. Gerhard Westerburg of Cologne, the brother-in-law of Carlstadt (Chs. 4.2; 8.3), likewise became a ducal counselor.

Despite the strong favor that the Anabaptist colonists enjoyed at court under the influence of Heydeck, Entfelder,[37] Gnapheus, and Westerburg, in 1543 all the Netherlandish settlers who refused to conform to the Prussian Lutheran Church order in respect to baptism and the sacrament of the altar were, under pressure from Bishop Speratus, driven from ducal Prussia, though they could not easily be kept from returning. Entfelder himself withdrew from the ducal court in 1546. In the same year, as it happened, an unnamed Flemish anti-Trinitarian (possibly the unitarian Mennonite Adam Pastor) visited Cracow.

By the summer of 1549, Menno Simons himself visited royal Prussia, laboring a number of weeks to settle differences among his far-flung followers and organize them.[38] His interest extended, no doubt, to the settlements of Netherlandish Anabaptists, who by now populated the whole region from Danzig and Elbing south to Toruń and Chełmno; for it was in 1547 that a new phase in ducal Prussian Anabaptism opened with the extensive drainage operations in the delta.

By the death of Sigismund I in 1548 and Henry VIII in 1547, the Netherlandish Anabaptist diaspora, of which Menno Simons was the chief pastor, stretched along the Hanseatic Coast from Colchester in England and Cassel in French Flanders to Chełmno and Königsberg. During this same period the High German Anabaptist diaspora, now extending beyond Silesia, Moravia, and Slovakia, had penetrated Poland all along its western and southern borders to introduce and to blend, presumably in Polish speech, such beliefs and practices as were later to become the distinctive mark of Polish Anabaptism (Ch. 25.1), namely, immersion, Spiritualism, and anti-Trinitarianism.

---

[37] There is a letter of 1544 by Entfelder to John Łaski, printed by Veesenmeyer in Gabler's *Neuestes theologisches Journal*, IV, No. 4 (Nuremberg, 1800), 321–328.

[38] Letter of 7 October 1549; *Writings*, 1030.

CHAPTER 16

THE HUTTERITES, 1529–1540

We have followed the various reactions within the Radical Reformation to the Münsterite debacle, the renewed belligerence of the Batenburgers, the Spiritualism of the Davidjorists, the ethical rigorism of the Mennonites with their disavowal of the excesses of Münster and their characteristic stress upon the ban, the diaspora of the Dutch dissenters from England to Prussia, and the emergence in Silesia and Slovakia of immersionist, communitarian Anabaptism under Gabriel Ascherham and of Sabbatarian, anti-Trinitarian, communitarian Anabaptism under Oswald Glait and Andrew Fischer.

As we return now to the Anabaptists in Moravia among whom a pacifistic communism had even earlier found theological and practical expression by 1529 (Ch. 9.2.d), we should be prepared to find a consolidation and purification under way comparable to that which we have chronicled in the Netherlands. The analogue of the Mennonites are here the Hutterites, taking their name from the charismatic Tyrolean apostle Jacob Hutter, who succeeded in welding the disparate refugee factions into a solid fellowship of communistic colonies. Just as the first phase of Mennonitism came to a close with the *Foundation Book* of 1540, so the first phase of Hutteritism comes to a close with a comparably systematic summary of the faith and practice of Hutter's followers in the *Account of Faith* (*Rechenschaft*) of 1540, composed in prison by an ally of Hutter, Peter Riedemann.

We shall first follow the development in Moravia from the arrival of Hutter in 1529 until his death in the same year that Menno left the Roman obedience, 1536.

1. ANABAPTISTS IN MORAVIA FROM 1529 TO THE DEATH OF JACOB HUTTER IN 1536

It will be recalled that the pacifistic staff men under Jacob Wiedemann had withdrawn from Nicolsburg (and nearby

Bergen) and established by 1529 a completely communitarian colony to the north in Austerlitz.

The complicated and unedifying account which follows of the personal and ecclesiastical controversies growing out of differences in homeland usages of the refugees and divergent conceptions of the Anabaptist gospel can be visualized geographically by projecting a *Y* on the map of Moravia and thinking of Austerlitz at the tip of the right stem, Rossitz at the tip of the left stem, Auspitz at their juncture, and the original settlement of Nicolsburg at the base.

At Rossitz a colony of Grabriel Ascherham's followers was established as early as 1527, and, when the Gabrielites as a body were driven from Silesia, the colony was greatly expanded in 1529 and flourished there until driven back into Silesia in 1535. Alongside the Gabrielites there were an earlier colony of the *Unitas Fratrum* and a community under the leadership of Philip Plener,[1] called after him Philippites.

Auspitz, at the juncture in our *Y,* was also to have two communitarian Anabaptist colonies. The first was established by Philip Plener, who in 1529 led most of his loyal band of Hessian and Palatinate converts to lands near Auspitz opened up to him by the abbess of Maria Saal. The second was a Tyrolese community established by Jacob Hutter and placed under the immediate direction of his deputy, George Zaunring. But this is to anticipate.

Jacob Hutter in the double task of reconciling the quarreling factions in Moravia and converting and shepherding in the valleys of the Tyrol was to emerge as the inspirer and reorganizer of the new kind of rigoristically communistic Anabaptism that would take his name and principles and slowly adopt and assimilate all the bands and clans whom he had molded together as a new people of destiny.[2]

A native of the hamlet of Moos, Hutter was given the rudiments of an education at the school in Bruneck in the Puster

---

[1] Philip Plener, called also Blauärmel and Weber, should not be confused with Philip Jäger Weber, the associate of Wiedemann in the trek from Nicolsburg to Austerlitz.

[2] The most recent study is that of Hans Fischer, *Jakob Huter: Leben, Frömmigkeit, Briefe,* Mennonite Historical Series, No. 4 (Newton, Kansas, 1956). Quotations from Hutter's letters are translations from the collection of seven edited in modern German in this book. Several of these are also printed in Beck, *Geschichts-Bücher,* Müller, *Glaubenszeugnisse (QGT,* III), and the Zieglschmid and the Wolkan editions of the Hutterite *Chronicle.*

Valley before going on to Prague to learn the trade of hatter,
whence his name. He might have heard Müntzer's Prague
Manifesto in 1529 or come to know Kalenec, leader of the Minor
Unity then living there. After his journeyman's travels, Hutter
settled down at Spittal in Carinthia.

It was probably at Klagenfurt that he first became acquainted
with Anabaptists. It is not known by whom he was baptized. Confirmed as an elder and evangelist, he first served the congregation
at Welsperg in the Puster Valley, and barely escaped when it was
surprised by sleuths in May 1529. With the burning at Klausen
nearby of Blaurock in September 1529, the last of the original
Zurich triumvirate, Hutter became in effect the chief pastor of
the Tyrolese Anabaptists.

Hutter and Simon Schützinger visited Austerlitz to size up the
situation in Moravia. Favorably impressed by the possibility of
extensive and safe colonization for his hard-pressed Tyrolese converts, he returned to the Tyrol to organize the bands of refugees.
Over them he placed the already mentioned George Zaunring,
who at first got on well with the original founder of the Austerlitz colony, Wiedemann. It is possible that the communitarian
church order of 1529, already characterized in Ch. 9.2.d, represents the articles of agreement drawn up between Wiedemann
and Zaunring.

At this point William Reublin now enters the Hutterite
chronicle. We have encountered him many times in the course
of our narrative as people's priest in St. Alban's in Basel, as associate of Grebel from his base in Wytikon, as baptizer of Hubmaier in Waldshut, as the commissioner of Sattler at Rottenburg,
and as the associate of Kautz and Marpeck in Strassburg. He arrived in Austerlitz in 1530 and found that the company was so
large that in winter, when they could no longer hold their services
out of doors, they were meeting in three different shelters concurrently. These discussion groups were developing into factions.
Reublin was becoming the vigorous spokesman of the faction
who were vexed by old Wiedemann's authoritarian administration of Christian communism. Reublin in his popular sermons
and Biblical explications after supper was arousing the enmity of
Wiedemann and the other elders, until at length he was formally banned.

Among those who sided with Reublin were Zaunring and a
Bohemian Brother, David by name. In the last tense encounter
with Wiedemann, each side hurling the charge of false prophet,
Reublin drew up some ten serious charges of maladministration,

defective theology, and want of elementary humane consideration. All of this he rehearsed in a lengthy letter to Marpeck back
in Strassburg, dated 26 January 1531.[3]

Among the specific charges were the cruelty and unfairness
of Wiedemann and the other elders in the administration of the
common property: for example, the fact that more than twenty
infants had died for want of milk when their parents had, on
entering the community, turned over in some cases as much as
fifty guilders; that the elders, and particularly their wives, were
better fed and better clothed than the ordinary members; that
girls were often obliged to accept as husbands whomever the
elders designated as though by divine decree; that the elders
refused to turn over a fair share in taxes for the war against the
Turk despite their promise to their patrons, the lords of Kaunitz;
and such doctrinal aberrations as Wiedemann's allegedly holding
that water baptism is absolutely essential to salvation; that infants who die prior to accepting the covenant of baptismal grace
are condemned to hell; and that it is no longer necessary to recite
the Lord's Prayer. Since Reublin will not have been unpartisan
in his report to Marpeck, we are fortunate in having an authoritative account from the other side, not from Wiedemann
himself, but from Ulrich Stadler. His *Cherished Instructions on
Sin, Excommunication, and the Community of Goods,*[4] though
coming from a slightly later date, is a good specimen of the way
in which the conception of *Gelassenheit,* derived from Denck and
Hut, could indeed be combined with a starkly authoritarian
eldership, with a high view of apostolic baptism administered by
the elders as requisite to salvation, and with a communism of
production in which yielding to the disciplines of labor becomes
spiritually more important than sharing lovingly in the fruits of
labor.

In any event, the acrimonious dispute reached its climax when
in the dead of winter Reublin and Zaunring, with three hundred
and fifty followers, many of them sick, trudged toward Auspitz,
leaving perhaps two hundred and fifty in Austerlitz under Wiedemann.

At this season of bitterness, when the experiment in Christian
communism was being blasted by factionalism, both sides were
prompted to send letters to Hutter in the Tyrol, imploring him
to intervene and if possible to undo the disruption. Hutter

---

[3] Printed by C. A. Cornelius, *Geschichte des Münsterischen Aufruhrs,* II
(Leipzig, 1855), Beilage, V, 253–259.
[4] *SAW,* 274–284.

responded to the appeals and on investigation "found that the Austerlitz group was most to be blamed."

He returned to the Tyrol satisfied with his work of reconciliation and prepared to urge further immigration thither from the hard-pressed valleys under the direct control of Ferdinand and the equally fierce prince-bishops of Brixen and Salzburg. Then messengers arrived with the bad news of further disruption in Austerlitz and between Austerlitz and Auspitz. It was discovered that Reublin was not wholeheartedly practicing apostolic communism. He had retained several guilders for emergency use. On the charge of being a false Ananias, he was removed from office, and Zaunring was elevated to the foremost place in the eldership at Auspitz. But Zaunring, too, failed to live up to the standards of leadership. His wife was taken in adultery. Even more grievous was his failure to bring her before the assembled brethren to be rebuked and banned as any other sinner would have been. Because the congregation was unsympathetic to Zaunring's leniency and "could not suffer the vice of adultery and whore's work to be so lightly punished," they excommunicated him. Once more Hutter and Schützinger came from the Tyrol to reorder the settlers. Schützinger was appointed pastor.

At this point, a federation was effected between the two communities in Auspitz, that now led by Schützinger and that led by Philip Plener. The federation was expanded at Hutter's instigation to include the Gabrielites at Rossitz; and Gabriel Ascherham himself was named bishop of the three groups.

Meanwhile, Zaunring, repenting of his charitable indiscipline, was received back into communion. Dispatched as a missionary into Franconia, he was subsequently beheaded by the bishop of Bamberg. Reublin for his part was through with communitarian Anabaptism and was back in Swabia, in July 1531, reorganizing remnants of his former congregation near Esslingen. Eventually he was to abandon his Anabaptism altogether, seek to recover his inheritance in his native Rottenburg, and live to old age with his wife, successively in Znaim in Moravia, and in Zurich and Basel.

On 11 August 1533, Jacob Hutter returned to Moravia for his fourth, last, and longest sojourn. In his opening address before the federated colonists or representatives in the case of the Gabrielites of Rossitz, he pointed out that the succession of major and minor failings among the chosen of God had been due to remnants of family ties and insufficient separation from worldly considerations, when the elect should have been mindful that their only citizenship was in heaven. By now, Hutter was completely convinced that he was called of God in a unique way to guide the federated groups into the way of the Lord. He visited Rossitz with a view to assuming supremacy there with the consent of Ascherham and his people, persuaded as he was of his own apostolic mission. In this he was temporarily unsuccessful. Back in Auspitz he sought in several assemblies to be acknowledged as chief elder, but both Schützinger and Plener defended their place in the eldership, and their followers urged upon Hutter that for the sake of harmony he not press for such unwanted plenitude of power.

The change from respectful reserve toward him to ready acceptance of his apostolic claim came about in connection with the admission of two recent converts after an unusually powerful sermon by Hutter. It was discovered that, like Ananias and Sapphira, this couple had retained for themselves something by way of personal security in case of disaster. While the *Diener der Notdurft* were investigating the case, Hutter raised the question of whether Schützinger's wife might not also be a Sapphira. The incredulous congregation at last consented to a search of the Schützinger bedroom on condition that Hutter's bed and drawers be inspected too. To the shocked surprise of the faithful, Schützinger himself proved to have stashed away several articles, including four pounds of Bernese silver coins. When Schützinger admitted his guilt before the whole congregation, there was enough indignation and chagrin to sweep Hutter into the position of chief elder or *Vorsteher* of the three federated colonies. For standing by Schützinger, Ascherham and Plener were also deposed. Each of the triumvirate of deposed elders retained portions of their respective followings.

Hutter was undaunted by the great split (*die grosse Zerspaltung*). He set out at once to implement on the ground, and no longer through deputies, his communistic plans. Convincing his followers that they were indeed God's elect apart from whom there could be no salvation at the advent of Christ, and among whom as sojourners in the world there could be expected now only suffering and hardship, he released the energies and channeled the skills of his people into the building up of an economically durable and socially cohesive organization with the capacity to colonize and missionize more vigorously and steadfastly than had ever been possible before.

For the perhaps envious Philippites and Gabrielites, communism—leaving homeland and kindred to share with fellow pilgrims what they might bring or produce—was but an exquisite form of resignation, *Gelassenheit*, an advanced expression of suffering as a way of life leading to an inner clarity and peace (*Abgeklärtheit*). With Hutter it was not the inner peace of a sectarian convent that was the goal of communal production and sharing but the discipline of spiritual warriors persevering against all obstacles until their vindication at the second advent of Christ.

Hutter's direct leadership in Moravia lasted from August 1533 until the late spring of 1535. At the Moravian diet in Znaim, which King Ferdinand attended, the magnates were forced to comply with his demand that all Anabaptists be routed from the margraviate in order to forestall a development in Moravia comparable to the disaster in Münster.

Driven from their homes by the often reluctant nobles, the Hutterites, Philippites, Gabrielites, and all the other Anabaptists who had sought asylum in Moravia spent Easter in the fields and forests.

At Whitsuntide, Hutter yielded to the entreaties of his followers to seek personal safety in the familiar recesses of the Tyrol and from there to continue to guide them. Forty guilders had been placed on his head by Ferdinand. While his people were wandering about without shelter, Hutter wrote his vehement *Remonstrance* to the governor of Moravia, in which he movingly reassured the lords of the peaceful intentions of the brethren and pleaded for a plot of the God-created earth where they might sojourn. And then he rebuked the lords for yielding "to that horrible tyrant and enemy of divine truth, Ferdinand."[5]

Back in the Tyrol, Hutter wrote another letter, referring to the "horrible, raging dragon [who] has opened his craw and jaws . . . to swallow the woman clothed with the sun, who is the bride and spouse of our Lord Jesus Christ" (Rev. 12:1).[6]

More significant than this identification of the persecuted remnant with the woman of the wilderness and of the persecutor with Satan or Antichrist in the apocalyptic language of the seer of The Revelation was Hutter's assurance that he himself was an apostle of the latter days. In two of his letters he even used the Pauline gesture: "With my own hand have I written this." The letter just quoted, his last to the Moravians, opens with the following assimilation of the apostolic epistolary style which must be quoted in full to convey Hutter's own sense of mission and the Hutterite conception that they were themselves the righteous remnant:

Jacob, servant of God and apostle of Jesus Christ and servant of all

[5] Letter IV; Fischer, *op. cit.,* 26 ff.
[6] Letter VIII; *ibid.,* 62 f.

His elect saints everywhere far and wide in the land of Moravia, called [to this office] in the powerful grace and unutterable mercy of God, elected and made worthy thereof by His grace and groundless mercy without any merit of mine own but rather solely by reason of His overwhelming faithfulness and magnanimity, who has esteemed me faithful and made me worthy as His servant of the eternal and new covenant, which God first established and made with Abraham and his seed forever, and has given and entrusted to me His divine, eternal Word, [placing it] in my heart and on my lips along with the heavenly riches of His divinity and His Holy Spirit which lie [otherwise] hidden above in the tabernacle of the eternal and invisible God in heaven, who is there as Lord and King of kings and who has blessed me with His eternal and heavenly blessing and has through me quickened and activated His divine and eternal Word and His will in letting me proclaim it, giving testimony thereto in the sharing and co-operation of the Holy Spirit, evidenced in powerful miracles and signs [in me] whom He has established as watchman, shepherd, and guardian over His holy people, over His elect, holy, Christian congregation, which is the bride and spouse, the beloved and gracious partner of our dear Lord Jesus Christ—purchased, purified, and washed through His precious blood . . . to [you] the called and chosen saints, the fighters and witnesses of God and of our dear Lord Jesus Christ, to [you] my most beloved brethren and sisters and to [you] my longed-for and elect dear little children whom I have borne and planted through God's Word, grace, and gift from on high . . . from the bottom (*Abgrund*) of my heart I wish for you grace, peace, and eternal life and eternal mercy from Almighty God and great love and faith, victory, strength, and the overcoming of the world.[7]

Perhaps in no other passage from the literature of the Radical Reformation can one come so close to the overwhelming sense of divine election and vocation in the face of all principalities and powers as in Hutter's final apostolic salutation.

In the main body of this letter and the others there is no assuagement of the suffering. The burden, rather, of this last epistle and all the others is that suffering is the expected lot of all who truly follow Christ, alike the prophets who were stoned before him and the apostles who have been martyred after him. The assurance of ultimate vindication after "battles and struggles," preceding and accompanying Christ's imminent return on clouds of glory from heaven, is that "pillar of fire" within, which is faith in Christ and a burning resolution to persevere until the glorious end.

Hutter himself, sustained by convictions, was steadfast to the end. In the night of 19 November 1535 he and his wife were captured in the house of a former sexton in Klausen, the very

[7] Full English text, R. Friedmann, *Hutterite Studies* (Goshen, 1961), 203–213.

town in which Blaurock had been martyred. The tremendous value of the testimony of the long-hunted heresiarch prompted the authorities to transfer him under reinforced guard to Innsbruck, while his wife was held for a hearing before the local magistrates.

Between repeated hearings with the application of torture and discussions with a series of Catholic clerics, Hutter remained obdurate in his refusal to yield the names of his associates or to discuss the manner of conducting his mission. He seems to have been less interested in particularizing the articles of his faith than other Anabaptist prisoners, because he was as certain that he was dealing with a minion of Satan as were his interrogators. In fact, they became so vexed by his claim to have the sole truth of the gospel that, to exorcise the devil from him, as they said, they resorted to the unusual torture of placing him bound and gagged in freezing water and then after he was partly frozen placing him in a warm room where they poured brandy on his lacerated flesh and set it aflame. Though there was a consensus among the local magistrates that for fear of popular sympathy he should be beheaded in secret, Ferdinand personally intervened to insist upon a public burning 25 February 1536.

2. FROM THE DEATH OF HUTTER IN 1536 TO THE "ACCOUNT" OF PETER RIEDEMANN IN 1540

After Jacob Hutter left Moravia, he was succeeded in Auspitz by John Amon, a strong and inspiring leader. Amon, a cloth weaver by trade, had come from Bavaria. He was among some eighty persons who left Böhmisch-Kromau in 1529 to settle in Austerlitz. He worked under Jacob Hutter's direction in the Tyrol from 1530 to 1534, when the persecutions there were at their height. After the fearful times which Hutter describes in his *Remonstrance*, Amon rallied the stricken Hutterite people from the forests and fields, and on Easter, 1536, after exactly a year of tribulation and homelessness, they celebrated their semiannual Lord's Supper in a forest. Then the elders deliberated on their problems, and decided to divide themselves into small groups of six or eight, and severally to find work and a place to stay. In this they were soon successful, as the nobles were eager to have them back, once the insistent demands of Ferdinand had abated. Within a decade of their expulsion from Auspitz and elsewhere they were able to establish many new communities.

The years after 1536 are obscure. The Moravian nobles outwardly complied with King Ferdinand's demands, and yet they must have secretly obeyed their own hearts and made places for the returning Brethren, for in the next decade we hear less of persecution. In 1537, Ulrich Stadler returned from a brief experiment in Poland, and together with former Auspitz and Austerlitz brethren, began to rebuild the desolated sites at Austerlitz.

During Amon's administration, missionaries (*Sendboten*) were sent to many places in Europe, with a view to systematic coverage. Four fifths of these missionaries died as martyrs. Amon's extant writings include, besides several hymns, an epistle of comfort to brethren enslaved in Admiral Andrea Doria's galleys.

Among the most prominent and more fortunate of the Hutterite missionaries was Peter Riedemann, an outstanding doctrinal writer, called by some the second founder of the brotherhood. Born in 1506 in the town of Hirschberg in Silesia, he was a cobbler by trade. We first encounter him in 1529 in Gmunden, imprisoned for his Anabaptist faith. He had apparently joined the brethren in Upper Austria, where John Hut and Wolfgang Brandhuber had been preaching. He was ordained a servant of the Word in 1529. During his three years' imprisonment in Gmunden he wrote a major doctrinal work, his first *Rechenschaft*,[8] a deeply spiritual work that placed him doctrinally close to his contemporary brethren Leonard Schiemer and John Schlaffer (Ch. 7.5). Even though at this time he was not yet a Hutterite, the Hutterites faithfully preserved this early *Account* in numerous manuscript codices. Besides its main part, it also contains two separate pieces of great beauty: "How to Build the House of God" and "Concerning the Seven Pillars of This House" (Prov. 9:1).[9]

In 1532, Riedemann escaped from the prison and went to work first with the Anabaptists in Linz, but soon thereafter went to Moravia to join the Hutterite brotherhood, then still in its formative years. About this time he married, and six beautiful letters that he wrote to his wife have been preserved.[10] In 1533 he was sent as a missionary to Franconia, where he was again imprisoned (1533–1537). In 1537 he was released on his promise not to preach further in Nuremberg, and he returned to Moravia, again by way of Upper Austria, where he met remnants of the Philippite Brethren.

[8] The completed title reads *Rechenschaft unseres Glaubens geschrieben zu Gmunden im Land ob der Enns im Gefängnis*. This work, which is not to be confused with the later Confession (*Rechenschaft:* below, n. 14) written in Hesse, awaits publication.

[9] *ME*, IV, 326.

[10] *ME*, III, 327.

This group stemmed from the Philippite mission before 1535, and now, as a result of Plener's flight from Moravia, was isolated and cut off from the original source of spiritual direction. Riedemann willingly shepherded them. He later wrote a number of epistles to the Philippites in Linz, Steyr, and Gmunden.

In 1535 the Hutterite brethren sent him on a mission to Hesse, in an attempt to straighten out John Bott, Hessian friend of Melchior Rinck (Ch. 17.1), who had joined the Hutterites for a time, but had later been expelled for denying the existence of angels and devils, and was now issuing harmful propaganda in Hesse. Riedemann returned to Moravia just after the arrest of a number of brethren at Steinabrunn (Lower Austria), to whom he wrote several letters of comfort in their imprisonment. Two months later he set out again, visiting all the groups he could in the Austrias, the Tyrol, Swabia, and Württemberg on the way back to Hesse. He induced many to migrate to Moravia. Some of these emigrants were captured, and Riedemann wrote letters of comfort to them.

Soon he himself was captured in Hesse, probably in February 1540. He was at first chained and kept in a dark dungeon in Marburg. In spite of all imperial edicts, Landgrave Philip consistently refused to execute Anabaptists for their faith (Ch. 17.1). In keeping with this reluctance to persecute on religious grounds, Riedemann's confinement was soon eased. He was transferred to the castle at Wolkersdorf, and kept in the castle. It was here that he wrote in 1540 his great doctrinal work, the *Account* (*Rechenschaft*), taking his title from I Peter 3:15: "Always be prepared to make a defense to any one who calls you to account for the hope that is in you." This second *Rechenschaft* is a consciously Hutterite document.[11] Riedemann was prompted to write it in the hope that the landgrave, who had never interrogated him personally, might "at least know why he is keeping us imprisoned."[12] Although the work of only one man, the *Account* was quickly accepted by the Hutterites as a definitive statement of their faith, and was later to be submitted as such by them to the lords of Moravia in 1545.[13]

The *Account* is divided into two parts, a longer one on the twelve essentials of faith, and a shorter section of seven special

[11] It was contemporaneously better known to the outside world than the *Article Book* of 1547 (and 1577) because it is one of the few printed Hutterite writings (1565).
[12] Epistle 21, of 1540/1541, sent to John Amon and Leonard Lanzenstiel, *ME*, IV, 260.
[13] *Ibid.*

meditations. The confessional part is based on the Apostles' Creed, but does not follow it systematically, nor does it correspond exactly to the Twelve Articles (which Hubmaier wrote in Zurich and had printed in Nicolsburg, Ch. 9.2.a). The *Account* goes on to discuss faith, doctrine, the Creation, original sin, law and gospel, baptism, the ministry, the Lord's Supper, the community of goods, marriage, governmental authority, whether rulers can be Christians (they can, but only if they will divest themselves of their worldly glory), warfare, taxation, the manner of worship, the ban, and the whole life, walk, dress, and adornment of Christians. Little emphasis is placed on original sin, none at all on justification by faith, but rather on the Spirit of Christ working in the regenerate.

Riedemann emphasizes disobedience as the source of sin, and sanctification of life as the proof of inner rebirth and obedience. There is but one reference to Lutherans, who, "if they say that Christ is their righteousness while continuing to live in all abomination and lasciviousness, draw near to God with the mouth while the heart is far from him." He passionately refutes the charge that the Brethren teach works righteousness, "for we know that all our work, insofar as it is *our* work, is naught but sin and unrighteousness; but insofar as it is of Christ and done by Christ in us, so far is it truth—just and good, loved of God and well-pleasing to him."[14] Riedemann uses traditional language to describe the atonement,[15] placing, however, the emphasis upon the personal experience of being "grafted into Christ,"[16] and thereby becoming "the children of his covenant."[17]

The *Account* gives a good idea of Riedemann's view of the church: "We also are the children [of the covenant of freedom] if we let ourselves be sealed by it and submit and surrender ourselves to its working."[18] "The Church of Christ is the basis and ground of truth, a lantern of righteousness, in which the light of grace is borne and held before the whole world . . . that men may also see and know the way of life."[19] The church for Riedemann is not only passively the congregation of the saints but it also has a regenerative assignment in the world. To discharge this function, the church must be preserved free from all spots and

[14] *Account of our Religion, Doctrine, and Faith Given by Peter Rideman of the Brothers Whom Men Call Hutterians,* translated by Kathleen Hasenberg (London, 1950), 35 ff.
[15] *Ibid.,* 34 ff.
[16] *Ibid.,* 61.
[17] *Ibid.,* 63.
[18] *Ibid.,* 68.
[19] *Ibid.,* 39.

wrinkles, which means the use of the ban for the exclusion of backsliders.[20]

Some of Riedemann's ideas come from Hubmaier, including specifically the points in refutation of infant baptism. Denck, Hut, and Stadler contributed to his thought, but since the *Account* was written in prison without access to works and references, it is unwarranted to deny Riedemann a high degree of originality and literary skill in its composition. His chief source was, of course, the Bible, to which over eighteen hundred references are made. Its moving synthesis of Scriptural phrasings commended the *Account* in the eyes of the Brethren.

The Philippites, whom Riedemann had befriended, produced during their imprisonment in Passau, at about the same time he was composing his *Account* in a Hessian prison, fifty-one hymns which have become the nucleus of the *Ausbund,* the oldest Anabaptist hymnbook. It is still used today by the Amish Mennonites of North America.[21] Besides the Philippite core, there were several hymns written by Felix Mantz, Michael Sattler, and John Hut. The hymns besing the suffering church in a pitiless world, enhearten the pilgrims, and look forward to martyrdom as the fate of sincere Christians everywhere.

The death of Ulrich Stadler in 1540 and of John Amon in Schäkowitz two years later left the Hutterites without a leader. They naturally turned to Riedemann, who was still a "prisoner" in Hesse. Although his confinement was so mild that escape would have been easy, he was reluctant to violate the friendship and trust of his lenient jailers. The story of his eventual decision to do so, of his return to Moravia, and of the history of the Hutterites after 1540 will be told in Ch. 26.1.

3. Theology and Institutions of Hutterite Communism

At this point it is appropriate to turn our attention to the idea for which early Anabaptists in Canton Zurich had been reproached, which the Münsterites under Rothmann and John Beukels of Leiden had built into their abortive new Jerusalem, and which now Jacob Hutter, in a saner, quieter, and lasting way had made the distinguishing mark of Moravian Anabaptism, namely, Christian communism, the sharing of goods and production. We have already noted the earliest communistic development in Moravia (Ch. 9.2.d), based partly on the necessity of mutual aid, partly on the pattern of Acts 2:44. It remains to discuss the

[20] *Ibid.,* 131 f.
[21] First printed in 1564.

peculiar features of the Hutterite communism of production and the theology and source of the idea.

The simple sharing of goods must be distinguished from the programmatic communism of production which we encounter in Hutter and his followers. Through the ages there have been repeated attempts to assert the communistic principle, based in some cases on an ascetic contempt for the world (the monks) or else on a very practical understanding of the Dominical injunction to sell all and give to the poor (the Waldensians). Communism was, of course, practiced by all the monastic orders with their vow of poverty. But personal poverty was ever and again vitiated by corporate wealth. It remained for the original (and later the Spiritual) Franciscan friars to go farther than communism of production and to seek to hold down production, in order to achieve not merely a common life but a common poverty. When the Spirituals, at the close of the thirteenth and beginning of the fourteenth centuries, tried to assert that, like Adam in Paradise, neither Jesus nor the apostles had owned anything, Pope John XXII condemned this teaching as heretical. Significantly, a copy of the Postil on the Apocalypse, by one of the condemned Spiritual Franciscans, Petrus Olivi (d. 1298), survives among the Hutterite codices.[22] We have also seen how pacifistic communism was endemic in Bohemian and Moravian sectarianism throughout the fifteenth century (Ch. 9.1).

The majority of the monks and even the friars, although they shared a common life and a common goal, were religious individualists, each man working for his own salvation. The Hutterite coenobites, besides being a covenantal sect of wedded couples with their progeny, claimed to be the true church, i.e., the community of redemption, outside of whose fellowship (*Gemeinde*) there could be no salvation. The Hutterites were more than married coenobites. They were a household (*Haushaben*) of faith. Theirs was a communism of love and production, marked by a readiness to suffer in *Gelassenheit* and by hope in ultimate vindication.[23]

At some earlier stage in the development of their communal theology, they must have become acquainted with a number of communitarian efforts in ancient church history besides the communism of the church in Jerusalem recorded in The Acts. Their principal sources were no doubt Sebastian Franck's *Chronica,* Eusebius' *Ecclesiastical History,* and the writings of Hubmaier against Zwingli.

They came in due course to adopt as spiritual ancestors the

[22] *ME,* IV, 1113.
[23] Robert Friedmann, "Christian Communism," *ARG,* XLVI (1955), 203.

Therapeutae described favorably by Philo of Alexandria in his *On the Contemplative Life* and excerpted by Eusebius as though descriptive of early ascetic Christians.[24] The Hutterites could not know, as do we, that the Therapeutae were none other than the Essenes, the Egyptian counterpart of the Qumrân community. The Hutterites also found substantiation for their communism in the Pseudo-Clementine Epistle IV, allegedly written by Peter's successor in Rome, Clement, to James the Lord's brother and first bishop of Jerusalem.

This spurious letter belongs to the Pseudo-Clementine cycle of literature which developed in Ebionite, anti-Pauline circles. Neo-Pythagorean and Stoic ideas of a golden age were here conflated with the memory of a primitive communism in the early church of Jerusalem. In the ninth century the Clementine letters were incorporated into the Pseudo-Isidorean Decretals, long an authoritative collection of canon law. Pseudo-Isidore was no doubt confident that in this case he had at his disposal authentic decretals of the apostolic see. In 1526, Clement's Epistle was separately published by John Sichard in Basel as a valuable testimony to apostolic institutions. Franck excerpted the letter in his *Chronica* of 1531. It is quite probably from Franck that a later Hutterite article quotes "Clement," supposedly writing in A.D. 92, as follows:

A common life is necessary for all, especially for such as fight, blameless, for God and desire to follow the life of the apostles and their disciples; for truly in this world things should be held in common by all men, but through acquired wickedness, one saith: This is mine, and another: That is mine, and thus a division takes place among men—but not out of the counsel of God. Therefore hath the wisest of the Greeks (Pythagoras) said and recognized: Just as the sunlight cannot be divided, and the air—even so should one have all other things common in this life, and not divide them.[25]

---

[24] Eusebius, *Ecclesiastical History*, II, xvii. The reference to the Therapeutae is in a Hutterite document of a date beyond the limits of the present section, but there can be no doubt that the Hutterites knew this and the following material to be adduced, well before 1577, the date of *The Great Article Book*, article iii of which is translated and introduced by Kathleen Hasenberg and Robert Friedmann respectively, "A Notable Hutterite Document Concerning True Surrender and Christian Community of Goods," *MQR*, XXXI (1957), 22–61, especially in item 147. A fuller study of *The Great Article Book* was presented by Robert Friedmann in "Eine dogmatische Hauptschrift," *ARG*, XXVIII (1931), 80–111, 207–240; XXIX (1932), 1–17.

[25] Hasenberg and Friedmann, "A Notable Hutterite Document," *loc. cit.*, 61. The wording in Franck and the Hutterite article differ. Friedmann puts the two versions in parallel columns in "Hauptschrift," 235. It is of interest that it was the Hutterite version that indicates in the margin that the wise Greek was Pythagoras.

The same section goes on to quote Augustine (Epistle XLVIII), Chrysostom, and *Theologia Germanica* to the same effect.

It would be a mistake to infer from all this that Hutterite (or Münsterite) communism derived directly from a third-century forgery. The communitarian impulse was in fact present from the beginning of Anabaptism in 1525 and had found complete implementation in Moravia under Wiedemann in 1529 well before the publication of Franck's *Chronica* and among the Unity of the Brethren sixty years before that; but once communism was established, the Hutterites eagerly extended their ancient pedigree and with considerable cunning in fact identified a large number of surprisingly communitarian passages and allusions in the whole of the New Testament and Old Testament in substantiation of their claim to represent the faithful *Gemeinde,* the community of God's elect.[26]

The Hutterites believed that God from the beginning had commanded the communitarian way of life, in which all of man's activities could be considered sacred. In the Epistles of Hutter and Stadler, and in the *Account* of Riedemann, and the articles of the later Hutterites, one can distinguish a fourfold motivation in Hutterite communism.

First, there was the eschatological, paradisic interpretation of the community as the true church, driven into the wilderness (Rev. 12:6), which by spiritual diligence and self-discipline, could be converted into a garden. The church is thus a provisional paradise in which, writes Ulrich Stadler, c. 1537, there is no *his, mine, thine:*

The children of God should group themselves and hold together here in misery after they have been driven out. . . .

In this time a place has been given to the bride of the Lamb in which to dwell amid the wasteland of this world, there to put on the beautiful bright linen garment and thus to await the Lord until he leads her after him here in tribulation and afterward receives her with eternal joy. The time is now. . . . The Roman Church . . . spews out all the children of God and only drives them into the wilderness. . . . We are never for ourselves but for the Lord. We have in truth nothing for ourselves but of the Lord. We have in truth nothing of our own, but rather all gifts in common, be they temporal or spiritual. . . . So judge all ordinances according to propriety and opportunity for the good of the saints and take hold with strength and bring it to pass that property, that is, *his, mine, thine,* will not be dis-

[26] Most of the items preceding the reference to Clement are in fact careful analyses of Biblical texts susceptible of a communitarian interpretation against detractors of the Hutterites, especially among the Lutherans.

closed in the house of the Lord, but rather equal love, equal care and distribution, and true community in all the goods of the Father according to his will.[27]

Secondly, there was the motive of brotherly love, the strong longing for sharing, togetherness, and unity, even as with the Father and the Son. Riedemann put it this way, on the basis of John, ch. 17, and related texts:

Community, however, is naught else than that those who have fellowship have all things in common together, none having aught for himself, but each having all things with the others, even as the Father hath nothing for himself, but all that he hath he hath with the Son, and again, the Son hath nothing for himself, but all that he hath, he hath with the Father and all who have fellowship with him.

Thus all those who have fellowship with him likewise have nothing for themselves, but have all things with their Master and with all those who have fellowship with them, that they might be one in the Son as the Son is in the Father. It is called the communion of saints because they have fellowship in holy things, yea, in those things whereby they are sanctified, that is in the Father and the Son, who himself sanctifieth them with all that he hath given them. Thus everything serveth to the betterment and building up of one's neighbour and to the praise and glory of God the Father.[28]

The true imitation of Christ was attained through brotherly love in the overcoming of selfishness. Without giving up private property, the Hutterites argued, such a unity could not be achieved. The community was all-important. The Hutterites' *Gemeinschaft* had the double connotation of fellowship and community of goods. *Gemeinde* meant both the congregation and the community or commonwealth.

Thirdly, there was the mystical principle of *Gelassenheit*, resignation, which could be variously understood as "surrender," "yielding to God," or even as "conquest of self." "Not hard the word of God would be / If from self-interest men were free."[29] Ulrich Stadler regarded the vexations and squalor of living closely together as the best test of resignation.

Fourthly, there was full and absolute obedience toward God and the eldership, for in the community, outside of which there could be no salvation, was embodied the whole will of God. When all selfish desires had been destroyed in *Gelassenheit*, God's posi-

[27] *Cherished Instructions on Sin, Excommunication, and the Community of Goods, SAW*, 280 ff.

[28] Riedemann, *Account, loc. cit.,* 43. In the last paragraph I have altered the translation from "community" to "communion."

[29] *The Great Article Book*, article iii, *loc. cit.,* 34.

tive commandments and those of the church could be obeyed as one.[30] Obedience became the means to freedom in Christ, just as it was for the monks. Living co-operatively was the Hutterite alternative to the "holy poverty" of the Franciscans. There was a clarity of perception about their communism, a conviction that it involved not only surrender but in the end real fulfillment:

Now, because what is temporal doth not belong to us, but is foreign to our true nature, the law commandeth that none covet strange possessions, that is, set his heart upon and cleave to that which is temporal and alien. Therefore, whosoever will cleave to Christ and follow him must forsake the taking of created things and property, as he himself also saith [Luke 14:33]: "Whosoever forsaketh not all that he hath cannot be my disciple." For if a man is to be renewed again into the likeness of God, he must put off all that leadeth him from him—that is, the grasping and drawing to himself of created things—for he cannot otherwise attain God's likeness.[31]

In evangelical communism, man is freed from this world and from self-love and thus is enabled to realize his true nature.

[30] Stadler, *Cherished Instructions, SAW*, 284.
[31] Riedemann, *Account, loc. cit.*, 89.

CHAPTER 17

ANABAPTISM IN MIDDLE GERMANY, 1527–1538

Our study of the interweaving strands of radical thought and action in the Reformation Era has carried us around the margins of the Empire from Switzerland and South Germany to the Austrias and Moravia; from Alsace to the Netherlands along the Hanseatic Coast to Poland and back to Moravia. We have overlooked thus far the development at the hub since we were last in central Germany in the course of the Peasants' War. We must therefore drop back in our narrative to carry forward the account of Anabaptism in Middle Germany.

The specific territories under consideration are, from west to east, the landgraviate of Hesse, then a solid cluster of four ecclesiastical territories, notably Fulda and Würzburg, then the two Saxonies. The rulers of Ducal Saxony (roughly the equivalent of late medieval Thuringia) and Electoral Saxony, the one Catholic and the other Lutheran, were throughout the whole period under discussion in vigorous opposition to the lenient landgrave of Hesse as to the best way of coping with the sectaries or, as Luther called them indiscriminately, fanatics (*Schwärmer*).[1]

In this region thus defined there were at least three major currents of Anabaptism that swirled and eddied.[2] In eastern Hesse and Thuringia the leading figure was Melchior Rinck (Ch. 17.1). In the portions of Hesse exposed to the direct or indirect influence

---

[1] The most recent studies of Luther and Melanchthon on the Radicals are those of Karl G. Steck, *Luther und die Schwärmer* (Zurich, 1955), and John Oyer, "The Writings of Luther Against the Anabaptists," *MQR*, XXVII (1953), 100 ff., and "The Writings of Melanchthon Against the Anabaptists," *MQR*, XXVI (1952), 259–276.

[2] The main modern collection of source materials for the region is that of Günther Franz *et al.*, *Wiedertäuferakten 1527–1626*, Urkundliche Quellen zur hessischen Reformationsgeschichte, IV (Marburg, 1951). The most

of Hofmann and the Münsterites the leading figure was perhaps Peter Tasch (Ch. 17.2). The third current was made up of Hutterite emissaries and recruits, of whom Peter Riedemann (Ch. 16.2), imprisoned in Hesse, may be mentioned as the most distinguished representative. Besides these three evangelical Anabaptist currents, there came to the surface in central Germany a rather large number of sectarian vagaries and excesses. Because of the extraordinary tolerance of Philip and the consequent concentration of Anabaptist propagation in his realm, the bulk of the ensuing narrative will be centered in Hesse and the borderlands toward the two Saxonies; and a whole section (Ch. 17.3) will be devoted to the consolidation of the Hessian territorial church as the result of the great Marburg disputation with the Anabaptists in 1538.

1. PHILIP OF HESSE AND MELCHIOR RINCK: THE LEGACY OF JOHN HUT IN MIDDLE GERMANY FROM THE END OF THE PEASANTS' WAR TO THE FALL OF MÜNSTER

Landgrave Philip I of Hesse (1504–1567) began in 1518 his rule of the varied dominions of Hesse at the age of fourteen. A decisive military leader and tactician, Philip had been primarily responsible for bringing to a close the Franconian-Thuringian phase of the Peasants' War at Frankenhausen (Ch. 4.2.c) in 1525. In 1526 he introduced the Reformation at a combined diet and synod gathered in Homberg. He had been reluctant to call a territorial diet before this because his nobles had strong ties with the Ernestine house of Electoral Saxony, while he himself stood in closer relationship to the Albertine branch in Ducal Saxony. The moment Philip came forward to espouse the Reformation, he had a religious reason to favor the Ernestine Saxons protecting Luther and thus a new basis for co-operation with the Hessian nobility in other matters that might come before the diet.

Philip's chief divine at the synod-diet was Francis Lambert of

recent comprehensive studies with the literature are by Ruth Weiss, "Die Herkunft der osthessischen Täufer," *ARG*, L (1959), 1–16; 182–199; and John Oyer, "Anabaptism in Central Germany," *MQR*, XXXIV (1960), 219 –248; "Faith and Life," *ibid.*, XXXV (1961), 5–17. The major earlier interpretations for this region are those of Paul Wappler, *Die Stellung Kursachsens und des Landgrafen Philipp von Hessen zur Täuferbewegung* (Münster, 1910) and *Die Täuferbewegung in Thüringen* (Jena, 1913), both with considerable documentation. For the influence of Jacob Strauss in this region and his help in securing for Rinck his pastorate at Eckartshausen, see Joachim Rogge, *Der Beitrag des Jacob Strauss zur frühen Reformationsgeschichte* (Berlin, 1957).

Avignon (c. 1487–1530).[3] Son of a papal official, Lambert had entered the Observant branch of the Franciscan order at the age of fifteen. A good preacher, he was marked for promotion by his superiors, but provoked considerable enmity among his fellow friars. He was caught up in the reform current which in Italy brought forth the Capuchins (Ch. 1.3.b). For a while he considered joining the stricter Carthusians. On a preaching tour, he passed through the Swiss Confederation to Zurich, where, still in his cowl, he engaged in conversations with Zwingli in 1522 and preached in defense of the invocation of Mary and the saints. A bitter disputation with Zwingli followed in the canons' salon of the Great Minster. From Zurich he went on to Basel, where he was inwardly won over. He then visited Wittenberg, met Luther, and married. From Wittenberg he went as a reformer to Metz, then to Strassburg, where he came to know Jacob Sturm, who recommended him to Philip for the reformation of the church in Hesse.

The result of Lambert's application to the new assignment was Philip's calling in 1526 the synod in Homberg, which was at once the first territorial diet of Philip's regime and an emergency provincial synod that only on an *ad hoc* basis fulfilled Lambert's ideal of representation by congregations. The legal basis of the Homberg reforming synod-diet was the decision of the imperial diet of Speyer earlier in the year to tolerate territorial changes pending a general council. The theological, or more specifically the ecclesiological, basis of the synod-diet was the congregationalist pattern suggested by Luther as a "third form" of the church in his introduction to *Deutsche Messe und Ordnung des Gottesdiensts* of 1526. Influenced by Schwenckfeld, Luther had outlined the *ecclesiola*: "those who mean to be Christians in earnest," centered about the Word of God and practicing discipline according to the rule of Matt., ch. 18.[4] To the synod-diet, Lambert presented his own *Paradoxa*. Despite opposition from the local Franciscan superior, the estates of Hesse joined the Reformation.

In the very year that Philip introduced the Reformation into his territory, 1526, Luther had also written:

God has established two kinds of rule among men, namely, the spiritual, through the Word and without the sword, that men might become pious and just . . . and the handling of such righteousness he has entrusted to preachers; the other is worldly rule, by the sword, to

[3] Roy L. Winters, *Francis Lambert of Avignon* (Philadelphia, 1938); Gerhard Müller, *Franz von Lambert von Avignon und die Reformation in Hessen* (Marburg, 1958).
[4] John O. Evjen, "Luther's Ideas Concerning Polity," *Lutheran Church Review*, XIV (1926), 207 ff. On Schwenckfeld and a third form, Pietz, Ch. 31, n. 1.

the end that all those who do not desire to become pious and just through the Word, will nevertheless be forced by the worldly rule to be pious and just before the world.[5]

Here and elsewhere Luther had programmatically eliminated all forms of coercion apart from that of the magistrate. This meant in Hesse, for example, the disappearance of the several bishops and archbishops who had hitherto exercised jurisdiction in the territory, of monastic chapters, and eventually of noble patrons and their right of presentation. This meant the repudiation of canon law and all permanent canonical or legal structures interposed between the vocational righteousness of the territorial prince and the forensic righteousness of his Christian subjects saved by faith alone. Thus Luther was fundamentally impatient with all efforts to substitute for the law and discipline of the Old Church any comparable organs that might temporarily be formed to take their place, including the congregational and synodal provisions urged by Lambert, to say nothing of the congregationally administered ban as urged by the Anabaptists. To Lambert's great disappointment Luther expressly repudiated the Homberg ideal which Lambert had thought he had faithfully transcribed from Luther's own works.

The influence, however, of Lambert and the Homberg congregationally oriented church order idealized in *Reformatio Ecclesiarum Hassiae* of 1526 persisted in Philip's dominions despite Luther's disparagement of the efforts. Something too of Lambert's legacy is apparent in the unusual treatment accorded the proponents of radical congregationalism, namely, the Anabaptists, throughout the reign of Philip.

The conflicts attendant upon the setting up in Hesse of a model evangelical territory as a fragment of the medieval *corpus christianum* liberated from its canon law makes the early history of the Hessian Reformation especially significant,[6] as also the protracted conflict with the Anabaptists, who with their separatist Christian organization and discipline were soon to swarm within the domain of the tolerant landgrave.

In 1527, Philip founded the first Protestant university at his principal seat, Marburg. Lambert became the professor of theology and henceforth, because of his failure to master German, was largely confined to the classroom and the council chamber. He soon died of the plague (1530).

Philip, who strove valiantly in 1529 to be the patron of irenic unity among the Magisterial Protestants in convening the Mar-

[5] *Ob Kriegsleute auch in seligem Stande sein können, WA, XIX, 629.*
[6] Admirably and succinctly recounted and analyzed by W. Sohm, *Territorium und Reformation in der hessischen Geschichte, 1526–1555* (Marburg, 1915).

burg colloquy, may also with respect to the Radical Reformation be entitled "the Magnanimous." He was one of the few Protestant princes to recognize the need for interchanges among all evangelical groups, including the Anabaptists and the Spiritualists.[7] Philip looked upon Anabaptism as an error in faith; but, since he also held that true faith was a gift of God, he was indisposed to punish error with undue severity as though it were the fault of the misled adherent. He could not always be sure of his own faith. Moreover, he noted the courage and the upright lives of the bulk of the Anabaptists, and, as chief magistrate under God, he knew that he would be held to a final accounting for the way he treated his Christian subjects.

Philip's first important encounter with Anabaptism was in the person of Melchior Rinck, former pastor at Eckhardtshausen, former follower of Müntzer in the Peasants' War (Ch. 4.2.d). In conjunction with John Denck and Jacob Kautz, Rinck had once helped formulate the Seven Articles of Worms in 1527 (Ch. 7.3). Banished from Worms, Rinck, erudite, passionate, and irascible, evangelized in Hersfeld territory between the Hessian and the Ducal Saxon borders. By 1528 his following was so large that he made bold to request permission to preach before the parish in Hersfeld. It was as a result of his persistence and the resistance of the local Lutheran pastor, Balthasar Raidt, that the problem came to Philip's personal attention, and Rinck was summoned for an interview at the landgrave's hunting lodge in Friedewald. Rinck held fervently to his convictions, and Philip judged the case worthy of the attention of his university theologians.

Accordingly, a cross-examination was conducted by the new theological faculty at Marburg in August 1528.[8] For the occasion, Rinck prepared a statement of faith in five articles. His Hersfeld antagonist, Raidt, prepared a set of twelve charges. The most heated debate arose over Raidt's charge that Rinck had openly declared that an infant at baptism received not Christ but the devil. Since no agreement could be reached as to the validity of the charges, Rinck was simply banished. Elector John (1525–1532), a much less temperate prince than Philip, was angered at Hessian dalliance with heresy, blasphemy, and sedition.

Soon thereafter Rinck was seized on Hessian soil. This time Philip put him in prison at Haina. From April 1529 to May 1531, he disputed with visitors who came to change his views, com-

---

[7] For Philip's policy of toleration, see A. Heidenhain, *Die Unionspolitik Landgraf Philipps von Hessen, 1557–1562* (Halle, 1890), and especially Franklin Littell, *Landgraf Philip und die Toleranz* (Bad Neuheim, 1957).

[8] Franz, *Wiedertäuferakten*, pp. 4–15.

municated with his followers, wrote a small piece on baptism,[9] and became involved in extended altercation with his wife and his Lutheran father-in-law, refusing to grant her a divorce.[10] When released on promising not to re-enter either Hesse or Electoral Saxony, he almost at once returned to his old haunts as evangelist. It was his conviction that it was contrary to God's dominion over all the world and his will for his children to banish any child of God from any territory or for a child of God permanently to accept such a usurpation.[11] In November 1531, Rinck was seized with eleven others.

By this time the divines and magistrates of Electoral Saxony were exacerbated by Philip's policy. Back in 1530, Justus Menius, Lutheran superintendent at Eisenach, for example, had pointedly dedicated to Philip a booklet on the Anabaptist danger with a preface by Luther: *Der Wiedertäufer Lehre und Geheimnis aus heiliger Schrift widerlegt* in which Menius justified the elector's execution of six Anabaptists who refused to recant at Gotha. He traced their origin to Müntzer and threatened personally to stone one of the recalcitrants publicly.[12]

The divergent policies of the two Protestant states were notably in conflict in certain areas jointly administered as a condominium or protectorate, such as the Hausbreitenbach district and Mühlhausen. Here the contradictory policies of repression and suasion succeeding each other in the alternations of the local administration of justice caused disorder, encouraged defiance, and emboldened the sectarian denizens in their claim that, after all, so-called Christian government was only a matter of human convention and not of divine law. As Rinck himself once declared in addressing a Saxon magistrate, the prince might indeed repress Christians and even kill them for reasons of state but he had no right to claim that he was thus discharging a Christian duty.

The specific case of the rearrested Rinck and therewith the fundamental problem of the divergent policies of Hesse and Electoral Saxony came before the diet of the Smalcald League early in December 1531. The Saxons demanded the death penalty in accordance with the mandate of Speyer (Ch. 10.1), but the Hessians, like the Smalcald Swabians in the humane Memmingen Resolutions of the same year (Ch. 8.3), argued with the support of the irenic Marburg theologians, Simon Goldenhauer and Adam

---

[9] Preserved in a manuscript codex of the Marpeck circle; translated by J. C. Wenger, *MQR*, XXI (1947), 282–284.
[10] Oyer, "Central Germany," 233.
[11] Wappler, *Thüringen*, 335; Oyer, "Central Germany," 237.
[12] Oyer, "Central Germany," 228, n. 26.

Kraft, that it was the open sin and the hypocrisy found in the established churches which made the Anabaptists persevere in their separation. Philip said that if they could not be persuaded from their belief, they should suffer no more than having "their hearth fire extinguished," that is, being forced to migrate.[13]

The case of Rinck, of course, was by now notorious; and on 3 January 1532, Philip informed John that Rinck had been sentenced to life imprisonment. He was to be visited several times by state-church divines and converted separatists with a view to persuading him; but Rinck persisted in his theological separatism, dying after more than a dozen years of confinement.

At this point we may introduce a lesser figure, Fritz Erbe, who was to endure imprisonment for eighteen years. Arrested in October 1531 in a raid in the Hausbreitenbach district, Erbe recanted. He had never been as insistent on believers' baptism as most converts. When rearrested in 1532, however, he remained steadfast. After a long time in the tower of the Eisenach town wall and much effort to persuade him of his error, he was transferred to the prison in the tower of the Wartburg. As to a kind of latter-day pillar saint, devotees came to him under the cover of darkness to receive his comfort and counsel.

The version of Anabaptism professed by several of these night visitors after capture deserves notice. It appears to have been a deformation of John Hut's gospel of all creatures. In effect, Hut's conception of baptism as the initiation into lifelong suffering culminating in a final baptism in blood or fire and his correlative conception of the Lord's Supper as a mutual pledge to lay down one's life for the brethren were transformed by Erbe's sympathizers to the point where they were prepared to call suffering itself the true Lord's Supper, the true Communion. A more extreme development along this line is represented in the later deposition of three of Erbe's visitors who made bold to call the bread, even of the evangelical commemorative Supper, "the bite of Judas," and the cup, "the curse of the Whore of Babylon" (Rev. 17:6), drunken with the blood of the saints.[14]

In July 1533, when another batch of Anabaptists, most of them followers of Rinck, were seized in the condominium of Hausbreitenbach, the new elector, John Frederick, renewed the Saxon

[13] Littell, *Philip,* 33, 52. Philip's regulations toward the end of 1531 and Smalcald discussion, Franz, *Wiedertäuferakten,* Nos. 15, 18.

[14] There were two arrests and two trials, November 1537 and June 1539. Though of a later date, the depositions no doubt faithfully record an attitude in radical Hutian circles from near the beginning. These are not the only evidence of the transmutation in this region. Wappler, *Stellung,* 196–204.

appeal to Philip for exemplary execution. The landgrave refused with the words: "Our Lord will give grace, that they may be
converted." When Philip's turn came as protector of Mühlhausen,
he immediately sent pastor Raidt, by now a specialist in reconversion, who succeeded in persuading all the Anabaptists imprisoned there to recant. Thereupon they were released.[15] The
large Anabaptist conventicle originally gathered in Sorga, near
Hersfeld, was raided in August. This group of prisoners, now
under John Bott, did not yield to suasion and entreaty. Philip,
however, could find nothing seditious about them except their
stubborn separatism, and they were banished in September 1533.[16]
They sought asylum in Moravia. The Hutterites considered them
tainted by Spiritualism. They continued to live apart, unprepared
to yield completely to the communal way of life, but associated
themselves with the Gabrielites and the followers of Plener (Ch.
16.1).

Besides the already mentioned Peter Riedemann, there were
many other Hutterite emissaries successfully recruiting pilgrims
for the Moravian commonwealths, the most notable being George
Zaunring (Ch. 16.1) and Christopher Gschäl.[17]

Philip's lenient and constructive policy of orderly, unvindictive
emigration, of suasion and disputation, firmed up by an occasional
life sentence for the defiantly obdurate and concurrently made
more agreeable by renewed efforts at moral reform in the state
church, had borne enough fruit to induce some of the lesser magistrates of the central German territories to emulate the landgrave
in leniency. But the increasing ugliness of the development in
Münster and the fascination it exercised over the imaginations of
separatists and restive elements of the population far and wide
put that policy to an impossible test. Philip was in correspondence
with the bishop of Münster, Francis of Waldeck, and the city
council.[18] We have already seen two of his conciliatory divines in
Münster, vainly trying to settle the dispute between the Rothmannites and the conservative Lutherans (Ch. 13.1).

Besides the distant Münsterites, Philip and the other central
German magistrates had to contend with a rather large assortment
of eccentric and even violent sectaries, several of them claiming to
be Anabaptists. We have elsewhere mentioned the libertarian
Blood Brethren in the region between Gotha and Mühlhausen
(Ch. 7.4). There was also a John Römer, former fighter under
Müntzer in the uprising of the peasants, who was subsequently

[15] Wappler, *Thüringen*, 101.
[16] *Ibid.*, 102; Franz, *Wiedertäuferakten*, No. 28.
[17] *Wiedertäuferakten*, Nos. 5, 13a, 14a.
[18] Cornelius, *op. cit.*, II, 244, *et passim*.

converted by Hut to Anabaptism. As much carried along by his socially revolutionary followers as he was leading them, Römer had resorted to force and in 1528 had undertaken an assault on the walls of Erfurt.[19] Nearby was a prophet in the abbatial territory of Fulda whose rebaptized followers, excited by mass hypnosis, experienced healings, glossolalia, contortions, and the other manifestations of a camp-meeting revival, similar to the Pentecostal outbreaks among the St. Gall Anabaptists of an earlier date (Ch. 6.2). A large and determined group of these revivalists were besieged in their fortified house for six months in 1532. When finally captured, several were beheaded.[20]

The following year in the same territory a much more aggressive group under the leadership of John Krug, John of Fulda, and Peter the Baptist pillaged, burned, raped, and murdered over a considerable terrain before they were captured. They remind one of the Batenburgers (Ch. 13.5); but unlike this berserk breed of Münsterites, the Anabaptist arsonists under John Krug still made baptism the badge of admittance to their violent gang. In fact, Krug freely acknowledged his rape of a villager who refused to accept rebaptism at his hands.[21]

After the collapse of Münster and Philip's attempt to reconvert the wretched survivors with the aid of two Hessian divines (Antonius Corvinus and Johann Kymeus), the Elector John Frederick (1532–1547), with malicious satisfaction, demanded that Philip at long last give up his fatuous policy. The Elector's adviser, Melanchthon, prepared the new, sharp mandate issued for Saxony, 10 April 1536, and also composed a refutation of certain "unchristian articles" which were to be expounded from every pulpit in Saxony on every third Sunday of the month.

Most of the central German Anabaptism discussed thus far is traceable to the apocalyptic spiritualism of John Hut. Römer, Rinck, Bott, and Erbe in various aspects of their teaching and conduct bore the permanent impress of the fiery apostle of Bavaria and Austria. Alongside this current, there flowed, as we have already remarked, the Hofmannite version of Anabaptism, to which we now turn.

2. PETER TASCH AND GEORGE SCHNABEL: THE HOFMANNITE LEGACY IN CENTRAL GERMANY AFTER 1535

On one of his evangelistic tours between Strassburg and the Netherlands, Melchior Hofmann gave expression to his intensely

[19] Wappler, *Thüringen*, 25–37; Oyer, "Central Germany," 227, n. 24.
[20] Wappler, *Thüringen*, 81–85; Oyer, "Central Germany," 241 f.
[21] Franz, *Wiedertäuferakten*, pp. 71–73.

eschatological version of Anabaptism in the presence of Landgrave Philip himself.[2] The principal Hessian Melchiorites were Peter Tasch and George Schnabel. Tasch considered the collapse of Münster as condign punishment for the deformation of Hofmann's original message. But the failure of imprisoned Hofmann's prophecy to be realized even in Strassburg also prompted Tasch and Schnabel to rethink Melchiorite theology in somewhat the same way as Menno Simons and Dietrich Philips were doing in their region. Tasch continued to use Hofmann's conception of a spiritual temple, which he now thought of as being mysteriously built up throughout Christendom, rather than being limited to any one locality. He tacitly acknowledged earlier miscalculations about the identity of the two prophet witnesses foretold in Rev. 11:3. He retained in full Hofmann's doctrine of the celestial flesh of Christ, restated in a tract, *Von der Menschwerdung*. He wrote at least two other locally influential tracts, *Von der Taufordnung Christi* and *Vom Eid*. The fact that he was in correspondence with a circle who still practiced Münsterite polygamy would indicate that he was not only engaged in reconceiving Melchiorite theology but also actively involved in rewinning the refugees from, and partisans of, Münster for a version of Anabaptism closer to the norms of the South Germans and the Swiss Brethren.

In 1536, George Schnabel and some thirty other Anabaptists were overtaken as a conventicle at worship in an abandoned church in the Cassel district. Ten of them were imprisoned at Wolkersdorf. They were destined to play an important role in the gradual alteration and hardening of Philip's policy toward all the separatists.

He intended that their incarceration be mild to make them physically and mentally receptive to efforts at persuasion. In addition to the leniency of their incarceration, the prisoners contrived an extraordinary freedom of movement. By means of a saw they enlarged the hole through which they were fed and through which they returned like homing pigeons after a day's or even a week's evangelistic tour. Provision was made to maintain for the benign or duped custodian the semblance of continuous occupancy and compliance with the law!

Several of these prisoners had been previously banished; and it was because these irrepressible evangelists had been at work again in his territory that they had been selected for an incarceration milder than even Philip at the moment realized. It was with special reference to the Wolkersdorf prisoners that Philip in May 1536 requested the judgment of the magistrates of Strassburg and

[22] Krebs and Rott, *Elsass*, II (*QGT*, VIII), No. 407.

Ulm, the dukes of Württemberg and Brunswick-Lüneburg, and the professors of the theological faculties of Marburg and Wittenberg, with a view to drawing up comprehensive regulations for ordering the state church of Hesse and for disposing of the separatist threat.[23]

In response, the hitherto moderate chancellor of Hesse, a jurist, now came out for enhanced severity, including the death penalty for those foreign Anabaptists who should make bold to return a third time after banishment. Sharp opinions were also expressed by the two Lutheran theologians, Tilman Schnabel and Justus Winter, who again demanded the implementation of the imperial mandate. Johann Lening, however, Philip's former emissary to Münster, still upheld the older policy when he called upon "God to correct the errors in his own life and [urged his fellow divines] to admonish the Anabaptists kindly and in a friendly spirit . . . and not to make use of the sword until all other means had been tried."[24]

It was the milder counsel that prevailed. The result of the renewed consideration was to place the problem of the separatists in the larger context of establishing the doctrinal and disciplinary norms for the whole of the territorial church. This was a procedure which had been followed in the Strassburg synod of 1533 (Ch. 10.4); and before the completion of that process in Hesse, Bucer was called from Strassburg to bring to bear his great experience with synods and separatists in the work of building up the state church of Hesse. For the moment, the first result of the new efforts of the landgrave was the drawing up of the Visitation Order of 1537, which expressly recognized the legitimacy of some of the Anabaptist criticisms. The mandate accordingly insisted on the abolition of open vices among members of the state church. It sharpened, however, the previous regulation of the Anabaptists by requiring that their foreign preachers be beaten with rods, have a sign burned into their cheeks, and be threatened with death if they should ever return. Native Anabaptists were again ordered to sell all their goods and leave. For returned natives, the penalty was torture; for foreigners and natives returned a second time, the penalty was death. Philip left an opening even in this sharpest mandate: "But no Anabaptists shall be put to death, even after the sentence has been passed, without previously notifying us."[25] Moreover, if in the face of death an Anabaptist recanted, he should be taken back for further consultation and not be killed. Actually,

[23] Franz, *Wiedertäuferakten*, No. 47.
[24] *ME*, IV, 165.
[25] *Ibid.*

the severe measures of the mandate of 1537 were never put into effect. Philip never confirmed a death sentence. The Anabaptists who were imprisoned were given humane treatment. Riedemann's famous *Account of Our Religion,* it will be recalled (Ch. 16.2), was produced in one of Philip's prisons.

It was against the Visitation Order of 1537 that George Schnabel, lieutenant of Peter Tasch, wrote his booklet *Verantwortung und Widerlegung* (1538),[26] in order to clarify for his own fellow believers some eleven articles and to help the magistrates to distinguish the evangelical Anabaptists from those guilty of certain apparently quite common aberrations.

He had been town treasurer in Allendorf near Cassel before joining the movement. Schnabel, perhaps more energetically than Tasch, was determined to dissociate the peaceful, law-abiding Anabaptists, among whom he was to be numbered, from the belligerent and occasionally polygamous survivors of the Münsterite movement and also from the radically spiritualist Anabaptists like those around Fritz Erbe. A glance at his eleven articles will enable us to picture a large body of Middle German Anabaptists in the aftermath of Münster.

The booklet, incidentally, is remarkable for the large number of quotations from the Apocrypha (Tobit, Judith, III and IV Esdras, Ecclesiasticus, and Baruch). Of special interest among the arguments justifying meetings in private homes is Schnabel's appeal to the "third form" of Luther's preface to the German Mass.[27] Biblical and moral justification of secret meetings in homes, heaths, and forests constitutes one of the eleven articles. His conception of baptism, which he expressly derived in part from the Melchiorite Tasch, is richly defined as "a bath of rebirth," "a covenant of the good conscience," "a sepulture with Christ," whereby the believer is separated from any association with the children of the world, "an incorporation into the body of Christ, which is the fellowship of the saints," "a going into the wilderness or the forecourt of the service of God," "a putting on of Christ," in such a way that one "follows Christ's footsteps." Melchiorite on baptism, Schnabel was Melchiorite also in his doctrine of the celestial flesh of Christ and for the same reason:

For Christ comes not *of* the world nor from Adam's flesh and blood, but rather he comes *into* the world, for were he of the world, he could not have saved the world.[28]

[26] Franz, *Wiedertäuferakten,* No. 63, pp. 165 ff.
[27] *Ibid.,* article 9, p. 178.
[28] *Ibid.,* p. 173.

Schnabel's conception of Christ as "the true bread of heaven," who brought "his flesh from heaven," is expressly dependent upon Tasch's booklet on the incarnation. In contrast to the Servetian and Schwenckfeldian view (Ch. 11.3) and somewhat more clearly stated than with Melchior Hofmann, God the Father sent his Word to be received aurally by the Virgin.

On the related questions of magistracy, war, oath, and taxes, Schnabel appealed to the Melchiorite exegetical principle of the cloven hoof[29] (Ch. 32.1.c) and again expressly to the larger tract of Tasch on the oath. Schnabel was against aggressive wars and other military action involving bloodshed, except when the territory was invaded and women and children were in immediate danger. He warned against any military action that would make more widows and orphans than it protected.

On the question of polygamy, Schnabel was unequivocally monogamous. He refuted the charge of communism, justified private property by Biblical citations, but argued in favor of sharing any surplus for the good of the brethren and became indignant on the question of usury. He cited in his favor the work of Dr. Johannes Eisermann (Montanus), professor in the faculty of law, *Vom gemeinen Nutz* (Marburg, 1533).[30]

It was to Schnabel in prison at Wolkersdorf that Peter Tasch sent the letter intercepted by Philip. It will be recalled (Ch. 14.4) that this document gave the landgrave a sense of alarm at the vast geographical scope of the Anabaptist movement and induced him to join with Elector John Frederick in warning Henry VIII and other princes of the dangers. But even then he insisted on distinguishing the bellicose from the evangelical Anabaptists and expressed his sorrow that so many of the latter had perished because of the evil name of the others.

It was in this mood that Philip decided to convene a great Anabaptist-Protestant colloquy at Marburg.

3. Schnabel Before Bucer and Eisermann: The Marburg Anabaptist Disputation of 1538

Philip, after seeking several times to induce the Wolkersdorf Anabaptists to recant, sent them a letter in his own hand,[31] expressing his anger at their exploitation of their lenient imprisonment, but at the same time apprising them generously of his plan

---

[29] *Ibid.*, p. 171.
[30] On this particular book and the extensive interest in Hesse in the problem, see Sohm, *op. cit.*, 82–92.
[31] Franz, *Wiedertäuferakten*, No. 76, p. 213.

to have Bucer come from Strassburg to dispute with them on the outstanding issues.

The promised confrontation took place in Marburg in a series of sessions between 30 October and 3 November 1538.[32] Schnabel led the Wolkersdorf prisoners in the debate. Arrayed against them were the Hessian divines, headed by a distinguished foreigner who had successfully organized the territorial church of Strassburg after a similar confrontation with dissenters (Ch. 10.4), leading jurists and magistrates, among them Dr. Eisermann, and the representatives of the guilds of the town of Marburg. The Marburg disputation, which was to result in very significant accommodations to the dissenters in return for their submission, was outstanding also for the fact that it centered in such questions as usury, the ban, and the commonweal rather than in baptism.

The reason for the prominence of social justice in the Marburg Anabaptist disputation was the fact that both Eisermann and Schnabel were especially interested in the social implications of evangelical Christianity. We recall that Schnabel had earlier cited the Marburg jurist favorably.

Eisermann, sometime rector of the university, had valiantly sought in his book *Vom gemeinen Nutz* (as he was to do later in *De republica bene instituenda*, 1556) to work through the problem of creating a just and Christian commonweal within the context of Luther's programmatic elimination of works righteousness and his vigorous disparagement of any visible, catholic church, with its various means of rewarding and punishing and its hierarchy of ascending grades of accomplished Christians, from pious laymen to canonized saints. With Luther's proclamation of salvation by faith alone and its correlate, the priesthood of all believers, religious hierarchies lost their sanction in an evangelical state (Ch. 17.1). To fill this void, Eisermann sought to spell out how the citizens of an evangelical territory under its prince should each in his special vocation strive to live out a Christian life for the commonweal in uncalculating, even prodigal, and, above all, joyful acts of good will in the inner assurance of divine justification, while the evangelical prince himself and his magistrates would, in the discharge of their duties, see to it that subjects who could not yet willingly and joyfully perform would at least prudentially conform! There was no place in Eisermann's Christian commonweal for separatists with a separate church law. His was a unitary, territorial state in which "all who love God co-operate in the common good" and in which those who do not are properly constrained by the conscientious prince to "imitate," at least, "that inner

[32] The protocol is printed as No. 77, *Wiedertäuferakten,* pp. 213 ff.

righteousness." Justification in a theological sense and justice in a civil sense had thus come very close together.

Anabaptist Schnabel was, it is clear, pitted in debate with a man of law who was no less concerned than the conscientious dissenters with practical righteousness. Schnabel, too, had once espoused Luther's ideas. As the treasurer of his native parish he had been in charge of the church loans to the poor and the rentals of church lands. In the presence of Eisermann, Bucer, and the guildsmen, Schnabel described how he had become deeply distressed by the unbiblical spirit of his former pastor and by the prosperous members of the reformed church who remorselessly extracted interest from the poor and needy. Schnabel had come, he said, to the conclusion that the exploiters of God's poor should be banned. Finding his pastor utterly un-co-operative in any effort to make righteous the economic life of the parish, Schnabel separated and gathered about himself a loyal following of like-minded dissenters. There is in Schnabel's protest a trace of the political conviction that we noted in the religio-political articles proposed by Westerburg in Frankfurt, by Kautz and Rinck and others in Worms, and even by Grebel in Zurich, namely, that the saints should have a determining voice in the selection of godly magistrates and pastors who would not exploit the economically underprivileged in a reformed town or parish.

In any event, Schnabel, in his zeal for social justice, had come to the conclusion that righteousness could be best secured within small, self-recruiting, self-disciplining churches made up of explicit believers independent of prince and magistrate qua magistrate. Only when Christians were thus organized, he argued, could the ecclesiastical ban be distinguished from political banishment. At the present time, he said, the most conscientious evangelicals were being politically banished as separatists, while the state church in making only perfunctory use of the disciplinary ban was in effect compounding the dissatisfaction of the scrupulous and thereby augmenting the number of dissenters.

Besides Schnabel, there were on the Anabaptist side his fellow prisoners, the evangelists Leonard Fälber of Maastricht, Herman Bastian, and Peter Lose; and they joined in discussing the standard points at issue—baptism, the call and office of the pastor, and magistrates. In connection with baptism, they all so stressed the need for instruction as well as for explicit faith before baptism that Bucer was moved to acknowledge the need for instituting formal religious education and having the implicit baptismal vow of infancy made explicit in a ceremony of confirmation. Bucer also acknowledged the validity of the ban if used sparingly, pointing out how Paul with the flagrantly immoral and heady Corinthians was slow to exclude even egregious offenders.

The debate ended inconclusively. Each side, however, was perhaps more open to the insight, and responsive to the convictions, of the other than in any other debate of the Reformation Era thus far recounted.

After leaving Marburg for Wittenberg, Bucer wrote to Philip urging him so to reorganize the territorial church that it would commend itself to the dissidents and incorporate such features as a program of education for children and a judicious use of the ban.[33] The Anabaptist disputants recognized the seriousness of Bucer's efforts to meet their terms and the long-suffering magnanimity of the landgrave himself, and within less than a year of the disputation the Wolkersdorf prisoner-disputants, led by Schnabel and also Peter Tasch, submitted to Philip their Confession of Faith (11 December 1538).[34]

They acknowledged original sin, dealt with sin and those good works too little esteemed by the established church members in their solafideist stress, reiterated their conviction about baptism as the covenant of a good conscience to be undertaken by believers, but declared themselves henceforth ready to withhold their condemnation of infant baptism so long as every effort should be made to bring the child up in the faith. In their article on the Lord's Supper they stressed the exclusion of those living in open sin and proceeded to the ban, which they hoped would be more widely used throughout the territorial church.

Philip received the Confession and turned it over to his divines for analysis and comment. In their reply they did not argue vigorously against the moral charges leveled against the state-church pastors and lay members, but concentrated on the want of charity of those who had separated in pharisaical perfectionism. The submitting Anabaptists were, however, addressed as "brethren" and were promised that in returning to the established church and in accepting infant baptism, the civil oath, and military responsibilities, the divines and the magistrates would for their part renew their efforts to the best of their ability in respect to education and the ban, in order that "by the grace of God . . . men may see that we are concerned about Christian discipline."

By the end of November 1538 the territorial church had already met in synod at Ziegenheim and adopted a new church discipline.[35] Herein the state church provided, in response to the Anabaptist critique and in fulfillment of Bucer's promise at the Mar-

---

[33] Letter of 17 November 1538.
[34] Franz, *Wiedertäuferakten,* No. 85.
[35] Printed the following year.

burg disputation, that all "baptized children as soon as they are old enough should be sent for [instruction in] the catechism, which shall be arranged in every place at such a time convenient for everyone sending the children."[36] From this provision and the confirmation of the baptismal vow by the thus educated adolescents grew up a practice that spread over the years from the Hessian state church to Lutheranism elsewhere in Germany, a permanent legacy of the constructive interchange between the Anabaptists and the state-church divines in Hesse.

An accommodation equally important at the time but without permanent influence was the provision for the introduction of the ban in the order of discipline of 1538. In the earlier church order of 1537 there had been a provision for two of the three warnings to a wayward member according to the injunction of Matt., ch. 8.[37] But there had been no provision for the third warning and the ban for failure to comply. It was this that was now being urged by the state-church divines at Ziegenheim in order to meet the widespread criticism by the Anabaptists.

To the proposal Philip reacted cautiously. He foresaw misuse, as in former times under Catholic regimen, and feared that excommunication might not be applied "with Christian sympathy and modesty." He suggested, therefore, that the provisions not be published right away, and that experimentally the ban "should be applied in the cities and villages where the most able and most learned preachers are to be found," and designated Cassel and Marburg.

As a consequence of the good faith of the Magisterial Reformers and their prince, about two hundred Anabaptists rejoined the state church, at their head Peter Tasch, who thereupon went to Strassburg with Bucer. Already at Bucer's suggestion an effort had been made to use conforming Anabaptists to convert the rest.[38] It is disappointing to note that Tasch, once he had conformed, deteriorated in his ethical conviction and led at Strassburg an extravagant life, falling into debt and deceiving his creditors.[39]

[36] The order is printed in *Sammlung Fürstlich Hessischer Landesordnungen*, edited by C. L. Kleinschmid (Cassel, 1767), I, 109 ff.; W. Diehl, *Zur Geschichte der Konfirmation* (Giessen, 1897), 17; discussed by Sohm, *op. cit.*, 150–168.

[37] Sohm, *ibid.*, 158.

[38] Letter of Bucer to Philip, 4 November 1538; Franz, *Wiedertäuferakten*, No. 81.

[39] Rembert, *Jülich*, 457. There was, however, an ongoing concern within the established church of Strassburg for the disciplines and the piety cherished by evangelical Radicals. See Werner Bellardi, *Die Geschichte der "christlichen Gemeinschaft" in Strassburg (1546/50): Der Versuch einer "zweiten Reformation," QFRG*, XVIII (Leipzig, 1934). For some later developments in Strassburg sectarian history, see Ch. 19 at n. 48.

Beginning in 1535, Philip had been carrying on an intermittent correspondence with another spokesman for toleration, Schwenckfeld.[40] Contact was no doubt established through Schwenckfeld's friend and protector, the mayor of Ulm, Bernard Besserer, on good terms both with Philip and Duke Ulrich, whom Philip (thereby earning the title "Magnanimous") had restored, against Ferdinand, to the ducal throne of Württemberg without exacting any personal or territorial compensation.

The first epistolary contact between Philip and Schwenckfeld related to the Anabaptist crisis in Münster. Once again, Schwenckfeld was fatefully implicated with Hofmann, whose doctrine of the celestial flesh had now been writ large even on the coins and the tokens of the Kingdom of Münster. Philip, whom King John Beukels had accorded the doubtful privilege of being selected as one of the few princes to survive alongside his twelve apostolic dukes, sent to Schwenckfeld three Münsterite writings, among them Rothmann's *Restitution*. Schwenckfeld in Ulm was at that very moment seeking to defend his own variant of the celestial-flesh Christology against the orthodox Lutheran divines (Ch. 18.2). Schwenckfeld was therefore at first hard pressed to clear himself of any Münsterite taint while so stating his position on Christology, baptism, and the Supper, that he might in the end win over Philip to support him against his detractors among the divines of the Smalcald League. Philip remained friendly toward him, but never accepted his ideas, and confined himself to expressions of esteem.

We may at this juncture leave Philip and the Anabaptists of Middle Germany to pick up the story of Anabaptism in South Germany and its great conflict with Spiritualism in the extended controversy between the two major antagonists, Caspar Schwenckfeld and Pilgram Marpeck.

---

[40] James L. French, *The Correspondence of Caspar Schwenckfeld of Ossig and the Landgrave Philip of Hesse* (Leipzig, 1908).

CHAPTER 18

THE DEFINITIVE ENCOUNTER BETWEEN EVANGELICAL ANABAPTISM AND EVANGELICAL SPIRITUALISM: MARPECK VS. SCHWENCKFELD

The spiritualizing and the sectarian impulses in the Radical Reformation are found in varying intensities not only within the various regional and confessional groupings but also even within a given individual in the changing course of his religious career. In the latter case, the shift would more commonly be from the sectarian to the spiritualizing mood, as for example in John Denck, Christian Entfelder, Obbe Philips, David Joris, and Gabriel Ascherham. The Radical Reformation as a whole, however, may be said to have moved from the spiritualism of late medieval mysticism, the solafideism of the young Luther, and the charismatic apocalypticism of the first-generation prophets of Zwickau, Allstedt, Strassburg, and St. Gall, to the ever-increasing ecclesiological firmness betokened by the expanded and intensified use of the ban, by the enhanced authority of the written word and codified custom over inspiration and exaltation, by the emergence of duly authorized, ordained, and functionally differentiated ministers, and by the reordering of the external life of the communities of believers with increased attention to the problems and needs, such as religious education, of an increasing birthright membership.

It was inevitable that innumerable lesser conflicts over grace and works, spirit and letter, should find their cumulative outburst in an extended controversy between major and consistent spokesmen of the two opposed tendencies which in the inchoate state of the Radical Reformation had existed side by side. The controversy between Schwenckfeld and Marpeck signified the definitive clarification, at least for the Radical Reformation in South Germany and Switzerland, of the inherent incompatibility of the two impulses which had from the beginning confused not only many of the proponents of the Radical Reformation but also many of their opponents as well. Schwenckfeld had always

453

been a Spiritualist, though friendly to both the Anabaptists and the Magisterial Reformers, wherever he was not rebuffed, and Marpeck had from the beginning been a sober and constructive sectarian! Marpeck and Schwenckfeld in the literary deposit of their extended controversy, which began late in 1542, make very clear the great differences between evangelical Anabaptism and evangelical Spiritualism.

Before entering into the intricacies of the controversy, we must recount the careers of the antagonists from their last contact in Strassburg a decade earlier.

1. Marpeck in the Decade Before the Great Debate, 1532–1542

We were last with Pilgram Marpeck in Strassburg when he was obliged to leave for religious reasons in 1532 (Ch. 10.3.h). Martin Bucer and Ambrose Blaurer congratulated each other on having rid the city of the leader of (the moderate party among) the Strassburg Anabaptists. Ambrose Blaurer from Esslingen wrote to Bucer:

Your report concerning Marpeck will be dear and useful to all our people, but still more your earnest reply to his nonsense. . . . An evil of this kind usually sticks obstinately with people who have once been spotted by it, but superstition knows how to deceive simple people by a pious bearing. I am glad about the swift dispatch of the trinitarian question.[1]

The last part alludes, no doubt, to Servetus. Among the "simple people" whom Bucer had to reconcile to Marpeck's departure was Margaret, Blaurer's sister.

Marpeck may first have gone back to his old haunts around Rattenberg. Later he made his headquarters at Ulm.[2] In 1534, he reappeared in Strassburg, but was not permitted to remain. A letter written by him in 1540 places him in the Grisons, so that it is reasonable to assume that he found the territory of the Three Leagues (Ch. 18.4) to be a welcome haven when he was not traveling in the service of a unified pan-German Anabaptism.

Marpeck visited the Anabaptist minister and hymn writer Wolfgang Sailer at Austerlitz in Moravia during the first part of 1540.[3] He came again to Moravia in 1541, hopeful that a union of the several radical groups might be effected. He and his fol-

---

[1] Schiess, *Briefwechsel: Blaurer*, I, 319.
[2] John C. Wenger, "The Life and Work of Pilgram Marpeck," *MQR*, XII (1938), 137–166.
[3] According to Schwenckfeld, *CS*, VII, 161; Kiwiet, *Pilgram Marpeck*, 55.

lowers represented a less programmatic attitude than either the Swiss Brethren regarding the ban or the Hutterites regarding the community of goods.

The Hutterite chronicler records the visit:

He gave out that he had come to this land in order to bring together all factions (*völcker*), regardless of how many pieces and how disunited in the country they be and to make them one.[4]

After some discussion, in which strong feelings were expressed on both sides, Marpeck, when the community knelt for prayer, himself offered prayer. The chronicler, calling him a scoffer, reports that he was prevented from doing so by the whole congregation. Embittered by so bold a rejection of his gesture of good will, Marpeck left saying publicly that he "would rather unite with the Turk or the pope than with such a church," and stomped away in great anger.

Back in South Germany, Marpeck resumed even more earnestly his task of building up a circle of followers calling themselves, by 1541, "the Christ-believing comrades of the covenant of the tribulation that is in Christ."[5] Marpeck, rebuffed by the communitarian Anabaptists of Moravia, found in the same year that in South Germany the greatest danger to his cause lay in the defection of the moderate and, in a few notable cases, highborn Anabaptists to the Schwenckfeldians, whose spiritual yoke, without external sacraments or corporate discipline, was somewhat easier to bear. Before entering upon the details of the spirited encounter between Schwenckfeld and Marpeck beginning in 1541, we must recount the story of the Silesian after his departure from Strassburg, a little after Marpeck's expulsion.

2. SCHWENCKFELD, 1534–1541

It will be recalled (Ch. 17.3) that Schwenckfeld was involved in correspondence with Philip of Hesse in an effort to clear himself of the aberrations connected with the Christology of Münster. That was shortly after his being linked with Melchior Hofmann in the synodal hearings in Strassburg. Having received the advice of the leading magistrate of Strassburg, Jacob Sturm, as well as of the whole council, that he might remain in the city only if he agreed to keep silence, Schwenckfeld departed thence in the summer of 1534 (Ch. 10.4.c). After a visit to Speyer, he traveled to Frankfurt, and tarried also near Esslingen. On 28 May 1535 a colloquy was held at the castle at Tübingen in the hope that peace might be re-

---

[4] Zieglschmid, *Chronik*, 224.
[5] Kiwiet, *op. cit.*, 58.

stored between Schwenckfeld and his opponents—Bucer, Blaurer (now pastor in Constance), and Martin Frecht (Lutheran pastor in Ulm). The irenic intent of the colloquy was disrupted by Frecht's attack on Schwenckfeld's denial of Christ's creaturely humanity in the glorified state. Henceforth, Schwenckfeld's writings dealt more and more with Christology. However, a truce was managed, whereby the preachers of the Magisterial Reformation agreed to refrain from public expressions of animosity toward Schwenckfeld, while he agreed to desist from criticizing or disturbing their ministry and doctrine.

By September of 1535, Schwenckfeld had taken up residence in Ulm, as guest of the burgomaster Bernard Besserer, and had within the year clashed with Pastor Frecht on the matter of the Wittenberg *Concordia* of 26 May 1536. This unionistic attempt to remedy the failure of the Marburg colloquy to produce agreement on the interpretation of the Supper had been prepared by Melanchthon and Bucer, and signed by a number of German preachers, including Frecht. The town council of Ulm, however, was hesitant about accepting their pastor's recommendation, and Frecht encouraged Bucer to believe that the delay could be traced to the influence of Schwenckfeld on the burgomaster.[6] Ulm finally accepted the *Concordia,* but with reservations, thereby feeding the fire of Frecht's discontent with Schwenckfeld's presence. The city council in November ruled that respect for each other should prevail between the two men. Frecht had to content himself with making critical remarks about Schwenckfeld in his letters.

In 1538, the Lutheran minister came into possession of Schwenckfeld's works attacking the theory of Christ's creaturely humanity. Carefully adding personal comments, Frecht sent the offending piece to Schwenckfeld's host, Burgomaster Besserer. As a result, a commission was created to investigate Schwenckfeld. Upon receiving the commission's report, the city council ordered that Schwenckfeld should be permitted to live in Ulm, that his movements should not be hampered, and further, that those having criticisms to make of the Silesian should complain directly to him rather than attack him in their sermons.

On 13 January 1539, Schwenckfeld and Frecht publicly debated on the creaturehood of Christ's human nature before the council, Schwenckfeld following up his appearance with two

---

[6] Schultz, *op. cit.,* 240–242, concedes that the Silesian probably was invited by the burgomaster to render his views on the document; *CS,* V, Document CCXVIII.

books on the subject. The preachers of Ulm rallied to Frecht's side, threatening to resign on the ground that an unordained Silesian nobleman enjoyed greater freedom than they. Informed of this turn of events by Besserer, Schwenckfeld left the city on 13 September 1539. After his customary round of visits to familiar communities, he settled down for his seven-year sojourn at Justingen castle as the guest of George von Freyburg. Frecht, however, was not done with Schwenckfeld. In March of 1540 the Lutheran pastor of Ulm appeared before the convention at Smalcald and secured the condemnation of Schwenckfeld's Christology. (It was in connection with this development that Schwenckfeld carried on most of his correspondence with Philip of Hesse, Ch. 17.3.)

Frecht also secured the condemnation at Smalcald of another Spiritualist of Ulm, Sebastian Franck, who, incidentally, had been obliged to leave Strassburg about the same time as Marpeck and Schwenckfeld. We may here pick up his trail.

We reintroduce Franck at this juncture not only because his fate was intertwined with that of Schwenckfeld but also because he gave the Spiritualist conception of the church its typologically purest formulation.

3. SEBASTIAN FRANCK, 1531, TO HIS DEATH IN 1542

It was in his already mentioned letter from Strassburg to Campanus that Franck gave memorable expression to his spiritualizing view of the church, which went farther than Schwenckfeld's and constituted a continuing threat to the disciplined, tightly sectarian ecclesiology in normative evangelical Anabaptism.[7]

Franck, a pacifist, an opponent of the confusion of the Old and the New Testaments, an exponent of the celestial flesh of Christ as the substance of spiritual nourishment, was in various ways close to Servetus on the Trinity, to the spiritualizing Anabaptist Bünderlin on the relationship of true Christians to good pagans, and to Schwenckfeld especially on the invisible character of the church.

---

[7] The original Latin letter, dated Strassburg, 4 February 1531, is lost. It is printed in two surviving vernacular versions, Middle Netherlands and High German, in Krebs and Rott, *Elsass*, I (*QGT*, VII), No. 241. It appears in translation in *SAW*, 145–160. Alterations from this translation in the quotations which follow are emendations made possible in the light of the slightly larger and apparently more faithful Dutch translation that was only partly taken into account in the *SAW* version.

Franck was opposed to all attempts to restore the institutions of the primitive church, having come to regard the conservative reformation of the Lutherans and the radical restitution of the Anabaptists and of Servetus and Campanus as ill-advised because he regarded the constitution (polity), the sacraments, and even the written word (Bible) as the regulations, the nourishment, and the reading matter of infants and children:

God permitted, indeed gave, the outward signs to the church in its infancy, just like a doll to a child, not that they were necessary for the Kingdom of God, nor yet that God would require them of our hands. To be sure, the church in its childhood could not dispense with such things as a staff; and God therefore favored the infant church as a father gives something to a child so that it won't cry. But when the child is at length strong enough to throw the staff away, the father does not thereupon become angry, but rather the same is pleasing to the father.[8]

To change the metaphor, Franck thought of the ecclesiastical externals as the integuments sloughed off by a Christianity which after its spiritual maturation or metamorphosis no longer needs to crawl but can fly:

Therefore, I believe that the outward church of Christ, including all its gifts and sacraments, because of the breaking in and laying waste by Antichrist right after the death of the apostles, went up into heaven and lies concealed in the Spirit and in truth. I am thus quite certain that for fourteen hundred years now there has existed no gathered church nor any sacrament.[9]

At the very beginning, Antichrist, clutching at the husks or *cunabula* of Christianity, converted them into the appurtenances of an oppressive religiosity, while all the time God, foreseeing the maturation of his elect among all peoples, had provided inner ordinances for their spiritual comfort:

Since the holy and omniscient Spirit anticipated that all these outward ceremonies would go under because of Antichrist and would degenerate through misuse, he gladly yielded this victory to Satan and fed, gave to drink, baptized, and gathered the faithful with the Spirit and the truth in such a way that nothing would be lost to truth, although all outer transactions might pass away. . . .

God through the Spirit in truth provided by means of his Spiritual (*geystelicke; vnsichtbaren*) church all things which the signs and outward gifts merely betokened. He leaves it to the devil, who seeks

[8] *SAW*, 155.
[9] *SAW*, 149.

nothing other than the externals, to misuse the externals and control the sacraments.[10]

The *Ecclesia Spiritualis* includes not only devout Christians but also, as with Schwenckfeld, the saints before Christ and, as with Ziegler (and, as we shall see, also with certain of the Italian Evangelical Rationalists), the good Moslems and pagans who may know only the inner Word without having heard of the incarnate Word:

Therefore the unitary Spirit alone baptizes with fire and the Spirit all the faithful and all who are obedient to the inner Word in whatever part of the world they be. For God is no respecter of persons but instead is the same to the Greeks as to the Barbarian and the Turk, to the lord as to the servant, so long as they retain the light which has shone upon them and the joy in their heart (Ps. 4:6b-7).[11]

This Spiritual Church will remain scattered and hidden among the heathen (II Thess. 2:7) and the nominal Christians until Christ gathers his own at his second advent (Isa. 11:11 f.).[12]

It was not because of Franck's Spiritualist manifesto to Campanus, it will be recalled, but because of his *Chronica*, which enrolled so diverse a company of distinguished and vilified groups and persons among the "heretics," that Franck was expelled from Strassburg in 1531 (Ch. 10.3.d). From Strassburg he went to Kehl. In the spring of 1532 he addressed a petition to Strassburg, seeking permission to return and to have his *Weltbuch*, or universal geography, published as a fourth section of a revised and enlarged *Chronica*. Both requests were refused.

From Kehl, Franck went to Esslingen, where, while earning a livelihood by making soap, he engaged in some literary activity. He was molested by interference from the Strassburg authorities. He sold his product at the weekly market in Ulm, and decided to move there, establishing himself in April 1533, thanks to the support of Schwenckfeld's protector, Mayor Besserer, and obtained in October 1534 the right of the city. He associated himself with the printer Hans Warnier. The latter, however, declined to print Franck's *Weltbuch*. It was published instead at Tübingen (1534), the first comprehensive German geography. Its religious significance lies in its chapter entitled "Concerning the True Christian Faith," wherein Franck unfolded his religious convictions with greater moderation than in 1531, and contented himself with ridiculing Roman practices and the hierarchy. At Ulm,

[10] *SAW,* 152 f.
[11] *SAW,* 150.
[12] *SAW,* 150.

Warnier printed Franck's translation of Erasmus' *Praise of Folly* with three supplements, called collectively the *Kronbüchlein*, namely, a paraphrase of a book on the vanity of all knowledge and skill by Cornelius Agrippa of Nettesheim,[13] *The Forbidden Fruit,*[14] and *Ein Lob* in praise of the divine Word. The general idea of the translation with its supplements is the contrast between human wisdom and divine folly, between God and creation, freedom and sin, the Word of God and the Bible.

In the same year, 1534, defender of *Geist* against *Welt* (Ch. 32.1. b), Franck carried farther his idea of paradox, publishing with Warnier his *Paradoxa ducenta octoginta,* wherein, under the form of seeming contradictions, he pressed some of the main themes of his theological thought somewhat in the spirit of Denck. He once, it will be recalled (Ch. 10.3.d), mildly opposed Denck. The idea of paradox was in the air. The book drew heavily upon the dialectical mysticism of *Theologia Germanica.* Franck defined a paradox as an incredible thesis contrary to common sense but nevertheless true from a particular point of view. In the actual formulation of a paradox the thesis and antithesis were more commonly implied than stated.[15] An idea contained in his book that was particularly unacceptable to the preachers of Ulm appears in the preface: "Literal Scripture, the sword of Antichrist, kills Christ; heresies and sects [come from] the literal sense of Scripture."

While in Ulm, Franck made the acquaintance of the Augsburg patrician George Regel and his wife. It will be recalled that Anna Regel was involved, perhaps quite innocently, at Louis Haetzer's trial in Constance for bigamy (Ch. 8.3). Since then she had become a follower of Schwenckfeld. Thanks to the support of the Regels, Franck was able now to acquire his own printing press.

About this same time, January 1535, Besserer received a letter from Philip of Hesse, who counseled him to banish Franck as an "Anabaptist and revolutionary" if the town of Ulm wished to avoid conflict with the Emperor. Landgrave Philip had been prompted so to write by Melanchthon. Melanchthon for his part had been moved to act thus by Bucer, himself alerted by Frecht, the principal preacher in Ulm. In consequence of pressure from Marburg, Strassburg, and Wittenberg, Franck's press suspended

---

[13] *De incertitudine et vanitate omnium scientiarum et artium.*

[14] *Vom Baum des Wissens des Guten und Bösen,* English translation in 1640.

[15] Because of the formal inconclusiveness of his paradoxical approach, which never became systematically dialectical, Kurt Goldammer has characterized Franck as "Der dialektische Denker ohne Synthesis, der Mann der ungelösten Synthese," *ARG,* XLVII (1956), 184. But see a contrary view, Eugene Peters, "Sebastian Franck's Theory of Religious Knowledge," *MQR,* XXXV (1961), 267–281.

activity 25 January 1535, and on 3 March the town council demanded that Franck leave by 24 July. Franck endeavored to
refute the charge of being hostile to imperial authority. He
denied, moreover, that he was in accord with the Anabaptists,
many of whom, like the Regels, of Augsburg, he had converted
to his own Spiritualist views. He protested against the arbitrary
expulsion which would reduce him to misery, and with him his
pregnant wife and his young children. Besserer and George Regel
managed to get Franck out of difficulty by arguing that it was
necessary to give Franck a chance to earn enough money to pay
back his creditors. Besserer indicated that he himself was willing
to give up his personal claims in favor of the claims of the city
of Ulm. Franck was permitted to explain his situation and his
views before the commission of five censors presided over by
Frecht, who made the final report. The *Chronica* of 1531 was
cited twice with an indication of the folio. Since the edition had
been completely destroyed at Strassburg, one must conclude that
it was Bucer who furnished these references. Franck was asked
to reply to a questionary under seven points, and this resulted in
his *Deklaration,* presented to the censors of Ulm on 3 September
1535.

We may form some picture of the widespread opposition to
Franck at this moment by attending to his response to the seven
points against him. Firstly, he distinguished the Word, of which
the Evangelist speaks at the opening of the Fourth Gospel and
which is not, of course, a book, from the written Word, which is
created and which must not be placed in the room of God. As
the basis of this distinction Franck established the differences
between the interior word and the exterior word. He cited in
support the preface written by Luther to the new edition of the
Theologia Germanica of 1518.

Secondly, as to the question whether an impious person without vocation might preach, Franck asserted that in reproducing
the distinction of Luther between the *peccator* and the *impius*
he merely had in mind the Lutheran view that the preacher is
always, of course, like every other Christian, *simul justus et peccator,* but could not be manifestly impious and continue in his
preaching office. A probing criticism of the Lutheran Church and
its institutions is implied in this reply.

Thirdly, as to whether arts and sciences, apart from grace, are
diabolical (in allusion to Franck's paraphrase of Agrippa), he
responded that they might be quite useful to pious people but
might also contribute to the perdition of the wicked because
everything is impure to those who are impure, as the nectar of a
flower becomes poisoned in the body of a spider.

Fourthly, there is no possibility that meritorious works can render man acceptable in God's sight. Franck's is thus a clear endorsement of the Pauline-Lutheran conception of justification by faith alone.

Fifthly, as to the charges which Bucer had made against Franck in connection with printing his *Chronica,* he distinguishes between outright lies and errors of judgment (or miscalculation), which are not reprehensible.

Sixthly, Franck denies the charge that his social teaching (including his favorable citation of IV Clement, Ch. 16.3) had implied an enforced community of goods. He simply wishes to exhort Christians to help one another in mutual aid.

Seventhly, in dealing with the peace of the church, Franck takes occasion to express his personal conviction and confession of faith. It is not possible to have complete agreement in faith with the whole world, because faith is not a matter for all; and, in any event, coercion is impotent to produce conformity. The state should not intervene in order to bring it about. Woe unto him who confesses the truth before dogs and swine! Such a one deserves being torn to pieces. In fact, it is sometimes necessary to conceal the word of God. Franck indicates that he had no vocation to assemble the Israel of God dispersed among the faithless. Only God is able to unite believers by his word, and this union is purely spiritual.

On 15 October the censors of Ulm declared that Franck had responded satisfactorily to certain points, and that concerning others new questions should be asked of him. But the preachers insisted that he should sign his name to a confession of faith in ten articles, prepared by Bucer. The confession was to concern itself with, among other things, the necessity of the exterior word in preaching, the Bible, and the baptism of infants.

The town council, as it turned out, took the side of Franck. Franck responded with a statement promising not to publish anything under his own name and as a printer to submit the works of other authors to the censors. At the same time he insisted on not being required to take any special oath, for faith should not be constrained. Franck was supported by Burgomaster Besserer, who at the session on 5 November insisted that the ten-point confession of faith made out by Bucer for Regensburg would not have the force of law in Ulm, that it was not possible for the council to accede to the demands of the pastors in every respect, and that Franck should simply promise not to print anything without the authorization of the censors, a somewhat more liberal arrangement than Franck's own offer.

Nevertheless, Franck did not publish anything more of his own at Ulm except for the second edition of his *Chronica* in 1536. The so-called lies, in so far as they were errors, disappeared.[16]

While printing for his livelihood in Ulm, he had his own works published elsewhere. His *Die goldene Arche,* for example, which was a compilation of Biblical, patristic, and pagan texts concerning certain points of faith, appeared in Augsburg in 1538. It aroused loud protests because in the foreword he rebuked theologians for their long commentaries and acrimonious disputes about the sacraments while neglecting their practical religious life and because he made bold to declare that pious Christians needed to know no more doctrine than that contained in the Ten Commandments and the Apostles' Creed. His compilation of Biblical texts, *Das . . . mit sieben Siegeln verschlossene Buch* (1539), picked up the idea of Denck's in his work attacked by the *Diallage* of Althamer. A good example of what Franck assembles as Biblical contradiction is the following: The sins of one cannot implicate another; but the guilt of Adam condemns the whole world. Or again, Christ brings peace; Christ brings the sword.

Franck's *Chronicon Germaniae* was accepted by the censors of Frankfurt for publication in 1539. The sources of this *Chronicon* are more numerous than those of the *Chronica.* Franck, in fact, compared the two and gave his judgment about each one. It is significant that his earlier pessimism had passed into the background, for he was now writing about the glory of Germany.

Already before the appearance of the *Chronicon* the preachers of Ulm had denounced Franck before the town council in respect to a number of small books for which, they said, he had no permit from the censors. As it happened, these works were not by him, except for the preface in the case of a piece of satirical poetry. The denunciation referred to the works which appeared outside of Ulm, and consequently on 15 June, Franck received a notice of expulsion with no indication of why. He wrote one more appeal, protesting that he had honestly kept his promise. He argued that the *Arche* had been bought by learned men and that the censors at Augsburg had judged the book a good one. He pointed out that if he were to be banished from Ulm for having published books in other towns, Ulm might itself fall into trouble with the towns thus defamed. Consequently, the censors of Ulm were required to draw up a new list of his works and those published by him since November 1535. But Frecht

---

[16] Franck added by way of appeasement that the fierce eagle was also the emblem of John the Evangelist, as well as of the Roman Emperor.

refused to hold himself to that date and repeated the old complaints. He suggested that Franck's personal life was not above suspicion, making insinuations about the fact that he lived above a tavern. Frecht, moreover, pretended to hold that the decision of 1535 had been quite simply an interdict of all the works of Franck. Thus, despite everything, Franck was defeated by Frecht, and the council decreed his expulsion on 8 January 1539, to be effective on 23 April. Schwenckfeld was banished at the same time.

Leaving his wife and children provisionally in Ulm, Franck set out for Basel in search of a new position. Finding that at Basel there was quite an oversupply of printers, he wrote to a magistrate in Bern, who had read some of his works, asking whether it would be possible for him to establish himself there as a printer. But nothing resulted from this effort. Frecht apparently compassed the ruin of Franck's prospects in Bern by writing to Sebastian Münster. Since Franck's wife was about to have another child, he was accorded further delay; and the removal to Basel did not take place until July. He required several carriages to transport his printing equipment. On his departure Franck addressed a letter to the council of Ulm, wherein he charged Frecht with literary jealousy. He also published in 1539 his *Kriegsbüchlein,* attacking the magisterial chaplains who defended warfare.

In the meantime, the divines of central and southwest Germany, among them Melanchthon, Bucer, and several of the Hessian theologians, assembling March 1540 at Smalcald,[17] moved at the instigation of Martin Frecht to condemn the two Spiritualists of Ulm, Schwenckfeld and Franck, and also all Anabaptists. Burgomaster Besserer was present to vouch for the good conduct of both, but in vain.

Schwenckfeld referred to the Smalcald declaration as "the new bull of excommunication." Against the Anabaptists, called "the new Donatists," the declaration renewed the complaint of the state churches against separatism and sectarian perfectionism. Against the two Spiritualists specifically it leveled the charges of indifference to the outstanding points at issue for the evangelical church of the Magisterial Reformation as it sought to establish itself between the conventicles of the sectaries on the one side and the monstrous perversion of Christianity on the Catholic side. These Spiritualist "vagabonds" in their individualistic relativism,

---

[17] Teufel, *op. cit.,* 90, on the basis of a letter of Blaurer, 6 June 1543, argues that Frecht was present at Smalcald as the major opponent of Schwenckfeld and Franck, even though his name does not appear among the twelve signatories of the Smalcald articles. Compare *CR,* II, c. 986.

declared the Smalcald divines, class all three as fragments or factions of the one true, invisible church and in their irenic spiritualizing justify their absence from attendance upon the divine services of any church! Since "faith comes from what one hears," they continued, all citizens must attend upon the preaching of the Word in the territories and towns of which they are inhabitants. Skeptics who criticize the evangelical institutions and attenuate the significance of the preached word and the written Word, taking their perverse directions from an alleged inner Word, fail to realize that the Holy Spirit acts exclusively through the exterior word (literal and preached). Thus, at Smalcald the Spiritualist element so prominent in the young Luther himself was programmatically repudiated.[18]

Soon after Franck's establishment in Basel his wife died, and he remarried, this time Barbara Beck, daughter of his editor in Strassburg. She brought to the marriage a considerable dowry, and as a consequence Franck was able to purchase a house in Basel, 21 November 1541. On 11 May 1541 he paid his tax for the right of citizenship and was on 24 June enrolled as a member of the spice guild, which appropriately enough included the printers! He was associated with Nicholas Brylinger and edited with him in 1541 a Latin-Greek New Testament, which was republished the following year.

It is possible that Franck was evading the censors of Basel by having his controversial works printed elsewhere. It was at Frankfurt that he published in 1541 his big collection of proverbs in two parts.

Franck died in the autumn of 1542, and the archives at Basel preserve an inventory of his possessions, apparently prepared 31 October of that year.[19]

We resume our account of Schwenckfeld and Marpeck, bearing in mind that the individualistic conception of both Franck and Schwenckfeld of a Spiritual Church—without baptism, Eucharistic bread, or ban (as with the much later Quakers)—is what Marpeck regarded as the principal temptation and threat to South German Anabaptism of which he had become the principal spokesman in the middle third of our century. The controversy between Marpeck and the spiritualizers, symbolized by Schwenckfeld, will prove to be all the more arduous for the reason that Marpeck shared something of the "ecumenical" vision of the spiritualizers and was in continuous conflict with the Hutterites and other completely exclusivistic Anabaptists to the right.

---

[18] Teufel holds Frecht and Bucer responsible for this action against Franck and Schwenckfeld.

[19] Teufel, *op. cit.*, reproduces a list of the books in his library.

4. THE "DAMENKRIEG" OF THE RADICAL REFORMATION: MARPECK AND SCHWENCKFELD, 1542

It will be recalled that despite the good will of Burgomaster Besserer, both Franck and Schwenckfeld had been obliged to leave Ulm and had fallen under condemnation of the Smalcald divines, led by Martin Frecht.

Others besides the Lutherans at Smalcald were attacking Schwenckfeld's doctrines. In July of 1539, Bullinger's *Orthodoxa Epistola* had appeared, maintaining that in respect to his humanity Christ was a creature.[20] In 1540, the burgomaster Reformer of St. Gall, Vadian, produced his *Antilogia*, following the path marked out by Bullinger, and in the following year another work in the same vein, *Anacephaleosis*. Schwenckfeld's reply was his major Christological book, *Vom Fleische Christi* (1540), and the great *Confession*.[21] They were probably written in the library of the Benedictines in Kempten, copied, and then sent not only to Vadian but also to Philip of Hesse, the city councils of Ulm, Nuremberg, and Strassburg, the clergy of Zurich, and indirectly to Luther and Melanchthon.[22] At about the same time, a schoolmaster of Schwäbisch-Hall entered the literary lists against Schwenckfeld by publishing the first of four books against the Schwenckfeldian Christology.[23] Schwenckfeld discerned here as his real opponent the preacher at Hall, John Brenz, who provided one of the prefaces.[24]

While domiciled for seven years in Justingen castle, Schwenckfeld was engaged not only in extended literary controversy but also in innumerable "pastoral" visits to his friends and sympathizers throughout the whole of the southwest quadrant of the Empire,[25] where conventicles gathered to hear his messages. Of such groups, Schwenckfeld wrote:

When some of us meet together, we pray together, also for our enemies who persecute Christ in us, some perhaps unwittingly, that God convert them, raise up his kingdom, and increase the number of his believers. Furthermore, we instruct each other, consult one another, question each other about Christ and the mystery of the divine Trinity, and the kingdom of God, etc. We, who are as yet poor souls, inexperienced in divine things, poor and weak in the spirit and faith, hope

[20] Maier, *op. cit.*, 39–40.
[21] *CS*, VII, 281–361, and 451–884, respectively.
[22] Maier, *op. cit.*, 39–40.
[23] The other books appeared in 1543 and 1546.
[24] He was not, however, to reply to Brenz until 1553, by which time he would already be engaged in controversy with Matthias Flacius Illyricus on the Word of God.
[25] Ulm, Speyer, Esslinger, Kaufbeuren, Kempten, Memmingen, etc.

that God the Lord will in time help us and others further, as it may please Him. Meanwhile we are zealous in the pure wholesome doctrine about the Lord Jesus Christ and endeavor through Him to live piously in His grace. . . . We also are zealous in the correct understanding and interpretation of the Scriptures after the Spirit, as much as we are able through prayer and the revelation of His Spirit. Our books are an exposition of Scripture and an elucidation of the twelve articles of our Christian faith. This is our calling and the reason for our teachings.

Our alliance does not rest on ceremonies, but alone on the doctrine of the knowledge of Christ according to his two natures, with all who acknowledge in their hearts our doctrine . . . as divine truth. . . . We hope that the Lord through this pure, wholesome doctrine of his saving knowledge, because it came out of his divine revelation in the Holy Spirit, will build his chosen Church and through it will gather the children of God which are scattered over all the earth. . . . And although we know of no new Apostolic Pentecost, we do not wish to wait for it to repent and better our lives, but while it is today, to work out our salvation with fear and trembling, and endeavor daily to prepare ourselves for the coming of the Lord. Nor can we wait here on earth for a golden age. We hope to attain to the perfect knowledge of Christ yonder in the fatherland. Here we know only in part.[26]

Such was the kind of conventicle of study, prayer, and prophecy which was attracting the bruised and battered Anabaptists of South Germany. In such wise was Schwenckfeld occupied when the appearance in 1542 of an anonymous *Vermahnung* (Admonition) involved him in a controversy, this time within the Radical Reformation itself.

It was early in 1542 out of his efforts to unite the several Anabaptist parties and to prevent further defections to the Schwenckfeldian conventicles that Pilgram Marpeck had prepared the *Vermahnung*,[27] also known as the *Taufbüchlein* and as *Das Buch der Bundesbezeugung*. Much of it is a translation and revision of Bernard Rothmann's *Bekenntnisse van beyden Sacramenten* (Chs. 12.1; 13.1), published at Münster in 1533.[28] Marpeck's adaptive appropriation would indicate more than a casual exchange between the Lower and Upper German Anabaptist groups.[29] The authors of the *Vermahnung* signed themselves simply "the Christ-believing comrades of the covenant of the tribulation that is in Christ," but their treatment of Baptism and the Supper at once

[26] *CS*, XVI, Document MCLXVI; translated in Schultz, *op. cit.*, 280 f.

[27] Edited by Johann Loserth (Vienna, 1929).

[28] Edited by H. Detmer and R. Krumbholtz, *Zwei Schriften des münsterischen Wiedertäufers Bernard Rothmann* (Dortmund, 1904).

[29] See Frank J. Wray, "The 'Vermanung' of 1542 and Rothmann's 'Bekenntnisse,'" *ARG*, XLVII (1956), 243–251.

identified it as a product of Marpeck's circle. Chiefly concerned with the sacraments of Baptism and the Supper, the *Vermahnung* opens with the matter closest to Marpeck's heart: a lament over the separation of Anabaptism into divergent groups and a call for reunion.

Marpeck and his co-workers make a much sharper distinction between the Old and New Testaments than did Rothmann in his *Bekenntnisse* and reject the Münsterite hermeneutical principles. On original sin, on baptism by pouring as well as by immersion, on persevering unto the end, in a reworking of the covenant idea, and in the rejection of violence, the *Vermahnung* also differs from Rothmann's work. Marpeck's views on the Supper show the persistence of Carlstadt's Eucharistic theology.

Helen Streicher, the widow of an Ulm shopkeeper, coming into possession of a copy of this *Vermahnung*, delivered it (together with one of Marpeck's letters to her) to her spiritual mentor, Schwenckfeld. The receipt of these writings marked the beginning of a new episode in the relations between Schwenckfeld and Marpeck, which, because of the prominence of the patronesses, we are with some exaggeration calling the war of radical ladies. Over against Schwenckfeld's ally, Frau Streicher, stood Lady Magdalene von Pappenheim, the protectress of Marpeck. The two women themselves were actually friends and were drawn together in the common pursuit of evangelical truth amidst the welter of religious claims.

Schwenckfeld found doctrinal errors in Marpeck's *Vermahnung*, as well as in the letter to Helen Streicher, and in another epistle from the Grisons thought to be from Marpeck, which reached him at about the same time.[30] Schwenckfeld conceived himself to be the object of concerted Anabaptist attack. Since Helen was among Schwenckfeld's most fervent disciples, he understandably resented Marpeck's obtruding himself into the Ulm circle of which she was the fostering mother.

The widow Streicher, her five daughters, and one son were all members of the Schwenckfeldian conventicle in Ulm, and often the itinerant Silesian would come to dwell with them. Since one daughter, Agathe, and the son were physicians (the latter eventually becoming Ulm's city doctor), Schwenckfeld, who was in-

---

[30] 25 September 1542. The Grisons letter is lost, but is mentioned here as having been particularly distressing to Schwenckfeld. Torsten Bergsten, "Pilgram Marpeck und seine Auseinandersetzung mit Caspar Schwenckfeld," *Kyrkohistorisk Årsskrift*, LVII (1957), 52 ff., LVIII (1958), 53 ff., questions Marpeck's authorship. It was more likely written by Leopold Scharnschlager (Ch. 22.1).

creasingly troubled with gravel, found the Streichers' hospitality beneficial medically and spiritually.

Schwenckfeld lost no time in meeting the Anabaptist challenge to his theology and evangelical leadership. On 21 August 1542 he wrote to Marpeck's sympathizer, Lady Magdalene von Pappenheim, that "several brethren" had persuaded him to refute Marpeck's *Vermahnung*.[31]

A word about the von Pappenheims. The first of the family to meet Marpeck was Joachim (d. 1536), who had early been drawn to Protestantism. Magdalene, his sister, had been a Benedictine nun. She and Helen Streicher were now fated to play major roles in the contest between Spiritualism and Sectarianism being waged between Schwenckfeld and Marpeck. Magdalene had expressed a desire to meet the Silesian, but he chose to write her rather than pay a visit. In reply she sent a letter,[32] which Schwenckfeld rightly suspected to have been written by Marpeck. Schwenckfeld was understandably displeased and called Marpeck a "chief disrupter."[33]

Marpeck, for his part, suspected Schwenckfeld of being more concerned about the threat to his influence on the ladies than with the theological points at issue.[34] The strained loyalties of Frau Streicher and Lady Magdalene for Junker Schwenckfeld and Werkmeister Marpeck are an indication that the class lines and the theological issues between Anabaptism and Spiritualism were not yet clearly drawn.

Helen Streicher's correspondence reveals that Schwenckfeld had not hesitated to disparage Anabaptist developments. She wrote in a Schwenckfeldian spirit to Marpeck, observing that "since Christ's work and teaching are spirit and life, one must rise to it and must not make earthly elements, baptism or anything else, a condition for salvation."

In replying to Frau Streicher's call for a Spiritualist approach, Marpeck had sent his argumentation to Lady Magdalene to send on to Frau Streicher, for the two women had been for some time in correspondence. Marpeck's reply in due course reached the widow Streicher, who turned it over to Schwenckfeld. Marpeck in this much-handled epistle insisted that because baptism had been commanded by Christ, and because the internal and external sacrament could not be divided, as Schwenckfeld thought,

[31] *CS*, VIII, 222.
[32] *CS*, VIII, 214.
[33] *CS*, VIII, 219.
[34] Loserth, *Quellen*, 63 f. Many modern scholars agree. Loserth, *ML*, III, 29 f.; Wenger, "The Life and Work of Pilgram Marpeck," *MQR*, XII (1938), 158 f.; Kiwiet, *op. cit.*, 60.

he would not even entertain Frau Streicher's suggestion that they discuss the suspension of all the (unfortunately) divisive ordinances.

In the meantime, by 21 August 1542, Schwenckfeld had completed his retort to the main Anabaptist document, the *Vermahnung*. This was his *Judicium*.[35] After composing it, Schwenckfeld wrote to Magdalene explaining his action. He told her of his chagrin that she no longer wished to meet him, and of his regret that she based her opinion of him on disparaging remarks by Marpeck. Schwenckfeld enclosed a tract by his supporter Valentine Ickelsamer, against Marpeck's alleged position that it would have been possible for Christ to sin. Finally, explained the Silesian, he had composed his *Judicium* not merely because his teachings had been attacked in the *Vermahnung* but because certain brethren had urged him to make reply.[36]

Magdalene's response was a spirited defense of sectarian Marpeck, suggesting that spiritualizing Schwenckfeld reread the New Testament. Meanwhile, Marpeck himself wrote to Schwenckfeld, bitterly complaining that the charges made in the *Judicium* were unjust and that Schwenckfeld had presented Marpeck's ideas in perverted form. On 25 September 1542, Schwenckfeld wrote to Marpeck, explaining how he had composed the *Judicium* in the spirit of Christian freedom in order that the errors of the Anabaptists might be corrected and truth be served. He reminded Marpeck how often he had himself been charged with specific traits of the Anabaptists simply because he had defended their rights. The author(s) of the *Vermahnung*, Schwenckfeld charged, evidently held that any who did not accept the Anabaptist doctrine of baptism were not Christians but deniers of Christ.[37] As for Magdalene, he went on, before whom Marpeck had disparaged the Middle Way, he had shown her (by sending her Ickelsamer's tract) a correct understanding of the two natures of Christ. The same day (25 September 1542), Schwenckfeld wrote again to Magdalene herself, listing twelve of Marpeck's errors. Although the lady did write once more to Helen Streicher (and thus, indirectly to Schwenckfeld), this may be considered the end of the Pappenheim-Schwenckfeld correspondence.

On 29 September 1542, Schwenckfeld wrote directly to Marpeck concerning whether Christ, though of course sinless in the eyes of both contenders, had such a nature and will that he could have sinned. He received no immediate answer.

---

[35] The full title reads *Über das neue Büchlein der Taufbrüder . . . Judicium; CS*, VII, 161–214.
[36] Letter in *CS*, VIII, 217–222.
[37] Schultz, *op. cit.*, 284.

The *Judicium*, to which Marpeck had taken such angry exception,[38] began with a preface on baptism and proceeded to criticize
Anabaptism under the following rubrics: the word "sacrament,"
whether external baptism is a sign of grace, the Spirit of God and
the spirit of error, original sin, adoption, the Word of God, the
church, the faith of the Old Testament prophets and patriarchs,
the source of the *Vermahnung*'s errors, the Lord's Supper, the
words of institution, an address to the Anabaptists, and the true
baptism of Christ. Some of Schwenckfeld's criticisms were in
response to matters outside the *Vermahnung*, for example,
Ickelsamer's charge that Marpeck held it to have been possible
for Christ to sin, the report that Marpeck believed Christ to
have suffered in hell after the crucifixion, together with the Anabaptist emphasis on the cross, on a too "creaturely" Christ, and
the church as exclusively visible.

Marpeck realized that formal refutation of the *Judicium*
should be produced as soon as possible, lest some of his followers
be drawn to Schwenckfeld's side. He was aware, for example, that
another devoted patroness of the Anabaptist cause, the Baroness
Helen von Freyburg, sister-in-law of Schwenckfeld's host (at the
time in hiding because of her religious beliefs) was in correspondence with Schwenckfeld. By 1 January 1544, Marpeck had
completed the first part of his answer to the *Judicium*. This was
the *Verantwortung*,[39] which circulated in manuscript form.

Treating fifty-four of the hundred *Reden* (of which the
Judicium was composed), Part I of the *Verantwortung* was
prefaced by an open letter to Schwenckfeld, defending the
Vermahnung against the Silesian's charge that its authors were
incompetent and presumptuous. A copy of the work was sent to
Schwenckfeld, with a note promising that Part II would be written
if Part I did not have the desired effect. On 31 January, Marpeck
wrote directly to his antagonist:

I would not have thought it of you that you would behind my back
send letters into the world against me, and without asking or informing me would make charges against me, since you in the earlier
days dealt with me so much in matters of faith. . . . Now you have
composed a whole book [the *Judicium*] against me and selected in
particular thirty-eight articles . . . and sent them out everywhere so
that I must defend myself about them toward many who know my
teaching.[40]

[38] Later it called forth from the Lutheran theologian Matthias Flacius his
Antwort auf das Stenckfeldische Büchlein.
[39] Edited by Johann Loserth as *Pilgram Marbecks Antwort auf Kaspar
Schwenckfelds Beurteiling des Buches der Bundesbezeugung von 1542*
(Vienna/Leipzig, 1929).
[40] *Ibid.,* 58.

Late in 1544, Marpeck took up permanent residence in Augsburg. Schwenckfeld still had three comparatively peaceful years ahead of him as the guest of Baron George von Freyburg. Other matters claimed Marpeck's attention for some years and he could give only sporadic attention to the production of Part II of the *Verantwortung* (Ch. 31.1).

Although Marpeck had broken off his personal relationship with Schwenckfeld, he continued his campaign against him in letters and admonitions to his own followers. Marpeck apparently forbade his people to dispute with Schwenckfeld in 1546, in an effort to put an end to the mingling between Anabaptists and Spiritualists.[41] Occasional flare-ups and reconciliations between their followers are reported from time to time.

5. The Basic Points at Issue

The conflict between Schwenckfeld and Marpeck, although probably touched off by concern for the influential *Damen,* was, of course, motivated by compelling theological differences separating Evangelical Anabaptism and Evangelical Spiritualism.

We may here summarize the points at issue. Although the controversy between Marpeck and Schwenckfeld centered in baptism, it involved the whole range of theological and ecclesiological concern. For the exponent of baptismal theology, with its stress upon the new covenant in Christ, the Old and the New Testaments could not be taken as equally authoritative. For the exponent of Eucharistic theology, Schwenckfeld, the celestial Christ was present to the worthies ("fathers") of the Old Covenant no less than to the saints of the New Covenant. Schwenckfeld was quite explicit about the implications of the Anabaptist refusal to make Christian baptism the equivalent of Jewish circumcision, namely, the exclusion of the Old Testament worthies from any knowledge of the eternal Christ.[42] Schwenckfeld asserted that Abraham was "a Christian" before he was circumcised a Jew.[43]

For Marpeck, Abraham and the Old Testament worthies had only the promise of Christ, and hence even circumcision had only a promissory meaning. Marpeck held that there was a considerable difference between the promissory (*zukünftig*) faith of yesterday of the Old Testament worthies and the present (*heutig*) faith of today of the Christian. The Old Testament worthies had as the object of their faith the promise of God. The New Testa-

---

[41] Bergsten, *op. cit.,* 67.
[42] Marpeck, *Verantwortung,* in Loserth, *op. cit.,* 317, 325.
[43] *CS,* VIII, 198.

ment people have as their object the justifying and sanctifying realities or rebirth and the Holy Spirit.[44] The Spirit of the Old Testament was also different from that in the New Covenant. The fathers were baptized in the cloud and in the sea, but not in the (Holy) Spirit.[45]

The core of the controversy between Schwenckfeld and Marpeck was, of course, over baptism.

Schwenckfeld, like Marpeck, had been from the beginning of his reforming career opposed to infant baptism. As early as 1527, he had written that he regarded "the baptism of infants to be the beginning of papistry and the foundation of all error and ignorance in the churches of Christ."[46] Later he had declared that although the command of Christ to baptize could not be denied, the correct external baptism had not been observed for a thousand years, and he gave the impression that it ought to be suspended until further divine authorization should be forthcoming, for the conflict with and even among the Anabaptists was evidence that there was no certainty about the true visible church into which baptism admitted one.[47] In fact, Schwenckfeld was content with an "inner baptism of the Spirit" which "comforts, strengthens, and assures the believing soul or inner man."[48] Schwenckfeld was interested not so much in the inner washing as in the inner eating of the body of Christ. His whole theology, in fact, can be characterized as Eucharistic rather than baptismal.

Marpeck in his baptismal theology not only demarcated his position over against Schwenckfeld but also went somewhat beyond the baptismal theology of the first leaders (Ch. 11.1). To be sure, with them he describes baptism as the "covenant of the good conscience," but also as the "certain knowledge of the good conscience."[49] With these two expressions he describes the unity which he sees in the baptismal action. Holding that the soul and the body of man are distinguished as the inner and outer aspects

---

[44] Bergsten, op. cit., 84.

[45] Marpeck, Verantwortung, in Loserth, op. cit., 351.

[46] CS, III, 858. Quoted by Maier, op. cit., who has a small, useful section on baptism, 23–25. Larger treatments are those of Urner, "Die Taufe bei Caspar Schwenckfeld," loc. cit., and Karl Ecke, Das Rätsel der Taufe (Gütersloh, 1952), 21 ff.

[47] CS, VII, 252.

[48] CS, VII, 450.

[49] The following five paragraphs are a summary of Pilgram Marpeck's baptismal theology extracted by Rollin Armour from his Harvard Th.D. dissertation on "The Theology and Practice of Baptism in Selected Representatives of the Radical Reformation," Cambridge, 1962, ch. iv.

of one reality, he maintains that inner baptism of the Holy Spirit (the cleansing of the conscience and the new birth) is incomplete without the subsequent external baptism of water. The latter is bestowed by the church, which, as the yet unglorified social body of Christ, acts with the power of the glorified Christ. In fact, Marpeck says that Christ is actually present in baptism, provided baptism be received with true faith and commitment. Thus external baptism (and the Lord's Supper as well) "is no sign, but the external work and reality (*wesen*) of the son."[50] In the *Vermahnung* the wholeness of baptism is also based on the unity of the Godhead, whereby, according to Marpeck, the internal action is performed by the Father through the Spirit, while the external work is by the Son through the church. This latter argument gives way in the *Verantwortung* to the anthropological argument, however, due largely to the fact that Schwenckfeld challenged Marpeck's view of the unity of man's nature.

The covenantal element is described in two ways. It is Jeremiah's covenant written upon the heart by God's Spirit, i.e., "the covenant of the good conscience," a conscience created by the Holy Spirit cleansing the heart of sin. It is at the same moment the believer's pledge to God and dedication to the Christian life, specifically to the redemptive suffering which Marpeck says the members of the body of Christ must continually bear. He states that throughout Scripture water is used as a symbol of anguish and tribulation, and that one who receives it in baptism thereby publicly avows his entering into the fellowship of the sufferings of Christ, which are actually the pangs of the new birth. The pains persist up to the advent of the Kingdom of God.

Neither the Strassburg *Bekenntnis* of 1531[51] nor the *Vermahnung*, in contrast to the teaching of John Denck and John Hut (Ch. 11.1), stresses the constitutional (ecclesiological) significance of the baptismal covenant. The *Verantwortung*, in reaction to Schwenckfeld's Spiritualism, merely repeats the view that baptism is also a submission to the discipline of the Christian congregation, together with a promise of Christian love for the brethren.

Marpeck's favorite term for baptism is "witness" or "co-witness," whereby he means that the rite possesses a revelatory character according to which the baptizand receives the "certain knowledge of the good conscience." Together with the Spirit and the blood of Christ (I John 5:8), it witnesses to the believer that his soul is cleansed and righteous before God.

[50] *Vermahnung*, 207.
[51] Krebs and Rott, *Elsass*, I (*QGT*, VII), No. 302.

Infant baptism is attacked along two different lines: (1) infants are incapable of knowledge and faith, and (2) they have no need of baptism. Marpeck retains the former position throughout his writings. The latter he alters somewhat, in the course of debate with Schwenckfeld. In the *Bekenntnis* he had said simply that infants were freed from the guilt of original sin (*Erbsünde*) by the command of Christ, who said, "Of such is the kingdom of heaven." In the *Vermahnung* he drops this argument, but says that infants enjoy a countervailing inherited grace (*Erbgnade*) and are in a state of "creaturely innocence," an expression which he applies also to the unfallen Adam and Eve. Sensitive to Schwenckfeld's charge of Pelagianism, Marpeck then goes on in the *Verant-wortung* to clarify his view that this "creaturely innocence" is the result of the atoning sufferings of Christ. He now defines original sin according to the Zwinglian conception of *Erbrest,* that is, a defect for which one becomes guilty only when it bursts forth into conscious, "actual" sin.

The anthropology of the two men clearly differed. The heart of the dispute concerned the relationship between the outer and inner man. Marpeck had a tripartite view of man (somewhat like Hubmaier's; see Ch. 9.2.a), but stressed contrariwise the unity of body, soul, and spirit. For him, "the whole, undivided man" is incorporated into the body of Christ or the church, henceforth living by the Word and destined to rise from the dead to glory.[52] Schwenckfeld had a dualistic anthropology which stressed the distinction between body and soul-spirit. For him, the chief charge against the Anabaptists was that they were too much concerned with externals.[53] According to Schwenckfeld, the outer word (Scripture and preaching) must be distinguished from the inner word of the Spirit. There is a parallel between them, but not identity. For Schwenckfeld, the Word of God proceeds out of God's revelation in Christ and in the Bible.

According to Marpeck, evangelical preaching of the Word is directed to the whole man—spirit, soul, and body. Marpeck agrees with Luther that faith and the Holy Spirit come "through hearing bodily preaching."[54]

It is of interest that Schwenckfeld, who was relatively pessimistic in respect to the sinfulness of man, was more positive than Marpeck on the divine significance of the state, which he saw as divinely appointed, not only to check and punish sin, but

---

[52] Marpeck, *Verantwortung,* in Loserth, *op. cit.,* 123, 467.
[53] *Ibid.,* 166, margin.
[54] Marpeck, *Testamenterläuterung* (n.d.), Berlin copy, 222b, cited by Bergsten, *op. cit.,* 97.

also to engage in eleemosynary and educational activities and in such other positive works as building roads and bridges, draining swamps, and improving the common life of man. His *Office and Scope of Civil Government* (1548) is a noble plea for the separation of church and state and at the same time a vindication of the magistrate's vocation as a Christian and a call for Christian involvement in the welfare of society as a whole.[55] The concern of Schwenckfeld to find in the Old Testament essentially the same faith as in the New was an integral part of his concern for vindicating the universal character of the church and the Christian significance of the magistrate, including the sword.

Marpeck, on the sword and civil authority, holds that the civil law should be heeded by all and that it is indeed necessary for the majority of citizens who still live under the law, even when they purport to be Christians under the gospel. True Christians, however, as subjects of the Kingdom of God, although they obey the temporal magistrate may themselves never exercise authority or use the sword. When later asked about the centurion of Acts 10:1, he said that, to be sure, he was converted while a magistrate, but that it is not recorded how long "the Holy Spirit and his conscience" permitted him to remain a magistrate.

The difference between Marpeck the Sectarian and Schwenckfeld the Spiritualist was profound. Marpeck insisted on the unity between the inner and outer man, the unity of spirit, soul, and body, the unity of the inner and the outer word. Schwenckfeld was a Spiritualist alike in his anthropology and his theology.

We may, during this lull in the controversy between a major proponent of evangelical Anabaptism and the principal proponent of evangelical Spiritualism, make a few concluding observations about the latter. Within a few months of each other, three important spokesmen of German Spiritualism passed from the scene. Carlstadt, who had in fact become more conservative, ending his days as professor of theology in Basel, was stricken by the plague and died in 1541. In the same year at Salzburg, Paracelsus, a kind of sacramental Spiritualist, was pushed to his death from a high place by rival physicians. In 1542, as we have already noted, the wandering Spiritualist printer-preacher, Sebastian Franck, died in Basel. The most significant career of Spiritualism lies ahead in the Netherlands, where Franck's influence was to be extensive (Ch. 19.3).

---

[55] *CS*, XI, Document DCLXVII, 604–625; printed in part in English by David Parke, *The Epic of Unitarianism: Original Writings* (Boston, 1957).

Chapter 19

SPIRITUALISM AND RIGORISM AMONG THE NETHER-
LANDERS AND LOWER GERMANS, 1540/1543–1568

We were last with the Netherlanders in Ch. 14, where we followed the consolidation of Menno Simons' leadership of the
pacifistic Melchiorite Anabaptists, and the literary embodiment
of his practical churchmanship in *The Foundation Book* of 1540.

In the score of years after 1540, evangelical Anabaptism (Mennonitism) in the Netherlands consolidated itself between various
expressions of evangelical Spiritualism on the left, and extremely
exclusivistic Anabaptism on the right, much as was also happening in South Germany. The developments in the two
areas roughly parallel each other in chronology and in the points
at issue. The score of years in Germany between the Schwenckfeld-Marpeck controversy begun in 1542 and Schwenckfeld's
death in 1561 corresponds in the Netherlands to the consolidation of Mennonitism between the defection of Obbe Philips as a
spiritualizer c. 1540 and the death of Menno in 1561.

Spiritualism among the Netherlanders and Lower Germans,
after the departures of David Joris and Obbe Philips, centered in
the translations of Sebastian Franck into Dutch, in the rise of the
liberal Waterlanders (*Doopsgezinden*), and in the emergence of
the Familists under Henry Niclaes. Since the Familists were a
group quite distinct, we shall consider them first, before taking
up the other Spiritualist trends against which the Anabaptists
under Menno, Dietrich Philips, and Leonard Bouwens took an
increasingly rigorous position.

1. Netherlandish Spiritualism: Henry Niclaes and the
Familists; the Dissimulation of David Joris

About the year 1540 there came to Emden a prosperous mercer,
Henry Niclaes, a native of Münster, who, having left his city of

477

birth c. 1530, now found it expedient to leave his second home, Amsterdam, where he had fallen under suspicion because of his unusual religious views.

Henry Niclaes[1] was born the son of a Münster merchant in 1502. The somewhat solitary and brooding child of devout Catholic parents, Niclaes is reported to have been taken daily to Mass and to have displayed early evidences of a precocious interest in religious matters. One day the child asked his father what he thanked God for, to be told that he thanked God for forgiveness of sins through Jesus Christ and for the true life of godliness established by him. Thereupon, Henry announced to his startled parent that he could not see that sin in man had been bettered by Christ's coming. Before the father could remonstrate, Henry, then only eight or nine, continued, saying that he did not at all doubt that through the death of Christ the door to the Kingdom of God had been opened for all, but that for him, faith was meaningless without an imitation of Christ's Passion, and that he could think of no restoration to the perfect state of godliness until sin itself was destroyed. Unable to cope with this theological precocity, the father took his son to talk with a Franciscan confessor, but the child was not satisfied by the friar's replies. Not long afterward, Henry began to experience those visions which in later life caused him to call himself "a begodded man." Outwardly, his life conformed to that of the son of a prosperous merchant. For three years he attended the local Latin school and eventually joined the mercers' guild. At the age of twenty, Niclaes wedded a virtuous lady of plain and simple family.

Niclaes was twenty-seven when, under the authority of the bishop of Münster, he was arrested on suspicion of holding Lutheran views. Niclaes had indeed read much of Luther, but he disagreed with the former monk on several points. He did not approve of Luther's attack upon the Roman Catholic priesthood. He felt that Luther had failed to teach the ground of true righteousness and sanctification in Christ. He believed further that Luther erred in not insisting upon a church composed of sanctified believers. Shortly after his arrest and release, Niclaes and his family moved from Münster to Amsterdam, where he continued to prosper. His religious convictions were perhaps given a Spiritualist turn through his friendship with David Joris.

---

[1] The basic study is that of Friedrich Nippold, "Heinrich Niclaes und das Haus der Liebe," *Zeitschrift für die historische Theologie*, XXXII (1862), 321–402, reworked by Rufus M. Jones, *Studies in Mystical Religion* (London, 1909). See also Allen C. Thomas, "The Family of Love or the Familists," *Haverford College Studies*, XII (Fifth Month, 1893), 1–46.

"David George layde the egg and Henry Niclaes brought forth the chicken," an opponent of Niclaes was to say.[2]

Niclaes was not long in Amsterdam before he suffered arrest on suspicion of being a Münsterite Anabaptist. On being released, he remained in the city until his removal to Emden.

Once Emden had become his base of mercantile operations (which involved him in much traveling), Niclaes began to sign himself by his initials, "H.N.," in calculated reference to his being a new man, *homo novus*. A charismatic personality, Niclaes was to be described in his later years as being "of reasonable tall stature, somewhat grosse of bodie," and "brave in his apparell," of a "crimson satin doublet" and long beard.[3]

Certain that he and his followers were living in the latter days, Niclaes rejoiced in his experience of divinization and his call as prophet to communicate the gospel of spiritualization through divine love. In his *Evangelium,* he wrote:

So hath God at the last, remembred the Desolate/ heard the Sighing and Prayer of the Poore/ and for his Chosens-sake (to thend that his Trueth/ and what his Will is, mought; before all Louers of the Trueth; be made-manifest or declared/ and the Scripture fulfilled) shortened the Dayes/ according to his Promises, and; through the heartie Mercifulnes of his Loue; wrought a great[4] and wonderfull Woorke vpon Earth, out of his holie Heauen, and raised-upp Mee HN, the Least among the Holyons of God (which laye altogether dead/ and, without Breath and Life,[5] among the Dead) from the Death/ and made mee aliue, through Christ, as [sic] also anointed mee with his godlie Beeing, manned himself with Mee/ and godded[6] Mee with him/ to a liuing Tabernacle or howse for his Dwelling/ and to a Seate of his Christ, the Seede of Dauid, To-thend that his wonderful-woorkes mought now in the last time, be knowen 'the Light of his Glorie; with full Cleernes and Instruction; revealed' and the Coming of his Kingdom; to an Euangelie of the same Kingdom/ and to the Blessing of all Generations of the Earth.[7]

Central to all of Niclaes' thought and underlining all his writings (most of which were composed during the Emden

---

[2] John Rogers, *The Displaying of an Horrible Sect* (London, 1579).

[3] Charlotte Fell-Smith, collecting contemporaneous reminiscences in "Henry Nicholas," *Dictionary of National Biography,* XIV. See also Ernest A. Payne, "The Familists," *The Chronicle,* XVI (1953), 28–33.

[4] Habakkuk 1:1 ff.; Acts 13:32–34.

[5] Ezekiel 37:7–10.

[6] John 17:20–26; II Peter 1:3 f.

[7] *Evangelivm Regni. A Joyfull Message of the Kingdom, published by the holie Spirit of the Loue of Jesu Christ, and sent-fourth unto all Nations of People, which loue the Trueth in Jesu Christ,* translated by C. Vitell (Amsterdam ?, 1574 ?).

period) was his insistence on actual righteousness and a physical
or experiential holiness, as contrasted with the imputed or
forensic righteousness of classical Protestantism.[8] In this he was
close to Netherlandish Anabaptism of the Melchiorite-Mennonite
strain and to Schwenckfeldian Spiritualism. But whereas the
divinization in both these otherwise distinct movements had in
common the adherence to the doctrine of the celestial flesh of
Christ available for inward assimilation (with or without the external Eucharistic elements), the divinization in Familist Spiritualism, akin to and perhaps dependent upon the earlier Netherlandish Libertinism (Ch. 12.2), was conceived in analogy to the
descent of the Holy Spirit from the Father tabernacling with the
Son on the banks of Jordan. In the Familist Articles of Faith,
belief is professed in "God the Father Almighty, maker of
heaven and earth," "a mighty Spirit, a perfect, clear Light," who
as "God and Saviour" "manneth himself, according to the inward
man with us, and who becomes likewise with the clearness of his
godly light . . . godded or made conformable in a good-willing
spirit."[9] Niclaes expressly dissociates sin and any divine sanction
for antinomian behavior so near the surface in all forms of
Libertinism, stipulating, for example, in the foregoing ellipsis,
that "He with the law of His chastising is always against us in
sin." Niclaes elsewhere completes his thought on the relationships
of the three Persons in the redemptive "manning" within each
individual believer:

For yee shall evidentlie see/ and in maner-of-suffering; through the
Sufferinge of Christ; right-well perceaue/ and finde-in-experience/
that God/ with his Christ/ and Holye-gost/ and with the heauenlie
Fellowship of all the Holyōs / will inhabit with you / and lyue and
walke in you. and that Hee assuredlie is your God/ and yee his Peo-
ple. For Hee hath chosen none other Howse nor Temple/ for his
Habitation/ but you O yee godlye Children/ or Communialite of the
Loue.[10]

The love of God tabernacling among men of the Spirit in the
latter days was forming under Niclaes' winsome ministry the
Huis der Liefde or *Familia Caritatis*. The House or Family of
Love was later to become an international fellowship of Familists,
spreading from Emden throughout Frisia, into Holland, Brabant,
Flanders, and, somewhat later, into France and into England,
where much later it would be absorbed into Quakerism (Ch.
30.3). Members of the fellowship were drawn from, and might

---

[8] Cf. Jones, *Mystical Religion*, 433.
[9] *Exhortatio*, I (c. 1574), fo. 10b and 11b.
[10] *Ibid.*, cap. xx, fo. 48b.

continue to conform outwardly to, the parochial life of the surrounding Catholics or Protestants, and possibly Anabaptists (cf.
Nicodemism: Ch. 22.4).

While "God-services" and "ceremonies" were mere "vain
husks" apart from "experience," the Familists appear to have
been uncommonly well organized in their private and often
clandestine prayer meetings.

Since membership and leadership among the Familists depended upon the degree of enlightenment or divinization, theirs
was a charismatic hierarchy and an apostolic succession of the
Spirit. Under the highest bishop or elder,[11] Niclaes, there was
a group of elders. The conversion (Familist) names of the first
three "begodded" elders are preserved.[12] Beneath the elders was
the Familist priesthood, consisting in three not otherwise
described levels of enlightenment. The elders and priests of
Familism were not allowed to hold personal property.[13]

Niclaes viewed marriage as a Christian ordinance, advised the
married to destroy the lusts of the flesh, and held that conjugal
life should always be consistent with enlightened love.[14]

Discipline within the Familist conventicles appears to have
been nominally in the hands of the whole brotherhood, although
the elders and priests as "fathers of a family [conventicle]" were
generally at the fore in this aspect of the life of the fellowship
and led in worship. Niclaes wrote, for example, in his *Introduction to the Holy Understanding of the Glasse of Righteousnes,*
c. 1560:

For every Father of a Familie vnder the Loue hath doubtles the
Libertie in his Familie to vse Seruices and Ceremonies/ according as
he perceiueth out of the Testimonies of the Holy Spirit of Loue that
they are most-profitablest or necessariest for his Houshold/ to the
Life of Peace/ for to keepe his Houshold/ therby/ in Discipline and
Peace: Trayning them vp therwith, that they may learne to practise
and use thatt which is right and equall./ For to manifest vnto them
therby, the true Righteousnes which God esteemeth.[15]

Though the elders and priests were foremost in worship and
discipline, Niclaes secured a place in his service for the inspired
utterance of every believer: "If any man therefore has ob-

[11] Jones, *Mystical Religion,* 442, claims that the Familists themselves never
used the word "bishop."

[12] Daniel, Elidad, and Tobias. The change of name suggests not only monastic
but also Waldensian practice.

[13] Payne, "The Familists," *loc. cit.*

[14] Charges of moral laxity brought against the House of Love by sixteenth-
century authorities are now generally held to have been erroneous.

[15] *Introduction* (London, c. 1574), cap. xxiv., secs. 22 f.

tained . . . any gifts of God, or if any man has any heavenly revelation, or if any man use any service of the priestly ordinance, let him with us be serviceable to the Love therewith, to the intent that it may all be agreeable with the Love, and may all be done to concord in the service of Love."[16]

Because of the recurrent danger of "strife, dissention, and schisme," Niclaes enjoined his followers in case of uncertainty to obey their spiritual superiors:

Give-eare to the Elders of the Holy Vnderstanding: and followe not the Will or Counsell of your owne Mynde: but; with the Elders, vnder/ the Seruice of the Loue; followe the Mynde and Counsell of the Wisdom: and alwaies keepe yourselues; with the Elders in the Family of Loue; to the Concorde/ and to the Multiplying in the Good/ and of the peaceable Kingdome in all Loue.[17]

Niclaes, using the term "service of love" very much as the Anabaptists used *Gelassenheit* (yieldedness), urged prospective converts to yield their wills to the elders and to be subject to them in faith or trustfulness in order to be freed from self and be saved:

Men may fynde Diuers that will take very great heed to themselues/ least they should be deceiued or beguyled. and so will stay onely vpon themselues. But because they; so staying vpon themselues; giue no heed to the Grace vnder the Obedience of the Loue/ therefore re-mayne they/ such as they are and come not at any tyme to the Light of Life or the Day of Loue . . . Others will in their Unregenerate estate and Depriuation/ account themselues free/ and will not be subject vnto anything, neither to the Scripture/ nor to any teaching/ nor yet to the Seruice of Loue: and therefore; in that Sort, do neuer come to the Freedome of the Children of God.[18]

Of Niclaes' life, apart from his thought, after coming to Emden, not much is known. He may have visited England in 1552–1553 (toward the end of Edward VI's reign, when there were many foreign visitors in England). We shall meet his followers in England in Ch. 30.4. He died probably in Cologne, c. 1580.[19]

Familism was not much of a threat to Mennonitism. It was otherwise with the kindred movement of Davidjorism, for the latter shared with Mennonitism in part a common ancestry from Melchior Hofmann.

[16] *Ibid.*
[17] *Ibid.*, secs. 41 ff.
[18] *Ibid.*
[19] Another reckoning places his death in 1570.

We were last with David Joris in Ch. 13.5, on the occasion of the decapitation of his mother at Delft and the martyrdom of his devotee, Anneken Jansdochter, at Rotterdam. Obliged to leave the Netherlands, David Joris carried on a wide correspondence, sending a self-defense to the court of justice in Holland and a prophetic writing to Philip of Hesse. In 1542 he published his *'tWonderboeck*. In the same year a bitter dispute arose between him and Menno Simons, who accused Joris of being a false prophet, the Antichrist, the "deceiver and falsifier of divine truth." Joris tried to convince Menno of his divine authorization, but Menno rejected his claims and after a certain point declined to have anything further to do with him.

Hunted from city to city, in constant danger of arrest and execution, indeed having many very close brushes with his pursuers, Joris developed distinctive ideas on the question of religious tolerance. The purpose of religion, he said, is not to argue over the relation of the Persons of the Trinity, about which, in any case, man can have no sure knowledge, but to achieve unity with God, a unity which comes only by the inner re-enacting of the incarnation and Passion of Christ. Faith is an inner experience, not something proved by assent to a written creed. In the light of this, the whole concept of heresy and orthodoxy becomes greatly altered and reduced in importance and the authority of the magistrate in matters of religion is abolished. A heretic is now defined by Joris as one who lacks the new birth, "who is proud toward God, who for a single error in an article or belief will deprive another of his goods and honor and even his life."[20] The Spirit alone is of prime importance, and without it nothing else is of any use. As to polity, the sacraments, the creed, and even martyrdom, they are all externalities.

In 1543, Joris, his wife and family, and a large number of followers settled in Basel. Joris, under the pseudonym of John of Bruges, represented himself vaguely as "a fugitive for the gospel." He and his followers were welcomed there, especially since they were apparently people of dignity and substance, and they purchased property in the city. Joris spent his time writing prolifically,[21] painting, and devoting himself to his family and the colony of his followers. He became allied by marriage with several Basel families and directed by letters and personal emissaries his Netherlandish following.

An important Dutch follower was Nicholas Meynderts van Blesdijk. He had attached himself to Menno in 1536, but in 1546

[20] Bainton, *Travail,* 138.
[21] His writings were published in the Netherlands.

turned to David Joris. An educated man, he found satisfaction in the writings of Joris, which seemed to him "to come from the divine Spirit."[22] He defended the Jorist position in 1546 at Lübeck against Menno and others, and wrote out his convictions in *Christelijcke Verantwoordinghe*.[23] Presently, Blesdijk went to Basel and married the eldest of David's daughters. In close contact with the great Spiritualist, Blesdijk began to wonder whether Joris might not be, after all, a hypocrite.

Blesdijk at length openly accused Joris of soft living and the desertion of his own mission. Joris admitted that his personal claims had been exaggerated. Dissension broke out among the colony, some disillusioned, as was Blesdijk, with the prophet, others still regarding him as the true, though temporizing, Messiah. When he died in 1556, rumors were already being spread about him. He was given an honorable burial, but after his death the banning of his secretary, van Schor, from the colony led to the latter's testimony that the old gentleman had kept concubines, a fact which he himself, he said, had only just discovered.[24] Stories, perhaps fanciful, perhaps partly true, began to circulate, but no action was taken until March, when several men of the colony were arrested and their houses searched. Blesdijk finally admitted that van Brugge was none other than the infamous Joris. In accordance with Roman law, the university ordered that the heretical Joris should be exhumed and burned. On 13 May, the body was tied to a stake and burned, and at the same time a box filled with his writings was given to the flames.

His followers were not persecuted, and after they publicly recanted in the cathedral their errors and those of their leader and subscribed to the Basel confession, they suffered no further, except for chagrin.

Though we last glimpse the red beard of David Joris amid the flames of a posthumous pyre in Basel, the spiritual flames which he had himself ignited burned longest in the Netherlands, where an endemic Spiritualism was continuously being rekindled.[25]

It was this recurrent Spiritualistic tendency from without and

---

[22] Friedrich Nippold prints some of Blesdijk's work in "David Joris von Delft," *Zeitschrift für die historische Theologie*, XXXIII (1863), 3–166; XXXIV (1864), 483–673; XXXVIII (1868), 475–591.

[23] *Ibid.*, XXXVIII (1868), 534–544.

[24] Bainton points out that van Schor had lived in Joris' house, and that it was unlikely that such a thing could have been kept secret from him for fifteen years.

[25] H. W. Meihuizen, "Spiritualistic Tendencies and Movements among the Dutch Mennonites of the 16th and 17th Centuries," *MQR*, XXVII (1953), 259–304.

within his flock that made Menno Simons and his lieutenants conspicuously devoted to the use of the ban.

2. NETHERLANDISH ANABAPTISM BECOMES "ANABANISM"

The ban, which in the medieval church had been the prerogative of the pope, was ascribed, in the Schleitheim Confession (Ch. 8.1), to the local congregation, and became one of the seven basic articles of the Swiss Brethren. Exactly thirty years later, in 1557, the stern and repetitive use of the ban on the part of the Lower Germans was a major reason for the formalization, at a synod in Strassburg, of the schism between the Upper and the Lower Germans, and, in the Netherlands itself, the withdrawal of one group of moderates, known as the Waterlanders. The frequency and ferocity of banning among the most disciplined of the Lower Germans under the leadership of Dietrich Philips and Leonard Bouwens, with the somewhat reluctant sanction of the more charitable Menno, tempt one to pun in characterizing the main theme of this section, in observing that in the second generation Anabaptism in the Netherlands and in Lower Germany became "Anabanism."

No longer made up predominantly of fresh recruits from Catholicism or Protestantism, the Anabaptists in the period between 1540 and 1557 were using the ban and the equally formalized solemn reinstatement into membership as the ethical, psychological, and constitutional equivalent of believers' baptism for the increasingly numerous "birthright" members, who in routinized baptism in adolescence were no longer undergoing the great formative experience of the public *re*baptism of the heroic days of the first apostles of the new evangel. The ban had come to replace baptism as the new focal point of Anabaptist ecclesiology.

In Menno himself we can follow the emergence of the ban to its pre-eminence.

a. Menno: From His Exile from the Netherlands in 1543 to the Wismar Resolutions of 1554. We were last with Menno when he was driven from the Low Countries in 1543 (Ch. 14.1), though we also caught a glimpse of him on one of his extensive journeys along the Hanseatic Coast as far as Livonia (Ch. 15.4).

Menno is thought of as Dutch. Yet he spent all told only a few years of his evangelical ministry of twenty-five years in the Dutch provinces proper. To northwest Germany he devoted his last eighteen years, building up churches in East Frisia, around Cologne, in the duchy of Holstein and along the coast, and returning to the Netherlands proper only on visits.

Early in the winter of 1543–1544 Menno and his family appeared in East Frisia, where the tolerant Countess Anna ruled. She had just appointed Erasmian-Reformed John Łaski (1499–1560)[26] to superintend the state church. A Polish nobleman, he had studied in Bologna, Padua, Rome, and Basel; had taken part with his brother Jerome (Ch. 15.4) in the fierce campaign against Ferdinand and had been made titular bishop of Veszprém in Hapsburg Hungary, royal secretary, dean of Gniezno, and archdeacon of Warsaw; had visited Melanchthon and then joined the Brethren of the Common Life in Louvain. In 1542, after a furtive return to Poland to visit his dying brother, he had renounced his Catholic preferments in Poland and therewith abandoned the career of the prospective successor of his uncle as primate of Poland to espouse the Reformation. After his encounter with Menno Simons in Emden, we shall next overtake him in this narrative as he seeks to cope with the radical wing of the Reformed Church of Little Poland (Ch. 25), whither he will return as superintendent in 1556.

Łaski found a considerable number of Anabaptists in East Frisia, including the bellicose Batenburgers and the spiritualizing Davidjorists. This perceptive Pole soon distinguished the revolutionary and peaceful strands among the Radicals. Intending to treat all fairly, he was pleased to learn of the arrival of Menno, whom he invited to meet with him in Emden, the East Frisian capital. There a semipublic interview was held with Anna's permission from 28 to 31 January 1544, at which Łaski and Gellius Faber (Ch. 12.1) went over with Menno the familiar points at issue, namely, original sin, the incarnation, baptism, sanctification, and the calling of preachers. Agreement was reached on original sin and sanctification, but not on the other points. Menno testifies that he was treated with kindness, and was required only to submit a statement of faith which might be presented to the authorities. This he did three months later in his *Brief and Clear Confession and Scriptural Instruction*[27] (1544), although he covered only two of the three disputed points, omitting infant baptism. Łaski subsequently published this confession without Menno's permission, and wrote a refutation in his *Defensio verae . . . doctrinae de Christi Domini incarnatione* (Bonn, 1545). Menno was hurt by this apparent abuse of his confidence, for he had thought that the *Confession* would serve as a basis of *rapprochement*.

Łaski seems to have been of two minds toward Menno and his followers. He used his influence to protect them from the severe

[26] Oskar Bartel, *Jan Łaski,* I (Warsaw, 1955).
[27] *Writings,* 419–454.

measures enacted against the revolutionary group. It was, in fact, Łaski who helped draft the first official document (1545) to use the expression "Mennonites" (*Mennisten*) to distinguish the peaceful party among the Anabaptists (Ch. 14.1). His toleration was motivated largely by the hope of bringing the more reasonable Mennonites over to his Reformed position; and, when this hope proved vain, he showed that he had no intention of permitting them permanently to maintain a separate church apart from his own.

In 1548 the discussions between Łaski and Menno were suspended when Archbishop Thomas Cranmer invited the former archdeacon of Warsaw and Zwinglian pastor of Emden to become superintendent of the international Reformed Strangers' Church in London, with filiates in the adjoining counties. Then, with the accession of Catholic Mary in 1553, Łaski and many of his Dutch members had to flee in midwinter. When their ship was frozen in Wismar harbor, it was Menno's followers who ministered to them in their distress.

The theological debate on the incarnation between Łaski and Menno resumed in 1554, when Menno replied to Łaski's *Defensio* in a tract, *The Incarnation of Our Lord* (1554).

Menno also debated with Martin Micron in Emden, and between 6 and 15 February 1554 a conversation with considerable literary consequences was carried on between them. Micron, an alumnus of Basel, had become associated with Łaski in the Strangers' Church in London, and had been expelled at the same time. Micron published an account of the debate with Menno on 18 June 1556, *Een waerachtigh Verhaal der t'zammensprekinghe,* which was followed by *Menno's Reply to Martin Micron* (1556)[28] and an *Epistle to Martin Micron.*[29] Micron then turned for counsel to his colleagues in South Germany and Switzerland, notably to his old teacher Bullinger and to Calvin.[30] Calvin owed his low estimate of Menno to Micron, for whom, in response, he prepared an extensive refutation of the celestial-flesh doctrine, *Contra Mennonem.*[31]

The third person with whom Menno fell into dispute in 1554 was Gellius Faber (Jelle Smit), whom we met as a Roman priest of Jelsum near Leeuwarden. Like Menno, he had early turned Sacramentist (Ch. 2.2), and had left the Roman priesthood in the

[28] *Ibid.,* 835–913.
[29] *Ibid.,* 915–943.
[30] Calvin, *Opera,* XVI, Ep. 2642, col. 5. Ep. 2818, coll. 67 f.
[31] *Ibid.,* X, coll. 167–176. Calvin said of Menno that he could imagine nothing "prouder than this ass or more impudent than this dog."

same year as Menno, 1536, but continued as a Sacramentist, in due course serving as Reformed (or "Zwinglian") pastor under Łaski in Emden. Here he had participated in the extended public interview with Menno in 1544. A decade later he had become particularly irritated by an Anabaptist letter, printed in Magdeburg, which had fallen into his hands, and to which he replied bitterly in a booklet (1552).

It was to this work, now lost, that Menno addressed himself in his longest work, *Reply to Gellius Faber* (1554).[32] Containing the already cited spiritual autobiography, which Menno wrote in connection with his extended discussion of the vocation of preachers and the need for reordination, the book deals also with baptism, the Supper, the ban, the differentiation of the church of Christ and that of Antichrist, and a large number of specific refutations of points made by Gellius. The book is especially interesting, not only because of the autobiographical section, the "Renunciation of the Church of Rome," but also because in it we see pitted against each other two former priests from the same region about Leeuwarden, both of whom had passed through a Sacramentist phase, the one ending in Anabaptism, and the other in "Zwinglianism." Baptism, free will, Christology, the nature of the church, and the place of the magistracy were the issues that now divided them. Menno's *Reply* was printed in Lübeck, whither he had gone from Wismar.

Before the banishment of Anabaptists from Wismar by the town council in November 1554, Menno had called a synod of seven elders, among them Dietrich Philips, Leonard Bouwens, and Giles of Aachen (Ch. 14.3), to discuss several of the aforementioned issues set forth in the nine Wismar resolutions.[33] The first five dealt with the ban and shunning. Of interest is the mitigation of avoidance of the banned in trade if the dire necessity of the tradesman prompts sympathetic purchases. The sixth dealt with the superior authority of the congregation over against unbelieving parents in the case of a young member wishing to get married and being unable to secure parental consent. The seventh item permitted members to make use of courts and magistrates in legal cases. The eighth permitted Anabaptists on a journey to carry a saber or sword as a matter of elementary precaution against robbers, but only as camouflage, for it was not to be employed. The same article permitted Anabaptists who were called up for watch and ward and other duties to present arms at the

[32] *Writings*, 625–781.
[33] Printed in *BRN*, VII, 51–53.

regular inspections, but, again, they were not to use them. The ninth article ordered that no one be permitted to go about among the congregations teaching and admonishing without being "sent or ordained by the congregation or the elders."

When the Anabaptists were driven from Wismar, Menno led them to one of the estates of the nobleman Bartholomäus von Ahlefeldt near the town of Oldesloe in Holstein. Von Ahlefeldt had soldiered in the Netherlands, and, witnessing the execution of many peaceful Anabaptists, had resolved to convert his estate of Wüstenfelde into an asylum for them. In the year that Menno and his group moved in, certain otherwise unidentified Anabaptists with a great quantity of Bibles and other books from the Anabaptist print shop in Lübeck were overtaken en route to Oldesloe and their books confiscated.[34]

Leaving Menno in Wüstenfelde to continue his synodal, pastoral, and literary activities from his new home in Holstein, we return to the situation which he left behind him in the Netherlands, and to its rigoristic development under other leaders. Menno had recognized and promoted the rise of a younger colleague who was to play an increasingly important role in his absence.

b. *Dietrich Philips.* Dietrich Philips (1504–1568), already familiar to us as Obbe's younger brother, had become increasingly important in the movement after his ordination as an elder by Obbe. He emerged as a leader second only to Menno in his influence, and was considered by some superior to Menno in his basic learning, his vigor of writing, and his steadfastness in leadership. Trained as a Franciscan friar, and perhaps intending to become a priest, he had a command of Latin, and knew Greek and some Hebrew. In his works he quoted, for example, from Horace and used certain Greek and Hebrew expressions; and although these instances would not of themselves prove great familiarity with the ancient tongues, when taken together with the statements of writers generally antagonistic to him, they do indicate some degree of formal theological training.[35]

Dietrich had been baptized by Peter Houtzagher, one of the apostles commissioned by John Mathijs in Leeuwarden between Christmas, 1533, and 2 January 1534, and ordained or commis-

---

[34] *ME*, I, 27; IV, 54.
[35] Because his *Evangelical Ban and Ordinance* survives only in French, some have thought that he knew that language too, but the tract is probably a translation from a lost Dutch original. William Keeney, "Dirk Philips' Life," *MQR*, XXXII (1958), 174.

sioned by his own brother. Obbe reports that Dietrich was the only one who would help him oppose the revolutionary tendencies of the Münsterite Anabaptists.[36] Dietrich wrote against the vagaries of the Münsterites, for example, in his *Van de Geestelijcke Restitution,* in which he answered Rothmann's defense of Münster of similar title.[37] Although Dietrich indirectly derived his ordination from the Münsterites, he did not share their belligerence. He preferred the ban in the building up of a righteous remnant.

As early as 1537, he had risen to a certain prominence, engaging in a debate with Joachim Kükenbieter, Lutheran divine of Schwerin, in that year. He participated with Menno in 1542 in the ordination of the Flemish evangelist Giles of Aachen (Ch. 14.3) and of Adam Pastor (Ch. 19.2.c). This ordination was part of an attempt by what we might call the "direct line" of Dutch Anabaptists, i.e., those who sought to consolidate their pacifism and to extrude what they were coming to regard as abnormalities in regard to Spiritualism, marriage, and the Trinity.

Dietrich also participated in the already mentioned Lübeck parley of 1546 (Ch. 19.1) in which Menno, Giles, Adam Pastor and he opposed Nicholas Blesdijk. Nicholas espoused the view of David Joris that one who believed in Anabaptist principles might prudentially conform to the established churches. He opposed specifically the action of the Jorists in having their infants inconspicuously baptized in the Reformed churches. (It will be recalled that the father of Dutch Anabaptism, Hofmann himself, once advocated a temporary suspension of baptism.) The following year Blesdijk published another book dealing with five points of controversy between Jorist Spiritualism (Anabaptist Nicodemism) and Mennonitism, including the Jorist suspension of the rites of Baptism and the Supper in their conventicles. Here the argument was not merely prudential. It partook of the Spiritualism of Sebastian Franck, for whom, likewise, the sacraments belonged to the childhood of the church.

But Spiritualism in the form of Jorism was not the only explosive element at the interior of Mennonitism in the process of sectarian coagulation.

c. Adam Pastor: Unitarian Anabaptist. At the Lübeck dispute of 1546, Adam Pastor, who sided with Menno and Dietrich on the sacraments, revealed his dissatisfaction with the Melchiorite-Mennonite doctrine of the celestial flesh of Christ. He also challenged the doctrine of the Trinity, adhered to by the Anabaptists with a few exceptions, but seldom at the center of attention.

[36] Keeney, *loc. cit.,* 175.
[37] Printed as a section of the *Enchiridion or Handbook,* 323; *BRN,* X. 342.

Pastor[38] (born Rudolph Martens), like Menno, had been a priest before his conversion. He had joined the Anabaptists about 1533, probably in Münster, and had become one of John Mathijs' emissaries, but soon went over to the peaceful party, co-operating with them also against the influence of David Joris. In the course of the dispute at Lübeck, it became apparent that Adam Pastor differed markedly, however, from Menno on the Melchiorite Christology; Pastor held Christ to be only human, though the bearer of God's Word. The controversy broke out into the open at Emden in 1547, at a momentous meeting attended by Menno, Dietrich Philips, Giles of Aachen, and Adam Pastor, where the doctrines of the incarnation, infant baptism, and avoidance in marriage were discussed. At Emden it became quite clear how precarious the Anabaptist consensus was, for the Frisian elder Francis de Cuiper and Adam Pastor, who had been supporting Menno against the Davidjorists, now came out sharply against him. Adam Pastor held that Christ did not exist as the Son of God previous to his coming into the world, and was divine after his incarnation only in the sense that God dwelt in him.

At the Emden meeting, the direct-line Mennonite leaders, now virtually reduced to Menno himself and Dietrich Philips, still hoped that Adam might be won back. The discussion was privately resumed at Goch near Düsseldorf, where Adam had actively preached and had brought many to rebaptism. At Goch it could no longer be concealed that Adam Pastor held a widely "aberrant" Christology. Dietrich Philips, with Menno's concurrence, led in excommunicating him in 1547. Adam Pastor was expelled chiefly for his views of Christ and the Trinity, but it had also become clear that he was much less rigorous on the ban and separation from the state than the main body of the Mennonites.

Even the zealous Dietrich Philips himself, of course, also held to an "aberrant" Christology, which, involving him in a subordination of the Son to the Father, made him in turn unwittingly anti-Nicene in his doctrine of the Trinity. We see this in the letter he sent to Anthony of Cologne,[39] who was troubled by the Trinitarian controversy among the Mennonites on the Lower Rhine, caused by Adam Pastor's excommunication, and also by

[38] Wilbur, *Unitarianism*, 41 f.; A. H. Newman, "Adam Pastor, Antitrinitarian Antipaedobaptist," *Papers of the American Society of Church History*, 2d series, V (1917), 73–99; Dunin-Borkowski, "Untersuchungen," esp. 102 ff.

[39] The letter, written between 1547 and 1550, is edited and interpreted by J. ten Doornkaat-Koolman, "Een onbekende brief van Dirk Philips," *NAK*, n.s., XLIII (1959), 15–21.

the difficulties recently experienced by Anthony's associates in some otherwise unidentified debate with certain "Zwinglians" (possibly the local name for the Rhenish Calvinists) on the doctrine of the Trinity. When we examine the doctrine as it was understood by the man who instigated the excommunication of Pastor, we see at once the subordination of the Son (as distinguished from the *impersonal* Word) implicit in all Melchiorite theology.

Unusual in Dietrich's brief exposition of the doctrine of the Trinity is the appeal to Heb. 10:5, where Christ the Son, addressing the eternal Father, says, "A body hast thou prepared for me [before the world]." Dietrich brings this passage into relation with John 1:1; Col. 1:9; and II Cor. 5:19; and, being *as a Melchiorite* disposed to equate (the pre-existent) Christ and the Son, he subordinates Christ the Son to the Father (in Nicene terminology: eternal), for the reason that God or God the *Word* gave the Son his body. Dietrich infers from this that, though Christ the Son with his divine soul and his celestial body was entirely from God the Father and the Word, still he may not be called God in the fullest sense, for God is without beginning or end; but Christ the Son had a beginning when before creation he received "from the *Word*" his celestial body. Dietrich makes the following extraordinary statement:

Thus the body of Christ cannot really be regarded as God; but, rather, in that body [before the creation of the world and then visibly from the earthly nativity to the crucifixion] dwelt the fulness of the Godhead bodily; and God was in Christ reconciling the world unto himself.

Dietrich's Christology, although he held to two natures (apparently in the sense of soul and body), was defective in terms of the Chalcedonian standard because neither nature was derived from Mary; and hence also his doctrine of the Trinity was deficient in terms of the Nicene standard because he postulated a time before creation when the Son came into being on receiving a body (and soul) from the *impersonal* eternal Word of God. It is understandable that Dietrich prudently counseled Anthony not to become unnecessarily involved with the "Zwinglians" in controversy on these doctrines.

In the meantime, Adam Pastor, with his unequivocal adoptionism freed from all traces of the Melchiorite legacy, secured a goodly number of followers, especially in the region between Münster and Cologne. They called themselves Adamites (not to be confused with the medieval sect) or Adam-Pastorians.

Their vigor and persistence called forth Menno's tract in 1550, *Confession of the Triune God*.[40] Menno and Adam met for a last debate at Lübeck in 1552, in the hope that a reconciliation could be brought about, but this hope proved vain. It was probably in connection with the debate in 1552 that Adam published his *Underscheit tusschen rechte unde valsche leer*.[41]

The treatise outlines thirteen points of difference between right and false doctrine, namely: (1) on the true and the false God; (2) the incarnation; (3) the atonement, forgiveness, and salvation; (4) mediation and intercession; (5) the time of grace; (6) God-sent and self-running preachers; (7) repentance; (8) faith, new birth, and the church; (9) baptism; (10) the Supper; (11) human institutions and divine instructions; (12) true and false brethren, the Kingdom of God, polygamy, true and false freedom; and (13) true and false books.

The section on God is a listing of the unitarian texts of the Old and New Testament with a minimum of comment. In the second section, on the incarnation and Christology, Pastor vindicated for Mary her full role as mother of Jesus from whom he took Adamic flesh as any other child of woman. In challenging Menno's faulty biology, Pastor pointed out that God, in commanding both Adam and Eve to be fruitful and multiply, used the plural imperative, a construction which would not have been employed if the male seed alone were fruitful of new life. As the unique and miraculously conceived Son of God as Father, all power and glory was given to Christ; but Pastor insisted that not one of the contested New Treatment passages indicated that the Son was, before the incarnation, independently and eternally God.

Pastor's eighth section disconnects regenerative faith from baptism, which is reduced to a sign of covenantal membership.

Adam Pastor, in the Trinitarian controversy, was earnest and critical, but remained mild, reverent, and comprehensive in his arguments against the Nicene formulations.

His influence may have spread up the Vistula river to Cracow, where his name and ideas, arguments and patterns of Scriptural analysis, appear to have been known to the Polish unitarian Anabaptists (Ch. 25.2).

d. *Leonard Bouwens and the Withdrawal of the Waterlanders*. The Lübeck dispute of 1546, which brought out Adam Pastor's unitarianism, also introduces us to a rising leader in the direct line, Leonard Bouwens. Born in Sommelsdyk in 1515, he had

---

[40] *Writings*, 487–498.
[41] *BRN*, V, 315–581.

been in his youth a member of a chamber of rhetoric. After his ordination as an elder by Menno in 1551 at Emden, his influence spread from Harlingen, near which he resided, through East and West Frisia and the North Sea islands. He soon rivaled, even challenged, his older colleagues.

Bouwens was the most rigoristic of all the Netherlandish leaders in the use of the ban, and it was his excesses that caused the defection of the Waterlanders. Leonard progressively sharpened his views on the use of the ban, extending Paul's injunction not to eat with the faithless, i.e., the banned (I Cor. 5:11), to include all social intercourse with the banned and even avoidance in marriage. In most cases, Bouwens supported the application of the ban even without preliminary admonition. There are instances where the elders, or those commissioned by them, made bold to enter by night the house of an adulterous or otherwise unfaithful and therefore banned husband, to seize his wife from him and her screaming children in brute enforcement of the ban.[42]

Menno's last years were troubled by the increasing bitterness and seriousness of the controversy among the Netherlandish congregations. We have already seen how at Wismar five of the nine resolutions of 1554 were devoted to the ban. Menno, Dietrich, and Bouwens had already reached a provisional accord.

The first indication of the seriousness of the fresh trouble in the Netherlands reached Menno by letter in 1555.[43] Five brethren of the congregation of Franeker explained the division of their West Frisian church over the issue of whether it was proper, in the case of gross public sin, to abide by the Matthaean (ch. 18:15–18) injunction to give three warnings, and, if not, whether the ban should not be as swift and inexorable also for lesser offenses. Menno in his reply[44] insisted that "some sins, as for instance murder, witchcraft, arson, theft, and other like criminal deeds, which eventually require and imply punishment at the hands of the magistracy," should be the occasion of swift banning. In dealing with lesser sins and repentant sinners, however, Menno defended the traditional moderate procedure in the spirit of his earlier writings. He found "wholly frightful" and an "unheard-of fanaticism" the demand of some of the Franeker rigorists that even a transgressor in a minor matter, who had already in pain

[42] Y. Buruma, *Het huwelijk der Doopsgezinden in de zestiende eeuw* (Amsterdam, 1911).
[43] Printed in *BRN*, VII, 444–447.
[44] *Instruction on Discipline to the Church at Franeker; Writings*, 1043–1045.

and sorrow lamented his sin to a brother, be obliged still to confess before the whole congregation or else be banned with the guiltiest of hardened transgressors.

Leonard Bouwens brought on the crisis when he threatened to ban a married woman in Emden because she refused to shun her husband, who had been abruptly excommunicated for an unspecified reason. Menno reacted with a letter which spoke out vigorously against such a practice,[45] expressing the hope that wherever the banned spouse did nothing otherwise to interfere with the spiritual life and churchly duties of the other, banning should not necessarily lead to marital avoidance.

Yet Menno's stand, though less strict than that of Leonard, was by no means lenient. Indeed, he was becoming involved at almost the same time (April 1556) with two brethren, Zylis Jacobs of Monschau (Eifel) and Lemke Bruerren of Maastricht, one active from Cologne south to Strassburg, the other in Jülich, both of whom considered Menno too rigorous. The Middle and South Germans excluded banned persons from Communion, but did not shun them. Caught between two fires, Menno inclined more and more to the camp of Leonard, impelled by "the lack of discipline" of the South Germans and badgered by Leonard's threat of using the ban against him! Menno resolved to preserve church discipline intact, even if it meant allying himself with the extremism of Bouwens and, under pressure, finally took the position that all human ties, including those of marriage and the family, must give way under the ban of the church. This attitude called forth opposition from the Middle Rhenish brethren; and Menno's last extant writing, *Reply to Zylis and Lemke* (1560),[46] was a defense of his newly hardened position. There is no doubt that he was deeply grieved by the whole controversy and regretted the extreme view into which he had been maneuvered.

Leonard Bouwens, pressing his advantage, banned the leaders of the moderate faction in the churches of Franeker and Emden. To Henry Naaldeman in Franeker, the proponent of the formerly normative and apostolic triple warning, Menno wrote with the hope of reconciling him and his followers, but the break was definitive in 1556, despite a colloquy in Harlingen in 1557. Naaldeman, heading the moderate "Franekers," joined with similar "liberal" factions in Emden, such as that of Jacob Jans

---

[45] *Writings*, 1051 f.
[46] *Ibid.*, 999–1015. The regional background of Zyl and Lemke is filled in by Ernest Crous, "Anabaptism in Schleiden-in-the-Eifel," *MQR*, XXXIV (1960), 188–191.

Scheedemaker, and with the other communities in the Waterland district of Holland and West Frisia, to be known presently as Waterlanders. The designation was destined to be primarily a religious rather than a regional label. Bouwens and his followers called them "Scheedemakers," after the Emden elder, with a punning allusion also to their being "division-makers." Actually, of course, the rigorists were, in one sense, the innovators and hence the cause of the factionalism.

The Waterlanders were the least rigoristic and soon turned out to be the most "progressive" or culturally accommodative group of Dutch Mennonites. From the outset they maintained contact with the "world," countenancing intermarriage with members of other churches, and eventually accepting lesser magisterial offices which would not involve them in the use of the sword. Feeling it inappropriate to be named for a man, they came to prefer to be called "Doopsgezinden" (baptism-favorers) rather than Mennonites.[47] The Waterlanders quietly built up their congregationally ordered brotherhoods, with no place for dominating elders or bishops. They soon achieved a sober, well-organized congregational life, and an arrangement for mutual assistance in preaching. They recognized as Christians all who had experienced the regeneration of the inner man through the power of God by faith in Jesus Christ. In spite of Leonard's view that they were a "garbage wagon," the Waterlanders were to be the only Anabaptist group in the Netherlands to avoid further schism in the years ahead.

In the meantime, the disagreement of the Swiss and South German Brethren with the extreme views on shunning and the incarnation (celestial flesh) came to a head, and at two, possibly three, conferences (cf. Ch. 31.1) in Strassburg in 1554 (about which almost nothing is known), 1555, and 1557 (before and after consulting Menno) they repudiated the Mennonite position. The "Second Strassburg Conference," held in August 1555, was attended by High German Anabaptists (Swiss Brethren, Hutterites, and South German Pilgramites) and by a small number of Mennonites (called locally Hofmannites). At this meeting (about which we know only through a circular letter which the group sent to the Netherlands)[48] the discussion was confined to the doctrine of the incarnation. It was observed that the New Testament

[47] In 1796, this word became the official designation for all Dutch Mennonites.
[48] Hulshof, *op. cit.*, 219–222. Harold Bender helpfully orders and characterizes those synods in "Strasbourg Conferences," *ME*, IV, 642–644. Conference I, March 1554 attended by six hundred Anabaptists; Conference II, August 1555; Conference III, 1557; Conference IV, 1568. It is not certain that the Netherlanders were involved in the scantly documented Conference I.

spoke inconclusively as to whether Christ's nature was celestial or Adamic. The decision reached was that both Upper and Lower Germans should limit themselves to the expressions of the New Testament, and should avoid speculative elaborations of them. On the question whether Christ was capable of sin, the two factions were not agreed, for the letter urges the participants "to work for peace."[49]

Before the Third Strassburg Conference, Leonard Bouwens, who as we have seen had in the meantime secured Menno's adherence to his strict view of the ban, thought that with Menno's influential support he could win the High Germans over to his position. Accordingly he summoned a conference to meet at Cologne in the spring of 1557. The High Germans, however, with their plans for another Strassburg conference that same year, did not show up at Cologne. Rather than go in person to Strassburg and become involved in the great debate on original sin, Leonard chose to rely upon a strong letter from Menno to the High Germans on "common" shunning. "Common" shunning for him, as we have seen, consisted in the avoidance of conversation, even civil greeting, also of trade, and (where one spouse was under the ban) of marital intercourse. The Third Strassburg Conference of 1557 was attended by representatives from possibly as far away as Moravia.[50]

Menno's letter did not have the desired result but, rather, the contrary. The High German Anabaptists were completely unsympathetic to Menno's proposal; and, although they couched their reply to him in fraternal and apologetic language, they were firm in their refusal. They begged the Netherlanders not to press the issue to the breaking point, but in vain, for that was precisely what Leonard was determined to do. The proffered hand of reconciliation was rejected, and at a meeting later that same year, the Netherlandish elders banned the High Germans, and refused to recognize the validity of their baptism. The rigoristic ban was on the way to becoming the basis for Anabaptist anabaptisms.

Strassburg, whence Melchior Hofmann had set out in 1530 for

---

[49] Hulshof, *op. cit.*, 223.

[50] There were representatives *"van der Eyfelt aen tot Maerlant toe."* Maerlant is not quite Mähren, and Moravia does not necessarily mean Hutterites, as Kiwiet, *Marpeck*, 68, says. He refers to Timotheus Röhrich, *Geschichte der Reformation in Elsass*, III (Strassburg, 1832), 139, who refers in turn to Johann Ottius, *Annales Anabaptistici* (Basel, 1672), 120, 127. Röhrich incidentally mentions a Martin Steinbach living at this time, calling himself Elias and a leader of a group called *Lichtseher*, with a confused reference to Jer. 48:12.

Emden to proclaim to the Low Germans the Anabaptist gospel of baptism as the covenant or betrothal of the believer with Christ, was thus, a quarter of a century thereafter, 1555 and 1557, the scene of the formalized break between the Low and the High Germans on the ecclesiological implications (pure church and the rigorous ban) of precisely the two doctrines which Hofmann had elaborated while in Strassburg. His doctrine of the celestial flesh of Christ, with its perfectionist thrust in ecclesiology, had led to the rigoristic banning of all who, because of spiritual adultery, were disqualified from participation in the corporate life of the one celestial body. We have thus come full circle in that part of our narrative on baptismal-nuptial theology which began in Ch. 11.1, from Strassburg 1530 to Strassburg 1557.

The discussion in Ch. 14.1 will have made it clear that Menno began by looking on the ban as an instrument of reformation and a means of reconciliation. Even after he had yielded to Leonard Bouwens' influence, he was still very acute in his analysis of the danger of a false show of repentance by the sinner on the one hand, and of pharisaical self-righteousness in the banners on the other. His last words on the subject, written after the break with the High Germans, still close on a note of cure rather than condemnation:

[Let the church] bring him to the altar of the Lord, sprinkle him with the spiritual hyssop of God, declare to him the grace of Christ, and so receive him again as a beloved brother in Christ Jesus and greet him with the salutation of His holy peace, for the Lord . . . does not desire the death of the wicked, but that he repent.[51]

The spirit in which this admonition is intended can be sensed from the following account of the by now formalized ceremony of readmission. The banned and now repentant brother or sister in question would appear before the whole Mennonite congregation, where he would be asked publicly to confess that he had aroused the anger of God by his transgressions and sin, which had been the cause of his excommunication. This done, a short message by one of the elders would point out the importance of repentance and the consciousness of guilt. The one seeking reinstatement was thereupon asked whether he truly repented of his wrongs with all his heart, and whether he hoped, by his grace, to serve God in the future. With an affirmative answer, the elder would proceed: "If you have reformed and have been honestly converted, we proclaim to you the grace of God." This was followed by a verse of Scripture; and the brother was asked whether

[51] *Instruction on Excommunication; Writings,* 961–998.

the church should pray for him. At his request the congregation would pray, and finally the elder would conclude: "As Paul [Rom. 15:7] commanded that we should receive one another as Christ received us, so we receive you . . . also." The reinstated brother was thereupon dismissed with a special admonition.[52]

The frequency with which the ban was used makes it clear that readmission was also frequent, which was formalized in the Mennonite penitential cycle of sin-ban-repentance-readmission, roughly corresponding to the Roman cycle of sin-confession-penitence-absolution.

3. FROM THE DEATH OF MENNO IN 1561 TO THE DEATH OF DIETRICH IN 1568: THE INFLUENCE OF SEBASTIAN FRANCK

Menno Simons, saddened by controversy, crippled, and bereaved of his wife, died 31 January 1561 at Wüstenfelde, exactly a quarter of a century to the month after his leaving the Catholic parish of his native Witmarsum.

Between his death in 1561 and that of his closest associate, Dietrich Philips, in 1568, the major literary achievements among the Netherlanders and Low Germans were the publication of what might loosely be called the first edition of the *Martyrs' Mirror* in 1562 and the collected works of Dietrich in the *Enchiridion* in 1564. The major developments were the renewed struggle with Spiritualism occasioned by the publication, in Dutch translation, of two letters by Sebastian Franck in 1564, and the division on the issue of rigorism in the use of the ban between the Frisians and the Flemings in 1567. As the latter development is connected with the flight of the Flemings and the rise of nationalist Calvinism in 1566, we shall postpone that story until Ch. 30.1.

a. *"Het Offer des Herren," 1562.* As we devote our attention to the theological and organizational developments among the Anabaptists in the Netherlands, we do not forget that this growth and controversy took place in the face of severe and systematic persecution. The Anabaptists early produced a theology of martyrdom and thought of themselves as the suffering church in succession to the righteous remnant from the days of the prophets. *The Offering of the Lord,* which we have already cited several times in its final form, the *Martyrs' Mirror* of 1660, was a compilation of reports on the Netherlandish Anabaptist martyrs, although it includes only a fraction of the martyrdoms. Interest-

[52] Anna Brons, *Ursprung, Entwickelung und Schicksale der altevangelischen Taufgesinnten oder Mennoniten* (Norden, 1884), 121 f.; Frank C. Peters, "The Ban in the Writings of Menno Simons," *MQR*, XXIX (1955), 31 f.

ingly, it contains an account of the cross-examination of one Upper German martyr, Michael Sattler (Ch. 8.2). All of its editions include a songbook (*Een Lietboecxken*), with songs of comfort and courage, retelling the story of the martyrs. Besides accounts of the trials and imprisonments, *Het Offer* often gives the final letters of the martyrs to next of kin and to the brethren, the reminiscences of eyewitnesses, and many hymns. Some of these pieces, written by the prisoners themselves, vividly testify to their steadfast courage, earnest Christian conviction, charity, and even their "gallows humor." The date of the appearance of the collection is also a good indication of the inner development of the Mennonite community.

By 1562, a year after Menno's death, the Netherlandish Anabaptists could look back on a tradition gradually emerging into clarity. They had reached the point where they could catch their breath and recall their martyrs. Martyrdoms were still taking place, but they were those of loyal followers, not of the first heralds of the faith. Second-generation Anabaptists were beginning to speak of martyrdom as the normal pattern for Christian life at just about the time that it was no longer being forced upon them by a hostile government. By 1566 the Netherlands under William the Silent would be in arms against the Spanish oppressors.

b. The Spiritualist Crisis of 1564–1567. Besides the withdrawal of the Waterlander Baptists in 1557, who preferred the South German and more Scriptural use of the ban with a triple warning; besides the rejection a decade earlier in 1547 of the unitarian Adamites; besides the rejection of the Jorists' overtures for union a second time at Lübeck in 1546; besides the defection of Obbe Philips in Amsterdam and the emergence of the Familists in Emden about 1541, there was one more manifestation of the struggle between Spiritualism and Anabaptism within the Radical Reformation, namely, the wide circulation of the works of Sebastian Franck and their repeated translation into Dutch[53] and reissue well into the next century. The Spiritualist challenge to main-line Mennonitism may be said to have become acute in 1564, when two letters, earlier addressed by Franck to his sympa-

[53] Bruno Becker, "Nederlandsche Vertalingen van Sebastiaan Francks Geschriften," *NAK*, n.s., XXI (1928), 149–160. Three of his works survive intact only in later Dutch translations: *The Kingdom of Christ* (Gouda, 1611, 1617), which is his most systematic work; *Of the World which is the Devil's Kingdom* (Gouda, 1618), and *The Communion of Saints* (Gouda, 1618). A sermon against "Herr Omnes," which is included in the second of these three Dutch translations under the title of "Treatise Concerning the People," had been refused by the censors in Ulm in 1538.

thizers in Lower Germany, were, because of their great appeal, published and circulated in a Dutch translation by Peter de Zuttere. The temptation to go spiritual was as great in the Netherlands as in South Germany, when Marpeck was fighting Schwenckfeld (Ch. 18). The Dutch edition of Franck's letters was symptomatic of a widespread reaction to the rigorism of Bouwens.

The first of these two popular letters was Franck's manifesto on the *Ecclesia Spiritualis* written to Campanus in 1531 (Ch. 18.3). Franck's other letter was addressed to Christians in Lower Germany, who "live like sheep among wolves." It had been written at the request of one John of Bekesteyn of Oldersum (Ch. 14.1), that renowned asylum near Emden for refugee Sacramentists, Anabaptists, and now Spiritualists. Bekesteyn had visited Franck in Basel c. 1541. Another person in the Netherlands to have been demonstrably influenced by Franck was David Joris. To be sure, Joris wrote both before and after Franck. But in the principal work of Joris, *'t Wonderboek* of 1542, it is apparent that he had passed, under the influence of Franck's Spiritualism, from ecstatic prophetism to quietistic mysticism. Henry Niclaes had also made use of Franck's writings.[54]

The "national-reformed" Sacramentist Anastasius Velanus, in *Leken Wechwyser* (*The Layman's Guide*), denounced Franck in 1554 as impure and sullied with dangerous errors in every article of his faith, and in 1557 in his treatise on the Supper he referred to the presence of "Sebastianists," and in his *Confession* of 1561, to "Franckists." By 1564 it was thus clear that Franck's individualistic Spiritualism was attractive to professed Mennonites, and in 1567, Dietrich took up the challenge of the two popular Franckist letters and warned his congregations against the Spiritualist menace.[55]

Philips was dealing with a major threat to the disciplined communities of the Anabaptists at the very moment in Dutch history when a new belligerence, no longer apocalyptic, as with the Münsterites, but nationalistic, had emerged under the banner of predestinarian Calvinism to free the Netherlands of the Hapsburg yoke. The Calvinists, too, had their clandestine conventicles and had adopted a national confession of faith at Antwerp in 1566, the *Confessio Belgica*. The Anabaptists, having completely purged their membership of fighting saints, as a pacifistic and patient remnant, could not afford, under the influence of the Spiritualizers, to let their only weapons tarnish and their only sup-

[54] Bruno Becker, "Nicolais inlassching over de Franckisten," *NAK*, n.s., XVIII (1925).
[55] *BRN*, X, 473 ff.

plies spoil, namely, their believers' baptism as a sign, their Eucharistic banquet with the risen Christ, and their stern and swiftly executed ban.

It was in the same year that Franck's popular letters were published in Dutch that Philips published his systematic theology.

c. The "Enchiridion" of 1564. Dietrich Philips' *Enchiridion or Handbook for the Christian Soldier* of 1564[56] corresponded in magnitude as a systematic, collected work to Menno's *Foundation Book* of 1540. It was in the Dutch- and German-speaking parts of Poland that Dietrich had the time to pull together his diverse writings as an enchiridion. He had followed Menno to the delta of the Vistula; and, from 1555 to his death in 1568, his base was Danzig and then Schottland, the latter a region just outside the jurisdiction of the town, whence he continued to make frequent trips by sea to the Netherlands and Emden.

The *Enchiridion* contains close to 650 pages, comprising almost all his writings to date.[57] Some of its component treatises are of especial interest to us at this point.

In the line of Hofmann and Menno, Dietrich Philips stressed the Eucharistic and soteriological implications of the celestial flesh of Christ.[58] Dietrich became even more explicit than Menno on the identity of the heavenly flesh and the manna of Communion:

Christ says much, according to John, of the eating of his flesh and the drinking of his blood. It therefore behooves us to see and consider, how the flesh of Christ shall and must be eaten and his blood drunk, namely thus, that we accept and obey the word of God with pure hearts and in true faith. . . . And the living bread (which is Christ and his flesh) is beyond all doubt and contradiction the Word of God, and therefore if any man believes and obeys the Word of God, he receives Christ, the Word of life and the bread of heaven, yea, he eats the flesh and drinks the blood of Christ. And because of this, Jesus calls his flesh "meat indeed," and his blood "drink indeed," because the Word of God is really meat for the soul.

Philips, like Hofmann (Ch. 11.3), appealed to the dew-pearl analogy of medieval mysticism:

---

[56] *BRN*, X; translated by Abraham B. Kolb (Elkhart, Indiana, 1910). See also William Keeney, "The Writings of Dirk Philips," *MQR*, XXXII (1958).

[57] Writings not included are the refutation of the two epistles of Franck (1567), the *Short but Thorough Account* (1567) about the quarrels between the Flemish and the Frisians, and *Christian Matrimony* posthumously printed in 1569.

[58] Cf. Cornelius J. Dyck, "The Christology of Dirk Philips," *MQR*, XXXI (1957), 147–155.

Christ Jesus is the living bread which came like dew or manna from heaven, and what was the food of angels has also become the food of men [Ps. 78:25]. But the bread, which he is himself, and gives men—that is, believers—to eat, is his flesh, which he has given for the life of the world.

In *Regeneration and the New Creature,* from which the foregoing has been quoted, Dietrich clarified his conception of salvation as the progressive restitution of the image of God among men through regenerative baptism and Eucharistic nourishment. In Christ, the image of the invisible God, in Christ, the new Adam, the faithful are reborn to become partakers of the divine nature, of the celestial and holy flesh of Christ, and, with qualifications, to become gods:

Now although men become participant in the divine nature, gods and children of the Most High, they yet do not become in being and person what God and Christ alone are. Oh no! The creature will never become the Creator, and flesh will never become eternal spirit, which God is, for this would be impossible. But the believers become gods and children of the Most High through the new birth, the impartation and fellowship of the divine nature, righteousness, glory, purity, and eternal life.[59]

To sum up the development from Hofmann through Philips: For Hofmann, the doctrine of the heavenly flesh was the sanction of a new order which he conceived both experientially and eschatologically. For Menno, the new order was seen primarily in the church of the regenerate, faithfully employing the ban to maintain a spotless community in the world of evil. For Philips (as with Schwenckfeld, the Spiritualist!), the emphasis was on the mystical eating of the heavenly flesh of Christ in Communion and gradual divinization.

Dietrich was not, however, a perfectionist in his ecclesiology. He knew that there would always be backsliders and even hypocrites. But the church must use the ban to help itself remain as pure as possible.

Although it is the whole congregation which loosens or binds in the name of God, nevertheless the preachers and teachers have an important role. They are commissioned directly through God or through the operation of the whole church. Their heroic functions are discussed in *The Sending of Preachers and Teachers.* In this treatise on polity, it is clear that the primary oppo-

---

[59] *Van der Menschwerdinghe ons heeren Jesu Christi, BRN,* X, 148 f., translated by Alvin J. Beachy in his unpublished doctoral dissertation, "The Concept of Grace in the Radical Reformation," Harvard, 1960, 171 f.

nents of Dietrich are the Spiritualists like his own brother Obbe, Franck, and Schwenckfeld. Herein also Dietrich emphasizes the importance of the proclamation of the law in preparation for the proclamation of the grace of God. "Elders" and "bishops" seem to be used interchangeably in early Mennonite literature. We have already remarked that former priests among the Anabaptists, such as Menno, Dietrich, and Adam Pastor, felt it incumbent upon themselves to seek reordination as well as rebaptism. This, however, is an obscure chapter in Mennonite history. Theirs was a Spiritual succession in the Melchiorite sense of a succession of rebaptized converts who were in turn set aside by the charismatic leaders as elders by the laying on of hands.

In still another treatise, *The Church of God*,[60] Dietrich states most fully and in lofty language the evangelical Anabaptist conception of the true church, which was first gathered among the angels in heaven, which was reconstituted in Paradise, and which, though it suffered defection and corruption from the fall of the angels and the fall of Adam up to the most recent present, nevertheless has been one great succession of faithful men and women wending their way like a caravan through the centuries. Among the members of this band, the image of Christ has been restored.

Dietrich extended the paradisic ideal to marriage. The paradisic character of Christian monogamy, propounded in his earlier work on *Spiritual Restitution,* was amplified in *Christian Matrimony,* wherein he closely related marriage to the relationship of the Second Adam to the Second Eve, the church, and propounded the view that only the reborn who partake of the divine nature of Christ can be joined in holy wedlock, and that separation (divorce) is obligatory when one spouse is banned.

Dietrich's book on matrimony was his last. It was published posthumously. The importance of the covenant of marriage in the Radical Reformation, replacing the sacrament of marriage in the Old Church, has been suggested several times in the course of our narrative. It is perhaps appropriate that we pass from a chapter on Familism and stern banning with respect to bed and board to a chapter dealing comprehensively with marriage in the Radical Reformation.

[60] Translated in *SAW,* 226 ff.

CHAPTER 20

MARRIAGE IN THE RADICAL REFORMATION

We may take Dietrich Philips' last work, *On Christian Matrimony* (1568), as the occasion to discuss the conception of marriage and divorce for the whole of the Radical Reformation.

It was inevitable that Netherlandish Anabaptism, which derived in large measure from Melchior Hofmann, who likened baptism to betrothal (Ch. 11.1), and which, passing through the Münsterite phase, came temporarily to espouse polygamy, should have become theologically and ethically the most articulate of any branch or region of the Radical Reformation about the Christian or Biblical meaning of marriage and divorce. But to understand the preoccupation of any group of Anabaptists with marriage and divorce we must see their particular formulations and practices in the larger context of the Radical Reformation.

It was inevitable that a movement which sought to restore the church as a provisional paradise in the wilderness of the world should not only propose to rebaptize and to reordain but also to rethink the bonds of matrimony and discover in the renewal of marriage a covenantal means of redemption, as an ordinance appointed by the Second Adam for the recovery of the pristine harmony of Adam and Eve before their fall.

For Luther (e.g., *Vom ehelichen Leben*, 1522),[1] the family belonged to the order of fallen creation, as did the state. For Zwingli and Calvin, the children of Christian parents belonged to the covenant. Hence the equation of circumcision and pedobaptism; but for them both as for Luther, marriage itself was neither sacramental nor covenantal.

The Council of Trent, challenged by the programmatic Protestant desacramentalizing of marriage, prepared to make the two ways of life, marriage and celibacy, at least equally valid and equally sacramental. The *locus classicus* for the sacramental character of marriage was Eph. 5:31 f., where the Vulgate renders

---

[1] C. Olavi Lähteenmäki, *Sexus und Ehe bei Luther* (Turku, 1955).

the Greek term for the relationship of man and wife, Christ and his church, as a *sacramentum*. Though from the days of Paul the married state was held by the fathers, the monastic divines, and the scholastics as implicitly inferior to celibacy,[2] the passage in Ephesians and many kindred expressions in the Old Testament and the New were always there to make possible, after a millennium and a half of Christian experience, the restoration of the original Hebraic esteem for conjugal love and the divine injunction to be fruitful and multiply, to a place co-ordinate in significance with the Hellenistic-ascetic esteem for celibacy. At the Council of Trent the Catholic Church, redefining marriage as one of the seven sacraments, no longer implicitly inferior to the clerical vow of celibacy, insisted that to be valid henceforth it had to be consecrated in the presence of a priest.

The Radical Reformation shared with Catholicism the resolution to perpetuate or indeed to intensify the Christian sense of marriage as an ordinance of the church, but it shared with the Magisterial Reformation the repudiation of both the sacramental character of marriage and the Christianization of celibacy as an alternative and implicitly superior way. In interpreting matrimony in the language of the covenant with Christ, the Radical Reformation found a new theological basis for marriage as an ordinance of Christ within the purview of the church. Needless to say, excesses and aberrations attended the theological realignment of the most fundamental of human institutions and relationships.

Both the Protestants and the Radicals were prepared to repudiate vows taken to celibacy within the Old Church, but the former would never have theologically countenanced the disavowal of any marriage contracted in the Old Church.[3] In contrast, the Anabaptists were not only rebaptizers and reordinationists, they were also, on principle (though not always in practice), "re-trothers," in the sense that they reaffirmed their marital relationship in Christ or remarried in faith. Instances of formal remarriage of a banned and reinstated spouse with the faithful spouse are preserved.[4]

Nowhere else in the Reformation Era were women so nearly the peers and companions in the faith, and mates in missionary

---

[2] The best-known example is Jerome's view that marriage was useful chiefly to produce more virgins; *Epistle* XXII to Eustochium, CXXX to Demetrias.

[3] The divorces and marriages of that Magisterial Reformer par excellence and Defender of the Faith cannot be entered into at this point in the generalization.

[4] *ME*, III, "Marriage," 502–510, and specifically 506.

enterprise and readiness for martyrdom, as among those for whom believers' baptism was an equalizing covenant, consummated in terms readily employing the language of betrothal and the marriage bed.[5] The Anabaptist insistence on the covenantal principle of the freedom of conscience for all adult believers and thereby the extension of the priesthood of the Christophorous laity to women constituted a major breach in patriarchalism and a momentous step in the Western emancipation of women. Besides numerous patronesses, protectresses, and martyrs, the Radical Reformation acknowledged several prophetesses, at least two women apostles, and one redemptress (William Postel's Venetian virgin).[6]

As a consequence of the covenantal understanding of marriage as a conjugal relationship between a man and a woman as responsible believers under Christ, the Anabaptists, sociologically "sectarian" though they were, took a position closer to the sociologically "churchly" Catholics than to the (no less, in the sociological sense) "churchly" Protestants. But precisely because marriage was, for them, a covenant, as their relationship with Christ was a "betrothal," they found a basis both for greater personal loyalty within the covenantal bond than in sacramental Catholicism, and for greater freedom of divorce and remarriage.

At the same time, uncertainty as to the binding character of the Old Testament marital precepts and practices (notably the polygamy of the patriarchs), the fascination exercised by late medieval Adamite speculation concerning the original intention of God for the sexes before the Fall, the baleful influence of IV Clement (below), innocently regarded as apostolic, the Dominical injunction (Matt. 10:35 ff. and 19:29) to leave kith and kin and carry the cross,[7] and the eschatological urgency to procreate in covenantal purity the saints foreseen in Rev. 7:4— all these marginal matters delayed or turmoiled the eventual clarification of the basically new conception of marriage which the Anabaptists had come to espouse. To the theological confusion caused by conflicting Scriptures must be added the strains in the hearts of loving spouses separated by persecution, flight, imprisonment, missionary duty, and altering convictions as to the requirements of faith.

---

[5] Roland Bainton, *What Christianity Says About Sex, Love, and Marriage* (New York, 1957).

[6] The generalization is that of Max Weber, *Die protestantische Ethik und der "Geist" des Kapitalismus*, Gesammelte Aufsätze, I (Tübingen, 1922), 171. For the two *Apostelinnen*, see Crous, "Eifel,"*loc. cit.,* 189.

[7] Schornbaum, *Bayern,* I (*QGT,* II), Nos. 15, 16, 353.

In its conjugal aspects the Radical Reformation was admittedly more prone to excesses than the Magisterial Reformation, which put the cleric on the same level and roughly in the same circumstances of life as the layman, which placed the contractual aspect of marriage itself under the civil authorities, and which only in a few notorious cases contrived sanctions for bigamy or divorce as the lesser of two evils in notably political situations. Although more turbulent, nevertheless, the Radical Reformation was perhaps also religiously more creative than normative Protestantism because it went beyond placing the minister and the layman on the same level. Refusing to consider marriage, thus reconceived, as solely of nature or the natural estate, it found new ways of construing the marriage of Christians as a relationship superior to, and also religiously more hazardous than, civil matrimony. The excesses with respect to marriage in the Radical Reformation, the outcropping of polygamy, the self-righteous desertion of unbelieving spouses by converts, and here and there the explicit espousal of sexual communism within the confines of the conventicle must be understood not only (1) as concomitants of the disruption of the medieval sacramental conception of marriage but also (2) as the earnest aberrations of Biblical literalists who could, after all, find several passages in support of their theory and practice, and (3), finally, as the syndrome of the eschatologically intense turning away from attachment to previous property, inheritance, civil and social status, and from the state as their support and sanction. Embracing as their own literal way of life the love of the brethren and the sharing in all things recorded in so many passages of the New Testament, the Radicals almost inevitably at times approached the border where *agapē* and *erōs* became confused. For all that, the post-Reformation conception and practice of marriage cannot be understood without full recognition of the sectarian, covenantal impulse, mediated to the modern world in part by Anabaptism directly, in large measure, however, indirectly by way of the sectarianized forms of Puritanism.

1. The Comprehensive and Conflicting Views of Paracelsus

If we wish to examine in further detail the correlation between the bridal theology and marital practice in the Radical Reformation, we may turn first to Paracelsus, who perhaps best of all illustrates the possibilities in the transition from the medieval Catholic to the Anabaptist view, and who wrote specifically on the subject both as a physician and as a theologian in five works

and several sermons, notably *De nupta* and *De thoro legitimo.*[8]
He embodied the extremes of medieval sacramentalism and the
covenantal ideal of the Radicals. At one point he advocated
polygamy; at another, he justified only monogamy. In his defense of polygamy, he wrote as a physician defending plural marriage as against promiscuity:

God ordained that marriage be sacred, but he did not prescribe the
number of wives, neither a high nor a low one. He commanded: thou
shalt be faithful to thy marriage vow, and thou shalt not break it.
Now it so happens that God has always created many more women
than men. And He makes men die far more readily than women.
And He always lets the women survive and not the men. . . . And if
there is such a surplus of women, let it be taken care of by marriage,
so that the meaning of God's commandment may be heeded. . . . If
this cannot be achieved by giving each man one wife, he should have
two, or whatever number may be required to take care of the surplus. And all this should be done in a just way, not in the spirit of
partisanship. . . . For human laws must be adapted to the needs of
the times, and accordingly can be abrogated and replaced by others.[9]

Presumably at a later date, Paracelsus defended monogamy in
the unusual form of divinely preordained coupling:

And although in former times—that is, in the Old Testament—some
had more than one [wife], that does not mean that it was right. . . .
Rather, it is right that each man belong to his wife only and each
woman to her husband. . . . No man shall take another man's predestined spouse (*geborne gemahel*), even if the couple have not yet
been joined together in the presence of other men, but only before
God. When the right hour has come, God will reveal to the people
the identity of their intended mates. This is in accordance with the
providence and foreknowledge of God, which is hidden from man.
Accordingly, [when] Christ says [cf. Matt. 19:6; Mark 10:9]: "Those
whom God joins together"—that is to say, those whom he [by anticipation already] joins together in the mother's womb . . .[10]

On the surface, at least, Paracelsus reversed himself on the question of monogamy and polygamy. The two quoted passages
agree, however, in that the principal sin is adultery; that the
standard of true marriage is God's initial monogamous command in Genesis and the restitution of this pre-Mosaic ideal by
Jesus; and that the permanent and the essential in true marriage

---

[8] Goldammer, *Paracelsus: Offenbarung,* conveniently classifies and lists the
Paracelsian works, *Schriften,* 113 f.
[9] Paracelsus, *Selected Writings,* edited by Jolandi Jacobi, translated by Norbert Guterman, Bollingen Series XXVIII (New York, 1951), 109 f.
[10] *De Nupta;* quoted in Goldammer, *Schriften,* 281 f.

is the divine commandment, what Paracelsus calls the "metaphysic of marriage."[11]

Paracelsus did not recognize divorce as valid on any grounds. Here he followed Mark 10:9 rather than Matt. 19:6, holding that the latter, which permits divorce in the case of a wife's adultery, was addressed to Jews and made the concession to them only and not to Christians.[12] But while Paracelsus did not permit full divorce, that is, separation with the right to remarry, he did justify separation without the right to remarry; namely, in the case of one especially called to be an apostle.[13] Divorce thereupon was mandatory, not because Paracelsus held celibacy to be a superior state, but because, as missionary to the world, the apostle should not be burdened by family responsibilities. Paracelsus required the apostles, if already married, to forsake their wives. Like many of his contemporaries, Paracelsus conceived of the age in which he lived as one of impending doom. An apostle had to imitate Paul (I Cor. 7:7) and be prepared for martyrdom, incompatible with family obligations.[14]

Insistence on apostolic celibacy did not, of course, in any way detract from marriage. On the contrary, Paracelsus valued marriage as a holy estate "so high that all lords of the world shall be abandoned for the sake of its commands,"[15] and in a characteristically spiritualizing sense he still called it a sacrament:

Marriage is a sacrament, for, taken from its original Latin context, the word "sacrament" equals "sacra mens"—in other words, a holy disposition. Or, to put it differently, [marriage] shall take place with a pure heart according to the command of God, and not the command of men.[16]

Indeed, next to the office of apostle, there is no higher office than that of spouse. Because monasticism undermined marriage, Paracelsus attacked it and blamed the devil, himself a "despicable virgin":

He whom God loves is no virgin; for whoever would be a virgin, whether man or woman, must belong to a better estate than the

---

11 The term is Kurt Goldammer's in "Neues zur Lebensgeschichte und Persönlichkeit des Theophrastus Paracelsus," *Theologische Zeitschrift,* III (1947), 215.

12 *Ibid.,* 209, n. 11, quoting *De thoro legitimo.*

13 Cf. *ibid., passim,* on Paracelsus' concept of office and its relation to the question of celibacy. Apostles included also prophets and teachers, but not bishops, the last considered by Paracelsus as noncharismatic officers.

14 Cf. Goldammer, *Schriften,* 282. When Paul said he wished all were, like himself, unmarried, he addressed, not Christians in general, according to Paracelsus, but apostles.

15 Quoted by Goldammer, "Lebensgeschichte," 208, n. 7.

16 *De thoro legitimo;* quoted *ibid.,* n. 8.

estate of marriage. "Which one is that?" you ask. Only the office of apostle, which is the smallest of all, having few members. If, however, you are not a true apostle, and yet profess virginity, consider how greatly you will be accused before God on the day of judgment; for the estate of marriage is, in God's view, the greatest there is. It has a merit in his sight which is richly rewarded. Indeed, nothing else on earth enables us to achieve a merit. On the contrary, everything which is not matrimonially based is negligible as far as God is concerned. Thus marriage is the greatest ministry (*ampt*) which God has endowed.[17]

Paracelsus has set the terms of our discussion in their highest form: charitable polygamy, predestined and androgynously conceived monogamy, and vocational divorce (and celibacy).

2. POLYGAMY

Polygamy, or the plurality of wives, was the distinctive feature of the practice of the Münsterites in their final phase and of several other groups and individuals in the Radical Reformation, drawing upon patriarchal precedent and impelled by the Melchiorite eschatological requirement to be fruitful and multiply in covenantal purity without fleshly lust to fill out as speedily as possible the requisite number of one hundred forty-four thousand elect saints for the Kingdom of God (Gen. 1:22; Rev. 7:4).[18] Plural marriage (including bigamy) was theologically defended also among such representatives of the Radical Reformation as the above-cited Paracelsus, the sometime Capuchin general turned Evangelical Rationalist, Bernardine Ochino (Ch. 24.2.c), and here and there a South or Middle German Anabaptist. David Joris himself argued for monogamy in the second age, that of the Son, but it is evident that there were polygamists among his correspondents, who contended that because the patriarchs were close to God, polygamy must be superior to monogamy.[19] Community of wives was the distinctive feature of the Batenburgers, drawing upon the paradisic speculations of the medieval Adamites and emboldened by the restitution of polygamy in Münster. Fleshly mingling as the true and sole sacrament, called *Christerie* or *Christirung*, was the distinctive feature of a small group of Thur-

---

[17] *Auslegung über die zehn Geboten Gottes*, c. 1533; quoted in Goldammer, *Schriften*, 292 f.
[18] Gerhard Zschäbitz, *Zur mitteldeutschen Wiedertäuferbewegung nach dem grossen Bauernkrieg*, Leipziger Übersetzungen und Abhandlungen zum Mittelalter, Band I (Berlin, 1958), has a good section, "Frau und Ehe," 106–121.
[19] Bainton, *Joris*, 66–70.

ingian and Hessian Dreamers or Blood Friends, led by one Louis of Tüngeda, who around 1550 renounced baptism as the covenantal sign in favor of a sexual spiritualism that "sacramentally" unified the fellowship by a *single* dream-inspired coition all around.[20] Adultery was the formal charge against Louis Haetzer, put to death at Constance (Ch. 8.3), and Nicholas Frey in Strassburg (Ch. 10.4), the latter, at least, maintaining to the end a Biblical justification for the desertion of his first wife. Promiscuity cropped out in many places among the excesses of the evangelistic revival, notably in St. Gall (Ch. 6.2) in the group around Hut's deputy in Franconian Königsberg, George Volk (Ch. 7.4), and in the communitarian, Sabbatarian Anabaptism of Andrew Fischer in Zip (Ch. 15.4).

In recounting the rise and fall of the bellicose and polygamous Bibliocracy of Münster (Ch. 13.1), we actually confined our brief canvass of the factors leading to the institution of polygamy to the fact that the Münsterites based their practice principally on God's command to man in Gen. 1:22 to "be fruitful and multiply," which they reinforced by citing, as a secondary authorization, the example of the Old Testament patriarchs. As Bernard Rothmann, in a sermon in the Münster cathedral, proclaimed enthusiastically, it was the will of the Lord that the saints should multiply as the sands of the sea. There is substantial evidence that the Melchiorite Münsterites were concerned to eliminate lust in order that their numerous progeny, procreated in the covenant, would by their purity qualify for a place among the one hundred forty-four thousand in the Holy City.

Bernard Rothmann may have come into contact, either through Sebastian Franck or John Sichard (below), or directly in the Münster cathedral library, with a certain epistle ascribed to Clement of Rome, which urges the community of goods (Ch. 16.3), including wives.[21] We recall that this letter was printed separately from the collection of canon law by John Sichard in Basel in August of 1526, and was considered authentically apos-

---

[20] On the *Träumer* and *Blutsfreunde*, see further, Paul Wappler, *Die Stellung Kursachsens und des Landgrafen Philipp von Hessen*, 13/14 Reformationsgeschichtliche Studien und Texte (Münster, 1910), 429, 481; Zschäbitz, *op. cit.*, 111–115. On George Volk's practice, see Joseph Jurg, *Deutschland in der Revolutionsperiode* (Freiburg/B, 1851), 682.

[21] "*Denique Graecorum quidem sapientissimus* [Pythagoras or Plato], *nec ita sciens esse, ait communia amicorum omnia. In omnibus autem sunt sine dubio et conjuges.*" Paulus Hinschius, editor, *Decretales Pseudo-Isidorianae* (Leipzig, 1863), 65. This is the Latin text behind the Hutterite passage on Clementine communism quoted in Ch. 16.3 at n. 25.

tolic. Some of its decisive passages were taken over almost verbatim into Franck's *Chronica*.[22] This odd document, though surely not the major factor in the emergence of "evangelical" polygamy in the sixteenth century, may well have provided an "apostolic" sanction for the aberrant developments in Münster and elsewhere.[23]

3. COVENANTAL MARRIAGE

In the eyes of their enemies all Anabaptists were basically Münsterites. Accordingly, despite the fact that Menno and Dietrich Philips had recoiled from the fanaticism typified by Münster, one of the charges that they had to deny was that their followers practiced polygamy.

In his refutation of the charges, Menno dealt with the very incidents in the Old Testament which the Münsterites had cited in support of polygamy and, like Dietrich Philips, appealed to the paradisic exemplars of marriage:

As to polygamy, we would say the Scriptures show that before the Law some of the patriarchs had many wives, yet they did not have the same liberty under the Law that they had before the Law. For Abraham who was before the Law had his own sister for wife, as he himself testifies before Abimelech, the king, saying, "And yet she is my sister. . . ." Jacob had two sisters for wives, Leah and Rachel, the daughters of Laban, his mother's brother. These liberties to marry their own sister and to marry two sisters at once were afterwards strictly forbidden Israel. . . .

Each era had its own liberty and usage according to the Scriptures, in the matter of marriage. And under the New Testament we are not pointed by the Lord to the usage of the patriarchs before the Law nor under the Law, but to the beginning of creation, to Adam and Eve. . . . Therefore we teach, practice, and consent to no other arrangement than the one which was in vogue in the beginning with Adam and Eve, namely, one husband and one wife, as the Lord's mouth has ordained.[24]

The Hutterites, too, though like the Münsterites communistically organized, stoutly opposed polygamy. Peter Riedemann's argument to this effect is noteworthy because it illustrates the close relation, to which reference has previously been made, between bridal theology and covenantal marriage:

[22] Strassburg, 1531, 496a.
[23] Von Schubert, *loc. cit.*
[24] *Reply to False Accusations; Writings,* 560.

The man should also be the husband of only one wife, even as Christ is the head of the one Church. For, since marriage is a picture of the same, the likeness and indication must resemble what it indicateth. Therefore must a man have no more than one wife.[25]

One's wife among the Hutterites and among many other Anabaptists was most commonly called "marital sister," that is, she and her spouse were primarily members of the brotherhood or congregation of the saved and only secondarily related to each other as husband and wife. So strongly was this conviction sustained that it was the elders, representing the will of God, who by various arrangements reduced the personal choice of a life's partner to a formalized minimum and eliminated courtship. Riedemann wrote, in his *Account:*

One should in no case choose from the flesh but await such a gift from God, and with all diligence pray that God in accordance with his divine will might send what he from the beginning hath provided, serving to one's salvation and life. Then, after such a prayer, one should ask not his flesh but the elders that God might show him through them what he hath appointed for him. This, then, one should take with real gratitude as a gift from God, whether young or old, poor or rich, even as God hath shown through their counsel. What, therefore, God hath joined together, man should not sever. They should, however, be married openly in the presence of the Church, by an ordained minister of the Word.[26]

Riedemann distinguished three levels of marriage, the lower a reflection of the higher:

Marriage is . . . in three grades or steps. First is that of God with the soul or spirit, then that of the spirit with the body, and thirdly that of one body with another, that is, the marriage of man with woman; which is not the first but the last and lowest grade, and is therefore visible, recognizable and to be understood by all. Now, because it is visible, recognizable and to be understood, it is a picture, an instruction and indication of what is invisible, that is of the middle and highest grades. For as man is head of the woman, so is the spirit the head of the body, and God is the head of the spirit.[27]

From plural and monogamous marriage we turn to divorce.

4. Separation and Divorce

The first formalized expression of Anabaptist conviction on divorce appears in close connection with the Schleitheim Con-

---

[25] Riedemann, *Account,* 100. See also, *ME,* III, "Marriage, Hutterite Practices," 510 f.
[26] Riedemann, *Account,* 100.
[27] *Ibid.,* 98.

fession of 1527 (Ch. 8.1), in an anonymous tract on divorce, possibly written by Michael Sattler in 1527.[28] The basic points were the permanence of the marriage covenant undertaken within the conventicle of the faithful, the supremacy of the believer's obligation to Christ over obligation to one's spouse, adultery as the only ground of divorce, the transfer of the sin of fornication to a person who would willingly marry a fornicator, and the implicit sanction of remarriage on the part of the innocent party in a divorce. Thus, bound up with the betrothal-bridal image of the Anabaptist covenant was the conviction that adultery could exist on the spiritual level, and that marriage on the human level should be dissolved if it conflicted with one's spiritual marriage:

> The spiritual marriage and obligation to Christ, yea faith, love and obedience to God, . . . takes precedence over the earthly marriage, and one ought rather forsake such earthly companion than the spiritual companion (Gemahel). And by not removing the designated one from the bond of marriage we care more for earthly than for spiritual obligations and debts, as it is written [cf. Matt. 10:37], He who loveth father or mother, wife or child, more than me is not worthy of me.[29]

The anonymous Swiss tract required divorce of believers from nonbelievers only if the nonbeliever was an impediment to the believer's faith and dutifulness.

The Rothmannites in Münster, holding marriage an image of the relation of Christ to his community of the faithful, could think of Christ with many individual brides, and hence each husband with a plurality of wives. But since plural marriage was also bound up with faith, the marriage of believers with unbelievers was not true marriage, but the equivalent of adultery, and therefore to be annulled by a rigid, communal discipline.

The Biblical basis for the Münsterite and also the stern Mennonite regulations in respect to separation and divorce was Ezra 10:11 f. Ezra broke the marriages contracted between the returned Israelites and the "foreign wives."

For Dietrich Philips, of course, all non-Mennonites, including other Anabaptists formally excommunicated or not in communion with them, were "foreign," and it was in this very tight context that he forbade mixed marriage:

> In view of the fact that such unclean matrimonial alliances and mixed marriages between the children of God and unbelievers could

---

[28] John C. Wenger, "Concerning Divorce: A Swiss Brethren Tract on the Primacy of Loyalty to Christ and the Right to Divorce and Remarriage," MQR, XXI (1947), passim.

[29] Ibid., 118 f. The reference is to marriage between believers and unbelievers.

not stand under the imperfect dispensation of the Law, how could it stand before God and His church under the perfect dispensation of the Christian age of the Gospel? Let everyone meditate upon and consider this matter.[30]

But over against Ezra's injunction to divorce "foreign wives," applied here by Dietrich to non-Mennonites, was the New Covenantal injunction of Paul in I Cor. 7:10–15 that there be no divorce and that a believing spouse could make holy the children of a mixed marriage, and the injunction of Jesus that what God had joined should not be put asunder. To be sure, Jesus, in the Matthean version (ch. 19:9) of his injunction, permitted divorce on the ground of adultery, and Paul permitted the *unbelieving* spouse to separate (I Cor. 10:15) on the ground of spiritual incompatibility. In their effort at harmonization the Anabaptists, using Ezra 10:11 f. as a precedent and stressing the conjugal relationship as an analogue of the covenantal relationship of the believer and Christ, made bold to reverse Paul's dictum and permitted, indeed often enjoined, the *believing,* i.e., Anabaptist, spouse to separate from the unbelieving partner, and to interpret adultery in Jesus' dictum as spiritual.

For example, the fifth article of the Mennonite Wismar resolutions of 1554 enjoins divorce for spiritual adultery and legitimizes remarriage in the case of physical adultery:

Concerning a believer and a non-believer—if the non-believer wishes to separate for reasons of the faith, then the believer shall conduct himself honestly without contracting a marriage, for as long a time as the non-believer is not remarried. But if the non-believer marries or commits adultery, then the believing mate may also marry, subject to the advice of the elders of the congregation.[31]

Menno Simons confirmed this view in his *Instruction on Excommunication,* asking rhetorically (1558):

Is there a man under heaven, no matter who, learned or unlearned, young or old, without us or within, man or woman, who can instruct us with the Word of truth that the spiritual marriage bond, made with Christ through faith, may yield to the external marriage bond, made in the flesh with man? . . . Ponder whether spiritual love has to yield to carnal love?[32]

Riedemann, the Hutterite, likewise extended the meaning of adultery theologically and ethically to the advantage of the husband:

Where . . . the man doeth his part, but his wife acteth not but without his counsel, she transgresseth her marriage and union in

[30] *Enchiridion,* 358.
[31] Menno, *Writings,* 1042.
[32] *Ibid.,* 970.

small things as well as in great things, and taketh from her husband his honour and lordship. If the man permit her to do this, he sinneth with her as Adam did with Eve, in that he consented to eat of the forbidden fruit, and both fell to death. For they broke marriage with their creator and transgressed his order.[33]

The Hutterite Five Articles of 1547, by Peter Walpot, accord a sensibly preferred status to the wife:

Nothing can break the marriage bond but adultery. Where, however, a brother has an unbelieving wife, and she agrees to live with him, he may not divorce her (nor vice versa). But where she is endangered in her faith or is hindered by the unbelieving husband in the training of her children in the true faith, she may divorce her husband, but must remain unmarried as long as her husband lives.[34]

We have dealt recently (Ch. 19.1) with the similar conjugal views of such a Spiritualist as Niclaes the Familist. (Such an important evangelical Spiritualist as Schwenckfeld apparently did not express himself on the subject of marriage, nor did such an important revolutionary Spiritualist as Müntzer. The view of the Transylvanian Unitarians has not been explored.) Although the Italian Evangelical Rationalists lie ahead of us in our narrative, we can anticipate them to the extent of observing that their views on marriage were much the same as those of the evangelical Anabaptists, and we now proceed to sum up the evidence for the whole of the Radical Reformation.

Apart from certain excesses, it is clear that the Netherlandish, Hutterite, Swiss, and South German Anabaptists, and the Italian-Polish, anti-Nicene Anabaptists all shared a common view of marriage as a covenant under God the Father or in Christ and that they sanctioned divorce as a possible, as a preferred, or even as an enjoined alternative to infidelity to him. At the same time that the evangelical Anabaptists insisted on the precedence of theological faithfulness over conjugal fidelity they were also aware that Christ had done away with the old divorcing, no longer permitting hardness of heart to be a valid occasion for divorce, and that he had in effect renewed the regulation of his Heavenly Father for the perpetual monogamy of Paradise before the Fall.[35] The restorationist impulse in the Radical Reformation had thus the effect of replacing the sacrament of marriage with the mystical-covenantal idea of spiritual wedlock reinforced further by the cosmic covenant of primal man and woman before their Garden had become a wilderness.

[33] Riedemann, *Account,* 101 f.
[34] *Chronik,* 308–316, article 5.
[35] Wenger, "Concerning Divorce," 117.

CHAPTER 21

WALDENSIANS IN ITALY: 1510–1532; ITALIAN EVANGELICALS: 1530–1542

In trying to follow the developments of the Radical Reformation genetically, and yet in so far as feasible synoptically and synchronously, we have, by way of exception (Ch. 19), for one region, the Netherlands, and for almost an entire generation, 1540–1568, gone well beyond the general chronological framework of the rest of the narrative. For the Swiss Brethren the account has been brought forward only to the death of Zwingli in 1531 (Ch. 8); for England and Poland, to the deaths, respectively, of Henry VIII and Sigismund I; for the Hutterites, to the composition of Riedemann's *Account;* and for Middle and South German Anabaptism and Spiritualism, through the Marpeck-Schwenckfeld controversy of 1542.

In the following two chapters we pass through the Alps into Italy[1] and step back in time to carry our account forward in this region from the point where we left off in 1530 (Ch. 1).

In the dozen years between the *rapprochement* of the Emperor and the pope in 1530 (symbolized by the imperial coronation) and the re-establishment in 1542 of the Roman Inquisition, modeled on that of Charles for his Spanish dominions, Italy was brimming over with divergent religious currents, alongside and within the ancient ecclesiastical system and in either case largely independent of the pope. For each pope in his turn was preoccupied with his position as a major prince of the peninsula and baffled by the recalcitrance of the fomenters of the religious revolt in Germany. The dozen years between 1530 and 1542 are in Italy, as in Germany, religiously well defined.

---

[1] Recent works on Italian Protestantism and sectarianism are Frederic C. Church, *The Italian Reformers, 1534–1564* (New York, 1932); George Kenneth Brown, *Italy and the Reformation to 1550* (Oxford, 1933); Delio Cantimori, *Eretici Italiani del Cinquecento: Ricerche Storiche* (Florence, 1939).

In 1530, after his coronation in Bologna, Charles attended the diet of Augsburg to hear, among other things, the Augsburg Confession, in which Melanchthon, in Luther's absence, made as many concessions to traditional theology and institutions as the Lutheran party, which had readily disavowed the extremism of the sacramentarian Swiss, could faithfully yield.

In 1542, Contarini died in sorrow and despair after the failure the year before of the colloquy of Regensburg, at which the Evangelical Cardinal had formulated his great concession on grace in terms of double justification in the last hope of saving the unity of Western Christendom. In the same year, Bernardine Ochino, the general of the Capuchin Order and Italy's greatest preacher of penitence, along with many other leading Italian Evangelicals and Protestants, fled from the peninsula. The year before, 1541, John de Valdés had died in Naples. He had given his name to the Italian form of Evangelism.

Italian Evangelicals after the introduction of the Inquisition in 1542 either conformed as "Nicodemites" or fled to Protestant lands, or threw themselves with somewhat altered enthusiasm into the current driving toward the reform Council of Trent.

Within the eddying currents of reform, piety, and dissent in these fateful dozen years, there were in addition to Catholic Evangelism (Valdesianism) at least five other religious currents, namely, Waldensianism, Lutheranism, Calvinism, Evangelical Rationalism, and Anabaptism. In Italy with its extremes of piety and indifference, of poverty and splendor; with its practical toleration until 1542 of greater diversity than elsewhere; with its long habituation to manifold expressions of medieval and then Renaissance sectarianism, heresy, devout fanaticism, and skepticism—sixteenth-century "radicals" were often carried over from one current to another, for all these currents of the sixteenth century were in Italy most difficult to keep from flowing one into the other.

One major current, of course—Protestantism (Lutheranism and Calvinism)—is excluded on principle from our narrative as elsewhere except as it clarifies the more radical trends, whereas Catholic Evangelism remains a part of our story so long as it endures, because the radical movements in Italy become its residuary legatee. The Waldensians in the sixteenth century are also part of our narrative up to the general synod of Mérindol in 1530, when they fall under the influence and direction of the Swiss Reformers. We reserve for the following chapter (Ch. 22) the account of Italian Anabaptism and Evangelical Rationalism.

1. THE ITALIAN WALDENSIANS

Waldensians interrogated in Paesana at the headwaters of the Po in 1510 declared their fervent hope

that at the head of a great army, a king of the Bohemians would come, belonging to their sect, subjugating the provinces, cities, and villages, destroying the churches; that he would kill all the clerics and take from them their temporal possessions, abolishing tolls and all sorts of exploitation; and that he would impose a single tax per person, introduce the community of goods, and make all conform to his law.[2]

The belligerent hope in the imminent advent of a Bohemian messiah seems out of place in the Cottian Alps among the pastoral followers of Peter Waldo of Lyons, who had originally been content to seek papal and then archiepiscopal approval of his demand that laymen, when called of God, be permitted to proclaim the gospel in the vernacular in the squares and elsewhere in the open. It was only when Waldo was excommunicated by the synod of Verona in 1184 that Waldensianism began its long history as a sectarian movement, spreading throughout central Europe and *absorbing*, in different regions, *the local heresies in ever new combinations.*[3]

The French and Italian Waldensians of the Cottian Alps in the second half of the fifteenth century had rallied their strength and engaged in extensive missionary activity, establishing colonies as far south as Calabria and Apulia. In 1483 they had risen against Duke Charles I of Savoy. Pope Innocent VIII had authorized a crusade against them in 1487, under the direction of the marquis of Saluzzo, the king of France, and Duke Charles. The new king of France, Louis XII, brought the crusade to a close in 1501 in the valleys he controlled, and ordered the restoration of confiscated properties. But the widow of the marquis of Saluzzo, purchasing the rights of the bishop and the inquisitor to the property of the Waldensians in the upper Po valley, extended the persecution in the neighborhood of Paesana. We have

---

[2] The Latin text, from the MS. "Errores Valdensium" (Turin), is quoted by Giovanni Gonnet, "Il movimento valdese in Europa secondo le più recenti ricerche," *Bollettino della Società di Studi Valdesi*, LVIII, No. 100 (1956), 26. The text is described as item 756 by Giovanni Gonnet and Augusto Armand-Hugon, *Bibliografia Valdese* (Torre Pellice, 1953), *Bollettino*, LXXIII, No. 93 (1953).

[3] The newest interpretations of Waldensianism are brought together magisterially by Giovanni Gonnet, "Delle varie tappe e correnti della protesta valdese in Europa da Lione a Chanforan: Problemi vecchi e nuovi (1176–1532)," *Bollettino*, LVI, No. 102 (1957), 19–28; and "Nuovi studi sul valdismo nel medio evo," *Bollettino*, LVIII, No. 100 (1956), 60–62.

already overheard the voices of the six Waldensians captured in 1510, preserved in the inquisitorial transcript quoted above, and it remains only to note that four of them escaped during the snowy night before the execution, and that the remaining two were burned on the banks of the Po, 12 May 1510.

It was in 1498 that Brother Luke of Prague, chief spokesman of the Major Party of the Unity (Ch. 9.1), who had already visited the Byzantine East and Armenia in search of the authentic apostolic tradition, arrived in Florence, where there was a Waldensian conventicle. At the time, Savonarola was being put to death for excoriating the apostolic see of Rome. It is not likely that Brother Luke visited the Waldensian communities in the Cottian Alps, although, since the rigid Minor Party of the *Unitas* in Bohemia claimed precisely the sanction of Waldensian predecessors for their opposition to his revisions in sacramental theology and polity, one might have expected Brother Luke to seek out the support of the Italian Waldensians on his trip.[4] He seems, rather, to have visited Italy, primarily to assure himself at first hand that Rome was in as wretched an estate as the Hussites had always maintained. But if he did not visit the Alpine sectaries in 1498, a relationship between them and the *Unitas* was at least well established in the dozen years following, for in 1510 the tortured Waldensians of Paesana gave voice to their great hope of relief coming to them from the "king of the Bohemians." A number of Luke's writings—for example, his famous letter of 4 December 1507, protesting to Ladislas Jagellon, king of Bohemia and Hungary, against the edict of expulsion—were translated into the Cottian vernacular.[5]

By 1526 three factions had developed in the Israel of the Alps— the Swiss, the Saxon, and the Bohemian sympathizers among the Waldensians. At a synod in September of that year at Laus (Vallon du Laux) in the valley of Cluson, one hundred and forty pastors (barbs) met to consider their own traditions in relation to the *Unitas* and the Protestants of Switzerland and Saxony. William Farel had been working in Dauphiny in 1523, and news of his preaching attracted many Waldensians. The synod delegated barb Martin Gonin, with the assistance of George of Calabria, to visit Germany and bring back copies of Luther's

---

[4] That Luke visited the Cottian Waldensians in 1498 is the traditional view, now altered, in the light of the recently worked Prague manuscripts, by Amadeo Molnár, "Les Vaudois et la Réforme," summary by the author of two articles in Czech, *Bollettino*, LXXV, No. 96 (1954), 45–47.

[5] Amadeo Molnár, "Luc de Prague et les Vaudois d'Italie," *Bollettino*, LXX, No. 90 (1949), 40–64.

writings.[6] Gonin's labors created a Protestant party, over against those who espoused closer bonds with the *Unitas* in Bohemia.

In 1530, at the synod in Mérindol in Provence it was decided to seek the counsel of the Reformed pastors of Switzerland. Accordingly, barbs George Morel (Maurel) of Freissinières Valley and Peter Masson of Burgundy were sent with letters for Farel in Neuchâtel, Haller in Bern, Oecolampadius in Basel, and Bucer in Strassburg. To Bucer they carried a document containing forty-seven points of belief and practice about which they had questions.[7] For Oecolampadius, they limited themselves to a selection of twelve.[8] With their first authorized contact with sacramentarian Protestantism the Cottian Waldensians found themselves defending Waldensian traditions, interlarded with some Hussite (*Unitas*) doctrine and practice which they had only incompletely assimilated. In fact, we have overtaken the Italian Waldensians at that moment in their long history when they are in the process of interacting with the latest antipapal movement. In the past the inveterately syncretistic Waldensians, depending on the locality, had taken over elements from the Albigensians, the Beghards, and the followers of the *Devotio Moderna*. It is well, therefore, to pause at this point to examine the amalgam as we find it described by barbs Martin Gonin, George Morel, and Peter Masson (c. 1530) in connection with their first Protestant contacts.

The Waldensian leaders of the first quarter of the Reformation century were called "barbs."[9] The designation (French, *barbe;*

---

[6] J. Jalla, *Histoire des Vaudois* (Pinerolo, 1922), 70. One of the most recent works on the relations of the Waldensians to the Magisterial Reformers is that of Giovanni Gonnet, "Beziehungen der Waldenser zu den oberdeutschen Reformatoren vor Calvin," *ZKG,* LXIV (1952/1953), 308–311.

[7] All forty-seven items, with variations in Romansh and Latin versions where available, and the German translation, are given by Johann Herzog, *Die romanischen Waldenser* (Halle, 1853), 350–362.

[8] The twelve are not worded exactly the same as in the communication with Bucer. Letter of Morel and Masson to Oecolampadius, October 1530; Staehelin, *Briefe und Akten,* II, item 787. Since the letter was written after the visit to the Reformer in Basel, it is possible that the barbs limited their queries to items still under discussion. But a comparison of their relations with Bucer and Oecolampadius would indicate that the Cottian Waldensians were more forthright with Bucer about their practices.

[9] In the fourteenth century, three orders of clergy were found among the Waldensians in both the Romance and Germanic areas, namely, bishops, presbyters, and deacons. In the fifteenth century, these orders had pretty much disappeared in both areas, although there was still uncertainty about ministerial grades in the Cottian Alps. Staehelin, *Briefe und Akten,* II, p. 507; Emilio Comba, *History of the Waldensians in Italy* (London, 1889), 254–256.

Italian, *barba*) comes from the medieval Latin *barbanus,* in the sense of "uncle."[10] The itinerant barbs, exercising moral authority, were often also called "teachers." In Italy a strong central organization of barbs and superintendents was maintained into the Reformation Era. Their main school was in Milan.[11] The Lombard Waldensian barbs (unlike their French counterparts) prided themselves on having a trade, generally that of medicine and surgery. Recruits for ordination were to begin with almost always young shepherds or husbandmen, usually illiterate. While yet living in the parental household they would seek admission to the pastoral fraternity on their knees, with the object of performing thus an act of humility, and asking the ordained barbs to pray for them that they might be rendered worthy. The barbs thereupon communicated the request to the assembled brethren; and if the applicants were well thought of, they would be admitted by general consent to receive instruction.

The candidates were kept on trial during two or three winter months for three or four years at most, in order that the barbs could be satisfied as to their irreproachable conduct. The recruits were given elementary instruction in reading and spelling and made to learn by heart the Gospels of Matthew and John, and many of the epistles. About halfway through their tutelage the candidates were transferred to a certain place where consecrated Waldensian women, called sisters, lived a cloistered life. Here the candidates lived for one or two years, helping with the more rugged chores of such an establishment. Finally, they were admitted to the pastoral office by the laying on of hands and the celebrating of the sacrament of the Eucharist. At ordination, the chief barb or master would assemble the other barbs, and the candidates would then be required to respond by oath to the following formula:

Thou, [N.], swear upon thy faith to maintain, multiply, and increase our law, and not to betray the same to any person in the world; and here promise that thou wilt not swear by God in any manner, but observe the Lord's day; and that thou wilt not do anything to thy neighbor, which thou wouldst not have him to do to thee; and that thou dost believe in God, who made the sun and moon, heaven and earth, cherubim and seraphim, and all that thou seest.[12]

---

[10] It may also have derived from *barba,* "bearded." In lands of Germanic speech, the pastors were more commonly called "masters."

[11] Comba, *op. cit.,* 151–153.

[12] Latin original in Peter Allix, *Some Remarks upon the Ecclesiastical History of the Ancient Churches of Piedmont* (London, 1690), 313; English translation, *ibid.,* 276.

Having taken the vow, the candidate was handed a cup by the master, who at that moment assigned him a new name, saying: "Henceforth thou shalt be called thus." This ceremony, in the eyes of the community and particularly of the ordained *perfecti* themselves, effectually superseded rather than confirmed the baptism which the recruit had usually been obliged to receive at infancy in his Catholic parish.[13]

Duly instructed and ordained, the young barbs were sent out in pairs to the work of evangelization.[14] Once a member of the Waldensian ministry, the ordained found that precedence depended solely upon seniority. He who preceded in the order of consecration was the master; he who followed was the disciple. The latter did nothing without the former's permission, even the most insignificant thing, such as drinking a cup of water. As a rule, the barbs did not marry, although chastity was not always the better kept for that. Bread and clothing in sufficient quantities were furnished gratuitously by the people who received their instruction, although the barbs worked at different trades, to please the people and avoid idleness. The pastoral self-discipline was prescribed. The barbs prayed, kneeling, morning, noon, and evening, before and after supper, and sometimes also during the night. The prayers lasted about a quarter of an hour. Before eating or drinking, they generally repeated the Lord's Prayer. Once a year, all the barbs of a given jurisdiction assembled in general council, to talk over affairs and to change residence in pairs (every two or three years), except in the case of old men, who were permitted to have a fixed residence for the remainder of their lives. Their temporal goods were managed in common. All that was received from the people in the way of alms was handed over to the general council and placed in the common treasury, in the hands of the central leaders. Some of the money was used to cover the expense of traveling; a portion was reserved for the poor. The barbs united annually in the mutual confession of sins. If one of the barbs had in the course of the year fallen into carnal sin, he was excluded from the fellowship, forbidden to preach further, and directed to earn his bread by the sweat of his brow.[15]

In Germany, Apulia, Calabria, and many Piedmontese colonies, the Waldensian laity regularly attended Catholic worship. Only where they were in the majority, as in the Cottian Alps, could they confess to one another and regularly to the barbs and com-

---

[13] Barb Martin, for example, had earlier been called François.
[14] Letter of Oecolampadius, *loc. cit.*
[15] Letter to Oecolampadius, *loc. cit.*, and Morel's "Memoirs" in Herzog, *Die romanischen Waldenser*, 340 ff.

mune apart from the Catholic parishes. The Waldensians in the
Cottian Alps and middle Italy had been receiving the Eucharist
from their own barbs up to the crusade of 1487. They commonly
called it the *consolamentum*, which shows the extent of the
Cathar influence even in the Italian Alps, where syncretism was
generally less advanced than in the more populous and accessible
areas.[16] After 1487, even in the Alps, Waldensians usually received Communion from Catholic priests, except at the annual
ordinations of their barbs.[17]

Waldensian worship centered in the visit of the barbs in pairs.
When the senior barb and his assistant arrived and were recognized by the conventicular sign, lodging would be prepared for
them. The evening meal took on the character of a love feast,
recalling the daily communion of apostolic times. For the period
before 1487 when the Waldensian Eucharist was more commonly
and openly observed, we learn that before the barbs sat down to
table, they blessed the food, saying: *"Benedicite, Kyrie eleison,
Christe eleison, Kyrie eleison, Pater noster."* Thereupon, the
senior barb would say, in his own dialect: "God, who blessed the
five barley loaves and two fishes for his disciples in the wilderness,
bless this table, whatever is upon it, and whatever may be brought
to it." Then, making the sign of the cross, the junior barb blessed
it in the name of the Triune God. In the same manner, when
the company rose from table, they returned thanks in the words
of Rev. 7:12, pronounced by the senior barb present in his
own dialect, adding: "May God grant ample reward and good
return to all those who do us good and bless us, and after having
given us material bread, may He give us spiritual food. God be
with us, and we with Him for ever." Thereupon the rest answered "Amen," often joining hands and lifting them up toward
heaven.[18]

Worship followed the meal, the three basic elements being
prayer, the reading of Scripture, and the reception of the consecrated bread and wine, understood in the symbolic sense.[19] The
more complicated Eucharistic theology of the *Unitas* had not
been readily assimilated. Prayer was confined almost exclusively
to the Lord's Prayer, repeated silently as often as forty times.

---

[16] Evidence for the use of the Catharist term *consolamentum* in the Inquisi-
tions of 1335–1387 and 1451 is brought in by Gonnet, "Delle varie tappe
e correnti," 26.

[17] On the rare Waldensian custom of taking fish along with the bread and
wine, see the newer literature brought in incidentally but nevertheless
profusely in Kurt Goldammer, "Der Naumburger Meister und die
Häretiker," *ZKG*, LXIV (1952/1953), esp. 97–102.

[18] Comba, *op. cit.*, 258.

[19] *Ibid.*, 269.

Since the Waldensians trained themselves in the memorization of Scripture, the assembly easily followed the barb's reading. In the sermon, the two seated ministers, the older and then the younger, quoted maxims of certain apostles or of such saints or doctors of the church as might strengthen the presentation. The sermon concentrated upon virtues, vices, good works, the Golden Rule, and the avoidance of lying, swearing, or shedding blood, and concluded with the exhortation: "The time is short; confess your sins, and do penance."

As to sacramental beliefs and practices, although Waldo himself had been traditionally Catholic, by the opening of the Reformation Era all seven sacraments were greatly weakened or altered. One of the seven sacraments, ordination, was firmly in the hands of the *perfecti* of the sectarian brotherhood. Infant baptism, which commonly linked the Waldensians to the Catholic parish, was still widely regarded as desirable for salvation, but some held that it might be administered by anyone, including women. By 1530 the Waldensians had come to hold that it was better to confess to a pious layman than to an unworthy priest. Solemn confession of the laity took place at least once a year as occasion offered.[20] After absolution, the penitents fasted and prayed.

Waldensians rejected purgatory as a priestly invention, as they did the doctrine of the intercession of the saints. They believed that in the afterlife there is a place of abode of the elect, Paradise, and of the rejected, called hell. Believing in a God in three Persons, and a Christ fully human and fully divine, the Waldensians held that faith must be combined with works. Lutheran and Zwinglian justification by faith alone did not appeal to them, and they found it hard to accept in all its rigor the doctrine of predestination espoused by the Magisterial Reformers.

When, among the barbs, a proponent of free will angrily tried to shake the conviction of a convert to predestinarianism, throwing a saltcellar from the table with the angry ejaculation that he had proved his free will, the Swiss and Saxon-instructed barb retorted in effect: "Yes, you can very well do a wicked work on your own, but now try to put the broken pieces together and reassemble the grains of salt, and you will see that without the grace of God, you can do no good work."[21]

Their general repugnance to the doctrine of predestination is

---

[20] Letter to Oecolampadius, *loc. cit.*, 505.

[21] The anecdote, referring to our period, was recounted by barb Girolamo Miolo of Pinerolo, *Historia breve e vera degl'affari dei Valdesi delle Valli* (1587), reported by Gonnet, "Il movimento valdese," *loc. cit.*, 27 f.

the twelfth and last of the disputed points raised in Morel and Masson's letter to Oecolampadius in 1530. Just to mention several of the others among the twelve brought up with Oecolampadius and the forty-seven brought up with Bucer rounds out the picture of the Cottian Waldensians in the first third of the Reformation century. They were troubled about whether they should in any respect submit to those set in authority over the world, for example, in the adjudication of altercations among Waldensians; whether the capital punishment of murderers, thieves, and other malefactors was Christian in view of the prophetic declaration (Ezek. 33:11) that God desires not the death of the sinner but that he be saved and live; whether the civil authority is of God; whether it be permitted to counsel the brethren to kill a false brother who turns informer and discloses to the inquisitors or magistrates the place of sojourn of the barbs and thereby threatens the whole community.[22]

With the foregoing characterization of the theology and practices of the Cottian Waldensians on the eve of their turning Protestant, we may resume our narrative.

Masson was arrested on the way to Neuchâtel, but Morel escaped to confer with Farel and Anthony Saunier (Saulnier) at Neuchâtel and Morat. Returning to Provence, Morel worked energetically in behalf of the Swiss Protestant cause. Numerous debates were held among the distinguishable parties, namely, the traditionalists, the "Hussites," and the "Protestants," by now largely Reformed in orientation. On 12 September 1532, many barbs gathered in assembly under the chestnut trees of Cianforan in the Angrogna Valley, with Farel, Saulnier, and Peter Robert Olivétan in attendance.[23] Morel's work had been thorough, and the synod adopted a new confession of faith which included the Reformed doctrine of predestination. The assembly formally renounced all recognition of the Roman Church, accepted clerical marriage, and ordered communal worship to be henceforth open and public in defiance of Rome. Farel was the dominant figure at Cianforan, persuading the barbs to accept the Zwinglian interpretation of the Supper. The Cottian Waldensians, on becoming Protestants, preserved certain older practices, for example, the name "barb" and some of his traditional functions, and also their pacifism. Fifteen hundred gold écus were set aside for the publication of a new French translation of the Bible. To Olivétan was delegated the task of preparing it.

[22] Letter to Oecolampadius, *loc. cit.*, 507; Herzog, *op. cit.*, 350 f.

[23] The most recent accounts of this major event are by Jean Jalla, "Le Synode de Chanforan," *Bollettino,* No. 58 (1932), 34–48; Ernesto Buonaiuti, "Il Sinodo di Chanforan," *Ricerche Religiose,* X (1934), 85.

A conservative minority, headed by two barbs, Daniel of Valence and John of Molinos, broke away in exasperation, and took with them the ancient documents of the Waldensian brotherhood. Going to Mladá-Boleslav in Bohemia, they prevailed upon the leaders of the *Unitas Fratrum* (Luke was by now dead) to write a letter reproaching the Alpine Waldensians for their infidelity. But another synod confirmed the decisions reached at Cianforan.

Olivétan's preface to the new translation of the Bible is dated "The Alps, 12 February 1535." This became the model of all subsequent French versions.[24] In the Cottian Alps, the Protestant faction had prevailed. The former Waldensians now received French pastors from the academy of Lausanne, who gradually remodeled the services in the Cottian Alps after those in Switzerland.

Not all the Italian Waldensians were able to make the abrupt transition from medieval sectarianism to Protestantism. Some conventicles in the lower Po valley from Paesana to Venice and all of the Waldensian colonies in Calabria and Apulia until 1556 declined to comply with the decision of the majority congregated in the Alps. More exposed than their Alpine confreres to the hazards of municipal, episcopal, and (after 1542) papal inquisition, they could not afford to make so public their testimony, and chose to survive as a loose network of popular dissent. These remnants of late medieval conventicular life, receptive alike to Protestant, Anabaptist, Spiritualist, and Servetian (Ch. 21.4) theology and speculation, may be characterized as the most likely seedbeds for the anti-Trinitarian anabaptism that becomes part of our narrative in Ch. 22.

This loose and still incompletely understood analogue to what we have seen developing alongside the Magisterial Reformation, as in Switzerland, or in an officially Catholic environment, as in the Netherlands, came to stress in the Po valley and the encircling Alpine valleys certain Italian features which tended to be marginal elsewhere in the Radical Reformation, namely, predestinarianism, Eucharistic fellowship meals, psychopannychism, and anti-Trinitarianism.

Though the relationship of the Waldensians and the Radical Reformation is still a moot question, it is of interest to note that the Waldensians before their conversion to Protestantism held much the same view as the Anabaptists did of the atoning work of Christ, and this would have remained true in all likelihood of those who refused to come under direct Helvetic tutelage. For

[24] Olivétan died in 1538, in Ferrara.

the Cottian Waldensians, Christ's Passion removed the guilt of original sin from all mankind, leaving the forgiveness of actual sins to such Dominically instituted means as confession to a barb or mutual confession of the barbs among themselves.[25] Hence, for many of the Cottian Waldensians the baptism of infants without actual sins was regarded as unnecessary for their salvation in the case of premature death.

As one reflects further on the continuity between Waldensianism and Italian Anabaptism, one is prompted to conjecture that it would have been only a step from the Waldensian ordination of a young barb as a pastoral *perfectus* on confession of faith to the Anabaptist penitential rebaptism (cf. that of Blaurock, from the Grisons, Ch. 6). The first Anabaptists, to speak schematically, needed only to combine the Zwinglian-Lutheran stress on sin and faith with (1) the clerical Waldensian practice of mutual confession, (2) the *Unitas* practice of rebaptism, and (3) the Waldensian ordination of the *perfectus* as a roving missionary under discipline and thereby produce the penitential outcry of the typical Anabaptist convert, his martyr-missionary zeal, and his covenantal vow to lead a righteous life. On this view, anabaptism would be a kind of reordination to the priesthood of the perfect or the elect. It is almost certain that the assumption of the quasiministerial duty of public testimony among the Anabaptists and the missionary mobility of their charismatic leaders, traveling about in pairs, especially in Italy, along with the occasional practice of acquiring at rebaptism or regeneration a new name, again very common among the Italian Anabaptists, perpetuate in a new guise long familiar Waldensian usage.

We turn now from the Waldensians, not, however, directly to the Anabaptists, but to the Valdesians; from the Cottian Alps we go to the Bay of Naples.

2. JOHN DE VALDÉS

The principal spokesman of Evangelism in the peninsula was John de Valdés. Another name for Evangelism in Italy might well be Valdesianism (to be distinguished from Waldensianism, Ch. 21.1). We last met the twin brothers John and Alphonse in Ch. 1.2.c, when the latter with Servetus was in attendance at the imperial coronation in Bologna in 1530.

John, it will be recalled, left Spain because of the heretical character of his *Dialogue*. On his arrival in Rome he was engaged some time before August 1531 as secretary to Pope Clement VII. Here he made the acquaintance of the papal prothonotary

25 Letter to Oecolampadius, *loc. cit.*, 505.

Peter Carnesecchi, destined to be martyred as an Evangelical. He visited the imperial court in Mantua after Alphonse died in October 1532, and there met Cardinal Ercole Gonzaga, who became an intimate friend. Returning to Rome, he continued as papal secretary until the death of Clement, September 1534.

Valdés thereupon departed for Naples, the scene of his greatest literary and religious activity. Here he served as Spanish imperial inspector of fortifications.[26] Through Cardinal Gonzaga he came into contact with the latter's sister, Lady Julia Gonzaga, widowed for eight years and still only twenty-two. She was renowned for her beauty and personality, her fame having received additional luster in 1534 when the pirate Barbarossa attempted to kidnap her to present her to the Sultan. Admired and courted, she persevered in her religious quest, and knew how to maintain her masculine friendships on an elevated plane, overcoming and spiritualizing the emotions which she involuntarily engendered. She was the presiding spirit of an evangelical salon when Valdés became her spiritual adviser in 1536.

After a Lenten sermon by Bernardine Ochino in San Giovanni Maggiore, Lady Julia Gonzaga and Valdés engaged in a dialogue, set down later that evening from memory by Valdés and at her request. It was translated into Tuscan and presented to her as the renowned *Christian Alphabet* (1536), an introduction to the way of "Christian perfection."[27] In his Spanish *Dialogue*, John had addressed the whole Christian world; in the *Alphabet*, a single soul. This handbook of the Christian life propounds a simple, ethical, Erasmian piety. There is little in the *Alphabet* that would be unacceptable to orthodox Roman Catholics. It was in his later work, the *CX Considerations*, that Valdés introduced his distinctive ideas.[28] In Valdés' theological piety, doctrine was not a concept, but an ethical reality and a psychological experience. In order to understand dogma, one dare not rely on reason alone, for the lights of reason, if they are not brought into focus together with the divine illumination, can easily lead to error. Valdés considers human prudence an adversary on the road to Christian perfection. Those who follow Holy Scripture alone walk with a single candle; those who are illuminated by the Spirit of God walk in the full light of the sun. After establishing the principle of right understanding, he goes on to consider the nature and meaning of the atonement.

Among the seminal ideas in the *Considerations* are his re-

[26] It is possible that this was not his only or his major office.
[27] *Alfabeto Cristiano;* translated in *SAW*, 351–390.
[28] Written sometime after 1536, published posthumously in Basel in 1550; *Considerations I–X* in *SAW*, 335–350.

flections on the atonement, destined to be developed by several Italians, notably Bernardine Ochino and Faustus Socinus, and to become the distinctive mark of Socinianism (Ch. 29.7). For Valdés, the atonement is considered from two aspects: (1) as the divine good work in forgiving and redeeming man (*beneficio de Cristo, beneficium*); and (2) as the human experience and assurance of this forgiveness and the change which it works within the individual man, the "Christian transaction" (*negocio cristiano*).[29]

When he takes up, in the latter part of the *Considerations,* the objective nature of the atonement, we shall see that Valdés has a completely orthodox, patristic Christology. But it is important to note that theology is not his point of departure, but rather the personal appropriation of redemption, the transaction, the *negocio cristiano.* The objective *beneficio,* which is the radical justification[30] of mankind, is first understood psychologically. He twice gives a related parable of the fall and redemption of mankind.

It is as though subjects rebelled against their king and he cast them out of his kingdom and condemned them to death; but moved by compassion, he executed the rigor of his justice upon his son, and announced a patent (*patente*) of amnesty to the reprobates, by which he invites them to return to the kingdom from which they have been exiled. Instead of their trusting in the satisfaction which his son has offered for them,[31] instead of their accepting the patent and returning joyfully, too many of them in their skeptical rationalism scrutinize it to ascertain whether the seal is of gold or copper, while others, excessively prone to the piety of external works, occupy themselves with adorning and adoring it, and in effect remain deprived of the kingdom and of the grace of the king. Failing to make use of the patent as divinely intended, they solicit by other means to obtain the boon which the king has already granted them. Too many false Christians, forgetting the original sense of the "patent," fail to see that since Christ died for the sin of mankind, the immutable justice of God is the guarantee of salvation because God, being just, will not exact double punishment.[32] The death of Christ has the character of a guarantee or a seal (*señal, sello*) of man's justification. The psychological and ethical effect of the atonement is paramount in Valdés' analysis. The objective divine action is the indubitable divine guarantee (*garantía*) of man's justification:

[29] *CX Considerations,* xlvi.
[30] Domingo de Santa Teresa, *op. cit.,* 169.
[31] *CX Considerations,* xiii and xxxviii.
[32] *Ibid.,* xi.

It was necessary that Christ should manifest and feel all this weakness, in order that I might be certain that God executed the rigour of His justice, which should have been executed upon my flesh, upon a flesh as passible as my own, and that He should thus confirm me in the faith of the gospel, that I should believe that things actually are, as they are intimated to me in the gospel, which intimation is based upon Christ's suffering; whilst the foundation or basis is so much the firmer, in proportion as the suffering was the more rigourous.[33]

The pledge that the punishment has been once for all exacted and will not be demanded of mankind a second time is the good news (gospel) of truly evangelical preaching. The comparison above of the king and his son, he writes,

ought to be made at once by the man who is coming to know evangelical preaching which is like a patent (*patente*), by which God graciously and freely pardons all the unworthiness on account of which we are in exile and outside his kingdom; and whereby he enables us to turn (*volvér*) to enter into it and to recover his grace and with it his image and likeness.[34]

Valdés repeatedly asserts the importance of the guarantee *to man* implied in the crucifixion: "God in executing the rigour of His justice upon Christ, was more intent upon *giving me assurance, than satisfaction to Himself.*"[35]

The atonement as an objective fact was effected through Christ as very God (although human reason cannot comprehend the manner of the divine generation, any more than the worm can understand human generation).[36] According to this divine generation, Christ is the Word of God, the Son of God, of the same substance as the Father, one with the Father, coeternal. Indeed, not only man is restored by his sacrifice, but also the whole created world, which should intone a hymn of thanksgiving to God for the favor of Christ: "As the first Adam in submitting all men to misery and to death estranged all creatures, so the second Adam . . . leading all men to felicity and to eternal life will restore all creatures."[37]

At the same time, Christ is man, and his humanity has gone through three stages, the ignominy of death, the resurrection, and glorification in heaven. Valdés begins his analysis of man with

---

[33] *On St. Matthew's Gospel,* translated by John T. Betts (London, 1882), 487 f.
[34] *Consideration* xxxviii.
[35] *On St. Matthew's Gospel,* 457.
[36] *Consideration* cix.
[37] *Consideration* lxxxvii. In the reference to the restoration of all creatures, Valdés does not specify how this may take place for animals.

a description of man's original perfection in Paradise,[38] in which state he was impassible and immortal. Having lost this through sin, he can regain it only by sharing with Christ in Christ's three stages of humanity. Valdés speaks of a threefold covenant[39] which binds believers to Christ throughout each stage of the objective and subjective redemptive process, by means of which a reascent to the original glory *ante peccatum* is achieved, but not fully, until the Kingdom of Heaven is reached. The Christian, through incorporation into Christ, dies with him, rises with him to the new life of the Christian on earth, and the perfected life with him in glory in eternity. Commenting on Rom., ch. 4, Valdés writes:

> And as much as they believe in Christ, they believe in him in the pact (*pacto*) and covenant (*confederación*) which he interposed (*puso*) between God [the Father] and those men who are washed in his blood; and, believing this, they are held justified, and without holding back from the love and obedience of justice, they hope for its fulfilment, which is the resurrection, the glorification, and the life eternal.[40]

Though Valdés here mentions the new covenant, he does not always clearly specify the manner of incorporation into the covenanted community, whether by baptism, by the Eucharist, by faith, or by various combinations of devout and sacramental actions.

Of baptism he wrote that Christians are "incorporated by faith and by baptism into the only-begotten Son of God."[41] As to how he understood that baptism, by virtue of the covenant which consists in faith and in baptism, is a constituent in justification, he wrote:

> that we, who have been baptized as infants, then begin inwardly to feel the fruit of baptism, when through divine inspiration, we with the heart accept the grace of the gospel, and so approve of our having been baptized; that had we not been baptized, we would be baptized; we resolve to live Christianly, and we imitate Christ by putting an end to all ambition and personal satisfaction.[42]

Valdés was aware of the prevailing practice of the ancient church in giving extended instruction before baptism, and it was his counsel that, ideally, baptism should be given only after adequate instruction and exercise in the devout life. In the case of the

---

[38] *Consideration* i.
[39] *Consideration* viii.
[40] *Reformistas antiguos españoles*, X (1856), 61.
[41] *On St. Matthew's Gospel*, 508.
[42] *Ibid.*, 505 f.

majority of Christians, baptized in infancy, he urged, as we have seen, that the growing knowledge of the faith should be sealed by some inner act of grateful acceptance and resolution "to live Christianly," "by imitating Christ."

It is clear that the relationship with Christ is not limited to the once-for-all redemption of all men by his sacrificial death. Christ is in a continuous, vital, and dynamic communication with those who in fact attain personal justification, i.e., sanctification. Valdés symbolizes the relation with numerous metaphors, some of which indicate a particular function of Christ, others of which refer to the spiritual life of the individual soul. Christ is the pastor, the gate of piety, the way of the knowledge of God, the physician. He is, above all, the king of the people of God and the head of the church.[43]

Valdés loves most of all the metaphor of Christ as the head:

Exactly as my head sends power (*virtúd*) through all my members, which are sustained and governed thereby, so from Christ comes the power to all those who belong to the Church, so that they are all sustained and governed by those divine gifts which are imparted to them by Christ.[44]

Significantly, this Iberian individualist does not stress the idea that all the members form a single mystical body, concentrating instead on Christ as the head of the assembly of devout individuals.[45]

The *beneficio* of Christ has radically justified mankind, but it is necessary to examine the manner in which this justification is enjoyed by the individual. Radical justification needs to be converted into actual and personal justification by the above-mentioned communication. In his last books, Valdés devotes considerable attention to the problem of how general justification becomes sanctification of the individual. Negatively, it consists in the forgiveness of sins. On the positive side, man, once justified and reconciled with God, is no longer a son of wrath and a son of Adam, but is reborn a son of God, and again obtains and shows forth the image of God which he had lost, together with the right to receive eternal life by "grace of inheritance."[46]

For Valdés, justification means, in effect, regeneration. Incorporation into Christ through faith (and baptism) has tangible results in the life of the regenerate. One cannot obtain the grace of regeneration through one's own labors; but once one has been

---

[43] Domingo de Santa Teresa, *op. cit.*, 170.
[44] *Consideration* lxxv.
[45] Domingo de Santa Teresa, *op. cit.*, 171.
[46] *Trattatelli sul principio della dottrina cristiana*, edited by Eduard Böhmer (Halle an der Saale, 1870), 55.

granted it, one must, *por necessidad,* bring forth fruits of repentance. Again and again, Valdés stresses the origin of justification in a phrase which is found in all his last works: the believer enjoys justification "through the justice of God, executed in Christ." The act of justification which Christ *offered*[47] to God is entirely sufficient without ecclesiastical addenda. Valdés speaks, however, ambiguously of the manner in which one becomes justified, saying at times that justification is freely given by Christ, and at other times that man must personally appropriate it by meritorious behavior. In the same passage in which he says, "God makes them just," he also says that they are "accepted by God as just."[48]

In the *Dialogue* and *Alphabet* he had spoken of faith as *living* faith; in his later works, it is *inspired* faith, with the stress on its supernatural origin, without the possibility of its being earned by human industry.

In his circle of friends in Naples, Valdés contributed greatly to the impulse of an evangelical Catholicism which came close to some of the doctrines of classical Protestantism. He had perhaps even more in common with Schwenckfeldian evangelical Spiritualism, except that he never found occasion to advocate suspension of the sacramental life of the church. But his devotional focus was outside the official sanctuaries of Catholicism. Members of his circle met at his house at Chiaja, near Naples, on Sundays for prayers and Bible study.[49] As to the regular observances of the Catholic Church, Valdés advised Julia to attend them on the obligatory days[50] but to avoid preachers who did not preach Christ. "Make use of abstinence," he told her, "so far as you are conscious that it is necessary to you."[51]

In his final years, Valdés translated at least most of the New Testament and all the psalms, and wrote commentaries on Matthew, Romans, and I Corinthians.[52] Three major and five minor tracts,[53] also dating from this period, stress justification by faith and encourage a purification of the church by the threefold admonition, and excommunication if necessary, of those who live in

[47] Preterit tense with the emphasis of "once for all."
[48] *La Epistola de San Pablo a los Romanos,* in *Reformistas antiguos españoles,* X (1856), 44.
[49] *Alfabeto Cristiano,* edited by Benjamin Wiffen (London, 1861), xxxvii ff. (this portion not in *SAW*).
[50] *Ibid.,* 161.
[51] *Ibid.,* 167.
[52] Allegedly on all the Gospels and all of the Pauline epistles except Hebrews, and on I and II Peter, but all these except the ones listed above have been lost.
[53] Printed posthumously at Rome in 1545

open sin or solely according to vain ceremonies and superstitious customs.[54] In the midst of this literary productivity and fruitful religious speculation and discussion, John—who like his brother, Alphonse, was never very hardy—died in July 1541, just after receiving word of the failure of the diet of Regensburg to bring about a *rapprochement* between Catholics and Protestants. The next year the Spanish Inquisition came to Naples.

3. NORTHERN ITALIAN EVANGELISM 1530–1542: CARDINAL CONTARINI AND BERNARDINE OCHINO

Besides the extensive and united Spanish kingdoms of Sicily and Naples, near the capital of which Valdés guided his Evangelical circle until 1541, the rest of the peninsula was divided into a patchwork of competing principalities in which variations in courtly and civic culture and in monastic and episcopal attitudes toward reform and piety were sufficiently great to constrain us from making facile generalizations about Italian Protestantism and dissent during the two middle quarters of the sixteenth century.

The Papal States gripped the peninsula from Rome to Bologna. Depending upon the fortunes of papal alliance and warfare, the apostolic temporalities bordered or did not quite border on the Republic of Venice. The latter, in addition to its extensive maritime dominion, extended from the island capital to Bergamo in the shadow of the Alps.

Technically within the boundaries of the Holy Roman Empire were seven other leading principalities extending from the boundaries of the Swiss Confederation to the borders of the Papal States. We have already visited one of them, the duchy of Savoy, extending from Neuchâtel to Nice (Ch. 21:1). It was lost to the French by Duke Charles III in 1535 and reorganized in 1557 under his son Emanuel Filibert with Piedmont as the Italian-speaking core and the center of the modern Italian state of Savoy. Savoy bordered on the Italian side the duchy of Milan, the duchy of Parma, and the city republic of Genoa.

South of the Po lay the cluster of smaller states, of which the city republic of Florence (absorbing the republic of Siena in 1557) was the most powerful and religiously the most important.

Throughout Italy, Catholic Evangelism or Valdesianism moved not only devout ladies like Julia Gonzaga (d. 1566) but also prelates. Two such may be introduced to represent a whole gen-

[54] Eduard Böhmer, "Lives of the Twin Brothers Juan and Alfonso de Valdés," *On St. Matthew's Gospel*, 21.

eration of pious and theologically earnest Italian clerics who sought to come to terms with the German religious challenge: Cardinal Contarini, and Minister General of the Capuchins, Bernardine Ochino.

a. Cardinal Contarini. The Venetian Gasparo Contarini (1483–1542), belonging to one of the foremost families of Venice, may be taken as representative of the highly placed Italian ecclesiastic concerned with the theological and ethical challenge of the Lutheran Reformation with special reference to the doctrine of justification.[55] He enters the narrative of the Radical Reformation only as he helps to establish a frame of reference for the various groups and personalities to his left. By innumerable gradations one can move in Italy before 1542 from him as an Evangelical hierarch of the Roman Church devoted to the cause of *rapprochement* with Protestantism, through the two forms of Protestantism (Lutheran and Calvinist), all the way to the various persons and conventicles constituting the proper subject of a history of the Radical Reformation.

Contarini, who once rebuked the pope for his preoccupation with the "morsels of worldly dominion," earnestly strove for universal reform. In 1530, after the diet of Augsburg, he published against Luther his *Confutatio Articulorum,* a polemical examination of the *Confessio Augustina.* This work closes the first period of his life, and prepares for the second.

His popularity at Rome led him, while still a layman in various ambassadorial roles for the Republic of Venice, to be created a cardinal by Paul III in 1535. In 1536 he was put on the commission which was to prepare the way for the reforming Council of Trent, and with it issued the confidential reforming manifesto *Consilium de emendanda ecclesia.* In the same year he was assigned the bishopric of Belluno. In this second phase, Contarini was influenced by Calvin—whose *Institutes* were published in the year of his *Consilium,* filling him, as he declared, with mingled admiration and dread—and by Valdés, whose *Christian Alphabet* was composed that same year for Lady Julia Gonzaga (Ch. 21.2). Contarini, introduced to Valdesianism by Lady Victoria Colonna, found himself impressed by the way both predestination and justification were being thought through in the Neapolitan circle around Valdés. On the vexing issues between Catholics and Protestants in the realm of grace, Contarini found a position intermediate between grace and merit, and subscribed to the theory of a single predestination, namely, to salvation only. For

[55] The most recent theological study is that of Hanns Rückert, *Die theologische Entwicklung Gasparo Contarinis* (Bonn, 1926).

the damned, the divine prescience took the place of explicit reprobation.

In a third period of much shorter duration, the outstanding literary deposit of his thinking was the *Epistola de justificatione,* which Contarini sent from the colloquy at Regensburg to Cardinal Ercole Gonzaga, 25 May 1541. In it he put forward his theory of "double justice." Although his accentuation of justification was not so great as Luther's, he certainly approached the Protestant view. There was, in his brief exposition of the theory, the same feeling for human misery and the same conception of divine majesty as in Luther and Calvin. In practice, at least, it was upon the imputed or forensic justice that Contarini laid stress. He differed from Luther primarily in interposing a period of purgation and an inner gesture of inadequacy before one's acceptance of God's forensic justification by faith. Not so emphatically as Luther, but nevertheless animated by a similar idea, Contarini said that human justice (*inherentem*) "is inchoate and imperfect, which cannot save us." In order to reinforce his theory of "double justice," he drew particularly upon two texts: Ps. 17:21 (Vulgate), "The Lord has dealt with me according to my justice," and Deut. 6:25 (Vulgate), "He will be merciful to us, if we keep and do all his precepts." His own words are:

We may add that there is a *double righteousness* or justice, the one *inherent* by which we begin to be righteous and are made partakers of the divine nature and His love is spread abroad in our hearts: the other not inherent but given to us with Christ and his merits and righteousness. We receive both of these by faith; which of them is first is rather a scholastic question.[57]

Contarini's concern was pre-eminently practical:

This justification can be said to be by works (*ex operibus*) and can be called justification by works. . . . Works, however, which follow this justification and this faith are perfected or formed and efficacious for charity, as said James in his Epistle [ch. 2:14–26]. For if good works do not follow, imperfect and infertile was that faith.[56]

Contarini was believed by many to have compromised the Catholic position at Regensburg in 1541. He died, in anguish at his failure, in Bologna in 1542.

b. Bernardine Ochino. Just before his death at Bologna, Cardinal Contarini was sought out by Bernardine Ochino, Minister General of the Capuchins, who had been summoned to Rome.

---

[56] *Epistola; Gasparo Contarini: Gegenreformatorische Schriften,* edited by Friedrich Hünermann (Münster, 1923).
[57] *Ibid.*

There are three versions of what took place on that occasion. Contarini's secretary says that Ochino had to force his way into the cardinal's presence, and that Contarini, whose condition before his death had grown suddenly worse, said to Ochino: "Father, you see the state I am in; excuse me, and pray to God for me. *Buon viaggio!*"[58] Ochino himself says that Contarini spoke with him, telling him that since his return to Italy he had been accused of appropriating, in a secret manner veiled under generalizations, the doctrine of justification through Christ, despite his opposition to Protestant doctrine at the diet.[59] Although we cannot assume from Ochino's account alone that the dying cardinal discussed his position at Regensburg with him, the account of Girolamo Muzio, Ochino's violent opponent, if not exactly like Ochino's, does say that "the cardinal received him and told him to go to rest until the following morning."[60]

The scene has been fixed upon the memory of posterity, for it symbolized the farewell of the Evangelical cause in Italy. Both the cardinal and the preacher were under the influence of Valdesian Evangelism, the cardinal on the point of death after his last great effort at Regensburg, the friar on his way to the lands of the Reformation.

We last encountered Ochino as the newly elected minister general of the new order of the Capuchins (Ch. 1.3.b). He had been born in Siena in the section dell'Oca (hence, Ochino).[61] He had entered the order of Observantine Friars, the strictest sect of the Franciscans, c. 1504, and then gone to Perugia, c. 1510, giving himself over to the study of medicine, then to the Bible and scholastic philosophy (especially that of Bonaventura), and had then risen to be provincial of the order in Siena (1523), and finally vicar for the Cisalpine province (1533). Craving yet a stricter rule, he had transferred himself in 1534 to the newly founded order of the Capuchin Franciscans, of which he was elected third vicar-general in 1538. Under the patronage of the Capuchins, the medieval practice of having special sermons during the forty days of Lent and in seasons of calamity was greatly extended and intensified.

As a Lenten preacher the gaunt ascetic, of such resonant voice

---

[58] Giovanni della Casa, *Opera* (Venice, 1728), IV, 123.
[59] Ochino, *Prediche* (Venice, 1541), I, treatise X.
[60] Girolamo Muzio, *Le Mentite Ochiniane* (Venice, 1551), fo. 22b.
[61] The two most recent studies are Roland H. Bainton, *Bernardino Ochino, Esule e Reformatore Senese del Cinquecento 1487–1563* (Florence, 1940), and Benedetto Nicolini, *Il Pensiero di Bernardino Ochino* (Naples, 1939). See also *idem*, "Bernardino Ochino: Esule a Ginevra," *Ginevra e l'Italia*, 137–147.

and terrifying directness, was so eagerly sought by competing towns and bishops that the pope himself had sometimes to intervene and fix an acceptable itinerary. At Rome he once had almost all the resident cardinals in his Lenten congregation.

Combining the traits of Francis of Assisi and Savonarola, the barefoot preacher was papally commissioned to study Protestant books in order to refute them. Inwardly, Ochino was soon converted to the Reformation. Calvinism seemed to him the most valid imitation of Christ. But remaining in his order, Ochino hoped that he might be the chosen instrument for the conversion of Italy.

It was his Lenten sermon in Naples in 1535 which was the occasion of the dialogue between Lady Gonzaga and Valdés eventuating in the *Christian Alphabet*. Several of his later sermons are popularizations of the works of Valdés. In 1539, Ochino delivered at Venice a remarkable course of *Prediche*,[62] showing a tendency to the doctrine of justification by faith, all under the guise of opposing the Protestant theory and deriving the doctrine solely from the teachings of Christ in the New Testament. This is more marked in his *Dialogi VII*.[63] The *Dialogi*, in which the Valdesian Duchess Catherine Cibo serves as interlocutress, deal with the nature and the conditions of perfection.

Already under suspicion, Ochino was invited to Rome in 1542 but was probably deterred from presenting himself in the end by the advice of Peter Martyr Vermigli at Florence. Ochino later considered his decision to flee Italy a direct inspiration of the Holy Spirit.

He escaped across the Alps to Geneva. He was cordially received by Calvin. He married a lady of Lucca who had once heard him as the renowned Capuchin preacher. He undertook preaching to the Italian refugee and merchant community domiciled there, and writing. He published in 1544 his *Apologhi,* a collection of one hundred and ten reminiscences and satirical anecdotes about popes, cardinals, priests, and friars. As an example, there is the retort of the converted Jewish merchant to his Italian priest that he would continue his reckonings in Hebrew so long as his pastor continued praying in Latin. Ochino also wrote in Italian and saw first published in French his *L'Image d'Antichrist* (1544) and his *Exposition of Romans* (1545) and *Exposition of Galatians* (1546).

He was minister of the Italian Protestant congregation at Augsburg from 1545 until 1547, when the city was occupied by the

[62] Subsequently printed in Venice in 1541. See n. 59 above.
[63] Published in Venice in 1540 and 1542.

imperial forces in the Smalcaldic War. Escaping by way of Basel and Strassburg, he found asylum in England, where he was made a prebendary of Canterbury, preacher to the Italians in London, and pensionary of Edward VI. While in England, he composed his chief work, *A Tragoedie or Dialogue of the injuste usurped primacie of the Bishop of Rome.*[64]

While Bernardine Ochino was still in Basel, he engaged under the assumed name of Corvinus in an epistolary exchange with Schwenckfeld, who opposed him in a number of writings dealing particularly with the incarnation and salvation by progressive deification.[65]

The writings and thought of Ochino were brought to Schwenckfeld's attention by Valentine Ickelsamer, who, after his vigorous espousal of Carlstadt against Luther, was now a major supporter of Schwenckfeld's irenic Spiritualism *against* Marpeck,[66] and yet would in due course be favorably represented in the cherished *Kunstbuch* of the Marpeck circle (Ch. 31.2)!

4. The Influence of the Radical Reformers in Italy, 1539–1553

We may take the occasion of Schwenckfeld's interchange with the refugee Ochino to bring together the small bits of information we have about the influence of the Radical Reformers outside of Italy upon the Reformation, dissent, and heretical ferment and speculation in the Po valley.

We have already in this chapter recounted the influence on the Italian Waldensians of the Bohemian Brother Luke of the Major Party of the *Unitas* (Ch. 21.1) and the influence of the Spaniard Valdés on the Catholic Evangelicals (Ch. 21.2 and 3). It remains to mention what little there is about the influence of Schwenckfeld and Servetus, and, for good measure, a word about the Venetian sojourn of William Postel.

It would be extremely interesting to establish connections between Schwenckfeld and Italian Evangelicals more radical than Ochino; for, as we shall see in the next chapter, the Spiritualist Anabaptism of many of the Italians, especially in the Grisons (Ch. 22.1), seems to have had in it a Schwenckfeldian strain. Per-

---

[64] Originally written in Latin, it is extant only in the translation of Bishop John Ponet (London, 1549). The conception of the *Tragoedie* bears a remarkable resemblance to that of *Paradise Lost*. It is almost certain that John Milton, whose sympathies with the Italian dissenters were so strong, was acquainted with it, as also with some of Ochino's later works.

[65] See especially Document CCCCXXXI of February 1544, *CS*, VIII.

[66] Cf. Introduction to Document CCCCXXX, *CS*, VIII.

haps Valentine Ickelsamer was in this respect a more important intermediary than the documentation would indicate.

Schwenckfeld may have had direct contact with, and influence upon, the Italian evangelical refugees in the Grisons. Marpeck's stout ally against Schwenckfeld, Leopold Scharnschlager, was from 1547 to his death a resident of Ilanz in the Grisons and may well have had local motivation for his struggle against the Spiritualists (Ch. 31.1 and 2).

No less characteristic than Schwenckfeld's vigorous Christological polemic with Ochino in disguise was his philanthropic activity in behalf of certain Italian Evangelicals in Venetia who had not been able to evade their persecutors in Italy. Through the services of German merchants and agents active in Venice, word of the existence of an evangelical community and of its difficulty reached the ears of Schwenckfeld and many German Protestant divines and princes. It is of interest that one of these German travelers—the humanist, geographer, and theological dilettante Jacob Ziegler (1470–1549)—who had been extremely active in Northern Italy in the years 1521–1531 (especially in Venice and Ferrara), on moving to Strassburg (1531–1534) had sided with Schwenckfeld in the synod of July 1533.[67] It is difficult to assess the extent to which men like Ziegler might have spread Schwenckfeldian ideas in Italy. Schwenckfeld made inquiries of Sibilla Eisler about the religious situation in Venice as early as April 1547.[68] She was presumably in contact with Philip Walther, who traveled commercially between Venice and Augsburg. In August 1548, Walther was a guest in her house in Augsburg at the colloquy with some of the Augsburg preachers, at which he defended Schwenckfeld's doctrine.[69]

Beginning in 1549, Philip Walther, diplomatic representative of Philip of Hesse and Elector John Frederick of Saxony, and an incumbent of other commercial and diplomatic posts, corresponded with Schwenckfeld about two evangelical prisoners, Peter of Cittadella and Baldo Lupetino, who were still in a dungeon, though they were allowed a certain freedom to develop and propagate their ideas. Walther sent Schwenckfeld sixteen articles drawn up by Lupetino, and Schwenckfeld took sufficient exception to Lupetino's traditionalist views on the Eucharist to

---

[67] Karl Schottenloher, *Jakob Ziegler* (Münster, 1910), 286 ff. Before going to Italy, Ziegler had traveled in Bohemia and Hungary, and made the acquaintance of the *Unitas,* and had written a book (1512) to refute their views.

[68] *CS,* XI, Document DCXIV.

[69] *Ibid.,* 489.

write a refutation of them and send it to Walther. He also forwarded his postils to Italy.[70]

Schwenckfeld disagreed with Lupetino's views on the veneration of the cross, the saints, and the Virgin, as "too crude and idolatrous to discuss."[71] But at many points he found much with which to sympathize.[72] He referred to Lupetino as "the captive brother."[73] He forwarded twenty guilders to Walther as a contribution and encouraged others to aid the Italian Evangelicals.

As for Michael Servetus, his ideas about the Trinity circulated in Venice as early as 1539, as evidenced in a letter addressed to the Venetian Senate over the name of Melanchthon.[74] Though not actually written by the *praeceptor Germaniae,* the letter refuted Servetus for the benefit of the Venetians with the same arguments used by Melanchthon in his *Loci communes.* The letter would indicate that some Venetian student or visitor in Wittenberg had been aware of a sufficiently large circle of Italians favorably disposed to Servetus to warrant the detailed warning in the name of the Saxon divine. Further notices of Servetian influence in Italy do not reappear until the eve of Servetus' execution in Geneva (Chs. 23.4; 24).

The Norman-born William Postel (1510–1581),[75] missionary, polyhistorian, cabalist, sometime Jesuit, acquaintance of David Joris, correspondent of Schwenckfeld, and defender of Servetus, was in Venice in 1537 on his way back from Turkey and again from 1547 to 1549. It was in Venice that he translated the cabalist *Zohar* and was strangely converted to cosmic feminism by an illiterate Venetian virgin of about fifty who was giving her life in ministry to the sick and the poor, and possessed occult powers of healing and spiritual discernment. When after her death Mère Jehanne took possession of Postel in 1551, and "her spiritual body and substance sensibly descended into" him, he considered himself reborn as the Shekinah, the Holy Spirit; and he felt driven to proclaim a new gospel of the restoration of all things in a millennium, the advent of which he fixed in frenzied excitement for the year 1556. Among Postel's fifty-five printed books and broadsheets, his *Panthenosia* (?Basel, ?1547), his *Restitutio rerum omnium* (Paris, 1552), and *La doctrine du Siècle Doré ou de*

---

[70] CS, XII, Documents DCCXLVI, DCCXLIX, DCCLI, DCCLVII, DCCLVIII.
[71] CS, XI, 493.
[72] CS, XI, 498.
[73] *Ibid.*
[74] Melanchthon, *Opera Omnia,* III (Halle, 1836), N. 1831.
[75] William J. Bouwsma, *Concordia Mundi: The Career and Thought of Guillaume Postel (1510–1581)* (Cambridge, 1957).

l'evangélique règne de Jésus Roi des Rois (Paris, 1553) came closest to the major themes of the Radical Reformation. Postel twice wrote to Schwenckfeld on the restitution. Postel's extraordinary theory about the Golden Age of Noah and the role of Italy and France in the divine plan of restitution might very well have appealed to the Italian Spiritualists and Evangelical Rationalists. Camillo Renato's vision of the return of the Golden Age "under the fair auspices of Christ" (Ch. 22.1) may represent an appropriation of Postel's ideas.

In any event, with a sketch of Waldensianism, Valdesianism, and the influence of foreign Radicals on the Italians behind us, we are ready to turn to the Italian Radical Reformers themselves.

CHAPTER 22

THE RADICAL REFORMATION IN ITALY AND THE RHAETIAN REPUBLIC

We have already indicated the difficulty of distinguishing within the Italian context what should be identified as belonging properly to the local Catholic reform movements, what in turn should be identified as the reanimation and transformation under the influence of northern Protestantism of indigenous Italian sectarianism surviving from the Middle Ages, what should be identified as the Italian appropriation of specifically Lutheran or Reformed impulses, and finally, what should be segregated from all this to be validly labeled the Radical Reformation in Italy. In the last chapter we saw that elements in both Valdesianism (Evangelism) and Waldensianism in its sixteenth-century transmutations could be seen as tributary to the Italian Radical Reformation. Similarly, normative Protestantism, when its principles took effect in various Italian milieux, precisely because it never gained the open support of princes or town magistrates and was therefore by necessity organized in conventicles, quickly lost the conservative reforming character of the Magisterial Reformation in the north. What the fiery Italian apostles of the Reformation and their captors and their inquisitors alike called "Lutheran" would often have been repudiated by Luther himself. Moreover, it was not the Lutheran version of Protestantism that made the greatest appeal to the Italians anyway, but, rather, the inherently more radical and potentially more sectarian Reformed version. And Bullinger, Bucer, and Calvin, who were the main exponents of Protestanism for the Italians on the eve of the re-establishment of the Inquisition in 1542, found themselves in lively correspondence with many an Italian admirer who, had he been living in Zurich, Strassburg, or Geneva under the eyes of these leading Protestant divines, would have been rather swiftly dismissed as uncongenial, or harried—or worse, as heretical!

Besides the difficulty of defining the Reformation in Italian terms and hence that of differentiating from it the Radical Reformation in Italy, there is the additional difficulty of transposing to the Italian phase of the Radical Reformation, however segregated and defined, the religio-sociological typology which has been largely derived from the situation to the north. To refer only to the three main thrusts of the Radical Reformation, it must be said at once that the Italian Anabaptists were not primarily interested in penitential, covenantal rebaptism and the purifying ban but, rather, in repudiating papal baptism and in modifying the doctrine of the Trinity, and that the Italian Spiritualists for their part were not so much interested in mystical contemplation or in exegetical inspiration as in predestination and the death (or the sleep) of the soul pending the resurrection. As for the third main thrust of the Radical Reformation, we have already recognized that Evangelical Rationalism was pre-eminently and distinctively the Italian element in our typology. Evangelical Rationalism has, in fact, already been defined as a fusion of Italian humanism or critical Rationalism with selected ingredients of Anabaptism and Spiritualism, rendered thus capable of expressing itself in organized churches and even synods—experimentally in Rhaetia, with more enduring results in Poland (Ch. 25) and Transylvania (Ch. 28).

In the present chapter we shall first look at the early life and thought of Camillo Renato (c. 1500 to c. 1572), in whom all the aforementioned radical Italian currents flowed; then at the rise of Italian Anabaptism, which in part stemmed from him; then at Laelius Socinus (1525–1562), the progenitor of Socinianism; then at the plight and extinction of Italian Anabaptism after the synod of Venice in 1550 and the defection of its leader Peter Manelfi in 1551; and finally at the attenuation and deformation of Italian Spiritualism and Evangelism as Spiritual Libertinism and Nicodemism. We shall reserve for another chapter our presentation of other Evangelical Rationalists whose life and thought unfolded to a large extent in the Italian diaspora (Ch. 24).

This Italian diaspora was the dispersion of Italian refugees into Protestant lands, among people of other tongues. There was also one region to which Italian Evangelicals could flee for religio-political asylum which was Italian in speech and also in culture—the Italian and Ladin valleys of the Rhaetian Republic. Small though this area was, it was the one place in Christendom where a Reformed Italian Christianity could take form more or less freely on, so to speak, Italian soil. Allied with the Swiss Confederation and hence the meeting place of Germanic and Italian ideas, the Rhaetian Republic becomes a focal point for the history of the Italian phase of the Radical Reformation all out of proportion to its size. The relatively tolerant and humane Venetian Republic, as a consequence of its intensive trade relations with partly Protestantized Germany and its maritime vision of the larger world, also bulks large in our narrative along with the duchy of Ferrara, where Duchess Renée once received Calvin, sponsored a circle of reform-minded humanists, and introduced in her private chapel the simplified Mass modeled on that at Navarre with Communion in both kinds.

It was in Ferrara, Venice, and Rhaetia that major events in the life and influence of Camillo Renato were recorded.

1. CAMILLO RENATO: RADICALISM IN RHAETIA TO 1552

Camillo Renato began his tempestuous career as a Franciscan in Naples, where he may have come into contact with the circle of John de Valdés. "A big man and well formed," a master in theology and accomplished in classical literature, Camillo, under the name of Lisia Phileno or of Paul Ricci, moved easily in courtly and academic circles, and by his powerful preaching appealed also to popular audiences.[1]

Camillo appeared in Bologna a year or two, perhaps, before the death of Valdés, and in 1540 he fled to Modena, where he won a large number of converts to his radical views in the academy of *letterati*, by whom he was esteemed for his humanistic flourishes; in the court, where the count found the friar to be for "incomparable magnanimity and love . . . far from any personal ambition and quest of glory"; and among the members of the local Protestant conventicle gathered before his arrival and at one time in epistolary contact with Bucer. Despite Camillo's local popularity, he was arrested by orders from the duke in Ferrara, in turn under pressure from the Dominican inquisitors at Bologna. The trial which took place in Ferrara toward the end of the year made it clear that he was in fact egregiously heretical and seditious, even

[1] The first to have suggested the identification of Phileno and Camillo was Church, *Italian Reformers,* 39, n. The identification was virtually proved by Alfredo Casadei, "Lisia Fileno e Camillo Renato," *Religio,* XV (1939), 356–440. The identification was accepted by Cantimori, *Eretici,* with a few amplifications. The presentation here is based upon my much larger study, "Camillo Renato," *Reformation Biographies,* edited by Charles Garside, Jr., for 1962. In the following summary, documentation is minimized. For new light on Camillo in Modena, see the forthcoming study of Antonio Rotondò.

if not guilty of rascality, according to rumors picked up both by Cardinal Contarini in Rome and Cardinal Morone, the bishop of Modena, at the time on a mission in Germany.

The nine accusations brought against him at the trial, which Duke Ercole II and possibly also Duchess Renée attended as observers, may be brought together under three main headings: namely, that salvation depends utterly upon divine election, with no meritorious use of one's will in the process; that the souls of both the righteous and the wicked expire at the death of the body and have no abiding place until the resurrection and the Last Judgment; and hence that all the liturgical and penitential practices based on the alleged existence of a purgatory filled with sinners and of a paradise filled with saints are not only a religious deception but also the occasion for an intolerable social exploitation by the professionally religious. After at first arguing as a Spiritual Franciscan that the monks and friars should give more for the poor than the Christians in the world, Camillo had moved on to undercut the economic basis of many a chapel, monastery, and convent by insisting that the foundation for the saying of Masses for the dead was fatuous and also that vows taken before God and the saints were no longer binding once the truly liberating gospel had been heard.

Camillo's doctrine of predestination and the bondage of the will unto salvation, and his allegedly apostolic doctrine of the provisional death of the soul pending the resurrection, constituted together a highly sharpened sword which Camillo had been wielding with frightening skill in cutting away the whole ecclesiastical merit system. But, under trial, Camillo agreed to sheath it in a complete abjuration and even promised to give the names of any persons who held similar views or circulated works containing such doctrines. He was conducted in solemn procession through the town, mitred, and sentenced to life imprisonment as an act of clemency.

It is possible that his penalty was graciously interpreted as something much less than solitary confinement in a dungeon, and that it was under the influence of the beneficent Duchess Renée that he was enabled to escape from the prison in Bologna to which he was removed in the spring of 1541.

There may even be a gallant allusion to Renée as liberatress (Italian: Renata) in the name which Camillo Renato chose for himself and may have used for the first time when, writing from the Italian section of the Rhaetian Republic, 9 November 1542, he signed his first letter to Henry Bullinger, the leading Swiss divine at the time.[2] Camillo said he was emboldened by Coelius Secundus Curio, who was a friend of Bullinger's, to write (Ch. 24.2.d). It is of interest that the latter was in Ferrara shortly after the trial of Camillo and had been encouraged to leave by Duchess Renée, anxious for his future. In Camillo's letter to Bullinger, he gave little indication of his radical views, confining his personal remarks to a few vague reminiscences about his sufferings, imprisonments, and escape.

Nevertheless, the very name he had now chosen for himself at the outset of his Rhaetian career was theologically programmatic. Camillus was the ancient Roman hero who had brought back to Rome the *signa* captured by the Gauls; and it was the conviction of Camillo, the Reborn, that he was the consistent restorer of the original meaning of the so-called sacraments as *signa*. In his subsequent correspondence with Bullinger and in his efforts to reform the Italian churches in the Rhaetian Republic according to his idea, Camillo steadfastly rejected the very word "sacrament," first, because it implied an oath and hence a commitment, and secondly, because the *segni,* as he preferred to call them, were, even by the Protestants, too readily administered and interpreted as though the believer or the church could in some way confirm or ratify what God had already done through the Spirit in awakening in the elect the realization of their salvation.

The center of Camillo's "sacramental" theology was the Lord's Supper. At Caspano, the ancestral seat of the powerful Paravicini family, by whom Camillo was retained as a tutor of classical languages for the numerous household, the Lord's Supper was observed in the local church according to Camillo's unusual arrangements. Paulinist that he professed to be in his doctrine of election and in his conception of the Holy Spirit in the reborn or redeemed, Camillo was also exclusively "Pauline" in his Eucharistic theology. Noting that Paul (I Cor. 11:23) had instituted the ordinance "as it had been transmitted to him by the Lord," Camillo introduced a full meal, which he called an *epulum* preceding what he liked to call the *libatio.* There is evidence that the nourishing *epulum (agapē),* sponsored no doubt by the hospitable Paravicini, united the residents and the refugees, the rich and the poor, men and women of all degrees.

When Camillo came to explain further to Bullinger the

[2] Letter No. 51; edited by Traugott Schiess, *Bullingers Korrespondenz mit den Graubündnern*, 3 vols., Quellen zur Schweizer Geschichte, XXIII (1904), XXIV (1905), XXV (1906).

theology behind this usage, he drew a clear distinction between the Last Supper, when Jesus asked the incredulous apostles to eat the bread as an act of faith, and all the suppers to be observed ever thereafter by Christians till he come again. Camillo detached the dutiful and faithful *manducatio* of the first and precrucifixion supper, which was once for all (*semel*), and converted it into his technical term for the individual appropriation in faith of the salvation proffered in Christ by the Spirit. This inward eating reminds one of the similar doctrine of Schwenckfeld and was in effect a Eucharistic metaphor for that which is in a baptismal metaphor more commonly called rebirth or *regeneratio*. Unlike Schwenckfeld, however, Camillo did not hold because of the pre-eminence of the unique inward experience that the outward rite should be suspended. Rather should it be reinterpreted and then *frequently* observed as a corporate *commemoratio* in great joy (*recordatio*) in the prospect of Christ's imminent advent to vindicate his elect. Camillo was not content to have the local church or churches under the patronage of the Paravicini adopt his interpretation. He wished the use of Caspano to spread throughout Rhaetia and beyond.

The impending schism in the Rhaetian Reformed Church stems partly from this effort. It is now the place to say something further about the extraordinary constitutional and religious character of the Rhaetian Republic.

The Rhaetian Republic, roughly the modern Swiss Grisons and coterminous with the bishopric of Chur as it existed then, was a federation of three component Alpine federations: The Grey League proper, with its important center, Ilanz, was the principal federation, and often lent its name to the Republic as a whole (Grigioni, Grisons, Graubünden). The other two component federations were the League of the House of God, with its capital at Chur, and the League of the Ten Jurisdictions, with its chief city, Davos. The three federations constituting the Rhaetian Republic were linked closely with the Swiss Confederation. In 1512, the Rhaetian Republic had jointly come into possession of subject territory received as indemnification for their joint military service in Italy. This fringe of subject territory, roughly the valleys of the Mera and the Adda from Bormio down to Lake Como, was administered by appointive Rhaetian functionaries. The principal subdivisions of this federal jurisdiction were the district around Bormio, the Valtellina (German: Veltlin), and the district around Chiavenna. Valtellina, the largest region, was itself subdivided into three main administrative districts. The whole of the federal jurisdiction was Italian or Ladin (Romansh) in speech, as indeed were many of the valleys within all three of the component federations of the Rhaetian Republic, particularly the Grey League. Italian, Ladin, and German constituted the three official languages of the Republic.

The Republic was also divided religiously. At the federal diet in Ilanz in 1526 mutual religious toleration of Catholics and Evangelicals (Protestants) had been decreed, with the provision that whichever party had the majority in any parish or district would also have the use of the ecclesiastical edifices. Anabaptists, who at that time were being recruited in all classes under the powerful preaching of Blaurock, Mantz, and Castelberger (Ch. 6.1), had been expressly excluded from the provisions of the edict of Ilanz.[3]

Despite this restriction of the Anabaptists, the valleys of Rhaetia, trilingual, biconfessional, and voluntaristic, were seed-beds of sectarianism, especially after the renewal of the Inquisition in the Italian principalities to the south by the bull *Licet ab initio* of 21 July 1542 and the flight of hundreds of evangelical monks, friars, priests, bishops, and pious laymen into this readily accessible asylum.

Let Camillo Renato speak for all of them. Like all the Italian refugees, he bore in his heart a great love and esteem for the Swiss and Rhaetian Reformers who, in their "temples in the mountains," were preparing that house of God to which all the nations in the latter days might flow (Isa. 2:2). Confident that under their spiritual leadership and the protection afforded by the Swiss and the Rhaetian confederations the "Golden Age under the fair auspices of Christ" would soon return, Camillo described the plight and the pluckiness of fellow clerical exiles from Ausonia under papal domination and inquisition. We who are "reborn," he says, "are children of God and followers of Christ!"

For that reason we have departed from the Ausonian shore; and, embracing exile, we live in foreign lands. Poverty is our only companion. Our condition in life is hard. Work cheats us on some days, but constant labor pays us our tutor's fees, worn though we be. We have proclaimed the gospel whenever occasion offered, prompted neither by ambition for advancement nor adequately recompensed.

[3] See John Comander's letter to Zwingli for the situation in Chur in 1528; Petrus Dominicus Rosius de Porta, *Historia Reformationis ecclesiarum Raeticarum*, 2 vols. (Chur, 1771/1774), 1:1, 94, n. The principal source behind De Porta is Ulrich Campell, *Historia Raetica*, edited in two volumes by P. Plattner, Quellen zur Schweizer Geschichte, VIII (1887), IX (1890).

Advancing through the usual dangers of life wherever the divine im-
pels us, where a blessed hope calls us, ever willing, with a mighty
force we have laid low the opposing foes. Those whom providence
predestined and whom the Spirit drove within, we have snatched from
Satan and joined as new souls to Christ.[4]

The key figure among these refugees in Rhaetia was Augustine
Mainardo, the pastor in Chiavenna. He had succeeded Francis
Negri, the founder of the Protestant community there, who then
stayed on as a tutor and was eventually drawn into the faction
fomented by Camillo. When Camillo first arrived in Chiavenna,
he was well received by both the pastor and the teacher and
apparently prevailed upon them and the local presbyterial council
to adopt the rite of Caspano with its *epulum* preceding the
libatio. Mainardo was not enthusiastic about the idea, however,
and wrote Bullinger to ask him what he thought about it. Camillo
visited several other communities—for example, Vicosoprano—
gaining some support for his ideas among the established Italian
pastors.

In the meantime his interest in sacramental theology was
shifting from the observance of the Lord's Supper to the problem of baptism and the associated question of the Triune formula. By early 1548, Camillo had moved to the radical position
of repudiating baptism as received under the papal Antichrist in
his book *Adversus baptismum*, which was later edited by the
grandson of Faustus Socinus. There is a basic ambiguity in this
book which goes far to account for the difference between Italo-
Polish Anabaptism (Ch. 25.2) and Germanic Anabaptism. On
the one hand, Camillo stressed the invalidity of papal baptism,
its unreconstructed continuation in a Protestant context, and the
equation of circumcision and pedobaptism. On the other hand,
as with the Eucharist, Camillo's views were so Spiritualist that
he himself may have been altogether satisfied with what he would
have called an inward baptism. Although many of his followers
submitted to an evangelical rebaptism, there is no evidence that
he himself did.

He was not, however, the only proponent of radical Anabaptist
ideas in the Rhaetian Republic. To mention first the German-
speaking valleys, after the original propagation of Anabaptism
under the leadership of Blaurock, Mantz, and Castelberger in
Chur (Ch. 6.1), there was the activity of Leopold Scharnschlager in

---

[4] The *Carmen* of Camillo against Calvin; Friedrich Trechsel, *Die protestant-
ischen Antitrinitarier vor Faustus Socin,* 2 vols. (Heidelberg, 1939/1944),
I, *Beilage,* IV, lines 81–98.

Ilanz.[5] Between 1546 to his death in 1563, Scharnschlager served unobtrusively as the teacher in the local school of Ilanz, while carrying on by correspondence and visitations the duties of a major leader of South German Anabaptism. Scharnschlager had been successively an associate and successor of Marpeck in Strassburg, a missionary in South and Middle Germany and in Moravia, and would be a participant in the long disputation with Schwenckfeld (Ch. 31.1 and 2) and a major contributor to the important doctrinal collection, the *Kunstbuch.* While Scharnschlager was publicly teaching school in Ilanz and privately directing the local Anabaptist conventicle and carrying on a wide correspondence, his devoted wife, who belonged to a prominent Tyrolese family, was seeking to recover her confiscated estate after the two had been converted to Anabaptism. It is quite probable that the well-to-do Scharnschlagers were able to give hospitality and counsel to many Italian Radicals.

Much closer to our present interest are the Italian-speaking Anabaptists, two of whom antedate Camillo in their propagation of Spiritualist, anti-Nicene Anabaptism in Rhaetia, and specifically in the Ladin-speaking Engadine. The one, Francis of Calabria, had been called to the Protestant parish of Vetto; the other, Jerome of Milan, had been called to Lavin. They both claimed to be followers of Ochino.

In their stress on predestination, their minimizing of the atonement, and their antipedobaptism, they may with Camillo be taken as representative figures in whom the Protestant, (Catholic) Evangelical, and proto-Anabaptist currents flowed at that point in Italian religious history where, after intermingling, they would soon redivide and become two distinctive Italian movements, Evangelical Anabaptism and anti-Trinitarian Evangelical Rationalism.

Francis and Jerome[6]—the former enthusiastically supported by his congregation; the latter, however, rejected by his—so stressed the doctrine of predestination that they were prepared to say that no matter how grievous or monstrous his sin or crime, if a person were predestined to salvation, he would be saved by the grace of God. They virtually deprived Christ of a redemptive

---

[5] For his presence in Ilanz, see the letter to him edited by J. ten Doornkaat-Koolman, "Leupold Scharnschlager und die verborgene Täufergemeinde in Graubünden," *Zwingliana,* IV (1921–1928), 329–337. The fullest account is in *ME,* IV, 443–446.

[6] The views are summarized hostilely by De Porta, *op. cit.,* 1:1, 68 ff., based upon Campell, *Historia,* II, 297–309.

role. Because it was to God's grace alone that the elect owed their salvation, the incarnation and the death of Christ were not necessary.

The sacraments, for these radical Evangelicals, were not essential to salvation. They were signs only, as with Camillo, of the public acknowledgment of one's salvation. Accordingly, Francis and Jerome were opposed to infant baptism, which had no more significance, they stated, "than if administered to a horse." In order to mitigate the rigor of their predestinarianism for those not favored by God, they denied the existence of eternal punishment for the reprobate, and like Camillo, espoused the death of the soul pending the resurrection, with the single exception of the forgiven thief at the crucifixion, who, as they acknowledged, had been vouchsafed a unique privilege among mortals in his direct admission to paradise.

Francis and Jerome were required in 1544 to give an account of themselves before a mixed Ladin synod of Protestants and Catholics, divines and magistrates, in a disputation lasting two days in Zuoz. Many of Francis' parishioners from Vetto were present to sustain him, participating actively in the debate.

Francis at first sought to ridicule the Protestants for having to bring in Catholics to support them. He was told promptly that he himself was not regarded as an ordained minister of the Evangelical confession. In one place, Francis argued his main Christological point by showing how absurd it would be for a shivering beggar (the believer), instead of giving praise to the donor (God) of a coat (salvation), to thank the coat itself (*corpus Christi*). At this, the aged magnate and warrior John Travers could contain himself no longer, and, mounting the pulpit, charged Francis with having been grievously corrupted either by Manichaeus, or by Arius, or by the Turk.[7] Francis was condemned as an Anabaptist, and therefore made subject to banishment under the edict of Ilanz. His parishioners urged another meeting, but when they were told that they would have to bear the expenses they reluctantly acquiesced in the condemnation of their pastor.

The debate at Zuoz in 1544 helps place the bitter controversy between Camillo and Mainardo at Chiavenna in 1548 in the context of the whole Rhaetian Reformed Church. Chur was the virtual headquarters of the general synod. It was the seat also of a theological gymnasium (the old Dominican convent) for the training of a new Rhaetian clergy. Chiavenna was the natural center of the Italian-speaking Reformed churches. It must have occurred to more than one among the many former prelates,

[7] De Porta, *op. cit.*, 1:1, 73.

priors, and preachers exiled from Italy that a semiautonomous Italian-speaking synod in Rhaetia, supplementing the work of the general synod, with its preponderantly Germanic character, would fulfill the legitimate aspirations of these heroic churchmen for independence. Needless to say, all aspirants for leadership in the Italian Reformed community desired the approval of Bullinger and the divines of the other Swiss cantons to offset the influence of Chur. In fact, at least four of the antagonists in the growing schism in the church of Chiavenna were at one stage or another to be in epistolary or personal contact with Bullinger.

At the center of the controversy stood beleaguered Mainardo, who was in continuous contact with the divines of both Chur and Zurich. Stubborn and unimaginative, Mainardo smarted under the local charge of being neglectful of his pastoral duties and too much concerned to impose his own will. He had drawn up a confession of faith in twenty articles which he wished to have approved by the authorities to the north and subscribed to locally, as in effect the creed of the Italian churches. Nothing of this confession survives except the twenty-two anathemas directed against Camillo and his followers. These were drawn from Camillo's public statements and his writings, one of which, *De sacramentis*, appears to be identical with a now partly edited Bern manuscript, *Trattato sul Battesimo e sulla Eucaristia*. From these two documents it is clear indeed that Mainardo was, as the leading pastor of Italian Rhaetia, faced with a major threat to the integrity of the whole Italian Reformed community. Camillo had clearly resumed the preaching of all the doctrines for which he had been condemned at Ferrara; and even in a fully Reformed context, these doctrines constituted a threat, notably Camillo's conception of election, regeneration, and eschatology. Mainardo, speaking for himself and the majority of the church in Chiavenna, anathematized Camillo and his followers and allies, such as Francis of Calabria:

We damn those [the Renatians] who say that the rational soul is mortal, and dies with the body, but will be raised at the Last Day with the body, and that the whole man will be made immortal . . . ; who say that the souls of the dead live in such wise that they sleep until the Last Day, and then will be raised from sleep; . . . that impious men are not bodily resurrected at the Last Day; [and] that those men who are not born again of God are irrational like the brutes, so long as they are not yet translated by the Spirit of God into the Kingdom of Christ.[8]

[8] These are articles I, II, XII, and XVIII of Mainardo's confession of faith, printed by De Porta, *op. cit.*, I:2, 83–86.

Camillo apparently distinguished between the *anima* and the *animus*. The clearest indication of this is in the statement of one of Camillo's students, Gianandrea Paravicini. The *anima*, shared with the unregenerate and with animals, perishes at death. The *animus*, or rational soul (*anima rationalis*), or universal intellect, is that which is present in the intellectually reborn or the elect animated by the Holy Spirit. The originality of Camillo lay in having constructed a fully New Testament anthropology and eschatology within the framework of medical-humanistic Averroism (endemic in the Italian university towns where he had sojourned). By identifying the world soul with the human *ratio* purified or endowed by the visitation of the Holy Spirit to the thus reborn or illuminated elect, he was able to go beyond a purely Averroistic conception of an impersonal immortality of absorption into the world soul and to reaffirm the Pauline hope of the resurrection in spiritual bodies. The *renati* are accordingly the elect who have been reborn in the Spirit and await the resurrection of the just. Camillo's eschatologically reinterpreted Averroism—it must be put down in passing—was one of the very important impulses in the new religious interpretation of the role of reason in what we have called Evangelical Rationalism.

Mainardo sought to prevail upon Camillo to confess a belief in the natural immortality of the soul if he wished to be considered a Christian and a member of the local church. Mainardo was equally opposed to that other variant of psychopannychism found among his foes, the belief in the sleep of the soul pending resurrection, the view favored by some of the German Anabaptists and represented also among the Italian Radicals (Ch. 22.2).

The combination of Camillo's conception of election and his view of the experience of spiritual regeneration led some of his followers and associates to an antinomianism which, claiming Paul for patron, went so far as to claim that there is no natural law in man by which can be discerned the things that should be done and the things that should not be done, and therefore that believers, for their part, have no need of the natural law or even of the Ten Commandments, for the reborn are spiritual men, judging all things. One readily sees how this heady combination of predestination and spiritualism could lead to Spiritual Libertinism, increasingly corrosive of the traditional values and motivations, fostered by the moralistic sects no less than by the established churches, in the measure that its adherents could stress alongside their spiritual liberty the elimination of hell and purgatory and even a last judgment for the wicked among whom they might indeed in the end be counted. Already aware of this implicit threat in Spiritualist "Anabaptism," Curio had, back in 1541 in Lucca, written his *De immortalite animorum* "against Anabaptists, Sadducees, and Epicureans."[9]

As for Camillo's "sacramental" theology at this stage of the conflict with Mainardo, one can only remark that he persisted in strenuously denying that the two ordinances were sacraments and in depriving them of any confirmatory or ratifying power. In the *Trattato,* for example, he wrote:

As to the effect of baptism and of the Lord's Supper, I state and affirm that it is not the function, either primary or secondary, of either one of them, that they be confirmatory or certifying seals (*suggelli*), firstly, because such designations (*nomi*) do not suit them. . . . Secondly, we do not find in the scriptures that Christ instituted them for such a purpose. And yet if we wish to call them signs (*segni*), because they do signify something, this does not mean that they are certifications or confirmations any more than any other name because it signifies the thing named. It is one thing to signify something, another to confirm it.[10]

At this point in the conflict with Mainardo, Camillo did not stress his interest in the *agapē* (*epulum*). As for baptism, he regarded papal baptism as invalid, and was opposed to the Bullingerian equation of circumcision and pedobaptism; but he did not stress rebaptism, although rebaptisms are everywhere documented among his followers. He called the church by preference the company of Christ (*compagnia*) and espoused the principle of local autonomy (congregationalism).

Like the Germanic Anabaptists, Camillo believed in the threefold warning and the ban of Matt. 18:15 ff., as well as in the effort to persuade and heal in Matt. 17:14 ff. He opposed the use of magisterial coercion in the realm of conscience. He regretted that the wholesome principle of loving and prayerful excommunication, with a readiness to readmit the penitent, had given way to the use of magisterially enforced exile and capital punishment.[11]

In the mounting schism in the church of Chiavenna and the environing cluster of churches, Mainardo found himself opposed not only by Camillo and the other Radicals but also by the founder of the church, Francis Negri, and by Francis Stancaro, a

---

[9] Markus Kutter, *Celio Secondo Curione* (Basel, 1955), 44.
[10] *The Trattato* is edited by Delio Cantimori and Elizabeth Feist, *Per la Storia degli Eretici Italiani del Secolo XVI in Europa: Testi Raccolti* (Rome, 1937), 47–54.
[11] In the *Carmen, loc. cit., passim*

refugee Hebraist from Venice (Ch. 22.3). The latter, although he was not in agreement with Camillo on many points, went as the spokesman of the Chiavenna dissidents to Zurich, whither Mainardo also went, each side hoping to gain the support of Bullinger. Although Bullinger had by now been prompted to call Camillo "the worst of heretics," it is significant that Camillo himself could still, as late as 12 May 1549, write to Bullinger, demanding an explanation for the charge in the name of Christian forthrightness and love and in keeping with their mutually professed friendship, signing his name "hopefully thine."

Bullinger was instrumental in getting a Rhaetian synodal visitation organized to hear the charges and countercharges in the residence of one of the patrons of the Chiavenna church, December 1549. It was reported hostilely of Camillo that he was so filled with alarm at the prospect of four evangelical pastors coming down from Chur to ferret out his "warrens" that he considered escaping this Protestant "inquisition." But he finally resolved to stand his ground and prepare his defenses, including one hundred and twenty-five articles of what he called the errors, ineptitudes, and scandals of Mainardo. At the hearing, the old pastor was largely vindicated by the visitors, who went home, after drawing up twenty-one points of agreement, feeling that the dangerous Chiavenna schism had been healed by a few concessions to the sensibilities of the Renatians and by the constraint of Camillo Renato himself from further agitation. But Renato could not contain himself and was formally excommunicated 6 July 1550. He proceeded to organize "a church of the Anabaptists."

At this juncture Peter Paul Vergerio entered the controversy from his newly acquired base as the pastor in tiny Vicosoprano. Having laid down his episcopal crozier in Capodistria in 1549, this former prelate of noble birth and wide experience in missions for the Holy See in France and Germany was no doubt alert to the possibility of replacing Mainardo as the chief spokesman of the Italian-speaking Reformed Church of Rhaetia. Styling himself "the authorized visitor of the synod," he came to preside over the formal recantation of Camillo, 21 January 1551. There is no documentation for collusion between Camillo and Vergerio, but it is strange that Camillo, in signing this second recantation with none of the fear of fire or imprisonment which understandably gripped him in inquisitorial Ferrara a decade earlier, did not attempt to safeguard even the more moderate of his doctrines and those which might still be discussible in a Reformed context. Vergerio, for his part, had the capacity to sympathize with or tolerate positions ranging from Catholic Evangelism through Lutheranism to anti-Trinitarian Spiritualism. In return for Camillo's real renunciation of the radical and divisive principle of believers' baptism and rebaptism and a formal rejection of the rest of his teachings, Vergerio no doubt momentarily hoped to present himself to the northern divines as a successful healer of schism and with a moderate Camillo to work for the building up of a comprehensive latitudinarian Italian Church on Rhaetian soil. He was soon to defend his policy of comprehension, expressing the hope that Rhaetia might earn thereby a reputation in the world for proceeding prudently and with great gentleness, "as indeed God our Lord deals with us." The agreement with Camillo, if one there was, did not last long. Camillo resumed his sectarian activities and was presently captured on a sally out of his Rhaetian sanctuary in Bergamo, in the fall of 1552. We can leave him there, reassured, however, that he will again make good his escape, and we turn to the Italian Anabaptist movement outside Rhaetia.

2. THE ITALIAN ANABAPTIST MOVEMENT OUTSIDE RHAETIA, 1542–1554

Italian Anabaptism was said by two relapsed Anabaptists to have been derived from Renato.[12] But there were surely other ingredients in the movement, and other personalities. It is not at all unlikely that, by way of Venice and Rhaetia, German Anabaptist refugees spread their ideas and practices. Waldensian conventicles will have formed the original seedbeds of propagation. Apocalyptic Spiritualists in the tradition of Savonarola and stray Catholic Evangelicals will have been among the recruits.

In any event, Italian Anabaptism had a strong rationalistic bent, and was programmatically critical of both the Nicene and Chalcedonian formulations. In contrast to northern Anabaptism, it stressed predestination to saving faith, and it was in this context that the atoning role and hence the Lordship of Christ in the churches was minimized or neglected. Its actual practices with respect to rebaptism—for example, immersion—may have perpetuated local Catholic usage, for immersion or partial immersion and pouring in the baptisteries survived from antiquity in several parts of this more clement region of Christendom. Otherwise than in the north, the Italian Anabaptists regarded believers' baptism as a sign of predestination to salvation more than as an incorporative covenant. Italian Anabaptists formed

---

[12] Reported by Vergerio in a letter of ˙o January 1553; Schiess, *Korrespondenz*, I, No. 199:2.

conventicles and they convened synods. Their local gathering was called variously a *consorcio, congregatione, unione, compagnia,* and collectively, God's *"santa e immaculata chiesa in quelli che sono ordinati . . . a vita eterna."*[13] In the Italian Anabaptist conventicle, despite the environing Renaissance mood, there was little of that yearning to restore in its primitive perfection the church of apostolic times. The stress was eschatological rather than restorationist, if one may distinguish these two closely interrelated sectarian moods (Ch. 13.3). At the same time, the Italian Anabaptists readily called their itinerant pastors *apostoli.* They were more individualistic than their northern counterparts. At the same time, their womenfolk were not so prominent as in Switzerland, Germany, and the Netherlands. On the whole, the Italian Anabaptists found little occasion for, or interest in, developing such a conventicular instrument as the ban.

It was in August 1549 that we first learn of Tiziano, the mediator of Camillo's ideas.[14] It was about then that he was extruded from the Rhaetian synod and expelled "by the secular arm" from Rhaetia, presumably in accordance with the provision of the edict of Ilanz, which did not extend toleration to Anabaptists.

In Florence, Tiziano met the former priest Peter Manelfi, who in San Vito and then Ancona c. 1540 had been moved by several Capuchins, including Ochino. After about a year he had given up his priestly duties on the advice of a former Capuchin (one Giulio). Some three years later Manelfi left for Padua, where he preached clandestinely as a Lutheran. He then traveled about for some time in northern Italy, visiting evangelical communities. In Florence, Tiziano, with two other converts, Lawrence Niccoluzzo of Modiano and Joseph (Iseppo) of Asolo, acquainted Manelfi with Anabaptist views. These included the Renatian view that sacraments are signs only, that only adults may be baptized, that Christians cannot hold magistracies, that the Bible alone is the basis of Christian doctrine, and that the Catholic Church is diabolical and its baptism invalid. There is no mention of anti-Trinitarian teachings. Some months later Tiziano rebaptized Manelfi and three others at Ferrara. Manelfi

---

[13] These phrases have been assembled from the Venetian inquisitorial archives by E. Pommer, "L'idée d'Eglise chez les anabaptistes italiens au XVI siècle," *Atti del X Congresso internazionale 1955;* Comitato Internazionale di Scienze Storiche (Rome, 1957), 791–793. The most comprehensive recent account is that of Henry A. De Wind, "Anabaptism in Italy," *CH,* XXI (1951), 20–38.

[14] Letter of Vergerio to Bullinger, *Korrespondenz,* I, No. 199:2. The fullest account of Tiziano is that of Henry A. De Wind, *ME,* IV, 729 f.

clearly believed that Tiziano was responsible for the introduction of Anabaptist teachings into Italy. Together they formed Anabaptist conventicles in the Republic of Venice.

In the same year, 1549, Manelfi, with Benedict of Asolo, bribed the guards at a prison in Venice and persuaded a Lutheran prisoner, Peter Speziale of Cittadella, to undergo rebaptism at their hands. In other cases, they helped prisoners to escape. Theirs was a well-organized underground network and communication system, continuous, perhaps, with that of the surviving Waldensians in the valleys of the Po and Adige.

In this region dominated by the Venetian Republic during the first half of the sixteenth century, the persecution of heretics had been deliberately restrained in order that there might be no interference in trade relations with the German merchants. In fact, at one point the hope had spread that the whole of the Republic would turn Protestant. Not until 1546 did the Inquisition begin to make itself effectual in Venice.[15]

After the termination of the Lutheran meetings in Venetia, the more radical sectaries continued to flourish, especially around Vicenza. Through the efforts of Tiziano, Manelfi, and their sympathizers, by the middle of the century Anabaptists were known to dwell in many localities. Very numerous, with ordained clergy under ten or more itinerant "apostolic bishops," these Radicals, who were chiefly artisans, met secretly in the homes of the members of the fellowships. On matters of doctrine they were in some disagreement.

In the conventicle at Vicenza, anti-Trinitarian and Christological questions came to the fore, requiring the calling of a synod for the establishment of consensus among the far-flung brethren. There may have been a proto-Unitarian, proto-Anabaptist conventicle in Vicenza as early as 1546. A vague Socinian memory places here and at this time a fellowship made up, among others, of Laelius Socinus (Ch. 22.3), Nicholas Paruta (Ch. 29.5), John Valentine Gentile (Ch. 24.3), Francis Negri (Ch. 22.1), Julius of Treviso, and Francis della Sega (Ch. 22.4).[16] Not all these men would have been in Vicenza on the eve of the great Anabaptist synod of 1550; but it was precisely in this

---

[15] Karl Benrath, *Geschichte der Reformation in Venedig* (Halle, 1886), "Wiedertäufer im Venetianischen um die Mitte des 16. Jahrhunderts," *Theologische Studien und Kritiken*, LVIII (1885), 9–67.

[16] Andrew Wiszowaty, grandson of Faustus Socinus, supplies this information about the *collegia vicentina* in his *Narratio Compendiosa*, printed in Christopher Sandius, *Bibliotheca Antitrinitariorum* (Amsterdam, 1684), 207–217. For the learned dissolution of this composite phantom academy, see Wilbur, *Socinianism*, 80–83.

community of divergent trends that the sense of urgency for the calling of such a synod was generated. To settle the disputed points, it was decided to hold the council of the leaders of the movement in Venice, with two delegates from each congregation. Tiziano and Joseph of Asolo recruited the delegates in northern Italy, the Rhaetian Republic, and the Swiss cantons. Manelfi had part of the responsibility for seeking funds and providing housing for the delegates. Some sixty persons, all Italians and representing around thirty conventicles, gathered in synod at Venice in September 1550. Francis Negri may have come from Chiavenna. There was even a delegate from St. Gall. They met for forty days,[17] opening their sessions with prayer. The Lord's Supper was three times observed in the course of the forty days.

Manelfi was apparently very forceful in moving the synod to adopt as their own a nearly unanimous statement on ten disputed points, strongly supporting the kind of theology represented by Renato, Francis of Calabria, and Tiziano. The ten points can be condensed thus: Jesus was not God, but an exceptional man, the natural child of Joseph and Mary; Mary had other sons and daughters after Jesus; human seed has the God-given power to produce both body and soul. The elect are justified by the eternal mercy of God; the "benefit" of Christ consisted solely in his giving instruction in the good life and in his self-sacrificial testimony to the love of God. There are no angels. There is no devil other than human prudence. The latter claim, possibly a Waldensian note, is based on Rom. 1:18–23 and the general Biblical observation that "we do not find anything in Scripture created by God as his enemy except human prudence." The Radicals had eliminated, besides the devil of course, also the idea of hell. They held that the souls of the wicked die with their bodies; that for the unrighteous, there is no hell except the grave, and that after the death of the elect their souls sleep till the Day of Judgment. This point represents a rejection of Renato's starker conception of the expiration of the soul pending the resurrection.

The delegates of the congregation of Cittadella refused to accept all these points, and were henceforth excluded from the

[17] Emilio Comba, "Un sinodo Anabattista a Venezia anno 1550," *Rivista Cristiana*, XIII (1885), 21–24, 83–87; *id., I nostri Protestanti* (Firenze, 1895–1897), II, ch. xiii. The sources are the records of the heresy trials held by the Inquisition in the Frari Archives and the State Archives at Venice, in the latter notably, Busta IX, *Processi del Sant'Uffizio*, explored by Benrath, Comba, and De Wind.

fellowship. But for the most part the Venetian synod clearly represented a triumph of the radical leaders of Italian Anabaptism.

At the conclusion of the synod several participants were designated as "apostolic bishops" to bring the synodal decisions to the constituent and related congregations. They moved about in pairs reminiscent of the Waldensian barbs. Manelfi, with Marcantonio of Asolo, for example, traveled to Vicenza, Padua, Treviso, and Istria. Another pair of emissaries was Lawrence Niccoluzzo and Pasqualino of Asolo, who visited the Romagna, Ferrara, and Tuscany. These synodal tactics brought about a schism between the congregations willing to accept the ten Venetian points and those which held to a more moderate course.

In September 1551, Manelfi was asked by the brethren in Verona to explain the ten Venetian points of agreement. A Sunday meeting attended by some twenty-five members in a secluded spot broke up in disagreement over his reassertion of the Venetian point that Christ was merely a prophetic teacher, a man born of the seed of Joseph.

Suddenly, in October, Manelfi decided to return to the Catholic Church and told his companion of his startling decision. In Bologna he turned himself over to the Inquisition and on 17 October made his first deposition, describing his "aberrations," disclosing the deliberations of the synod in Venice, and recounting the history of the movement from radical "Lutheranism" to radical Anabaptism during the preceding decade.[18] The case was transferred, because of its obvious importance, to Rome, where Manelfi prepared three more statements, enabling the Inquisition very shortly thereafter to wipe out most of the Anabaptist movement in Italy. In a deposition of 12 November, he gave further details about his work as bishop and about the teachings of Renato and Tiziano. He pointed out that the stress on Christ's humanity had not been so prominent in the conventicles until his own urging of it in Venice. On 13 November he provided further information about the synod and named several participants and some of the other apostolic bishops. Manelfi also listed as many members of the sect as he could recall and added the names of a number of Lutherans in Venetia. In his final deposition on 14 November he described several occasions on which he and other evangelists had narrowly escaped capture and how they had entered prisons to comfort fellow believers, winning also new converts.

---

[18] His reference to "ten or eleven years ago" would mean about 1539 or 1540, the years of Camillo's activity in Bologna, Modena, and Ferrara.

The Inquisition moved swiftly against the Anabaptists and related nonconformists. The orders for the arrest of the persons named by Manelfi were sent to the authorities at Padua, Vicenza, Treviso, and Asolo. Arrests and recantations followed. The fate of Manelfi, the informer, is not known.

A former Franciscan, Lawrence Tizzano, was tried before the Inquisition in Venice in 1553, where he confessed to having been a member of the Valdesian circle in Naples for several years,[19] then a Lutheran, then an Anabaptist, and finally a member of the "diabolical" sect, by which he may have meant the Spiritual Libertines (Ch. 22.5).

Another radical Sicilian figure who may be mentioned here, though not an Anabaptist, was George Siculo.[20] A hostile Italian refugee in Rhaetia said of him that he had combined papism and Anabaptism and contributed to the establishment of a third sect.[21]

A former Benedictine monk, Siculo was a prophetic preacher, active in the same cities and perhaps among the same sectaries as Renato a decade earlier. Like Renato, Siculo believed in a regeneration in the Spirit, but over against Renato and in company with most Germanic Anabaptists in opposition to the Protestants, he believed in the freedom of the will unto salvation, and took the occasion of the vacillation and the execution in Padua of the Protestant jurisconsult Francesco Spiera to compose a doctrinal *Epistola* which was printed in Bologna in 1550. It contained in substance what Siculo had preached for forty days at Riva di Trento. He had gone to Riva, possibly with the hope of preaching before the council a bit farther up the river, of exhorting it prophetically to turn from predestinarian Protestantism (!) and to return to the true catholic and apostolic tradition. But he was denounced and summoned before the magistrates of Riva. The same year he was again in Ferrara, where he attained a number of followers, still preaching against the Lutheran predestination and bondage of the will. The Inquisition at Ferrara was well aware that his opposition to Luther shielded a heresy even more dangerous. Siculo was in prison by the beginning of April 1551. On May 23 he was executed, according to some sources, without a trial; according to others, after he had refused to recant. His followers were numerous in Italy and Rhaetia. He was so much appreciated by some of the Italian residents in Geneva that Calvin wrote against him, saying of his books and

---

[19] Tiziano and Tizzano are not identical. The confession of Tizzano is printed by Francesco Lemmi, *La Riforma in Italia* (Milan, 1939), 68 ff.
[20] Cantimori, *Eretici*, VIII. Siculo is mentioned twice by Bartolommeo Fontana, *Renata di Francia,* II (Rome, 1893), 279 and 421.
[21] A letter of Guilio Milanese of Poschiavo; *ibid.,* citing Comba.

ideas that "passing swiftly throughout Italy, they corrupt many people."

3. CONTINUED SCHISM AND HERESY IN RHAETIA, 1552—1561: LAELIUS SOCINUS

Tiziano escaped to the relative security of Rhaetia, from which he had been banished in 1547. His preaching brought him a renewed following. In June 1554, the authorities at Chur had him imprisoned and questioned about his beliefs. He answered in ambiguous language, claiming to be guided only by the Holy Spirit. Fear of capital punishment moved him, however, to sign in the presence of assembled elders and other Christians a confession prepared by Philip Gallicius, pastor at Chur.[22] This confession implies that Tiziano had denied the Trinity and the divine nature of Christ (as an Ebionite), had suspected the tendentious corruption of the genealogies and Nativity narratives by Jerome (as a Helvidian), had placed the authority of the Holy Spirit above that of the Bible, had rejected infant baptism, and had said that Christians might not serve as magistrates. As to the alleged corruption of Scripture, we know from another source that his followers specifically rejected as Jerome's interpolations the first two chapters of Matthew and the corresponding sections of Luke. After his recantation, Tiziano was driven by rods from the town, exiled (a second time) from the Rhaetian Republic. Gallicius, in his letter to Bullinger, felt obliged to justify his relative leniency in the treatment of Tiziano by pointing out that a recantation would be demoralizing for his followers, whereas another martyrdom (Gallicius refers to the martyrdom of Servetus, Ch. 23.4) would but raise their devotion to a new pitch.

Camillo Renato, for his part, had found that not even two recantations could damn the ardor of his followers. We were last with him when he was captured by the constables in Bergamo in September of 1551, the year after the Anabaptist synod in Venice. Cardinal Innocenzo del Monte, formerly a secretary to Cardinal Contarini and now to Pope Julius III, was almost at once in possession of the information that the notorious "Sicilian heresiarch" had been captured, and he sought, through the papal nuncio in Venice, to gain possession of the escapee from the inquisitorial prison in Bologna—but in vain. With the aid of "powerful supporters who are able to use shields of gold," and with a formal renunciation once again of all his heretical views, Camillo

---

[22] Letters to Bullinger, 2 and 25 June 1554; *Korrespondenz,* I, No. 261:1, 2.

returned to Rhaetia, where as a "poisonous bladder" (Bullinger's phrase) he began to "infect the whole of the Valtellina with his poison" (Vergerio's report). Camillo even made bold to seek the headship of the evangelical school in Sondrio as a counterweight to the seminary in Chur. "Here Camillo reigns," wrote Vergerio with alarmed exaggeration.

The principal document surviving from this period is Camillo's long, flamboyant, passionate indictment of Calvin for burning Servetus. The *Carmen,* composed in Traona in September 1554 for the anniversary of the execution, mingled Biblical and mythological language in highly mannered, humanistic verse.[23] It was a great plea for religious toleration. Distinguishing between the two dispensations, that of the New and that of the Old, Camillo associated the Roman priesthood with that of the Hebraic covenant, since both stressed law and sacrifice; and he appealed for a gentler conception of religion as proclaimed and practiced by Jesus himself, who healed, who forgave, and who was slow to anger. Nowhere else do we have in Camillo's writings such stress upon the apostolic ban as the only means of force allowable to Christians. He laments the fact that in the so-called Reformed Church the wholesome apostolic ban has itself been banned.

After this we hear relatively little about Camillo. Something should be said about those who continued or communicated his ideas.

We can single out Laelius Socinus (1525–1562) and Michelangelo Floris, pastor in Soglio: the one primarily a covert carrier of Camillo's ideas to another age and area, the other primarily an implementer of Camillo's tactics on the Rhaetian scene during the lifetime of the heresiarch.

It was Michelangelo, with four other Italian refugee pastors, who, in perpetuating some of Camillo's teachings, widened the schism in the Italian Reformed community of Rhaetia and renewed the attack in Chiavenna. They published in Milan a selection of Camillo's one hundred and twenty-five articles against Mainardo, and led a vigorous fight against Mainardo's continuing efforts to impose his personal confession upon the Italian churches and to make personal subscription to it a condition of membership in the local congregation and of participation in its offices and in its ministrations. To Mainardo's confession were attached not only the twenty-two anathemas already dealt with against the Renatians and other Anabaptists but also the Nicene and Athanasian Creeds and the very controversial Tome of Pope Damasus (c. 380). The antisubscriptionists headed by Michel-

----

[23] The *Carmen* is translated in my larger study of Camillo.

angelo wanted no more than the Apostles' Creed. They were at once latitudinarian in doctrine and congregationalist in polity in their redoubled determination not to allow Nicene and Chalcedonian formulations to define the Christian message and in their unwillingness to permit any synod of churches to impose any confession of faith on any congregation without the consent of the latter duly assembled. Michelangelo carried the problem before Bullinger, presenting him and his colleagues in Zurich with twenty-six questions, 24 May 1561.[24] The effort of the five latitudinarian pastors was doomed to failure. In fact, their *démarche* precipitated the decision of the general synod in Chur, strongly abetted by Bullinger, to oblige the five recalcitrant pastors to sign a confession, no longer to be called "that of Mainardo but rather that of the Rhaetian Church."[25]

Camillo had lost in Rhaetia. The tolerant Evangelical Rationalism of his later years was to be perpetuated outside Rhaetia in the tradition of Laelius Socinus operating largely through the work of his nephew in Poland.

Laelius Socinus (1525–1562)[26] was born in Siena of a distinguished line of patrician lawyers which provided Italy in the course of a century with its three most celebrated jurisconsults. Mariano Sozzini, the elder, was the first and the most famous. A founder of the academy, he influenced the young Aeneas Sylvius Piccolomini (Pius II). Strongly flowing in the family was that current of Italian thought, more philosophical than religious, which found expression in the dialectic of Lorenzo Valla, and which was characterized by sober philological observation, subtle and almost perverse doubting, persistent uncertainty, and diffidence in the face of all allegedly final solutions, and yet recurrently prompted to demand proof. We may call this current, somewhat colorlessly, humanist Rationalism.

Laelius was the sixth son of Mariano Sozzini, the younger. From the age of five, Laelius lived in Padua and was educated to become a jurist under his father's eye. He came to be interested in learning Hebrew, Greek, and Arabic. The motivation may have been his ecumenical concern for the eventual union of the three great religions, an eschatological hope widespread among the seekers of this age. Despite the weight of the legal tradition in his family, Laelius' interests were primarily religious. He later told Melanchthon that his desire to reach the *fontes juris*

---

[24] Printed in Trechsel, *op. cit.*, II, *Beilage*, V.

[25] Letter of Johannes Fabricius to Bullinger, 6 June 1561; *Korrespondenz*, II, No. 349.

[26] The most recent accounts are Cantimori, *Eretici*, Chs. 14, 17, and 21, and Wilbur, *Socinianism*.

had led him into Biblical research, and thence to rejection of "the idolatry of Rome." His conversion to Protestantism, with a disposition to favor the spiritualizing Anabaptists, dates roughly from the introduction of the Inquisition and the dashing of the hopes of the Evangelicals. He studied in Padua and went on to Venice. In Vicenza he joined perhaps as early as 1546 in colloquies with the exponents of various radical trends.[27]

Several of these radical currents were revolving in the mind of young Laelius as he set forth for study in Basel in the summer of 1547. Stopping at Chiavenna, he came under the influence of Francis Negri and particularly of Camillo Renato in the midst of the conflict with Mainardo. Carrying Renato's ideas, with respect to psychopannychism and to the sacraments as signs only, Socinus left Chiavenna for Basel, where he found congenial company in Castellio, Ochino, and Curio, perhaps introduced to the latter (Ch. 24.2.d) by a letter from Camillo. Laelius registered in the university in the fall of 1547[28] under the rectorship of the Hebraist Sebastian Münster and made the acquaintance of Boniface Amerbach, a sometime colleague of his father's.

From the end of 1547, documentation for Laelius becomes scarce,[29] but he traveled in Switzerland (probably Geneva), France (Nérac, the court of Margaret of Navarre), England, where he was to make the acquaintance of Peter Vermigli, John Łaski and the Fleming John Utenhove,[30] and possibly Holland, where he may have come into contact with Anabaptists.[31] He was in Geneva the winter of 1548–1549.[32]

Laelius' queries took a sacramental turn after Curio in Basel made known his opinions concerning the *Consensus Tigurinus* of August 1549, the attempt of Calvin and Bullinger to unite the Swiss Protestants doctrinally and with special reference to the Lord's Supper. Laelius returned to Basel briefly, then withdrew to Zurich, lodging with the Hebraist Conrad Pellican. He went to Wittenberg (July 1550 to June 1551), first as Melanchthon's

---

[27] For Laelius' role in the Valdesian circle of Vicenza (cf. n. 16), see the forthcoming study of the trial of Abbot Matteo Busale by Aldo Stella.

[28] Hans Georg Wachernagel, *Die Matrikel der Universität Basel* (Basel, 1956).

[29] The basic biography is that of C. F. Illgen, *Vita Laelii Socini* (Leipzig, 1826), who used sources in the Socinian tradition.

[30] With Utenhove, confident of Łaski, Laelius was not long afterward in correspondence, which is the only and quite indirect confirmation of the tradition that he went to England.

[31] There is no documentation for a Dutch sojourn, a part of the itinerary in the traditional biography. The sojourn, however, was accepted by Eugène Burnat, *Lélio Socin* (Vevey, 1894).

[32] J. H. Hottinger, *Historia ecclesiastica Novi Testamenti*, IX (Zurich, 1657), 436.

guest, then with Johann Forster for the improvement of his Hebrew. With the Lutherans, he vigorously argued for Bullinger's views. Despite his outspoken spiritualism with respect to the sacraments, he received a favoring testimony from Melanchthon. By way of Breslau and Prague, Laelius visited Cracow, staying with Francis Lismanino, head of the Polish Franciscans and confessor of the queen. From here he wrote Calvin on the state of Protestantism in Poland. In the Polish university town of Cracow, rationalist opinions were beginning to challenge the orthodox doctrine of the Trinity (Ch. 25.1).

After Laelius returned to Zurich he learned about the summary imprisonment of an opponent of Calvin on predestination (Jerome Bolsec). Calvin had long before become vexed by Laelius' "darling vice of curiosity" and admonished him to "lay aside the foolish itch for inquiry" and for meddling in theological abstrusities.[33] Besides the question of predestination, Socinus had raised with Calvin, Bullinger, and others the problems of baptism and the resurrection. He asked, for example, whether a Turk, just converted to Christianity, should have his children baptized at once, to which Calvin programmatically responded in the affirmative, but obviously ill at ease with a question which was asked to cast doubt on the claim of the Magisterial Reformers that circumcision and baptism were correlative ordinances. As to the resurrection,[34] Laelius, presumably secure in his psychopannychist conviction as he had derived it from Camillo, plagued Calvin with detailed questions about the organs, members, and functions of the bodies of the resurrected saints.

Presently, Laelius set out in 1552 to visit Italy at peril of body and soul. He may have been prompted by a desire to regulate family affairs. As it turned out, his father died the following year. It is possible that he harbored the hope that the whole republic of Siena might turn Protestant.[35] Coming south, he stopped at Vicosoprano with Vergerio, and the two of them traversed the Valtellina during the late summer.[36] He was actually in Siena at the time of the uprising against the Medici. He left for Bologna, with at least one work by Camillo, to be with his father through the winter. He returned to Siena, conducting himself freely as an Evangelical, because the Inquisition was not effec-

---

[33] Calvin to Socinus, 1 January 1552; *Opera*, XIV, Epistle 1578, coll. 229–230.
[34] *De resurrectione;* Trechsel, *op. cit.*, II, *Beilage*, VII, pp. 445 f.
[35] Cantimori, *Eretici*, XIV, n. 10.
[36] Letter of Vergerio to Bullinger, 1 November 1552; Schiess, *Korrespondenz*, I, No. 195:1. In this letter he said that Camillo was spreading his doctrine everywhere. This will not have disturbed Laelius so much as Vergerio.

tive.[37] In the fall he stayed for two months in Padua in the home of the crypto-Protestant professor of law, Matthew Gribaldi (Ch. 24.2). On his way north he may have sought out Camillo. It was not, however, until he was back in Zurich with Julius of Milan, pastor in Poschiavo (with whom Curio stayed for a while that very summer), that Laelius was vigorously accused of being both a Renatian and a Servetian.[38]

In Ch. 24.2 we shall see how he sought to defend himself before the incredulous and benign Bullinger.

No disciple of Camillo, but for a brief period his ally, was another Italian refugee in Rhaetia, Francis Stancaro,[39] whom we have already met briefly as a spokesman of the factions lined up against Mainardo in Chiavenna (Ch. 22.1). No narrative of the Radical Reformation would be complete without something more than passing reference to Stancaro, because, although never himself a heretic from the point of magisterial Protestantism, he was ever and again to be found in the midst of mounting tension and radical schism.

Born in Mantua, c. 1501, he had won fame as a Hebrew scholar, publishing his *De modo legendi Hebraice institutio brevissima* at Venice in 1530. Successively a monk, a priest, and a proponent of Evangelism, Stancaro had a talent for stirring up antagonism wherever he appeared. A Venetian with whom Stancaro lived for a while compared him with "a snail which leaves behind it a trail of slime." A syndic of Venice who also played host to Stancaro for a time described his boarder as unreliable, egotistical, and selfish in all that he did, adding that although Stancaro looked like a Jew, he was not, and that in Venice the Hebraist married a woman of doubtful reputation. Stancaro, who may have begun his teaching career at Friuli, became a teacher of language at Padua in 1540, at which time he left the Roman Church. He suffered eight months' imprisonment for certain of his writings in Mantua and Venice, and then escaped to the Valtellina in 1542.

The summer of 1544, Stancaro was in Vienna, and there in

---

[37] Letter of Vergerio to Bullinger, 10 March 1553; Schiess, *Korrespondenz*, I, No. 207:1. The editor has mistakenly given the date as 1553.

[38] The evidence for the time of Laelius' arrival in Switzerland, first Zurich and then Basel, is Curio's letter to Bullinger, 19 January 1554. Laelius is mentioned by Curio in a number of letters, Kutter, *op. cit.*, *Briefe*, 49, 99, 123, 155, 158 (*ibid.*, p. 170, n. 57). Julius' first extant letter concerning Laelius' heresy is dated 4 November 1555.

[39] The most recent study is that of Francesco Ruffini, *Francesco Stancaro, Studi sui Riformatori Italiani*, edited by Arnaldo Bertola, Luigi Firpo, and Edoardo Ruffini, III (Turin, 1955), 165–406.

October he was given the university chair of Hebrew. After a time, popular suspicion directed the attention of the Inquisition toward him. At the command of King Ferdinand he was dismissed March 1546.

Not waiting for the formal dismissal, Stancaro went to Regensburg, where he may have met Ochino, who, in any event, invited him to Augsburg. In Augsburg, he accepted a professorship in Greek and Hebrew offered him by the town council.

In 1547, Curio attempted to get Stancaro a position on the faculty of the university in Basel, but failed. Stancaro therefore busied himself with the publication of his Hebrew grammar (1547) and a commentary on James, receiving in due course his doctorate in theology at Basel. It was from Basel that he sent a treatise on the Reformation to the *signoria* of Venice. The papal nuncio at Venice wanted Stancaro prosecuted. The *signoria,* however, put him off, suggesting that he write to Cardinal Farnese at Augsburg and demand Stancaro's arrest on the spot.

Nothing came of the nuncio's appeal. Stancaro reappeared in the Rhaetian Leagues and found work as a teacher, becoming further acquainted with John Comander of Chur and with Francis Negri in Chiavenna. We have already noted how he became involved in the dispute (1547–1548) between Camillo and Mainardo. When Mainardo attempted to straighten matters out by forcing the Renato party to sign an orthodox confession, Stancaro produced a counterconfession, which was approved by the two leading Reformed pastors of Chur. In November 1547, it will be recalled, Mainardo and Camillo were summoned before the general synod of Rhaetia at Chur. Camillo, failing to appear, was condemned *in absentia* and commanded henceforth to keep silence. Mainardo and Stancaro, as spokesmen, went separately to Zurich in order to consult Bullinger. On 7 June 1548, Bullinger and the other divines rendered their decision in favor of Mainardo. Stancaro, who had attempted to put Mainardo in a bad light, was eliminated from the controversy. He returned to teach for a few months in the Valtellina (having brought Francis Negri's young son, George, back with him from Zurich); but a letter from Mainardo to Bullinger,[40] containing some of the adverse characterizations already quoted, widely discredited Stancaro, and he left the country. We shall next meet him as the founder of the first Reformed parish in Poland (Ch. 25.1).

The close relation of Francis Stancaro and Laelius Socinus to Camillo Renato, a father of Italian Anabaptism, has justified the

[40] Letter of 22 September 1548, Schiess, *Korrespondenz,* I, No. 102.

interruption of our Anabaptist narrative, to which we return in the wake of the persecution caused by Manelfi's desertion of the cause.

4. ITALIAN ANABAPTISTS, 1554–1565: RELATIONS WITH THE HUTTERITES

Three important survivors of the first wave of persecution were the Venetians Julius Gherlandi, Francis della Sega, and Anthony Rizzetto. All of them sought asylum with the Hutterites in Moravia and led many of their followers thither. Around them can be told the remainder of the Anabaptist story in Italy.[41]

Julius Gherlandi (also, in Hutterite records, Klemperer) was born c. 1520 near Treviso in Venetian territory and was intended by his father for the Catholic priesthood. He was troubled in conscience by the contradiction between his Christian professions and his own actual achievements and failings. It is quite possible that he belonged for a season to the circle in Vicenza and that his memory was preserved in Socinian records as "Julius of Treviso." In reading Matt. 7:15 f. about false prophets and bad fruit trees, he was led to break from the Roman Church[42] to join the Anabaptists. He was baptized by one Nicholas of Alessandria, a member of the conventicle in Treviso. He baptized several persons himself. When the renegade Manelfi exposed the whole movement to the Inquisition, Gherlandi and Francis della Sega, on learning about the Hutterite colonies, journeyed to Moravia and were admitted to the Bruderhof at Pausram (just west of Auspitz). Significantly, they were not required to be rebaptized. Among the Hutterites, Gherlandi engaged in his new craft of making lanterns, but soon asked permission to bring word of the Hutterites to his former associates in Italy.

In March 1559, Gherlandi arrived in Italy, bearing a letter from della Sega to a fellow believer in Vicenza, as well as a general letter of introduction from the Hutterites to the Italian Anabaptists. The letter describes Hutterites as communitarian Anabaptists, and makes clear that only those Italian Evangelicals would be welcomed as members whose minds were not contaminated with false doctrines about the nature of Christ, the resurrection from the dead, angels, devils, or other matters (in obvious reference to the doctrines approved by the Venetian council of 1550). Gherlandi also carried a list of more than a hundred

---

[41] Henry A. De Wind, "Italian Hutterites Martyrs," *MQR*, XXVIII (1954), 164–171; *ME*, II, 514.
[42] De Wind says between 1549 and 1551.

Italians living in over sixty localities in northern Italy and the Rhaetian Leagues.

On 21 March 1559, Gherlandi came to official attention when on arriving in Venice he refused, as every other Anabaptist did, to swear by oath: in this instance, to the port authorities that he had no disease! On being released, he appeared a few days later in his native Treviso, publicly criticizing the Roman Church. He was arrested and examined at Treviso and was then transferred to prison in Venice, from which he managed to escape and return to Moravia.

He was back in Italy by Christmas of 1560, and in October 1561 was captured once again at Treviso and imprisoned at San Giovanni in Bragora in Venice. From his prison he wrote, 4 or 14 October 1561, a letter[43] to Bishop Leonard Lanzenstiel (Ch. 26:1) in Moravia. It explains his predicament, and breathes a courageous spirit, firm in the faith: "Do not for a moment doubt that there will be given to me in that hour, according to the true divine promise, wisdom against which all the adversaries shall not be able to prevail." A few days later Gherlandi prepared a comprehensive confession of faith, recounted the reasons which had prompted him to leave Catholicism and eventually to join the Hutterites. He closed thus: "That is my simple confession. I ask that it be accepted with indulgence, for I am no orator, writer or historian, but only a poor lantern-maker—I am however not truly poor, since I am indeed content with my fate." On 16 November 1561, Gherlandi was examined by three theologians. The issue between the inquisitors and the Hutterite concerned the relative authority of church, tradition, and the Scriptures. The Catholics found that he remained "obstinate in the crime of heresy," and he was left to languish in the prison, where he sought to convert his fellow prisoners. When admonished by a priest to beg pardon from the court for proclaiming his gospel in prison, he replied: "To God alone ought I to bend the knee and not to worldly men."

It is at this point that we pick up the story of the already mentioned Francis della Sega. Della Sega was born at Rovigo (1528 or 1532) in the Republic of Venice. He studied civil law in Padua. Stricken with illness brought on by his gay life as a student, and chided by a pious craftsman, he turned to the New Testament, determined to model his life on that of Christ. His conversion was complete. He abandoned law and became a tailor, incurring the ridicule of family and friends. He joined the Ana-

---

[43] It was never delivered and is now in the archives of Venice.

baptist movement. He is remembered in the Socinian tradition as among the refugees in the Grisons after 1551.

Around 1557 he was in Vienna and then traveled with a Hungarian friend through Hungary and Slovakia. Learning of the Hutterites from their Moravian servant, he visited several communities in Moravia. He was admitted to membership, perhaps first in Slovakia, but later in Pausram in Moravia. There he married a woman from the Engadine and settled down as a tailor. He never became ordained as a Hutterite evangelist. Shortly after the departure of Gherlandi with the letter of introduction to his former associates, della Sega himself, on receiving news of his father's death, returned to Italy to see about his inheritance. Other trips followed. Like Gherlandi, he carried word of the Hutterite way of life to friends.

In 1562, on one of these expeditions to Italy in the company of one Nicholas Buccella, a physician of Padua, and of Anthony Rizzetto, of Vicenza, he was leading to Moravia some twenty members of the Cittadella conventicle. It will be recalled that a large part of this group had not assented to the Venetian ten points. The company were overtaken at Capodistria just as they were embarking for Trieste. The charge against them was for the moment unrelated to heresy. But the *podestà* soon realized that he had stumbled upon a band of Anabaptists, and at once sent his prisoners to the Inquisition at Venice for further examination. They were put in the prison where Gherlandi, who had fallen into the hands of the Inquisition the preceding year, was held. The Italian Hutterites quickly made contact and were able to reinforce one another in the difficult weeks ahead.

Rizzetto is as interesting a personality as Gherlandi and della Sega. He had been rebaptized about 1551 in Vicenza by the apostle Marcantonio of Asolo, the companion of Manelfi. Rizzetto and Bartholomew of Padua, with the wife and daughter of the latter, were among those who had chosen to flee the persecution by taking ship to Thessalonica. When Bartholomew died, Rizzetto married the widow, and after returning to Italy, he visited the Hutterites. It was on his return trip from Moravia to bring back his wife and family that he had joined della Sega's company and been overtaken with him by the *podestà* at Capodistria.[44] Della Sega and Rizzetto prepared a confession, dated 20 October 1562.[45]

The principal points of their testimony were that salvation is

---

[44] The episode leading to the arrest of della Sega and Rizzetto is told by Benrath, "Wiedertäufer," 46 f.
[45] They are the source of much of the foregoing information.

by faith alone, that baptism should be reserved for believers, that confession should be to God and not to priests, that one should seek to obey God's commandments.[46] During their imprisonment, there was a series of examinations conducted, by the Jesuit theologian Alfonso Salmeron, among others. Throughout, della Sega stressed his devotion to Scripture.

In the meantime, on 15 October 1562, the court had sentenced Gherlandi to be drowned. When informed of his fate, he prepared a last word of greeting to the Moravians. It was necessary first to degrade him formally from his rank as ordained subdeacon of the Roman Church before turning him over to the secular arm. Under the cover of darkness his boat set forth into the *Laguna* to meet another one which was waiting for it. A plank was thrown between the two boats, he was tied upon it and weighted with stones, and the boats thereupon grimly returned separately to their ports. The martyrdom of Gherlandi in Venetian waters took place sometime after 23 October 1562.

Early the next year, della Sega directed a letter to Bishop Leonard Sailer Lanzenstiel, Peter Scherer Walpot, and the whole community in Moravia. Unlike the one written earlier by Gherlandi, it was somehow delivered.[47] Of exceptional interest, it transmits Gherlandi's last words and speaks movingly of his martyrdom. It breathes a pure faith and devotion to Christ:

I would not [writes della Sega] let the occasion pass while I am yet in this tabernacle of desiring for you the grace of the salvation of the omnipotent God. I have loved you all sincerely; but I love you even more now that I have been deprived of your presence, which deprivation is a great tribulation to me. And when the end comes, I will love you with the love that I have through Christ himself, because you are of his flesh, yea, bone and limbs of Christ. And you have loved me sincerely. Through you I have received of God innumerable benefits for which I have not repaid you, and thus I remain your debtor. But I desire to bear this my humiliation with patience, for love of you; yea, I would bear being rejected and cast out and finally led to execution on account of my love of you.[48]

Della Sega exhorts the pastors and the community as a whole, and has special words to his fellow Italians who, in Christ, had been so hospitably received by the Hutterites:

I say to you, my dear ones, above all love and fear the Lord and see to it that you never forsake the brotherhood and church but keep

---

[46] There is here none of the anti-Trinitarianism to which they both had been exposed earlier in Venice.
[47] Letter in the Hutterite Codices under date of 1563.
[48] Benrath, "Wiedertäufer," 49; De Wind, *ME*, IV, 495–496.

always before your eyes Christ's parable of the vine. . . . Think what grace you have received from God through being led from the deepest shadows to his marvelous light, and love one another with a pure heart, with all sincerity and fullness of heart, without pretense.

He closes with greetings to his friends, to his beloved and loyal wife, Ursula, from the Engadine, and to his mother-in-law, who had accompanied them to Moravia.

A decree of the Venetian Council of Ten, issued 7 April 1564, providing for the expulsion of heretics,[49] momentarily raised in della Sega and Rizzetto the hope that it might apply to them. Della Sega wrote the court 18 July 1564, praising the authorities for what seemed an enlightened policy, reminding them that Jesus would have approved of allowing such alleged heretics as the Hutterites to grow up until the harvest, and asking release from imprisonment to return to his wife and family in Moravia.[50]

His arguments were ignored, perhaps because Rome itself was rebuking Venice for its relative leniency. In November, the inquisitor Fra Adriano reported the case, listing the chief heresies of della Sega and Rizzetto—namely, their rejection of the Roman Church, of infant baptism, and of confession to priests; and their union with the Hutterites as the allegedly true church. An interrogation of 12 December 1564 showed della Sega and Rizzetto still firm in their faith despite the abjuration one week earlier of their companion Buccella.

It must have been around this time that della Sega addressed a letter or testament to his Catholic mother and brothers. This undelivered letter is remarkable in being directed to next of kin who had disowned him and would do nothing to relieve the anguish and physical wretchedness of one who for his faith was enduring the dank, sunless squalor in nearby Venice. He lovingly reproached them for ignoring his efforts to bring them to see the spiritual light:

May God pardon you and summon you to repentance. I pray you for the last time to consider why you have come into the world, and calling yourselves Christians, to do what Christ teaches. . . . I exhort you still to desire His grace and to observe His commandments. I pray it of you with all my heart, now that I am about to die. In place of my last testament, since I have no money to leave, that which I have and know for divine grace I manifest to you, and anew with great sorrow of heart and with tears in my eyes, I plead you to seek God while He is to be found. . . . And do not put off your conversion, because we do not know what tomorrow will bring. Think that if God

[49] Cantù, *Eretici*, III, 139.
[50] Della Sega's letter is printed in full in Benrath, "Wiedertäufer," 64–67.

is merciful, His wrath is great toward the rebellious. . . . Now, if this letter should not please you, I know nought else to say. God will not save you by force. It remains to me, in this case, to ask you only to pass this letter to some other who may have the desire to do good and live a Christian life.[51]

Sentence was passed on della Sega and Rizzetto on 8 February 1565. Della Sega wavered momentarily. When the executioner told this to Rizzetto, the latter replied: "Unhappy soul! But if he has lost his soul, I do not want to lose mine. What I have said, I have said."[52] Della Sega still appeared undecided in the presence of Salmeron, and he was reproved for his indecision, but in the end he remained true to his faith. The two Hutterite heretics were spared the usual fiery punishment[53] for heresy which prevailed beyond the confines of watery and more clement Venice. At ten o'clock of the night of Monday, 26 February 1565, after refusing to kiss the crucifix pressed to their lips, they were cast, weighted, from planks into the depths of the sea. "But the sea will give up its dead at the Judgment Day of God," the Hutterite *Chronicle* reminds its readers.[54]

In passing from Italy to Slavic Moravia, the Italian Hutterites found their way no doubt through or very close to Slavic Slovenia and Croatia. And we therefore mention here in passing, for want of a better place, the possibility that the social unrest connected with the peasant leaders Matthew Gubec (martyred in Zagreb, 1573), John Pasanec, Ily Gregoric, and also the highly emotional Skakalci ("jumpers") may be someday shown to belong to the general diffusion of the Radical Reformation.[55]

5. Italian Libertinism and Nicodemism

We turn from three Italian Anabaptist martyrs to the Italian Nicodemites and Spiritual Libertines, who, out of the same general movement of spiritual unrest in Italy, had, after the stern implementation of the Inquisition, decided to stay in Italy and outwardly conform.

[51] This whole testamentary letter is characterized by Benrath, "Wiedertäufer," 49, as "one of the most moving documents to come out of the whole Anabaptist movement." The MS. was re-examined and translated in part by De Wind, *ME*, IV, 496.

[52] De Wind, *ME*, IV, 346.

[53] The adjustment of the sentence "for special reasons" is signed by the Bishop of Vercelli in his capacity as papal legate, by the Patriarch of Venice, and by the inquisitor general; Benrath, "Wiedertäufer," 53.

[54] Zieglschmid, *Chronik*, 413. The specific reference here is to the previous death of Gherlandi.

[55] See the article of B. Grafenauer, "Gubec," *Yugoslavian Encyclopedia*.

Bucer and Calvin called "Nicodemites" those in Catholic lands who sympathized with the evangelical cause and yet refused to avow their faith publicly. Nicodemus, who secretly asked Jesus about rebirth (John 3:1 ff.), was considered by the stern Reformer of Geneva as the type of ineffectual and fainthearted convert who should be castigated for timidity. Calvin, of course, knew that the well-stationed interrogator is also recorded as having circumspectly and vainly sought a proper hearing for Jesus with his own party (John 7:50 f.), after having first come to him by night, and then, after the crucifixion, as having brought a mixture of myrrh and aloes (John 19:39). The traits of Nicodemus have suggested to modern scholarship the useful term "Nicodemism" for that irenic, prudential Spiritualism in Romance countries and other Catholic lands where people of high station were unable to make common cause either with the belligerent Protestants, protected by their magistrates, or with the martyr-minded sectaries, usually recruited from the classes of a humbler station than that of the cultured or mercantile Nicodemites.[56] The Nicodemites, many of whom were to hold that their spiritual rebirth (John 3:1 ff.) was on principle invisible (as election was!), were all the more loathe to break with the established church for the reason that in their instinctive espousal of the inwardness of Spiritualism they could not take polity and other externalities so seriously as either the Catholics or the Calvinists or the Anabaptists did. Nor could they accept predestination and salvation *sola fide* with as much confidence as did both the Swiss and the Lutheran Protestants. Although the Nicodemites were very much concerned with the devout and sanctified life, they could not, perhaps because of a difference of temperament, take so seriously as did the sectarians the disciplines and the demands of conventicular perfectionism.

Thus in its broadest sense, Nicodemism in Italy could include timid Protestants, conformist Waldensians, Valdesians, and other Evangelicals, but not the Anabaptists. Nicodemism is probably best defined, however, in the more restricted sense as the remnant of Italian Evangelism which persisted after that thrice-fateful year for Italian Evangelism, 1542, which saw the death of Conta-

---

[56] Delio Cantimori has defined the term in a succession of studies, *Eretici Italiani del Cinquecento* (Florence, 1939), 57, 120; "La Riforma in Italia," sec. 10, "*Il Nicodemismo,*" *Problemi Storici e Orientamenti Storiografici,* edited by Ettore Rota (Como, 1942), 574–576; "Nicodemismo e speranze conciliari nel Cinquecento Italiano," *Quaderni di "Belfagor,"* edited by Luigi Russo; *Contributi alla Storia di Concilio di Trento e della Controriforma* (Florence, 1948), 12–23.

rini, the establishment of the Roman Inquisition, and the defection of Ochino to Protestantism. In this more limited sense, Nicodemism was the camouflage and "degeneration of Evangelism, of its principles of a purely internal, individual devotion."[57] In Nicodemism, the original humanistic indifference to dogma was transformed by the exigencies of the Inquisition "into practical indifference and hypocritical submissiveness."

Related to Nicodemism was Spiritual Libertinism, which may be defined as the psychopannychist, predestinarian Spiritualism (Camillo, in Ferrara) in an advanced stage in which the original reforming ardor had become largely dissipated and in which its inherent antinomianism had here and there given way to license as a result of the disappearance of all fear of hell. (Cf. Ch. 12.2 for the same phenomenon in the Netherlands.)

Calvin was vigorously opposed alike to the Nicodemites, the Libertines, and the Anabaptists. His majestic figure has been towering for some time above our narrative of religious developments and aberrations in Rhaetia and the Italian states. It is time to return to Switzerland and see the whole of the Radical Reformation from the perspective of the principal spokesman for Protestantism after the death of Luther.

[57] Eva-Maria Jung, *op. cit.,* 519.

CHAPTER 23

CALVIN AND THE RADICAL REFORMATION

The Reformer who had published the first edition of his *Institutes* in Basel in the year of the collapse of the Anabaptist restitution in Münster, who in his dedicatory letter to Francis I had warned the French monarch against confusing the vagaries of a spurious restitution with a politically responsible institution of Reformed Christianity, and who that same year, 1536, had been made Farel's coadjutor in Geneva, entered most directly into contact with the representatives of the Radical Reformation in 1538. In that year, exiled from Geneva, he became pastor of the French congregation in Strassburg, the city where Hofmann lay in prison and where Schwenckfeld and Servetus, among many others, had but recently debated and published.[1]

After his recall to Geneva in 1541 and his introduction of the *Ecclesiastical Ordinances,* which embodied certain religio-political and disciplinary features suggestive of Anabaptist influence—such as the lay eldership and the fencing of the Communion—Calvin began a series of letters, tracts, and larger works directed against various manifestations within the Radical Reformation, from which he intended to safeguard the Reformed Church. It was in 1542 that he published his first edition of the long-worked-over treatise *Psychopannychia.*[2] Then in 1544 he wrote directly against the Anabaptists, whom he had included in part in the earlier writing, and also against the Nicodemites, especially in Italy. In 1545 he assailed the Libertines, especially in France and the Netherlands. Despite his diversified ecumenical contacts, Calvin never clearly distinguished among these four trends, which

---

[1] To be sure, Calvin had had contact earlier with Servetus in Paris (Ch. 23.4) and as early as 4 September 1532 had written Bucer about somebody whom he knew in Noyon from Strassburg charged, but falsely, said Calvin, with Anabaptism. Calvin, *Opera,* X:2, No. 16.

[2] Edited by Walther Zimmerli, *Quellenschriften zur Geschichte des Protestantismus,* XIII (Leipzig, 1932).

is all the more remarkable for the reason that he had taken to wife in 1540 the converted widow of an Anabaptist leader, John Stordeur.

Although Calvin absorbed into his ecclesiastical practice, if not into his theological system, more ingredients of the Radical Reformation than any other Magisterial Reformer, with the possible exception of Bucer, we shall in his case as in the others have to confine our treatment to those moments in the Reformer's life when, in consolidating his theocracy and seeking to promote its extension, he turned his attention to what he considered the grievous aberrations or failings of the psychopannychists, the Libertines, the Anabaptists, the Nicodemites, and the anti-Trinitarians.

1. CALVIN'S PERSONAL CONTACTS WITH PSYCHOPANNYCHISTS, ANABAPTISTS, AND SPIRITUALISTS, 1534–1544

It will be recalled that the problem of the sleep of the soul and, in the more extreme form, of the outright death of the soul, along with the challenge embodied in the alleged philosophical proof of the soul's natural mortality, had come before the Fifth Lateran Council (Ch. 1.3.c). It will be recalled that we have allowed the etymologically ambiguous word "psychopannychism" to serve as the generic term for the two variants "soul sleep" and the "mortalist" heresy within the Christian framework of a belief in the resurrection of all men for final judgment or of the saints alone for their reward. It is, in fact, the eschatological context that makes the Christian psychopannychism of the sectaries differ fundamentally from the Averroistic and Aristotelian demonstration of the mortality of the soul or its absorption at death into the world soul, propounded by the Italian philosophers and condemned by the Fifth Lateran Council. In the course of our narrative we have several times seen how one or the other form of psychopannychism was adopted by such Spiritualists as Carlstadt and by such Anabaptists as Westerburg (Ch. 5.4) in many quarters of the Radical Reformation, from the mouth of the Rhine to the valley of the Po. Psychopannychism obviously fitted best into that interpretation of Christianity and of ecclesiastical reformation which was prepared to stress the imminence of the Kingdom and of the general resurrection of the dead. It is now our task to show how Calvin, at this point in company with the Catholics, became prominently involved in opposing the soul-sleepers and the mortalists.

Calvin, building up a Reformed Church that would endure,

perpetuated and defended the medieval Christian tradition, formalized by the Fifth Lateran Council, as to the susceptibility of the departed soul to bliss: philosophically, on the ground of his Platonism; theologically, within the context of his stress on predestination.[3] In his anthropology, Calvin, as we have elsewhere noted, differed notably from Luther. Where Luther was a traducianist, Calvin was a creationist, holding that each soul is created by God in the fetal stage. Where Luther stressed the Pauline conflict between flesh and spirit (and found the Spiritualists and symbolist sacramentarians often "carnal"), Calvin emphasized the Platonic conflict between body and spirit-soul. In somewhat the same way as Hubmaier, Calvin considered the spirit-soul the exclusive bearer of the image of God and the essence of human personality to the disparagement of the body and its drives.

As a Platonist, Calvin therefore found it easier than Luther, who was, of course, also a firm predestinarian, to hold to a natural persistence of the soul after death. Calvin thought of the afterlife as a *watchful* wake of the righteous soul in an unspecified realm, blissfully anticipating the resurrection of its body and the final judgment of both the elect and the reprobate. He was therefore impassioned in his opposition to the adherents of the death or the unconscious sleep of the soul pending the resurrection. As a creationist he was opposed also to the Libertine (Averroistic) conception of the soul-spirit as an emanation of the essence of the divine rather than as an immortal individualized creation by the divine.

Etymologically, "psychopannychia," it will be recalled, means precisely a watchful or sentient "wake" of the soul, and would ordinarily be used to designate the position of Calvin himself. Recognizing that the wakeful soul is also at peace and therefore in a kind of sleep, Calvin in fact says: "In the main, like them [the psychosomnolents] we call this rest 'sleep.' And we would not be afraid of the word 'sleep' had it not been corrupted and sullied by their lies."[4] As a consequence of this admission, the very title of Calvin's book has come to be attached to the doctrine he opposed rather than to the formulation he defended. In the course of debate, "psychopannychism" has come to designate both the doctrine of the death of the soul (thnetopsychism, mortalism) and the unconscious sleep of the soul (psychosom-

---

[3] The main study here is that of Heinrich Quistorp, *Calvin's Doctrine of the Last Things,* translated from the German of 1941 by Harold Knight (London, 1955).

[4] *Psychopannychia,* edited by Zimmerli, 41.

nolence) pending the resurrection. Though we thereby perpetuate an ineptness of nomenclature, we have already agreed to call
the proponents of both versions "psychopannychists" since it
is useful to have a generic term for both of the sectarian Christian
variants opposed to *natural* immortality.

Calvin first become interested in the problem of psychopannychism in Orleans in 1534 when he put his thoughts down in an
unpublished draft of *Psychopannychia*. We presuppose that what
he later published preserves intact his earliest views,[5] in this,
his oldest writing as a Protestant.

The hypnologists, as Calvin also called the psychopannychists,
were "babblers, madmen, dreamers, and drunkards." But this
does not make it certain who the *hypnologi* were whom Calvin
first opposed in Orleans. It is, in fact, not entirely certain
whether Calvin, at the time of his composition, had fully broken
with the Catholic Church.[6] In any event, his arguments for immortality were still closer to those of Pope Leo than to the views
of Luther.[7]

According to Calvin, there were in Orleans, Paris, and else-

---

[5] *Psychopannychia* is properly the title of the 1545 edition, which is printed
in *Opera*, V, 170–232. It is a second, slightly revised edition of the first edition, 1542, entitled *Vivere apud Christum non dormire animos sanctos, qui
in fide Christi decedunt: assertio*. Both editions appeared in Strassburg. With
both editions, Calvin printed the prefaces of 1534 and 1536. These prefaces
are the sole basis for the earlier assumption that the work had actually been
twice printed before 1542 in supposedly lost editions. A full account of the
editions is given by Zimmerli, *op. cit.*

[6] John T. McNeill, *The History and Character of Calvinism* (New York, 1957),
107–118, holds that Calvin's sudden "conversion" came as the climactic rupture with the Old Church after a period of Evangelical Catholic preparation
and that it probably fell between 6 April and 4 May 1534. The interview
between Calvin and Jacques Lefèvre around 6 April was the decisive factor.
The surrender of his clerical benefices at Noyon on 4 May marked the
formal break with Rome.

[7] Émile Doumergue, *Jean Calvin, Les hommes et les choses de son temps*, I
(Lausanne, 1889), 584 f. Doumergue (*op. cit.*, 468) argues that since the
preface of 1534 makes it clear that Calvin was spokesman for a large number—namely, for the Reformed Church (or *nouvaux Evangéliques*)—he must
have been converted for some time prior to 1534. But the sleep of the soul
which he opposed was actually a Lutheran view in 1534. Hulshof in *stelling*
ii of his doctoral dissertation *Geschiedenis van de Doopsgezinden te Straatsburg* held that the second part of Calvin's *Brève instruction*, which may
well come close to the original draft of his *Psychopannychia* of 1534, was
directed, not against the Anabaptists, but rather against *"eine sekte onder
de Hervormingsgezinden in Frankrijk."* An old theory of Father François
Garasse, that Calvin in the original version of *Psychopannychia* was writing
on this point *against* Luther, may have something in its favor. Henri Busson,
Le Rationalisme dans la littérature française de la Renaissance (2d edition.
Paris, 1957), 321, n. 3.

where in France, two groups among the *hypnologi*.[8] One group (psychosomnolents) conceded that the soul was an enduring substance but that it fell asleep at death and lost memory and feeling. The other group (thnetopsychists) believed that the soul was merely a vital power which could not subsist without the body, though it might rise again with it at the resurrection. Here are his words:

Our controversy, then, relates to the human soul. Some, while admitting it to have a real existence, imagine that it sleeps in a state of insensibility from death to the judgment day, when it will awake from its sleep; while others will sooner admit anything than its real existence, maintaining that it is merely a vital power which is derived from arterial spirit on the action of the lungs (*ex spiritu arteriae aut pulmonum agitatione*), and being unable to exist without the body, perishes along with the body, and vanishes away and becomes evanescent till the period when the whole man shall be raised again. We, on the other hand, maintain both that it is a substance, and after the death of the body truly lives, being endued both with sense and understanding. Both these points we undertake to prove by clear passages of scripture.[9]

It does not appear that either group of *hypnologi*, numbering at this point in the thousands, were French Lutherans. This surely was not the doctrine that would have been the distinguishing mark of Luther's French followers in 1534.[10]

Calvin may have composed his first draft of *Psychopannychia* in connection with the protracted excitement over the return of the spirit of the deceased wife of an Orleans magistrate.[11] She had insisted by testament on a simple requiem, which deprived

---

[8] The term appears, for example, in *Opera*, V, col. 211. In the version annexed to *Briève instruction*, he has the same characterization, but calls both groups "Anabaptists."

[9] *Psychopannychia;* printed in Calvin, *Tracts*, III (Edinburgh, 1851), 419 f. On Calvin's Platonic-Patristic *sentient* separable soul, see Harry Wolfson, *Religious Philosophy* (Cambridge, 1961), 91; *passim* on why Libertines and other psychopannychist Spiritualists were dubbed Epicureans (Ch. 22, n. 9).

[10] Busson, in *Rationalisme*, 320 f., postulates a group of Augustinians or Anabaptists in Orleans, but he is here simply transferring to Calvin's opponents in 1534 a designation Florimond Raemond gives (in 1605) to certain *hypnologi* in Bohemia, *Histoire de la naissance, progrès, et décadence de l'hérésie* (Paris, 1605), ii, cap. xv:1, "Des Augustinians et Stancariens." It should be noted, however, that there were medieval Augustinians who would be so styled in the sixteenth century. Bainton uses the term in his discussion of "New Documents on Early Protestant Rationalism," *CH*, VII (1938), 179–187. For psychopannychist Augustinians, see Ch. 26.2 at n. 9.

[11] It was the theory of Paul de Félice, *La tragédie des Cordeliers d'Orleans, 1534–1535, épisode de l'historie monastique orléanaise au XVIᵉ siècle* (1887), and before him of Archdeacon Blackburne, *An Historical Controversy con-*

the local Franciscan priory of its accustomed revenues. The Franciscans, in revenge, thereupon secreted a novice in the vault of the church to play the role of revenant and by ghostly signs disclose that "she" had died a Lutheran, to the great embarrassment of her widower. The scandal was exposed and the guilty friars were condemned to imprisonment. Locally there was much sympathy for the punished friars. But surely Calvin's *Psychopannychia* is too serious a work to have been primarily written because of the local scandal. In any event his argument would have tended to support the mendicants and surely would not have satisfactorily exculpated the local Lutherans!

Neither Lutherans nor fraudulent Franciscan revenants, Calvin's opponents in the first instance must have been French Paduans, the Netherlandish Libertines, and Anabaptist refugees, if such there were in France at the time. In the two prefaces of 1534 and 1536 but only once in the body of the *Psychopannychia* are his *hypnologi* called also "Catabaptistes."[12]

As for the "French evangelical Paduans,"[13] the Libertines, and the radical Evangelicals among his original opponents, it will be recalled that the Libertine Anthony Pocquet (Ch. 12.2) taught psychopannychism at this time in France and Navarre. Calvin would later be attacking him and other Libertines expressly on this point. We know, moreover, that Calvin had become acquainted with Pocquet's convert and most renowned spokesman, one Quintin of Picardy, in Paris in 1533 or 1534. The Libertines in Paris and at the court of Queen Margaret at Nérac, which Calvin visited in the course of the year, would probably have been one of the two groupings of *hypnologi* attacked in 1534. With their Anabaptist affiliations, it is not unnatural for Calvin to have called them incidentally also Anabaptists.

And who were the second grouping, those who had a more physiological argument for the sleep of the soul? Our best surmise is that it was made up originally of Michael Servetus and his presumably small circle in Paris, who could with even greater

---

cerning the Intermediate State (2d edition, London, 1772). The whole episode is recounted by John Sleidan (d. 1556), who was in Orleans at the time. *Commentarii,* ix, under date. See Doumergue, *op. cit.,* 466, n. 3, and Félice, *op. cit.,* 464.

[12] *Briève instruction* (1544), *Opera,* V, col. 232.

[13] Busson, against his own preference for the hypothetical "Augustinians of Orleans," suggests this when he writes in *Rationalisme,* 321: "Possibly the early Libertines had already propagated this heresy. Did Calvin perhaps begin with the purpose of refuting the Italian rationalists rather than Anabaptist dreamers? Since the book had been modified several times, it is impossible to affirm this with any certainty."

propriety be called by Calvin "Anabaptists," in view of Servetus' sojourn among them in Strassburg. (In Calvin's revision of 1542 the group would have been enlarged to include Renato and his followers in the Grisons.) We know that Calvin had a rendezvous with the author of *De Trinitatis erroribus* in Paris in 1534, shortly before the writing of the first draft of the *Psychopannychia*. Servetus, for some reason, failed to show up for the secret discussion.[14] Note, however, the garbled but perhaps telltale allusion to the pulmonary circulation of the blood in the foregoing quotation. We shall return to its implications in Ch. 23.4. Calvin carried the unpublished draft of *Psychopannychia* along with the much more important first draft of the *Institutes* as he journeyed into exile by way of Metz to Strassburg, en route to Basel.

In Strassburg, Capito persuaded[15] Calvin (at some date prior to the publication of the *Institutes*) not to print the *Psychopannychia,* alleging that it would but intensify interest in the subject and might indeed offend Luther, who on this point stood closer to the Radicals. In 1537, Peter Caroli, then Reformed pastor at Lausanne, began to revive the doctrine of purgatory, which represented a view of the afterlife no less abhorrent to Calvin[16] than psychopannychism at the other extreme. Moreover, in Geneva itself the psychopannychist Anabaptists were becoming a problem.

Early in 1537, several Netherlandish Anabaptists came to Geneva; and, to the dismay of Calvin, they found the people responsive to their preaching. Two of them, Herman of Gerbehaye (near Liège)[17] and Andrew Benoît of Engelen (now in Dutch Brabant), were taken before the council 9 March 1537. They sought a public disputation with Calvin and Farel. After some hesitation the council so ordered. The disputation, lasting for two days in March, took place in the Franciscan convent church of Rive. Along with the usual points of baptism and the ban, the disputants dealt with psychosomnolence. Calvin did not partici-

---

[14] Bainton, *Hunted Heretic,* 218.

[15] Calvin, *Opera,* X:2, 45, dates Capito's letter in 1535. A. L. Herminjard, *Correspondances des Reformateurs dans les pays de langue française* (Geneva/ Paris, 1866 ff.), III, 242, dates it 1534. That Calvin had been moved to revise the Orleans draft substantially is evident from his letter to his friend Libertet, 3 September 1535, *Opera,* Xb, No. 29, col. 52; Herminjard, *op. cit.,* III, 349 f.

[16] Calvin reported this to Megander, 20 February 1537. Peter Viret, also pastor at Lausanne, undertook to refute Caroli twice, the second time arguing against him for two days, 28 February to 1 March 1537. Letter from Megander to Bullinger, Herminjard, *op. cit.,* IV, No. 616.

[17] Hulshof, *op. cit.,* 187, note. The text has "Gerbihan."

pate directly.[18] The two Anabaptists withstood Farel with some success, even though they expressed themselves awkwardly; but the council declared them defeated and expelled them from the city. In a second disputation the same month, Calvin himself took part, this time with two Anabaptists—John Bomeromenus, a printer, formerly of Strassburg, and John Stordeur, a turner, of Liège. They were no theological match for the great lawyer-reformer. After defending their faith with courage, they both were banished (30 March). There were several Anabaptist inhabitants of the city reported that autumn.[19]

By the following Easter, Calvin, who shared with the Anabaptists their conviction that only the outwardly righteous should be permitted to partake of the Communion, found also that he could agree with them about the independence of the church from the state. The Bernese Church Order had recently been adopted by the magistrates in Geneva.[20] Ideally, Calvin would have given to the elected lay elders of the parishes, together with their pastors, the whole authority for congregational discipline which the magistrates found in themselves and in the elders as their appointed deputies. Calvin was, of all the Protestants, the least "magisterial" and much closer to the Radicals on the principle of ecclesiastical autonomy than Zwingli, Luther, or Cranmer.

On such lesser issues as whether the Communion should be observed with wafers or broken bread, whether Christmas, Easter, Ascension Day, and Pentecost should be retained in the liturgical year, the great issue of whether it was the magistrates or the divines who should decide ecclesiastical matters was being fought out. Calvin and his associates, liturgically and religio-politically more radical than the Bernese, refused to distribute the Sacrament on Easter as instructed. The following Thursday (23 April), Calvin, by vote of the whole people in civic assembly, was obliged to leave. The charge of Caroli in Lausanne, that

---

[18] *Ibid.,* 186 ff.
[19] Report to the council by the clergy, 7 September 1537. For other names, see Herminjard, *op. cit.,* IV, 272, n. 6.
[20] 11 March 1538. Cf. Doumergue, *op. cit.,* II, 277. The foregoing characterization of Calvin as the least "magisterial" of the classical Protestants, and with special reference to the lay but congregational eldership, is applicable to the period before his exile, although it became more explicit in connection with the *Ecclesiastical Ordinances* of 1541, when Calvin fought hard to preserve the congregational election and accountability of the elders over against the magisterial prerogative. McNeill, *op. cit.,* 160 ff. See also Bryan Hatchett, Jr., "On the Relationship of the Strasbourg Reformation to Church Discipline in Calvin's Thought," dissertation, Emory University, 1960.

Calvin was weak on the doctrine of the Trinity, compounded the Reformer's difficulties at the end.

The importance of the charge of being anti-Nicene in his doctrine of the Godhead is so important in the career of Calvin, Servetus, and later the whole Polish Reformed Church that we must interrupt our narrative about psychopannychism and Anabaptism to examine Caroli[21] and his allegation.

Caroli was one of the first French clerics to go over to the Reformation. After winning his doctorate in theology at the University of Paris, he had attracted a considerable audience, expounding the Pauline epistles in a popular homiletical manner at Paris, for which he was admonished and finally ordered by the Sorbonne to cease preaching (1525). After having held a living at Alençon under appointment by Queen Margaret of Navarre for almost a decade, Caroli was suspected of being party to the affair of the placards against the Mass in Paris, and fled to Geneva in January of 1535.

He almost immediately fell out with Farel and Peter Viret (who may have suspected the authenticity of his conversion to Protestantism), and moved to Basel and then Neuchâtel, where he was given a parish in the spring of 1536. Ambitious for advancement, Caroli next won the pastorate at Lausanne, November 1536.

As he had pushed ahead of Viret for this post, the Genevan pastors made loud complaint, urging against Caroli his peculiar teaching that prayers for the dead would ensure an earlier resurrection. In February of 1537, Calvin came to Viret's aid, only to be confronted by Caroli's accusation that Viret, Calvin, and Farel were Arians, and that the Genevan Catechism was doctrinally defective. Calvin's obdurate refusal to assent to the Athanasian Creed (as distinguished from the earlier and less specific Nicene and Apostolic Creeds) and to consign to oblivion the Genevan Catechism appeared to Caroli to be the proof of Calvin's Trinitarian aberration.

A colloquy was held at Bern (28 February to 1 March 1537) to resolve the matter. Caroli pressed his charge of Arianism, only to drop it when Calvin made an impassioned defense of his own position. Calvin refused to dissociate his cause from that of Farel and pressed for a synod. On 15 May it met at Lausanne. It resulted in Calvin's vindication, whereas Caroli was deprived of his ministry. On 31 May, a parallel synod at Bern heard Farel

---

[21] Originally from Rosay en Brie, prior of the Sorbonne, canon of Sens, Caroli was early attracted to Jacques Lefèvre d'Étaples. Doumergue, *op. cit.,* II, 252 ff.; Herminjard, *op. cit.,* IV, No. 611.

launch a bitter attack on Caroli's personal life and doctrinal eccentricities. As a result, Caroli was also forbidden to preach in Bernese territory.

Calvin and Caroli were alike exiles, respectively from Geneva and Lausanne.

Caroli removed to French territory, returned to the Catholic Church, and signalized his reconversion by writing an impudent letter to the council of Lausanne. We shall see him next in Strassburg, whither we now go with Calvin.[22]

It was in Strassburg that Calvin was alerted to the geographical and doctrinal magnitude of the Radical Reformation. On the matter of psychosomnolence he learned that at Metz, in 1538, two psychopannychists had been drowned in the Moselle and a third exiled, and that all three were Anabaptists. One, somewhat educated, a barber[23] from Lille, had been in the company of the Netherlandish Anabaptists who had been with Herman of Gerbehaye in Geneva. Another was from Mouzon (near Sédan), the third, from Montlhéry (south of Paris). All three had been preaching the sleep of the soul, including that of the Virgin Mary.[24] Bucer, who until that time had dissuaded him from it, now pressed Calvin to publish his book against the sleep of the soul. On 1 October 1538, Calvin informed Antoine Pignet,[25] a pastor near Geneva and a fellow student with him at Orleans, that he was indeed going to publish his *Psychopannychia* against the "somnolent hypnosophists." Pignet encouraged him,[26] but for some reason Calvin put it off.

It is quite possible that Calvin, while in Strassburg, came into contact with Hofmannites. Increased specificity in references to the celestial-flesh doctrine in the second Latin edition of the *Institutes*[27] (Strassburg, 1539) could be traceable to Calvin's direct encounter with Hofmann's Christology.

During the same October of 1539, as it chanced, Caroli sought out Calvin at Strassburg to mend their relationship; but he was still unable to forget Calvin's former treatment of him in the

---

[22] Cf. McNeill, *op. cit.*, 141.
[23] The text has *"barbier."* In view of his education, he might have been a Waldensian barb. J. F. Huguenin, *Chroniques de Metz* (1839), 839; quoted Herminjard, *op. cit.*, p. 112, n. 12.
[24] Calvin from Strassburg to Farel, now at Neuchâtel, 11 September 1538; Herminjard, *op. cit.*, V, No. 743.
[25] Herminjard, *op. cit.*, V, No. 749.
[26] *Ibid.*, VI, No. 821.
[27] II:xii, 1–3; xiii, 1 f.; xiv, 1–4, 6 f. This is the observation of William Keeney in his Hartford Seminary multigraphed seminar paper, "An Analysis of Calvin's Treatment of the Anabaptists in the *Institutes*," 4.

matter of the Lausanne appointment. Caroli had not been welcomed with open arms by the Catholics and he reappeared in Switzerland, professing again the Reformed faith and seeking the friendship of Calvin, Farel, and Viret! The Strassburg divines talked the matter over and exonerated Calvin of any blame in Caroli's misfortunes. However, they attempted to bring peace by writing a long document of reconciliation which Calvin and Caroli were to sign. Strange to relate, among those framing the document was Caroli himself. When it was brought to Calvin in the home of Mathew Zell, late in the evening, Calvin at once discovered the implication that he and Farel had been to blame for Caroli's ejection from Bernese territory. Calvin was shaken to the point of hysteria, and refused to sign the document under any circumstances. He would henceforth be very sensitive about the creedal formulations of the doctrine of the Trinity. (Caroli departed from the scene, to reappear at Metz in 1543 as a Roman Catholic![28])

Still in Strassburg, Calvin was asked by the local authorities to deal with the French-speaking Anabaptists in and around the city. At the synod in 1539 he persuaded John Stordeur, or John Bomeromenus, and Herman of Gerbehaye, whom he had already met in Geneva, to renounce their faith in favor of the Reformed confession. Calvin supplies the details of the submission in his letter to Farel, recalling[29] that it was Herman who had asked him for the conference:

He [now] grants that he was in serious error on infant baptism, Christ's humanity [the problem of the celestial flesh], and many other points. On some other questions he still has some doubts, but he is hopeful because he has already overcome so much. His companion John [Stordeur][30] has finally brought his boy, who is already quite large, for baptism. I hesitated a while because of his frailty, since he said that was the principal reason for postponing the baptism. Finally he said he would not stop the people whose obstinate insistence on baptism he could by no means withstand.

Three weeks later,[31] Calvin evaluated the conversion thus:

---

[28] Beza claims that he eventually went to Rome and there died most miserably. Another tradition, however, suggests that from Rome, Caroli came back to France, that he occupied himself by teaching the Tridentine catechisms, and that he was assassinated in 1575. The foregoing account is taken from Doumergue, *op. cit.*, II, 258–268.

[29] 6 February 1540. Herminjard, *op. cit.*, VI, No. 846.

[30] Or John Bomeromenus. If, however, the reference is to John Stordeur, Tordeur (tournier), of Liège, the boy baptized would be, in effect, Calvin's future step-son. See below, n. 32.

[31] Calvin to Farel, 27 February; Herminjard *op. cit.*, VI, No. 854.

Herman has, if I am not mistaken, in good faith returned to the fellowship of the Church. He has confessed that outside the Church there is no salvation, and that the true Church is with us. Therefore, it was defection when he belonged to a sect separated from it. Confessing that he was guilty of this crime, he asked forgiveness. He accepted instruction on the freedom of the will, the deity and humanity of Christ, rebirth, infant baptism, and other things. Only on the question of predestination did he hesitate. Yet he almost subscribed to this too, except that he could not understand the difference between prescience and providence. But he asked that this might not prevent his being received into the communion of the church with his children. I received him with fitting readiness, and when he asked forgiveness I gave him my hand in the name of the church. Then I baptized his little daughter, who was over two years old. If my judgment does not deceive me, he is a pious man. When I admonished him to lead others back to the right way, he said: "That is the least that I can do, to exert myself no less in building up than I did before in tearing down."

Calvin goes on to mention "John," either Stordeur or Bomeromenus, now of Ulm, as likewise having "come to his senses."[32] Early in August 1540, Calvin was married by Farel to the ailing Idolette de Bure, recently widowed by the death of John Stordeur.

A major achievement of Calvin in Strassburg in respect to the Radicals was the reconversion of the former preacher of St. Nicholas' Church, Paul Volz. He had for a season joined the Schwenckfeldians.[33]

Calvin, only momentarily pleased with his local conversions and still horrified by the extent of the Anabaptist and Spiritualist movements, rushed ahead with the publication of his old draft of the *Psychopannychia*, along with the earlier, unused prefaces (Orleans, 1534, and Basel, 1537). It appeared at Strassburg in 1542. By then Calvin, having served Strassburg as a deputy at the fateful colloquy of Regensburg, had returned triumphantly to Geneva in September 1541.

Since we have already characterized Calvin's own view of the afterlife in the *Psychopannychia*, assuming for this purpose that it had not been significantly reworked since 1534, we shall take up instead another work which, in touching freshly upon psychosomnolence, more clearly than the belatedly published *Psychopannychia*, will give us Calvin's thoughts on the problem and in

---

[32] It is more probable that it was Bomeromenus (Hulshof, *op. cit.*, 106), who had been banished from Strassburg in 1537 and gone to Metz, than Jean Stordeur, whose widow Calvin would be marrying that very August.

[33] Hulshof, *op. cit.*, 197; Röhrich, *Mitteilungen*, III, 215.

the broader context of his struggle with Anabaptism, but we must first carry the story of the whole of Swiss Anabaptism forward to this point.

2. SWISS ANABAPTISM FROM THE DEATH OF ZWINGLI TO CALVIN'S MAJOR ATTACK, 1531–1544

As we return with Calvin from Strassburg to Geneva, we pass through Bernese territory. Bern was at the time the largest canton of the Confederation, stretching from the Rhine on the borders of the urban canton of Basel to the city republic of Geneva. Geneva had secured independence from its prince-bishop and the duke of Savoy through the armed aid of Bern, had introduced the Bern Church Order, and was in every respect closely linked to the powerful canton which, at the time, controlled both German- and French-speaking areas and towns, including Lausanne. Although we have mentioned in passing a few encounters of the Genevans with the Anabaptists, it is well to have before us the whole sectarian situation as it developed after our taking leave of Swiss Anabaptism in 1531 (Ch. 8). The story now centers in the canton of Bern.

The Bernese Reformation had been formulated in the synod of January 1532 under the theological leadership of Wolfgang Capito, who skillfully managed to implement Strassburg's Unionistic policy of holding the Swiss as closely as possible to the Saxons.[34] The Bern Church Order in forty-four articles, composed chiefly by Capito and promulgated as a result of the synod, was liturgically conservative and yet full of those Spiritualist traits which no doubt reflected Capito's penchant for the ideas of Schwenckfeld, Servetus, and other assorted seekers whom he had but recently entertained in Strassburg. On the relationship of baptism to circumcision, it is of interest that Capito induced the Bernese synod to yield, by implication, to the Anabaptists in eschewing that equation of the two rites which had been approved by Zwingli, Bullinger, and Bucer, and in laying great stress also on infant baptism as merely a sign of the promise to be progressively substantiated through the Christian nurture of the baptizand in the midst of the congregation.

Despite reticence on the doctrine of the Trinity, despite a strong stress upon the clarifying and sanctifying roles of the Holy Spirit, despite modifications in baptismal theology, the effect of the Bern Church Order—which after all must be seen primarily

---

[34] For Capito's participation in the synod see Strasser, *Capitos Beziehungen zu Bern,* 67–121.

in the pan-Protestant context of Unionistic urgency on the morrow of the Second Peace of Cappel—was a consolidation of the
Bernese attempt to end the threat of sectarian separatism. In consequence, the Bern council decided to convene a major colloquy
with the Anabaptists.[35] A strong effort would be made to regain
the Anabaptists in sufficient numbers in order to win their
allegiance for a completely reformed canton. Without their good
will, the Bernese government might have found itself in a very
serious situation vis-à-vis the ardently Catholic cantons. To ensure attendance and fair play, a safe-conduct was offered to all
the Anabaptists participating in the disputation. It was, furthermore, to be held outside Bernese territory in Zofingen, in the
condominium of the Aargau (governed jointly by Bern and other
cantons), in order that the dissenters might feel especially secure.
In addition, it was decided that no Magisterial Reformers from
outside Bern, not even Bullinger himself, should be asked, lest
the Anabaptists say that the Reformed Church could only debate
with them by summoning its most learned disputants from great
distances. The disputation was set for 1 July 1532 and extended
until July 9.

Although Bullinger could not participate, he contributed considerable advice by letter. He warned his colleagues that half the
battle in disputing with Anabaptists was to secure orderly
procedure and to confine the dispute to one question at a time,
being careful not to be drawn off the subject onto side issues.[36] It
is necessary, he warned, to make sure that they accept the authority of the Scriptures of both the Old and the New Testaments, without in any way disparaging the former. Bullinger
presented a great many texts and arguments to show that the Old
Testament was fully authoritative, but he did not satisfactorily
refute the Anabaptist view that the New Testament represents a
later and hence a higher level of the divine disclosure. Restating
the common sixteenth-century position that one must interpret
the obscure passages of Scripture by the clear ones, he went on to
stress "faith" and "love" as the canons of interpretation, which
might well lead to "another meaning than the one yielded by the
words themselves." The divine injunction to love was interpreted,
for example, as to be concerned for the best interest of the social
order and the peace of the whole Christian society.

When the disputation began, there were twenty-three Ana-

[35] Heinold Fast and John H. Yoder, "How to Deal with Anabaptists," *MQR*,
XXXIII (1959), 83–95.
[36] Bullinger to Haller, *Quomodo agendum et disputandum sit cum Catabap-
tistis;* printed in translation; see n 35 above.

baptists present, of whom Martin Weniger of Schaffhausen and John Hotz were the main speakers. Haller and Caspar Megander of Bern and Sebastian Hofmeister (formerly of Schaffhausen, then of Zurich, now of Zofingen) led the eight-man Reformed delegation, which included the erstwhile Anabaptist leader Pfistermeyer (Ch. 8.4.c). Four delegates of the Aargau and the city of Bern were designated as chairmen and instructed to guard against any possible impropriety. The result of these efforts was a tactful and courtly exchange of views. The minutes were kept by three secretaries and submitted to all parties involved for verification before being printed in Zurich and made available for distribution at the expense of Bern.

Eleven points were selected for discussion: (1) whether love is, in fact, the final arbiter of all Scriptural disagreements (Bullinger's stress); (2) whose sending, or ministerial vocation, is valid; (3) where the true church is; (4) whether the ban may rightly be administered by magistrates in their role as Christian officers of the commonweal; (5) whether, in fact, the magistracy can be Christian; (6) whether the Christian should pay tithes and taxes; (7) whether the civil oath is legitimate; (8) whether preachers should be called by the town council or the church members; (9) whether preachers should be supported by the ancient endowments; (10) whether a Christian may charge interest; and (11) last of all, whether infants may be baptized. There was some superficial agreement reached on certain points, but real progress was not made. Both parties, as usual, claimed victory in the debate.

The colloquy in Zofingen was, nevertheless, the most significant of the Anabaptist disputations in Switzerland, since it clarified the Reformed principle of love as a concern for the unity and peace of Christian society and as a major exegetical standard. The formal acknowledgment of Bullinger's hermeneutical principle was taking the Reformed pastors away from the strict Biblicism to which they had been accustomed to appeal all in the interest of preserving a harmonious relationship between church and government and of securing an integral reform of the territorial *corpus christianum*.

Three quarters of a year after the Zofingen disputation, the government of Bern issued another mandate (2 March 1533) against the Anabaptists, who had obviously not been hampered by their "defeat" at Zofingen. It provided protection for the Anabaptists if they would keep quiet and hold their faith to themselves, but threatened agitators with imprisonment, at the prisoner's expense, or on bread and water. The authorities began to demand, however, that those who applied for protection under the provisions of the mandate publicly attend the Reformed services every Sunday and have their infants baptized. Over a year later, on 8 November 1534, another mandate appeared against both Anabaptists and Catholics, providing for Communion three times a year. Marriages were to be performed only by state pastors. Anyone who could not conscientiously conform to these regulations by oath was to leave the canton at once. An appendix was added a few months later, providing eight days' imprisonment for recalcitrants in order to give them time to consider; whereupon, if they still refused compliance, they should be banished with the threat of death if they should return. The Bernese government continued to increase the severity of the measures against the Anabaptists, corporally punishing many and executing several. Constables were especially commissioned to "hunt" Anabaptists and to round them up wherever they could.

Despite this show of force, or, rather, in the light of its manifest failure as a policy, the government convened another important *Gespräch* between the separatists and the established preachers, this time in the town of Bern itself, March 1538.[37] The Anabaptists appeared in large numbers, though with the exception of John Hotz from the district of Grüningen, who had been at the earlier Zofingen disputation, they were all minor figures. They acquitted themselves well in the debates, earnestly professing their willingness to be convinced by Scripture and exhibiting their confidence that in forthright, committed conversation, under the headship of Christ, with the inspiration of the Holy Spirit, and by the authority of Scripture, all the participants could emerge from a full and fair discussion in possession of a common truth which neither side had had at the beginning. The established controversialists in Bern as elsewhere were annoyed by this principle of mutability in debate.[38]

The immediate effect of the disputation was a stiffening of the earlier mandates. Then in September a still more severe mandate was issued, providing for the execution of the leaders and the torture of the others as a means of inducing recantation. How-

---

[37] There is a typewritten copy of the *Acta des gesprächs zwüschenn predicannten Vnnd Tauffbrüderenn Erganngen Inn der Statt Bern* in the Mennonite Historical Library in Goshen, Indiana. For another Swiss statement from this period, see J. C. Wenger, "Martin Weninger's Vindication of Anabaptism," *MQR*, XXII (1948), 180–187.

[38] The major work on the Swiss disputations is that of John Yoder, *Die Gespräche zwischen Täufern und Reformatoren in der Schweiz, 1523–1538* (Basel, 1960). Franklin Littell has written a number of works touching upon the Anabaptist conception of mutability in theological conversation, most recently in "The Laity in the Radical Reformation," *The Laity in Historical Perspective*, edited by Hans-Ruedi Weber (in press).

ever, three years later, 28 November 1541, the government reversed its policy when it came to deal with the question again, thanks to the skillful advocacy of the bailiff Hans Nägeli, who pointed out how the Anabaptists owed their origin to very real weaknesses and inconsistencies in the Reformed position, particularly the religious indifference of the masses, the unbecoming conduct of the pastors, and especially the lack of unity among the Protestants on the question of the Lord's Supper. The council decided thereupon to reduce the severity of the legislation against the Anabaptists, limiting punishment to the stocks for such Anabaptists as those who, having once sworn obedience to the previous mandate, should violate it anew. Severer penalties were to be introduced only after the third relapse. This leniency provided the Anabaptists in the canton of Bern with a modicum of peace.

With the Bernese background filled in, we may with Calvin in 1541 re-enter Geneva, where he immediately introduced the new *Ecclesiastical Ordinances.* Had the autonomy of the congregationally elected elders, the fencing of the Communion table, and the exercise of the ban by the church rather than by the state originally proposed by Calvin been accepted by the governing councils of Geneva, Calvinism on the disciplinary side would have appeared closer to Anabaptism than to magisterial Lutheranism.

In 1544 on 10 November, the entire Confederation adopted a stringent policy against the Anabaptists. In this same year, Farel, urging Calvin to translate his *Psychopannychia* into French,[39] enclosed also a translated copy of Hubmaier's *Von der christlichen Taufe der Gläubigen,* and referred disparagingly to Michael Sattler's martyrdom (Ch. 8.2). Calvin now turned his attention to the problem of psychosomnolence in relation to the whole problem of Anabaptism so much in the minds of all Swiss churchmen and magistrates. The result was his *Brière instruction pour armer tous bons fidèles contre . . . la secte commune des anabaptistes* (Geneva, 1544).[40]

The *Brière instruction* is a formal refutation of Anabaptism as represented in the seven articles adopted in Schleitheim in 1527, and is thus the French equivalent of Zwingli's *Elenchus.* Convinced by his recent encounters with both French- and German-speaking Anabaptists in Strassburg and Geneva that two other articles of comparable significance should be included in his refutation, Calvin turned at the close of the *Brière instruction* to

[39] Letter of 23 February 1544; Herminjard, *op. cit.,* IX, No. 1332.
[40] *Opera,* VII, coll. 103–142.

what he pilloried as the Marcionite-Gnostic doctrine of the celestial flesh or heavenly body of Christ and psychosomnolence.[41] Calvin suspected that the denial of a fully Adamic flesh in Christ was related to the denial of a substantial soul susceptible of wakeful existence after the death of the body, with the capacity to look forward with pleasure to the Last Judgment. He thereupon proceeded to summarize his old *Psychopannychia*, freely speaking now of Anabaptists, where earlier he had spoken of *hypnologi*.[42] We need not repeat familiar arguments here.

Calvin's last personal encounter with evangelical Anabaptism seems to have occurred two years later, when an otherwise unknown Belot came to Geneva and laid out tracts for sale. Calvin had him arrested.[43] Once the colporteur was in the grip of the civil authorities, Calvin was prepared to speak politely with him "as is my custom." Belot was as conscious of his divine mission as Calvin, who describes him mockingly as "giving himself with raised head and rolling eyes the majestic aspect of a prophet" and says that he "answered if it suited him with a few words the questions directed to him." The discussion turned on the legitimacy of the civic oath, perfectionism, and the public maintenance of the Reformed pastors. Belot was apparently quite obnoxious in accusing Calvin of luxuriating at the expense of the poor, with his substantial annual salary of five hundred florins, twelve measures of wheat, and some two hundred and fifty gallons of wine, apportioned no doubt with a view to the demands of pastoral hospitality! Belot was expelled from the city. When apprehended two days later, he was beaten for his defiance,

[41] It is curious that the Mennonites (Neff in *ME;* Hulshof, *Geschiedenis*) claim that the doctrine was never held by them or the German Anabaptists, and that Karl Müller, the general church historian who seems to have given the most attention to this doctrine, claims only that it was the view of the French Anabaptists, whoever they might have been, apart from the few mentioned above. *Kirchengeschichte,* II (Tübingen, 1919), 121 and *passim.*

[42] He dealt more briefly with the sleepers and their dreams in the 1560 French edition of the *Institutes,* III, v. 10: *"Ces nouveaux prophets veulent qu'on tienne leur songe pour article de foy, duquel il ne soit licite de s'enquerir."* *Opera,* IV, col. 176. At about the same time, it may be mentioned, a parallel defense of natural immortality was set forth (cf. Ch. 22 at n. 9) by Celio Secondo Curione, *De immortalitate animorum oratio* (1543), printed in Basel at the end of his *Araneus.* He sought to replace the arguments of Plato with texts from Paul. He does scarcely more than change the names, beginning with I Thess. 5:23: "And may your *spirit* and *soul* and body be kept sound and blameless at the coming of our Lord Jesus Christ," and then interpreting the *spiritus* as the *mens* of the philosophers and the *anima* as the sensitive soul.

[43] Calvin himself tells of the incident in a letter to Farel, 21 January 1546. *Opera,* XII, No. 752.

his books were publicly burned, and he was threatened with the gallows if he should return.

The episode is not important in itself except as it confirmed Calvin's caricature of the Anabaptists; and, when he touched upon Anabaptist views in his several reworkings of the *Institutes*, it is certain that his pen was envenomed by his unpleasant recollections of this and other encounters.

We may now turn to Calvin's attacks on the Libertines near and far.

3. THE LIBERTINES AND THE NICODEMITES

We have already noted that Calvin did not clearly distinguish among his opponents. The psychopannychists against whom he wrote in Orleans in 1534 were, in his mind, much the same as those whom he later called Libertines and Anabaptists.

We last took leave of the Libertines and Loists in the Netherlands (Ch. 12.2) when some of their leaders, notably Pocquet and Quintin, were on their way to the castle of Nérac, where they had reason to expect protection under Queen Margaret.

Margaret of Angoulême (1492–1549), sister of Francis I, had, by her second marriage in 1527, become queen of the truncated Basque kingdom of Lower Navarre,[44] mistress of the several courts of the interrelated dependent French fiefs including Nérac, and in due course grandmother of that spiritualizing "Protestant" who would in one momentous hour agree that it was worth a Mass to become king of France as Henry IV. Margaret's religious life, expressed by patronage and poetry, moved easily from Christian humanism, Platonic mysticism, through the Evangelical Catholicism of Gérard Roussel, Jacques Lèfevre (whom as a centenarian Biblicist she was protecting when Calvin visited him in 1534), and William Briçonnet of Meaux (her spiritual director), all the way to a "Spiritualized" Protestantism.[45] She was at once devout and indiscreet. Her racy yarns about courtly gallantries and convent indiscretions were widely savored. Her more evangelical *Mirror of a Sinful Soul* was censured in 1532 by the Sorbonne despite her royal dignity and the spirited defense of her by Nicholas Cop.

It is understandable that the spiritualism, the antinomianism, and even the quakery of the Netherlandish Libertines might well

---

[44] The largely Iberian and ethnically Basque kingdom of Navarre (of which, incidentally, Servetus, born in Tudela, was a native) was in 1512 absorbed into the amalgamating kingdom of Spain.

[45] Well characterized with the literature by Busson, *Rationalisme,* 306–311.

intrigue her. She made Anthony Pocquet a chaplain. Quintin[46] as *huissier* and Bertrand of Moulins as *valet de chambre* may have begun their service at Nérac in the early thirties.

In 1538, Bucer wrote Margaret about the Libertines in Navarre and France, without specifically naming them, but characterizing them as "timid Nicodemites," confident in the sinlessness of the perfected as a cover for their license.[47]

Calvin, who had met Quintin in Paris, no doubt knew at first hand something of his imbalance and that of the other Libertines, who were commonly called after him "Quintinists." A Flemish-French Spiritualist, Quintin thought little of the New Testament apostles because they had lived before the now-dawning age of the perfection of the world. He held, indeed, that every Christian becomes, in a pantheistic or mystical sense, a Christ. In Paris, Calvin had been told[48] that both Quintin and Bertrand were driven from their homeland because of license. As early as in the 1539 version of his *Institutes*, Calvin was prompted to take issue with the Quintinist perversion of the concept of divine omnipotence.[49]

Strange to relate, the Libertine leaders—Pocquet, Perceval, and Bertrand of Moulins—actually stayed in Bucer's home (sometime between September 1541 and September 1544)[50] along with Peter Brully, the preacher to the French Protestants in Strassburg in succession to Calvin.

Calvin himself first became directly acquainted with Anthony Pocquet in 1542 or 1543, when Margaret's protégé was in Geneva and asked Calvin for a recommendation. Pocquet was driven from Geneva. The gravity of the Libertine threat to the sobriety of the development at Nérac under Margaret and to the Reformed parishes in the Low Countries was especially borne in upon Calvin when two Netherlanders, visiting Strassburg and Geneva in 1544, reported the spiritual havoc being wrought by the Libertines (perhaps also by the Loists).

Specifically, in May 1544, Valérand Poullain of Strassburg wrote to Calvin,[51] importuning him to write a letter of counsel

---

[46] *Biographie universelle*, LIV, col. 664.
[47] Letter of 5 July 1538; *Opera*, Xb, 215.
[48] By Stephen de la Forge, martyred in 1535, the Piedmontes Waldensian with whom Calvin lived in Paris when working on Seneca.
[49] Wilhelm Niesel, "Calvin und die Libertiner," *ZKG*, XLVIII (1929), 64.
[50] This is the reconstruction of Karl Müller, *op. cit.*, 127. The evidence for the presence of the three Libertines in Bucer's house is supplied by the records of Brully's trial. See n. 72 below.
[51] Letter of 26 May 1544; Herminjard, *op. cit.*, IX, No. 1358.

and consolation to the brethren in Valenciennes plagued by the Quintinists. On 5 September 1544, Peter Viret wrote to Rudolph Gwalter, pastor in Zurich, apprising him of the scourge of a sect in Lower Germany, and in Valenciennes, Liège, and Tournai, worse than the Anabaptists, namely, the Libertines.[52] William Farel, 5 October 1544,[53] also wrote to Calvin, urging him to speak out against the sons of Simon Magus in Valenciennes. In the same month (13 October), Poullain expressed joy that at length Calvin was intending to take up arms against the Quintinists and the followers of David Joris and Loy Pruystinck.[54]

Long disturbed by the Libertines and the Spiritualists generally since his Paris and Nérac days, and estimating their number between four and ten thousand,[55] Calvin now resolved to write the already mentioned *Contre la secte phantastique et furieuse des Libertins qui se nomment Spirituels* (Geneva, 1545) in double concern to warn Margaret, discreetly and yet emphatically, that she had been nourishing at her court a monstrous heresy, and not piety, and at the same time to vindicate his successor at the French church in Strassburg, Peter Brully. For in the meantime Brully had been captured on a visitation in northern France and in the French-speaking Netherlands, at Tournai, and burned by the Catholic authorities 19 February 1545 as a heretic. In the trial, Brully had had to defend himself against the charges that linked his Protestant solafideism with the antinomianism of Pocquet, Perceval, and Bertrand of Moulins.

Calvin directed his attack principally against Pocquet, whose treatise, as we have noted (Ch. 12.2), is quoted in virtual completeness for refutation. Pocquet, at the time of Calvin's *Contre la secte,* was presumably at the court of Margaret, serving as almoner. The refutation of the Spiritualist Pocquet by the disciplined Calvin in 1542 was *mutatis mutandis* a morphological analogue to the answer of Pilgram Marpeck to Spiritualist Schwenckfeld in the same year (Ch. 18.4), and the parallel extends psychologically and strategically to the concern of both the Anabaptist and the Reformer to circumvent the alienation of a patroness by a courtly Spiritualizer!

[52] *Ibid.,* No. 1392.
[53] *Ibid.,* No. 1395.
[54] *Ibid.,* No. 1398.
[55] In *Contre la secte phantastique,* already analyzed in connection with Pocquet in Ch. 12.2. For later French and English developments of libertinage, see George L. Mosse, "Puritan Radicalism and the Enlightenment," *CH,* XXIX (1960), 424–439.

In 1547, Calvin continued his attack on the Libertines, this time warning the Reformed community of Rouen against a former Franciscan, Duchumin, who expounded the dogma of predestination after the manner of Pocquet and Quintin.[56] Duchumin had been Calvin's associate in the *Antapologia* (1531) against Andrew Alciati. Calvin also had known of that restless and even more eccentric Norman Libertine, William Postel (Ch. 21.4). Among the known followers in Rouen of the Libertine way was Pierre du Val, poet and playwright,[57] author of the *Théâtre mystique* (six pieces, of which five were morality plays). It is quite possible that it was due to Calvin's polemic against the Libertine Franciscan that du Val was converted to Calvinism (c. 1550) and afterward became a Reformed preacher to the French-speaking congregation in Emden. In two other writings, Calvin dealt with Libertines and their associates, namely, in a letter to the Reformed congregation at Corbigny[58] and in a response to Dirck Volkerts Coornhert (Ch. 30.2.b), whom Calvin, however, left unnamed. Calvin wrote also about two anonymous French writings, which he ascribed neither to Quintin nor to Pocquet, but which seem to have been of a mystical Libertine cast.[59]

A Spiritualist of Rouen of another type, whom we may mention at this point, was John Cotin.[60] He might be best described at the end as a Revolutionary Spiritualist, the French counterpart of Thomas Müntzer, though with only a local following. A native of Gisors, he became a Protestant citizen of Geneva (1554), es-

---

[56] *Epistre contre un certain Cordelier. Opera*, VII, 341–364. François Wendel discusses the work and the literature thereon in *Calvin, sources et évolution de sa pensée religieuse* (Strassburg, 1950), 59, 132–134.

[57] V. L. Saulnier, "L'Evangelisme de Pierre du Val et le problème des Libertins spirituels," *BHR*, XIV (1952), 205–218.

[58] *Opera*, XX, 503 ff.

[59] Some writings of this character were collected by C. Schmidt, *Traités mystiques ecrits . . . 1547/1549* (Geneva, 1876), and by E. Picot, *Théâtre mystique de Pierre du Val et des Libertins spirituels de Rouen au 16me siècle* (Paris, 1882); G. Jaujard, *Essai sur les Libertins spirituels de Genève* (Paris, 1890). Bainton, *David Joris*, has shown that some of the French Libertine tracts were translations of the work of David Joris.

[60] Louis Régnier de la Planche, *Histoire de l'estat de France* (n. p., 1576), 323–329.

The Libertine spirit must have lingered in Rouen, for as late as 1561 the Reformed community there found it expedient to print (for the first time in French) Luther's *On Christian Liberty*, obviously directed, not against the Catholics, but against the Spiritual Libertines. Henri Hauser, "Petits livres du XVI siècle," *Études sur la réforme française* (Paris, 1909), 289–292.

teemed as a teacher of Hebrew, Greek, Latin, and French. His Biblical studies drove him from the classroom into preaching. Given to "dreams and revelations" and "ecstatic grimaces," as were some "of the Anabaptists," he gathered a following from among the humbler and more excitable members of the evangelical circle in Rouen. Excommunicated by the local Reformed church, he declared to his followers that the Spirit of God had revealed to him the imminent destruction of the papacy and that God would choose him to head the army of the saints against Antichrist. With two of his disciples he was burned at the stake in Rouen in 1559. His indiscipline and his vagaries endangered the Reform movement in Normandy and readily explain how the Calvinist pastors could acquiesce with relief in the capital punishment meted out by the Catholic authorities.

In effect, Libertinism may be defined at a certain point as a predestinarian or speculative Spiritualism which threatened the ecclesiological and ethical discipline and solidarity of international Calvinism, particularly in Romance countries.

In Calvin's estimate, many of the Libertines near and far were Spiritualists justifying their conformity to their Catholic environment by appealing to Nicodemus (Ch. 22.4). Four works of Calvin's stand out in his opposition to the Nicodemites, the most important in 1544. The Nicodemites, like the Libertines, were Spiritualizers but seem not to have expressed the peculiar doctrines of such Flemish-French Spiritualists as Pocquet, Joris, and Niclaes or of such German Spiritualists as Ziegler (second phase), Schwenckfeld, and Valentine Weigel (Ch. 31.4). The great failing of the Nicodemites was their timidity. It is just possible that Calvin was especially severe with the Nicodemites because he himself in the still obscure days of his conversion knew something of the temptations of the Nicodemites.[61]

The first tract against the Italian Nicodemites was written in 1537 while Calvin was among the Evangelicals at the court of Margaret of Navarre's cousin, Duchess Renée, in Ferrara. There he had been distressed by the way the gospel could be disguised by well-intentioned conformists. In response to an inquiry, he wrote forthrightly to the layman Nicholas Duchemin a work later printed in the security of Basel as *De fugiendis impiorum illicitis sacris, et puritate Christianae religionis observanda.*[62] In

[61] The most recent study of Calvin's conversion has a chapter, "War Calvin 'Nikodemit'?" Paul Sprenger, *Das Rätsel um die Bekehrung Calvins* (Neukirchen, 1960).
[62] *Opera*, V., coll. 239–278.

it, Calvin attacked the Catholic Church as at once an Egypt and a Babylon. He did not, on this occasion, actually employ the term "Nicodemite," nor did he in his second letter to Gérard Roussel on his election, under the patronage of Margaret of Navarre, to the episcopate in Oloron, published subsequently as *De sacerdotio papali abiiciendo*.[63] Calvin became imperious in his *Petite traité montrant que c'est que doit faire un homme fidèle connaissant la verité de l'Evangile quand il est entre les papistes* (1543).[64] Herein, Calvin again wrote of the idolatrous worship of Egypt and Babylon and made it specific that, however much he might sympathize with the Protestants in "bondage" or "exile," he felt called to summon to acts of valorous forthrightness "all the faithful who are scattered throughout France, Italy, England, Flanders, and other places."[65] He concluded by urging the faithful to flee, and, when this was impossible, to stand fast, even if it meant death; and, if the believer could not do this, he should at least not rationalize his conformity but implore God daily for forgiveness and strength finally to prevail against idolatry. It was to this that Coornhert, the Dutch "Libertine," would react with his plea for moderation (Ch. 30.2.b).

Following this, Calvin proceeded to write specifically against those who in fact sought to justify their conformism precisely by appealing to Nicodemus. This was his *Excuse à messieurs les Nicodemites*, 1544,[66] his most serious work against Nicodemite Spiritualism. Calvin's basic argument is repeated movingly, namely, that God is the Lord of the body no less than of the soul of his elect, that the believer—mind, soul, and body—must honor God by public worship, by an upright life, and by abstention from idolatrous conformity to the Papal Church. An Anabaptist could scarcely have been more imperious in his demand for accountability in the face of the Gentiles! Calvin excoriates all those in Catholic lands who, under the patronage of Nicodemus, seek to justify their blasphemous evasion, their prostituting of the temple in which God's Spirit dwells, by appealing quite improperly to "this sainted personage."

Including the incompletely converted Evangelical Catholics, there are, according to Calvin, four kinds of self-styled Nicodemites, actually unworthy of the name of Nicodemus.

---

[63] *Ibid.*, coll. 279–312.
[64] *Ibid.*, VI, coll. 541–578. It was printed with a letter to the same effect composed in Strassburg, 1540.
[65] *Ibid.*, coll. 574 f.
[66] *Ibid.*, coll. 589–614.

There are, first of all, the Evangelical priests and bishops who preach from Catholic pulpits the Evangelical message but give these people the impression that they have thereby made acceptable the whole superstition-encrusted ecclesiastical carapace in which the unreformed church hobbles. Calvin, at this point, is looking to the Catholic Evangelicals of France, such as Roussel.[67]

Secondly, there is the "sect of delicate prothonotaries" (an allusion to the profession of Nicodemus) who play religion with the ladies at court and beguile them with sweet theological niceties, all of them condemning with one voice the too-great austerity of Geneva. He seems, here, to be looking to the theological salons of Nérac and Ferrara, and to such practitioners of the devout life for ladies at court as John de Valdés and perhaps also the Silesian nobleman Caspar Schwenckfeld.[68]

The third kind of Nicodemites are men of letters, given to philosophy and tolerant of the foolish superstitions of the papacy. Many men of the study, Calvin insists, feel that it is enough to know God by books and contemplation in their cabinets, without becoming strained or sullied by involvement in the organization of the community of faith, worship, and Christian action.[69]

There is the fourth group of Nicodemites—merchants and the common people—who would prefer that their pastors or priests not become so much involved in the fine points of doctrine and thereby disturb commerce and the workaday tasks and satisfactions.[70]

Nicodemism, or prudential Spiritualism, would long continue to be a problem for Calvin in dealing with would-be Protestants in lands that were in the grip of the Spanish or Roman Inquisition.

Religious Libertinism, however, in so far as it can be distinguished from Nicodemism, largely disappeared as a religiously motivated movement among people of means and political status, and became in the second half of the century frankly political in the cities and regions that were controlled by the Reformation itself.

Specifically, the term was appropriated by Calvin for the political party in Geneva led by Ami Perrin, hence known also as Perrinists, who opposed Calvin in his efforts to reform the morals of the city and maintain his strict Biblical regimen. Before the Reformation, this faction and its antecedents had striven

[67] *Ibid.*, col. 597.
[68] *Ibid.*, coll. 598 f.
[69] *Ibid.*, col. 600.
[70] *Ibid.*, col. 601.

for the liberty of the city against the Roman Catholic bishop and the duke of Savoy. Under the rule of Calvin, they especially opposed the excommunication by the consistory (made up of pastors and elders elected by the magistrates) of those it deemed unworthy to partake of the Lord's Supper. They also contended against the admission of French refugees as burghers of the city with voting rights. In May 1555, the political Libertines endeavored in vain to lead a violent protest against the influence of these refugees and the French preachers. Defeated, some of the leaders fled, others were sentenced to death, and thus the party was completely disrupted.[71] It was this group who, in 1553, were alleged to have supported Servetus against Calvin.[72]

To this anti-Nicene anabaptist, psychopannychist, and his fiery fate in Geneva at the hands of Calvin, we now turn.

4. CALVIN AND SERVETUS

Except for a glimpse of Servetus in Paris, we were last with him as he was about to leave Basel for Lyons (Ch. 10.3 f.), where, living under the name of Villanovanus, he was an editor of geographical, scientific, and Biblical texts. He had found a patron in Dr. Symphorien Champier (d. 1539), and in 1536 he went again to Paris to study medicine. He published a widely consulted pharmacological treatise on sirups, devoted in large part to the theory of digestion, which ran through several lucrative editions. He became interested in astrology and astronomy as an adjunct to his medicine, because of the supposed influence of the stars on physiology. This brought him under fire from members of the medical faculty, partly for scientific reasons, partly out of professional jealousy. Although reprimanded by the Parlement of Paris, he was not condemned, nor was his true identity discovered.

He thereupon left Paris to practice medicine successively in Lyons, Avignon, Charlieu, and Vienne. In Vienne he had an apartment within the palace precincts of Archbishop Peter Palmier. He continued to copy-edit geographical books and in 1542 he published a one-volume edition of the Bible. This he followed in 1545 with the seven volumes, with glosses, of the so-called Pagnini Bible. He enjoyed a tranquil and respected life, engaging in covert theological speculation and writing, but out-

---

[71] Subsequently the term was used with similar purport by the strict Calvinists in Holland for their opponents.

[72] Roland Bainton, "Servetus and the Genevan Libertines," *CH*, V (1936), 141–149; Müller, "Calvin und die 'Libertiner,' " *loc. cit.*

wardly conforming to the Roman Church. He would later justify his Nicodemism by appealing to the willingness of Paul himself to conform to outward Jewish practices in the Temple when in Jerusalem (Acts 21:26).

The intellectually omnivorous Servetus procured some of the writings of Calvin, which he read eagerly but critically, with the mounting conviction that he could instruct the Genevan Reformer. He therefore resolved to press his own view upon Calvin, sending him in 1546 drafts of his *Restitutio Christianismi,* and submitting three oddly framed questions about Christology, regeneration and the Kingdom, and the relationship of faith to Baptism and the Lord's Supper.[73] Calvin, recalling the earlier and "hazardous" effort he had made at Paris "to win him for Christ,"[74] deemed it appropriate to reply in full, though as he said, he wearied of writing a book for a single reader. Servetus was dissatisfied with the answers, for he was really intent upon informing Calvin more fully, not upon learning from him. In all, he sent Calvin thirty epistolary discourses besides the manuscript of his *Restitutio.*

Calvin decided that he did not have time to answer Servetus in further detail, but sent him a copy of his *Institutes,* which, he observed, adequately explained his position. At this point he also wrote to Farel: "Servetus has just sent me, together with his letters, a long volume of his ravings. If I consent, he will come here, but I will not give my word; for, should he come, if my authority is of any avail, I will not suffer him to get out alive."[75] Servetus sent back the *Institutes* with critical comments, but Calvin kept the draft of the *Restitutio.*

In the four years after the correspondence ended in mutual recrimination, Servetus busied himself with the revision of his magnum opus for publication. He sent a copy to Cellarius in Basel, with the hope of getting it printed there, but learned that it would be unsafe. Buoyed by his sense that it was his destiny to fight under the Archangel Michael (Dan. 12:1; Rev. 12:7) for the restoration of the church so long bedeviled by Antichrist, he now made bold to have an issue of one thousand copies secretly printed at Vienne. The lot was baled in January 1553, and arrangements were made in Lyons for sales at the Easter fairs in Italy, Frankfurt, and even Geneva. Calvin was in possession of a copy by February, perhaps a gift of the bold and eager author.

Servetus' exposure in Vienne came about as an incidental con-

---

[73] Calvin, *Opera,* VIII, col. 482.
[74] *Refutatio errorum Michaelis Serveti, ibid.,* col. 481, n. 1.
[75] *Opera,* XII, coll. 282–284, esp. 283.

sequence of a quarrel between two cousins, the Catholic Anthony Arneys of Lyons and the distinguished Protestant refugee, William de Trie, resident in Geneva since 1549. Arneys had written to William in an attempt to persuade him to abandon the Reformed faith and return to Lyons. De Trie's reply, 26 February, was to assert that, far from being a citadel of orthodoxy, Lyons with Vienne nearby was a haven for the rankest form of heresy! He enclosed several pages of Servetus' printed *Restitutio* by way of proof. Arneys immediately turned to the inquisitor-general, Matthew Ory, who dictated to him a letter requesting further documentation. Calvin, pressed by William de Trie, reluctantly[76] gave him several letters from Servetus, the handwriting of which would at once incriminate the esteemed physician living under the assumed name of Dr. Villeneuve.

   The Inquisition in Lyons acted promptly. Servetus was haled before it. He delayed appearing long enough to conceal the evidence at his apartment. The court treated him with courtesy until the publication and authorship of his book in Vienne was placed beyond doubt. Taking advantage of the mild confinement he enjoyed as a gentleman, he slipped away in the early-morning hours of 7 April 1553. The tribunal continued the proceedings against him and on 17 June condemned him to be burned. The sentence was executed in effigy.

   For four months Servetus remained out of sight, until he made bold to take the route via Geneva to Venice or Naples. On Sunday, 13 August, he put up at an inn in Geneva, awaiting transportation by boat toward Zurich. Since he could not leave until Monday, he went to an afternoon service, possibly at St. Magdalene's, which he thought would be less conspicuous than staying away.

   He was recognized despite some attempt at disguise, and immediately denounced by Calvin.

   The only way that the magistrate could legally arrest the transient was for Calvin to arrange to have his servant, Nicholas de la Fontaine, also submit to imprisonment as the formal accuser in what was a capital charge (the *poena talionis*). Accordingly, the young servant and Servetus were arrested the very next day.

   It was not hard for Calvin to enable his stand-in to substantiate "his" charges of heresy and blasphemy, gaining thereby immediate release and supplying the evidence necessary for the court

---

[76] Servetus later charged that Calvin supervised the correspondence to compass his downfall. For the Catholic trial, see Pierre Cavard, *Le procès de Michel Servet à Vienne* (Vienne, 1953).

to proceed to further hearings and to a trial. Without going into the procedural details of the five phases of the trial,[77] we may set forth the struggle between Calvin and Servetus on three levels.

If Calvin has been called theologically cruel, Servetus may be called theologically vainglorious. In the clash between personalities, each man exhibited his ugliest traits, aggravated by the memory of that obscure personal encounter in Paris in 1534 when Calvin may have been closer to Servetus than he would later care to admit, and by the recollection of their violent epistolary interchanges, broken off in 1546. A Picard and a Basque, a relentless canonist with chronic dyspepsia and an enigmatic doctor with a rupture, baited each other remorselessly on theology and ethics, and growled.

On the religio-political level, allegations were made[78] that Servetus was involved in a conspiracy with the political Libertines, or Patriots (Ch. 23.3), of Geneva, who hated Calvin and his repressive regimen based in part upon the growing voting strength of Protestant refugees so promptly accorded the rights of citizenship. Servetus arrived in Geneva just as the struggle between Calvin and the political Libertines was reaching its peak.

The Libertine councilor Philibert Berthelier had been excommunicated at Calvin's initiative, although the magistrates in council attempted to override the decision of the pastors and elders in consistory. The Servetus case had been on for more than a month when Calvin, expecting Berthelier to present himself brazenly for Communion, announced, "If any one comes to this table, who has been excluded by the consistory, I will do my duty with my life."[79] Berthelier did not come: Calvin had won this phase of the struggle. But with the trial of "Libertine" Servetus in progress, intensifying the local constitutional struggle and obliging Calvin to preach and speak frequently on the Servetian challenge, it is evident that he was not yet certain that he would finally surmount the crisis. The Libertines, whose objective was

[77] The most recent interpretation of the encounter between Calvin and Servetus goes beyond making it symbolic of the conflict between Reformation and Renaissance and construes it as Calvin's struggle with secularism in the sense of unbelief camouflaged by heretical sophistry. Richard Nürnberger, "Calvin und Servet: eine Begegnung zwischen reformatorischem Glauben und modernem Unglauben im 16. Jahrhundert," *ARG*, XLIX (1958), 177–204. But Servetus' immersionist doctrine of rebirth was surely something quite different from both humanistic renascence and modern secularism. The day-by-day account of the trial and execution is vividly rehearsed by Bainton, *Hunted Heretic*, chs. 10–11; Wilbur, *Unitarianism*, ch. 12; and James MacKinnon, *Calvin and the Reformation* (London, 1936).

[78] Discussed by Bainton, *Hunted Heretic*, 173 f.

[79] Doumergue, *op. cit.*, VI, 332–334.

their own personal and civil liberty, probably did no more for
Servetus than give him fatuously the hope that in his theological
and legal argumentation he might win his case, thereby unwittingly inflating his vehemence and substantiating Calvin's
caricature of him as a theological megalomaniac.

Still on the religio-political level, but in a much broader context than the constitutional struggle within the city-state, Calvin
and his associates, abetted by communications, notably from
Bern, Zurich, and Basel, had come to recognize that the orthodoxy
of the whole Swiss Reformed community was at stake in the eyes
of the Lutherans and Catholics alike. The Reformer of Geneva,
who had not long ago been condemned by Caroli as being un-
sound on the doctrine of the Trinity (Ch. 23.1), could not afford
to be less severe with blasphemy and heresy with respect to the
great conciliar dogmas of the Trinity and Christ than Catholic
Lyons.

Thus on the highest level, the struggle between Servetus and
Calvin was passionately theological; and, although the conditions
of Servetus' confinement rapidly deteriorated, he was never put
to the rack, as was Dr. Hubmaier by Zwingli (Ch. 6.4). Servetus
was able to say as much as he would. Moreover, the public debate
which Servetus demanded as his right would have been arranged
by Calvin but for the council's adamant stand against it.

We may conveniently bring together at this juncture the principal points of Servetus' matured theological system as it may be
extracted from his recent correspondence with Calvin, from the
court records and related documents, and especially from the
Restitutio itself. The four main charges of heresy were anabaptism, anti-Trinitarianism, "pantheism" (redemption by deification), and pyschopannychism.

The last charge is of interest in that we have already found
occasion to suggest that the original version of Calvin's *Psychopannychia* may have been directed against Servetus in Paris, c.
1534, among other "Libertines" and "Anabaptists." At the trial,
Calvin pressed him on psychopannychism, and it is clear from
Calvin's summary of the interrogation that Servetus' deep eschatological convictions were misunderstood.[80]

We have also already anticipated Servetus' baptismal theology
as embodied in the *Restitutio* (Ch. 11.1.d). But his matured views
on the Godhead remain to be discussed, for Servetus had in fact
come to change his formulations since the days of his two Alsatian
works on the Trinity (Ch. 11.2). He was so much opposed to the
doctrine of the Trinity, which he considered a sophisticated

[80] See responses 27 and 29; Calvin, *Opera*, VIII, coll. 739 f.

abstraction, that he had coined the term *Trinitarii* for the devotees of this "unscriptural" concept. Nevertheless, in the final version of the *Restitutio,* he was prepared to go much farther than in Alsace with the traditional language.

Whereas formerly he had restricted himself to the term *prolatio* for the relationship between the Word and God, he was now prepared to call that relationship one of *generatio,* admitting that the eternal Word, generated before the creation of the world, might be called not only the Son of God but also Christ. The Prologue of John was seen to be a parallel to the prologue of Genesis, and the identification of the Word with Light had now made it possible for Servetus to think of the Word itself (cf. Dietrich Philips, Ch. 19.2.c) before the mundane incarnation as also a kind of celestial flesh. In arguing thus, he appealed to the Hebraic text, pointing out that whereas the Word in Spanish, Latin, or German can be only spoken or heard, in Hebrew the Word "comes," "goes," "runs," "appears," etc. It became visible in the fiery bush; audible in the still, small voice; visible and palpable in the pillar of fire. The self-revelation of God as a Person took place exclusively through Christ,[81] but for Servetus, as of 1553, Christ was also the eternal idea of man in the mind of God.

Servetus fantastically accused Calvin, in the course of their earlier correspondence, of making three sons: the human nature, the divine nature, and the whole Christ (a "third son"). In a way this characterization was truer of his own view, except that he would have called them stages in Sonship, namely: (1) the man Jesus who was the Christ; (2) the man Jesus who had been miraculously generated of the substance of God as his only Son; and (3) the Christ who is, was, and will be the redemptive epiphany or impersonation of the divine. Jesus was the Messiah as the son of Mary, and, as the Christ, he was concurrently the Son of God and hence derivatively God. Servetus argued this schema from Christ's declaration in John 10:30, *"Ego et pater unum sumus."* Christ was here able to say *sumus* because he was "God as well as man," and *unum* because "there is one godhead (*deitas*), one power, one consensus, one will of the Man with God." Servetus could even say that Christ was consubstantial with the Father, using the term *homoousios.* The premundane substance was in some sense the "flesh" which the *Logos* brought down to be joined with the flesh derived from the womb of Mary (Ch. 11.3). This flesh, this spiritual body from heaven, was the

[81] Ernst Wolf, "Deus omniformis," *Theologische Aufsätze Karl Barth zum 50. Geburtstag* (Munich, 1936), 453.

panis caelestis, de substantia Dei; and the soul of the Son was also from heaven.[82]

Servetus was now prepared to call the Word interchangeably the Son, the eternal idea of Man, and hence the "eternal" Christ, so long as his basic proposition was safeguarded, namely, that there were not three intradeical Persons: the Word as a *substantiale verbum* was an oracle that appeared, a "personification" of God (*personatus Deus*).

In all this new speculation, Servetus was going beyond the Nativity accounts in the Gospels, beyond the Prologue in John, beyond Paul's declaration that Christ was the first-born before all creatures, beyond the Johannine assertion that he was present before the laying of the foundation of the world, to the declaration that the Messiah had been born from eternity; for, essential to the idea of man, is mind, spirit, and substance, however rarefied these conceptions may be. Therefore, the wholeness of Christ the Man must have been present from the beginning in the mind of God.

Servetus stated this in parallel terms: there have been three stages in the Christological descent and the consequent deification of the world and the "mundification" of God: Christ was *filius personalis* in the covenantal manifestation of God, *filius realis* through the incarnation, and since his resurrection and glorification, *filius futurus*,[83] the Judge yet to execute his judgment.

In respect to the first, Servetus could say that Christ was to the omniformality or pervasive yet transcendent essence of God as was Elohim to Jehovah. The person of Christ or the face (*vultus*) of Elohim was more than an image. Christ (*Elohim*) was not merely the representative countenance of God; he was also himself the creator and pattern of the created order.

Servetus, moreover, thought that he had "solved" the problem of why it was the Word, rather than the Spirit of God, which became incarnate as *filius realis*. Referring again to the Hebrew usage, he pointed out that the Spirit is inward, whereas the Word is compatible with the visibility, the motion, and the vitality of a human body.

---

[82] *"Anima Christi est Deus, caro Christi est Deus, sicut spiritus Christi est Deus, et sicut Christus est Deus." Restitutio,* 231.

[83] One is again reminded not only of the speculations of the Cabala but also of the Paulicians (Ch. 11.1.d). Servetus cites Hermes Trismegistus: *"Deus lux ita omnia fabricavit, ut eum in omnibus fulgentem cernamus," Restitutio,* 152.

As for the continuous but invisible outpouring of the Spirit of God, Servetus was aware of it everywhere as the mundification of the divine *substantia* in all creatures, which could therefore be considered full of divinity. Hence, all things, from the heavenly bodies to the smallest flowers, could be looked upon as gods.[84]

It was in connection with Servetus' effort to show how the divine Spirit was communicated to man and all creatures that he appealed to the medical analogy of the living spirit in each person produced by a mixture in the lungs of inspired air with blood, going on to state for the first time in print his discovery of the lesser or pulmonary circulation of the blood. It was this medical explanation of the spirit-soul, it will be recalled, which had disturbed Calvin back in 1534 (Ch. 23.1) when he wrote his *Psychopannychia*.

According to Servetus, God's Spirit is present in a special way at baptismal regeneration or deification to clarify the mind of the convert and to prepare him for the second sacrament of the church, the participation in the Eucharistic body of the incarnate Word.

Closer at this point to the Anabaptist Hofmann than to the Spiritualist Schwenckfeld, Servetus attached pre-eminent importance to the Eucharistic nutriment (Ch. 11.4) that comes from the celestial body of the Word he worshiped. The Lord's Supper, for Servetus the physician, was the only way in which God could become tangible in the interval between the incarnation and the Last Judgment. It was for this God, thus visible in the countenance of the historic Jesus, audible in Scripture preached, and palpable in the breaking of the Eucharistic body, that Servetus was prepared to die a martyr.

It should be added that Servetus, the anti-Nicene, anti-Chalcedonian Anabaptist, was not a pacifist. He expressly recognized the state as ordained *by Christ,* and he legitimated as proper to a Christian magistrate the punishment of obstinate or blasphemous heretics by death, although he counseled exile as more humane. He had earlier pointed out in one letter to Calvin, for example, that Paul included *potestates* and *gubernatores* in the church (I Cor. 12:28), and that Peter killed Ananias and Sapphira through divine intervention and with divine sanction when they appeared otherwise incorrigible.[85]

As the trial ran its course, Servetus was variously headstrong, truculent, and plaintive. He pled several times for a change of

---

[84] Cf. Calvin's account in *Opera,* VIII, col. 496. Cf. Christian Entfelder, Ch. 11.2.

[85] Undated letter, *apud* Calvin, *Opera,* VIII, col. 708.

apparel and relief from the vermin and the unspeakable wretchedness caused by the dampness and cold aggravating his colic and rupture. In his exacerbation he demanded that Calvin be imprisoned likewise, with death to one or the other under the *poena talionis.* The council ignored Servetus' petition and charges.

While the trial was in progress, the Genevans appealed to the ministers and magistrates of other Swiss towns for their opinions, and all replied that Servetus should be punished, mostly without specifying how. The replies of the Swiss divines were rather brief. The magistrates were aghast at Servetus' conduct and doctrine as described to them; but, since the fine points of doctrine largely went over their heads, they left the details to the ministers. Typical was the attitude of the Schaffhausen clergy: "We do not doubt that you, in your wisdom, will repress his attempts lest his blasphemies like a cancer despoil the members of Christ."[86] More specific was Bullinger, of Zurich, who asked for the death penalty. The ministers of Bern sent a long reply in German, defining Servetus' errors in twelve points.[87] The condemnation of Servetus' doctrine was unanimous among the established Protestants, making the punishment almost a Confederal action, for, needless to say, the Catholic cantons would have agreed with Lyons and hence with Geneva. The uniform replies of the Protestant cantons made it virtually impossible for Geneva to do other than convict Servetus, even had it not so desired. The public prosecutor Claude Rigot, himself a Libertine, accused Servetus of subverting the social order, of a dissolute life, and of affinity with Jews and Turks.

Many private persons, on the other hand, were distressed by the impending action against Servetus, since it so closely corresponded to the conduct of the Inquisition. A welcome exception to the general tenor of the official communications coming into Geneva was the letter of the Spiritualizer David Joris (Ch. 19. 1), then living a comfortable life in Basel but brave enough to write anonymously to the Genevan magistrates and divines, "as a member of the body of Christ." He asked them pointedly whether Jesus' prophecy in John 16:2 f.: "They will put you out of the synagogues; . . . [and] whoever kills you will think he is offering service to God," applied to "those who inflict or those who endure suffering." It is not known whether his eloquent appeal to the Genevan magistrates "to refrain from the sin against the Holy Spirit," "to refuse to join the Scribes, Pharisees, and Pilate

[86] Calvin, *Opera,* VIII, col. 810.
[87] *Ibid.,* coll. 811 ff.

against the anointed of God," ever reached the authorities in Geneva.[88]

After much argument and mutual vituperation, the court found Servetus guilty of anti-Trinitarianism and anabaptism, 26 October 1553, following the provisions of the Justinianian law, and condemned him to be burned at the stake. The allegations of pantheism, of psychopannychism, the doctrine of the celestial flesh of Christ, Servetus' errors about the Holy Land as partly a blasted wilderness, and his alleged moral offenses, were not mentioned. There was nothing about any political conspiracy: Servetus was condemned as an Anabaptist and a neo-Samosatenian.

Calvin intervened to secure an execution more merciful than death by burning, but the judgment was not changed. It was Farel who conducted Servetus to the place of execution at Champel outside the walls, urging him to recant. Servetus rejected all entreaties to repudiate his theology and thereby save his life. His last words at the stake were, "O Jesus, Son of the eternal God, have pity on me!" In his extremity he was explicit in his belief, still refusing to ascribe eternity to the person of Jesus Christ the Son.

[88] Printed in translation by Bainton, *Concerning Heretics*, 305–309.

Chapter 24

THE RADICAL ITALIAN EVANGELICAL DIASPORA AND THE REACTION TO THE EXECUTION OF SERVETUS

It will be recalled that Renato, the Reborn, with his compatriots in the land of the Renaissance, had looked forward to the return of the Golden Age "under the fair auspices of Christ" (Ch. 22.1) in the lands of the Reformation and the Restoration. For all Italian Evangelicals who broke from the Roman Church, the great liberating doctrine had been that enunciated like a clarion call by Luther. As it echoed over the Alps, it sounded like this: The elect are predestinated to salvation manifest in their faith. In the Italian context, without the backing of any magistracy, whether cantonal or princely, Lutheranism swiftly acquired, as we have seen, a radical character, becoming, for example, readily sacramentarian in line with the Swiss; and, when Calvin succeeded Luther in giving majestic and imperious leadership to the whole ecumenical Protestant cause, the Italians gravitated, usually by way of the half-evangelical, tolerant, and multilingual territory of the Three Leagues, to Switzerland and, with particular fascination, to Geneva itself. The word of an emigree, addressed indirectly to Calvin, evokes the feeling of many:

I have travelled far to distant lands and differing peoples for the Word of God, having chosen your church primarily and for no other reason than in order to meet and to hear M. Calvin face to face, whose fame I had hitherto held in utmost reverence.[1]

The Italian congregation in Geneva was particularly large, distinguished, and enthusiastic, but, from Calvin's point of view, also wayward in matters both of doctrine and discipline. It had been first assigned a chapel in St. Peter's. Outgrowing these accommodations, the refugees and resident merchants favoring the Reformation had been granted the use of St. Magdalene's, under the leadership of the marquis of Vico, Galeazzo Caracciolo, from

---

[1] John Valentine Gentile; *apud* Calvin, *Opera*, IX, col. 390.

Naples, who had been touched by the Valdesian spirit. Count Celso Martinengo, former canon of the Lateran Church, was the principal pastor. The volatile and passionate refugees met not only for the Sunday service but also for weekday Bible study and theological discussion.

In October 1553 the Italian Protestant community in Geneva and elsewhere in the diaspora were stunned by Calvin's action against Servetus. Some of their more radical spokesmen found the courage to rebuke the perpetrator of the most notorious auto-da-fé of magisterial Protestantism.

Camillo Renato, in his poem of 357 lines, mourned the sad destiny of the evangelical Christians of Italy, who beheld, to their great horror, a fiery stake erected where they had thought to discover a haven (Ch. 22.3). In this poem, Renato openly excoriated Calvin for his presumption in going far beyond Jesus, who readily sought out the wayward, who found good in the sinful, hypocrisy in the righteous, and who in any event gave specific instructions as to a threefold admonition (Matt. 18:15–18) and, in the case of the youth suffering from frenzy or disease (Luke 9:38–42), rebuked his own disciples for having dismissed the sick son and his sorrowing and hopeless father, instructing them further and showing that some ailments of the spirit or body can be cured only by loving prayer. He scorned Calvin, who, despite his claim to have renewed apostolic Christianity, had gone also far beyond Paul; for the apostle, even for the worst of sinners in Corinth, recommended no more than excommunication. Renato importuned all the other Swiss Reformers to become spiritual physicians, courageous prophets against evil, and magnanimous preachers of Christian brotherhood in imitation of God in his righteousness and of Christ in his loving calm, instead of turning into inquisitors and executioners as wicked as the minions of Antichrist.

A much more renowned and subsequently influential literary reaction to the execution of Servetus appeared pseudonymously in Basel, in 1554, entitled *Concerning Heretics*. We shall discuss it under the works of Sebastian Castellio (Ch. 24.2.b). Where Renato's poem argued passionately for Christlike benignity and long-suffering on the part of leaders of the Reformed Church, Castellio's anthology of patristic and contemporary pleas against coercion of conscience argued for a policy of broad toleration. But neither the poem nor the publicistic anthology openly espoused the specific tenets for which Servetus had been condemned.

In contrast, the *Apologia pro Michaele Serveto,* written pseu-

donymously by one calling himself Alphonsus Lyncurius Tarraconensis, was at once an argument for toleration, an appeal for
humaneness in dealing with recalcitrance, a spirited attack upon
the legality of the trial itself, and an unequivocal espousal of the
condemned doctrines of Servetus on the Trinity.

Throughout the whole expanse of the Italian diaspora, poems,
apologies, anthologies, and other materials for some time after
1553 tossed like flotsam on the ever-widening waves of despair
at what to these Italians appeared to be the foundering of the
Reformed Church under its reckless pilot, Calvin.

1. THE RELATIONSHIP OF ANABAPTISM AND ANTI-TRINITARIANISM

Before entering further into the contents of this material, we
should pause for an introductory generalization as to why it was
that, in contrast to the Germanic Radicals, the Italians, even
when they were also technically antipedobaptist, stressed not so
much the recovery of believers' baptism as the restitution of a
humane and kindly Christ and therewith the dissolution of the
Nicene doctrine of the Trinity, which, in the course of the
centuries, seemed to them to have immobilized his mercy within
the rigid carapace of a dogmatic formulation.

The more radical among the Italian conventicular Evangelicals,
who were indiscriminately called Anabaptists, building in part
upon the surviving organization and familiar usages of the non-
Protestantized Waldensians (Ch. 21.1), had much of the character
of the Germanic Anabaptists. But unlike their cousins north of
the Alps, the Italian Radicals adhered to the Protestant doctrine
of predestination, although they turned it in a potentially universalistic direction. In the end there were, to be sure, a number
of authentic Italian freewill Anabaptists, such as the Venetian
Hutterite martyrs noted in Ch. 22.4. But for the most part, rebaptism, when linked with the regent doctrinal principle of predestination to faith with its spiritualizing effect, would only here
and there become a distinguishing sign of the radical Italian
Evangelicals, whether they remained in Italy or joined the
diaspora.

Back in Italy, rebaptism could never have become ecclesiologically constitutive in a loose Catholic context where—in a
patchwork of diocesan, monastic, princely, and civic jurisdictions,
suffused with the Renaissance spirit and long accustomed to
sectarian expressions of Christianity among both the intellectuals
and the lower classes—the Italian come-outers were surrounded by
so many nominal Catholics that they did not have to mark them-

selves off by the act of believers' baptism. Instead, merely to join a circle of readers and earnest exhorters was itself the constitutive action. "Classical" (Germanic) Anabaptism, in contrast, presupposed either a predestinarian, solafideist state church or the old Catholic Church fiercely defended by Hapsburg princes and Catholic leagues. Italian radical Evangelicals, emerging in a situation that was until 1542 only languidly Catholic, where the church was only slowly assembling its strength to fight back, were, to be sure, consciously antipedobaptist because of the new stress on explicit faith; but these Italian Radicals could never make adult baptism the distinctive badge of their break with "Antichrist."

Nor could rebaptism be the distinctive mark of the Italian Radicals after their flight. Instead, as a consequence of their stress upon predestination to faith, when these liberated Italians entered Swiss territory, their most radical impulses were destined to find expression, not in anabaptism, but rather in anti-Trinitarianism. As refugees, they were already marked off from the indigenous parishioners by speech and theological accent. Rebaptism of Italians, already organized here and there into Italian-speaking congregations in French-speaking or German-speaking towns, could never have the programmatic significance it had for the indigenous German Radicals in the towns and parishes of their birth.

Common to both the Germanic Anabaptist and the Italian anti-Trinitarian impulses, however, was the radical pacifism in imitation of Christ and the ways of the early Christians. Like the German evangelical Anabaptists, almost all the Italian Evangelicals, whether Protestantized Waldensians, conservative Protestants, or Radicals, were opposed to war, to capital punishment, and to coercion in the realm of conscience. They espoused the separation of church and state, or at least the freedom of conscience and the withholding of coercion in the realm of religion.

Thus in October 1553 the Italian radical Evangelicals instinctively sensed that their special moral assignment was to attack the coercive ecclesio-political implication of the doctrine of the Trinity in the context of the Swiss magisterial Protestantism, which had been founded by a Reformer who died in armor on the battlefield at Cappel and which was now being given its most dynamic expression by a Reformer who, as they generally maintained, had vindictively connived at the burning of Servetus.

Their target for an assault upon inquisitorial ecclesiasticism in its new Protestant guise was thus marked out for them by Calvin's own insistence that the God of the Old Testament is the triune

Godhead of the creeds. Calvin, in this respect more explicit than the Nicene fathers, held that whenever the Father alone is mentioned in the Scriptures, the equally stern, consubstantial Son is implied correlatively; that there is therefore no essential difference between the revelation of the Old Covenant and that of the New; and that accordingly, as one of the practical consequences of this postulated equivalence, the Christian—as once the Hebraic —commonwealth is ordained and ruled with the full sanction of the triune God. As to this last asseveration, the Italian Evangelicals were especially baffled, given the seeming contradiction between Calvin's ceaseless concern to separate the Reformed Church of Christ from the control of the Genevan magistrates and at the same time his theological insistence upon the Christian role and the Christian vocation of these same magistrates.

Although many of the Italian Radicals were well-educated men —lawyers, physicians, former clerics, and men of station and substance—they could not share the subtle and profoundly Biblical conviction of Calvin that the Christian states were ordained and sustained by the triune God as much for the restraint of the sinful among the elect as for the temporal protection and encouragement of the civically virtuous among the reprobate! Thus, when in his religio-political anxiety Calvin fatefully persuaded himself that the brazen Spanish "reprobate" was also a criminal because he threatened the Triune basis and sanction of Christian magistracy, the Italian Radicals became certain that, for the safeguard of their Christian conscience and for the protection of the members of the Reformed churches of Christ from molestation in the name of Christ, their only recourse was to set about dismantling the doctrine of the Trinity. Calvin appeared to them to have appealed for sanction to a Christ from whose countenance he had effaced all the features of the forgiving and suffering Son of Man. Henceforth, disengagement of the Son from what seemed to them the pitiless iron vise of dogmatic formulations presented itself as the best means of securing the independence of the devotees of Christ. The simplification of the doctrine of the Trinity would thus serve roughly the same religio-political function for the Italian Radicals as the insistence upon believers' baptism among the German Radicals.

By distinguishing between the judicial Father, creator of the world and the ordainer of law and civil order, and the atoning Son, and by subordinating Christ, the Son, and thereby altering the Nicene-Genevan formulation, the radical Italian Evangelicals sought, still within the context of Protestant predestinarianism and solafideism, to safeguard freedom of conscience, to secure the elimination of coercion in religion, to foster Christian brother-hood, and to recover all those other apostolic institutions and ways of life for which the Germanic Radicals were striving in their insistence upon believers' baptism, upon free will, and upon sanctification.

Germanic Anabaptism, grounded in the freedom of the will, and Italian anti-Trinitarianism, grounded in an inclusive divine election and only *incidentally* receptive to the practice of adult rebaptism, had then this basic motif in common, namely, the con-cern to distinguish the two divine dispensations and to restore to pre-eminence the New Testament and the apostolic noncoercive Christian community of faith. But by separating the covenants, by distinguishing the Father and the Son, and then subordinating the Son to the Father, the radical Italian Evangelicals soon found themselves ascribing *to the Father* the features and some of the functions of the Son and, in the final devolution of the doctrine of the Trinity, they would find themselves lowering the Son to the rank of the greatest of the prophets and thereby obscuring once again, in a generalized ethical theism, the difference between the Old and the New Dispensation!

This displacement naturally altered also the doctrine of the atonement. Under the influence of John de Valdés, many Italian Evangelicals had early come to see in the crucifixion the demon-stration (or revelation) of the forgiving and re-creative love of both God the Father and the Son, expressed by Christ for fallen and lost humanity—not a sacrifice to appease or indemnify an exacting Ruler, not a cosmic penal transaction contrived by God himself to secure a token justification for sinful man. Thus, be-ginning within the framework of predestinarianism and proceed-ing to subordinate Christ to God (the Father), the Italian Radi-cals in their anti-Trinitarianism approximated the adjustment which the freewill Anabaptists, such as Denck, and the Spiritualists, such as Schwenckfeld or Franck, achieved by stressing, respectively, believers' baptism in the covenant of the good conscience with God or the contemplative penetration of self to the point where the inner spirit was experienced as identical with God's Word.

It will become apparent, therefore, in the course of the next chapters, that within Anabaptism, Spiritualism, and particularly Evangelical Rationalism, there was building up, more or less un-noticed, a strong pressure to rearticulate the conception of sal-vation and more specifically the atonement in such a way as to break from both the patristic and the Anselmian theories. The *De Jesu Christo servatore* of Faustus Socinus (Ch. 29.7), to be composed at the very end of our period in 1578, may be at this point anticipated as a specific formulation toward which many in the Radical Reformation as a whole were groping for half a century.

To sum up, the adherence to the doctrine of predestination did for the Italian Radicals almost exactly what the doctrine of the inner Word or the inner Christ or the listing Spirit accomplished for the German Spiritualists, and the doctrine of Christ's removal of original guilt on Calvary did for the German Anabaptists. That is, all three groups were more or less freed from the necessity of dealing with justification, sanctification, and hence personal salvation in terms of a historic atonement or propitiatory sacrifice of fulfilled righteousness. What the classical Protestant Reformers were trying to express in their revulsion from the idea of repetitive liturgical sacrifices or imitative acts of atonement on the Eucharistic altar and in their polemic against the elaborate system of works righteousness connected with the Mass, the Radicals had come to take for granted in their complete break with the Catholic past, the Italians in their confidence in election, and the Germans in their reliance on imitative suffering betokened by believers' baptism. The whole of their theological structure was erected, in fact, on this foundation, concealed as much to themselves as to others. As a consequence, when the radical evangelicals—whether Anabaptist, Spiritualist, or Rationalist—came to formulate a (new) doctrine of the atonement, since the *forensic* atonement of fulfilled righteousness or vicarious sacrifice was not only historically but also psychologically remote, theirs turned out to be an "experiential atonement," that is, in effect, a doctrine of progressive divinization, or spiritualization, or redemptive suffering, or divine imitation, or demonstrable sanctification, or perfectionism.

Only such a generalization about this, the central transaction in Christian theology, will give meaning to the Trinitarian and Christological speculations and vagaries in the Radical Reformation as a whole and, more to the point of the present chapter, make some sense of the restless movements and tragic encounters of the radical evangelical refugees from Italy as they spread out in a vast diaspora stretching from Edwardian England to Jagellon Poland and to Transylvania under the shadow of Suleiman the Magnificent, often to end their theological careers as explicit Unitarians.

2. ITALIAN EVANGELICAL RATIONALISTS IN THE DIASPORA

There must have been considerable Servetian sentiment among the Italian Rationalists well before the anti-Nicene Anabaptist's name was on the lips of all, following his execution in the fall of 1553. We have already noted "Melanchthon's" letter of warning to the Venetian Senate in 1539 (Ch. 21.4). We have also seen how readily the Anabaptist synod in Venice in 1550 subscribed to extreme views on Christology and the doctrine of the Trinity which went even beyond Servetus (Ch. 22.2). In the July before Servetus' fateful entry into Geneva, Paul Gaddi wrote Calvin about the alarming spread of the theology of "that proud and diabolic man," in the Grisons and northern Italy.[2] Then two years after the execution of Servetus it will be possible for William Postel (Ch. 21.4) to speak of the considerable and well-established following of Servetus in Venice.[3]

In any event, several Italian Rationalists, when they came to rebuke Calvin for his inhumanity and unapostolic behavior, were prepared to defend the specific doctrines of Servetus as well. This seems to have been especially noteworthy in the case of the Paduan jurist Matthew Gribaldi, who apparently had connections with the radical circle in Vicenza antedating the execution of Servetus.

a. Matthew Gribaldi. Matthew Gribaldi (1506–1564), professor of civil law at Padua, was vacationing at his wife's estate at Farges, in Bernese territory, at the time of Servetus' trial. He was among the very first to declare that the execution of Servetus was an indelible blot on the Reformation, and that the death penalty was never justified in cases of divergent religious opinion. He presently became a major spokesman of Servetian theology. Furthermore, as lord of the château of Farges in Gex,[4] he was able to make of his summer retreat an asylum for anti-Trinitarianism. We should therefore take a closer look at him.

Born in Piedmontese Chieri, Gribaldi had begun an illustrious career in civil law, successively ornamenting the faculties at Perugia, Toulouse, Valence, and Grenoble (1535–1545). It was during his tenure at Valence that Gribaldi published his well-known textbook in civil law, *De methodo et ratione studendi,* 1541. Calvinist by 1542, in 1548, he accepted a professorship at Padua and soon won a large following among the students. He

---

[2] Gaddi to Calvin from Zurich, 23 July 1553; *Opera,* XIV, No. 1763.

[3] Postel's *Apologia pro Serveto Villanovano* is largely taken up with his own theory of the Trinity of *potentia, sapientia,* and *clementia;* his idea of the world soul; the restoration of all things through regeneration; and the role of the aged Venetian nurse Mère Jehanne as the virgin redemptress, coordinate with the male principle embodied in Christ. The *Apologia* is printed by J. L. von Mosheim, *Versuch einer unpartheyischen und gründlichen Ketzergeschichte* (Helmstedt, 1748), II, 466–499.

[4] Gex, formerly under the dukes of Savoy, was conquered by Bern in 1536 and ceded in 1601 to France. It is now in the department of Ain.

became associated with the "Lutheranism" openly espoused by the students, many of them German or Swiss. Numbering more than six hundred, they were a power in their own right, conducting military drills, sending embassies to the doge, and defending their university freedoms.

The popular Gribaldi, as we have already hinted, may have as well been for some time attracted to Italian or even Servetian anti-Trinitarianism. During his vacation at Farges, he will surely have taken great interest, as a civil lawyer, in the *ad hoc* use of the penalties of Justinian against the physician on trial in nearby Geneva. Even in September, before the execution in October, he wrote a letter about it to the "brethren of Vicenza," a center of radical evangelicalism with an anti-Trinitarian and anabaptist reputation (Ch. 22.2).[5] Soon thereafter he was publicly defending Servetus and criticizing Geneva for the conduct of the trial.[6] To be sure, he is said to have first read Servetus' *On the Errors of the Trinity* when Pietro Perna presented him with a copy in Padua the winter after the execution.[7] But it is also possible that he knew of and perhaps corresponded with Servetus himself before the physician's fateful encounter with the head of the church in Geneva. Gribaldi could, for example, have come into contact with Servetus, the editor-physician, in Lyons and Vienne when his own textbook was printed in Lyons. Moreover, Gribaldi's summer estate and all his university posts were rather close to Lyons, and we know that another anti-Trinitarian, Laelius Socinus, was actually staying with Gribaldi at Farges during the early stages of the trial of Servetus.

It is quite possible, therefore, that Gribaldi made bold to visit Servetus in prison in Geneva when he passed through the city on his way back to his classes in Padua. We know that he made a conspicuous but unsuccessful effort to intercede with Calvin, who would not clasp his hand. Calvin alluded bitingly to the jurist's well-known theological evasions in the discussions held by the local Italian congregation. It is therefore possible that the spirited *Apologia* of "Lyncurius" was actually written by Gribaldi himself sometime after 15 January 1554.[8]

Whoever the author, he surely had firsthand knowledge of

---

[5] Church, *op. cit.,* 154. It will be recalled that the later Socinian tradition located a very important radical conventicle in Vicenza as of 1546.

[6] Wilbur, *Unitarianism,* 216.

[7] Church, *op. cit.,* 206.

[8] The work is published *apud* Calvin, *Opera,* XV, No. 1918. The allusion to Calvin's published *Libellus,* col. 62, gives a *terminus a quo* for the *Apologia.* The authorship of this work has been variously assigned: to Martin Cellarius of Basel because he is known to have possessed a copy of Servetus' work; to

Servetus' plans to go from Lyons via Geneva to Venice and there to edit a commentary to the Hebrew Bible.[9] The *Apologia* is also distinctive in that it enters extensively into alleged legal improprieties connected with the trial of Servetus. The apologist was, moreover, evidently well acquainted with the circumstances of the Genevan prisoner.[10] It is noteworthy, therefore, in seeking to identify the advocate, that he says that Servetus entrusted to him

Curione because his handwriting has been identified in the marginalia of the Basel MS., and because he is known to have passed on to his son a copy of the *Restitutio;* and to Laelius Socinus, partly because the Greek behind Lyncurius is the equivalent of Latin *soccinum* (amber), in alleged allusion to Laelius' family name. Cantimori, *Eretici*, 175, has proposed Laelius as the author. Kutter, *Curione,* agrees with him in at least "exonerating" Curione of all but the marginalia. Neither man knew of the reinforcement to be given to the Curione hypothesis by Kot's work in Becker, *Autour de Servet et Castellion,* 113, on the preface to Servetus' *Declaratio* (Ch. 11.1), written by the same "Alphonsus Lyncurius" in possession of the same personal information about Servetus as the apologist. Since all these theories more or less cancel each other out, I am here assuming that Gribaldi was the author, for his known views, style, career, profession, and itinerary comport well with the presence of a "Lyncurius" MS. in both Basel and Tübingen.

There is further circumstantial evidence in that when in 1567 Blandrata, who knew Gribaldi very well, came to list great leaders after Erasmus, Valdés, and Servetus, mentioning among others Laelius Socinus, Cellarius, and Gentile, he included "Lyncurius," and perhaps thereby left room for the lord of Farges to be understood under that pseudonym. Writing in Transylvania, Blandrata might well have been unaware of Gribaldi's death in 1564 and thereby sought to protect him. Cf. Kot, in Becker, *op. cit.,* 87.

Quite recently, Alain Dufour has shown that Peter Viret and perhaps even Calvin were in correspondence with Gribaldi as convert to Protestantism as early as January 1542, which would further increase the probability of Gribaldi's authorship of the *Apologia,* the work of a jurist for a jurist. "Deux Lettres de Pierre Viret," *Revue de théologie et de philosophie,* 3rd series XI (1961), 222–235. Dufour has also suggested that Curione was the possible author of the poetic *Epitaphium Michaelis Serveti,* "Vers latins pour Servet," *Mélanges offerts à M. Paul-E. Martin* (Geneva, 1961), 483–496.

[9] This information is supplied both by the *Apologia* and by Lyncurius' Tübingen preface to the *Declaratio,* Kot, in Becker, *op. cit.,* 113.

[10] The proximity of the composition to the execution is inferred from such evidence as (1) the absence of any reference to the *Restitutio,* only one copy of which will have been available in Geneva in 1553, as distinguished from the earlier Alsatian works, (2) the absence of any reference to the connivance of Calvin in the trial at Lyons, which only later became generally known, and (3) the vivid interest in the manner of Servetus' entry into the city, his imprisonment, and his trial—the kind of details that would recede into the background with the passage of time and with some distance between the writer and the place of the event. That the author was an Italian is of course only a conjecture—a composite of all the figures suggested by modern scholarship—Cellarius being the only non-Italian candidate among them. The impassioned style is much closer to the known works of Gribaldi than to those of the more placid and dry Socinus or the humanistically mannered Curione.

not only his plans in respect to Venice but also some of his writings.[11]

We know that in a very short time the lawyer Gribaldi had absorbed so much of Servetus' abstruse theology that he could expound not only his doctrine of God but also his peculiar Christology. In Gribaldi's known theological utterances, in the *De vera cognitione Dei*, for example, he would presently declare the three Persons to be three distinct Gods, holding that "God the highest is like Jove, the first among them," the Son and the Spirit being subordinate Gods, and that "the divine seed of the Son of God or the Word took form as a human being in the Virgin Mother, *without*, however, *taking a human nature from her.*"[12] Here is the only known instance among Italian Radicals of the explicit appropriation of Servetus' doctrine of the celestial flesh of Christ, along with his more widely adopted alteration in the doctrine of the Trinity.

Whether or not from Gribaldi's pen, the *Apologia* is the oldest fully explicit presentation of Servetian "unitarian" thought by an Italian in our era. The overwhelming theological conviction of the Apologist (Gribaldi) is that the Protestant divines have concentrated on the "tail" of the complex theological body of Catholicism, and dealt with such matters as "the Mass, purgatory, sacraments, penance, satisfaction, fasting, the invocation of saints, images, monastic vows, celibacy, free will, and predestination," claiming that all these are entirely or in part corrupted by the papal Antichrist, but that they have refused to examine the "head": namely, the capital doctrines concerning God, Christ, and the Spirit! Traditional formulations here have been taken over by the timid Reformers, unexamined, unchallenged. Yet the doctrine of the Trinity is blasphemous to begin with, a feminine *trinitas* being put in the place of God the Father, creator of heaven and earth. The "Trinity" is an imaginary construct introduced by the Greeks, elaborated in papal hallucinations, a chimera of the Scholastics, not to be found in the Scriptures. Servetus, in fact, was not far off when in his reported conversation he called it a hideous Cerberus. This dogma blasphemes God the Father, caricatures Christ, and judges the Holy Spirit, who judges all things and should be judged by none! Servetus was no less inspired by the Spirit than Luther. The Catholic Church, shaken by the challenge of Luther, acted vigorously, not moving to burn him but, rather, to argue with him. The Spirit perhaps inspired Zwingli also; and, in his sacramentarian extreme, he was in turn

[11] Namely, the *Declaratio,* the preface to which is printed by Kot, in Becker, *op. cit.,* 113.

[12] Haller to Bullinger, 14 September 1557; *apud* Calvin, *Opera,* XVI, No. 2711.

obnoxious to Luther. Did Luther rally the princes to compass
Zwingli's execution? No, he personally debated the problems at
Marburg.

Calvin, the Apologist goes on, unscripturally and illegally, contrived Servetus' death under the pretext of defending the Trinity
but actually in "private revenge." In committing Servetus to the
flames, Calvin confirmed the Catholics in their disposition to use
flames on heretics, and the concept of "heretics" among them was
to be broadly defined! What kind of Christianity is that which
proclaims its "good news with flames"? Where in the Genevan
Reformation is the God who said that he wanted not the death
of a sinner but that he repent, who warned that in any event
vengeance was his, not man's? Where in the so-called recovery
of evangelical Christianity in Geneva is the "humility, patience,
benignity, long-suffering, and mercy of the Lord Jesus Christ,"
who enjoined love for one another and prayer for those that
despitefully use one? Did he not instruct his closest followers to
await the Final Judgment for the separation of the tares from
the wheat? Where in the so-called apostolic Christianity in Geneva
are the precepts and examples observed of such apostolic spokesmen as Paul and John, Ignatius and Irenaeus? They seem entirely
unknown in Geneva in so far as their principles would apply in
the realm of human conduct. Even the Neros of history would be
horrified if they should learn that Christians were now burning
Christians in the public arena of Christendom!

God is not a substance, the Apologist goes on, affirming his
own convictions as identical with those of Servetus, but he is
the Creator and Father, who commissioned his only-begotten Son
to redeem the world and has sent forth his Spirit to work in the
hearts of men, performing the miracles of a thief's conversion, of
a blind man's illumination, and of a wanderer's return. Let Calvin
follow Gamaliel if he cannot follow Christ and Paul, and at least
wait and see whether this new thing be of God!

In comparison with the *Apologia*, the publicly avowed views of
Gribaldi on the Trinity are relatively vague or guarded. Whenever he passed through Geneva, it was presumably his custom to
attend the services of the Italian congregation there. His sympathies with Servetus were sufficiently well known to call forth at
one time a lively discussion. Gribaldi expressed himself cautiously
but clearly enough afterward in his letter to the Genevese
Italian congregation.[13] He strove to use orthodox language but

---

[13] Trechsel, *Antitrinitarier*, II, *Beilage*, XI, 460 f.; Calvin, *Opera*, XV, No.
2018.

could go no farther than a monarchian Trinity comparable to the unity of three apostles, such as Peter, Paul, and Apollos, in the same apostolate.[14] He was willing to speak of the Father and Son as *"due cose substantiali"* or even as *"due hypostasi realmente et veramente distinte,"* but avoided the equivalent of "consubtantial." Unable to accept as rational that *"in concreto et individuo, uno sia tre et tre uno,"* he came out, in effect, for tritheism, or actually for ditheism, since he neglected to speak of the third Person.

Back in Padua, the intensification of the Inquisition under the newly elected Pope Paul IV (1555–1559) prompted Gribaldi to resign his position. In Zurich, former Bishop Peter Paul Vergerio of Capodistria, whom Gribaldi had recommended to Calvin as a convert to the Reformation in 1549[15] and with whom he had talked freely in defense of Servetus at the residence of the French envoy in Chur, now recommended him in turn to Duke Christopher for a position at the University of Tübingen. As to the effectiveness of his voicing his increasingly radical religious beliefs, one may simply note that two Polish students, Peter Gonesius and Michael Salecki (the former soon to play an important role in the spread of Servetian Anabaptism in Poland and Lithuania, Ch. 25.2), followed Gribaldi to the University of Tübingen in 1555.

In 1557, Gribaldi suffered an attempt on his life by the disgruntled loser in a lawsuit and then dismissal from his post for refusing to clear himself of charges of anti-Trinitarian sympathies. Gribaldi fled to Farges, leaving behind his books and papers. These were searched. Among them was discovered his incriminating *De vera cognitione Dei.*

b. Sebastian Castellio. The Savoyard Sebastian Castellio[16] (1509/1515–1563) stands out with his *De haereticis an sint persequendi* (Basel, 1554) even more boldly than Gribaldi in giving systematic public expression to the revulsion shared by most Spiritualists and Evangelical Rationalists against persecution for reasons of faith and conscience.

Born of prosperous farmers in St. Martin-du-Fresne near Nantua in Savoy, Castellio had studied at Lyons and been converted to Protestantism on reading Calvin's *Institutes.* He had gone to Strassburg to confer with the author and stayed in his home in 1540. When Calvin was recalled to Geneva, Castellio accompanied him and was given charge of the new college. For

---

[14] A somewhat tendentious Scriptural allusion!
[15] Letter of Gribaldi to Calvin; Calvin, *Opera,* XIII, No. 1304.
[16] A recent brief biography is that of Bainton, *Travail,* 97–124.

his students, he rendered in classical Latin expurgated abridg-ments of the Bible, his oft-reprinted *Dialogi sacri*, 1541.

After his marriage, in order to supplement his college stipend from parish work, Castellio in 1544 requested ordination. Calvin, despite a shortage of trained pastors, refused to admit him to the ministry because, among other things, he denied the divine inspiration of the Song of Songs and refused to accept, in respect to Christ's descent into hell, Calvin's allegorization of hell in the *Genevan Catechism* (1545)[17] as the consummation of Christ's anguish and the experience of utter desertion by God the Father. Castellio, like many others in the Radical Reformation (Ch. 32.2), insisted on the literal descent of Christ into hell as the only means of redeeming the Old Testament saints. Calvin, though a sober, searching exegete in his commentaries on the Bible, evaded at this point in the Apostles' Creed the literal sense.

Calvin still thought well of Castellio as a teacher, if not as a minister, and sought to find another position for him. Castellio removed to Basel. There he suffered extreme poverty. For a while he supported himself and his family by capturing stray timber floating down the Rhine. He was at length rescued from penury for intellectual activity more worthy of his training. He got work as a proofreader on Biblical and classical texts and received his master of arts degree at the University of Basel. Castellio, in 1554, under the pseudonym of Martin Bellius, challenged the thesis that heretics should be burned, in his famous *De haereticis an sint persequendi*,[18] defending Servetus.

On Heretics immediately won acclaim from the many who deplored Calvin's deed. Seeing the work soon after its publication, Theodore Beza at once surmised that it was from Castellio, adding that also Laelius Socinus and Curione might well have been in-volved. To these identifications, Calvin added the name of Martin Borrhaus (Cellarius), who had long stood on the shifting bound-aries between Spiritualism and Anabaptism (Ch. 3.2). Borrhaus, now well established at the university, was certainly not directly involved.[19] The collaboration of Curione and Socinus is unlikely, except in matters of compilation and translation.

This farrago or anthology (depending on the point of view) excerpted Lactantius, Chrysostom, Jerome, and Augustine against

---

[17] Calvin, *Opera*, VI, coll. 29 ff.
[18] Translated by Roland Bainton, with other pertinent documents and ex-cerpts, *Concerning Heretics*, Records of Civilization, Sources and Studies, XXII (New York, 1935).
[19] Bainton suggests that he prepared the German translations; *Concerning Heretics*, 7.

the execution of heretics, added the testimony of Erasmus, and quoted similar statements from Luther, John Brenz (Ch. 10.1), Urbanus Rhegius, and even Calvin; from the "Erasmian" Protestant liberals[20] Caspar Hedio, Conrad Pellican, Curione, and Otto Brunfels (Ch. 8.4.b); and from the religious Radicals Sebastian Franck and Castellio himself! In the dedication of De haereticis to Duke Christopher of Württemberg (prince over John Brenz, whose tract of 1528 protesting the brutality of Austrian persecution of the Anabaptists was incorporated into Castellio's book), "Bellius" first defined heretics as those "with whom we disagree." Showing how difficult it is to judge of doctrine (as compared to the judging of conduct), he appealed for a common-sense approach:

Let not the Jews or Turks condemn the Christians, nor let the Christians condemn the Jews or Turks, but rather teach and win them by true religion and justice, and let us, who are Christians, not condemn one another, but, if we are wiser than they, let us also be better and more merciful. This is certain: that the better a man knows the truth, the less is he inclined to condemn, as appears in the case of Christ and the apostles. But he who lightly condemns others shows thereby that he knows nothing precisely, because he cannot bear others, for to know is to know how to put into practice. He who does not know how to act mercifully and kindly does not know the nature of shame.[21]

Christians who delude themselves so as to justify religious persecution become worse than the Jews and Turks they would convert:

Who would wish to be a Christian, when he saw that those who confessed the name of Christ were destroyed by Christians themselves with fire, water, and the sword without mercy and more cruelly treated than brigands and murderers? Who would not think Christ a Moloch, or some such god, if he wished that men should be immolated to him and burned alive? Who would wish to serve Christ on condition that a difference of opinion on a controversial point with those in authority should be punished by burning alive at the command of Christ himself more cruelly than in the bull of Phalaris, even though from the midst of the flames he should call with a loud voice upon Christ, and should cry out that he believed in Him? Imagine Christ, the judge of all, present. Imagine Him pronouncing the sentence and applying the torch. Who would not hold Christ for a Satan? What more could Satan do than burn those who call upon the name of Christ?[22]

[20] Cf. ibid., 79 ff.
[21] Ibid., 132 f.
[22] Ibid., 133 f.

After the publication of *Concerning Heretics,* the Magisterial Reformers never ceased to hound Castellio. Beza, outraged, at once retorted with his *De haereticis a civili magistratu puniendis.* Calvin wrote *A Defense of the Faith against the Errors of Michael Servetus.* Both Calvin and Beza tried to bring about Castellio's dismissal from the University at Basel, but a party rallied to his support. Calvin demanded a public debate, which took place at Bern in 1555. In the same year, Castellio was busy translating the Bible into French.

Other religious refugees who were outspoken in their criticism of Calvin's execution of Servetus were Bernardine Ochino and Laelius Socinus.

c. Ochino and Laelius Socinus. On the morrow of the execution of Servetus, with the ashes still warm, Bernardine Ochino (Ch. 21.3.b) arrived in Geneva, en route from the England of Bloody Mary, and gave Calvin his opinion in outrage and sorrow. He went on to Chiavenna, then to Basel, where in the home of Curione he met a number of Polish students, and then to Zurich. Here, through the influence of Laelius Socinus, he was called as pastor of the Italian congregation, which was made up of about a hundred refugees from Locarno. The smallness of the congregation, regarded as provisional until the members should have time to learn German and become part of the regular Zurich parishes, gave Ochino leisure to write.

Laelius Socinus, who had left Italy after Ochino and before the defection of the Anabaptist Manelfi, was, as a layman, freer to come and go than the clerical evangelicals. He had reached Padua by the time Servetus was executed, but both Beza and Calvin, as noted above, suspected that Laelius had collaborated with Castellio in *De haereticis.* The fate of Servetus now focused Socinus' inquiring mind on the Trinity. After living successively in Basel (January 1554) and Geneva (April 1554), where he made incautious remarks, Socinus resumed his residence in Zurich, where he now found himself constrained by Bullinger (at the instance of Calvin and others) to reaffirm his orthodoxy in a *Confessio de Deo* (15 July 1555).[23] Herein he asseverated his right to the "holy liberty of inquiring from my elders and disputing modestly and reverently in order to enhance my knowledge of divine things." He spoke respectfully of the three great creeds; but, while abhorring "the errors of Servetus and the whole Arian theology" and that of the Anabaptists as well, he continued to avoid saying in what precisely these errors consisted. On the

[23] English translation by Edward M. Hulme in *Persecution and Liberty, Essays in Honor of George Lincoln Burr* (New York, 1931), 221–225.

question of the sleep of the soul, he was equivocal, but his Renatian eschatological convictions are suggested when he concluded: "May all my desire be directed to this end—the resurrection [of the righteous] from the dead, that caught up in the clouds I may meet my Lord in the air and ever live with him, praising our God and Father world without end." Bullinger allowed himself to be convinced that Laelius was orthodox, and the two shook hands in confirmation. Only Julius of Milan, to whom Bullinger reported the confession in detail, was wary, reminding Bullinger that all who had once imbibed the doctrine of Servetus, Renato, and the Anabaptists in general, found it "impossible to get rid of their indelible impressions."[24] A fellow Italian, who remained unswervingly Protestant, Jerome Zanchi, once said of Socinus that he was "a man full of divine heresies," which, however, he never put forward for the sake of disputations, but always questioningly, with the desire to learn.[25]

The death of his father involved Socinus, beginning in August 1556, in an effort to vindicate his patrimony, impounded by order of the Inquisition. He visited Wittenberg, and, armed with letters of recommendation from Melanchthon, went on a long tour of German, Polish, and Hapsburg courts, purportedly in order to obtain princely support for an appeal to Cosimo at Florence for the recovery of his own and his family's estates. He was well received by Maximilian of Austria, who presented him with a letter of commendation. Socinus did not proceed beyond Venice. The Inquisition had its eyes on the whole family. His brother Cornelio was imprisoned at Rome. His other brothers, Celso and Camillo, and his nephew Faustus were *"reputati Luterani."* In August 1559, Socinus returned to Zurich, without having secured his estate, to live with a silk manufacturer.

Besides the *Confessio* and several letters, there survive from the pen of Laelius the *Brevis explicatio in primum Johannis caput*,[26] *Theses de Filio Dei et Trinitate*,[27] and *Dissertatio de sacramentis ad Ligurinos et Genevenses scripta* (1560 or 1561).

Several times his nephew Faustus visited him, coming from Lyons. Then, after Laelius' death on 14 May 1562, Faustus gathered up his papers and library and converted the work of his uncle into a major religious movement in Poland (Ch. 29.7).

It is clear that the minds of Socinus and of Ochino, the pastor

---

[24] The letters between Bullinger and Julius are printed in *Bullingers Korrespondenz*, Nos. 290 and 296.
[25] Quoted by Illgen, *op. cit.*, 65.
[26] Edited by Cantimori and Feist, *Testi*, 61.
[27] *Ibid.*, 57.

of the Italian church at Zurich, acted powerfully on each other. In 1556, Ochino had published his *Dialogo del Purgatorio* (also in Latin and German), in which he (as Deodatus), after initial bantering with a Dominican to the effect that surely one of the omnipotent pontiffs of Rome would have, in a moment of charity, emptied purgatory of its wretched denizens, went on to uphold, against the serious defenders of the Catholic dogma, the view that the sole purgatory was Jesus himself, who purified man of his sins. In the same year, Ochino published, against an extreme Lutheran, the *Syncerae et verae doctrinae de coena Domini defensio,* in which he defended the essential unity of the Swiss sacramentarians and declared that the belligerent Lutheran's appeal to the sword instead of working further at the Eucharistic problem with his pen reminded one of Mohammed. Ochino described the Supper as a commemoration of the exemplary death of Christ without its having been a payment for sin, and suggested thereby a Valdesian doctrine of the atonement.[28] None of the Swiss Reformers were pleased with Ochino's officious presentation of their sacramentarianism.

Ochino's other Zurich works were, because of the problem of possible censorship, published in Basel in 1561. One was *Tractatio de conciliatione inter reformatas Ecclesias.* Another was *Disputa intorno alla presenza del Corpo di Gesù Cristo nel sacramento della Cena,* dedicated to the Valdesian exile Lady Isabelle Breseña. Rejecting, of course, the Catholic doctrine of transubstantiation, Ochino herein also challenged the Calvinist Eucharistic theology of the communication of the believer *per fidem.* Ochino, in a moving passage, describes the love of Christ for his fellow men and of God his Father in giving him, his only-begotten Son, an action that in a Valdesian spirit made of the physical commemoration of the Lord's Supper an adiaphoron, for the forgiven thief was saved directly from his cross without any Eucharistic theology and the Apostles' Creed had no reference to the Eucharist. The book is of special interest as a Spiritualist manifesto, in which the refugee ex-Capuchin pointed out to the exiled Valdesian lady that it was not necessarily evil to remain in a Catholic land and to observe the required external acts of piety, since wherever one is there are always external aspects of the Christian cultus and community which one cannot wholeheartedly endorse. Even the primitive church had its Judas. Ochino was writing not only against Calvin's Eucharistic theology but also against Calvin's tract on the allegedly evasive Nicodemites (Ch. 23.3).

[28] Bainton, *Ochino,* 44.

From Eucharistic theology and the forgiven thief, Ochino moved into the very center of Reformation theology, the problem of predestination and free will. He published his Italian sermons on the subject and also a Latin translation in 1561 under the title *Laberinti*, both versions dedicated to Queen Elizabeth. Although he was certain that faith was a gift of grace, he did not feel that theological precision in respect to the doctrine of predestination was necessary for salvation.[29] Also in 1561 he published for his congregation *Il Catechismo*, with anti-Trinitarian undertones. In respect to the doctrine of the descent of Christ into hell, he rejected Calvin's interpretation of it as a symbol of consummate suffering in favor of a literal descent, the view also of Castellio and most Anabaptists (Ch. 32.2.c). In 1562, Ochino published a series of sermons in which he deplored the exclusiveness of the various Protestant churches alongside the equally intolerant Church of Rome, mentioning also the conventicles of the Anabaptists and the Libertines, among the countless new contenders for having the "true" church. Fighting Christians cannot be true Christians, nor their gospel the authentic good news, was his message.

Then, in 1563, he published, also in Basel, his *Dialogi XXX* in a Latin translation by Castellio. Herein the former Capuchin who had in his Lenten sermons in Italy cried, "Woe unto Venice, woe Siena," was saying, "Woe unto Zurich, woe Geneva," but in more subdued tones, for he was now a married minister, not a friar, and the pastor of a small and immigrant congregation. The drift of the dialogues, for example, between imprisoned Cardinal Morone and Pope Pius IV, was the impropriety of using force in the realm of faith. Ochino denounced the burning of Servetus in Geneva and the drowning of Anabaptists in Zurich. A lost sheep should be brought back lovingly to the ninety and nine, not slaughtered. No one should die for denying the Nicene formulation of the Trinity or for any other doctrine unless that person himself believed it to be essential for salvation!

Ochino's adversaries maintained that, besides being weak on the Trinity, Ochino had also justified polygamy[30] under color of a pretended refutation. This led to his banishment. A hearing subsequent to the banishment uncovered further theological

---

[29] This is Bainton's view, *Ochino*, 123, as against Erich Hassinger, who argued that Ochino was Calvinistic in his doctrine of predestination to the very end. *Studien zu Jakobus Acontius*, Abhandlungen zur mittleren und neueren Geschichte, LXXXVI (1934), Exkurs über die Theologie Bernadino Ochinos, 97–109.

[30] In *Dialogue*, XXIX.

deviations in the *Dialogi* regarding the doctrines of justification, the atonement, and baptism. Ochino fled to Basel, but found no haven. Mühlhausen proved inhospitable. He took refuge at Nuremberg until the spring of 1564, where he wrote his defense, *La Prudenza humana e Ochino,* against the charges which had led to his banishment from Zurich. He gathered up his children at Frankfurt, and removed to Poland, about which Socinus had given him a good report, and settled briefly near Cracow.

   d. Blandrata and Curione. A major figure in that section of the Italian diaspora destined to move, within Evangelical Rationalism, all the way to explicit Unitarianism was the Piedmontese physician George Blandrata (c. 1515 to c. 1585).[31] A specialist in female diseases, he had been invited to Poland a quarter of a century before the arrival of Ochino. Court physician, he became a friend of Francis Lismanino, the confessor of Queen Bona Sforza at Cracow. He had then gone to Transylvania and served as court physician to the widow of John Zápolya. Returning to Italy, he sojourned in Pavia (1553–1556), where he became an object of suspicion on account of his doctrinal utterances and escaped the Inquisition in 1556 by going to Geneva. Here, shortly after his arrival, he was elected an elder of the Italian congregation under Martinengo, with whom he debated. He was soon engaging Calvin himself with countless doctrinal questions, especially concerning the Trinity. His persistent queries finally won from Calvin a reprimand,[32] and in fear of Calvin's further displeasure he left the city.

   Celio Secundo Curione (1503–1569),[33] who first saw Christianity in the perspective of the Reformation when he read Melanchthon's *Loci Communes,* given to him by an Austin friar in Turin, was professor successively at Milan, Vicenza, Pavia, Venice, Ferrara and Lucca. Upon receiving a summons to Rome in 1542, he fled across the Alps, first to Lausanne, then to Basel. Like Ochino, in his relief at having escaped, he produced an antipapal satire in the form of a dialogue, *Pasquillus exstaticus* (Basel, 1544). He was appointed professor at Basel in 1547, composed his doctrinal *Christianae religionis institutio* in 1549, translated the *Considerationes* of Valdés the following year, and published his major theological work, *De amplitudine beati regni Dei,* at Poschiavo. 1554. The last, dedicated to the king of Poland, sought to prove

---

[31] Delio Cantimori, "Profilo di Giorgio Biandrata saluzzese," *Bollettino storicobibliografico subalpino,* XXXVIII (1936), 352–402.
[32] Trechsel, *Antitrinitarier,* II, 467; Calvin, *Opera,* XVII, No. 2871.
[33] Kutter, *Curione.* See also Delio Cantimori, *Italiani a Basilea e a Zurigo nel Cinquecento* (Rome/Bellinzona, 1947).

that God's predestination to salvation included many more than was commonly supposed.

For the most part, Curione conformed to the established church of Basel, but he stood close to Castellio. He became the father-in-law of conservative professor Zanchi in Heidelberg and a friend of Bullinger in Zurich, but also of the two Italian liberals dwelling there, Laelius Socinus and Ochino. He seems to have read and critically evaluated Socinus' *Theses de filio Dei et Trinitate.*[34] Curione also made marginal notations in the manuscript of the *Apologia pro Serveto*[35] and Gribaldi's *De vera cognitione Dei,* which was discovered among the jurist's belongings at Tübingen in 1557. Curione was disturbed by the treatment meted out to the Jorists by the University of Basel in 1559, but with revulsion dissociated himself from Joris' views.

It is clear from his own family catechism and especially from his *De amplitudine* that Curione was an Erasmian "Protestant." Uneasy about the traditional formulation of the doctrine of the Trinity, disposed to favor believers' baptism preceded by Christian nurture and education, he opposed coercion in the realm of conscience; but he was not a Radical and conformed to the outward symbols and usages appropriate to a professor and citizen in Basel.[36]

3. CALVIN'S SECOND MAJOR CONTACT WITH ANTI-TRINI-TARIANISM: JOHN VALENTINE GENTILE

In 1558, Calvin, troubled by the death of the local Italian pastor Martinengo, the absence of Caracciolo, and the continuing influence of Gribaldi and Blandrata, determined to obtain from the remaining Italian residents of Geneva assent to an unequivocally orthodox confession of faith (18 May 1558).[37]

The confession was wholly devoted to the Trinity and Christology and restated in Italian and Latin the eternal generation of the Son, at once the wisdom and the Word of God, and con-

---

[34] Edited by Cantimori and Feist, *Testi;* the emendations of Cantimori's text of Curione's marginalia are given by Kutter, *op. cit.,* where he observes that Cantimori misconstrued somewhat Curione's *monendus:* the author, presumably Socinus, should be warned against going to such untenable extremes.

[35] For the marginalia as copy editor of the Basel MS. of the *Apologia,* see Kutter, *op. cit.,* 183. See also Dufour's suggestion, above, n. 8.

[36] The remainder of Curione's life found him repeatedly refusing invitations to teach elsewhere and saddened by the deaths of his children: daughter Violante (Zanchi's wife) in 1556, three other daughters, son Orazio (an imperial privy-councilor) in 1564, and son Agostino (who held the chair of rhetoric at Basel) in 1566. Curione died in Basel on 25 November 1569.

[37] Calvin, *Opera,* IX, coll. 385–388.

demned those who said it was the Father only who generated the Son, and not the whole Godhead, and who did so in such a way that the Son and the Holy Spirit proceeded from God the Father by a dividing and a separating of the essential unity of the whole Godhead. The full significance, however, of what Calvin was insisting on and to which the spirited Italians were objecting had come out more explicitly in Calvin's *Confessio* occasioned by his strife with Caroli, in which he had spoken of Christ as Jehovah, and now in a *Responsum* to Blandrata.[38] The more moderate among the radical Italian Evangelicals did not originally object to the language of the creeds, but they preferred a monarchian rather than a consubstantialist formulation of the unity of the three Persons, and above all sought to guard against what they considered a quaternity of one divine substance, the Godhead, and three distinct Persons.

The opinionated members of the Italian congregation were given complete freedom to discuss their points of view with Calvin. The leading spirit among those who protested against signing the confession was the Piedmontese John Paul Alciati de la Motta di Savignola (not to be confused with the humanist scholar Andrea Alciati). John Alciati (1515/1520–1573), who left Piedmont at mid-century because of the rigorous policy of King Henry II of France toward heretics, had in 1552 joined the Genevan congregation of Italians (elected deacon in 1555 and elder the next year). In 1555, he had been granted Genevan citizenship. Described by Calvin as frenzied in speech, he had earlier criticized the treatment given Servetus, and he not only refused to sign Calvin's confession, but also persuaded several others to resist.[39] Calvin, however, was not to be swerved from his policy with respect to Italian denizens. Though Alciati and Gribaldi managed to escape, Calvin secured submission from most of the remaining recalcitrants.

Conspicuous by his absence from the first session with Calvin on 18 May 1558, at which the latter sought to bring the Italian congregation of Geneva into line, was John Valentine Gentile, who pleaded ill-health.[40]

[38] *Confessio, Opera*, IX, col. 708; *Responsum*, cf. Ch. 25, n. 27.

[39] The others were Silvio Tellio, Francis Porcellino of Padua, Philip Rustici the physician, Nicholas Gallo the Sardinian, and Hippolytus of Carignano. Blandrata had already left Geneva for safety's sake.

[40] The most recent study is that of T. R. Castiglione, "Valentino contra Calvino," *Studia nad Arianizmem*, edited by Ludwik Chmaj (Warsaw, 1959), 49–71; idem, "La 'Impietas Valentini Gentilis' e il corruccio di Calvino," *Ginevra e l'Italia: Raccolta di Studi*, edited by Delio Cantimori et al. (Florence, [1959]), 149–176.

A native of Scigliano in the province of Cosenza (Calabria), Gentile had come under the influence of Valdés, had sought refuge in the Rhaetian Leagues, and then had come to Geneva about 1556, where he entered Gribaldi's circle. Although he eventually signed Calvin's confession, Gentile continued his study of Servetus, begun after the execution, and spoke his mind in "a school in secret." Calvin described him as having a "portion of pride, hypocrisy, malice and obstinate impudence greater than any other."[41] For his temerity, Gentile was cast into prison, and with him Nicholas Gallo of Sardinia, whom he had won over from subscribing to the Calvin's confession. Once in prison, 9 July 1558, Gentile worked on a Second Confession and a letter with patristic citations,[42] holding that God the Father in his *aseitas* is the *principium* of the substance (*essentia*) of the other two Persons, that as their *essentiator* and *informator* he is also "sole monarch," and that among these "three eternal spirits of one and the same dominion and rule," the Son as Mediator is of the same substance with, but as it were of less substance than, the Father.

Gentile could look out from prison to St. Peter's, where Calvin ruled and had compassed the death of Servetus. With such a prospect, Gentile steeled himself. When Calvin visited him, in the company of the councilors of the city-church-republic, Gentile, holding his ground with courage, requested the help of a theologian, and specified the orthodox Peter Martyr Vermigli. The council turned down his request, but granted a delay to enable Gentile to prepare his case. Realizing that his judges were committed to Calvin's views, the Calabrian agreed to make a public recantation (the ancient *amende honorable*) rather than risk the death penalty demanded by his accusers. Bareheaded and clad only in a shirt, carrying a lighted torch in his hand, he was led through the city to the sound of a trumpet, having first confessed his errors and burned his writings.

In the meantime, ill fortune had pursued Gribaldi from Tübingen to Farges. The bailiff of Gex, forewarned by the Bernese authorities, soon apprehended Gribaldi and conducted him to Bern along with some of the tracts he had been distributing. The jurist was finally sentenced to banishment from Bernese soil, once he had signed a Reformed confession. Gribaldi at length complied (20 September), and retired to Freiburg.

[41] Letter to Caracciolo; Calvin, *Opera*, VIII, No. 2919, coll. 257 f.
[42] Second Confession, *ibid.* IX, coll. 389 f.; letter, 390–399; letter to bailiff, Trechsel, *op. cit.*, II, 471–486; for his patristic sources, Ignatius, Justin, Irenaeus, Tertullian, see Jan Koopmans, *Het oudkerkelijk Dogma in de Reformatie* (Wageningen, 1938), 64–66.

Following the death of his wife (24 April 1558), he was permitted by the Bernese authorities to return to Farges on the condition that he keep doctrinal silence.

Shortly after Gentile humiliated himself in Geneva, he joined Alciati and Blandrata with Gribaldi at Farges. The bailiff of Gex now required Gentile to make a fresh profession of orthodoxy. Instead, he wrote a letter to the bailiff with notes on *Quicunque Vult* (destined in printed form to foster tritheism in Polish Reformed circles, Ch. 25.3). Proceeding to Lyons, he dedicated his *Antidota* to the Polish king, sharply parrying Calvin's attacks in the recently completed, definitive Latin edition of the *Institutes* of 1559 (cf. I. xiii. 23; II. vi. 4).

At Grenoble, where in the meantime Gribaldi had accepted anew a university position, Gentile was examined by the Catholic authorities, who found him gratifyingly anti-Calvinist. A trip to Farges resulted in his being briefly imprisoned. Released, Gentile returned to Lyons, there to be jailed and again released.

As for Alciati, the magistrates of Geneva pronounced him a foe of the Reformed faith, commanded his friends to cease visiting him on pain of banishment, and finally sequestered his property. After a brief stay in Chiavenna, he appeared for the winter term at the University of Basel. In the spring of 1559 he was stirring up doctrinal controversy in Turin. Returning to Farges, Alciati next proceeded to slight Calvin in a letter to the Genevan magistrates, setting down his religious beliefs in a statement far less offensive to the Reformed than earlier utterances.

As for Gribaldi, it was not long before his abstention from Mass (which he justified on the ground that his property was held by the Bernese, whom he dared not offend) rendered him an object of renewed suspicion, as did his hospitality toward Gentile. Gribaldi was dismissed from his Grenoble post in 1560. He made his way back to Farges, where he was to die of the plague in 1564, the same year as Ochino, and a year after Castellio.

In 1562, Gentile and Alciati set out for Poland. At about the same time, Francis Negri traveled the same route. Negri, a friend of Laelius Socinus and Renato, who had been living since 1559 at Tirano and Chiavenna, had won renown for his tragedy on free will, a dramatic presentation entitled *Il Libero Arbitro*, dedicated to Prince Nicholas Radvila of Lithuania. Negri's journey was motivated by his desire to visit his son George, who had become pastor of the Italian congregation at Pińczów in Little Poland.

CHAPTER 25

ANTI-TRINITARIAN ANABAPTISM IN POLAND, 1548–1565

We were last in the kingdom of Poland in Ch. 15 when we traced Schwenckfeldian Spiritualism alongside Lutheranism in ducal Prussia, and followed the colonization of the valley of the Vistula by the Netherlandish Sacramentists and Anabaptists from Danzig to Toruń, ending our account with the death of King Sigismund in 1548.

As we return to Poland, this time in the company of Alciati, Gentile, and Francis Negri, from Switzerland in 1562, we find an entirely new situation under King Sigismund II Augustus (1548–1572). Numerous others—Catholics, Protestants, and Radicals—have already preceded these Italian wanderers into the hospitable land. Among the non-Catholics, we have had occasion to mention Blandrata, who came as court physician in 1540; Stancaro, as professor of Hebrew at Cracow in 1549 (returning in 1559); and Laelius Socinus, who came in 1551 (returning with Blandrata in 1558). Peter Paul Vergerio had been in Lithuania and Poland several times, beginning in 1556.

The Lutheranism of which we took note earlier is still largely limited to ducal Prussia. Vergerio's effort at royal Lutheranization has proved abortive (Ch. 25.1). There has been some agitation among the Erasmian prelates to organize a national Catholic Church on the model of Henrician England. The great Protestant force in Poland and Lithuania is, of course, the synodally organized Reformed Church under the distant tutelage of Calvin and other Swiss Reformers, but also very much under the direct influence and leadership of emigree Italian intellectuals and thus already well on its way toward that permanent schism between the orthodox Major (Reformed) Church and the anti-Trinitarian, largely anabaptist Minor (Reformed) Church destined in the next century to be known by the name of Laelius and his nephew, Faustus Socinus, as Socinian.

639

1. The Radical Thrust of the Polish and the Lithuanian Reformed Churches, 1550–1556

The Helvetic-Italian Reformed Church in Poland began in 1550 when Stancaro (Ch. 22.3.a) prevailed upon Lord Nicholas Oleśnicki to drive out the monks from his town of Pińczów and to support the organization of a synod of the Reformed Church.

By March 1555, there were enough Reformed pastors in Little Poland to elect Felix Cruciger as their superintendent. The attempts of the Poles to create order in their church were stimulated and encouraged by the presence of numerous Bohemian Brethren (*Unitas Fratrum*), who had begun to enter the kingdom in 1547, after their exile from Bohemia by Ferdinand. The Poles found in this venerable, Slavic, reformed community the disciplines and safeguards necessary for counteracting the greed of certain of the magnates espousing the Reformation in Poland for selfish reasons. After initial discussions, a synod was held at Koźminek, 24 August to 1 September 1555, for the purpose of uniting the Little Poles and the Unity. In general, the Poles accepted the confession and doctrine of the Bohemian Brethren, already much influenced by Luther and Zwingli (Ch. 9.1), reserving independency of ecclesiastical jurisdiction and certain divergent usages to themselves.

In the same year, at the diet of Warsaw, permission was granted to every Polish lord to introduce into his house and estate any Scriptural mode of worship he desired. This Polish "Interim" allowed for much more individualism and conventicular Christianity than did the contemporary Peace of Augsburg (1555) in the Empire, which extended the religion of the prince beyond his private chapels to the whole of his territory (*cuius regio, eius religio*).

Almost immediately after the Polish "Interim" and the federal union with the refugee Bohemians, the Little Poles took up direct contact with the Swiss. The adherence of the Little Poles to the Calvinists was signaled by the unanimous election at Pińczów (15 September 1555) of one Francis Lismanino, to be cosuperintendent with Cruciger.[1]

---

[1] Theodor Wotschke, *Die Geschichte der Reformation in Polen* (Leipzig, 1911), 133 ff. The main source is Stanislas Lubieniecki, *Historia Reformationis Polonicae* (Amsterdam, 1685), translated by E. Morse Wilbur and revised and edited by Marek Wajsblum, to be Volume XXI of *Harvard Theological Studies*. See also the survey by Janusz Tazbir, "Research on Anti-Trinitarianism in Poland," *Studia z Dziejów ideologii Religijnej xvi i xvii w.* (Warsaw, 1960), 183–198.

Lismanino was, at the moment of his election, in Geneva. He had left Poland in 1553 as court preacher and provincial general of the Franciscan Order. It was word of his conversion to the Reformation that prompted his sudden election as coleader of the newly formed Polish Reformed Church. Born of Italian parentage on the island of Corfu, he had been brought as a boy to Cracow, and, on becoming a Franciscan, in due course was made Italian preacher and confessor to Queen Bona Sforza. She had given him Ochino's sermons to read, and from there he went to Calvin's *Institutes*. It was while on a royal mission to purchase books for the king's library that he had come out for Calvinism, hoping perhaps that on his return his monarch might embrace both him and the new cause.

Constitutional antagonisms, however, were casting their shadow on the development of the Reformation. The unruly gentry (*szlachta*), in their pressure on the king, came out against the privileges of the senatorial magnates. This drove even the Protestant senatorial nobles, who had been instrumental in securing the temporary religious freedom, over to the side of the almost despondent bishops, and enabled the king to repress the activities of the Reformers. Thus, on his return, Lismanino found that his hopes of royal support were vain. In fact, he had to go into hiding and could not give public leadership to the young church he had been elected to serve.

To aid the cosuperintendents, Lismanino and Cruciger, pastor at Secymin (Secemin), the synod convening in this town in January 1556 elected three clerical *seniores*, who were expected to counterbalance the pressure from the lay *seniores* from among the gentry. Two of these coadjutor pastors, Gregory Paul and Stanislas Sarnicki, were, without yet realizing it, destined to become spokesmen of the two factions that end in the schism into the Minor and the Major Reformed Churches. At this very synod Peter Gonesius (Ch. 25.3) gave expression to his Servetian convictions. At the synod of Pińczów that spring the greatly strengthened Reformed Church of Little Poland summoned John Łaski from his disputations with Menno Simons (Ch. 19.2.a) to return to the land over which his uncle had once ruled spiritually as the primate to serve Polish Protestantism as its irenic and ecumenical chief.

Thus far we have been talking about the Polish realm of the Jagellon (Lithuanian) King Sigismund II. We must also take note of his geographically vaster territory under the royal chancellor for Lithuania, the mighty voivode of Vilnius (Vilna),

Nicholas Radvila (Radziwiłł) the Black. It was in this grand duchy stretching beyond the Dnieper River that much of our Eastern narrative of the Radical Reformation unfolds.

The grand duchy, like Poland, was divided into palatinates. The seigneury of Samogitia was still largely barbaric. Here and in the adjacent palatinates of Lithuania proper the language of the peasant population was Lithuanian. The other palatinates of the grand duchy used Byelo-Russian and Ruthenian (Ukrainian). The official language of the courts of the grand duchy was a form of Byelo-Russian; in the homes of the gentry the Polish language was spoken, and at the Reformed synods either Polish or Latin.

Most of the population of the grand duchy was Orthodox. The metropolitans of Kiev in the westward expansion of Orthodoxy had since 1415 made Nowogródek and later Vilnius one of their official residences. There was an Armenian bishop for the Armenian mercantile community centered in Lwów.

Protestant, Judaizing, rationalizing, and otherwise revolutionary trends had so far penetrated or indigenously arisen in Russia itself that Ivan IV the Terrible in 1553 called a synod in Moscow to condemn the new sectaries.

Precisely because so much of Lithuania was congenitally anti-Roman and anti-Muscovite, the Reformation could present itself with an unusual appeal, for it made possible at once the purification of Christianity, the appropriation of church lands, the institution of new schools and printing presses, and all in the name of an evangelical humanism freed from subservience both to Rome and to Moscow.

It was mediately from Cracow that the Lithuanian gentry acquired their taste for evangelical humanism and from Polish-trained or Polish-speaking clerics that they recruited their pastors. The consequent pre-eminence of Polish along with the Latin over Lithuanian and Ruthenian in the reformation of the grand duchy should not be allowed to obscure the Oriental or "Orthodox" features of the Lithuanian development in the swift radicalization of the Lithuanian Brethren as a distinctive group within the Radical Reformation. Specifically, it was a Judaizing trend within certain sections of Russian Orthodoxy, the preservation of the Nicene formula without the filioque, and the practice of baptismal immersion that operated in Lithuania to raise questions about certain "papal" formulations and practices once the Calvinist movement was accelerated in the direction of radical apostolicity.

Radvila called the former Cracow priest Simon Zacius (Żak) to head up the reform; and, when the king was in Brest-Litovsk in 1554, Radvila encouraged Zacius to celebrate the Mass in Polish and to offer Communion in both kinds.[2]

Before Radvila went over completely to Calvinism, Vergerio, the former bishop of Capodistria (whom we met briefly in connection with Camillo Renato, Ch. 21.1), sought, singlehanded, to bring about the formation of a royal Lutheran Church in Poland and Lithuania under Sigismund.[3] Radvila, the chancellor and, as such, vicegerent for Lithuania, was essential to the plan. Vergerio had conferred with Lismanino in Basel about his efforts in behalf of ecumenical Protestant reform. In the meantime, Pope Paul IV had dispatched to Poland his nuncio Alois Lipomani. The nuncio's influence with such vital figures as Nicholas Radvila disturbed the Protestants and moved Duke Albert of Prussia to recommend Vergerio's plan. Vergerio published his Italian rendition of the Württemberg Confession (1 January 1556) with a dedication to the new queen of the Poles, his godchild. On 11 July, the ex-bishop arrived in Königsberg, there publishing his critique of clerical laxity, *Catalogus haereticorum,* dedicated to Radvila. In September he visited the prince at Vilnius, and dedicated to Radvila's young son a Polish translation of Valdés' *Spiritual Milk.*

Anticipating an invitation to attend the forthcoming diet, Vergerio moved to the border town of Soldau in ducal Prussia, and there waited for the summons to join battle with the papal nuncio. When the invitation failed to materialize, he had to content himself with the discharge of literary barrages. After the diet concluded its meeting, he briefly visited Warsaw. He spent a fortnight with Łaski and Lismanino at Cracow, vainly attempting to persuade them to condemn Curione's *De amplitudine beati regni Dei,* dedicated to the Polish sovereign.

Impatient at having his advice consistently ignored, the ex-bishop returned to Württemberg to gain princely backing in Germany with which to sway Sigismund and Radvila into accepting his vision of a Lutheranized Poland. After Vergerio's failure, reformation by convinced magnates and lesser lords was

---

[2] At this time he had also anticipated perhaps his interest in baptismal theology in ordering a great silken tapestry from the Netherlands, picturing Luther and his protective elector on one side and the baptism of Christ at Jordan on the other.

[3] Jan Sembrzycki, *Die Reise des Vergerius nach Polen* (Königsberg, 1890).

henceforth the way of reform in Poland. Radvila, for his part, was already moving from standard Calvinism to a much more radical reordering of religion in his vast realm, inspired by the hope of lifting the region culturally and bringing closer the Orthodox and Latin traditions in an ecumenical, apostolic, humanistic reform.

The congeries of aristocratically supported Helvetic churches by now strewn through Lithuania and especially Poland had much the character of gathered conventicles of the sectarian type. They were perhaps most like the Huguenot churches in Catholic France. No part of Poland, except for ducal Prussia, and no part of Lithuania, unless it be the palatinate of Radvila, ever knew a truly Magisterial Reformation of the kind that has given classical Protestantism its norm.

In Poland the sponsoring noblemen were frequently elders. It was in their great homes or in spireless, whitewashed stone meetinghouses constructed on their estates or in the towns they governed as starosts that the Reformed met for worship and synodal discussion. The strong stress on the Biblical sanction for the authority of the king, prince, or town council in religion characteristic of Anglican, Reformed, and Lutheran Protestantism was not in place where the royal central authority was Catholic and where the gentry sponsored Protestantism more as leading laymen in a royal republic than as magistrates. And unlike the corresponding Huguenot conventicles, likewise sponsored by aristocrats as well as by burghers, the Polish Reformed churches did not think of themselves as a *militia Christi* in hostile tension with the Catholic king, but rather as a righteous remnant committed to supporting a policy of royal toleration.

In addition to the distinctively Polish-Lithuanian constitutional and sociological factors, we must reckon with both the spiritual contagion from immigrant and indigenous Anabaptism and the infiltration of anti-Trinitarian Evangelical Rationalism. The proponents of each of these currents—the one originally German and Dutch; the other, largely Italian—had in common the experience of, and predilection for, a conventicular Christian life because of their common stress on moral reformation and personal sanctification.

Under the influence of Anabaptists from the humbler classes, drawn into Reformed conventicles by their Polish or Lithuanian lords, a large minority of the Polish gentry came to espouse an irenic and even pacifistic view of the corporate claims of the radically Reformed churches, until at length some of the gentry carried out completely the anabaptist renunciation of political power.[4]

At the same time, the aristocratic sponsors and their pastoral associates in Polish Reformed circles were, far more than their Huguenot counterparts, exposed "from above" to the rational challenge to traditional dogmas, especially the Trinity and Christology, because of the omnipresence of articulate, well-trained clerical and lay refugees from Italy.

Although the Anabaptists and the anti-Trinitarian Rationalists were kindred spirits in their dislike, or programmatic rejection, of force in the realm of church and conscience, be the coercion Catholic or Calvinist, the representatives of these two currents converging in Poland commonly differed on the question of free will and predestination and, as a consequence, on the relative importance of believers' baptism and the corporate ban. The Italian Rationalists could never be wholehearted about believers' baptism and especially about rebaptism. Faustus Socinus, for example, will in the course of our narrative (Ch. 29.8) refuse to be rebaptized despite the importuning of the very group at Raków whose cause he would otherwise be vigorously defending.

It is well at this point to anticipate schematically the devolution of the two doctrines whereby the Radicals sought to recover what they regarded as the simplicities of a pre-Constantinian theology and churchmanship, here earlier, there later, in the course of Polish and Lithuanian synodal debate.

Since in antiquity there had been a very close collaboration of church and state in the formulation of both the Nicene-Constantinopolitan doctrine of the Trinity and the Chalcedonian formulation of the two natures of Christ, and again in the imperial sanction of the patristically evolved theory of the indelibility of baptism, brought into close association with civic loyalty, it was perhaps inevitable in a conventicular type of Calvinism, in isolation from the monarchy, that the traditional doctrines concerning Christ and baptism should be seriously challenged. In any event, the intermingling of the Anabaptist and

---

[4] Zbigniew Ogonowski, *Arianie Polscy* (Warsaw, 1952), 82, *et passim*. A more Marxist writer, Zanna Kormanowa, deprecates the contribution of the nobility and emphasizes the revolutionary aspects of the movement, "Arianie polscy," *Nowe Drogi*, III (1949), 107–118. See further, Henrk Barycz, "U kolebki małopolskiego ruchu reformacyjnego," *ORP*, I (1956), 9–12, and Wacław Urban, *Chłopi wobec reformacji w Małopolsce w drugiej połowie xvi w.* (Cracow, 1959), also *idem*, "Activité pratique des frères polonais envers les paysans," *ORP*, V (1960), 109–126.

anti-Nicene motifs is the distinguishing mark of the Radical Reformation in Poland and Lithuania.

As in the rise of Germanic Anabaptism, one moved in Poland from pedobaptism by sprinkling, to antipedobaptism, to rebaptism (by means of total immersion—a distinctively Servetian, Silesian, and Polish trait) on the model of Christ at Jordan, to the renunciation of baptism altogether (except optionally or in welcoming converts from Judaism or Islam, respectively the views of Jacob Palaeologus and Faustus Socinus). The roughly corresponding sequence for the other doctrine in Poland and Lithuania was from traditional trinitarianism through tritheism, by eschewing the concept of consubstantiality; ditheism, by rejecting the deity of the Holy Spirit, considered rather as a force or gift; adoptionism (Ebionitism); on to pure unitarianism.

2. ANABAPTISM IN POLAND AND LITHUANIA, 1548–1565

Even from the perspective of the seventeenth century it seemed appropriate for the grandson of Faustus Socinus to look back and assign to Menno Simons the penultimate glory due to him in the recovery of evangelical Christianity from Luther to Socinus:

The appearance of Luther, Zwingli, Calvin, and Menno came first, as of daybreak and dawn; and this was then followed by the brighter days of the returning sun.[5]

The rise of Polish-speaking Anabaptists in between the arrival of Menno Simons in royal Prussia in 1549 to settle differences among his far-flung followers in the delta of the Vistula (Ch. 15.4) and the definitive organization of the antipedobaptist, pacifistic, anti-Trinitarian Minor Church in 1565 can be only sketchily recounted because of the paucity of documentation.

In 1548 a new wave of Silesian immersionist Anabaptists had found refuge in Poland. Somewhat later three Silesian Brethren— Alexander Vitrelin, George Schomann, and Daniel Bieliński[6]— destined to play an important part in the formation of the Polish Minor Church, left Silesia. By around 1551, Menno's spiritual lieutenant, Dietrich Philips, was established as chief pastor of the

---

[5] Wiszowaty, *Narratio compendiosa, loc. cit.,* 209; translated by Wilbur and Wajsblum, *Historia.*

[6] The Silesian Brethren as a group are treated by Ludwik Chmaj, *Bracia Polscy: Ludzie, Idee, Wpływy (Warsaw,* 1957), 9–49. Lech Szczucki in his study of one Silesian, John Licinius, feels that the Silesians as a group cannot be assigned a special role in the radicalization of the Polish Reformed Church. *Studia nad Arianizmem* (Warsaw, 1959), esp. 149 and n. 70, with the literature.

Dutch Anabaptists of the estuary of the Vistula, with his base in or near Danzig, much to the irritation of the guildsmen there and in other towns, who had long complained to the king that their town councils were tolerating these Anabaptist outlaws and economic competitors. The penetration of Polish society by Anabaptist ideas was recorded indignantly by Jacob Przyłuski in Cracow in 1553, when he deplored "the madness of the fanatics who make it a matter of doubt whether Christians may hold office or possess anything as property." A certain cobbler, Michael, was openly proclaiming Anabaptist teachings in Poznań in 1554. (Schwenckfeldians were in Danzig in 1555, while in the same year a number of bound copies of Schwenckfeld's books were received by King Sigismund in Cracow.) At the Prussian diet in 1556, Sigismund made known the widespread complaints that had reached him to the effect that many towns in Prussia against his express orders had not only tolerated Anabaptists, "Picardians" (Bohemian Brethren), and other heretics, but had even encouraged them.[7]

Then, momentously, at the Reformed synod of Secymin in (Ch. 25.1) January 1556, the Podlachian Peter of Goniądz (Gonesius), who as a student of Gribaldi in Padua and Tübingen had made the acquaintance of the works of Servetus and who on his way home had visited the Hutterites in Moravia, now spoke out, the first time on record in the Polish tongue, against the Trinity as formulated in the Nicene and Athanasian Creeds. Gonesius, with credentials from Prince Nicholas Radvila, had not yet fully stated his own anabaptist views, but he now went girt with the wooden sword of the Minor Party among the Unity and the Hutterites as a token of his pacifism.[8] The agitated colleagues of Gonesius insisted in synod that he travel to Wittenberg to be strengthened on the Nicene dogma, but he returned unconvinced and wrote a (no longer extant) book on the Trinity. At the joint synod of the Reformed and the *Unitas* at Pińczów in April 1556, Lismanino was instrumental in having Gonesius excluded as an Arian.

Although not recorded, Gonesius' baptismal theology must also have found ready supporters. In any event, the indignant Simon Zacius, superintendent of the conservative Reformed congregation in and about Vilnius, writing in 1557, indicates the rapid spread of Anabaptism and anti-Trinitarianism among several other heresies in both Poland and Lithuania:

[7] Szper, *op. cit.,* 66, 198.
[8] Actually, the first evidence of the wooden sword dates from 30 May 1566; Łaski's letter to Beza; Wotschke, *Briefwechsel,* No. 350, p. 271.

The Evil One swells so powerful his bagpipe—the Anabaptists, the Libertines, the Enthusiasts, the followers of Schwenckfeld, Servetus, and Gonesius, the neo-Arians—that he depresses by their deafening yelps the spirit of the many pious and virtuous Christians.[9]

The groups and individuals here pilloried are not mutually exclusive. Anabaptism and anti-Trinitarianism were beginning to fuse. About this time, several local synods moved to an antipedobaptist position. The synod of Włodzisław (between Kielce and Cracow) in September 1558, after condemning Gonesius with Servetus, and obliging their followers to repudiate them, went on to declare in alarm, lest the Anabaptists undermine the authority of the state: "We must beware the superstition of the Anabaptists, who do not even drive off a biting dog!"[10]

Then, at the Lithuanian synod of Brest-Litovsk, 15 December 1558, Peter Gonesius made clear the full extent of his anabaptist as well as his anti-Trinitarian convictions in reading from his (lost) *Libri contra paedobaptismum*.[11] During the synod, Jerome Piekarski, pastor of Biała, who with two others had been forced to conform at Włodzisław, sided again with Gonesius against the majority. Anne Kiszka, sister to Prince Radvila, temporarily set him up as pastor on the estate of the magnate of Kiszka at Węgrów. Servetian in his view of the Trinity, Gonesius was Servetian in his insistence on immersion but he combined it with a doctrine of predestination that reminds one of Renato (Ch. 22.1).

We have already suggested that the usage of the Russian Orthodox Church served to reinforce the immersionist conviction. A possible further factor contributing to the notable baptist sentiment in Poland and Lithuania may be traceable to the Bohemian Brethren with whom the Reformed Church was affiliated. Since the Bohemians had originally practiced the rebaptism of converts from Catholicism, although under Luther's influence (Ch. 9.1) they had allowed this peculiarity to lapse in 1534 (lest they be confused with the Münsterites), the memory of the older practice must have persisted among them and contributed in a general way to unsettling those in the Helvetic tradition on the question of pedobaptism. Moreover, the Minor Unity under Kalenec may still have continued the practice. At

---

[9] *Monumenta Reformationis Poloniae et Lithuaniae,* quoted by Kot in Becker, *Autour de Michel Servet,* 78, n. 19.

[10] Hermann Dalton, *Lasciana nebst den ältesten evangelischen Synodenprotokollen Polens 1555–1561* (Berlin, 1898), 463.

[11] Wiszowaty, *apud* Sandius, *op. cit.,* 211; John Stoiński, *ibid.,* 187; cf. Konrad Górski, "Humanizm i antytrynitaryzm," *Studia nad dziejami polskiej literatury antytrynitarskiej, XVI Wieku* (Cracow, 1949), 67–69.

the joint synods of Pińczów, 1556 and 1559, the *Unitas* ministers were specifically asked by their Polish colleagues about their practice of baptism with respect to those coming over "from the papacy" and to children presented to them for baptism by parents who remained Catholic. The Reformed ministers on the estates and in the villages and towns owned by Reform-minded gentry were willing to baptize the infants of serfs and others (and to solemnize their marriages) in lieu of the displaced priests of the old order, even though these infants would not be brought up Reformed by their stubbornly traditionalist parents. The *Unitas* ministers would baptize only the children of serfs who covenanted to bring them up as members of the Brethren.

Whatever the sources of the immersionist practice of the Polish and Lithuanian Brethren—whether Bohemian, Silesian, Servetian, or Ruthenian, or a combination of these—Gonesius for his part was insistent that rebaptism be an immersion, for he did not regard a pouring or a sprinkling as a true baptism. In outlining here his immersionist anabaptist theology, we must reach ahead to the fullest extant treatment, but there is no reason to suppose that his later views differed much from the convictions he espoused in 1558.[12]

People misunderstand the name "Christian," he says. The designation "Christian" does not derive indirectly from christening (*chrzest*) but directly from Christ. If there is an error made in such a simple matter, how much greater the error must be in the greater mysteries of theology! One becomes a Christian from being submerged or immersed with Christ, not from having had a little water sprinkled on the head in infancy.

Antichrist or the papacy purposely gave the equivocal name to the sacrament of infancy in order to mislead people into thinking they were Christians by a mere formality. When the Catholic priest or Reformed pastor repeats the ancient formula, "*Ego te baptizo*," he says, "I submerge you"; but actually he only pours water over the head and is therefore boldly lying. Whoever acts in this manner is not a minister of Christ, but a minister of Antichrist. Whoever adds or detracts from the word of God serves Satan. Those who are "baptized" according to Antichrist are clearly not baptized; by having introduced a new kind of baptism, the papists and the Protestants following them are the ana-baptists! The Orthodox Church is here more apos-

---

[12] The work upon which we draw is *O ponurzaniu chrystajańskim* (Węgrów, 1570). It is vol. iii of *Doctrina pura et clara de praecipuis Christianae religionis articulis* surviving in a unique copy in Paris. Parts ii and iii are reprinted in part by Szczucki in *Literatura Ariańska*, 259–273 and in full in *Biblioteka Pisarzy Reformacyjnych*, Nos. 2 and 3 (Warsaw, 1960–1961).

tolic in its practice. Those who are submerged, according to Christ's original ruling, should not be considered as being rebaptized, since they have not been hitherto baptized, that is, submerged.

It is nonsense to require baptism of children, since they cannot have faith. Gonesius quotes Tertullian: *"Fiunt, non nascuntur Christiani."*[13] God ordered only those who already had faith to be baptized. Moreover, since not all who are born are predestined to be spiritually reborn, it is all the more inappropriate that the words and signs of God should be fruitlessly given to infants. God grants his grace only to a certain number of predestined individuals, who at a given moment will feel called to submit to immersion as a seal of their faith and salvation. Any seal which does not certify a gift is useless. God would be giving a useless gift if he allowed his valid sacrament to be given to those who will reject his grace and salvation.

Such, in brief, is the baptismal theology of Gonesius, the Polish Servetian-Hutterite, pastor at Węgrów under the protection of a Lithuanian magnate.

On the estates of Kiszka's even more powerful brother-in-law Radvila, there were two other Reformed clerics, Martin Czechowic and Simon Budny.[14] Radvila had called Martin Czechowic to Lithuania in 1559 as a teacher in his new Reformed school at Vilnius; he was destined to play an increasingly important role in the Radical Reformation.

Czechowic was born c. 1532 of humble parents on the westernmost (Brandenburg-Silesian) border of the kingdom in Zbąszyn (Bentschen) between Międzyrzecz and Wschowa, which feature in Silesian Anabaptist history. (It is plausible to conjecture that Czechowic might have heard in his youth about Anabaptism of the Hutterite-Gabrielite type.) He had intended to enter the Catholic priesthood, but was converted to the Reformation at Leipzig in 1554. After his appearance as a Reformed pastor at the synod of Gołuchów in 1555, Prince Radvila called him to Vilnius. In 1561, Radvila made Czechowic his personal representative to carry out a survey of Swiss ecclesiastical institutions, and specifically to seek to reconcile Calvin and Blandrata, both of whom Radvila admired. It is probable that on his way back

---

[13] *Apologia,* xviii, 4.

[14] Stanislaw Kot, "Szymon Budny: Der grösste Häretiker Litauens im 16. Jahrhundert," *Wiener Archiv für Geschichte des Slaventums und Osteuropas,* II (1956); "La Réforme dans le Grand-Duché de Lithuanie: Facteur d'occidentalisation culturelle," *Annuaire de l'Institut de Philologie et d'Histoire Orientales et Slaves,* XII (1952), 201–261; "Ausbruch und Niedergang des Täufertums in Wilna, *ARG,* XLIX (1958), 212–226.

from his unsuccessful mission of reconciliation, Czechowic also visited the Hutterites in Moravia.

Simon Budny, born c. 1533, the son of a Masovian squire, was trained at Cracow in Biblical languages. Familiar with Russian and a master of Polish prose, he came to Kleck in the palatinate of Nowogródek in 1559 to teach and catechize on Sundays, Tuesdays, Fridays, and holidays, and to board in the house of Jacob Kurnicki. Radvila's design to win his numerous Eastern Orthodox serfs, lords, and clerics to Protestantism involved the closure of both Orthodox and Roman churches on his vast estates. He was gratified by the defection of a number of Orthodox monks. To further Radvila's plan, Budny almost immediately began publishing works in Byelo-Russian, the first of which[15] concerned the justification of the sinner before God, published in 1562. Although at this point he was still in line with orthodox Protestantism, in another Byelo-Russian book later that same year, *Katichisis,* he revealed his awareness of the problem of believers' baptism. He directed his attack, however, not at Latin but at Greek orthodoxy. In the Polish catechism he edited the next year, he stated that the Protestants had not yet begun to deal with the problem of the procession of the Holy Spirit. In the same year (1563), he broke with Reformed orthodoxy, primarily on the doctrine of the Trinity. But with Czechowic he would (later) move to immersionism, although he would never go so far in advocating the social radicalism of Gonesian Anabaptism.

By 1563 the Anabaptist sentiment had so far spread in Radvila's domain that Simon Zacius in indignation left Vilnius. Nicholas Wędrogowski, at the moment favorably disposed toward the anabaptist, anti-Nicene movement, replaced him. The appearance of the Brest Bible in Polish late in 1563 gave added impetus to the anabaptist movement by making it clear to large numbers of people just what the practice of the first disciples had been.[16]

It was in this revolutionary situation that George Witzel sounded the alarm. Born in Nuremberg, he had gone, as Andrew Osiander had (Ch. 25.3), to Königsberg but had been driven out in 1562 because of his sympathies for Melanchthon's eclecticism, and had found asylum in Vilnius. As a pensionary of Radvila, he had been given the opportunity to study in Basel and Zurich, and on his return vigorously attacked the local anti-Nicene Anabaptist leaders in two writings: *Necessaria consideratio . . . de confusa multitudine Vilnae . . . quam hypocritae Anabaptistae*

---

[15] *O opravdanii gresnago celoveka pered Bogom.* The work is lost.
[16] Wotschke, *Reformation,* 218 ff.

duo vel tres homines profani regunt tacite, addressed to the religiously conservative regency council established by Radvila shortly before his death; and *De confusionibus et scandalis,* alerting the Lithuanian magnates at large.[17] Witzel was enraged that the social and theological Radicals had the hardihood to promote their program from within the sumptuous sanctuary of the palatine palace which Radvila had turned over to them in Vilnius, unaware of the blasphemy and sedition they would soon be propagating!

Witzel's specific charges were that the new leaders had scant respect for the clerical office and formal theological training, that they were observing the Lord's Supper too infrequently, that they were fencing it with too many impertinent questions about the worthiness of the communicants, that in celebrating the Lord's Supper they so arranged the seating of the communicants that gentry and commoners were rubbing elbows in liturgical confusion (cf. Servetus on the Communion service, Ch. 11.4), that in encouraging all the communicants to address one another in and out of meeting as brethren in Christ they were destroying the fabric of society and disparaging the dignity and authority of the magistrates, that they were coming close to an insistence upon the manumission of serfs and the espousal of the community of goods, that they were destroying the structure of the liturgical year, and by eliminating the observance of feast days were incidentally making it difficult for magistrates to keep their court records and for readers of history to visualize the time of the year of past events, and finally, that in eliminating Christmas and Easter as special days in the liturgical year they were derogating from the significance of both the incarnation and the atonement.

By 1565, Vilnius was an Anabaptist center as much as Zurich or Augsburg had once been. On 6 January 1565, Czechowic had printed at Radvila's press in Nieśwież an annotated transcript of a three-day colloquy on pedobaptism in which he reflected the widespread disposition of the Lithuanian clergy to postpone the baptism of children at least until their seventh year. Prince Radvila could have tolerated this adjustment had it not been associated with the more radical social ideals pilloried by Witzel. Radvila's uneasiness about the movement he had been fostering among his clergy is evidenced in the character of the regents he appointed for his son and the executors of his will. They included his cousin Nicholas Radvila the Red, the Reformed bishop of Kiev, Nicholas Pac, and the Ruthenian Prince Con-

---

[17] The two sets of Latin articles against the Radicals of Vilnius are published and interpreted by Kot, "Ausbruch," *loc. cit.*

stantine Ostrogski. It was their coming into power immediately upon Radvila's death on 28 May 1565 that cut short the development of Lithuanian Anabaptism. We shall meet the refugees from Vilnius after this council assumed power of regency, as we resume the Anabaptist aspect of our narrative in Ch. 27.2. We now turn back to pick up the bypassed details of the anti-Nicene aspect of the movement.

3. Trinitarians and Anti-Trinitarians, 1556–1565

Peter Gonesius' synodal avowal of the Servetian view of the Trinity in 1556 might have remained an isolated episode in Poland had it not been for the tremendous controversy stirred up by Stancaro and Blandrata, both purporting to be defenders of the Trinity and both in the end to be denounced by Calvin. The devolution of the doctrine of the Trinity began in Poland in a spirited defense of the divinity of Christ in his role of mediator in the atonement. It was the Italian Stancaro who occasioned the controversy.

Before his founding of the Reformed Church in Pińczów, we were last with Stancaro as an associate of Laelius Socinus and Camillo Renato (Ch. 22.3.a) in the Valtellina in the fall of 1548. Stancaro next appeared in Transylvania, where he won favor with Isabella, the widow of King John Zápolya. Through her influence, in 1549, he was received at the court of her brother, King Sigismund II Augustus, and made professor of Hebrew at the University of Cracow by Bishop Maciejowski, who had no notion of Stancaro's theological idiosyncrasies. Within a short time, however, Stanislas Hosius, bishop of Chełmno, sent a disparaging report on his performance in Vienna. Stancaro's lectures on the psalms caused an uproar, in which, incidentally, Peter Gonesius, still at the time a student, had taken part against the Hebraist. Stancaro was deposed by the bishop and imprisoned in the episcopal palace.

Stancaro had favorably impressed certain Polish nobles, who managed after eight months to smuggle a rope ladder into his cell and effect his escape. He took refuge in Pińczów, and then, as we have already noted, persuaded the owner of the town to set up Reformed worship in 1550. To this end, Stancaro met informally with seven reforming pastors and discussed a reformed order of worship. Lord Oleśnicki's involvement brought criticism from the king and resulted in the temporary banishment by royal decree of Stancaro, who thereupon went to ducal Prussia. Under the patronage of Duke Albert of Prussia, Stancaro now became professor of Hebrew at the University of Königsberg.

Stancaro, a born controversialist, arrived at the moment when this new Lutheran university was engaged in controversy over justification and the doctrine of the atonement. Andrew Osiander, whom we last encountered in Nuremberg as a foe of John Denck (Ch. 7.1), had converted Duke Albert to Protestantism when the latter was in attendance at a diet in Nuremberg. Osiander diverged from the prevailing Lutheran view of justification in distinguishing the historic act of redemption, whereby Christ reconciled God to mankind by fulfilling the law and dying for mankind's aboriginal sin, and the ongoing experiential-*sanctificatory* justification whereby the eternal Word regenerates individual believers in a continuous infusion of his divine nature into the believer. According to Osiander, justification was not only a forensic imputation of the righteousness of Christ, the standard Lutheran position, but a palpable regeneration. The Christian was justified because of the justice of Christ dwelling in him by faith.[18] The divines of the Smalcald League Lutherans tended in their stress upon the individual appropriation of salvation by faith to blur the distinction between the historic atoning action and personal justification by faith. Irritated both by Osiander's mysticism and his vulgar violence in debate, they made things so hard for him in Nuremberg that he sought in 1549 protection from his ducal convert in Königsberg.

Duke Albert requested Stancaro to help settle the controversy. The new professor of Hebrew became involved in a debate so fierce that the disputants took to carrying firearms to the lecture hall.

Neither contestant realized the extent to which the controversy in Lutheran Prussia, with echoes in Geneva and in the heart of Germany, had implications for Christology and especially for the doctrine of the Trinity, which would have a lasting effect within the Reformed community in Little Poland. In brief, Osiander, perhaps under Schwenckfeldian influence, was so much concerned for a physical sanctification that he was prepared to involve the divine nature of Christ in the "atoning" action of justification.[19]

Osiander's physical justification resulted from his previously expressed view of man as created in the image of the eternal idea of the God-Man operative in the Old Testament theophanies

---

[18] *De unico mediatore Jesu Christo et justificatione fidei confessio* (Königsberg, 1551), discussed by Albrecht Ritschl, *Die christliche Lehre von der Rechtfertigung*, I (3d edition, Bonn, 1889), 236 ff.

[19] The medieval, deificatory mystical element is fully recognized by Marinus Johann Arntzen, *Mystieke Rechtvaardigingsleer: Een bijdrag ter beoordeling van de Theologie van Andreas Osiander* (Kampen, 1956).

and finally incarnate in Jesus.[20] This image of God the Son who from all eternity was destined to become man in Jesus Christ was, according to Osiander, also to be re-formed in supralapsarian perfection in every true believer in Christ. The effectual salvation of each man could, in fact, be realized only by the regenerative indwelling of the Son of God. Since objective salvation is appropriated personally when the eternal Word comes in the words of preaching and communicates the experience of forgiveness unto salvation, mediation is thus intimately tied up with the action of the indwelling *divine* Christ. Christ mediated historically in his humanity, but operates in his divinity as eternal Word, in the atoning mediation of regenerative justification.

In opposition to Osiander, Stancaro asserted, on the scholastic authority of Peter Lombard and Anselm, that Christ was mediator only according to his human nature. Far away in Geneva, Calvin, preparing the definitive Latin edition of the *Institutes* (II. xiv), likewise opposed Osiander's confusion of righteousness and sanctification (I Cor. 1:30); *but like* Osiander, Calvin had his own antischolastic conviction as to the involvement of the two natures of the Mediator, which he would presently explain to his Polish followers in their impending debate with Stancaro. Meanwhile, Stancaro, after wandering in Germany and stopping briefly in Poland, went on to promote his idea among the Reformed in Transylvania (Ch. 28.1).

In May of 1559, however, Stancaro returned for his third visit to Poland. He had met Andreas Musculus at Frankfort on the Oder, and there Musculus had argued that Christ, mediator both as God and as man, not only effects justification by virtue of his divine nature (with Osiander) but also that he has effected the historic atonement in the same way and thus that Christ had died as God. Stancaro now argued further that only on his terms could one avoid the subordination of the eternal Son of God to God the Father. It was not Christ in his Godhead who mediated with the Godhead of the Father, for a mediator is inferior to him with whom he intercedes.

To safeguard the orthodox conception of the impassibility of the Godhead, Stancaro was so insistent on the exclusion of Christ's divine nature from the propitiatory action that he unwittingly involved his opponents in defending the divine role in the atonement even at the risk of subordinating the divinity of the mediatorial Son to that of the appeased Father and therewith dissolving the Nicene formula.

[20] *An filius Dei fuerit incarnandus . . . de imagine Dei quid sit* (Königsberg, 1550).

Stancaro, in his implicit modalism, called forth in Poland tritheism, a brief phase or episode in the devolution of the doctrine of the Trinity within the Polish Reformed community. In this tritheism, God the Son was inferior to God the Father. Stancaro wrote in consternation to Calvin, assuming that Geneva was on his side, and described the Polish "Calvinist" tritheists, actually, of course, spiritual kinsmen of Gribaldi and Gentile:

The Arians here teach that the Father, the Son, and Holy Spirit are not one God but three Gods in such a way that they are separate from each other as three men are separate and that these three Gods are three substances, three wills, and three separate operations.[21]

Settling at Pińczów, Stancaro published a bitter ten-page pamphlet against Melanchthon (who died that year, 1560, long a favorite among the Polish Reformed clergy because of his eclecticism), calling him the "Arius of the North," and charging him and the Polish Calvinists with subordinating the eternal Son to the Father. This *Summarium doctrinae Arii et Melanchthonis* enraged not only Łaski and Christopher Tretius (founder of Cracow's Reformed school) but also such incipient anti-Nicenes as Gregory Paul, Martin Krowicki, Stanislas Lutomirski, and George Schomann.[22] To defend themselves against the charge of Arian subordinationism, the Polish Calvinists in their turn charged Stancaro with Sabellian modalism. They burned all the copies of his pamphlet they could find and took his printer to task. Stancaro fulminated.

Of the aforementioned incipient anti-Nicenes, one stands out above all the rest, Gregory Paul (1526–1591). Soon to become an advocate of millennialism, immersionism, and communism, as well as of outright unitarianism, Gregory Paul was at this point in our narrative the Reformed pastor of Cracow, ministering to more than a thousand communicants. Born in Brzeziny, Gregory Paul (Paweł) had earlier earned his master's degree in Cracow. Thence he had gone for further study to Königsberg and then to Wittenberg (1549). After serving as pastor in Poznań, he returned in 1551 to his native town as Reformed pastor. After defending himself against the archbishop of Gniezno and defending the Reformation itself against his expropriating patron bent primarily upon private gain, Gregory Paul went once again to Königsberg and then resumed pastoral duties in a small manorial church. It was while so engaged that the synod of Secymin in 1556, it will be recalled,

---

[21] On 4 December 1560; Wotschke, *Briefwechsel*, No. 208; Calvin, *Opera*, XVIII, No. 3288, coll. 260 f. See Stanislas von Dunin-Borkowski "Die Gruppierung der Antitrinitarier im XVI. Jahrhundert," *Scholastik*, VII (1932), 493 f.

[22] Wotschke, *Reformation*, 179 f.

elected him as one of the three coadjutor pastors of the Reformed Church of Little Poland. It was in 1558, promoted by his patron General Stanislas Cikowski, that he returned to Cracow, this time as its first Protestant pastor.

At the synod of Pińczów, August 1559, called to deal with Stancaro after his attack on Melanchthon, Stancaro managed to provoke a shouting disputation, despite the law forbidding religious debates except by royal permission. Under the direction of Łaski and Lismanino, the controversy was so heated that Łaski threw a heavy Bible at Stancaro's head, failing in his rage even then to impress the Word of God on the disagreeable, loquacious, but technically the more orthodox theologian.[23] Stancaro refused to submit a confession of faith, but presented some of his polemical tracts. The synod excommunicated him, and decreed that any pastor following him should be deprived of his office. Lismanino wrote to all the churches of Great Poland, Lithuania, Masovia, and Prussia, sending Stancaro's tract and describing his behavior. In consequence, most of his supporters among the clergy and gentry abandoned him. Lord Stanislas Studnicki of Nieświcż and Dubiecko, however, resisted the importunities of his pastor in Nieświcż, Stanislas Sarnicki, and gave Stancaro his protection. Sarnicki, himself of noble birth, hoped to advance in the Reformed Church by means of his zeal against the perverters of pure doctrine.

Stancaro's oratorical talent, his deluge of words, and his cascade of dialectical brilliance always made an impression. He could have successfully defended even an absurd cause; in fact, however, on the doctrine of the atonement and the Trinity he was nearer Augustine, Anselm, and Peter Lombard than Calvin or any of his Polish opponents. It was exceedingly difficult for them to oppose him when he seemed always to convict them of the heresy of Arianism. His allegations were not unfounded. How far to the anti-Nicene left at least one participant in the Pińczów synod was by 1559 can be seen from George Schomann's later *Testamentum:*

There [at Pińczów] I clearly recognized that the full equality of the persons of the Trinity is not a Christian dogma of faith, but rather an error: there is one God-Father, one Son of God, and one Holy Spirit.[24]

The behavior of Stancaro at Pińczów convinced Łaski, Lismanino, and Cruciger of the necessity of opposing him with every means at their disposal. Late in 1559, they published a series of

[23] Francesco Ruffini, *Studi,* 214.
[24] Sandius, *Bibliotheca Antitrinitariorum,* 193.

letters, as well as a confession, designed to confute him. This was Łaski's last effort, for he died on 8 January 1560 (the same year as Melanchthon). A macabre note was struck when Stancaro's Pińczów supporter, Gregory Orsatius, declared that the dead Łaski's lips had grown together as a sign that God wanted his mouth stopped. The casket was opened in order to disprove the charge. Calvin and Bullinger at their distance had little enthusiasm or understanding for the struggle. "Our Polish brothers," Bullinger complained, "are very wondrous and burdensome."

The Poles, indeed, were toughened fighters. Sarnicki and John Karniński hastened to Chełmno and persuaded the synod at Bychawa on 24 April 1560 to condemn Stancaro. In Little Poland similar steps were urged at Pińczów (5 May) and Włodzisław (28 May), in the presence of delegates from Lithuania. But at those two places, Stancaro received powerful support from the national-reformed Catholic Erasmian and royal secretary, Andrew Frycz Modrzewski,[25] who was about to publish *De mediatore* and who, though sharing Stancaro's Anselmian view, urged the synods to preserve at least the appearance of harmony. Stancaro's violence would allow no peace, however, and he was again condemned. Orsatius was deposed for continuing to support him, and in retaliation Lord Studnicki ejected Sarnicki from his pastorate at Nieświcz.

It was George Blandrata who turned the confusion occasioned by the Stancaro controversy into inchoate unitarianism by suggesting that Stancaro could be defeated best by abandoning the exotic philosophical vocabulary of the scholastics and reverting to the simple language of the Bible, especially Matt. 28:19 and the Apostles' Creed, with the Father and the Son and the Holy Spirit as three divine beings. In this way he was provisionally a spokesman of tritheism as orthodox because apostolic.[26]

Before long the opponents of Stancaro would be called Blandratists. Blandrata's pre-eminence in the emergence of the Minor Church, theologically and organizationally, requires that we pause to reintroduce him at this juncture. We were last with him in Ch. 24.2.d when he left the Italian congregation of Geneva to avoid further altercations with Calvin. In the meantime he has

[25] The *Opera Omnia* have been edited by Kasimir Kumaniecki, in 5 volumes (Warsaw, 1953–1955). His role in the rise of Arianism has been most recently recounted by Konrad Górski, "The Evolution of the Religious Views of Frycz Modrzewski," *Studia nad Arianizmem,* edited by Ludwik Chmaj (Warsaw, 1959), 9–47, summarized in English, 533 f.

[26] The significance of Blandrata at this juncture has been analyzed by Konrad Górski, "Humanizm i antytrynitaryzm," 70.

been a second time in Poland, arriving in the same year as Laelius Socinus, 1558, has gone to Transylvania (Ch. 28.1) to serve Queen Isabelle in her last illness and received Calvin's *Responsum* (1558), and has now returned to Poland for the third time.

He attended the synod of Książ in September 1560 and was at once recognized as an illustrious personage of tremendous vitality and great devotion to the radical reformation of Christianity. In the course of the deliberation on the polity of the Reformed Church, Blandrata expressed himself vigorously in an effort to distinguish the duties of the ministers as pastors and teachers from the office of the lay elders, and would have confined the government of the churches solely to the latter. He expressed at Książ the fear, no doubt intensified by his observations in Geneva, that the Reformed ministers, unless checked, might "wish to dominate us as once the Pope through his bishops," adding that for their own good "the ministers of the word should not be implicated in political matters." The synod rejected his proposal, however, and it was the high chamberlain of Cracow, Stanislas Cikowski, who pointed out that the elders had great need of the ministers in their deliberations.[27] The same synod, in a move to harmonize the ministers and the magnates, elected Blandrata as lay coadjutor to superintendent Cruciger to supplement the services of Lismanino, who was having difficulty functioning publicly because of the royal disfavor.

A major task at Książ was again the condemnation of Stancaro. To this end Calvin's *Responsum ad Fratres Polonos quo-Mediator sit Christus* was read. In it, as in his just completed definitive edition of the *Institutes* (cf. II. xiv. 3, 6), Calvin declared that "by the decree of the Father" Christ is "Mediator from the beginning of creation" "with regard to his deity" "unto eternity."[27] This was almost enough to condemn Stancaro; but Lord Jerome Ossoliński led a protest, insisting on silence for four months, pending further word from Calvin and other arbiters. It would have been helpful if at this juncture someone could have risen to explain clearly the difference between mediation in creation (the concern of Arius), mediation in atonement (the concern of Calvin and his Polish would-be followers), and mediation in regenerative or essential justification (the concern of Osiander and the most radical among the Polish Reformed).

---

[27] The *Responsum* is in *Opera,* IX, coll. 333–342; that earlier to Blandrata, in which Calvin speaks of Jehovah as a name common to the Son no less than the Father, *ibid.,* coll. 321–332; cf. echoes of the Polish controversy, *Institutes,* I. xiii. 3 and II. xiv, esp. in *LCC,* XX, p. 485 at n. 7; for the *novum* in Calvin, see Koopmans, *op. cit.,* 86.

The temporary truce allowed the Swiss correspondence to be resumed, while a synod at Pińczów in January 1561 gave a definitive form to the Reformed Church of Little Poland, now subdivided into five districts, each under one clerical coadjutor and several lay *seniores*. The former, charged exclusively with the right, elected as the new superintendent of all the pastors the illustrious former priest Stanislas Lutomirski.

In the meantime, Blandrata, for his part still stressing the ethical aspects of Christianity, avoided whenever possible the vexing theological and Christological problems. His evangelical, disciplined, irenic rationalism was well expressed in his letter of 19 September 1561, written in his capacity as physician and as coadjutor of the Reformed churches of Little Poland meeting in synod at Cracow, and addressed to confreres in Lublin.[28] It is filled with concern for practical Christianity and organization. Nevertheless, he and Gentile, who had gone to Lithuania, were being denounced to Calvin by Sarnicki for their attempt to cope with Stancaro by "paganly introducing the plurality of gods."[29]

For a time, Stancaro belligerently maintained his position as virtually the only authentic Nicene Calvinist in Poland, insisting that the letters favorable to the Poles from Calvin, Bullinger, and Peter Martyr Vermigli were forgeries. Finally, Stancaro "realized" that even Calvin and Bullinger were "Arians"; and in 1562, in *Contra i ministri di Ginevra e di Zurigo,* he ejaculated:

Peter Lombard alone is worth more than a hundred Luthers, two hundred Melanchthons, three hundred Bullingers, four hundred Peter Martyrs, and five hundred Calvins, and all of them ground in a mortar with a pestle would not amount to an ounce of true theology.[30]

To repeat, the significance for the history of the Radical Reformation of Stancaro's controversy, first with Osiander and Musculus and then with Łaski and Blandrata over the mediation of Christ, lies in the fact that some would-be orthodox Polish Calvinists were forced into a provisional tritheism to defend Christ's *divine* mediation in redemption against Stancaro's modalism and to parry the charge against them of Arianism, while others, along with programmatically anti-Nicene churchmen such as Blandrata and George Schomann, were pleased to carry the devolution to

---

[28] Stanisław Zachorowski, "Najstarsze synody Arjan Polskich," *Reformacja w Polsce,* I (1922), 214 f.

[29] Letter of 1 September 1561; Wotschke, *Briefwechsel,* No. 226; Calvin, *Opera,* XVIII, No. 3506.

[30] Against *Ad nobiles Polonos,* ibid., IX, 345; Cantù, *Eretici,* II, 500.

another stage. Calvin himself recognized the danger, and would presently warn his Polish followers of the implications of their unorthodox defense of orthodoxy in *Brevis admonitio ad fratres Polonos*.[31] Of one Blandratist, Gregory Paul in Cracow, Calvin wrote that "in order to avoid the absurdity of Stancaro [he] falls into the more fetid error of tritheism," promoted "by that imposter Blandrata."

Although coupled by Calvin with Stancaro as equally aberrant,[32] Blandrata was able now to clear himself in a succession of synods, notably at Książ in March 1562, which accepted his confession of faith as orthodox, even though it was limited to the language of the Bible and the Apostles' Creed,[33] and yet sought at the same time to appease Calvin. At a synod in Pińczów the next month, the problem was discussed again. Lismanino and Blandrata agreed again to rule out nonscriptural terminology in order to cope with Stancaro and preserve the peace of the Reformed Church.[34] Blandrata had thus succeeded in establishing, among local Calvinists, against distant Calvin, the momentous principle that Scriptural language with that of the Apostles' Creed was adequate for the expression of all necessary theological truth. The disintegration of the Nicene formulation had received synodal sanction.

Calvinist-Nicene orthodoxy had, of course, its vigorous and informed indigenous defenders, despite the action of the synod of Pińczów in the crucial spring of 1562. With Łaski dead (1560) and Lismanino softened up, Christopher Tretius and Stanislas Sarnicki remained the most determined spokesmen for orthodox Calvinism. Sarnicki, an elder without a position since his expulsion from Nieświcz, was ambitious for ecclesiastical advancement in Cracow and for recognition abroad as a stout defender of Helvetic orthodoxy. He hoped, by exposing Gregory Paul as heretical, to be able to replace him as pastor of the Reformed Church in suburban Cracow, under the protection of the governor of the castle. As early as 1561, in letters to Calvin, he had picked Gregory Paul along with Blandrata and Lismanino as targets for vituperative attacks. It was while Blandrata was involved in "clearing" himself from Sarnicki's charges of anti-Trini-

---

[31] Letter of 16 January 1563; Wotschke, *Briefwechsel*, No. 266; Calvin, *Opera*, IX, coll. 633 f.

[32] *Opera*, XVIII, col. 158.

[33] Text edited by H. P. C. Henke as *Georgii Blandratae Confessio Antitrinitaria* (Helmstadt, 1794).

[34] Zachorowski, "Najstarsze synody," *loc. cit.*, 213 and 216.

tarianism that Sarnicki visited Italy, there to enlist at Padua the services of Tretius against the Radicals within the Polish Helvetic Church.[35]

At a gathering in July 1562 at Rogów in the manor house of the former Italian, Prosper Provana, who had become naturalized as a member of the Polish gentry, on his estate between Cracow and Pińczów, the problem of the Trinity was debated with a view to reconciling Sarnicki and Gregory Paul. In the course of the discussion the problem of the Trinity was intensified by the receipt from Moravia of some twenty propositions originally prepared by one Darius Socinus, in association with the Venetian refugee Nicholas Paruta (Ch. 29.5). These were disseminated in the area by Provana's steward,[36] who took the liberty of copying the propositions, which in due course came to the attention of the receptive Stanislas Lutomirski, cosuperintendent of the Reformed Church in Little Poland.

A general synod of the Reformed Church was an urgent necessity. In anticipation, a lesser synod was called at Balice, 12 August 1562,[37] in order, if possible, to reconcile Sarnicki and Gregory Paul, the latter being the clerical "standard bearer" of the Blandratists. The twenty propositions of Paruta at Rogów no doubt reappear in the twelve articles of the Blandratists at Balice, set forth hostilely, but no doubt accurately, by Sarnicki (who attended) in a letter to Tretius.

It is clear that the Blandratists or, with equal propriety, the Gregory-Paulinists, opposed what they called Stancaro's (Sabellian) *Deus conflatus,* his *Deus Turcicus sine filio.* The Blandratists held further that wherever God is spoken of in the Bible without further qualification, it is of God the Father and Creator. The Son was God, but a lesser God than the Father, precisely because he was a mediator in his divine nature no less than in his human nature and could not have discharged this office if he had been in his deity equal to him with whom he interceded.

To insist upon their orthodoxy in making a soteriologically adequate distinction between both the role and the divine rank of the Father and the Son, the Blandratists resorted to the Greek Nicene formulation, which distinguishes among the intradeical functions in postulating the procession of the Spirit *from* the

---

[35] Wotschke, *Briefwechsel,* No. 201.

[36] The later Socinian historian Stanislas Budziński.

[37] Zachorowski, "Najstarsze synody," *loc cit.,* 217 f.; described by Sarnicki to Tretius; Wotschke, *Briefwechsel,* No. 260; Calvin, *Opera,* XIX, No. 3875; Marek Wajsblum, "Dyteiści małopolscy," *Reformacja w Polsce,* V (1928), 39–42.

primordial Father *through* the generated Son. Soon after the meeting, George Schomann, pastor at Pińczów, came out in Cracow in open support of Blandrata and Gregory Paul, going even further, however, in rejecting as papist the words "Trinity," "Person," and "essence."

At the general synod in Pińczów in August, called because of the growing antagonism between Sarnicki and Gregory Paul, the two men fought out their differences, the one resorting to the creedal terminology of the ecumenical councils, the other confining himself to the language of Scripture and the Apostles' Creed. The synod unanimously upheld the agreement (*scheda*) [38] of the synod in the same place (Pińczów) that April to refrain from the use of traditional theological language in referring to the Trinity. At the same time, in communicating their common faith briefly to the churches in Switzerland[39] and Strassburg,[40] they nevertheless, inconsistently or prudentially, found occasion to use in fact creedal language. Condemning Servetus, Arius, Stancaro, and Sabellius alike, the Pinczovians declared that they did not confuse the Three, as did Stancaro and before him Sabellius, and at the same time they abhorred "a plurality of Gods"; and, upholding "the unity of the divine *natura*," they even described "the Son as *homoousios*" with the Father. The letters were signed by, among others, Gregory Paul and Lutomirski.

The Radicals were now commonly referred to not only as Blandratists but also as Pinczovians. The pastor of the Italians congregated in Pińczów was George Negri, son of Francis Negri, the friend of Renato in Chiavenna. Here in Pińczów the first non-Catholic press in Poland had been established (1558). Here the naturalized Frenchman Peter Statorius[41] directed the already mentioned (Ch. 25.2) first Protestant translation of the Bible into Polish. The unstable situation in Pińczów was now being complicated by Alciati and Gentile, with whose arrival in 1562 we began this chapter. Neither of them, after their rough encounter with Calvin, hesitated to declare their beliefs publicly.

During this time, Sarnicki took every opportunity to divide the Reformed parish in Cracow ministered to by Gregory Paul. He found support among prominent citizens, and the governor of the castle, John Bonar, took alarm at the charge that he was protecting heresy. He found Gregory Paul adamant in his views

---

[38] Referred to in the letter of Sarnicki to Tretius, *loc. cit.*, col. 574.
[39] On 18 August 1562; Wotschke, *Briefwechsel*, No. 254.
[40] *Ibid.*, No. 255.
[41] Pierre Pfoertner of Thionville in Lorraine. He eventually Polonized his name as Stoiński.

and withdrew the use of his house for Paul's meetings. In order to reconcile the factions, Bonar called the clergy together on two occasions.

Lismanino was horrified at the interpretation being given his own views on the Trinity and sought to muzzle the tritheists with a fully orthodox confession. This measure was futile; for, although the Nicene confession, which Lismanino drew up for the synod at Cracow, was accepted on 20 August, it did not really represent the view of the majority, even at this opposition synod.[42] One of them, Superintendent Stanislas Paclesius (Paklepka) of Lublin wrote to his old teacher Peter Martyr Vermigli, complaining bitterly of Stancaro's *confusus Deus,* and warning, "If you keep silent, the stones will speak."[43]

A few weeks later John Bonar suddenly died (17 September), and his funeral became the occasion for an "opposition synod" of the orthodox, i.e., Genevan-Nicene ministers and gentry, at Cracow, on 16 October 1562.[44] Although the assembly affirmed the conciliar creeds and the XV Articles imposed by the Zurich church on resident Italians, amplified by parts of the confession of Łaski's London congregation, Beza's Geneva confession, and some lines from the Pińczów confession against Stancaro, they were careful not to condemn by name any of their former colleagues. Except for Servetus, Gonesius, and Stancaro, only the Italian tritheists Gribaldi, Gentile, and Alciati were mentioned by name.[45]

Despite Sarnicki's efforts, the Radicals maintained their advantage. Within his own residence in Cracow, General Stanislas Cikowski arranged for Gregory Paul a new place to preach. The dauntless Sarnicki had his orthodox confession printed and distributed from house to house and sold before the doors of Gregory Paul's new place of meeting. In November 1562, Gregory Paul published his *Tabula de Trinitate* against Stancaro. Although this important document has been lost, we do have the author's own summary, in a letter written to the magistrates of Zurich in indignant repudiation of their charge of Arianism.

Gregory Paul agreed with the purpose of the Nicene Creed, which was to vindicate the deity of Christ as the only-begotten Son of God. He wished, however, to vindicate also the personality

---

[42] Wotschke, *Reformation,* 20 f.
[43] Pińczów, 18 August 1562; Wotschke, *Briefwechsel,* No. 253.
[44] Wotschke, *Reformation,* 203. See also Roman Żelewski, "Troubles confessionnels à Cracovie ... 1551–1573," *ORP,* VI (1961), 91–111.
[45] *Ibid.*

and mediatorial function of the divine Christ, even if he had to go beyond the Nicene formulation in terms that could make sufficiently explicit not only Christ's filial but also his mediatorial relationship to God the Father: "There is the God who begets and there is the God who is begotten and *mediates* and is made man." Gregory Paul appealed to the scene at Jordan: "This day have I begotten thee." It was no abstract *deitas* that generated an abstract *deitatem,* but rather a personal *Deus Pater* who generated a *deum filium,* a mediatorial Son: "There is one deity (*deitas*) of the Three, but there is no one God in three." Gregory Paul insisted: "The three are of one nature or divinity, but these three are never *unus,* but three." Sabellian Stancaro, he said, had no mediator, because he denied the generation of the mediator, or had a fictitious incarnation of his one God. Stancaro subverted the adequacy of the atonement by having in effect merely three phases of God or three names, without three distinguishable functions:

This one God of the sophists, unknown to all—alike to the prophets, Christ, and the apostles—which is called an essence and is said to be triune, never begat or had a Son, and hence no mediator either. He did not create us or redeem us.[46]

Stancaro, Gregory Paul said, was no better than the papacy, which had various gods and mediators, "but among them not one is that God, nor that mediator, the Son of God, the Word made flesh." Whether the mediating Son made flesh was *coeternal* with the Father or merely premundane (as with Arius), Gregory Paul did not say.

The publication of the *Tabula* enabled Sarnicki to demonstrate anew to orthodox Calvinists at home and especially abroad the unsoundness of Gregory Paul's doctrine, and with him the whole Blandratist or Pinczovian faction. Both parties sought influential support. The Radicals succeeded in winning judge John Niemojewski, while the ferocious Sarnicki denounced his former brethren as tritheists and therefore pagans, who should be executed according to Ladislas Jagiello's law of 1424. By this, he wanted the king to turn the ancient law, which the pope had urged in vain against the Reformers, upon his former comrades in reform. Since Sarnicki and his followers were in the minority among the ministers and gentry, it is possible that his vigorous attack was the only way to avoid complete submersion. Sarnicki called an irregular synod in Cracow of the conservatives, intended

46 Wotschke, *Briefwechsel,* No. 297.

to be secret; but it was known to, and resented by, the Pinc-zovians.[47] In reporting to the Swiss, the conservatives pointed out that although the Blandratists were willing to use traditional language and would never acknowledge themselves to be tritheists, nevertheless when they said the three are one, they meant *unum* and not *unus*, unanimous not consubstantial.[48] Under the leadership of Lutomirski, a synod in June 1563 at Mordy in Podlachia under Prince Radvila's protection confirmed the Pinczovian position, despite the protests of Sarnicki.[49]

The Lithuanian Brethren, under the clerical leadership of Martin Czechowic and Simon Budny, had, as noted above, also begun to deal with the question of the procession of the Holy Spirit, and, under the influence of adjacent Russian Orthodoxy, to reject the filioque in the Western Nicene Creed.[50] Prince Nicholas Radvila attempted to unify the anti-Nicene Pinczovians and the Nicene Calvinists at a Communion service at Warsaw at Christmas 1563, intended to symbolize a reconciliation between the factions.[51] The more belligerent gentry on both sides, when Sarnicki's sermon aroused partisanship, were scarcely restrained from drawing swords at this melancholy love feast.

Back in Lithuania, Czechowic, after his return from Switzerland, was completely identified with the anti-Nicene cause, and it was no doubt his pen that prepared the long letter of Radvila of July 1564, urging Calvin to espouse the tritheistic solution against Stancaro the Sabellian. Czechowic, in the name of Radvila, charged that Stancaro had eliminated the divine mediator and his benefits. At the same time, Czechowic insisted that the Poles and Lithuanians were opposed to Arius, who denied that the Son of God, incarnate as Christ, was from the substance of God the Father.[52] Like Servetus, they held, no doubt, that Christ, the only-begotten Son of God, drew his substance not only from Mary but from the Father, and they were, with a procreative realism that was alien to the philosophically disciplined Nicene fathers themselves, quite earnest when they avowed their willingness to use consubstantial or *homoousios* in the procreative sense.

Czechowic's letter is of great interest in documenting the way in which the Greek Orthodox formulation of the Trinity helped the

[47] *Ibid.*, No. 294; *Reformation,* 206.
[48] Letter of Alexander Vitrelin to Bullinger, 24 June 1563; Wotschke, *Brief-wechsel,* No. 294.
[49] *Ibid.*
[50] *Ibid.*, No. 310.
[51] *Ibid.*
[52] *Ibid.;* Calvin, *Opera,* XX, No. 4125. The surmise that the letter was composed by Czechowic is that of Szczucki, *Literatura Ariańska,* 632.

proto-Unitarians in opposing what they scorned as the papal distortion of the original Nicene intention through the addition of the filioque, and therewith the obliteration of all effectual distinctions among the Persons, and the conversion of the Trinity into a quaternity by distinguishing the common *deitas* (i.e., *substantia*) from the three Persons. Czechowic, writing for Radvila, quoted from the Roman liturgy and prayer books of various kinds to show that the Latin Church was liturgically guilty of Patripassianism. He found support for the clear distinction between three divine beings, only one of whom was incarnate in Jesus, not only in the Bible but also in the *Adversus Arianos* of Hilary of Poitiers.[53]

The letter also describes the fierce fighting among the Reformed churchmen which imperiled the united Protestant cause in Poland and the grand duchy, and concludes with the *scheda* of Pińczów enjoining all parties to avoid philosophical and "papistical" terminology. At about this time a Polish translation of Justin Martyr's *Dialogue with Trypho* was published in Nieśwież in support of the subordinationist Trinitarianism of Czechowic and Budny.

It was clearly not possible that the Polish–Lithuanian Reformed churches should continue to embrace much longer the diverse doctrinal tendencies represented by George Blandrata, Gregory Paul, Martin Czechowic, and George Schomann on the one hand, and, on the other, those of the strict Nicene Calvinists; but by the summer of 1564, the Polish anti-Trinitarian and antipedobaptist movements within the Helvetic churches were temporarily checked. Under the guidance of Sarnicki and Tretius, a strict Calvinist reaction was growing, culminating in the expulsion of foreign Catholic apostates from Poland by the edict of Parczów, 7 August 1564. The edict, favored by the Nicene Calvinists, was formulated by spokesmen of the mounting Catholic reaction to the whole Reformation and received impetus from the king's alarm at the anti-Trinitarian and anabaptist ferment.

Among those who left the country as a direct consequence of the edict of expulsion were Alciati, Gentile, Negri, and Ochino. (The fate of these and others of the Italian diaspora will be brought together in Ch. 29.5.) The more radical wing thus suffered a tremendous loss in leadership. Blandrata had already been called again to Transylvania in 1563, where we shall have occasion, in Ch. 28, to pursue further his controversial career. Prince Nicholas Radvila died in 1565, obliging Czechowic and several others to leave; for the chancellor's son was an ardent Catholic,

53 Calvin, *Opera,* XX, col. 334.

and his regency council was well alerted to the radical character of the Reformers of Vilnius and Nieśwież (Ch. 25.2).

With the expulsion of the anti-Trinitarian foreigners from Poland and the flight of the Radicals from Vilnius, the conservatives now hoped to effect a reunion of the indigenous Reformed factions before the decrees of the Council of Trent should be presented to the next meeting of the diet. A major debate was therefore held at Piotrków in March 1565.[54] On the one side stood the anti-Trinitarian antipedobaptist Radicals, and on the other the Trinitarian pedobaptists led by Sarnicki and Tretius, pastor and teacher respectively at Cracow. Among the Radicals were Superintendent Stanislas Lutomirski; Gregory Paul, pastor of the radical congregation of Cracow; George Schomann, pastor in Lublin; John Niemojewski, judge of Inowrocław; John Lutomirski, castellan of Sieradz; Jerome Filipowski, treasurer of the palatinate of Cracow; and Marshal Nicholas Sienicki, speaker of the Chamber of Deputies. The disputants on either side defended their respective positions by appeal to the authority of the Scriptures, the early church fathers, and Christian history. Gradually, the exchanges became so heated that the strict Calvinist representatives broke off, refusing to participate further. Thus the breach that opened at Cracow in 1562 was hopelessly widened at Piotrków in 1565. The hope that reunion might somehow be effected through the compromise efforts of Modrzewski, author of the *Sylvae,* was doomed to disappointment.

This monumental posthumous work (first three parts finished in 1565) on the Trinitarian controversy is an invaluable source of information. Modrzewski admirably summarizes the development to date. He sets forth the Pinczovian view that the Godhead does not exist in itself, but only in the Father, Son, and Holy Spirit separately. The Pinczovians deny that the three Persons can be *unus,* but avow that they can be *unum.* The Three are monarchically but not ontologically one in *natura, deitas, potestas, amor,* and *concordia.* Modrzewski shows the ease with which the reasoning of the tritheists had been utilized by those who were pointing toward a distinctly unitarian theology. He preserves the following summary of the Pinczovian doctrine:

Jesus Christ, the son of God and of man, at once God and our Lord, has been born once and for all: the same [birth] was on earth from Mary the Virgin, neither did anything of his exist before he was born of her. For as God is one, without any beginning and end, of all things the cause and the beginning, thus was his only Son born of the Virgin, at the time designated by the Father, for indeed he is begotten

[54] Zachorowski, "Najstarsze synody," *loc. cit.,* 222.

once for all, and besides this one the Father has no other. For he does not have a duplex nature (*naturam duplicem*) but only the one which he derived from the Virgin, through the agency of the Holy Spirit.[55]

With this incipiently unitarian theology the two branches of the Reformed Church were definitively sundered. The radical anti-Trinitarian, antipedobaptist faction were first known as "the brethren in Poland and Lithuania who have rejected the Trinity."[56] While their Protestant and Catholic foes called them "Arians," they preferred the designation "Christians." The official title, however, was the Minor Reformed Church of Poland.

Before pursuing the history of the Minor Church, we must look to Moravia, whence the Hutterites had already begun to exercise an influence on the Polish Brethren.

[55] *Sylvae,* Book III, ch. 1, 158 ff., cited in Dunin-Borkowski, "Untersuchungen," *75 Jahre Stella Matutina, Festschrift,* II, 120. There is a useful survey of the recent literature on Modrzewski (c. 1503–1572) by Gottfried Schramm, "Modrevius-Forschungen," *Jahrbücher für Geschichte Osteuropas,* VI (1958), 352–373.

[56] At the synod in Brzeziny, 10 June 1565; Zachorowski, "Najstarsze synody," *loc. cit.,* 229.

CHAPTER 26

THE HUTTERITES IN MORAVIA, 1542–1578

As we return to Moravia, crossroads and asylum for the way-farers of the Radical Reformation, we are prepared to examine the consolidation of the most resolute and exclusivistic of the Ana-baptist groups, the communitarian Hutterites under Leonard Lanzenstiel (1542–1565) and Peter Walpot (1565–1578). We shall also have occasion to note several overtures of other radical churches, notably the Polish Brethren, the Italian Anabaptists, certain Paulicians, and the Germans of the Marpeck circle and their hopes of entering into communion with the Hutterites and forming an international federation of apostolic churches.

1. The Coepiscopate of Lanzenstiel and Riedemann, 1542–1556/1565

The death of Ulrich Stadler, bishop of the community in Bucovic to the east of Austerlitz, in 1540 deprived the Moravian Hutterites of one of their best theological thinkers. Two years later, early in February of 1542, the chief bishop of all the brethren in Moravia, John Amon, died at Schäkowitz, having nominated Leonard Lanzenstiel as his successor in the leadership of the whole brotherhood.

Lanzenstiel, often called Seiler from his work as ropemaker, was never to write a great theological or expository work. The *Chronicle* calls him "a pious pastor, gifted with hot enthusiasm, earnestness, and industry."[1] His leadership of the orphaned Hut-terites began under favorable auspices, because the serious perse-cution instigated by Ferdinand, king of Bohemia and Emperor (1556–1564), had temporarily abated. The brethren stood at the beginning of a period of sturdy growth, and year after year peo-ple continued to flock to Moravia from all quarters.

---

[1] Zieglschmid, *Chronik,* 228.

Lanzenstiel was born somewhere in Bavaria. In 1529 he was with Amon at Kromau, and afterward he went to Austerlitz, where he was ordained. Late in 1536 he was sent as a companion of the missionary George Fasser into the Tyrol. At Neudorf, in Lower Austria, they had the misfortune of falling in with rowdy company at the local inn. Their disapproval of the particularly barbaric amusement and their consequent decision to leave the inn attracted considerable attention, and in the ensuing discussion they were recognized as Anabaptists and arrested.[2] All the way from Neudorf to Mölding, where they were to be examined, they constantly talked and gave such eloquent testimony "that the judge and all the others were aghast and could not utter a single word against it." They were nevertheless promptly thrown into prison in Mölding along with such a company of "godless, shameful, wanton people" that they would, they wrote to Amon, rather have been in a cesspool. They were examined several times, and their letters relate their growing conviction that only death would deliver them from imprisonment. Somehow, they were released after a year. Fasser went on to a martyr's death. Lanzenstiel visited Lower Austria and the Tyrol, where his wife was apprehended near Brixen in 1539 and drowned. From the Tyrol he went on to Switzerland, where, in spite of the fact that the authorities were forewarned of his coming and had posted rewards for his arrest, he managed to elude their vigilance.

On his return to Moravia he was recognized by Amon as the natural successor. A man of energy and godly courage, Lanzenstiel nevertheless felt that he was not competent to handle the administrative and pastoral problems alone, and besought the brethren to write to Peter Riedemann, imprisoned in Hesse, that they "had need of him in great necessity." Riedemann, for his part, was reluctant to violate the confidence which his considerate jailer had placed in him, but he finally concluded that the good of the congregation justified his escape, and he returned to Moravia (Ch. 16.2). It was quickly decided that he and Lanzenstiel should together share the leadership of all the Moravian communities, a decision which proved very fruitful, for "the Lord gave blessing and growth to the congregation; the number of the faithful increased, and the people grew more and more day by day."[3]

Under the benevolent and practical administration of Lanzenstiel and the sound pastoral guidance of the author of the

---

[2] *Ibid.*, 163 f.
[3] *Ibid.*, 230.

Account, the Hutterites made economic and spiritual progress. New converts flocked to join them. Among the adherents were many weavers, who developed a flourishing craft. The Hutterites thereby contributed much to the economy of Moravia. Their industry and frugality strengthened the economic programs of the nobles. When in 1544 the Moravian estates issued an order prohibiting the purchase of wool anywhere but in the royal cities or on the baronial estates, the Hutterites willingly complied, because the barons were increasingly considerate of their interests. In 1545 they were granted a number of new households even though the persecution was officially still in force.

The prosperity of the Anabaptists could not pass unnoticed in Hapsburg Vienna. In the spring of 1545 another order was issued, demanding that the Hutterites be expelled. Some of the lords complied in part, compelling the Anabaptist colonists to give up their communal institutions. In consequence they submitted a solemn protest to the barons with an *Account,* a confession of their doctrine and life, the already discussed work of Peter Riedemann. The Bohemian revolt of 1547 in solidarity with the Protestants of the Smalcald War (1546–1547) and its suppression increased Ferdinand's power and his determination to crush all dissident elements in his dominions. Together Riedemann and Lanzenstiel guided the brotherhood in the difficult years 1545–1551, when they were so hounded by the authorities that they became as hunted game. They dug (or enlarged already existing prehistoric) tunnels (Czech: *lochy*) as temporary abodes. Many fell away, returning to their diverse homelands, but the core remained loyal and was augmented by the adhesion of Silesian Gabrielites. Fortunately, the Moravian magnates reasserted their rights to administer their domains according to their conscience and their economic advantage. By 1553 they had permitted the Hutterites to set up three new colonies.[4] This independent action marked the beginning of a turn for the better, "the good time of the brotherhood."

Peter Riedemann, who contributed so much to the theological and literary undergirding of the Hutterite version of apostolic institutions, was able to enjoy but three years of the upward-turning fortunes of the Moravian communities. In 1556, fifty years old, he composed his last hymn, which begins:

> Quit, clear and free of death and hell,
> The power of Christ has made us well.[5]

---

[4] Damborschitz and Schaidowitz in Moravia and Kuty in Slovakia.
[5] Zieglschmid, *Chronik,* 357.

Calling the brethren to his bedside, he admonished them with the words from Nehemiah (ch. 8:10, KJV): "Go your way, eat the fat, and drink the sweet, and send portions unto them for whom nothing is prepared: for this day is holy unto our Lord: neither be ye sorry; for the joy of the Lord is your strength." With this blessing, Peter Riedemann died, at the Slovakian *Bruderhof* of Protzko, in December 1556, in the same year as the principal South German Anabaptist leader, Pilgram Marpeck (Ch. 31.1).

2. DIVISIVENESS AMONG, AND ECUMENICAL OVERTURES TO, THE MORAVIAN ANABAPTISTS

In the very season that Riedemann and Marpeck died, a Hutterite missionary, John Schmidt (Raiffer), was successfully recruiting new colonists among disaffected Anabaptists in two conventicles, one in Kreuznach in the Palatinate and the other in Aachen. Schmidt's activity was typical, and his argument in converting Rhenish Anabaptists to the communitarian version in Moravia throws much-needed light on the mentality of the whole Hutterite Church in its subapostolic age. Schmidt contended on his mission that the Hutterite Church was not only a matter of faith and order. It was also a matter of place. At the end of his *Brüderliche Vereinigung* of 1556, Schmidt declared that the Moravian wilderness then being turned by pious colonists into fruitful farmland was manifestly the providentially determined place of refuge foreseen by the seer of The Revelation, ch. 12:6. Just as the brethren on the Rhine should be separated in conventicles from the parishes of the wicked, so also they should, to prosper, be separated from the territory of these churches in which a sham Christianity corrupts even the most devout and sturdy conventicle. He continues:

Since God through his Spirit has in all times led the pious according to his word and will to the place which has pleased him or which he had provided for them to dwell in and thus leads and separates them that he may be to them their ruler and governor, and has a special delight in dwelling in the midst of the pious, and accordingly since God especially with the primitive church had joy and pleasure in seeing his own drawn together from all tongues under heaven, wherein his heavenly work and rule was established on earth [so likewise that he] might see his bride in the place determined for her in the wilderness wherever it should please him on earth and wherever he should ordain that she might rest awhile from the dragon and might *bear her children* [Rev. 12:6]—for that reason God's Spirit has [implanted] in the hearts of the pious a yearning to dwell in that very place.[6]

[6] *Ibid.,* 365 f.

To satisfy this holy yearning, the *Vereinigung* goes on, God has sent forth apostles or missionaries to gather together the scattered sheep under the protection and discipline of his apostolic pastors in Moravia.

The foregoing selection from the *Vereinigung* is eloquent testimony to the missionary zeal and cosmic sense of exclusive mission that inspired the Hutterites well into the second half of the century, and goes far to explain the tremendous attraction exercised by the patriarchal Hutterites over other radical but less seasoned churches, and also to account for the uncompromising self-assurance of the Hutterites in their proud conduct of negotiations with other Anabaptists and with other Radicals who hesitated to submit to the apostolic patriarch of Neumühl and his copresbyters.

One of the reasons for the authoritarian exclusiveness of the Hutterites was the enervating lure of a score of related sects burgeoning on the margins of their stolid communes. Although the Hutterite *Chronicle* gives the impression of a fairly harmonious and unified development of their apostolic church and commonweal, the unity even among the communitarians is that of a chronicler looking back idealistically.

The early division of the group at Nicolsburg (Ch. 9.2), followed by the three-way "great split" (Ch. 16.1) of the Austerlitz-Rossitz-Auspitz Anabaptists into Philippites, Gabrielites, and Hutterites, is only part of the story. Moreover, besides the relatively cohesive Hutterites, there were numerous allied and hostile groups, some of which were eventually absorbed by the Hutterites. The enthusiasm and eschatological Biblicism of these seekers for the pure evangelical society, together with their responsiveness to charismatic leaders, led to divisions within divisions and a proliferation of factions and groups, sometimes numbering only a few members. In some places they lived amicably side by side, sometimes in stern and mutual excommunication, in a way which was puzzling even to contemporary commentators. Roman Catholic and magisterial Protestant accounts usually overstress the fragmentation and bickering, but even when allowance is made for polemical exaggeration, there still remains a bewildering multitude of sects and factions interspersed with the Hutterite colonies in Bohemia and Moravia.

One of the best pictures is given by a Venetian weaver of taffetas and painter of battle standards, Marcantonio Varotto (or Barotto), who in 1564 began a series of journeys that took him to Geneva, then to Vienna, and subsequently to Austerlitz in

Moravia, where he listened to Anabaptist teachings. In 1568, having made his way back to Venice, he decided to return to the Roman Catholic Church and made a vivid deposition on his geographical and spiritual peregrination:[7]

I left Moravia because during the two months I spent there I saw so many faiths and so many sects, the one contrary to the others and the one condemning the others, all drawing up catechisms, all desiring to be ministers, all pulling this way and that, all wishing to be the true church. In one place alone, and that small enough, called Austerlitz, there are thirteen or fourteen kinds of sects.

He continues a little farther on:

In Moravia are the following [sects]: the Picards [Bohemian Brethren], the Lutherans, the Calvinists, the Austerlitzians, the Cornelians, the Cappellarians [Hutterites], the Josephines, the Sabbatarians, the Arians, the Samosatians, the Swiss (whose minister is one Vidal, a Savoyard), and three others whose names I do not know because they have few followers and are excommunicated by the other eleven sects. . . . All these sects agree together on many things, but each has some particular article different from the others and they all have different catechisms.[8]

Varotto's is the earliest comprehensive reference to the proliferation of sects in the region where the Hutterites were established. But another roughly contemporary document, the *Evangelische Inquisition* of 1573, by the jurist George Eder (d. 1586), confirms the impression, enumerating forty sects of so-called "Anabaptists," not, however, confined to the one specific region. Christoph Erhard, parish priest of Nicolsburg (1583–1589), in a violent book, *Von der Münsterischen Wiedertaufe* (1589), also lists some forty sects. Eder lists Müntzerites, naked-running Adamites, secretive or garden brethren, open witnessers, devilers (who universalistically held that the devil would be saved on Judgment Day), Libertines (cohabiters), weeping Brethren (*Fratres flebiles,* who held highly emotional prayer meetings), silent ones (who had no preaching at their contemplative worship), Augustinians (who were psychopannychists), Münsterites of various kinds, Paulinists (called also "Scripturalists" because they purported to possess the original letters of Paul, probably Paulicians), priest-murderers, Antichristians (who worshiped a mythical harlot mother of the Antichrist), Judaizers, etc.[9]

[7] Henry A. De Wind, "A Sixteenth Century Description of Religious Sects in Austerlitz, Moravia," *MQR,* XXIX (1955), 44–53.
[8] *Ibid.,* 45 f.   [9] *Ibid.,* 48 ff.

Obviously this composite canvas is still a caricature of the sectarian development. Eder and Erhard are tempted to list *all* the sects of which they have any knowledge, regardless of whether they existed in Moravia or not. In some cases the same group appears under two different names. The purpose of the catalogues is clearly polemical. The authors wish to show the disorganization of the Anabaptist movement and to discredit the sober and pious groups by classing them with the utterly eccentric or immoral sects.[10] But even the relatively reliable and circumstantial Varotto gives an impressive testimony of the extraordinary degree of religious toleration practiced by the Moravian lords.

The Hutterites, enjoying both a measure of toleration and a high degree of prosperity, seemed to many suffering Anabaptists elsewhere to be living in the Promised Land. The well-organized and far-flung Hutterite community was therefore the recipient of many ecumenical overtures and visitations from widely scattered groups.

We have mentioned Oswald Glait's attempt, even before the formation of the Hutterites proper, to bring together Anabaptists and the Unity of the Brethren in 1526 (Ch. 9.1). The overture and rebuff of Pilgram Marpeck has also been described (Ch. 18.1). Leaving for the next chapter the whole story of the exchanges between the Hutterites and the Polish Brethren, we shall here concentrate on certain Italian and Greek evangelicals.

Having seen (in Ch. 22.4) the contact from the Venetian side after the defection of Manelfi in 1551, we are now interested in the visitors from Venice and Thessalonica as they were received in Moravia. We quote from one of Hutterite codices:

There was a people in Italy, around Venice, eager to serve God. Their teacher was one Francis della Sega, who preached against idolatry and the godless doings. For that reason they were persecuted; and, as they did not know where to turn, a number of them finally decided to go across the sea towards Thessalonica. There they settled under a Turkish pasha. But Francis remained in Italy. When he heard of our church here in Moravia, where the brethren live together, and keep Christian community of goods, he started together with some other brethren from Italy and came to us. He looked around and inquired . . . and found out that this people here is standing upon the right apostolic ground. Thereupon he returned to Italy to visit his brethren there. After hearing the news they came with him to our church. He also wrote from Italy to Thessalonica, and informed this people that he had found the right church. . . . They should come up confidently and see for themselves. Thus several brethren from Thessa-

[10] *Ibid.*, 51.

lonica made themselves ready and came to us and became our brethren.[11]

Having earlier told about Francis della Sega and Julius Gherlandi, persecuted after Manelfi's defection in 1551 (Ch. 22.2), we may here concentrate on the third refugee, Anthony Rizzetto, who had gone by ship with a number of other anti-Trinitarian Anabaptists to Thessalonica. While there, he received word from Francis della Sega about the Hutterites, and returned to Venice to make his way northward. Accepted into membership by the Hutterites, Rizzetto accompanied della Sega on the ill-fated journey to Venice, where he had hoped to make arrangements for the return of his wife and stepdaughter from Thessalonica in order that they might have an opportunity to join him and the church of Moravia. We have already told about his execution.[12]

It is possible that it was Rizzetto or the Venetian refugees in Thessalonica who told certain Greek nonconformists about the Hutterites. These Greek evangelicals may have set forth for Moravia in belated response to the much earlier visits of Brother Luke of the Unity of the Brethren (Ch. 9.1). In any event, about the time of the original flight of the Venetian Anabaptists to Greece, a delegation of three Greeks from Larissa appeared in Moravia. They purported to have in their possession back in Macedonia "the letters which the apostle Paul wrote to them with his own hands," a claim which would indicate that they were in fact Paulicians. Their journey is recorded, not by the Hutterites or the Germans whom they visited, but by the Dutch, in *Het Brilleken* (1630), incorporated into the *Martyrs' Mirror*.[13]

The three emissaries, who, if they were Paulicians, would be Greek-speaking survivors of ancient Samosatene Armenian Christianity, on their arrival sought out a priest (possibly a benign

[11] A Hutterite manuscript of 1615 preserves this letter dated 1601; Beck, *Geschichts-Bücher*, 211–212; Robert Friedmann, "Christian Sectarians in Thessalonica and Their Relationship to the Anabaptists," *MQR*, XXIX (1955), 55.

[12] Henry A. De Wind deals with all the manuscript evidence in "Anabaptists in Thessalonica?", *MQR*, XXIX (1955), 70–73. He recognizes the mildly anti-Trinitarian background of Rizzetto and conjectures that he may have dissociated himself from the Thessalonican conventicle of anti-Trinitarians and somewhat casually also from his second wife because of his return to Trinitarian orthodoxy and greater satisfaction in the Germanic type of Anabaptism.

[13] Van Braght, *Martyrs' Mirror*, 365–367. A variety of accounts, mostly going back to the same source, say that Moravians, captured by the Turks and sold into slavery in Greece, had discovered the existence of these old Evangelicals throughout Macedonia, and in turn informed them of the existence of the Hutterite brotherhood. Robert Friedmann is reserved as to this explanation of the contact. "Christian Sectarians" and also in *ME*, IV, 708.

Utraquist priest or a Unity pastor), who took them to the Hutterites in Pausram. After a discussion, which was conducted in Latin, they found that despite a common stress on believers' baptism, they were not in harmony with the Hutterites on shunning, the community of goods, and the retention of all the property of a withdrawn or excommunicated member.[14] The Paulicians left the Hutterites with tears in their eyes, fearing that they had made their long journey for naught. But their interlocutor took them to a group of "Swiss" Brethren[15] in the same locality, with whom they found themselves in perfect accord. The joyful Greek Brethren deposited a confession of their faith with these Anabaptists.[16]

The Paulician church is well known to have centered its theology in believers' baptism, a rite administered at thirty years of age in imitation of Christ at Jordan (cf. Ch. 11.1). It is of special interest therefore that article iii of the Greek emissaries reads as follows:

Concerning baptism we believe and confess a baptism upon confession of faith and not an infant baptism, and we understand that a baptismal candidate must be standing with his feet in water as Christ was standing in the river Jordan. Thus he is baptized in the name of the Father and of the Son and of the Holy Ghost.[17]

The Greek emissaries, according to one account, journeyed as far as the Netherlands before returning to Larissa.[18] The story of the meeting not only was recorded in the *Martyrs' Mirror* but also was besung in a hymn in the Anabaptist hymnal, the *Ausbund*.[19]

The hymn records the joy at the realization that for centuries

---

[14] Caspar Schwenckfeld also corroborates this tendency of the Hutterites to exploit rich converts, describing a disillusioned Swiss Anabaptist who had to forfeit four hundred guilders and wander around impoverished after his excommunication. *CS*, XII, 37 (1550).

[15] The record says the second group, the "Schweitzer Church," took their name from one brother, John Schweitzer. Nothing is known of him. Anabaptists who did not live in the community of goods as the Hutterites did were generally called *Schweitzer Brüder* or Swiss Brethren, even if they had very little contact with the original Swiss immigrants.

[16] Van Braght, *Martyrs' Mirror*, 366. The document, copied many times as virtually a transcript of apostolic Christianity, although it may have been here and there altered in accordance with Mennonite piety and phraseology, is preserved in the Goshen College Library and has been translated by Elizabeth Bender and printed. Friedmann, "Christian Sectarians," 64–66. Its Paulician character is not recognized by Friedmann, who rejects of course a Bogomile origin. The orthodox Paulicians were not dualists.

[17] Friedmann, "Christian Sectarians," 64.

[18] *Het Brilleken;* cited in Friedmann, *ME*, IV, 708.

[19] In all recent editions, 892–895.

there had been an evangelical group practicing adult baptism in one of the most ancient lands of Christendom. The composer, likening the three Greek pilgrims to the three Magi, recounts their disappointment with the Hutterites (at "Jerusalem") and their rejoicing at their discovery of the fully like-minded "Swiss" Brethren (at "Bethlehem"). The hymn in thirty-six stanzas is characteristic of the epic or narrative quality of much of Anabaptist hymnody:

> And as to break the bread they went
> With all the brethren duly;
> Confessed they there with one intent
> That God's church it was truly.

> Full well did they in truth proclaim
> That home in Thessalony
> God's people had remained the same
> Since the Apostles' passing.

> Their faith unchanged and stubborn,
> They still have every letter
> Which holy Paul with his own hand
> Did send to those dear brethren.[20]

3. THE GOOD YEARS UNDER THE PATRIARCH PETER WALPOT, 1565–1578

Peter Riedemann's death in December 1556 had left Lanzenstiel alone in the office of general bishop. The intellectual leadership of the brotherhood, however, soon passed into the hands of the more creative Peter Walpot (1521–1578). Walpot, a Tyrolese, born near Klausen, had at the age of eight witnessed the martyrdom of George Blaurock in nearby Gufidaun (1529). He was soon converted to Anabaptism, and by 1542 was a minister in Moravia. His trade was that of a cutter, for which reason he is often called Scherer or Tuchscherer. In 1545, at the age of twenty-four, he participated in the debate between the Hutterites and the Gabrielites. Gabriel Ascherham had died that year, and the surviving Gabrielites sought a basis for union. As a result of the controversy, Walpot set down the Hutterite views in Five Articles of the Greatest Controversy Between Us and the World, transcribed in the Hutterite *Chronicle* at the year 1547.[21] Walpot de-

---

[20] Verses 23–25, *Ausbund* (Lancaster, 1815), appendix, p. 41. The hymn allegedly dates from 1540 but is clearly later and derivative. Friedmann, "Christian Sectarians," 68 f.

[21] Zieglschmid, *Chronik*, 269–316; reprinted in Müller, *Glaubenszeugnisse* (*QGT*, III), 237–257.

voted much attention to the orphaned Gabrielites, and persuaded many of them to join the Hutterites.

When, a decade later (Ch. 31.2), the Lutheran theologians published an attack on all Anabaptists at Worms in 1557,[22] the Hutterites alone replied in the *Handbüchlein wider den Prozess*, largely drawn up by Walpot rather than by the titular head of the brotherhood.

When Lanzenstiel died on 3 March 1565, a decade after Riedemann, he left the brotherhood in good economic condition and high morale. To succeed Lanzenstiel as principal bishop, the representatives of the brotherhood naturally elevated Walpot. The administrative center of the brotherhood as a whole was where the principal bishop (*Hauptvorsteher*) lived. During Walpot's administration (1565–1578) it was the *Bruderhof* of Neumühl.[23] Under Walpot the brotherhood flourished and attained a membership of perhaps thirty thousand baptized adults. Walpot was a man of great and varied industry, extending his attention to all details of life. The community is idyllically described in these good years:

Thus they came to dwell in the land which God had ordained especially for them. . . . They assembled in peace and unity and preached the gospel and the Word of God twice weekly, . . . making common prayer to God for all the needs of the brotherhood and splendid thanksgiving for all their blessings, praying also for the Emperor, the king, the princes, and the civil authorities. . . . They used the Christian ban with the sinful . . . , celebrating Christian baptism according to the Lord's command, and the Lord's Supper. . . . They practised the Christian community of goods as Christ taught and held with his disciples. . . . Their swords and spears were forged into pruning-knives, saws, and other useful instruments . . . , being obedient to the civil authority for good works. . . . The offices were filled with elders, special men who preached the Word of God, reading, teaching, exhorting . . . , exercising the office of reconciliation. . . . Chosen men directed the people at their work. . . . Other specialists were attached to the school. . . . There were not a few carpenters and builders, who made many millhouses, breweries and other buildings for the lords, noblemen, burghers and other people . . . , not a few millers. In short, there was no one who went idle; everyone did something which was assigned to him, which was within his ability, whether he

---

[22] Chapter 31.3. *Prozess, wie es soll gehalten werden mit den Wiedertäufern.*

[23] Walpot's influence was so great that when he died and the ordained men of the brotherhood met at Neumühl to elect his successor, the new bishop, Hänsel Kräl of Kitzbühel, took up his residence there and Neumühl thereafter remained the administrative center until the Thirty Years' War.

had been noble, rich, or poor. Even the priests who came learned like the apostle Paul how to work at an honest craft.[24]

Walpot took advantage of the economic upsurge of the Hutterite community to systematize the crafts and working teams and to prepare manuals of discipline for the various vocations. The manual for cobblers had been worked out by his predecessor. Among Walpot's own verified productions was a manual of school discipline and an address to the schoolmasters. This *School Discipline* is the second oldest of the Hutterite *Gemeindeordnungen*. Disciplines for other vocations followed.

Of all the sixteenth-century groups of Germanic Anabaptists, the Hutterites had the best opportunity for a systematic Christian upbringing of their youth, for in their *Bruderhofs* in Moravia and Slovakia, with a discipline embracing the whole community, they could systematically organize education and instruction, from nursery school up through several grades. Education beyond adolescence was rejected as not promoting the fear of God, which was the prime objective of education. Within the limits set, Hutterite education was of a high quality, and promoted, among other skills, the beautiful penmanship to which their numerous manuscript codices testify. Their writings evidence extensive knowledge of the Bible and a clarity of exposition unusual among peasants and artisans in the sixteenth century. Among the Hutterites, illiteracy was almost unknown, although it was very high among the rest of the people of Moravia.

The schools also served as homes for the children between the age of two years and the age of learning a trade. In effect the Hutterites with their "small school" anticipated by three centuries the modern kindergarten. Peter Walpot's *School Discipline*[25] of 1578 seems to be a model of practical psychology:

The brethren in the schools have already been instructed by the elders that they shall not manifest wrath towards the children and shall not strike the children on the head with the fist nor with rods, nor shall they strike on the bare limb, but moderately on the proper place. It is necessary to exercise great discretion and discernment in disciplining children, for often a child can be better trained and corrected and taught by kind words when harshness would be altogether in vain, while another can be overcome by gifts. A third, however, cannot be disciplined without severity, and does not accept correction. Therefore the exercise of discipline of children requires the fear of

[24] Zieglschmid, *Chronik*, 431–435 (abridged).
[25] Translated by Harold S. Bender in "A Hutterite School Discipline of 1578 and Peter Scherer's Address of 1568 to the Schoolmasters," *MQR*, V (1931), 231–241.

God. One should show sympathy to the little folk who have just started attending school, and should not undertake all at once to break the self-will, lest injury come therefrom. For the children who are a bit larger one must also always exercise very diligent care so that one can always have a good conscience.

Hygiene was emphasized in the schools, with constant inspection. The task of being a teacher was a high vocation, and teachers were not to busy themselves with "trifling things," such as going to market, but were to delegate such tasks while they devoted themselves to their paramount work.[26] The thoroughness and uniformity of Hutterite education, based on a brief *Kinderbericht*,[27] accounts for the fact that when, on coming of age, these earnest graduates of catechetical schools for martyrdom fell into the hands of persecutors, they, like the early Christian confessors, always had a ready and concordant answer.

Besides the *Kinderbericht*, presumably printed, Walpot also had Riedemann's *Account* printed at the Hutterite press in Neumühl. He commissioned an increasing number of missionaries who went into all dominions of the Empire (cf. Ch. 31.2) and acted as living links between the Moravian center and the recruiting grounds. Walpot's tireless industry and leadership are evident from the way in which he created and preserved a harmonious order and discipline among the many newcomers who continued to arrive. The enormous correspondence brought in almost daily by returning brethren was read before the assembled company and answered "in the sense of the congregation."

The protocol of the Frankenthal colloquy of 1571 (Ch. 31.2) claims that one Peter Scherer (?Walpot) and two other Hutterite brothers attended, but there is no other evidence of Walpot's having participated. Moreover, no one responded when the spokesman for the Reformed Church asked if there were any Hutterites present. In the peaceful years of the "Golden Age," Walpot was able to elaborate his earlier anti-Protestant *Five Articles* into the very large work, the *Great Article Book*.[28] This enlarged work, Riedemann's *Account,* and the considerably later *Sendbrief* of Andreas Ehrenpreis are the three basic Hutterite constitutional and theological texts, along with the great manuscript *Chronicle,* in which they are imbedded. Toward the end of his administration, Walpot encouraged Caspar Braitmichel, servant of the Word, to delve in the archives of the brethren at

---

[26] *Ibid.,* 239.
[27] Existing only in manuscript.
[28] *Ein schön lustig Büchlein etliche Hauptartikel unseres christlichen Glaubens,* etc., to be edited by Robert Friedmann in the second volume of *Glaubenszeugnisse.*

Neumühl and Austerlitz and to bring together a *Chronicle* of the history of God's people.[29] Braitmichel was able to carry his account down to the year 1542.[30] Apologizing for his failing eyesight, he thereby suggests that he may have undertaken the work toward the end of his life. He died in 1573, which may therefore be put down as the approximate date of the first comprehensive church history from the pen of an Anabaptist. From its pages, already much cited in the present work, we have an indication of how the subapostolic generation thought of itself in relation not only to the Protestant Reformation but also to the whole of human history.

Braitmichel began his *Chronicle* with Genesis in the elevated style of one who, with the medieval monastic chroniclers, was drawn to paraphrase the inspired words of Scripture in his narrative of God's creation of the world. Braitmichel was especially interested in the genealogy of the righteous remnant from the patriarchs, through bondage in Egypt and the exile, to the birth of Christ, and through the book of The Acts. From here on, he draws upon Josephus, Eusebius, and the Spiritualist Sebastian Franck. With their aid he carries the story of the righteous remnant alongside the ancient and medieval church. With Franck, he dates the fall of the church about fourteeen hundred years before the beginning of the restoration,[31] for which Wyclif and Hus prepared the way. Then came Luther and Zwingli, but because they defended with the sword the false teaching of pedobaptism, and thereby came to stand with Antichrist and Pilate, God once again separated his own from the world:

But because God wished to have his own people, separated from all peoples, he willed for this purpose to bring in the right true morning star of his truth to shine in fullness in the final age of this world, especially in the German nation and lands, the same to strike home with his Word and to reveal the ground of divine truth. In order that his holy work might be made known and revealed before everyman, there developed first in Switzerland an extraordinary awakening and preparation by God.[32]

Here follows an account of the momentous beginnings of the Anabaptist church in Zurich when George Blaurock (whom Walpot saw put to death) was rebaptized by Grebel (Ch. 6.1).[33]

[29] The MS. Codex of this work, much quoted in the present narrative, was first printed by Rudolf Wolkan in 1923, and again by A. J. F. Zieglschmid in 1943. It is the cherished possession of the Hutterite *Bruderhof* at Bon Homme in South Dakota.

[30] It was carried on by a succession of chroniclers to 1665.

[31] *ME*, I, 590; Beck, *Geschichts-Bücher*.

[32] *SAW*, 42.

[33] This section of the *Chronicle* is translated in *SAW*, 39–46.

The cosmic setting in which Braitmichel beheld the pilgrimage of his spiritual ancestors and the gathering of the Bride of the Lord in the wilderness of Moravia, bearing saints and waxing strong in the faith and communal discipline of true believers, extended the imaginations of his readers far beyond the parochial, the territorial, and the provincial horizons. Theirs was the confidence of being the one, holy, catholic church even though still largely hidden from the world.

It is noteworthy that it was at approximately this same time that from within the far-flung Mennonite community a similar grand design was beheld by Dietrich Philips in *The Church of God*.[34] In this work, too, without any of Braitmichel's ancient and medieval episodes or details, the Dutch Anabaptist, in an Augustinian framework of history, likewise presupposed a continuity of God's righteous remnant through history, and then, appropriating the spangling attributes of the church of the Apocalypse, described the Anabaptist church militant in the bright terms of the church triumphant. It would appear that the Mennonite-Hutterite-Marpeckian sense of history was a correlate of an intensely Johannine eschatology.

On 30 January 1578, Walpot died after having called the elders of the church to his bedside for a final instruction and blessing. The *Chronicle* says of him: "He was a faithful shepherd, a very well experienced man in all things . . . richly blessed by God in his word and doctrine, so that he richly caused the congregation of God to rejoice and edified it, so that it was indeed very downcast at his departure."[35]

During Walpot's pontificate the Greek, Rhenish, and Italian ecumenical contacts remained isolated events. A longer relationship was that sustained with the Polish Brethren, initiated indirectly perhaps by the Italians, who had passed through Moravia on their way to Cracow. Radical Christianity, as we have seen, was assuming a different form in Poland from the Anabaptism of South Germany and Moravia (Ch. 25); and the Poles, as we have said in anticipation, were by 1565, the year of Walpot's accession to the patriarchate, on the point of turning to the resourceful Hutterites for mutual support. The story of their visit to Peter Walpot's settlement and their eventual disillusionment with what they were to come to consider the autocracy of the Hutterites can now be told as an integral part of the second phase in the history of the Minor Church of Poland, to which we now return.

[34] *SAW*, 226–260.
[35] Zieglschmid, *Chronik*, 499.

CHAPTER 27

THE ANTIPEDOBAPTIST, ANTI-NICENE MINOR CHURCH, 1565–1572

As we return from Hutterite Moravia to the Minor Church in Poland, we find that the opening of the new phase in the history of the Radical Reformation in Poland and Lithuania is marked by three interrelated events: the death of the Lithuanian patron of the Radicals, Prince Radvila (27 May 1565), their headlong dispersion from Vilnius now under the conservative regimen of the regency council, and the convening of the first general synod of the new Minor Church at Brzeziny, 10 June 1565, to consolidate their anti-Nicene, anabaptist position. The phase thus opened will come to an end with the death of the king in 1572 without an heir and the consequent elevation to prominence, in all branches of Reformed Christianity in Poland, of the complex issues relating to church and government, attendant upon the constitutional crisis.

To refer in 1565 to the antipedobaptist and anti-Nicene dissenters from the orthodox Major Church as the Minor Church of Poland and Lithuania gives a premature impression of theological homogeneity and synodal inclusiveness. Such was not the case until the disparate or incompletely harmonized impulses within the Radical Reformation in Poland and Lithuania could be brought together in a well-organized church under the leadership of Faustus Socinus, beyond the limits of the present chapter.

1. EARLY STRAINS AND STRESSES IN THE MINOR CHURCH

On baptism the Minor Church, as of 1565, embraced both mere antipedobaptists and programmatic immersionists. By the arrival of Socinus in 1579 it will be almost completely anabaptist. On the doctrine of the Godhead and on Christology the range was equally great, namely, from tritheists still using the Nicene terminology equivocally, all the way to avowed unitarians, who refused to invoke Christ in prayer.

685

It was in the recovery of Jesus as Messiah and King in his fully human nature that the Polish "Arians" grounded their claim to exemption from discharging some of the customary duties toward their earthly king and lords, such as the waging of war. An Arian medal struck in the sixteenth century shows on one side the purely human teacher Jesus with plaited ringlets suggestive of a Polish rabbi and, on the obverse, the royal inscription in Hebrew characters.[1]

The Judaizing and unitarian stress within the Minor Church was concentrated from near the beginning in Lithuania, where several magnates, reminding us of the lords of Liechtenstein and their kin in Moravia, supported anti-Trinitarian Anabaptism in part as subaltern magistrates, and were therefore indisposed to renounce fully the *jus gladii* in their temporalities. In contrast, pacifism and the stress on the pre-existent Christ who was to be invoked in prayer were traits much more pronounced in Little Poland. It is therefore appropriate to speak distinguishingly of Polish Brethren and Lithuanian Brethren within the Minor Church, stressing, however, thereby not the ethnic and linguistic but rather the theological and ethical differentiation.

Thus, on whether a Christian might be a magistrate, on the oath, and on the use of arms in self-defense and in nonaggressive war, the Minor Church embraced such extremes as the Arian general of the army of Poland in the Livonian War against Russia, Stanislas Cikowski (Ch. 25.3), who promoted in 1565 the preaching of antipedobaptist Arianism in his camps and bivouacs all the way to the gates of Moscow,[2] and the absolute, communitarian pacifists of the colony at Raków in 1569, such as Gregory Paul and Martin Czechowic (after 1570 in Lublin). Along with the deep cleavage over the Christian magistracy within the Minor Church, which reminds us of the cleavage between the *Stäbler* and *Schwertler* at Nicolsburg (Ch. 9.2.b), there was in Polish-Lithuanian Anabaptism before the coming of Socinus also the already mentioned strong Judaizing trend, which found expression in Sabbatarianism and in the occasional identification of the Lord's Supper as at once a kiddush and a passover commemoration.

Polish and Lithuanian Anabaptism was much more open to

---

[1] See the plate in Szczucki, *Literatura Ariańska,* opp. 178.
[2] Tretius to Bullinger, Cracow, August 1565; Wotschke, *Briefwechsel,* No. 343, pp. 250 f. In 1570 the Bohemian Brother John Rokyta with a Polish embassy had an audience with Ivan IV the Terrible. Müller, *Brüder,* III, 145–149.

Spiritualism than its Germanic counterpart. In the end, this Spiritualism was to merge with the Evangelical Rationalism of Faustus Socinus and ultimately to deprive the ordinance of Baptism of the significance it had when immersionism was first being introduced. But in the realm of Eucharistic practice, this Spiritualist thrust would only here and there lead in the Schwenckfeldian or Palaeologian direction (Ch. 28.3) of the suspension of the ordinance, or its transformation into a love feast. Nor did the Spiritualist influence in Poland manifest itself, as it had in Germany with Sebastian Franck and John Denck, in a contrast between inner and outer Word. The principal effect of Polish Spiritualism was rather, as it turned out, in the sphere of the ministry.

There were, it will be recalled, leaders in Swiss, German, and Netherlandish Anabaptism and Spiritualism who came to doubt the validity of their own vocation to the apostolate or to the local ministry—for example, Carlstadt, John Denck, Sebastian Franck, and Obbe Philips. There was indeed a strong disposition within the Germanic phase of the Radical Reformation to question the legitimacy of any ordination deriving from the *ancien régime*. Thus, several former Catholic priests, such as Menno Simons, are recorded as having submitted to a reordination, as well as to a rebaptism, on becoming clerical leaders in the Radical Reformation, in marked contrast to the clerics of the Magisterial Reformation, who on principle, as anti-Donatists, refused to countenance the thought that their clerical authorization from the Old Church might be invalid in the Reformation context, for they felt themselves to be called precisely to reform, not to reinstitute, the church.

In the first years of the Reformation Era, the question of the old ordination would have necessarily centered, in any event, in the validity of an earlier Catholic ordination; but in Poland in the third quarter of the century, many of the ministers of the Minor Church were repudiating not only a Catholic call and ordination but also a Reformed call and installation. The temporary dissolution of the ministry in the Minor Church and the temporary exaltation of certain inspired but unlettered people as oracles of the will of God is thus a notable feature of a section of the Minor Church in the first years after the schism with the Major Church.

Albinus of Iwanowice and Daniel Bieliński, for example, are known to have claimed in some stage of their career "that nobody was fit to officiate or instruct unless he had had a divine revelation and had either witnessed miracles or performed them."[3] A disaffected Anabaptist who returned to the Major Church recalls the situation around 1565 tauntingly:

You [ministers of the Minor Church] remember when you debased yourselves and gave up your ministries, expecting that the Lord God would inspire more worthy men, and you gave place to shoemakers and tailors, highly praising their teaching and marveling at it, and saying that you learned more in one hour while listening to them than in all the ages from books. You can hardly deny this. But being unable to stand it, you had to turn again to books and order the cobblers and millers to keep silence. For you observed to what these dear, strange prophets were leading, and what a confusion they made, of which you are ashamed to this day.[4]

So much, then, for the strains within the inchoate Minor Church around 1565. In the following presentation we shall stress the baptismal theology of the anti-Trinitarian Minor Church and leave for Ch. 29.1 the polemic over the Christian magistracy.

2. Adjustments in Anti-Nicene Baptismal Theology, 1565–1569

At the first general synod of the Minor Church, which convened at Brzeziny, in a castellany near Warsaw, 10 June 1565,[5] baptism was the chief matter under discussion. It is notable that the first synod within the purview of the tradition of the Minor Church should have taken place fairly close to the lower Vistula extensively permeated by Dutch Anabaptists. Stanislas Lutomirski, reporting the synod to the Lithuanians, was, to be sure, careful to say that although the anabaptist sentiment prevailed, the term *Anabaptista* (with its Münsterite and hence seditious connotations) was eschewed; but, significantly, a typically Anabaptist interest in the judgment of the *sisters* as well as the brethren appears twice in this letter. Stanislas Lubieniecki, the later Socinian historian, recalls: "There is a tradition that the

---

[3] The source is the MS. "Polonoeutychia" of Andrew Lubieniecki, excerpted by S. Kot and I. Chrzanowski, *Humanizm i Reformacja w Polsce* (Lwów, 1927), 421.

[4] Kasper Wilkowski, *Przyczyny nawrócenia do wiary powszechnej* (Vilnius, 1583); printed in Szczucki, *Literatura Ariańska*, 557–575; translated in Kot, *Socinianism in Poland*, 51.

[5] Stanislas Lubieniecki's text reads "Braesinia." Wilbur interprets "Braesinia" as "Brest-Litovsk." In my essay in *Studia nad Arianizmem*, 235, I have given it as Brest-Kujawy, or Brzeziny near Łowicz, the birthplace of Gregory Paul. The most recent surmise is that it was the latter. See Jan Albertrandi, *Listy J. F. Commendoniego do Karola Boromeusza* (Vilnius, 1851), II, 217 f.

Cujavians, whose palatinate borders on Prussia, were the first to oppose infant baptism under the leadership of Martin Czechowic, who, besides other doctrines, had also imbibed this about the baptism of adults from Peter Gonesius."[6]

Altogether, there were thirty-two ministers and eighteen listeners at the synod of Brzeziny, at least two of them from Lithuania. Among them there were the following: Stanislas Lutomirski, Martin Czechowic, Gregory Paul, Daniel Bieliński, and Martin Krowicki. Nicholas Żytno, himself an anti-Trinitarian, but not an antipedobaptist at the time, observed bitterly that the stolid "anabaptist wolves" triumphed in Kujawy. Orthodox Calvinist Christopher Tretius, in referring hostilely to the synod in Brzeziny, says that "Anabaptists from Lithuania, Moravia, and other parts" attended, which, if he was correctly informed, means that possibly communitarian Hutterites were present as observers along with representatives of the Netherlandish Anabaptists from the nearby Dutch colonies in royal and ducal Prussia. Besides the five participants in the synod of Brzeziny mentioned above, two or three others should be characterized.

Present at Brzeziny was Superintendent Stanislas Paplepka, pastor of the congregation in Lublin, who was the first in his area[7] to oppose the doctrine of the Trinity and of pedobaptism. He was later quoted on baptism by Martin Czechowic. Matthew Albinus, pastor of the congregation in Iwanowice (near Cracow), though he remained steadfastly a Trinitarian to his death (as did the majority of Anabaptists outside of Poland), very early came to oppose pedobaptism and argued "that no one ought to be baptized unless believing and repentant."[8] Following Albinus was the German Peter Pulchranin, a schoolmaster who introduced immersion at Bychawa (which is significantly within eight miles of Kraśnik, where we know a Hutterite colony existed at least in 1536, Ch. 15.2). While engaged in the baptismal rite, the schoolmaster was severely beaten by an aristocratic bystander and thrown into a deep pond, barely escaping with his life.[9]

---

[6] S. Lubieniecki, op. cit., 177.

[7] Erasmus Otwinowski (fl. 1564) in Heroes christiani.

[8] S. Lubieniecki, op. cit., 152, 176.

[9] The fact is that there are thus quite a number of "firsts" on the question of antipedobaptism and rebaptism in the tradition and records of the immersionist, anti-Trinitarian Minor Church of Poland and Lithuania. The discrepancies could well be accounted for, however, by the probability that Anabaptism cropped out in many localities at about the same time and that the local traditions were only partly harmonized in the Synoptic account as seen from the later Racovian-Socinian perspective.

With Anabaptist convictions springing up all over, here and there moving over into the practice of adult immersion, the congregations of Great Poland (especially Kujawy), Little Poland, and Lithuania had agreed at Brzeziny in June to convene again in synod in December 1565, at Węgrów in Podlasie (east of Warsaw, north of Lublin), as an accommodation to Lithuanians who had earlier in the year journeyed to Brzeziny in order to prevent a schism opening up *within* the anti-Trinitarian Minor Church over the issue of baptism.

George Blandrata, writing since 1563 as spokesman of the unitarians in Transylvania, urged in a letter to Gregory Paul, 21 September 1565,[10] that the immersionists be as irenic as possible at the forthcoming synod in Węgrów; for surely the international unity of the anti-Trinitarian fellowship should not be imperiled by a secondary issue such as baptism. Blandrata reminded Gregory Paul of the bad reputation of Anabaptism, and deplored his stubbornness in allowing the great issue of the unity of God to be confused with rebaptism. The letter in respect to the Sonship of Christ is of special interest because, following Servetus, Blandrata makes it very clear that he does not object to an eternal and indeed consubstantial Word thought of as God's will, or as God's arm in creation, or as God's idea of Christ, or perhaps even as the soul of the future Christ as mediator; but he rejects the conception of a Son before the incarnation. There was only one Son, foreseen by the prophets of the seed of David, the Word historically incarnate, but not an eternal Son incarnate in a man. In a Servetian manner, Blandrata argued that the Three were as distinct as the Three heard and seen at the baptism at Jordan. Up to the incarnation there was the eternal Word of God and the Spirit of God, but not a Son of God, the mediator. Other anti-Trinitarians wrote from Transylvania to the Polish Brethren, complaining "that baptism was being made a sort of new saviour and even an idol like the brazen serpent . . . as if one would seek to get possession of Noah's Ark."[11]

From Austerlitz in sectarian Moravia, however, Alciati wrote to Gregory Paul, describing the Hutterites, and argued for believers' baptism.[12] At a somewhat later date in the baptismal controversy in Poland another Italian, Nicholas Paruta (Ch. 29.5), who was also living among the Moravian Anabaptists in Austerlitz, reproached Lutomirski for allowing the baptismal controversy to threaten the unity of the Minor Church because when

10 Wajsblum, *op. cit.*, 42.
11 S. Lubieniecki, *op. cit.*, 189.
12 Sandius, *op. cit.*, 28.

the fundamental "error about original sin is done away, its con-sequence, absolution, that is, its washing away through baptism, is also done away . . . [or at least] to be taken with a grain of salt."[13] Stanislas Budziński (who had been present at Rogów in 1562, where anti-Trinitarian propositions from the Italians sojourning among the Moravian Anabaptists had excited such intense in-terest) now tried to explain away, in his manuscript *Historia*, Nicholas Paruta's disparagement of the whole theology and prac-tice of baptism as it was coming to the fore among Polish anti-Trinitarians. He explained that what Paruta really intended was "that although they, the non-Polish anti-Trinitarians, considered rebaptism necessary to salvation, it should be performed by a washing *(absolutionem) in the church* building lest, by immers-ing *in public,* they immerse themselves for the sake of the rite alone *(ob solum ritum)*."[14] Clearly, the preoccupation of the native Polish anti-Trinitarians with rebaptism cannot be at-tributed to Italian influences.

At the long-anticipated Węgrów synod, when it convened from 25 to 30 December 1565, the two anti-Trinitarian factions were divided not only on the issue of the redemptive (as distinguished from the initiatory) significance of believers' baptism by total immersion, but also on such social and political issues as the degree to which true Christians might be involved in the affairs of the world, including the conduct of public office; and, while there were notable aristocratic converts to the immersionist-pacifist position, on the whole the class lines were fairly clear; and the humbler adherents of anti-Trinitarianism were also the more ardent proponents of pacifism and the other tenets of evangelical Anabaptism.

At Węgrów a great effort was made to reconcile anti-Nicene anabaptist Martin Czechowic and Gregory Paul with the anti-Nicene pedobaptists. This was urged by letter from Vilnius by Nicholas Wędrogowski. But a great majority of the forty-seven ministers, headed by Lutomirski, fourteen members of the nobility, headed by Lord Jerome Filipowski, and many com-moners, voted against pedobaptism, only eight voting for its retention.

Lutomirski, who presided at Brzeziny, and now at Węgrów, reporting on the debate, remarked that "when some were found who brought forward the wicked deeds of those [Anabaptists] at Münster, with a view to causing repugnance to the *recently in-troduced view* (about baptizing catechumens) and to leading us

13 S. Lubieniecki, *op. cit.,* 13.
14 *Ibid.*

to reject it upon consideration of those base deeds, then those at whom that suspicion was aimed" asserted their loyalty to the government (citing Rom., ch. 13), as indeed evangelical Anabaptists everywhere would do.[15] The temperate decision of the general Polish-Lithuanian synod of Węgrów allowed for the continuance of amicable disagreement and publication; but the delegations from Szydłów, Lublin, Chełmno, and Brest-Litovsk favored the immediate "abandonment of the baptism of infants and the restoration of that of catechumens and believers." The compromise decision was vigorously rejected, however, by the anti-Nicene but pedobaptist faction (led by George Weigel) at Vilnius, whose sharp letter to the anti-Trinitarian anabaptists of Brest-Litovsk of early 1566 is preserved:

For we see how these *poor little men* are proceeding in their plan. They declared formerly [at Brzeziny?] that they would assent if they may baptize only adults at the dictation of a good conscience. At present, now advancing from strength to strength, they have called their own baptism in question, openly saying that they have not been [truly] baptized. But after they have attained their wish, they will suppose that by such baptism they were made free and truly spiritual. Thus they will extend their schemes further and further, so that these good *Spirituales* consign to eternal damnation and the pains of hell those that have fallen away from their ranks or have sinned [a reference to the ban], denying them repentance. . . . Flee far from this Anabaptist plague![16]

At about this time a Catholic foe gloatingly published a secretly obtained letter in which George Weigel in Vilnius, writing to Zacius now in Cracow, deplored the excesses of the radically Reformed, that is, the anti-Trinitarian Anabaptists, who "tell their dreams and visions . . . introduce plurality of wives, community of goods, contempt of the magistrate, of the courts, and of every rank," "while serfs, writing to a master or to the magistrate, use the title 'brother.' "[17] Here are all the stock charges brought against all Anabaptists applied afresh to the Lithuanian Brethren, but without doubt more or less accurately, except for the plurality of wives.

It is apparent—from Weigel's remarks, such as "poor little men," and from the counsel of such anti-Nicene but socially conservative Italians as Paruta and Blandrata—that the Polish

---

[15] Lutomirski, *apud* S. Lubieniecki, *op. cit.*, 183.
[16] *Ibid.*, 185 f.; cf. Nicholas Żytno in L. Szczucki, *Studia z Dziejów*, 230.
[17] Quoted by Benedict Herbest, *Chrześciańska porządna odpowiedź* (1567), and quoted by Kot, *Socinianism*, 21, n.; Weigel's "letter" may well be the same as the document cited in Ch. 25.2.

anti-Trinitarians commonly disdained the anabaptists in their midst as being of lowly origin. The anabaptists of Lublin and Śmigiel were called by a Catholic priest, "peasants, turners, planers, skinners, linen-weavers, blockheads and other dregs of the human race," who meet "under Lublin wall near the water and almost by the reeds."[18]

The Anabaptist conviction nevertheless spread among the anti-Nicenes, especially now in Poland. Martin Czechowic spent the spring of 1566 recruiting members for the immersionist movement in the province of his birth, Poznań. Gregory Paul, pastor of the anti-Trinitarian congregation at Cracow, immersed many in the Vistula the same spring.[19] About this time the courtier Stanislas Żółkiewski was converted to immersionism; and, leaving the court at Cracow, "while splendidly clothed [he] received the genuine rite of baptism" and joined the Anabaptist congregation to the great astonishment of the court. At the diet of Lublin in May 1566, nobleman John Niemojewski, judge of the district court of Inowrocław, recently immersed by Czechowic at his own home in Kujawy on Christmas Day, 1565, was conspicuous "in a mean gray garment, without sword, without attendant."

Cardinal Hosius [the hostile observer continues] had long conversations with him several times, trying to turn him from his delusion, but he steadfastly insisted that the Holy Spirit taught him that the doctrine that he confessed was true and from God; indeed, that the voice of the Father had been heard from heaven: "Whosoever shall believe and receive baptism, shall be saved."[20]

During the sessions, Niemojewski's fellow believers, immersionist *trideistae,* were delivering sermons in the gardens in the suburbs, attracting many from among the Nicene Calvinists—sermons in which, according to a hostile account, "disregard for the magistrate was openly taught, for, said they, Christians ought to recognize only one, the king bedecked with the crown of thorns."[21]

The bishops, lords, and other gentry participating in the diet of Lublin in the spring of 1566, were all the more troubled by the local outcropping of Anabaptism for the reason that Stanislas Cardinal Hosius, bishop of Warmia, had received during the ses-

---

[18] The Catholic priest Jerome Powodowski; cited by Kot, *Socinianism,* 96.
[19] Łaski to Theodore Beza, 30 May 1566; Wotschke, *Briefwechsel,* 271. Łaski refers to the spirit of the Anabaptists of *Flandria* as having flown across (via Danzig?) to Poland.
[20] S. Rescius, *De Atheismis et Phalarismis evangelicorum* (Naples, 1596), 225; quoted by Kot, *Socinianism,* 28.
[21] 31 May 1566; Wotschke, *Briefwechsel,* 272, n. 1.

sions the alarming news that serfs in Sochaczów near Poznań had risen up and killed their lord on the pretext that "Christ suffered for us because he wished us to be free and equal and to be our king."[22] Though these rebellious serfs were not expressly Anabaptist, their conduct gave color to the charge that all Anabaptists were either passively or actively seditious. The usually tolerant king temporarily approved on 13 June 1566 a draft of an edict that, had it been passed, would have driven from the kingdom all Anabaptists and *"Trinitarii"* (as the Catholics called the members of the Minor Church). But at the end of the deliberations, on the principle that in "war among the heretics is the peace of the [Catholic] Church," Catholic deputies voted against the exile of "these two sects [*Anabaptistae et Trinitarii*]," though Lord Jerome Filipowski had to fear for his life for venturing "openly to protect the Anabaptists," when he implied that the King of Kings would defend his own.

Antipedobaptist and anti-Trinitarian currents within the Minor Church had not yet completely merged. Not all antipedobaptists became anabaptists. Not all tritheists became ditheists and then unitarians, but this was the inner logic of the forces at work in the Minor Church.

The question of the pre-existence of Christ was uppermost at the synod of Łańcut (a hundred miles east of Cracow) in the spring of 1567, dividing the more conservative ditheist followers of Gonesius and Stanislas Farnowski (Farnovians, Ch. 29.6) from the outright unitarians. Against the latter the Farnovians spoke bitterly. Despite the irenic efforts of chairman Filipowski, clamor reigned. The "blasphemy" of the unitarians so upset Lord Stanislas John Karniński, one of the earliest Minor Church supporters, that he withdrew from the anti-Trinitarians and again became a Nicene Calvinist. The debate grew violent, and was adjourned to Skrzynno (seventy-five miles southwest of Warsaw) 24 June. There, in the presence of one hundred and ten nobles and ministers, the pre-existence of Christ was supported by ditheists Farnowski, Niemojewski, and Czechowic; the fully unitarian view, by Gregory Paul, George Schomann, and Simon Budny. These three, though they denied the deity of the Holy Spirit and held only to the adoptive Sonship of Christ, agreed to tolerate a trinitarian phrasing in so far as it could be couched in Biblical and apostolic language. The Anabaptists, for their part, reluc-

---

[22] Urban, *Chłopi*, 67. Hosius' views may be read in a contemporaneous English version, *Beginnings of Heresy* (Antwerp, 1565).

tantly consented at Skrzynno to the coexistence of the practice of both believers' and infant baptism in the Minor Church.

In the fall of this year an anti-Trinitarian, communitarian, Anabaptist treatise was published in Polish at Grodno.[23]

At the synod of Iwie (near Vilnius) in 1568, unitarian Budny, giving expression to his relative conservatism in the social implication of the gospel, contended for the legitimacy of defensive war, capital punishment, and even class distinctions within the brotherhood. Over against Niemojewski and Czechowic, who stood by the Sermon on the Mount, Budny appealed to the authority of the Old Testament. A number of Lithuanian Anabaptists, shocked at Budny's social conservatism, left for Little Poland, among them Jacob of Kalinowka, Paul of Wizna, and Lucas Mundius. At the same time, Budny upheld believers' baptism against Calvin on the ground that baptism could not be assimilated to circumcision (and against Luther on the ground that an infant could not be said to have even implicit faith). Budny somewhat later wrote to John Foxe in England, confidently contending that pedobaptism had no more place in his church than the triune God or the twofold Christ.[24] About this time Gregory Paul published in Cracow a number of tracts, including several chapters of Servetus' *Restitutio* in Polish translation, entitled *Signa sexagenta regni Antichristi et revelatio eius iam nunc praesens,* and another not deriving from Servetus on the differences between the Testaments and between Judaism and Christianity.[25]

In October 1568 a synod convened in Pełsznica in the district of Cracow, during which the anabaptist Cujavians, led by Czechowic, demanded that the Little Polish antipedobaptists follow out the implications of the synod of Węgrów of 1565 and proceed to actual rebaptism as it had for some time been practiced in Kujawy by the followers of Czechowic and in Cracow, since the spring of 1566, by Gregory Paul. Besides Czechowic and Gregory Paul, George Schomann,[26] John Albinus, Peter Gonesius, and Stanislas Farnowski were present. Among the lay participants

---

[23] The letter reporting the publication is dated 13 September 1567; quoted by Kot, *Socinianism,* 24, n. 18.

[24] Letter of 1574; edited by Stanislas Kot, *Oddziaływanie Braci Polskich zwanych Socynjanami w Anglji* (Warsaw, 1936), 37.

[25] *Rozdział Starego Testamentu od Nowego.* On this work, see Kot in *Autour de Michel Servet,* 99.

[26] Also: Alexander Vitrelin, John Siekierzyński, John Kalinowski, Paul (of Wizna), superintendent in Lithuania, Martin Krowicki, Adalbert Kościeński, Daniel Bieliński, and Stanislas Wiśniowski.

were lords Jerome Filipowski and John Niemojewski, and the apothecary Simon Ronemberg. There was indeed a good deal of hilarity at the synod over the fact that of the antipedobaptist brethren of Little Poland who had for several years been talking about immersion, up to the present not a single *minister* had been submerged. The Little Poles thereupon promised the Cujavians that they would move to the introduction of immersion in their ranks. John Siekierzyński of Koryto (near Pińczów) appears to have been the first *minister* among the Little Poles to have had this decision carried out for himself.

Concurrently with the question of immersion, a basic problem of Christian polity was attacked, namely, the distinction of the gathered Christian people into clerics and laymen, nobles and serfs. Some of the Cujavians held that ministers should give up their tithes and earn their bread by manual labor and that the gentry should give up their estates, to which they held title only by right of ancestral conquest. There was strong but amicable disagreement on these problems of polity and the relationship of the church to the society. In the course of the deliberations Lucas Mundius, who had been a member of the town council of Vilnius, "enthusiastically recommended the sect of the [Moravian] communists, both for their government, and for the fact that they were said to be of one mind with our people *de Deo et Christo,* and for their devoutness."[27] There followed further dispute among the brethren about the Moravians; and "not until Mundius promised messengers from them to the brethren did they become quiet."

It is to be noted that the immersionist Cujavians with Peter Gonesius persevered at this time in holding to the pre-existence of Christ, and had still not moved on to the more radical positions as to the Godhead, as had the Pinczovians; and that, like the Prussian Mennonites, they exercised the rigorous discipline of the ban. There is some evidence that even at this time certain Polish Anabaptists, probably Cujavians, had tried to bring about some union with the Dutch Anabaptists of ducal and royal Prussia, but without success. The Minor Church synod of Pełsznica thus represents a fusion of the conservatively anti-Trinitarian anabaptists of Kujawy, undoubtedly under the influence of the Vistula Mennonites, and the irresolutely antipedobaptist anti-Trinitarians of the palatinate of Cracow, more noticeably under the influence of Italian rationalism, with its tendency to minimize the use of baptism.

Mundius, apparently with the endorsement of the synod of

27 Zachorowski, "Najstarsze synody," *loc. cit.,* 233.

Pełsznica, now took a journey to Moravia to request a delegation from the Hutterites. Lubieniecki, writing from another perspective, but we assume, with a correct dating, says of Mundius:

Leaving his office . . . [in Vilnius, early in 1568 and attending the synod at Pełsznica in the autumn] and yielding to a religious impulse, [he] used to like to travel through various places; and thus [early] in 1569 he came upon . . . the Moravian Brethren. . . . Living with them several weeks, he recommended the Polish churches as agreeing with them *in everything* save the holding of public offices.[28]

Apparently on the basis of an epistolary appeal, the Hutterites sent a certain brother Louis Dörker and three companions, who arrived in Cracow in September 1569; and, after discussions, led back four young Poles to learn the communal way of life.

In the meantime, at a synod in Bełżyce (southeast of Lublin) in March 1569, attended not only by the extreme Radicals but also by ditheists, tritheists, and even by Nicene Calvinists, an effort was made to bring together the factions of the Major and Minor Churches. When this final attempt at mending the schism in the Helvetic community failed, the more conservative anti-Trinitarians moved farther in the unitarian direction, while among all the anti-Trinitarians the radical communitarian spirit of the Moravian Anabaptists (and no doubt also the Minor Party of the Unity in Moravia), as earlier reported by Mundius, had so far prevailed since the synod at Pełsznica that pastors such as Gregory Paul, George Schomann, and Peter Gonesius, indeed all except Czechowic, were prepared to lay down their ministries and undergo reordination at the hands of the apostolic brethren in Moravia. Lay leaders, such as John Niemojewski and Simon Ronemberg, were prepared to abandon their callings in response to the common needs. Niemojewski, Simon Siemianowski, and Lawrence Brzeziński sold their estates in Kujawy and distributed the proceeds among the poorer brethren. One nobleman simply turned back to the king his jurisdiction over a district in the palatinate of Lublin.

At this confluence of the anti-Nicene and the anabaptist currents flowing with accelerated swiftness, we must take note of a major religio-constitutional development in Polish history that tended to constrict the flow of life in the Minor Church in sectarian narrows.

At the diet of Lublin in 1569, with a view to providing for an orderly succession on the death of the childless king, the Lithuanians and Poles, whose realms had been long united in the per-

---

[28] S. Lubieniecki, *op. cit.*, 227.

sonal union of the Lithuanian Jagellons as kings of Poland, proceeded to make kingship henceforth elective, and to preserve the traditional union by making it constitutional and federative rather than dynastic. In the deliberations, the Catholics promised the Protestants that, if they would agree among themselves, some permanent arrangements could be worked out religiously for the united kingdom. This encouraged the Protestants, gathering at Sandomir in the spring of 1570, to draw up a *Consensus* agreeable alike to Lutherans, the *Unitas,* and the Nicene Calvinists. We need not go into the fierce controversies among the three groups leading to the agreement. They were at least united in excluding the anti-Nicene antipedobaptist Minor Church from participation in the united Protestant front.

Nevertheless, the Minor Church was capable of considerable independent growth and alas also further controversy. At Węgrów, Gonesius published his comprehensive *Doctrina pura et clara* in 1572. In the same year the king legalized the erection of a meetinghouse for Gregory Paul's congregation in Cracow; but by far the most important development was the organization of a communistic colony in Raków in 1569.

3. THE FOUNDING OF RAKÓW, 1569

It was in the very year of the Union of Lublin, 1569, that an anti-Trinitarian, anabaptist communal experiment was established by Gregory Paul on wooded lands belonging to the castellan of Żarnów in the palatinate of Sandomir at Raków, destined a decade later to become the spiritual capital of Socinianism, with its prolific press eventually publishing the famous Racovian Catechism (1605). To Raków in 1569 came the rebaptized nobles who had sold their lands, especially those from Kujawy, along with many anabaptist anti-Trinitarian ministers whom we have thus far encountered.

At Raków the baptism of adolescents by immersion was introduced in 1570, but there remained some hesitation as to the rebaptism of adults. The community of goods was introduced. Some in the colony propounded psychopannychism and looked to the imminent advent of the Kingdom of God and the resurrection of the dead. There is clear indication also that some of the psychopannychists were under the influence of Paduan Averroism in denying that there is a distinct soul in a person apart from the universal Mind.

Tretius wrote scornfully of "Gregory Paul and very poor little associates in the ministry" who profited immensely by the device of Christian communism."[29] Even Transylvanian Unitarians disparagingly referred to "the Racovian secession and madness," and to "the conventicles of little old demented women."[30]

Czechowic and his noble convert Niemojewski tarried only a year in Raków and went on together to Lublin, the former to succeed Paplepka. There they could give more disciplined expression to their radical and consistent Anabaptist convictions on the necessity of rebaptism and an ordained ministry.

In the chaotic spiritualism and collectivism of Raków, the Cracow apothecary and lay elder Simon Ronemberg stands out, very much as Jacob Hutter did at a corresponding state of inchoateness among the Anabaptists in Moravia. In the decade from the founding in 1569 to the coming of Faustus Socinus in 1579, Ronemberg was like the "Ezra" of the new Zion; and he turned his eyes to Moravia for inspiration.

It was important for the leading spirits among the Anabaptists of the Minor Church to inspect the Moravian colonies. The purpose of some in the delegation, alarmed by their more parlous situation as a consequence of the consensus of Sandomir, appears to have been to effect a union with the Hutterites for their mutual reinforcement. Each group was conscious of being the restored apostolic church. There may have been more than one delegation in the period 1569–1571. The Hutterite and Racovian sources do not entirely agree.

George Schomann dates the departure of a Polish delegation to the Hutterites soon after the birth of his daughter, after sunset, 20 August 1569, namely, just about the time (September) that Dörker arrived in Cracow; and he describes it thus:

At about this time we had gone with Lord [Jerome] Filipowski, Master Simon [Ronemberg], the apothecary, and several others to Moravia to compare doctrines and morals with the Moravian brethren. We found the government of God's people there most excellent, but all parties passionately maintained a triune God.[31]

The Hutterite *Chronicle* records that Simon Ronemberg arrived at the Hutterite administrative headquarters at Neumühl near Nicolsburg on 25 January 1570, with an otherwise unidentified lord by the name of Janckowski (possibly Jerome Filipowski) regarded by the Hutterites as head of the delegation, and three unnamed preachers (including, possibly, Schomann). The Hut-

---

[29] Tretius to Josias Semler, February 1570; Wotschke, *Briefwechsel,* No. 408, p. 319.
[30] Marcello Squarcialupi to Socinus, 15 September 1581, *BFP,* 1, 360.
[31] Sandius, *op. cit,* 195.

terites rightly saw in Ronemberg the driving spirit behind the mission.

The Hutterites took note of the preference of the Polish Anabaptists for the practice of immersion rather than pouring. They made the *Rechenschaft* of Peter Riedemann the basis of their theological discussion. It is clear from this record that they differed from the Poles on the doctrine of the Godhead and the community of goods. That Filipowski and Schomann would have stressed Christology and the Trinity in deliberating with the Moravian communitarian Anabaptists is all the more natural for the reason that they had both recently come close to the adoptionist position; and Filipowski had recently been rebuffed by the Helvetic Trinitarians at Cracow in 1568, despite his moving and irenic address (in the hall of the palatine), calling for reunion. But it is notable that in the interchanges between the Polish and the Moravian Anabaptists, the subject of the Trinity was not conspicuous in the extant records on either side as the issue on which they failed to agree. The Polish delegation returned to Poland with the four youths who had accompanied Louis Dörker from Cracow to learn Hutterite crafts and doctrine.

Lubieniecki, writing from a later perspective, stresses the disappointment of the Polish delegates:

While these two men [Schomann and Filipowski; Lubieniecki does not mention Ronemberg] found much that was excellent, yet they unexpectedly found them [the Hutterites] holding obstinately to the common doctrine of the Trinity, and persecuting with hatred any that denied it, and shrinking from them. For they dared call pagan worshipers (*cultores Ethnicos*) us who by the grace of God confess the pure truth [in God]. . . . So that the journey and effort of these two men was in vain, for those good men would not depart a finger's breadth.[32]

On the Hutterite charge of "paganism" it is important to observe that the Poles did not interpret this as a reference to their view about the Godhead but to their view on property:

In the first place they [the Hutterites] lie when they claim that anyone who owns a house, land or money and does not bring it to their community is not a Christian but a pagan and cannot be saved.[33]

The Polish author of the acrimonious *Treatise not against the Apostolic Community . . . but against the Communists in Moravia*

[32] S. Lubieniecki, *op. cit.*, 223.
[33] *A Treatise*, Kot, *Socinianism*, 93. Cf. 97: "They [the early Christians] did not divest themselves of possessions, neither did the Apostles urge them to do so nor did they tell them that they were Pagans because of their possessions, as these 'economists' are now trying to convince others."

(c. 1570), from which we have just quoted, cannot have been any of the three members of the aforementioned delegation, because he expressly says his information is based upon this delegation's report and the conversations with the Hutterites in Cracow in September 1569. It is the work of one who speaks with authority in his own circle, possibly Stanislas Budziński.[34]

From the point of view of the Racovians, such as Ronemberg, negotiations and mutual instruction leading to union must still have seemed desirable, however much they were chagrined by the claim to exclusive apostolicity on the part of the Hutterites; for after the return of Ronemberg to Raków, he apparently besought the community there to dispatch two other messengers, namely, John Baptista (Swięwicki) and John Italus. At Olkusz, northwest of Cracow, they picked up a volunteer from the congregation of Daniel Bieliński, one Jerzy (George) Müller; and the three carried a letter of credentials and commission from Raków dated at Olkusz, 25 May 1570, and preserved in the Hutterite *Chronicle*.[35] It begins with a salutation that is programmatically anti-Trinitarian while at the same time giving immediate evidence that the delegates are taking earnestly the doctrine of the suffering Christ stressed by the Hutterites in an earlier interchange. The three bearers of the letter remain very respectful of Hutterite spiritual and disciplinary achievements and are prepared to learn more about the "holy institution" with a view no doubt to implementing further the practices and principles in Raków; but according to the Hutterites, they looked around "with cold heart," unable to unite with the Hutterites; and thus "little fruit came of it," from the Hutterite point of view.

Presently, Peter Walpot addressed a letter[36] to five named Poles, who had recently inspected the Hutterite colonies, and John Italus, who had come with Müller and John Baptista. It is quite possible that all these were Polish anti-Trinitarians of the Italian type without close connection with the Racovians. It appears from the Hutterite catalogue of imperfections among these otherwise serious visitors that they had not sufficiently broken from the

---

[34] Kot's conjecture; *Socinianism*, 99, n. 4.

[35] Zieglschmid, *Chronik*, 443. That one of these Johns was the Lithuanian Swięcicki is Kot's surmise, *Socinianism*, 33; but one may well have been Johannes Baptista Italus, the prophet of penitence last met in Ch. 10.3.a.

[36] Zieglschmid, *Chronik*, 444. The social significance of Walpot's epistle, along with related documents, has been admirably analyzed by Kot, *Socinianism*, and thoroughly studied by Robert Friedmann for doctrinal differences between Hutterites and the (proto-) Socinians, "Reason and Obedience: An Old Anabaptist Letter of Peter Walpot (1571) and Its Meaning," with complete translation in English by Harold Bender, *MQR*, XIX (1945), 27–40.

world and, above all, had "no proper or true baptism." They irritated the Hutterites because of their cultural superiority in languages, their overbearing manner, their Latinized names, and their "presumption" that they could also teach the Hutterites! Walpot's letter stresses their unwillingness to submit to the apostolic authority of the Hutterite Church and urges them not to "postpone or delay your conversion."

It is possible that Walpot could not clearly distinguish between merely antipedobaptist anti-Trinitarians (as this delegation may have been) and the immersionist anti-Trinitarians of Raków and elsewhere.

A second and long letter from Walpot is, however, clearly directed to Racovians in response to an inquiry from Simon Ronemberg. Ronemberg had written Walpot, 1 November 1570, about eleven months after his visit at Neumühl and presumably after he had tried to implement some of the Hutterite principles in Raków. Apparently, Ronemberg, as apothecary, had not yet fully decided to abandon his profession for the community of goods at Raków.

He is chastised by Walpot for wavering, the more so for the reason that Ronemberg has freely acknowledged that Walpot is "the builder of Noah's Ark" of salvation, and yet Ronemberg's people "have not reached the first step of the ladder of the will of God, namely, that of true submission and union with His people [the Hutterites, outside of whose Ark there is no salvation]." Walpot warns Ronemberg of the wrath to come, of the fate of Lot's wife and of the rich young ruler who turned away sorrowfully from the only redemption, communitarian *Gelassenheit*. In sternly dissociating himself from the Polish Brethren, Walpot enumerates some of the many differences, but significantly nowhere mentions the Trinity:

We cannot recognize you [Polish Anabaptists] as a people of God or as our brethren, for you are lacking in righteousness. . . . For where is your true submission in baptism, your new birth and renunciation of the world, sin, devil, repentance from dead works, faith in God, your own flesh and self-will . . . ? How do you exercise among yourselves and in your midst the Christian and proper ban, excommunication . . . ? According to you the [true, the Hutterite] Church would have had to adapt itself to *you* and learn from *you, you* who are not yet on the right foundation of God, and yourselves needed to be taught the very first beginning of the divine word, to lay the foundations, namely, repentance from dead works and faith in God, baptism [at the hands of the Hutterites], doctrine, the laying on of hands, the resurrection from the dead, and the eternal judgment.[37]

[37] Zieglschmid, *Chronik*, 446–455.

The principal objection of Walpot was that the Poles did not recognize "that the Lord Christ after his resurrection gave authority to his [communitarian] church, and that his authority thereafter was not broken." Saul, after his conversion, was bidden to go to Ananias, "who had to lay hands on him and baptize him," and Walpot and his fellow ministers regarded themselves as the only authorized servants of Jesus Christ and his church, guiding the new Ark of the new Moses, and prepared to baptize and lay hands on the Poles in return for their submission to the apostolic authority of the suffering church, outside of which there was no salvation.[38]

4. THE RACOVIAN "CATECHESIS"

In the light of such comings and goings, it is understandable that the image of the Ark shortly became especially prominent also at Raków, when, rejected by the authoritarian Hutterites, the Racovians sought to create their own somewhat less exclusivistic Polish *Bruderhof*. This new conception of the Polish Anabaptists is documented in the *Catechesis et confessio fidei* of 1574, composed by George Schomann.[39]

Schomann, for some time an antipedobaptist, had taken the momentous step for himself when he was rebaptized 31 August 1572 at the age of forty. In the *Catechesis* he gives full expression, largely in Biblical quotations, to the whole of the communitarian baptismal theology as accepted by himself and Ronemberg at Raków. "Flee from Babylonian faith," it exhorts, "and Sodomistic life, having entered into the Ark of Noah; for the Lord will in a short time inflict punishment on that wicked and ungrateful world by the final deluge, not of water but of fire, which will devour all the impious and those unmindful of repentance."

The *Catechesis* was designed both as an *apologetic* to correct the prejudices against "the little and afflicted company of those in Poland" "known by the Anabaptist name which Satan has sought in his wiles to make disreputable and hated," and as a *catechism* for young catechumens with brief questions and responses almost entirely made up of Biblical quotations.

A prominent structural principle in the organization of the material is the doctrine of the threefold office of Christ as prophet, king, and priest—a classification which, though earlier found, for example, in Eusebius of Caesarea, was revived in the Reformation Era primarily by John Calvin;[40] and its prominence in both

[38] For the use of the Cyprianic phrase, see Ch. 16.3.
[39] The full title is *Catechesis et confessio fidei, coetus per Poloniam congregati, in nomine Jesu Christi, Domini nostri crucifixi et resuscitati* (Cracow, 1574).
[40] I have traced Calvin's phrase in the "Excursus" to *The Harvard Divinity School* (Boston, 1954), esp. 340–348.

Schomann's *Catechesis* and the later Racovian catechisms must be seen as a Calvinist legacy to the Minor Church. Schomann understood Jesus Christ as highest prophet on the basis of such texts as: John 1:1, "In the beginning was the *Verbum*"; Matt. 23:8, "For only one is your *magister*"; Rev. 19:11 f., "And I saw a white horse and the name of him who sat thereon is called the *sermo Dei*"; and Heb. 1:1, "God who aforetime spoke through the prophets in our times has spoken with us by his Son."

It was the conviction of the early Racovians as expressed by Schomann that true Christians *imitate* Christ as prophet, priest, and king in a way which involves suffering: He "having suffered for us left us an example" that Christians might become "an elect race, kings and priests" (I Peter 2:9).

The Holy Spirit in the *Catechesis* is very pervasive, but, as with Servetus, as a power (*virtus*) rather than as a person, as "the spirit of truth," a divine "gift," "the finger of God," the divine "energy," as "fire" and "water." There can be no adoration of the Spirit, since the Spirit dwells in the believer himself and the disciplined community, but for that reason is closely connected with, indeed, instrumental in, the effectiveness of the whole of Schomann's baptismal theology.

Baptism, reminding us of the sacrament as defined by Servetus (Ch. 11.1), is described as:

the immersion in water and the emersion of a person who believes the gospel and exercises repentance in the name of the Father and Son and Holy Spirit, or in the name of Jesus Christ, whereby he publicly professes that by the grace of God the Father he has been washed in the blood of Christ by the aid of the Holy Spirit from all his sins; so that being ingrafted into the body of Christ he may mortify the old Adam and be transformed into the celestial Adam in the firm assurance of eternal life after the resurrection.

In a somewhat later formulation of the baptismal theology of the Minor Church, baptism is closely related to Christ in his role as re-creator. Though Christ in this unitarian theology was not thought of as pre-existent and, as Logos, the creator of the world, he is the author of the new creation of baptismal regeneration. The plunge into the waters of redemption is stressed:

Where there is no immersion there is no true external baptism (*Taufe*). *Taufen* is old German and means the same as *teufen*, "dip in." Ask . . . the Mennonites about it who call both *doopen* in their language. Moreover, where you don't dip or immerse in the water, you can have no understanding of baptizing unto the death, burial, and resurrection of the Lord Jesus Christ. Look also to scripture where it is the same. The word *baptizare*, which in Greek is *baptizein*, is in Latin *immergere,* in German *eindauchen, verschwemmen.* From this it comes about that Paul [I Cor. 10:1] can compare baptismal immersion with [passage through] the Red Sea; and Peter [I Peter 3:21] with the flood. And this immersion takes place publicly with us in water courses or rivers (where this is possible) with public confession of sins and forgiveness.[41]

At Raków public immersion was so prominent that long after the Racovians had been banished, their principal theological monument in the dilapidated colony was the large baptismal trench or pit (perhaps intentionally similar to an open grave) and their cemetery mound without markers.[42]

As to the afterlife, we have already observed that the Racovians, like the Anabaptists at the Council of Venice (Ch. 22.2), adhered to the doctrine of psychopannychism. Gregory Paul wrote on this subject as early as 1568, *Of the True Death.*[43]

As to the second sacrament or ordinance of the Racovian community, the Lord's Supper appears to have had a somewhat more than sacramentarian commemorative significance. The Holy Spirit was essential to its observance:

It is a sacred action instituted by Christ the Lord in which the proven disciples of Christ, sitting down in sacred assembly to the table of the Lord, give thanks from the heart to God the Father for his benefits in Christ, and breaking the bread eat, and from the cup of the Lord drink, in devout recollection of the body of Christ the Lord given for us unto death and of his blood shed in remission of our sins, stirring up one another to constant suffering under the cross and to sincere brotherly love.

As to how Christ is present, though in heaven, the answer is through the Holy Spirit, *non carnaliter, sed spiritu suo sancto* (John, ch. 14).

From another somewhat later source, the extraordinary frequency of the observation of the Supper among certain Polish Brethren is described thus:

The Lord's Supper we attend often and, indeed, where possible every day. . . . We seek the body and blood of the Lord [however] not in

---

[41] This is a description of baptism among the Dutch-German-Polish unitarian anabaptists in communion with the Racovians as described by Christopher Ostorodt, immersed at Chmielnik in 1584. His letter is addressed to the Strassburg Anabaptists, edited by Theodor Wotschke, *ARG* (1915), 145, 147.

[42] *Schicksale der polnischen Dissidenten,* II (Königsberg, 1768), 138.

[43] *O prawdziwej śmierci, zmartwychwstaniu* (Nieśwież, 1568), edited by Konrad Górski and W. Kuraskiewicz (Breslau, 1954). See also on Laelius and Faustus Socinus, Lech Szczucki, "Z Eschatologii Braci Polsckich," *Archiwum historii filozofii,* I (1957), 5–41.

the bread and wine, but rather the bread and wine in the body and blood of the Lord, that is, in his congregation [I Cor. 10:16], although we do not consider the bread and wine and the table of the Lord like other bread and wine, but as the Lord's bread and wine and the Lord's table, that is, consecrated or blessed, at which it is not fitting that an unclean person (as also no uncircumcised person could eat of the paschal lamb) should sit and eat with the others, from which indeed not only the unimmersed but also the immersed, if they have soiled themselves by sin, are to be withheld.[44]

The writer goes on to discuss the unitarian anabaptist Supper as a *pascha*, that is, a passing over or passing through; and he seems to be thinking of the unitarian commemoration as modeled on contemporary Jewish usage of the evocation of redemption from bondage to Egypt in the formalized paschal query of the Jewish child addressed to his parents at the Passover table.

The ban in the Racovian *Catechesis* of 1574 is, so to speak, as with all Anabaptists, the sacrament of discipline in love. It is "the frequent reminder of individuals of their duty and the admonition of such as sin against God or their neighbor, first privately, and then also publicly before the whole assembly; and finally, the rejection of the pertinacious from the communion of saints, that so being ashamed, they may repent, or if they will not, may be damned eternally." The moral discipline of the Racovian Anabaptists was such that they eschewed superfluity of personal possessions. They wore a simple gray garb and, intentionally, poor clothing.

On the polity of the Racovian community the *Catechesis* is remarkably complete. The offices of bishop, deacon, elder (*senior*), and widow are Biblically grounded and characterized.

Such was the communitarian, immersionist, anti-Nicene Anabaptism in the most radical center of the Minor Church. At the end of the reign of Sigismund II Augustus, negation of the traditional formulation of the triune Godhead had found positive expression in the vigorous and purportedly apostolic formulation of the threefold office of Jesus Christ as man, the adoptive son of God. Exclusive in their claims, though not so intolerant as the communitarian Anabaptists of Moravia, the Racovians, stressing the importance of dying to the world in immersion and rising with Christ in faith, called themselves *christiani* and all other Christians in Poland disparagingly *chrześciani* (from *chrzest*, "pedobaptist christening," as distinguished from the true baptism of immersion).

---

[44] Christopher Ostorodt of Danzig to the Strassburg Anabaptists, *loc. cit.*, 153.

We now leave the Polish Brethren for Transylvania, where we shall find a comparable radical tide at full flood, within the Reformed Church but with few traces of the pacifism, anabaptism, and psychopannychism prominent in Raków and elsewhere in Poland.

CHAPTER 28

THE RISE OF UNITARIANISM IN TRANSYLVANIA

By 1564 the Reformation in the riven kingdom of Hungary had, as in the neighboring kingdom of Poland, passed through a Lutheran and a Helvetic phase and was on the point of engendering an antipedobaptist unitarian movement. Francis Dávid (c. 1510–1579), successively superintendent of the Lutheran Church of Transylvania (1557), of the Calvinist Church (1564), and of the Unitarian Church (1576), embodied in his career the three Reformation phases experienced by the tripartite kingdom.[1]

The kingdom of Hungary was first bisected by a double election to the throne of St. Stephen after the defeat of King Louis II by the Turks at the battle of Mohács in 1526. One party among the nobility elected Ferdinand as his successor in the expectation that they could count on his brother, Emperor Charles V, to support them against further assaults from Suleiman I the Magnificent (1520–1566). The more nationalist party, fearing German and Hapsburg domination, preferred to cast their lot in the crisis with John Zápolya, a Hungarian. After two years of civil war, Zápolya was defeated; and, turning to the Sultan for support, he became a Turkish vassal. It is of incidental interest that for eight years, Jerome Łaski served as his prime minister and that the latter's brother John, still an Erasmian, for his service as diplomat was awarded with one of Hungary's nine bishoprics, that of Veszprém. By the Peace of Nagyvárad the rival kings of Hungary recognized each other; and an agreement as to the reunification was worked out depending on which of the two should die first. But instead, on the death of John Zápolya in 1540, the realm underwent in effect a tripartition.

Zápolya had married Isabelle, daughter of King Sigismund I of Poland. Just before Zápolya's death, an heir was born whom

[1] Recent accounts of Unitarianism in this area are those of Earl Morse Wilbur, *A History of Unitarianism in Transylvania, England, and America* (Cambridge, 1952); William Toth, "Trinitarianism versus Antitrinitarianism in

708

the nobles at once elected as king of all Hungary. Suleiman recognized the claims put forward for the infant heir John II Sigismund Zápolya (1540–1571). Ferdinand, protesting, invaded eastern Hungary, but was defeated. Thereupon the central Hungarian plain was organized in pashaliks, granted in military fief, subjected to heavy taxation, and perhaps somewhat maliciously accorded religious toleration. There were now three Hungarys: that of the Hapsburg Ferdinand, who even then was obliged to pay tribute for his narrow fringe; that directly under Turkish control (Central and Lower Hungary); and the vassal state of Transylvania, over which the "demonic monk" Bishop George Martinuzzi[2] governed, while the Queen Regent Isabelle lived the life of a frustrated widow over whom Martinuzzi tyrannized. Steadfastly Catholic, but a soldier more than an ecclesiastic, a diplomat more than a soldier, Martinuzzi basically sought the reunification of dismembered Hungary, while outwardly protesting obeisance to the Sultan. Then, for a brief period, while Isabelle and her son were exiled (1551 to her restoration in 1556), Ferdinand was elected king of Transylvania. Martinuzzi as voivode and cardinal was assassinated in 1551.[3] It was under John Sigismund, recalled from exile in Poland in 1556 and destined to be history's only Unitarian king, that Francis Dávid became successively confidant and court chaplain.

Here in the relative security of the Carpathian bastion, a

the Hungarian Reformation," *CH,* XIII (1944), 255–268; Heinrich Fodor, "Ferenc David, der Apostel der religiösen Duldung," Archiv für Kulturgeschichte, XXXVI (1954), 18–29. The latter, based upon recent and standard works in the Continental languages, does not cite Wilbur and differs from him considerably at many points. A major source is the MS. *Historia Ecclesiastica Unitariorum in Transylvania,* 2 vols., deposited by Alexander St.-Iványi in Houghton Library. Dr. St.-Iványi, who is preparing a life of Francis Dávid, has recently shown that the *Historia,* existing in several slightly variant manuscripts and photographs was primarily the work of John Tözser Kenosi, supplemented or continued by Stephen Foszto Uzoni, and thereafter by members of the Kozma family. Though commonly cited under the name of the second compiler, it is now clear that the first volume, and the one dealing with the formative period, was the work of Kenosi (d. 1772). See St.-Iványi, *The "Historia" and Its Authors,* American Hungarian Library, No. 3 (New York, 1960). The most recent study is that of Antal Pirnát, *Die Ideologie der Siebenbürger Antitrinitarier* (Budapest, 1961).

[2] Bishop of Nagyvárad, he was made archbishop of Gran and cardinal at the very end of his ill-fated career, 1551.

[3] He was cowardly put to death on orders from the Spanish general of the imperial troops and with the prior authorization from Ferdinand himself. The role of Martinuzzi and the social and political situation, with helpful maps, are described by Ladislas Makkai, *Histoire de Transylvania* (Paris, 1946), 133 ff.

buffer state between the Catholics under the Hapsburgs and the Moslems under the Sultan, the increasingly radical church of Transylvania developed the confidence that "it was ordained of the Lord that a pillar of great strength should be raised through us and placed in [these] inaccessible mountains."[4]

How one third of the realm of St. Stephen became largely Protestant under a cardinal and how a large number of the Transylvania Protestants became antipedobaptist Unitarians under the preaching of a sometime Lutheran and Calvinist bishop, filled with a sense of providential mission for his church and his people in their mountain fastness, is the burden of the present chapter.

As in Poland, we can distinguish, though in different proportions, three reformatory impulses: the two-pronged German-Swiss Protestant, the Italian Evangelical-Rationalist, and the Anabaptist-Spiritualist. The development of the Radical Reformation in divided Hungary was more complicated than in Poland. The vassal kingdom of Transylvania, consolidating usages from the period when it was a principality (voivodedom) of the larger realm, was constitutionally reorganized by Martinuzzi. There were three constitutionally recognized ethnic groups, namely: the Szeklers (Latin: *Siculi;* Hungarian: *Székely,* the original Huns), a proud yeomanry living in unwalled towns; the closely related Magyars (tenth-century invaders); and the Saxons (twelfth-century colonists). The most recent entrants into Transylvania, the Wallachs (Vlachs) in the thirteenth century were shepherd immigrants, later known as Romanians, who in the sixteenth century were without any constitutional voice. Spokesmen for the three incorporated nations met in different towns in a diet in a "general" or a "partial" state at the call of the voivode or king. The diet, made up of the nobility (chiefly Magyars), representatives of the Szekler and Saxon nations, and the "regalists" (men of the hour especially designated by the rulers), received the ruler's *propositions,* explicated by the ruler's spokesman; and, after debating them, returned their answer in a *replica* with resolutions. The diet could initiate legislation by sending a *supplicatio* to the ruler, who could in turn give it the status of an *articulus* by signing it. The diet also had the power to elect the ruler. The internal organization of these nations need not detain us, except to observe that the Saxon nation enjoyed the

---

[4] George Blandrata reports this as a widespread conviction in his letter from Transylvania to the churches of Little Poland, 27 January 1568; S. Lubieniecki, *Historia,* 230. Cf. Isa. 2:2 and Micah 4:1.

largest measure of autonomy (based on the *privilegium Andrea-num* of 1224 and extended in 1486). Governed by a corporation (*universitas Saxonum*) headed by the Saxon-elected mayor of the town of Hermannstadt (Nagyszeben), the Germans met at least annually to discuss matters pertaining to the government and welfare of their community.

1. THE ACCELERATION OF RADICAL TRENDS IN THE TRANSYL-VANIAN REFORMATION TO 1557

As early as 1520, Saxon merchants returned from the Leipzig fair to Hermannstadt in Transylvania with Luther's books. Laws were passed, beginning in 1523, against Lutherans in the hope that the Emperor would be encouraged by this token of ortho-doxy to aid Hungary against the Turks. However, by 1529 Her-mannstadt was completely Lutheran and by 1535 the German burghers in much of Hapsburg Hungary and the entire Saxon nation in Transylvania had become Lutheran, adopting the Augsburg Confession in 1544. In Transylvania, the Magyars rapidly followed the Saxons. Until 1557 the three Transylvanian nations were united in one Lutheran Church under a general superintendent or bishop; but divided into a German- and a Hungarian-speaking section (Magyars and Szeklers).[5] So rapidly did the Roman Catholic cause lose support that the diocese of Transylvania was secularized in 1542 and the see left vacant for a decade; and then, on 11 June 1556, the bishop left Transyl-vania. His see was not to have another incumbent for a century and a half.

Lutheranism in Turkish Hungary and in Transylvania began to develop a sacramentarian sentiment under the influence of the Swiss. By 1550, Lutheran congregations in Turkish Hungary were becoming avowedly Helvetic or Calvinist. In Transylvania, Calvinism eventually won most of the Hungarian-speaking Mag-yars and Szeklers who preferred it, partly perhaps, as in the case of the Slavic Poles, because it was not German. In passing, it may be mentioned that Anabaptist refugees early found that Turkish-controlled territory offered a haven for those persecuted by Roman Catholicism and magisterial Protestantism.

The return of the young king, John Sigismund, and the Polish-born queen mother to Transylvania in 1556 after the assassina-

---

[5] Fodor, however, says that Szeklers largely remained Catholic, *loc. cit.*, 23. For the Lutheran Saxons, the most recent account is that of Karl Reinerth, *Die Reformation der siebenbürgisch-sächsischen Kirche* (Gütersloh, 1956).

tion of Cardinal Martinuzzi had been engineered by the most influential man in the land, the voivode of Transylvania, Peter Petrovics. A Calvinist, he saw to it that the Reformed religion was well ensconced before the Catholic queen should return. The royal council, of which he was the leading figure, was the agency for formulating and expressing the royal will. It was composed chiefly of Magyars, half of them appointed by the ruler and half elected by the diet. (Not until Isabelle's sudden death in 1559 would John himself assume direct rule.)

When the general diet convened on 25 November 1556, at Kolozsvár, John II's Catholic tutor, the Pole Albertus Novicampianus, urged against Petrovics that the body re-establish Catholicism as the only faith in Transylvania, a motion doubtless approved by Queen Mother Isabelle. The diet, consisting largely of Lutherans and Calvinists, rejected Novicampianus' plea, and sent instead a *supplicatio* to Isabelle, requesting freedom of worship for the two Protestant confessions on an equality with Catholicism. Isabelle complied, perhaps regarding this as an interim arrangement.[6]

The next year, the general diet met at Torda from 1 to 14 June 1557 and submitted another *supplicatio* to the queen mother. Before convening, the parties of the diet had made elaborate preparations. The Transylvanian Saxons had declared themselves members of the Lutheran Church of the Wittenberg Confession. The Hungarians in the vicinity of Kolozsvár, also Lutherans, electing Francis Dávid as the superintendent of the Hungarian-speaking Lutherans, were at this point already well on their way to becoming sacramentarian and antipedobaptist. The Calvinists (as elsewhere, often called "sacramentarians") rallied about their head, Martin Kálmáncsehi, and trusted to the political protection of Petrovics. The Catholics concentrated on circulating Novicampianus' books. The queen's reply to the diet's *supplicatio,* going beyond the Polish Interim of two years before, constituted, in its wording, a notably nonsectarian grant of religious freedom in the history of the Reformation Era:

Inasmuch as We and Our Most Serene Son have assented to the most instant supplication of the Peers of the Realm, that each person maintain whatever religious faith he wishes, with old or new rituals, while We at the same time leave it to their judgment to do as they please in the matter of their faith, just so long, however, as they bring

[6] On the markedly divergent historical judgments on Isabelle, see Wilbur, *Transylvania,* 12, n. 24. The same divergences are to be seen in the treatments of Bishop Martinuzzi. Wilbur speaks of him as crafty and deceitful, Makkai as humane and devotedly Catholic.

no harm to bear on anyone at all, lest the followers of a new religion be a source of irritation to the old profession of faith or become in some way injurious to its followers—therefore, Peers of the Realm, for the sake of procuring the peace of the churches and of stilling the controversies that have arisen in the gospel teaching, We have decreed to establish a national synod, wherein, in the presence of devoted ministers of the Word of God as well as of other men of rank, genuine comparisons of doctrine may be made and, under God's guidance, dissensions and differences of opinion in religion may be removed.[7]

Despite the generous terms of this constitutional article, the diet at Torda the following year (27 March 1558), however, alarmed at the iconoclasm perpetrated by the sacramentarians, legislated against the Calvinists. The Reformed (sacramentarian) leader, Martin Kálmáncsehi, on 15 June 1558 suffered defeat in debate with nominally Lutheran Francis Dávid and left Transylvania. When the Calvinists became less extreme in their views and practices, the diet at Gyulafehérvár tacitly included them once again in the implementation of the article of toleration.

Kálmáncsehi's victorious opponent, the recently elected superintendent of the Hungarian Lutherans, Francis Dávid, had been born at Kolozsvár (Cluj, Klausenburg) about 1510.[8] His bootmaker father was a Saxon, his mother a Hungarian. Dávid was first educated at the school of the Franciscan friars in Kolozsvár, then at the cathedral school at Gyulafehérvár.[9] He studied at the University of Wittenberg (1545–1548),[10] and then returned to Transylvania in the year of Martinuzzi's assassination to become, successively, rector of a school at Bestercze, Lutheran pastor in the village of Péterfalva, rector of the Lutheran school at Kolozsvár, and pastor of the Lutheran church in the same town (1556). Francis Dávid was not yet an anti-Trinitarian.

[7] Alexander St.-Iványi, *Freedom Legislation in Hungary, 1557–1571* (New York, 1957), 30 f. St.-Iványi notes that the grant of religious liberty made by the Rhaetian diet of Ilanz in 1526 (Ch. 22.1) merely prevented mutual oppression between Roman Catholicism and the Reformed churches, while giving no relief to other bodies. The Polish "Interim" in 1555 did not lead to the repeal of the old heresy laws or go beyond the realm of private worship. St.-Iványi, *op. cit.*, 24 ff., holds that the queen included the Reformed, over against Wilbur, *Transylvania*, 22, who limits the toleration to Lutherans. The Latin text is in Sándor Szilágyi, *Records of the Transylvanian Diets* (Budapest, 1876–1899), II, 78.

[8] Toth says 1520.

[9] Fodor, *loc. cit.*, 20, implausibly says that in 1538 Dávid served as secretary to Transylvanian Bishop Statileo in France.

[10] Fodor says 1545–1546 and, without heeding Pirnát *et alii*, adds Padua. Toth adds Frankfurt.

The history of anti-Trinitarianism in Transylvania had begun[11] when Stancaro, the bellicose Anselmian, smarting from his controversy with Andrew Osiander at Königsberg on the doctrines of justification and the atonement (Ch. 25.3), came to Transylvania late in 1554. After becoming physician at Petrovics' court, he took occasion to develop and publicize his doctrine of Christ's mediation through his human nature alone. Stancaro's crypto-Nestorianism (the radical separation of the two natures of Christ) was decried at three Saxon Lutheran synods, beginning in 1554, and attacked in print by Caspar Heltai, Francis Dávid, and Peter Melius. As in his earlier efforts, Stancaro attempted to safeguard the divine majesty of the Son, at the same time maintaining the doctrine of the Trinity inviolate, by excluding the divine nature of Christ from any participation in the redemptive work. It will be recalled that Stancaro charged that Lutheranism in general, and Melanchthon and Osiander in particular, subordinated the Son to the Father in an Arian fashion by allowing the divine nature of the Son to participate in the mediation between God and man. As in Poland, so in Transylvania, Stancaro disturbed the ministers especially at Kolozsvár, causing them to publish a confession expressly repudiating his doctrine (published at Wittenberg, 1555). His theology was also condemned by a Lutheran synod at Óvár in 1556. He was refused a teaching position and was permitted to take up residence in Hermannstadt only on condition that he refrain from controversy. Unable to comply, he was expelled. Toward the end of 1557, Stancaro appeared in Kolozsvár, there to be challenged by the ministers, among them Dávid, in debate. Utterly defeated locally, Stancaro failed to find support elsewhere, and demanded of the queen that the Kolozsvár ministers who had opposed him should be put to death for heresy! The Kolozsvár pastors responded in their *Apologia adversus maledicentiam et calumnias Francisci Stancari* (1558).

Meanwhile, Melius had won "Lutheran" Dávid for the Reformed side. The two continued in their opposition to the views of Stancaro. Melius, so important in Dávid's religious development, had succeeded Kálmáncsehi as the chief spokesman for Calvinism in Hungary, and for a while also in Transylvania. He had been born at Horhi, and received his education at Tolna (formerly a Lutheran school, but, under the influence of Stephen Kis of Szeged in Turkish Hungary, Calvinistic) and then, briefly, at the University of Wittenberg (1556). He became pastor of the church at Debreczen, also in Turkish Hungary, and continued to imbibe

[11] Traditionally and according to Toth, but Wilbur differs.

and defend the faith of his old master. Having won Dávid to his sacramentarian view, Melius collaborated with him to produce the first confession of faith in the Hungarian language regarding the Reformed view of the Lord's Supper (1559).[12]

In 1559,[13] Stancaro returned to Poland, leaving behind him a few disciples and[14] the germ of an idea that the received formulations of Christology and the doctrine of the Trinity might be revised.

2. Unitarianism Becomes Explicit

The first direct attack on the Trinity came in Hungary from Thomas Aran (Arany) of Köröspeterd, who preached specifically that Christ is not God, but only the Son of God and a son of man; that the Holy Spirit is not God, but only the love of God; that there are not three Persons in the Trinity; and that Christ is not mediator between God and man in both of his natures.[15] Late in 1561, Aran appeared in Debreczen, where Calvinist superintendent Peter Melius decisively worsted him in debate and extracted from him a confession of error. From Hungary, Aran went to Transylvania, where, undaunted, he continued to argue against the received doctrine of the Trinity.

In the meantime, Dávid was expelled as a sacramentarian by the Saxon section of the joint Hungarian-Saxon Lutheran synod at Medgyes in 1560. Dávid kept his pastorate in Kolozsvár. He dealt with Aran's ideas critically at this time in *Capita consensus doctrinae de vera Trinitate*.[16] In 1561, Dávid, still head of the Hungarian "Lutherans" but now fully sacramentarian and opposed to the Eucharistically conservative Saxon Lutherans, held a heated debate at a second joint synod in Medgyes. To prevent a formal division in Transylvania of the Hungarian (Szekler-Magyar) and the Saxon Lutherans, John Sigismund renewed at the

---

[12] Melius, together with Gregory Szegedi and George Cseglédi, composed the Confession of Debreczen (1562), stating the Reformed attitude toward the faith of Rome. In the same year Melius published a hymnbook and a Hungarian translation of Calvin's Genevan catechism. Constantly in touch with Szegedi, Beza, Bullinger, Simler, and Tretius, Melius continued to engage in debate with the Hungarian Lutherans, in 1564 writing a book against the Lutheran superintendent, Matthew Hebler. Toth, *loc. cit.*, 260–264.

[13] 1556, according to Fodor, *loc. cit.*, 22.

[14] Traditionally, and according to Toth, but Wilbur says no.

[15] Révész, links Aran's ideas with North Italian anti-Trinitarianism. Toth contradicts Wilbur's claim that Aran "in 1558 wrote a clear and bold book denying the Trinity." Fodor deals with Aran, *loc. cit.*, 25.

[16] Fodor has Dávid developing his anti-Trinitarian ideas in this work. Wilbur postpones the onset of Unitarianism, *Transylvania*, 25 f.

diet of Torda in 1563 his mother's great edict of toleration of discrepant forms of worship and faith.

Thus far Dávid was arguing as a sacramentarian about the Lord's Supper and not about the Trinity except as he had opposed Stancaro's version of Trinitarianism.

Unitarian doctrine would not so suddenly have made headway against Calvinist and Lutheran opposition but for the backing and leadership of George Blandrata of Padua, Geneva, and Cracow (Chs. 24.2; 25.3), whose career as a physician had made him an intimate of Queen Bona of Poland, of Queen Isabelle of Transylvania, and of her son, John Sigismund. In 1563, proto-unitarian Blandrata became John's personal physician and private counselor. Despite his ease at court, Blandrata, like many another physician in our narrative, had a feeling for the poor. A humane humanist, he had transferred to the realm of Christology his conviction that the *Christus dives* of orthodoxy was false. He preferred the *Christus pauper,* whom the pious poor, despised by the world, follow. It was Blandrata who represented the king in 1564 at the general synod at Nagyenyed, where Lutheran Saxons and Calvinist Hungarians finally parted company.

Dávid emerged as the Reformed (Calvinist) superintendent of Transylvania, the counterpart of Melius in Turkish Hungary, and, at the suggestion of Blandrata, also court preacher at the Transylvanian capital, Gyulafehérvár.

Precisely when the new Reformed superintendent, Dávid, himself began to question the doctrine of the Trinity cannot be stated, although one tradition has it that he put forth some objections in 1560 while still a nominal Lutheran, though already converted to sacramentarianism.[17] Certainly, in conversation with Blandrata, Dávid's thought developed rapidly. But where Blandrata moved cautiously and diplomatically, Dávid was impatient to proclaim the truth as he perceived it at the moment.

In 1565, Dávid began to preach openly against the doctrine of the Trinity, gathering support from such colleagues as Stephen Basilius and Luke Égri. It was not long before the impetuous convert to unitarianism was charged by the rector of the Kolozsvár school, Peter Károli, with heresy and was reported on to Melius in Turkish Hungary. The indignant, increasingly radical superintendent of the Reformed Church of Transylvania now made bold to remove Károli from his position.[18] Károli thereupon moved to Turkish Hungary, joining forces with the Reformed

---

[17] See above; cf. Wilbur, *Transylvania,* 29.
[18] Wilbur dates Dávid's open attacks on the Trinity *after* the Károli incident, Toth *before*.

superintendent there, Melius. In concert, Károli and Melius sent warnings which they had solicited from Calvin and Beza to the king of Transylvania. Decrying the heretical views of both the court physician and the court preacher, Melius requested that a synod of all Reformed Hungarians be called to debate the issues.

The first pitched battle on the doctrine of the Trinity, as it happened, took place outside Transylvania, where the orthodox party had the advantage of numbers. Luke Égri, formerly like Dávid, a student at Wittenberg and his associate at Kolozsvár, had by now returned to his native Égér. It was Égri's anti-Trinitarianism that occasioned the calling of a synod at Göncz in January of 1566. Although Égri avoided formal criticism of the doctrine of the Trinity in his defense, he irritated the orthodox Reformed by his tritheistic explanations. (Two years later, 1568, Égri was to be brought, on the authority of a Hapsburg general and a Lutheran, before another Calvinist synod at Kassa and condemned.[19])

In Transylvania, one month after Égri's comparition at Göncz, Superintendent Dávid for his part likewise called a synod. Meeting with the king's consent, in Gyulafehérvár in February 1566, it dealt with the doctrine of the Trinity, and thereby publicly opened the Unitarian controversy in Transylvania. Several lesser synods and ministerial meetings followed. Throughout, Blandrata contrived to preserve as much of the traditional language as possible in his *Seven Theses and Antitheses.*

Then in April of 1566, again at Gyulafehérvár, King John II Sigismund, in accordance with Melius' request, called a joint synod of the Transylvanian and the Central (Turkish) Hungarian churches. Blandrata, as earlier in Poland (Ch. 25.3), forthrightly requested that philosophical and theological terms be eschewed and that only Biblical and apostolic language be employed, to which Melius (like his counterpart Lismanini in Poland) unaccountably agreed. Blandrata and Dávid for their part thereupon warmly expressed high regard for the Apostles' Creed, and acknowledged the equality of the three Persons; but they rejected the term and the idea of a common *substantia* or *essentia* on the ground that along with the three *personae* it made for a "papal and idolatrous quaternity." Shortly after the synod adjourned, Dávid and his supporters published a revision of the Heidelberg Catechism, at Maros-Vásárhely, called a *Catechismus ecclesiarum Dei in natione Hungarica per Transylvaniam: XIII articuli*

[19] Refusing to recant, he was thrown into prison, where he languished for five years. Finally, he signed a recantation, was released, and disappeared from the scene.

christiani consensus,[20] which rejected *"essentia"* in a simple avowal of the equality of the Father, the Son, and the Holy Spirit.

In February of 1567, at a synod at Torda, Dávid and Blandrata went even farther, rejecting the statements of Maros-Vásárhely and Dávid's revision of the Catechism in favor of an Arian statement of faith. They identified the one God as the Father, subjected the Son to the Father, and interpreted the Spirit not as a third Person, but as a power of God.[21] A week later, Melius convened a synod of his own forces at Debreczen to strengthen the battle lines against anti-Trinitarianism. This gathering issued two confessions:[22] one in Latin and dedicated to John Sigismund; the other in Hungarian and dedicated to the people of commerce "in order that wherever their business should take them, they might fight against the besetting heresy of the [Reformed] church." The Nicene Calvinist minority went on to suggest that Dávid, son of a sutor and spouse of an ambitious rich woman, should be stoned for his sophistry.[23]

Dávid, likening himself to much maligned Origen, replied in two books. His *Refutatio scripti Petri Melii* argued that the one God is the Father of the Lord Jesus Christ; that the Word was not, prior to the incarnation, the Son of God; and that the Holy Spirit was only the power of God. The other work was prepared jointly by Dávid and Blandrata, *De falsa et vera unius Dei Patris Filii et Spiritus Sancti cognitione*. It argued that the eradication of the doctrine of the Trinity should be considered the consummation of the Reformation begun in Luther, Zwingli, and Calvin, and that this consummation would occur with the second coming of Christ in 1570.[24] The theological and eschatological influence of Servetus is clear. The work ridiculed the alleged absurdities of the doctrine of the Trinity, printing eight woodcut renditions of sculpture and paintings of the Trinity taken from orthodox churches, together with appropriate anti-Trinitarian comments.[25]

Dávid's concern for the application of religious toleration to the anti-Trinitarian party found favor with his king; and, at the

---

[20] Printed by Friedrich Lampe, *Historia ecclesiae Reformatae in Hungaria et Transylvania* (Utrecht, 1728), 159 ff.
[21] Toth, *loc. cit.*, 261–262.
[22] Wilbur states that it adopted the Helvetic Confession.
[23] Fodor, *loc. cit.*, 26.
[24] Gyulafehérvár, 1567. Next year they published *De Mediatoris Jesu Christi divinitate*, including a chapter, "De restauratione ecclesiae," from *De operibus Dei* (Ch. 10.2) by Cellarius (d. 1564). Uzone, *op. cit.*, I, 129, 504.
[25] Reproduced by Górski, *Grzegorz Paweł*, 202–207; cf. Ch. 11, n. 55.

ensuing diet of Torda, after his impassioned appeal,[26] the toleration edicts of 1557 and 1563 were renewed and strengthened
28 January 1568, to secure by implication the toleration of both
the unitarian and the trinitarian parties of the much divided
Reformed Church, alongside the Lutheran and the Catholic
Churches:

Our Royal Highness, as he has decreed—together with the Diet—in
the matter of religion, now again confirms that in every place the
preachers shall preach and explain the gospel each according to his
understanding of it, and if the congregation like it, well; if not, no
one shall compel them, but they shall keep the preachers whose
doctrine they approve. Therefore none of the Superintendents or
others shall annoy or abuse the preachers on account of their religion,
according to the previous resolutions of the Diet, or allow any to be
imprisoned or be punished by removal from his post on account of his
teaching, for faith is a gift of God. This comes from hearing, and
hearing by the word of God.[27]

This law long stood as the most advanced step in toleration yet
taken in Europe.[28]

 Melius, displeased with the way things were running, now
sought to stem the tide by inviting his adversaries among the
Transylvanian clergy to a debate at Debreczen in Turkish
Hungary in 1568. Blandrata suspected an orthodox trap and
advised the Transylvanians to ignore the invitation. The king
himself thereupon summoned a general synod of the ministers
of both Turkish Hungary and Transylvania to meet in his palace
at Gyulafehérvár, to debate the doctrine of the Trinity. Five
debaters, led by Blandrata and Dávid, represented the Unitarian
side, whereas on the Calvinist side there were six debaters, led by
Peter Melius. At five in the morning on 3 March 1568, the great
debate (in Latin) began with solemn prayers on each side, continuing for ten days thereafter. Melius appealed to the authority
of the Bible, the creeds, the fathers, and the orthodox theologians; Dávid, to the Bible alone. The discussion began with heat.
On the ninth day the Calvinists asked to be excused from listening further. The king intimated that this would be confessing
defeat, and they remained; but as nothing new was being accomplished to bring the parties to agree, the king ended the debate
the next day, recommending that the ministers give themselves

[26] The scene is represented in the painting by Aladar Körösföi-Kriesch, which
 hangs in the town hall of Torda and has been frequently reproduced in
 Hungary and the United States.
[27] St.-Iványi, op. cit., 34.
[28] Fodor, loc. cit., 26.

to prayer, seek harmony, and refrain from mutual abuse as unbecoming.

The debate was generally regarded as a victory for the Unitarians, whose side the king favored. During the synod, Blandrata showed himself a poor debater, and he did not enter public discussion again. Dávid, who had opened and was ready with a convincing answer to every question or objection, now returned home to Kolozsvár to be received as a conquering hero. Many of the Lutheran Saxons left the town, and the Saxon federation of the seven fortified towns (Siebenbürgen) removed Kolozsvár from the rights and constitutional privileges of the Saxon corporation. For many years thereafter Kolozsvár was practically a Unitarian city.

Dávid was determined to carry the battle to the Hungarian people at large in their own language. He obtained the king's consent to hold a synod in Hungarian at Nagyvárad (Grosswardein) on the western frontier of Transylvania, on 20 October 1569. Although the Calvinists at first demurred, they were finally persuaded to attend. They would have preferred a duly called synod rather than a royally instigated colloquium. The king's most intimate counselor, Caspar Békés, presided. The king himself attended, with many generals and magnates, and the leading clergy of both Transylvania and Turkish Hungary. There were nine disputants on each side, but the debate for six days was mainly between Dávid and Melius and was carried on with the greatest intensity.

Dávid presented twelve anti-Trinitarian propositions.[29] He went much farther than before, contending, for example, that what the Calvinists were defending was, in fact, a papal quinity of three Persons, one substance, and a deified man. The only God is the Father of Christ, at once divine and human; Christ is the only-begotten Son of God. Though the Son was, as indeed all things have been, present in the mind of God from all eternity, he can be said to be only temporally begotten, not eternally. The Holy Spirit is the vivifying power or grace of God and Christ.

When, in the heat of battle, Melius attacked Dávid with unwonted violence, the king rebuked him, saying: "Inasmuch as we know that faith is the gift of God, and that conscience cannot be forced, if one cannot comply with these conditions, let him go beyond the Tisza [River]."[30] On the morning of one

[29] Printed, along with Dávid's call for a debate in Hungarian, by Lampe, op. cit., 224–230.
[30] Quoted by Wilbur, Transylvania, 40.

session, Melius declared: "May your Serene Highness hear me, and all of you here present. For in the night the Lord revealed to me anew who is and how he is his true and proper Son, to whom I give undying thanks!" In the midst of the disorder that ensued, the king chided Melius perhaps too humorously in view of the situation: "Pastor Peter, if last night you were instructed as to who is the Son of God, what, I ask, have you been preaching before? Certainly up to this moment you have been misleading the people!"[31]

The king saw that nothing further could be gained by fostering unity or unitarianism, and having charged the orthodox Reformed with evading the real issue, he closed the debate. The orthodox drew up a confession of faith of their own, the *Sententia catholica seu consensus ministrorum,* signed by fifty-nine pastors, condemning Dávid and his views.[32] Dávid drew up the entire text of the debate, which was read and amended by the king and several peers before it was published as the *Disputatio.*

The debate at Nagyvárad of 1569 marked the definitive schism between the trinitarian and the unitarian Reformed Hungarians and thereby corresponds to the Piotrków Synod of 1565 in Poland (Ch. 25.3), except that in Transylvania it was the radical party which constituted in effect the major (Hungarian) Reformed Church with both royal and popular support. It will be recalled that the Hungarians as Reformed and the Saxons as Lutherans had already in 1564 split Transylvanian Protestantism. There were now as many confessions in Transylvania as there were nations, although ecclesiastical and ethnic lines did not everywhere coincide. Some of the Szeklers, for example, remained Catholic.

The debate at Nagyvárad launched Transylvanian Unitarianism upon its golden age. With the conversion of the king, scarcely a Magyar family of importance remained outside the unitarian Reformed fold. Heltai's press at Kolozsvár was unceasing in the cause. Dávid secured able professors, some of them distinguished refugees from persecution in other lands, to teach in thirteen higher schools and colleges, chief of which was the

[31] The episode is recounted savoringly by Blandrata in his letter to the Polish Brethren, 31 October 1569; printed by Theodor Wotschke, "Zur Geschichte des Antitrinitarismus," *ARG,* XXIII (1926), 95 f. Fodor, *loc. cit.,* 27, citing Elek Jakab, *Dávid Ferencz Emléke* [Memoirs] (Budapest, 1879), cap. xxvii, Epp. B and C, speaks of Dávid as much less effective than does Wilbur, *Transylvania,* 40 f., who, using the same work by Jakab, calls the synod another victory for Dávid.
[32] Reported by Lampe, *op cit.,* 246–249.

college at Kolozsvár, occupying the buildings of an abandoned convent. Dávid's son-in-law, John Sommer from Pirna in Saxony, rector of the school at Kolozsvár, set down seven orthodox theses on the Trinity and cleverly proved them exclusively with texts taken from Plato, Aristotle, Plotinus, and Marsiglio Ficino, making it uncomfortably clear to the local Calvinists and the distant Wittenbergers that they had really abandoned "theology" and resorted to "pagan philosophy," and had thereby converted the Lord God of Hosts into an abstract *Jehovalitas!*[33]

Without at first a distinctive name, Unitarianism, as the major Reformed Hungarian party in Transylvania, emerged in the schism of 1569 as a well-organized church with several distinctive tenets besides its cardinal affirmation—a people's church with a powerful preacher and a shrewd spokesman at the royal court. Radically sacramentarian, it was sustained by an eschatological fervor and tended toward anabaptism.

Just before or after the Nagyvárad debate, Dávid and Blandrata printed anonymously but in the name "of the ministers and elders of the churches confessing one God the Father" a dual work, *De regno Christi* and *De regno Antichristi*. Dedicated to John II Sigismund, it was an anthology of chapters and sections from the *Restitutio* of Servetus without naming him.[34] To the publication was attached a tract against infant baptism, *Tractatus de paedobaptismo et circumcisione*. The anonymous authors at this point chose not to reproduce the full baptismal and Eucharistic theology of Servetus for fear of arousing opposition. Moreover, one of the two compilers, Blandrata, was not favorably disposed toward the sacramental aspect of Servetus' work.[35] The antipedobaptism in the dual publication must have been the work of Dávid.

Although there seems to have been nothing on baptism in Dávid's dispute with Melius at Nagyvárad, Dávid had earlier (at least before 1568) preached against infant baptism in several sermons which were published in 1569, wherein he took the familiar position that infant baptism was a papal invention and that true baptism depended for its significance upon "conscious faith." In the aforementioned excursus *De paedobaptismo,*

---

[33] Letter to Hallopegius in Wittenberg, 15 May 1571; preserved by S. Lubieniecki, *Historia*, 233 ff. It is of interest that Sommer in this letter shows familiarity with the work of William Postel.

[34] Stanislas Kot has arranged in parallel columns the contents of the work and the corresponding sections of the *Restitutio*, *Autour de Michel Servet*, 100–102.

[35] *Ibid.*, 103, n. 65.

Dávid went farther, moving from antipedobaptism to a qualified anabaptism. He now contended that all who had been baptized under Roman Catholicism should be rebaptized by the Evangelicals (Unitarians), on the ground that the popish baptism had been performed in the name of a "tritheistic substance" and a tripersonal Godhead. Dávid was not averse to punning on the Hungarian equivalent for substance (*állat*), which could also mean "animal" and suggest the "brutish" basis for the traditional christening.

In 1570, Dávid published *A Little Book on the True Baptism*.[36] This unequivocally Anabaptist book was published at Heltai's press in Kolozsvár in both Hungarian and German. It deserves more than passing notice.[37]

The book was originally written by a Flemish martyr not otherwise identified. A Polish physician in Warsaw, Dr. Alexander Vilini, who may have procured it from the Mennonites of the Lower Vistula (Ch. 15), translated it into "pure German" and sent the translation to Dávid, asking him to have it printed in both German and Hungarian. In the translation into Hungarian, Dávid coins new terms when necessary, corrects some sources of the quotations, but occasionally shows an inability to express theological problems concisely. Dávid does not seem to have "improved" or added much to the original text, but the fact that he went to the trouble of translating it and publishing it in two languages shows that he approved of the book and identified himself with its arguments. A large section of the original book of sixty-six pages attacks the dogma of original sin, maintains that children do not know the difference between good and evil, and concludes that infant baptism is unnecessary, since original sin has been "washed away" in Christ's atonement.

Thus far we have been largely concerned with the formulation and consolidation of antipedobaptist, sacramentarian Unitarianism within the Carpathian sanctuary under a benevolent Unitarian king. Unitarianism also won the allegiance of many Hungarian Reformed parishes outside Transylvania. Though King John Sigismund's claim was disputed, he largely controlled ten or twelve neighboring counties in Turkish and in Hapsburg Hungary to the west and north. The trinitarian party was there

---

[36] *Könyvecske Az Igaz Keresztényi Keresztségröl.*
[37] The story of Dávid's translation and the discovery of a portion of the German text in a soaked-out binding of another sixteenth-century book is told by Antal Pirnát in *Irodalomtörténeti Közlemények,* Publications in the History of Literature, LVIII (1954), 299-308.

strongly in the majority among the Reformed churches; but the unitarian Reformed were not in danger of being persecuted so long as the king of Transylvania favored them.

At Nagyvárad itself, the scene of the great debate, Stephen Basilius converted about three thousand to Dávid's persuasion. Unitarianism was also preached even in Debreczen, the citadel of the orthodox Reformed. In Turkish Hungary there were over sixty Unitarian churches (many of them with schools). At the old university town of Pécs the Helvetic church became Unitarian in 1570. Important magistrates joined the movement and assisted it with their wealth. When these churches became organizationally separated from those of Transylvania, they chose a close friend of Dávid's, the missionary Paul Kárádi, to be their superintendent.

Here on the Moslem frontier of Christendom the fierceness of religious feeling is grimly reflected in a famous incident, a Calvinist-Unitarian debate in which death was the prearranged penalty for the losing side. The Unitarian disputants were Luke Tolnai and George Alvinczi. When the Calvinist side won, Alvinczi was duly hanged. Tolnai escaped to the safety of Unitarianized Pécs.[38] A wealthy Unitarian living in the vicinity, indignant at this theological barbarity, thereupon complained to the pasha at Buda, demanding as satisfaction that the responsible Calvinist superintendent likewise be put to death! The pasha ordered a public disputation and, in the end, decided that the execution of Alvinczi had indeed been inhuman, thereupon condemning three Calvinists (including the superintendent) who had disputed before him to be executed. The orthodox petitioned that their spokesmen be spared; the Unitarians supported their plea, saying they had no wish for revenge. In time, the three Calvinists were released from imprisonment upon payment of a large ransom; and a supplementary annual tribute was levied on the Christians of the whole pashalik.

Let us return to the safer realm of the Unitarian King John Sigismund. For all his royal favor, he had not yet accorded the Unitarian Church in Transylvania a sure constitutional standing except as it was a "Reformed" Church. With Dávid's urging, the king at the diet of Maros-Vásárhely early in 1571 granted the people and church of Kolozsvár certain privileges which had been impaired by the withdrawal of the Lutheran Saxons. He strengthened the legal equality of all the rival churches of his realm by provisions against resorts to ecclesiastical violence or

[38] Toth, loc. cit., 266. The episode dates from the year 1574.

coercion by either of the superintendents of the two Reformed Churches and their respective ministerial retainers. Royal assent to the following *replica* was obtained:

Our Lord Jesus Christ orders us to seek first the Kingdom of God and its righteousness; therefore it was resolved in the matter of the preaching and hearing of the word of God, that—as Your Highness with the Diet had resolved in the past—the word of God shall be preached freely everywhere; no one shall be harmed for any creed, neither preachers nor listeners; if, however, any minister would go to criminal extremes, the Superintendent shall be permitted to judge and suspend him, after which he may be expelled from the country.[39]

Dávid's successful entreaty had come none too soon. Two months later, 15 March 1571, John Sigismund, injured in a fall from his horse, died. He was deeply mourned by all, for, despite animosities arising out of the disparate religions, he himself had been popular with his subjects for his personal qualities, his justice and mercy. Henceforth, all rulers of Transylvania would be bound to take an oath at coronation to preserve the equal rights secured by his articles of toleration.

3. ANTIPEDOBAPTIST UNITARIANISM IN TRANSYLVANIA FROM THE DEATH OF JOHN SIGISMUND TO THE DEATH OF DÁVID, 1571–1579

The Unitarian royal counselor Caspar Békés (who thought he might succeed to the Transylvanian throne) was on a royal mission in Vienna to arrange for an "orderly" succession when news of John Sigismund's death reached him. Békés' enemies had intrigued against him, criticizing his religion, his arrogance, his too swift rise to power, and his part-Wallach parentage. Christopher Báthory was made interim ruler, pending the election. Heeding the advice of Christopher and the Sultan, and fearful that Békés might have traded some of their liberties for imperial backing, the nobles thereupon chose Christopher's younger brother, Stephen, one of the three magnates in Transylvania who had remained Catholic. The election was confirmed by the Emperor and the Sultan; and, according to the new treaty, the title of the prince of Transylvania was that merely of voivode.

Educated at the University of Padua, an able commander in the field, Voivode Stephen Báthory pursued a policy of religious toleration; and when urged to show less consideration for non-

[39] Reprinted in St.-Iványi, *Freedom Legislation in Hungary,* 35.

Catholics, he replied that he was ruler of the people, not of their consciences. He promoted Calvinists and Lutherans to public office without prejudice. His rule was, however, hateful to the Szeklers. Presently the Unitarians, especially among the Szeklers, rallied to Békés and his stubborn opposition to the new rule. Stephen naturally became increasingly suspicious of the Unitarians, removing them from court and high public office. He forbade them to print books without his permission and thereby he cut off one of their chief means of spreading their faith. In 1572, at the diet of Torda, Stephen, although confirming his predecessors' edicts of religious freedom, decreed also that any Unitarians introducing further reforms or innovations and altering the faith of the late king should be excommunicated or otherwise punished, at the discretion of the prince.

As early as the end of 1572 there is evidence of an extremely radical sentiment on the margins of the Unitarian Reformed community. At least three students, among them presumably the later Unitarian pastor Andrew Erdödi, had returned from the University of Padua, espousing views in many respects similar to those of Gregory Paul and particularly of Camillo Renato: a spiritualist antipedobaptism; a description of the Eucharist as a fellowship meal; a disparagement of set prayers including even the Lord's Prayer and a disparagement of Sunday as the chief day of worship; frugality, self-discipline, and pacifism; a large concern for social justice and the sharing of goods with perhaps special reference to the large number of refugees from Turkish Hungary; and psychopannychism with a lively expectation of being resurrected in ultimate vindication of their having taken up the cross to follow after Christ.[40] Francis Dávid himself would not long remain untouched by some of these radical views.

Unitarian prospects began to cloud over. Dávid had divorced his wife. In 1574 both his divorce and his doctrine were investigated at the synod of Nagyenyed in order, if possible, to discover some scandal that might humiliate the Unitarian spokesman and impair his influence. Then in 1575, when the insurgent Békés was utterly defeated by Báthory and many of his followers were killed in battle, more than twoscore of the Szekler nobles, not a few of them Unitarians, were executed as rebels, more were mutilated,

---

[40] The first references are in a letter from Heidelberg, 4 December 1572; but the most complete documentation comes from the records of the Lutheran Saxon synod held at Gyulafehérvár in 1575. Printed in full by Pirnát, *Ideologie*, 135–160.

and a large number were imprisoned, degraded from their rank, and had their property confiscated.[41]

All this time, Blandrata had managed to retain his high position as court physician and counselor. When the throne of the kingdom of Poland fell vacant in 1574 (Ch. 29.1), Stephen Báthory sent Blandrata thither to work for his election. Against the other principal contender, the Emperor Maximilian (1564–1576), Stephen was elected. Thereupon, Christopher, his elder brother, was confirmed as voivode in Transylvania. For his dynastic contribution, Blandrata was awarded several villages near Kolozsvár. Christopher Báthory, though more prone than Stephen to promote Catholic interests, retained Blandrata in his service at court. But for Blandrata, the Unitarians might have fared worse than they did under the mounting pressure of the Hungarian phase of the Counter Reformation.

At the diet of Medgyes in 1576, Dávid's superintendency of the Unitarian Hungarians in Transylvania received constitutional recognition on a par with the already formally legitimated superintendencies of the Calvinist Hungarians and the Lutheran Saxons. The Unitarian superintendent or bishop Dávid thus stands out as having served successively as the spokesman of three of the four received religions of the land. The diet of Torda the next year, however, restrained the now formally recognized Unitarian superintendent from visiting his churches and limited the holding of the synods of the Unitarian Reformed Church to two towns, Kolozsvár and nearby Torda. Moreover, the oversight or superintendency over the Unitarian parishes beyond this circumscription was given to the Calvinist superintendent, who had leave to attempt their reconversion to Calvinism. (This unfair arrangement remained in force among the Szeklers for over a century.)

In spite of the defeats which Unitarianism suffered after the death of John Sigismund, the internal life of the churches went on much as before until the Jesuits found Dávid advocating that prayer to Christ be abandoned—an innovation that would clearly place the Unitarians beyond the embrace of the late king's article of toleration.

A logical development from the denial of Christ's deity, this viewpoint had been expressed by the Unitarian superintendent

---

[41] Békés, who fled to Poland, was there thrust into prison. Curiously, when Stephen Báthory ascended the Polish throne, Békés was released and his losses compensated for by gifts. Further, he was given command of Stephen's bodyguard and became his tentmate in the war against Muscovy. Wilbur, *Transylvania,* 56.

as early as 1572, perhaps at the suggestion of the Heidelberg refugee Adam Neuser (Ch. 31.3) and certainly with the agreement of the rectors of the Kolozsvár school, John Sommer and Jacob Palaeologus.[42]

The latter, who had come from Cracow (1571–1572; see further, Ch. 29.1), taught at Kolozsvár 1573–1574. A Greek from Chios, claiming descent from the Byzantine imperial family, he had become a Dominican in Rome, dedicated a commentary on the book of The Revelation to the Dominican general, Vincent Giustiniano, and then fled from the Inquisition in 1559. His movements for a decade thereafter are obscure, but by 1570 he had appeared in Prague as a learned Orientalist, well acquainted with the Koran. Because of his erudition or his allegedly imperial descent he was made a pensionary of the Hapsburg court until driven out when he fell under suspicion. He went to Cracow and Warsaw, then briefly to Transylvania (February), then back to Cracow, where he published *De discrimine Veteris et Novi Testamenti* (28 June 1572). He had been in epistolary contact with Dávid since September 1570. His recent visit and his new book must have inspired the disputations in Transylvania. In January 1573 he was again in Kolozsvár. While awaiting the spring to make a trip into Turkey, he elaborated his radical views on nonadorantism (which he mistakenly thought he was deriving from Servetus) and on the suspension of the sacraments in eight short treatises for the Unitarian seminary at Kolozsvár. Some of these were reworked by Sommer and copied by the students. Three of these of special interest are *Dissolutio de sacramentis, De eucharistia,* and *De baptismo.*[43]

In effect, Palaeologus argued that there were no sacraments in the ecclesiastical sense. The Bible does not mention them. As for baptism, it may be administered as a formality, but it has no significance. The last supper of Jesus was a regular meal at which the disciples took a lamb with sauce and spices, etc., not bread and wine only. The first Christians also ate regular suppers, introducing or following them by prayers and thanksgiving.

---

[42] Karl Landsteiner, *Jacobus Palaeologus: Eine Studie* (Vienna, 1873); Stanislas Kot, "Jacques Paléologue, défenseur de Servet," *Autour de Michel Servet,* 104–106; Antal Pirnát, "Jacobus Palaeologus," *Studia nad Arianizmem,* 72–129. Luigi Firpo, drawing upon D. Orano, mentions in passing the original name of Palaeologus as Giacomo Massilara. "Christian Francken antitrinitario," *Bolletino,* LXVIII (1960), 29, n. 8.

[43] It is not known whether they were ever printed. They have been preserved by Gervasius Lisznyai, George Enyedi, and Bishop Matthew Thoroczkai. They are described by Pirnát, "Palaeologus," *loc. cit.,* 91 f.

It is the task of the ministers to re-establish the original meaning of the Lord's Supper as an *agapē* (cf. Renato, Ch. 22.1) carefully and without shocking their parishioners' feelings. Jesus' command: "This do in remembrance of me" meant simply that whenever Christians thereafter should eat together, they ought to be mindful of him, his teachings, and God his Father. The fact that these treatises were used for teaching in the Kolozsvár school shows that Sommer and Dávid agreed with Palaeologus. Accordingly, the Lord's Supper, even in its sacramentarian form, was suspended in Kolozsvár.

Blandrata was alarmed at such innovations. Hounded by Blandrata, Palaeologus in the spring went to Turkey as planned. In May he visited the isle of his birth, Chios, and from 14 June to 8 July he was in Constantinople. By 12 August he was back in Kolozsvár, where he wrote a description of his trip.

Through this discussion, Palaeologus sought to regain the favor of the Emperor, as well as to allay all suspicions about his legitimate claim to descent in the Constantinopolitan imperial line. He claimed a fantastic number of connections in the East,[44] and refuted the assertion of Gregory Paul in Poland that he had become a Mohammedan and lived a profligate life in Constantinople.

He also took up his literary battle with Gregory Paul on the question of the magistrate and war. Palaeologus prepared an answer to Gregory Paul's polemic eight days after receiving it, and probably immediately set out with it to Poland. From Poland he returned to Transylvania at least once in 1573. But by 27 December, he had bounded back to Cracow, where (Ch. 29) we shall recount the remaining episodes and achievements of his life.

Nonadorantism and the suspension or radical alteration of the significance of the sacraments continued to concern Transylvanians after his departure.

At the Unitarian synod at Torda in March 1578, with 322 pastors present, Blandrata, as chief elder and court physician, aware of the great danger of innovation, and Dávid, the intrepid innovator, faced each other in tragic conflict on the issues of antipedobaptism and nonadorantism. The synod authorized *communis prophetia,* "which gave all the ministers liberty without

---

[44] With the voivode of Wallachia, the Patriarch of Constantinople, many Turkish officials and Mohammedan priests, and Aga Amurath, the son of the commander of the Turkish fleet. He said that he had received offers of high positions from the Turks, the Patriarch, and Cardinal Giustiniano, as well as from the Turkish vicegerent for Jews on the Aegean Islands.

danger to discuss with one another and to investigate matters that have not yet been decided and settled by the general synod, but to which serious consideration might be given . . . in good order and under rules suited to our times."[45] Dávid spoke persuasively on the idolatry implicit in the worship of Christ, the Man. Infant baptism, against which Dávid had long preached and written, was now synodally abolished as unscriptural.

That Francis Dávid had himself been practicing believers' baptism earlier than the official action is implied by his publication of the Dutch Anabaptist treatise in Hungarian and German translations in 1570 (Ch. 28.2) and is attested by a Jesuit heading Stephen Báthory's preparations for the Catholic recovery of Transylvania, who wrote that Dávid "had abolished [infant] baptism."[46]

Antipedobaptism and nonadorantism were certainly innovations in the faith of the deceased Unitarian king. Despite the growing aggressiveness of Catholicism and continued warning from the diet, Dávid pushed for further innovation in respect to the invocation of Christ. After calling another synod at Torda in the fall of 1578, he promulgated his views in three and then in thirty Theses. Blandrata, contesting each set, now proceeded to publish sixteen of Dávid's most Judaizing views, perhaps editing them tendentiously.[47] Báthory and his subjects were thereby informed that Dávid had gone so far as to hold that Jesus was of the seed of Joseph, the Messiah foretold by the prophets but rejected by the Jews, who from "a life of undisturbed repose" will soon come again to rule as king of God's people from Jerusalem, but that in the meantime he discharges neither a royal nor a priestly office and is therefore not to be invoked in prayer; for he is not God and even his precepts, though they should be heeded, are not to be construed in a way to derogate from the law of Moses.

Blandrata at court saw clearly that the prince, under Jesuit pressure, could legally take action against Unitarianism and urged Dávid to be discreet. The court physician went so far as to suggest that two or three Unitarian ministers who had most zealously promoted the new teachings ought to be tried for heresy, to show Unitarian good faith! Dávid rejected the proposal as dishonorable, and the ways of the two former allies sharply divided. Blandrata now sought the aid of the nephew of

---

[45] Palaeologus, *Defensio Francisci Davidis in negotio de non invocando Jesu Christi in precibus,* printed in Socinus, *Opera,* II, 229; quoted by Wilbur, *Transylvania,* 68 f.

[46] John Leleszi, 1579. Endre Veress, *Epistolae et acta Jesuitarum Transylvaniae,* I (Leipzig/Vienna, 1911), item 22, p. 7.

[47] Printed by Lampe, *op. cit.,* 306–311; in *BFR,* II, 801–803; by Robert Wallace, *Antitrinitarian Biography* (London, 1850), II, 248–255.

Laelius Socinus, Faustus Socinus. Of his debate at Basel (Ch. 29.7) early that year on Christ the Savior, Blandrata had heard. He prevailed on Socinus to come to Transylvania and argue Dávid back to the propriety of worshiping Christ and thereby preventing any further devolution of Unitarianism in the direction of Judaism. Socinus came, via Poland, bearing recommendations from the Polish churches, and lodged at Dávid's house, but at Blandrata's expense.

Dávid remained unmoved. Then Blandrata had Dávid's income from the church cut down. Dávid protested that this was comparable to Calvin's persecution of Servetus. Blandrata warned Dávid that he must abandon his offensive nonadorantism or else be accused and tried for innovation at the next meeting of the diet. The problem was referred to a committee of ministers, who in turn put it over until a general synod. Blandrata also proposed that the Polish Brethren be asked to judge the views of both sides, in writing, and that Dávid should preserve silence in the meantime. Dávid agreed, but presently, as superintendent, called a synod at Torda, in defiance of Blandrata and without waiting for a reply from the Polish churches.

Blandrata then decided that Dávid was incorrigible. He was able, by virtue of his standing in the Minor Church of Poland and his strategic position at the now Catholic court of Transylvania, to summon fifty of the clergy, to whom he made plain that Dávid's innovation would come before the diet. He gave them a summary of Dávid's views which seriously misrepresented the superintendent, and applied pressure by implying that if they, the pastors in synod, did not vote the right way, they could be removed from office and banished. At the same time, he wrote Socinus to inform Dávid that, although he had up to then defended him before the prince, he would now take sides against him. The Catholic voivode obligingly ordered the Kolozsvár town council to remove Dávid from his pastorate and put him under house arrest.

Suspecting Socinus of treachery, Dávid ordered him from his home. The next day Dávid preached in the two Kolozsvár churches, informed the people of what impended, and defended all the Unitarian doctrines, declaring the worship of Christ to be no more legitimate than the invocation of the Virgin or the saints. It was to be his last sermon.

Angered by Dávid's action, Báthory bade him appear before the diet in Torda in April 1579; but, taking note of the menacing sympathizers among the attendant nobles, he postponed the problem of innovation and sent Dávid back for incarceration. Blandrata's feeling toward Dávid had now become one of bitter personal enmity. He would not allow anything to be done to allay Dávid's physical sufferings. He had him kept under very strict guard and only rarely permitted his family to see him. Finally, Dávid, in extremely poor health, was brought to the prince's court at Gyulafehérvár. In the hearing, evidence was put forward to show that Dávid's views on the worship of Christ, far from being an "innovation," had at one time been held by Blandrata himself. The clergy demurred, with only one exception. The nobles supported Dávid. The Jesuits, of course, condemned him. The complainants asked mercy for him, but the Calvinist Hungarian ministers demanded his life. Pronouncing him guilty, the prince ordered him to be imprisoned in the castle at Déva. He did not long survive his hardships and died in prison, 15 November 1579.

Already in July, right after Dávid's trial, the conservative Unitarians had adopted in general synod a Confession in four articles,[48] safeguarding the office of the living Christ as "King of the churches," who is to be "worshiped and adored" and "who rules his faithful by his spirit." Thus did Blandrata hope to check the radical Davidians or Judaizers. But soon this group, drawing inspiration from one of Dávid's converts, Andrew Eössi, a wealthy Szekler, would move from nonadorantism and the suspension of the sacraments to the revival of Mosaic dietary and other ordinances, including worship on the Sabbath.[49] In resisting the Judaizers, Blandrata was glad to have the support of the Polish Brethren, hoping that under the protection of the Báthorys in Poland and Transylvania an international Unitarian Reformed Church could be permanently legalized. To this end he had the belated *Judicium ecclesiarum Polonicarum* (Ch. 29.7) against Dávid's radicalism printed in Kolozsvár.

Blandrata was also concerned to reorganize his church and safeguard its sacraments. He was instrumental in having Demetrius Hunyadi, administratively efficient and theologically conservative, imposed by Báthory upon the Unitarians as their new superintendent (1579–1592). At the synod in Kolozsvár in 1580 all the Unitarian pastors, except for eighteen steadfast Davidians, reluctantly embraced Blandrata's *Disciplina ecclesiastica,* restoring pedobaptism and a regular commemorative Lord's Supper.

[48] Latin text in Wallace, *op. cit.,* III, 556 f.

[49] The Sabbatarians, persisting within and without the Unitarian fold, would be formally excluded in 1618; and in 1638 the diet at Deés would enforce the *Complanatio Deesiana,* a confession which elaborates the document of 1579 and proceeds to cover the whole range of doctrine and discipline as the official standard of the church to the present day. Latin text, Wallace, *op. cit.,* III, 585–587.

Chapter 29

SECTARIANISM AND SPIRITUALISM IN POLAND, 1572–1582

One year after the death in Transylvania of the childless Unitarian king, John II Sigismund (1540–1571), in Poland, his uncle, the last Jagellon king, Sigismund II Augustus (1548–1572) died, likewise leaving no heir. For the Polish throne, the houses of Hapsburg, Valois, Muscovy, and Báthory were eager to provide a successor. The alarmed Polish senate ordered preparations for war in anticipation of aggression. In 1573, after extracting a promise that would forestall in Poland a repetition of the Saint Bartholomew's Day Massacre in France, the Polish senate elected Henry of Valois. When after a few months' rule he abdicated to succeed his brother as Henry III of France, the senate, made up of Catholic bishops and Protestant magnates, proceeded to elect the Catholic voivode of Unitarian-Reformed, Lutheran Transylvania, Stephen Báthory, as the king of Poland (1575–1586). We have already noted (Ch. 28.3) the important part played by the Italian physician of the courts of Cracow and Gyulafehérvár, George Blandrata, in securing the election of Stephen, who was related to the Jagellon house through marriage to the late King Sigismund's sister.

The constitutional struggle, 1572–1575, made actual the much mooted question within the Minor Church concerning the sword (Ch. 29.1), intensified the quest for a theological basis for religious toleration in a multiconfessional state (Ch. 29.2), and placed in a critical political context the Polish phase of nonadorantism (Ch. 29.3). The radical unitarian rejection of prayers addressed to Christ made the whole of the Minor Church appear now triply subversive; for, besides their denial of the validity of the baptism of the majority of the citizens and their withdrawal of the use of the sword, the extremists were now withholding from the state even the sanctions and the suffrages of the liturgy. Such, at least, would have been the charges against the Minor Church. After dealing with these closely interrelated developments, we shall pass from Judaizing nonadorantism to a discussion of several extraordinary theories of interfaith toleration espoused on the margins of the Minor Church (Ch. 29.4), to conclude with a section on the theology of Socinus (Ch. 29.7) and the beginnings of organized Socinianism on the site of the anti-Nicene, anabaptist colony of Raków (Ch. 29.8).

1. The Controversy Over the Sword, 1572–1575

The controversy in Poland over the sword was at once social and political. The social issue was whether the evangelical converts among the *szlachta* should renounce the use of the sword over their serfs and become their brothers in Christ. The political issue was whether these same lords should also renounce the use of the sword in the defense of the republic. As we shall come to see, there were anti-Trinitarians who insisted on the right of ownership of their villages and on their duty in time of war, others who freed their serfs but acknowledged their duty in the event of a just war, and finally a solid core of lords and their divines who went the whole way in the renunciation of the sword socially and politically.

There was, to be sure, no movement in Poland comparable to the Great Peasants' War in Germany, in which the peasants, artisans, and miners demanded a new status. In Poland the Christian social revolution[1] began, instead, when a number of anabaptist, anti-Nicene pastors—not all of them recruited from the humbler classes—converted to an evangelical Christianity certain lords and members of the gentry, who in turn were moved by a feeling of evangelical brotherhood to free their serfs and to recognize in them joint heirs in Christ. The stand of the majority among the Polish radical Reformed Brethren (the Minor Church) on Christian fraternity and pacifism was not the attempt of an underprivileged class to avoid entanglement in the pretensions and the conflicts of the great. It was in part, at least, the work of the lords themselves, the Polish and Lithuanian counterparts of such radical nobles as Lord Liechtenstein and Schwenckfeld. These partisans of pacifism were members of the headstrong and independent *szlachta*—some wealthy, others only

---

[1] It is too early to evaluate the extensive research now going on in Poland on the social origins of the leaders of the Minor Church and the class factors in synodal debates on the sword. Gottfried Schramm has admirably analyzed the recent Polish monographs, "Antitrinitarier in Polen, 1556–1658," *BHR*, XXI (1959), 473–511 esp., 496 ff.

moderately so—possessed of goods and of rights to defend as well as of dependents to protect, and with a code which required of them an almost quixotic readiness to do so whenever the mass levy of the gentry (*pospolite ruszenie*) was proclaimed. The conversion of these lords of the manor to pacifism entailed a social revolution for their families, their retainers, and their serfs. A nobleman such as Judge John Niemojewski, owner of twenty villages, with a family tradition of conspicuous gallantry in wars against the Teutonic knights, the Turks, and the Muscovites, could not escape the obloquy of his peers and even sometimes the disparagement of those (in the other confessional camps) whom he would now in Christ refuse to consider of low degree.

In 1572, the danger of dynastic war exposed the anabaptist, anti-Trinitarian, pacifist gentry of the Minor Church and their divines to violent attacks from Catholics and Major Churchmen and caused considerable dissension within the Minor Church itself. The issue of the sword in 1572, following hard upon the controversy over believers' baptism, bade fair to split the Minor Church, as a decade earlier in 1562 the issue of the "Constantinian" formulation of the doctrine of the Trinity had opened what was to become a permanent schism within the young Polish-Lithuanian Reformed Church as a whole.

In August 1572, a month after the extinction of the Jagellon dynasty, the enterprising, traveling theologian-publicist Jacob Palaeologus, whom we have but recently met in the important disputations in Kolozsvár (Ch. 28.3), published in part his work on the magisterial sword and the just war, *Defensio verae sententiae de magistratu politico*. Palaeologus, alarmed at what he considered the political irresponsibility of the Racovians and the other pacifists in the Minor Church of Poland, with whom he was otherwise sympathetic, strongly asserted the obligation of Christians to accept public office and to serve in the armed forces, because, said he, refusal to do so "always smoothes the road to power for the godless."[2] This challenge aroused the pacifist majority of the Polish Brethren, who felt that a cardinal tenet of evangelical Christianity was being placed in jeopardy. Their reply was formulated by Gregory Paul, *Adversus Jacobi Palaeologi de bello sententiam Responsio* (Raków, 1572).[3] It was not a closely reasoned argument, as the cosmopolitan Greek's was, but an impetuous, emotional appeal to the example of the humble Christ,

[2] Pirnát, "Palaeologus," *loc. cit.*, 84 f.
[3] Printed by Szczucki, *Literatura Ariańska*, 33–58; analyzed in Kot, *Socinianism*, 56–60.

Gregory Paul's caution in his *Responsio* is evidence of the danger involved in expressing pacifist sentiments during the interregnum of 1572–1573.

It was mostly at Raków that the Brethren espoused the extreme or evangelically consistent view on war. Stanislas Budziński, writing[4] from Cracow, criticized the Racovian position to the synod of Lutomierz in 1573; and the aged Martin Krowicki, learning that the synod had appointed Czechowic to reply to Budziński, himself wrote to the latter, encouraging him to resist the fatuous pacifism[5] of both Czechowic and Gregory Paul.

The principal theological blast against the Racovians came, however, from the man who had touched off the controversy. On 18 August 1573, the very day on which he received in Transylvania Gregory Paul's *Responsio*, Jacob Palaeologus sat down to write a thorough refutation.[6] He dealt with the fundamental question of the magistrate's right to use the sword and of the Christian's right to go to court in litigation. He upheld the civil power, and condemned what he called the Racovians' greater offense, their practice of excommunication, which deprived a man of eternal life. Palaeologus deplored what he considered the sectarian tendency of the Polish Brethren to isolate themselves from society. The arguments of the self-styled scion of the vanished Emperors of the East, abetted by the pleading of the Lithuanian scholar Simon Budny, did not dissuade the Racovians.

2. THE "PAX DISSIDENTIUM"

In addition to agitating the question of war and the role of the magistrate, not a few among the late king's subjects had been looking apprehensively to the day when a royal successor might reactivate the old penalties for holding dissenting beliefs. News of thousands of French Protestants slain in the Saint Bartholomew's night massacre alarmed Polish Protestants of all confessions. They all agreed that no diet should be convened to elect a new king until provision for their own safety could be secured. In January of 1573 the senate and the chamber of deputies assembled jointly in Warsaw, and there inserted in the "confederation,"[7] prepared by a mixed Protestant-Catholic committee and

---

[4] Kot, *Socinianism,* 61.

[5] *Ibid.* Krowicki's letter was published by Budny in his *Urząd miecza.*

[6] *Ad scriptum fratrum Racoviensium de bello et judiciis forensibus Responsio;* discussed by Kot, *Socinianism,* 62–66.

[7] "Confederation is the name given to the comprehensive preliminary basis of action with regard to the election of the king, agreed upon by the joint assembly at Warsaw, January 28, 1573 " Wilbur, *Socinianism,* 363, n. 26.

approved by almost all the senators, lay and clerical, an article to prevent in future any religiously incited persecution or civil strife:

Since there is in our Republic no little disagreement on the subject of religion, in order to prevent any such hurtful strife from beginning among our people on this account as we plainly see in other realms, we mutually promise for ourselves and our successors forever, under the bond of our oath, faith, honor and conscience, that we who differ with regard to religion (*dissidentes de religione*) will keep the peace with one another, and will not for a different faith or a change of churches shed blood nor punish one another by confiscation of property, infamy, imprisonment or banishment, and will not in any way assist any magistrate or officer in such an act.[8]

Accordingly, the new king, when he should be elected, would have to swear that he would "preserve and maintain peace and quiet among those that differ with regard to religion" and suffer none "to be influenced or oppressed by reason of his religion."[9] Opposition to this *Pax dissidentium* was immediately expressed by Archbishop Uchánski; and all the Catholic bishops withdrew their names but one,[10] who made bold to go along with the greater number of nobles present, *propter bonum pacis*. In 1573 the term "dissidents" was clearly understood to apply to all Christian groups, including the Catholics.[11]

When Henry of Valois was elected king, he was accordingly required to sign the so-called Henrician Articles, which guaranteed the political liberty of the *szlachta,* the responsibility of the king to the diet, and toleration among the *dissidentes.* These agreements were signed on Henry's behalf by the French envoy. When the Polish primate Hosius and his episcopal envoy vehemently objected to the king-elect's indirect acquiescence in toleration, it was the Lutheran noble John Zborowski who told Henry that he could not become king without personally reaffirming the agreements. Later in Warsaw, when the bishops again advised Henry to leave the liberal article out of his oath, it was the Calvinist grand marshal John Firlej who insisted that he include it.

A few months after ascending the Polish throne, Henry of Valois abdicated in order to claim the throne of France, left vacant at the death of his brother, Charles IX. His elected successor as king of Poland, Stephen Báthory, readily agreed to the

---

[8] *Volumina Legum* (Petersburg, 1859–1860), II, 124; given in English in Wilbur, *Socinianism,* 363–364.
[9] *Volumina Legum,* II, 135; Wilbur, *Socinianism,* 364.
[10] Bishop Krasiński of Cracow.
[11] By the end of the century, it came to mean only non-Roman Catholics.

Warsaw Confederation. Loyal to his Catholic faith, he steadfastly treated his new Protestant and radical subjects fairly, committed as he was to a great plan for the union of eastern Europe in preparation for a concerted attack upon Moslem Turkey. During his reign, the opposition of the Catholic bishops[12] to the *Pax dissidentium* and to Protestantism concentrated on the vagaries of the pacifistic, anti-Trinitarian Minor Church and with special reference to their Judaizing trend.

3. THE CONTROVERSY OVER THE ADORATION OF CHRIST: BUDNY'S RADICAL THEOLOGY

The inner life of the anti-Trinitarian, antipedobaptist churches in Little Poland and particularly in Lithuania was being disturbed by the Judaizing tendencies of certain leaders in contact with advanced radical thought among the Transylvanian Unitarians. Like Francis Dávid, they questioned the propriety of invoking Christ in prayer.

In Lithuania an endemic proselytizing spirit in Judaism had for a number of years reinforced, perhaps by contagion, a Judaizing trend within Calvinism. Simon Budny, chief spokesman for this trend, gave the Christocentric leaders of the Minor Church in Little Poland and elsewhere cause to fear that they would all soon be identified as Jews and would hence lose the benefits of the *Pax dissidentium*. We have already indicated that the Catholic opponents of this Warsaw Confederation of 1573 (corresponding to the Constitution of Maros-Vásárhely signed by the Unitarian king of Transylvania in 1571) were on the lookout for any "innovation" that would legitimize their placing the Radicals beyond the protection of the *Pax dissidentium* and thereby begin the breaching of the Protestant front.

The controversy within the Minor Church over nonadorantism and also over its adverse effects on the constitutional status of the Radicals and of the Protestant mission in Poland as a whole would eventuate in a schism, in effect, two churches or brotherhoods. The nonadorant or fully unitarian, nonpacifistic Lithuanian Brethren would, in the process of regional and theological polarization, become very much like the Transylvanian Unitarians under Francis Dávid. The pacifistic and more Christocentric Polish Brethren of Raków and Lublin, up until the arrival

---

[12] Some fourteen debates between Minor Church and Catholic theologians (1579–1620) are described by Stanislas Kot in "Dysputacje Arjan Polskich" (Disputations of the Polish Arians), *Reformacja w Polsce,* VIII (1936), 341–370; cited by Wilbur, *Socinianism,* 386.

of Faustus Socinus, would remain close to the pattern of the Germanic Anabaptists.

To further the cause of nonadorantism, Budny produced in 1574 a critical edition of the New Testament, from which he eliminated such passages as appeared to him to be later interpolations made to strengthen a philosophical doctrine of the Trinity.[13] Opposing not only Protestants and Catholics, but also the remaining Arians or ditheists within the Minor Church of Lithuania and especially of Little Poland, Budny rejected alike the pre-existence of the Word and the divinity of Christ. To the charges of Gonesius, Czechowic, and Farnowski (all now of Little Poland) that he had crossed the line into Judaism, Budny replied by enumerating his unitarian convictions in *De principalibus fidei christianae articulis*,[14] vigorously defending, as Francis Dávid had, his nonadorantism. Budny praised Servetus and Gentile for the progress they had made, but observed that they could not be expected to grasp the whole truth at once.[15]

Budny had already joined Palaeologus, as we have observed (Ch. 29.1), in vindicating the right of a Christian to hold office, to employ the sword in the fulfillment of justice, to own property, to defend himself, and to engage in warfare. Among his other *principalia fidei*, Budny also revealed his attitude on the controversial question of psychopannychism (Chs. 1.3.c; 5.4; etc.).

This issue was perhaps first raised for the Poles by Laelius Socinus, who left in his papers a work *De resurrectione*, which, following Camillo Renato (Ch. 22.1), attempted to replace the Catholic teaching of the natural immortality of the soul. Gregory Paul had followed Laelius and, since 1568, had taught that the soul, like the body, is mortal, awaiting the resurrection. Budny expressly espoused in his *De principalibus*, 1576, the extreme position, thnetopsychism, stating that the soul is nothing more than the life of the body and has no independent existence.[16] He found some followers among the White Russian gentry.[17]

In 1576, Budny printed his translation of the Huguenot Francis Hotman's description of the Saint Bartholomew's Day Massacre, originally prepared for the Poles as a warning against electing Henry of Valois king.

[13] Kot, "La Réforme," *loc. cit.,* 225.
[14] *O przedniejszych wiary Chrystyańskiej artykulech* . . . (1576); printed in Szczucki, *Literatura Ariańska*, 317–336.
[15] Kot, "Szymon Budny," *loc. cit.,* 91.
[16] *Ibid.,* 94.
[17] There is a record that Sigismund III dismissed the nobleman Stefan Łowdu from his post of judge in Mozyr for holding that there is no abiding soul in man. Kot, "Szymon Budny," *loc. cit.,* 95.

In 1578, Budny submitted to rebaptism. However, like the Anabaptist Balthasar Hubmaier at Waldshut (Ch. 6.3) and at Nicolsburg (Ch. 9.2.a), Budny still refused so to withdraw the Christian believer from the world as to sanction the neglect of his duty in respect to the whole of society. He also argued from the Bible that Jesus esteemed poverty and the poor and would not have insisted on social equality between lord and serf but would have been content to preach magnanimity to the one and resignation to the other. The learned, zealous, and enterprising Reformed Unitarian-Anabaptist from his base in Lithuania prevented the Minor Church in Little Poland from completely closing off the discussion of the full range of sociopolitical issues.

The charge that Simon Budny was a neo-Israelite was not unfounded. Moreover, in addition to espousing an Ebionite Christology, Budny placed his unitarian Christianity in the context of interfaith ecumenicity. In this he followed Palaeologus in promoting the universalistic idea of a sort of pan-Semitic redemptive action which amalgamated race and creed in a process of justification.[18] To the latter he gave a rather specialized definition (Ch. 29.4).

Budny's religious, humanistic, and social dynamism engendered important intellectual and spiritual currents in Lithuania. He brought Lithuanian and Ruthenian intellectuals into contact with the thought of the West. It is significant that the Counter Reformation, when it later gained control of his Lithuanian printing establishments after the sons of the Protestants Radvila and Kiszka were reconverted to Romanism, followed Budny's example by bringing out a great number of books and pamphlets in Polish, Lithuanian, and Ruthenian, as well as Latin. Budny's memory would long persist in these parts, held in odium by Catholics, Orthodox, and Calvinist Protestants alike, all of whom recognized the threat of his eccentric combination of philological and speculative talent with religious, social, and cultural reform.

4. THE INTERPRETATION AND TOLERATION OF NON-CHRISTIAN RELIGIONS

Against Czechowic and Gregory Paul, both Budny and Palaeologus were concerned to establish a Biblical basis, not only for the

[18] This idea of Budny and Palaeologus must not be confused with the older Judaizing movement which began in the Kiev area after 1470 and which persisted in Russia well into the sixteenth century. These people had gone much farther than Budny ever would, having entirely rejected the New Testament and based their religion on the Decalogue. Budny expressly rejected any connection with them, although it is very likely that their ideas prepared the ground for his own semi-Judaizing movement.

maintenance of social and international peace and justice, but also for a universalistic or interfaith toleration. Palaeologus, the much-traveled and speculative friar, felt about him not only the surge of radical reform in Latin Christianity but also the stirrings of new energies in Judaism, Orthodoxy, and Mohammedanism. Living and thinking on the frontier and at the crossroads of several religions, Palaeologus resolved to demonstrate how Lithuanian and Transylvanian Unitarianism, on becoming a bridge from Christianity, could discharge a unifying or at least an irenic role in relation to both Judaism and Mohammedanism. He had produced an interesting tract on this subject at Cracow as early as 1572, *De tribus gentibus*. Herein he unfolded his concept of salvation and his peculiar idea of justification, and ended with an impassioned plea for religious tolerance.

His idea of salvation (*salus*) is best translated as "blessedness." For the infant, it consists in food and warmth; for the natural man, in possessions and power; for the noble pagan, in perfection of the soul. All these are but fragmentary aspects of the highest *salus*, known only through revelation. Revelation was given only to the Jews, as the people of God. Therefore, in order to be justified, one must belong to one of the three extant branches of the people of God: either to the Jews by race, or to the Christians, or to the "Christian Turks." His idea of membership in these groups is curious.

The Jews are all blood descendants of Abraham. Through inheritance, they have a justice *per fidem imputata* which, however, is no longer sufficient for salvation, for they must also believe in Jesus as the Messiah. Thus the "Jews" are divided into the Mosaic Jews, who still reject Jesus, and those who have accepted him, namely, the Christians of Jewish race, specifically "the Coptic and the Syrian Christians." The second group, the "Christians," thus include only Gentile Christians, as well as all their descendants; for justice *per fidem imputata* is inherited by all children of baptized Christians, just as it is inherited among Jews. Among this second people are all uncircumcised Christians, i.e., Romanists, the Greek Orthodox, the Armenians, and the Protestants. The offspring alike of baptized Christian converts and of (circumcised) Jews have no need of being baptized. Baptism or circumcision is an ordinance reserved solely for converts from paganism. The "Christian Turks," by whom Palaeologus means all Mohammendans, are Christians because they occupy the lands and therefore are descendants (by inevitable racial intermixture) of former Christians! Their rite of circumcision does not make them racially Jews, because they practice it for reason of hygiene, not of religion. As to their faith, they have a *fides promissionis,* a trust in the promises of God, although they do not have a *fides narrationis,* faith in the narrative of the Bible. Nor, indeed, do many Christians, he adds, since they know little about the Bible. Mohammedans, at least, acknowledge the prophetic office of Jesus Christ and are to this extent Christians. Thus, in general, "Jewish," Gentile, and "Turkish" Christians are on an equal plane and should treat each other accordingly. The tract ends with a moving call for universal religious toleration, based on both natural theology and the Scriptures.

Palaeologus pushed on to Transylvania in January 1573, where, as we saw (Ch. 28.3), he worked for a while in Kolozsvár, until he was driven out by the hostility of Blandrata, the meagerness of his stipend, and the plague. Toward the end of 1574 he became the guest of the noble family of the Gerendi in Heltau.

While in Heltau, Palaeologus wrote his most interesting and colorful work, the *Disputatio scholastica,* an allegory which begins by describing the indignation of Jesus, the four-and-twenty elders, and all the angels and archangels at the attempts of the Papists and the Protestants to prove his divinity, attempts which eventuate in a great synod, for which prominent contemporary, medieval, and ancient teachers are summoned by the new Josiah (the Unitarian king John II Sigismund of Transylvania) to discuss the problem of ecumenicity at a special city built for the purpose (Janopolis). The account of the attempted co-operation between famous Romanists and leading Protestants against the anti-Trinitarians, the vain arguments and squabbles among the orthodox themselves, is quite humorous in its imagined disorder. Athanasius, for example, has to set Calvin right on the Athanasian Creed; and, when Aquinas attempts to conciliate and Scotus confuses the discussion on *essentia* and *natura,* it is Francis Dávid, of all persons, who helps the scholastics straighten out their terms! This work was never printed, and the available manuscripts are incomplete.[19]

Another very interesting work by Palaeologus, the *Catechesis Christiana* (1574), involved the conversion of a Jew and a Mexican Indian in an extended argument among a Romanist, a Lutheran, and a Calvinist, whose mutual strife resulted in their defeat by the Unitarians.[20]

In two other works of about this period, *De providentia* and *De peccato originali* (1573?), Palaeologus took issue with Calvin, denied predestination, and insisted that divine providence does

---

[19] Pirnát, "Palaeologus," *loc. cit.,* 120.

[20] The extensive dialogue in three hundred MS. folios, preserved by Bishop Matthew Thoroczkai, is intended as a compend of anti-Trinitarian theology.

not inhibit the freedom of men. Sin is not an act, but an intention (*concupiscentia*), the coveting of something which according to the law of God is not to be desired. Palaeologus distinguished between the sin of Adam and the sin of Eve, but in both cases denied that their culpability could be inherited, since children inherit only the nature of Adam and Eve, and it was not the nature which sinned, but two persons. Moreover, he argued in another tract, *An omnes ab uno Adamo descenderint,* that Adam and Eve were not the ancestors of all the people God created from the dust of the earth, and that accordingly not all of mankind could have inherited their sin.

Palaeologus' views on sin, the sword, and salvation were shared, as we have seen, by Budny, who printed several of his works in Lithuania.[21] Palaeologus lived in Poland after 1575, but withdrawn from religious affairs. He subsequently moved to Moravia and was arrested by the bishop of Olmütz.

With the arrest of Palaeologus in 1581 and his subsequent trial and execution in Rome in 1585 as a renegade Dominican and heretic, we find occasion to interrupt our narrative and mention the closing careers of a number of other religious refugees who played such a notable role in the Radical Reformation of both Poland and Transylvania.

5. The Italian Epilogue

Before proceeding to a delineation of the Sienese Faustus Socinus and a characterization of his role in transforming the Polish antipedobaptist, anti-Nicene Minor Church into the "Socinian" movement, we should take account in a kind of epilogue of several of the other radical Evangelical Rationalists of the Italian diaspora, who, exiled from Poland by the decree of Parczów back in 1564, have by now ended or will soon end their lives in varying degrees of obscurity and frustration. Since their impress even as exiles shaped the contours of a later international Socinianism, we do well at this juncture to speak briefly of their closing careers outside of Poland.

George Negri, pastor of the Italian congregation at Pińczów, had originally accompanied Stancaro around 1550 to Hungary, and then to Poland, and had been received by the Pinczovians in 1557, and appointed in 1558 private chaplain to Prosper Provana. George Negri also resided for some time at Radvila's court at Vilnius. In 1563, his father, Francis Negri, came to visit him (Ch. 24.3). Francis preached to the Italian congregation at Pińczów, made the friendship of Lismanini, and even contributed to the

21 All in 1580.

latter's *Explicatio de Trinitate*. The father was on the point of returning to his family in Chiavenna when death claimed him in May of 1564, at Cracow, as he was readying himself for an appearance before the Reformers of Zurich and Geneva to defend Lismanini's book. George Negri was prevented from serving as secretary at the decisive colloquy of Piotrków in 1565 because, though long in Poland, he was technically under the decree of Parczów.

Bernardine Ochino was likewise dislodged by the edict of Parczów. The aged ex-Capuchin general and his young family were stricken by the plague. Nursed at the home of Filipowski in Pińczów, Ochino gradually recovered, but his two sons and a daughter died. Near Christmastide, Ochino traveled wearily to Moravia with the one remaining child, finding his last home with Nicholas Paruta at Austerlitz. Three weeks later he died.

Paruta, a nobleman of Lucca and Venice, possibly related to the historian of Venice, Paolo Paruta,[22] had joined the Anabaptists at Venice (Ch. 22.2), had left for Geneva, and, after visiting Poland, had settled near a Hutterite colony in Moravia. He had a large library of Hebrew, Greek, and Latin books. Here he at long range assisted Blandrata in preparing a catechism for Transylvania. We have already taken note of the twenty theses on the Trinity sent by Paruta to the synod at Rogów in Poland (Ch. 25.3). Paruta had passed from inchoate anti-Trinitarianism to the ancient heresy of Paul of Samosata. He finally denied entirely the deity of the Holy Spirit, as Servetus had, speaking of that *virtù d'Iddio* which enlightens and inspires the heart to believe the promises. Paruta also, in a modification appropriate to his culture, espoused a kind of communism akin to that of the neighboring Hutterites. Paruta imprudently returned to Venice, and was arrested and executed in 1567.

It was in the last year of the Council of Trent that John Valentine Gentile had come to Poland (Ch. 24.3), hoping, in his narrow escape from Geneva, to find a community which would endorse his tritheistic solution to the problem of Christ's divine mediatorship (Ch. 25.3). When Cracow proved to be unsafe, Gentile removed to Pińczów; but with the edict of 1564 he fled, first to Moravia, thence to Vienna, and finally back to Savoy, thinking perhaps to lodge with Gribaldi (who, however, had, in the meantime, succumbed to the plague).

---

[22] The father of Nicholas was Giovan Giacomo, a rich citizen of Venice and a Catholic, according to the MS. deposition of Antonio Varotto (Barotto), who had visited Nicholas and Ochino in Moravia. The deposition is quoted in ample excerpts by Bainton, *Ochino*, 159 f.

Gentile now approached the bailiff at Gex, announcing that he would willingly debate three theses on God and Christ with the Protestant divines, the loser to suffer the death penalty! The governor promptly jailed Gentile (1566) and asked for instructions from Bern, where it was decided to try him for heresy, specifically for seven errors regarding the Trinity and for reproaching the Reformed Churches of Switzerland. For about a month, the ministers argued with Gentile, but this time he steadfastly refused to change his beliefs. At length, despairing of ever convincing him, the council ordered his death by the sword.

In Poland, Stanislas Wiśniowski in his *Demonstratio falsationis* (1572) vigorously defended the "second Servetus" in a well-organized plea for toleration directed to the Swiss.[23]

Peter Paul Vergerio, who had sought to organize a royal Polish Lutheran Church, died in Tübingen in 1565. Francis Lismanini, sometime superintendent of the Reformed Church of Little Poland before the definitive schism, had, by reason of the edict of Parczów, sought refuge at the court of Duke Albert in Königsberg. In 1566 he drowned in a well during a fit of epilepsy. His theological enemy Francis Stancaro, with his fellow Stancarians, was, without much grace on either side, reconciled to the Major Church in connection with the Consensus of Sandomir. Stancaro died four years thereafter in 1574 at the home of his noble patron at Stopnica, not far south of Pińczów, where, a quarter of a century before, he had organized the first Reformed parish of Poland. Among Stancaro's most determined foes during the synodal debates on the Trinity between 1562 and 1564 had been Alciati della Motta, sometime elder of the Italian congregation in Geneva.

During his brief Polish sojourn, John Paul Alciati is reported to have escaped manhandling by some Cracow students when he quickwittedly described his theology as not "Arian" but "Marian." He believed, he told the students, in Jesus Christ, Son of the living God and of Mary.[24] When non-Catholic aliens were expelled in 1564, Alciati made his way to Moravia. From there he wrote to Gregory Paul, denying the pre-existence of Christ. From Austerlitz, he made his way to Danzig, and practiced medicine there, dying sometime after 1573.[25]

George Blandrata, lay elder and influential theologian of the Minor Church of Poland (1558–1559; 1560–1563) and courtly mentor and, after the death of Francis Dávid in prison, conserva-

---

[23] Printed in part in Szczucki, *Literatura Ariańska*, 423–438; Wiśniowski's life is given briefly, *ibid.*, 651–653.
[24] Church, *op. cit.*, 385.
[25] *Ibid.*

tive reorganizer of the Unitarian Church of Transylvania (1563–
1579), became increasingly isolated from both the Hungarian Unitarians and the Polish Socinians. Consorting more and more with
the Jesuits of the Transylvanian court, and "in the end given to
no religion," he died in bed, 1588, leaving behind considerable
wealth to his adopted nephew.[26]

We return to the Minor Church of Poland shortly before the
arrival of the most influential of all the émigré Italian Radicals.

6. The Development of the Polish Brethren from 1575 to the Advent of Faustus Socinus in 1579

We took leave (Ch. 27.4) of the communitarian, anabaptist,
anti-Nicene colony of Raków with the rounding out of its theology
and discipline as formulated in Schomann's *Catechesis* of 1574.
With Schomann now pastor at Pińczów, the chief spokesman at
Raków was the apothecary Simon Ronemberg, who had been
prominent in the exchanges with the Hutterites. We have more
recently (Ch. 29.1 and 3) filled out two aspects of the struggle
between the Christocentric, sectarian, pacifistic Racovians along
with their sympathizers outside the colony and the nonadorant,
magisterial, universalistic Budnyites.

Whatever chance the socially and theologically radical but inwardly divided Minor Church might have had was largely ground
to pieces in a period of national crisis (1572–1575) between the
upper millstone of the natural aristocratic conservatism of the
majority of the Protestant, to say nothing of the Catholic, lords,
and the nether millstone of a radicalism fissured by theological
and ethical extremists. In short, the schism over nonadorantism
and the sword within the Minor Church had riven it, at the same
time providing the Catholics and the orthodox Reformed with
ample materials for substantiating their charges of Judaizing and
sedition. Thus, though quite unfairly, the Lithuanian Brethren,
who were in fact conscientiously concerned for the proper uses of
the magisterial sword, were being labeled as traitors, whereas
the Polish Brethren, who were in fact much concerned to preserve the invocation of Christ in prayer as divine, were being
called Jews. Before showing how Faustus Socinus was to combine the pacifism and the piety of the Racovians and the Spiritualist universalism of the Budnyites in a new school of thought,
Socinian Evangelical Rationalism, we may take note of a few
other developments in the riven radical churches between 1575
and 1579.

[26] Wilbur, *Socinianism,* 321.

One of the lesser schisms within the tradition of the Minor Church was that of the Farnovians. They took their name from their chief spokesman, Stanislas Farnowski, pastor of Sącz on the Hungarian frontier. The Farnovians had withdrawn from the synod of Skrzynno in 1567 and perpetuated in their midst the ditheistic stage in the devolution of the doctrine of the Trinity. The Farnovian sect with its printing press and school at Sącz was to maintain its existence until absorbed, after its leader's death, by the Minor Church in 1617. In 1575 both Farnowski and another important spokesman of the position, Stanislas Wiśniowski, pastor in Lucławice, presented their "Arian" or ditheist views: the former in *De cognitione et confessione Dei semper unius;* the latter in *Colloquium de sincera cognitione Dei.*

Martin Czechowic, now pastor in Lublin, who had once shared the "Arian" view but who had at Skrzynno moved on with the rest to an *adoptionist* unitarian position, was at the same time conspicuously identified with the struggle to prevent, from quarters still farther to the left, the spread of a *nonadorant* unitarianism, which locally was associated with Esias of Moscow, a Judaizing Russian priest and his sponsor, a Lublin merchant, who was presumably in contact with such leading nonadorants as Simon Budny in Lithuania and Francis Dávid in Transylvania. The catechetical *Colloquia christiana*[27] published by Czechowic at Lublin in 1575 was concerned to safeguard for the oncoming generation the devout Christocentric pacifism of the Minor Church against those from within who were refusing to invoke the adoptive Son of God in prayer and who were also seeking to legitimize war—in both cases by appealing to Old Testament texts.

The work, though it must be seen as a part of the great debate on the sword between the pacifistic Polish Brethren and the Budnyites, has its special place in our narrative as a representative piece of pedagogical literature designed for the instruction of the young, rather than as a polemic with peers. The teacher (Czechowic) explains to his spirited catechumen: (1) that the Christian may resist evil only by spiritual means; (2) that the Christian has no need of recourse to protection or arbitration at the hands of the temporal authorities; and (3) that the Christian cannot in any way join in the waging of war. Czechowic's pacifism is prudential and humanitarian, and does not suggest the *via crucis* of Germanic Anabaptism. The believer may obey the command of authority, but not to the extent of going out to the

---

[27] *Rozmowy Chrystyjańskie* (Raków, 1575), printed in Szczucki, *Literatura Ariańska,* 59–120; summarized by Kot, *Socinianism,* 70–77.

battlefield, or of striking a blow. "But if I also," the pupil asks his teacher, "having gone out to war at the king's command, should yet strike no one when others struck, and moreover even bore no arms, should I then be doing wrong?" The answer is yes, for one may not be yoked together with unbelievers (II Cor. 6:14). On the other hand, the state may, indeed must, wage war, which presupposes that magistrates, along with the great mass of the population, can never be evangelical Christians. Christians may provide money by way of taxation, the teacher says, and there will never be a want of soldiers.

A lengthy Latin appendix, *De vita et moribus christianorum primitivae ecclesiae,* supplements Czechowic's Scriptural arguments with the testimonies of Justin Martyr, Tertullian, Cyprian, Lactantius, Athanasius, Basil the Great, and Hilary of Poitiers.[28]

The stepping up of Polish military operations in the second phase of the Livonian War (1579–1582) was to make all the sentiments voiced by Czechowic, as those spoken earlier by Gregory Paul, a continuous problem, not only for the Protestants in general but also for those nobles within the Minor Church who, unlike the chivalric pacifist Niemojewski, could not endure the Catholic and Calvinist charges of treason or cowardice. The effort of Czechowic and Niemojewski in Lublin, of Gregory Paul and Ronemberg in Raków, to consolidate pacifistic anti-Nicene anabaptism within the Minor Church did not, for example, suffice to sustain the loyalty of the once passionately anabaptist Daniel Bieliński, who in 1576 left the settlement at Raków and defected to the Major Church, publishing a recantation (*Odwołanie*).

Nevertheless, the Racovian mentality gained adherents even in high circles. A settlement akin to Raków was established at about this time at Lucławice, south of Cracow. In 1577 the three Lubienieckis, Andrew, Stanislas, and Christopher (the accounts of two of whom we have been drawing upon), left the Polish court to devote themselves to the anti-Trinitarian anabaptist way.

In 1578 at the synod of Łosk, finally even Budny submitted to immersion, but he persisted in rejecting the pacifistic implications drawn from the rite by the Racovians and the Lubliners. Czechowic and the Silesian Alexander Vitrelin, pastor successively in Pińczów and now Węgrów, strenuously sought to connect baptismal rebirth with the rejection of the sword. Though under the patronage of the same Prince John Kiszka, Budny and Vitrelin opposed each other at Łosk like Hubmaier and Hut under Lord Liechtenstein at Nicolsburg (Ch. 9.2.b). Budny

---

[28] Kot, *Socinianism,* 76.

and the Ruthenian Prince Basil Ciapiński, leader of the immersed nobles in the grand duchy of Lithuania, declared that, despite the *theologically* radical character of the Brethren, it was not contrary to the gospel for a true Christian to hold office, to possess estates with serfs (so long as they were fairly treated), to resort to courts of law in adjudication, and to engage in defensive war. Czechowic, seconded by the devoutly pacifist nobleman John Niemojewski, lay *senior,* concerned to impose the order and discipline of the Lublin congregation upon the whole of the loosely synodal Minor Church in Lithuania and Poland, argued not only for pacifism but also for the manumission of serfs; and they together insisted that pastors, even though drawn from the gentry, should divest themselves of the manners of men to the manor born and live apostolically by the voluntary offerings of the faithful.

In the following year, in Bełżyce near Lublin, Vitrelin, at the request of Blandrata, drafted the Judgment of the Polish Churches (Ch. 28.3) against Francis Dávid because of his nonadorantism.

By 1578, the Racovians were in contact with the nephew of Laelius Socinus, Faustus, en route from Basel to Kolozsvár to defend the practice of invoking Christ in prayer. The Racovians were especially eager to encounter the distinguished Italian, because like them, Faustus Socinus was a pacifist and could well become their ally against the Budnyites. But on the issue of baptism and especially rebaptism, the Racovians had reason to believe that Faustus was not of their persuasion. To make his acquaintance, Czechowic, Schomann, and several Racovians arranged a conference.

Before we take up the second phase of the baptismal controversy in the Minor Church, a controversy now to be fought out in terms of immersion vs. the complete suspension of baptism (for born Christians), we must recount the career and thought of Socinus, the proponent of baptismal suspension, up to his settlement in Poland among the Radicals, who would in due course adopt the main features of his sacramental, soteriological, and Christological system.

7. Faustus Socinus

Faustus Socinus was born in Siena on 5 December 1539, the only son of Alexander Sozzini, by Agnes Petrucci, related to the papal house of Piccolomini. His father (who died in 1541) and his grandfather had both been famous as jurists. Fatherless at the age of two, he had no regular education. With his two sisters he was raised by his mother and grandmother. He spent his youth in casual reading at the family villa. His early intellectual stimulus came from his uncle Celso, a nominal Catholic, founder of a short-lived academy of which Faustus became a member. When another uncle, Laelius (Ch. 22.3.a), was pursued by the Inquisition, Faustus considered it advisable to leave Italy for Lyons, 1561–1563,[29] where he engaged in business. In 1562, perhaps in transit, he identified himself with the Italian congregation in Geneva, and went to Zurich at the death of Laelius in May 1562, to gather up his uncle's papers and settle his affairs. Returning to Lyons, he composed his *Explicatio* of the Prologue of Saint John, which was no doubt suggested by an earlier work of his uncle's of approximately the same title. Herein, Faustus enunciated the basic theme of his Christology in defining Christ as divine by office rather than by nature. In a letter from Lyons, dated 1563, to an Italian, he announced the second basic principle of his theology, the natural mortality of man.[30]

Toward the end of 1563, Faustus returned to Italy, outwardly conforming to the Catholic Church, and for twelve years he was in Florence in the service of Isabella de' Medici, daughter of the grand duke of Tuscany. He may have studied law at this time. At the instance of "a great personage," Faustus began in 1570 his treatise *De sacrae scripturae auctoritate*.[31] This work came to be published allegedly in Spain and somewhat implausibly by "The Reverend Father Dominicus Lopez, S.J." (Seville, 1588).[32]

Socinus held that the Bible is a revelation of God but that although it may contain things above reason (for example, that God is a creator and mankind his creation), it does not contain anything contrary to reason. Accordingly, the Bible reader must be at pains to ascertain the rational sense of Scripture, for upon his success in doctrine, linked with his achievement in the ethical realm of following evangelical precepts, depends his ultimate salvation from natural mortality to a resurrection in a spiritual body at the second advent of Christ.

Socinus opened his study with an inquiry into the authenticity of the canon. Like Calvin, Socinus found reasons to ascribe Hebrews to another than Paul. After some discussion, he in the

---

[29] Wilbur, *Socinianism*, 389.

[30] Faust Socyn, *Listy* (Letters), two volumes, edited by Ludwik Chmaj (Warsaw, 1959), 35–40.

[31] Available in English translation by Edward Combe, *An Argument for the Authority of Holy Scripture* (London, 1731).

[32] Wilbur, *Socinianism*, 390, holds that these data are fictitious and that it was printed at Amsterdam by sympathizers who wished to conceal its heretical origin.

end confirmed the traditional ascription of The Revelation to John the Evangelist. He dealt with miracles and inspiration as the credentials of the canon. Since the purpose of divinely inspired Scriptures was to enable the righteous to secure the reward of eternal life in following the precepts of patriarchal and Mosaic theology, confirmed by the life, teaching, and resurrection of the Righteous One, Socinus concluded his examination of the obscurities and seeming contradictions of the Bible by declaring that it was the wisdom of God not to propose the reward of eternal life so evidently that the merely prudential readers might, despite their bad inclinations, succeed in simulating a perfection that would entitle them to immortality!

Most wisely therefore, Almighty God thought not fit that the reward of immortality, . . . by Him proposed to all men who obey His only-begotten Son Jesus Christ, should appear self-evident and unquestionable . . . but [He] was pleased to think it enough that these writings and other arguments of this reward, wherever to be collected, should appear to be such . . . to anyone who is of honest principles, or so well disposed as easily to become so . . . but to him who is dishonest, and from bad inclinations not to be reclaimed, insufficient; that hereby the probity of the one, and the improbity of the other, being openly discovered, God might have the most just cause of inflicting punishments and conferring His favors (which seems agreeable to divine justice) and by this means exercise His sovereign mercy on the one, His righteous severity on the other, hereby making His wonderful power, universal dominion, and empire, to His infinite and immortal glory known to all; which is indeed the chief aim of God in proposing the doctrine of the gospel to the world, by His only-begotten Son, as in the New Testament is frequently declared.[33]

Socinus had with these words finished his book; but then, for a kind of peroration, he reached back to the authority of another great lay theologian in Florence, where he was sojourning at the time, and quoted in Latin translation *Il Paradiso,* canto xxiv. Socinus had found in the reply to Saint Peter on the part of Dante, like a queried university bachelor before a rigorous master, a poetic summary of his own convictions about "the infallible truth of God, . . . the heavenly shower of the Holy Spirit most liberally poured out upon the Old and the New parchments . . . which produces in me [Dante and now Socinus] firm and stable faith and convinces me of the truth of the Christian religion."[34]

[33] Socinus, *De auctoritate,* cap. v; *BFP,* I, 280; English translation, Combe, *op. cit.,* 157 f.
[34] Socinus, *De auctoritate,* cap. vi; *BFP,* I, 280.

In 1571, Socinus was in Rome, probably with his patroness. He suddenly left Italy after the death of Grand Duke Cosimo I in 1574, never to return, although he remained on good terms with the second grand duke, and until the latter's death[35] received from him regularly the income on his Sienese properties.

Socinus settled at Basel. Here he was to become involved in the discussion leading to his magnum opus on Christology and salvation. *De Jesu Christo servatore* grew out of Socinus' Paduan view of the death of the soul with the body (thnetopsychism), which he had formulated several times before and assumed in his work on Scriptures. He wrote out his convictions about the resurrection of the righteous, dependent no doubt on Renato and mediated perhaps by his uncle Laelius (Ch. 24.2.c), and gave the paper to one Jerome Marlian, declaring his readiness to debate the issue. At the request of Marlian, one John Baptist Rota from Padua, later pastor of a conventicle there, went on to Geneva with Socinus' paper and failed to return it.

Concurrently, Socinus was involved in debate with Francis Pucci (1540–1595), who after the Saint Bartholomew's Day Massacre had gone over to the Reformation. With Calvin and the Catholics, Pucci was defending the natural immortality of the soul, and, more like the Catholics than Calvin, he also denied the impairment of reason by the Fall. These and related ideas Pucci presented in ten theses in Basel in June 1577. To them Socinus responded. Thereupon Pucci replied in a letter of 1 July 1577. Socinus' long answer to this letter was the treatise later published under the title *De statu primi hominis ante lapsum*,[36] wherein he contended that man even before the Fall was liable to death.

During this period Jacques Couvet, pastor of the Huguenot Church in Paris, became another of Socinus' antagonists, when he heard that the traditional doctrines of the atonement and of immortality were being denied. Socinus, at the request of Couvet, obligingly wrote out his thoughts. Couvet replied after a few weeks. Whereupon Socinus sent to Paris the manuscript of *De Jesu Christo servatore*, finished 12 July 1578.

In *De servatore*, as earlier in the *Explicatio*, Socinus denied Christ's essential deity. The Word or will of God appeared in the form of flesh—a man. After the death and resurrection, Christ ascended to take a place at the right hand of God, sharing henceforth in God's power. Thus Christ was God, though in nature purely human, namely, as he on whom God Almighty bestowed

---

[35] Grand Duke Francesco I died in 1587.
[36] *BFP*, II, 253 ff.

after the ascension the government of the world, in cosmic vindication of the righteousness of his Suffering Servant.

Socinus was able to assert that Christ, though wholly human, is nevertheless *verus deus* because the Father shared his power with him at the ascension (Acts 13:33) and at this moment assigned to Christ an adoptive deity as coregent in the government of the world. Socinus thus gave a monarchian solution to the problem of the unity of the Godhead and thereby not only rejected the Nicene ontological solution, which made the Son consubstantial with the Father, but also the Chalcedonian physical solution of the full deity and the full humanity of Christ, as also the physiological solution of Servetus and others adhering to the doctrine of the celestial flesh of Christ (Ch. 11.2 and 3).[37]

Socinus, unlike Servetus, did not allow two natures in Christ. He derived the single nature of Christ from the Virgin. Against the Chalcedonian postulate, he insisted that Christ would not have acknowledged ignorance (Mark 13:32) if, by a second, divine nature, he had known the Day of Judgment. Passionately concerned for the full humanity of Christ, Socinus replaced the doctrine of the two natures with the idea of a higher degree of susceptibility to exaltation to the divine dignity on the part of Christ's human nature.[38] As possessed of the divine dignity, office, and power of the Father, Socinus considered Christ, the ascended Son, as entitled to divine adoration. It will be recalled that it was this asseveration which commended Socinus to Blandrata in the struggle of the latter with the liturgical and doctrinal innovation of Francis Dávid in Transylvania (Ch. 28.3).

Socinus, in his comprehensive theology, of which his distinctive soteriology was the core, defined Christianity as the divinely revealed way of reaching eternal life. Holding, as did Pomponazzi and the Paduans condemned by the Fifth Lateran Council (Ch. 1.3.c), to man's natural mortality, quite apart from any punishment for his transgression in Paradise, Socinus considered Christ, the Second Man, as likewise mortal. In fact, it was essential to Socinus' system to prove from the Bible that Christ was passible and mortal and hence fully human, except for his miraculous birth. The virgin birth was but the first of his many credentials

---

[37] Cf. Stanislàs von Dunin-Borkowski, "Untersuchungen zum Schrifttum der Unitarier vor Faustus Socini," *75 Jahre Stella Matutina, Festschrift,* II (Feldkirch, 1931), 115 f.

[38] Cf. J. A. Dorner, *History of the Development of the Doctrine of the Person of Christ,* translated by D. W. Simon (Edinburgh, 1870), Division II, Vol. II, 249 ff. There is a discussion of Socinus in Hans Emil Weber, *Reformation, Orthodoxie und Rationalismus* (Gütersloh, 1951).

in preparing mankind for the disclosure of his uniquely soteriological purpose. Therefore, unlike the exponents of all forms of
the doctrine of the atonement hitherto,[39] Socinus stressed not
the death of Christ as the work of salvation but rather (1) the
resurrection of Christ as an earnest of the eventual salvation of
his brethren in the fullness of time, and (2) the ascension of Christ
and the bestowal upon him of the governance of the world in
confirmation of the Old Testament prophetic declaration that
the prevailing disposition of God is his loving-kindness toward
his creatures.

Socinus set himself against what he regarded as the irrational
(as distinguished from suprarational) contradiction inherent in
the traditional formulations of Christ's role as Savior, all of which
presuppose in the Godhead both a concern for the maintenance
of justice (with a horror of sin) and such a degree of "mercy"
that God accepts the death of his innocent Son as a substitute for
the punishment of the wicked. Over against the view that love
and wrath are aspects of the ambivalent being of God, Socinus
spoke rather of the will of God, and declared that God had
manifestly willed to provide the means for saving mankind from
eternal death. Socinus' arguments were directed against what
he considered the contradiction in the inherited views of the
atonement that postulated at once the necessity for, and contrived
the implementation of, a penal satisfaction. The necessity for
penal satisfaction, in the traditional theory of the atonement was,
according to Socinus, founded on the consideration that God was
necessitated by his concern for cosmic righteousness to punish
sin, and that if he did not punish the guilty directly, he had at
least to punish an innocent representative of mankind, his own
Son made flesh.

Socinus, in his contrary theory of an atonement limited, not
by God's reprobation but by man's demerit, maintained that God
is always at liberty to punish or to forgive sins, that his justice
as expressed in his wrath and his loving-kindness as expressed in
his mercy are not inherent in his essence but only alternating acts
of his righteous will in the government of the world. Sin, Socinus
argued, is analogous to an insult or a debt, which like these can
be overlooked or forgiven without any further condition. Surely
God forgives under the New Covenant no less freely than he once
forgave under the Old Covenant, namely, without receiving
infinite satisfaction. Moreover, God's justice cannot be regarded

[39] The doctrine of the atonement has been under consideration at several
points in this book, beginning with Valdés in Ch. 1.2.c.

as having in any way to be safeguarded, even with a token satisfaction made infinite by the hypostatic union of the postulated human and divine natures, the latter provided by himself, because it would be in any case unjust for God to let all the guilty go unpunished, and to punish even one willing, representative but innocent person in their stead.

That the atonement was not, after all, a penal satisfaction is clear, for Socinus, in two respects. First of all, the Bible asserts that God's purpose was to forgive the sins of the whole world. There should, therefore, be no such palpable contradiction between the purpose proposed and the supposed means. A debt cannot be both remitted and satisfactorily repaid, for in remission of a debt the debtor is freed from his obligation and the creditor renounces his claim to satisfaction.

That a penal satisfaction to God is also impossible is all the more manifest when the analogy of redemption moves from pecuniary debt to a penalty involving life. A person other than the debtor can, to be sure, pay a debt, but he cannot endure for another capital punishment leading to *eternal* death. Transference of a capital penalty to an innocent person is intolerably unjust and, when writ large in terms of the divine redemption, mocks the very idea of a righteous God. That the one innocent Man, according to orthodox theory, who did die was also restored to life does not, for Socinus, attenuate the basic injustices of the original, divine exaction postulated.

Furthermore, Socinus continues, the orthodox doctrine, which stresses Christ's redemptive death, cannot support itself by the assertion that Christ as head of the church was qualified to take punishment upon himself in place of his members; for precisely that relationship first came into existence by virtue of his resurrection and psychopompal ascension. Before this ascension Christ did not stand in any special relationship to other men; and his death, therefore, did not deliver his disciples from the necessity of undergoing death. His personal fulfillment of the law could not have substitutionary value for others. He, like all men, was bound to fulfill the law for himself; and thus neither the effects of his obedience, nor those of his Passion, could be transferred to others.

Finally, even Christ's adoptive divinity, assigned to him at his ascension, could not enhance, even retroactively, the value of his Passion; for, as even the orthodox would agree, Christ suffered as man. Even if a postulated divine nature in Christ had suffered or been involved in the redemptive action, as Gregory Paul and

Osiander, each in his own way, had once said or implied (Ch. 25.3), still, according to Socinus, the infinite value of Christ's adoptive divinity could not be attributed to his temporal acts or moments of human suffering.

The significance of Socinus' theological system and notably of his *De Jesu Christo servatore,* of 1578, is that it brings to a close the efforts of the Radical Reformation to restate, in departure from traditional formulations, a new doctrine of salvation.

In his Christology, thnetopsychism, and conception of sanctification Socinus brings together with memorable clarity and baffling simplicity a doctrine of the atonement and justification which (more than any other work thus far discussed) shows how the whole of the Radical Reformation, in various thrusts and tentative endeavors, differed profoundly from the Magisterial Reformation.

We may state the difference succinctly, by way of a provisional summary. The Magisterial Reformers, in their concern for divine justice and the maintenance of human justice in the Christian commonwealth—that is, in the, for them, still essentially unbroken *conception* of a Catholic *corpus christianum*—were at pains to preserve in some fashion the combination of (1) God's loving-kindness, which they themselves had experienced and formulated in their insistence on salvation by faith alone (against ecclesiastical works, righteousness), and (2) God's horror of sin, crime, and disorder in creation generally, in mankind specifically, and in the church itself most grievously. The Radical Reformers, in contrast, with their generally individualistic view of sin, with their proclivity to loosen the conception of the solidarity of mankind in Adam and with their consequent dismantling of the conception of a universal church embodying the Second Adam as its head, were also disposed to stress God's love more than his justice. All the Radicals found God's demand for a responsive human justice better realized in the self-disciplined conventicle (separated from both the support and the coercion of the state) than in the forensic justification of intermingled saints and sinners in a coercive territorial or papal church.

Socinus, reflecting these sectarian views, had in Padua, Florence, and Basel formulated a doctrine of the atonement which may be said to mark the natural closing of the Radical Reformation in one of the main articles of theology.

Such was his theology when Socinus arrived from Transylvania in Poland, destined to reshape the Racovian anti-Trinitarian anabaptist Minor Church into a new school of Christianity. Thus far, however, he had not expressed himself on sacramental theology.

8. THE BEGINNINGS OF ORGANIZED SOCINIANISM: THE SECOND
   BAPTISMAL CONTROVERSY IN THE MINOR CHURCH

The substance of Socinus' soteriology, which had been formulated in his debate with Jacques Clouet in Basel, would in due
course be printed in Poland.

Ordinarily, *De Jesu Christo servatore*[40] is set forth as the beginning of a major movement, Socinianism, the first phase of
which would be made to extend from its composition in Basel or
from the arrival of Socinus with it in Poland to the death of
Socinus in 1604 in the midst of his work on *Christianae religionis
brevissima institutio*,[41] which would become the basis for the
first edition of the Racovian Catechism in 1605. But the Socinianism embodied in the Racovian Catechism was a school of religious
thought and corporate discipline quite different in the end from
the faith and order of the anabaptist, anti-Trinitarian Racovian
community which had produced the Racovian *Catechesis* of 1574
(Ch. 27.4). Indeed, the two Racovian communities, though continuous, so far differed from each other as to warrant their separate classification in the typology of religion. And since organized Socinianism, belonging as it does to the end of the sixteenth century and to the first half of the next, would carry us
beyond the chronological frame set for the present narrative, we
shall here limit our consideration to the first encounters of Faustus
Socinus with the Minor Church.

When Socinus from Transylvania "moved on into Poland,"
writes his grandson Andrew Wiszowaty, and "asked at the synod
of Raków in 1580 to be publicly admitted to the churches that
confessed that only the Father of Jesus Christ is God most high,
he was refused admission for disagreeing on certain doctrines
which he did not conceal (as on the satisfaction of Christ, on
justification without works, on predestination and free will, and
on baptism by immersion); nor was he admitted to the holy
Supper; yet in defense of these churches he contended actively in
his writings against their antagonists."[42]

Although Wiszowaty names a number of doctrinal differences,
the accent must have come down on baptismal theology, for it
was to the composition of his lengthy and tedious *De baptismo
aquae disputatio* (1580) that Socinus immediately turned.[43] In a
word, like Palaeologus, he held that an external baptism with
water was not enjoined or even always practiced by the apostles.

[40] *BFP*, I, 115–252.
[41] *BFP*, I, 657–676.
[42] Sandius, *op. cit.*, 607.
[43] *BFP*, I, 709–752.

Socinus saw in it therefore solely a rite, analogous to Jewish proselyte baptism, and argued that, though probably useful for marking the entry of ancient pagans into the New Israel, it had no present utility among those born in a Christian environment, except as it might formalize the occasional conversion of a Jew or a Turk to Christianity. Born Christians, wrote Socinus, regardless of the communion out of which they may come into the Minor Church, need not be baptized, and surely should not be rebaptized.

Simon Ronemberg at Raków requested a copy of *De baptismo* and wrote to Socinus, pleading with him to reconsider his decision and submit to immersion.[44] Ronemberg was surely not unmindful of how he and his delegation had themselves once smarted from unyielding and exclusivistic instructions when they had been at Hutterite Neumühl with Walpot just about a decade before (Ch. 27.3); and yet he was deeply convinced that the building up at Raków of the "collapsed house of God," the construction of an ark of salvation, had been effected precisely through insistence on baptism by immersion and on the ban; and, since Faustus Socinus was in so many other respects of one spirit with the old Racovians and regarded baptism as indeed something indifferent, could he not unobtrusively submit to immersion as the other good folk at Raków had, who had been prepared not only for a public profession of their Christianity by baptism in water, but also for the sufferings of this world, even detestable death itself.

In a friendly, even deferential, but very firm reply,[45] Socinus in effect summarized his *De baptismo* in eight points and contended that precisely because baptism, from his point of view, was indeed a matter of indifference, he could not bring himself to go through a ceremony which by its deliberately public and solemn character at Raków inevitably enhanced its importance, and that precisely because he, along with many other sympathizers with the Racovian movement, could not do so, they were all unwisely being kept away from both the wholesome discipline of the community and the spiritual benefits of the Supper.

Socinus was refuting, among others, a major baptismal treatise written in Lublin by Czechowic about this time, *De paedobaptistarum errorum origine*.[46] In it Czechowic brought together the

---

[44] *BFP*, I, 482 f.
[45] *BFP*, 429–431.
[46] The dedicatory foreword is available in Szczucki, *Literatura Ariańska*, 165–182. Socinus asked Czechowic for a copy of his baptismal treatise in a friendly letter 20 June 1580.

whole of his thinking on baptism for the purpose of preparing the powerful Lithuanian magnate, John Kiszka, for immersion. Kiszka, following Budny (as Lord Liechtenstein at Nicolsburg had followed Hubmaier), was prepared to submit to rebaptism, but did not feel that the rite committed him to abandoning his vocation as a magistrate.

In writing the treatise for Kiszka, Czechowic had in mind to counteract the influence of all Spiritualists and Rationalists, who were disparaging or minimizing what he regarded as *the* redemptive ordinance. "Since you wish to be baptized and you earnestly call upon God that he by baptism might bury you together with Christ," he began his appeal to Kiszka, "it is necessary that you, whom I see as one especially exposed to the greatest perils and temptations on all sides, be fully armed." Czechowic proceeded to deal with fourteen errors. Then, in an appendix,[47] he took up some 128 items dealing with what he regarded as a false spiritualizing or interiorizing of the sacraments and ordinances of the church.

Czechowic's polemic in this book was directed not so much against Calvinists and Lutherans as against Spiritualists like the Italians Faustus Socinus and Nicholas Paruta, and the Germans Caspar Schwenckfeld and Christian Entfelder, and the radical Poles who had been converted to Spiritualism in the first stages of the Racovian colonization. His opponents were all those who for any reason rejected or minimized the importance of the Lord's Supper, the ban, and the ordained ministry, not to mention baptism. Czechowic called them the "dreamers," "who believe they are pure." Thus, with special reference to baptism, Czechowic was facing, in his book, a Spiritualist challenge to Anabaptist discipline in Poland comparable to the Schwenckfeld-Marpeck struggle in South Germany (Ch. 18).

Andrew Lubieniecki tendentiously confirms the presence of Schwenckfeldian as well as other spiritualizing influences when he writes of those "who spoke of scripture as a dead letter and a daub of printer's ink, and, wishing to imitate Schwenckfeld, held that dreams, visions, and ideas were the things most necessary in religious practice for salvation."[48] Czechowic was thus also recalling encounters with Spiritualizers and Sacraments in Kujawy and

---

[47] Later refuted by Faustus Socinus and published as an appendix to *De baptismo; BFP,* I, 748–752, where Socinus quotes a phrase or two from each of the 128 items in the appendix of Czechowic's book. On the incorrect date of the foreword, and the relationship of Czechowic's book to other writings, see Szczucki, *Literatura Ariańska,* p. 182, n. 36.

[48] "Polonoeutychia," *loc. cit.*

"those who condemned all officiating at any religious service, claiming that nobody was fit to officiate or instruct unless he had a divine revelation and had either witnessed miracles or performed them."[49]

In defending believers' baptism by immersion, Czechowic insisted that it is a seal of faith; a symbol of dying with Christ and, for the Christ-imitating believer, the counterpart of the blood streaming down the sides of the Crucified; a public giving of one's name to Christ in contrast to an infant's being given a Christian name at a christening;[50] a putting on of Christ; an ablution from sin and a veritable cure or medicament (*medela*) for sin; and, indeed, a remission of sin inseparably linked to the preaching and the hearing of the Word.

The opposition of Czechowic, Ronemberg, and Schomann to any spiritualizing or other attempts to minimize baptism caused them to resist Faustus Socinus, even though Socinus dissociated himself from the Spiritualists on all other points, especially on the significance of the Supper.

No sooner, in fact, had Socinus sought to refute the immersionist anabaptism of the Lubliners and the Racovians than he turned about to defend their pacifism in his even more massive refutation of Palaeologus' *De Magistratu politico* (Ch. 29.1) in *Ad Palaeologi librum . . . pro Racoviensibus responsio*. With aging Gregory Paul nearly blind and no longer up to the task of a (second) refutation, it was the scion of a distinguished Sienese house of jurisconsults and the sometime Florentine courtier who responded to the call of the Polish pacifists. With his text on the new creation in Christ, II Cor. 5:17, "Behold all things are become new," Socinus attended the synod of Chmielnik in January 1581 to get the direct counsel of the Brethren and had his manuscript published in Cracow the following August.

On the issues of Christology and magistracy, Socinus found himself much closer to the Racovians than to the Lithuanian Brethren under the ever-mounting influence of unitarian, nonpacifist Simon Budny, recently rebaptized. At the synod of Lubecz (near Nowogródek) in March 1582, Czechowic, Niemojewski, and Nicholas Żytno, among others, contended once again for the principle of absolute pacifism against Budny.

To defend himself and his cause, Budny published his major

---

[49] Such as Sleszyński, Bieliński, Albinus, John Baptista, and many others. "Polonoeutychia," *loc. cit.*

[50] Item 9, and by inference from Socinus' responses to 19, 98, 99, 124.

work, *On the Sword*.[51] This is really a confession in the name of "the church of Christ the Lord in Lithuania" on the part of a "conscientious participant" in the society of the sword and judicial order; and it gives a vivid picture of the tension between the civic-minded Lithuanian anabaptist Unitarians and the Polish Brethren. A concluding section refutes some twenty-two arguments of Czechowic. (Eventually the Scriptural arguments that remind one of Hubmaier will be taken over by the Socinians, at Raków by Socinus himself.)

At the synod of Lucławice in May 1582,[52] the Polish Brethren with their consistently pacifist position received a delegate from the Mennonites in Danzig. The visitor appears to have come from the same group of unitarian Mennonites from Holland with whom one Matthew Radecke was associated.[53]

Born in Danzig, secretary to the town council, Radecke had become a Mennonite and gone to Holland whence he was driven in 1582 on account of his views on the Trinity.[54] In response to Radecke, the Lucławice synod of 1582 sent Czechowic, Alexander Vitrelin (rather recently converted from the Major Church), and Matthew Krokier as a delegation to Danzig. One of the differences, as it developed, was over predestination, the Danzig Mennonites holding to the freedom of the will, while Czechowic, for example, in his later report on Rom., ch. 7, insisted that, like Paul, no Christian is entirely free.

There is no direct evidence that the peculiar Mennonite doctrine of the celestial flesh of Christ was under discussion at Lucławice or in Danzig. There is, however, from the pen of Socinus the undated tract, *Disputatio brevissima de Christi carne adversus Mennonitas*.[55]

Czechowic reported the failure of the mission to the Mennonites at the general synod in Węgrów, May 1584. This synod excommunicated[56] Simon Budny on the issue of the pre-existence of Christ and the propriety of rendering him worship. The cleav-

---

[51] *O urzędzie miecza używającym* (Łosk, 1583), edited by S. Kot (Warsaw, 1932).

[52] The town was the residence of Socinus after 1583.

[53] F. S. Bock, *Memorabilia Unitariorum acta in Prussia* (Königsberg, 1753), 13 ff.; Wotschke, *Reformation*, 145.

[54] For the life of the unitarian anabaptist Radecke, who in the end was to undergo three baptisms, Catholic, Mennonite, and Unitarian, see my "Anabaptism and Spiritualism in Poland," *loc. cit.*, 258 f.

[55] *BFP*, II, 461–463.

[56] Wilbur gives the date of Budny's excommunication as 1582, *Socinianism*, 349. Górski, *Studia*, 155, places the excommunication in 1584.

age was now complete between the fully unitarian but politically positive Lithuanian Brethren under Budny and the Christocentric, pacifistic Polish Brethren, now under the influence of Socinus.

We are obliged to terminate our account of the evolution of pacifistic, anti-Nicene anabaptism into Socinianism at mid-career. Socinianism, as a distinctive amalgam of Anabaptism and Evangelical Rationalism within the Radical Reformation is a development of the last quarter of the sixteenth century, and falls therefore outside the chronological framework of the present narrative.

Suffice it to say that almost all of the theology of Socinus would soon be taken over by the Minor Church and would be elaborated in many a tract and tome and published by the new Racovians as their own, notably Socinus' hermeneutical and epistemological principles, his doctrine of natural mortality with the resurrection of the righteous only (psychopannychism), and his doctrine of Christ's atoning work as that of a psychopomp rather than that of a sacrifice. On the adoration of the risen Christ, on the impropriety of the use of the sword by Christians, and on related social doctrines, Socinus and the Racovians had from the beginning been in accord. It was only on the question of believers' baptism that the Anabaptist and the Rationalist currents failed to merge. Although, to be sure, the first neo-Racovian Catechism published in the year after the death of Socinus provisionally accepted his idea of baptism as a rite for "Gentile" converts only, in the succeeding editions of the Catechism the current springing from Gonesius and Czechowic flowed afresh. Thereafter, immersionism, Socinus to the contrary, became one of the marks of Socinianism.

The stress on believers' baptism at Raków had led to a great interest in the colony in the catechetical instruction of the young. Out of the catechetical literature and the increasingly elaborate catechetical instruction grew the school and the press of Raków. The latter printed some five hundred books before its dissolution. Catechetical schools outside the colony likewise took on a larger and larger cultural assignment as the catechetical impulse of the original Racovians merged with the Rationalist approach to Christianity embodied in Socinus, to bring about an influential reform of education.[57]

With the formal exchanges, beginning in 1582, between the Dutch unitarian Mennonites of the delta of the Vistula and the immersionist Polish Brethren, we have almost come full circle.

[57] Cf. Łukasz Kurdybacha, Z dziejów pedagogiki ariańskiej (Warsaw, 1958).

Eventually, a large body of the Polish Brethren, presently to be called Socinians, will seek refuge in Holland itself and introduce among the Rijnsburg Collegiants, and in their turn among certain Waterlander Mennonites (Ch. 19.2.d), the practice of immersion, which will eventually[58] be taken over by certain English sectarian refugees sojourning in Holland, and will become in due course quite general throughout the far-flung community of Anglo-American Baptists.

It is convenient at this juncture to return to the Netherlands and pick up the developments there, on the eve of the conversion of Holland to Calvinism (1566).

[58] The first overture from the unitarian Socinians in Poland to the Waterlander Mennonites in Holland came in 1598. Briefly discussed in my "Anabaptism and Spiritualism in Poland," *loc. cit.,* 261.

CHAPTER 30

DEVELOPMENTS IN THE NETHERLANDS, 1566–1578, AND IN ENGLAND

As we return to the Netherlands we must be prepared to find Mennonitism divided into numerous factions ranging from the very strict Frisians to the liberal Waterlanders, all trying to consolidate their position at the very moment in Netherlandish history when all dissenters were being driven headlong from the southern provinces under the ruthless new governor, Duke Ferdinand of Alva (1567–1573), and when the new revolutionary-nationalist movement in the northern provinces was being borne by a new class of insurgents, the Calvinists. No less disciplined and conventicular than the Münsterites, no less belligerent than the Münsterites had been a generation before, the Calvinists represent the third Reformation thrust (1566–1609) in the Netherlands in succession to the dominance of the Sacramentists (1500–1530) and that of the Anabaptists (1530–1566). The story of the Anabaptist fission in the first period of Calvinist ascendancy is a somewhat tedious chronicle of acculturation and further schism.

1. THE FLIGHT OF THE FLEMINGS AND THE FLEMISH-FRISIAN SCHISM

Anabaptism in the southern Netherlands was widespread and vigorous. In its second phase, extending from 1550 to 1576, Antwerp had become the recognized metropole of the "Belgian" Anabaptists. The brotherhood faced a storm of violent Catholic persecution that did not let up until the Calvinists replaced the Anabaptists as the main target of the Hapsburg attack. Antwerp, Ghent, Ypres, and Courtrai were so full of Anabaptists that the inquisitor appealed, in 1561, to the regent to put the armed forces in a state of readiness, so great was the fear of an uprising.[1]

---

[1] V. Gaillard, *Archives du conseil de Flandres* (Ghent, 1856), 206. The main martyrologies for Ghent, Bruges, Courtrai, Brussels, and Antwerp are brought together in my bibliographical "Studies in the Radical Reformation," *loc. cit.,* iv, 5. To this should be added "Les Martyrs Anabaptistes en

764

The details concerning the inner life of the community, however, are obscure.[2] It was in 1565 that the Belgian Calvinist Guy de Brès, himself to be a victim of Catholic persecution, published against the Anabaptists his *La racine, source, et fondement des anabaptistes ou rebaptisés de notre temps.* The evangelist Giles of Aachen has already been named (Ch. 14.3). Leonard Bouwens and Menno visited the southern provinces, and Bouwens baptized 292 converts in Antwerp before 1565, 242 in Ghent, and 187 more in other Flemish towns. Many of the converts were weavers, some of them prosperous. The statements of the inquisitors that there were seven hundred Anabaptists in Bruges in 1568 and two thousand in Antwerp in 1566 are probably not exaggerated.[3]

Persecution of the Anabaptists in the southern Netherlands (Belgium) had been especially severe from the outset, because of their greater proximity to the seat of the Spanish administration for the Low Countries, Brussels. By 1566 the responsibility for the search and the prosecution of dissenters was removed from the local magistracies and concentrated in Brussels. Henceforth it was directed with ruthless cunning against the leaders. In the period covered by our narrative the number of Belgian martyrs was about three thousand,[4] of whom the majority were Anabaptists. The latter were usually burned, the Protestants (Lutherans and Calvinists) hanged or beheaded. With their leaders imprisoned or burned, the orphaned Anabaptist flocks fled by the hundreds. Many Flemish localities lost their entire Mennonite population. By the end of our period some fifty thousand dissidents[5] had been driven from the Hapsburg Netherlands (mainly Flanders), the majority being Anabaptists.

When the Flemish Anabaptist refugees streamed into the northern provinces, by preference West Frisia, they found that they differed from their hosts in temperament and in spirit. Friction arose. The Frisian Anabaptists considered the Flemings ostentatious in dress and self-indulgent in their eating and drink-

Flandres et dans le Brabant méridional," *Annales du Congrès Archéologique et Historique de Tournai* (1949); "Notes au sujet de la Réforme en Flandres au XVIme siècle," *Bulletin de la Société d'Histoire du Protestantisme Belge* (1951), 506–521. All these regional martyrologies have been brought together comprehensively by Alphonse Verheyden, *Le martyrologe protestant des Pays-Bas du Sud au XVIème siècle* (Brussels, 1960).

[2] In the first decade of the prolonged war against Spain, 1575–1585, the southern congregations and their records were completely wiped out.

[3] *ME*, I, 271.

[4] Estimate of Verheyden, *Le martyrologe,* a third of which is a listing of all known Belgian martyrs.

[5] *Ibid.*

ing. The Flemings found the Frisians dour about insignificant matters, yet given to worldliness in such things as houses and linens. What the Frisians considered their virtue, the thrift which led to comfortable households, the Flemings thought vanity.

This unavoidable and trivial conflict was focused when the Flemings came into contact with an unusual experiment undertaken by some of the Frisians in 1560. The four congregations of Harlingen, Franeker, Dokkum, and Leeuwarden had formed a union on the basis of nineteen articles on various items of congregational life (*Ordinantie der vier steden*), which provided that a preacher chosen by one of the congregations had to be approved by all the others. All controversies arising in one church should be settled by the ministers of the four churches in concert, and the care of the poor and of the refugees was to be handled in common. Numerous incoming Flemings began to express dissatisfaction with this arrangement, which they thought abrogated a fundamental Anabaptist principle, the autonomy of the local congregation. The differences of taste and principle finally led to a schism.

When the occasion presented itself, the congregation at Franeker, where the Flemish refugees were concentrated, chose as their minister one Jerome Tinnegieter from the province of Hainaut. The Frisian majority in the federated congregation at Harlingen under Ebbe Pieters objected to this choice, as was its right under the terms of the covenant among the four churches. A council of ministers was called at Harlingen to deal with the problem which was destined to divide conservative Mennonitism into two mutually exclusive denominations. The single most distinguishable theological point at issue between the immigrant Flemings and the indigenous Frisians was that of congregational authority over against its monopolization by a congregational council (*kerkrad*) and the regional eldership (*oudsten*), but the issue was quickly obscured and confounded by the actions of both sides. The ethnic, cultural, and constitutional antagonism was intensified by the conflict between the two chief leaders, both of them Frisians by birth: Leonard Bouwens from his base in Emden; Dietrich Philips from his headquarters in or near Danzig.

The year before the flare-up among the four federated congregations, namely, in 1565, Dietrich had voyaged to Emden to adjudicate a quarrel between Leonard himself and his own congregation. The causes are not entirely clear, but it seems that Leonard made too many voyages over to West Frisia, neglecting his flock; that he there partook too readily of the alcoholic hospitality of his Flemish hosts accustomed to better fare than the frugal Frisians; and that when he was waited upon by a delegation of his congregation, he claimed that as an elder he had every right to come and go as his supervisory duties required. The basic point at issue was thus whether his *"vry-dienen"* or the principle of congregational control over their chief servant was the approved apostolic pattern. Leonard's own earlier implacable stand on moral questions and his perhaps capricious authoritarianism had engendered antagonisms that now worked against him. Seven ministers sat on his case, presided over by Dietrich, and as a result Leonard was suspended from his position as elder, though not banned. Leonard withdrew to a spot near Harlingen, and shortly afterward, perhaps as a result of his direct efforts, several members of the commission of seven withdrew their condemnation.

It was at this juncture that the grievances of the Frisian-born suspended elder and those of the frustrated Flemish refugee, Jerome Tinnegieter, reinforced each other in fateful intensity. Smarting at the insult inflicted on him by the three other covenanted parishes, Jerome had not promptly called a meeting of his own congregation to ratify the covenant of the four towns. Just before the time set, Jerome hastily called a meeting, but only about thirty out of three hundred members were able to be present. Because they were so few, they agreed to leave the decision with the congregational council. At Jerome's instigation *and utterly at variance with the professed Flemish preference for full congregational participation in a major decision,* the small council proceeded to repudiate the union of the four congregations. The majority, which was opposed to this action, on being apprised of Jerome's tactics, tried in vain to have the decision reviewed and rescinded. Soon the two factions in Franeker were holding separate services, and were being distinguished from one another by the names "Flemish" and "Frisian." Jerome went so far as spitefully to attack and malign Ebbe Pieters, the moderate Frisian pastor in Harlingen. More controversy and recrimination followed.

The sounds of the ugly feud reached Dietrich Philips in Danzig. He wrote from Prussia,[6] telling of his concern and sorrow at the new outbreak of strife while the Reformed Church was growing in power and influence, and would profit from disunity among the Mennonites. Dietrich exhorted the quarreling parties to harmony, and hinted that he would be glad to come and adjudicate the case; but his appeal was unsuccessful.

The two factions agreed, instead, to accept two ministers from

[6] 19 September 1566.

outside the affected region as arbitrators, John Willems and Lubbert Gerrits from Hoorn. These in turn chose ten others to help. They demanded that the parties in dispute sign an agreement to abide by their arbitration; and, after extended hearings and investigations, they called a solemn meeting for 1 February 1567 at Harlingen, attended by delegations from near and far. After a formal report of their findings, the arbitrators required both parties to kneel, to confess their guilt, and to ask forgiveness. The Frisians knelt first and rose. When the Flemish group in their turn, after kneeling and confessing their sin, started to rise also, they were told that they had to be lifted by the hands of the Frisians for bearing the larger burden of guilt. The humiliated Flemings, who felt that they had been tricked, furiously denounced both the commitment and their confession of guilt; and needless to say, the situation was worse than before.[7]

In this impasse, the Frisians appealed to Dietrich Philips to intervene personally, but their letter[8] was so ingratiating that Dietrich suspected their sincerity. Dietrich himself was in a quandary. Basically disposed to favor the church councils and the elders over whom he presided as the chief bishop, he was found in the course of the quarrel reversing himself as to just which faction were the Amalekites! He had already expressed his disapproval of the Frisians' yoked-church compact, as a nonapostolic arrangement, and he now let it be known that he considered the two arbitrators chosen, John Willems and Lubbert Gerrits (whom he himself had earlier ordained), as too young to wield the authority with which they had been invested. In response to th' Frisians, Dietrich set out toward Emden on what was to be his last journey, and he asked the contending parties to appear there before him. John and Lubbert excused themselves on the ground that their congregation at Hoorn would not permit them to leave. Thereupon Dietrich, who took this as evidence of a bad conscience, wrote to Hoorn, reminding the young elders that they owed their standing to him, and in effect suspending them until they should have freed themselves from the suspicion brought on them by their failure to appear before him in Emden. Thus pressed, the Frisians dispatched a delegation of nine, but not the requested pair. This action antagonized Dietrich all the more. He was certain that he had to bring the Flemings and the Frisians face to face in his presence. He sent the unbidden nine away, and wrote another letter announcing again the suspension of the

[7] Keeney, "Dirk Philips," *loc. cit.*, 189.
[8] Written by Hoyte Renix, 17 April 1567.

reluctant ministers of Hoorn. They, however, had in the meantime thought better of the matter, and set out with others[9] toward Emden. Meeting the returning nine on the way, they joined them and all went to Emden.

In Emden, they found that the old bishop would not budge from his demand that the two men in question, John and Lubbert, face the Flemings in his presence without the rest of their delegation, and this they were unwilling to do. Impatiently, Dietrich responded with an ultimatum,[10] which the Frisians interpreted as an excommunication, and to which they replied by banning Dietrich himself on 8 July 1567!

This sad split was the final outcome of Dietrich's attempts at reconciliation. In view of the rancor of the contending parties, which colors their accounts, it is hard to see at whose feet the greater charge of stubbornness and self-will is to be laid. It is ironical that in the end it was Dietrich who found himself allied with the laxer Flemings and banned by the Frisians, whereas Leonard Bouwens, who had started the whole affair by his too ready enjoyment of Flemish hospitality and spirits, was now aligned with the Frisians and banned by the Flemings. Despite this final incongruity, the Flemish had, after all moved away from the Frisians because of the rigorism and extreme "episcopal" authority of Dietrich Philips among the Frisians.[11] Thus, Dietrich Philips' work as chief bishop of the Anabaptists of the Hanseatic Coast in succession to Menno ended in a second major schism in 1567, comparable in proportions and issues to that occasioned by the defection of the Waterlanders a decade earlier (Ch. 19.2.d). Dietrich's last days were spent in writing a vindication of his conduct in the controversy. Shortly afterward he died, sometime in 1568, near Emden.

A number of Netherlandish Mennonites had sought to stay out of this controversy as *stilstaanders,* remaining neutral and chiding both parties for the lack of brotherliness. For their pains they were excommunicated by both the Flemish and the Frisians.[12]

The tensions between spiritualism and rigorism, congregationalism and clericalism, compounded by persecution, emigration, and personal animosities among the leaders, had led to successive fissions in Netherlandish Anabaptism. In 1567, besides numerous

---

[9] Hoyte Renix and Peter Willems Bogart.
[10] Cf. Kühler, *Geschiednis,* 425.
[11] Meihuizen, "Spiritualistic Tendencies," 274.
[12] The majority of this group eventually went over to the Flemish.

smaller factions, there were four major Mennonite groups, namely, the Frisians, the Flemish, the Waterlanders, and the unitarian Adamites.

The next year, 1568, the Waterlanders held a major meeting in Emden, with twelve congregations represented, including Ghent, Antwerp, Rotterdam, and Amsterdam,[13] and there reasserted the rights of the local congregations with respect both to their own elected spokesmen (*voorgangers*) and to any actions these servants of the church (*leeraars, vermaners, dienaars, oudsten*) might take in the absence of the congregation. On the constitutional side the Flemish schism and the Waterlander fellowship were in large agreement.

The strong affirmation of congregationalism or independency by two influential branches of Netherlandish Anabaptism occurred at the very moment when Calvinism, with its capacity for strong synodal articulation and cohesion, was emerging as the new fighting faith in the great national uprising against Spain.

2. The Rise of the Calvinists and the Achievement of Toleration for the Mennonites, 1566–1578

While the Netherlandish Mennonites were falling prey to internal strife and schism, another reforming group, which had come late to the scene, was beginning to perfect its organization and to grow in strength and influence in the Low Countries. In 1566 the Reformed Church organized itself at the synod of Antwerp and adopted the *Confessio Belgica* as the Netherlandish statement of Calvinist faith. The militant spirit of the Reformed movement is attested by the hardihood of the Walloon Guy de Brès, the author of the *Confessio,* who had sent it to Philip II in 1561 with the request that, having learned of their beliefs, he would either increase his tortures and burnings or become the support and refuge of his loyal subjects. De Brès paid for his proposal with his life in 1567.

Even before receiving this bold-faced challenge, Philip II (1555–1598) had learned much about the stubbornness and independent will of his Netherlandish subjects. His imperial father, Charles V, had sought to establish an efficient inquisition in the Netherlands on the Spanish model, but had met with nothing but frustration through the indifference or actual opposition of the native magistrates. On 25 October 1555, though only in the fifty-fifth year of his life, he had owned himself beaten, and had turned over the reins of his Spanish and Burgundian

---

[13] Minutes in *Doopsgezinde Bijdragen* (1877), 69–75.

dominions to his son Philip, in order to retire the following year to a monastery in Spain.

Unlike his father, who had been born in Brabant, Philip was a thorough Spaniard, spoke neither Flemish nor French, and neither understood nor wanted to understand the genius of his Netherlandish subjects. Even less than his father was he able to appreciate the unique industry and mentality of the Low Countries, which had provided Charles with two fifths of his annual revenue of five million gold crowns. He was zealous for the Catholic faith, and jealous of his own absolute power, even if he had to protect them at the cost of all his revenue from the Netherlands.

Philip's first ecclesiastical move in the Netherlands was the attempt actually to enforce Charles V's earlier edict[14] establishing the Inquisition. To this end he had effected, through a papal bull of 1559 (Paul IV), the episcopal reorganization of the provinces. Instead of the four old bishoprics of Arras, Cambrai, Tournai, and Utrecht (the first three under the archbishop of Rheims, the last under Cologne), there were to be three archbishoprics, namely: Mechlin with six dioceses, Cambrai with four, and Utrecht with five. This measure was odious to the evangelicals of all parties because it represented a strengthening of the Roman administrative system; repugnant to many of the towns because it represented a violation of their ancient charters and the installation of foreign prelates; and hazardous to the great monasteries, whose ample revenues were to be confiscated to support the new dioceses. Thus when Philip left the Netherlands for Spain in the same year, there was a strong body of opposition to his policy within the council of state.

The year of his diocesan reorganization and departure, 1559, was, it will be recalled, also the year of Calvin's final edition of the *Institutes,* the year of the adoption of the French confession of faith, and the year in which William of Orange, not yet a Protestant, formed the secret resolution "to drive the Spanish vermin from the land," which earned him the sobriquet "the Silent."

In 1566 a group of noblemen submitted a petition to the regent Margaret of Parma, requesting abolition of the edicts against the heretics and the summoning of the Estates-General. A frenzy of great religious excitement inundated the country, with preachers appearing everywhere, and a furious outbreak of iconoclasm, which destroyed thousands of works of art in Antwerp and elsewhere. Margaret originally made some concessions, but soon

[14] Of 1550.

put down the disorder and retracted them. Then, much to her displeasure and against her advice and entreaties, began the ruthless dictatorship of the Duke of Alva. A man who had fought the pope in the service of the Rey Católicissimo could by no means be less savage toward the Netherlandish heretics. His rule brought death to thousands of them and also to highly placed Catholic patriots such as Counts Hoorn and Egmont. This ill-advised Hispanic severity, instead of crushing the mercantile Dutch, succeeded in uniting the vast majority of the Netherlanders against Philip's rule, and in making the originally limited insurrection widespread and profound.

The various Mennonite parties, because of their common belief that Christians might not use the sword, were largely isolated from the main stream of this patriotic and religious uprising. With the memory of Münster, they wanted nothing to do with violence, even in the cause of driving out Antichrist in Spanish garb. There were exceptions. In 1572 the Waterlanders Peter Willems Bogart (whom we met as a companion of John Willems and Lubbert Gerrits in the Flemish-Frisian controversy, Ch. 30.1) and Dietrich Jans Cortenbosch presented William of Orange with one thousand and sixty guilders collected from Waterlander congregations for the promotion of the war against the common Spanish foe. But the Anabaptists could not share actively in the effort, much less become its real motive spirit, as the Calvinists were doing.

The Calvinists, who had come upon the scene late, in the third phase of the Reformation in the Netherlands, possessed a militant spirit which distinguished them from the withdrawn Mennonites. Dynamic preachers, trained in the teachings of the Genevan Academy, proclaimed their acutely formulated dogmatics with an irresistible enthusiasm. With their faith in a divine mission to establish the true church with the word and the sword, and with their excellent synodal organization, they were the men of the hour. They adopted the conventicular and covenanting impulse of the Anabaptists and gave it a new dogmatic, nationalist impetus.[15] From 1566 they held outdoor meetings for preaching and psalm-singing, under voluntary armed guard, something the Anabaptists had begun to do at the time of the Münsterite episode but had quickly abandoned. By combining the two powerful motives of religious and national freedom, the Calvinists were able to draw off from the pacifistic and yet factional Anabaptists a good measure of the social energies which had formerly been discharged in the great Münsterite movement among the dispossessed.

[15] Knappert, *De opkomst*, 205.

The vigorously organized Calvinist Church opposed the Mennonites of all factions. The Reformed synod at Dordrecht in 1574 even recommended that Reformed ministers enter the Mennonite meetinghouses to refute the preachers and to convince them of their false teachings. A more appealing course was that of arranging public disputations.[16]

a. *The Emden Disputation, 1578*. The most impressive of these meetings was the debate in one hundred and twenty sessions held at Emden in 1578.[17] A thousand Anabaptists from Holland had but recently arrived in Emden to live. An entry of 20 January 1577 in the records of the Dutch Reformed Church at Emden reveals that the ministers planned to approach Count Edward II and urge him to issue a mandate restraining the Anabaptists from preaching on the ground that they were not willing to defend their faith in public disputation. Naturally, the Mennonites, both the new arrivals and the older denizens, were not willing to let this challenge go unanswered; and, accordingly, a debate was arranged between several Reformed preachers and several representatives of the Flemish branch of the Mennonites, of whom the most important were John Busschaert, Peter of Cologne, and Brixius Gerrits.[18] Of the Flemings, only Brixius Gerrits knew the classical languages of theology. The Frisians and the Waterlanders declined the invitation.

The topics for the Emden debate should be recorded, since they indicate at once the issues between the "Flemish" Mennonites and the Reformed at the close of our period. Significantly, the doctrine of the Trinity heads the agenda, which may suggest the continuing influence of Adam Pastor (and possibly Racovian influence by way of Danzig). The other items concerned the creation and fall of man, original sin and the loss of the freedom of the will, the human nature of Christ, justification and sanctification over against second birth, good works, the church of God, the election and call of preachers, the proper use and misuse of the ban, the oath and the meaning of the Sermon on the Mount with special reference to divorce, and the resurrection of the flesh.[19]

The debate, as had been customary in Emden since the days of Łaski and Menno, was carried on in a spirit of charity, although the Mennonites were not given complete equality. On the other

---

[16] The fullest account of the issues is that of J. Wessel, *De leerstillige strijd tusschen Nederlandsche Gereformeerden en Doopsgezinden in de zestiende eeuw* (1945).

[17] Cornelius Krahn, "The Emden Disputation of 1578," *MQR*, XXX (1956), 256.

[18] Others were Paul Backer, Christian Arends, and John van Ophoorn (of Emden).

[19] *ME*, II, 201 f.

hand, they themselves were responsible for publishing the first and rather biased account of the proceedings, *Een Christelicke ende voorloopende Waerschouwinge.*

b. *Coornhert and Civil Liberty for Conscience.* The cause of liberty of conscience received a fresh impulse from a man closely associated with the liberator of the Netherlands, Dirk Volkerts Coornhert.[20] Coornhert, born in Amsterdam in 1522, was a mysterious but active figure in the period we are now considering, although it is chiefly in the theological speculation and thought of a later period that his ideas will make themselves strongly felt. A trained engraver and etcher of copperplates, he was led, by a desire to go back to the sources of religious truth, to learn Greek and Latin after he was already thirty-five years of age. An heir of Erasmus and the Dutch humanists, devoted to classical Stoic literature, he was especially concerned with ethics and the art of good living, expressed in his most famous work *Zedekunst, dat is wellevenkunst.*[21] Coornhert knew the works of Sebastian Franck. His thought resembles that of Franck. He was in fact a Catholic Spiritualist. He was a friend of the Familist Niclaes (Ch. 19.1) but an opponent of the vagaries of the Jorists. His early travels and exiles brought him into contact with the Spanish Inquisition and Genevan Calvinism, both of which he detested.

Like John de Valdés, he never formally left the Roman Church, although spiritually he was far beyond its boundaries. He strongly opposed the Calvinist stress on predestination and the depravity of man, and held that, in spite of the Fall, man was still possessed of native gifts and graces and of an unlost central being which remained in communion with God. He taught that it was possible for a regenerate man to lead a perfect life without any of the sacraments, and that in this life of perfection consisted the true discipleship of Christ. He was a perfectionist.[22] Calvin would call him a Libertine. He was offended by the iconoclastic violence of the Calvinists and the dogmatism of Calvin. We have already noted Calvin's tracts against the Nicodemites and Libertines (Ch. 23.3). Among these was the already mentioned *Petit traité montrant que c'est que doit faire un homme fidèle . . . quand il est entre les papistes* (1543). To this, Coornhert was indirectly and belatedly replying in his *Verschooninghe van de Roomsche Afgoderye* (1562). He charges Calvin, because of his rigorism, with

---

[20] H. Bonger, *Dirck Volckertszoon Coornhert: Studie over een nuchter en vroom Nederlander* (Lochem [1941]).

[21] Edited by Bruno Becker, Leiden, 1942.

[22] Bruno Becker, "Cornhert, de 16 de eeuwsche apostel der volmaaktheid," *NAK,* n. s. XIX (1926), 59–84.

the responsibility for unnecessary martyrdoms, coupling him with Menno Simons in his imposition of a baleful discipline upon his faithful followers. To this Calvin in turn replied in his *Réponse à un certain Hollandais lequel sous ombre de faire les chrétiens tout Spirituels, leur permet de polluer leur corps en toutes idolatries.*[23]

Coornhert's ideas on the possibility of achieving evangelical perfection and on the comprehensiveness of the true church of the Spirit influenced the Waterlanders, especially "the God-loving friend," John de Ries.[24] In Coornhert's opinion, all of the existing churches were in error, and he refused to receive the sacrament of Communion from any of them, because they set the sacrament itself above the love which is the characteristic mark of a Christian. Like Schwenckfeld, he held that the sacraments could not be rightly administered under the prevailing circumstances of disunity and mistrust among the churches. He advocated the formation of an interim church (*stilstandskerk*) while awaiting new apostles who would really reform the existing churches. This interim church would be based on all that is plainly and clearly taught in the canonical Scriptures, but would reject all commentaries and glosses made by men.

Pleading for the "Christianity above confessional diversity," Coornhert repeatedly urged toleration for Catholics and Mennonites. His ideas may well have influenced William of Orange, who made him his secretary to the Estates-General in 1572. He engaged in debates on toleration in 1578 with the Reformed preacher Thomas van Til, first in Delft, then publicly in Leiden, and published his great work on religious toleration in 1579, *Van de aangheheven dwangh in der conscientien.*[25] Before taking up the guarantee of religious freedom by William of Orange, we must take note of Coornhert's spirit at work among the Waterlanders.

c. The Waterlanders, 1568–1581. Coornhert, who dedicated several of his writings to de Ries and his associates, would one day even attend an important disciplinary meeting of the Waterlanders, and though not a member, carry the day on the issue before that assembly. That a major branch of Netherlandish Ana-

---

[23] Calvin, *Opera,* IX, coll. 581–628. The letter is summarized in Karl Müller, *op. cit.,* 87, n. 6. The anonymous Dutch Libertine addressed is an enthusiastic follower of Sebastian Franck, opposed to, or better, indifferent to the "ceremonies" and sacraments.

[24] It was with John de Ries that the unitarian Christopher Ostorodt of Danzig was in correspondence in 1598.

[25] See further H. Bonger, *De Motiviering van de Godsdienstvrijheid bij Coornhert* (Arhem, 1954).

baptism should be that receptive to a spokesman of Spiritualism, and of the world, measures the distance traversed in a generation after the arrival of Hofmann in Emden in 1530.

Soon after the general meeting of the Waterlander Doops-gezinden in Emden in 1568, where the authority of the local congregation was reasserted and moderation in doctrinal formulation was the order of the day, the Waterlanders admitted to their fellowship a gifted convert destined to wield an abiding influence upon this liberal brotherhood.

It was in 1575 or the year after, near De Rijp, that the Waterlander elder, Simon Michiels, baptized John de Ries and ordained him to the ministry. John de Ries (1553–1638) had, before this, considered joining the new Calvinists; but he was held back by his conscientious disapproval of their carrying swords to protect themselves at meetings in the fields and woods. Later he gravitated toward the Anabaptist community in Antwerp, where he was working as a bookkeeper for an Italian merchant; but, thinking always of the Christian way as an imitation of Christ, he was anguished by and finally disgusted with the mutual recriminations and the factionalism that he observed.

Soon after uniting with the Waterlanders who fulfilled his yearnings, he joined with Jacob Jans Scheedemaker, Simon Michiels, and two other *leeraars* to draw up at Alkmaar what proved to be the first formal Anabaptist Confession of Faith in the Netherlands, September 1577. It was intentionally imprecise in order thereby to accommodate the conservative and the liberal wings of the growing coalition of congregations, united in their opposition to the clerical authoritarianism and the disciplinary rigorism of the other factions. Though the Confession retained the traditional Mennonite articles on the ban and avoidance, the true church was so defined in a quasi-Spiritualist sense that these stern ordinances were largely deprived of their motive power. The church was defined as made up of all reborn and loving people who have been renewed in the Spirit of God and have resolved to lead a new life. This is the church of God on earth, though it be scattered in all corners of the world, of which church Christ is the only head, built up in the power and Spirit of God, also by the preaching of the godly Word, but never by force, never by persecution, never by the worldly sword of the rulers of the earth, but only by those ministers (*dienaars*) whom God has sent by his Spirit and whom the congregation have also called to this work.

With this Confession and policy the Waterlanders sought to recruit more members and to draw other independent congregations into their fellowship. Long before, it had been their willingness to accept into membership the banned and bruised from the more stringent factions that had prompted the rigorists to call them abusively the garbage wagon (*drekwagen*). In 1579, overtures were made between the Waterlanders and the more liberal congregation in Emden. The doctrine of the celestial flesh of Christ, which the more conservative Mennonites of Emden insisted on, would have prevented the federation, had not a committee of seven worked out a compromise in the Waterlander spirit, according to which the doctrine might be held by members of the fellowship so long as it was not made binding upon those in the majority who had come to a simpler view.

A major assembly of Waterlander congregations took place in Amsterdam in March 1581, with the representation of affiliated congregations from far beyond the Waterland district, even from Ghent and Antwerp. With de Ries the moving spirit, the assembly agreed about principles and practices that were long to mark the Waterlander tradition into modern times. The practice of rather solemn baptisms in the home was formally eliminated and the rite, simplified, was restored to the congregational meeting. De Ries attached importance to his practice of observing the Lord's Supper seated at tables, and the assembly made this the accepted usage of the whole Waterlander fellowship, involving, in the larger communities, several sittings. There was a very strong Spiritualist sentiment in the assembly, some of the participants openly expressing their desire to be freed of all outward ordinances such as preaching, baptism, and Communion in a preference for silent meditation together, which in any case had been a feature of the prayer in certain Mennonite groups. The Amsterdam assembly did not endorse this Spiritualism, but it made important concessions in two other sectors. The traditional stricture against marriage with outsiders was relaxed, and the members were also allowed to accept public office. The Waterlander assembly of 1581 marks the opening of a new epoch, as the participants themselves well realized when, in their final message, they declared that nothing in their deliberations was intended to bind the future. The liberal ferment among the Waterlander Anabaptists had its counterpart in the policy of William of Orange.

d. *The Mennonites Achieve Toleration: The End of an Epoch, 1577.* While the Reformed clergy of the Low Countries were industrious in their attempts to refute or convert the Anabaptists, the civil authorities were providing them with a greater measure of security than they had received from any others, with the exception of the Moravian and Polish magnates. In the very midst of his struggle with Alva, William of Orange wrote a letter to the governor of North Holland, requiring that no one be hindered in preaching the Word of God (20 April 1572). Later the same year (15 July), very possibly under the influence of Coornhert, he proposed to the Estates-General that religious freedom be guaranteed throughout the Netherlands, but this proposal was not at once accepted, due to the opposition from the Reformed side. In 1577, he was finally able to award the Anabaptists civil and religious freedom.[26]

With this action toward the Anabaptists on the part of the founder of modern Holland in 1577, subsequently confirmed and extended, with the mutually respectful Emden disputation of 1578, with the treatise of Coornhert, the Spiritualist, on tolerance in 1579, and with the accommodating Waterlander assembly of Amsterdam in 1581, our account of the Radical Reformation in the Netherlands comes naturally to a close.

We may now cross the Channel for one more visit to England, where so much of the legacy of the Radical Reformation on the Continent in the sixteenth century (1520–1580) was to be reworked by the Parties of the Left in the second English Reformation in the seventeenth century (1620–1688).

3. ANTI-TRINITARIANISM, ANABAPTISM, AND FAMILISM IN ENGLAND, 1547–1579

We were last in England at the end of Henry's headship of the church (Ch. 14.4). During Edward VI's reign, English radicalism emerged from its rather secret existence into the light of day. Although Edward's regents were committed to promotion of the Magisterial Reformation along the lines of Zurich and Geneva, Cranmer pursued the policy of argumentation with, rather than outright suppression of, the Radicals. Other positive measures were adopted. A license was granted in 1550 for the establishment of a church for aliens at London (the Austin Friars), where Łaski served as the first superintendent. The king recorded in his journal that the Strangers' Church was organized "for the avoyding of al sectes of Anabaptistes and such like."

A distinctive feature of the radical movement in England was the close interrelationship of Libertinism, anti-Trinitarianism, Anabaptism of the Melchiorite strain, and Spiritualism.

At hearings before Archbishop Cranmer at the beginning of

---

[26] J. Reitsma, *Geschiedenis van de Hervorming en de Hervormde Kerk der Nederlanden* (5th edition, The Hague, 1949), 59.

Edward's reign, we have successively the confession of a Libertine,
John Champneis, of Stratford on the Bowe,[27] who declared "that
a man after he is regenerate in Christe, cannot synne," which reminds us of Pocquet's theology (Ch. 12.2); the confession of the
Melchiorite Anabaptist tailor Michael Tombe, who espoused believers' baptism and the view that "Christ toke no flesh of our
lady";[28] and the confession of the unitarian priest John Assheton,
of Shiltelington in the diocese of Lincoln, who, on being denounced by two other priests, admitted that:

in tymes past I thought, believed, said, . . . that the trinitie of persons
was established by the confession of Athanasius declared by a psalm,
"quicunque vult," etc. and that the hollie Ghoste is not God, but only
a certeyn power of the Father; secundarilye, that Jesus Christ, that
was conceived of the virgyn Mary, was a holy prophet and speciallie
beloved of God the Father, but that he was not the true and lyving
God, for as much as he was seen and leved, hungred and thirsted;
thirdly, that this onley is the fruite of Jesus Christes passion, that
whereas we were straungers from God, and had no knowledge of his
testament, hit pleased God by Christ to bring us to th'acknowledging
of his hollie power by the testament.[29]

With such explicit unitarianism, which reminds one more of
Faustus Socinus than of Michael Servetus, it is clear that radical
alterations in theology were quite as far along in England as on
the Continent.

At the same series of hearings before Archbishop Cranmer in
the beginning of Edward's reign, there was the notable case of
Joan Boucher, a woman of some social standing. The charge
against her was the same as that against the tailor Tombe, but
its Melchiorite specificity should be quoted. The accusation:

That you beleve that the worde was made fleshe in the virgyn's belly,
but that Christe toke fleshe of the virgyn you beleve not; because the
flesh of the virgyn being the outward man synfully gotten, and bourne
in synne, but the worde by the consent of the inward man of the
virgyn was made fleshe.[30]

Refusing to surrender her Melchiorite faith (unlike the Libertine, the Unitarian, and the other Melchiorite), Joan was condemned to die at the stake, 2 May 1550.

A unitarian surgeon, Dr. George van Parris, a Fleming by

[27] David Wilkins, *Concilia Magnae Britanniae et Hiberniae*, IV (London,
1737), 39.
[28] *Ibid.*, 42.
[29] *Ibid.*, 41.
[30] *Ibid.*, 43.

birth and a member of the Strangers' Church, like Joan Boucher, refused to abjure his faith. Miles Coverdale served as interpreter in the hearing before Cranmer and, summarizing the Fleming's conviction, said "that he beleveth, that God the Father is only God, and that Christ is not very God."[31] Despite powerful intercessions in his behalf, he was burned at Smithfield, 25 April 1551.[32]

The spread of radical ideas at the outset of Edward's reign was so great that in alarm the ecclesiastical authorities saw to the translation into English of several Swiss treatises against the Radical Reformation, namely: Calvin's *A Short Instruction for to Arme All Good Christian People* (Ch. 23.2) in 1549, together with several items from Bullinger's pen, *An Holsome Antidotus or Counterpoysen* (London, 1548), *A Moste Sure and Strong Defence of the Baptisme of Children* (Worcester, 1551), and *A Most Necessary and Frutefull Dialogue between ye Seditious Libertin or Rebel Anabaptist, and the True Obedient Christian* (Worcester, 1551). Bucer, who had come to England in 1549, had considerable influence in the shaping of the Edwardian Ordinal of 1550. The formularies in the rite of confirmation in the Church of England indirectly reflect Bucer's extended efforts to cope with the demands of the Strassburg and the Hessian Anabaptists.

An influential leader of English Anabaptism was Henry Hart of Kent, whose people were "the first that made separation from the reformed church in England," and who produced two admonitory tracts, *A Godly Newe Short Treatyse* (1548) and *A Godlie Exhortation* (1549). Except for Hart's group, much of English Anabaptism up to and during Edward's reign appears to have been nonseparatist in aspiration, possibly because of the precedent set by Lollardy.

Cranmer's judicial leniency toward the Radicals found little favor with such hard-pressed clerics as John Hooper, who as chaplain to the Protector Somerset in 1549 complained to Bullinger that "Anabaptists flock to the place [where Hooper lectured in London] and give me much trouble with their opinions respecting the incarnation of the Lord." The next year, Hooper reported that the counties of Kent and Sussex were hotbeds of Anabaptist activity.[33] When the government took alarm at the growth of English Anabaptism toward the end of Edward's reign,

---

[31] *Ibid.*, 44.

[32] Wilbur, *Transylvania*, 171. The whole of ch. x is devoted to "Precursors of Unitarianism in England."

[33] As early as 1547, Thomas Ridley and Hugh Latimer had been assigned to the task of dealing with certain Anabaptists in Kent.

it quite naturally turned to men like Hooper (and John Knox) to battle the menace of radicalism. Hooper's *A Lesson of the Incarnation of Christe,* aimed at confuting the doctrine of the celestial flesh, went through at least three editions in 1549–1550.

Another opponent of Anabaptism was the French Reformed prebendary at Worcester, Jean Veron, who, in addition to translating and prefacing some of Bullinger's tracts, during the reign of Elizabeth, engaged in controversy with the well-known English Anabaptist, Robert Cooche. Cooche also debated with William Turner, "doctor of physick" and dean of Wells, on the doctrines of original sin (cf. Turner's *A Preeseruatiue,* 1551) and infant baptism. Cooche wrote *The Confutation of the Errors of the Careless by Necessity* (c. 1557).[34] A book by Cooche later prompted John Knox to publish *An answer to a great nomber of blasphemous cauillations written by an Anabaptist* (Geneva, 1560). Another literary opponent of the Radicals was their former sympathizer, Thomas Cole, who in 1553 published his *A Godly and Frutefull Sermon . . . against the Anabaptistes and others.*

The story of the English Anabaptists under Mary Tudor can hardly be separated from the general narrative of Protestant misfortune. Among sixty conventiclers of Faversham and Bocking, espousing free will against original sin, were two antipedobaptist leaders. Henry Hart, author of two tracts, debated in prison with Edward's chaplain (John Bradford, martyred in January 1555). Another Anabaptist minister, Humphrey Middleton, died for his beliefs in July of 1555. Although John Foxe's *Martyrology* (1570) is imprecise, those identified by him as "lay ministers" may in many instances have been Anabaptists. The greater percentage of the Marian martyrs came from the eastern counties and from the artisan class.

Under Elizabeth (1558–1603), Anabaptism became once more distinguishable from English Protestantism. In 1559, when Matthew Parker was chosen and consecrated as archbishop of Canterbury, he advised Bullinger that the realm was overrun with Anabaptists and other heretics. In November of the next year, Bishop John Jewel of Salisbury, but recently returned to England from his Marian exile in Frankfurt, wrote to his old friend, Peter Martyr Vermigli:

We found at the beginning of the reign of Elizabeth a large and inauspicious crop of Arians, Anabaptists, and other pests, which I know not how, but as mushrooms spring up in the night and in

[34] Baptist Historical Society, *Transactions,* IV, 2 (1915), 88.

darkness, so these sprang up in that darkness and unhappy night of the Marian times.[35]

Jewel's coupling of Arians and Anabaptists again suggest the closer relationship between anti-Trinitarianism and Anabaptism in England than anywhere else except Poland. In 1562, Jewel published his *Apologia Ecclesiae Anglicanae* to defend the newly re-established Church of England from both the Puritans and the Catholics. Spokesman of the latter was Thomas Harding (d. 1572), whose extended sneer at the alleged martyrdom of thousands of Protestants at the hands of Catholics induced Jewel rather savagely to distinguish between true Protestant confessors and "your anabaptists and Zwenkfeldians" who "find harbour amongst you [Roman Catholics] in Austria, Slesia, Moravia . . . where the [Protestant] gospel of Christ is suppressed." Jewell also ascribes the errors of "David George and Servete the Arian" to their Catholic upbringing.[36]

In 1560, Elizabeth (in a reinforcement of the Act of Uniformity) had decreed that all Anabaptists must conform to her Establishment or else leave the country, on pain of imprisonment and confiscation of their goods, specifically singling out "the Anabaptists and such Hereticks, which had flocked to the Coast-Towns of England from the parts beyond the Seas, under the colour of shunning Persecution." Furthermore, an ecclesiastical commission was created to register and bring to trial all those tainted with the Anabaptist doctrines.

A notable case of heresy in London was that centering in the Dutch-speaking congregation affiliated with the Strangers' Church, which had been re-established by Elizabeth in 1559 and now placed directly under the bishop of London. The successor of Łaski as superintendent of the diverse, foreign-language congregations was John Utenhove.

In 1562, Adrian Haemstede, a minister of London's Dutch congregation, former Reformed pastor in Antwerp and then Aachen, author of the oldest Dutch martyrology,[37] was asked by the local Anabaptists to petition the bishop for the right to meet separately outside the precincts of the Strangers' Church. He supported their efforts, recognizing "the Anabaptists as his brethren and as weak members of Christ."[38] Haemstede's willingness to befriend the

---

[35] Jewel's *Works,* edited by John Ayre (Cambridge, 1850), IV, 1240 f.

[36] Jewel's *Works,* III, 188 f.

[37] *Geschiedenisse ende den Doot der vroomen Martelaren* (1559).

[38] A. A. van Schelven, *Kerkeraads-protocollen der nederduitsche vluchteling-enkerk te London* (Amsterdam, 1921), 447. See also *idem, De nederduitsche vluchtelingenkerken de xvi° eeuw* (The Hague, 1909).

Anabaptists proved, on further investigation, to be based, in part, on sympathy with their Melchiorite doctrine of the celestial flesh of Christ. But more hazardous was his Spiritualist espousal of all earnest expressions of Christian faith as equally entitled to protection. He refused on principle to dispute with the Anabaptists, declaring that theologians had for all too long cast lots for the external garments of Christianity (Matt. 27:35), leaving the body of Christ, the solid core of true divinity, to suffer. For Haemstede, even the exact formulation of so important a doctrine as the incarnation could be regarded as an adiaphoron. His case soon involved the French congregation and finally Bishop Grindal, who excommunicated him and banished him from England.[39]

An eminent Italian member of the Strangers' Church, Jacob Acontius, had sympathized openly with Pastor Adrian Haemstede and was likewise excommunicated. The wide range of confessional, national, and temperamental differences represented by the Strangers' Church was, in fact, the immediate background of Acontius' famous *Stratagems of Satan,* published in Basel in 1565.[40] The *Stratagems* of Acontius takes its place alongside the other great sixteenth-century pleas for toleration within the Rationalist-Spiritualist context, Castellio's *On Heretics* a decade earlier and Coornhert's *Van de dwangh in der conscientien* a dozen years later.

Acontius, a Valdesian Catholic and secretary to the lenient Cardinal Christopher Modruzzo, had fled from Italy on the accession of the stringent Paul IV, had made the acquaintance of Marian exiles in Strassburg, and had gone to England with them in the capacity of an engineer. His great work on toleration was begun before the Haemstede case, but is closely connected with it in spirit. Acontius summarized what he himself regarded as the essential minimum for toleration in six intentionally imprecise and subsequently influential articles:

(1) That there is one true God and he whom he sent, Jesus Christ, and the Holy Spirit. And that it is not right to deny that the Father is one and the Son another, because Jesus Christ is truly the Son of God.

(2) That man is subject to the wrath and judgment of God. And that the dead will come to life again, the just to everlasting happiness, but the wicked to everlasting torments.

[39] He died the same year in Frisia.

[40] *Stratagems of Satan,* translated, with an introduction, by Charles D. O'Malley, Occasional Papers of the Sutro Branch, California State Library, English Series No. 5 (San Francisco, 1940). The most recent study is that of O'Malley, *Jacopo Acontio, Uomini e Dottrine,* No. 2 (Rome, 1955). Appendice II, 56–65, is also the fullest account of the case of Haemstede.

(3) That God sent his Son Jesus Christ into the world, who, being made man, died for our sins and was raised from the dead for our justification.

(4) That if we believe in the Son of God, we shall obtain life through his name.

(5) That there is salvation in none other; not in the blessed virgin, or in Peter, or in Paul, or in any other saint, or any other name whatever. And that there is no righteousness in the law or in the commandments or inventions of men.

(6) That there is one baptism in the name of the Father and of the Son and of the Holy Spirit.[41]

The Acontian six articles were the sixteenth-century Spiritualist forerunners of the five articles of Deism in the seventeenth century.

Radicals continued to flee to England, especially after the Duke of Alva assumed power in the Netherlands in 1567. By 1571, Norwich alone could number 3,925 Dutch and Walloons among its residents,[42] and sixteen years later these immigrants constituted a majority of the town's population.[43] Within a year after Alva's accession to power, the queen's government was well aware of the staggering increase in the number of Dutch and Flemish Anabaptists on English soil. Bad enough that these strangers were holding clandestine meetings; it was worse that they appeared to be exerting some influence on native-born English subjects. Once again, regulations were framed to expedite the investigation of English subjects, regardless of their origin. Refusal of Anabaptist suspects to conform to the Establishment meant leaving England within twenty days. Thus, in 1574, some sixteen Anabaptists were handed over to the mayor of London for deportation.

In 1575 the ancient law *De haeretico comburendo* was reluctantly revived again and employed in the best-known incident involving Anabaptism on English soil. According to the several versions given in the *Martyrs' Mirror*,[44] although the versions do not agree on all details, the sequence of events was as follows. On Easter, 3 April 1575, a group of Flemish Anabaptists was gathered for worship in a house beyond the Aldersgate ("on the way leading to Mirror Court"). During the meeting, a constable entered, questioned those there assembled in an insolent manner, and then took their names. Warning some twenty-five worshipers[45]

---

[41] *Stratagems,* vii; *loc. cit.,* 201 f.

[42] C. Norman Kraus, "Anabaptist Influence on English Separatism as Seen in Robert Browne," *MQR,* XXXIV (1960), 5–19, esp., 6.

[43] Henry M. Dexter, *The Congregationalism of the Last Three Hundred Years* (New York, 1880), 72.

[44] English edition, 1008–1024. See also Wilbur, *Transylvania,* 175 f.

[45] One version says seventeen, another thirty.

to remain until he should come for them, the constable left to find reinforcement. Either at this moment, or later as the group was being shepherded to prison, two of the Anabaptists made a quiet escape. The rest, however, were imprisoned for two days and nights in the South Fort in the Mersey, briefly released on bail, and then brought before Bishop Edwin Sandys of London for questioning.[46] With the bishop were a Mr. George, James King, John Wheelwright, two aldermen, and a French preacher.[47]

The interrogation centered on four points:[48] (1) whether Christ had assumed his flesh and blood from the Virgin Mary; (2) whether infants should be baptized; (3) whether a Christian might administer the office of magistrate; and (4) whether a Christian, in case of necessity, might swear an oath. These four points became the center of a literary exchange between a Puritan baker, William White, and "an English Anabaptist" carpenter known only as "S.B."[49] One of the younger men, by speaking too boldly, offended the bishop and was sent off to prison at Westminster; the rest were returned to the Mersey.[50]

On 25 May, five men among the Anabaptists recanted. They were exposed to public view in St. Paul's churchyard "with a fagot tied on their shoulders, as a token that they were worthy of burning," while the bishop preached a sermon. Thereupon, the apostates were permitted to be put on bail, being commanded that they should at once join the Dutch Reformed Church. The rest of the Anabaptists, unmoved by the episcopal threats and promises, were condemned to death "in the ecclesiastical court of St. Paul's church." To this end some fourteen women and one youth were removed to Newgate Prison, while the remaining five men were returned to the Mersey. Eventually, the fifteen at Newgate had their sentences commuted. The youth was scourged behind a cart, then he and the women were taken by ship to the Continent, to settle in Holland and Zealand.

Five members of the congregation now remained: Christian

---

[46] One account places the questioning at St. Paul's, another at the bishop's house.

[47] It appears that certain of the aforenamed were ministers of the Austin Friars Church in London, and that like the French cleric, they acted as interpreters.

[48] Here we follow the account of one of the prisoners, Gerrit van Byler.

[49] The text of their dispute (1575) has been edited and published by Albert Peel under the title "A Conscientious Objector of 1575," in *Transactions of the Baptist Historical Society*, VII (1920), 78–128. Except to show the acrimonious spirit of the Puritan toward the Anabaptist, the text reveals nothing concerning English Anabaptist beliefs not recorded in the *Mirror* account of the martyrs of 1575.

[50] According to the account of Jacques de Somere, some ten or twelve of the Anabaptists escaped from the Mersey, but later voluntarily surrendered themselves.

Kemels, Henry Terwoort, John Pieters, Gerrit van Byler, and John van Straten. On 2 June, these were questioned a third time by the bishop and his aides, and then sent to Newgate. There, about a week later, Kemels died. The other four, refusing to recant, were frequently advised of their impending deaths at the stake. Certain sympathizers, among them the Reformed layman Jacques de Somere, assisted the prisoners in framing a petition. Elizabeth refused to receive the document and "severely repri- manded the maids of honor who presented it to her." Another petition was forwarded to Sir Thomas Bodley,[51] who conferred fruitlessly on the matter with the bishop of London. Indeed, the bishop now required the aliens in his diocese to subscribe to a set of articles stating that a Christian magistrate might punish obstinate heretics with the sword. Members of the Strangers' Church as well as the martyrologist, John Foxe, continued to be active in the prisoners' behalf. Among the several confessions of faith produced by the members of this Anabaptist congregation is one addressed to Foxe, in which the prisoners sturdily defend their adherence to the doctrine of the celestial flesh of Christ.

On 22 July 1575, Henry Terwoort and John Pieters were led to the stake at Smithfield. Terwoort was a handsome man of some thirty-five years of age, by occupation a goldsmith. Pieters was a poor man of better than fifty years. His first wife had gone to the stake in Ghent as had the husband of his present wife. He was the father of nine young children. Such attenuations as strangling, suffocation, and the sack of gunpowder around the neck were omitted, and the two men died in unrelieved agony amidst the flames.[52] Van Byler and van Straten, although they languished in prison for some time (and were further disciplined for attempting to file through the iron bars of their cell window), were eventually released. No more is known of these last two members of the Aldersgate congregation.

Mention may be made of one Hans Bret who, in 1577, died at the stake in Antwerp. The son of an Englishman, Thomas Bret, Hans was perhaps twenty-one years of age when he was appre- hended, tried, and convicted. Letters written during his imprison- ment reveal that he had a brother, David, still living in England "who had not yet come to the knowledge of the truth." During one examination, Hans admitted that he himself had once visited England, and he testified that persons recently executed there were not Puritans but rather, "Menno's people."[53]

---

[51] The diplomat and later endower of the Bodleian Library.
[52] According to one hostile report, "in great terror, weeping and crying."
[53] *Martyrs' Mirror,* 1037–1054.

Between 1575 and 1580, English Anabaptism entered a new phase, in which it was virtually succeeded by Brownism and Barrowism. Those very areas where Anabaptism had counted its greatest number of adherents—London, and the southeast and middle-east counties—now witnessed the emergence of Separatist congregations. To establish proof of historical connections between these two movements it is necessary to demonstrate some connection between the person and teaching of Robert Browne (c. 1550–1633), founder of a Separatist conventicle at Norwich, which in 1581 removed to Middelburg in the Netherlands, and the Anabaptists of Norwich and London.

Browne, while a student at Corpus Christi College, Cambridge, came under the influence of Thomas Cartwright (1535–1603). Cartwright's vigorous defense of the antiepiscopal *Admonition to Parliament* (1572) won him the enmity of the dean of Lincoln (later archbishop of Canterbury), John Whitgift.[54] Whitgift contended that Cartwright's views were one with those of the Anabaptists at three crucial points: the separation of church and state, the doctrine of the ministry, the sacraments and their relation to preaching. While Cartwright's actual position was *not* so close as Whitgift assumed,[55] it appears that Whitgift's published charges against Cartwright must have called at least these Anabaptist tenets to the attention of the reading public. Certainly among those readers would have been Cartwright's student, Browne. Nor is it likely that Browne was ignorant of the sufferings of the London Anabaptist congregation in 1575.

The Separatism of Browne and Anabaptism were similar on the question of magisterial authority. Browne held that the magistrate's duty was to keep civil peace, and that only when this was threatened might he interfere in ecclesiastical matters. Like the Anabaptists, he was concerned to establish the church as a freely covenanted, disciplined fellowship apart from the state.

Browne's Scriptural foundation, however, unlike that of the Netherlandish Anabaptists, presupposed the parity of the Old and

---

[54] The full story is given by Donald Joseph McGinn in *The Admonition Controversy* (New Brunswick, 1949).

[55] In this connection, to know Cartwright's own assessment of his position vis-à-vis Anabaptism, mention may be made of his *Two Very Godly and Comfortable Letters, written Ouer into England. The One To A Godly and Zealous Lady: Wherin the Annabaptists errour is Confuted; and the Sinne against the Holye Ghoste Plainly Declared . . .* (London, 1589), which criticizes the error, attributed to the Anabaptists, of holding that there is no second chance following (believers') baptism and subsequent sin to the loss of salvation. Letter printed in *Cartwrightiana*, edited by Albert Peel and Leland H. Carlson (London, 1951), 75–88.

New Testaments, in keeping with Puritan hermeneutics. More-over, a comparison of names and publications of the English Ana-baptists with Browne's known contacts and sources reveals no trace of any connection between this Separatist and the Men-nonites. Browne, in fact, disclaimed any relationship to Ana-baptism.[56] Browne's Separatism and Dutch Anabaptism were analogous, rather than genetically related, movements.

But if Browne and the Brownists grew up independently of the Netherlandish Anabaptists, it is probable that other Separatist groups were influenced by the Dutch, particularly during their sojourn in Holland, the center of the English sectarian diaspora.

John Smyth (c. 1554–1612), the "Se-baptist" pastor of the Gains-borough-Amsterdam congregation and father of the English Gen-eral Baptists, held to a view of predestination and free will comparable to that of the Mennonites; and after regretting his precipitate act of baptizing himself in 1608, sought to join the Waterlander Mennonite congregation in Amsterdam. Three years after his death, in 1615, his whole congregation were ad-mitted to fellowship. Similarly, Richard Blunt, of the English Particular Baptists, on being convinced that baptism "ought to be by dipping the body into water, resembling burial and rising again," went to Rijnsburg (near Leiden), the center of the Col-legiants (seventeenth-century Spiritualists similar to the Schwenck-feldians) and submitted in 1641 to immersion at the hands of John Batten, and in turn introduced the practice in England.[57] The adoption by English Baptists of the practice of immersion, ultimately derived from the Minor Church of Poland and intro-duced into Holland by the Socinians, ties together with other loose threads to make a neat selvage along the upper chrono-logical border of our narrative.

It remains, however, to weave in the story of the English fol-lowers of Henry Niclaes. The English Familists were communi-tarian, pacifistic Anabaptists who, like the Paulicians and the Servetians (Ch. 11.1), received believers' baptism at the age of thirty. Morphologically and to a certain extent genetically, the

---

[56] Of course, had there been such a connection, it is not likely that Browne would have advertised the fact.

[57] Robert G. Torbet, on the basis of new manuscript evidence, says that it is more likely that Blunt was given instruction concerning the administration of immersion, but that as a Calvinist in respect to the doctrine of the will and grace, he would not personally have submitted to the Rijnsburg rite. *A History of the Baptists* (Philadelphia, 1950), 711; "Collegiants," *ME*, I, 639 f. See also A. A. van Schelven, "Engelsche Vroeg–Independentisme en Hollandsch Anabaptisme," *Uit den Strijd der Geesten* (Amsterdam, 1944), 72–89.

English Familists represent a transitional stage between evangelical Anabaptism and the completely nonsacramental Spiritualism of Quakerism. Many of the early Quaker recruits had, in fact, Familist antecedents; and some of them bore traces also of a Melchiorite (Valentinian) Christology.

As noted earlier (Ch. 19.1), the Familists gained their greatest following in England. If Niclaes himself did not visit England until 1560/1561, the person primarily responsible for the spread of Familism in England must have been a certain joiner from Delft, Christopher Vittels, who appeared in Colchester as early as 1555 as a Familist missionary and elder. He translated many of Niclaes' pamphlets into English. By 1574, the sect had made considerable headway in the counties of Norfolk, Suffolk, Cambridge, and Essex.

In 1579, one John Rogers published at London *The Displaying of an Horible Secte of Grosse and Wicked Heretiques, naming themselves the Family of Love*. Rogers claims to have been informed by members of the House of Love that at that time they had approximately a thousand members in England. Rogers cites a confession made by two Familists before a justice which conveniently summarizes English Familism:

They [the Familists] are all unlearned, save some who can read English and are made bishops, elders, and deacons, who call them to one of the disciples' houses; thirty in number assemble to hear the Scriptures expounded. They have goods in common, new members are received with a kiss, all have meat, drink, and lodging found by the owner of the house where they meet. They knock, saying, "Here is a Brother or Sister in Christ." The congregation does not speak until admitted so to do. They go to [the established] church, but object to the Litany that says "Lord have mercy upon us miserable sinners," as if they could never be amended. They may not say "God speed, God morrow, or God even." They did prohibit bearing of weapons, but at length allowed the bearing of staves. When a question is demanded of any, they stay a great while ere they answer, and commonly their word shall be "Surely" or "So." . . . The marriage is made by the brethren, who sometimes bring them together who live over a hundred miles asunder, as Thomas Chaundler of Woneherst, Surrey, who sent for a wife from the Isle of Ely by two of the congregation. These had never met before, and in a year they, upon a disliking, did divorce themselves asunder before certain of the congregation. No man is to be baptized before the age of thirty. Until then he is an infant. Heaven and hell are present in this world among us. They are bound to give alms only to their own sect. . . . All men not of their congregation or revolted from them are as dead. Bishops and ministers should not remain still in one place but should wander from country to country. They hold there was a world before Adam's time. No man should be put to death for his opinions, and they therefore condemn Cranmer and Ridley for burning Joan [Boucher] of Kent. They expound Scripture according to their own minds, comparing one place with another.

They brag very much of their own sincere lives, justifying themselves, saying, "mark how purely we live." If they have anything to do touching their temporal things, they must do it by advice, viz., ask counsel of the Lord through one of their bishops or elders. They give their alms by putting under a hat upon a table what they are disposed to give, and the money is secretly distributed by the bishops or elders.[58]

In the same year that John Rogers published his exposé, 1579, the Familists were also attacked by John Knewstub and by William Wilkinson. The next year, Queen Elizabeth issued a proclamation against the disciples of Henry Niclaes. In order to survive, the Familists went "underground."[59]

In bringing to a close our section on English radical trends in the third quarter of the Reformation Era, we may observe that England's Anabaptism was exclusively Melchiorite, that its Spiritualism was likewise of Netherlandish origin (Libertinism, Familism), that its anti-Trinitarianism seems to have been proportionately more prominent than in the Netherlands, and that except for the still unclarified relationship with indigenous Lollardry, the radical trends in England appear to have been largely an importation and as such an extension of the radical movements engendered in the Hanseatic zone of Low German speech.

We turn now to the comparable developments in the same quarter of a century in the area of High German speech and the homeland of Anabaptism.

[58] Confession before a justice of Surrey 28 May 1561; Jones, *Mystical Religion*, 441 f.

[59] At the accession of James I, the Familists who petitioned him for protection described themselves as "a people but few in number and yet most of us very poor." Payne, "The Familists," *loc. cit.,* 31. The Family of Love survived in England to about the end of the seventeenth century, leaping momentarily into prominence during the Commonwealth (when Giles Randall was its leading light) but destined to be absorbed by the Quakers. In this connection it is of interest that the doctrine of the celestial flesh of Christ persisted in Quakerism, for example, in the such notable apologists as Robert Barclay and George Keith. See Maurice Creasey, "Early Quaker Christology," University of Leeds Thesis, 1956.

CHAPTER 31

GERMAN AND SWISS ANABAPTISM, SPIRITUALISM, AND RATIONALISM, 1542–1578

In Ch. 18 we charted the course of the conflict between Spiritualist Caspar Schwenckfeld and Anabaptist Pilgram Marpeck. Before turning to a concluding survey of the fate of the Anabaptists in the lands of their birth, Switzerland and South Germany, and the emergence of German Unitarianism, we should pursue to its conclusion the second phase of the Schwenckfeld-Marpeck controversy.

1. THE SCHWENCKFELD-MARPECK DEBATE, PHASE II

From 1544 until his death in 1556, Marpeck remained a resident of Augsburg, being employed by the city in the capacity of engineer, to improve the municipal water system. During the last ten years of his life, he was paid the annual salary of one hundred and fifty florins. His activities in behalf of the Anabaptist brotherhood were well known to the city authorities; but, though he was periodically warned against such connections by the council, Marpeck's importance to the life of the city enabled him to escape serious discomfort.

Schwenckfeld, for his part, had by now left the haven of Justingen castle, when his host lost it to the imperial troops in the Smalcaldic War, in 1547, and had found a refuge in the Franciscan convent at Esslingen, where he was known to the brothers simply as "Eliander" (Elijah).

Further direct communication between Schwenckfeld and Marpeck was not necessary for the continuation of their argument. Schwenckfeld's *Judicium* had been answered thus far only in part. Marpeck's decision of 1546 to place Schwenckfeld under the ban was simply a matter of formalizing an attitude long held by the Anabaptist toward the Spiritualist.

The continuing conflict between Marpeck and Schwenckfeld is all the more poignant for the reason that the two leaders had much in common in their spiritual vision and in their ethical earnestness. Schwenckfeld, a knight of faith, who had from the beginning resolved as a consecrated *laicus* "to seek the glory of the gospel" as a chivalric exponent of the love of Christ, was no less concerned for the disciplines of the spirit than the theologian-engineer of Augsburg. Neither Marpeck nor Schwenckfeld was to die as martyrs, but both were acquainted with suffering and grief. Schwenckfeld, in hiding during the Augsburg Interim (1548–1552), was destined, for example, to spend a whole year and a half without once leaving the house of his protector; but never downcast, he was ever true to his life's motto: "Whoever has received Christ can never be sad." Schwenckfeld in his Christocentric piety, in his sustaining experience of regeneration and sustenance in the eternal Christ, in his lifelong prayer for the unity of the true Church of the Friends of God, in his prophetic lament over the wasting of this Zion by heedless resort to confessional war, in his compassion for both the humble and the great caught up and crushed in the cruel vagaries of religious strife, in his steadfastness in the devout life, in his more than spiritualizing concern for the continuity of the sacramental life despite his despairing suspension of the sacrament of the altar because of its incitement to contention or its misuse as a sanction of cheap grace, in his yearning to comfort and bind together disciplined communities of fellow seekers and emulators of the loving Christ—in all these ways Schwenckfeld was closer to Marpeck's kind of Anabaptism than he was to the rational Spiritualism of Franck or to the misty and sometimes antinomian theosophy of Libertine Spiritualism.[1] Yet the two men also differed profoundly; for, while Schwenckfeld asseverated the Lutheran doctrines of original sin and salvation by faith alone and accused the Anabaptists of a Pelagian construction of their lives upon their own faith in Christ rather than upon the Rock as the source of that faith, nevertheless he had so suffused and reordered his own theology with the patristic and partly Neoplatonic conviction about the sanctifying, indeed almost deificatory, presence of the divine Christ that he was in effect closer to medieval and patristic Catholicism in his confidence in the possibility of personal sanctification than Marpeck, whose attachment

---

[1] Such is the trend of interpretation in the most recent evaluations of the life's work of Schwenckfeld: Reinhold Pietz, "Die Gestalt der zukünftigen Kirche," *Calwer Heft*, XXV (Stuttgart, 1959); Walter Knoke, "Schwenckfelds Sakramentsverständnis," *Zeitschrift für Religions- und Geistesgeschichte*, XI (1959), 314–327; Gottfried Maron, *Individualismus und Gemeinschaft bei Caspar Schwenckfeld* (Stuttgart, 1961); Joachim H. Seyppel, *Schwenckfeld, Knight of Faith* (Pennsburg, 1961).

to the suffering "gospel of all creatures" and his acknowledgment of the persistence of sin in the justified made him somewhat closer to Luther.

Before composing Part II of the *Verantwortung*, Marpeck decided to construct an Anabaptist concordance of the Scriptures, to which reference might be made in works requiring the citation of proof texts. The concordance, the *Testamentserläuterung*, was evidently completed in 1550.[2] Leopold Scharnschlager, Marpeck's successor as leader of the Strassburg moderates, and from 1547 a teacher in the Grisons (Ch. 22.1.b) may have been primarily responsible for the production of the *Testamentserläuterung*. The preface promises that the concordance will indicate the difference between the Old and New Covenants. Accordingly, the concordance sets forth Scriptural references to certain doctrinal concepts under the headings "Yesterday," "Today," "Promised Yesterday."[3]

Authorship of Part II of the *Verantwortung* may likewise be assigned jointly to Marpeck and to Scharnschlager.[4] The measure of unity gained during the Anabaptist Second Strassburg Conference in 1555 meant that *Verantwortung* II might not be released for general circulation until all the brethren in Marpeck's far-flung circle had approved it.[5]

Against Schwenckfeld's charge that the Anabaptist doctrine of original sin falls into Pelagianism, *Verantwortung* II now argued that God does not hold a person accountable for either originai sin or actual sin, until he has obtained the knowledge of good and evil and then willfully abandons good and chooses evil. Baptism is not for children, for whom inherited grace (*Erbgnade*) provisionally suffices until they are old enough to believe, confess their sins, profess their faith, and submit to the covenantal ordinance.

As to the prophets and patriarchs of the Old Testament, Schwenckfeld's contention that they were "Christian" is false. These worthies, say Marpeck and Scharnschlager, died in faith but were effectually redeemed only when Christ descended into Hades (on which more in Ch. 32.2.c).

---

[2] Kiwiet's thesis in *Marbeck,* 77. The older view of Wenger, that it was finished in 1544, is no longer accepted.

[3] This concordance is cited over ninety times in Part II of the *Verantwortung*.

[4] The latter may have picked up the task at Marpeck's death (1566), completing it in March of 1588. Klassen, however (*ME*, IV, 808 f.), holds that Kiwiet's evidence is too slender to support this rather elaborate analysis of the authorship of the document.

[5] A copy was sent to Moravia for inspection. General publication of the completed *Verantwortung* did not come until 1571.

When Schwenckfeld laments that, according to the Anabaptists, "no Christian can be a magistrate or worldly ruler, nor can assume authority over cities or countries or people, since such authority belongs to earthly rulers and not to true Christians," *Verantwortung* II restates the Anabaptist view that, while indeed no true Christian may exercise such authority, there is no need for such temporal authority among true Christians.[6]

Against the Spiritualist's tendency to depreciate the visible church, and against Schwenckfeld's specific charge that in their sectarian ecclesiasticism the Anabaptists build on Peter rather than on Christ, *Verantwortung* II, of course, vindicated Christ's headship of their conventicles. Schwenckfeld did not deign to reply to Marpeck's *Verantwortung* II. References to Marpeck in the Silesian's letters after this date are uniformly bitter.

Marpeck's great concern to unify the various factions of evangelical Anabaptism and to protect them from Schwenckfeldian Spiritualism found expression in two Strassburg conferences, which brought together representatives from Moravia, the Netherlands, Switzerland, and South Germany. We have already taken note of the second in 1555 from the perspective of the Netherlanders' struggle over hard and soft banning (Ch. 19.2.d). It will be recalled that besides the ban a second point at issue was the Melchiorite doctrine of the celestial flesh of Christ, in which the southern and northern groups agreed to differ in charity.

The theology of the Marpeck circle in the middle years is best preserved in a unique codex, which may have been assembled in preparation for the Strassburg conferences. The codex, *Das Kunstbuch*,[7] contains forty-two letters and documents cherished by the community over the years from 1527 to 1555.[8] The great value of the collection is its preservation in one cherished volume of the literary connective tissues of South German Anabaptist piety.

The early letters are clearly influenced by Müntzer, Hut, Schiemer, Schlaffer, and Entfelder. They develop the theology of suffering discipleship, interpreting baptism as the life of suf-

---

[6] *Verantwortung*, II, *loc. cit.*, 304.
[7] A detailed analysis is given by Fast, "Pilgram Marpeck und das oberdeutsche Täufertum: Ein neuer Handschriftenfund [the *Kunstbuch*]," *ARG*, XLVII (1956), 212–242.
[8] Edited by George Maler of Augsburg and dated 4 September 1561. All these documents, with the exception of three, are unknown from any other source.

fering. There are letters by Marpeck himself, Leopold Scharnschlager, the editor George Maler, Sigmund Bosch, Helen von
Freyberg, the Lutheran John Has, and Valentine Ickelsamer.
The latter is of interest as a sometime defender of Carlstadt and
subsequent ally of Schwenckfeld in the dispute with Marpeck!
It is Ickelsamer's *Die Gelehrten die Verkehrten* that appears
in rhyme at the beginning of the codex and, along with the
decoration, gives the codex its name. The collection brings out
the many-sidedness and extent of the missionary and organizational activities of Marpeck and Scharnschlager, and the distressing fact that everywhere they found the Anabaptists split
into bickering factions. In their persistent attempts to establish
unity, Marpeck and Scharnschlager opposed the Swiss Brethren
for their tendency to rely on works righteousness more than
faith; the Hutterites for their stand on the ban and an exclusivistic coercive community of goods; the Low Germans for their
Christology. Marpeck and Scharnschlager maintained that undue
severity among the banners, shunners, and communitarians in
the Netherlands, Switzerland, and Moravia was inconsistent with
the freedom of the gospel. Their success in mediation and reunification was probably limited to winning small numbers to
the Marpeck party (including George Maler, the transcriber of
the codex).

It was Scharnschlager who in seven articles gave fullest expression in the *Kunstbuch* to the Marpeckian ideal community.
In this church order[9] we see a community with a common
treasury for the sustenance of the needy members and an order
of worship beginning with prayer and ending with the admonition to steadfastness, a service in which, besides the *Vorsteher,*
all the members one after another rise to read the Scriptures or
the communal writings, to discourse, and to prophesy.

Although the letters do not specifically refer to the First and
Second Strassburg Conferences of 1554 and 1555 with the Netherlanders (Ch. 19.2), it is probable, as already noted, that they
prepared the ground for them; for among the doctrines discussed
is the celestial flesh of Christ.[10] It is of interest that Marpeck
was able to say as of 1550 that it would be a matter of indifference before the judgment seat whether Christ had taken his
flesh from the Virgin or brought it with him from heaven to
earth and back to heaven. On this doctrine, central to the
theology of Spiritualist Schwenckfeld, as well as to the Melchior-

[9] Item 19 in the codex; described by Fast, *loc. cit.,* 237 f.
[10] Marpeck, 24 August 1550, "Von fünferlei Frucht wahrer Busse," *Kunstbuch,*
    174.

ite Anabaptists of the Netherlands, Marpeck was apparently willing to limit himself to the ambiguities of Scripture itself. This also was, it will be recalled, the decision of the Second and Third Strassburg Conferences. The corresponding doctrine of inward and outward Communion receives considerable attention in the *Kunstbuch.*

Marpeck himself was not able to participate in the Third Strassburg Conference of 1557. In Augsburg's *Baumeisterbuch* the first three quarterly payments of his salary are recorded; but under the payment date of 16 December 1556 there is the simple notation: "Is dead."

2. Anabaptism from the Death of Marpeck to the Translation of Menno Into German, 1556–1575

In the year of Marpeck's death, throughout the whole Rhine valley and the upper Danube with their tributaries, Hutterite missionaries were active in recruiting colonists for Moravia, and one of them in 1556 was successful in enlisting the majority of two conventicles of Swiss Brethren, the one in the Palatinate (Kreuznach, near Mainz) and the other in Aachen. Quarrels had developed in both communities, which prepared the way for Hutterite proselytization among their disaffected.

In Kreuznach, the quarrel may have been initially between the local leader, one Farwendel, and Diebold Winter, head of the congregation in Worms and overseer of the brotherhood in the whole region. The dispute concerned original sin and the sin of the soul and the sin of the flesh. About fifteen hundred brethren gathered at Worms to discuss the doctrine of original sin (and, no doubt, related topics). Farwendel had the support of the brethren, but both leaders were deposed, and the problem was put on the agenda for the Third Strassburg Conference in 1557.

Well before this company could assemble, the disaffected within the Kreuznach community had separated from the deposed Farwendel, under the leadership of Lawrence Hueff, and to the problem of original sin several largely communal issues were added. The brethren under Hueff were dissatisfied with voluntary giving to the poor and espoused the complete community of goods; they were against paying taxes for war; they insisted on public disciplining for misdeeds (however imprudent this might be in view of a hostile society), and at the same time they insisted on a more stringent separation from the people of the world. It was at this juncture that the Hutterite missionary

John Schmidt arrived and turned the communal-minded brethren toward the promised land of the Hutterites.

He dealt concurrently with a similar outbreak in Aachen, where one John Arbeiter, who had been an elder both in Kreuznach and in Worms, was the counterpart of Lawrence Hueff in leading the disaffected into Moravian communism.

For each group plying the Hutterite emissary with many questions, John Schmidt prepared two tracts, the one for Aachen in seventeen points, the other for Kreuznach in seven. This was the *Brüderliche Vereinigung*,[11] reminiscent of the *Vereinigung* or Confession of Schleitheim up the Rhine written exactly a generation before. We have already quoted from its summons to the providentially prepared wilderness of Moravia (Ch. 26.2) as evidence of continuing conflict and competition among the Moravian, the Swiss, and the Marpeckian versions of evangelical Anabaptism extending in each case far beyond the region of origin.

In the year after Marpeck's death, on 25 August 1557, Diebold Winter of Worms as head of the less sectarian of his brotherhood led some forty Anabaptists in a general disputation arranged by the Elector Otto Henry of the Palatinate (1556–1559), to bring together representatives of the Lutherans and the Anabaptists at Pfeddersheim. The Lutherans were headed by the Strassburg theologian, Dr. Johannes Marbuch, by John Brenz of Stuttgart, and Jacob Andreae of Göppingen. Five familiar topics were discussed at this disputation: infant baptism, the state, the oath, leaving the state church, and the ban. The result of the Pfeddersheim meeting was that the state church announced itself the victor, and thereupon commanded the "defeated" Anabaptists to relinquish their views.

In the fall of the same year,[12] a group of Catholic and Lutheran theologians debated together at Worms, hoping to promote a reconciliation of the Protestant and Catholic parties. Failing to arrive at any satisfactory conclusions, they took notice of the recent events at Pfeddersheim and thereupon proceeded to recommend a more stringent attitude toward Anabaptism by governmental authorities. Melanchthon, Brenz, Andreae, and others printed the results of the talks at Worms[13] and drew up in a record of the proceedings called a *Prozess* the list of what

[11] Zieglschmid, *Chronik*, 359–367; *ME*, I, 448, and related biographical and topographical articles.
[12] From 11 September to 7 October 1557.
[13] Under the title, *Prozess wie es soll gehalten werden mit den Wiedertäufern;* printed in Bossert, *Württemberg* (*QGT*, I), 161–168.

they considered seditious or merely heretical "lies." Among the charges were unitarianism, indifference to the preached Word, divorce from non-Baptist spouses, and "obscene cruelty" in separating children from their parents in the Hutterite nurseries under specialized sisters as guardians and teachers. Diebold Winter later declared that things had been printed about the Anabaptists at Pfeddersheim which they "never thought, much less spoke":

Also we protest [he continues] that thereupon a very sharp mandate was issued. If we were such people as represented in the *Prozess,* we would not be fit to stand before your eyes. We want to record this for our defense. This is our complaint and protest that we were dealt with unjustly at Pfeddersheim.[14]

As a result of the Worms discussions, the elector issued a mandate against the Radicals, threatening them with punishment according to imperial decree if they should fail henceforth to conform. However, the mandate was not enforced with much strictness.[15]

All groups of Anabaptists felt the challenge of the allegations in the *Prozess,* including the Dutch and Swiss Brethren. However, it was of all groups the Hutterites who systematically replied to the charge of Melanchthon and the other Lutheran theologians in their *Handbüchlein wider den Prozess* (1558), probably drawn up by Peter Walpot.[16] This Hutterite *Handbüchlein* dealt with all the topics under dispute with the Magisterial Reformation, but the most significant part is that devoted to the problem of original sin, which had already divided Anabaptists in Worms and then at the Third Strassburg Conference in 1557 when some fifty gathered in a public tavern to debate the great issue of original sin, in the meantime not forgetting their bellies, says the Hutterite *Chronicle* sarcastically,[17] to the extent of several hundred guilders.

It is clear from several documents at mid-century that the problem of original sin was becoming much more pressing for the second generation leaders with the large proportion of birthright members in their conventicles than it was in the first flush of the conventicular movement. The question of original sin and the solidarity of the human race was inextricably tied up with the more specialized problems of separation from the world,

14 *ME*, IV, 158.
15 Cf. *ML*, II, 594, on "Neues Mandat."
16 Wilhelm Wiswedel and Robert Friedmann, "The Anabaptists Answer Melanchthon," *MQR*, XXIX (1955), 212–231.
17 Zieglschmid, *Chronik*, 358.

war taxes, and voluntary giving as distinguished from apostolic communism.

It is appropriate therefore that we pause briefly to consider the concept of sin and especially of original sin at a point in our narrative far beyond our systematic coverage of baptism, the Dominical ordinance for the washing away of sins so prominent in the first generation of the movement.

It will be recalled that Marpeck in the earlier phase of the controversy with Schwenckfeld had at length come to acknowledge original sin in the sense of the *Erbbrest* of Zwingli. He was in this respect almost alone among the Anabaptist theologians in working systematically at a basic doctrine of the Magisterial Reformers and of the whole Western Church in the Pauline-Augustinian tradition.[18] We have already observed, however, that under a different rubric, namely, the "gospel of all creatures" (Ch. 11.1.a), something of the same perception of the world as fallen and suffering was shared by all Anabaptists in the tradition of Denck and Hut, to which indeed Marpeck himself belonged. But even this suffering was viewed *positively*. Indeed, in *Gelassenheit* it was to be accepted as the first stage in redemption. Moreover, despite the solidarity of the race in Adam's fall proclaimed in Genesis and also in IV Esdras, chs. 3, and 7 (widely cited among the Anabaptists), and I Cor., ch. 15, there was the countervailing innate impulse (*Gegenerb*) which pressed mankind toward the freewill acceptance of the gospel of reconciliation in Christ. This made it possible for the Anabaptists, when they came seriously to consider the problem of original sin, to break it down, as it were, into manageable parts. In the first place, almost all of the responsible statements among the leaders give evidence of the widespread conviction that Christ took away Adamic or original sin from the whole world and, for that reason, children were in no need of baptism for salvation. The evangelical Anabaptists were willing to admit the persistence of evil after regeneration (in contrast to the Netherlandish Libertines and certain other Spiritualists).

It is in dealing with these postbaptismal impulses that the Hutterite answer to Melanchthon, the *Handbüchlein*, stands out in having achieved unusual clarity of distinction. Based to some degree on the tripartite anthropology of Hubmaier, which refused to implicate the *spiritus* in the fall of the *anima* and *corpus* of Adam, Walpot above the original guilt of Adam dis-

[18] Robert Friedmann and N. van der Zijpp, "Original Sin," *ME*, IV, 79–83.

tinguished the sinful inclination which, if it is not yielded to so that the believer remains in Christ (Rom. 8:1; I John 3:9), does not condemn or lead to eternal death. The believer can compel the flesh to obey the spirit, for the power of the original inclination has been broken by Christ, and thereby the word of Ezekiel (ch. 18:20) has been fulfilled that "the children shall not bear the iniquities of the fathers."[19]

In the year of the *Handbüchlein* a notable Anabaptist of the second generation, the Lower Rhenish leader Thomas of Imbroich, was put to death. His confession and letters likewise reveal the mood of German Anabaptism in the process of regional differentiation and consolidation.

Thomas was born in 1533 near Aachen.[20] As a young man, he was apprenticed to a printer. Coming to Cologne in 1554, he associated himself with the local conventicle, and soon became acknowledged as a leader of the Lower Rhenish Anabaptists. On 23 December 1557, Thomas was imprisoned and questioned on his beliefs regarding baptism and marriage. Transferred to another prison, he sharply refuted the arguments of two priests regarding the baptism of his own children. He was thrice brought to the rack, but evidently not tortured, because the authorities were not agreed among themselves. After this, Thomas was haled before the count, who feared the imperial decree and the archbishop's displeasure. The young apprentice refused to relinquish his beliefs and was thereupon sentenced to death.

During his imprisonment, he set down his baptismal convictions in a confession.[21] Here he reasserted the familiar view that, since "the sin of Adam and of the whole world is reconciled through the sacrifice of Christ," children die blameless. Baptism is for those who choose to enter the spiritual ark of Noah and are thereby saved from the sins committed after they have been awakened to the knowledge of good and evil. Thomas also composed seven letters, which were published with his Confession, two of which are printed in the *Martyrs' Mirror*.

The second of these breathes a spirit of compassionate concern for his wife and children. Thomas reminds her that God is a jealous God. Perhaps they have loved one another so much that they have slighted God. Now, both of them will be able to love God the more. She is not to grieve for him unduly. She is, instead, to continue serving and loving God and caring for their

---

[19] Quoted from the somewhat earlier *Account* of Peter Riedemann, p. 58.
[20] He was also known as Thomas Drucker or Thomas of Truden. *ME*, III, 12.
[21] Printed in *Martyrs' Mirror*, 367–371; his letter, 578–582.

children. Like Esther (!), Frau von Imbroich must avoid costly wearing apparel and persons given to such worldly trifles.

With regard to the children, Thomas writes in stern solicitude:

Hence be of good courage, and bring up thy children in good manners, and in the fear of God, that their natural propensities may be mortified; and take an example from thyself, how thou bringest them up in their weakness, with great labor and trouble, and give the breast to them to whom the Lord has commanded milk to be given. Thou art also to give them the rod, according to the command of the Lord, when they transgress and are obstinate; for this is also food for the soul, and drives out the folly which is bound up in their hearts. . . .

I also pray that they, as far as possible, be kept away from intractable children; do not allow them to run about in the streets, but keep them with thee as much as possible, that thou mayest have joy and sorrow with them; and forget not the kind of widow mentioned by Paul in his letter to Timothy [I Tim. 5:4]; but place thy hope firmly in the Lord, and wait for him with patience.

In closing, Thomas commends her to the fellowship and care of the pious, whom she is to greet for him "with the kiss of love." Moreover, she is to remind them to take care of the novices or "neophytes" in the faith, which phrase, along with the instruction concerning the necessity of isolating the children from the progeny of the unbelievers, marks the beginning of a major concern with the special problems of "birthright" membership. We may compare his concern for the discipline and rearing of his children with the contemporaneous description of the Hutterite *kindergartens* in the *Handbüchlein* and with Menno Simons' *The Nurture of Children*.[22]

While on the lower Rhine we may note the well-known exchange in Catholic Cologne between another Rhenish Anabaptist leader, Matthew Servaes (1536–1565), and George Cassander, an irenic Romanist scholar and ecumenical churchman akin to the earlier Evangelical Catholics. In 1565, while conducting a meeting of Anabaptists in Cologne, Servaes, a linen weaver, was betrayed to the authorities and arrested. During his imprisonment he was subjected to torture in the usually unsuccessful attempt to get him to implicate others. But "I pressed my lips together, yielded myself to God, suffered patiently and thought of the word of the Lord (John 15:13): Greater love hath no man than this, that he lay down his life for his friends." He composed several hymns and letters, which continued to inspire genera-

---

22 For Menno's work c. 1557, see *Writings*, 945. Imbroich's confession and letters, many times reprinted for the edification of followers, called forth an edict against all Anabaptist books by the Duke of Jülich in 1560.

tions of Mennonites. The judges, favorably impressed by him, requested that Cassander try to win him back to the traditional faith by patient exploration of the differences, ethical and doctrinal, that separated them. Cassander found that one of the points at issue was psychopannychism. He was deeply impressed by Servaes, and deplored the severity of the imperial law, but despite his attempts he failed to persuade the stalwart Anabaptist or to protect him from the consequences of his steadfastness in the faith. Servaes was executed on 30 June 1565, having uncomplainingly endured all the trials and torments to which he had been subjected.

In nearby Hesse, Landgrave Philip remained tolerant, and in his testament to his four sons, among whom he divided his territory, he wrote at the end of his life (1567): "To kill people for the reason that they believed an error, we have never done, and wish to admonish our sons not to do so, for we consider that it is contrary to God, as is clearly shown in the gospel."[23] Philip's four sons continued his policy in spite of attempts by church authorities and other rulers to get them to change it. One son, the landgrave William, heir to Lower Hesse, in the *Reformationsordnung* of 1572, limited the penalty for Anabaptism to expulsion from his territory. As under his father, persons convicted of recalcitrance were permitted to profit from the sale or rental of their Hessian properties. The other three brothers were similarly benign in their domains.

In Württemberg, whither many Hutterites returned when driven from Moravia,[24] Duke Christopher (1550–1568) decided that the state church councils and superintendents should consult together quarterly about the Schwenckfeldians and the Anabaptists. Thus the Lutheran Church of Württemberg indirectly owes its synodal organization to the need to deal with the Radicals. Christopher issued a mandate in 1554 against Schwenckfeld. In 1558, he set up the canons of examination and treatment of suspected sectaries, including Anabaptists. Torture might be employed to loosen tongues. Those who recanted had to confess their error in the parish church. Those who persisted were to be jailed and their property sold to support them and their innocent children. Attention was given to distinctions between Anabaptist leaders and followers, consideration being paid to problems relating to the family life of the Anabaptists. The death penalty was not invoked, although after 1571 Anabaptists were often

---

[23] Franz, *Wiedertäuferakten*, No. 148.
[24] Gerhard Neumann shows that the ratio was two to one in favor of the returners, "Nach und von Mähren," *ARG*, I I (1960), 75–90.

branded or imprisoned for their faith. The census of 1570 showed only 129 Anabaptists in the duchy, the majority in Lorch. Varieties of Radicals familiar to the Württemberg authorities included Servetians, Davidjorists, Hutterites, the Hofer Brethren (an offshoot of the Hutterites), Moserites (who appear to have been the local Swiss Brethren), and probably Pilgramites, or followers of Marpeck.[25]

The Lutheran general superintendent at Göppingen, Jacob Andreae (1528–1590), was set against all sectarians and was responsible for Duke Christopher's stringent attitude. Andreae was instrumental in drawing up the Lutheran Formula of Concord of 1576, revised in 1577, which contained a chapter listing Anabaptist errors on church, government, and economics. It was primarily directed against the Hutterites and indicates that their missionaries were still threatening. Ironically, Andreae's grandson, John Valentine Andreae, born in 1568, was to become a forerunner of the Pietist movement and to produce much of the early literature of the Rosicrucians.

In the divided duchy of Baden, different attitudes toward the Radicals were held. Baden-Baden, which had embraced Protestantism under its first independent ruler, had been officially recatholicized by the guardians of the second duke. Under the third duke, Philibert, the cause of the Reformation was again favored, but at his death in 1569, the territory fell to Duke Albert of Bavaria. Albert determined to recatholicize the duchy, and so enforced the imperial mandates against the Anabaptists. One Radical, John Geiger of Zell, is known to have been executed in 1571.

Baden-Pforzheim[26] had been first ruled by the moderate duke Ernest, whose sympathy for Schwenckfeldianism made the land temporarily safe also for Anabaptists. In 1556, Duke Charles II (with the help of Jacob Andreae and the court chaplain of Heidelberg, Michael Diller) espoused the Reformation with the consequence that the Radicals were no longer tolerated. With the ascendancy of Duke Albert of Bavaria recatholicization proceeded apace. The change of policy was symbolized by the baptism of an infant child of Anabaptist parentage on Christmas Day in 1570.[27]

For Switzerland, the homeland of Anabaptism, there is little to recount that belongs to general, as distinguished from purely regional or denominational, history after the Confederation

25 Bossert, *Württemberg* (*QGT*, I), 276, 296.
26 In 1565, Baden-Durlach.
27 *ME*, I, 206.

Edict against Anabaptists and Calvin's major work against them in 1544 (Ch. 23.2). In 1560, Bullinger summarized a whole generation of polemic against the Radical Reformation in his *Der Wiedertaüfer Ursprung* (Ch. 33). With a succession of famines and plagues (1563–1571) and a series of mandates and repressive measures in the cantons, the Anabaptists continued to flee, especially to Moravia. In 1576, emigration from Zurich was forbidden because of the loss to the economy. All the Reformed cantons enacted the same ruling in 1577. These regulations, however, were applied not only to Anabaptists but also to Catholics. Emigration nevertheless continued. The final Zurich effort to settle the problem was the promulgation in 1580 of the great Christian ordinance which was intended to regulate conduct along lines consonant with sobriety and edification, and thus to eliminate the moral abuses against which the Anabaptists had been protesting. Thus at the end of our period, the canton of Zurich, hearth of evangelical Anabaptism, was belatedly adopting measures which seemed to be a response to a favorite Anabaptist admonition: "Be ye doers of the word, and not hearers only, deceiving yourselves" (James 1:22).[28]

During these years, which witnessed the ebbing of the Anabaptist mission in the Rhineland, Hesse, Württemberg, Baden, and Switzerland, and the consolidation of the remnants into a unified denomination of second-generation believers, a major conference was held in Strassburg (1568) and a major disputation was held in Frankenthal (1571).

The Fourth Strassburg Conference, which took place in 1568, was called when it became evident that the breach between the South German and Swiss Brethren on the one hand, and the North German and Dutch on the other, was going to be permanent.[29] The three earlier conferences (1554, 1555, 1557) of Strassburg had failed to heal it, and the meeting in 1568 marks the recognition of this split on the part of the South Germans and Swiss, and their adoption of a definitive discipline for their own group independent of that of the Low Germans and Dutch.

The Strassburg *Discipline* of 1568, twoscore years after the exploratory attempts at Schleitheim (Ch. 8.1), shows us a community which has developed a settled social and group consciousness, an awareness of themselves as a distinctly different

---

[28] Cornelius Bermann, *Die Täuferbewegung im Canton Zürich bis 1660*, Quellen und Abhandlungen zur schweizerischen Reformations-Geschichte, II (Leipzig, 1916), 50.

[29] Harold S. Bender, "The Discipline Adopted by the Strassburg Conference of 1568," *MQR*, I (1927), 57–66.

element in an unregenerate society, and a program for preserving their distinctiveness. Moderate but firm, the *Discipline* deals with the practical problems of a subapostolic generation. The only theological question treated is that of the nature of Christ (the question of the celestial flesh), where the admonition of the earlier Strassburg conferences is repeated, to hold fast to Scriptural language (without further precision as to the two natures), and to avoid further discussion and dissension. The *Discipline* reveals the existence of ordained bishops (*Aelteste*), who are to visit the various congregations, "filling the offices" where there are vacancies, ordaining (*bestätigen*) ministers (*Diener*) and bishops by the laying on of hands. These bishops also are to have care for the wives and children of imprisoned ministers, as well as for widows and orphans. There is counsel for the proper care of orphans and a rule forbidding marriage outside the community of faith. Other rules also illustrate the sense of exclusiveness. Brethren are to be greeted with the kiss of peace, but those outside the community simply with the words: "The Lord help you." Money should be deposited with a brother or sister, and while debts already contracted to the world must be paid, no more should be incurred outside the brotherhood. Significant of their self-consciousness as a group apart are the regulations forbidding hunting and trapping, the making and wearing of proud clothes, and serving as armed watchmen. The *Discipline* seeks to promote a modest, godly, and sober life of a separated group within a larger, hostile society, making provision both for inward sustenance and for protection from outside contamination.

The climax of the series of disputations designed to win the Anabaptists to the orthodox faith took place at Frankenthal in the Palatinate in 1571. Like the Pfeddersheim debate of 1557, it was arranged by the count palatine, now Frederick III (1559–1576). Frederick, the first German prince to embrace Calvinism, had sought to lead all his people into the same fold. With the Lutherans and Catholics he was fairly successful, but the Anabaptists, of course, proved recalcitrant. Like his predecessor, Otto Henry, Frederick thought that a public disputation would be good for all, and would convert the Anabaptists. He was extremely open-minded and fair about the disputation, promising safe-conducts to all participants for fourteen days before and after the dispute, and free board and lodging during the sessions. Foreign preachers were invited, and prisoners might take part on the condition that they refrain from preaching and baptizing.

Nevertheless, in spite of his assurance, relatively few Anabaptists came, fearing that participation would involve them in eventual persecution. In all, only fifteen Anabaptists arrived, mostly "Swiss" Brethren. One report says that there were three Moravians (Hutterites) present.[30] The Palatine representatives were reserved, and the chief burden of the discussion was borne by Diebold Winter of Weissenburg in Alsace, who had attended the Pfeddersheim meeting.[31] John Rannich and Nicholas Simmerer were brought from prison to Frankenthal and repeatedly cross-examined before the disputation began, in order to obtain statements to use in the public discussion and in the hope of discovering divergences.

The confrontation lasted for nineteen days, excluding Sundays (28 May to 19 June), with two sessions daily. The elector showed his interest by attending the opening session. Several of the questions were familiar. Others indicated the new stage of Anabaptist-Protestant relations after four decades of coexistence. The old question of the authority of the Old Testament compared to the New was brought up. The Anabaptists replied that they gave preference to the New without neglecting the Old. The second question concerned the doctrine of the Trinity, which the Anabaptists embraced. The third question, on the celestial flesh of Christ, they refused to answer, feeling that they had no information on this subtle point of doctrine.

On the fourth point, whether children were born in original sin and were therefore by nature deserving of death, the Brethren admitted the sinfulness of infants, but were not willing to say anything about their damnation. To the fifth question, about the magistracy, the Anabaptists gave their usual answers. On the sixth article, whether justification was by faith or by works, the Brethren agreed with the magisterial churchmen. On the seventh, concerning the resurrection of the body, the Reformed insisted that the substance of the present body would be resurrected, whereas the Anabaptists believed a new and glorified body would replace it. The eighth question, on excommunication and divorce, drew attention to the harsh regulations of the Mennonite and Hutterite Churches, and revealed the distance that still separated them from the Swiss and South German Anabaptists. The ninth question, on the corporate ownership of property, referred to the Hutterites, who, however, if indeed there were any present, did not respond. The tenth question dealt again with government, the eleventh with the oath, the twelfth with believers' baptism, and the thirteenth with the Lord's Supper.

The Frankenthal disputation, which had begun with high

[30] See the forthcoming *MQR* article by Jesse Yoder on Frankenthal.
[31] For additional names, see *ME*, II, 374.

hopes, ended, having drawn the parties no closer together than they were at the outset. The elector closed with a speech emphasizing his regard for the Anabaptists and his hope that they might yet be won back to the state church. They were henceforth forbidden, however, to teach in his domain, "in order not to confuse our subjects."[32] Anyone failing to observe this order would be banished.[33]

In the disputation it had become clear, despite differences between South German–Swiss Anabaptists and Dutch–Low German Mennonites in respect to the ban and the celestial flesh of Christ, that they were drawing together in opposition to the Hutterites. The North German and Netherlandish Anabaptists had adopted the name "Mennonite" before Menno's death in 1561, but the South Germans and Swiss were not to do so until later, taking advantage of its peaceful connotations. Significantly, however, already in 1575 Menno Simons' *Foundation Book* appeared in High German translation.

The Rhine was at length beginning to unite the Anabaptist sacramentarians at its headwaters with those at its mouth. Eventually the term "Mennonite" would embrace all the survivors of Anabaptism within the boundaries of the old Empire, except for the Moravian Hutterites, who had repeatedly rejected all ecumenical overtures from within the Radical Reformation.

We turn now to other branches of the denominational delta into which the great current of the Radical Reformation was debouching on its way into the seventeenth century.

3. GERMAN UNITARIANISM

The Unitarians in Germany were represented by only a handful. The principal Unitarian episode within the framework of our narrative likewise unfolds in the Palatinate.

At the universities of Germany, opposition to the doctrines of left-wing rationalism was on the rise. It will be recalled that when Gribaldi came to teach law at Tübingen in 1555 (Ch. 24.2.a), he was accompanied by two Polish students, Peter

---

[32] *ME*, II, 375.

[33] *Protocoll, das ist Alle Handlung des gesprechs zu Frankenthal* (Heidelberg, 1571).

[34] For Gribaldi's career at Tübingen, see Delio Cantimori, "Matteo Gribaldi Mofa et l'università de Tubinga," *Bollettino Storico-Bibliographico Subalpino*, XXXV (1933), 492–504. The whole story of the MS. and related material is told by Stanislas Kot, "L'influence de Michel Servet sur le Mouvement Antitrinitarien en Pologne et en Transylvanie," *Autour de Michel Servet*, 72–115. Kot holds that Curione, whose marginalia have been identified, wrote the preface under the pseudonym.

Gonesius and Michael Salecki (Zaleski). In 1559, as the latter was packing up to return to Poland, he was assailed by adventurers and stabbed. The case, arousing the Polish colony of a half dozen students, was investigated by the ducal authorities of Württemberg, and in the examination of the nobleman's effects, it turned out that some of the Poles had been reading in secret the *Declarationis Jesu Christi filii Dei libri V* of Michael Servetus. It had been brought from Basel via Strassburg and edited for publication with a preface by "Alphonsus Lyncurius Tarraconensis." We have already suggested that Gribaldi may have received this directly from Servetus in Geneva (Ch. 24.2.a).

The interest in Servetus must have extended beyond the Italian expatriates and the Polish student body, for in 1560 Jacob Scheck of Tübingen attacked Servetus, and possibly also Campanus and Adam Pastor. He characterized the position of his opponent as a purely monarchian view of the Trinity as a unity of three, not in essence, but of powers.[35] The scope and intensity of Scheck's defense of the Nicene and Chalcedonian formulations testify to the presence in Germany, and particularly, as he says, in the North, of fully developed unitarianism well in advance of Faustus Socinus and even Francis Dávid.

We have already noted the Wittenberg reaction to the Transylvanians. Professor George Major in 1569 directed expressly against Dávid and Blandrata his *De uno Deo et tribus personis;* and other weighty volumes followed.

At Heidelberg, Professor Girolamo Zanchi was to write against them and others his *De tribus Elohim,* 1572.

When Caspar Olevianus, leader of the Reformed Church at Heidelberg (*Heidelberg Catechism,* 1562), began advocating the introduction of a discipline like that in Geneva, he was opposed by the outspoken first preacher at St. Peter's, Adam Neuser—eloquent and well liked by the congregation, but emotional and unstable. Neuser's vehement criticism caused the elector to dismiss him from his post, c. 1570, and to give him an insignificant assignment in the country. This humiliation turned him even more openly against orthodoxy. He claimed that the new ideas which he brought forward came strictly from his own study of

---

[35] Cf. Scheck's *Contra Antitrinitarios negantes Patrem, Filium et Spiritum S. Unum numero et essentia esse Deum* (Tübingen, 1566). Further examples may be found in Stanislas von Dunin-Borkowski, "Untersuchungen," *loc. cit.,* 132 f. An old and bellicose Servetian disputant at Stuttgart, Hans Hottmann. is recorded in Bossert, *Württemberg* (*QGT,* I), 433.

the Bible, although we have reason to suppose that he learned of them through the Poles.[36]

Neuser won over three other local Reformed pastors—namely, John Sylvan,[37] Jacob Suter,[38] and Matthew Vehe.[39] In his reaction to the new Calvinist orthodoxy of Heidelberg, Neuser was delighted to learn of the Transylvanian Unitarians, who enjoyed the patronage of their prince. While Sylvan wrote to Blandrata, Neuser looked beyond Transylvania to Constantinople, and wrote to Sultan Selim II, commending him for his religious views and assuring him of wide support in Germany if his conquests should carry him so far![40] Neuser's Unitarianism was thus combined with a political irresponsibility calculated to alarm even the most tolerant German ruler. When the Transylvanian envoy, Caspar Békés, appeared at the diet of Speyer in June 1570, Neuser and Sylvan offered their services to the Unitarian Church in Transylvania. Békés, however, betrayed their confidence to the Emperor Maximilian II (1564–1576), in an effort to put John II Sigismund of Transylvania in a good light in the eyes of the Emperor. The Hapsburg thereupon informed the elector of the Palatinate of the offer, and he in turn ordered all four Unitarian preachers arrested.

Neuser had set out for Hungary before the order was issued, but when he learned of the arrest of Sylvan, he bravely returned and was himself arrested. Later he escaped. Suter and Vehe were eventually released, the latter to become in due course rector of the Unitarian college at Kolozsvár. Sylvan, after some delay, was beheaded. Neuser traveled first to London, in the hope of securing a position with the Strangers' Church, but presented no credentials, since he was using an assumed name, and when he was rebuffed went to Paris. He eventually reached Constantinople, via Cracow and Kolozsvár, having submitted to circumcision and become a Mohammedan on the way. This conversion grew out of difficulties with the pasha of Temésvar, who could not understand why Neuser, a Christian, wanted to set up a printing press on Turkish territory, and suspected him of being an imperial agent. When Neuser explained that, like the Turks, he believed in one unipersonal God, and that this had involved

[36] Stanislas Farnowski, prominent among the ditheists (Farnovians) in Poland, had had to leave the University of Heidelberg in 1564 because of his similar views.
[37] Of Ladenburg.
[38] Of Weinheim.
[39] Of Lautern.
[40] Wilbur, *Unitarianism*, 259.

him in difficulties with the imperial government, the pasha challenged him either to prove it by becoming a Turk, or to be sent to the Sultan in Constantinople for a thorough examination on suspicion of spying. Neuser chose Mohammedanism, and traveled to Constantinople of his own accord. Here, after embroiling himself with the Mohammedan religious leaders and leading a dissipated life, he died in 1576.[41] He claimed, while in Transylvania, to have persuaded Francis Dávid that it was an error to worship Christ.[42] It was Neuser who also observed: "No one known to me in our time has become an Arian who was not first a Calvinist—therefore if any one fears that he may fall into Arianism, he should avoid Calvinism."[43] Neuser is rare among sixteenth-century anti-Trinitarians in having readily accepted and adopted the name Arian to describe his position.[44]

4. German Spiritualism and Proto-Pietism, 1542–1578

Caspar Schwenckfeld, who must by now seem to the reader to be the only constant figure amid the swirling litter of an autumnal storm, watched his friends and foes pass from the scene. His own ardor for the Middle Way may have been flagging in the face of the hardened positions of the Roman, Lutheran, and Reformed Churches and the various Anabaptists.

After the strife of 1547 his contacts with Anabaptism were marginal. Schwenckfeld's correspondence mentions a former disciple, Daniel Graff, who eventually swung over to Marpeck's camp. At another point, Schwenckfeld was requested by a sister to reply for her to an Anabaptist missionary's letter urging immediate rebaptism. He speaks in a letter concerning certain *Schweiger* (silent ones) among the Anabaptists. Schwenckfeld's contact with other branches of the Reformation were also almost entirely negative.

Much of the three years as Eliander at Esslingen after 1547 Schwenckfeld spent in writing and visiting friends nearby. The confusion created by the Augsburg Interim of 1548 permitted him to break his self-imposed confinement and to visit and strengthen his little groups of followers in several localities.

[41] Gotthold Ephraim Lessing, *Von Adam Neusern, einige authentische Nachrichten* (Braunschweig, 1774), in *Sämtliche Schriften* (Leipzig, 1897), XII, 202–254, esp. 220 ff.

[42] Letter of Adam Neuser from Constantinople, Wednesday before Easter, 1574, to "Caspar," published in Lessing, *op. cit.*, 207 ff.

[43] Stephen Gerlach sr., *Tage-Buch* (Frankfurt, 1674), 254. Gerlach also relates that Neuser designed an automobile, the model of which worked well, although the full-size was defective.

[44] Lessing, *op. cit.*, 207 ff.

By 1551, however, he was once more engaged in controversy with the Lutheran camp, this time with Matthias Flacius Illyricus, who violently attacked Schwenckfeld's nonliteral doctrine of the Word of God. During the next six years, Flacius penned perhaps a dozen books against the Silesian's position on this and allied doctrines, while Schwenckfeld and his aide George Mayer (Theophilus Agricola) produced fourteen works defending their conception and attacking the Flacian position.

Between 1552 and 1554, Schwenckfeld lived secretly with the younger Streichers at Ulm, and in Oepfingen at a former residence of the von Freyburgs. On 14 June 1554, Duke Cristopher of Württemberg issued the already mentioned mandate calling for his arrest. At almost the same time, certain Reformers and theologians met at Naumburg under the leadership of Melanchthon and produced a document accusing Schwenckfeld of a variety of blasphemies. Even though Philip of Hesse intervened on his behalf with Melanchthon, the gentle Reformer refused to become reconciled with the Silesian, despite Schwenckfeld's great attempt in 1557.

In 1558, Schwenckfeld visited Strassburg and the vicinity of Heidelberg. In 1560 he was asked by one Lucas Pomisius of Nuremberg to deal with questions raised by Laelius Socinus.[45] The questions are not extant. He requests Pomisius to beg Laelius Socinus not to be offended for his not replying to him directly. He warns Pomisius that Laelius sounds very much like Servetus and Gribaldi. He expresses the hope that Pomisius will read the letter to Castellio and Curione in Basel.

Schwenckfeld returned to the Streicher residence in Ulm in August of 1561, when dysentery (probably complicated by tuberculosis) made him seek the medical assistance of Agatha Streicher. Schwenckfeld grew progressively weaker, and finally died on 10 December 1561. He was presumably buried beneath the house of his associates of so many years, the Streichers.

Schwenckfeld was a "Protestant" Spiritualist who, however, separated from all organized churches. In the course of the history of the Reformation, we have encountered several Catholic Spiritualists and Evangelicals, such as Erasmus, Valdés, Campanus, Paracelsus, William Postel, Coornhert, and George Witzel, who, remaining within or returning to the Roman Church, were spiritually closer to Schwenckfeld and to such spiritualizing Anabaptists as Entfelder and Bünderlin.

As the Reformation Era comes to a close, we begin to en-

---

[45] February 1560; *CS*, XVII, Document MCXXIII.

counter a phenomenon within the established Protestant territorial and civic churches comparable to Catholic Evangelism and
Nicodemism, namely, a Protestant conformist Spiritualism. John
Denck, conforming at the end of his life to the established church
at Basel, was perhaps the first of the conforming Protestant
Spiritualists, to be succeeded in the same city by David Joris.
At the end of our epoch, we may mention another whose subsequent influence on German Pietism, mysticism, and anthro-
posophy was great, Valentine Weigel.

Weigel was born in 1533 near Dresden,[46] of Catholic parents
who went over to Lutheranism in 1539 on the death of Duke
George of Saxony. In 1554 he attended the University of Leipzig,
and in 1563 he went to Wittenberg, where Melanchthon's
moderate spirit still prevailed.[47] In 1567 he became preacher in
the small Saxon town of Zschopau, and married in the following year. His sparkling oratorical talent won him great popularity among the people. He was much opposed to the Lutheran
Formula of Concord (1577), with its emphasis on formal dogma
and its strait-jacketing of inner spiritual movement.[48]

During his life he published only one small work;[49] all his
other books were published posthumously.[50] He wrote in 1578
Of the Life of Christ.[51] After 1578, influenced by the works of
Paracelsus, he produced a number of writings dedicated to the
concept of incorporation (Verleiblichung). He finally (somewhat as Obbe Philips had) came to consider his own calling
vain, indeed the whole of the ordained ministry as the work of
the Antichrist. But he concealed most of his radical ideas during
his lifetime (d. 1588) and continued to preach relatively orthodox Lutheranism. He was never attacked, and the periodic
reports of the visitations by his superintendent always commented favorably upon his preaching and charitable endeavors.

Following the Pauline-Origenistic tripartite anthropology held
also by Hubmaier, Weigel correspondingly envisaged three
worlds, namely, the material world or world of darkness, the
invisible or angelic world, and the world of God. God is the
summum bonum and blessedness. When a person accepts salva-

---

[46] In the town of Hain.
[47] Julius Otto Opel, *Valentin Weigel* (Leipzig, 1864).
[48] Winfried Zeller, *Die Schriften Valentin Weigels*, Historische Studien, 370 (Berlin, 1940).
[49] *Eulogy for Lady von Ruxleben*, 1576.
[50] His extensive edifying and moralizing works of the years 1572 to 1576 are catalogued in his *Informatorium oder Soli Deo Gloria* (Newenstadt, 1616, 1618).
[51] So translated and published in London, 1648.

tion, be becomes a god. Weigel held the doctrine of the celestial flesh of Christ.

In Weigel's theosophic vision, elaborately worked out, we have the theosophical reworking of orthodox Christian theology. Weigel's system of thought, complex but not systematic, exercised an influence on later thinkers, especially Johann Arndt (1555–1621) and the Pietist mystic, Jacob Boehme (1575–1620). Weigel may, with some justice, be denominated a proto-Pietist. His writings, reworked by the father of German Pietism, Johann Arndt of Anhalt, provided much of the rationale for that later movement.

In seventeenth-century Pietism, the quieter currents from Anabaptism, Spiritualism, and Evangelical Rationalism merged.[52] It is not surprising that Pietism has been called "a grandchild of Anabaptism."[53] The same area where Anabaptism was strongest, the southwest quadrant of the Empire, eventually witnessed the development of Pietism.

Schwenckfeldianism and Pietism are even more closely akin, if not genetically, at least morphologically. It may be possible to construct a connecting chain of influence from Schwenckfeld through Weigel and Arndt (both of whom were accused of Schwenckfeldianism) and Jacob Boehme (who acknowledged his indebtedness to Schwenckfeld, Paracelsus, and Franck) and, by way of the Brecklings, father and son, and Christian Hoburg (a Schwenckfeldian exiled to Holland) to Philip Spener, educated at Strassburg.[54] The birthplace of Spener, Rappoltsweiler (Ribeauvillé) in upper Alsace, had earlier been part of an area —Strassburg, Landau, Speyer, Rappoltsweiler[55]—where Schwenckfeld commanded a considerable following.

While the Mennonites of a century after our period will become known as the *Stille im Lande,* closely allied to Pietist development,[56] the evangelical Anabaptism of the first two formative generations differed markedly from the later Pietism in

---

[52] Cf. Robert Friedmann, "Anabaptism and Protestantism," *MQR,* XXIV (1950), 12 f., "Anabaptism and Pietism," *MQR,* XIV (1940), 90, 149, and *Mennonite Piety Through the Centuries* (Goshen, 1949); and Heinrich Bornkamm, *Mystik, Spiritualismus, und der Pietismus* (Giessen, 1926).

[53] Maximilian Gobel, *Geschichte des kirchlichen Lebens in der rheinisch-westfälischen evangelischen Kirche* (Koblenz, 1849–1860).

[54] Schultz, *Schwenckfeld,* 404.

[55] Schultz, *op. cit.,* 177, 404; F. Fritz, "Die Wiedertäufer und der württembergische Pietismus," *Blätter für Württembergische Kirchengeschichte,* XLIIII (1939), 81 ff.

[56] Ernst Crous, "Mennonitentum und Pietismus," *Theologische Zeitschrift,* VIII (1952), 279–296.

several important respects.[57] Though both movements rejected
the coercion of conscience in the state church, though both were
impatient with dogmatic subtleties, though both were conventicular expressions of Christianity, though both generated a
deep missionary urge, Anabaptism stressed the "bitter Christ" of
suffering, sending its rebaptized converts out into the dangerous
struggle of life and possible martyrdom, while Pietism emphasized the "sweet Christ" of the devout life and philanthropy.

[57] As was recognized in an early work treating the relationship between the two
movements, J. J. Wolleb's *Gespräch zwischen einem Pietisten und einem
Wiedertäufer* (Basel, 1722).

CHAPTER 32

LAW AND GOSPEL: SECTARIAN ECUMENICITY

Before we bring to a close our narrative and analysis of the Radical Reformation on the point of breaking up into denominations and regional communions as rigidly separated as were the state churches of the Magisterial Reformation, it will be useful to round out two topics which we have thus far treated only on an *ad hoc* basis. These are (Ch. 32.1) the relationship between Word and Spirit and the corresponding tension between law and gospel and (Ch. 32.2) the missionary motif seen in the perspective of what may be called sectarian ecumenicity. Incidentally the wording of the latter topic is not as facile a modernization as it might be thought. Ecumenicity in the sixteenth-century Radicals was a combination of the sense of the imminence of the Kingdom of God, the experience of the universality of the work of the Holy Spirit, the impatience with the territorial particularization of the Reformation, and the overwhelming conviction as to the actuality of the New Covenant. The experience of the new creation in the Spirit gave all the Radicals a feeling of comradeship in Christ and a longing to share their Christian fellowship in solidarity with saints and would-be saints of all times and in all climes. Just as there was a "unitive Protestantism"[1] of the Magisterial Reformation that cut across the territorial boundaries, although nationalism and princely particularism were the main thrusts, so likewise there was an underlying catholicity in the Radical Reformation,[2] even though divisive sectarianism and conventicular fission seem to have bulked very large in our narrative.

---

[1] John T. McNeill, *Unitive Protestantism* (New York, 1930).
[2] Something of this is suggested by the title and several of the essays in the collected work, edited by Guy Hershberger, *The Recovery of the Anabaptist Vision* (Scottdale, Pennsylvania, 1957).

In any event the two topics, "Bible" and "Church," are plausibly brought together here in the same chapter since there was a very close connection between the way the Radicals conceived of the two Testaments and the way they conceived of the nature and the mission of the church and the solidarity and destiny of all mankind.

1. WORD AND SPIRIT: THE BIBLE IN THE RADICAL REFORMATION

The Radical Reformation stood for the most part with the Magisterial Reformation and was indeed largely at this point dependent upon it in the recovery of the Bible and in the rejection of the medieval synthesis of Scripture, tradition, and papal authority. This synthesis had already been largely dissolved by the end of the Middle Ages.[3] At the same time the Radicals differed with the classical Protestant divines, here more, there less, in respect to (*a*) the canonical problem of the authority of the Apocrypha and related ancient writings; (*b*) the theological problem of the two covenants, the inner and the outer word, the letter and the Spirit; and (*c*) the hermeneutical problem of the validity of allegory, concordance, and typology. Into roughly these three subtopics we shall divide the present section.

a. Translations and the Canon. We recall the Sacramentist study groups in the Netherlands: the proto-Anabaptist gatherings for Bible-reading and exposition in Strassburg under Ziegler, in Augsburg under Haetzer, in Zurich under Grebel; and also the prophesyings by women as well as the dreams and the visions of young men and old in conventicles from London to Modena. These gatherings of study and mutual exhortation grounded the sixteenth-century nonconformist in the fundamentals of his faith, opened to him the awesome vistas of other times and nations, exercised him in Scriptural accountability (I Peter 4:5), and promoted in him that Scriptural cunning and inspired readiness of answer (Luke 12:11) that alternatively baffled and impressed the magistrates and divines before whose tribunals he was summoned to appear.

Except for the occasional humanist, the rank and file cited the Bible in a vernacular version. The relationship among the translations of Scripture employed in the Radical Reformation should therefore be clarified. The Upper and Lower German Anabaptists relied largely on the High German Froschauer Bible of Zurich, the Strassburg Bible, and the Liesveldt Bible of Antwerp.

Jacob van Liesveldt of Antwerp printed in 1522 an edition of

---

[3] Cf. Georges H. Tavard, *Holy Writ or Holy Church: The Crisis of the Protestant Reformation* (London, 1959).

the gospels from the Vulgate. When he came into possession of Luther's translations, he put together his complete Dutch Bible in 1526, relying upon translation from the Vulgate to fill the gaps in Luther's work.

It was the fact that Luther had not as yet produced a translation of the Old Testament prophets that induced Haetzer and Denck (Ch. 7.3), perhaps with encouragement from the Strassburg Hebraist, Capito, to publish in Worms in 1527 a widely distributed version of the prophets. It went through twelve editions by 1531. Luther was stimulated to complete his translation of the whole Bible (1532) to counter the popularity of "The Worms Prophets" which so frequently cited Jewish authorities.

The Zurich New Testament (1524) and the complete Bible (1529) printed by Christopher Froschauer was based on Luther's translations to date, with some alterations in the word order and vocabulary and with Swiss vocalization until 1527. At first Froschauer used "The Worms Prophets" to fill the gaps in Luther's translations. So widely popular were the early editions of the Froschauer New Testaments, with their Swiss diphthongs and other cherished *idiotica,* among the Swiss Brethren that under the Bernese authorities they were for a while subject to confiscation as "Anabaptist books."

On the French side, we have had occasion to observe the emergence of a new French text prepared by Peter Olivétan for the Protestantized Waldensians, beginning in 1532 (Ch. 21.1) with prefaces supplied by Calvin, but, of course, this cannot be considered an achievement of Radicals. The Scriptural interest of Servetus was in critical editions rather than in translation. We have mentioned his contribution in Lyons as editor of the Santes Pagnini Bible (1542 and 1545) and his plan to move to Venice by way of Geneva (!) to work on a polyglot edition. We have also mentioned Castellio's translation from the original tongues into humanistic Latin: of the Pentateuch (1547) and of the whole Bible (1551, dedicated to Edward VI), and of the whole Bible afresh into French (1555). In 1562, in his *Defensio translationum bibliorum,* Castellio admitted a number of stylistic and philological errors in his works but reasserted his contentions about free will and predestination, defending himself against the charge of Theodore Beza that he had been tendentious and impious.[4] With a sharp critical sense, Castellio did not hesitate to make clear the original character of the Song of Songs. He

---

[4] For the strongest statement on free will censored by Cellarius, see Sape van der Woude, "Censured Passages from Sebastian Castellio's Defensio Suarum Translationum," *Autour de Michel Servet,* 259–279.

was pleased to think of the Bible as a library in which God and man might meet.

Besides the earlier Dutch translations, mention should be made of *Den Bibel in Duyts* in 1556. This was the work of Stephen Mierdman, a native of Antwerp, who, settling in Emden, combined Liesveldt for the historical books of the Old Testament and Froschauer for the rest of the Bible. The translation was done by the Fleming John Gheylliaert. In 1557 a new Dutch New Testament was printed by Matthew Jacobs. In 1560, the Mennonite Nicholas Biestkens published a Dutch Bible. Drawing on the phrasings of Liesveldt and Mierdman, it was essentially Luther's version in Dutch with certain words reflecting Mennonite usage and experience.

As for the translation into English of the New Testament and large parts of the Old by William Tyndale, the martyr of Vilvoorde, 1536 (while a sojourner and refugee in Marburg and the Netherlands), it is only by extension that it can be claimed in part as an achievement of Radical Protestantism. In only one sector of the Radical Reformation was there truly pioneer work in vernacular translation—Poland. To be sure, the Brest Bible of 1563, a Polish translation under the direction of the French Reformed *émigré*, Peter Statorius (Stoiński) of Pińczów, can be ascribed with equal propriety to the Major and the Minor Church, since it was completed before the definitive schism. But Simon Budny's Polish Bibles of 1572 and 1589 clearly reflected the radical spirit in theological scholarship and evangelical zeal. Budny had learned Hebrew from Stancaro and local rabbis. His translation won high praise from rabbis for the rendition of the Old Testament. In the New Testament, Budny stressed the full humanity of Christ. He even altered Luke 3:23 to insist on Joseph's paternity. Because of its Judaizing trend, Martin Czechowic of the Minor Church in Lublin brought out a counter-version of the New Testament in 1577. Budny's translation was the basis of a Ruthenian New Testament published in 1580 by Basil Ciapiński. At the end of his life Budny withdrew some of his most radical ideas and even found reasons to reascribe Hebrews to Paul.

A word is in order concerning the use of the Apocrypha and related writings in the Radical Reformation. In the Middle Ages the Bible was, of course, seldom seen as a single codex. Besides the difficulty of containing between two boards the manuscript of the whole Bible, there were the varied liturgical and devotional uses of the several parts of the Bible which also encouraged the edition of the Bible in manageable units. In addition to these canonical books, apocryphal books were circulated separately and were popular in medieval spirituality and iconography. It was only gradually that the Protestant principle of the centrality of the Word of God found tangible and visible expression in large, printed, vernacular Bibles; and even then, there was some difference among the classical Protestants as to whether the Old Testament Apocrypha should be included or not. It is therefore understandable that a popular movement such as the Radical Reformation, drawing on several streams of late medieval piety, should continue to make use of the little books of the Apocrypha.

This tendency is particularly noteworthy among the Anabaptists of all persuasions. To be sure, when Luther first proclaimed his doctrine of *sola scriptura* over against tradition and papal authority in parallel to his doctrine of *sola fides* over against works or merits, most of his admirers in what would prove to be the camp of the Radicals hailed him and for a while followed him. But when Luther proceeded to criticize certain writings within the canon as not sufficiently solafideist, as for example, the "straw" epistle of James, many of the Radical Reformers balked and in the end most of them in the sixteenth century fell back upon the pre-Reformation canon *in toto,* and by extension, upon the pseudepigraphical writings of the New as well.

This tendency was particularly marked in the Melchiorite line, where a special exegetical method (Ch. 32.1c) made it possible for Hofmann himself, Menno Simons, Dietrich Philips, and Peter Tasch to use parts of the Old Testament and its Apocrypha which the South Germans and the Swiss Brethren with their greater stress on the disparate character of the two Testaments had reason to neglect or eschew. But the Apocrypha were used in the South too and among the Hutterites. Michael Sattler, for example, quoted IV Esdras extensively in his letter (1527) to the Anabaptists at Horb. Peter Riedemann often cited it in his *Account* (1540). Although neither used it for the purpose, it was IV Esdras 7:32 which served other Anabaptists as a proof text for psychopannychism. Marpeck four times cited *The Testament of the Twelve Patriarchs.* The Amish Mennonites to this day use Tobit as the basis of the marriage sermon.[5]

As for the writings of the New Covenant, it is of interest that the Radicals readily ranged alongside them as of virtually equivalent testimony other documents that they had reason to believe were comparably ancient and apostolic.

[5] John Umble, "An Amish Minister's Manual," *MQR,* XV (1941), 95–117.

The whole of the Radical Reformation, for example, tacitly or programmatically put the creeds of Athanasius and Nicaea to the test of the simpler creed which they confidently ascribed to the twelve apostles. Many of the most valuable and systematic theological tracts of the Anabaptists from Rattenberg to Raków were, in fact, commentaries on the twelve articles of the Apostles' Creed.

Radical restitutionists that they were, the Anabaptists felt that all the early documents preserved by Eusebius in his *Ecclesiastical History,* and particularly the fragments of Hegesippus, were grist for their mill. There can be no doubt but that what Eusebius wrote in dependence upon Philo and Josephus about the Therapeutae and the Essenes served as a sanction and as a model for the communal organization of sectarian Christianity, particularly among the Hutterites. Also, what Eusebius wrote,[6] in dependence on the early Apologists, about the men of righteousness from Abraham back to Adam as Christians, exercised an abiding influence on the whole of the Radical Reformation in reinforcing its paradisic, restitutionist, and universalistic impulses from Renato to Riedemann, from Schwenckfeld to Socinus. The pseudo-Clementine, pseudo-Isidorian IV Epistle of Clement was thought of as an authentic letter of Clement of Rome to James in Jerusalem and as such furnished a supplement to Acts for Münsterite and Hutterite communism (Ch. 16.3). Polderman is known to have brought a copy of the Shepherd of Hermas to Hofmann imprisoned in Strassburg (Ch. 10.4). The prominence of the Gospel of Nicodemus (The Acts of Pilate) in the Radical Reformation, as also earlier among the Lollards, is due to the fact that it stressed the literal descent of Christ into hell, thereby supplementing the corresponding article in the Apostles' Creed. The Apocryphal gospel was cited, for example by Marpeck, who was concerned to oppose the tendency of Bucer and others in the Magisterial Reformation to allegorize at this point (Ch. 32.2.c).

It will not be forgotten that many of the letters, prophecies, martyr acts, hymns, and histories produced by the Radical Reformation were written in a style imitative of the corresponding apostolic documents. One thinks here, for example, of the epistles of Hutter, the published prophecies of Leonard and Ursula Jost, *The Martyrs' Mirror,* Braitmichel's *Chronicle,* and the *Ausbund.* These neoapostolic writings were preserved, copied, distributed, and employed at worship much as were the canonical writings.

Many an Anabaptist theological tract was really a beautiful

[6] Eusebius, *Ecclesiastical History,* I, iv, 6.

mosaic of Scriptural texts, an original work only in the exquisite craftsmanship exhibited in the laying and pointing. In expediting this kind of work and in all their exegetical activity, the Anabaptists were given to building up concordances, of which the *Testamentserläuterung* (Ch. 31.1) was the most ambitious.[7]

We turn now from concordances, canons, and translations to the problem of holy words, the Word, and the Holy Spirit.

b. Word and Spirit. A whole complex of Biblical and theological problems is suggested by the contrast between Word and Spirit.[8] The outer word can range in meaning all the way from the written words of the Bible in vernacular translation, through the audible and tangible word of salvation in the sermons and the sacraments of the established churches or the radical conventicles, to the incarnate Word, which was, of course, the historic Christ. The inner Word can likewise range in meaning, all the way from the inner abyss of self (*Abgrund*), superficially identifiable with conscience, then the coherent principle of Scripture ("that which drives Christ into one"), to that eternal Word which is consubstantial with the Godhead of the Father.

In the controversies between the Radicals and the exponents of classical Protestantism the uniqueness of the incarnate was almost never directly under discussion. The controverted question of the two natures belongs in any event to the chapter on Christology (Ch. 11.3). Under discussion and at issue were (*a*) the relationship between the historic Jesus Christ, including his recorded words, and the inner Word either as the illumination of conscience or as made present by faith or by mystical exaltation, and (*b*) the relationship between all the words of Scripture, collectively the Bible, and the eternal, consubstantial Word, active in creation and revelation, and hence perceived at least darkly by men of the Old Covenant and of enlightened paganism before the incarnation. The theological and epistemological problems involved in these two relationships led naturally to a third and a fourth issue: (*c*) the relationship between the role of the consubstantial Word and the Holy Spirit in the inspiration of Scripture, and (*d*) the relationship of these two Persons of the Trinity to the inner Word and/or to the inner spirit of man, as also to the objective, verifiable experience of an external

---

[7] For a preliminary survey of the concordances, see the long excursus by Friedmann, "Dogmatische Hauptschrift," *loc. cit.*

[8] See, for example, Wilhelm Wiswedel, "Zum Problem: inneres und äusseres Wort bei den Täufern," *ARG*, XLVI (1955), 1–19; Gordon Rupp, "Word and Spirit in the First Years of the Reformation," *ARG*, XLIX (1958), 13–26.

spirit, for example in justification, religious exaltation, and corporate inspiration.

We are well reminded at this point that these four aspects of the problematic Word and Spirit were under discussion not only between the Radical Reformation and normative Protestantism but also and very intensely within the Radical Reformation itself. For, to the strong rationalist current in one sector of the Radical Reformation and to the strong ingredient of medieval mysticism in the other two sectors, there was added that multiform and pervasive spiritualism which was at once the reflection and the interpretation of the widespread pentecostal or revivalistic and charismatic experience of the new, largely popular, conventicular forms of Christianity. This unencumbered spiritualism, separated from the wise restraints of the sacramental life and traditional usages of the variously reformed but always established parishes, was often eccentric and fantastic. But these vagaries should not obscure from view the fact that a large element in the spiritualism of the Radical Reformation goes back to Luther himself and, to a lesser extent, Zwingli.[9]

Luther, however, always guarded his position. Solafideist that he was by origin and proclamation, he fully recognized the power of the inward and the spiritual; but he insisted that God always deals with man in a twofold manner: "The inward comes after and through the outward, and it is God's will to give nobody the inward without the outward signs which he has instituted," such as the sacraments and preaching.[10] It was Luther's frequent observation that our Spiritualists and the spiritualist Anabaptists, many of whom expressly appealed to Luther as their source and inspiration, had in fact taken the inner, the invisible, and the spiritual out of the context of Scripture, Christian solidarity, and sacrament and were, in fact, "carnal," by which Luther meant subjective. He was grossly picturesque when he complained that the Spiritualist talks facilely about *"Geist, Geist, Geist"* and then "kicks away the very bridge by which the Holy Spirit can come . . . namely, the outward ordinances of God like the bodily sign of baptism and the preached Word of God."[11] The Spiritualists whom Luther most vigorously opposed were, of course, Carlstadt, Müntzer, and then Schwenckfeld.

Carlstadt's Spiritualism was a compound of elements derived from Luther himself, reinforced by the predestinarianism and symbolism of Augustine and the *Gelassenheit* of the Rhenish

[9] See Karl Steck, *Luther und die Schwärmer* (Zurich, 1955).
[10] Quoted by Rupp, *loc. cit.,* 25.
[11] *WA,* XVIII, 137; pointed out by Rupp, *loc. cit.,* 24.

mystics. Carlstadt, in fact, edited Augustine's *De spiritu et littera*.[12] In another of his already cited works, Carlstadt wrote of the relationship of the Scriptural word and the Spirit in a way just the opposite of that which we have quoted from Luther:

As far as I am concerned, I do not need the outward witness. I want to have the testimony of the Spirit within me, as it was promised by Christ. . . . This is the way it was with the apostles, who were assured inwardly by the testimony of the Spirit, and who afterwards preached Christ outwardly, and reinforced by writings that Christ had to suffer for us.[13]

Some Spiritualists, seeking in addition to the Bible another sanction for their break from the medieval church, found it in a combination of the mysticism[14] of the inner Word and the immediate experience of the Spirit of God taking possession of them as once the prophets of the Old Testament in their oracular exaltation. The revolutionary Spiritualist Thomas Müntzer came in the end to attribute to "the *whole* Scripture" only a propaedeutic utility in "slaying" the believer so that he might awaken to the inner Word and respond to the Spirit: "The Word upon which the faithful hangs is not 100,000 miles from us." Every elect person is the temple of the Holy Spirit. In him is the eternal Word. "The living Word of God," he wrote, "is where the Father bespeaks the Son in the heart of man."[15] Without the Spirit within, one "does not know how to say anything deeply about God, even if he had eaten through a hundred Bibles!"[16]

Less radically than Müntzer, the rational and evangelical Spiritualists were satisfied to say that the written Word, with all its paradoxes and seeming contradictions, could not be grasped without the Holy Spirit, virtually identical with the inner Word. Fearing that men would be led so to revere the letter of the Bible that they might neglect the living God who gave it, Sebastian Franck, Clement Ziegler, Caspar Schwenckfeld, the Strassburg "Epicurean prelate" Wolfgang Schultheiss, and to a lesser extent such contemplative or spiritualist Anabaptists as John Denck and the Hutterite Ulrich Stadler tended to consider Scripture as witness to faith or as a means of nourishing an already formed faith.

[12] E. Köhler, *Karlstadt und Augustin* (Halle, 1952).
[13] *Vom greulichen Missbrauch des heiligen Abendmahls;* Walch, *Luthers Werke*, XX, 2893; mentioned by Rupp, *loc. cit.*, 20.
[14] A major source was, of course, the *Theologia Germanica*, popularized by Luther himself. See Albert Auer, *Leidenstheologie im späten Mittelalter* (St. Ottilien, 1952).
[15] Böhmer and Kirn, *Briefwechsel*, 145.
[16] *SAW*, 58.

The views of a rational Spiritualist, Sebastian Franck, may be summarized here in his own words:

Scripture and [another] person can only give to a person and a believing brother some testimony, but cannot teach what is divine [directly]. However holy they may be, they are nevertheless not teachers, only witnesses and testimony. Faith is not learned out of books nor from a person, however saintly he may be, but rather it is learned and poured in by God in the School of the Lord, that is, under the cross.[17]

Franck, contrasting mere appearance (*Schein*) as the world with ultimate reality (*Sein*) as spirit, holds that faith or the spirit of man expressed as faith, being the interior Word or the divine Christ within, enables the true believer *lovingly* to perceive that deeper meaning which remains concealed to the worldly—including the loveless scribes and orthodox theologians bound to the external or Scriptural word.

The interior Word is the motif which reappears with most constancy in Franck's thought. Actually, the Word and the Holy Spirit within each individual are interchangeable at times, and yet sometimes distinguished. The proper role of the interior Word is to clarify, that of the Holy Spirit to dispose the will. But in effect, the Spirit becomes a mode of the Word. This Word is the divine light within each individual (John 1:9) consubstantial with God. Within this interior or living Word, man finds all that is necessary for his salvation. The literal Word of the Bible and the incarnate Word which was Jesus Christ have no other purpose than to awaken "the seed" of redemption which sleeps within the individual, and to give testimony of the eternal truth which each individual carries about within himself. True faith does not have as its principal object the facts of redemptive history recorded in the Bible. By faith a devout person may encounter this redemptive Word within himself in any land, and at all times, "for God is no respecter of persons."

The evangelical Spiritualist Caspar Schwenckfeld was also, in his way, on guard against elevating the outer Word of Scripture above the living Word (inner Word) that is the Christ within. His position was that the Scriptures "indicate, indeed, who and what the Word of God is but do not pass themselves off for that Word. They always point beyond themselves to Christ, pre-existent and now regnant, who must preach and utter himself into the believing heart through the Holy Spirit, and who

[17] *Ibid.*, 157.

alone is the Word, Power, and Wisdom of God."[18] According to
Schwenckfeld, the Bible is understood Christocentrically. Its
meaning is revealed by the inner Word as witness to the Christian
faith in the historic Word in visible, celestial flesh.[19] With this
spiritualist reservation, Schwenckfeld was glad to suggest that
Scripture answers four needs. It provides man with innumerable
examples of holy life (the patriarchs, prophets, Christ, and the
disciples); secondly, it provides the basis of discipline for those
who are disobedient, erring, or seditious; thirdly, Scriptural
witness to the grace of God permits man to improve what is right
and correct what is wrong; and fourthly, by Scripture man may
be strengthened and educated to live according to Christ's will
and righteousness.

The same spiritualist impulse of the spiritualizers found expression among those who counted themselves Anabaptists and
found themselves, as such, in contrast to the pure Spiritualists,
bound by covenant and discipline to organized conventicular life.
We have already dealt with Denck's constructive view of Scriptural paradox (Ch. 7.1), and seen also how he identified law and
grace as two aspects of the same reality and was thus able to
write: "The lamb and the lion are together the Word of God
. . . which is in our hearts."[20] A spiritualist Anabaptist of the
Denckian type, one Umblauft of Regensburg, may here speak
for him, and others of the same tendency. Concerned alike for
the pious before Moses wrote the Bible and for the illiterate
since, Umblauft said that the Scriptures are the witness and
lamp for an inner Word revealed by God to all. A man can be
saved without preaching and the Scriptures; otherwise, illiterates
or imbeciles could never be saved. God is understood as redeemer,
not through the letter, but through the indwelling Christ. To
the scribes and Pharisees the written Word turned out to be,
not a guide to Christ, but a hindrance. Salvation should be
ascribed alone to the inner Word of God. We encountered a
quite similar view, in the heterodox Lutheran Osiander (Ch. 25.3),
of the redemptive role of Christ in justification. It will be
recalled that this Lutheran antagonist of Denck in Nuremberg
developed in Königsberg a view similar to that of Denck and
Schwenckfeld in the controversy with Stancaro.

Surprisingly, this same kind of hermeneutical Spiritualism can

[18] *CS*, V, 126; translation by Maier, *Schwenckfeld*, 27. See another statement by
Schwenckfeld about the Christ within him (Ch. 10.3.b).
[19] *CS*, XII, 428, 431.
[20] Baring and Fellmann, *Schriften* (*QGT*, VI:2), 95.

be documented among Anabaptists as rigorously conventicular as the Hutterites. Thus, for example, the mystical-spiritualist principle is clearly articulated in so conservative and representative a Hutterite as Ulrich Stadler:

The outward Word is what Christ commanded his apostles to preach when he said [cf. Mark 16:15]: "Preach the gospel of all creatures. . . ." But a properly equipped preacher must have the true Word of God in the abyss (*Abgrund*) of his soul and overcome through much tribulation. . . . The eternal Word is not written either on paper or tables, is not spoken or preached either, only a man is assured of it by himself from God in the soul's abyss; and it is written in his fleshly heart by the finger of God. This difference [between the inner and the outer Word] is suggested by St. John when he writes [I John 2:7]: "Beloved, I am writing you no new commandment, but an old commandment which you had from the beginning. The old commandment is the word which you have heard." That shows that all that one reads in books, or hears, or sees in men or in creation is not the living Word of God but rather a letter or imitative sign or testimony of the inward and eternal or living Word.[21]

Over against such expressions of the Spiritualist legacy on the margins and even, as we have just seen, at the interior of Anabaptism, it was the great task of such sober and resourceful exponents of normative evangelical Anabaptism as Hubmaier, Marpeck, Scharnschlager, Riedemann, Walpot, and Menno Simons to recover and firmly undergird what was in effect the Protestant co-ordination of Word and Spirit. To be sure, in so doing, these main-line Anabaptists still differed from Luther, Zwingli, and Calvin in insisting upon the pre-eminence of the New Covenantal word.

Among the Evangelical Rationalists, Sebastian Castellio and Faustus Socinus were perhaps the most explicit in formulating their view of Scriptures. We have already dealt with Socinus' influential *De sacrae scripturae auctoritate* and his idea that the complexities of the Bible as a whole were, like the parables as defined by Jesus, intended by God to be understood only by the initiated or the elect (Ch. 29.7). We may let Castellio speak here for the Evangelical Rationalist noting simply that he was more moralistic and less literalistic than Socinus.

Castellio's parallel to Luther's criterion that Scripture was "*was Christum treibet*" was the ethical theistic view that Scriptural truth was whatever drove toward human betterment. For Castellio, morality was the sum of Scriptural content, whereas reason was the formal principle, understood as at once the com-

---

[21] Müller, *Glaubenszeugnisse* (*QGT*, III), 212.

mon sense of untutored humanity (over against the ratiocina-
tions of Catholic scholastics and Protestant "scribes") and the
eternal, pre-existent Logos or Wisdom of the literature of the
Old Testament, the Apologists, and the Stoics. Reason, with
its sanctifying intention, was in effect for Castellio one with
Spirit. Interchangeably he assigned them the same attributes
and the same tasks. The Spirit behind Scriptures and the reason
of the interpreter thereof occupied in Castellio's ethical theism
the place of Christ as *opus Dei* in Luther's theology. *Ratio* and
spiritus replaced Luther's *sola fides* and *sola scriptura*.

Somewhat differently from Socinus, Castellio declared that
what could not be understood by reason was unnecessary for
salvation and might be freely discussed and debated. Castellio
replaced objective truth with moral truth: "For truth is to say
what you think, even if you err."[22] For Castellio, morally understood *justitia* was the hermeneutical principle. This justice
grounded, limited, and demarcated all that was essential in
Scripture. He so emphasized the moral sense as the "inner light"
by which the individual judged Scripture that he was prepared
to say that Spirit and reason could together lead one to a knowledge of saving truth even without Scripture. Castellio's view
made truth a moral category dependent on the intention of the
interpreter and represented a divergence from the views of most
Radical Reformers, who were generally more concrete in their
approach.[23]

We may summarize our observations about the Word and
the Spirit in the Radical Reformation in terms of the extremes
to which the impulses inherent in each sector might lead a
particularly bold and articulate exponent. If in general we can
say that the temptation of magisterial Protestantism in this
regard was to define the Scriptural Word and the experienced
Spirit in terms primarily of pure doctrine (the Lutherans) or
of pure doctrine and polity (the Reformed) or of the purified national church under the written Word and with royal headship
of the episcopate (the Anglicans),[24] we may correspondingly characterize the three extremes in the Radical Reformation. It was,
for example, the temptation of the Spiritualists to identify the
Scriptural Word and the inner spirit to the point of experiential

---

[22] *"Nam veritas est, dicere quae sentias, etiamsi erres,"* De calumnia (1613),
425; cited by Heinz Leibing, "Die Frage nach einem hermeneutischen
Prinzip bei Sebastian Castellio," *Autour de Michel Servet*, 214.

[23] *Defensio translationum bibliorum*, 216 f., *De arte dubitandi*, 363; cited by
Leibing, *loc. cit.*, 220.

[24] See the frontispiece of the Cranmer Bible.

subjectivism or Maccabean violence. It was the temptation of the Evangelical Rationalists to impose upon the Scriptural Word the canons of reason and conscience (scruple), converting worship into study, the church into a school of ethics. The great hazard of the Anabaptists was to identify the saving Word of Scripture, valid for them as evangelical Christians, with the words of the New Testament converted into a new law.

c. *Anabaptist Hermeneutical Principles.* For the Radical Reformation, the core of the hermeneutical problem was how to interpret the Old Testament evangelically, because for the most part, unlike the classical Protestants, the Radicals did not accept the Scriptures of the Old Convenant without a radical reconception of their meaning for reborn Christians.

Without going into detail about the appropriation of the Old Testament by normative Protestantism, we can simply say that the Magisterial Reformers rejected on principle the Catholic (Hieronymic) legitimation of several nonliteral senses of Scripture. They approached the Bible as a unity and with a view to interpreting it *literally*. In contrast, the Anabaptists, like the Catholics, sought by several hermeneutical means and dispensational schemes to utilize and yet to distinguish the Old from the New Testament. Spiritualists and Evangelical Rationalists in this respect were closer to the Magisterial Reformers than to the Anabaptists, but these two other kinds of Radicals accomplished much the same effect as the Anabaptists by stressing, as we have noted above, an active principle transcending the limits of the written Word in both a Godward and a manward direction. With Maccabean Müntzer, there had been, of course, no problem— the unitive principle was the Spirit of God common to the Old and the New Testaments taking possession of the reader or of the charismatic leader; for "the will of God is the *whole* over all the parts." With Schwenckfeld the unity was ascribed to the eternal Christ behind his various manifestations and infusions. With Franck the unity stemmed from the eternal Word within every reborn reader and behind the various Scriptures. With spiritualizing Denck, the unitive principle was the inner Word which, with the help of the external Holy Spirit, orders and appropriates the words of Scripture. With Castellio and Socinus it was the Wisdom of God commanding his righteousness from above in progressive disclosures, supplementary, but not contrary, to reason or humane justice.

There is one principle or practice—group study and reverent disputation—common to the entire Radical Reformation which goes far to explain the spirit of the movement as a whole. We have already remarked that the Radicals, especially the Anabaptists, took earnestly the instruction of Jesus in Luke 12:11 about looking to the Holy Spirit to teach them in moments of crisis what to say before the tribunal and inquisitorial ecclesiastics. But this confidence did not restrain them from an intensive study of Scriptures in preparing for the crucial moment! Confidence that the Holy Spirit would infuse their exegetical deliberations and also that the same Spirit would bridge the gulf between themselves and their Protestant opponents accounts for the frequency of the Biblical colloquies or disputations (*Gespräche*) so eagerly attended by the Anabaptists. Confident in the ultimate unity of the true church of Christ, the sectarians long persisted in the hope that the colloquies with the magisterial divines would be eventually consummated by some fresh illumination leading to oneness of mind and heart.[25] Many an Anabaptist disputant or prisoner before a judicial hearing sincerely avowed his willingness to be convinced from Scripture. Hubmaier, with his strong conviction about the church outside of which there could be no salvation, even expressed his willingness to submit to the inspired consensus of an ecumenical council. Doctrinal synods under the Spirit (Acts, ch. 2) or Christ (Matt. 18:20), sanctioned by Calvin, bulked large with Polish and Magyar Radicals who fancied themselves reviving a pre-Constantinian conciliar tradition.

The yearning for Scriptural concord to be found in the inspired solidarity of the questing faithful under the guidance of the Spirit found its most formal expression, not among the Anabaptists, but among such marginal figures as the binitarian John Campanus (Ch. 10.3.g) and the "Epicurean prelate," Wolfgang Schultheiss (Ch. 10.4.a). Both of these spiritualizers appealed to what they thought of as the *lex sedentium (Sitzerrecht)*, based on I Cor. 14:23 ff. and with some support from II Peter 1:19 ff., the right of the whole Christian congregation, the laity with the divines, to judge difficult passages of Scripture together, not individualistically or professionally. The principle of inspired corporate interpretation of the Bible was the presupposition of much of the committed conversation (*Gespräch*) within Anabaptism and between Anabaptism and magisterial Protestantism, but this interesting theological formalization of it was comparatively isolated.

With respect to the New Testament, the Anabaptists, as we have remarked, could be and were literalists. Grebel wrote to Müntzer:

Therefore we beg and admonish thee as a brother by the name, the power, the word, the spirit, and the salvation, which has come to all

[25] John Yoder, *Die Gespräche zwischen Täufern und Reformatoren in der Schweiz, 1523–1538* (Basel, 1960).

Christians through Jesus Christ our Master and Savior, that thou wilt take earnest heed to preach only the divine Word without fear, to set up and guard only divine institutions, to esteem as good and right only what may be found in pure and clear Scripture.[26]

Some Anabaptists were indeed so literal in their use of the New Testament that in St. Gall, for example (Ch. 6.2), in the Netherlands (according to Guy de Brès), and elsewhere, some of them, in strict obedience to Matt. 10:9 ff., wandered about the countryside without weapons, girdle, or money; others, following Matt. 10:27, preached literally from the roof tops; still others, taking Jesus' many references to children as their guide, played, babbled, or whimpered like infants. Sober exegetes, however, such as Hubmaier, Marpeck, and Menno Simons were on their guard against such erratic literalism.

Also in their use of the Old Testament, the Anabaptists were generally not literalistic in their religious appropriation of Scripture except where the plain sense was also consonant with their idea of themselves as the righteous remnant of Israel. For the rest, the Anabaptists, not denying, of course, the literal or historical sense, resorted to a variety of devices to assimilate the otherwise incongruent parts of the Old Testament. Most of these efforts were a continuation or recombination of the traditional Catholic or medieval sectarian resort to allegory, concordance, typology, and the other nonliteral interpretations. The Anabaptists, needless to say, were eclectic, and elements of the several systems of interpretation—Catholic, normative Protestant, Spiritualist, and Rationalist—are to be found in their tracts and sermons alongside their more characteristic efforts.

The Anabaptists were especially given to typology in terms of shadow and light (Schiemer), prophecy and fulfillment, "yesterday" and "today" (Marpeck),[27] and such principles as the Key of David and "the cloven hoof," "moonlight" and "sunlight" (Melchior Hofmann).

It was in order to construe the Old and New Testaments as one that Melchior Hofmann, with the Magisterial Reformers, developed the odd theory that they were one from God, as two clefts constitute the one hoof of a clean cloven-hoofed beast. The term itself derives from Lev. 11:3 and Deut. 14:6. Carrying out the bovine image, Hofmann declared that the interpreter

---

[26] *SAW*, 75.

[27] There are two related, unpublished doctoral dissertations on Anabaptist hermeneutics: William Klassen, "The Hermeneutics of Pilgram Marpeck," Princeton Theological Seminary, 1960; Walter Klassen, "Word, Spirit, and Scripture in Early Anabaptist Thought," Oxford, 1960.

must walk through the Old Testament clearly mindful of the division. All events in the Old Testament are images to which some happenings in the New Testament, or yet to take place, correspond. Everyone must take cognizance of the "cloven hoof" (*gespaltenen clawen; gespauwde klawe*), for all God's words are double or twofold. Hofmann held, however, that only the especially called leaders and prophets might undertake the difficult exegesis: "The cloven claws and horn [only] the true apostolic heralds can bear because [to explicate] the Scripture is not a matter for everybody, to unravel all such involved snarls and cables, to untie such knots, but only for those to whom God has given [the power]."[28] Convinced at length that the Holy Spirit abode within him as with other prophets and prophetesses at Strassburg and elsewhere, Hofmann in opposition to the *lex sedentium* considered himself in his oracular ecstasy authorized to interpret Scripture and to resolve the contradictions involved in the two clefts: "For all words of God are of equal weight, also just and free, to him who acquires the right understanding of God and the Key of David." Hubmaier drew upon the same exegetical theory when he wrote: "He who thus cannot divide judgment on the Scriptures eats of the unclean beasts which divide not the hoof."[29]

The Hofmannite principle was notably in dispute in 1534 at Amsterdam, when Jacob van Campen, who had taken over Hofmann's typological hermeneutics, came into conflict with Obbe Philips and John Scheerder. Obbe, a follower of Hofmann in other respects, was unable to accept the idea that there was a double meaning to the Old Testament. He argued quaintly that the writings of the two Testaments stand upon "one hoof" and are not to be fancifully allegorized. Obbe's objections cast doubt on the way the belligerent Hofmannites at Münster were using the prophet's principle to justify the Maccabean violence; and this colloquy over the cloven hoof led the moderate Münsterite Jacob van Campen to refuse to participate in the abortive attempt at sympathetic revolt in Amsterdam (Ch. 12.3). Hofmannite hermeneutics had triumphed at Münster, but not all who took over the principle of the "cloven hoof" were revolutionaries. Dietrich Philips, for example, made it a part of his teaching. For Dietrich, the "hiddenness" of the gospel, stressed by Hofmann, was a hiddenness restricted to the Old Testament, which, with the help of the Spirit, could be harmonized with the New.

[28] See *SAW*, 202 f. and n. 42.
[29] *SAW*, 115.

To sum up, the Anabaptists continually distinguished between the covenant of servitude and that of sonship. Above all concerned to give Christ the honor due to him alone, they for the greater part did not care to stress the Old Testament except where it accorded literally or by nonliteral interpretation with the New, justifying the division by the formula of Christ himself in Matt., ch. 5, "You have heard that it was said to the men of old, . . . But I say to you," and by the claim made for the superiority of the Christian dispensation over the Mosaic in the epistle to the Hebrews. In their insistence upon the superiority of the New Testament and the New Covenant over the Old Testament and its law the Anabaptists even within the New Testament often seemed to have predilections—some for the Synoptic Gospels; others, such as Marpeck, for John's Gospel and Paul's letters; others for the Johannine Gospel, epistles, and Revelation (which they took, of course, to be from the same writer).[30] In any event, the Anabaptists were all earnestly sectarian as were the primitive Christians in distinguishing themselves as the children of light from the children of darkness. At the same time, the Anabaptists scarcely less than the Spiritualists and the Evangelical Rationalists had in their theological systems universalist or ecumenical ingredients. We turn, then, to our second topic, the ecumenical or ethically universalistic thrust of the Radical Reformation.

2. SECTARIAN ECUMENICITY

The Radicals, for the most part distinguishing sharply between the Old and the New Covenants, also considered themselves a righteous remnant separated from Christendom at large. By the end of our period they had come to think of the schism between magisterial Protestantism and papal Catholicism (confirmed by the Council of Trent, 1563) as roughly comparable to the ancient division between Judah and Israel, later between Judea and Samaria. Both forms of territorial or churchly Christianity were, from the point of view of the sectarians, still living under one version or another of "the law," while they, in their innumerable conventicles and factions, were severally laying claim to being the righteous remnant living by the covenant written on the heart. The evangelical Radicals consequently considered Catho-

---

[30] Robert Friedmann has suggested a left-wing typology based precisely upon these predilections, "Conception of the Anabaptists," *CH,* IX (1940), 341–365.

lics and Protestants, no less than Jews, Turks, and pagans, as the objective of their divinely sanctioned, neoapostolic mission. This, of course, is the all too familiar sectarian side of our narrative. But here is the place to point out also that in thus putting unregenerate Protestants and Catholics on the level of adherents of the Old Covenant and of the infidels, the Radicals were not only reconceiving the church but also the world beyond the confines of Christendom; and by implication they were enhancing the status of infidels relative to the beneficiaries of cultural Christianity.

Denying the parity of the two Testaments and the unity of the Old and the New Covenantal people, which was implied in the Protestant stress on election, and the equation of circumcision and baptism, the Radicals not only challenged the reorganization of a gospel church by magistrates under "the law," but also went on to challenge some of the doctrines which they felt were holdovers of a superseded conception of the validity of the law. The Radicals felt instinctively, if not always articulately, the palpable evasion of the consequences of the newness or rebirth in Christ on the part of the Magisterial Reformers when the latter were at theological pains to sustain in dialectical tension the law and the gospel, justice and love, justification and sanctification, state and church. Severing, or in their own way identifying, these pairs of opposites, the Radicals were on the move away from such doctrinal correlates or supports of the law-grace tension as the doctrine of predestination, the Anselmian view of the atonement, and the Nicene doctrine of the Trinity in so far as the last was regarded as a formula for projecting into the Godhead the sanction for the alleged unity of justice and love.

Separated from the territorial churches and on principle repudiating the whole conception of God's renewed people being controlled by magistrates however benevolent, the radical sectarians fanned out in utter disregard of territorial boundaries and local laws, emissaries and exemplars that they were of a gospel at once new and old, to be shared by the whole world. With imaginations excited by the vistas opened before them in Bible study, from apocalyptic rumor, and through wide travel, the Radicals pondered what might be the providential and redemptive significance of the persistence of the Jews, the military successes of the Turks, and the opening up of whole continents of aborigines who had never heard either of Adam and his fall or of the Second Adam and a provisional redemption.

We shall bring together the vaguely ecumenical catholic, universalistic, along with the intensely missionary, impulses in the Radical Reformation, under five headings.

   a. Pagans, Jews, and Mohammedans in the Perspective of the Radical Reformation. A universalistic and ecumenical note in the Radical Reformation was the eschatological interpretation of the destiny of the Jews, the prophetic interpretation of the current military successes of the Turks, and the ambivalent primitivist-missionary interpretation of the aboriginal pagans. Generally speaking, there were three ways of looking upon these three main non-Christian groups.

   As to the relationship with Jews, the Radicals displayed a considerable range of attitude from the gross anti-Semitism of Balthasar Hubmaier (before his avowal of Anabaptism, Ch. 4.2.a), to the interfaith ecumenicity of Jacob Palaeologus (Ch. 29.4) with his vision of a Jewish, a Turkish, and a Gentile church.

   As for the antipathy for the Jewish community of which there are traces, particularly in Anabaptism, it was in part a legacy of the social aspiration of the Peasants' War, an expression of the radical protest against tithes and usury, and in part a theological correlate of the greater sense of spiritual distance from the claims of the Old Testament than was true of the proponents of classical Protestantism. The latter, of course, were as much concerned to recover the exact meaning of the Hebrew as of the Greek text of the Bible, whereas in general the Radicals were concerned with the vernacular versions.

   If, however, the Protestant Reformation represented an acute Judaizing of Christianity, especially in the Reformed tradition (cf. the observation of Valentine Crautwald, Ch. 15.3), the same could also be said in a different sense for the Radical Reformation. It was the difference, in effect, of their Judaizing on the model of the suffering remnant. Moreover, by distinguishing sharply between the covenant of the law and the covenant of the gospel, the Radicals escaped the legalism of the Old only to become in many cases more tightly bound by a legalism based on the New. The self-identification of the radical sectarians with the suffering righteous remnant in Israel facilitated this transmutation of the gospel into law. The radical sectarians were therefore commonly charged by the classical Protestant divines not only with prolonging medieval Catholicism in the form of married "monkery" but also of being Judaizers and losing the benefits of salvation by faith.

   Besides the unconscious "Judaizing" of sectarian legalism, there were, of course, in the Radical Reformation many programmatic attempts to reproduce in Christian form various aspects of the life and thought of the chosen people. At this point in our narrative it will suffice to recall and group together these attempts. There were the Pentateuchalists in Strassburg (Ch. 10.2). There were the anti-Trinitarian, anabaptist Sabbatarians inspired by Oswald Glait and Andrew Fischer in Silesia (Ch. 15) and in Moravia (Ch. 26.2). Even the restorationist gaze, which ordinarily fixed upon the primitive church or Paradise as the ideal, in Münster concentrated on Davidic, Solomonic, and Maccabean Israel. There was the patriarchalism of the Hutterites, the apocalyptic messianism of two sorts represented by Augustine Bader and Melchior Hofmann, and the Maccabean Spiritualism of Thomas Müntzer based on Daniel more than upon Revelation. There was the predilection for the Old Testament on the part of such nonadorant ethical theists as Simon Budny and the *semi-Judaeus* Matthew Vehe (Glirius) of Heidelberg and Kolozsvár, of Unitarian John Sommer and his father-in-law Francis Dávid. These four divines and teachers found enhanced significance in the Old Testament, in contrast to most Anabaptists and Rationalists, considering it in no important way superseded by the New Testament, which they of course construed in a psychopannychist and Ebionite sense.

As for the Moslems, the Radical Reformers regarded them variously and sometimes interchangeably as (1) the instrument of God's wrath (Hofmann); as (2) the instrument of his redemption, Suleiman being the new Cyrus (Hut); as (3) the objective (along with the Jews) of their missionary proclamation in the Latter Days (Ziegler, Bader, John Baptista Italus, Servetus); as (4) already constitutive of an interfaith church of spiritual Semites (Palaeologus, Budny, Neuser); and as (5), along with Jews and righteous pagans, already a part of the *Ecclesia spiritualis* in so far as they conformed to the inner Word (Franck, Castellio, Coornhert, and, with reserve, Denck). Whatever the stress, whether tutelary chastisement or missionary conversion or interfaith concord, the Radical Reformation as a whole differed from the Magisterial Reformation in breaking away from the territorial or political aspects of the Moslem challenge in an effort to make a religious or specifically theological adjustment to the new world-situation characterized by the Turkish military advances on Christendom.

As for the third group, the pagans, only the Catholics, recovering from the onslaughts of Protestantism in their Counter Reformation, actually sought them out for conversion; but the Radicals, even though not strategically located or equipped to carry out a world mission, were, far more than the Magisterial Reformers, concerned for the salvation of pagans near and far. In various theological adjustments they had taken account, not only of the pagan races beyond Islam in dark Africa, India, Cathay, and the Americas, but also of the pagans who lived before the accomplishment of Christ's redeeming work. The concern of the Radicals for the latter found notable expression in their efforts to safeguard the literal descent of Christ *ad inferos* (Ch. 32.2.c).

There were two other medieval impulses, surviving among some of the Radical Reformers and here and there already noted in the course of our narrative, which notably contributed to the enlargement of their vision. These were the "gospel of all creatures" and the idea of the true believers everywhere as the Friends of God.[31] Although quite disparate in origin (despite their being in part mediated by the same late medieval mystical circles), these two impulses had the effect of encouraging the Radicals to perceive the revelation and the call of God beyond and prior to the Bible and to Christendom. It is well known that the Friends of God of the Upper Rhine brought together Biblical, classical, patristic, and mystical traditions concerning the universal company of all those who by obedience, by faith, by love, by sacrifice, by martyrdom, or by knowledge through faith had come into a special relationship with God, such as, notably, Abraham, the friend of God by faith with a covenant written upon the heart (James 2:23; Isa. 41:8) and the other ancient worthies before Abraham back to Adam who were as *christi* (Ps. 105:15), "Christians before they were Jews," "few in number, wandering from nation to nation." In John 15:14, the Friends of God were they who in Christ had passed from bondage to friendship. The classical philosophical ideal of the sharing of goods among friends became tributary to this evolving concept of divine friendship, while Clement of Rome, Justin Martyr, Irenaeus, among others, and notably Eusebius of Caesarea found in Abraham's faith before his circumcision the basis for their attempt to descry the outlines of the ongoing company of the companions of the eternal Christ the Word. By various channels, for example among the followers of Francis of Assisi, *verus amicus*

---

[31] For these two themes, see Erik Peterson, "Der Gottesfreund: Beiträge zur Geschichte eines religiösen Terminus," *ZKG*, XLII (1923), 161–202, and Gordon Rupp, "Thomas Müntzer, Hans Huth, and the 'Gospel of All Creatures,'" *Bulletin of the John Rylands Library*, XLIII (1960/1961), 492–519. In the latter, Rupp advances reasons why *Vom Geheimnis der Taufe,* ascribed in Ch. 7.4 to Hut, may have been the reworking of a late work of Müntzer.

Christi, this potentially universalistic concept reached that company of Upper Rhenish *Gottesfreunde* around Rulman Merswin.

Revolutionary Spiritualists like Müntzer who stressed the suffering of the "elect friends of God," rational Spiritualists like Franck who stressed the inner Word common to all mankind, contemplative Anabaptists like Denck who stressed regeneration in Christ, and evangelical Spiritualists like Schwenckfeld who stressed the regenerative visitation and spiritual sustenance of the eternal Christ—all of them were drawing upon the ancient tradition of the Friends of God, which encouraged them to seek that choice company drawn out of many nations, the spiritual predecessors and heirs of Abraham. Schwenckfeld, for example, was drawing on Eusebius and the *Gottesfreunde,* when in his *Judicium* (1542), seeking to counter the sharp dispensationalism of Marpeck, he declared: "Thus did the Church of Christ begin soon after the creation of the world (though in a hidden manner) . . . and Adam, Abel, Enoch, Noah, and all the elect faithful fathers were members of the Church and were Christians; for the Church of Christ is much older than that of the Jews . . . ; Abraham was faithful and righteous, which is to say that he was a Christian before he was circumcised." Therefore, continues Schwenckfeld, all "the holy fathers . . . and patriarchs were Christians and the children of God and the Friends of God."

Related, yet distinct from the idea of divine friendship before and, by implication apart from, the visible covenants, by reason of the action of the eternal Christ, the same yesterday, today, and tomorrow (Schwenckfeld, Clement Ziegler, Franck) was the conception of the Book of Nature as the primer of all believers, open to all perceptive souls whether within or without Christendom.

This "gospel of all creatures" as propounded by some of the Radicals, notably Müntzer, Denck, Entfelder (Ch. 11.2), Servetus (Ch. 23.4), Hut, Schiemer, Schlaffer, and Spittelmaier (Ch. 7.3 and 4), Franck, Marpeck, and Stadler (Ch. 32.1.b) took the *whole* of creation or nature as filled with divine emblems, instructing man as to the universality, the solidarity in, and the purposefulness of suffering, the whole of creation groaning in travail. As the baker kneads the dough, as the wheelwright bends his staves, as the butcher dresses an animal all for the service of man, so God kneads, bends, and breaks man by the law and reshapes him by grace for the still higher service of God. Some radical preachers even sought to teach the common man directly from the scrutiny of natural things about him, appealing to the example of the homely parables of Jesus.

The Biblical basis of their "gospel of all creatures" was not only the already noted Mark 16:15, "the gospel *aller Kreatur*" (the Greek dative construed in German as genitive) but also an equally strained Col. 1:23 and, on much surer grounds, Rom. 1:20 on the visibility of the invisible God in his creation. The "gospel of all creatures" in the special sense of the propaedeutic message of universally suffering creation came to the Radicals by way of the mystics and especially by way of the *Liber naturae sive creaturarum*, written originally in Spanish by the Catalan Franciscan Raymond of Sebonde, professor at the University of Toulouse. Latin versions of this work were entitled simply *Theologia naturalis*, reprinted several times, for example, at Deventer in 1484, at Strassburg in 1496, at Nuremberg in 1502, and at Paris in 1509. It was, at the end of our period, translated into French by Michel de Montaigne in 1569. The Radicals, much more somber than the French essayist or the Franciscan natural theologian, chose to stress in the Book of Nature the lesson of suffering. It will be recalled, for example, that Müntzer, who had in his voracious reading read not only Tauler and Suso and other mystical and visionary authors but also the Koran, elaborated a three-grade progression in the school of Christ. The beginning (*Ankunft*) of faith was for him the perception of God's Word in creation and in Scripture as a whole with its continuous lesson, not of purgative but of propaedeutic suffering, culminating in the experience of the "bitter Christ," in nature as on Calvary. This apprehension of the solidarity and purposefulness of suffering in all creation led on through the motion (*Bewegung*) of the Spirit through temptation (*Anfechtung*) to genuine faith (contrasted with Luther's allegedly verbal or forensic or "scribal" or "fatuous" faith) and on to a life of redemptive tribulation *in the name and for the sake of Christ.* Müntzer's Anabaptist successors, such as Denck and Hut, interposed between this genuine faith and the life of suffering the act of believers' baptism as the covenantal transaction of a personal and corporate pledge of commitment to the way of tribulation. It is not, however, to rehearse the meaning of baptismal theology that we recall this theology of martyrdom at this juncture but, rather, to suggest in this gospel of the universality of suffering that many of the Radicals were aware of the common bond that connected them with all creation and with all mankind. Thus Müntzer could write: "I preach such a Christian faith as does not agree with that of Luther, but which is in conformity with the hearts of the elect in all the world. And even though he were born a Turk, a man might yet have the *Ankunft* of this same faith, that is, the *Bewegung* of the Holy Spirit, as it is written of Cornelius (Acts, ch. 10)."

b. The Belief that Christ Died for the Salvation of All Mankind. Most of the Radical Reformation broke away from the Protestant pattern in a universalistic direction in abandoning or revising the doctrine of predestination and in holding that the work of Christ, in taking from mankind the burden of Adam's guilt, made possible the recovery, for all men everywhere, of that freedom of the will which Adam lost in Paradise.

In the first place, all Anabaptists maintained that God fulfilled his promise to Abraham that in his seed all the nations of the earth would be blessed by effectuating in Christ, of the lineage of David and the seed of Abraham, the removal of the sins of the whole world. The whole of Anabaptist soteriology presupposed the forensic atonement of all mankind through the work of Christ on Calvary, something different from the forensic justification of the individual believer, as in Lutheranism: hence the refusal of the Anabaptists to impose a purificatory baptism on new-born infants, already cleared of Adamic sin by the will of God and the deed of Christ. As recently as the last chapter we came upon Anabaptists arguing for Christ's expiatory removal for all mankind of original guilt, even if they acknowledged the persistence of a sinful proclivity, as for example, Marpeck in his debate with Schwenckfeld (Ch. 18.5) and Walpot in his *Büchlein* against Melanchthon (Ch. 31.2).

The universalist note among Anabaptists, it should be recalled, was most clearly struck by Melchior Hofmann after he had broken away from Luther's conception of the bondage of the will of fallen man. Hofmann confidently asserted that Christ, the Second Adam, had restored to all men everywhere the freedom of the will lost by the first Adam. Basing his thought on John 8:36, "So if the Son makes you free, you will be free indeed," Hofmann wrote:

The noble and high testimony of God is this: that God is no respecter of persons . . . and has brought him [every man] true enlightenment and knowledge, and has placed his will again in his own hands so that it came to pass that from then on [the advent of Christ, the Second Adam] man became a truly free creature, . . . that he from this time on might be prepared to have his own choice or election whether he would now taste of good or evil, whether he would choose life or death, whether he would walk in the way of God or remain the property of Satan.[32]

The Anabaptists, like Hofmann in their appeal to the univer-

[32] *BRN,* V, 188, 194; noted and evaluated by Beachy, *op. cit.,* 125.

sality of Christ's redemptive action, like the Spiritualists and the Evangelical Rationalists in their appeal to the universal scope of the inner Word and of the Spirit which bloweth where it listeth, had a vision of the universal scope of God's benignity. Schiemer, it will be recalled (Ch. 7.5), considered Luther wrong in applying the above-cited text, John 1:9, to those alone who knew and responded to the gospel of the incarnate Word: for Christ, the eternal Word, he said, illumines all men everywhere, whether or no they acknowledge Christ personally. Menno Simons and Dietrich Philips were also confident as to the theoretical extension of the work of Christ to the infants of Jews and Turks, even though there was no explicit Scriptural text.

   c. *The Doctrine of Christ's Redemptive Descent Into Hades.* We have already anticipated another expression of the ecumenical or "catholic" urge in the Radical Reformation, in time no less than in space: the doctrine of Christ's redemptive descent into Hades. Common to all the Radical Reformers was a great interest in safeguarding the literal sense of Christ's descent into Hades to redeem the worthies of the Old Covenant and, by implication, in some instances at least, the good pagans.

   To understand the significance of this stress, we must have before us the conception of hell in late medieval Christendom. Actually there were two locations, the hell of the demons in the zone of the fiery atmosphere above and the hell of the nether world in which Satan and these fiery demons exercised their rule over the departed dead as over prisoners. This subterranean hell was itself divided into four parts: the hell proper of the damned, the *limbus patrum* for the pre-Christian worthies, the *limbus infantium* for unbaptized but otherwise innocent children, and purgatory.

   Medieval popular piety, scholastic theology, and Rhenish (Eckhardtian) mysticism differed as to the manner in which Christ descended into hell (whether or not only as a soul separated from his mortal body), and as to the extent, purpose, and effect of his penetration. The detailed differences of opinion need not detain us. Suffice it to say that alongside the literal interpretation of normative scholasticism and of popular piety, there was the mystical view that both heaven and hell were but spatial metaphors for the proximity or absence of the divine, and hence that the *descensus* of the Apostles' Creed was but an intensification and amplification of the reference to Christ's suffering under Pontius Pilate to include the spiritual anguish of his sense of being utterly forsaken by God his Father.

With minor differences the classical Protestant theologians Luther, Melanchthon, Bucer, and Calvin accepted the *descensus* in the tradition of the mystics as a spiritual *resignatio ad infernum (ad inferos)*.[33] In contrast, representatives of all three of the main typological sectors of the Radical Reformation vigorously argued for the literal descent of Christ to the nether world in their manifest concern to safeguard the conviction that Christ in the fullness of time saved all who had lived by faith in anticipation of his advent, just as he, aboveground, saved from the consequences of Adam's defection all of mankind, coeval with and subsequent to his atoning act on Calvary. *Descensus* and *crucifixio* were for the Radicals correlative redemptive terms.

The Spiritualist Valentine Crautwald opposed Bucer's view that Hades meant simply the grave.[34] Schwenckfeld wrote frequently on the subject, though in view of his conception of "Christians before Christ," the article was more traditional than essential to his system, unless by chance he intended to preserve the literal descent not primarily for the Old Testament worthies, who had, according to him, been regularly sustained by the eternal and celestial flesh of Christ (manna), but for the sake of the righteous pagans. Servetus implied that Christ descended into hell for the sake of baptizing the worthies into salvation and suggested a second *descensus* at the second advent for the sake of baptizing the unimmersed (Ch. 11.1). Castellio defended the literal *descensus* against Calvin's interpretation of it as the equivalent of anguish.

To be sure, Hut, Schiemer, Schlaffer (Ch. 7.5), and Marpeck also knew and used Meister Eckhardt's language and likened the suffering of the true follower of Christ to descent in the sense of the anguish of dereliction. Marpeck, for example, in his manuscript tract *Von der Tiefe Christi* (1547)[35] likened baptism to the *descensus Christi:* "Whoever finds not Christ in the deep [of baptism] will not find him on high in joy and glory forevermore." But Marpeck from the very beginning also insisted on the literal *descensus,* maintaining that Christ preached the gospel of forgiveness in hell.[36]

---

[33] Erich Vogelsang, "Weltbild und Kreuzestheologie in den Höllenfahrtsstreitigkeiten der Reformationszeit," *ARG*, XXXVIII (1941), 90–132.

[34] Letter of 29 June 1528; Krebs and Rott, *Elsass,* I (*QGT,* VII), No. 141, p. 171; No. 144, p. 175.

[35] *Kunstbuch* (see n. 37), 278a–301a.

[36] "Pilgram Marpeck's Confession of Faith," edited by John C. Wenger, *MQR* XII (1938), 167–202; Krebs and Rott, *Elsass,* I (*QGT,* VII), No. 302.

In the course of the controversy with Marpeck beginning in 1542, Schwenckfeld expressed the view that Christ descended into Hades as *triumphator,* preaching and perhaps in some mystical way sharing his celestial flesh Eucharistically (cf. Rupert of Deutz, Ch. 2.1). He accused Marpeck of teaching that Christ's redemptive suffering on the cross had not been complete until he also descended into hell to be tortured by Satan and thereafter made High Priest.[37] Schwenckfeld here made a useful theological observation to the discredit of neither the one nor the other antagonist. There were, in fact, in Marpeck's soteriology two works of Christ. Though never expressly stated, it would appear that Christ suffered on the cross for the sins of all mankind who were to come after him, and *suffered* at the hands of Satan in hell for the sins of all who had died before his advent.

d. The Doctrine of Election to Salvation. Ordinarily the doctrine of predestination represents a restriction rather than an extension of the scope of salvation. Yet in that sector of the Radical Reformation which welcomed the Protestant emphasis on predestination, the doctrine was turned in a potentially universalistic sense.

The doctrine of predestination was, of course, the very core of the theological systems of Lutheranism and Calvinism. It was for the classical Protestant Reformers co-ordinate with the doctrine of salvation by faith alone. The two doctrines of predestination and solafideism constituted respectively the Godward and the manward side of the same fundamental spiritual reality at the base of the Protestant revolt against every expression of the idea of human merit in the joyful proclamation of the experience and the theology of the wholly unmerited grace of God. Classical Protestantism not only opposed the gross forms of works righteousness like the indulgence system. It was also sensitized against the importation of the slightest trace of meritoriousness, as for example, any attempt to make sanctification a visible demonstration of salvation. Hence the common charge of the Protestant Reformers hurled against the "new monkery" of the Radicals.

Yet in lands destined to remain Catholic and notably among the spiritualist Rationalists of Italy the severe Protestant doctrine

---

[37] Letter of 24 March 1549; *CS,* XII, 797–803. Johann Loserth says that Marpeck never taught such a thing, whereas Heinold Fast says that Schwenckfeld simply exaggerates. "Ein neuer Handschriftenfund [the *Kunstbuch*]," 215, n. 100.

of predestination was picked up and propounded with a sense of liberating joy. This is the place to remind ourselves of Camillo Renato and those who, though dependent on him, took their name from another Italian, Faustus Socinus. Renato (Ch. 22.1) in his doctrine of predestination went far beyond Paul, Augustine, and Calvin in completely dissociating election from membership in the true visible church of the saints so long, as the reborn separated himself from the Old Covenantal church of the Jews and its counterpart, the oppressively sacramental church of Antichrist. For Renato, predestination was a liberating doctrine in respect to the Catholic Church, without involving the believer in further ecclesiastical commitments. For Renato and after him Socinus, the church of Christ's elect was present wherever virtue, defined as human love or concern for one's fellow men, was manifest. Thus predestination to salvation was for the Evangelical Rationalist confirmed in humaneness. As for other Italian Spiritualists, such as Johannes Baptista Italus, who visited Strassburg (Ch. 10.3.a), the church of the predestined could embrace also good pagans, Turks, and Jews.

Closely related to the universalistic reworking of the Biblical texts on predestination was the postulation of an invisible church known only to God and embracing many who know not the name of Christ. Like other Spiritualist excesses, it could claim descent from the thought of the young Luther. Although this doctrine of the invisible church appears in two forms, the church of the hidden elect and the church of humanity in all its diversity, it was in either case inclusivistic in its intention and spirit. Though most commonly formulated by such Spiritualists as Schwenckfeld, Ziegler (Ch. 10.2), Franck (Ch. 18.3), Coornhert (Ch. 30.2), Postel (Ch. 21.4), and by such spokesmen of interfaith toleration in Poland and Transylvania as Palaeologus and Budny (Ch. 29.4), it was also formulated by such spiritualizing Anabaptists as Bünderlin, Entfelder (Ch. 10:3), and Jacob Kautz.[38]

A recurrent feature of this kind of thinking, for example in the spiritualist Anabaptist Denck, the Spiritualist Ziegler, the messianic Anabaptist Bader, and the Libertine Pocquet (Ch. 12.2), was the appeal to the New Testament *apokatastasis* or *restitutio omnium* (Acts 3:21) in arguing for the possibility of the eventual redemption even of the demons. Ziegler expressly cited Origen in support of his conviction that pagans and devils,

---

[38] There is a good deal about Kautz's conception of the invisible Church in Bucer's refutation of him, Krebs and Rott, *Elsass*, I (*QGT*, VII), No. 171.

even without their knowledge of the earthly work of Christ, would be saved before the Last Judgment.[39]

For the most part, the spiritualism and the rationalism in the Radical Reformation actually undercut the last of our "ecumenical" thrusts, the missionary impulse. But what the Spiritualists and the spiritualizing Rationalists partly or wholly lacked, the Anabaptists displayed in redoubled intensity.

   e. The Missionary Impulse of the Radical Reformation.[40] Magisterial Protestantism was concerned with the reformation of Christendom along civic, territorial, and national lines—to be sure, as a second-best to the unitive reformation of the whole of Christendom in head and members. Magisterial Protestantism acknowledged, so to speak, the prophetic function of criticism of the medieval church, but it found no place formally in its theory of polity or the ministry for the prophet and no place whatsoever for the apostle. In contrast, the proponents of the Radical Reformation, in a sectarian identification of the whole of territorial Christianity—Protestant scarcely less than Catholic —as anti-Christian or sub-Christian, turned with vehemence to the pentecostal task of converting Christendom and the world to Christianity as they variously understood it. Even the Münsterites, for all their ferocity, in espousing and adopting the Hofmannite version of election, combined it with an "ecumenical" view of the world mission symbolized by King John's global orb. In the first generation every believer was a prophet or prophetess, or even an apostle, or at least a responsible disciple of Christ, ready to propagate his faith by his martyrdom.

   A new kind of Christian had emerged in the course of the Radical Reformation, a composite of the medieval pilgrim to Jerusalem, the ancient martyr of the heavenly Jerusalem, and the emissary of the neoapostolic Jerusalem. This new kind of Christian was not a reformer but a converter, not a parishioner but, reviving the original meaning of that New Testament word, a sojourner (paroikos) in this world whose true citizenship was

---

[39] Elsass, I, No. 8, p. 13. There is considerable reference to salvation for the devils in the antiradical polemic in Strassburg, for example, Elsass, I, Nos. 285, 358. For the restitution of all things, including devils, see the comprehensive essay of Ernst Staehelin, Die Wiederkehr aller Dinge: Rektoralrede (Basel, 1960). For an isolated and original English universalist who, in appealing to Rom. 8:22, envisaged the salvation of all creatures, including the animals and birds, see my reference to Edward's chaplain, John Bradford, burned as a heretic in 1555, in my Wilderness and Paradise in Christian Thought, ch. iii, 2.

[40] Franklin Littell, "The Anabaptist Theology of Missions," MQR, XXI (1947), 5 ff.

in heaven (Heb. 11:9; Phil. 3:20) and who looked forward to the imminent descent of the Heavenly City, like a Bride prepared for the Bridegroom at his Second Advent. This new kind of Christian was no longer primarily a German or a Gentile, no longer primarily a husband or a wife, a nobleman or a peasant, but a saint (Müntzer), a fellow of the covenant (Denck), a bride of Christ (Hofmann), an *electus* (Renato), a baptized *christus* (Servetus), a god (Menno), a begodded man (Niclaes), a friend of God (Schwenckfeld).

The same sectarian claim of the regenerate in Christ to be superior to the world induced within the conventicles themselves a social revolution comparable to that in the ancient church, where charismatic slaves might emerge as bishops, and converts from the higher classes could find no greater joy than in placing their worldly goods and influence at the disposal of the beloved elect in Christ. And as in the ancient church, so in all sectors of the Radical Reformation, one is impressed by the mobility, the purposefulness, and the testimonial missionary urgency of every convert, whether a commissioned elder or the steadfast wife of a weaver evangelist. In the stress upon personal accountability and explicit faith, the whole of the Radical Reformation pushed the Lutheran doctrine of the priesthood of all believers in the direction of a universal lay apostolate.

CHAPTER 33

THE RADICAL REFORMATION: A NEW PERSPECTIVE

The Radical Reformation was a tremendous movement at the core of Christendom during the threescore years following Luther's three great Reformation tracts of 1520. Embracing peasants and princes, artisans and aristocrats, devout wives and disillusioned humanists, it was as much an entity as the Reformation itself and the Counter Reformation. To be sure, only by assimilation to the nomenclature imposed by these other two religious movements of the age can it be itself called a reformation. It was, rather, a radical break from the existing institutions and theologies in the interrelated drives to restore primitive Christianity, to reconstruct, and to sublimate.

Pedobaptism, equated with circumcision and with imperfectly defined sacramental effectiveness, remained the ultimate symbol for the Magisterial Reformers of the continuity of their churches with the Old Church and through it with old Israel. Conversely, for the largest of the three components of the Radical Reformation, believers' baptism was the symbol and the constitutive principle of the church reconceived, not as a *corpus christianum,* but as a people in covenant, a scattered remnant ever anew being assembled by God's Spirit and his Word.

Though Spiritualism, Anabaptism, and Evangelical Rationalism were by the end of our epoch clearly distinguishable interpretations of Christianity, the cumulative impression is massive and overwhelming that these same three thrusts were themselves part of a still larger upheaval of the strata of late medieval Christendom. The Radical Reformation drained the brackish pools and opened the sluices for innumerable religious currents long impounded in the interstices of late medieval Christendom, which were set in torrential motion by the upthrust of solid blocks of Reformed territories under kings, princes, and the magistrates of numerous city-states. Within the turmoiled flood of radical reform or restitution the fresh vitalities of the Ref-

846

ormation, such as solafideism, Biblicism, predestinarianism, and the doctrine of the priesthood of all believers, were borne along swiftly to radical extremes. We have stressed the transmutation of these Protestant principles in conventicle, fellowship, and synod; but we have also been aware of the quickened flow of late medieval piety below the surface.

To be sure, we have not solved the problem of the relationship of the Radical Reformation to the Middle Ages. In fact, we have only here and there reached back to developments before 1520 with respect to certain regions, institutions, and doctrines.

We reached back in the Netherlands, for example, and into the thought of Wessel Gansfort, who died in 1489, to suggest the way in which late medieval Eucharistic piety could lead to sacramentism (Ch. 2.1), and elsewhere (Ch. 11.3) how it could lead to the formulation of a peculiar doctrine of the celestial flesh of Christ. We reached back in Bohemia to 1467 (Ch. 9.1) to show in that region certain analogues of Hutterite proselyte rebaptism and the community of goods, especially among the Minor Party of the Unity of the Brethren. In Italy we reached back to catch something of the eschatological fervor in the train of Savonarola and of the philanthropic ardor of the proto-Evangelicals (Ch. 1.3) and later (Ch. 21.1) we penetrated the Cottian Alps as of 1498 to take note of the syncretistic accommodation of the Waldensians in this one representative region, finding in the non-Protestantized dissidents among them plausible recruits for the radical evangelical movement in Italy. We reached back in Germany to the Bundschuh of 1493 to ascertain the religious character and motivation of the social unrest that erupted catastrophically in the Great Peasants' War (Ch. 4.1).

We did not recount the history of the Reformed Savoyard Waldensians from the synod of Cianforan in 1532 to the limited guarantee of their embattled caves and cabins in the upper Alpine valleys in the Treaty of Cavour in 1561, nor did we recount the history of the Lutheranized Bohemian Brethren (*Unitas*) after the death of Brother Luke in 1528 to the *Confessio Bohemica* of 1575 and therewith Maximilian's grant of toleration in the same year and their relocation in Moravia (whence their more common subsequent designation as the Moravian Brethren). Otherwise our comprehensive narrative of the Radical Reformation within the interstices of a Christendom reshaped by Magisterial Protestantism and the Council of Trent (1545–1563) has been schematically complete.

We have followed the development of German Anabaptism to the Frankenthal Disputation in 1571; of Italian radicalism in the peninsula and in the diaspora to the deaths of Camillo Renato c.

1572, John Paul Alciati in 1573, and Francis Stancaro in 1574; of English radicalism to the fiery extinction of the London Anabaptist congregation in 1575 and the rise of Barrowism and Brownism; of the Lithuanian Brethren to the publication of Simon Budny's evangelical Rationalist, unitarian, psychopannychist, socially conservative *De principalibus fidei christianae* in 1576; of Mennonitism to William the Silent's first act of toleration in 1577; of Hutteritism to the death of Peter Walpot in 1578; of Transylvanian Unitarianism to the death in prison of Francis Dávid in 1579; of evangelical Spiritualism to the death of Henry Niclaes c. 1580; and of the Polish Brethren down to Faustus Socinus' massive *Responsio* in defense of the Racovian pacifists in 1581.

Thus with only a few exceptions we have confined ourselves to the years 1520–1580, following in considerable regional, biographical, and doctrinal detail the extension of the Radical Reformation as it took shape over against magisterial Protestantism; and we may therefore in conclusion simply observe that the Radical Reformation separated on principle from the reforming and reformed territorial churches of Protestantism because it was carried along by two generations of earnest men and women *already deeply alienated* from the medieval Christendom that the papacy had so long neglected and which magisterial Protestantism was now seeking piecemeal to reform. The Radical Reformation contained impulses which were at once more primitive and more modern than the driving forces of classical Protestantism.

Henry Bullinger (Ch. 31.2), the most comprehensive of the contemporary interpreters of the Radical Reformation, was tendentious in *Der Wiedertäufer Ursprung* of 1560, in trying to derive the whole movement from a single source, which he subsumed under the name of one only of its components, for the Radical Reformation clearly sprang from many sources; but he was right in apprehending it as a unity despite its diversity, of which he himself, as the first major typologist of radicalism, was quite aware.

Anabaptism in the proper sense, as we now know, did not begin until 1525, in Zurich. Bullinger, however, found its origin in Saxon Zwickau, and ultimately in Satan.[1] His magisterial

---

[1] *"Non e nostris intemperiis, sed ex malita propria et suggestione diaboli, contra puritatem doctrinae et nostrum ministerium, exortos esse Anabaptistas."* The following analysis of Bullinger's work is based upon Heinold Fast, *Heinrich Bullinger* (Weierhof, Pfalz, 1959). The foregoing quotation and others are to be found on p. 93.

interpretation was translated into Latin for the international community of clerics and scholars, and also translated, with amplification, for Dutch readers. Even a French version was projected. His earlier works against Anabaptists and Libertines had already appeared in several English translations. Bullinger continued, moreover, to write and publish on the subject right up to his death in 1575.

The ecclesio-politically tendentious historiography of Zwingli's successor in Zurich at the close of our period may therefore serve as the point of vantage for a concluding glance at the Radical Reformation as a whole, because it was Bullinger's work that established the basic pattern for the interpretation of the Radical Reformation by scholars in the traditions of the European state churches down to most recent times. Moreover, as a literary product falling well within the chronological frame of our narrative and as a historiographical achievement of immense subsequent influence, Bullinger's work will help us measure the extent of present-day reassessment of the sixteenth-century role of the Anabaptists and facilitate our concluding effort to set the whole Radical Reformation more clearly over against the Magisterial Reformation in a fresh perspective.

Admittedly, to select as our elevated ground Bullinger's final polemic, which by its very title was limited to "Anabaptists," would seem to exclude from our concluding survey of the scene some two thirds of what we had originally defined as constitutive of the Radical Reformation, or alternatively to give indirect credence to his description of an ill-assorted band of pretentious or pathetic sectaries or come-outers lumped together without differentiation, no longer, to be sure, as "Anabaptists" but to the same effect as "Radicals."

Such, of course, cannot be our intention in view of the great effort which has been made in the preceding chapters to distinguish adequately several kinds of Anabaptists, Spiritualists, and at least three Reformed churches permeated and regrouped under the impact of (Italian) Evangelical Rationalism.

The usefulness of Bullinger's historiography, apart from its serving as the foil for measuring the extent of our revisions, is precisely that Bullinger after all took seriously, within the limitations imposed by his polemical and ecclesiastically parlous age, the full range of the Radical Reformation. Bullinger was right in seeing the Radical Reformation as a whole, even though he misnamed it, overlooked the diversity of its origins, and failed to heed the important differences among the groupings within the purview of his polemic. He had, however, the advantage of his geographically central position and was hence well acquainted with much more than the indigenous Swiss form of Anabaptism. He was in extensive correspondence and personal contact with Lower Rhenish, Frisian, and English Reformers. The last especially hung on his words when they came to deal with the outcroppings of the Radical Reformation in England. He was in continuous correspondence also with the Poles concerning Anabaptism and Arianism, and with the Italian Protestants in the Grisons and elsewhere who were coping with the Radicals, and he even, unwittingly, befriended some of the Radicals, for example, Camillo Renato and Laelius Socinus. Moreover, the problem of anabaptist, anti-Nicene Servetus was fresh in his mind when he wrote his last major work against the Radicals. He played a role in the process that led to the decapitation of tritheist Gentile. He had long been familiar with the tenets of Schwenckfeld, and in the last year of his life was occupied with the problem of a certain Schwenckfeldian who persisted in holding back from the Reformed communion. Finally, the Zwickau prophets, Müntzer, Münsterites, and Libertines had long provided him, along with the other Magisterial Reformers, with an inexhaustible supply of epithets and examples with which to supplement and reinforce the normal patristic and scholastic vocabulary of abuse, invective, and theological incrimination.

Even though Bullinger was inadequate in his classification and typology, and wrong also about the genesis and the interrelationship among the main groupings of the Radical Reformation, he was right in sensing that however great the variety, there was in fact something at work among all the Radicals that set them apart from the Magisterial Reformers and the Tridentine Catholics.

What was, then, his conception of the Radical Reformation which he firmly fixed in the minds of his contemporaries who read his several works and advisory letters and which he stamped upon the historiography of Reformation sectarianism into the present century?

Strange to relate, Bullinger, as spokesman for Germanic Swiss Protestantism, felt obliged up to the end of his life to defend Zwingli from Luther's charge that the Swiss sacramentarians were essentially of the same spirit as the Anabaptists! Luther had in mind, of course, the fact that Carlstadt (connected with sacramentarianism in Wittenberg, fanaticism in Orlamünde, and sponsorship in Rothenburg of the cause of the peasants in their war) was well received in Zurich and ended his career as professor at Basel. Yet Luther himself never specifically derived Swiss Anabaptism from Carlstadt or even Müntzer.

It was, rather, Melanchthon who first made the connection in a statement preserved uniquely in the *De anabaptismi exordio,* published by Deacon John Gast of Basel in 1544.[2] Melanchthon singled out Nicholas Storch of Zwickau as the first to have scattered in Germany "the poisonous doctrines" about divine dreams, direct revelation to the elect, the imminence of the Kingdom, and the disparagement of the external word and sacraments in preference to direct leadings from the Holy Spirit. For these Spiritualists, Bullinger himself used the term *"Spiritöuser."*[3]

It was Bullinger's epoch-making decision, as a pre-eminent authority on Swiss Anabaptism, to pick up this clue from Melanchthon as mediated by Gast. He also utilized clues from Sebastian Franck, who had said that Müntzer preached although he did not practice rebaptism,[4] and from Caspar Hedio, who had connected Müntzer, the revolutionary Spiritualist, with Grebel, the Anabaptist.[5] Bullinger proceeded to his scholarly loom and wove these strands into a pattern plausible enough to exonerate Zwingli and Switzerland from primary responsibility for the rise of radicalism! He was confident that he had so well pieced together the clues and testimonies, some of the evidence being drawn from Lutherans themselves, that he could justify his relocation of the beginnings of all sectarian opposition alike to Luther and Cranmer, to Calvin and himself, in Saxon Zwickau— in the spiritual environs of Wittenberg itself! Saxony, not Switzerland, was the spawning ground of a closely interrelated conspiracy of libertines, revolutionaries, fanatics, visionaries, blasphemers, and communists!

It was not, then, primarily the self-centeredness of early Lutheran divines and later scholars that has made the Saxony of Storch, Carlstadt, and Müntzer the original hearth of counter-Protestant sectarianism, but rather the scholarly and yet adroitly ecclesio-political effort of Henry Bullinger to vindicate the Swiss Reformation and to dissociate the Swiss sacramentarian Magisterial Reformation from the charges and insinuations that per-

---

[2] Fast, *Bullinger,* 94, says that there can be no doubt that the crucial fragment from Melanchthon is authentic and unaltered by Gast, although he cannot locate it in Melanchthon's known works.

[3] *Ibid.,* 19.

[4] *Chronica,* 1531; Fast, *Bullinger,* 95.

[5] The *Paralipomena* annexed to *Chronicon abbatis Urspergensesis,* edited by Hedio in 1537; Fast, *Bullinger,* 96 f., and reprint of relevant excerpt in the appendix, 172 f.

turbed him to the end of his life. The fact that Bullinger sent copies of his *Ursprung* to many princes, and even Queen Elizabeth, accompanied by letters expressly dissociating Zwingli and the Swiss churches from "the Anabaptists and other sectaries," shows the extent to which the Lutheran charge weighed on him and his Swiss colleagues and also the satisfaction which he felt in proving massively that Swiss Anabaptism was derivative and not indigenous.[6]

The defensive character of Bullinger's historiography was not an isolated phenomenon, but fitted into the Baslean, Genevan, and Bernese actions against Joris, Servetus, and Gentile to vindicate the orthodoxy of the whole Swiss Reformation; for it would not be until the Peace of Westphalia in 1648 that the Reformed Church would be fully secure in its constitutional place in the by then completely fragmented Empire, and that the Reformed churches in and outside the Empire would enjoy ecclesiastical parity with the Lutheran territorial and national churches.

In attacking the Radical Reformation as at once diabolic and Saxon, Bullinger also manifested the characteristic concern of a territorial churchman to pillory the come-outer attitude of Radicals who either withheld themselves from participating corporately in the life and sacraments of the Reformed churches or who withdrew into separatist conventicles, and who in either case pharisaically dissociated themselves from the fullness of responsibility in Christian society at large.

Bullinger divided the Anabaptists into the "general" (evangelical) group, largely defined in terms of the Swiss Brethren he knew best, and the "special" or marginal Anabaptists, among whom he distinguished twelve kinds.

From the perspective gained after four centuries of polemic, *apologia,* and research since Bullinger's reflections and compilation down to his death in 1575, we should be able to clarify the respects in which the Radical Reformation, despite its inherent divergencies, was in fact a historic entity. We should be able to see how it was comparable to and distinguishable from the Magisterial Reformation and as such of tremendous interest not only in its own right but also as a hitherto theologically misunderstood and sociopolitically underestimated force, the proper description and analysis of which enhances our understanding of classical Protestantism in all its achievement and otherwise unaccountable one-sidedness.

---

[6] Fast, *op. cit.,* 65 f.

In helping us to understand normative Protestantism, a fair delineation of the Radical Reformation is indeed as requisite as a grasp of the Magisterial Reformation for our comprehension of the direction taken by Tridentine Catholicism.

Let us first recall to the stage the main groups and individuals in what—if for no other reason than because of the thousands of martyrdoms—may be considered as the tragedy of the Radical Reformation (1520–1580). After glimpsing once again the *dramatis personae* as a company, we may spend the remainder of the chapter in reflecting upon the themes which have made of the three far-flung actions—the Anabaptist, the Spiritualist, and the Rationalist—a coherent, gripping, and dramatic unity.

Regionally defined, we have seen how the Anabaptists grouped themselves into Swiss Brethren; South German and Austrian Anabaptists in the line of John Denck, John Hut, and Pilgram Marpeck; the communitarian Hutterites; the Melchiorite (anti-Chalcedonian) Lower German, Netherlandish, English, and Prussian Anabaptists in the line of Melchior Hofmann and Menno Simons; the revolutionary Münsterites in the line of Hofmann and John Mathijs; the predestinarian, psychopannychist, anti-Nicene North Italian Anabaptists; and the increasingly anti-Nicene Polish and Lithuanian Brethren (before the arrival of Faustus Socinus). The chronological priority of the Swiss Brethren, who happen also to have retained more or less intact but unspeculatively both a Chalcedonian Christology and a Nicene doctrine of the Trinity, does not entitle them to be considered alone normative for sixteenth-century Anabaptism to the exclusion of those other self-disciplining rebaptizers, who were, for example, anti-Chalcedonian (the Mennonites), anti-Nicene (the early Polish Brethren), and anti-Lateran (the Italian sectaries).

These seven primarily regional groupings with their variously associated doctrinal and disciplinary traits have also been brought schematically under three morphological types. For the most part the typology given at our point of departure has been confirmed in our detailed explorations. The Evangelical Anabaptists were the pacifistic Grebelians, Mennonites, Hutterites, Marpeckians, and Racovians. The Revolutionary or Maccabean Anabaptists thought of themselves in their eschatological zeal as especially summoned to use force in advancing the Kingdom. Besides the Münsterites in their last phase, there were in this category only the small following of Augustine Bader, who had messianic dreams, though he did not resort to force. The Batenburgers seem to have been Münsterites who had lost most of the Melchiorite vision of the original covenanters and were calculatingly violent. The Spiritualizing Anabaptists accentuated the mystical, sacramentarian, or predestinarian thrusts within the Radical Reformation as a whole and therefore came to minimize all the ordinances of conventicular Christianity, including even baptism and the ban—for example, John Denck, Christian Entfelder, Adam Pastor, Gabriel Ascherham, John de Ries, and Camillo Renato, who, especially in the last phases of their careers, bordered on or indeed passed over into evangelical Spiritualism or anti-Trinitarian Rationalism. Michael Servetus, who influenced the Gonesians, is hard to classify because he was at once a speculative brooder and a proponent of the redemptive significance of the sacraments.

These three socioreligious types of Anabaptism and the corresponding psychological dispositions among the leaders have been recognized throughout our narrative. Our terminology has been confirmed as to its validity in helping to distinguish the suffering servants, the militant heralds, and the watchful brooders among the Anabaptists.

At close range, however, the simply geographical designations have more often proved convenient because they have freed us from the necessity of being tediously specific as to the precise tenets, traits, and tempers of a given group at a given moment; for these clusters of characteristics which are determinative for our over-all morphological classification have, in fact, in the shifting phases or in unrepresentative individuals, appeared ephemerally or sporadically and by contagion and interaction within just about all of the regional developments.

By the end of our period, except for scattered pockets of survivors, all but the Evangelical Anabaptists had disappeared or been converted into something else. These Evangelical Anabaptists were well on their way toward "denominational" or confessional isolation, namely, the Mennonites (themselves divided into several mutually exclusive groups), the Swiss Brethren, and the Hutterites.

More even than with Anabaptism, the nature of Spiritualism has emerged from our narrative and analysis as variegated and complex. Here, too, we have observed diverse regional expressions of the phenomena which we have been willing to recognize as a recurrent tendency, without insisting always on demonstrable genetic relationships. Here, in fact, more than with Anabaptism, we have been content to point to analogies and temperamental types. For, unlike true sectarianism (i.e., Anabaptism), which is ecclesiological or constitutional in its external thrust, spiritualization, akin to mysticism, is a tendency which is largely dependent upon personal endowment and disposition and which therefore makes its appearance in diverse ecclesiastical settings. We have, however, recognized here also three recurrent morphological variants, namely, the evangelical or conventicular spiritualizers along with the speculative and solitary brooders, the conformist spiritualizers, and the prophetic or revolutionary Spiritualists. This classification represents a slight adjustment and refinement of the terminology with which we opened our account.[7]

Common to all Spiritualists was the stress on the divine immediacy either by way of the celestial flesh of Christ, the inner Word, or a Spirit-possession. Common to most Spiritualists likewise was an antinomian streak which could in its mildest form be simply a stress on grace over against law but which could become excessive in an inner repudiation of all organization in church life, sometimes under the camouflage of prudential conformity, sometimes in the cultic flouting of normal ethical behavior. In respect to law, however, the prophetic Spiritualists stood apart from both the conformist and the conventicular spiritualizers in that these eschatologically intense revolutionary Spiritualists repudiated, not the laws of Moses and Christ, but the canons and ordinances of what they considered a moribund Christendom. With the zeal of prophets driven by the Spirit, they took very seriously indeed the corporate ordinances of the Kingdom they were seeking to usher in.

The evangelical or conventicular spiritualizers met in conventicles apart but had little use for the traditional sacraments and ordinances. Such were the Dutch Sacramentists, the Schwenckfeldians, and the Loists, and the speculative solitaries such as Franck.

The conformist spiritualizers, while they might have conventicles of their own, also conformed in principle to the locally established churches. Such were the Libertines, the Nicodemites, and the Familists, and speculative brooders such as Weigel.

Finally, there were the revolutionary Spiritualists, who, unlike the Libertines, were sensible of a great gulf fixed between God and man, and yet, like Müntzer, Carlstadt (in his middle period), Postel (in his last phase), Palaeologus, and many lesser charismatic figures, felt called by the Holy Spirit or possessed of the Spirit in discharging a prophetic role; who in contrast to all other kinds of Spiritualists took seriously the structures of church

---

[7] In the Introduction and in the introduction to *SAW*, the terms were "Evangelical Spiritualists," "Rational Spiritualists," and "Revolutionary Spiritualists."

and society; and who felt uniquely summoned as instruments of the Holy Spirit to usher in the social righteousness of the millennium under the fifth age of Christ or the third age of the Holy Spirit.

In the third main sector of the Radical Reformation the Evangelical Rationalists stressed the rational approach to Christianity. They were seen to have been at the start akin to the prophetic Spiritualists in their eschatology based, however, more on the doctrine of election than on the experience of the Spirit, and also akin in their sober Biblicism to the evangelical Anabaptists. They were somewhat less diversified than either the Spiritualists or the Anabaptists, although they displayed several of the traits of both groups. They were, to begin with, that party among the Italian Evangelicals who, as Valdesian "Protestants," broke from the Catholic Church, and in time became also disillusioned with the Helvetic form of Protestantism. They were a loose band of ethical theists, commonly of aristocratic or clerical background, who were sustained by a predominantly individualistic piety and who shared (1) with the evangelical Anabaptists their pacificism, (2) with many Anabaptists and with the Libertines among the Spiritualists their eschatological confidence in the resurrection of the dead or the sleeping souls of the elect to rule with Christ at his imminent advent, and (3) with the evangelical Spiritualists generally their minimizing or eliminating the sacraments and other ordinances of organized Christianity. Characteristic, though not entirely distinctive, of these Evangelical Rationalists was their gradual elimination of the divine nature of Christ and their vindication of Christ's humanity and adoptive Sonship, whereby they hoped to remove his image from the heavy dogmatic framework wrought by the Nicene formulation and to point to Christ as fully and solely a man, the first fruits of that promised resurrection for all who would follow in his way and be saved and also vindicated in return for their pacifistic, tolerant, and philanthropic endeavors.

We have seen how these Evangelical Rationalists in the Italian diaspora succeeded in transforming, in varying degrees, three eastern Reformed churches into what constituted, by the end of our narrative, a third major geographical sector of the Radical Reformation, made up of the Transylvanian Unitarians under Francis Dávid, the Lithuanian Brethren under Simon Budny, and the Socinians in Poland (the latter being the Polish Brethren with both Anabaptist and Calvinist residues transformed by Faustus Socinus). In some respects, the Socinian or later Racovian Church was in the end an amalgam of the three main ingredients of the Radical Reformation, for even Spiritualism found expression in Socinus' personal elimination of the ordinance of Baptism and in his programmatic reconstruction of the Minor Church into a school. This Spiritualist tendency was later reinforced by the banishment of the Socinians from Poland (in 1658). Thereafter, Socinianism moved about as a disembodied spirit capable of permeating diverse churches and fellowships in Holland, Germany, and England in the course of that and the following century.

The Radical Reformation in its three major divisions was thus comparable to the Magisterial Reformation, which was likewise, as it happens, tripartite: Lutheran, Reformed, and Elizabethan.

Thus far we have reviewed the important differences and gradations from Anabaptism through Spiritualism to Evangelical Rationalism. We have made a special effort in the course of the narrative to interrelate the three-pronged movement and the lives of the leaders and to connect them up with the lives and developments of the Protestant leaders and churches. Now, in this concluding chapter, we point up the inner coherence of the tripartite Radical Reformation and show how it was at least as much an entity as tripartitely divided Protestantism itself, and, as such, a movement to be ranged alongside the Magisterial Reformation, the Counter Reformation, Renaissance Humanism, and Nationalism as one of five major forces in the great age of discovery, reform, and revolt.

The Radicals were, first of all, engaged not in a reformation of the church but, rather, in the restitution of the church. The radical movement, the career of which we have followed in diverse forms and regions, has been called a Radical Reformation, as we have said, primarily to vindicate its place among the major movements of the Reformation Era. Actually, it differed from both the Magisterial and the Counter Reformation in its impatience with mere reform. It espoused, rather, a radical rupture with the immediate past and all its institutions and was bent upon either the restoration of the primitive church or the assembling of a new church, all in an eschatological mood far more intense than anything to be found in normative Protestantism or Catholicism.

This intense expectancy, which marked almost the whole of the Radical Reformation and cut it off from the Catholics and Protestants, resulted from the widespread abandonment of the traditional view that the church was living in the sixth age of the world. Since the time of Augustine this age had been thought of as the millennium of Rev., ch. 20, during which the powers of Satan were being held in partial check by Christian magistrates. Its replacement by several competing and vexingly unharmonized eschatologies raised the hopes of the Radicals in some phases and some localities to a feverish pitch.

We do well at this point to recall these various eschatologies by setting them before us systematically.

The Trinitarian scheme of Joachim of Flora (d. 1202) was especially pervasive. Working with the hermeneutical principle of concordance or typology (which presupposed the unity of God's people) rather than mere allegory, Joachim had reworked and shifted Paul's division of world history into three ages, *ante legem, sub lege,* and *sub gratia,* in terms of three typologically related and partly overlapping dispensations (1) of the Father, (2) of the Son, and (3) of the Holy Spirit. On the basis of calculations which would harmonize prophecies in Daniel and Revelation, Joachimites assigned to each age a partially overlapping total duration of 1260 years.

The beginning of the age of the Spirit for the neo-Joachimites could be variously reckoned from whatever event in the past could be construed as the moment of the fall of the apostolic church. For such a neo-Joachimite as Servetus, for example, the fall came with the accession of Constantine or with his Council of Nicaea in 325, which, in the latter case, would make 1585 the eschatological moment. For David Joris, Anthony Pocquet, and William Postel, the third age had begun with their respective conversions or rebirths.

Another reckoning, conspicuous in the prophetic Spiritualist Thomas Müntzer and in evangelical Anabaptists John Hut and Melchior Hofmann, is that based upon the Danielic-Hieronymic conception of four empires or monarchies, of which the Roman was the last, leading to a Fifth Monarchy or Age, that of Christ's direct rule of the saints.

Especially interesting was the eschatology which saw in the woman seeking refuge in the wilderness of Rev. 12:6, the true church identical with the beloved of the Bridegroom coming up out of the wilderness in Canticles 8:5. Proponents of this eschatology found solace in the cultivation of their remnant church as a provisional paradise precariously maintained pending the advent of the millennium.

We have also found the idea of the return of a combined Golden Age, Paradise, and primitive church in varying strengths and permutations, in Balthasar Hubmaier, John Hut, Melchior Hofmann, Menno Simons, Dietrich Philips, Jacob Hutter,

Michael Servetus, Camillo Renato, William Postel, and George Schomann.

A more generalized millennialism, based upon a harmonization of Scriptural and Apocryphal prophecies, reinforced by various medieval prognostications, was the most common eschatology, because it was always amorphously amenable to fresh calculations in the light of current signs and developments.

Whether as a provisional paradise or garden enclosed, as the harbinger of the third Age of the Spirit or of Christ, as the outpost of the Fifth Monarchy of Christ the King, or as the gateway to the millennium, the churches of the Radical Reformation were sustained and emboldened by the conviction that they and their charismatic leaders were the instruments of the Lord of history in the latter days.

It was this intense conviction within the Radical Reformation as to the imminent end of the age which encouraged Laelius Socinus, Servetus, Gregory Paul, and Francis Dávid, no less than Schwenckfeld (called Eliander), Joris (the third David), and Thomas Müntzer (the prophet of the Fifth Monarchy). It was in this apocalyptic mood that John Hut, the revivalist, baptized, using the cross as a sign upon the forehead in seeking to recruit the one hundred and forty-four thousand saints of the imminent millennial Kingdom; that Melchior Hofmann, the new Elijah, prophesied the descent of the heavenly Jerusalem in Strassburg; and that Camillo Renato described the outlines of the returning Golden Age under the fair auspices of Christ. Everywhere about them the Radicals experienced the outpouring of the Spirit and beheld the other signs foretold by Isaiah, IV Esdras, Daniel, Joel, Malachi, and the seer of The Revelation. It was their intense expectancy which warranted the repudiation by all of the infant baptism of the Old Church and justified the call for a final Johannine repentance, a complete change of mind and an avowal of sinfulness, and a regeneration of true believers, in order to escape the wrath to come.

It was this same pervasive hope and fear that encouraged all the Radicals to break completely from the inherent idea in, and the historically elaborated organs of, the medieval *corpus christianum* and to assume, as the early Christians did, either an attitude of indifference to the state as belonging to an aeon that was passing or an attitude of mingled hostility and provocativeness toward that which, even as it bore down in persecution and perpetrated martyrdoms, could but serve to confirm them in their conviction that they were at once pilgrims toward, missionaries of, and martyrs for that City which would momentarily descend from heaven or emerge messianically from the debris of an age that was breaking asunder. Hence, almost all the Radicals insisted on the utter separation of the church from the state and found in the willingness of the Magisterial Reformers to use the coercive power of princes, kings, and town councilors an aberration from apostolic Christianity no less grievous than papal pretensions.

It was again this apocalyptic confidence in an age over which Christ or the Holy Spirit would soon preside that called for the formation of new organs of self-discipline among true Christians as a substitute both for papal and episcopal excommunication and inquisition and for magisterial sanctions and oversight, namely, the restitution and practice of the congregational ban in conjunction with the observance of the most sacred meal of the New Covenant in Christ.

It was, furthermore, this overwhelming sense of the dawn of the millennium or the final age that warranted the commissioning of new apostles to proclaim the acceptable time of the Lord. Not only the Anabaptists but also the less institutionally minded spiritualizers, such as Loy Pruystinck, Anthony Pocquet, and Henry Niclaes, regarded themselves as apostolic emissaries. Such diverse spokesmen of the Radical Reformation as Hut, Marpeck, Hutter, Menno, Schwenckfeld, Paracelsus, Servetus, Gherlandi, Postel, Palaeologus, Dávid, Tiziano, and Czechowic moved about and otherwise conducted themselves as commissioned from on high to proclaim a message of liberation to those who still sat in darkness, and emboldened them to act as apostles, however much several of these very leaders themselves might have decried the ecclesiastical pretensions of both the Protestant Reformers and the self-styled apostles among their fellow sectarians.

Only among the proponents of the Radical Reformation, as we saw, were the ordinations and divine commissions of the clergy of the Old Church scrutinized and found deficient. Like the earliest Christians, the Radicals counted the priesthood of the old Temple as having lapsed with the completion of the redemptive work of Christ as the only High Priest, and they therefore proceeded to reordain and otherwise reconstitute the polity of God's ongoing Israel, a priesthood no longer according to the flesh, a priesthood likewise no longer legitimized through the sacramental conduits of apostolic grace, clogged, as they would have said, with corruption.

Perhaps it was the repudiation of the older ordination, the prominence of "laymen," and the conversion of the whole believing fellowship into a new people of God, a royal priesthood, a lay apostolate that most clearly set all the Radical Reformers off from the Magisterial Reformers. Although the latter moved readily from colloquy to diet and disputation, and corresponded with a wide range of magistrates and fellow clerics outside their own territories, they never felt called upon to evangelize or conduct missions, some of them expressly declaring that the apostolic office had lapsed in antiquity, while others were satisfied to think of the nationalized bishops as the only authorized successors of the apostles. In any event, the Magisterial Reformers were concerned with reform and not with missionary expansion. In contrast, like the awakened Catholics, the Radical Reformers glimpsed the mission beyond Christendom.

With the overriding conviction that they were living at the opening of a new age, the Radical Reformers had begun, moreover, to alter their conception of the redemptive role of Christ, without being themselves at first fully conscious of the extent of the displacement. No longer a self-sacrificing High Priest, Christ was to them primarily the suffering exemplar and the vindicating Lord, or the inner self-substantiating Word. In their intensely eschatological mood, the basic conception of the Radicals as to what constituted salvation and as to what constituted Christ's role in their redemption was being transformed. Without at first expressly repudiating the Anselmian doctrine of the atonement, but increasingly distressed by Luther's preoccupation with justification at the practical expense of sanctification, and in any event disposed to look back to the humble Christ rather as exemplar than as sacrifice and to look forward to his imminent return as vindicator, they neglected or but routinely repeated the thought of Christ's death as a ransom to the devil or as a sacrificial appeasement of Deity and concentrated, rather, on fresh surmises concerning, or substitutes for, the traditional versions of the doctrine of the atonement. Competing or complementary formulations with respect to the objective atonement jostled alongside each other in the ferment of fresh speculation and experience, from subjective justification and observable sanctification, all the way to the conception of physical regeneration and Eucharistic or baptismal deification. All these formulations could purport to be no more than provisional, for definitive salvation lay ahead for the Radicals no less than for the classical Protestant Reformers, the latter more sober in their prognostication of the Last Judgment. Some of the Radicals concentrated on the achievement of the state or experience of *Gelassenheit;* others on variously conceived mortifications and regenerations;

others on contemplative identification of the inner and eternal
Word; others on the gospel of all creatures in redemptive suffering leading to clarification; others on the progressive deification
through an immersionist rebirth in Christ or through sustenance
upon the celestial flesh of Christ, either through inward masti-
cation or through a disciplined Lord's Supper; others on utter
obedience to Christ and vindication at the imminent advent
and resurrection; and still others on immediate enrollment in the
true church militant as the outpost and recruiting station for
the advancing millennial rule.

Anabaptism has been called an "Abortive Counter Revolt
within the Reformation."[8] Indeed, the whole of the Radical
Reformation might be called abortive. It was surely incomplete.
Its utter repudiation of any sense of the sacramental solidarity
of the church through the centuries has today a limited appeal
even to the direct descendants of the movement who today
cherish above all their own spiritual lineage. But the Radical

---

[8] The title of an article by Lowell H. Zuck, CH, XXVI (1957), 221–226. The
most recent evaluation of Anabaptism is that of Hans J. Hillerbrand, "Anabaptism and the Reformation: Another Look," CH, XXIX (1960), 404–423.
With the main thesis of this important essay the present writer is in sympathy. This study, which appeared after my book was in press, is especially
useful in concentrating on justification as a key theological category in distinguishing the Radical from the authentically Protestant Reformation.
However, the evidence and point of view of Alvin Beachy, op. cit., as to the
concept and experience of grace in Anabaptism, should be adduced to avoid
too sharp a distinction.

As to Hillerbrand's provisional conclusion that the Anabaptist did not so
much "radicalize" the Reformation as present "a Christian tradition in its
own right," we have already in this chapter advanced the reason for retaining
the word "Reformation" for the Radicals surveyed in this book. There is no
doubt that for Anabaptism alone, Franklin Littell's preferred designation,
"the Restitution," would be the most apposite; but the comprehensive term
"Radical Reformation" seems by far the best to cover the whole of the three-
pronged movement, to permit of significant differentiation within it, and
to situate it in and relate it to the two other Reformations in the sixteenth
century. The term has already been favorably received and employed by two
major American scholars in the field, Franklin Littell and Robert Friedmann. The latter discusses the term in an article so entitled in ME, IV.

This final note of the book may appropriately carry two references to the
future. Hans Hillerbrand has prepared a comprehensive "Bibliography of
Anabaptist History, 1520–1630." The fact that the project was sponsored
by a grant of the largely Lutheran-endowed Foundation for Reformation
Research in St. Louis and that it will be printed by the Institute of Mennonite Studies in Elkhart is a fitting symbol of the progress of Christian
scholarship in our ecumenical age. The monograph of Torsten Bergsten,
*Balthasar Hubmaier: Seine Stellung zu Reformation und Täufertum, 1521–
1528* (Kassel, 1961), also promises to be a substantial contribution to our
understanding of the relation of Anabaptism to Protestantism.

Reformation had a feeling for cosmic time and an intuition of the essential unity of all mankind, prospectively redeemed by Christ at Calvary. The Radicals had a gripping conviction as to individual responsibility to witness to Christ in the world and a fresh awareness of covenantal responsibilities accompanying the radical Christianization of ecclesiastically hitherto neglected areas of human relationship so basic as the brotherhood of men of all classes, the equality of men and women, and the solidarity of all races of mankind before a God who is not a respecter of persons. They had an emboldened sense of personal answerability (*Verantwortlichkeit*) both before God and man in the implementation of the disciplined life of the churches independent of the organs of civil society; and a new range of diversified experience and theory in the realm of that basic Christian transaction which is salvation.

There were bigots, mountebanks, and scoundrels in the Radical Reformation. But the great majority of the mighty host of men and women whose lives we have sketched communicate an overwhelming sense of their earnestness, their lonely courage, and their conviction. They were aware of a providential purpose that informed their deeds. The bleakness, squalor, brutality, and frenzy of the vast scene in which they played their parts was relieved for them—as for us, the spectators—by the intense assurance which these people had that within the shadow of their crosses God stood keeping watch above his own. The cumulative effect of their testimony is that Christianity is not child's play, that to be a Christian is to be commissioned.

Despite the intolerant exclusiveness of the churchmanship on the part of some, or the serious alterations in dogma on the part of others, or their sublimation of the sacraments, the brave men and women of the Radical Reformation deserve to have their testimony taken down anew before the less partisan tribunals of another age.

As to two of four tenets widely held in the Radical Reformation, namely believers' baptism and the sleep of the souls of the dead pending the resurrection, it is a poignant fact that the greatest modern Protestant theologian who is the counterpart and in a sense the successor of Zwingli or Calvin—who teaches, as it happens, not in Zurich or Geneva but in Basel—is in accord with the once despised antipedobaptists and psychopannychists. With respect to a third tenet, it is a commonplace that the programmatic separation of church and state has long been accepted by American Christianity as a basic principle, a boon both for the churches and the state. Above all, with respect to a fourth tenet, the Great Commission, it is clear that the Protestant missionary of the eighteenth, nineteenth, and twentieth centuries, with his concern for education, medical care, and personal conversions in Asia, Africa, and also at home in the domestic missions of the established churches and denominations, is as much the heir of Marpeck, Schwenckfeld, and Budny, with their doctrine of free will, personal accountability, and their conviction as to the church's transcendence of nation and local culture, as he is of Luther, Zwingli, or Cranmer, with their doctrine of predestination, their preoccupation with and almost exclusively corporate conception of reform, and their consequent neglect of the great commission to build up the waste places of Zion within and beyond the borders of historic Christendom.

In the fullness of time the true martyrs among the Radicals may come to be counted by all as revered members of that larger church which is the communion of saints, the elect of every nation.

Constitutionally, in the larger perspective of the history of central Europe, the revolutionary thrust of the Radical Reformation also proved abortive.

From the Sacramentist fellowships, through the peasant camp meetings and parliaments, to the self-disciplining Anabaptist conventicles, and the great and small synodal deliberations, from Venice to Vilnius, the Radical Reformation in its main drive was at once individualistic, conventicular, and universalistic. It was the last great effort of the yeomen and burghers within the late medieval Empire and on the marches to reorder Christendom according to evangelical precepts and on the basis of free association and individual accountability.

That which was to be in England constitutionally a permanent legacy of the age of the Civil Wars and the Commonwealth and a major resource in the evolution of modern Christian democratic critical pluralism was, in the aging Empire, ground up between the nether millstone of particularistic territorialism under the princes and with the sanction of Magisterial Protestantism and the upper millstone of the Hapsburg domination of the Empire in the interest of one dynasty and a tightly defined Catholicism. The ruthless suppression of the Radical Reformation by the Protestant and Catholic princes alike led to the permanent disfigurement of the social and constitutional structure of central Europe, culminating in the treaties of Münster and Osnabrück, with their sanction of the complete disintegration of the great medieval ideal of a universal Christian society.

One need not agree with all the religious tenets of the Puritans in the English seventeenth century and the religious parties to their left, such as the Levellers and the Diggers, to recognize their indispensable contribution to the evolution of modern democratic society with its voluntarist groups, party systems, and the concept of a loyal political opposition. Similarly, without being necessarily a Mennonite, a Schwenckfeldian, or a Unitarian, one can readily perceive and acknowledge the unrealized constitutional potential of the Radical Reformation. It is a tragedy of central European constitutional history down into modern times, with two ill-fated attempts to restore the Empire in purely nationalistic terms, that back in the sixteenth century the evangelically motivated revolution of peasants, petty burghers, some knights, and some scholars, after being persecuted and crushed, did not at least undergo a belated and constitutionally significant sublimation in some kind of glorious central European revolution.

To be sure, the Radical Reformation of the sixteenth century had no Oliver Cromwell. Indeed, it did not for the most part believe in the use of force except here and there when baited into self-defense. The Radical Reformers in almost all camps were pacifists. Moreover, unlike their English counterparts a century later and indeed the Calvinist freedom fighters in Holland at the end of the very same century, the Radical Reformers for the most part eschewed the doctrine of predestination, a theological monopoly of normative Protestantism. They stressed instead sanctification and aspired, within their limits, to imitate Christ and the martyr-minded members of the primitive church. Unwilling to resort to force, they gave themselves over instead to the refinement of the disciplines of the spirit in the fellowships of covenanters in a good conscience with God.

The Radical Reformation was thus also an abortive constitutional revolution. But even when the echo of the theological testimony of these Radicals fails to reach our inward ear across the centuries—either because we have formally more beliefs or fewer beliefs than they—it will be our recollection of their anguished courage in the face of the stern tribunals of their age that will prompt us humbly to salute them from afar as honored citizens of that larger community which is the commonwealth of all mankind. They who read the *Liber creaturarum,* the *Liber sapientiae,* and the *Evangelium* in the School of Christ, assured by various tokens of renewal that they were covenanters of the ongoing Israel of faith, died confident in their election to live obediently at the suffering center of redemptive history in imitation of Him who taketh away the sins of the world.

INDEXES

The topics are indexed analytically but not exhaustively, supplementing the table of contents and the cross references within the narrative. In contrast, the entries for persons and places are intended to be complete. Places which in the text are given by preference in the English form, if there is one, or in the form appropriate to the political and linguistic provinces of the sixteenth century, in the index are often supplemented in parentheses and in some cases cross-referenced by the modern spellings or forms of the names when notably different, in order to facilitate their being located on modern maps. Personal names, which in the text are usually Anglicized with respect to the first name, are occasionally in the index supplemented in parentheses by the modernized national spelling. Patronymics, vocational names, and names derived from the place of birth or principal activity are, in the index, for convenience, regularly treated as surnames even when, as for example in the case of the Dutch patronymics and trade names, they were not so treated in the sixteenth century and therefore are usually not so treated in modern works. In a few notable cases the personal name (like Jacob, or Menno, or John) is entered as a cross reference to a trade name (like Hutter) or patronymic (like Simons, i.e., Simonszoon) or a place name (like Leiden). When a person has two or three of these "incipient" surnames, unless one of them has clearly established itself as customary, the patronymic is allowed to take precedence over the trade name, and the trade name over the place name, especially when the latter is that of a well-known city. While in the text Latinized names have been preferred to vernacular names, in the index by means of cross reference and parentheses selected vernacular names (and also Latin names for one reason or another eschewed in the text) are included for ready reference. In the topical entries, the analytical subdivisions are, depending upon the matter, arranged sequentially (as presented in the book), logically (as in a dictionary), alphabetically (as, for example, the various cities listed under "University"), and chronologically (as, for example, various ecumenical councils listed under "Council"). Individual cathedral, parish, or monastic churches, like St. Lambert's in Münster, are listed under the town. Special attention is drawn to the topical entry "Sources Quoted," where the larger quotations from sixteenth-century writers are listed alphabetically according to author; also to the entry "Rulers," where the principal dynasts and the popes are listed with their regnal dates.

867

Belgium. *See* Netherlands: southern,
342, 398, 765
Bellius, Martin. *See* Castellio, Sebastian, 628
Belluno, Italy, 537
Belot, 597
Bełżyce, Poland, 697, 749
Benedetto of Mantova, xxvi
Benedict of Asolo, 561
Benfeld, France, 248
Benoît, Andrew, 586
Bentschen. *See* Zbąszyń
Berg, Germany, 83n, 342
Bergamo, Italy, 536, 559, 565
Bergen, Czechoslovakia, 224, 230, 418
Berger, George, 144
Bergklooster, Holland, 370
Bergzabern, Germany, 160
Bern, Switzerland, 61, 143, 146–148,
181, 199–201, 251, 270, 280, 464, 522,
588, 592–596, 608, 613, 622n, 637,
745; Church Order, 587, 592
Bernard of Asti, 20
Bernard, prior of Luxemburg, 266
Berner, Alexander, 257
Berthelier, Philibert, 608
Bertrand of Moulins, 354, 599, 600
Besserer, Bernard, 452, 456 f., 459–462,
464, 466
Bestercze (Bistriţa), Rumania, 713
Bethesda, 313
Bethlehem, metaphorically, 679
Betrothal imagery. *See under* Baptism; Church; Eucharist; Mysticism
Beuditz bei Weissenfels, Germany,
45n
Beukels, John of Leiden, king of Münster, 358 f., 363, 368–375, 377–379,
380 f., 390 f., 393, 399, 429, 452
Bewegung, 52
Beza, Theodore, 590n, 628, 630, 647,
664, 693n, 715n, 717, 817
Biała, Poland, 648
Biberach, Germany, 190
Bible, xxvii, 750 f.
emphasis on whole Bible, 823, 828
Apocrypha, 446, 819
New Testament, concentration on
and differentiation from Old,
194, 457, 468, 472 f., 593, 728,
816
translations of, 2, 9, 12, 39, 159, 161,
192, 527 f., 628–663, 816–820;
Latin-Greek edition, 465

alone authoritative (*sola scriptura*),
95, 125, 153, 214, 240
rejection of certain passages or
books, 493, 564
hermeneutics, 55n, 151, 153, 158,
377, 750 f., 828–832; concordances for, 793, 816, 821; love
and faith as canons of, 593 f.;
Key of David in, 830; divided
hoof in, 831; moonlight and
sunlight, 830; sword of the
Spirit in, 247, hazard of, 267;
yesterday and today, 472, 830.
See also Paradox
See also Council: theory of, among
Radicals; *Sitzerrecht;* Word:
Scripture, Spirit
Bibra, Germany, 79, 156, 164, 178
Bieliński, Daniel, 646, 687, 689, 695,
701, 748, 760n
Biestkens, Nicholas, 818
Billicanus, Theobald, 389
Binder, Eucharius Kellermann, 164,
167
Bischofszell, Switzerland, 193
Bithynia, 237
Bitter Christ, contrasted with sweet,
48, 51, 99, 100
Blandrata (Biandrata), George, 329n,
624n, 634–636, 638, 650, 653, 658–
661, 663, 667, 690, 692, 710n, 716,
717, 718, 719, 720, 721, 722, 727,
729, 730, 731, 732, 733, 742, 744, 745,
749, 753, 808, 809
Blandratists. *See* Polish Brethren
Blaurer, Ambrose, 185n, 191, 193, 241,
272n, 454, 456, 464n
Blaurer, Margaret, 454
Blaurer, Thomas, 185n, 193
Blaurock, George Cajacob, 120–126,
128n, 129, 134, 137–139, 141 f., 144–
146, 166, 184, 200, 234, 529, 550, 552,
679, 683
Blesdijk, Nicholas Meynderts van,
483 f., 490
Blood Friends or Brethren (*Träumer*),
164, 442, 511 f.
Blunt, Richard, 788
Bluntschli, the widow, 139
Böblingen, Germany, 731
Bocholt, Germany, 381–383, 401 f.
Bocking, England, 781
Bodenstein, Andreas. *See* Carlstadt
Bodley, Sir Thomas, 785, 786

145 f., 148, 199, 201–203, 297, 389, 466, 487, 545, 548 f., 555, 558, 560n, 565, 567–571, 586, 592–594, 613, 625n, 630, 631n, 635, 658, 660, 666, 686n, 715n, 780, 804, 848, 849, 850, 851, 852

Bünderlin, John, 156, 167, 178, 255, 265, 267 f., 273 f., 281, 338, 408, 412, 457, 811, 843

Bundesgenossen. See Covenanters

Bundschuh, 63, 245

Bure, Idolette de, 581, 591

Burgundy, 342n, 522

Burial. *See* Cemetery

Burian, Sobek, Lord of Konicý, 48, 222

Busale, Abbot Matteo, 568n

Busschaert, John, 773

Bychawa, U.S.S.R. (?), 658, 689

Byler, Gerrit van, 785n, 786

Cabalism, 325n, 543

Cadolzburg, Austria, 169

Calabria, Italy, 520, 524, 528, 637

Calvary, 338, 863

Calvin, John, 3 f., 9, 21, 104, 181, 199, 235, 269, 272, 323, 350, 351n, 354, 375, 395, 408, 487, 505, 522, 537 f., 540, 545, 547, 552, 564, 566, 568 f., 578 f., 580–614, 615–619, 622, 624n, 626–630, 632, 635–638, 641, 646, 650, 653, 655–661, 663, 666 f., 695, 703, 715n, 717, 718, 730, 742, 750, 752, 771, 774 f., 780, 804, 817, 826, 829, 841, 843, 851, 863. *See also Institutes*

Cambrai, France, 771

Cambridge, England, 789

Camerino, Italy, 20

Camillus, 549. *See also* Renato

Campano, Italy, 549

Campanus, John, 265, 268, 272 f., 282, 304, 309–311, 324, 361, 375, 377, 457–459, 501, 808, 811, 829

Campbell, Ulrich, 551n, 553n

Campen, Jacob van, 359, 831

Campen, John van, 262

Canon law, 258

Canterbury, England, 541, 781, 787

Capital punishment, 239, 695; opposition to, 200; acceptance of as legitimate, 224, 612; Waldensian view of, 527

Capito, Wolfgang, 135 f., 139n, 140n,

160n, 185, 187, 199 f., 244, 248 f., 251, 254–257, 269 f., 278–281, 286n, 290n, 291 f., 294, 347, 364, 410, 586, 592, 817

Capodistria, Yugoslavia, 558, 574, 627, 643

Cappel (Kappel), Switzerland, 81, 200, 296, 618

Caracciolo, Galeazzo, marquis of Vico, 615, 635, 637

Carinthia (Kärnten), Austria, 62, 166, 206, 419

Carlstadt, Andreas Bodenstein of, 28, 35, 38–44, 57–59, 64, 68–75, 78, 81, 83, 85, 91 f., 97 f., 100–107, 112, 150–152, 154, 157, 223, 245, 251, 260–262, 349, 392, 416, 468, 476, 541, 687, 795, 822, 823, 850, 851, 853

Carnesecchi, Peter, 530

Caroli, Peter, 588–590, 609, 636

Cartwright, Thomas, 787

Casimir, margrave of Brandenburg, 70

Cassander, George, 2, 801, 802

Cassel, France, 400, 416

Cassel, Germany, 444, 446, 451

Castelberger, Andrew, 121, 129, 550, 552

Castellio, Sebastian (pseudonym: Martin Bellius), 9n, 25, 568, 616, 642n, 627–630, 632, 635, 638, 783, 811, 817, 826, 827, 828, 835, 841

Catechesis, Catechism. *See* Heidelberg; Raków

Catechetical instruction. *See* Schools

Cathars, 240, 325n, 327. *See also* Bogomiles; Paulicians

Catherine of Gaunt, queen of Castile, 7

Catholic Evangelism, xxvi, 2, 8–16, 18, 19, 87, 360–361, 536–541, 559, 578 f., 602, 604, 801

Catholicism. *See* Catholic Evangelism; Council: of Trent; Counter Reformation; Orders: religious; Papacy

Cavour, Treaty of, 847

Celestial flesh of Christ, xxvi, 88, 107, 197, 246, 265, 269, 285 f., 325–337, 339, 377, 394–396, 398, 403, 444, 446 f., 457, 466, 486 f., 492, 496, 498, 502, 589, 597, 761, 779, 785 f., 789 f., 795 f.; as manna, 336, 472, 502 f.

Celibacy, apostolic, 510

Langenmantel, Eitelhans, 164 f., 178, 188
Lanzenstiel, Bishop Leonard, Seiler (Sailer), 427n, 573, 575, 670–672, 679 f.
Larissa, Greece, 317, 677 f.
Łaski, Jerome, 415, 486, 708
Łaski (à Lasco), John, 415 f., 486–488, 568, 641, 643, 647, 656–658, 660 f., 664, 693n, 708, 773, 778, 782
Last Judgment, 174, 189, 221n, 275 f.
Lateran Council. See Council
Latimer, Hugh, 780n
Latter Days, 48, 56, 163, 169 f., 172–174, 217, 225, 227, 245, 345 f., 383, 424. See also Apocalypticism; Kingdom of God; Last Judgment; Resurrection
Laufenburg, Germany, 136n
Laus, Italy, 521
Lausanne, Switzerland, 528, 586–590, 592, 634
Lautern, Germany, 189
Lavin, Italy, 553
Law. See under Canon; Code, Roman; Common; Divine; Germanic
Law (theological sense) and grace, 150, 153, 170 f., 275, 410, 475, 815. See also Antinomianism
Laymen. See Priesthood of all believers
League, of the Ten Jurisdictions, of House of God, Grey, see Rhaetia; Swabian, see Swabian League
Leber, Oswald, 189
Leeuwarden, Holland, 357 f., 387–389, 392 f., 487–489, 766
Lefèvre d'Étaples, Jacques, 93, 583n, 598
Legnica. See Liegnitz
Leiden, Holland, 346, 349, 373, 383, 429, 775, 788
Leiden, John of. See Beukels
Leipheim, Germany, 68
Leipzig, Germany, 38 f., 45, 65, 80, 121n, 213, 215, 650, 711
Leisure from self, 268. See also Gelassenheit; Separation
Lemoine, Cardinal, 93
Lening, John, 445
Leo X, pope, 11, 17, 18n, 20, 23, 104, 583
Leonard, Lord of Liechtenstein, 205,

218 f., 224–227, 229–231, 257, 410, 414, 734, 749, 759
Letovice, Czechoslovakia, 218
Leubel, Michael, 295
Leuterhofen, Germany, 188
Leutschau, Czechoslovakia, 414
Lhotka, Czechoslovakia, 211
Libertet, 586n
Libertinism, spiritual, 7, 24, 35; in the Netherlands, 351–355, 480; in Italy, 564, 577–579, 774 f.; in Moravia, 675; opposed by Calvin, 598–605; political, 604 f., 608. See also Batenburgers; Familists; Jorists; Loists; cf. Nicodemism; Quietism; Quintists; Spiritualism
Licinius, John, 646n
Liechtenstein. See Leonard, Lord of
Liège, Belgium, 272, 341, 342n, 379, 399, 587, 590n, 600
Liegnitz (Legnica), Silesia, Poland, 108 f., 111, 114 f., 410–412
Liesveldt, Jacob van, 816, 818
Lille (Rijssel), France, 354, 400, 589
Limburg, Holland, 379, 399
Lincoln, England, 779, 787
Lindau, Germany, 190
Linz, Austria, 156, 165, 167, 169, 255, 408, 426 f.
Lipany (Böhmischbrod), Czechoslovakia, 209
Lipomani, Alois, 643
Lismanino (Lismanini), Francis, 569, 634, 640 f., 643, 647, 657, 659, 661, 664, 743–745
Lithuania, Grand Duchy of, general orientation, 404–407, 639, 642–644, 646–650, 657 f., 660, 666, 669, 685 f., 689 f., 695n, 738–740, 743, 747–749, 761
Liturgical year (also happenings significantly related to), 50, 76; elimination of, 652; Christmas, 379, 587, 693, 803; Epiphany, 368; Lent, 539; Maundy Thursday, 136; Easter, 129, 136, 188, 371, 379, 423, 425, 587; Passover, 706; Ascension, 248, 587; Pentecost (Whitsun), 161–163, 176, 225, 246, 423, 467, 587; Corpus Christi Day, 29, 328, 346; Assumption of Mary, 346; St. Bartholomews', 176, 736, 739, 752. See also Music; Sabbatarianism; Worship
Livonia, 260

Messianism *for* apostolic prophetic king; apostle (emissary), 37, 164, 175, 212, 236, 368, 376, 422 f., 560, 563, 860; prophet, 49, 124, 164, 175, 255, 353, 357, 373, 479, 597; *for* eschatological impersonations of an ancient prophet, *see under* Elijah, Enoch, Daniel, David, *also* Michael; evangelist, 175; elder, lay, 641, 644, 659 f.; missionary, 421, 426, 529; bishop or superintendent, 640 f.; patriarch, 674, 789 f.; in Familism, 481–482; 12 elders in Münster, 373; teacher (*Lehrer*), 402; deacon, 230, 790; itineracy, 212, 259, 488, 522, 529, 560; divine commission, 360, 368, 392, 492, 503 f., 773; (re)ordination, xxix f., 122, 176, 184, 211, 215, 230, 393, 488, 490, 504, 523, 529, 687, 697, 759, 860; deposition, 422; congregational control of election to, 60, 74, 398, 438, 449, 488, 503, 594, 766 f., 770; voluntary support of, 63, 184, 594, 597; women in, 123, 393; criticism of Protestants, 55, 195
Minor Church (Party), defined for Unity of Brethren, 219; for Polish Reformed, 639, 669. *See primarily* Polish Brethren; Unity
Miolo, Girolamo, 526n
Missions, xxv, 3, 245, 682, 844, 859; Great Commission (to baptize), 127, 303, 844 f. *See also under* Moslems
Mladá-Boleslav, Czechoslovakia, 528
Modena, Italy, 547, 563n, 816
Modiano, Italy, 560
Mödling, Austria, 671
Modrevius. *See* Modrzewski
Modruzzo, Cardinal Christopher, 783
Modrzewski (Modrevius), Andrew Frycz, 2, 658, 668, 669n
Moeseke, Lauken van, 34
Mohács, Hungary, 108, 206, 234
Mohammedans. *See* Moslems
Molinos, John of, 528
Mollenhecke, Henry, 372
Moloch, Christ compared to, 629
Mondsee, Austria, 167
Monninkendam, Holland, 345, 370
Montaigne, Michel de, 838
Monte, Cardinal Innocenzo del, 565
Montlhéry, France, 589
Moos, Austria, 418
Morat, Switzerland, 527

Moravia, 60, 84, 132, 141, 156, 165–168, 178, 191, 198, 202–206, 218–234, 254 f., 267, 295, 306 f., 404, 406, 412, 414–419, 421, 423–427, 429, 432, 435, 442, 454 f., 553, 572–577, 647, 651, 662, 670–684, 686, 689, 697, 699, 706, 743–745, 782, 793–797, 802, 804, 835, 847
Moravian Brethren. *See* Unity
Mordy, Poland, 666
More, Thomas, 401
Morel (Maurel), George, 522, 524n, 527
Morone, Cardinal, bishop of Modena, 548, 633
Mortality of the soul. *See* Psychopannychism
Mortification, 171, 704, 861. *See also Gelassenheit*
Moscow, U.S.S.R., 642, 686, 747
Moses, 170, 189, 312–315, 410, 731, 825, 855
Moslems, 283, 834–838; as enemies to be fought, 226, 234; as instrument of divine chastisement, 163, 164, 189; as objects of irenic mission, 224, 246, 255; as capable of salvation by eternal word, 56, 170, 459, 629, 740–743, 838, 843; as exemplary, 265; conversions to the, 729, 809; Turks, 46, 56, 163, 170, 186, 226, 246, 255, 265, 613, 708–732. *See also* Universalism
Motta Alciati della. *See* Alciati della Motta
Mouzon, France, 589
Mozyr, U.S.S.R., 739n
Mühlhausen (Thuringia), Germany, 56n, 68 f., 75–78, 81, 151, 155, 164, 440, 442. *See also* Mulhouse
Mulaer, William, 400
Mulhouse (Mülhausen), Alsace, France, 634
Müller, Hans, 64
Müller, Jerzy (George), 701
Mundius, Lucas, 695–697
Munich, Germany, 165, 198
Münster, Germany, xxiii, 45, 74, 83, 268, 294, 297 f., 307, 342 f., 348 f., 358–391, 400–402, 416 f., 423, 442–447, 452, 455, 467, 477–478, 490–492, 511–513, 515, 580, 691, 772, 831, 835, 864; St. Lambert's, 365–367; St. Giles's, 348, 365; St. Maurice's, 364

Empire, Ottoman, *see:*
  Selim I (1512–1520)
  Suleiman I, the Magnificent
    (1520–1566)
  Selim II (1566–1574)
Austria, Upper and Lower, arch-
    duke of, *see:*
  Ferdinand (1521–1564; in Em-
    pire, I)
  Maximilian (1564–1576; in Em-
    pire, II)
Aragon, Spain, king of, *see:*
  Ferdinand II (1479–1516)
  Charles I (1516–1556; in Em-
    pire, V)
  Philip II (1556–1598)
Bohemia, king of, *see:*
  Sigismund (1419–1437)
  Albert II (1437–1439)
  Ladislas Posthumus (1440–
    1457)
  George Poděbrady (1458–
    1471)
  Ladislas II Jagellon (1471–
    1516)
  Louis (1516–1526)
  Ferdinand (in Austria, 1526–
    1564; in Empire, I)
  Maximilian (in Austria, 1564–
    1576; in Empire, II)
Cleve-Jülich, duke of, *see:*
  John II (1481–1521)
  John III (1521–1539)
  William (1539–1592)
Denmark and Norway, *see:*
  Frederick I (1523–1533)
  Christian III (1534–1558)
  Frederick II (1558–1588)
England, king or queen of, *see:*
  Henry VIII (1509–1547)
  Edward VI (1547–1553)
  Mary (1553–1558)
  Elizabeth I (1558–1603)
France, king of, *see:*
  Louis XII (1498–1515)
  Francis I (1515–1547)
  Henry II (1547–1559)
  Francis II (1559–1560)
  Charles IX (1560–1574)
  Henry III, Valois (1574–1589;
    in Poland, I)
Hesse, landgrave of, *see:*
  Philip I, the Magnanimous
    (1509–1567)

Hungary, king of, *see:*
  Louis II (1516–1526)
  John Zápolya (1526/28–1540)
  Ferdinand (1526/28–1564; in
    Empire, I)
  Maximilian (1564–1578; in Em-
    pire, II)
Muscovy, grand duke of, *see:*
  Ivan IV the Terrible (1533–
    1584; Czar in 1547)
Netherlands, seventeen Hapsburg
    provinces of, definitively di-
    vided
  divided between north and
    south in 1579, *see:*
  Mary, duchess of Burgundy,
    direct rule (1477–1482)
  Maximilian, her spouse, re-
    gent for their son Philip
    (1482–1494)
  Philip the Fair, direct rule
    (1494–1506)
  Maximilian again, for his
    grandson Charles (1506–
    1515)
  Charles, direct rule (1515–
    1519; in Empire, V)
  Margaret of Austria, widow
    of Duke Philibert *of Savoy,*
    regent (1519–1530)
  Mary of Austria, widow of
    King Louis *of Hungary,*
    regent (1530–1555)
  Philip, direct rule (1555–
    1559; in Spain, II)
  Margaret of Austria, duchess
    of *Parma,* half-sister of
    Charles, regent (1559–
    1567)
  Ferdinand, duke of Alva, re-
    gent (1567–1573)
  Luis de Requessens y Zúñiga,
    regent (1573–1576)
  Don Juan d'Austria, (1576–
    1578)
  Alessandro Farnese, duke of
    Parma (1578–1592)
  William I, the Silent, of
    Orange, sovereign stad-
    holder in the north (1576/
    79–1584)
Palatinate, elector of, *see:*
  Louis V (1508–1544)
  Frederick II (1544–1556)

Sources Quoted

MODERN AUTHORS

BIBLICAL REFERENCES